Sixteenth Edition
Antique Trader Books
ANTIQUES & COLLECTIBLES
PRICE GUIDE

2000 ANNUAL EDITION

ANTIQUE TRADER BOOKS
Antiques & Collectibles
Price Guide

Edited by
Kyle Husfloen

An illustrated comprehensive price guide to the entire field of antiques
and collectibles for the 2000 market

ISBN: 1-58221-017-9
ISSN: 1083-8430

Editor: *Kyle Husfloen*
Assistant Editor: *Ruth Willis*
Book Designer: *Virginia Hill*
Design Assistants: *Lynn Bradshaw, Janell Edwards, Vicki Rohrssen*
Photographic Technician: *Tom Emery*
Cover Design & Color Technician: *Aaron Roeth*

Cover photo credits:

Front cover: clockwise from top: Chippendale Revival mahogany tall chest of drawers, by R.J. Horner, late 19th - early 20th c., $1,000, courtesy of Slawinski
Auction Co., Felton, California; Nippon porcelain 9½" d. plaque painted with
portrait of a monk, $660, courtesy of Jackson's Auctions, Cedar Falls, Iowa;
Watling "Treasury" slot machine, $2,600, courtesy of Slawinski Auction Co.,
Felton, California; Czechoslovakian blown glass vase in deep red with dark blue
serpentine trim, $145, courtesy of Ruth Forsythe, Galena, Ohio.

Back cover: top to bottom: carved & painted wood figural bird trump indicator, $85,
courtesy of Ellen Bercovici, Bethesda, Maryland; Heintz Art Metal vase with single silver rose, $345, courtesy of David Surgan, Brooklyn, New York.

Printed in the United States of America

For information about ***Antique Trader Weekly*** subscriptions or
Antique Trader Online Price Guides contact:

Antique Trader Publications
P.O. Box 1050
Dubuque, Iowa 52004
1-800-334-7165

Antique Trader Books
A division of Krause Publications

A WORD TO THE READER

For the past thirty years The Antique Trader has been producing detailed, authoritative pricing guides to the world of antiques and collectibles and we're proud to present our most current effort which will lead readers into the realm of collecting in the new Millennium. Thirty years is just a blip on the screen when scanning the time line of a thousand years, but the past three decades have been momentous in terms of changes reflected in the collecting field. If one stretches their imagination and envisions the Western world at the dawn of the first Millennium in 1000 A.D. you will realize that collecting in the modern sense was nearly unheard of. Perhaps a few wealthy monarchs or merchants cherished rarities from exotic locales, but most of humanity was just coming out of the Dark Ages and was more concerned about mere survival and the prospect of the Apocolypse which many expected to arrive any moment.

Nine hundred years later, at the dawning of this past century we find that the birth of collecting in the modern sense had arrived. As Emyl Jenkins, noted author and appraiser, explains in our special 32 page supplement in this edition there was a growing interest and appreciation of American history and cultural artifacts by 1900. As our country boomed forward into an exciting new century our forebears were becoming more and more aware of the heirlooms handed down from their ancestors and if you hadn't inherited a Queen Anne chest or a Chippendale chair you could still purchase an original or even a modern "adaptation" of those pieces. Popular magazines of that day were quickly disseminating information about antiques, where to find them, what pieces were choicest and how to decorate with them. By the 1920s, as our economy boomed, antiques became a serious business across the country and "Early American" became a synonym for all things quaint, charming and worthy of collecting. The past eighty years have seen vast changes in the way Americans collect and what they collect and Ms. Jenkins' fascinating and informative feature will give you a wonderful overview of the last century of collecting as well as what may lie ahead in 2000 and beyond.

In addition to the special feature we're proud to include a comprehensive listing of major collecting categories in today's market. Some of these are well-established and long-popular areas of collecting such as Furniture, Pattern Glass and antique ceramics, but we have also worked diligently to include newer currently "hot" categories such as Costume Jewelry, Kitchenwares, Czechoslovakian Collectibles, Television Sets, Sports Memorabilia and more.

Even some unique and very new areas for budding collectors are presented such as Melmac Ware, Trump Indicators and Wall Pockets. We hope you'll agree that there's something here for every collecting interest and budget.

As always we take great care to offer the most accurate and up-to-date information with careful descriptions and thorough indexing and cross-referencing. This year we have expanded the offerings of Special Contributors in numerous collecting categories which ensures we have the most authoritative, current data available. I want to offer special thanks to all these people and organizations for their great efforts and you'll find a complete listing of them on the following pages.

Most people who use antiques price guides also find that good photos are an invaluable part of the book and we've also included this year an even larger variety of photographs to highlight the price listings as well as including a brief introduction to most categories and information on good reference books covering the topics. In the Glass and Ceramics sections we are also including sketches of many of the factory or artists' marks which will be an aid in identification.

As thorough and authoritative as our price listings are, we do want to remind readers that this book should be used only as a guide to pricing. What makes collecting so fun and fascinating is that each item you find is actually unique in terms of condition and local market demand. What may sell for hundreds of dollars in "mint in box" condition may only bring a few dollars in "used, average" condition. Regional demand and tastes will also have an impact on the market for certain items and must be kept in mind. In today's shrinking world it is often quite easy to reach collectors around the country or in far corners of the world, but if you wish to sell something in your local market, keep in mind that interest and demand, as well as rarity and condition, will play a part in what value your item may have. Also, the values listed here, as in most price guides, reflect a retail value range, in other words, what you would have to pay to purchase or replace a similar item in the general market.

Antique Trader's Antiques & Collectibles Price Guide follows a basically alphabetical format for most categories. However, we have arranged the larger categories of Ceramics, Furniture and Glass into their own sections where each specific type or maker will be listed alphabetically within that section. If you have a question about where a specific category is to be found please refer to the detailed INDEX we provide at the back of this book. We will cross-reference as many of the categories as possible to also help in your research.

I want to remind you that although our descriptions, prices and illustrations have been double-checked and every effort has been made to ensure accuracy, neither the editor nor publisher can assume responsibility for any losses that might be incurred as a result of consulting this guide, or of typographical or other errors.

Photographers who have contributed to this issue include: E. A. Babka, East Dubuque, Illinois; Stanley L. Baker, Minneapolis, Minnesota; Dorothy Beckwith, Platteville, Wisconsin; Johanna S. Billings, Danielsville, Pennsylvania; Donna Bruun, Galena, Illinois; Herman C. Carter, Tulsa, Oklahoma; Susan N. Cox, El Cajon, California; J. D. Dalessandro, Cincinnati, Ohio; Ruth Eaves, Marmora, New Jersey; Susan Eberman, Bedford, Indiana; Bill Freeman, Smyrna, Georgia; Scott Green, Manchester, New Hampshire; Jeff Grunewald, Chicago, Illinois; Vance Hall, Wichita, Kansas; Joe Hallahan, Dubuque, Iowa; Robert G. Jason-Ickes, Olympia, Washington; Marlyn Margulis, Cherry Hill, New Jersey; Kevin McConnell, Pilot Point, Texas; Louise Paradis, Sparta, Wisconsin; Joyce Roerig, Waltersboro, South Carolina; David H. Surgan, Brooklyn, New York; and Tom Wallace, Chicago, Illinois.

For other photographs, artwork, data or permission to photograph in their shops, we sincerely express appreciation to the following auctioneers, galleries, museums, individuals and shops: Albrecht Auction Service, Vassar, Michigan; Alderfers, Hatfield, Pennsylvania; American Social History and Social Movements, Pittsburgh, Pennsylvania; Auction Team Koln, Cologne, Germany; Bertoia Sales, Vineland, New Jersey; Donna Bauerly, Dubuque, Iowa; Block's Box, Trumball, Connecticut; Burns Auction Service, Bath, New York; Charles Casad, Monticello, Illinois; Norm & Diana Charles, Hagerstown, Indiana; Frank Chiarenza, Newington, Connecticut; Christie's, New York, New York; Cincinnati Art Galleries, Cincinnati, Ohio; Collector's Auction Services, Oil City, Pennsylvania; Collector's Sales & Services, Middletown, Rhode Island; Copake Country Auction, Copake, New York; Bill Correll, Bedford, Indiana; S. Davis, Williamsburg, Ohio; DeFina Auctions, Austenburg, Ohio; William Doyle Galleries, New York, New York; Early American History Auctions, Inc., La Jolla, California; T. Ermert, Cincinnati, Ohio; John Fontaine Auction, Pittsfield, Massachusetts; Garth's Auctions, Inc., Delaware, Ohio; Glass-Works Auctions, East Greenville, Pennsylvania; Glick's Antiques, Galena, Illinois; Green Valley Auctions, Mt. Crawford, Virginia; Grunewald Antiques, Hillsborough, North Carolina; and Guyette and Schmidt, West Farmington, Maine.

Also to Vicki Harmon, San Marcos, California; the Gene Harris Antique Auction Center, Marshalltown, Iowa; the late William Heacock, Marietta, Ohio; The House in the Woods Auction Gallery, Eagle, Wisconsin; International Carnival Glass Association, Mentone, Indiana; International Toy Collectors Association, Athens, Illinois; Jackson's Auctions, Cedar Falls, Iowa; James Julia, Fairfield, Maine; Sherry Klabo, Seattle, Washington; Peter Kroll, Sun Prairie, Wisconsin; Lang's Sporting Collectibles, Raymond, Maine; Leland's Auctions, New York, New York; Jim Ludescher, Dubuque, Iowa; J. Martin, Mt. Orab, Ohio; Mastro & Steinbach Fine Sports Auctions, Oakbrook, Illinois; Russ McCall, Auctioneer, Onawa, Iowa; Randall McKee, Kenosha, Wisconsin; McMasters Doll Auctions, Cambridge, Ohio; Dr. James Measell, Marietta, Ohio; Wm. Morford Auctions, Cazenovia, New York; Northeast Auctions, Portsmouth, New Hampshire; O'Gallerie, Inc., Portland, Oregon; Pacific Glass Auctions, Sacramento, California; Past Tyme Pleasures, Los Altos, California; Pettigrew Auctions, Colorado Springs, Colorado; Dave Rago Arts & Crafts, Lambertville, New Jersey; Jane Rosenow, Galva, Illinois; Tammy Roth, East Dubuque, Illinois; L.H. Selman, Ltd., Santa Cruz, California; Skinner, Inc., Bolton, Massachusetts; Slawinski Auction Company, Felton, California; Ron Smith, Yelm, Washington; Sotheby's, New York, New York; Doris Spahn, East Dubuque, Illinois; George and Judy Swan, Dubuque, Iowa; Temples Antiques, Eden Prairie, Minnesota; Theriault's, Annapolis, Maryland; Patrick Thomas Auctions, Saugerties, New York; Time & Again Antiques, Linden, New Jersey; Tin Pan Alley Antiques, Galena, Illinois; Tradewinds Antiques, Manchester-by-the-Sea, Massachusetts; Treadway Gallery, Cincinnati, Ohio; Victorian Images, Marlton, New Jersey; Lee Vines, Hewlett, New York; Doris Virtue, Galena, Illinois; Web Wilson's Antique Hardware Auctions, Portsmouth, Rhode Island; Wolf's Auctioneers and Appraisers, Cleveland Ohio; Woody Auctions, Douglass, Kansas; The Yankee Peddler Antiques, Denton, Texas; and Yesterday's Treasures, Galena, Illinois.

We hope that everyone who consults our Antiques & Collectibles Price Guide will find it the most thorough, accurate and informative guide on the ever-changing world of collecting.

The staff of Antique Trader's Antiques & Collectibles Price Guide welcomes all letters from readers, especially those of constructive critique, and we make every effort to respond personally.

–Kyle Husfloen, Editor

SPECIAL CATEGORY CONTRIBUTORS

GENERAL CATEGORIES

Autographs
Bill Butts, Main Street Fine Books & Manuscripts, 206 N. Main, Galena, IL 61036

Avon Collectibles
Connie Clark, President, National Assoc. of Avon Collectors, Inc., P.O. Box 7006, Kansas City, MO 64113

Bakelite
Treadway Gallery, Inc., Cincinnati, OH, in association with The John Toomey Gallery of Oak Park, IL

Bootjacks
Harry A. Zuber, Houston, TX

Bottle Openers
Charles Reynolds, Reynold's Toys, 2836 Monroe St., Falls Church, VA 22042

Bottles
Mike Pollack, P.O. Box 30328, Long Beach, CA 90853, (562) 438-9209

Buttons
Millicent Safro, Tender Buttons, 143 E. 62nd St., New York, NY 10021, (212) 758-7004, Fax: (212) 319-8474

Candy Containers
Terry Whitmeyer, 88 Woodbine Dr., Hershey, PA 17033-2668

Cat Collectibles
Marilyn Dipboye, 33161 Wendy Dr., Sterling Heights, MI 48310

Children's Books
General:
Bill Butts, Main Street Fine Books & Manuscripts, 206 N. Main, Galena, IL 61036

Little Golden Books:
Steve Santi, 19626 Ricardo Ave., Hayward, CA 94541, e-mail: lgb-steve@aol.com, Author: *Collecting Little Golden Books*

Youth Books:
James D. Keeline, The Prince & the Pauper Collectible Children's Books, 3201 Adams T., San Diego, CA 92116-1554, (619) 283-4380, Fax: 619) 283-4380 e-mail: books@old-kidsbooks.com, Web: www.oldkidsbooks.com, Author: *Stratemeyer Syndicate Ghostwriters*

Christmas Collectibles

General
Pamela Apkarian-Russel, Box 499, Winchester, NH 03470, (603) 239-8875, e-mail: halloweenqueen@top.morad.net, Author: *More Halloween Collectibles*

Hallmark Keepsake Ornaments
Rosie Wells Enterprises, Inc., 22341 E. Wells Rd., Canton, IL 61520, e-mail: rosie@rosiewells.com

Coca-Cola Items
Allan Petretti, 21 S. Lake Dr., Hackensack, NJ 07601

Comic Books
Antique Trader Book's, Annual 1999 Comic Values, by Alex Malloy & Sotheby's, New York, NY

Compacts & Vanity Cases
Roselyn Gerson, P.O. Box 40, Lynbrook, NY 11563, Author: *Ladies' Compacts of the Nineteenth & Twentieth Centuries and Vintage & Contemporary Purse Accessories (Lipsticks, Mirrors and Solid Perfumes)*

Czechoslovakian Collectibles
Ruth A. Forsythe, Box 327, Galena, OH 43021

Disney Collectibles
Robert G. Jason-Ickes, 3600 Elizabeth Ave. S.E., #19-203, Olympia, WA 98501

Farm Collectibles
Philip Whitney, 303 Fisher Rd., Fitchburg, MA 01420-1548, (978) 342-1350

Fire Fighting Collectibles
H. Thomas Laun, Little Century, 215 Paul Ave., Syracuse, NY 13206, (315) 437-4156

Fishing Collectibles
Lang's Sporting Collectibles, Inc., 14 Fishermans Lane, Raymond, ME 04071, Phone/Fax: (207) 655-4265

Golf Clubs—Wooden Shafted
Peter Georgiady, 6101 O'Bryant Ct., Greensboro, NC 27410, Fax: (336) 668-7260, ahp@greensboro.com, Author: *Wood Shafted Golf Clubs* (Airlie Hall Press)

Graniteware
Jo Allers, Cedar Rapids, IA

Heintz Art Metal Shop Wares
David Surgan, 328 Flatbush Ave., Suite 123, Brooklyn, NY 11238, (718) 638-3768

Indian Artifacts
Bob Sleeper Auction Service, 920 N. Elm, Higginsville, MO 64037, (660) 584-7019, Fax: (660) 584-2239, e-mail: sleeper@ctcis.net, Web: www.bobsleeper.com
Dick & Terry Engel, P.O. Box 1429, Ennis, MT 59729, (406) 682-4499

Jewelry (Costume)
Marion Cohen, P.O. Box 39, Albertson, NY 11507

Kitchenwares

General
Carol Bohn, KOOKS, 501 Mark St., Mifflinburg, PA 17844, (717) 966-1198

Egg Timers, Pie Birds & String Holders
Ellen Bercovici, 5118 Hampden La., Bethesda, MD 20814, (301) 652-1140

Juice Reamers & Napkin Dolls
Bobbie Zucker Bryson, 1 St. Eleanoras La., Tuckahoe, NY 10707, e-mail: Napkindoll@aol.com, (914) 779-1405

Kitchen Glassware
Kate Trabue, 1603 Pine St., #1, Eureka, CA 95501-2280, (707) 444-3326

Laundry Room Items

Irons
David Irons, 223 Covered Bridge Rd., Northampton, PA 18607, Fax: (610) 262-2853, Author: *Irons by Irons, More Irons by Irons* and *Pressing Iron Patents*
Jimmy & Carol Walker, Iron Talk, P.O. Box 68, Waelder, TX 78959-0068

Sprinkling Bottles
Ellen Bercovici, 5118 Hampden La., Bethesda, MD 20814, (301) 652-1140

Lipstick Holder Ladies
Ellen Bercovici, 5118 Hampden La., Bethesda, MD 20814, (301) 652-1140

Magazines

Denis C. Jackson, P.O. Box 1958, Sequim, WA 98392, (360) 683-2559, e-mail: ticn@olypen.com

Melmac

Michael J. Goldberg, 823 SE 25th Ave., Portland, OR 97214, e-mail:emjaygee@inetarena.com, Author: Several books & articles including *I Remember Melmac*

Militaria & Wartime Memorabilia

Jim Trautman, R.R. 1, Orton, Ontario, Canada L0N 1N0, (519) 855-6077

Nutting (Wallace) Collectibles & Print Artists - 20th Century

Michael Ivankovich, P.O. Box 2458, Doylestown, PA 18901, (215) 345-6094, Fax: (215) 345-6692, wnutting@comcat.com

Playing Cards

Rhonda Hawes, Secretary/Treasurer, 52 Plus Joker, 204 Gorham Ave., Hamden, CT 06514, Web: www.52plusjoker.org

Political & Campaign Memorabilia

Rich Friz, P.O. Box 472, Peterborough, NH 03458, (603) 563-8155, Author: *House of Collectibles Official Price Guide to Civil War Memorabilia*

Postcards

Susan Brown Nicholson, P.O. Box 595, Lisle, IL 60532, (630) 964-5240, Author: *Encyclopedia of Antique Post Cards*

Salt & Pepper Shakers (Novelty)

Sylvia Tompkins & Larry Carrey, c/o Novelty Salt & Pepper Shakers Club, Lula Fuller P.O. Box 3617, Lantana, FL 33462, (561) 588-5368

Sewing Adjuncts

Beth Pulsipher, Prairie Home Antiques, 240 N. Grand, Schoolcraft, MI 49087, (616) 679-2062

Sports Collectibles

Leland's Auctions, 36 East 22nd St., New York, NY 10010

Mastro Fine Sports Auctions, 1515 W. 22nd St., Suite 125, Oak Brook, IL 60523

Television Sets

Harry Poster, P.O. Box 1883, S. Hackensack, NJ 07606 (201) 794-9606, Fax: (201) 794-9553, e-mail: hposter@worldnet.att.net

Tools

Martin & Kathy Donnelly, Donnelly Antique Tools, 31 Rumsey St., P.O. Box 281, Bath, NY 14810, Fax: (607) 776-6064, e-mail: mjd@mjdtool.com, Author: *The Catalogue of Antique Tools*

Toys, Character Collectibles

Bill Bruegman, Toy Scouts, 137 Casterton Ave., Akron, OH 44303, (330) 836-0668, Fax: (330) 869-8668, e-mail: toyscout@newreach.net

Tramp Art

Clifford Wallach & Michael Cornish, 277 W. 10th St., New York, NY 10014, Authors: *Tramp Art: One Notch At a Time*

Trump Indicators

Ellen Bercovici, 5118 Hampden La., Bethesda, MD 20814, (301) 652-1140

Watches

Barbara Stevens, 4490 Cricket Ridge Dr., #204, Holt, MI 48842, Fax: (517) 337-4560, e-mail: stevens44@aol.com

World's Fair Collectibles

Jim Trautman, R.R. 1, Orton, Ontario, Canada L0N 1N0, (519) 855-6077

Writing Accessories

Ray & Bevy Jaegers, P.O. Box 29396, St. Louis, MO 63126, e-mail: upsisquad@aol.com, Publications: *The Write Stuff*

CERAMICS

American Painted Porcelain

Dorothy Kamm, P.O. Box 7460, Port St. Lucie, FL 34985-7460, (561) 465-4008, e-mail: dorothy.kamm@usa.net, Author: *American Painted Porcelain: Collector's Identification & Value Guide; Comprehensive Guide to American Painted Porcelain* and the bimonthly newsletter, *Dorothy Kamm's Porcelain Collector's Companion*

Blue & White Pottery

Stephen E. Stone, 18102 East Oxford Dr., Aurora, CO 80013

Flow Blue & Mulberry

Ellen Hill, Mulberry Hill South, 655 - 10th Ave. N.E., Apt. 5, St. Petersburg, FL 33701

Lefton China

Loretta DeLozier, 1101 Polk St., Bedford, IA 50833, (712) 523-2289, e-mail: LeftonLady@aol.com, Author: *Collector's Encyclopedia of Lefton China (Books I & II)*

Red Wing

Charles W. Casad, 801 Tyler Court, Monticello, IL 61856-2246

Stoneware

Vicki & Bruce Waasdorp, P.O. Box 434, Clarence, NY 14031

GLASS

Carnival Glass

Bruce Dooley, 2571 7th Ave., Sweetwater, NJ 08037, (609) 965-2535

Cut Glass

Vance Hall, A Touch of Glass, Ltd., 9107 Autumn Chase, Wichita, KS 67206, (316) 634-2220

Imperial 'Candlewick'

Mary M. Wetzel-Tomalka, P.O. Box 594, Notre Dame, IN 46556, (219) 254-9817, Author: *Candlewick—The Jewel of Imperial*

Milk Glass

Frank Chiarenza, National Milk Glass Collectors Society, 80 Crestview, Newington, CT 06111-2405, (860) 666-5576

Pattern

Iris Cottage Interiors, Andrea & Alan Koppel, Rt. 295 & County Rt. 5, P.O. Box 254, Canaan, NY 12029, (518) 781-4379

Tim Timmerman, 11655 S.W. Allen Blvd., #31, Beaverton, OR 97005, (U.S. Coin pattern)

Rose Bowls and Jack-in-the-Pulpit Vases

Johanna S. Billings, P.O. Box 244, Danielsville, PA 18038-0244, e-mail: bankie@concentric.net, Author: *Collectible Glass Rose Bowls*

Early Horlick's Postcard

ADVERTISING ITEMS

Thousands of objects made in various materials, some intended as gifts with purchases, others used for display or given away for publicity are now being collected. Also see various other categories.

Ashtray, "Andes Stoves & Ranges," tin, one-sided w/striker, on shield-shaped die-cut cardboard w/illustration of young dark haired woman wearing a flower trimmed bonnet w/large bow under chin above "Use ANDES STOVES and RANGES - For Sale By Hessler & Schafer, 512 & 516 N. Salina St., Syracuse, N.Y. - Best in the World - Always Give Satisfaction," 4⅝" w., 6¼" h. (minor fading & water stain, scratches & denting to match strike) . . **$171**

Bartels Brewing Co. Ashtray

Ashtray, "Bartels Brewing Co.," tin, cone-shaped w/removable match holder w/metal striker on top, three cigarette holes around sides w/"Bartels Malt Extract" beneath alternating w/scenes of man holding mug of beer, crazing, fading, scratches & soiling, 4⅝" d., 4" h. (ILLUS.) **660**

Ashtray, "Champion Spark Plugs," ceramic, a round black-glazed dish w/two swirled indentations around the top w/two cigarette indentations at the rim, a real "Champion Ford" spark plug standing upright in the center, base stamped "Champion Sill - Manite," 5" d., 3½" h. (scratches, soiling & rust spotting on plug). . . . **132**

Fisk Tires Advertising Ashtray

Ashtray, "Fisk Tires," rubber tire-type w/clear glass insert printed under the bottom w/a full-color design of the Fisk tire boy & "Time to Re-tire" - "Get A Fisk" in black all on a yellow ground, soiling, cracking to rubber, some paint loss, 6½" d. (ILLUS.)........................ 209

Ashtray, "Kelly Tires," rubber tire-type w/glass insert & decal w/"Kelly Tires," 6" d. 20

Ashtray, "Michelin Tires," plastic, round black tray w/notched rim, the seated Michelin man in white on one rim, marked "Made in USA," 5 x 5½", 4¾" h. (minor scratches, soiling)...................... 110

Ashtray, "Phillips 66," rubber tire-type w/clear glass insert printed under the bottom in orange & black w/company logo & name & address of dealer, w/original box, 6½" d. (scratches & wear to box) 132

Ashtray, "Smoke Kools," milk glass, w/penguins trademark, ... 20

Bank, "Phillips 66," square clear glass block, embossed on one side "Phill-up with - Phillips 66 (in logo) - See What You Save," soiling, 3" w., 4¾" sq. 149

Bank, "Texaco," plastic, figural gas pump, Texaco logo & "Sky Chief " on front, 1⅝" w., 4¾" h., (top of gas hose broken off, front panel loose) 302

Blotter, "Pan - Am" logo w/imprint "Keep Pace With Pan - Am Gasoline," illustration of airplane flying over countryside, 6¼" w., 3" h. (minor creases, fading & soiling, rounded edges) 176

Booklet, "Cracker Jack," riddles, ca. 1896 75

Booklet, "Historic Tours in Socony Land," 1925, very good condition 22

Horlick's Miniature Bottles

Bottle, miniature, "Horlick's - The Original Malted Milk - Sweet Chocolate Flavor Lunch Tablets...," cow shown on bottom of paper wrapper, unopened, 1½" d., 3" h. (ILLUS. right) 32

Bottle, miniature, in original wrapping printed w/"Horlick's Sweet Chocolate Flavor Malted Milk...," unopened, 1½" d., 3" h. (ILLUS. left) 32

Box, "Baby Bunting Oats," cardboard, 1 lb. **1,430**

Broom holder, "Bond Bread," wooden stand below porcelain sign w/"Fresh Bond Bread," holds six brooms, gold, red & white, 19" w., 40½" h. (wood frame

soiled, small pieces missing on base & holes on top, paint loss to base, edge chips to porcelain) **220**

Calendar, 1900, "Hood's Sarsaparillas," die-cut, pictures two little girls, complete 95

Calendar, 1901, "Hood's Sarsaparilla," entitled "Patience, " heavy paper, full pad, matted & framed, "Hood's Sarsaparilla - Calendar 1901" in corner above young girl w/blonde bangs & curly hair dressed in white long-sleeved ruffled dress sitting w/hands folded in lap & leaning against a white & blue ruffled pillow w/floral decoration, "Copyright 1900 by C.I. Hood & Co. Lowell Mass." in bottom corner, 9¾" w., 6¾" h., w/frame 10" w., 13½" h. (small creases & tears to edges & corners, very minor rust to staples) 110

1903 Hood's Sarsaparilla Calendar

Calendar, 1903, "Hood's Sarsaparilla," color-printed paper, scene depicts young girl in a pink dress w/a bow in her long blonde hair playing w/two dogs & a horse, full pad w/top cover sheet missing, wooden frame w/glass front & back, w/advertising information on back, picture titled "Four Friends" & marked "Copyright 1902 By C.I. Hood Company, Lowell, Mass.," edge wear & tears, fold mark across center, 6" w., 16½" h. (ILLUS.) 99

Calendar, 1917, "Hall's Chocolates," paper, "Hall's Chocolates Tease the Taste" above a colorful scene of a man seated & writing at a table w/a plate of chocolates nearby, a young woman leaning over his shoulder, calendar pad December only, signed, newer frame, 16¾" w., 30" h. (soiling & scuffs along right side) 121

Calendar, 1928, "Lydia E. Pinkham Vegetable Compound," paper in newer frame w/matte, "Bringing You Health" above beautiful color illustration of airplane flying over countryside, Lydia Pinkham's portrait in center below w/short history of her background, full calendar pad, "Ask Your Neighbor" at bottom border, Litho U.S.A., 15" w., 22¾" h. (minor water staining on edges) **121**

Calendar, 1935, "De Laval Cream Separators" . . . **50**

Calendar, 1936, "De Laval Cream Separators" . . . **40**

Calendar, 1939, "De Laval Cream Separators" . . . **40**

1940 Hercules Powder Calendar

Calendar, 1940, "Hercules Powder Co.," color lithographed paper, scene of young family in wagon covered wagon, picture titled "Pioneers," copyright Hercules Powder Co. Inc. 1939, Litho in U.S.A., unused, minor creases & soiling, 14½" w., 31½" h. (ILLUS.) **358**

Calendar, 1951, "De Laval Cream Separators" . . . **20**

Cane, "Gulf Refining Co." wood w/rubber base, "Gulf Refining Co." debossed on front top, 39" l. (minor scratches, small chips at bottom, rubber tip worn on one side) **28**

Aluminum Horlick's Canister

Canister, cov., "Horlick's," cylindrical aluminum container w/low domed fitted cover w/tall central knob, name stamped in circle & highlighted in red, 6" d., 6" h. (ILLUS.) **55**

Chalkboard, "Bubble-Up," self-framed tin, 19⅝ x 30" **100**

Chalkboard w/thermometer, "Nor'Way Antifreeze," rectangular self-framed tin, a tall chalkboard w/a blue thermometer down one side, cartoon mechanic holding a can of the product in the lower left corner, advertising across the bottom in blue & white "Nor'way Reliable Service Anti-Freeze," w/original thermometer tube, 15¼ x 22, 14" h. (minor fading, scratches & soiling) **132**

Rare Pulver's Kola-Pepsin Gum Box

Chewing gum box, "Pulver's Kola-Pepsin Chewing Gum," cardboard, tall red vending machine shown on left, ornate black & pink wording on white ground on right, early 20th c. (ILLUS.) **3,300**

Cigarette lighter, "Dodge," chrome w/Dodge pickup truck imprint & "From Pickups to Diesel Power" on one side, "Dodge Builds Tough Trucks" & semi truck on other side, 2⅜" h. (rust spotting on bottom) **33**

Cigarette lighter, "Sinclair Gasoline," debossed metal, Sinclair logo above "Powell C. Heiskell - Sinclair Products," 2¼" h. (scratches) **105**

Clock, "Black Cat Shoe Polish," key-wind, rectangular tin advertisement w/wooden frame, illustration of black cat below clock & near product containers w/"Black Cat Shoe Dressing & Superba Polish Challenges the World - The Nonsuch Mfg. Co., Limited Toronto. McDonald Mfg. Co., Limited, Toronto," 17½" w., 23½" h. (soiling & paint loss overall, minor touch up, key missing) **990**

Clock, "Champion," battery-operated, plastic w/glass front, die cut steering wheel w/clock in center w/Champion trademark & Spark Plug illustration, by "Spendia -

Champion Steering Wheel Clock

Paris," minor scratches, soiling & staining
w/corrosion in battery compartment,
11½" d. (ILLUS.)........................ **380**

Harley-Davidson Advertising Clock

Clock, "Harley-Davidson Motor Cycles,"
square electric wall model w/glass face &
dial & metal body, square dial w/numbers
only at the "12," "3," "6," & "9," the other
numbers represented by small company
logos, a large orange, black & white
company logo across the center, sweep
seconds hand, minor body wear,
15¼" sq. (ILLUS.)...................... **770**

Clock, "Honeymoon Chewing Gum," cast
iron, wall-mounted.................... **2,860**

Clock, "International Harvester," square
electric wall model w/glass face & front &
metal body, square white dial w/black
Arabic numerals around the border, large
black & red "IH" logo in center over
"International Harvester," marked "Pam
Clock Co., Rochelle, N.Y.C. '60," sweep
seconds hand, 15½" sq................. **358**

Clock, "Monroe-Matic Shock Absorbers,"
round 'double bubble' electric wall-type,
glass face & front, metal body, the dial
w/an outer band of Arabic numerals on
white, yellow center w/black wording
"Monroe-Matic Shock Absorbers -
Monroe - Load Levelers," like new, 16" d. **550**

Clock, "Phillips 66," electric wall-type, round
glass & metal 'double bubble' type,
Arabic numerals around the outer ring
border, the inner circle w/a large orange

& black "Phillips 66" shield logo w/"Tires"
in black above & "Batteries" in black
below, w/sweep seconds hand, by
Advertising Products, Inc., Cincinnati,
Ohio, 15" d. (small scratch above shield,
paint flaking near "6," seconds hand worn) ... **990**

Coffeepot, cov., "Monroe-Matic Shock
Absorbers," painted metal, footed
cylindrical shape w/tab handles, "Is Your
Car Safe - We Offer Complete Safety
Inspection (Monroe logo) - Let Us Check
Your - Shock Absorbers Now," working
condition, 12" w., 14½" h. (scratches,
soiling & inside staining)................ **165**

Comic book, "The Mighty Atom," starring
Reddy Kilowatt, 1965 .... **40**

Counter display, "Burgess Batteries,"
painted metal, hinged top has zebra
holding battery & advertising & slot
w/original business reply card, "Here are
Burgess Batteries to fit Every Size
Flashlight" in white letters at top, "New
Burgess Batteries" at bottom &
"Advertising Metal Display Co. Chgo &
NY - Made in U.S.A." on back, 10¾ x
11¾", 14¾" h. (chips w/minor rust on
bottom section, some soiling, scratches &
paint loss)............................ **33**

Counter display, "Clarks Thread" spool
holder w/suffragette theme **1,430**

Counter display, "Dr. Morse's Indian Root
Pills," die-cut cardboard, three-section,
colorful scene depicts river in background
w/tents & Native American sitting near
camp fire & marked "Dr. Morse's Indian
Root Pills - Favored for 50 Years - for
Constipation and Biliousness," John
Igelstoem Co., Masillon, Ohio, 41½" l.,
27" h. (edge wear & soiling) **605**

Counter display, "Kodak Film," metal,
painted yellow w/"don' t forget ... Kodak
Film" in black & red letters above
lithograph of Ed Sullivan saying "Hold it!
Got film" & "See the Ed Sullivan Show -
Buy 2 and have enough!," plastic cover
above film slots, "Made in U.S.A." on
back, 7½ x 12½", 15" h. (soiling, minor
fading, chips & scratches, surface rust
inside back) **55**

Counter display, "Master Padlock," wood
w/12 hangers for displaying locks,
embossed lion head w/Master logo in
mouth top right corner, one padlock
sample, marked "Master Lock Co.,
Milwaukee, Wisconsin, U.S.A.," 11⅝" w.,
23¼" h. (wood soiled & metal holders
have some rust, soiling & scratches, one
hook missing & one loose) **39**

Counter display, "Red Goose Shoes,"
model of goose drops egg & toys,
1950s-60s **185**

Florida Chewing Gum Display

Counter display box, "Florida Chewing Gum," scene of woman reclining on lounge w/packs of gum around her, marked "Florida Chewing Gum - 3 Flavors - 5¢" w/"This Box Contains 20 Packages" on bottom edge of box, along w/20 unopened packages of gum (ILLUS.) **2,530**

Counter display cabinet, "Dr. Daniels' Veterinary Medicines," wood w/tin front, depicts likeness of the doctor w/"Dr. Daniels' Warranted Veterinary Medicines - Home Treatment for Horses and Cattle Dr. Daniels' Famous Dog Remedies" & illustrations of various product containers, original contents included, 8 x 21½", 28¾" h. (edge wear, rust spotting, scratches, soiling & staining) **3,630**

Counter display cabinet, "Munyon's Homeopathic Remedies," wood w/tin front & back w/original product contents, lists products & cost on front, by Economy Sign Co., N.E. Or. Broad & Race, Phila., 17" w., 8" l., 23¾" h. (edge wear, rust spotting, scratches, soiling & staining) **990**

Counter display cabinet, "Rainbow Dyes," rectangular w/arched top, wood w/paper decals, w/original contents, marked on top, "Rainbow (over colored rainbow) - Beautifully Brilliant" & written below "One Dye For All Fabrics - No Fading - No Poison - No Ripping - No Odor - No Crocking - No Acid - Easiest - Simplest - Cleanest - Most Economical For Home Use - 10¢ a Package," 6" w., 12½" l., 16¾" h. (edge wear, scratches, soiling, staining, front edge of base missing) **825**

Counter display cabinet, "Rit Dye," tin, "New Improved Rit - Guaranteed to Fast Dye or Tint - Washes as it Dyes" on side, area in front w/slot for message to be inserted, three drawers in rear each w/three compartments, other product information on top & side, 11¼ x 14", 8¼" h. (minor denting, soiling & staining) **88**

Counter display case, "Crowley's Needles," wood, wide drawers across top & bottom w/two center rows of five small drawers, all w/original porcelain knobs, decal letters "Crowley's" across top drawer & "Needles" across bottom drawer, 9⅝ x 18¾", 9½" h. (soiling, staining, six small drawers new) **253**

Counter display case, "Feen-a-mint," tin w/oval mirror top center w/"Feen-a-mint" above woman pictured holding a tablet w/"The Chewing Laxative - Chew it Like Gum" above a picture of the product in a box, wooden base, one shelf in back for product storage, 5½ x 7½", 16¼" h. (scratches & minor paint chips & dents) **501**

Freihofer's Cakes Display Case

Counter display case, "Freihofer's Cakes," tin w/glass front & front portion of sides, three metal shelves w/wood frame, sign on top reads "Freihofer's Quality Cakes" w/"Freihofer's Quality Cakes - A cake for every taste - Pound - Sponge - Fruit" on side, minor denting, rust spotting, scratches & soiling, 24¾" w., 17" l., 27½" h. (ILLUS.) **660**

Counter display case, "Rusco Fan Belts," upright rectangular metal case w/three open shelves at the back, w/a slant-front printed w/a black ground & "Rusco Fan Belts" in white above a small red parrot saying in red "Carry a spare in your tool box," lower front panel reads "A Rusco Product...," top & sides in maroon, wood base, w/two belts, 12½ x 22", 16¾" h. (some denting, spotting, scratches & soiling) **193**

Short Horlick's Glass Display Jar

Counter display jar, cov., "Horlick's,"
cylindrical clear glass w/low domed
cover, printed in dark blue "Horlick's - The
Original Malted Milk," on both sides,
4½" d., 5¾" h. (ILLUS.). 75

Rare Early Horlick's Jar

Counter display jar, cov., "Horlick's Malted
Milk...," clear glass, tall squared footed
w/a fitted ground-rimmed domed cover
w/thumbprint border, label under glass in
white w/dark blue & red printing & gold
border, bottom embossed "Patent Applied
1889," 9¼" h. (ILLUS.) 295

Horlick's Shipping Crates

Crate, "Horlick's Malted Milk - 1/6 Doz.
Original - Genuine - Hospital - Beware of
Imitations," machine-dovetailed wood,
black lettering & red logo, held packages
for hospital use, early 20th c., 9 x 16",
13" h. (ILLUS. bottom) 145
Crate, "Horlick's Malted Milk - Racine, Wis.,"
machine-dovetailed wood, black lettering
& red logo, made to hold one dozen glass
flasks, early 20th c. (ILLUS. upper left) 80
Crate, "Horlick's Malted Milk Sample
Packages," machine-dovetailed wood
w/black printing & red logo, early 20th c.,
7 x 9", 4½" h. (ILLUS. upper right) 55
Doll, "Malto Rice," cloth, uncut, shown
w/curly dark hair, high neck top, long
sleeves, knee pants & long stockings,
instructions to side, "Copyrighted
November 1899 By The American Rice
Food And Manufacturing Co. Matawan,
N.J.," 17½" w., 34½" h. (soiling &
fold marks) 143

Michelin Man Baby Doll

Doll, "Michelin," rubber, wearing a blue bib
embossed "Michelin" & holding a Michelin
Man doll, some soil, dirt & paint loss,
4¾" w., 7" h. (ILLUS.). 138
Door push, "Bunny Bread," metal
w/"Everybody Loves (imprint of bunny
head) Bunny Enriched Bread" &
"Copyright American Bakers Cooperative,
Inc. 4.17.56," 28" w., 3" h. (some soiling
& minor paint chips) 242
Door transom window, "Mobil Gasoline,"
reverse-painted glass, rectangular long
glass panel w/an early red flying Pegasus
logo against a solid black ground w/a red
stripe across the top, set in a green-
painted wood frame, 15 x 37½" (edge
flaking, soiling & some fading) 264
Fan, "Hudson Gasoline," two-sided
cardboard w/wooden handle w/scene of
gas station w/electric pumps & tanker
trucks, "Economical Transportation with
Hudson Gasoline and Oils" & "'Always

Less' (logo) At This Sign," company blurb on reverse, 8" w., 13½" h. (staining & soiling, minor paper separation at top of fan, minor chips to fan) 176

Fire chief's hat, "Texaco," child's size, mint in box 195

Fly swatter, "Socony Oil," wire handle & bound wire mesh, "Socony Kerosene Oil Safest and Best," 17" l. (edge wear). 55

Knife sharpener, "Winchester," on original cardboard 40

Lamp, "Poll-Parrot Shoes," electric, metal base w/ "Quality speaks for itself" decal label, wood parrot cut out w/slightly curling decal & perched on an oval sign marked "Poll - Parrot - Shoes," plastic "stained glass" shade w/"Poll - Parrot - Shoes" in oval, 8" d., 19" h. (cord has small nicks) 77

Light or fan pull, "Wrigley's Gum," die-cut cardboard, figural Santa Claus, made to slide real pack of gum under his arm, shows packs of gum in Santa's pack, 6½" h. 135

Mailbox, "Standard Oil," metal, Santa Claus-type, rectangular upright green box w/curved-back letter slot at the top, locked fold-down front opening, letter slot reads "Be Sure Your Letters Are Stamped," a red, white & blue Standard oval logo above the fold-down door w/a yellow frame around red & green wording "Santa Claus Mailbox," side w/white circle at the top reading "Santa Claus, Ind. - Dec. 25 7 A.M.," lower rectangular scroll frame around wording "Letters mailed here will be postmarked with the famous Santa Claus, Ind. Postmark," contains form letter from Santa, 7¾ x 12½", 17" h. (some spotting, scratches, soiling) 253

Cerosota Flour Match Holder

Match holder, "Ceresota Flour," die-cut tin, embossed one-sided, depicts boy wearing large hat sitting on a small bench

& cutting a loaf of bread w/a knife above a barrel-shaped holder w/"Ceresota - Prize Bread Flour - of the World," minor chips, staining & scratches, 2½" w., 5½" h. (ILLUS.) 303

Matchbook, "Keen Kutter" 15

Menu, "Borden," depicts Elsie the Cow, 2 pp. 14

Mirror, "Angelus Marshmallows," round pocket-type 100

Mirror, "Big Joe Flour," round pocket-type 40

Mirror, "Excelsior Gasoline," round pocket-type, celluloid on metal back, celluloid printed across the upper border w/white stars on a blue ground & around the lower border w/red & white stripes, a large gilt scroll-bordered white center reserve printed in red & blue "EXCELSIOR - Motor Oils & Grease - GASOLINE - Lubricating Oils - For All Purposes," the lower border overprinted in black "C. E. Mills Oil Co., Syracuse, N.Y.," 2" d. (scratches on mirror, soiling & scratches on back) 83

Horlick's Pocket Mirror w/White Border

Mirror, "Horlick's Malted Milk," round pocket-type, celluloid, the top w/a round central scene of a young dairy maid holding a can of the product & standing beside Jersey cow printed w/"Ask For Horlick's at all Fountains," white outer border band w/blue letters reading "The Original Malted Milk - Ask For Horlick's Avoid Substitutions," 2" d. (ILLUS.) 85

Horlick's Pocket Mirror w/Gold Border

Mirror, "Horlick's Malted Milk," round pocket-type, celluloid, the top w/a round central scene of a young dairy maid holding a can of the product & standing beside Jersey cow printed w/"Ask for Horlick's at all Druggists," the gold outer border band printed in blue w/"The Diet for Infants Invalids and Nursing Mothers - The Original Malted Milk - Ask For Horlick's - Avoid Substitutions," 2" d. (ILLUS.) 85

Mirror, "Kansas Expansion Flour," round pocket-type 45

Old Reliable Coffee Mirror

Mirror, "Old Reliable Coffee," round pocket-type, celluloid over metal, figure of man smoking cigar leaning on an Old Reliable coffee can, minor scratches & soiling, chips & soiling to edges, 2" d. (ILLUS.) 94

Red Goose Shoes Mirror

Mirror, "Red Goose Shoes," counter-type, reverse-painted glass in wood frame, metal handle at top w/metal stand on sides to allow mirror to stand up on counter, logo near top, paint loss, scratches & wear to frame, very minor cracking of paint to goose, 15½" w., 21¾" h. (ILLUS.) 303

Mirror, "Traveler's Insurance," round pocket-type 35

Ceramic Horlicks Mixer

Mixer, "Horlicks," tall cylindrical ceramic body w/a small rim spout & C-form strap handle, w/metal interior mixer mechanism, white w/blue label on the side w/white wording "Horlicks Mixer," made by Alfred Meakin, England, early 20th c., 3" d., 7¾" h. (ILLUS.) 60

Moving picture book, "Kellogg's Funny Jungleland," dated 1932, 6½ x 8" 48

Horlicks Restaurant Ware Mug

Mug, "Horlicks," ceramic, heavy duty restaurant ware in beige w/brown script name on side, made by Shenango China, Newcastle, Pennsylvania, 20th c. (ILLUS.) 25

English Horlicks Mug

Mug, "Horlicks," ceramic, tall swelled cylindrical form w/ear handle, white w/orange lettering, made in England, 20th c., 3" h. (ILLUS.) 20

Early Horlick's Advertising Pamphlet

Pamphlet, "Horlick's Malted Milk," printed paper, black & white printing on cover w/scene of a dairy maid standing beside a cow in a meadow, back cover showing a factory scene & three sizes of the powder available, late 19th - early 20th c., matted & framed open (ILLUS.) 6

Paper clip, "Culter Proctor Stoves," w/celluloid picture 65

Paperweight, "Bell Telephone Company," bell-shaped, cobalt blue glass w/fired on white lettering on two sides, 3¼" d., 3" h. 209

Paperweight, "Chalmers Motor Company," rectangular, brass, "Chalmers" embossed top center flanked by embossed automobiles, center embossed scene of factory w/"The Home Of The - Chalmers Motor Company - Detroit, Mich." embossed at bottom flanked by logos, 3½" w., 2¼" h. 132

Paperweight, "Violet Ray Lens," cornflower colored glass w/figure of baby on base imprinted w/"Safety First" & "Use Violet Ray Lens," 3⅛" h. plus base (some soiling & dirt in engraved areas) 110

Pencil, "Lion Head Motor Oil," plastic & metal, yellow & red w/"Lion (logo) Head," sample of oil sealed in top, 5½" l. (wear to pocket clip, scratches) 66

Pinback button, "Empire Cream Separator," white celluloid over metal, cream separator in center w/"I Chirp for the EMPIRE Because It Makes the Most Dollars For Me" around top blue border & "Empire Cream Separator Co. - Bloomfield, N.J." at bottom, paper on back w/"Empire Cream Separator Co. Bloomfield, New Jersey," 1¼" d., (minor soiling) 44

Pinback button, "Westfield Steam Laundry," celluloid over metal, depicts horse pulling wagon above "Carrington & Grout - Proprietors" w/"Compliments of - Westfield Steam Laundry Westfield, Mass." in white lettering around blue border, 1¾" d. (minor soiling) 11

Esso "Drip" Pins

Pins, "Esso," enameled metal, figural "Happy" & girlfriend waving, pr. (ILLUS.) 94

Newer Horlicks Pitcher

Pitcher, "Horlicks," ceramic, bulbous body tapering to a flat rim w/wide spout, large C-form handle, royal blue ground printed w/thin red swirled lines alternating w/yellow grain heads, name printed in white, base marked "Churchill England," 4½" h. (ILLUS.) 27

Old Smuggler & Pinch Bar Pitchers

Pitcher, "Old Smuggler Scotch Whiskey," bar-type, ceramic, figural toby-style, all-white bust of man wearing tricorn hat w/wording & gold trim (ILLUS. left) 121

Pitcher, "Pinch - The Dimple," bar-type, ceramic, flattened ovoid form w/indented sides & short flaring neck, all-white w/gold printed logo near the base (ILLUS. right) 69

Advertising Bar Pitchers

Pitcher, "Plymouth Gin," bar-type, ceramic, figural fish w/wide open mouth forming spout & tail forming handle, embossed wording, dark green glaze (ILLUS. left) **32**

Pitcher, "White Horse Scotch Whiskey," bar-type, ceramic, triangular foot & body w/long spout & angled handle, dark blue w/white wording & profile of a horse (ILLUS. right) **66**

Plates, 8" d., "Esso," ceramic, center cartoon illustration of dog w/small Esso logo by front paws, black & white, pr. (minor soiling & small chips on back) **55**

Playing cards, "Planters," w/Mr. Peanut, complete deck **1,375**

Pocket knife, "Esso Gasoline," debossed metal, gas pump-shaped w/"Standard" on globe & "Essoline" on base, 2½" l. (minor wear & scratches) **165**

Early Horlick's Postcard

Postcard, "Horlick's Malted Milk," color-tinted card showing herd of cows in a wooded meadow, wording in red & blue "Homeward Bound - Original - Genuine - HORLICK'S MALTED MILK - FOR ALL AGES," reverse printed w/offer "Send 10 cents for a Speedy Mixer," early 20th c. (ILLUS.) **8**

Poster, "Eveready Radio Batteries," lithographed paper w/archival backing, colorful outdoor scene of group of young boys in makeshift "Broadcasting Studio" w/box marked "Eveready Radio Batteries," dated "1930" & signed

Eveready Radio Batteries Poster

"Jackson," fold marks, creases, scuffs, thumbtack marks at top touched up, 24" w., 32" h. (ILLUS.) **242**

Poster, "Satin Skin," lithographed paper w/archival backing w/"Satin Skin Powder - 4 Tints, Flesh, White, Pink, Brunet." above a colorful bust portrait of a young brunette lady w/flowers in her upswept hair holding a fan which reads "Don't You Want Satin Skin," flanked by two containers & "Satin Skin Cream - Copyright, 1903 by Albert F. Wood. MFR. The Satin Toilet Specialties, Detroit, Mich." below, gold, red, white, & green w/black lettering, 30¾" w., 45" h. (very minor soiling) **110**

Poster, "Kickapoo Joy Juice," lithographed paper, 22 x 28¾" **170**

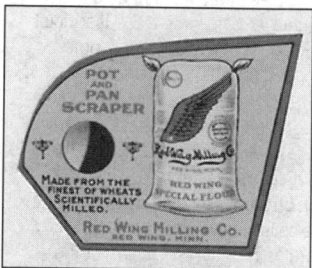

Rare Red Wing Flour Pot Scraper

Pot scraper, "Red Wing Special Flour," printed metal, blade-form w/finger hole, dark yellow ground w/red border printed w/white flour sack w/red & black printing, red & black printing around the sack reads "Pot and Pan Scraper - Made from the Finest of Wheats - Scientifically Milled - Red Wing Milling Co. - Red Wing, Minn.," early 20th c. (ILLUS.) **1,155**

Puzzle, "Hills Bros.Coffee," jig saw-type, model of a black coffeepot, steam rising from spout & sitting on yellow & orange flames, can of coffee in center w/logo & "Hills Bros. Coffee," various colorful scenes of people at different times of day w/"Where's the fire?" near the handle & beneath the flames "It's under a pot of Hills Bros Coffee ...No One Can Resist That Marvelous Aroma, Copyright 1933 by Hills Bros," framed under glass, along w/original box, 14" w., 16" h. (box has edge wear & fading overall) **99**

Puzzle, "Kellogg," jig saw-type, lithographed on cardboard, depicts boy on scooter w/dog running beside, "No 3398 Corp. 1933 Kellogg Co" bottom left corner & "Printed U.S.A." right corner, matted & in newer frame, 8¾" w., 10¾" h. (minor fading, soiling, scuff mark under boy's elbow, sticker residue on glass bottom right corner) **72**

Radio, "Champion Spark Plug," plastic model of spark plug on pyamid-shaped base, working condition, 5 x 8½", 15" h. **220**

Radio, "Poll-Parrot Shoes," brown plastic cube-shaped, battery-operated w/"Poll-Parrot Shoes - For Boys And Girls" in white letters on one side, w/"Quality Speaks for Itself" on opposite side, other sides w/battery compartment, tuning & volume controls & speaker & on/off switch, colorful composition parrot sits on top on a yellow perch w/"Poll-Parrot Shoes" in black letters, radio by General Electric, 3¾" w., 11" h. (soiling) **105**

Rug, "Buster Brown Shoes," round Acrilan Acrylic, center design of Buster Brown & his dog Tige in red, blue, orange, yellow & blue on yellow ground, blue border w/five yellow stars, marked "Carpet by Magee Pattern C189-2C SS5-8" AA Permanently mothproof, Bloomsburg, PA Perry, GA.," 47½" d. **770**

Ruler, "Peters Shoes," wooden **18**

Ruler, "Breyer's Ice Cream," brass edge, ca. 1951, 85th anniversary commemorative, 12" l. . . **5**

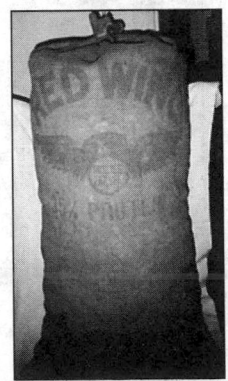
Red Wing Gunny Sack

Sack, "Red Wing," 100 lb. gunny sack, marked "Red Wing - 35% Protein Linseed Meal, Red Wing, Minn." (ILLUS.) **75**

Salt & pepper shakers, "Borden Company," ceramic, figural bust of cows, Elmer & Elsie, shaded brown, "C Borden" on base, 2⅜" w., 4" h. pr. (corks missing, Elmer w/small marks on right arm) **99**

Plastic Gas Pump Shakers

Salt & pepper shakers, "Co-Op Gasoline," plastic gas pump-shaped, one pale green, one cream, each w/advertising decals on the sides, one side resembling a gas pump, the opposite side reading "See your Co-Op first," ragged edges to decals, 2¾" h., pr. (ILLUS.) **143**

Salt & pepper shakers, "Sealtest Milk," glass bottle-shaped, pr. **40**

Scale, "Purina Cow Chow," rectangular, brass front, metal back, w/hanging loop at top & S-hook at bottom, "Cow Chow Makes More Milk" at top w/"Don 't Guess Use This Purina Milk Scale" at the bottom, 4½" w., 15½" h. (minor edge wear, scratches & soiling) **66**

Screen door, "Sunbeam Bread," painted on lettering "Reach For - Sunbeam - Bread with a Bonus" w/tin door push w/"Reach for Sunbeam Bread," wooden frame & wagon wheel trim, 34" w., 82" h. (overall wear from use, door push & handle scratched, paint loss & rust) **468**

Shipping box, "Doublemint Gum," cardboard, lithographed to resemble Doublemint labels, ca. 1950s, 9 x 13½ x 16" . . . **65**

Sign, "Borden Company," one-sided die-cut porcelain on wooden platform w/easel support, yellow & white neon lights, head w/ring of flowers around neck & front paws of Elsie (porcelain chips around edges, corners & along bottom edge, creases, denting, fading, scratches, soiling & staining) **1,870**

Buster Brown Shoes Sign

Sign, "Buster Brown Shoes," silk-screened cloth, cushioned & mounted on die-cut wood, "Buster Brown" & "Tige" the dog, two separate pieces added together for 3D effect, green, red & brown, edge wear, tips have fabric wear, 24" w., 20" h. (ILLUS.) **385**

Sign, "Captain Kidd Beverages," lithographed tin **1,650**

Sign, "Finck's Overalls," stand up-type, die-cut painted cardboard w/easel back, pig shape w/"Finck's - Detroit-Special - Overalls - 'Wear Like a Pig's Nose.'" w/"For Sale Here" & "'Union Made'" on base, 34¾" w., 14½" h. (creases, edge wear, scratches, soiling & warped). **198**

Honey-Fruit Gum Sign

Sign, "Honey-Fruit Gum," tin over cardboard, rectangular, black ground printed w/white package of gum, white wording "Nothing Like It - Delightful Flavor" (ILLUS.). **2,750**

Sign, "King Cole Tea & Coffee," one-sided die-cut porcelain w/colorful illustration of King Cole character wearing large crown, ruffles at neck & wrists, holding a steaming cup in one hand, saucer in the other, blue, red, black, white & yellow, 9" w., 15" h. (minor rust spotting on back, staining & scratches to front) **1,430**

Sign, "Kodak Camera" window display w/scene of a couple in a canoe. **1,650**

Sign, "Moxie Soda," cardboard, stand-up w/Ted Williams **1,925**

Sign, "National Biscuit," colored-paper, pictures silent film star of 1920s, Diana Allen, holding a plate of cookies above "National Biscuit Company Does My Baking," newer frame, 20" w., 27" h. (minor tears & wear to edges, fold mark across center) **1,650**

Wise Potato Chip Sign

Sign, "Wise Potato Chips," die-cut stand-up cardboard, lithographed figure of owl perched on log, "Wise Potato Chips" in white lettering on breast & bag of chips near wing, copyright Wise Delicatessen Co. Litho in U.S.A., tape repair to edges, corner on back & to vertical crease at end of log, ears w/bent tips, piece of cardboard added for support on easel, 20" w., 29½" h. (ILLUS.). **715**

Wonder Bread Howdy Doody Sign

Sign, "Wonder Bread," die-cut heavy paper, jointed Howdy Doody character, plaid shirt, jeans & boots, "C Kagran printed in U.S.A.," 1" d. top layer paper in hair missing, very minor wear to edges, some fading, 5½" w., 13" h. (ILLUS.) . . . . **200 to 300**

Spool holder, "Corticelli Silk Thread," metal, rotates **65**

Rare Texaco Stained Glass Window

Stained glass window, "Texaco," round
  w/wire frame, large red logo star w/green
  "T" surrounded by white & w/"Texaco"
  painted in black across the top, some
  cracks to glass "T," one piece of star
  replaced, 21¾" d. (ILLUS.) **1,375**

Rare Stick of Yellow Kid Chewing Gum

Stick of chewing gum, "Yellow Kid
  Chewing Gum," wrapper in white
  w/center picture of Yellow Kid dressed in
  yellow, lettering in black w/red trim, early
  20th c. (ILLUS.) **1,265**
Store display, "Model Smoking Tobacco,"
  die-cut cardboard w/"Model Man," as a
  cigar store Indian, ca. 1940s, 12" h. **65**
Store display box, "Wrigley's Spearmint
  Gum," cardboard, looks like oversized
  pack of gum, ca. 1950s, 8½ x 10 x 36" **175**
Store display rack, "Poll-Parrot Shoes,"
  metal cage, post & shoe holders w/green,
  yellow & red plastic parrot in center,
  wooden sign base & red oval sign on top
  w/"Poll-Parrot," separate motor unit,
  metal case & cardboard cover attaches to
  metal housing unit to make parrot &
  shoes spin, 20" w., 33" h. (paint chips to
  post, soiling & small paint chips to cage,
  shoe holders & parrot) **160**

Phillips 66 Stovepipe

Stovepipe, "Phillips 66," tall metal cylinder
  printed w/orange ground w/thin white
  pinstripes & wide white band printed in
  black "Motor Oil" below white circle
  w/orange & black company logo, denting,
  rust spotting, scratches, soiling, 8" d.,
  21¼" h. (ILLUS.) **110**

Sunbeam Bread String Holder

String holder "Sunbeam Bread," painted tin,
  both sides w/Little Miss Sunbeam eating
  a slice of bread, string mounted inside on
  metal rod, red, blue, yellow & white, paint
  chips & loss w/cracking of paint overall,
  90% paint loss on reverse side, 13" w.,
  16" h. (ILLUS.) **105**
Table, "Calumet Baking Powder," child's,
  wooden body & legs w/white porcelain
  top w/letters of the alphabet in a semi-
  circle at the top above the red & blue
  Calumet logo & "The Kind Mother Uses"
  & the numbers 1 through 10 below, blue
  lettering, numbers & edge, 16" w., 20" l.,
  18" h. (one leg loose, rust spotting on
  edges, cracking to porcelain, minor
  fading, scratches, soiling & staining) **721**

Thermometer, "Birley's Orange Drink," tin, 4½ x 19¾" 350

Thermometer, "Clark Bar," rectangular, wood w/glass bulb & metal fasteners, image of Clark bar over a clock w/"4PM - 'Clark Bar O'Clock'" & "Clark Bar - Join The Millions In This Mid-Afternoon Candy Delight," 5½" w., 19" h. (paint loss, fading & soiling 204

Thermometer, "Hills Bros. Coffee," one sided porcelain, an Arab man wearing a long yellow robe drinking coffee, red, yellow, white & black, 8½" w., 20½" h. (touch up to mounting holes, edges & around lip of thermometer edge, very minor surface rust on back) 495

Thermometer, "Mobil," tin & glass, large round tin disk in white printed w/black numbers around the border, the center w/a grey & red rectangular reserve w/"Mobil" in black letters over a small red Pegasus logo, round glass front, ca. 1957, 12" d. (soiling denting in back, minor paint cracking near top) 440

Thermometer, "NuGrape Soda," tin, oblong w/rounded ends, glass tube in center w/"Drink NuGrape Soda" above a row of six bottles & "A Flavor You Can't Forget" below, 6¾" w., 16" h. (soiling, denting & paint chips, some white paint drops) 99

Thermometer, "Peters Weatherbird Shoes," oblong porcelain w/glass tube, bird logo at top over "Peters - Weatherbird," & "Peters - Diamond - Brand - Shoes - Solid Leather Footwear" at the bottom, "Pat. March 16, 1915 Beach, Coshocton, O.," white, black & red, 7" w., 27" h. (soiling & chips to mounting holes & edges) 176

Thermometer, "Sauer's Flavoring Extracts," wood w/glass tube, "Sauer's Flavoring Extracts" in red above "None Better - 10 and 25¢ - Sixteen Highest Awards and Gold Medals - Purity Strength and Fine Flavor - The G.F. Sauer Co., Richmond, VA" in black letters, ¾ x 7", 23½" h. (some rust to brackets holding glass, soiling & paint chips, does not work) 193

Thermometer, "Shell Gasoline," porcelain, narrow oblong form w/orange printing on dark yellow ground, a shell logo at the top reading "Shell Gasoline," & another at the bottom reading "Shell Motor Oil," w/original tube, patent-dated in 1915, strong luster, 7¼" w., 27" h. (chips at mounting holes & edges). 1,980

Toy, "Colt," pewter toy six-gun on original cardboard advertising, early 45

Toy, "Planters Peanuts," rubber squeeze-type, model of standing Mr. Peanut in tan, black & white, early 20th c. (ILLUS. top next column). 1,870

Rare Mr. Peanut Squeeze Toy

Toy, "Winchester," toy pewter rifle w/Winchester clown on small display board, ca. 1953 45

Texaco Fire Chief Hat

Toy fire chief hat, "Texaco," plastic w/microphone & speaker attached, shield in front w/ logo & "Texaco Fire Chief" held by eagle on top of hat, original box & instructions, box w/tears, faded & pieces missing on edges, 14¼" l., 8" h. (ILLUS.). 110

Toy truck, "Sunshine Biscuits," metal, battery-operated, yellow w/"Sunshine Biscuits" in red lettering, Goodrich Silvertown tires, Metalcraft Corp. St. Louis, U.S.A., insert batteries through front, 12" l. (front replaced, back doors missing, lights not working) 176

Toys, "Winchester," pewter red hunter & moose on original cardboard advertising display, ca. 1953, the set 150

Tray, "Howertown Sanitary Dairy," metal, square, "Howertown Sanitary Dairy - Clarified and Pasteurized Milk and Cream" above milk bottle w/image of baby & a circle reading "Mothers Darling Fine as Silk - Because She Uses Our Milk" & flanked by "Grade A Guernsey Butter & Cottage Cheese" on right side & "Phone 644 - Northampton, PA. - R.F.D.

Howertown Sanitary Dairy Tray

No. 1" on the left, Wm. H. Kleppinger
Prop, Northampton, Pa., paint chips to
edges, minor denting, edge wear,
scratches & soiling, 13¼" sq. (ILLUS.) **72**
Yardstick, "Hi-Park Guernsey Milk, Red
Wing, Minn.," wooden. **50**

ARCHITECTURAL ITEMS

*In recent years the growing interest in and
support for historic preservation has spawned a
greater appreciation of the fine architectural
elements which were an integral part of early
building, both public and private. Where, in
decades past, structures might be razed and
doors, fireplace mantels, windows, etc., hauled to
the dump, today all interior and exterior details
from unrestorable buildings are salvaged to be
offered to home restorers, museums and even
builders who want to include a bit of history in a
new construction project.*

Ornate Copper Building Finial

Building finial, molded copper, a flaring
square pedestal w/a small square
stepped platform supporting a tall urn
flanked by long S-scroll handles & w/a
scroll & fleur-de-lis finial, fine verdigris, on
modern wood base, repair, minor dents &
seam splits, America, 19th c., 61½" h.
(ILLUS.) **$3,220**
Door, painted pine, four-paneled door w/two
small raised panels over two long raised
panels, old dark patina & a daub of blue
paint, Shaker-made, from the Whitewater,
Ohio Community, 30 x 77¼" **330**
Fan-carved panel, for a window or
doorway, in a half-round frame,
weathered surface w/black & yellow
repaint, 19th c., 36" w., 18" h. **330**
Fireplace mantel, painted pine, Federal
style, the flaring top shelf w/molded
edges above a stepped narrow dentil-
carved band over a wide frieze band
w/reeded & swag-carved end & center
blocks above a molded opening frame
flanked by reeded pilasters ending
stepped block feet, old black paint, early
19th c., 58¾" w., 52¾" h. (piece of end
molding on shelf replaced) **1,100**

Ornate Renaissance Revival Mantel

Fireplace mantel, Victorian Renaissance
Revival substyle, gilt-lined walnut & burl
walnut, the molded blocked top shelf
w/heavy deeply blocked front posts
w/rondels & gilt-trimmed line incising
flanking the recessed central frieze band
w/narrow rectangular panels w/raised
beaded molding flanking central blocks
w/a central carved head, the side blocks
over ornate scroll-, shell-, knob- and
block-turned pilasters w/stepped block
bases all w/gilt-incised trim, outer side
framing w/quarter-round columns
w/further gilt-trimmed incised decoration,
third quarter 19th c., American (ILLUS.) **2,310**
Gate, wrought iron, an arched top centered
by S-scrolls & a spearpoint finial above
two smaller arches enclosing spearpoints
all above seven vertical bars supported
by three cross bars, shield-shaped center
label reads "Cincinnati Iron Fence Co.,"
old black & silver paint, second half
19th c., w/latch & hinges, 31" w., 46" h. **358**

Wall panels, painted & decorated wood, narrow rectangular form w/molded frame border darkly painted & enclosing a cream-colored ground outlined in green paint w/painted ovolu corners, centered by red birds w/a green-eaved branch w/red berries, central Massachusetts, ca. 1810, 11 x 48¾" & 12 x 46⅞", pr. (minor paint imperfections, molding losses) **27,600**

Window, round w/eight divided lights, white painted frame, America, 19th c., 33½" d. (minor imperfections) **431**

Window grill, painted wood, rectangular molding w/eight triangular panes formed by rayed muntins joined to a central oval axis, weathered old green & white repaint, 21¼ x 46½" **182**

Window valances, relief carved & painted wood w/stylized acanthus blossoms & leafage, painted dark brown, highlighted w/gilding, 19th c., 40½" l., 5½" h. **632**

ART DECO

Interest in Art Deco, a name given an art movement stemming from the Paris International Exhibition of 1925, continues to grow today. This style flowered in the 1930s and actually continued into the 1940s. A mood of flippancy is found in its varied characteristics: zigzag lines resembling the lightning bolt, sometimes steps, often the use of sharply contrasting colors such as black and white and others. Look for prices for the best examples of Art Deco design to continue to rise. Also see JEWELRY, MODERN.

Book ends, patinated metal, figural nude dancing maidens on a felted half-oval base, impressed "203" near base, ca. 1930, 6½" h., pr. **$230**

Clock, mantel-type, alabaster, onyx & patinated metal, a long rectangular white & black onyx base centered by a round white alabaster frame around the dial w/Arabic numerals, dial flanked on the base by large brass patinated metal models of peacocks, 3½ x 23½", 9" h. **143**

Clock, table model, amber Bakelite case, marked "Lackner, Neon-Glo Clock, Cincinnati," 3 x 6¼", 6½" h. **345**

Cocktail shaker, figural, ruby red glass model of a tall lady's boot mounted in chrome straps, 1930s, 6½" w., 15" h. (some metal pitting) **173**

Art Deco Sculpture

Figure group, alabaster, stylized female nude kneeling near reclining fawn, Italy, 14" l., 14" h. (ILLUS.) **253**

Figure of a woman, cast metal w/silvered enamel finish, the nude dancer w/one leg raised, her head tilted to one side & one arm raised & bent at the elbow, on a square foot, 13" h. **127**

Floor lamps, silver-leaf, architectonic-style, a tall slender tapering hexagonal standard above a flaring stepped base on eight ball feet, American-made, ca. 1930, 68½" h., pr. **5,750**

Lamp, accent-type, a cast-metal enameled bronze-finished figure of a seated nude woman w/her head leaning forward to rest on one raised knee, on a stepped rectangular plinth in front of a fan-shaped caramel slag glass lighted panel, 12½" l. **144**

Lamp, table model, bronze, geometric perched bird, unsigned, 1930s, 5½" w., 23½" h. **374**

Lamp, table model, ceramic globular form glazed in black & silver w/a geometric design, inscribed "Alsy—Made in France," mid-20th c., 9" h. **402**

Art Deco Lamp

Lamp, table model, green crackle glass globe on rectangular base flanked by kneeling female nudes (ILLUS.) **400**

Panel, wrought iron, rectangular openwork design w/a stylized standing mountain lion above a stylized leaping horse above a band of large graduated scrolls, all within a hammered scrollwork border, in the manner of William Hunt Diederich, ca. 1920s, 26½ x 38¼" **1,840**

Table, side-type, wrought iron, a circular marble top raised on double square iron legs, France, ca. 1930, 20" d., 27" h......... **747**

Tea & coffee set: cov. teapot, cov. coffeepot, cov. sugar bowl & creamer; silver, each on a stepped round foot, the teapot, creamer & sugar w/half-round flat-topped bodies, the coffeepot w/a tall slightly tapering cylindrical body w/a long narrow spout down the front, angled & curved handles, ca. 1930s, coffeepot 10" h., the set **690**

Art Deco Vase

Vase, 6½" h., 6½" d., ceramic, spherical form w/green & black geometric design, marked "Sevres," France (ILLUS.) **489**

Wall sconces, molded glass & gilt-bronze, each w/two panels of grey glass molded in low-relief w/foliage, teardrops & serpentine channels fitting into a stepped tapering gilt-bronze frame cast w/serpentine channels, teardrops & swags, impressed "LB 16224," France, ca. 1928, 15¾" w., 26" h., pr. **4,025**

Wall scones, bronze, each w/a shaped rectangular back plate supporting a single curved socket arm, polished, in the manner of Emile-Jacques Ruhlmann, unsigned, France, ca. 1925, 18" h, pr. **3,335**

ART NOUVEAU

Art Nouveau's primary thrust was between 1890 and 1905, but commercial Art Nouveau productions continued until about World War I. This style was a rebellion against historic tradition in art. Using natural forms as inspiration, it is primarily characterized by undulating or wave-like lines and whiplashes.

Many objects were made in materials ranging from glass to metals. Figural pieces with seductive maidens with long, flowing hair are especially popular in this style. Interest in Art Nouveau remains high, with the best pieces by well known designers bringing strong prices. Also see FURNITURE, JEWELRY (ANTIQUE), and MUCHA ARTWORK.

Armchairs, carved mahogany, each w/carved flaring corners centering an upholstered back & seat raised on tapering legs, upholstered in yellow fabric, designed by Louis Majorelle, France, ca. 1900, pr. **$1,380**

Bar cabinet, oak, of simple rectangular form, the door decorated w/a bust of a woman & poppies, Europe, ca. 1900, 17 x 17¾", 71" h. **488**

Box, cov., wood & brass, a rectangular two-drawer box w/embossed flower & vine design in brass, inset w/colored glass flower centers, signed "Daguet," Europe, early 20th c., 8 x 14½", 5½" h. **345**

Bust of a maiden, porcelain, wearing a diaphanous gown w/grape clusters in her hair & on her shoulder, raised on a rectangular blue lustre base, impressed marks, Europe, ca. 1900, 24" h. **1,380**

Candelabra, gilt-metal, figural, three-light, the stem modeled as a young Art Nouveau maiden w/long flowing hair & wearing a long swirling gown gathering at the bottom to form the foot, her arms behind her head where three serpentine candlearms extend out & upward, each terminating in an iris-form candle cup, Europe, ca. 1900, 13" h. (gilt wear) **632**

Clock, figural table model, enameled cast white metal, relief-cast design w/a head of a woman w/flowing hair, leaves & thistles, Seth Thomas movement, round dial w/Roman numerals, ca. 1900, 12½" h. (some minor wear) **288**

Art Nouveau Silver Desk Set

Desk set: pen tray, letter opener, rocker
blotter, stamp box, inkstand, candlestick,
picture frame, letter scale, match holder &
letter rack; silver, each piece decorated
w/a stylized clover design, in original
fitted case, Europe, ca. 1900, inkstand
13" l., the set (ILLUS.) **2,300**

English Art Nouveau Fireplace Mantel

Fireplace mantel, cast iron, the whole of
keyhole outline, cast above w/a nude
maiden seated among waves & within a
shell, flanked by tendrils & stylized plants,
surmounted by a shaped shelf cast w/a
fish, all above a rectangular opening
hung w/a panel cast w/a fish & mounted
w/a grate flanked by stylized plants, the
back molded "No. 509 - 14 FIRE - Rd.
No. 458335," England, ca. 1900,
37½" w., 67" h. (ILLUS.) **7,475**

Lamp, oil-type, brass, of goblet form,
worked overall in a thistle design, signed
"Lalou," France, ca. 1900, 17" h. **460**

Lamp, table model, figural, silvered metal,
the base depicting a standing woman
gazing into a mirror, signed "P. Philippe,"
ca. 1900, 25" h. **1,840**

Pitcher, cov., copper & brass, the tall gently
waisted copper body w/a stepped base &
the side panels w/raised geometric linear
designs, a brass rim spout, hinged
paneled cover w/loop handle & thumb
rest attached to a long slender looped
brass handle down one side, possibly
French, marked on the base w/a shield &
"C.D.E.," late 19th to early 20th c.,
15" h., 7" w. **595**

Majorelle Art Nouveau Table

Table, carved mahogany & ormolu-
mounted burled walnut, triangular
shaped top w/molded sides raised
on three slender tapering shaped legs
w/floral & scrolled leaf ormolu mounts,
joined by a triangular medial shelf,
designed by Louis Majorelle, France,
ca. 1900, 22½" w., 30½" h. (ILLUS.) **8,050**

Tea & coffee service: cov. teapot, cov.
coffeepot, open sugar bowl & creamer;
silver, each piece of bulbous inverted
pear shape w/a squared flaring base &
the corners impressed w/scrolling foliage
centering buds, bud finials on the covers,
Germany, ca. 1900, coffeepot 9¾" h.,
the set **2,070**

Tray, pierced mixed-metal frame holding a
porcelain insert decorated w/yellow water
iris & lily pads against a green, blue &
white ground, late 19th c., Europe **575**

Umbrella stand, silvered metal, figural,
cylindrical form w/a semi-nude maiden
holding flowers, signed "Piguemal,"
France, ca. 1900, 28" h. **1,955**

Vase, cut glass & silver plate, of shaped
square section, the vase cut w/stylized
flowers, set in a frame set w/panels
depicting women picking flowers, signed
"W.M.F.," Germany, early 20th c., 16" h. **1,380**

Vase, porcelain, figural, a pedestal base
supporting a tall ovoid body all entwined
w/long leafy stems & a trumpet flower,
applied at the shoulder w/a seated Art
Nouveau maiden wearing a diaphanous
robe, glazed in shades of green, yellow &
purple, ivory, rush & gilt, underglaze-blue
maker's mark, impressed "9790-16,"
Europe, ca. 1900, 20" h. **2,530**

AUDUBON PRINTS

John James Audubon, American ornithologist and artist, is considered the finest nature artist in history. About 1820 he conceived the idea of having a full color book published portraying every known species of American bird in its natural habitat. He spent years in the wilderness capturing their beauty in vivid color only to have great difficulty finding a publisher. In 1826 he visited England, received immediate acclaim, and selected Robert Havell as his engraver. "Birds of America," when completed, consisted of four volumes of 435 individual plates, double-elephant folio size, which are a combination of aquatint, etching and line engraving. W. H. Lizars of Edinburgh engraved the first ten plates of this four volume series. These were later retouched by Havell who produced the complete set between 1827 and early 1839. In the 1840s, another definitive work, "Viviparous Quadrupeds of North America," containing 150 plates, was published in America. Prices for Audubon's original double-elephant folio size prints are very high and beyond the means of the average collector. Subsequent editions of "Birds of America," especially the chromolithographs done by Julius Bien in New York (1859-60) and the smaller octavo (7 x 10½") edition of prints done by J. T. Bowen of Philadelphia in the 1840s, are those that are most frequently offered for sale. Anyone interested in Audubon prints needs to be aware that many photographically-produced copies of the prints have been issued during this century for use on calendars or as decorative accessories, so it is best to check with a print expert before spending a large sum on an Audubon purported to be from an early edition.

American Bison or Buffalo - Plate LVI, hand-colored lithograph by J.T. Bowen, Philadelphia, ca. 1845, framed, 21¼ x 27⅛" (slight discoloration at sheet edges). . **$9,200**

American Bison or Buffalo - Plate LVII, hand-colored lithograph by J.T. Bowen, Philadelphia, ca. 1845, framed, 22 x 28½" (slight mat stain & minor soiling at sheet edges) **9,200**

Annulated Marmot Squirrel - Plate LXXIX, hand-colored lithograph by J.T. Bowen, Philadelphia, ca. 1845, framed, 21⅞ x 28" (mat stain, foxing & a few repaired tears, primarily in margins) **690**

Bay-Winged Bunting, Male - Plate 94, hand-colored etching, engraving & aquatint by Robert Havell, Jr., London, 1827-38, framed, 22⅛ x 32⅝" (faint light- and mat stain & a few inconspicuous specks of foxing) **920**

Bewick's Wren - Plate XVIII, hand-colored etching, engraving & aquatint by Robert Havell, Jr., London, 1827-38, 17½ x 24⅞" **345**

Black Vulture or Carrion Crow - Plate 3, chromolithograph by J. Bien, New York, 1860, framed, 26 x 38½" (tears in sheet edges, few pin holes in margins, faint damp staining & few specks of foxing along lower sheet edge) **345**

Black Warrior - Plate LXXXVI, hand-colored etching, engraving & aquatint by Robert Havell, Jr., London, 1827-38, framed, 26⅜ x 39" (foxing, few tiny tears in sheet edges, small loss in lower right corner - sheet somewhat rippled) **4,887**

Boat Tailed Grackle

Boat Tailed Grackle - Plate CLXXXVII, hand-colored etching, engraving & aquatint by Robert Havell, Jr., London, 1827-38, framed, slight discoloration at sheet edges & short tear in bottom margin, 6 x 35⅜" (ILLUS.) **3,105**

Brown Pelican

Brown Pelican - Plate CCLI, hand-colored etching, engraving & aquatint by Robert Havell, London, 1827-38, two tiny tears in

upper sheet edges, few pale specks of
foxing, primarily in background at right,
25¼ x 38" (ILLUS.) **63,000**

Carolina Parrot - Plate 278,
chromolithograph by J. Bien, New York,
New York, 1860, framed, 26 x 38⅜"
(light-stain, foxing & a few repaired tears
along the sheet edges) **5,750**

Fish Hawk

Fish Hawk - Plate 81, hand-colored etching,
engraving & aquatint by Robert Havell,
Jr., London, 1827-38, framed, 25⅝ x
38½" (foxing) **46,000**

Glossy Ibis - Plate 385, chromolithograph
by J. Bien, New York, New York, 1860,
framed, 26 x 32⅞" (tears & losses in
lower outer margin, faint foxing &
discoloration in margins, faint backboard
stain on verso, masking tape stain in
lower & upper edges, verso) **2,415**

**Golden-Winged Warbler, Cape May
Warbler - Plate CCCXIV,** hand-colored
etching, engraving & aquatint by Robert
Havell, London, 1827-38, 26 x 39¼"
(sheet edges w/slight discoloration, tiny
loss at bottom sheet edge w/faint offprint
& stitch holes along disbound sheet edge) . . **1,725**

**Golden-Winged Warbler, Cape May
Warbler - Plate CCCXIV,** hand-colored
etching, engraving & aquatint by Robert
Havell, London, 1827-38, framed, 20⅛ x
28" (foxing, margins folded back
w/discoloration along creases) **345**

Great American Cock Male (Plate 1)

Cock of the Plains

Cock of the Plains - Plate CCCLXXI, hand-
colored etching, engraving & aquatint by
Robert Havell, London, 1827-38, framed,
water stains lower left & 2" scratch in
upper right, 25⅛ x 38" (ILLUS.) **4,025**

Common Flying Squirrel - Plate XXVIII,
hand-colored lithograph by J.T. Bowen,
Philadelphia, ca. 1843, framed,
21½ x 27⅜" (small tear in lower
sheet edge) **1,725**

Common Gull - Plate CCXII, hand-colored
etching, engraving & aquatint by Robert
Havell, London, 1827-38, framed,
25 x 36" (fox marks in image - paper
tone discolored) **805**

Connecticut Warbler - Plate CXXXVIII,
hand-colored etching, engraving &
aquatint by Robert Havell, Jr., London,
1827-38, framed, 22⅛ x 32⅜" (faint light-
& mat stain & a few inconspicuous
specks of foxing) **1,265**

Cow-Pen Bird - Plate XCIX, hand-colored
etching, engraving & aquatint by Robert
Havell, London, 1827-38, framed,
25¼ x 38⅛" (foxing throughout) **1,380**

Curlew Sandpiper - Plate 333, color
chromolithograph by Julius Bien, New
York, 1860, framed, 15 x 18¾" (toning) **230**

**Double Crested Cormorant - Plate
CCLVII,** hand-colored etching, engraving
& aquatint by Robert Havell, London,
1827-38, framed, 25 x 37⅝" (pale mat
stain & mottled discoloration) **2,990**

Esquimaux Curlew - Plate CCVIII, hand-
colored etching, engraving & aquatint by
Robert Havell, London, 1827-38, framed,
25 x 37⅞" (discoloration at sheet edges) . . . **1,610**

Great American Cock Male - Plate 1, (similar to Wild Turkey Male - Plate 1), hand-colored etching, engraving & aquatint by Robert Havell, Jr., London, 1827-38, few tiny specks of foxing, traces of discoloration at sheet edges, few repaired tears, stitch holes along disbound edge, 26 x 38⅜" (ILLUS.) **71,250**

Hooping Crane - Plate CCLXI, hand-colored etching, engraving & aquatint by Robert Havell, London, 1827-38, framed, 22⅞ x 35⅜" (light-stain, surface nicks & scratches, several repaired tears, trimmed to image) **8,625**

House Wren - Plate 83, hand-colored etching, engraving & aquatint by Robert Havell, Jr., London, 1827-38, framed, 25⅝ x 38" (foxing, repaired loss below text, w/associated discoloration, traces of damp staining, repaired tear in left sheet edge, small loss in lower left corner) **33,335**

Hutchin's Barnacle Goose - Plate CCLXXVII, hand-colored etching, engraving & aquatint by Robert Havell, London, 1827-38, 24⅛ x 36¾" (slightly darkened paper tone, tiny, inconspicuous pinholes along left sheet edge) **3,450**

Kildeer Plover - Plate CCXXV, hand-colored etching, engraving & aquatint by Robert Havell, London, 1827-38, framed, 18⅜ x 26" (light-stain, foxing, margins folded under) **1,265**

Lazuli Finch, Clay-Colored Finch, Oregon Snow Finch - Plate CCCXCVIII, hand-colored etching, engraving & aquatint by Robert Havell, London, 1827-38, framed, 20⅛ x 28" (foxing & margins folded back w/discoloration along creases) **1,610**

Leopard Spermophile - Plate XXXIX, hand-colored lithograph by J.T. Bowen, Philadelphia, ca. 1844, framed, 21½ x 27⅜" (small tear in lower sheet edge) **230**

Lepus Bachmani, Waterhouse, hand-colored lithograph by J.T. Bowen, Philadelphia, ca. 1847, framed, 20 x 27" (mottled fox marks in background, light soiling along upper sheet) **920**

Little Sandpiper - Plate CCCXX, hand-colored etching, engraving & aquatint by Robert Havell, London, 1827-38, framed, 25⅜ x 38" (tears in outer margins, three repaired w/associated tape discoloration on recto, few small losses in extreme sheet edges - sheet very slightly rippled) . . . **1,840**

Long-Tailed Deer - Plate CXVIII, hand-colored lithograph by J.T. Bowen, Philadelphia, ca. 1847, framed, 21½ x 27⅛" (stitch holes along disbound edge) . . . **2,645**

Mallard Duck - Plate CCXXI, hand-colored etching, engraving & aquatint by Robert Havell, London, 1827-38, 25⅝ x 38⅞" (inconspicuous skillfully repaired tear in image & verso, few traces of staining) **71,250**

Marsh Hare - Plate XVII, hand-colored lithograph by J.T. Bowen, Philadelphia, ca. 1843, 19⅞ x 26¼" (165 mm tear into image at lower left, slight mat stain in outer margins, two small losses in upper edge, handling creases) **1,495**

Marsh Hawk - Plate CCCLVI, hand-colored etching, engraving & aquatint by Robert Havell, London, 1827-38, framed, 25⅝ x 38¼" (foxing, slight sheet discoloration, one short repaired tear in margin & one small repaired puncture) **9,775**

Mexican Marmot-Squirrel - Plate CXXIV, hand-colored lithograph by J.T. Bowen, Philadelphia, ca. 1847, framed, 21⅞ x 27¾" (horizontal tear left sheet edge, small loss lower left corner, pale foxing in background & margins) **460**

Moose Deer: Old Male and Young - Plate LXXVI, hand-colored lithograph by J.T. Bowen, Philadelphia, ca. 1845, framed, 21⅞ x 28" (sheet edges w/repaired tear & slight discoloration) **2,645**

Musk-Rat, Musquash - Plate XIII, hand-colored lithograph by J.T. Bowen, Philadelphia, ca. 1843, framed, 20⅞ x 26⅞" (light-stain, foxing & slight rippling in sheet) **920**

Olive Sided Flycatcher - Plate CLXXIV, hand-colored etching, engraving & aquatint by Robert Havell, London, 1827-38, 25⅝ x 38⅞" (foxing on sheet edges, slight discoloration & a few short tears). **1,610**

Orchard Oriole - Plate 42, hand-colored etching, engraving & aquatint by Robert Havell, Jr., London, 1827-38, framed, 24⅞ x 37" (foxing, discoloration in margins, few handling creases, tiny nicks in edges) **4,312**

Pine Finch - Plate CLXXX, hand-colored etching, engraving & aquatint by Robert Havell, Jr., London, 1827-38, framed, 20⅛ x 28" (foxing, margins folded back w/discoloration along creases) **1,380**

Pine Grosbeak - Plate CCCLVIII, hand-colored etching, engraving & aquatint by Robert Havell, London, 1827-38, framed, 16⅛ x 22¼" (light-stain, foxing). **1,840**

Prairie Wolf - Plate LXXI, hand-colored lithograph by J.T. Bowen, Philadelphia, ca. 1845, 21¾ x 27⅞" (tears & losses in margins, slight light-stain, discoloration on verso) **2,530**

Purple Sandpiper - Plate CCLXXXIV, hand-colored etching, engraving & aquatint by Robert Havell, London, 1827-38, framed, 22 x 28" (paper tone discolored, light foxing in margins throughout) **690**

Red Texan Wolf

Red Texan Wolf - Plate LXXXII, hand-colored lithograph by J.T. Bowen, Philadelphia, ca. 1845, mat stain & a few small tears at sheet edges, 21⅝ x 27½" (ILLUS.) **3,910**

Red-Shouldered Hawk

Red-Shouldered Hawk - Plate 56, hand-colored etching, engraving & aquatint by Robert Havell, Jr., London, 1827-38, framed, slight discoloration, few specks of foxing & few short tears at sheet edges, 25½ x 38⅛" (ILLUS.) **11,500**

The Jaguar, Female

The Jaguar, Female - Plate CL, hand-colored lithograph by J.T. Bowen, Philadelphia, ca. 1846, framed, few small specks of discoloration, 21⅜ x 26⅞" (ILLUS.) **10,350**

Trumpeter Swan - Plate CCCVI, hand-colored etching, engraving & aquatint by Robert Havell, London, 1827-38, framed, 26 x 39" (few short skillfully repaired tears, stitch holes along disbound edge) . . . **93,250**

Wild Turkey Male (Plate 1), hand-colored etching & engraving by W.H. Lizars, 24⅞ x 38¼" (skillfully repaired vertical crease & attendant tear through image & repaired horizontal tear in foliage at left, sheet edges w/minor soiling, few short tears) **23,000**

Wilson's Plover - Plate CCIX, hand-colored etching, engraving & aquatint by Robert Havell, London, 1827-38, framed, 22 x 28" (foxing & slight sheet discoloration, primarily at sheet edges) **460**

Yellow Shank - Plate CCLXXXVIII, hand-colored etching, engraving & aquatint by Robert Havell, London, 1827-38, framed, 24⅛ x 36¾" (slightly darkened paper tone, tiny, inconspicuous pinholes along left sheet edge) **8,625**

AUTOGRAPHS

What follows are 99 desirable autographs from noteworthy persons from all walks of life— a miniscule sampling given the scope of human endeavor, to be sure, but enough to give an idea of the range of sought-after autographs. This is not a "best of" list, but merely a sampling representing some of the more popular collecting areas: U.S. presidents, military figures, authors, composers, entertainers, scientists, etc. Keep in mind that supply and demand, not relative fame, is the major factor in determining an autograph's value, and that collectors favor good content letters and documents over mere signatures.

These specific items all sold in recent auctions at major auction houses, and were selected for their representative nature and average price; sizes given are approximations.

Basic abbreviations:

ALS="Autograph Letter Signed" (body of letter entirely in the person's hand)

TLS="Typed Letter Signed"

LS="Letter Signed" (body of letter in secretarial hand)

ADS="Autograph Document Signed"

DS="Document Signed"

ANS="Autograph Note Signed"

AQS="Autograph Quotation Signed"

PS="Photograph Signed"

Abbott, Bud (1894-1974) & Costello, Lou (1906-59), film comedy duo, PS, signed by both & inscribed by Costello, undated, 8 x 10" (quite worn) **$300**

Adams, Ansel (1902-84), renowned landscape photographer of the American West, LS, discusses photography w/a high school teacher, December 3, 1963, 1 page, 5 x 7" **200**

Adams, John Quincy (1767-1848), sixth U.S. president, DS, ship's passport, countersigned by Henry Clay, dated November 28, 1825, 1 page, 8 x 12" **950**

Alcott, Louisa May (1832-88), famed New England author of "Little Women" (1868), ALS, discusses a school, w/original envelope, dated October 28, no year, 1 page, 6 x 8" **900**

Arnold, Benedict (1741-1801), American Revolutionary War officer who betrayed his country to the British, ALS, requests clothing for his troops, mentions a wound received during the siege of Quebec, dated January 24, 1776, 1 page, 8 x 10" **4,800**

Austin, Stephen F. (1793-1836), founder of the first American settlement in Texas, which bears his name, DS, Texas Loan Certificate, dated January 11, 1836, 1 page, 9 x 11" **1,400**

Barnum, P.T. (1810-91), the greatest circus showman & marketer of all time, ALS, discusses his new museum & requests free shipping, dated July 18, 1865, 1 page, 6 x 8" **500**

Beardsley, Aubrey (1872-98), British illustrator controversial for his erotic images, ALS, discusses mutual friends, dated February 7, 1897, 4 pages, no size noted **6,000**

Ben-Gurion, David (1886-1973), first prime minister of Israel, LS, regrets he cannot attend a convention in Tel-Aviv, dated June 17, 1954, 1 page, 6 x 8". **700**

Booth, John Wilkes (1838-65), actor who assassinated Abraham Lincoln, ALS, discusses Baltimore's summer social life, dated June 18, 1855, 3 pages, 10 x 14" . . . **19,000**

Brown, John (1800-59), fiery abolitionist who led the famed raid at Harper's Ferry, ALS, writes his wife & children about his return home, dated June 19, 1839, 1 page, 9 x 12" **2,750**

Burnside, Ambrose E. (1824-81), Union general after whom "sideburns" are named, DS, stock certificate for 500 shares in the Indianapolis & Vincennes Railroad, dated January 8, 1869, 1 page, 9 x 12" **210**

Burr, Aaron (1756-1836), Thomas Jefferson's vice president, who shot & killed Alexander Hamilton in an 1804 duel, ALS, reviews travel plans w/his wife, dated November 25, 1792, 1 page, framed, 7 x 12" (condition poor) **1,100**

Carter, Jimmy (born 1924), 39th U.S. president, TLA, excellent content to a powerful Congressman regarding the American hostages in Iran—the issue that helped Carter lose reelection—dated April 29, 1980, 1 page, 8½ x 11" **1,800**

Carver, George Washington (1864-1943), agricultural chemist & educator who discovered numerous industrial uses for peanuts, soybeans & sweet potatoes, PS, undated, 4 x 5" **1,200**

Charles (born 1948) & Diana (1961-97), Prince & Princess of Wales, PS, dated 1983, matted & framed, 3 x 4". **2,600**

Christie, Agatha (1891-1976), popular British mystery novelist famed for Miss Marple & Hercule Poirot, ALS, answers personal questions, dated July 8, 1945, 2 pages, 6 x 8" **700**

Cooper, Gary (1901-61), Oscar-winning actor remembered for "Sergeant York," "High Noon," "Meet John Doe," etc., DS, amends an agreement regarding billing for "It's a Big Country," 4 pages, 8½ x 11" **275**

Cooper, James Fenimore (1789-1851), notable 19th-century novelist whose numerous works include "The Pathfinder" & "The Last of the Mohicans," ADS, check written out & signed for $20.56, dated January 18, 1840, 1 page, 3 x 8" **210**

Dali, Salvador (1904-89), influential Spanish surrealist artist, ink sketch, untitled, inscribed original drawing, dated 1975, 1 page, 6½ x 9" (stained & creased) . . **2,000**

Dalton, Emmett (1871-1937), Old West outlaw turned realtor & screenwriter, TLS, concerns right to his 1931 book "When the Daltons Rode," dated April 7, 1937, 1 page, 8½ x 11" **1,600**

Darwin, Charles (1809-82), British naturalist who developed the theory of evolution through natural selection, PS, choice personal inscription, also signed by noted photographer Julia Margaret Cameron, dated 1868, 9 x 11½" **8,000**

Dillinger, John (1903-34), daring "Public Enemy Number One," ALS, from prison, discusses a cryptic legal matter, undated, 2 pages, 6 x 8". **5,500**

Disney, Walt (1901-66), cartoonist who created Mickey Mouse & founded an entertainment empire, DS, transfers interests in four films to another company, dated June 6, 1961, 2 pages, 8½ x 14" **2,500**

Dodgson, Charles L. ("Lewis Carroll") (1832-98), English author of the children's classic "Alice's Adventures in Wonderland," ALS, letter of introduction, dated April 6, 1873, 2 pages, 6 x 8" **2,200**

Doubleday, Abner (1819-93), supposed creator of baseball, DS, two bank shares in the Bank of Binghamton, signed by bank president Doubleday, dated May 4, 1855, 1 page, no size given 220

Earp, Wyatt (1848-1929), legendary Dodge City lawman who survived the OK Corral gunfight, ANS, notes that summons has been served & dockets verso, dated September 26, 1870, 2-page summons, 6 x 8" 9,500

Eiffel, Gustave (1832-1923), French engineer of Eiffel Tower fame, ALS, discusses possible scientific uses for the Eiffel Tower, dated August 27, 1906, 2 pages, 6 x 8" 1,100

Eliot, George (1819-80), female novelist noted for "The Mill on the Floss," ALS, about the paper on which one of her books was printed, dated May 4, 1874, 1 page, 6 x 8" 1,300

Elizabeth I (1533-1603), British monarch after whom her period of reign (1558-1603) was named, DS, in Latin, on vellum, regarding a manor in Somerset, dated June 25, 1572, 11 x 18½" 1,500

Ferdinand V (1452-1516) & Isabella I (1451-1504), Spanish rulers who supported Columbus, DS, rewards a knighthood & property to a captain, dated January 3, 1491, 1 page, 11 x 14" 3,000

Fields, W.C. (1880-1946), film & vaudeville comedian famed for his love of liquor & dislike of children, DS, check for $25, dated October 10, 1925, 1 page, 4 x 8" 750

Garfield, James A. (1831-81), 20th U.S. president, assassinated by Charles J. Guiteau, LS, as a congressman, recommends a job seeker to President Grant, also signed by another congressman, dated December 1876, 1 page, 8½ x 11" 600

Garland, Judy (1922-69), actress & singer best remembered as Dorothy in "The Wizard of Oz," PS, nicely inscribed portrait, undated, 10 x 13" (condition poor) . . . 300

Goethe, Johann (1749-1832), German dramatist & author of "Faust" (1808), LS, expresses his dislike of rowdy students, dated May 31, 1796, 7 pages, 4½ x 7½" 3,500

Grant, Cary (1904-86), debonair British leading man, TLS, thanks a magazine editor for an award, dated September 9, 1965, 1 page, 8½ x 11" 250

Grey, Zane (1875-1939), the best-selling Western novelist of all time, PS, small portrait, also inscribed on verso, undated, 3½ x 7" 300

Hamilton, Alexander (1739-1802), first U.S. treasury secretary, killed in a duel by Aaron Burr, LS, concerns freight imported from various countries, dated September 8, 1792, 1 page, 9 x 13" 1,500

Hart, William S. (1870-1946), star of silent Western films known for his deadpan expression, PS, profile portrait in Western garb, undated, 7½ x 9½" 200

Hawthorne, Nathaniel (1804-64), novelist, ALS, responds to a request, dated March 29, 1860, 1 page, 6 x 8" 1,100

Henry, Patrick (1736-99), "Give me liberty or give me death" Revolutionary War patriot, ALS, consults a lawyer about a legal matter, dated June 2, 1792, 1 page, 9 x 12" 3,200

Himmler, Heinrich (1900-45), infamous head of the Nazi SS, PS, undated, no size given 800

Holmes, Oliver Wendell (1809-94), the first dean of Harvard Medical School was better known as a poet & man of letters, AQS, brief excerpt from his most famous poem, "The Last Leaf," dated August 13, 1881, 1 page, 3 x 5" 300

Houdini, Harry (1874-1926), America's most famous magician & escape artist, DS, stock certificate for 20 shares in the short-lived Houdini Picture Corporation, dated January 23, 1922, 1 page, 9 x 12". . . . 4,500

Houston, Samuel (1793-1862), first president of the Republic of Texas & namesake of the city, DS, legal affidavit, dated June 14, 1853, 1 page, 9 x 14" 1,000

Hughes, Langston (1902-67), "Harlem Renaissance" poet & author, TLS, discusses how important his high school education was to him as a writer, dated August 1, 1957, 1 page, 8½ x 11" 325

Irving, Washington (1783-1859), author of such classics as "Rip Van Winkle" & "The Legend of Sleepy Hollow," ALS, writes the U.S. Madrid Legation regarding wine, dated July 27, 1845, 1 page, 9 x 12" 300

Jackson, Andrew (1767-1845), hero of the War of 1812 & later the 7th U.S. president (& first Democratic president), DS, land grant on vellum awarding 80 acres in Missouri, dated January 1, 1831, 1 page, 11 x 14" 700

Jackson, Thomas "Stonewall" (1824-63), brilliant Confederate general who defeated the Union at the second Battle of Bull Run, clipped signature, undated, no size given 2,200

Johnson, Andrew (1808-75), Lincoln's second vice president, then 17th U.S. president, barely surviving impeachment, DS, authorizes the secretary of state to affix the U.S. seal to a presidential pardon, dated December 24, 1867, 1 page, 9 x 12" **750**

Johnson, Lyndon B. (1908-73), Kennedy's vice president, then 36th U.S. president, TLS, expresses sorrow over the death of President Kennedy, dated December 11, 1963, 1 page, 8½ x 11" **1,100**

Kafka, Franz (1883-1924), German author of grim, bizarre short stories & novels, ALS, praises author Franz Werfel's writing, undated, 1 page, no size given **12,000**

Karloff, Boris (1887-1969), British-born film star who played the definitive monster in "Frankenstein," DS, contract w/MCA Artists, dated August 29, 1956, 6 pages, 8½ x 11" **250**

Kern, Jerome (1885-1945), composer of musical comedies such as "Show Boat" (1927), ALS, gracious thank you letter, undated, 1 page, 8½ x 11" **450**

Lafayette, Marquis de (1757-1834), French officer who aided the American Revolution & became a close friend of George Washington, ALS, tells General Nathanael Greene of being pursued by Cornwallis, dated June 3, 1781, 4 pages, 9 x 12" **14,000**

London, Jack (1876-1916), author of such popular tales as "The Call of the Wild," ALS, gives his views of graphology, dated September 17, 1905, 3 pages, no size given, framed. **1,100**

MacArthur, Douglas (1880-1964), controversial American Army officer who accepted the Japanese surrender in 1945, later dismissed by Truman, PS, silver print portrait, undated, 9 x 12" **425**

Madison, "Dolly" (1768-1849), First Lady, ALS, thanks an author for a book, free franked by James Madison, dated March 8, 1828, 1 page, 9 x 11" **1,700**

Marconi, Guglielmo (1874-1937), inventor of the wireless telegraph, PS, undated, 6 x 10" (stained & damaged) **900**

Marx, Karl (1818-83), German philosopher who originated the idea of communism, rare ALS, choice content discussing Richard Wagner's music, revolt in Russia & more, dated January 21, 1877, 2 pages, 5 x 8". **17,000**

McKinley, William (1843-1901), 25th U.S. president, assassinated, PS, profile portrait, dated July 22, 1896, 6 x 8" **375**

Mussolini, Benito (1883-1945), Italian fascist part leader & later prime minister who allied his country w/Hitler, DS, proclamation, countersigned by King Vittorio Emmanuel III, dated January 28, 1926, 1 page, 9 x 12" **225**

Nelson, Horatio (1758-1805), English naval officer who defeated the French at Trafalgar, ALS, informs a vice admiral of his plans to deceive the French w/a prison ship, dated October 4, 1803, 3 pages, 9 x 12". **1,600**

O'Keeffe, Georgia (1887-1986), artist famed for her large canvases depicting bleached animal skulls & flowers, ALS, thanks a friend for a book & record & discusses a New York art exhibit, dated June 10, 1961, 2 pages, 8½ x 11". **1,100**

O'Neill, Eugene (1888-1953), Nobel Prize- & Pulitzer Prize-winning American playwright, ALS, discusses the screenplay for his play "The Emperor Jones," dated August 7, 1933, 2 pages, 6 x 8" **2,600**

Oakley, Annie (1860-1926), sharpshooter who performed in Buffalo Bill's Wild West show, rare PS, signed on verso, undated, 4 x 4½" **4,000**

Peary, Robert E. (1856-1920), American explorer who was the first to reach the North Pole, LS, discusses steel cable needed for his ship, dated June 8, 1905, 1 page, 8½ x 11" **325**

Penn, William (1644-1718), English colonizer after whom Pennsylvania is named, DS, land grant, dated September 11, 1681, 1 page, 9 x 12" **2,100**

Pickford, Mary (1893-1979), one of the first silent film stars, known as "America's Sweetheart," PS, sepia-tone portrait, undated, 5 x 8" **120**

Poe, Edgar Allan (1809-49), American writer celebrated for macabre poems such as "The Raven" & short stories such as "The Cask of Amontillado," rare ALS, writes a newspaper editor regarding contributions, dated May 21, 1844, 1 page, 6 x 8" **26,000**

Presidents, U.S.: Richard Nixon (1913-95), Gerald Ford (born 1913), Ronald Reagan (born 1911), & George Bush (born 1924), color PS, group portrait at the opening of the Nixon Library, signed by all four, dated July 19, 1990, 8 x 10" **1,500**

Rackham, Arthur (1867-1939), English book illustrator famous for his "Winnie the Pooh" & other children's book drawings, ink & watercolor sketch titled "Santa Claus at the Chimney," dated 1931, 1 page, 5½ x 7" **7,000**

Reagan, Ronald (born 1911), actor & later 40th U.S. president, ALS, declines to attend a conference, citing fear of flying, dated March 6, 1962, 1 page, 8½ x 11" **700**

Remington, Frederic (1861-1909), renowned painter & sculptor of Old West scenes, ALS, says his "Harper's Weekly" prints are not reproduced elsewhere, dated January 30 (no year), 1 page, no size given **900**

Revere, Paul (1735-1818), Revolutionary War patriot & silversmith, DS, masonry certificate, undated, 1 page, framed, 6 x 8" (well worn) **4,500**

Rickenbacker, Edward V. (1890-1973), race car driver turned Medal of Honor-winning aviator turned Eastern Airlines executive, PS, dated 1933, 8 x 10" **400**

Robeson, Paul (1898-1976), stage actor & singer, PS, sepia-tone portrait, undated, 5 x 7" **160**

Robinson, Jackie (1919-72), the first black baseball player to enter the major leagues, TLS, promises to sign a baseball sent to him, dated June 16, 1949, 1 page, 8½ x 11" **650**

Ruby, Jack (1911-67), Dallas nightclub owner who shot & killed JFK assassin Lee Harvey Oswald in 1963, DS, waiver of notice for first board of directors meeting of the Min-I-Ron Company, dated May 15, 1957, 1 page, 8½ x 11" **150**

Selznick, David O. (1902-65), "Gone With the Wind" producer, TLS, grants use of a film clip from "Song of Bernadette," which is then discussed, dated June 30, 1962, 1 page, 8½ x 11" **200**

Shaw, George Bernard (1856-1950), prolific Nobel Prize-winning British playwright & critic, ALS, encouraging remarks to an actress, dated October 1, 1927, 2 pages, 6 x 8" (heavily worn) **375**

Stevenson, Robert Louis (1850-94), Scottish novelist of such classics as "Treasure Island," "Dr. Jekyll and Mr. Hyde" & much more, DS, requests that a payment of nine shillings be made to a third party, dated October 1, 1892, 1 page, 5 x 7" (worn & damaged) **700**

Stravinsky, Igor (1882-1971), influential Russian-born composer noted for his ballets, PS, postcard portrait, undated, no size given **575**

Taft, William H. (1857-1930), 27th U.S. president & later Supreme Court chief justice, PS, sepia-tone portrait, dated July 13, 1912, 11 x 14" **300**

Tesla, Nikola (1856-1943), Austrian-born electrical engineer & inventor, LS, responds to technical questions about electrical equipment, dated November 22, 1911, 1 page, 8½ x 11" **750**

Thurber, James (1894-1961), humorous "New Yorker" short story writer, humorist & cartoonist, TLS, asks playwright George S. Kaufman for data on "New Yorker" editor Harold Ross for an "Atlantic Monthly" article, dated March 28, 1958, 2 pages, 8½ x 11". **450**

Toscanini, Arturo (1867-1957), director of LaScala Opera House in Milan & one of the most renowned conductors of his day, PS, undated, 7 x 10". **325**

Trotsky, Leon (1879-1940), Communist leader who organized the 1917 Russian Revolution, rare PS, undated, 7 x 9" **2,000**

Truman, Harry S (1884-1972), 33rd U.S. president, PS, inscribed to a Roman Catholic cardinal, dated December 20, 1947, 6 x 9" **375**

Van Buren, Martin (1782-1862), 8th U.S. president, DS, appoints a captain in the Second Infantry Regiment, dated July 10, 1838, 1 page, 11 x 14". **650**

Verne, Jules (1828-1905), French "Founder of Science Fiction," author of "Twenty Thousand Leagues Under the Sea," among numerous other titles, ALS, excellent content about translating one of his books into English, dated May 10, 1890, 1 page, 6 x 8" **850**

Wagner, Richard (1813-83), German composer & librettist, ALS, discusses w/a stage designer the layout for "Tristan and Isolde," dated February 18, 1866, 1 page, framed, 5 x 8" **1,600**

Washington, Booker T. (1856-1915), prominent black educator who founded Tuskegee Institute in 1881, LS, concerns a fund-raising appeal, dated November 13, 1899, 1 page, 6 x 8" **550**

Wilde, Oscar (1854-1900), Irish playwright noted for "The Importance of Being Earnest" imprisoned for homosexual acts, ALS, thanks a correspondent for a poem on the Irish famine, undated, 3 pages, 6 x 8" **3,300**

Wilson, Woodrow (1856-1924), Nobel Peace Prize-winning 28th U.S. president, DS, appoints an officer in the Medical Reserve Corps, dated March 18, 1913, 1 page, 9 x 12" **300**

Wolfe, Thomas (1900-38), "You Can't Go Home Again" novelist, TLS, replies to an admirer, dated May 21, 1933, 1 page, 8½ x 11" **800**

Yeats, W.B. (1865-1939), leading Irish poet & playwright, ALS, discusses censorship, dated February 22, 1932, 1 page, 8½ x 11" **1,400**

York, Alvin C. (1887-1964), World War One hero whose memoir was turned into the 1941 Gary Cooper film, ALS, comments about a suggestion he run for president, dated October 23, 1951, 1 page, 8½ x 11". . . . **260**

Zola, Emile (1840-1902), French novelist known for his defense of Dreyfus, ALS, thanks a critic, dated July 6, 1866, 1 page, 6 x 8" **300**

AUTOMOBILES

1924 Dodge Touring Car

Dodge, 1924, four-door touring car w/canvas top **$9,000**

Ford, 1929 AA 1½ ton truck, originally used as an ice truck **9,000**

Ford Truck with Una-Fon Bell Unit

Ford, 1929 truck w/Deagon Una-Fon bell unit **12,500**

Mercedes Benz, 1961 Model 300D, six-cylinder, blue exterior, red upholstery, odometer reads 19,831 miles **23,650**

AUTOMOTIVE COLLECTIBLES

Also see ADVERTISING ITEMS and CANS & CONTAINERS

Air pump stand, Gilbert & Barker, cast iron, a square stepped base below gently curved paneled sides supporting a slender tall fluted pedestal w/square top, painted red, earliest known base for a Gilbert & Barker Gilbarco Air Meter, No. 4-6598X, restored, 12" sq., 41" h. **$303**

Attendant's cap, "Mobil," light brown cloth w/black plastic rim & visor, red, white & blue Mobil patch on the front, 10 x 11", 5" h. (some soiling, wear to inside edge) **149**

Gas Station Attendant's Hat

Attendant's hat, "Phillips 66," tan cloth top w/embroidered black & orange logo patch & black vinyl bill, side loops hold advertising plastic mechanical pencil w/name & address of gas station, minor wear & cracking on pencil decal, hat size 7⅜, 2 pcs. (ILLUS.) **231**

Baby Feeding Dish with Auto Scene

Baby feeding dish, china, rounded w/flattened rim transfer-printed w/red letters of the alphabet & small animals, the center w/a scene of two young boys driving an early red open auto, marked by Three Crown China, Germany, minor scratches & soiling, early 20th c. (ILLUS.) **182**

Book ends, cast metal, three slender long bars joining hinged end rectangular pierced metal panels w/arched & rounded top above a side view of a man driving an early open auto, early 20th c., 7½ x 11¾", 5" h. (some rust spotting, scratches & soiling). **143**

Booklet, "The Arizona Sheriff," ca. 1925, Studebaker Corp. **48**

Bottle rack, "Mobiloil," rectangular metal crate on wire stretcher legged base painted dark orange w/white wording "Mobiloil 'AF'" or "Mobiloil 'AF' Filpruf," holds eight diamond-shaped clear glass quarter bottles w/metal top but no caps, 10 x 18¾", 22" h. (one bottle repainted, crate w/some paint chipping, denting, rust spotting, scratches & soiling). **1,210**

Brochure, 1958 Plymouth, colorful
illustrations 55
Chauffeur's badge, 1922, Illinois. 28
Chauffeur's badge, 1922, Kentucky 60
Chauffeur's badge, 1931, Virginia. 45

Rare Packard Presentation Clock

Clock, Packard presentation model,
cloisonné on metal, rectangular front
w/rounded top & notched bottom corners,
white enamel outer band w/black wording
across the bottom "Master Salesman -
1926," grey enamel central panel w/inlaid
Packard logo above the round brass
bezel & steel dial w/the numbers replaced
w/incised letters spelling "Packard Motor,"
plate below the dial engraved "J.E. Land,"
Seth Thomas model, four jewels, small
chip at bottom corner & one at "P" in dial,
4 x 5¼" (ILLUS.) 2,750
Creamer, porcelain, bulbous ovoid form w/a
wide rim & small rim spout, C-form
handle, white decorated w/a color
transfer of a lady & gentleman riding in an
early open auto w/various animals
running to get out of the way, early
20th c., 2½" h. 99
Credit card, "The Texaco Company," paper,
pale bluish green w/recipient's name &
address, issued for May, June, July &
August 1940, tire & battery purchase
coupons still attached, 3½ x 6¼" (some
soiling & staining) 176

Old Indianapolis Speedway Item

Desk accessory, advertising-type,
"Indianapolis Motor Speedway," plaster
model of a race car molded into a domed

oblong base w/raised wording, gold paint,
back side of base embossed w/"500 Mile
Race - May 30, 1931," some scratches,
soiling & edge wear, 3 x 7½", 3" h.
(ILLUS.) 237
Gas pump nozzle, heavy metal, raised
marking "K-721-1," 14" l. (wear, scratches) 66
Gas station floor display, "Mobil," painted
wood life-sized cut-out figure of a gas
station attendant in uniform, easel-
backed, red logo on his cap & jacket
pocket, 21" w., 72" h. 715

Early Shell Station Soap Dispenser

Gas station soap dispenser, "Shell,"
silvered cast metal, a deep rounded
container w/paneled sides & notched
corners w/a matching domed cover
w/hinged flap w/Shell logo over dispenser
opening, swings between knob-topped
end bar uprights joined by a flat
rectangular base, some pitting & minor
rust on base, 5" h. (ILLUS.) 165
Gasoline pump, Bennett Model 646 B/W,
restored to Dino Gasoline, curved top,
painted white border & green center w/a
small round dial over the gas metering
face, lights up, reproduction globe,
18 x 29", 73" h. (small chips to "Contains
Lead" signs) 880

Restored Early Pennsylvania Pump

Gasoline pump, Pennsylvania Pump Co. model, red-painted metal body w/"Tydol Ethyl" pump signs, black domed top & metal dial within black ring, chips to pump signs, fading to face, lights up, reproduction globe w/"Flying A" symbol on lens, 18 x 24", 68" h. (ILLUS.) **1,045**

Gasoline pump, "Sharmeter" by Neptune Meter Co., black roof-shaped top in black overhangs the red-painted body w/black rectangular plate w/half-round ribbed "roof" projecting over the round clock dial-style gallon register, white dial w/black numbers & "Sharmeter" in red, smaller black rectangular plate below reads "Motor," restored, 22 x 25", 68" h. (plate not attached, reproduction globe w/Flying A symbol) **1,210**

Gasoline pump, Wayne Model 60, restored to Atlantic gasoline, rounded top & step-sided Art Deco style, red body w/a white arched dial face w/two "Hi-Arc" insert signs, white vertical stripes down the front w/"Atlantic" in red, 18 x 27", 75" h. (chips & staining to pump signs) **935**

Gasoline pump globe, "Ashland Kerosene," wide hull body w/two milk glass lenses, red & black lettering, 13½" d. (very minor inside rim chips) **605**

Rare Independent Gasoline Globe

Gasoline pump globe, "Independent Gasoline," high profile metal body w/two milk glass lenses, red frame, black lettering in ring around central round color scene of marching Minutemen based on "The Spirit of '76," minor flaking on one lens, other w/water stain & paint loss, very rare, 15" d. (ILLUS.) **5,500**

Gasoline pump globe, "Mobilgas Ethyl," high profile metal body w/two milk glass lenses, red Pegasus logo above blue & red wording, 16½" d. (minor fading, paint chips & soiling to body) **495**

Gasoline pump globe, "National White Rose Gas," wide round milk glass hull body, dark blue & red printing, minor

National White Rose Gas Globe

chips inside base rim, overall interior spotting in the making, 13½" d. (ILLUS.) **413**

Figural Red Crown Ethyl Globe

Gasoline pump globe, "Red Crown Ethyl," crown-shaped one-piece milk glass, embossed lettering painted red around the lower rim, minor scratches, 17½" d. (ILLUS.) **1,210**

Gasoline pump globe, "Red Pepper Ethyl," metal body in blue mounted on a wooden light-up base, two milk glass lenses w/"Red Pepper" in red above "Ethyl" & other printing in a black & yellow triangle, label on base reads "Cinti Ball Crank Co. Balcrank Cincinnati, Ohio," 15½" d. (scratches on body) **1,788**

Gasoline pump globe, "Rice Oil Co. - Johnstown, O.," high profile metal body w/two milk glass lenses, black wording in outer ring around center monogram of colored, overlapping letters, red frame, 15" d. (display lens w/paint loss & fading to edges, reverse lens w/cracks & two glued pieces, soiling to both) **1,320**

Gasoline pump globe, "Sinclair Pennant," narrow hull body w/two milk glass lenses, red ground w/white fluttering pennant & lettering in white & black, 13½" d. (lenses glued in) **990**

Solene Gasoline Pump Globe

Gasoline pump globe, "Solene No-Knock Gasoline," wide milk glass round body w/two lenses, printing in red & green, cracks in back lens, body scratches, 13½" d. (ILLUS.). **880**

Gasoline pump globe, "Super Kant-Nock Gasoline," wide milk glass hull body w/two lenses, black & red printing within thin yellow ring, 13½" d. (soiling) **468**

Gasoline pump globe lens set, "Ben Franklin," depicts Ben Franklin w/yellow & black Ethyl logo at bottom center, "Ben Franklin" in white lettering w/black border on red outer rim, minor scratches, 13½" d., the set **5,500**

Hood ornament, Pierce Arrow, die-cut metal w/raised lettering, a ring w/wording pierced w/a hexagonal opening showing the front of a car, a small wing at the top of the ring & an arrow tip & feathered end on each side, 5½" w., 4" h. (some soiling & use wear) **187**

"The Wiggler" Hood Ornament

Hood ornament, "The Wiggler" spinner-type, metal w/rubber-coated base, composed of a large shiny top center orb above half-round cupped orbs w/alternating red or green center 'jewels' & mounted to spin on a central short rod above a domed foot, marked "The Wiggler Co., Buffalo, N.Y. , Pat. Dec. 8,

1925 - June 29, 1926 Made in U.S.A.," some rust spotting, scratching & soiling, wear on base, 4" d., 3¾" h. (ILLUS.) **253**

Hood ornament, "Thomas Flyer," cast silvered metal, spread-winged eagle perched atop a realistic globe on a base ring atop a notch-edged cap, 2¾ x 5", 4¾" h. (some edge wear & scratches) **380**

Ink blotter, "Gargoyle Lubricants," leather rocker-type, the flat top stamped in gold "Gargoyle Lubricants" w/gargoyle logo, foreign-made, 2 x 6¾", 3¼" h. (minor scratches & soiling) **66**

License plate, New Jersey, 1911, one-sided porcelain, rectangular w/white ground & red lettering "10846 - NJ - 11," embossed tin medallion w/registration number at one end, stamped on back "Horace E. Fine Co. Ing-rich Auto Tags, Trenton, N.J.," 6 x 13" (chips, edge rust, water stain, scratches) **143**

Light bulb kit, "The Pep Boys Handy Bulb Kit," rectangular tin w/advertising on the lid w/cartoon depictions of "Manny, Moe & Jack," advertising for Cornell Tires on one side & Cadet Batteries on the other, red ground w/red, white & black printing, 2¼ x 4", 2½" h. (minor fading, scratches & crazing of paint) **83**

Motor oil can, "Conoco," tin, man in Revolutionary period clothing next to "Conoco, Motorine, Medium, The Continental Oil Company" on pale yellow & light blue striped background, minor surface rust, paint chipping & scratches, ½ gal., 8" w., 6¼" h. **275**

Motor oil jar, "Longlife Motor Oil," 1 qt., features airplane. **230**

Trop-Artic Oil Cup

Oil cup, "Trop-Artic Auto Oil," cylindrical tin form w/wide strap handle, printed in color around the sides w/landscape scenes w/an early open touring car in the summer & winter, advertising in red & also marked "Manhattan Oil Co.," very minor scratches, 3¾" d., 2¾" h. (ILLUS.) **440**

Oil dispenser, "Associated Oil Company," 1 qt. w/swingspout **70**

Oil dispenser, metal floor model, pedestal flared base below the clear glass tall cylinder for oil below a tall pumping mechanism w/the spigot near the top of the glass cylinder, S.F. Bowser & Co., Inc., Fort Wayne, Indiana, Pump No. 46077, Figure 115, repainted red, 11 x 18", 55" h. (minor scratches & soiling) **303**

Owner's guide, 1953 Buick **20**

Pamphlet, 1967 Ford taxicab **25**

Paperweight, "Husky," advertising-type, metal, figural husky dog on rectangular platform, embossed "Western Oil & Fuel Company" on front of base, 4½" w., 3¾" h. **193**

Paperweight, "Packard," advertising-type, brass, flat squared form w/rounded top, slanted sides & notched lower corners, embossed scene of people riding in an open car below the wording "Ask the Man Who Owns One," back marked "Packard Motor Car Co. Detroit, Mich.," early 20th c., 3½" x 3½" (minor tarnish) **358**

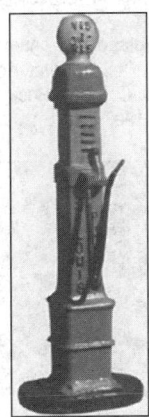

St. Louis Pumps Paperweight

Paperweight, "St. Louis Pumps," advertising-type, cast-iron model of an early slender gas pump w/copper hose & nozzle, painted red w/white globe at the top & black lettering down the side, repainted, some chipping, 7¾" h. (ILLUS.) **550**

Parts book, Indian Motorcycle, 1928 . . . . **40**

Picnic set, running board-type, a rectangular black leatherette-covered trunk holding six knives, six white graniteware plates, five graniteware cups, two graniteware coffee mugs, three tin cups, two tin compartments w/leather straps, one spoon, six various forks, one sharp knife & one can opener, outside straps for attaching to the car, made in Sweden, early 20th c., the set **330**

Postcard, advertising,1967 Mercury **3**

Program, 1933 Elgin National Auto Races **46**

Pump sign, "Pate Challenge," one-sided porcelain, rectangular, design in red, black & white of knight's helmet above a large shield w/"Pate" above a black narrow rectangle w/"Challenge" in white, 12 x 15" (some fading, minor edge chips & scratches) **495**

Pump sign, "Sky Chief Su-preme," one-sided porcelain, rectangular, upper band w/"Sky Chief Su-preme" in red & black on white over a green ground w/large red wing & "Texaco" star logo & "Gasoline," bottom white band printed in black & red "Super-Charged With Petrox," 12 x 18" (minor chips & water stain) **110**

Rare "Wings" Gas Pump Sign

Pump sign, "Wings Regular Gasoline," one-side porcelain, rectangular, blue & red on a white ground, "Wings" printed in red across the top above a blue design of three geese flying in formation above clouds above "Regular Gasoline" in red at the bottom, chips at edges & mounting holes, minor scratches, 6 x 7" (ILLUS.) **1,870**

Racing pennant, felt, long pointed red felt w/white wording "Nat. Road Races - Aug. 29-30, 1913 - Elgin," w/printed blue & white scene of a speeding race car, 29½" l., 11½" h. (piece missing from one letter, some fading) **385**

Radiator shield, Mobilgas, two-sided Socony vacuum shield w/Pegasus & "For Friendly Service," 1920s, rare, 12 x 19" **125**

Sign, car dealer, "Dodge - Plymouth," rectangular porcelain neon-type w/stepped lower corners, dark blue ground w/white word "Dodge" in larger letters over "Plymouth" in smaller letters, the narrow white border band set off w/a neon band, lights white, newer transformer, 28 x 60" (repair to neon, water stain & chips to sign) **1,650**

Sign, "Igol," die-cut plastic, figure of an attractive young blonde woman walking & holding a can of the product aloft in one hand, wearing white short shorts & tight short-sleeved shirt w/wide black belt, red lace-up sandals, 11½" h. (minor scratches) . . . **275**

Jaguar Dealer Sign

Sign, "Jaguar Sales & Service," one-sided
die-cut porcelain, rounded shield form,
jaguar head logo at top, creamy wording
on a maroon ground, good luster, minor
chips to mounting holes & edges,
18¾ x 19¾" (ILLUS.). **1,650**

Ticket brochure, 1935 Indianapolis
Speedway. **32**

Toy tea set: cov. teapot, cov. sugar bowl,
creamer & four cups & saucers;
porcelain, each piece decorated w/a
chauffeur-driven open auto w/two
ladies in the back seat in red, yellow &
green, a running boy on the reverse,
marked "Made in Japan," the set
(various minor damages) **242**

Vase with Early Auto Scene

Vase, china, a flattened ovoid body tapering
to a short flaring neck flanked by ornate
scrolled handles, cobalt blue ground w/a
front reserve w/pointed white floral
clusters forming a ring around an oval
reserve w/a color scene of seashore
w/two women, a boy & a dog in an early
open automobile, early 20th c., worn gilt
trim, 4½" h. (ILLUS.). **275**

AVIATION COLLECTIBLES

*Recently much interest has been shown in
collecting items associated with the early days of
the "flying machine." In addition to relics, flying
adjuncts and literature relating to the early days
of flight, collectors also seek out items that
picture the more renowned early pilots, some of
whom became folk-heros in their own lifetimes,
as well as the early planes themselves.*

Command-Aire Biplane

Command-Aire Biplane, serial number 1,
90 hp Curtiss engine, OX5 water-cooled,
Arkansas Aircraft Co., Little Rock AR,
flying condition, 1928 (ILLUS.) **$200,000**

Fleet Biplane

Fleet Biplane, serial number 234 N684M,
125 hp Kinner motor, 2 seats, Brewister
Aircraft Co., Buffalo, NY, flying condition,
1930 (ILLUS.) **125,000**

Flying Helmet

Flying Helmet, leather, w/earphones, Model
NAF1092, Slote & Klein, New York, 1930,
size 7½ (ILLUS.). **300**

Height Gauge

Height gauge, model mark VIII, out of 1930
British Spitfire Aircraft, Ort & Mason,
England (ILLUS.) **500**

Rare Airplane Oil Can

Motor oil can, Zerolene Aircraft Oil 1 gal.
can, rectangular upright w/strap handle &
spout w/cap on top, one side w/a large
rectangular panel w/a black ground
printed w/advertising & surrounding a
smaller color rectangular scene of a blue
sky w/clouds & two small white planes &
one blimp & a large grey tri-motor plane
in the foreground, orange circle near
base above line reading "Standard Oil
Company of California," very minor
scratches, 3 x 7½", 11" h. (ILLUS.) **2,750**

Propeller

Propeller, wood, Sensenich Propellers,
Lancaster, PA, 1941, 90" l. (ILLUS.) **1,200**

AVON COLLECTIBLES

*Avon got its start in June 1886 when the
California Perfume Company began selling "The
Little Dot" perfume set. Suggesting a California
beginning, the company was actually located in
New York City. By 1929, the Avon cosmetic line
was presented to representatives and customers,*

*and the rest is history. Avon collectibles are not
limited to just the cosmetic line. From dolls to
plates, steins, glassware, Christmas ornaments
and much more, collecting Avon is proving to be
one of the fastest growing hobbies of the day. The
listings below include collectible bottles and
miscellaneous Avon products. All prices reflect
mint condition.*

381 Locomotive

1955 Ford Thunderbird, bottle, blue glass,
1995 . . . . **$15**
381E Locomotive, Lionel Classic Train
Collection, 1995 (ILLUS.) **35**
700E Hudson Locomotive, men's figural,
black porcelain train, ca. 1993, 9" l. **45**
Ballet Recital Doll, Childhood Dreams
Collection, porcelain **35**
Bay Rum, glass bottle w/stopper, California
Perfume Co., ca. 1896, 4 oz. **150**
Bay Rum Keg, men's figural, brown & silver
paint over clear glass, ca. 1965-67, 6 oz. **15**
Bear Cookie Jar, ceramic, brown, ca. 1985. . . . . . **25**
Best Friend Soap, children's, blue dog
soap, ca. 1956 . . . . **60**
Betsy Ross, women's decanter, white
painted over clear glass, holds cologne,
ca. 1976, 4 oz. **7**
Bunny Mates, salt & pepper shakers, white,
ca. 1983 . . . . **12**

Century of Basketball Stein

Century of Basketball Stein, ca. 1995 (ILLUS.) . . **40**
Charisma, soap set, ca. 1975 . . . . **8**

Christmas 1994 Plate

Christmas Plate, depicts Victorian Santa
holding young girl, w/"Christmas 1994"
below (ILLUS.) **25**

Close Harmony, men's figural, barber
bottle, white glass w/after shave,
ca. 1963, 8 oz. **25**

Coleman Lantern, men's figural, green
painted over clear glass, ca. 1977-79, 5 oz. **10**

Cotillion Always Sweet Set: cream lotion,
talc & perfume set, pink & white box
w/straw handbag w/green & yellow
ribbon, ca. 1950, 5/8 dram perfume, the set . . . **95**

Cotillion Debutante Set: cologne mist &
beauty dust in pink, white & gold box,
ca. 1963, the set **20**

Country & Western Stein, embossed "Wild
West" & features Western characters,
sitting Indian finial, ca. 1995 . . . . **40**

Crystal Cat Collection

Crystal Cat Collection, cat on back w/ball,
lead crystal, 1995 (ILLUS.) **15**

Crystal Cat Collection, sitting cat, lead
crystal, ca. 1995 . . . . **15**

Daisies Won't Tell Blossoms Set: cologne
w/blue ribbon & gold pomade, ca. 1956,
2 oz., the set **28**

Daisy Soap on a Rope, yellow rope,
includes pink, white & yellow box, ca. 1963-64. . **20**

Daisy Treasures Set: nail polish & file, pink
box w/yellow slide-open cover, includes
three bottles polish, ca. 1959, the set. **60**

Electric Charger, men's figural, black glass
w/red cap & red side decals, ca. 1970-72,
5 oz. **10**

Father Christmas, porcelain Santa figurine,
ca. 1994 . . . . **30**

"First School Play" Doll, white dress
w/gold stars & ribbon, wings, halo & harp,
Tender Memories, 1995 . . . . **35**

Seasons Treasures Eggs

Floral Bouquet Egg, bouquet centered in
lilac-colored ribbon, diamond & floral
design, Seasons Treasures Egg
Collection, ca. 1995 (ILLUS. right) **15**

Floral Fantasy Bell, 24% lead crystal **20**

Fragrance Baby Set: toilet water, baby
soap bar & can of baby powder,
California Perfume Co., ca. 1923, the set **125**

Fruit Harvest Egg, pears w/leaf surround
on cream background, Seasons
Treasures Egg Collection, 1995
(ILLUS. left) **15**

Garden Girl, women's decanter, sprayed
frosted glass w/yellow plastic top, holds
cologne, ca. 1975, 4 oz. **11**

Garden of Love, perfume w/glass stopper &
gold tag, ca. 1948, 3 drams **120**

Gingerbread Soap Twins Set: children's,
two blue plastic gingerbread cookie
cutters w/two yellow bars of soap in pink,
white & brown box, ca. 1965, the set **30**

Golden Promise, powder sachet, ca. 1952-56 . . . **12**

Here's My Heart, perfume oil, ca. 1970-71 . . . . . . **15**

Images of Hollywood, ca. 1983-84 . . . . **25**

Jasmine, soap set, ca. 1946-53 . . . . **400**

Kasey Kangaroo, children's, stuffed toy
w/socks in pouch, ca. 1991, 12" h. **15**

Lavender, powder sachet, ca. 1961-68 . . . . **20**

Lavender, soap set, ca. 1945. . . . . **60**

Liberty Dollar, men's figural, silver paint
over glass w/after shave, ca. 1970-72, 6 oz. **1**

Lil Folks Time, children's, yellow & white
plastic clock, holds non-tear bubble bath,
ca. 1961-64, 8 oz. **11**

Major League Mitt, children's decanter, non-tear shampoo, plastic baseball glove w/blue cap, ca. 1993 6
Mickey Mouse, children's, bubble bath, plastic, ca. 1969-71, 4½ oz. 7
Moon Flight Game, children's, white space capsule w/non-tear shampoo, ca. 1970-72, 4 oz. 5

Mother's Love Figurine

Mother's Love, figural, mother holding child on lap & dog at side, ca. 1995 (ILLUS.) 15

Mother's Love Plate

Mother's Love, plate, depicts mother holding child on lap w/"Mother's Day 1995" below (ILLUS.) 15
Mr. Robottle, children's, bubble bath, plastic bottle w/blue body, red arms & legs, ca. 1971-72, 8" h. 6
Nativity figurine, white, ca. 1983-1993 15-20
Peace Rose, yellow porcelain, ca. 1987, 7" l. 35
Peanuts Gang Soap, children's, Lucy, Charlie Brown & Snoopy, ca. 1970-72 12
Persian Wood, baby powder, ca. 1961-63 10
Precious Slipper, women's decanter, frosted glass bottle w/cap, ca. 1973-74, ¼ oz. .. 7
"Pur-fect Love" Figurine, Tender Memories, porcelain, 1992, each (ILLUS.) 10
Quaintance, beauty dust, red rose on tin lid, white paper sides, ca.1948-57 18
Quaintance, perfume, red rose cap & painted label, ca.1948-50, 1 dram 70
Reo Depot Wagon, men's figural, amber glass w/black plastic top, ca. 1972-73, 5" l. 12

Pur-fect Love Figurines

Rose Geranium, bath oil, four flower-shaped soaps, ca. 1966-67 18
Skating Party Doll, Childhood Dreams Collection, porcelain 35

"Sleigh Ride" Christmas Ornament

"Sleigh Ride" ornament, silver plate, 1991 (ILLUS.) 10
Spring Bouquet Vase, women's decanter, glass w/scented outside coating, ca. 1981, 6" h. 6
Stanley Steamer, men's figural, blue glass w/black plastic seats & tire cap, ca. 1971-72, 5 oz. 10
Strawberry Candlette Set: porcelain, includes 2¼" h. cup w/strawberry design & 4" saucer, w/box, ca. 1979-80 7
Touring T Silver, men's figural, silver plated over clear glass, ca. 1978, 6 oz. 12
Trailing Arbutus, cold cream in small sample tube, California Perfume Co., ca. 1925 .. 40
Trailing Arbutus, face powder, blue box, California Perfume Co., ca. 1925 40
Trailing Arbutus, perfume w/glass stopper, includes embossed box, California Perfume Co., ca. 1915 140
Ulysses the Unicyclist, Circus Bear Collection, bisque porcelain, ca. 1993, 4½" ... 20
Vernafleur, toilet water, California Perfume Co., ca. 1928 110
Washington Fostoria Goblet, blue glass, candleholder 15

BABY MEMENTOES

Everyone dotes on the new baby and through many generations some exquisite and unique gifts have been carefully selected with a special infant in mind. Collectors now seek items from a varied assortment of baby mementoes, once tokens of affection to the newborn babe. Also see CHILDREN'S BOOKS and CHILDREN'S MUGS.

MISCELLANEOUS

Victorian Wood & Leather Carriage

Baby carriage, painted & decorated wood, leather & cast iron, the convertible leatherette top above a faille tufted & upholstered seat, on wooden spoked wheels w/iron rims & a long arched wooden handle, the body's yellow paint w/dark blue & orange striping, the wheels in cream w/similar accents, America, ca. 1860, imperfections, 24 x 55", 41" h. (ILLUS.) **$460**

Ornate Wicker Twin Baby Carriage

Baby carriage, twin-style, woven wicker, two upholstered seats w/diamond-woven outer sides w/rolled arms & a central woven wicker divider, deep scrolled wicker foot rests, scrolled wooden handles, adjustable iron bar support for parasol, on wire-spoked wheels w/hard rubber rims, late 19th c. (ILLUS.) **850**

Unusual Baby Vehicle

Baby vehicle, painted wood, a blue seat w/U-form crestrail on ring-turned spindles over a block base w/red striping, on a long shaped wooden platform fitted at the front w/a small model of a mohair-covered horse, straight iron handles at the back w/a turned wooden grip, hard rubber-rimmed wire-spoked rear wheels & a small cast-iron front wheel, some paint wear & fabric loss, early 20th c., 39" l., w/handle 21" h. (ILLUS.) **690**

Victorian Stick-and-Ball Crib

Crib, stick- and ball-turned, the headboard, footboard & sides composed of slender crisscrossed ball-turned spindles w/bobbin-turned stiles & knob finials, a slatted bottom, late 19th c., 24 x 45", 36" h. (ILLUS.) **182**

Cup, hand-hammered sterling silver w/elephant handle, engraved "Hilda," Watrous Co., ca. 1900 . . . . **109**

RATTLES

Baby rattles have been a part of every civilization for thousands of years. They are a reflection of how a particular culture lived and cared for their children. Collectors can find rattles made of all types of materials, including: straw, reed, wood, ivory, silver, mother-of-pearl, animal claws, tin, leather, plastic, paper, cloth, gourds and shells. The craftsmanship varies from highly-skilled gold and silversmiths to homemade creations. The rattle's initial purpose was to calm and soothe an upset child. The addition of protective powers, like amulets and charms, were the next logical step. From the beginning of their use until today the gift of a rattle symbolizes the wish for good health and fortune.

Bamboo, drum-shaped, bright colored paper on a bamboo frame w/bead clappers & a wooden handle, w/purpose of warding off evil, Thailand, ca. 1970s, 2½" d. . . **1**

Brass, foot scraper-type, w/a scored & weighted bottom, a bird & rabbit are on top, India, 20th c., 3" w. **350**

Celluloid, model of cocker spaniel, w/painted face atop a pedestal which forms the handle, England, ca. 1920s, 4½" h. . . **90**

Celluloid, model of little girl in sports attire holding tennis racquet, traces of bright color remain, U.S., 1930s, 3" h. **75**

Celluloid, model of Santa Claus, marked "Made in Occupied Japan," intended for the American market, Santa has a face reminiscent of the Japanese sage who symbolizes long life, Japan, ca. 1945-55, 4½" h. **75**

Celluloid, Native American boy & girl paddling canoe, U.S., 1930s, 5¼" l. **35**

Celluloid, boy & girl holding removable umbrella, Japan, 2¾" **80**

Clay, models of seven painted faces strung on a cord, purchased at the Tokyo Folk Art Museum, Japan, ca. 1970s, ¾" d. each bell **20**

Cloth, stuffed cloth doll w/beads or pebbles inside, brightly painted in typical Orissa face & costume style of South India, India, ca. 1970, 9" h. **6**

Cotton, stuffed doll-type, square cotton pillow w/bells attached at corners, painted doll face, Scotland, ca. 1940, 4½" sq. **20**

Cowrie Shell, clustered shells attached to hemp rope, Philippines, early 20th c., 4" l. **20**

Gold, Empire period, w/scrolled buttress design, whistle tip, iridescent mother-of-pearl handle, three original bells, French hallmark, France, ca. 1803, 6" l. **5,000**

Gourd, low relief crocodile design on one side & a human face on the other, from an Akan tribe, Ivory Coast, Africa, early 20th c., 4⅞" d. **700**

Gourd Rattle

Gourd, modern museum reproduction of an antique rattle w/incised figures of the sages, which signify wisdom, China, 2" l. (ILLUS.) **3**

Ivory, Art Deco style, octagonal watchcase shape w/ivory ring, France, c. 1920s-1930s, 2¼" d. **75**

Ivory, doll-type, pierce-work, France, ca. 1900, 1¾" l. **60**

Ivory, dumbell-shaped, w/inlaid multicolored decoration, typical of the Jaipur area, India, ca. 1910, 5" l. **225**

Ivory, openwork of "pom pom," French equivalent of pinchbeck, whistle tip & ivory handle, France, ca. 1900, 3" l. **350**

Ivory, pierce-work w/whistle tip & gold ring, France, ca. 1900, 2¼" l. **50**

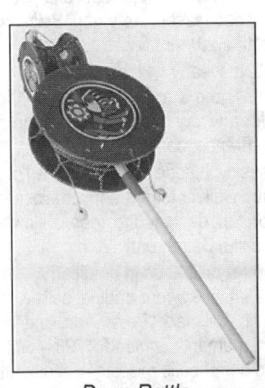

Prisoner's Work Rattle

Ivory, prisoner's work-type, pierced & carved ivory of fine workmanship, France, early 19th c., 5" l. (ILLUS.) **275**

Scrimshaw Rattle

Ivory or whalebone, scrimshaw-type, w/pierced & carved decoration & ivory ring, U.S., mid-19th c., 2" l. (ILLUS.) **500**

Leather, modern souvenir in classic drum-on-a-stick Oriental shape, painted w/wooden handle & pearl bead bangers, China, late 20th c., 6" l. **3**

Drum Rattle

Papier-mâché, model of drum w/painted
stylized cat design & two clappers,
miniature drum is set atop rattle, which is
on a wooden stick, Japan, ca. 1970s (ILLUS.)... **8**

Plastic, blow-up-type, model of popular
television character Miss Piggy, rattle is
weighed at the bottom w/sand or pebbles,
U.S., 1990s, 9½" h. **2**

Plastic, model of costume doll wearing a
European peasant dress, from series of
rattles showing costumes of the world,
France, 1930s, 5¾" h. **40**

Spinner Rattle

Plastic, spinner-type, model of mermaid
holding clear plastic ball w/tiny sea
creatures inside which rattle when spun,
probably designed as a bath toy, original
box showing price of 39¢, U.S.,
ca. 1940s, 7" l. (ILLUS.) **40**

Plastic, World War II period, ball rattle
w/painted design of child wearing an
American soldier's cap, painted
inscription "Sourire de France" meaning
"French smile," France, 1940s, 6" l. **50**

Reed, intricately woven version of the
classic straw rattle, Russia, ca. 1970s, 4½" l. ... **7**

Reed, woven twisted straw design echoing
basketry on rattles of many countries,
Russia, ca. 1970s, 4" l. **7**

Silver, Art Nouveau style, model of a pear
w/embossed leaves, ivory ring, Belgium,
early 20th c., 3" h. **100**

Silver, Art Nouveau style, spinner rattle,
woman's figure & arms in silver form the
frame for an ivory ball, w/carved ivory
handle, France, ca. 1910-15, 5½" l. **450**

Silver, classic Chinese bell-shaped, w/floral
decoration, silver loop & semiprecious
stone on top, designed to keep evil away
from a child, China, early 20th c., 1¾" h. **80**

Silver, coral & bells-type in modified
baluster shape, w/four original bells &
whistle tip, hallmark "Peter, Ann, and
Hester Bateman," England, 1793, 4⅞" l.
(second tier of bells missing, white coral
handle may be a replacement) **1,000**

Silver, coral & bells-type, original bells,
w/whistle tip & thick coral handle, delicate
brightwork decoration, hallmark "W.T."
(William Tookey), George II, England,
ca. 1735, 6½" l. **1,500**

Silver, crystal & bells-type, scrolled buttress
supports, crystal handle, Holland, early
18th c., 5½" l. **750**

Silver, design of Santa Claus descending
chimney on handle which is riveted to an
ivory ring, bells attached to ring have
Santa Clause faces, marked "Sterling,"
U.S., ca. 1910, 4" l. **200**

Silver, embossed, flattened circular shape,
w/whistle tip & its original three bells,
ivory handle, French hallmark, France,
ca. 1830-50, 6" l. **450**

Silver, European style, modified square
shape, w/Chinese character for
happiness engraved in center, w/two
silver bells on a chain, whistle tip & ivory
handle, China Export, China, early
twentieth c., 6⅜" l. **225**

Silver, European style, umbrella-shaped,
w/vermeil decoration & bells, China
Export, China, ca. 1900-10, 3½" l.
(ivory handle is missing)................ **200**

Silver, European style, w/floral engraving,
three bells, carved ivory handle, marked
"MK" for Canton, China Export, China,
mid-19th c., 5" l. **250**

Silver Rattle

Silver, finely engraved design on bulb-
shaped body, silver bells & mother-of-
pearl handle, marked "Sterling," U.S.,
1870-90, 5" l. (ILLUS.) **200**

Golliwog Rattle

Silver, Golliwog-type, figure of Bernice
Upton's storybook character, Birmingham
mark, England, 1917, missing ring, 2¼" h.
(ILLUS.) 200

Silver, hippocampus-type, figure of half-
man, half sea-monster, high relief
decoration w/whistle top & original bells,
Italian hallmark, Italy, mid-18th c., 3½" w.... **1,500**

Silver, lock-shaped, w/embossed floral
design, the lock symbolizes keeping
the child safe from harm, China, late
19th c., 1¾" d. 150

Silver, mallet-shaped, in the traditional style
of Shiva, god of good fortune, low relief
decoration w/clusters of small beads
attached, India, early 20th c., 6¼" l.......... 75

Silver, model of a cottage, high relief design
of typical alpine house with two bells & an
ivory handle, Munich hallmark, Germany,
ca. 1900, 6½" h....................... 175

Silver, model of Boy Scout in full uniform,
w/mother-of-pearl handle, Birmingham
mark, England, 1912-14, 4½" h.
(missing bells) 350

Silver, model of French horn, w/silver bells
& whistle tip, France, 1860-70, 2¼" d. 350

Silver, model of French horn, w/silver bells
& whistle tip, porcelain nipple in whistle
end, France, 1860-70, 3½" d............. 400

Silver, model of Medieval soldier wearing
cloak, probably St. Martin, whistle tip &
mother-of-pearl handle, one of few
religious personages depicted in baby
rattles, French hallmark, France, mid-
19th c., 5½" l. (ivory ring & bells missing)..... 300

Silver, model of owl, representing gift of
wisdom wished for the baby, pressed
design w/two bells, thin coral handle,
Birmingham mark, England, late 19th c.,
3" h. (missing ring) 175

Silver, model of stylized lion, symbol of
Venice, w/whistle at the mouth, original
bells & chain are attached, hallmark
unclear, but it has a Venetian stamping,
Italy, ca. 1750-1800, 2½" w. **1,000**

Silver, modified ball shape, w/floral & piece-
work decoration, Spain, 20th c., 1¾" d.
(ivory handle or ring has been replaced
w/an ivory bead)...................... 40

Silver, Regency style, w/restrained
decoration & original bells, Holland, ca.
1830, 4" l. (coral or crystal handle is
missing) 800

Silver, spinner-type in Moroccan-style
w/delicate filigree work, Spain, ca. 1950,
2" d. (missing ring) 30

Silver, spinner-type, stylized silver ball
w/silver frame & handle, ivory ring, Italy,
ca. 1940s, 4¾" l...................... 100

Silver, w/ivory handle & two silver bells, has
realistic cat's head emerging from barrell,
marked "Sterling," U.S., ca. 1910-15,
3½" l. 150

Silver plated, Art Deco style, w/raised
bowknot design, Belgium, ca. 1920s,
2" h. 30

Silver plated, model of stylized African
native head, ivory ring, Spain, ca. 1950s,
2" h. 25

Silver plated, set of clown rattles, identical
jester-head design on baby rattle, doll
rattle & dollhouse rattle, each w/ivory ring
in proportion, France, ca. 1900, 2½" d.
baby rattle, set of 3 250

Silver & silver gilt, coin-type, coin (called a
thaler) is stamped with the face of Maria
Theresa, valuable old coins were given
as engagement presents, bells were
added at the birth of first child, Austria,
early 20th c., 1⅝" d. coin 800

Straw, traditional woven twisted straw style,
painted in bright colors, 5½" l. 4

Straw & clay, tambourine-shaped, six clay
bells w/painted faces attached to a rigid
straw-wrapped frame, purchased at the
Kurashiki Folk Art Museum, Japan, ca.
1970s, 6½" d.......................... 20

Teak & ivory, Art Deco style, drum-shaped,
attributed to Jacques Ruhlman, who
used knobs of this style on his furniture,
France, ca. 1925, 6" l. 250

Terra cotta, Archaic period, model of
elephant, traces of kaolin, from the
Chandraketugarh region, India, second to
first century B.C., 5½" h. **1,500**

Pre-Columbian Rattle

Terra cotta, Pre-Columbian period, bird
head on rounded body, Costa Rica,
11th-13th c., 3" h. (ILLUS.)............... 350

Terra cotta, Pre-Columbian period,
polychromed terra cotta in the form of a
mythic animal, Costa Rica, 11th-13th c.,
3" h. 400

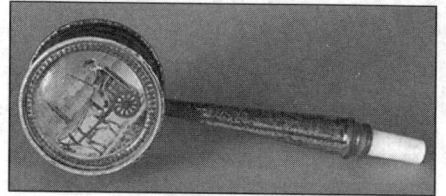

Painted Tin Rattle

Tin, drum-shaped, painted w/colorful scene showing child in a goatcart, tin handle & porcelain whistle tip, France, ca. 1903, 6" l. (ILLUS.)......................... 180

Tin, drum-shaped, painted w/face of Christ, reverse side has head of Pope, probably Benedict XV, who was Pope from 1914 to 1922, painted tin handle & whistle tip, Italy, ca. 1914, 6" l...................... 100

Vermeil, embossed & pierce-work decoration, w/extended whistle tip, ivory handle, France, 1830-50, 6" l. 600

Vermeil, Empire period, ivory handle, design is a reclining angel amid a cluster of bells, French hallmark, France, ca. 1800, 6" l....... 950

Wood, double drum-shaped, polished dark wood w/an incised design & wooden clappers, made by the Congo people, Zaire, Africa, 5" l. 450

Wood, educational toy style, bentwood frame w/brightly painted rings, a modern variation of the beads-on-a-string rattle form, U.S., 1980s, 3½" w.................. 15

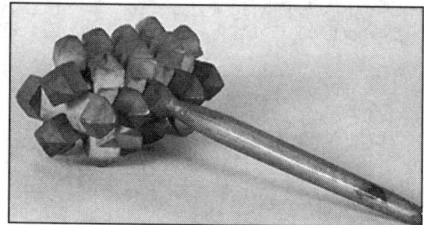

Folk Art Rattle

Wood, Folk Art style, carved wooden rattle similar in style to American tramp art, may have been made by an itinerant farm laborer, England, early 20th c., 5" l. (ILLUS.) 60

Wood, modern bell-shaped, wooden ring & a painted wooden bead are attached, created to ward off evil, China, late 20th c., 2¼" h. 20

Wood, poupard-type, clown w/bisque head (probably French or German) sits atop a wooden drum, wearing gauze & cotton costume, carrying brass cymbals & beating foot on drum, England, early 20th c., 13" h......................... 850

Sistrum Rattle

Wood, sistrum-shaped, w/wooden frame & brass discs in a classic form, Indian, 1997, 9" h. (ILLUS.) 10

Wood, Tramp art style, interlocking pieces of dark-stained wood w/sawtooth edging, U.S., ca. 1870, 7" l..................... 400

Wood, whimsy-style, center rod & sliding rings carved from one piece of dark-stained wood, U.S., early 20th c., 8" l........ 100

BAKELITE

Bakelite, a synthetic resin, was discovered & patented by Belgium born Leo Hendrick Baekeland, in 1907. Soon to replace amber, hard rubber and celluloid, Bakelite was first used industrially for electrical & machinery parts. With Baekeland's patent expiring in 1926, the hard, polished & lightweight substance took many shapes & forms. Today when one thinks of Bakelite, costume jewelry generally is the first thought to come to mind. The Bakelite items and photographs provided below were brought to us by Treadway Gallery, Cincinnati, Ohio, in association with the John Toomey Gallery of Oak Park, Illinois.

Bar pin, charm-style, deep amber carved bar w/three marbled red peppers & three green leaves, 4" w. **$1,760**

Cherries Bar Pin

Bar pin, charm-style, ivory color w/green overdye bar holding eight cherries on white chain w/leaves, 4" w. (ILLUS.) **413**

Bracelet, bangle-type, brown w/overall leaf carving, 2" w. **605**

Bracelet, bangle-type, marbled butterscotch inset w/six alternating marbled orange dots, 1" w. **358**

Bracelet, bangle-type, reverse-carved, apple juice w/ten gold & green fish swimming among waves around entire circumference, 1" w. **1,760**

Bracelet, cuff-style, laminated brown, green, yellow & red, 1" w. **176**

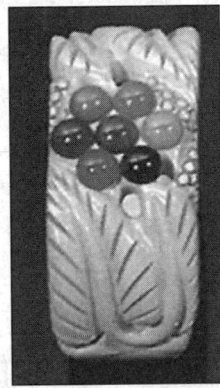

Hinge-style Bracelet with Bead Cluster

Bracelet, hinge-type, carved & reticulated butterscotch w/applied polychrome & bead cluster, 1¼" w. (ILLUS.). **990**

Buckle, figural afghan dog head, ivory colored w/brown painted nose, eye & collar, brass studs on collar, 5½" w. **264**

Crib toy, figural elephant, butterscotch beaded body w/celluloid head, 3¼" h. **88**

Napkin rings, figural elephants w/trunks up, red & butterscotch tones, inset eyes, 3" h., set of 6 . . . . **468**

Necklace, charm-style, fruit & leaves, marbled red strawberry & cherry, butterscotch lemon, orange, pear & apricot, green celluloid leaves, 13" l. **1,320**

Necklace, charm-style, ten ivory colored bowling pins w/red ring & centered black bowling ball on black chain, 8" l. **605**

Pin, charm-style, "1942" class pin, overdyed pen w/"1942" yearbook, ivory diploma, black mortarboard & ink bottle charms, 4" w. **2,860**

Pin, charm-style, butterscotch cruise ship w/wood & Bakelite suitcase charms, all w/painted details, 3" w. **2,200**

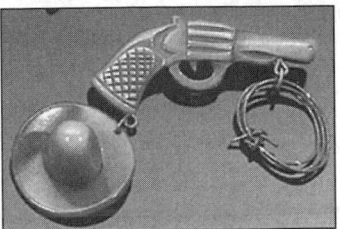

Western Charm Pin

Pin, charm-style, pistol bar w/cowboy hat & lasso charms, butterscotch w/rust overdye, 3" w. (ILLUS.) **264**

Pin, figural cat, marbled green w/pivoting tail & large red painted bow, 4" h. **6,050**

Pin, figural clown head, butterscotch w/painted hat, collar & face details, 3" h. **660**

Pin, figural dagger, marbled green w/carved & gilt detailing, brass bands, 4" l. **187**

Pin, figural flowers w/leaves, heavily carved leaves & two applied red flowers w/painted centers, 4" l. **358**

Pin, figural golfer w/golf bag, butterscotch w/painted details, 2½" h. **495**

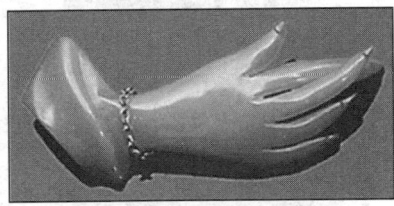

Figural Hand Pin

Pin, figural hand w/crossed fingers, orange w/red painted nails, brass bracelet & cuff, 3½" (ILLUS.) **2,090**

Pin, figural hanging heart & key, red, heart w/keyhole & brass links attaching key, 3". **935**

Pin, figural hat w/wide brim, green w/carved top, red band w/applied red cherries & green leaf, 3" **1,210**

Pin, figural hound dog head, overdyed marbled green w/inset eye & fabric flower decoration on ear, 3½" l. **1,100**

Lion Pin

Pin, figural lion, butterscotch w/painted red & black details, inset red felt mane, designed by Martha Sleeper, 3½" l. (ILLUS.) **2,750**

Owl Pin

Pin, figural owl, blue overdye on ivory w/deep carving & applied googly eyes, 3" h. (ILLUS.) **2,860**

Pin, figural pineapple, marbled butterscotch w/carved & painted details, 3" l. **1,100**

Scottie Dog Pin

Pin, figural Scottie dog, butterscotch w/red overdye & red painted bow, glass eye, 3" w. (ILLUS.) **935**

Pin, figural tiger, butterscotch w/red & black painted details, inset leather ears, designed by Martha Sleeper, 3½" l. **2,530**

"Moon Over Miami" Pin

Pin, "Moon Over Miami," figural, butterscotch man-in-the-moon w/palm tree, 3" w. (ILLUS.) **4,950**

Pin, "School Days," girl w/black yarn hair & white ribbons reading "ABC's" book, ivory w/light overdye, 4" w. **4,950**

Pin, "Victory," thick red heart w/applied black "V", 2½" **1,650**

Stick pin, figural tulip, marbled red w/carved details, screw-on stem, 5½" l. **33**

BANKS

Original early mechanical and cast-iron still banks are in great demand with collectors. Their scarcity has caused numerous reproductions of both types and the novice collector is urged to exercise caution. The early mechanical banks are especially scarce and some versions are seldom offered for sale but, rather, are traded with fellow collectors attempting to upgrade an existing collection. Numbers before mechanical banks refer to those in John Meyer's Handbook of Old Mechanical Banks. *However, another book* Penny Lane---A History of Antique Mechanical Toy Banks, *by Al Davidson, provides updated information and the number from this new volume is indicated in parenthesis at the end of each mechanical bank listing. In past years, our standard reference for cast-iron still banks was Hubert B. Whiting's book* Old Iron Still Banks, *but because this work is out of print and a beautiful new book,* The Penny Lane Bank Book---Collecting Still Banks *by Andy and Susan Moore pictures and describes numerous additional banks, we will use the Moore numbers as a reference preceding each listing and indicate the Whiting reference in parenthesis at the end. The still banks listed are old and in good original condition with good paint and no repair unless otherwise noted. An asterisk (*) indicates this bank has been reproduced at some time.*

MECHANICAL

1 Acrobat, w/blue base, swinging acrobat causing the clown to spin & the coin to fall, designed by Edward Morris of Boston, pat. Feb. 8, 1883 (some chipping especially to figures), 7¼" l. (PL 1) **$6,325**

Artillery Bank (round trap), soldier w/moving arm, mortar fires coin into opening of building, (lacking round trap), 8" w. (PL 12) **3,795**

Bank Teller Bank

10 "Bank" Teller, when coin is inserted in teller's extended hand, the weight causes him to lower his arm so coin drops into bank & he nods his head, (PL 24), rare (ILLUS.) **96,000**

23 Boy on Trapeze, w/red shirt & blue trousers, on lattice base, (damage to base top, considerable chipping to figure), 9½" h. (PL50) **1,495**

22 Boys Stealing Watermelons, dog house w/dog, two boys stealing watermelons, ca. 1885-95, 7" w. (PL 53) **4,543**

25 Buffalo - "Trick Buffalo Bank," semi-mechanical, w/removable head, 9½" l. (PL 60) **748**

65 Bull Dog - Standing, Coin on Tongue, w/moving tongue & tail, paint worn, 6½" l. (PL 66) **575**

Clown, Harlequin & Columbine Bank

119 Clown & Harlequin (The), & Columbine, pat. Nov. 13, 1877, after coin is inserted between figure of Harlequin & clown, press lever on right & the two figures reverse themselves, causing figure of Columbine to spin & coin to go into the bank (ILLUS.) **85,000**

Clown on Globe Bank

49 Clown on Globe, w/turning & flipping mechanism, red & orange outfit, blue sphere & tan base, (lacking trap), unextended 9" h. PL 127 (ILLUS.) **15,874**

53 "Creedmoor Bank," w/red trousers, w/firing rifle, moving head & bell, marked on the base, stamped "Bowden Series," 10" w. (PL 137) **728**

Darky And Watermelon

92 Darky and Watermelon, (Football Bank), place coin in the football & pull darky's right leg back until it locks; press lever on darky's back & he kicks the football dropping coin into bank, (PL 147), rare (ILLUS.) **354,500**

88 Elephant & Three Clowns on Tub, w/red blanket, the elephant's trunk knocks the coin into the base & the mounted clown turns, 5¾" h. (PL 170) . . **1,696**

82 Elephant Howdah (Man Pops Out), finished in gold, black & red, w/moving trunk causing the wood figure to pop out of the trunk, 6½" l. **920**

79 Elephant - "Three Stars," w/moving trunk & tail, ca. 1880s, paint loss & chipping, 9" l. (PL 183) **316**

91 Ferris Wheel, wheel finished in orange & black w/six yellow gondolas each carrying two male riders, base w/clockwork motor, coin-slot & on/off lever, finished in black w/red

Ferris Wheel Bank

highlights, underside marked "Bowen's Pat Apd For," (chipping to wheel & gondolas), 22" h., PL188 (ILLUS.)........................ **12,650**

Freedman's Bank

98 "Freedman's Bank," (wood, metal, cloth), after winding the spring in rear of bank, place coin on table by figure's left hand & press lever; figure will turn his head from side to side as he scoops coin into slot on top of table & raises his right hand to his face & thumb to his nose, moving each finger independently; then he lowers his hand & shakes his head, rare, historically important, (PL 198), excellent (ILLUS.) **321,500**

99 Frog Bank, two frogs - 1 lying on back, 1 sitting, w/opening mouth & remnants of paint, (lacking frog's leg), 8½" l. (PL 200) **920**

102 Frog on Round Lattice Base, w/foot operated mouth & eyes, (paint worn, retaining screw replaced), 4¼" d. (PL 204) **489**

146 Hall's Liliput Bank, w/tray, w/pivoting cashier & white domed building, ca. 1877, (lacking trap), 4½" h. (PL 230) **4,600**

121 Hen & Chick, cast iron, the brown hen opens its mouth & her chick pops up to deposit the coin, w/bellows making "clucking" sound, 9¾" w. (PL 236) **4,425**

127 Humpty Dumpty, clown figure depicts well-known pantomime G. L. Fox , w/moving arm, tongue & eyes, (chipping), 7½" h. (PL 248) **788**

132 "Jolly Nigger," w/red shirt, moving arm, tongue & rolling eyes, patented on March 14, 1882, 6½" h. (PL 275) **316**

133 "Jolly Nigger," w/moving eyes & tongue, red shirt & collar, yellow butterfly tie & buttons (considerable paint loss to arm), 4⅝" w.............. **201**

143 Leap Frog Bank, two boys play leap frog near fence & tree stump, one boy leaps over the other to hit a lever which causes the coin to fall into the tree, (considerable chipping especially to figures), 7½" w. (PL 292) .. **3,798**

Lion Hunter Bank

148 Lion Hunter, mica flakes make painted rocks more realistic, w/firing rifle, moving head, & rearing lion (rifle inoperative), 11" w., PL 301 (ILLUS.) ... **3,220**

150 Little Joe, bust w/extended right hand, w/moving eyes & tongue, red shirt, white collar, & blue tie, (arm broken, chipping), 3¾" h. (PL 304) **144**

Mosque Bank

168 Mosque, rotating gorilla figure inside building & hand crank at side, black w/blue wipe (lacking finial) 6¾" h., PL 340 (ILLUS.) **1,035**

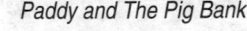

Old Woman in the Shoe Bank

242 Old Woman in the Shoe, woman raises her arm & boy leans forwards to deposit coin (PL 367), rare (ILLUS.). **426,000**

179 Organ Bank, in the form of a barrel organ, w/hand-turned mechanism causing the monkey to deposit the coin, tip his hat, & the bell to ring, (paint loss, lacking trap), 6½" h. (PL 371) **1,035**

184 Owl w/Book, w/coin-slot in book under wing causing the eyes to move, (lacking trap, paint loss), 5¾" h. (PL 373) **288**

Paddy and The Pig Bank

185 Paddy and the Pig, w/dark blue jacket, moving mouth & eyes, J. & E. Stevens Co., Aug. 8, 1882, 8" h., PL 376 (ILLUS.) **5,463**

186 Panorama Bank, house w/opening in front to reveal lithographed pictures mounted on wooden wheel which moves when coins are deposited, J.

Panorama Bank

& E. Stevens & Co., pat. March 7, 1876, (some repair & repaint to roof), PL 377 (ILLUS.) **18,400**

188 Peg Leg Beggar, w/off-white face, drop coin in slot in the hat & beggar nods his head in thanks, 5" h. (PL 380) **575**

194 Pig in High Chair, nickel plated, cast w/floral & foliate motifs, the pig lifts tray, swallows the coin & moves his tongue, pat. Aug. 24, 1897, 6" h. (PL 390) **1,380**

Preacher In The Pulpit Bank

197 Preacher in the Pulpit, when a coin is placed on the tray, the weight causes the preacher to lower his arm & the coin slides from the tray into the bank; simultaneously, he tilts his head forward, J. & E. Stevens Co. pat. Aug. 1, 1876 (PL 395), rare (ILLUS.). **233,500**

201 Professor Pug Frog's Great Bicycle Feat, Mother Goose reading w/frog riding bicycle & clown holding large basket, some flaking (PL 400) **3,025**

203 "Punch & Judy," figures in theater setting (PL 404). **7,198**

211 Roller Skating, two figures skating around rink, two have fallen & one stands (PL 417). **156,500**

212 **Rooster,** on base, w/moving head &
beak, ca. 1880-90, 6¼" h. (PL 419) **920**
220 **Squirrel & Tree Stump,** the squirrel
leaps to drop coin into stump,
(underside possibly replaced), 7" w.
(PL 452) **863**
224 **Tammany - "Little Fat Man,"** seated
man in suit, vest & bow tie, (chipping)
5½" h. (PL 455) **690**

![Teddy and the Bear Bank]

Teddy and the Bear Bank

226 **Teddy and the Bear,** w/brown tree,
Teddy shoots the bull's-eye, raises
his head & the bear pops out of the
tree, lacking trap, 10¼" w., PL 459
(ILLUS.). **2,760**
227 **Telephone - "Pay Phone Bank,"**
cast iron & sheet metal, semi-
mechanical, bell rings when coin is
deposited, finished in maroon, black
& silver, w/5, 10 & 25 cent slots,
(some chipping), 7¼" h.(PL 462) **3,220**
103 **Toad on Stump,** green painted
w/opening mouth, (base affected by
damp), 4" l. (PL 475) **489**
72 **Trick Dog Bank (solid base),** clown
w/hoop, barrel & dog, dog jumps
through the clown's hoop, modern
w/one-piece solid base, 8¾" w. (PL 482). . **690**
195 **"Tricky Pig Bank,"** cast brass, after
the Bismark bank, w/tail lever causing
the figure to emerge from the pig's
back, 8½" l. (PL 486) **690**

World's Fair Bank

244 **World's Fair Bank,** the Indian chief
appears after lever is pushed, then
hands Columbus a peace pipe as

Columbus salutes, w/"Columbus"
cast into base, "World's Fair Bank"
cast on front (finish worn on tree
trunk), 8¼" w., PL 573 (ILLUS.) **1,150**

POTTERY

![Human Bean Bank]

Human Bean Bank

Bean,"Human Bean," ceramic,
modern, Enesco (ILLUS.). **40**

![Entenmann's Chef Bank]

Entenmann's Chef Bank

Chef, marked "Entenmann's,"
ceramic, modern, made in China (ILLUS.). . **50**

Cool Cash Penguin Bank

Penguin, "Cool Cash," ceramic, modern, Hallmark (ILLUS.) 125

Warner Brothers Tour Bus Bank

Tour bus, Warner Brothers characters appear in windows of double decker tour bus, ceramic, modern (ILLUS.). 90

Uncle Sam bust, ceramic, ca. 1940s, made in Japan, 7" tall (ILLUS.) 35

Uncle Sam Bank

STILL

698 Bear - "Teddy" Bear, cast iron, "Teddy Bear" embossed on side, Arcade Mfg. Co., 1910-25, very good, 3⅞" l., 2½" h. (W. 331) 165

Bear Stealing Pig

693 Bear - Bear Stealing Pig, American-made, original gold paint, scarce, pristine, 5½" h. (ILLUS.) 1,430

81 "Billiken-Good Luck," gold w/green hair, 4" h. 316

676 Bird - Old Abe with Shield (eagle), cast iron, American-made, ca. 1880, good, 3⅞" h. (W. 255) 550

597 Bird - Owl, cast iron, orange & white, Vindex, 1930, pristine, 2½" w., 4¼" h. (W. 203) 275

"Be Wise Owl"

598 Bird - "Be Wise Owl," cast iron, "Be Wise - Save Money" on stump, A.C. Williams Co., 1912-20s, 2½" w., 4⅞" h., excellent (ILLUS.) 198

174 Black Man - Darkey (Sharecropper), cast iron, w/toes visible on both feet, American-made, early 1900s, pristine, 5¼" h. 352

556 Buffalo - Amherst Buffalo, cast iron, "Amherst Stoves" embossed on side of buffalo, has 5" slot for dollar bills, American-made, ca. 1930s, near mint, 8" l., 5¼" h. (W. 207) 418

1145 Building - Cupola Bank, cast iron, Vermont Novelty Works 1869 & J. & E. Stevens Co. 1872, w/red roof, gray/blue walls, & yellow & red details, 3⅜ x 4¼ x 5½" (W. 305) 1,150

Flat Iron Building Bank

1160 Building - "Flat Iron Building Bank," cast iron, small trap, Kenton Mfg. Co., 1904-26, triangular w/silver finish, lacking trap, paint wear, 4½ x 4¾ x 5¾" h. (ILLUS.) **230**

1237 Building - "Home Savings Bank" Dog Finial, cast iron, J. & E. Stevens Co., 1891, 3⁵⁄₁₆ x 4⅜ x 5¾" h. (W. 375) . . . **360**

1020 Building - Ironmaster's House, cast iron, w/combination trap, Kyser & Rex Co., 1884, 2¾ x 2⅞ x 4½" h. (W. 298) . . **2,530**

990 Building - Old South Church, cast iron, modeled after the Old South Church in Boston, Massachusetts, American-made, 1900, (damage to corner of one wall, spire top rusted), 4 x 6⅜", 9¼" h. to top of spire **4,025**

1122 Building - Roof "Bank," cast iron, J. & E. Stevens Co., 1887, w/mansard roof & gilt highlights, 3¼ x 3¾ x 5¼" h. (W. 366) **345**

1124 Building - Roof Bank, cast iron, Grey Iron Casting Co., 1903-28, w/triangular shingles & gilt highlights, 3¼ x 3¾ x 5¼" h. **201**

State Bank

1078 Building - State Bank, cast iron, w/cupola dormer windows & locking door, Kenton Mfg. Co., ca. 1900, 5½ x 7 x 8" h. (ILLUS.) **1,380**

Tower Bank

1198 Building - Tower Bank, cast iron, "Tower Bank" above door & "1890" on red door w/inner & outer door alphabetic combination door lock, Kyser & Rex Co., 1890, 6⅞" sq., W. 437 (ILLUS.) **1,035**

1179 Building - Villa, cast iron, two story building w/ornamental top & four corner towers, Kyser & Rex Co., ca. 1894, paint loss, especially to roof, 3 x 4⅞ x 5½" h. (W. 376) **403**

1242 Building - Independence Hall, cast iron, Enterprise Mfg. Co., 1875, w/removable tower, cast legends "Birthplace of American Independence" & "LIberty Proclaimed July 4, 1776," tied reed plinth w/gilt finish, 8 x 9⅜ x 10" h. (W. 447) **978**

Buster Brown & Tige

241 Buster Brown & Tige, cast iron, A.C. Williams Co., 1910-32, 5½" h. (W. 2), pristine (ILLUS.) **330**

770 Camel - Kneeling Camel, cast iron, scarce, wearing pack, Kyser & Rex Co., 1889, excellent, 2½" h., 4¹³⁄₁₆" l. (W. 256) **462**

163 "Campbell Kids," cast iron, A.C. Williams Co., 1910-21, pristine, 3¼" h. . . . **308**

952 Chest - Jewel Chest (Coffin Bank), nickel-plated cast iron, w/hinged lid, combination lock, embossed scrolls on footed coffin, American-made, 1889, 6⅛" l., 4⅝" h. **316**

544 Cow - Holstein Cow, cast iron, standing animal, white w/black markings, Arcade Mfg. Co., 1910-20, excellent, 2½" h., 4⅝" l. (W. 188) **220**

407 Dog - "Lost Dog," cast iron, Judd Mfg. Co.(?), ca 1890s(?), excellent, 5⅜" h. (W. 115) **418**

443 Dog - Fido on Pillow, cast iron, Hubley Mfg. Co., ca. 1920s, very good, 7⅜" base, 5¾" h. (W. 336) **220**

442 Dog - Puppo on Pillow, cast iron, w/bee on side, Hubley Mfg. Co., ca. 1920s, (chipping), 6" l., 5⅝" h. W. 336). **173**

428 Dog - Tiny Scottie, cast iron, black
overall, in seated position, American-
made, excellent, 3⅛" h. **165**

409 Dog - Spitz, cast iron, 1928, finished
in gold (paint wear), 4½" l., 4¼" h. **374**

St. Bernard with Pack Bank

437 Dog - St. Bernard with Pack (large),
cast iron, A.C. Williams Co.,
1901-30s, 7¾" l., 5½" h., W. 113 (ILLUS.). . **86**

500 Donkey (large), cast iron, A.C.
Williams Co., ca. 1920s, pristine,
6¼" l., 6¹³⁄₁₆" h. (W. 197). **385**

616 Duck - Duck on Tub, cast iron,
"Save for a Rainy Day," Hubley Mfg.
Co., 1930-36, near mint, 5⅜" h. (W. 323). . **220**

462 Elephant - Circus Elephant, cast
iron, seated animal wearing child's
straw hat w/ribbon, Hubley Mfg. Co.,
1930-40, 3⅞" h. **330**

Elephant on Wheels

446 Elephant - Elephant on Wheels,
cast iron, A.C. Williams Co., 1920s,
4⅛" h., 4⅜" l. (W. 75) pristine (ILLUS.) . . . **495**

General Butler

54 General Butler, cast iron, man in the
form of a frog reads "Bonds & Yachts
for Me - For the Masses This is
$1,000,000," J. & E. Stevens Co.,
1884, 6½" h., (lacking trap, paint
loss), W. 294 (ILLUS.). **2,828**

"Two Kids" Bank

594 Goat - "Two Kids," cast iron, base
embossed "Two Kids," Harper Mfg.
Co.(?), 4½" w., 4½" h., W. 262,
excellent (ILLUS.) **1,430**

610 Goose - "Red Goose Shoes," cast
iron, Arcade Mfg. Co., ca. 1920s,
very good, 3¾" h. **330**

532 Horse - "Beauty," cast iron, Arcade
Mfg. Co., 1910-32, excellent, 4⅛" h.,
4¾" l. (W. 82) **88**

**506 Horse - Prancing Horse with Belly
Band,** cast iron, American-made,
5" l., 4½" h. **190**

523 Horse - Saddle Horse, cast iron,
small, A.C. Williams Co., 1934, very
good, 3³⁄₁₆" l., 2¾" h. (W. 86) **132**

Tally Ho Bank

535 Horse - "Tally Ho," cast iron, horse
head framed by horseshoe w/fox hunt
items, Chamberlain & Hill, England,
4½" h., 4³⁄₁₆" l., (W. 168), pristine
(ILLUS.) **242**

Work Horse

533 Horse - Work Horse, cast iron, black, Arcade Mfg. Co., ca. 1910, 4⅛" h., 4¾" l. (W. 81) near mint (ILLUS.).. **220**

228 Indian - Indian with Tomahawk, cast iron, Hubley Mfg. Co., 1915-30s, pristine, 5⅞" h. (W. 39) **440**

Lion on Tub

746 Lion - Lion on Tub, cast iron, decorated, A.C. Williams Co., 1920s-34, tub 2½" d., 5½" h. (W. 57), near mint (ILLUS.) **165**

Three Wise Monkeys Bank

743 Monkeys - Three Wise Monkeys, cast iron, embossed "See, Hear & Speak No Evil" on base, A.C. Williams Co., 1910-12, excellent, 3¼" x 3½" (ILLUS.) **242**

177 Mulligan (Policeman), cast iron, A.C. Williams Co. 1905-32 & Hubley Mfg. Co. 1914, pristine, 5¾" h. (W. 8) **308**

1184 Multiplying Bank, cast iron, Gothic Revival house w/steps leading to glass paneled archway revealing interior fitted w/two mirrors which create the illusion of multiplying coins, J. & E. Stevens Co., 1883, (lacking trap), 5⅛ x 5¹⁄₁₆ x 6½" h. **5,031**

Mutt & Jeff Bank

157 "Mutt & Jeff," cast iron, A.C. Williams Co., 1912-31, 3½" x 4¼" h., w/worn gold paint, W. 13, (ILLUS.) **119**

613 Pig - "A Christmas Roast," cast iron, "Christmas Roast" embossed on side, American-made, pristine, 3¼" h., 7⅛" l., (W. 185) **357**

264 Pig - Porky Pig, cast iron, "Porky," on square base, Hubley Mfg. Co., ca. 1930, 5¾" h. (W. 27) **88**

311 Frog - Professor Pug Frog (Frog Bank), cast iron, A.C. Williams Co., 1905-12, 3¼" h. (W. 230)............. **132**

565 Rabbit - Rabbit Lying Down, cast iron, American-made, gold overall, pristine, 2⅛" h., 5⅛" l. (W. 101) **990**

819 Radio - Crosley Radio (large), cast iron, Kenton, US 1931-1936, excellent, 4½" l. x 5⅛" h. **605**

827 Radio - "Majestic" Radio, cast iron w/steel back, cabinet-style on legs, Arcade, US, 1932-34, original box, near mint, 4½" h. **462**

826 Radio - "Templetone Radio," cast iron w/steel sides, Kenton, US, 1930-34, pristine, 4⁵⁄₁₆" h............. **550**

721 Rhino, cast iron, gold overall, Arcade Mfg. Co., 1910-25, very good, 2⅝" h., 5" l. (W. 252) **330**

547 Rooster, cast iron, black w/red highlights & white eyes, Arcade Mfg. Co., 1910-25, pristine, 4⅝" h. (W. 187) ... **275**

882 Safe - "Arabian Safe," cast iron,
key-locked trap w/key, door & sides
w/Middle Eastern scenes, Kyser &
Rex Co., 1882, some corrosion &
discoloring, 4⅛ x 4¼ x 4⁹⁄₁₆" h. (W. 346) . . . 86

Safe "Bank of Industry," nickel-plated
iron, w/combination lock, door cast
w/blacksmith, top cast w/tools,
instruments & other technological
motifs, 5½" h. 86

"Fidelity Trust Vault" Safe Bank

901 Safe - "Fidelity Trust Vault" (with
Lord Fauntleroy), cast iron, Lord
Fauntleroy & his dog often mistaken
for Buster Brown & Tige, embossed
under each of four windows
"Security," "Fidelity," "Paying Teller,"
and "Cashier," J. Barton Smith Co.,
1890, 3⅞ x 4½ x 4⅞" h., W. 398 (ILLUS.). . 431

891 "Security Safe Deposit," cast iron,
Kyser & Rex Co.(?), ca. 1881,
w/inner & outer lettered combination
knobs & gilt highlights, 2⅜ x 2¹³⁄₁₆ x
3⅞" h. (latch bracket detached) 105

895 Safe "Time Safe," cast iron w/eagle
motif above clock face w/legend
"What Time Does It Open", door
opens at correct time setting.,
w/original instruction sheet,
3¾" l., 7¹⁄₁₆" h. (W. 397) 575

732 Sea Lion (Seal on Rock), cast iron,
black overall, Arcade Mfg. Co., 1910-
13, pristine, 3½" h. , 4¼" l. (W. 199) 528

154 Trust Bank (The), cast iron, figure of
old banker w/lettering on vest, J. & E.
Stevens Co., late 19th c., excellent,
7¼" h. (W. 317) 5,280

848 U.S. Mailbox - Air Mail Bank on
Base, cast iron, pedestal base, Dent
Hardware Do., ca. 1920, very good,
6⅜" h., 2⅝" w., base 2¾" d. 155

BARBERIANA

*A wide variety of antiques related to the
tonsorial arts have been highly collectible for
many years, especially 19th and early 20th-
century shaving mugs and barber bottles and,
more recently, razors. We are now combining
these closely related categories under one
heading for easier reference. A selection of other
varied pieces relating to barbering will also be
found below.*

BARBER BOTTLES

Amber, Coin Spot patt. w/orange, white &
yellow enamel decoration, pontil scarred
base, rolled lip, scarce pattern, ca.
1885-1925, 8⅛" h. $94

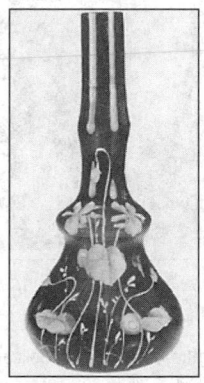

Amethyst Corset-waisted Barber Bottle

Amethyst, Optic Rib patt., corset waisted-
form, w/blue, orange & green enamel
floral decoration, pontil scarred base,
sheared lip, perfect, ca. 1885-1925,
7⅞" h. (ILLUS.) 770

Black amethyst, Optic Rib patt. w/white &
orange enamel floral decoration, pontil
scarred base, rolled lip, ca. 1885-1925, 7" h. . . . 105

Clear, cut shoulder & neck flutes,
multicolored enamel decoration of
golfers, polished pontil, sheared lip,
ca. 1885-1925, 7⅛" h. 1,210

Clear, detailed multicolored enamel
decoration showing a deer on winter
mountain scene, smooth base, applied
mouth, perfect, 8⅜" h. 413

Clear w/ruby red, laid on web design,
smooth base, polished lip, about perfect,
ca. 1885-1925, 7¾" h. (some light inside
haze rings) 688

Cobalt blue, Coin Spot patt. w/white
enamel, Mary Gregory cameo-style
decoration, pontil scarred base, rolled lip,
scarce pattern, ca. 1885-1925, 8¼" h. 770

Cobalt blue, Optic Rib patt. w/pleasing multicolored floral decoration & gilt lettering reading "Hair Tonic," pontil scarred base, rolled lip, perfect, 9" h. **990**

Cobalt blue, white enameled Mary Gregory boy tennis player decoration, pontil scarred base, rolled lip, ca. 1885-1925, perfect, 8" h. **385**

Cut clear, Diamond patt., smooth base, tooled lip, original sterling silver stopper w/screw off top, perfect, 8⅜" h. **231**

Deep pinkish amethyst, white enameled Mary Gregory woman holding basket of flowers, pontil scarred base, rolled lip, perfect, 7¼" h. (ILLUS.) **385**

Deep turquoise blue, Thumbprint patt., polished pontil, rolled lip, ca. 1885-1925, 7" h. (some light inside haze) **121**

Frosted apple green, Optic Rib patt., enameled Art Nouveau style "belt buckle" decoration, pontil scarred base, rolled lip, ca. 1885-1925, perfect, 8" h. **330**

From left:Cobalt Blue Mallet-Form Barber Bottle Cobalt Blue Bell-Shaped Barber Bottle

Deep cobalt blue, mallet form w/delicate orange, yellow, & white enamel decoration, pontil scarred base, rolled lip, perfect, ca. 1885-1925, 7¾" h. (ILLUS.) **187**

Deep cobalt blue, Optic Rib patt. bell form w/white & gilt enamel flower & butterfly design, pontil scarred base, sheared lip, 8" h. (ILLUS.) **1,155**

From left: Frosted Green "Art Nouveau" Design Frosted Pink Puce Barber Bottle

Frosted grass green, bell-form w/white & gilt Art Nouveau style leaf & flower decoration, pontil scarred base, sheared lip, perfect, 8" h. (ILLUS. left) **963**

Frosted pink puce, w/overall white enamel decoration, smooth base, polished lip, ca. 1885-1925, 7⅞" h. (ILLUS. right) **413**

Frosted topaz, Optic Rib patt. w/large, multicolored enameled rose decoration, pontil scarred base, sheared lip, ca. 1885-1925, 8⅛" h. **578**

Mary Gregory Woman Holding Basket

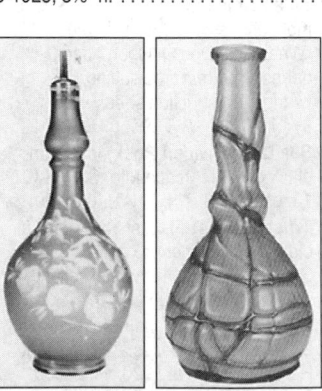

From left: Frosted Turquoise w/White Enamel Loetz-type Iridescent Pearl Barber Bottle

Frosted turquoise blue, w/white enamel floral decoration, smooth base, sheared lip, perfect, 8¾" h. (ILLUS. left) **176**

Frosted yellow green, Optic rib patt. w/white & gilt floral design, pontil scarred base, sheared lip, perfect, ca. 1885-1925, 7⅝" h. **220**

Iridescent pearl, Loetz-type, iridescent pearl w/heavy cobalt blue vine-type design throughout, smooth base, polished lip, applied mouth, ca. 1885-1925, 7¾" h. (ILLUS. right) **1,815**

Light cranberry red, Optic Rib patt. w/multicolored floral decoration, smooth base, rolled lip, perfect, ca. 1885-1925, 7¼" h. **385**

Light yellow green, Coin Spot patt. w/white, yellow & orange enamel decoration, pontil scarred base, rolled lip, perfect, ca. 1885-1925, 8" h. **116**

Light yellow green, Optic rib patt. w/red & white enamel decoration, corset-form, pontil scarred base, sheared lip, about perfect, ca. 1885-1925, 7⅝" h. (two crazing lines in edge of lip) **88**

Milk glass, w/multicolored cherub decoration, pontil scarred base, sheared lip, 7⅝" h. **303**

From left: Cranberry Daisy & Fern Pattern Bottle Cranberry Opalescent Swirl Bottle

Opalescent cranberry, melon-ribbed sides, ornate Daisy & Fern patt., smooth base, rolled lip, perfect, ca. 1885-1925, 7" h. (ILLUS. left) **231**

Opalescent cranberry, Swirl patt. to left, polished pontil, rolled lip, perfect, ca. 1885-1925, 6⅞" h. (ILLUS. right) **303**

Pink amethyst, bell-form w/white & gilt Art Nouveau floral decoration, sheared lip, pontil scarred base, ca. 1885-1925, 7⅝" h., .. **550**

Purple amethyst, Optic Rib patt. w/large white enamel floral decoration, pontil scarred base, sheared lip, perfect, 7⅞" h. **105**

Purple amethyst, Optic Rib patt. w/white enameled Mary Gregory-type cottage decoration & words "Witch Hazel," pontil scarred base, rolled lip, perfect, 7¾" h. **523**

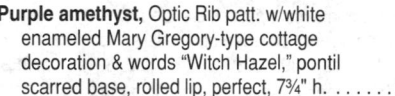

From left: Purple Amethyst Art Nouveau Bottle Bohemian-style Barber Bottle

Purple amethyst, Optic rib patt. w/yellow & gold Art Nouveau floral decoration, pontil scarred base, rolled lip, perfect, 7¾" h. (ILLUS.) **220**

Purple amethyst, w/white enamel, Mary Gregory style, bust portrait of woman w/"Vegederma," below , pontil scarred base, rolled lip, ca. 1885-1925, 7¾" h **523**

Ruby red cut to clear, Bohemian-style etched decoration of a deer, tower, etc., smooth base, polished lip, perfect, ca. 1885-1924, 8⅝" h. (ILLUS.) **495**

Spatter, clear, white & blue overall spatter, polished pontil, polished lip, perfect, ca. 1890-1930, 7¾" h. **330**

Cranberry Spatter Fountain Form Bottle

Spatter, opalescent pinkish cranberry, fountain-form, polished pontil, flared lip, perfect, ca. 1890-1930, 8¼" h. (ILLUS.) **853**

Teal blue, melon-ribbed sides w/Coin Spot patt., smooth base, rolled lip, ca. 1885-1925, 8½" h. **121**

Turquoise blue, Hobnail patt., polished pontil, rolled lip, ca. 1885-1925, 7" h. (one hobnail w/small chip) **105**

Yellowish green, Optic Rib patt. w/red & white enamel decoration, pontil scarred base, sheared lip, perfect, ca. 1885-1925, 7½" h. **88**

MUGS

FRATERNAL

Fraternal Order of the Elk Shaving Mug

Benevolent & Protective Order of the Elk, shows emblem w/owner's name below, good detail, 3⅝" h. (ILLUS.) **99**

Brotherhood of Firemen, shows a horseshoe w/the letters "B. of L.F.E.," colorful sprigs of flowers on either side of decoration, owner's name above, 3⅝" h. **198**

Brotherhood of Railroad Trainmen, shows a mail car w/letters "B. & O.R.R." (Baltimore & Ohio) on side, also decorated w/their emblem on side, owner's name above, base stamped "T & V Limoges France", 3⅝" h. **413**

GAR Ribbon Mug

Grand Army of the Republic, shows a GAR "Sons of the Republic" ribbon-medal, owner's name above, 3⅝" h. **385**

Junior Order of United Auto Mechanics, w/American flags on each side, owner's name below, mug has full blue wrap, some blue worn off wrap, 3⅞" h. **66**

Knights of Columbus, shows emblem, owner's name below, looks like never used, "Felda China Germany" marked on base, 3⅝" h. **176**

Modern Woodsmen of America, shows emblem surrounded by floral decoration, owner's name above, base marked "The Eugene Berninghaus Co., Cincinnati," perfect, 3⅝" h. **198**

Mystic Shrine, shows emblem, owner's name above in gilt, base marked "C.A. Smith Barber Supplies Philadelphia," 3⅝" h. . . . **242**

Odd Fellows, photographic mug for Glen Bunk w/Odd Fellows emblem below, All Seeing Eye all above photo, mug w/full mint green wrap, base marked "T & V Limoges France," perfect **1,265**

Order of Redmen, shows their emblem w/owner's name above, "E.J.M." in gold on base, 3⅝" h. (thin crack on outer part of handle) **94**

Patriotic Order of Sons of America, decorated w/their emblem & owner's name above on one side & a hand operating a telegraph key on the other, ca. 1885-1925, 3½" h. (professional repair exists on top of base rim beneath Fraternal logo) **275**

GENERAL

Cameo style, raised white cameo of a woman on blue background, ca. 1900-1930, 3⅝" h. **61**

Character Toby Mug

Character Toby, figural seated Mr. Toby, scuttle-type, white china w/multicolored glazes, ca. 1900-1925, 4⅛" h. **187**

Character-type, white china, model of a pig's head in pink, red & black, ca. 1900-1925, base marked "P.M. Bavaria," 3½" h. . . . **204**

Number, "13" in black w/gold outline, base marked "J.P.L. France," scarce room mug **121**

Portrait-type, decorative portrait of pretty
woman, owner's name above, 3½" h. **253**

OCCUPATIONAL

Artist, shows an artist's palette & several
small rose flowers, owner's name above
palette, perfect, 3½" h. **358**

Baker, scene of baker putting two loaves of
bread in oven, highly detailed & colorful,
other tools, etc. in background, "M.
Schneider" written above, base stamped
"P.B.S. Co." & "C.F.H. G.D.M.," 3⅞" h.
(sizable repair exists to left of decoration) **121**

"Conrad Baker" Mug with Bread Roll

Baker, shows a bread roll, leaf decoration
shaped around bread, "Conrad Baker"
written above, 3⅝" h. (ILLUS.) **440**

Bartender, scene of bar room w/two men &
the bartender, "John Connaghan" written
above, 3⅞" h. **330**

Blacksmith, scene of blacksmith shoeing a
horse, "H.W. Hemich" above, base
stamped "Limoges W.G. & Co., France" &
"The World Our Field Koken St. Louis
Trade Mark," detailed, perfect, 4" h. **550**

Brakeman, shows railroad brakeman's
wheel, name "A. B. Weil 1901" inside
spokes, colorful sprigs of flowers on each
side, base marked "Limoges W.G. & Co.
France" & "The World Our Field Koken
St. Louis Trade Mark," unusual, 3⅞" h. **572**

Brewer's Mug & Matching Beer Caps

Brewer, scene of beer keg w/brewers' tools
on top w/colorful sprigs of flowers on
each side, two beer caps w/identical
decoration included, "Eugene Schenk"
written above, 3½" h. **550**

Clerk, scene of grocery store w/male clerk
weighing sugar for woman customer,
"P.K. Graster, Jr." written above, base
stamped "K.P.M." & "Made in Germany,"
detailed, 3⅞" h. **1,018**

Clerk, scene of textile store w/male clerk
showing a yard of cloth to a woman
customer, floral sprigs on sides, "A.W.
Holman" written above, "The World Our
Field Koken St. Louis Trade Mark" on
base, 3⅞" h. **825**

Clock repairman, scene of clock or watch
repairman working at his bench, full pink
wrap w/birds on either side of the handle,
very detailed, "J.W. Locke" written above
(a badly discolored repair exists above
the handle on the rim) **358**

Trolley Conductor Mug

Conductor, scene of an electric trolley
w/conductor & driver, owner's name
below, base marked "T & V Limoges
France," 3⅝" h. (¾" flat chip off top of
base rim beneath the decoration). **248**

Engineer, large detailed scene of
locomotive & tender, "Peter Ritter" written
above faintly, "Leonard Vienna" marked
on base, 4" h. **385**

Engineer, shows a locomotive (No. 193) &
tender w/the letters "P.R.R."
(Pennsylvania Railroad) on side, "S.W.
Miller" written above, base stamped
"G.D.A. France," 3½" h. **330**

Fireman, shows a fireman's helmet,
decoration surrounding, "Geo. McVeigh"
written below, 3⅝" h. (repair to mug
handle) **330**

Fisherman, full maroon wrap, shows a fish
w/"Charles Zeller" written above, rare,
3¾" h. **1,595**

Grocery delivery man, scene of driver &
horse-drawn "Groceries" wagon, large,
well-detailed design, "Chas. K. Barnes"
written above, base marked "T & V
France," 3⅝" h. (professional repair to top
of base rim) **231**

Hardware store, "John W. Jones Hardware"
above "Hardware," gilt trim, "W.G. & Co.
France" marked on base, perfect, 3⅞" h. **275**

Harvester, scene showing a well-detailed harvesting machine, "J. O. Septer" written below, rare, excellent detail & color, 3⅝" h. **3,410**

Hunter, shows two hunting dogs on the point, owner's name above, base impressed "Germany," large, perfect, 4" h. ... **187**

Ice delivery man, scene of Mack "ICE" truck, owner's name illegible, full green wrap, "Germany" stamped on base, 3¾" h., (missing most of the gold trim) **1,018**

Ice Delivery Man Shaving Mug

Ice delivery man, scene of man taking block of ice out of horse-drawn "ICE" wagon w/building in background, for "W.M. Von Gilder" above scene, base marked "T & V France," perfect, 4" h. (ILLUS.) **798**

Mailman, floral sprigs frame scene of mailman holding a letter, owner's name above, "D & Co" stamped on base, perfect, 3⅝" h. **1,073**

Milk delivery man, scene of man next to horse-drawn "Pure Milk" wagon pumping water into a can w/word "Short" on the side, "A.A. Gifford" above scene, perfect, 3¾" h. **1,650**

Musician, large leaf decoration frames a violin & a guitar above owner's name, base marked "Koken B.S. Co. St. Louis," perfect, 4" h **358**

Musician, shows a French horn w/an urn to the right & "V.H. Haven" written above, entire scene surrounded by thick sprigs of flowers, 3½" h. **132**

Oyster fisherman, shows large basket of oysters, small floral decoration on each side, "J. Fralinder" written above, 3⅝" h. (two repairs on top rim) **385**

Painter, scene of "Paint" bucket & brushes, "J.W. White" written above, base marked "C.F.H. G.D.M." & "Candrian & Co. K.C. Mo.," 3¾" h. **358**

Painter, shows a well-detailed painter's bucket, owner's name above, perfect, 3⅝" h. **413**

Pharmacist, shows a mortar & pestle w/floral design on each side, "S.J. Jenkes" written above, base marked "T & V France," 3⅝" h. **165**

Photographer, shows a studio camera on a tripod w/owner's name above, 4" h. **688**

Pianist, upright piano, nicely decorated mug, "G.R. Colbath" written above, base marked w/"Limoges PHL France" & "The Ransom and Randolph Co. Toledo Ohio," 3⅝" h. **330**

Printer, shows a printer's block, "Will D. Fish" written below, "T & V Limoges France" marked on base, perfect, 3⅝" h. **121**

Printer, shows small printing press, "G.H. Haywood" written above, "T & V" stamped on base, 4" h. **468**

Railroad worker, shows railroad hand car, owner's name below, 3½" h. (two small repairs on base rim, one to the right of design, other to the left) **358**

Tailor, scene of tailor working at his bench, "R.P. Lee" written below, base stamped "Limoges W.G. & Co. France" & "R.H. Hegner Barber Supplies MInneapolis," 3⅞" h. **303**

Tailor, shows a pair of scissors & measuring tools, "J.W.Kable" written above, 3¾" h. **132**

Telegraph Operator Shaving Mug

Telegraph operator, shows telegraph receiving key, highly detailed, "F.A. Cook" written above, 3¼" h. (ILLUS.) **660**

Tinsmith, scene of tinsmith working at his bench, large colorful decoration, "T.F. Wall" written above, base stamped "P. German," 3⅝" h. **770**

Undertaker, scene of man driving horse-drawn hearse, made for "M.S. Bush," written above scene, base marked "K.F.", perfect, 3⅞" h. **176**

Wagon driver, scene of man driving horse-drawn stake wagon, "Wm. Soete" written above scene, base marked "Limoges W.G. & Co. France" & "The World Our Field Koken St. Louis Trade Mark," perfect, 3⅞" h. **468**

GENERAL ITEMS

Barber pole, early clockwork lighted pole, white & blue enamel on metal base & top, enameled red, white & blue revolving pole, heavy cast-iron hanging bracket, a crank is inserted in the side of the base to

Early Clockwork Lighted Barber Pole

wind the clockwork to make the pole turn, a brass plate covers the hole where crank is inserted & reads "Beardslly Mfg. Co. Chicago, Ill, Serial No. 1170", heavy clear glass around pole & milk glass light globe, very rare & early, excellent condition, 43" h. (ILLUS.) **688**

Barber pole, wooden, h.p. red, white & blue swirl design w/round gold top, flat bottom w/band of gold trim, on iron hanger, 35" h. (some cracking & loss of paint) **550**

Barber shop sign, red, white & blue enamel on metal, "Look Better Feel Better," made by the "William Marvy Company," made to be mounted on wall, 20th c., 4' h., 8" w. (some chipping around mounting holes but otherwise in excellent condition) **121**

Razor, straight razor, celluloid handle w/raised peacock decoration, original paint, made by "Golden Rule Cutlery Chicago," ca. 1890-1930, perfect **88**

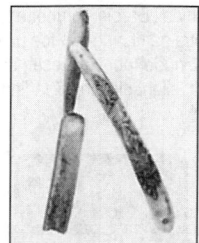

Straight Razor with Raised Stag Design

Razor, straight razor, celluloid handle w/raised stag decoration, made by "H. Boker & Co. No. 387 Germany," ca. 1890-1930, overall surface staining to blade, perfect (ILLUS.) **110**

Sharpening device, early mechanical honing or sharpening device, cast iron, made to clamp onto the end of a bench or table, chain driven sharpening wheel

Mechanical Sharpening Device

operated by turning a larger wheel, "Empire Impl't Manufa'g Co. Boston Mass Pat Pending" on crank wheel, perfect, unusual, appears to have never been used, ca. 1880-1900, 10" h. (ILLUS.) **121**

Shaving kit, brass chin tray, soap pot, & sterilizing container, ca. 1860-1880, soap pot & sterilizer w/soldered joints, set of 3 (½ x ¼" hole in side of the chin tray) **132**

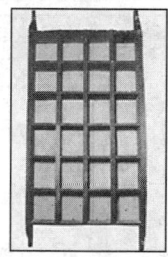

Wooden Shaving Mug Rack

Shaving mug rack, made to hang on a wall, painted wood, 24 holes, excellent condition, 20¼" w., 34½" h., 5½" d. (ILLUS.) . . **231**

"Barber Shop" Advertising Sign

Sign, enamel on metal advertising "Barber Shop," red, white & blue on metal, maker "William Marvy Company St. Paul Minn. No. 2418," bent to fit contour of a pole, original metal eyelets on either side, perfect, 14¾ x 24" (ILLUS.) **110**

Traveling shaving kit, hard wood w/fold-down mirror & three compartments w/lids & a set of seven straight razors w/black handles & makers mark "J.A. Henckel's Solingen, Germany," bone plaque on top w/initials "C.A.," early **242**

BARBIE DOLLS & COLLECTIBLES

At the time of her introduction in 1959, no one could have guessed that this statuesque doll would become a national phenomenon and eventually the most famous girl's plaything produced. Over the years, Barbie and her growing range of family and friends have evolved with the times, serving as an excellent mirror on the fashion and social changes taking place in American society. Today, after almost 40 years of continual production, Barbie's popularity goes on unabated among both young girls and older collectors. Early and rare Barbies can sell for remarkable prices and it is everyone's hope to find mint condition "#1 Barbie."

#1 Ponytail Barbie in Box

DOLLS

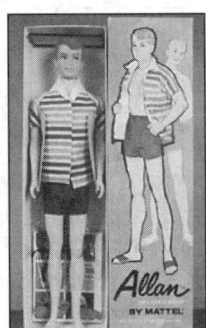

1964 Allan in Box

Allan, 1964, painted red hair, beige lips, straight legs, wearing original striped jacket, blue swim trunks, cork sandals w/blue straps, wrist tag, Exclusive Fashion Book 1 in cellophane bag, black wire stand, cardboard arm insert, near mint in box, wrist tag torn, slight wear & discoloration to box, small tear on lower box flap (ILLUS.) **$120**

Allan, 1965, painted red hair, pink lips, bendable legs, blue swim trunks & original red jacket with "A" (small split on top of left toes, faint ink dot on lower arm) **125**

Barbie, "#1 Ponytail Barbie," 1960, brunette hair reset into a ponytail, red lips, nostril paint, blue eyeshadow, finger & toe paint, straight legs, wearing black & white #1 striped swimsuit, hoop earrings, pink cover Barbie booklet & black open toed shoes w/holes in replaced cellophane bag, replaced plastic pedestal stand w/metal prongs, replaced cardboard box liner, hair slightly fuzzy, booklet worn, box in poor condition (ILLUS.) **2,700**

#1 Ponytail Barbie

Barbie, "#1 Ponytail Barbie," dark blonde hair, red lips, finger & toe paint, straight legs, wearing black & white striped swimsuit, played-with hair retied & fuzzy, some fading & rubbing, slight damage to one hip joint (ILLUS.) **1,550**

Barbie, "1920s Flapper Barbie," The Great Eras Collection, Second Edition, No. 4063, box dated 1993, never removed from box **205**

Barbie, "#4 Ponytail Barbie," brunette hair, red lips, nostril paint, finger & toe paint, straight legs, nude (ponytail reset, flat fuzzy bottom, slight staining & fading, ink stain on back) **185**

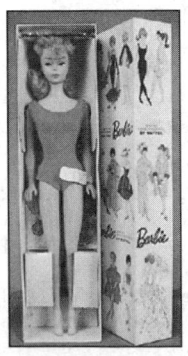

#6 Ponytail Barbie

Barbie, "#6 Ponytail Barbie," 1964, ash blonde hair, coral lips, finger & toe paint, straight legs, wearing red nylon swimsuit, wrist tag, white cover booklet & red open toed shoes in cellophane bag, black wire stand, cardboard box insert, near mint in box, bottom of hair loose & curly, wrist band torn, split at wrist area taped, small tears in arm & leg areas, slight box damage (ILLUS.) **405**

American Girl Barbie

Barbie, "American Girl Barbie," 1965, long ash blonde hair, pink lips, nostril paint, finger paint, bendable legs, nude, slight fading & rubbing, earring holes in ears (ILLUS.) **425**

Barbie, "Barbie as Dorothy in The Wizard of Oz," 1994, Hollywood Legends Collection Special Edition, No. 12701, never removed from box (box edges slightly worn) . . **200**

Barbie, "Benefit Ball Barbie," Classique Collection, first in series designed by Carol Spencer, No. 1521, box dated 1993, never removed from box **80**

Barbie, "Bubblecut Barbie," 1964, titian hair, coral lips, finger & toe paint, straight legs, wearing red nylon swimsuit, red open toed shoes, white cover booklet in cellophane bag, gold wire stand, cardboard box insert, near mint in box (slight fading, box slightly worn & faded) **225**

Barbie, "Color Magic Barbie," 1966, golden blonde hair w/blue barrette & original nylon head scarf, bright pink lips, nostril paint, cheek blush, finger paint, bendable legs, nude, near mint **300**

Barbie, "Gold Jubilee Barbie," 1994, Second in the Limited Edition Jubilee Series celebrating 35 years of Barbie, serial No. D3743 of 5,000 offered in the United States, No. 12009, never removed from box, including cardboard shipping box **455**

Barbie, "Living Barbie," 1970, brunette hair, pink lips, rooted eyelashes, bendable arms & legs, "Now Wow!" outfit including corduroy dress w/green crochet trim, matching hat, pale blue stockings, majorette boots, Paul David Collection (dress slightly soiled) **95**

Barbie, "Standard Barbie," 1967, brunette hair w/replaced ribbon tie, pink lips, painted eyes, face & toe paint, straight legs, original two-piece hot pink swim suit w/vinyl flower, hot pink open toe shoes (small amount of fingernail paint on left hand) **325**

Barbie, "Starlight Splendor," black Barbie, the second edition of Bob Mackie designed limited edition series, No. 2704, box dated 1991, mint in box (box corners slightly worn, small tear in upper left) **320**

Barbie, "Swirl Ponytail Barbie," 1964, titian hair in original set w/hairpin & yellow hair ribbon, coral lips, nostril, face & toe paint, straight legs, "Enchanted Evening" gown w/bead accents, white fur stole & newer hot pink shoes (dot of green discoloration on both ears, gown faded w/several stain lines on front) **425**

Barbie, "T'nT Barbie" artist doll, 1967, red hair rerooted by Mikelman, pink lips, cheek blush, rooted eyelashes, face & toe paint, pierced ears, straight legs, Dressed-Up pak dress w/gold brocade top w/belt & red satin skirt, plastic wedgies w/gold uppers, Mikelman wrist tag, Paul David Collection (discoloration on both ears) **75**

Casey, "Twist 'n Turn Casey," 1967, blonde hair wrapped w/clear plastic headband, pink lips w/teeth, rooted eyelashes, cheek blush, bendable legs, wearing original one-piece swimsuit, wrist tag, clear plastic stand, pink "Living Barbie" booklet, in box (earring missing, wrist tag creased & slightly worn, box corners slightly worn & cellophane missing) **195**

Francie, "Francie w/Growin' Pretty Hair," 1970, blonde hair in original set, pink lips, rooted eyelashes, bendable legs, original one-piece outfit, wrist tag, pink soft pumps, pink cover Living Barbie booklet, clear plastic stand, box insert (head light colored, small stain on front right leg, box discolored, worn, & creased) **95**

"Ken in Mexico" Doll

Ken, 1964, painted blond hair, pink lips, straight legs, wearing "Ken in Mexico" outfit including brown jacket w/trim, matching pants & sombrero w/necktie & adjuster, white shirt, black tie, green satin cummerbund, black boots, travel pamphlet, wrist tag, wire stand, box discolored w/edges & corners worn (ILLUS.) . . **170**

Ken, 1964, painted blond hair, beige lips, straight legs, original red & white jacket, red swim trunks, cork sandals w/red straps, Exclusive Fashion Book 1, wire stand, boxed (box discolored w/edges & corners worn) **90**

Ken, 1965, painted brunette hair, pink lips, bendable legs, blue jacket w/red trim & "K," red swim trunks, cork sandals w/red straps, wrist tag (box discolored w/edges & corners worn, box insert creased & torn, seam on back of box split) **145**

Midge, 1963, blonde hair, pink lips, finger & toe paint, straight legs, wearing Barbie in Switzerland outfit including dress w/embroidered apron, green felt corset w/tie, white hat w/necktie, white open toed shoes, original blue two piece swimsuit, flower bouquet w/ribbon accent, paper travel pamphlet, white cover booklet w/white open toed shoes in cellophane bag, black wire stand, near mint in box (box slightly discolored & worn) . . . **150**

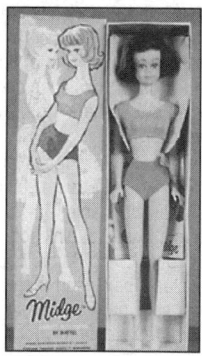

Original Midge in Box

Midge, brunette hair, coral lips, finger & toe paint, straight legs, wearing original pink & red two-piece swimsuit, wrist tag, white open toed shoes & white cover booklet in cellophane bag, black wire stand, cardboard box insert, near mint in box, cellophane headband split, wear & creases to swimsuit, slight wear & discoloration to box (ILLUS.) **255**

Ricky, painted red hair, beige lips, straight legs, original striped jacket, blue swim trunks, cork sandals w/red straps, wire stand, boxed w/insert (box discolored w/edges & corners worn) **185**

Skipper, 1965, blonde hair w/metal headband & plastic protective cover, beige lips, bendable legs, wearing original one piece nylon swimsuit, white cover Skipper booklet, Exclusive Fashions Book 1, red flat shoes & white plastic brush & comb in cellophane bag, gold wire stand, near mint in box (box slightly discolored & worn) **190**

Skipper, "Porcelain Skipper," 1994, blonde hair w/silver headband, blue & white dress, white socks, shoes & short gloves, hat, stand & accessories, Paul David Collection **70**

Skooter, 1964, blonde hair w/ribbon ties, pink lips, straight legs, original two-piece swim suit, red flat shoes, boxed w/insert (box discolored w/edges & corners worn) **75**

CLOTHING & ACCESSORIES

Barbie pak, a silk yellow sheath w/bow accent, paper label, hanger booklet, never removed from package (some discoloring to package, small tear on bottom of paper label) **70**

Bicycle, "Barbie's Ten Speeder" plastic model, yellow w/rear baskets, ca. 1970, mint in box **83**

Clothing set, Barbie, "Arabian Nights," pink satin blouse, pink long skirt w/gold trim, matching sari, gold & turquoise beaded necklace, bracelets including two turquoise & one gold, gold dangle earrings, gold plastic lamp, gold shoes, paper theater program, booklet, paper label, never removed from box (box discolored w/edges worn) **220**

Clothing set, Barbie, "Cinderella," No. 0872, poor dress w/laced bodice, broom, yellow satin gown w/silver design, silver & tulle collar & tulle skirt trim, silver headband w/attached white tulle veil, white nylon long gloves, clear open toed shoes w/silver glitter, paper program, booklet & cellophane, never removed from carton **230**

Clothing set, Barbie, "Dog 'n Duds," grey poodle w/felt eyes & tongue, red leash w/gold trim & chain, red & gold & pink & black dog coats, red & white ear muffs, white plastic collars w/black tie, pink tutu w/gold trim, yellow & black felt hat w/elastic chin strap, black mask, plastic dog bone, dog food box, wooden bowl w/dog food, booklet, cellophane, never removed from carton (dog food box discolored) **180**

Clothing set, Barbie, "Enchanted Evening," pink satin dress w/beaded accents, white fur stole, white nylon long gloves, three strand pearl necklace, clear open toed shoes w/gold glitter, booklet, paper label, never removed from box (necklace broken w/pearls loose in pkg., box discolored w/edges & corners worn) **200**

Clothing set, Barbie, "Tennis Anyone?," white sweater w/orange trim, white dress, socks, white tennis shoes, two tennis balls, tennis racquet, blue goggles, rules book, booklet & paper label, never removed from box **75**

Clothing set, Barbie, "The Yellow Go," No. 1816, Sears Exclusive, yellow coat w/button accents, matching yellow hood w/blue pompon & attached silk scarf, yellow lacy stockings, blue vinyl purse w/chin strap, blue shoes w/molded bow, hanger, booklet, cellophane, never removed from carton **1,100**

Clothing set, Francie, "Buckeroo Blues," No. 3449, blue suede skirt w/chain & button accents, matching vest, purse & boots, print nylon shirt, booklet, paper label, never removed from box (box discolored w/edges & corners worn & scuffed) **95**

Clothing set, Francie, "Style Setter," No. 1268, nylon print dress, matching stockings, aqua velveteen cape w/metal hooks, matching hood, greyish blue soft pointed toe shoes, hanger, cellophane, never removed from carton ("#1268" written in pen on corner of cellophane, booklet missing) **150**

Clothing set, Francie, "Victorian Wedding," satin wedding dress w/lace overdress, white veil w/metal headband & lace trim, white flower bouquet w/ribbon & green tulle accents, white cutouts, hanger, booklet, paper label, never removed from package (label discolored) **115**

Clothing set, Ken, "Best Buy Fashion," No. 9004, plaid pants, plaid & denim shirt, package dated 1962, never removed from package (backing slightly discolored, hanger partly perforated) **35**

Clothing set, Ken, "Cheerful Chef," white apron w/red trim & green & black printed design, white chef hat w/green "Ken" on band, metal spatula, spoon & fork w/red plastic handles, plastic hot dog, paper label, booklet (cardboard backing discolored & creased) **140**

Clothing set, Ken, "Drum Major," No. 0775, white jacket w/button accents, red & gold trim & accents, fur hat w/gold trim & plume, red pants w/stripe, white socks & shoes, gold baton, booklet, paper label, never removed from box (box discolored & corners worn, small stains on back of box) . . . **85**

Clothing set, Ken, "The Prince," gold & green brocade jacket w/button accents, white collar, tights, green velvet cape, green velvet slipper w/gold trim, gold

velvet hat w/feather & pearl & "emerald" accents ("emeralds" loose in package), velvet pillow w/gold trim & tassels, clear pointed toe shoes, theater program booklet, paper label, never removed from box (box discolored & corners worn) **215**

Clothing set, Ricky, "Skateboard Set," No. 1505, white shirt w/stripes & button accents, white shorts & socks, white tennis shoes, plastic skateboard, booklet, never removed from package. **40**

Clothing set, Skipper, "Wild 'n Wonderful," No. 1959, blue & green fur coat w/vinyl trim, blue & green striped knit dress, green fishnet stockings, blue vinyl cap & boots, paper label stapled to upper right cardboard backing & cellophane, hanger, booklet, cellophane, never removed from carton (tear in upper left of cellophane) **105**

Ken pak, "Lounging Around," a reddish brown sport shirt w/button accents, yellow shorts, paper label, booklet, never removed from pak (some pak discoloration, top of cellophane opened w/small tear, booklet loose) **20**

Tea set, Barbie, "35th Anniversary Barbie Tea Set," limited edition, box dated 1994, never removed from box (box slightly scuffed). **45**

Telephone, Barbie, "Solo in the Spotlight Barbie Telephone," box dated 1995, never removed from box (box slightly scuffed). **50**

Wrist watch, Barbie, "Charming Barbie Watch," in a jewelry box w/Certificate of Authenticity, 19548/20000 Limited Edition, box dated 1994 (flap wear on box) **70**

Wrist watch, Barbie, "Fossil Barbie Watch," 35th Anniversary, 1994, 03400/20000 Limited Edition, in hatbox w/scarf & Cert. of Authenticity **65**

BASEBALL MEMORABILIA

Baseball was named by Abner Doubleday as he laid out a diamond-shaped field with four bases at Cooperstown, New York. A popular game from its inception, by 1869 it was able to support its first all-professional team, the Cincinnati Red Stockings. The National League was organized in 1876 and though the American League was first formed in 1900, it was not officially recognized until 1903. Today, the "national pastime" has millions of fans and collecting baseball memorabilia has become a major hobby with enthusiastic collectors seeking out items associated with players such as Babe Ruth, Lou Gehrig, and others who became legends in their own lifetimes. Though baseball cards, issued as advertising premiums for bubble gum and other products, seem to dominate the field there are numerous other items available.

Yankee Stadium Original Ornament

Architectural ornament, original terra cotta rectangular block from the front of Yankee Stadium, The House that Ruth Built, molded w/two overlapping baseballs against a wide scroll background, 75 lbs. (ILLUS.). **$9,598**

Baseball, autographed by Mickey Mantle, late 1950s official American League model, inscribed in blue ink "To Pamela - My Best Wishes - Mickey Mantle" (some scuffing & staining) **345**

Baseball, from Mark McGwire's home run record-breaking series, signed by McGwire's hitting coach Dave Parker & inscribed "9 - 7 - 98 - Game Used Gall - Big Mac HR 61...," includes ticket stub for game **18,785**

Baseball, Pete Rose 4,200 hit baseball, Official Feeney model, hit by Rose after breaking Ty Cobb's record, signed by Rose on the sweet spot & inscribed "Base Hit 4200 - 9-21-95" & "Astros 9 - Reds 5," all writing in Rose's hand **9,356**

1929 N.Y. Yankees-Signed Baseball

Baseball, team-signed, 1929 New York Yankees model, includes Ruth, Gehrig, Combs, Dickey & others, also inscribed "N.Y. Yanks 1929 ... to Charlie Lotsch" (ILLUS.). **3,058**

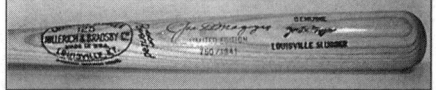

Joe Dimaggio-signed Bat

Baseball bat, limited edition model, signed by Joe DiMaggio, No. 720 of 1941, Hillerich & Bradsby w/stamped facsimile signature & actual autograph (ILLUS.) **1,310**

Baseball cap, New York Giants, game-worn, dark blue w/white & red overlapping "NY" initials on the front, by Goldsmith, stitched-in size "7⅜," 1940s (heavy wear inside & out, bill floppy) **505**

Baseball glove, 1940s Vince DiMaggio model, signed by the three DiMaggio brothers, one in silver marker, two in gold marker, recent signatures **1,012**

Baseball glove, leather workman-style, buttonback wrist strap, no webbing, smooth & pliable, unstained soft lining, 1890s, 9½" l. **18,975**

Bat, limited edition, No. 1 of 1,000 commemorating Nolan Ryan's 5th career no-hitter September 25, 1981, Louisville Slugger w/Astros logo, major league baseball insignia, date, location, score & stats, autographed in blue sharpie by Ryan, 34" l. **996**

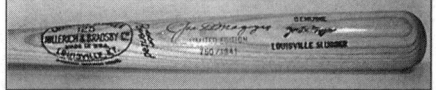

Maris & Mantle-signed Baseball Bat

Bat, signed by Roger Maris & Mickey Mantle celebrating the 1961 home run race, Hillerich & Bradsby M 110 model, stamped "LIMITED EDITION 88 of 115," from the mid-1980s, 35" l. (ILLUS.) **2,554**

Calendar, 1888, printed paper, adverting-type, a green & purple printed seasonal image w/each month, July featuring a baseball scene w/a portrait vignette of Albert G. Spalding in upper left corner, produced for the Walter H. Wood Machine Co., w/original hanging string **443**

Candy mold, molded tin, two-part model of a baseball impressed "National League Baseball" & "ROCKWOODS," all-original **821**

Catcher's mask, iron & leather, oval iron cage over original leather padding at the rim, single black strap, 1890s (light cage rust) **6,563**

Check, personal check signed by Babe Ruth, drawn from the Chemical Bank & Trust Co., dated May 6, 1940, matted & framed w/an action photo of Ruth batting, overall 14½ x 18". **2,885**

Cigar box, rectangular soft wood w/hinged lid, "Boyish Babe - Mild & Sweet," interior of lid centered by boyish image of Babe Ruth, early pendulum-style clasp, for five cent stogies, rare. **2,875**

Early Baseball Hand Fan

Fan, hand-type, color-printed cardboard, round baseball-printed top w/a central color head portrait of Larry Doyle above his facsimile signature, cream ground w/black printed seams & red wording at top "A Fan for A Fan," maker's address on the back, original wooden stapled-on handle, early 20th c. (ILLUS.)............. **673**

Gate sign, metal, flag-style, from Crosley Field, reddish orange ground w/white wording "Gate 5," on original pole, shows wear, 17½ x 24"...................... **840**

High school yearbook, 1937 issue from John Muir Technical High School, graduating class of Jackie Robinson, signed next to his photograph "Best of luck - Jack Robinson," two other of his signatures inside **920**

Income tax form, double-signed by Christy Mathewson, for the year 1918, half-sheet, 5 x 10" (small corner tears) **1,585**

Jersey, grey cloth road model, game-worn by Jimmy Piersall, "Boston" in raised blue felt on the front & "37" on the back, three tag on bottom read "Tim McAuliffe ...44...58," 1958 .... **1,793**

Jersey, grey flannel, game-worn by Max Bishop, blue felt letters spelling "Boston" on chest w/Bishop's "1" splits the back, "M. Bishop" sewn into collar & "35" year tag on tail, 1935.................... **15,687**

Letter, typed & signed thank you note from Tris Speaker, on his letterhead, dated "May 15, 1937," w/original envelope **575**

Magazine, "Sport Magazine," June, 1962, Mickey Mantle on cover **45**

Magazine, "The Elks," August 1933, cover of boy w/Babe Ruth shown at bat behind him. . **150**

Man's shirt, small short-sleeved button-down surfer style, tan printed in color w/baseball designs including "Dodgers" & Brooklyn Bridge logos, 1950s (slight wear) ... **463**

Movie poster, "Rawhide," starring Smith Ballew & Lou Gehrig, full-color w/portraits of the stars & vignettes from the movie, half-sheet, mounted on linen, 1938, 22 x 28"............................ **1,233**

Mug, ceramic, from Mickey Mantle's Southern restaurant, white printed in red "Mickey Mantle's Country Cookin'" (some light use marks) **201**

Early Brooklyn Dodgers Pennant

Pennant, felt, purple ground printed in gold w/"Brooklyn - Dodgers" w/Dodgers printed on the side of a stylized early trolley car, triangular, 8" l. (ILLUS.) **905**

Photograph, black & white group shot showing Ted Williams & John Sain receiving awards at a dinner banquet, signed by players & the two other men in the photo, ca. 1946, 7 x 9".............. **1,898**

Photograph, cabinet-size, team shot of the 1896 Providence Grays of the Eastern League, shows sixteen players in period uniform, w/pencil player notations, 4 x 6" **680**

Roberto Clemente Signed Photo

Photograph, color shot of Roberto Clemente, magazine image showing Clemente staring at the camera from behind the batting practice net, signed in blue ballpoint "Best Wishes - Roberto Clemente," matted & framed, 12 x 15" (ILLUS.)............................ **1,947**

Photograph, comic black & white shot of Babe Ruth seated & dressed as a baby w/long golden tresses & a baby nightgown & bonnet, signed & inscribed by Ruth "To my friend Margie Little - from

Candid Babe Ruth Photograph

Babe Ruth - Feb. 18th 1929," paperclip impression near Babe's shoulder, tack holes in corners, 8 x 10" (ILLUS.) **3,701**

Photograph, group shot of the three DiMaggio Brothers, signed by each, taken in the late 1960s or early 1970s, taken at a promotional event, matted & framed, 13½ x 17" **4,308**

1934 Babe Ruth Photograph

Photograph, signed by Babe Ruth, black & white full-length photo of Ruth standing & holding a pipe, a vintage auto in the background, framed w/plaque inscribed "Babe Ruth - March 17, 1934," photo 4 x 6" (ILLUS.) **1,020**

Photograph, Willie Mays signed small black & white shot from his 1951 rookie year, posed swinging a bat, vertically inscribed along one side "William Mays," 3 x 4" (slight creasing) **611**

Pinback button, commemorative, round printed metal, black & white w/center black & white bust photo of Lou Gehrig, black outer border printed in white "Never Forgotten - Lou Gehrig," 1940s, 1¾" d. **505**

Rare Maris & Mantle Pinback Buttons

Pinback buttons, round printed metal, one w/a printed black & white bust photo of Roger Maris on white w/red wording "I'm For Maris - 60 in '61," the other w/a bust photo of Mickey Mantle on white w/red wording "I'm for Mantle - 60 in '61," 1961, slight rust on backs, pr. (ILLUS.) **6,429**

Postcard, photo-type, signed by Tris Speaker, in Cleveland Indians uniform, ca. 1946, back addressed & mailed **616**

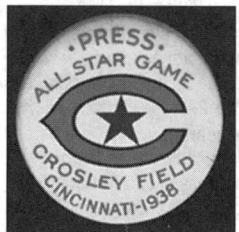

1938 Cincinnati All-Star Press Pin

Press pin, 1938 Cincinnati All-Star game, first All-Star press pin, round pinback-type in white printed w/red wording & red & blue Cincinnati logo, reads "Press - All Star Game - Crosley Field - Cincinnati - 1938," original paper backing w/maker's name (ILLUS.) **3,450**

1917 World Series Program

Program, 1917 World Series, printed in color w/red & white lettering & red, white & blue flag, photo cover scene of a grinning President Wilson throwing out

the first ball of the American League
season, team photos, score sheets, old
ads, 32 pp., minor paper loss on covers
(ILLUS.)............................. **1,807**
Scarf, printed silk, yellow w/center printed in
reddish brown Detroit Tigers tiger logo
surrounded by a ring of players including
Cobb, Crawford & Donovan, also printed
"We-A-A-Ah Champion Tigers - Pennant
Winners - 1907-1908," natural fading on
image, 18 x 18" (slight edge fraying)....... **2,385**
Schedule, newspaper premium, 1910
Boston Red Sox, rectangular sheet
w/monthly schedule printed in the center
& surrounded by black & white head
shots of the various players w/their name,
printed at the top "Boston American
League Red Sox," 12 x 15" (light pencil
marks above some players, some very
small tears at edges) **348**
Score card, 1945, Yankees at White Sox **15**
Score card, 1952, Philadelphia at Yankees...... **20**

Early Western League Season Pass

Season pass, 1899, printed paper, Western
League, yellow printed in green
w/vignette of early player at bat, front
reads "Season Annual Pass - To All
Grounds - The Western League of
Professional Base Ball Clubs -
Championship 1899 Games," printed
w/name of president & written name of
owner, excellent condition (ILLUS.) **316**
Season pass, sterling silver, 1929 New
York Giants, round-topped rectangular
form embossed w/a half-length comical
portrait of a hatted fan winking & hitching
a ride while holding a sign dated "1929,"
bottom reads "Giants - Chas. A.
Stoneham - Pres.," base inscribed
w/name of original owner along w/its
more recent owner **488**
Sheet music, "When A Cowboy Goes To
Town," purple, yellow & white cover
w/vignette photos of stars Lou Gehrig &
Smith Ballew against a mountainous
landscape, from the movie "Rawhide," hit
song "On the Sunny Side of the Rockies"

Lou Gehrig "Rawhide" Sheet Music

on the back, stamped on the front
"Complimentary Copy - Not For Sale,"
1938 (ILLUS.)......................... **616**

1927 World Series Ticket Stub

Ticket stub, 1927 World Series, printed
purple paper, game two at Forbes Field in
Pittsburgh, New York Yankees vs
Pittsburgh, dated "Oct. 6, 1927" (ILLUS.) ... **1,643**

BASKETS

The American Indians were the first basket weavers on this continent and, of necessity, the early Colonial settlers and their descendants pursued this artistic handicraft to provide essential containers for berries, eggs and endless other items to be carried or stored. Rye straw, split willow and reeds are but a few of the wide variety of materials used. The Nantucket baskets, plainly and sturdily constructed, along with those made by specialized groups, would seem to draw the greatest attention to this area of collecting.

Berry, splint-sided, wide slightly flaring
spaced splints joined at the rim & base by
narrow tin rims, traces of red, pint, 4¼" d.,
3⅞" h., pr............................. **$303**
Bushel basket, woven splint, deep rounded
sides w/a wrapped rim & bentwood rim
handles, old patina, 23" d., 13" h. (some
wear & damage)....................... **358**

Bushel basket, splint stave construction, the deep rounded sides of slightly space staves joined at the top by a bentwood band, small wire rim handles w/turned wood grips, old patina, 22½" d., 15½" h. **193**

"Buttocks" basket, woven splint & cane, 18-rib construction, long oval form w/wrapped rim, center bentwood handle w/Eye of God design, 16 x 20", 8" h. **193**

Large "Buttocks" Basket

"Buttocks" basket, woven splint, greyish patina, some damage, 10" d., 12" h. plus bentwood handle (ILLUS.) **149**

"Buttocks" sewing basket, woven splint, 22-rib construction, wrapped rim & center bentwood handle, worn cloth lining, 6" d., 4" h. plus handle. **110**

Cheese basket, woven splint, shallow round form w/wrapped rim & overall large honeycomb design, 9" d. **358**

Fruit basket, woven splint, round w/tapering sides, wrapped rim w/open rim handles, good patina, 16½" d., 11" h. **231**

Herb Drying Basket

Herb drying basket, woven splint, round, wrapped rim w/open rim handles, good patina, 21" d., 6¼" h. (ILLUS.) **248**

Laundry basket, woven splint, deep round sides tapering in to a base band, the wide wrapped rim w/small rim bentwood handles, bottom signed in Gothic letters "Harvard 1916," old patina, 22" d., 9" h. (rim wrap incomplete, some splint damage) **303**

Laundry basket, woven splint, rectangular bottom w/deep swelled sides & oblong wrapped rim, end-to-end hinged bentwood handle w/interesting laced end detail, old patina, 15" l. **138**

Market Basket

Market basket, woven splint, rectangular w/upright sides, fanned ribbing, wrapped rim, center bentwood handle, 15½ x 26", 10" h. plus handle (ILLUS.) **209**

Nantucket basket, finely woven splint, round, 19th c., 7¼" d., 3" h. (minor losses to basket & lashing). **1,150**

Nantucket basket, tightly woven splint, wide rounded form w/a narrow wrapped rim & bentwood swing handle, remnants of paper label, early 20th c., 8⅜" d., 4⅜" h. **1,265**

Nantucket basket, finely woven splint, round, w/paper label on base reading "I was made on Nantucket Island I am strong and stout Don't lose or burn me I'll never wear out," S.P. Boyer, 7½" d., 4½" h. **2,645**

Nantucket Basket

Nantucket basket, tightly woven splint, wide rounded form w/a narrow wrapped rim & bentwood swing handle, early 19th c., imperfections, 13¾" d., 9⅞" h. (ILLUS.) **1,265**

Peach basket, woven splint staves, wide thin staves in a woven diamond design forming the slightly tapering deep cylindrical sides, thin bentwood base & rim bands, old brown patina, 14½" d., 11½" h. **193**

"Picket fence" basket, tapering cylindrical form constructed of spaced fence-like picket slats w/rounded tops, joined by a galvanized metal band around the base & a wire ring around the top, old patina, 16" d., 10" h. **248**

Pie basket, cov., round lattice construction w/slender slats forming the sides, interior band & thin rim band w/scalloped edge, removable interior shelf, plywood bottom, 11½" d. **578**

Pie basket, cov., cylindrical oval lattice sides composed of thin wood lattice w/central interior band & thin, scalloped rim band, double bentwood swing handles at center of rim, removable interior shelf, plywood bottom, 15½" l. **468**

Storage basket, woven splint, deep oval sides w/four small bentwood rim handles, two at each side, lined w/burlap stenciled w/a label "C.H.H.," 19 x 25", 9" h. (minor damage) **303**

Storage Basket

Storage basket, woven splint, deep rectangular sides w/wrapped rim & center bentwood handle, red, blue & natural, 10½ x 17", 10½" h. plus handle (ILLUS.) **77**

Storage basket, cov., honeycomb design openwork woven splint, cylindrical sides w/flat fitted cover, 11" d. (damage, hole) **138**

Small Utility Basket

Utility basket, woven splint, round, wrapped rim & center handle, good patina, 8½" d., 6" h. plus handle (ILLUS.) **330**

Utility basket, woven splint, deep round cylindrical sides w/a wrapped rim & bentwood handle, old patina, 12" d., 6" h. plus handle **138**

Utility basket, woven splint, deep rounded rectangular form w/wrapped rim & bentwood swing handle, old greyish patina, 9½ x 13", 8¼" h. plus handle (wear, damage) **138**

Work basket, woven splint, wide shallow openwork round form w/small rim handles, flaking heavy green paint, 11" d. **385**

BELLS

Altar bells, brass, threaded scalloped removable base centered by a handle w/scrolled arms decorated w/leaves & grape clusters suspending four plain domed bells which represent the four gospels, overall 7½" w., 8" h. **$475**

Bell, metal, fitted w/an old replaced wrought-iron arm, arm extends 24", bell 10" d., 10½" h. **165**

Child's Rattle Bell

Child's rattle bell, silver w/ivory handle & metal chain to wear around the neck, whistle at top of rattle, ca. 1790, overall 5½" l. (ILLUS.) **2,550**

Figural bell, fist & bar finial, "angry god"-style body w/a grotesque growling face on each side, a flaring base band of rope-twist beard, 3½" h. **65**

Figural bell, Jacobean head finial, cylindrical sides w/embossed band of figures, flared rim w/embossed inscription, 4" h. **110**

Figural bell, painted brass, sculpted owl head w/glass eyes, table or door mount-type, mechanical, pressing nose rings the bell, spring winder in back, ca. 1870, Germany, 2¾" h. **700**

Figural bell, brass w/embossed detail & niello work, loop handle, type used by blind in India, ca. 1860, 3½" l. **205**

Figural bell, figure of a young Victorian girl in a long dress & bonnet, her arms held out from her sides, 3¾" h. **65**

Figural bell, metal, model of crawling turtle, damascene & niello work on shell w/Greek key design on border, pull tail to ring bell, ca. 1930, Germany, 4¼" l., 1¾" h. **395**

Figural bell, metal, model of a crawling turtle, shell w/etched scene of a horse & rider & a weary donkey on black ground, when tail is pushed both the head & tail move as bell is rung, ca. 1950, Spain, 5½" l., 2" h. **230**

Figural Dinner Bell

Figural bell, brass, dinner bell, domed bell
  w/paw feet supports cage w/one bear
  inside & one outside, pushing the outside
  bear rings bell & causes both bears to
  turn, textured fur-like finish on bears,
  inlaid ruby eyes, ca. 1880s, 6" h. (ILLUS.) **565**

Figural bell, silicon bronze, waisted
  cylindrical base w/scene of man on
  horseback & figure of Paul Revere
  standing & holding a large bell, hand-cast
  by the "lost wax" process by Gerald
  Ballantyne, ca. 1976, 6" h. **205**

Figural bell, brass, Italian Renaissance-type
  w/pendant clapper, DeVinci household
  crest, niello & damascene work, figural
  owl handle, ca. 1860, 7⅞" h. **780**

Oriental Floral Bell

Oriental bell, champleve & cloisonné,
  tapering cylindrical form w/peony & other
  floral & vine decoration, white jadite & red
  jade stem, green jade clapper, early to
  mid 19th c., 4⅝" h. (ILLUS.) **1,200**

Sleigh bells, brass, heavy graduated string
  of 40 keyed bells on original double
  leather strap, numbered 0 to 10, 19th c.,
  8½' l. **445**

Sleigh bells, a leather strap w/thirty-seven
  graduated round bells in steel w/worn
  nickel plate, 80" l. (leather worn, strap
  buckle damaged) **138**

Sleigh bells, brass set of twenty-nine
  graduated bells on a leather strap, late
  19th to early 20th c., 83" l. **336**

Hebrew Spice Box with Bells

Spice box w/bells, silver filigree, domed
  stepped base w/short pedestal supporting
  filigree box w/door opening & tall finial
  w/pennant, each corner of box
  suspending bell, ca. 1850-1860,
  Warsaw, 8¼" h. (ILLUS.) **1,050**

"St. Peter's Bell"

"St. Peter's Bell," heavy cast brass, raised
  figures of Apostles around bell, cross
  finial, 4" d., 7½" h. (ILLUS.) **125**

Tibetan Prayer Wheel

Tibetan prayer wheel, silver repoussé &
appliqued cylindrical wheel w/handle, bell
attached by a chain, weights facilitate
turning, prayers are written & placed
inside cylinder & each turn of the wheel
w/the bell ringing signifies a prayer told,
mid-19th c., 10¼" l. (ILLUS.) **1,800**

BICYCLES

Rare Early Boneshaker Bicycle

Boneshaker, early model w/32" d. front
wheel & 29" d. rear wheel, incorrect
pedals, ca. 1860 (ILLUS.) **$3,410**

1952 Boy's Columbia Five Star Superb

Columbia, boy's Five Star Superb, three-
speed, two-tone cream & maroon
w/original paint, fender tip over-painted
Hornet speedo, ca. 1952 (ILLUS.) **963**

Early Columbia Lady's "Century"

Columbia, lady's "Century" pneumatic
safety, complete w/rear brakes, front &
rear fenders, improper seat, fair
condition, patent-dated 1889 (ILLUS.) **1,760**
Columbia, man's "Century" model, split-
frame pneumatic safety-style, patent-
dated 1891 (needs brake hardware, no seat) . . **688**

Columbia Model 65 "Chainless"

Columbia, man's Model 65 "chainless"
safety, amateur restoration, late 19th c.
(ILLUS.) **770**
Columbia, Model 43, tandem safety
w/caliper brakes front & rear, needs
restoration, ca. 1900. . . . . **275**

Early Crawford Lady's Safety Bike

Crawford, lady's pneumatic safety model,
w/wooden fender & chain guard,
manufactured in Hagerstown, Maryland,
needs restoration, ca. 1898 (ILLUS.) **495**
Eagle, "Altair" HTS model, safety-type,
produced as either a hard tire or cushion
tire model, Eagle Mfg. Co., Torrington,
Connecticut, ca. 1891, Kennedy
restoration **1,375**

1940 Girl's Elgin Deluxe Bicycle

Elgin, girl's Deluxe model, w/horn tank,
headlight, illuminated rear rack & skirt
guards, good original condition, 1940
(ILLUS.) **220**
Elgin, girl's model, original rare pod stop-tail
light & Stewart Warner floating hub, fair
condition, ca. 1940s **413**

Firestone 1937 Streamline Bicycle

Firestone, Streamline model w/extended gooseneck, Dayton "Ashtray" speedo, Dayton deep fenders, twin silver ray lights, streamlined pedals, crossbar handlebars, long spring seat, chrome three-rib tank & three-rib chain guard, restored, 1937 (ILLUS.).................**3,190**

Griffith's Man's Safety Bicycle

Griffith's Corporation, man's pneumatic safety model, original paint & stenciling, unusual "Overland Roadster" tires, signed on tread pattern, needs cork grips & seat cover, late 19th c. (ILLUS.)................**248**

Harley Davidson Man's Bicycle

Harley Davidson, man's safety model, original name plate & sprocket, frame primed, good condition, ca. 1920 (ILLUS.) .. **1,045**

Hawthorn, "Flo-Cycle," exceptional original condition, ca. 1936 ....**2,200**

J.C. Higgins 1950s Boy's Bike

Higgins, boy's model w/"Wonderide Spring Fork," very clean restored condition, ca. 1957 (ILLUS.) **1,100**

Highwheel model, ordinary open head-style, radial spoked, original paint & striping, correct pedals, no seat, some

Early Highwheel Ordinary

brake hardware, moustache handlebars, as found, late 19th c., 50" (ILLUS.) **2,310**

Unusual "Inglo-bike"

Ingersoll Div., Borg Warner Corp., "Inglo-bike," invented by Phillip & Prescott Huyssen, produced 1934-37, good original condition (ILLUS.)...............**1,293**

1915 Iver Johnson Man's Bicycle

Iver Johnson, man's pneumatic safety model, period accessories include squash horn, "Twentieth Century" head lamp, handlebar bell, accessories rack, leather tool pouch, wood, leather & paint in excellent condition, ca. 1915 (ILLUS.) **605**

Monark Silver King Racing Bicycle

Monark, boy's Silver King Racing model,
original Gillette Road Racer tires,
replated, very original restoration,
ca. 1935 (ILLUS.) **1,485**

Girl's Monark 1936 Silver King

Monark, girl's Silver King model, open lug
frame, streamline seat & stainless
fenders, very good condition, 1936 (ILLUS.) . . **248**

Rare Monark Silver King Model 26-X

Monark, Silver King Model 26-X, pencil
spring fork, streamlined horn light, electric
tail light, stainless fenders rare & sought-
after w/26" d. wheels & 45" wheel base,
1939 (ILLUS.) **1,980**
Overman Wheel Co., man's "The Victor"
safety model, retro-fitted w/high-
pressure pneumatic tires, w/optional
spring saddle post, very original,
needs restoration, 1893. . . . . **1,265**
Raleigh, "Chopper" boy's bike, purple w/red
accents, 1970s **347**

Rare Early Rudge Highwheel

Rudge, highwheel model w/moustache
handlebars w/stirrup or spade handgrips,
excellent restored condition, late 19th c.,
52" (ILLUS.). **2,530**

1939 Schwinn Boy's Bike

Schwinn, boy's Model D97XE, w/horn tank,
headlight, nine-hole rack & drop stand,
original red & cream paint, Goodyear All
Weather whitewall tires, 1939 (ILLUS.) **1,155**

1960s Schwinn Boy's "Panther" Model

Schwinn, boy's "Panther" balloon model,
blue & white paint w/knee-action spring
fork, good condition, 1960s (ILLUS.) **220**
Schwinn, boy's "Scrambler" model, red
paint, excellent condition, ca. 1975, 20" **55**
Schwinn, boy's "Speedster" six-speed, blue
& chrome, ca. 1970s, 24" **83**

1970s Schwinn Stingray Boy's Bike

Schwinn, boy's Stingray five-speed model,
orange paint, excellent condition, ca.
1970 (ILLUS.). **413**

Stringray "Fast Back" Bicycle

Schwinn, boy's Stringray "Fast Back" model, five-speed, black & white paint, ca. 1960s, good condition, 20" (ILLUS.)...... **385**

Schwinn Jaguar Mark 2 Bicycle

Schwinn, Jaguar Mark 2 model, w/horn tank, phantom rack & tail light, book rack, three-speed, crashrail seat & Westwind white wall tires, excellent original condition, 1955 (ILLUS.)................. **495**

Schwinn Victory Sports Tourist Bike

Schwinn, Victory Sports Tourist model, very good condition, ca. 1947 (ILLUS.) **165**
Shelby, lady's "Speedline" Airflow model, very original, needs restoration, ca. 1939 .... **990**

Rare Model M137 Silver King

Silver King, Model M137 "Wing Bar," w/Bailey seat, otherwise correct & excellent condition, 1937 (ILLUS.) **3,025**
St. Nicholas, highwheel model w/early "T"-beam construction, late 19th c., restored, 46" h. **2,090**

Early Star Highwheel Ordinary

Star, safety highwheel ordinary, ca. 1880, poor condition, as found (ILLUS.) **1,540**
Swiss Army, rear wheel & lock key, complete w/two parcel bags, leather tool pouch w/tools, air pump, bell, generator & license plate, dated 1943 .... **1,485**
Syracuse, tall-frame pneumatic safety model, transfer-type head badge, original maroon & pinstripe paint in fair condition, original wheels, needs restoration, late 19th c. **275**

Early Lady's Waverly Safety Bike

Waverly, lady's pneumatic safety model, accessories include a "Search Light" head lamp, bell, wheel bell, tool pouch & ornate press-decorated wooden chain guard, made in Indianapolis, ca. 1898 (ILLUS.) **578**
Wolff (R.H.), matched pair of male & female pneumatic safety models, nice original condition w/matching name plates & good wheels, New York, late 19th c., pr.......... **990**

BLACK AMERICANA

Over the past decade or so, this field of collecting has rapidly grown and today almost anything that relates to Black culture or illustrates Black Americana is considered a desirable collectible. Although many representations of Blacks, especially on 19th and early 20th century advertising pieces and housewares, were cruel stereotypes, even these are collected as poignant reminders of how far American society has come since the dawning of the Civil Rights movement, and how far we still have to go. Other pieces related to this category will be found from time to time in such categories as Advertising Items, Banks, Character Collectibles, Kitchenwares, Cookie Jars, Signs and Signboards, Toys and several others. For a complete overview of this subject see Antique Trader Books' Black Americana Price Guide with a special introduction by Julian Bond.

Alarm clock, animated, silvered square metal case w/square white dial & black Arabic numerals, in the center an

Lux Animated Alarm Clock

animated black shoeshine man shines a standing lady's shoe, Lux Company, ca. 1930s, works, 3¾" w. (ILLUS.) **$220**

Autograph, Frederick Douglass, inscribed hardboard book, ink inscription "Very truly yours - Fedr. Douglass - 1876," from book belonging to Miss Lillian Pierce, Biddeford, Maine, book includes other signatures of friends & relatives 4 x 6½" **333**

Book, "History of the Negro Race in America, 1619-1880," by Geo. W. Williams, G.P. Putnam, New York, 1882-83, hardcover, 2 vols. (slight wear) **493**

"Memoirs of Elleanor Eldridge"

Book, "Memoirs of Elleanor Eldridge," Providence, Rhode Island, 1847, second edition, story of a free black woman in Providence, published to raise funds when she was ill & financially strapped, woodcut of author in front, hardcover, 128 pp., 3¾ x 5" (ILLUS.) **168**

Book, "Stride Toward Freedom - The Montgomery Story," by Martin Luther King, Jr., Harper & Row, New York, 1958, signed in ink by King "Best Wishes - Martin Luther King Jr.," hard cover w/dust jacket, 230 pp. **1,452**

Book, "The Day They Marched," edited by Doris E. Saunders, published by Johnson Publishing Co., Chicago, 1963, first edition, photographic documentation of the March on Washington, color cover, 88 pp., 8½ x 11" (ILLUS.) **41**

"The Day They Marched" Book

Booklet, "Sit Ins - the student report," produced by CORE in May 1960, letters from groups of students & sit-in participants, 16 pp., 6 x 8½" **69**

Booklet, "The Right To Vote," produced by CORE, documents voter registration drive in Sumter, South Carolina, 1962, slight soiling, 22 pp., 8½ x 11" **58**

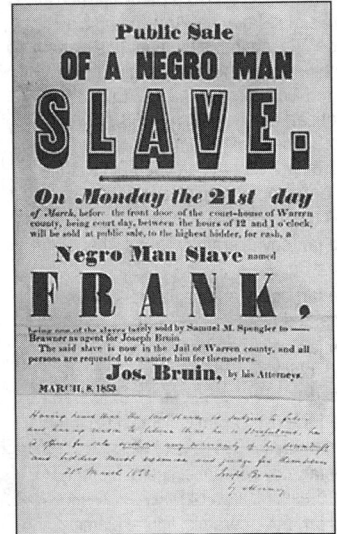

Rare Slave Sale Broadside

Broadside, printed paper, "Public Sale - Of A Negro Man Slave - On Monday the 21st day of March...Negro Man Slave named FRANK...., Jos. Bruin, by his Attorneys - March 8, 1853...," light even tone, few minor edge splits & folds, 7¾ x 10" (ILLUS.) **2,530**

Carte-de-Visite of Black Nursemaid

Carte-de-visite, photograph of a black Georgia nursemaid holding a white infant, by J.N. Wilson, Savannah, Georgia, ca. 1850s, tiny spots on infant's white dress (ILLUS.)............. **212**

Carte-de-visite, photograph of a black Virginia grandfather & two grandchildren, he seated in ragged cloths in the center w/a standing girl on one side & young boy on the other, possibly antebellum era, by W. Ogilvie, Norfolk, Virginia **605**

Certificate, lithographed & partly finished in manuscript, from the "American Bible Union" stating that a member has made a contribution of one dime to "give the Sacred Scriptures to the FREEDMEN of America," dated January 1868, New York, vignette of Freeman kneeling before Lady Liberty, an open Bible at the center bottom, completed in purple ink (light toning, small edge tear) **431**

Cookie jar, cov., ceramic, figural Chef, Pearl China Co. **850**

Cookie jar, cov., ceramic, figural Chef, unmarked **275**

Cookie jar, cov., ceramic, figural Chef's head, black w/gold features, white hat, unmarked **70**

Cookie jar, cov., ceramic, figural Luzianne Mammy............................ **650**

Cookie jar, cov., ceramic, figural Mammy, blue dress, Mosaic Tile.................. **485**

Cookie jar, cov., ceramic, figural Mammy, National Silver Co. (NASCO) **250**

Cookie jar, cov., ceramic, figural Mammy w/spoon, unmarked.................... **1,450**

Cookie jar, cov., ceramic, figural Mammy, yellow dress, Mosaic Tile **495**

Cookie jar, cov., plastic, figural Aunt Jemima, F & F Mold & Die Works **750**

Cracker jar, cov., ceramic, figural Mammy, Japan **500**

Cup & saucer, advertising, ceramic, "Coon Chicken Inn" **425**

Rare "Kneeling Slave" Cup & Saucer

Cup & saucer, handled, porcelain, white w/black transfer-printed design of the "Kneeling Slave" in chains, images outside & inside cup & on saucer, England, ca. 1830s, bowl 6" d. (ILLUS.) **1,035**

Doll, black man, stuffed cloth, wearing a cream-colored striped cotton shirt, rayon tie & black, white & purple polka dot shirt, early 20th c., 16¼" h. (scattered staining, minor fiber wear) **374**

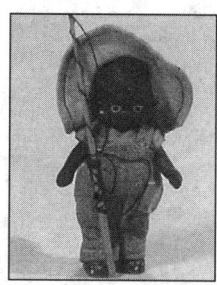

Miniature Bisque Black Doll

Doll, miniature, bisque, a black child dressed in blue overalls & red shirt wearing a large cloth hat, w/small wooden fishing pole, early 20th c., 3¾" h. (ILLUS.)........................ **110**

Large Black Girl Cloth Doll

Doll, stuffed cloth, figure of a black girl w/hooked hair through a burlap ground, the face embroidered w/brown & beige stitches, dressed in a hand-stitched petticoat, pinafore, shirt, skirt & apron, late 19th - early 20th c., 32½ " h. (ILLUS.) .. **1,380**

Doll, unsewn cloth, Aunt Jemima, framed, ca. 1929 .... **285**

Dresser box, cov., ceramic, figural Butler **375**

Election slate card, anti-black, lists candidates of the National Union Party opposing "Negro Suffrage," 1st Leg. District of Maryland, ca. 1865, before passage of the 15th Amendment, 3 x 7½ " (folded in quarters) **80**

Flour bag, cloth, Aunt Jemima decoration, 5 lb..... **8**

Flyer, printed paper, "Finish the Fight! against The Lynch Mob...," wording in red on white, produced by the NAACP, 1946, 8½ x 11"............................ **112**

Game, target-type, "Jolly Darkie" **325**

Figural Cast Iron Hitching Post

Hitching post, cast iron, figural, a standing black groom wearing ragged clothes & holding up the hitching ring, on a thick square cast base, marked "R. Wood & Co., Phila.," late 19th - early 20th c., 48" h. (ILLUS.)....................... **2,600**

Scarce Nippon Humidor

Humidor, cov., porcelain, h.p. colorful half-length portrait of a black minstrel playing a banjo, stylized geometric borders around base & rim of cover, Nippon, cover professionally restored, ca. 1900, 14¼" d., 6½ " h. (ILLUS.) **800**

Invitation, SNCC fundraising dinner, printed light board w/cover drawing by Ben Shahn of a black & white handshake, held at the New York City Hilton, April 25, 1965, many notables attending, 4 pp., 7 x 10" **28**

Lithographed photo, black & white group shot of male & female black students, printed across the bottom "Greetings from McKinley Normal and Industrial Institute, Meadville, Virginia," building in background, used to acknowledge a contribution, printed by "The News," South Boston, Virginia, 1909 (slight browning & edge wear) **67**

Magazine, "The Abolitionist," Volume 1, No. 1, first issue published by the New England Anti-Slavery Society, January 1833, string-bound w/a handbill "Prospectus of The Abolitionist," advertising for the magazine & November 1832 handbill, 16 pp., 6¼ x 10" (some soil & stains, edges unevenly cut & crumpled) **593**

Movie lobby cards, "The Crimson Skull," Western silent film w/an all-black cast, black & white scenes from the movie, shot in the all-black town of Boley, Oklahoma, published by Rotograph Co., New York, starred Bill Pickett & Anita Bush, 1921, 11 x 14", 2 pcs. (tack holes, soiling, foxing, top hole in one, edge tear in other) **132**

"Without Pity" Movie Poster

Movie poster, "Without Pity," printed in black & red on yellow, a 1948 Italian film concerning interracial relationship, written by Federico Fellini & produced by Carlo Ponti, starred John Kitzmiller, photo of two stars, printed across the top "Mercury Theatre - 565 Main St. - Buffalo, N.Y. - Starts Tues. May 9th...," horizontal fold, tack holes, some upper tears, 14 x 22" (ILLUS.) 133

Photograph, Booker T. Washington, print on card stock, name below & notation "From his best photograph," copyright 1915 by A. N. Jenkins, published by Austin-Jenkins Co., Washington, D.C., noted at bottom "Worth $1," perhaps some type of premium, framed, 11 x 14" (wrinkles & small tears around edges) 80

Photograph, cabinet-size, studio portrait of a standing young black woman, by Crier, Arch St., Philadelphia, back w/penciled name "Lottie Cooper - Melrow St." (some small spots) 41

Rare Carte de Visite of Colored Troops

Photograph, carte de visite image of Colored troops standing in uniform in lines between log camp buildings, arms stacked in the center foreground, noted as 64th U.S. Colored Infantry, photographed in Mississippi, 1864, upper corner bumped (ILLUS.) 1,485

Photograph, glossy black & white new photo of the Homestead Grays baseball team on the road, posed group shot w/the reverse stamped "Sockwell Studio, N. Braddock, PA," dated in ink "March 23, 1946," pencil notation of players including Hall of Famers, 8¼ x 10" (edge wear, slight tear). 396

Photograph, "Alligator Bait," ca. 1897, 9 x 24". . . 350

Pinback button, celluloid, "Aug. 28 - March On Washington - For Jobs and Freedom," light blue & cream, black & white hands shaking, for 1963 March on Washington, 1¾" d. 78

Pinback button, celluloid, "Black Is Beautiful - Black Panther Party," black on neon pink, stalking panther in the center, 1960s, 1½ " d. 18

Pinback button, celluloid, "Chicago Defender Defense Program," red, white & blue, late World War II "V" for Victory in center, also "Remember Pearl Harbor - and Sikeston Too - Fight to Save Democracy - Victory with Justice For All," 1" d. 182

March on Washington Pinback Button

Pinback button, celluloid, "National March For Freedom - I Was There - Aug. 28, 1963 - Washington, D.C.," blue & white w/sketch of the Capitol dome, 3" d. (ILLUS.) . . 127

Plate, paper, Aunt Jemina decoration. 36

Rosa Parks-signed Postal Cover

Postal cover, autographed by Rosa Parks, first-day issue honoring Planned Parenthood, postmarked "New York, NY - Mar. 18, 1972," signed in ink below the postmark (ILLUS.) 46

Black Big Band Show Poster

Poster, "Hartley Toots and His Famous Orchestra," printed in yellow, blue & black on heavy card stock, Black big band on

"A Close Shave" Comical Mug

Figural Souvenir Novelty

Early Abolitionist Token

Black Jockey on Donkey Pull Toy

Amos and Andy Freshair Taxi Toy

Toy, windup tin, "Amos and Andy Freshair Taxi," the two characters seated in an orange open taxi, complete, working, very good condition, Marx (ILLUS.) **825**

Ham and Sam Windup Tin Toy

Toy, windup tin, "Ham and Sam - The Minstrel Team," a colorful upright piano w/one man seated playing & another man standing beside him playing a banjo, Strauss, works, even overall wear, minor rust on banjo (ILLUS.) **715**

Blizzard Freezer Trade Card

Trade card, Blizzard Freezer, color front illustration of two children being served ice cream by a black Mammy, white border, advertising on the back (ILLUS.) **15**

Wall pocket, ceramic, figural Mammy on green stove. **70**

Whistle, ceramic, figural black man polishing a boot, blow hole hidden in top of head, sounding hole cut into middle of back, England, good paint, 4" l. **66**

BOOTJACKS

The Bootjack is a utilitarian device used to remove a boot, and often an American art form at the same time. As with so many everyday items created in the 19th and early 20th

centuries, the way something looked was as important to its creator as its use. United States patent records from 1790 to 1873 indicate the first patent for a bootjack was issued April 6, 1852 to Saris Thomson of Hartsville, Massachusetts (Patent #8865). Normally, the bootjack has been produced from cast iron or wood and ranges from extremely fine casting and carvings to crude ones-of-a kind. As with so many collectible items bootjacks are heavily reproduced, especially crickets and "Naughty Nellies"--castings are lightweight and of a poor quality. Prices on early fine castings and carvings have risen steadily in the last five years but prices for the more common varieties are still reasonable.

Brass, figural "Foxy Grandpa," ca. 1900-1910, 12" **$1,000**

Cast iron, adjustable cut-out arms w/wing nut on underside, marked "C. Parker, Pat. Oct. 7, 1873," 11" **450**

Cast iron, advertising, original gold paint, geometric & scroll design w/embossed words "Use - Musselmans - Bootjack - Plug - Tobacco," early 20th c., 9½" **165**

Cast iron, closed loop at the top to hold both boot & heel, cut-out wagon wheel in center, ca. 1880, 20½" **350**

Cast iron, cut-out lettering "BOSS," ca. 1880s, 15" **400**

Cast iron, cut-out scroll design w/cut-out wording "DOWNS & CO" in center ('N,' '&' 'S' in reverse), date unknown, 13½ " **200**

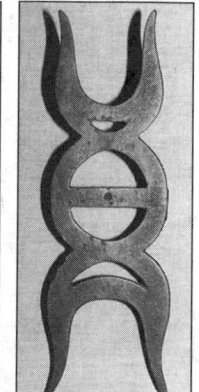

From left: Double-Ended "A. M. Mitchell" Bootjack Double-Ended Bootjack with Half-circles

Cast iron, double-ended, cut-out floral design w/"A. M. Mitchell" on one side & "Charleston, ILL." on reverse, 11⅝" (ILLUS.) . . **350**

Cast iron, double-ended w/half-circles in middle & quarter moon each end, early 20th c., 11¼" (ILLUS.) **175**

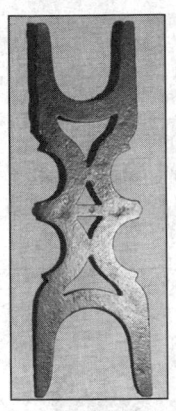 

From left: Double-Ended Bootjack with Triangles
Stylized Floral & Heart Bootjack

Cast iron, double-ended w/triangles in
center, Pennsylvania, early 20th c.,
13½ " (ILLUS.) **150**

Cast iron, embossed lettering "Wittier's"
above & "American Centennial Boot Jack
- 1876" around a cut-out star, above
another star circled by "Hyde Park" all
above "Mass - 1776," 13" **450**

Cast iron, fancy raised stylized floral design
w/heart at bottom, 14" (ILLUS.) **300**

Cast iron, figural Devil w/painted white
horns & arms, cut-out circular eyes &
triangular nose above a painted red
mouth & cut-out stomach, w/some
original paint, ca. 1880-90, 10½ " **300**

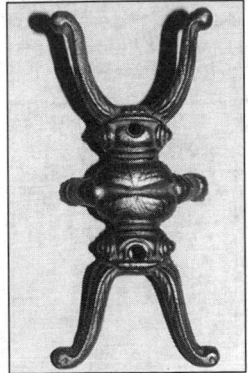

Double-Ended Beetle Bootjack

Cast iron, figural, double-ended beetle,
9½ " (ILLUS.) **270**

Cast iron, figural female weightlifter holding
barbell w/rope & rings in her outstretched
arms, late 19th c., 10" **1,000**

Cast iron, figural mermaid w/outstretched
arms lying atop green seaweed,
w/original paint, ca. 1900, 11" **500**

Cast iron, figural "Naughty Nellie" w/hands
away from her head, painted gold, date
unknown, crude casting, 10" **600**

Cast iron, figural "Naughty Nellie" w/head
slightly turned to left, w/original red paint,
fine detail, paint worn, 11½ " **300**

Cast iron, figural "Naughty Nellie" w/original
paint, late 19th c., 10½ " **650**

Cast iron, figural "Naughty Nellie" w/original
wine-red-painted dress & light brown
skin, ca. 1875-85, 9½ " **350**

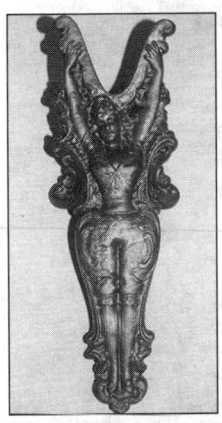 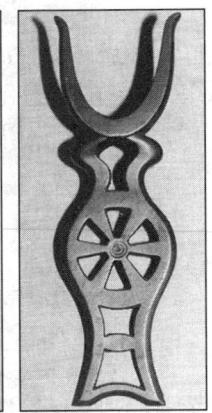

From left: Figural Woman In Bloomers Bootjack
Bootjack with Cut-Out Wheel At Center

Cast iron, figural, very finely cast, woman in
bloomers, made in Czechoslovakia, early
20th c., 13¼" (ILLUS.) **750**

Cast iron, finely cast w/cut-out wheel at
center, Pennsylvania, late 19th c.,
10¾" (ILLUS.) **650**

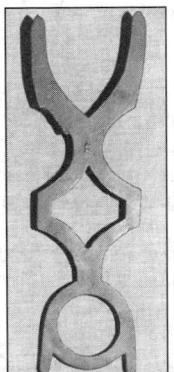

Early 20th Century Cast Iron Bootjack

Cast iron, forked at one end w/open
diamond central design & ring end
design, early 20th c., 12" (ILLUS.) **150**

Bootjack with Cut-out Heart & Hole

Cast iron, forked end w/cut-out heart at top
& hole at bottom, heavy, late 19th c.,
12¾" (ILLUS.). **175**

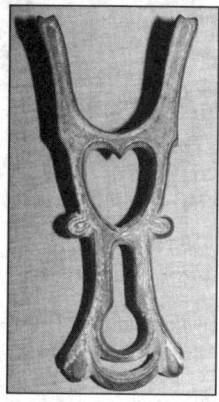

Bootjack with Heart & Keyhole Cut-Outs

Cast iron, forked end w/heart & keyhole cut-
outs, some gold & white paint, 9⅜" (ILLUS.) . . **175**

Cast iron, model of a cricket w/bulging black
eyes, painted all-over w/green & black
speckled paint, ca. 1920, 10½ " **125**

Cast iron, model of a cricket w/original
paint, decorated in brown, red, blue &
yellow on a black ground, ca. 1900 . . . . **125**

Cast iron, model of a folding pistol, marked
"Phelps Dodge - Palmer - Chicago,"
ca. 1890, 8½ " **400**

Cast iron, model of a lobster, marked "Keen
Kutter" on underside, w/some original
paint, 10¼" **125**

Cast iron, model of a lyre, ca. 1890, 12" **275**

Cast iron, model of a pair of upside-down
dress boots above two scrolls,
ca. 1870s, 13" **450**

Cast iron, model of a snail, date unknown, 13" . . **125**

Cast iron, model of a stag head above scroll
design, ca. 1880, 11" **650**

Cast iron, model of a steer head, marked
"101 Ranch" below w/Pat. Pend. on
underside, ca. 1910, 11½ " **700**

Cast iron, model of the Tree of LIfe
w/unusual vulture heads, cut-out heart at
base, ca. 1890, 11¾" **200**

Cast iron, original red paint, elaborate floral
& scroll designs w/inverted heart in center
& hole at bottom, ca. 1880-90, 12¼" **300**

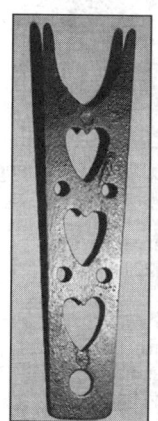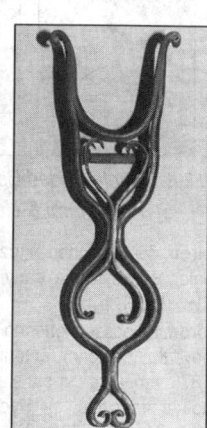

From left: Bootjack with Three Stylized Hearts
Bootjack with Cut-out Hearts & Circles

Cast iron, tapering flat wedge-shaped
w/three cut-out hearts & five cut-out
circles, 15⅝" (ILLUS.). **450**

Cast iron, traveling-type, pivoting arms fit
size of heel, cut-out vine design, style
pat'd. Oct. 29, 1867 by "A. P. Seymour,
Hecla Works, N. Y.," 8¾" open, 5⅛" closed **95**

Cast iron, U-form end & heavy shaped
frame w/three stylized hearts,
Pennsylvania, unique, 13" (ILLUS.) **750**

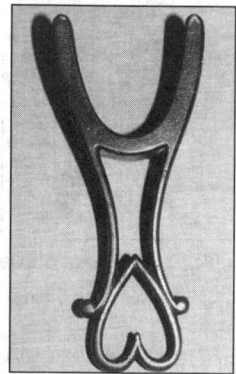

Bootjack with Upside-Down Heart

Cast iron, U-shaped forked end w/upside-
down heart at bottom, finely cast, late
19th-early 20th c., 8¼" (ILLUS.). **350**

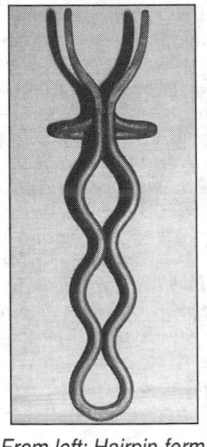

From left: Hairpin-form Pennsylvania Bootjack
Cast Iron "EZ -OFF" Bootjack

Cast iron, undulating hairpin-form,
Pennsylvania, probably unique, early
20th c., 17" (ILLUS.) **350**
Cast iron, Victorian scroll design, ca. 1900, 11" . . **450**
Cast iron, w/cut-out letters "EZ" above word
"OFF," nicely cast, 11½ " (ILLUS.) **250**

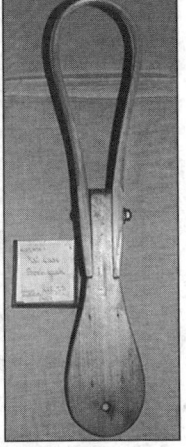

From left: Victorian Scroll & Shield Bootjack
Wooden Wheeler Case Co. Bootjack

Wooden, flattened board beetle-form
incised w/scrolls & a shield w/initials
"W.L.," Victorian, 13" (ILLUS.) **175**
Wooden, folding-type, hand-carved pistol,
brass hinges & pins, ca. 1860-70, 10" **350**
Wooden, folding-type, long narrow boards
w/brass hinges & pins, possibly Shaker,
ca. 1870-80, 10½ " **300**
Wooden, folding-type, w/closed loop,
original patent model for Wheeler Case
Co., 22¾" (ILLUS.) **1,000**

Wooden, folding-type, w/closed loop,
w/original label "Folding Boot-Jack -
Wheeler Case & Co." pat'd. Dec. 7, 1869,
Utica, New York, 23" open, 14¾" closed **200**

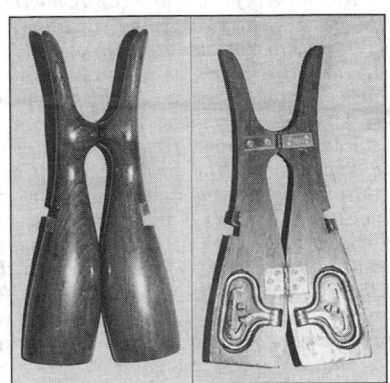

Wooden Lady's Leg Bootjack

Wooden, lady's-leg style, hinged brass
fittings & boot strap pulls inset
inside,early 20th c., 12" (ILLUS. of two views) . . **900**

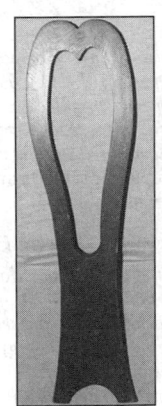

From left: Heart-Shaped Wooden Bootjack
Pennsylvania Folk Art Bootjack

Wooden, large heart-shaped loop at the top,
fork at opposite end, 25½ ." (ILLUS.) **125**
Wooden, original red paint w/black pin
striping, slender design w/small hole at
bottom, ca. 1850, 16" **250**
Wooden, tapering board w/incised
Pennsylvania Dutch folk art designs
including a star, pinwheel & heart, initials
"R.T.," at bottom, late 19th - early 20th c.,
Pennsylvania,13¼" (ILLUS.) **300**
Wooden, walnut, folding lady's legs
w/pointed toes, brass hinges & pins, ca.
1860-70, 10" **350**
Wooden & cast iron, mechanical, spring-
operated mechanism, oblong wood
platform on iron base, ca. 1900, 13½ " **125**

BOTTLE OPENERS

Before the turn of the century, the crown cap for bottled drinks was invented and immediately there was a need for a bottle cap remover or bottle opener. There are many variations of openers, some in combination with other tools, others are utilitarian with fancy handles. Perhaps the most important type of bottle opener today is the figural bottle opener. There are 22 classifications or types of figural bottle openers, with Type 1 being the most important and sought after by collectors. Figures for openers include people, animals, birds, pretzels, keys, etc. Wall-mount openers are mostly faces of people or animals with the opener located in or near the mouth. The important early producers (ca. 1940-50) of iron and pot-metal (zinc) figural openers were Wilton Products, John Wright Inc., Gadzik Sales and L&L Favors. Figural openers were made primarily as souvenirs from vacation spots around the country. Today, new original figural openers are produced in limited numbered editions and sold to collectors. Manufacturers such as Reynolds Toys have produced over 40 different figural bottle opener editions since 1988.

There are two clubs for bottle opener collectors: Figural Bottle Opener Collectors (F.B.O.C.) and Just For Openers (J.F.O.). J.F.O. is a club primarily for beer opener collectors, but includes collectors of figural openers, corkscrews and can openers. The numbers used at the end of the entries refer to Figural Bottle Openers Identification Guide, a new book printed by F.B.O.C.

Bottle openers by type: Type 1—Figural bottle openers, free-standing or in a natural position or wall-mounted, the opener an integral part of the figure. Type 2—Figural openers with corkscrew, lighter or nutcracker, etc. Type 3—Figural openers, three-dimensional on both sides but do not stand. Type 4—Figural openers with loop openers an integral part of design. Type 5—Figural openers with a loop inserted in the casting process. The loop or opener is not part of the casting process. Type 6—Same as Type 5 with an added can punch. Type 7—Same as Type 5 with an added corkscrew or lighter. Type 8—Flat, back not three-dimensional, loop part of casting. Type 9—Same as Type 8, loop inserted in the casting process. Type 10—Same as Type 8, with a corkscrew. Type 11—Openers are coin or medallion shape, one- or two-sided, with an insert or cast integral loop opener. (These are very common.) Type 12—Figural stamped openers, formed by the stamping process (steel, aluminum or brass). Type 13—Extruded metal openers. Type 14—Johnny guitars or figural holders. Johnny Guitars are figures made of wood, shells, string, etc.; they have a magnet that holds a stamped steel (Type 12) opener; figural holders or display holders are cast holders that have a clip that holds one or two cast figural openers. Type 15—Church keys with a figure riveted or cast on the opener. Some do not have a punch key. Type 16—Figural church-key openers with corkscrew. Type 17—Decorated church-key openers (church-key loop or wire loop openers with names and jewels attached). Type 18—Base opener (opener molded in bottom as integral part). Type 19—Base opener added (opener added to bottom by brazing or soldering). Type 20—Base-plate opener (opener screwed in base of figure). Type 21—Wooden openers / Syroco openers (metal insert, cast stamped or wire type). Type 22—Knives, hatchets, scissors, etc., with openers. Rarity: A—Most Common. B—Difficult. C—Very difficult. D—Very hard to find. E—Rare to Very Rare (few known).

FIGURAL (FULL DIMENSIONAL)

TYPE 1

All-American Bottle Opener

All-American, cast iron, figure of a man in an orange football jersey w/the letters "Z B T" across his chest, standing on base marked "Joe Alexander", rarity E, 4¼" h., F-38 (ILLUS.) . . . . **$600 to 950**

Alligator & boy w/hands up, cast iron, figural group of black boy w/his hands raised above his head, being bitten in the behind by an alligator, rarity B, 2¼" h., F-134 . . . . **150 to 250**

Barking at the moon, aluminum, figural group, a barking brown & white dog sitting at the base of a crescent moon, 2" h., N-529 . . . . **45 to 110**

Bear, baby, aluminum, model of baby bear wearing a red top, blue pants & holding a cap in his hand, rarity C, 3" h., N-562 . . . . **45 to 90**

Beer Drinker Bottle Opener

Beer drinker, cast iron, figure of a portly
man wearing a hat, blue shirt & brown
pants holding a bear mug, rare, 5½" h.,
F-192 (ILLUS.). . . . . **1,500+**

Billy goat, cast iron, figure of a goat w/head
tilted back, rarity C, 2¾" h., F-74. . . . . . **150 to 250**

Buffalo, aluminum, 2" h., N-595 . . . . **50 to 75**

Caddy, cast iron, figure of a black boy
wearing a red shirt, black pants & red
shoes, holding a golf bag w/clubs &
resting his hand on a white sign that
reads "19," rarity D, 5⅞" h., F-44 . . . . . **350 to 550**

Canvasback duck, cast iron, colorfully
painted duck w/red head & neck & a
yellowish white body, 1¹³/₁₆" h.,
F-107 . . . . **75 to 150**

Cockatoo, cast iron, colorfully painted,
3" h., F-121 . . . . **100 to 225**

Cocker Spaniel, cast iron, model of dog
w/white body & brown ears, neck & hind
end, standing w/one foot raised, rarity A,
2¾" h., F-80 . . . . **75 to 110**

Cool Penguin Bottle Opener

Cool penguin, zinc, model of walking
penguin wearing a top hat, rarity C,
4" h., (ILLUS.). . . . . **150 to 250**

Cowboy w/cactus, pot metal, figural group
of cowboy wearing cowboy hat & plaid
shirt clutching a cactus, rarity D,
4⅝" h., F-23 . . . . **350 to 650**

Crystal beetle, pot metal & crystal, model of
a beetle w/cut-crystal circular body
w/metal legs & head, rare, 4⅜" . . . . **550+**

Devil, aluminum, figure of Devil dressed in
red robes holding pitch fork, rarity B,
4" h., N-563 . . . . **100 to 150**

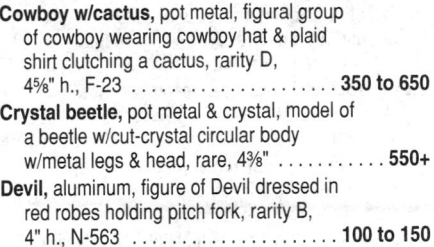

Standing Donkey Bottle Opener

Donkey, cast iron, figure of standing donkey
w/white teeth, rarity D, 3½" l, N-613
(ILLUS.). . . . . **250 to 350**

Donkey, brass, body of donkey marked
"Phila. - 1948," rarity D, 3¾" h. . . . . **500+**

Elephant, cast iron, model of walking
elephant w/mouth open & trunk raised,
rarity D, 4¼" l., N-616 . . . . **1,200+**

Eskimo ice, aluminum, figural group of
Eskimo dressed in a parka holding the
leash of the dog sitting in front of him,
3" h., N-575 . . . . **50 to 90**

Father Christmas Bottle Opener

Father Christmas, aluminum, rarity C,
4½" h., N-558 (ILLUS.) . . . . **150 to 250**

Flying fish, aluminum, model of a trout atop
a wave, rarity B, 4¾" h., N-656 . . . . **75 to 150**

Goat, cast iron, model of seated goat,
rarity A, 4⁵/₁₆" h., F-71 . . . . **60 to 100**

Gobbler, aluminum, model of gold-painted
turkey w/stern look on his face, wearing
suit w/arms crossed, 3" h., N-625 . . . . . . **45 to 75**

Indian chief, aluminum, figure of chief
wearing full headdress, standing w/legs
spread & hands on hips, 5" h., N-598 ... **50 to 75**

Key (large), stainless steel, marked "Powell
- White - Star Valves - are - Closers,"
rare, 9" l. .... **300 to 400**

Lady in kimono, cast iron, stylized figure of
woman wearing a kimono, entire figure is
black except for the red sash & light
brown hat, rarity D, 3⅞" h., N-580 .... **200 to 300**

Lamppost drunks, cast iron, figural,
common, 4⅛" h., F-1, 2, 11 .... **10 to 25**

Mexican with Cactus Bottle Opener

Mexican w/cactus, cast iron, figural group
of Mexican wearing sombrero, sitting
beside cactus, rarity E, 2⅞" h., F-24
(ILLUS.) .... **550 to 750**

Mighty Musky, cast iron, rarity B, 6⅛" l.,
N-659 .... **75 to 150**

Monkey, cast iron, model of seated monkey,
2⅝" h., F-89 .... **250 to 300**

Mother goose, aluminum, figure of woman
in a green dress & white apron holding a
goose, rarity A, 3¾" h., N-573 .... **50 to 75**

Motorcycle rider, aluminum, figural group
of man riding motorcycle wearing a red
helmet, goggles, white shirt & brown
pants, rarity B, 2¾" h., N-588 .... **75 to 150**

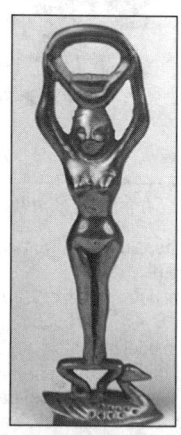

Nude on Swan Bottle Opener

Nude on swan iron, brass, rarity B, 6⅝" h.
(ILLUS.) .... **75 to 150**

Old pal, aluminum, model of a dog
w/head turned & paw raised, rarity B,
2¾" h., N-570 .... **45 to 90**

Owl, bronze, model of a stylized owl sitting
on a branch, rarity A, 2⅞" h., N-552 ..... **50 to 75**

Paddy the Pledgemaster, cast iron, figure
of a young man wearing a blue sweater &
white pants holding a paddle marked "Phi
Kappa Pi," standing on a base marked
"Dinner Dance '57," 3⅞" h., F-41 ..... **300 to 350**

Parrot on Perch Bottle Opener

Parrot on perch, cast iron, figure of yellow,
blue, green & red parrot on elaborate
perch, rarity E, 4⅝" h., F-114
(ILLUS.) .... **450 to 700**

Patty Pep, cast iron, figure of young woman
wearing a red cap & coat & a brown skirt,
buttons of coat marked w/Greek letters,
on a base marked "Pledge Dance '57,"
rarity E, 4" h., F-36 .... **1,200+**

Pelican, cast iron, model of a pelican
w/orange eyes, 3⅜" h., F-131 .... **250 to 350**

Pretzel, "Hauenstein Beer," rarity D, 2⅞" w.,
F-231 .... **250 to 350**

Red Riding Hood, aluminum, figure of Red
Riding Hood holding a basket w/the wolf
at her feet, 4" h, N-568 .... **50 to 75**

Rhino, cast iron, rarity E, 4", F-76 ...... **350 to 550**

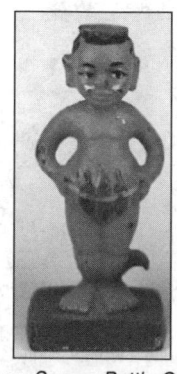

Sammy Somoa Bottle Opener

Sammy Somoa, cast iron, figure of a native
wearing leaves, rare, 4⁵⁄₁₆" h., F-39
(ILLUS.) . . . . **950 to 1,500**
Sawfish, cast iron, 5" l., F-157 . . . . **350 to 550**
Sea gull, cast iron, model of a sea gull on a
brown perch, 3" h., F-123 . . . . **50 to 75**
Setter dog, cast iron, model of a dog w/front
paw raised & straight tail, rarity A,
2½" h., F-79 . . . . **60 to 90**

Uncle Sam Bottle Opener

Uncle Sam, figural group of Uncle Sam
clutching sign post w/sign that reads
"Uncle Sam," 1 of 13, rarity D, 3⁷⁄₈" h.,
N-580 (ILLUS.) . . . . **250 to 350**

TYPE 2

Old Snifter, zinc, turns head & corkscrew
comes out **125**
Old Snifter, zinc, w/lighter & corkscrew **275**

TYPE 3

Dachshund, Wilton Flats, cast iron, three-
dimensional but does not stand . . . . **50 to 100**
Donkey, Wilton Flats, cast iron, three-
dimensional but does not stand . . . . **50 to 100**
Elephant, Wilton Flats, cast iron, three-
dimensional but does not stand . . . . **50 to 100**
Fish, Wilton Flats, cast iron, three-
dimensional but does not stand . . . . **50 to 100**
Scottie Dog, Wilton Flats, cast iron, three-
dimensional but does not stand . . . . **50 to 100**

TYPE 4

Drunk, Wilton, cast iron, three-dimensional
drunk wearing black top hat & suit, w/loop
top **65**
Mermaid, cast iron, three-dimensional,
marked "Chiquita," loop tail **110**

TYPE 8

Gemini, zinc, flat back **20**

Lobster, cast iron, flat back, red, claws
serve as loop **35**
Mad Man, zinc, flat back, depicts man
bending at the knees w/hands clasped,
legs serve as loop **75**

TYPE 9

Mermaid, lead & steel, depicts mermaid
w/tail curled under, her upraised arms
holding loop, loop inserted in casting
process **45**
Pretzel, large, lead & steel, top of pretzel
holds loop, loop inserted in casting
process **150**
Winston Churchill, aluminum & steel,
shows Churchill in front of hand giving a
victory sign, fingers of hand hold loop,
loop inserted in casting process **90**

TYPE 11

Coin in Holder Opener

Coin in holder, stainless steel & bronze,
bronze coin in rectangular holder, loop
cut out at top (ILLUS.) **20**

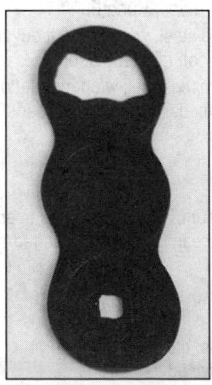

Three Coins Bottle Opener

Coins, cast iron, three Oriental coins joined
together w/loop cut out of top coin
(ILLUS.) **15**

Medallion Bottle Opener

Medallion, bronze, two-sided, w/loop at top
(ILLUS.) 10

TYPE 12

Ax-form Bottle Openers

Ax, stamped steel & wood, rectangular
wood handle, opener cut out of blade
(ILLUS left.) 10
Ax, stamped steel & wood, thin rounded
wood handle, opener cut out of blade
(ILLUS. right) 10
Fist, stamped steel, w/opener cut out of
palm, wrist reads "Kung-Fu" 12
Foot, stamped steel, w/opener cut out of the
ball of the foot, marked "Goon" 12
Football, stamped steel, w/opener cut out of
top, small medallion at bottom reads
"Clearwater" 12

TYPE 13

Shark, aluminum, mouth serves as opener,
marked "Ocean City, MD," attached to
key ring 3

TYPE 14

Bar & patrons, bar holds two figural
openers shaped as patrons .... 75 to 150
Golf bag & caddie, golf bag holder holds
figural caddie opener .... 75 to 150
Johnny Guitars, figures of old people
w/magnets that hold Type 12 openers,
each .... 45 to 75

Shield & Knight Bottle Opener

Shield & knight, shield holds figural knight
opener (ILLUS.) .... 75 to 90

TYPE 15

Cat, attached to church key-type opener,
depicts green cat w/crossed arms 25
Girl, attached to church key-type opener, girl
w/long hair & large red bow on top of
head 25
Violin case, attached to church key-type
opener, case marked "Beethoven's fifth" 25
Woman in bikini, attached to church key-
type opener, woman wearing red & white
polka-dotted cap & bikini 25

TYPE 17

Church keys & wire-type, w/scrolls,
medallions & decorations, each .... 15 to 20

TYPE 18

Boar's head, nickel silver, full-figured,
opener in bottom 110
Bull's head, bronze, full-figured, opener in
bottom 55

TYPE 19

Hats, bronze, opener soldered in bottom, each ... 35

TYPE 20

Dog's Head Bottle Opener

Dog's head, Syroco, base plate opener
screwed in bottom (ILLUS.) 55
Horse's head, zinc, base plate opener
screwed in bottom 35

TYPE 21

Syroco Butler Bottle Opener

Butler, Syroco, wearing black suit & white apron, holding green bottle, metal opener attached to head inside body (ILLUS.) **90**

Clown, Syroco, wearing white outfit w/blue collar, metal opener attached to head inside body **350**

Figure, wooden, figure of Viking w/beard & holding shield, horned hat serves as opener, Danish . . . . **10 to 30**

Figure, wooden w/metal lifter on face, figure wearing green scarf & hat, Danish . . . . . . **10 to 30**

Man by lamppost, wooden, carved, figure of man w/suitcase standing next to lamppost, music box in suitcase, metal opener attached to head inside body **225**

War-time Wooden Bottle Opener

Wooden, metal opener attached, marked "War-time Bottle Opener- With nail-head under cap, pull up...your bottle is open!," World War II era (ILLUS.) **90**

WALL MOUNT

Amish man, cast iron, w/long beard wearing Amish-style hat, rare, 4⅛" h., F-422 . . . . . . **1,900+**
Bear head, cast iron, 3" h, F-426 . . . . **150 to 250**

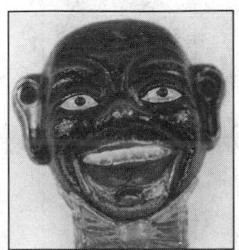

Black Face Bottle Opener

Black face, aluminum, black face wearing bow tie w/mouth open to reveal white teeth, rare, 5" h., F-401 (ILLUS.) . . . . **650+**

Boy winking, cast iron, freckle-faced winking boy w/two large front teeth, rare, 3⅞" h., F-418 . . . . **550+**

Clown head, cast iron, model of a clown head w/orange hair, red nose & mouth wearing red polka-dotted tie, 4½" h., F-417 . . . . **75 to 150**

Coyote, cast iron, gold-painted, rare, 3½" h., F-429 . . . . **850+**

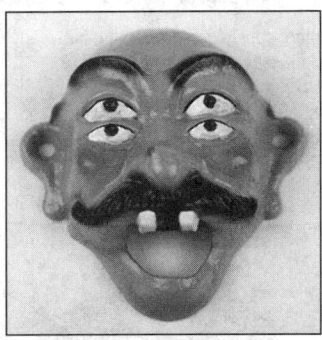

Double-eye Bottle Opener

Double-eye, cast iron, four-eyed bald-headed man, rarity A, 3⅞" h., F-414 (ILLUS.). . . . . **50 to 75**

Florida Pipe & Foundry, cast iron, four-eyed black woman w/red hair & lips, wearing bonnet that reads "Florida Pipe & Foundry," rare, 4⅛" h., F-410 . . . . **550+**

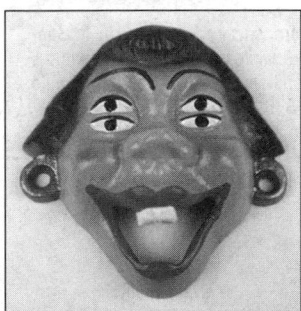

Miss Four Eyes Bottle Opener

Miss Four Eyes, cast iron, four-eyed woman w/brown hair, red lips & gold earrings, rarity B, 3¾" h., F-408 (ILLUS.) . **50 to 75**

Miss Two Eyes, zinc, two-eyed woman w/short hair & hoop earrings, rarity C, 3⅜" h., F-409 . . . . **150 to 250**

Moon, aluminum, smiling & winking black painted moon face w/silver painted eyebrows, eyes, nose, cheeks, teeth & chin, rarity B, 3½" h., N-664 . . . . **75 to 150**

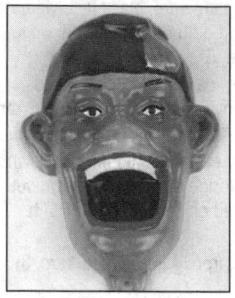

Norwegian Bottle Opener

Norwegian, cast iron, man wearing blue cap
  w/gold tassel, rarity D, 5¾" h., N-579
  (ILLUS.). . . . . **350 to 700**
Teeth, brass, model of teeth & gums marked
  "Bottle Chops," rarity B, 3¼" w.,
  F-420B . . . . **75 to 150**

Uncle Sam Wall Mount Opener

Uncle Sam, cast iron, head of Uncle Sam
  w/red & white painted top hat & white
  painted hair, eyebrows, teeth & bow tie,
  rarity B, 6⅛" h., N-537 (ILLUS.) . . . . **75 to 150**

BOTTLES

BITTERS

*(Numbers with some listings below refer to
those used in Carlyn Ring's* **For Bitters Only.***)*

African Stomach Bitters, cylindrical
  w/applied top, smooth base,
  dark amber, 9⅝" h. **$88**
**African Stomach Bitters - Spruance,
  Stanley & Co.,** cylindrical w/applied
  mouth, dark amber, 9⅝" h. (cleaned) **132**
**Allen's (Dr.) Stomach Bitters - Pittsburgh,
  PA,** cylindrical w/tall neck & applied
  mouth, aqua, 12¼" h. **330**

*From left: Appentine Bitters Bottle
Dr. Bell's Liver - Kidney Bitters*

**Appentine Bitters (under) Geo. Benz &
  Sons, St. Paul, Minn.,** w/"Pat. Nov. 23,
  1897" on base, square, scrolls along
  sides of label panel, medium amber,
  8¼" h. (ILLUS.). **385**
**Arabian Bitters - Lawrence &
  Weichselbaum, Savannah, Ga.,**
  medium amber, rectangular w/paneled
  sides & applied sloping collar, ca. 1870,
  9¾" h. (some light inside stain) **242**
Bell's (Dr.) Liver - Kidney Bitters, square
  w/beveled corners, applied sloping collar
  mouth, pale greenish aqua, 9" h. (ILLUS.) **105**
**Brown's Celebrated Indian Herb Bitters -
  Patented 1868,** figural Indian Queen,
  yellowish amber, rolled lip, 12⅛" h. **660**
Digestine Bitters, rectangular, sample size,
  ringed lower neck & tooled mouth,
  medium amber, 3½" h. (lightly cleaned) **853**
Doyle's - Hop - Bitters - 1872, around sides
  of sloping shoulder, square w/paneled
  sides w/raised clusters of hop berries &
  leaves, yellow w/green tone, 9⅝" h. **275**
**Drake's (S T) 1860 Plantation X Bitters -
  Patented 1862,** cabin-shaped, six-log,
  golden honey amber, 10" h. (D-105) **121**

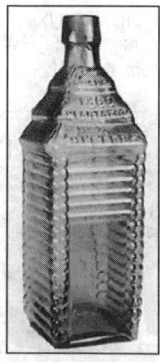

Rare Drake's Plantation Bitters

Drake's (S T) 1860 Plantation X Bitters -
Patented 1862, cabin-shaped, six-log,
light to medium yellowish olive, 10" h.,
D-108 (ILLUS.) 3,080

Drake's (S T) 1860 Plantation X Bitters -
Patented 1862, cabin-shaped, six-log,
medium copper puce, 10" h. (D-105) 231

Drake's (S T) 1860 Plantation X Bitters -
Patented 1862, cabin-shaped, six-log,
medium reddish puce, 10" h. (D-105)........ 156

Drake's (S T) 1860 Plantation X Bitters -
Patented 1862, cabin-shaped, six-log,
strawberry puce, 10" h. (D-105) 259

From left: Drakes Plantation Bitters Bottle
Rare German Balsam Bitters Bottle

Drakes Plantation Bitters - Patented 1862,
cabin-shaped, five-log, deep chocolate
amber, 10" h. (ILLUS.) 220

Fish (The) Bitters - W.H. Ware, Patented
1866, figural fish, dark amber, 11½" h....... 225

German Balsam Bitters, W.M. Watson &
Co., Sole Agents for U.S., square
w/applied tapering collar, rare opaque
blue, 9" h. (ILLUS.)..................... 825

Greeley's Bourbon Bitters

Greeley's Bourbon Bitters, barrel-shaped,
ten rings above & below center band,
medium smoky olive green, 9⅜", G-101
(ILLUS.).............................. 1,155

Henley's (Dr.) Wild Grape Root IXL
Bitters, cylindrical w/applied rim, aqua,
12" h. (slight haze) 121

Henley's (Dr.) Wild Grape Root IXL
Bitters, cylindrical w/applied rim, teal
blue, 12" h. (minor interior stain) 1,100

Henley's (Dr.) Wild Grape Root IXL
Bitters, cylindrical w/applied rim,
yellowish green, 12" h. (minor interior
stain) 2,090

Henley's (Dr.) Wild Grape Root - IXL (in
oval) Bitters, cylindrical w/tall neck &
applied mouth, smooth base, deep aqua,
ca. 1870, 12⅛" h. (light spots of stain) 88

Rare H.P. Herb Wild Cherry Bitters

Herb (H.P.) Wild Cherry Bitters, Reading,
Pa., cabin-shaped, square w/cherry tree
motif & roped corners, paper label
reading "H.P. Herb Wild Cherry Bark
Bitters," 99% of label, medium 7-Up
green, 8⅞" h. (ILLUS.)................. 5,060

Hertrichs Bitter, Einziger Fabrikant, Hans
Hertrich Hof Gesetzlich Geschutzt,
footed ball-shaped w/tall ringed neck,
applied double collar, deep olive
green, 9" h............................ 385

Lacour's Bitters - Sarsapariphere,
cylindrical w/ringed rim & sunken side
panels, amber, 9" h..................... 935

Langley's (Dr.) Root & Herb Bitters, J.O.
Langley, proprietor, cylindrical, deep
amber, 6" h. 121

Lash's Kidney and Liver Bitters - The
Best Cathartic and Blood Purifier,
square w/paneled sides & applied sloping
collar, deep red amber, 8¾" h.
(few haze spots)....................... 187

Lediard's Celebrated Stomach Bitters,
square w/beveled corners, applied
sloping double collar mouth, medium
bluish green, ca. 1865-70, 9½" h.
(lightly cleaned) 743

Litthauer Stomach Bitters (paper label),
Hartwig, Kantorowicz, Posen,
Germany, square case gin shape, milk
glass, 99% of label, 9½" h. 132

Mishler's Herb Bitters - Table Spoon Graduation (ruler marker) - Dr. S.B. Hartman & Co. - 40 Med. Doses, embossed on base "Stoeckels Grad. Pat. Feb. 6 '66W. McC. & Co. No. 2," square, strawberry, 9" h. (lightly cleaned) **385**

Mishler's Herb Bitters - Table Spoon Graduation (ruler marker) - Dr. S.B. Hartman & Co. - 40 Med. Doses, embossed on base "Stoeckels Grad. Pat. Feb. 6 '66W. McC. & Co. No. 2," square, medium peach or topaz, 9" h. **523**

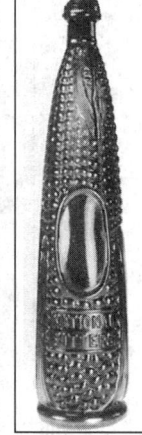

From left: Moffat Phoenix Bitters
National Bitters Ear of Corn Bottle

Moffat (John) - Phoenix Bitters - New York - 1-Dollar, rectangular w/beveled corners, medium olive amber, ½ pt., 5⅜" h. (ILLUS.) **908**

National Bitters - Patent 1867, figural ear of corn, medium amber, "Patent 1867" on base, applied mouth, 12⅝" h. (ILLUS.) **303**

Nibol Kidney and Liver Bitters

Nibol Kidney and Liver Bitters, square, 100% paper label reading "Nibol Tonic Laxative," w/contents, amber, 9½" h. (ILLUS.) . . **176**

Old Sachem Bitters and Wigwam Tonic, barrel-shaped, ten-rib, deep cherry puce, 9½" h. **660**

Old Sachem Bitters and Wigwam Tonic, barrel-shaped, ten-rib, deep reddish puce, 9½" h. **440**

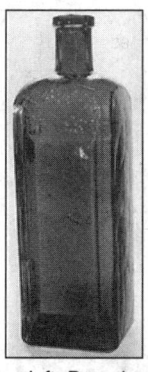

From left: Peruvian Bitters with Monogram
Roback's Stomach Bitters

Peruvian Bitters - "W & K" monogram in shield, applied top, smooth base, orangish red amber, 9⅛" h. (ILLUS.) **231**

Pharazyn (H.) Phila. Rights Secured, figural Indian Queen w/raised shield, golden amber **990**

Roback's (Dr. C.W.) Stomach Bitters, Cincinnati, O., barrel-shaped, yellow amber w/olive tone, some light inside haze, minor scratches on label panel, 9⅜" h. (ILLUS.) **743**

Rose's (E.J.) Magador Bitters For Stomach, Kidney & Liver - Superior Tonic, Cathartic and Blood Purifier, rectangular w/beveled corners & tooled lip, medium amber, ca. 1900, 8¾" h. **83**

Rare Royce's Sherry Wine Bitters

Royce's Sherry Wine Bitters, rectangular
w/beveled corners & rounded shoulders,
applied sloping collar, aqua, 8" h. (ILLUS.) . . **1,705**

Sahl'burgh, PA, rectangular w/indented
side panels, rounded shoulders, applied
sloping collar, root beer amber, 10¼" h. **3,960**

**Solomon's Strengthening & Invogorating
Bitters - Savannah, Georgia,** square,
crudely applied top, cobalt blue, 9⅝" h.
(lightly cleaned, tiny potstone in side) **715**

**Tippecanoe (birch bark & canoe design),
H.H. Warner & Co.,** cylindrical,
"Rochester N.Y." on base, applied disc
mouth, amber, 9¼" h. **121**

**Townsend's (Old Dr.) Magic Stomach
Bitters, New York,** rectangular
w/indented panels, applied sloping collar,
medium bluish green, 10" h. (shallow chip
on side of lip) **963**

**Uhler's Purifying & Strengthening Bitters,
Philada.,** rectangular w/indented side
panels, applied sloping mouth, aqua,
7⅞" h. (overall stain, spider crack) **143**

**Warner's Safe Bitters (design of safe),
Rochester, N.Y.,** "A. & D. H.C." on base,
rectangular w/rounded shoulders, applied
mouth, medium amber, 7½" h. **605**

Wheeler's - Berlin - Bitters - Baltimore,
hexagonal, applied mouth, pontil,
yellowish green citron, 9½" h.
(light exterior cleaning) **5,500**

Rare Dr. Wonser's Bitters Bottle

Wonser's (Dr.) U.S.A., Indian Root Bitters,
cylindrical w/applied mouth, ringed neck,
ribbed shoulder, amber, ¾ qt., 11" h.
(ILLUS.) **6,600**

**Woodcock Pepsin Bitters, Joseph C.
Schroeder Co., St. Louis, MO. U.S.A.,**
wide rectangular form w/rounded
shoulders, 90% original paper labels on
front & back, clear, ca. 1900, 8" h. **187**

FIGURALS

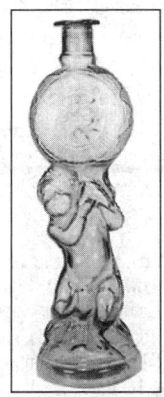

Cherub and Clock Bottle

Cherub holding clock, yellowish topaz,
kneeling figure holding a round clock on
one shoulder, short cylindrical neck
w/flared lip, ca. 1900-20, 13⅜" h. (ILLUS.). . . . **154**

Duck, milk glass, upright position w/neck
extending from bird's beak, Atterbury
Glass Co., ca. 1865-75, 11⅝" h.
(shallow chip on top of lip) **187**

Rare Man in the Moon Bottle

Man in the Moon, milk glass crescent moon
face w/original red, blue, black & pink
facial paint, original embossed metal wire
stand & end spigot, early 20th c., 9⅞" h.
(ILLUS.) **4,510**

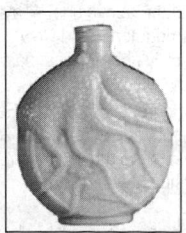

Octopus & Silver Dollar Bottle

Octopus on silver dollar, milk glass, relief-molded design w/short cylindrical neck & ground lip, dollar dated "1901," 4½" h. (ILLUS.) **413**

FLASKS

Flasks are listed according to the numbers provided in American Bottles & Flasks and Their Ancestry *by Helen McKearin and Kenneth M. Wilson.*

Chestnut, plain body, sheared lip, brilliant yellow green, Midwestern, ca. 1820-30, 5½" h. (small patch of exterior wear) **358**

Chestnut, twenty-four vertical ribs, sheared & inward-rolled rim, medium amber, Midwestern, ca. 1820-30, 5½" h. **330**

Chestnut, twenty broken ribs swirled to the left, small slender neck w/sheared lip, yellow olive, Midwestern, ca. 1820-30, 7⅜" h. **3,850**

Chestnut, "grandfather" type, twenty-four broken ribs swirled to the right, sheared lip, deep reddish amber, Midwestern, ca. 1820-30, 8¼" h. (some milky inside stain) . . **990**

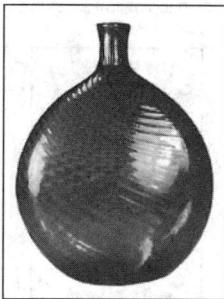

Rare Chestnut Flask

Chestnut, "grandfather" type, twenty-four ribs swirled to the left, sheared lip, golden amber, Midwestern, ca. 1820-30, few spots of inside haze, 8⅜" h. (ILLUS.) **3,850**

GI-11 - Washington bust below branches - American eagle w/head turned right & body curving, sunrays above eagle's head & 13 small stars, horizontal beading w/vertical medial rib, deep bluish aqua, pt. . . . **550**

GI-24 - "Washington" above bust - Taylor bust below "Bridgeton" [star] New Jersey," vertically ribbed sides, pale greenish aqua, pt. **110**

GI-26 - Washington bust - American Eagle w/shield w/eight vertical & two horizontal bars on breast, head turned to right, aqua, qt. (highpoint wear, spotty inside stain) **105**

GI-31 - "Washington" above bust - "Jackson" above bust, yellow amber w/olive tone, pt. **176**

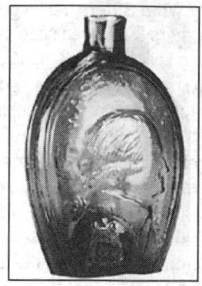

"Washington" - "Jackson" Flask

GI-34 - "Washington" above bust - "Jackson" above bust, vertically ribbed edges w/heavy medial rib, yellowish amber w/slight olive tone, pinhead flake on outer lip, bold impression, half-pint (ILLUS.) **385**

GI-40a - Washington bust below "The Father of His Country" - Taylor bust, "Gen Taylor Never Surrenders," smooth edges, applied double collared lip, aqua, pt. **66**

GI-55 - Washington bust w/short queue & plain toga - Taylor bust w/collar decoration missing, smooth edges, medium pale bluish green, pt. **440**

GI-71 - Taylor bust (facing left) w/"Rough and Ready" below - Ringgold bust (facing left) w/"Major" in semicircle above bust & "Ringgold" below bust, heavy vertical ribbing, aqua, pt. **165**

GI-80 - "Lafayette" above bust & "T.S." & bar below - "DeWitt Clinton" above bust & "Coventy C-T" below, horizontally corrugated edges, medium yellow olive w/amber tone, pt. **605**

GI-94 - "Where Liberty Dwells is My Country - Benjamin Franklin" over bust of Franklin - "Dyottville Glass Works Philadelphia - T.W. Dyott, M.D." over bust of Dyott, aqua, pt. **385**

GI-97 - Franklin bust obverse & reverse, vertical ribbing, pale greenish aqua, qt. **160**

GI-114 - Draped bust of Byron facing left - Draped bust of Scott facing right, vertically ribbed edges, dark amber, half pint (some inside stain) **176**

GI-114 - Draped bust of Byron facing left - Draped bust of Scott facing right, vertically ribbed edges, medium olive green, half-pint (some highpoint wear) **253**

GII-1 - American Eagle on oval, head turned to right obverse & reverse, horizontally beaded edges w/narrow vertical medial rib, sheared lip, open pontil, aqua, pt. **275**

GII-126 - American Eagle w/shield above laurel wreath, obverse & reverse, smooth edges, light pink amethyst, half pint **715**

GII-143 - American Eagle w/plain shield in talons & pennants in beak, calabash, four-flute edges, medium green, qt. **495**

GII-53 - American Eagle w/shield & furled flag - "For Our Country," wide bands of vertical edge ribbing, aqua, pt. **143**

GII-63 - American Eagle below "Liberty" - inscription in five lines "Willington - Glass - Co - West Willington - Conn.," smooth edges, deep amber w/olive tone, half pint **231**

GII-63 - American Eagle below "Liberty" - inscription in five lines "Willington - Glass - Co - West Willington - Conn.," smooth edges, deep bluish green, half pint **1,540**

GII-63 - American Eagle below "Liberty" - Willington Glass Co., smooth edges, applied lip, dark amber, half pint **143**

GII-64 - "Liberty" above American Eagle w/shield facing left on leafy branch - "Willington - Glass - Co - West Willington - Conn," smooth sides, olive green, pt. (tiny lip flake) **121**

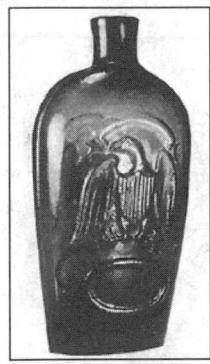

American Eagle Flask

GII-79 - American Eagle above oval obverse & reverse, edges w/single vertical rib, deep olive amber, qt. (ILLUS.) **275**

GII-81 - American Eagle above oval inscribed "Granite - Glass Co." obverse - reverse the same except inscription "Stoddard - NY," narrow vertical edge rib, sheared lip, tubular pontil, olive amber, pt. **209**

GII-86 - American Eagle above oval obverse & reverse, vertically ribbed edges, medium olive amber, half pint **143**

GIII-14 - Cornucopia with Produce & curled to right - Urn with Produce, vertically ribbed edges, deep bluish green, half pint **358**

GIV-18 - Masonic Arch, pillars & pavement w/Masonic emblems - American Eagle without shield on breast, plain oval frame below "KCCNE" inside, smooth edges w/single rib, medium yellowish amber, pt. **220**

GIV-19 - Masonic Arch, pillars & pavement w/Masonic emblems - American Eagle without shield on breast, plain oval frame below "KCCNE" inside, smooth edges

w/single rib, some design elements such as trowel, skull & beehive missing, yellowish amber green, pt. **204**

GIV-20 - Masonic arch, pillars & pavement w/Masonic emblems - American Eagle w/"KCCNC" in oval frame below, single vertical edge rib, medium yellowish amber, lots of seed bubbles, pt. **176**

GIV-43 - Masonic six-point star w/eye of God in center all above "A D" - six-point star w/arm in center all above "GRJA," sheared lip, vertical edge ribs, olive amber, pt. . . **198**

"Success to the Railroad" Flask

GV-5 - "Success to the Railroad" around embossed horse pulling cart - similar reverse, plain lip, vertically ribbed edges, medium moss green, light inside stain, pt. (ILLUS.) **385**

GV-6 - "Success to the Railroad" around embossed horse pulling cart obverse & reverse, w/"Success" above scene, sheared lip, pontil, olive green w/dark striations, pt. **242**

GV-10 - "Railroad" above horse-drawn cart on rail & "Lowell" below - American Eagle lengthwise & 13 five-point stars, vertically ribbed edges, plain lip, pontil, olive green, half pint (very minor lip flakes) **198**

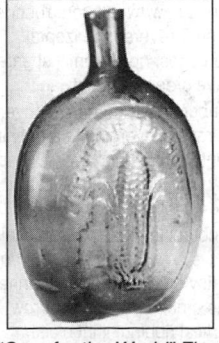

"Corn for the World" Flask

GVI-5 - "Corn for the World" above large ear of corn - Monument w/"Baltimore," crude pebbly glass, golden yellowish amber, qt. (ILLUS.). **1,600**

Rare Sunburst Flask

GVIII-7 - Sunburst w/twenty-four rounded rays flanked by a small circle on each side, obverse & reverse, horizontal corrugated edges & stepped lower neck, yellowish olive amber, pt. (ILLUS.) **1,380**

GVIII-8 - Sunburst w/twenty-eight triangular sectioned rays, obverse & reverse, center raised oval w/"KEEN" on obverse & w/"P & W" on reverse, yellowish olive amber, pt. . . **440**

GVIII-8 - Sunburst w/twenty-eight triangular sectioned rays obverse & reverse, center raised oval w/"KEEN" reading from top to bottom on obverse & "P & W" on reverse, sheared lip, open pontil, dark olive green, pt.. . **440**

GVIII-10 - Sunburst w/twenty-nine triangular sectioned rays, center raised oval w/"Keen" reading from top to bottom on obverse & reverse, yellowish olive green w/amber tone, half pint (some heavy highpoint wear). **231**

GVIII-14 - Sunburst w/twenty-one triangular sectioned rays, obverse & reverse, sunburst centered by ring w/a dot in middle, deep yellowish green, half pint (small iridescent inside lid bruise) **413**

GVIII-18 - Sunburst w/twenty-four rounded rays obverse & reverse, horizontal corrugated edges, open pontil, sheared lip, light olive green, half pint **440**

GVIII-28 - Sunburst w/sixteen rays obverse & reverse, rays converging to a definite point at center & covering entire sides, horizontally corrugated edges, light yellow green, half pint (some wear) **413**

GVIII-29 - Sunburst in small sunken oval w/twelve rays obverse & reverse, panel w/band of tiny ornaments around inner edge, sides around panels w/narrow spaced vertical ribbing, light bluish green, ¾ pt. **259**

GIX-1 - Scroll w/two six-point stars obverse & reverse, vertical medial rib, long neck w/sheared lip, graphite pontil, deep yellowish green, qt. (slight inside stain, small spot of interior lip roughness) **825**

GIX-10b - Scroll w/six-point stars, a small one in upper space & medium sized one in lower space obverse & reverse, vertical medial rib, dark olive amber, pt. **660**

GIX-11 - Scroll w/two eight-point stars obverse & reverse, tubular pontil, aqua, pt. (slight inside haze) **88**

GX-4 - Cannon framed by "Genl Taylor Never Surrenders," grapevine frame around "A Little More Grape Capt Bragg," vertically ribbed sides, copper color, pt. **4,950**

GX-15 - Summer Tree - Winter Tree, smooth edges, applied double lip, smooth base, deep aqua, pt. (inside haze). **66**

Spring Tree - Summer Tree Flask

GX-18 - Spring Tree (leaves & buds) - Summer Tree, smooth edges, light inside haze, deep bluish green, qt. (ILLUS.) **1,705**

GX-19 - Summer Tree - Winter Tree, smooth edges, deep bluish aqua, qt. **110**

GX-19 - Summer Tree - Winter Tree, smooth edges, yellow w/olive tone, qt.. . . . . **1,540**

GXI-26 - "For Pike's Peak" above a small miner w/tools above oval reserve - American Eagle above oval reserve, aqua, half pint. **143**

GXI-50 - "For Pike's Peak" above prospector w/tools & cane - Hunter shooting stag, plain edges, root beer amber, pt. **990**

GXII-13 - Clasped hands above oval w/"L.F. & Co." all inside shield w/"UNION" above - American Eagle above frame w/"Pittsburgh Pa.," yellow w/strong olive tone, qt.. . . . . **1,210**

GXII-18 - Clasped hands above oval, all inside shield - American Eagle w/plain shield above oval frame, base w/"L & W" inside disc-shaped frame, medium amber, pt.. . **187**

GXII-41 - Clasped hands above oval all inside shield w/"Union" above shield - Cannon, medium lime green, pt. (some overall inside milky stain) **798**

GXII-43 - Clasped hands above square & compass above oval w/"Union" all inside shield - American Eagle, calabash, greenish aqua, qt. **138**

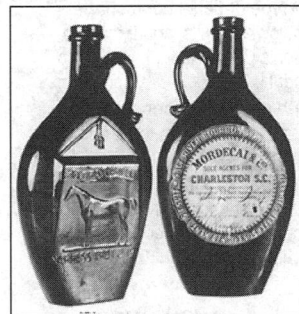

Rare "Flora Temple" Flask

GXIII-21 - "Flora Temple" above figure of a horse over "Harness Trot 219¾," plain reverse w/original round paper label reading "Salt River Bourbon Whiskey Distilleries, Jefferson County Kent'y...," rare w/label, applied shoulder handle, smoky copper, pt. (front & back ILLUS.) **1,925**

GXIII-35 - Sheaf of Grain w/rake & pitchfork crossed behind sheaf - "Westford Glass Co., Westford Conn," smooth edges, applied double collar w/large spillover, olive amber, pt. (slight inside stain) **143**

GXIII-35 - Sheaf of Grain w/rake & pitchfork crossed behind sheaf - "Westford Glass Co., Westford Conn," smooth edges, reddish amber, half pint **165**

GXIII-38 - Sheaf of Wheat w/rake & pitchfork crossed behind it - star, yellowish olive, qt. (minor inside content stain) **688**

GXIII-39 - Sheaf of Grain above crossed rake & pitchfork - large five-pointed star, smooth edges, applied double lip, deep green, pt. **1,210**

GXIII-48 - Anchor between fork-ended pennants inscribed "Baltimore" & "Glass Works" - Sheaf of Grain w/crossed rake & pitchfork, yellowish amber, qt. **935**

GXIV-7 - "Traveler's Companion" arched above & below stylized duck - eight-pointed star, smooth sides, medium amber, half pint. **578**

Pitkin, thirty-six broken ribs swirled to the left, sheared lip, deep root beer amber, ca. 1820-30, 6¼" h. **413**

Pitkin, thirty-two ribs swirled to the right, sheared lip, olive green, ca. 1790-1810, 7¼" h. **853**

INKS

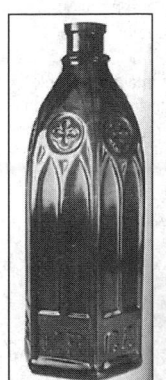

From left: Carter's "Cathedral" Master Ink Master "Carter's" Ink Bottle

Cathedral, master size, six Gothic arch panels, cobalt blue, ABM lip, smooth base marked "Carter's," ca. 1920, some inside stain, 9¾" h. (ILLUS.). **99**

Cylindrical, master-size, deep bluish green, applied sloping double collar w/pour spout, smooth base, 98% front & back original illustrated Carter's paper labels, ca. 1870-80, 8" h. (ILLUS.). **358**

Domed w/central neck, 12-sided form, deep olive amber, sheared lip, base pontil, 2" h. **660**

Figural, blown-molded head of Ben Franklin w/neck curving upward, aqua, sheared lip, smooth base, 2¾" h. (small flake on edge of base) **209**

House-shaped w/central neck, aqua, marked "S.I. - Comp.," tooled mouth, smooth base, 2¾" h. **132**

Igloo-form w/side neck, deep purple, sheared lip, smooth base, 2" h. **1,375**

Igloo-form w/side neck, reddish amber, ground lip, smooth base, 2" h. **242**

Rare "Teakettle" Inkwell

Teakettle-type fountain inkwell w/neck extending at angle from base, deep cobalt blue, ground lip, smooth base, original brass neck ring & hinged lid, 2" h. (ILLUS.) **660**

Teakettle-type fountain inkwell w/neck extending at angle from base, double dome-form body, lime green opaque, polished lip & base, possibly Boston & Sandwich Glass Co., 2" h. 880

Teakettle-type fountain inkwell w/neck extending up at angle from base, white porcelain w/multi-colored floral decoration on each panel, original brass hinged lid, 2⅜" h. 633

Rare "Turtle" Ink Bottle

Turtle-form, paneled sides, light yellow w/green tint, embossed letters on panels "J - & - I - E - M," sheared lip, smooth base, 1¾" h. (ILLUS.) 825

Unusual "J.S. Dunham" Ink

Twelve-sided w/central neck, aqua, embossed around panels "J.S. Dunham - St. Louis," rolled lip, open pontil, 2⅞" h. (ILLUS.) 385

Twelve-sided w/central neck, light ice blue, embossed around sides "Titcomb's Ink Cin.," rolled lip, base pontil, 2⅞" h. (lightly cleaned) 358

Umbrella-type (6-panel cone shape), light bluish green, rolled lip, open pontil, 2½" h. 149

Umbrella-type (8-panel cone shape), bright lime green, rolled lip, smooth base, 2⅝" h. (lightly cleaned) 468

Umbrella-type (8-panel cone shape), deep amber, sheared lip, smooth base w/pontil, probably New Hampshire, 2½" h. 187

Umbrella-type (8-panel cone shape), deep olive amber, sheared lip, base pontil, New England, 2½" h. 132

Umbrella-type (8-panel cone shape), medium emerald green, rolled lip, base pontil, 2½" h. 209

Umbrella-type (8-panel cone shape), sapphire blue, molded on four panels "B - B - & - Co.," deep olive amber, sheared lip, base pontil, New England, 2½" h. rolled lip, base pontil, 1¾" h. (overall light haze) 770

Umbrella-type (8-panel cone shape), straight lower panels, aqua, marked "Harrison's Columbian Ink," rolled lip, base pontil, 2" h. 154

Umbrella-type (8-panel cone shape), yellowish olive w/amber tone, rolled lip, open pontil, 2⅝" h. 330

Umbrella-type (16-panel cone shape), deep yellowish root beer amber, rolled lip, open pontil, possibly Stoddard glassworks, 2¼" h. 440

MEDICINES

Allan's Anti-Fat - Botanic Medicine Co. - Buffalo, N.Y., rectangular w/indented panels, applied sloping collar, medium sapphire or peacock blue, 7⅝" h. 358

Balm of Thousand Flowers - Fetridge & Co., New York, curved rectangular form w/beveled edges, applied rim, open pontil, crude, aqua, 4¾" h. 77

Birmingham's (Dr.) Antibilous Blood Purifier, paneled cylinder, applied mouth, teal blue green, 8⅝" h. 688

Bonpland's Fever and Ague Remedy, New York, rectangular w/applied top & open pontil, aqua, 5⅛" h. 44

Brown's Blood Cure

Brown's Blood Cure, Philadelphia, base marked "M.B.W. - U.S.A.," square w/beveled corners, tooled mouth, some milky stain inside, bright 7-Up green, 6¼" h. (ILLUS.) 121

Buckhout's (E.A.) Dutch Liniment (design of standing man) - Prepared at Machanicville Saratoga Co. N.Y., flattened rectangle w/rounded shoulders & rolled lip, ca. 1845-55, deep bluish aqua, 4¾" h. **440**

Copper's (Dr.) Ethereal Oil For Deafness, rectangular, rolled lip, deep bluish aqua, ca. 1840-55, 2⅝" h. **242**

Curtis & Perkin's Cramp and Pain Killer, cylindrical w/rolled lip & open pontil, aqua, 4⅞" h. **77**

Curtis & Perkins Wild Cherry Bitters, cylindrical w/applied mouth, open pontil, greenish aqua (slight mouth ding) **99**

Davis Vegetable Pain Killer, rectangular w/applied top & open pontil, aqua, 4⅝" h. **77**

Drink Dr. Radam's Microbe Killer (around shoulder), square w/rounded shoulder & tooled mouth, 45% original paper label, ca. 1890, medium amber, 10⅜" h. **121**

Ginseng - Panacea, rectangular w/paneled sides, rolled lip, ca. 1845-55, deep aqua, 4½" h. **176**

Hyatt's - Infallible - Life Balsam, N.Y., rectangular w/paneled sides & beveled corners, applied sloping double collar, medium bluish green, 9¾" h. **303**

Hyatt's - Pulmonic - Life Balsam - N-Y, rectangular w/paneled sides & sloping double collar mouth, ca. 1845-55, aqua, 9¾" h. (spots of faint inside haze) **468**

James (Dr. H.) Cannabis Indica, Crabbock & Co., Proprietors, Phila., Pa., cylindrical w/tooled mouth, clear, 7¾" h. (some minor stain) **209**

Kennedy's (Dr.) - Medical Discovery - Roxbury, Mass., rectangular w/paneled sides, applied mouth, open pontil, aqua, 8½" h. **88**

Kilmer's (Dr.) Cough Cure - Consumption Oil - Cartarrh Specific, rectangular w/tooled mouth, aqua, 8½" h. **715**

Lahnstoks (Dr.) Vermifuge, cylindrical vileform w/rolled lip & open pontil, aqua, small ... **110**

Liquid Opodeldoc, cylindrical, thin flared lip, pontil, aqua, 4½" h. **55**

Log Cabin Hops and Buchu Remedy

Log Cabin - Hops and Buchu - Remedy, paneled cylinder, applied mouth, base marked "Pat Sept 6/87," deep root beer amber, lightly cleaned, 10" h. (ILLUS.) **198**

McBride (Dr. J.J.) - King of Pain, rectangular w/paneled sides, applied top, deep aqua, 6¼" h. **88**

Mintie's (Dr.) Dephreticum, San Francisco, rectangular w/paneled sides, applied mouth, smooth base, aqua **209**

Mitchell's - Liniment - Pittsburgh, PA, rectangular w/paneled sides, rolled lip, ca. 1845-55, aqua, 4⅞" h. **358**

Murray's (Dr.) Magic Oil, S.F. - Cal., rectangular w/paneled sides, tooled top, aqua, 6" h. (tiny potstone in neck) **121**

Newell's - Pulmonary Syrup - Redington & Co., rectangular w/paneled sides, applied top, smooth base, aqua, 7⅝" h. **88**

Perkinson's (Dr.) Pain Killer - Balt., rectangular, rolled lip, ca. 1845-55, aqua, 3⅞" h. (overall stain)................... **330**

Perry's Magnetic Wine of Iron - Manchester, N.H., rectangular w/paneled sides & applied mouth, deep cobalt blue, 7" h......................... **231**

Pratt's Abolition Oil for Abolishing Pain, rectangular w/paneled sides, flared lip, smooth base, aqua, 5⅞" h. (tiny lip flakes)..... **55**

Radam's (Wm.) Microbe Killer, Germ, Bacteria or Fungus Destroyer, (design of man beating a skeleton), Registered Trade Mark Dec. 13, 1887, Cures All Diseases, square w/rounded shoulders, tooled mouth, medium amber, 10¼" h. **132**

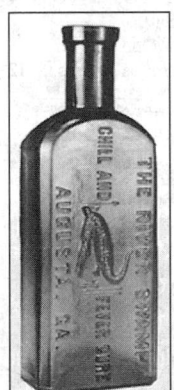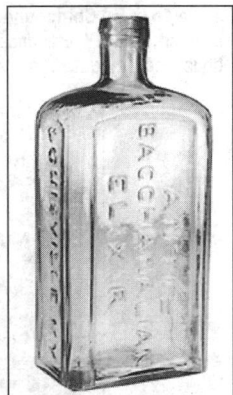

From left: River Swamp Chill & Fever Cure
Dr. Urban's Anti-Bacchanalian Elixir

River Swamp (The) Chill and Fever Cure, Augusta, GA (center design of alligator), rectangular w/beveled corners & rounded shoulders, tooled mouth, medium amber, light overall haze & scratches, ca. 1880, 6¼" h. (ILLUS.) **660**

Swaim's - Panacea - Philada, paneled
cylinder, applied sloping double collar,
medium to deep olive green, 8" h.......... 253

Swayne's (Dr.) Compound Syrup of Wild
Cherry, squared w/indented side panels,
flared lip & open pontil, aqua, 6" h.
(some staining)........................ 77

U.S.A. - Hosp. Dept., cylindrical w/applied
double collar, base marked "S.D.S.,"
reportedly dug, apricot yellow,
ca. 1860-70, 9⅜" h. 688

U.S.A. - Hosp. Dept., cylindrical w/applied
double collar, yellow w/olive tone, ca.
1860-70, 9¼" h. 660

U.S.A. - Hosp. Dept., cylindrical w/rounded
shoulder, tooled mouth, medium cobalt
blue, ca. 1865-80, 7¼" h. 1,650

U.S.A. - Hosp. Dept., oval w/rounded
shoulder, tooled mouth, deep cobalt blue,
ca. 1865-80, 2½" h. 688

Urban's (Dr.) - Anti - Bacchanalian Elixir -
Louisville, KY, rectangular w/paneled
sides, applied mouth, ca. 1845-55, deep
bluish aqua, lightly cleaned, 7¼" h. (ILLUS.) .. 990

Vanvleck & Johnsons (Drs. H. & W.G.)
Ague Conqueror, rectangular w/rounded
shoulders & rolled lip, ca. 1845-55, deep
bluish aqua (lightly cleaned).............. 176

Warners Safe Nervine (above design of a
safe), Rochester, N.Y., flattened
rectangle w/rounded shoulder & tooled
mouth, golden honey amber, 7⅜" h. 66

Westmoreland's - Calisaya Tonic,
rectangular w/paneled sides & tooled
mouth, base marked "A.G. Co.," golden
yellow amber, 8¼" h. 88

Wheatley's (J.B.) Compound Syrup,
Dallasburgh, NY, cylindrical w/applied
double collar, aqua, 6" h. 121

Wishart's Pine Tree Tar Cordial

Wishart's (L.Q.C.) - Pine Tree Tar Cordial,
Phila. - Patent (design of pine tree)
1859, square w/beveled corners, applied
sloping collar, emerald green, milky
inside base stain, 9⅜" h. (ILLUS.) 231

Wishart's (L.Q.C.) - Pine Tree Tar Cordial,
Phila. - Patent (design of pine tree)
1859, square w/beveled corners, applied
sloping collar, medium bluish green, 9¾" h.... 187

Wright (P.T.) & Co. Pectoral Syrup,
Philada., rectangular w/applied top &
open pontil, aqua, 6¼" h. (light stain)........ 110

Yerba Santa (in cross) - San Francisco,
California, rectangular w/paneled sides,
tooled mouth, aqua, large
(some milkiness on lip)................... 198

MINERAL WATERS, SODAS & SARSAPARILLAS

*From left: Rare Alfs Soda Water Bottle
Artesian Spring Co. Bottle*

Alfs (C.) - Soda Water - Charleston - This
Bottle To Be Returned, 8-paneled ten-
pin shape, yellowish olive green, applied
sloping collar mouth, iron pontil,
ca. 1845-55, cleaned, 7¼" h. (ILLUS.) 8,525

Artesian Spring Co. "AS" (monogram)
Ballston N.Y. - Ballston Spa "AS"
(monogram) Mineral Water, cylindrical
w/applied sloping double collar,
ca. 1865-75, green, pt., 7⅝" h. (ILLUS.)....... 83

Aufrecht (J.), Philada (in slug plate)
cylindrical w/applied sloping double
collar, ca. 1845-55, deep bluish green, 7¼" h... 77

B&G San Francisco Superior Mineral
Water, cylindrical w/ten-sided base,
applied flattened blob top, iron pontil,
cobalt blue, ca. 1852-56 (never cleaned,
typical wear) 358

B&G Soda San Francisco "Superior
Mineral Water," cylindrical w/ten-sided
base & applied blob top, iron pontil, dark
blue, 1850s (some scratching, little
roughness, lightly cleaned)............... 253

Blue Lick Water Co., KY, cylindrical
w/applied sloping double collar, ca. 1855-
65, deep bluish green, pt., 8" h. (minor
iridescent bruise) 688

Boley & Co. Sac City Cal. Union Glass Works, Philad., cylindrical w/applied blob top, iron pontil, small "c" variety, cobalt blue, 1850-52 (cleaned, small ding near base) **220**

Burt (W.H.) San Francisco, cylindrical w/applied blob top, iron pontil, deep green, . . . **165**

Burt (W.H.) San Francisco, cylindrical w/applied blob top, iron pontil, emerald green, 1852 (cleaned) **165**

From left: Rare Catell's Superior Mineral Water Chalybeate Water Bottle

Catell's Superior Mineral Water, ten-sided cylinder w/applied sloping mouth, some light outside stain, small bruise & chip on contour of lip, ca. 1845-55, sapphire blue, 6⅞" h. (ILLUS.) **1,595**

Chalybeate Water of the American Spa Spring Co. N.J., cylindrical w/applied mouth, light to medium bluish green, ca. 1865-75, pt. (ILLUS.) **495**

Clark (C.), Charleston (in slug plate), cylindrical, deep grass green, applied sloping collar, iron pontil, ca. 1845-55, 7½" h. (lightly cleaned) **303**

Clark (C.) Mineral Water, cylindrical w/applied sloping collar, iron pontil, deep emerald green, ca. 1845-55, 7¼" h. (cleaned). . **231**

Coca-Cola Bottling Co. In Binghamton, cylindrical w/tall tapering neck & tooled crown top, ca. 1900-10, medium olive yellow, 7¾" h. **176**

Congress & Empire Spring Co. E Saratoga, N.Y., cylindrical w/tall neck & applied sloping double collar, ca. 1865-75, deep olive green, qt., 9⅜" h. (small flake inside lip) **55**

Cosgrove (J.) Charleston 1866, cylindrical w/applied blob top, smooth base, aqua, ca. 1855-70, 7¼" h. (overall stain & dullness) . . **99**

Dawson & Blackman, Charleston, S.C. - Union Glass Works Philad Superior Mineral Water, cylindrical w/applied blob top, paneled mug base, deep cobalt blue, ca. 1845-55, 7½" h. (staining, small iridescent bruise) **550**

Dawson & Blackman, Charleston, S.C. - Union Glass Works Philad Superior Mineral Water, cylindrical w/applied blob top, paneled mug base, peacock blue, ca. 1845-55, 7⅝" h. (overall stain, small iridescent bruise inside edge of base) **825**

Eastern Cider Co., cylindrical w/applied blob top & smooth base, medium golden amber, 1877-82 . . . . **165**

Excelsior Spring, Saratoga, N.Y., cylindrical w/applied sloping double collar, ca. 1870-80, teal blue, pt., 7¾" h. **193**

Farrel & Co. Mineral Water, Evansville, I.A. - F. & Co., cylindrical w/applied blob mouth, ca. 1845-55, ice blue, 7⅜" h. **798**

Fields - Superior - Soda Water - Charleston, S.C., eight-sided ten-pin shape, cobalt blue, applied sloping collar, iron pontil, ca. 1845-55, 7⅝" h. (some overall ground lines & imperfections) **413**

Geo. Eagle, cylindrical w/spiral ribbed design on lower body w/plain band w/the name, applied sloping collar, ca. 1845-55, medium bluish green, 6⅞" h. **935**

Gettysburg Katalysine Water, cylindrical w/tall neck & applied sloping double collar, ca. 1865-80, medium emerald green, qt., 9⅝" h. **61**

Geyser Spring, Saratoga Spring, State of New York- The Saratoga Spouting Spring, cylindrical w/applied sloping double collar, ca. 1865-75, bluish aqua, pt., 7⅝" h. **61**

Geyser Spring, Saratoga Springs, State of New York, The Saratoga Spouting Spring, cylindrical w/applied sloping double collar, ca. 1865-75, deep bluish aqua, pt., 7¾" h. **61**

From left: Highrock Congress Spring Bottle Humboldt Mineral Water Bottle

Highrock Congress Spring (design of a rock), C. & W. Saratoga N.Y., cylindrical w/applied sloping double collar, ca. 1865-75, medium yellowish amber, pt. (ILLUS.) **264**

Humboldt Artesian Mineral Water - Eureka, Cal., cylindrical w/tooled lip, numerous seed bubbles, dark aqua, ca. 1895, 6⅞" h. (ILLUS.) **66**

Italian Soda Water Manufactory San Francisco, cylindrical w/applied blob top, dark green, late 1850s (cleaned, some superficial crazing) **143**

Ketner (M.M.) and Aulenbach (J.) Pottsville - Union Glass Works, Phila., cylindrical w/applied blob mouth, ca. 1845-55, deep bluish aqua, 7¼" h. **605**

Lithia Mineral Spring Co. Gloversville, cylindrical w/applied sloping collar, ca. 1865-80, bluish aqua, pt., 7¾" h. (very light haze, tiny flake on underside of collar) . . . **825**

Litton's Mineral Water Healdsburg, cylindrical w/applied mouth & smooth base, dark aqua, ca. 1870s (small ding on base) **358**

Lynde & Putnam Mineral Waters San Francisco Cala. Union Glass Works, Philad., cylindrical w/applied blob top & iron pontil, shaded cobalt blue, 1850-51 (cleaned) **303**

*From left: Rare M.R. "Sacrimento" Soda Bottle
McKinney Mineral Water Bottle*

M.R. Sacrimento (sic) Union Glass Works, Phila., cylindrical w/applied blob top & iron pontil, teal green, open bubble above the "R," 1850s (ILLUS.) **1,430**

McKinney Philada - Rice & Mineral Water, cylindrical w/applied blob mouth, ca. 1845-55, medium teal blue, 7" h. (ILLUS.). . **121**

Middletown Healing Springs, Grays & Clark, Middletown, Vt., cylindrical w/tall neck & applied sloping double collar, ca. 1865-75, amber w/olive tone, qt. **154**

O'Kane & Maginnis C. May, N.J., cylindrical w/applied sloping double collar, ca. 1855-70, medium teal blue, 6⅞" h. (light scratching) **88**

Oak Orchard Acid Springs, Address G.W. Merchant, Lockport, N.Y., cylindrical w/applied sloping collar, ca. 1865-75, Lockport green, qt., 9" h. **83**

Owen Casey Eagle Soda Works Sac City, cylindrical w/applied blob top & smooth base, medium green, 1867-71 . . . . **176**

Owen Casey Eagle Soda Works Sac City, cylindrical w/applied blob top & smooth base, sapphire blue w/green streaks, 1867-71 . . **88**

Pacific Congress Water, cylindrical w/applied blob top & smooth base, deep aqua, 1869-76 . . . . **66**

Saratoga (design of star) Spring, cylindrical w/tall neck & applied sloping double collar, ca. 1865-75, medium orangish amber, qt., 9⅜" h. **121**

Saratoga (design of star) Spring, cylindrical w/tall neck & applied sloping double collar, ca. 1865-75, deep olive green, qt., 9½" h. **143**

Saratoga Red Spring, cylindrical w/applied sloping double collar, ca. 1865-75, deep bluish green, qt., 9⅝" h. **110**

Smith (A.P.) Charleston, S.C., cylindrical w/applied sloping collar & iron pontil, deep sapphire blue, ca. 1845-55, 7½" h. (overall heavy stain, pick bruise inside lip) **264**

*From left: Smith & Co. Soda Water Bottle
Star Spring Co. Bottle*

Smith & Co. - Premium - Soda Water - Charleston, eight-sided ten-pin shape, deep green, applied blob top, iron pontil, ca. 1845-55, cleaned, 7½" h. (ILLUS.) **468**

Star Spring Co. (design of star) Saratoga, N.Y., cylindrical w/applied sloping double collar, ca. 1865-75, deep chocolate amber, pt., 7¾" h. **358**

Star Spring Co. (design of star) Saratoga,
N.Y., cylindrical w/applied sloping double
collar, ca. 1865-75, medium yellowish
olive amber, pt., 7⅝" h. (ILLUS.) 209

Star Spring Co. (design of star) Saratoga,
N.Y., cylindrical w/applied sloping double
collar, ca. 1865-75, root beer amber,
pt., 7⅝" h. 121

Steinke & Kornahrens - Soda Water -
Return This Bottle - Charleston, S.C.,
eight-sided ten-pin shape, deep cobalt
blue, applied sloping collar, ca. 1845-55,
8¼" h. (two shallow lip chips) 154

Superior Soda Water - design of a
spread-winged eagle & shield,
cylindrical w/applied sloping collar, iron
pontil, grass green, 7¾" h. (overall stain,
several chips & bruises around lip) 275

Superior Soda Water - design of a
spread-winged eagle & shield,
cylindrical w/applied sloping collar, iron
pontil, medium sapphire blue, 7⅞" h.
(Iridescent bruise on inside of lip, some
scratching & stain) 154

Taylor & Co. Soda Waters San Francisco,
Eureka, cylindrical w/applied blob top &
iron pontil, dark sapphire blue, 1850s
(wear, uncleaned). 341

Townsend's (Dr.) - Sarsaparilla - Albany,
N.Y., square w/beveled corners & applied
sloping collar, ca. 1845-55, deep emerald
green, 9½" h. 495

Townsend's (Dr.) - Sarsaparilla - Albany,
N.Y. - IIII, square w/beveled corners &
applied sloping collar, ca. 1845-55, deep
olive green, 9½" h. 413

Twedles' Celebrated Soda or Mineral
Waters - Courtland Street 38 New
York, cylindrical w/applied sloping collar,
ca. 1845-55, medium bluish green, 7" h.
(tiny lip flake) 66

Wagner (A.) & Co., Philada - W, cylindrical
w/applied blob mouth, ca. 1855-65, deep
emerald green, 7¼" h. 72

Washington Lithia Well Bottle

Washington Lithia Well Mineral Water,
Ballston Spa, N.Y., cylindrical w/applied
sloping double collar, ca. 1865-75, deep
bluish aqua, pt., 7¾" h. (ILLUS.) 468

Williams & Severance, cylindrical w/applied
blob top, iron pontil, sapphire blue,
ca. 1852-54 303

Williams & Severance San Francisco, Cal.
Soda and Mineral Waters, cylindrical
w/applied blob top, iron pontil, dark
green, ca. 1852-54 198

Young (Philip) & Co., Savannah, Ga. -
design of spread-winged eagle &
shield, cylindrical w/applied mouth,
smooth base, medium teal blue, 7⅜" h.
(lightly cleaned) 550

PEPPERSAUCES

Aqua, Cathedral-type, six-sided Gothic arch-
style, pebbly texture, applied top, iron
pontil, 8½" h. 121

Aqua, lobed cylindrical form w/tall ringed
neck, applied rim & open pontil, "Wells
Miller & Provost, No. 217 St. New York"
around the sides, 8" h. (cleaned) 99

Cobalt blue, tapering paneled sides w/spiral
ribbing, marked on base "S&P Pat. App.
4," tooled lip (minor dings) 66

Deep aqua, pyramidal-form w/roped
corners, slender neck w/applied sloping
collar, base pontil, ca. 1845-60, 11¼" h. 385

Light bluish green, six-sided Cathedral-
type w/Gothic arches, slender neck
w/applied double collar, open pontil,
ca. 1845-60, 9" h. 143

Medium bluish green, six-sided Cathedral-
type w/Gothic arch panels, slender neck
w/applied double collar, ca. 1855, 8¾" h. 165

Sapphire blue, Cathedral-type, four-sided,
Gothic arch panels, applied top, open pontil .. 264

PICKLE BOTTLES & JARS

Amber, six-sided cathedral-type, tooled
mouth, smooth base, ca. 1880-1890,
13⅜" h. 1,265

Apple green, four-sided cathedral-type
w/Gothic windows, applied mouth,
smooth base, ca. 1855-1865, light to
medium apple green, 10⅞" h. 440

Aqua, lobe-sided, iron pontil, "W.K.
Lewis & Co." 475

Aqua, square w/applied top, double neck
ring & shoulder scrolling, iron pontil,
embossed "W. D. Smith, N.Y.," lots of whittle .. 750

Aqua, cathedral shape, rolled lip, double
neck ring tapering to fishtail shoulder
scroll, iron pontil, embossed "Albany
Glass Works," ca. 1850-1860, 8⅝" h. 990

Aqua, square w/double neck ring, shoulder scrolling, obverse & reverse diamond panel embossing, W. D. Smith, N.Y., ca. 1839-1959, 8¾" h. **700**

Aqua, six-sided cathedral-type w/Gothic windows, rolled lip, open pontil, marked "T. Smith & Co." around shoulder, ca. 1850-1860, 9½" h. **688**

Aqua, square, rolled lip w/tapering shoulder collar, iron pontil, embossed "64 oz. William - Underwood - & Company - Boston," ca. 1850-1860, 12½" h. **187**

Bluish-green, four-sided cathedral-type w/Gothic windows, rolled lip, iron pontil, ca. 1855-1865, 11¾" h. **1,265**

Cathedral-type Pickle Jar

Citron, four-sided Cathedral-type, four Gothic arches, ringed wide applied neck, ca. 1855-65, 11⅝" h. (ILLUS.) **468**

Deep aqua, Cathedral-type, four Gothic arches w/ornate finials, wide ringed neck w/rolled lip, ca. 1855-65, 11¾" h. **253**

Deep bluish aqua, rectangular w/paneled sides & wide applied mouth, marked "Anchor Pickle And Vinegar Works," smooth base marked "H.N. & Co.," ca. 1880, 8" h. (potstone on one side w/small radiations) **44**

Emerald green, four-sided cathedral-type w/Gothic arch windows, rolled lip, iron pontil, ca. 1850-1860, 11½" h. **2,530**

Emerald green, four-sided cathedral-type w/Gothic arch windows, rolled lip, smooth base, ca. 1860-1870, 13¾" h. **143**

Green (deep to medium), square w/applied top, two neck rings & vertically ribbed, open pontil, ca. 1839-1859, 7½" h. **1,700**

Greenish aqua, square w/two rings & vertical ribs on neck, rolled lip, iron pontil, embossed "W.D.S. N.Y.," ca. 1855-1865, 7¾" h. **198**

Greenish-aqua, paneled body w/petal-style embossing on shoulder & base, rolled lip, ca. 1855-1865, 10⅝" h. **330**

From left: Ribbed Amber Pickle Jar
Skilton Foote & Cos. Pickle Bottle

Medium amber, square heavily ribbed sides w/rounded corners & wide applied mouth, tiny flake inside lip, ca. 1855-70, 8¼" h. (ILLUS.) **231**

Teal blue, cathedral-shaped, rolled lip, double neck ring tapering to fishtail shoulder scroll, iron pontil, embossed "J McCollick & Co New York," ca. 1850-1860, 8⅝" h. **1,650**

Yellow green, round, rolled lip, pontil-scarred base, ca. 1850-1860, embossed "Wm. Numsen & Sons Baltimore," 9¼" h. **330**

Yellow olive, round w/tooled mouth, smooth base, embossed "Skilton Foote & Co. S Trade [motif of monument] Mark Bunker Hill Pickles" on body, "Onions, from Skilton, Foote & Co., Bunker Hill Pickles" on 100% original label, 7⅜" h. **176**

Yellow w/amber tone, square w/cathedral panels, tooled mouth, smooth base, 98% original label marked "Arrow Brand Pickles, J. J. Wilson Chicago," ca. 1880-1900, 8⅝" h. **358**

Yellow w/olive amber tone, "Bunker Hill Pickles" w/embossed monument, 6½" h., Twilight Rose patt. **140**

Yellowish amber, cylindrical w/wide applied mouth, "Skilton Foote & Cos Bunker Hill Pickles" w/trademark, professionally cleaned, 7¾" h. (ILLUS.) **55**

POISONS

Clear, flask-form, flattened round body w/mold-blown swirled broken-rib design, base pontil, probably Europe, ca. 1800-40, 6½" h. **94**

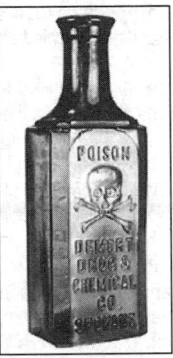

*From left: Rare Skull Poison Bottle
Rare Demert Poison Bottle*

Cobalt blue, small figural skull, marked
"Poison - Pat. Appl'd for," base marked
"Pat June 26th 1894," light milky overall
haze & crazing lines, 2⅞" h. (ILLUS.) **1,925**

Cobalt blue, square w/beveled corners,
tooled mouth, marked "Poison (skull &
crossbones) Demert Drug & Chemical
Co. Spokane," smooth bottom marked
"W.T. Co, U.S.A.," ca. 1890, 5⅝" h.
(ILLUS.)............................ **2,750**

Cobalt blue, square w/ribbed sides w/tooled
lip & original sawtooth-edged stopper,
plain front panel & side panels
w/"Poison," smooth base marked "E.R.S.
& S.," ca. 1890, 4⅝" h. (edge of
stopper chipped)....................... **440**

Cobalt blue, triangular w/rounded shoulder
& tooled mouth, marked "Poison -
[molded design of owl on mortar &
pestle] - The Owl Drug Co.," 8" h. **385**

Small Amber Poison Bottle

Yellowish amber, cylindrical w/tooled
mouth, overall latticework design w/a
central panel w/"Poison" on each side of
a skull & crossbones, a five-point star
above & below the skull, ca. 1890, 4¾" h.
(ILLUS.) **550**

WHISKEY & OTHER SPIRITS

Beer, "Bay View Brewing Co., Seattle,
Wash. - Not To Be Sold," cylindrical
w/applied mouth & original marked
porcelain stopper & wire bail, medium
olive green, ca. 1890, 11¾" h.
(wire bail broken) **303**

Beer, "C. Conrad & Co's Original Budweiser
U.S. Patent No. 6376," cylindrical
w/lady's-leg neck & applied mouth, aqua,
9¼" h. (lightly cleaned).................. **99**

*From left: Gambrinus Brewing Co. Bottle
Golden Gate Beer Bottle
Early Rainier Beer Bottle*

Beer, "Gambrinus Brewing Co., G.B. Co.,
Portland, Or.," cylindrical w/lady's-leg
neck & tooled mouth, "S.B. & G. Co." on
smooth base, amber, ca. 1890, some
inside stain, tiny "peck" mark on shoulder,
11¼" h. (ILLUS.)........................ **33**

Beer, "Golden Gate Bottling Works, Trade
(design of bear drinking from stein) Mark,
San Francisco," cylindrical w/tooled top &
original wire bail & porcelain stopper,
medium yellow amber, ca. 1900, 7¾" h.
(ILLUS.) **55**

Beer, "Rainier Beer, Seattle, U.S.A.,"
cylindrical w/lady's-leg neck & tooled lip,
amber, fragments of original foil wrapper
on neck, ca. 1900, 5½" h. (ILLUS.) **66**

Red Wing Brewing Co. Beer Bottle

Beer, "Red Wing Brewing Co., Red Wing, Minn.," attached porcelain stopper, rare, amber, embossed, 15" h. (ILLUS.) **95**

Bourbon, "Cutter (J.H.) Old Bourbon A.P. Hotaling & Co., Portland, O.," tapering flask form w/applied mouth, smoky clear, pt. (small pressure ding on top, stained) **330**

From left: Rare Dallimores Brandy Bottle Kiderlen Celebrated Old Gin

Brandy, "Dallimores - Celebrated - Brandy - 130 Broome St. - N.R. Broadway - New York," paneled cylinder w/applied straight double collar, small flake at base of one panel, ca. 1845-55, deep olive green, 7⅛" h. (ILLUS.) **2,860**

Cognac, "Cognac - W. & Co." (in seal), squatty bulbous tapering to a cylindrical neck w/applied mouth & neck handle, ca. 1860-70, medium amber, 5¾" h. **660**

Gin, "Kiderlen Rotterdam Celebrated Old Gin," barrel-shaped, tooled mouth, light olive green, crack down from lip, 8½" h. (ILLUS.) **176**

Mead, "Champagne Mead," eight-sided cylinder w/applied blob top, smooth base, greenish blue (few dings at bottom corners) . . **110**

Schnapps, "Udolpho Wolfe's Aromatic Schnapps, Schiedam," rectangular w/beveled corners, applied sloping collar mouth, olive green w/amber tone, 9⅜" h. **77**

Van Brunt's Aromatic Schnapps

Schnapps, "Van Brunt's Aromatic Schnapps, Schiedam," square w/beveled corners, applied sloping collar, deep olive green, some inside stain, 10" h. (ILLUS.) **132**

Spirits, club-form, tall neck w/applied rim, swirled broken-rib design, yellow olive, Midwestern, ca. 1820-30, 8⅛" h. **4,400**

Spirits, free-blown mallet-form, pontil w/deep kick-up, applied string lip, deep olive amber, England, ca. 1730-45, 8" h. **440**

Spirits, free-blown onion-form w/tall neck & applied string lip, pontilled base, medium yellowish olive green, Europe, ca. 1715-30, 6⅞" h. **143**

Early Zanesville Bottle with Handle

Spirits, globular, short neck w/rolled rim, applied strap handle w/end crimp, twenty-four ribs swirled to the left, medium amber, Zanesville, Ohio, ca. 1820-30, V-shaped stress crack from end of handle, 6½" h. (ILLUS.) **4,620**

Spirits, globular, tall neck w/rolled rim, twenty-four ribs swirled to the left, unusual wide neck, yellow w/strong olive tone, Midwestern, ca. 1820-30, 7⅜" h. **1,018**

Spirits, globular, tall ribbed neck, broken-rib patt., rolled lip, Midwestern, ca, 1820, medium amber, 7½" h. (some milky inside stain) **8,250**

Spirits, globular, plain body w/tall neck, rolled rim, medium yellowish amber, Midwestern, ca. 1820-30, 7⅞" h. **275**

Spirits, globular, tall neck w/rolled rim, twenty-four ribs swirled to the left, medium amber, Midwestern, ca. 1820-30, 8" h. . . . **468**

Spirits, club-form, tall neck w/applied rim, twenty-four broken ribs swirled to the right, medium sapphire blue, Midwestern, ca. 1820-30, 8¼" h. **8,525**

Spirits, globular, tall neck w/rolled lip, twenty-four ribs swirled to the left, lots of bubbles, yellowish amber, Midwestern, ca. 1820-30, 9⅝" h. **577**

Whiskey, "Binninger's Regulator, 19 Broad St., New York" around molded clock face, 100% paper label on reverse w/printed clock face & same inscription, applied double collar, medium amber, 6" h. **2,315**

Whiskey, "C.A. Richards & Co., 99 Washington St., Boston," square w/beveled corners, reversed "Ns" in molded text, applied sloping collar, deep reddish amber, 9½" h. **94**

From left: Chestnut Grove Whiskey Flask Rare E.G. Booz Whiskey Bottle

Whiskey, "Chestnut Grove Whiskey, C.W.," chestnut flask-shaped w/applied neck handle, applied mouth, medium amber, 8⅞" h. (ILLUS.) **154**

Whiskey, "Clinch & Co. Liquor Dealers, Grass Valley," coffin flask, applied sloping mouth, clear, half pint **303**

Whiskey, "Davy Crocket Pure Old Bourbon, Hey, Grauderholz & Co., S.F. Sole Agents," cylindrical w/tall neck & tooled mouth, ca. 1900, medium orangish amber, 12" h. **110**

Whiskey, "E.G. Booz's Old Cabin Whiskey - 1840 - E.G. Booz's Old Cabin Whiskey - 120 Walnut St., Philadelphia," cabin-shaped, straight roof, overall milky inside stain, deep amber, 7⅝" h. (ILLUS.) **3,300**

Whiskey, "From Wine House Liquors & Cigars Reno, Nev.," pumpkinseed flask, clear, half pint **1,540**

Whiskey, "G.W. Huntington" (on applied seal), cylindrical w/wide rounded shoulder w/seal, applied sloping collar, ca. 1855-65, medium bluish green, 11¾" h. **468**

Whiskey, "Gaines (W.A.) Old Crow Whiskey, The Capital, Cheyenne, Wyo.," flask-shaped w/neck screw threads, clear, half pint **264**

Whiskey, "Gilmor & Gibson, Importers, Baltimore" (on applied seal), cylindrical w/wide rounded shoulder, tall neck & applied sloping collar, ca. 1870-80, red amber, 9¾" h. **303**

Whiskey, "Melczer & Co. (Jos.) Wholesale Liquor Dealers San Francisco, Cal.," flask w/applied tapering mouth, clear, half pint **99**

Whiskey, "Mohawk Pure Rye Whiskey, Patented Feb. 11, 1868," figural Indian queen w/shield, rolled lip, golden amber, 12⅝" h. **2,315**

Whiskey, "Old Bourbon Castle Whiskey - F. Chevalier & Co., Sole Agents," cylindrical w/tall neck & tooled lip, medium orangish amber, 12" h. **231**

Old Monongahela Rye Whiskey

Whiskey, "Old Monongahela, C (sheaf of wheat) H, Rye Whiskey," cylindrical w/wide rounded shoulder w/seal, appled sloping collar, ca.1865-75, olive amber, 9½" h. (ILLUS.) **330**

Whiskey, "Old Velvet Brandy, S.M. & Co." (on applied seal w/necklace), conical w/tall neck & applied double collar, internally ribbed, ca. 1855-70, medium amber, 9⅞" h. **688**

Whiskey, "Peerless [in script] Whiskey [in banner], Wolf, Wreden Co. Sole Agents, S.F.," cylindrical w/tall neck & tooled lip, medium orangish gold, 11⅞" h. **440**

Whiskey, "Potts & Potts - Atlanta, Ga." (on applied seal), cylindrical w/tall neck w/applied sloping double collar, medium amber, ca. 1870, 9½" h. **264**

Whiskey, "R.B. Cutter, Louisville, KY," ovoid w/applied mouth & handle, partial paper label on reverse w/"Woodbury, New Jersey," golden amber, 8¾" h. **413**

Silkwood Whiskey Bottle

Whiskey, "Silkwood Whiskey, Laventhal
Bros., San Francisco, Cal.," cylindrical
w/swirled ribs at base of the tall neck
w/tooled lip, amber, ca. 1900, 11⅜" h.
(ILLUS.) **154**

Whiskey, "Sontaw's Old Cabinet Whiskey"
(one applied seal), cylindrical w/sloping
applied mouth, medium amber, 8⅜" h.
(cleaned) **183**

BOXES

Band box, wallpaper-covered cardboard,
oval, the flat fitted top & sides covered in
a paper w/a design of large shaded
arches, 19th c., 6⅝" l., 2¾" h.
(minor wear) **$546**

Rare Large Band Box

Band box, wallpaper-covered cardboard,
oval w/deep sides & narrow fitted cover,
the sides w/a scenic landscape w/figures,
trees & a building in brown, black & white
on a dark blue ground, building titled
"Castle Garden," signed "Joel Post" in
ink, 23" l. (ILLUS.) **3,300**

Bentwood, round w/fitted flat cover, lapped
seams, old green paint, 7½" d. (nail rust)..... **314**

Early Book-form Box

Book-form, carved wood, w/a slide top,
chip-carved borders on the covers
surrounding a high-relief male on one
side & female on the other, the binding
deeply carved w/a name & date "Michel
Thomas 1759," very minor losses, 3⅝" h.
(ILLUS.)........................... **1,610**

Bride's box, pine bentwood, oval w/deep
fitted cover, the sides w/original
polychrome decoration of large stylized
flowers on a brown ground, the flat cover
w/a large figure of a woman, laced
seams, Europe, late 18th - early 19th c.,
10¼ x 16¾" (some edge damage
w/repair & touch-up).................... **495**

Fancy European Bride's Box

Bride's box, pine bentwood, oval, deep
fitted cover, the sides w/the original
detailed polychrome floral decoration on
a blue ground, the flat cover w/a
polychrome scene of a youth pushing a
girl on a swing w/a German inscription,
partial decal on lid "Nederland...," laced
seams, Europe, 19th c., age cracks in
cover, 12 x 18¾" (ILLUS.) **2,035**

Candle box, hanging-type, painted poplar, a
low scalloped crestboard w/two metal
hanging loops above a hinged
rectangular top opening to the storage
well, staple hinges, old worn bluish green
paint, 4½ x 10¼", 4½" h. (repaired split in
back board) **198**

Chart box, painted pine & poplar,
rectangular hinged top on a dovetailed
box w/applied base, original grain paint in
brown & tan, lettered "R.E.B.," probably
Cape Cod, Massachusetts, first half
19th c., 12¾ x 48", 11" h................. **489**

Collar box, printed cardboard, oval w/flat
fitted top, the border of the top printed to
resemble large tacks, the side printed w/a
rectangular reserve showing to early
men's collars & the advertising "E. Stone
No. 116½ William-Street New York,"
19th c., 13" l., 5" h. (wear, minor losses) **575**

Document box, painted & decorated poplar,
rectangular w/deep hinged cover
w/central brass bail handle & iron hasp &
lock on the front, the cover opening to a
well & liddled till, the exterior decoration

Decorated Document Box

w/ochre painted on a red ground, gilt
initials "G.W.S.," American, 19th c., very
minor wear, 9½ x 18", 8¼" h. (ILLUS.) **1,150**

Glass Box with Landscape on Cover

Glass box, metal mounts w/hinged cover,
round, cobalt blue enameled on the cover
w/a winter farm scene in white, brown &
tan, the sides w/white enameled swag &
dot bands, late 19th c., 3" d., 2¼" h.
(ILLUS.) **165**

Glass box, gilt-metal mounts w/hinged
cover, squatty rounded body in sapphire
blue decorated w/small white & yellow
enameled blossoms, the flattened domed
cover w/large white & yellow daisy-like
flowers w/yellow leaves above a white
grass ground, 3⅜" d., 3" h. **175**

Scroll-decorated Blue Glass Box

Glass box, gilt-metal rim & footed base,
hinged cover, the cover decorated
w/white enamel leafly scrolls & small dot

blossoms, the sides w/delicate white
enamel scroll band, late 19th c., 4⅜" d.,
4" h. (ILLUS.) **225**

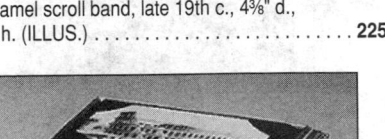

Italian Micromosaic Jewelry Box

Jewelry box, Micromosaic, rectangular
casket-form, gilt-metal beaded framework
& pierced bird & foliate feet, the sides &
top each set w/micromosaic landscape
scenes of Roman ruins, stamped
"C. Roccheggiani, Roma, Italy," late
19th c., 5 x 6", 4" h. (ILLUS.) **4,830**

Pipe box, painted cherry, shaped & pierced
backboard joining cutout sides & front
w/thumb molded drawer & turned knob
on molded base, old red paint, New
England, last half 18th c., 5⅙ x 6 x 20½" . . . **4,025**

Storage box, burl veneer, rectangular
w/hinged cover, the interior w/old gold
paint w/sponged colors & mirror in cover,
5¼" l. (some veneer damage) **193**

Storage box, cov., round bentwood
w/copper tacks in seam, flat fitted cover &
arched bentwood swing handle, old
varnish finish, 13½" d., 6½" h. plus
handle (some renailing) **193**

Storage box, cov., round bentwood w/side
seam & flat fitted cover, old black paint,
7" d. (minor edge damage) **275**

Storage box, cov., painted wood, dovetailed
construction w/molded base, original
yellow grain-painted surface, probably
Mid-Atlantic States, early 19th c.,
8¾ x 11¾", 9¾" h. (interior w/later
red paint, repair to base) **316**

Storage box, cov., round bentwood
w/lapped seams w/steel tacks, flat fitted
cover, wire bail handle w/turned wood
hand grip, old patina, 10½" d. **83**

Storage box, painted & decorated pine,
dovetailed case w/hinged cover, old
brown graining on a white ground,
19th c., 16" l. (wear, edge damage) **193**

Storage box, painted pine, a narrow top
shelf above a molded slant-lift lid opening
to a single compartmented interior,
dovetailed case w/applied molding,

Early Painted Pine Storage Box

original worn salmon red paint, New England, 18th c., 16½ x 25½", 17½" h. (ILLUS.) **5,175**

Wall box, pine, the wide & high backboard topped by a flat disk pierced w/a hanging hole above sharply sloping edges to flat sides above a narrow, shallow projecting base box w/shaped sides, the reverse inscribed w/a three-masted sailing ship, old refinish, New England, late 18th c., 3⅜ x 9¾", 17¾" h. (minor cracks & losses). **690**

Painted & Decorated Wood Box

Wood box, painted & decorated pine, rectangular hinged flat top w/breadboard ends lifts above a deep nailed box, decorated w/old mustard yellow paint w/a polychrome scroll-painted decoration on the front (added later), New England, 1830s, paint wear on top, 16 x 29", 23" h. (ILLUS.) **805**

BREWERIANA

Beer is still popular in this country, but the number of breweries has greatly diminished. More than 1,900 breweries were in operation in the 1870s, but we find fewer than 40 major breweries supply the demands of the country a century later, although micro-breweries have recently sprung up across the country. Advertising items used to promote various breweries, especially those issued prior to Prohibition, now attract an ever growing number of collectors. The breweriana items listed are a sampling of the many items available.

Advertisement, lighted, counter or wall mount, metal w/glass face, decorated w/fort in circle near top flanked by hops & banners reading "Choicest Malt" & "Finest Hops" w/"Fort Pitt - Special - Beer" in center w/"Fort Pitt Brewing Co., Pittsburgh, 15 Pennsylvania Epp-13," black & red lettering, 14½" d. (minor scratches). **$330**

Advertisement, die-cut cardboard w/3-D effect, depicts a light tan horse w/glossy coat standing on green ground & against dark brown background, brown frame w/"Special Kaier's Beer" at top & "First Prize Winner" on bottom & in white lettering at one side "Kaier Brewing Co. Mahanoy City, Pa. - Brussels 1950 Belgium," clear coating, 19½ " w., 16½ " h. **99**

Advertisement, "Al. S. Schorrs City Brewery," Hannibal, Missouri, embossed scene of clutch of dead game birds, lithograph by Gast, St. Louis, Missouri, ca. 1905-1910, matted & framed, 11 x 23" **308**

Anheuser-Busch Calendar

Calendar display, tin over cardboard w/chain to hang, "Budweiser" above tray holding a beer bottle & a pilsner glass filled w/beer, "Preferred Everywhere" below, cardboard calendar, months & days included, red & gold, Anheuser-Busch, Inc., minor scratches, denting & rust spotting, 12" w., 22½ " h. (ILLUS.) **248**

Clock, electric wall model, w/light, round glass & metal, white w/black Arabic numerals & hands, red seconds hand, bust of Indian over wide red banner w/"Leinenkugel's" & "made with Chippewa Water from the Big Eddy Springs" in black, Advertising Products, Inc., Cincinnati 23, Ohio for Jacob

Leinenkugel's Beer Clock

Leinenkugel Brewing Co., Chippewa Falls, Wisconsin, some scratches & soiling, 15" d. (ILLUS.) **534**

Clock, electric wall model, w/light, round molded embossed plastic w/metal back & hands, depicts embossed white bust of Indian in full headdress on red arrowhead design & advertising "Iroquois Beer-Ale" & marked "Since 1842," red & white lettering, 17" d. (paint chips to hands & soiling) **440**

Clock, w/light, Art Deco style, rectangular bar w/"Duquesne - The Finest Beer in Town" above stepped frame enclosing octagonal clock, reverse-painted glass w/metal housing, old clock starting mechanism, black & grey w/red numerals, red & yellow lettering, 5½ x 24½ ", 18½ " h. (very minor paint chips to hands, minor scratches & soiling & minor staining to white background) **468**

Coaster, "A-1 Pilsner Beer," tin, round tip-tray form, red outer rim w/white center marked "A-1 (below motif of eagle) Pilsner Beer Thank You," 3½ " d. **33**

Coaster, lithographed tin, round, tip tray-form, bottle in center flanked by "Valley Forge Special Beer" & "A Beer for Unsurpassed Quality" w/"Bottled Only at the Brewery" below, black, yellow & red, Adam Scheidt Brewing Co., Norristown, Pennsylvania, ca. 1954, wrapped in original paper, 4" d. **94**

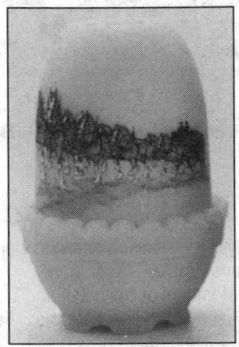

Budweiser Fairy Lamp by Fenton

Fairy lamp, creamy frosted glass shade w/transfer decoration of the Budweiser team of horses pulling a wagon, cupped matching footed base w/scalloped rim, Fenton (ILLUS.) **110**

"Grant's Farm" Mugs

Mug, "Grant's Farm" pottery, cylindrical shape, green ground decorated w/scene of brown & white horses & green trees in background, CS15, Budweiser (ILLUS. right) **294**

Mug, "Grant's Farm" pottery, wide cylindrical shape, tan & brown decorated w/colorful scene of brown & white horses & green trees in background, CS15, Budweiser, small (ILLUS. left) **340**

Budweiser Mugs

Mug, pottery, Budweiser "Label" model, CS 18 (ILLUS. far left) **605**

Mug, pottery, Budweiser series, Bud Girl, blue dress, w/filigree, CS20 (ILLUS. second from right) **457**

Mug, pottery, Budweiser series, Bud Girl, purple dress, no filigree, CS20 (ILLUS. second from left) **650**

Mug, pottery, cylindrical shape, Budweiser "Wurzburger" label model, CS39 (ILLUS. far right) **363**

Miniature German Pilique Mug

Mug, pottery, miniature German Pilique-style, tapering cylindrical form w/molded narrow bands around the top & base, in tan & brown, decorated w/tavern scene on dark blue background, Budweiser, CS5 (ILLUS.) **402**

Brewers Association Pin

Pin, "United States Brewers Association (1897)," convention souvenir w/embossed buffalo head in center, surrounded by enamel work & set stones, suspended from a scrolled bar pin inscribed "1897," Heintz Bros., Buffalo, New York, 1½ " l. (ILLUS.) **110**

Miller High Life Pinback Button

Pinback button w/hanger, celluloid logo above die-cut woman wearing dress w/flaring skirt & standing on sign reading "High Life - Milwaukee's Leading Bottled Beer," Miller Brewing Co., Milwaukee, Wisconsin, 1⁵⁄₁₆ x 4⅛" (ILLUS.) **116**

Print, "Westward Ho," lithographed paper by Oscar Berninghaus for Anheuser Busch, colorful scene of wagon trains, matted & framed, 13 x 21". **99**

"Schlitz" Salt & Pepper Shakers

Salt & pepper shakers, miniature bottle-shaped, "Schlitz," plastic w/plastic lids, 4" h., pr. (ILLUS.) **15**

Sign, neon-type, "Schaefer" in script & "Beer" in block letters, mounted on metal framework, 11" h. (soiling, cracks & wear to rubber tips) **170**

Sign, one-sided porcelain pillow-form, red w/center image of beer glass figural waiter carrying two glasses of beer on a tray, "Heineken" in white lettering above, logo below w/"Heineken Bier," 16" w., 23½ " h. (very minor scratches) **275**

Sign, one-sided porcelain w/rounded sides, depicts early steam engine below "Door County's Premium Lager" & "Cherryland Brewing, Ltd." below, rectangular white panel w/"Cherry Rail" across center, red, white & black w/red lettering 19" w., 14" h. **275**

Sign, tin over cardboard, Prohibition-era non-alcoholic drink, shows bottle on wooden case, Budweiser, 7 x 17" **750**

Fort Pitt Beer Sign

Sign, painted metal, embossed colorful scene of couple seated at table w/a bottle of beer & filled glasses, "Thanks to Our Courageous President and Sound Thinking Members of Congress and U.S. Senators" above, "for this Delicious - Fort Pitt Beer - Pittsburgh, Pennsylvania - Sharpsburg, Suburb" below, denting

around edges, touch-up to rust spotting &
nail holes overall, 26" w., 22¾" h.
(ILLUS.) **990**

Iroquois Beer Tray

Tray, lithographed metal, round, gold center
w/bust of Indian w/full headdress, red
border w/"Iroquois" above & "Buffalo"
below, gold rim, Iroquois Beverage Corp.,
Buffalo, New York, minor edge wear,
scratches & soiling, 5¼" d. (ILLUS.).......... **72**

BUTTER MOLDS & STAMPS

While they are sometimes found made of other materials, it is primarily the two-piece wooden butter mold and one-piece butter stamps that attract collectors. The molds are found in two basic styles, rounded cup-form and rectangular box-form. Butter stamps are usually round with a protruding knob handle on the back. Many were factory-made items with the print design made by forcing a metal die into the wood under great pressure, while others had the design chiseled out by hand. An important reference book in this field is Butter Prints and Molds, *by Paul E. Kindig (Schiffer Publishing, 1986).*

Chicken & house mold, cased carved
wood w/scene of house & large chicken,
hinged sides, 4½x 10" **$193**
Cow stamp, hardwood, carved design of a
cow & tree, old weathered finish w/age
cracks, turned one-piece handle, 4¼" d. **163**

Eagle & Star Stamp

Eagle & star stamp, round, carved
hardwood w/center design of large eagle
w/open wings & star near head, one
piece turned handle, old patina, age
crack, 4" d. (ILLUS.).................... **289**
Eagle & stars "lollipop" stamp, square,
pine w/primitively carved spread-winged
eagle in center w/stars in arc above head,
old patina, minor age cracks, 8½" l......... **275**

Flower & Heart Stamp

Flower & heart stamp, rectangular
w/rounded ends, carved pine w/deeply
cut stylized flower above a double heart,
soft worn patina, 3⅜ x 6⅛" (ILLUS.)........ **523**
Flowers & initials stamp, rectangular, pine
w/carved stylized pot of flowers w/"H.M."
in a cross-hatched design, "1823" carved
on back, old patina, 2⅝ x 4" **165**
Heart & star stamp, rectangular, carved
wood w/"The Union" above a large
double heart & stars, old scrubbed finish,
added tin hanger, 3⅛ x 5" **358**

Hearts Stamp

Hearts stamp, round, hardwood, carved
lines dividing surface into four sections,
each containing a carved heart w/cross-
hatching, zipper-notched border band, old
patina, square self handle, 4¾ x 4⅞"
(ILLUS.) **440**
Pomegranate w/foliage, round cased, good
patina, case stamped "Pat. Apr. 17,
1866," 4¾" d. **138**

Tulip Stamp

Tulip stamp, round, carved poplar
w/stylized deep cut tulip in center, carved
star on each side at top & one at bottom,
zipper-notched border band, old patina,
one-piece turned handle, 4⅞" d. (ILLUS.) **413**

Carved Tulip Stamp

Tulip stamp, rectangular, carved pine,
stylized tulip, old patina, added tin
hanger, 3 x 4⅞" (ILLUS.) **248**
Tulip stamp, round, poplar w/primitively
carved tulip & leaves, self handle dated
"1796," initials worn away, old black
finish, attributed to Ephrata,
Pennsylvania, 4½x 5" **550**

BUTTONS

Buttons have reflected the world around us
for more than two centuries. They have and
continue to give us insights to both social and
political movements throughout history.
Millicent Safro, author of Buttons notes buttons
with pictorial designs have been made in many
periods, but those known by collectors as "picture
buttons" came into vogue during the Victorian
era in the second half of the 19th century.
Usually metal with stamped designs, their
varied array of subjects included animals,
children, buildings, scenery, insects, fruit,
flowers, birds, people, mythology, theater and
opera. Many of the images are derived from
contemporary illustrations, trade cards and a
wide range of literary works including children's

stories and fairy tales. The following
photographs and listings include not only
buttons of the Victorian era, but a wide range of
other 18th and 19th century buttons.

Brass Bee Button

Brass, stamped, large bee decorated w/cut
steel, applied to darkened metal
background w/a white metal inner border
& embossed & scrolled outer border,
Victorian, ca. 1880-90, 1⅝" d. (ILLUS.).... **$50-75**
Brass, stamped, round, a large & small dog,
stamped w/inner white metal border
surrounded by a faceted brass rim, from
Sir Edwin Landseer painting titled "Dignity
& Impudence," Victorian, ca. 1870-80,
1¹⁵⁄₁₆" d. **35-125**
Brass, stamped, round, head of Cannio
from the opera "I Pigliacco" by
Leoncavello, surrounded by a ruff &
wearing a clown's hat, Victorian,
ca. 1890, 1⁷⁄₁₆" d. **40-50**

Neptune Brass & Wood Button

Brass, stamped, round, head of Neptune
holding trident, mounted on dark wood
background in a double rope border,
Victorian, ca. 1880-90, 1⁷⁄₁₆" d. (ILLUS.) **12-15**
Brass, stamped, round, head-on view of
horse-drawn carriage & driver, Victorian,
ca. 1880-90, 1½" d. **40-50**

"Gay Nineties" Brass Button

Brass, stamped, round, large Victorian "jeweled" design encasing an oval purple swirl glass center, known as "Gay Nineties" style, ca. 1880-1900, 1¹¹⁄₁₆" d. (ILLUS.) **50-75**

Brass, stamped, round, one-piece image of elephant on decorated beaded background & border, Victorian, ca. 1890-1900, 1¼" d. **20-25**

Stamped & Tinted Brass Button

Brass, stamped, round, tinted, two saddled horses outside stone building w/arched & mullioned windows, Victorian, ca. 1880-90, 1⅝" d. (ILLUS.) **65-70**

Celluloid Button

Celluloid, round, cream & browns in off-set oval w/gold half moon on side, darkened decorative brass trim, ca. 1880-1900, 1¼" d. (ILLUS.) **12-24**

Celluloid, round, mottled cream & browns w/floral starburst design & decorative brass trim, ca. 1880-1900, 1¼" d. **12-24**

Celluloid & Brass Button

Celluloid & brass, round, brass horseshoe center & trim w/variegated red background, ca. 1880-1900, 1" d. (ILLUS.) . . **12-24**

Large China Buttons

China, round, four-hole w/transfer printed calico designs, made in small ½" at $2.00, medium ⅝" at $4.00, & large ¹⁵⁄₁₆" at $75.00, ca. 1850, (ILLUS.) **75**

George Washington Inauguration Button

Copper, round, centered engraved "GW" & bordered by "linked states" representing 13 original colonies, made for George Washington's inauguration, ca. 1789, 1⅝" d. (ILLUS.) **1,500-2,000**

Enamel & Stone Button

Enamel, round, painted woman's head w/powdered hair, red dress embellished w/white lace & pink roses, set in painted brass border w/turquoise glass stones, France, ca. 1880, 1⅜" d. (ILLUS.) **150-200**

Enamel on brass, depicts young boy in 18th c. dress wearing a red waistcoat, yellow weskit & blue-green knee breeches, known as "Nut Tree Boy" from a nursery rhyme, ornate border of blues, green & red champleve enamel, France, ca. 1880-90, 1¼" d. **175**

Gilt & Copper Button

Gilt & copper, octagonal, engraved &
chased, late 18th c., 1⅜" d. (ILLUS.) **150-175**

Pressed Glass Flower Button

Glass, round, pressed clear glass flower
w/red, yellow & green paint applied to
back, decorated w/black paint between
flower petals, resembles "lacy glass"
produced by Boston & Sandwich
Glassworks, Czechoslovakia or Austria,
late 19th c. to early 20th c., 1¼" d. (ILLUS.)... **150**

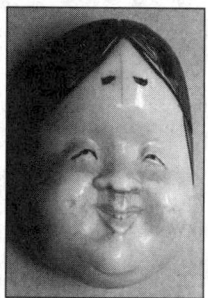

Carved Ivory Button

Ivory, carved figural head of woman
w/pigmented hair, brows & eyes, Japan,
ca. 1880-90, 1¹⁄₁₆" l. (ILLUS.)........... **100-150**
Ivory under glass, oval, depicts finely
detailed miniature painting of white, blue,
yellow & red bird on tree branch w/tree &
lake in background, beveled glass, set in
silver rope trim, England, mid-19th c.,
¹⁵⁄₁₆ l." **250-300**

Ivory Under Glass Button

Ivory under glass, oval, finely detailed
painted miniature of mosque, depicts
Indian monuments in realistic colors,
silver mount, travel souvenir,
ca. 1880-90, 1⁷⁄₁₆" d. (ILLUS.)......... **300-400**

Jasperware Button

Jasperware, round, white classical head on
blue background, mounted on gilded
copper, probably made by Josiah
Wedgwood, England, late 18th c.,
1⁷⁄₁₆" d. (ILLUS.) **400-500**
Micro-mosaic w/inlaid glass, round, shows
brown & white spotted spaniel, red border
& gilt cup setting, ca. 1880, 1³⁄₁₆" d. **75-85**

Paper Under Glass Button

Paper under glass, round, finely detailed
gouache painting, depicts man in tricorn
hat & orange jacket seated on white
horse w/landscaped background, France,
late 18th c., from set of 12, 1½" d. (ILLUS.) ... **400**
Pearl, round, cameo carved in 2-color ocean
pearl, depicts two figures in a ruin,
ca. 1880, 1¼" d. **100-125**

Porcelain Portrait Button

Porcelain, round, painted bust of young boy
in Italian Renaissance style, set in brass
w/a paste border, mid to late 19th c.,
1¼" d. (ILLUS.) **200-250**

Porcelain Butterfly Button

Porcelain, round, painted butterfly in blues, browns & reds w/thin gold paint border, England, late 18th c., 1⅜" d. (ILLUS.). . . . **300-350**

Japanese Satsuma Pottery Button

Pottery, round, h.p. Japanese Satsuma of woman wearing blue striped kimono, stippled gold background & dark blue border, encrusted w/gold, ca. 1890-1900, 1⅝ " d. (ILLUS.). **100-145**

Shell, round, black nautilus shell engraved & pigmented in black, depicts a horse & rider in 19th c. costume, England, 19th c., 2¼" d. **250-300**

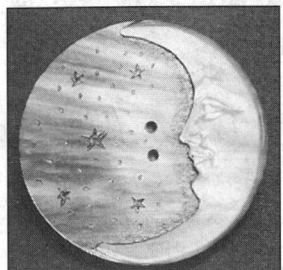

Crescent Moon on Shell Button

Shell, round, carved crescent moon applied to engraved & gold pigmented flat shell background, ca. 1880-90, 1⁹⁄₁₆" d. (ILLUS.). **200-250**

Silver, ball-shaped w/large domed knobs outlined w/rope-twist banding, Austria-Hungary, late 17th to early 18th c., 1⅛" d. (ILLUS.). **65-100**

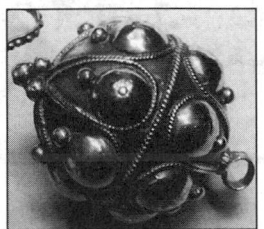

Ornate Silver Button

Silver Plated Cherub Button

Silver plated, round, pierced metal w/cherub surrounded by Art Nouveau floral border, Victorian, ca. 1895-1900, 1⁹⁄₁₆" d. (ILLUS.) **40-45**

Sterling silver, heart-shaped, depicts playful cherubs lighting a fire, Victorian, ca. 1890, 1⅜" d. **75-85**

Tortoiseshell Button

Tortoiseshell, round, inlaid w/three engraved abalone & silver birds in flight, ca. 1870-80, 1⁹⁄₁₆" d. (ILLUS.) **100-150**

Pierced White Metal Button

White metal, round, pierced w/crimped border showing Hop O' My Thumb in seven league boots, from the children's story, Victorian, ca. 1880, 1⁷⁄₁₆" d. (ILLUS.) **75**

CANDLESTICKS & CANDLEHOLDERS

Also see METALS and ROYCROFT ITEMS.

Candelabra, sterling silver, three-light, Colonial Revival paneled baluster-form standard, three convertible socket, early 20th c., Tiffany & Co., 17⅝" h., pr. **$3,738**

Candleholder, brass, Arts & Crafts style, three-light w/a tiered design, three square candle sockets w/square rims raised on a C-form squared upright & spaced along an angled flat bar w/a angular curled tall upper foot & a squared small curl at the lower end, impressed "Hand Wrought L.C. Shellbarger," early 20th c., 12" l., 6" h. **330**

Candleholder, wrought iron trammel-style, a thin bar w/a slender sawtooth trammel bar ending w/a short arm supporting a small oval pan w/two cylindrical candle sockets & a rush light holder, sockets w/push-ups, 27" l. **495**

Candleholder, wrought iron w/domed wooden base & handle w/old red paint, 5" h. . . **275**

Candleholders, brass, ship's gimbal spring-loaded holders, traces of original nickel finish, 19th c., 11" h., pr. **316**

Candlestand, wrought iron, a rounded arch tripod base w/penny feet centering a tall tapering turned & pointed bar mounted w/an adjustable double arm w/a candle socket at each end, squared iron brackets w/hooks below the arms, 19th c., 23¼" h. **1,815**

Candlestick, brass, domed base & baluster stem w/mid-drip pan, early Dutch, 12⅜" h. . . **3,520**

Candlestick, pressed flint glass, hexagonal, scalloped rim socket, opaque medium blue, Pittsburgh, 9⅝" h. (pewter socket missing, small edge chips) **220**

Candlestick, pressed flint glass, hexagonal w/flaring base & wafer, canary, 7½" h. (broken blister inside socket) **138**

Candlestick, pressed flint glass, round base, hexagonal knopped stem, opalescent tulip-shaped socket, canary, Pittsburgh, ca. 1860, 9¼" h. (pewter insert missing, chips & crack in socket) **110**

Candlestick, pressed flint glass, vase-shaped w/flared rim socket, cobalt blue, 15¾" h. **176**

Candlesticks, brass, Neo-classical w/pushups, 5½" h., pr. **105**

Candlesticks, brass, octagonal base w/turned standard, w/pushups, Victorian, 12" h., pr. **121**

Brass Pricket-type Candlestick

Candlesticks, brass, pricket-type spike above ring & turned column over wide drip pan above ring & turned baluster stem on domed circular ringed foot, Europe, late 17th to early 18th c., dents & repairs, 15" h., pr. (ILLUS. of one) **805**

Candlesticks, brass, Queen Ann style, scalloped base & baluster stem w/seam, 6¾" h., pr. (one has old repair). **990**

Candlesticks, brass, Queen Anne-style, square base w/invected corners, detailed stem w/scalloped lip, 8" h., pr. **1,045**

Candlesticks, brass, square base, knob turned column w/flaring socket, late 19th to early 20th c., 10½" h., pr. **110**

Candlesticks, brass, "The Diamond Prince" patt., central ring-turned shaft w/a diamond design section, domed base w/squared foot w/cut corners, w/pushups, 19th c., 11¾" h., pr. **358**

Early Brass Candlesticks

Candlesticks, brass, trumpet-form base tapering to wide drip pan below cylindrical sausage-turned column, England, late 17th c., 7⁹⁄₁₆" h., pr. (ILLUS.) **13,800**

Candlesticks, brass, Victorian w/pushups, diamond & beehive detail, 10¾" h., pr. **110**

Candlesticks, brass, wide domed base w/turned baluster stem, mid-drip plate, not seamed, one w/casting holes filled w/solder, 11¼" h., pr. **495**

Candlesticks, gilt-metal, Art Nouveau design w/floral & foliate decoration, ca. 1900, 8" h., pr. (minor scratches) **345**

Candlesticks, hand-hammered copper, Arts & Crafts style, each w/a cylindrical stem surmounted by a bowl-form drip pan centered by a cylindrical candle cup, all on a domed foot, applied trefoil mounts at joints, dark brown patina, ca. 1900, 11⅜" h., pr. 575

Candlesticks, pewter, capstan bases, knopped standard, 4¾" h., pr. (somewhat battered w/repair) 715

Candlesticks, pressed flint glass base & blown hollow socket w/baluster stem, clear, 8⅛" h., pr. (checks in base in the making, no inserts) 358

Candlesticks, silver on copper, telescoping design, Sheffield, England, 7¾" h., pr. (silver worn) 220

Candlesticks, silver, on shaped square base w/scrolling stylized dolphins to corners, stem w/flat leaf motifs, bell-shaped flat leaf sockets, Russian, 13¾" h., pr. 805

Candlesticks, silver-plated, each w/stepped square base w/canted corners & conforming baluster-form stem terminating in a spool-form candle cup, George II-Style, 20th c., 7¾" h., pr. 172

Candlesticks, sterling silver, square base w/gadrooned borders, the stem, sock & detachable bobêche also gadrooned, monogrammed to base, Robert Makepeace & Richard Carter makers, England, George III period, 9½" h., pr. 4,888

Chamberstick, sterling silver, circular dished form w/C-scroll handle, cylindrical turned stem, flared socket rim, London hallmarks for 1755-56, 4¼" h. (old repair, snuffer not marked) 633

Chamberstick, sterling silver, maker's mark "AK," ribbed borders, monogrammed, London, 1804, 2⅛" h. (extinguisher missing) 173

Chambersticks, tin w/riveted handles, old worn black paint, 6⅝" h., pr. 138

Bronze Girandoliers

Girandoliers, gilt bronze & crystal, relief-molded figure of a woman forms base beneath the three candle sockets, each w/a flower form bobeche & ten cut crystal prism pendants, 15" h., 19th c., pr. (ILLUS.) 173

CANDY CONTAINERS

* *Indicates the container might not have held candy originally.*
\+ *Indicates this container might also be found as a reproduction.*
‡ *Indicates this container was also made as a bank.*

All containers are clear glass unless otherwise indicated. Any candy container that retains the original paint is very desirable; readers should follow descriptions carefully, realizing that an identical candy container that lacks the original paint will be less valuable.

Airplane, left side rear door, 25% paint, original propeller, original cover $550

Airplane, "Spirit of St. Louis," clear glass, all original tin, original cover 517

Amos & Andy, open car, 80% paint, replaced cover 495

Baseball Player, 80% paint, original cover (minor nick) 825

Baseball Player on Base, 95% paint, original cover 688

Boat, "Submarine F6," all original tin, original cover (original flag on replaced pole, replaced periscope) 550

Bus, "Greyhound," 98% paint, original wheels, original cover 550

Bus, "Victory Glass Co." (no paint, replaced cover) 495

Camera on Tripod, all original parts, 98% paint, donkey picture, original cover 633

Candlestick, "Colonial," original cover 468

Carpet Sweeper, "Baby Sweeper," all original tin, original cover 440

Coach, "Angeline," replaced glass coupler projections, replaced wheels, some chipping 413

Flossie Fisher's Bed, original cover 4,125

Flossie Fisher's Chair, Borgfeldt & Company 825

Flossie Fisher's China Closet, original cover, minor edge wear (door tabs broken) ... 935

Flossie Fisher's Dresser, original cover, Borgfeldt & Co. 2,475

Flossie Fisher's Sideboard, original cover, Borgfeldt & Company (no mirror) 990

Flossie Fisher's Table, minor scratching, original cover 2,640

Jackie Coogan, 30% original paint, original cover 550

Kiddies Candy Filled Toy Assortment, original box, replaced liner, old containers inside, replaced original contents, the set 990

Lamp, "Christmas Lamp," original cover (replaced shade, small tears in label) 633

Locomotive, "Silver Link," original cover 1,815

Man on Motorcycle, w/sidecar, repainted, replaced cover **523**

Man on Motorcycle, w/sidecar, 20% trace of paint, original cover **644**

Opera Glass, "Victor," original candy, original cover, original box (some wear). **715**

Pocket watch, all-original w/candy, original packing box, original cover. **853**

Pumpkin Head Witch, 70% paint, original cover (minor thread roughness) **633**

Rabbit Family, 96% paint, replaced cover (minor chip) **715**

Rabbit Mother & Daughter, 25% paint, original cover **633**

Santa Claus, wearing long coat, replaced cover. **660**

Soldier w/Sword, 80% paint, red coat, grey pants, replaced cover. **880**

Soldier w/Sword, no paint, original cover **687**

Statue of Liberty, 90% gilded, no hole in upheld hand. **2,035**

Stop & Go Sign, no paint, original cover **687**

Swan Boat, w/rabbit & chick, 90% paint, replaced closure (small chip under top) **688**

Tree stump, w/cherry, no cover **1,265**

Windmill, "Teddy Wind Mill," all original tin, original cover. **1,155**

CANES & WALKING STICKS

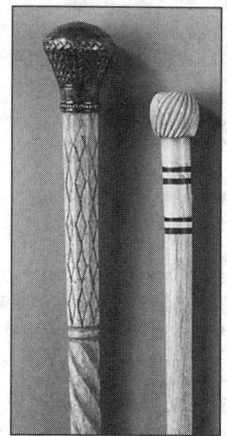

Carved Whalebone Canes

Carved Narwhal whalebone presentation cane, tapered silver knob handle decorated in a sailor's knot pattern, a band of bright-cut flowers in diamonds & beaded edge, the top w/Scottish coats of arms of crowned lion rampart, upper ribbon banner inscribed "pro regein tyrannos," lower ribbon inscribed "Victoria Velmors," edge ring inscribed "W.S. McDonnall 11 Blackford Road," above a paneled shaft w/diamond & ring-turned carving, continuing to spiral twist, a turned ring then tapering shaft, presented to Captain Duff of the Royal Navy, tip missing, pre-1836, 37½" l. (ILLUS. left). . . . **$2,530**

Carved softwood walking stick, fist-carved handle above a shaft carved in low-relief w/a snake wrapping around the sides, branded inscription "A.M. Gregg, Dec. 3, 1891, Waufpgy, Pike Co. Ohio," old worn crusty finish, 34¼" l. (some edge damage) **165**

Carved stag horn & malacca presentation cane, natural smooth round stag horn knob handle, carved as a scallop shell above a silver collar inscribed "Bryant P. Tilden to John Callender," full bark malacca shaft w/two silver oval eyelets terminating in a very long 8¼" brass & iron ferrule, American, ca. 1775, 35¾" h. **2,310**

Carved walrus tusk & whalebone cane, handle in the form of a lady's leg, above tapering shaft inset w/two baleen spacers, 19th c., 34¾" l. (minor age crack, slight warping) **920**

Three Ivory Canes

Carved walrus tusk & whalebone cane, octagonal handle w/ebony spacer, tapering shaft w/octagonal carving continuing to sailor's knots & spiral turning continuing to a fluted column, ring turnings & diamond points, 19th ca., age cracks, 35½ " l. (ILLUS. center). **2,645**

Carved whale ivory & whalebone cane, the ring-turned knopped handle w/traces of red sealing wax, top w/mother-of-pearl inlaid disk, baleen spacer, hexagonal top third of shaft inset w/abalone diamonds & dots & ring turnings continuing to round tapering form, 19th c., damage to spacer, tip end of shaft missing & broken, missing one diamond inlay, minor age cracks, warping, 31¼" l. (ILLUS. left) **748**

Carved whale ivory & whalebone cane, the L-shaped ivory handle carved in the form of a Victorian lady's leg w/high button shoe & black stocking w/scalloped edge above a long cylindrical plain silver collar w/whalebone shaft twist-carved & tapering to a smooth end in a plated copper ferrule, probably sailor-made, ca. 1860, 34½ " l. **1,320**

Carved whale ivory & whalebone cane, handle carved in the form of an eagle's head w/inset eyes, baleen spacers, one w/a silver ring, above a round tapering shaft, 19th c., 34¾" l. (one eye missing, minor age cracks) **2,530**

Carved whale ivory & whalebone cane, carved Turk's-head knot handle above the shaft w/spiral decoration extending midway then round tapering & inset w/baleen spacers, 19th c., minor cracks, slight warping, 35¼" l. (ILLUS. right) **1,073**

Carved whale ivory & whalebone cane, carved spiral knob handle w/four baleen spacers above a tapering round shaft, 19th c., age cracks, 36¾" l. (ILLUS. right w/Narwhal cane). **403**

Carved whale ivory & whalebone cane, L-shaped two-part handle decorated in a jockey motif of cap, horseshoe & stirrup above a paneled to round shaft, 19th c., 38" l. (repair, missing spacer, slight warping) **345**

Carved whale ivory & whalebone walking stick, w/polyhedron handle inlaid w/ebony dots resembling a die, above a tapering shaft inset w/ebony & metal spacers, 19th c., 34¾" l. (crack beneath the knob, one dot missing) **1,093**

Carved whalebone & white ivory walking stick, w/Turk's-head knot handle above a spiral carved tapering shaft, decorated w/a carved ivory woven ring & a single carved baleen spacer, 19th c., 34½ " l. (slight warping) **2,645**

Carved wood cane, the handle carved in the form of an antelope's head w/glass eyes, polychrome highlights, 19th c., 37" l. (minor cracks) **230**

Elephant ivory & hardwood walking stick, carved ivory head of a young girl wearing a large silver bonnet above a ribbed silver collar, the shaft of mahoganized hardwood w/horn ferrule, probably England, ca. 1880, 35½ " l. (ILLUS. top next column). . **3,740**

Elephant ivory & hardwood walking stick, Art Nouveau style handle, beautifully carved ivory depicting flowing design of broad leaves & a fully opened blossom w/delicate stem carved through-and-

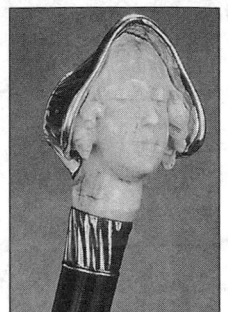

Ivory & Hardwood Walking Stick

through above a smooth silver collar on ebonized hardwood shaft w/horn ferrule, possibly France, ca. 1900, 36" l. **2,420**

Elephant ivory & malacca walking stick, a finely carved ivory hand w/a braided ring cuff, holding a knotted branch, small flat mushroom-shaped top, braided silver collar on a stopped malacca shaft w/white metal & iron ferrule, probably American, ca. 1850, 35¾" l. **1,155**

Glass cane, blue w/shepherd's crook handle, twisted white striping w/smooth rounded point, probably American, ca. 1890, 43½ " l. **330**

Ivory, brass & wood cane, the angled ivory handle carved in the form of a lady's leg wearing a brass boot, brass ferrule & hardwood shaft, 35" l. **403**

Ivory & hardwood cane, angled ivory handle w/finely detailed carved ivory full-bodied fox w/glass eyes, depicted in a crouched position, bushy tail fully extended, teeth bared & ears laid back, ebonized hardwood shaft w/thin decorated gilt collar & horn ferrule, probably England, ca. 1890, 36" l. **4,290**

Metal & exotic wood cane, the crook handle decorated at the shoulder in the form of relief-molded knight's head w/metal helmet elaborately decorated & a coat of mail protecting his throat & chest, two winged dragons flow from the back of his head onto the handle, shaft of tropical zebrawood w/a worn white metal ferrule, small Continental hallmarks, early 20th c., 33¼" h. **770**

Metal & snakewood cane, Art Nouveau style, silver figural duck fashioned in a half crook, the head of a duck depicted emerging from smooth flowing leaves, lightly figured snakewood shaft w/worn horn ferrule, Continental hallmarks, perhaps Vienna, ca. 1900, 34" l. (some denting at top of handle). **880**

Metal & snakewood walking stick, tapering cylindrical handle of English sterling decorated in C-scrolls w/smooth unmarked shield on the side, finely figured snakewood shaft w/horn ferrule, hallmarked London, England, 1892, 37¾" l. (areas of insect damage) **550**

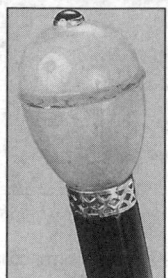

Quartz & Hardwood Walking Stick

Quartz & hardwood walking stick, egg-shaped rose quartz handle encircled by a faceted rock crystal ring w/cabochon garnet set in silver inlaid on top above a silver collar reticulated w/small diamond openwork, ebonized hardwood shaft w/horn ferrule, probably England, early 20th c., 36" l. (ILLUS.) **990**

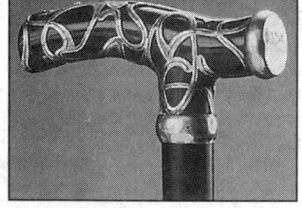

Tortoiseshell & Silver Overlay Cane

Tortoiseshell & hardwood cane, gently curved tortoiseshell handle decorated w/openwork silver overlay w/smooth silver end cap initialed & dated "1905," above sterling silver collar hallmarked London, England, 1905, ebonized hardwood shaft w/horn ferrule, 35¾" l. (ILLUS.) **1,100**

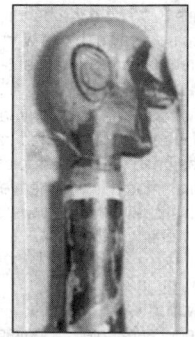

Folk Art Walking Stick

Wooden folk art walking stick, carved man's head forms handle, painted brown, black, red, yellow & orange, 20th c., 42" l. (ILLUS.) **165**

Wooden & metal walking stick, the handle cast in English sterling as a finely detailed full figural owl w/glass eyes perched atop a stump, hallmarked London, England, 1887, rosewood shaft w/worn brass & iron ferrule, 37" l. **1,210**

Wooden walking stick, carved black man's head forms handle, good detail w/glass eyes, black-grained shaft, 35" l. (some wear to head) **330**

Wooden walking stick, curved top carved & painted to resemble a diamond-back rattlesnake in brown w/gold & black diamonds, inset glass eyes, 37" l. **193**

CANS & CONTAINERS

The collecting of tin containers has become quite popular within the past several years. Airtight tins were first produced by hand to keep food fresh and, after the invention of the tin-printing machine in the 1870s, containers were manufactured in a wide variety of shapes and sizes with colorful designs. Also see: ADVERTISING, AUTOMOTIVE COLLECT-IBLES, COCA-COLA COLLECTIBLES and TOBACCIANA.

Baker's Delight Baking Powder Pail

Baking powder, Baker's Delight pail, round container w/side handles, lithographed Mammy holding a pan of baked goods, minor rust, soiling & chips to lithograph, 12¼" d., 14½" h. (ILLUS.) **$363**

Biscuit, Carr's tin, double decker motor bus model, partial box, 10⅛" l. (minor dent) **1,045**

Biscuit, Crawford tin, Yellow Sedan model, excellent, 8⅝" l. **10,450**

Biscuit, Crawford's tin, "Berengaria" cruise liner, includes advertisement card, excellent, 14¾" l. **3,080**

Biscuit, Crawford's tin, "General" double decker bus, 10¾" l. (surface wear to roof) . . . **4,400**

Biscuit, Crawford's tin, Rolls Royce model,11⅜" l., excellent **13,200**

Biscuit, Crawford's tin, service bus, very good, 11¾" l., (minor touchup) **2,420**

Biscuit, Crumpsall & Cardiff container, marble game w/the original steel balls, pristine, 4¾" x 6¾" **352**

Biscuit, Crumpsall & Cardiff container, motorcycle rider w/side car, 7" l. (minor scuffing to the driver). **4,620**

Biscuit, Crumpsall & Cardiff container, motorcycle rider w/side car, extremely rare, 7¼" l. (minor oxidation) **6,600**

Biscuit, Crumpsall & Cardiff tin, British telephone booth, rare, excellent, 6½ " h. **880**

Biscuit, Crumpsall & Cardiff tin, CWS Sedan w/clockwork mechanism, ca. 1926, excellent, 8¼" l. **11,000**

Biscuit, Crumpsall & Cardiff tin, elephant on wheels, excellent, 6" w., 4¾" h. **2,750**

Biscuit, Crumpsall & Cardiff tin, steam crane model, excellent, 7" l., 6¾" h. (minor wear to base & roof). **6,600**

Biscuit, G&R tin, Royal Mail delivery van model, excellent, 8" l. **990**

Biscuit, Gray & Dunn's tin, mailbox-shaped, shows young girl placing letter in mailbox, 5⅞" h. (minor scuffing & scratches) **330**

Biscuit, Gray & Dunn's container, motorcycle w/side car, extremely rare, 7¼" l. (minor oxidation) **16,500**

Biscuit, Gray & Dunn's tin, city bus, 7½ " l. (surface wear & minor scratches) **7,150**

Biscuit, Gray & Dunn's tin, racing car, 10" l. (minor scratch) **20,900**

Biscuit, Huntley & Palmers tin, Baby Carriage model, extremely rare, excellent, 4¾" h., 8½ " l. **7,150**

Biscuit, Huntley & Palmers tin, China Cabinet model, excellent , 5¾" x 7⅛" h. (minor denting) **1,100**

Biscuit, Huntley & Palmers tin, Grandfather Clock, excellent, 11½ " h. **1,100**

Biscuit, Jacob's tin, horse on wheels, rare original box, 8" w., 9⅛" h. **7,700**

Biscuit, Jacob's tin, locomotive, extremely rare, 9¼" l. (crazing to paint) **3,080**

Biscuit, LMS tin, trolley model, 9" l. (wear to roof & slight oxidation) **825**

Biscuit, Mailbox container, shows girl & dog delivering mail, excellent, 4⅞" h. **165**

Biscuit, Military Ambulance container, excellent, 7" l. **1,870**

Biscuit, Pascall's penny container, Punch & Judy design, excellent, 2⅞" h. **605**

Biscuit, Peek Frean Coconut Shies tin & game set, still w/wooden coconut shape pieces, 7½ " h. (some staining) **1,045**

Biscuit, Rowntrees tin, limousine-shaped, ca. 1926, excellent, 6⅛" l. **8,250**

Biscuit, William Crawford & Sons tin, model of a bus, original box, excellent, 10" l. **3,520**

Biscuit, William Crawford & Sons tin, model of a steamroller , extremely rare w/original box, 7¼" l., near mint **6,050**

Biscuits & cakes, John Hill & Son tin, delivery van, excellent, 7⅛" l. **2,750**

Buck shot, Winchester 1 lb. container, ca. 1939, full box **30**

Cigars, Dog-on-Good tin, paper label **2,310**

Cigars, Van Bibber pocket tin. **135**

Buell's Coffee Tin

Coffee, Buell's tin, round w/lithographed scene of lady drinking cup of coffee & marked "Buell's Brighton Blend Coffee - Merit - that's all!," George C. Burell & Co., Inc., "Rochester, N.Y. - Established 1846," embossed on lid, "turn to open," minor paint chips & overall soiling, 4½ " d., 6" h. (ILLUS.). **176**

Coffee, Comrade tin, round w/lithograph of dog's head & "Comrade Steel Cut Coffee" on one side & "Three pounds net weight vacuum packed J A Folger & Co., Kansas City San Francisco Trade Mark Reg. U.S. Pat. Off." on reverse, 6⅛" d., 7" h. (denting, scratches, soiling, surface rust & interior staining) **94**

Coffee, Golden West 2 lb. tin, cowgirl decoration. . **195**

Coffee, Log Cabin 1 lb. tin, key-wind. **1,705**

Coffee, Rose of Kansas 1 lb. tin **1,018**

Coffee, Sanico 1 lb. tin, Piggly Wiggly Store brand **1,485**

Coffee, Table King 1 lb. tin **963**

Coffee, Welcome Guest 1 lb. tin (missing lid) . . **1,705**

Condom, De-Luxe tin, shepherd dog decoration. . **798**

Dominion Condom Tin

Condom, Dominion tin, depicts young brunette woman (ILLUS.) **1,155**

Condom, Double Tip tin **825**

Condom, Gold Pak tin **440**

Condom, Nutex tin **935**

Condom, Silver Star tin **908**

Crackers, Crumpsall's Cream tin, delivery van model, ca. 1922, extremely rare, good, 7" l. (some repainting & one wheel replaced) **9,350**

Cup grease, MonaMotor 5 lb. tin, tapering cylinder w/fitted flat lid & wire bail handle, blue label printed in black & white "MonaMotor Hard Oil Cup Grease" above a black on blue scene of early car, motorcycle, farm machinery & airplane, 6" d., 6¾" h. (denting, rust spotting, scratches, soiling) **55**

Gelatine, Knox 1 lb. container, cardboard w/contents, "Knox U.S.P. Plain Sparkling" above head of cow flanked by "One - Pound" & "Gelatin - The Highest Quality - Charles B. Knox Gelatine Co., Inc., Johnstown, N.Y., Camden, N.J., U.S.A." below, side shows head of cow flanked by young girls holding plate w/gelatin mold, shrink-wrapped, 2¾ x 3½ ", 5" h. (very minor wear) **110**

Grease, Husky 25 lb. can, cylindrical w/clamp-on lid & metal & wooden bail handle, Husky dog logo & "Western Oil & Fuel Co. Minneapolis" on front & back, 12" d., 9½ " h. **358**

Gum, Hoadley's tin **770**

Gum & lozenges, Huntley, Boorne & Stevens, Ltd.container, Victory-V Grandfather clock model, circa 1922, clock operates, excellent, 5¾" x 18". **550**

Pure Canadian Honey Tin

Honey, Pure Canadian tin, round w/lid & bail handle, illustration of large beehive w/bees flying nearby, directions to liquefy the honey on back, some rust marks, 6¼" d., 6½ " h. (ILLUS.) **116**

Pep Boys Lighter Fluid Can

Lighter fluid, Pep Boys can, shows the Pep Boys, Manny, Joe & Jack, Philadelphia, Pennsylvania, scratches, soiling, 2¼" w., 1" l., 5" h. (ILLUS.) **132**

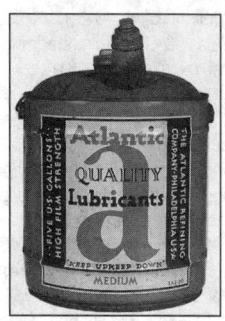

Atlantic Quality Lubricants Can

Lubricants, Atlantic Quality Lubricants 5 gal. can, wide cylindrical body w/low domed top w/spout & handles, the sides printed in red w/a large red, white & square center, printed "Atlantic Quality Lubricants" in red & blue over a large w/small white wording, white bottom band w/red word "Medium," minor soiling & scratches, 11½ " d., 16½ " h. (ILLUS.) **66**

Malted milk, Borden's metal can w/metal lid, "Borden's - Reg. U.S. Pat. Office" above triangle w/"Richer Malted Milk" appears three times around can, 6" d., 8½ " h. (denting to lid, minor scratches to can & lid) . . **121**

Horlicks Malted Milk Tins

Malted milk, Horlick's 10 lb. round tin, screw-on lid, marked "Horlick's Malted Milk - Fountain Brand - Manufactured by Horlick's Malted Milk Company - Racine, Wisconsin - Net Weight 10 Pounds" tan & black w/black & white lettering, Canco, 7¾" d., 9" h. (ILLUS. bottom left) **115**

Malted milk, Horlick's 10 lb. round tin w/handle over screw-on lid, scene w/cow, tan & black, 7½ " d., 9" h. (ILLUS. top left) **135**

Malted milk, Horlicks 25 lb. tin, screw-on lid, red, white & blue, Canco, 9" w., 13¾" h. (ILLUS. right) **275**

Motor oil, Camel Penn 1 qt. can, w/replaced top. . **798**

Motor oil, Clipper Penn 1 qt. can, name in large red letters w/a dark green four-engine plane flying between the words on a white ground, "Motor Oil" in green below name & above wave green bottom band w/"100% Pure Pennsylvania...," 5½" h. (top missing, minor scratches & denting) **1,100**

Motor oil, Conoco 1 gal. can, upright rectangular form, the sides w/ the name in large blue letters above & below the standing color profile of a Minuteman all on a cream ground, the rest of the can in dark yellow, original caps, 3 x 8", 11¼" h. (paint loss, scratches, soiling, denting) **1,375**

Motor oil, Ford & Sears, Roebuck 5 gal. can, upright square can w/a rectangular panel on one side w/an orange background & black wording & a black & white scene of two autos in a village, reads "Special - Automobile Oil - for - Ford Cars - Sears, Roebuck and Co.," 9¼" sq., 14½" h. (denting, rust spotting, scratches, soiling). **578**

Rare French Auto Oil 1 Gallon Can

Motor oil, French Auto Oil 1 gal. can, upright rectangular form w/two top spouts & ring handle, one side w/a large rectangular red-bordered yellow panel enclosed a green- and red-bordered white ring reading "Marshall Oil Co. - Distributers, U.S.A.," & enclosing a racing scene in green in black w/an early race car speeding past a grandstand, center

overprinted w/a large red arrow & "French Auto Oil," minor scratches & denting, 3 x 8", 10¾" h. (ILLUS.). **2,310**

Rare Husky Motor Oil Can

Motor oil, Husky Motor Oil 1 qt. can, color scene of a brown & black Husky in a snowy landscape w/Northern Lights behind him, product name in gold on blue around the top, very minor scratches (ILLUS.) **770**

Motor oil, Indian 1 gal. can, upright rectangular form w/top strap handle & spout w/cap, dark green ground w/a red, black & white profile of Native American in a circle over "Indian Oil" in large red letters above "100% Pure Pennsylvania - Especially Made by the Valvoline Oil Company - New York U.S.A. - for the - Indian Motocycle Company - Springfield, Mass." in small white & black lettering, 3 x 8", 11¼" h. (very minor scratches, denting & soiling). **2,090**

Motor oil, Opaline 1 gal. can, upright rectangular form w/spouts & strap handle on top, the sides w/a large rectangular reserve in cream bordered w/a thin green line, a large black, white & green early race car charging forward above "Opaline - Motor Oil - Sinclair Refining Company - Chicago" in green & blue lettering, 3 x 8", 11" h. (minor paint chips & soiling) **1,760**

Motor oil, Penn-Empire 5 gal. oil can, upright drum-shaped w/loop at bottom to keep from rolling, spout & loop handle at the top, the side printed w/a gold ring w/white wording reading "Penn-Empire Motor Oil" enclosing a black ring & an inner gold circle printed "Penn - Empire" & small wording, 8½ x 14", 16½ " h. (rust spotting, denting, scratches & soiling) **446**

Motor oil, Phillips Higrade ½ gal. can, long rectangular form, top strap handle & spout w/screw-on cap, the sides w/round logo above "Higrade Motor Oil" in red above "Medium" in black all on a white ground, 3¼ x 8", 6¼" h. (denting, rust spotting, scratches & soiling) **187**

Rare Phillips Trop-Artic Oil Can

Motor oil, Phillips Trop-Artic 1 qt. can, shaded striped pale green to orange ground w/a large center oval reserve w/an igloo scene above tall palm trees w/the Phillips shield logo in the center in green & black above "Motor Oil" in black, very minor denting & surface rust, soiling down spine, 5½ " h. (ILLUS.) **715**

Rare One Gallon Polarine Can

Motor oil, Polarine 1 gal. can, upright rectangular form w/hand grip, strap handle & spout w/cap on top, one side w/a large rectangular panel w/"Polarine - For Motor Lubrication" in large blue script & white letters in a blue banner above a pastel color hilly landscape scene w/a beachside village in the distance & an early long open roadster in the foreground, "Standard Oil Company - (New Jersey)" in blue at the bottom, early 20th c., denting, fading, paint chips, 3 x 7¾", 10¾" h. (ILLUS.) **2,090**

Motor oil, Red Hat 1 gal. can, upright rectangular can w/top strap handle & spout w/cap, the sides w/a dark blue ring around a red Uncle Sam-type top hat w/a blue hatband w/white stars, blue & white wording reads "Approved - Red Hat - Motor Oil," further wording in small letters at the bottom, 3 x 8", 11¼" h. (minor scratches & denting) **2,090**

Motor oil, Ronson 1 qt. tin **1,375**

Motor oil, Speedol 1 qt. can, a front-on view of an airplane above the name in large red letters all on a white ground, a wavy blue band at the bottom w/"Motor Oil," 5½" h. (minor scratches, soiling to top of rim) . . **341**

Motor oil, Trop-Artic 1 gal. can, upright rectangular can w/spout & cap & ring handle, one side w/a large rectangular color panel showing at the top a mountainous arctic landscape w/closed touring car & at the lower half a tropical landscape w/palm trees & a larger closed touring car, large red wording curves across the center, "Manhattan Oil Co." in black across the bottom, 3 x 8", 10½" h. (minor scratches & soiling) **3,520**

Planters Peanut Butter Tin

Peanut butter, Planters 1 lb. tin (ILLUS.) **5,170**

Veribest Peanut Butter Tin

Peanut butter, Veribest 12 oz. pail w/bail handle, marked in oval "Armour's Veribest Peanut Butter - Armour And Company - General Offices, Chicago," lithographed fairy tale characters shown around sides, product information on lid, Continental Can Co. Chicago, Illinois, minor edge wear rust spotting, scratches & soiling, 3½ " d., 3" h. (ILLUS.) **105**

Peanut oil, Planters Italian 1 gal. tin, decorated w/airplanes, ca. 1930s **963**

Society Brand Peanuts

Peanuts, Society Brand 10 lb. tin, scene of man wooing woman w/peanuts (ILLUS.) **963**

Potato chips, Gordon's tin, round, red panel delivery truck above "'Trucks Serving The Best' - Gordon's Fresh Potato Chips - Net

Gordon's Potato Chip Tin

Wt. One Pound - Made from Potatoes Cooked in Shortening - Salt Added" & "Mfg. by Gordon Foods Inc. Atlanta, Louisville, Birmingham, Memphis, Nashville, Chattanooga, Cincinnati, Roanoke," minor denting, fading, scratches & soiling, 7½ " d., 11½ " h. (ILLUS.). . **72**

Tea, Ferndell - Remus 1 lb.tin, colorful lithographed outdoor scene of Oriental woman on bridge, another woman standing below, many trees in background, marked "Net Weight One-Half Pound - Ferndell - Remus Brand - Tea - Distributed by Sprague, Warner & Co. Chicago, ILL. U.S.A." & "U.S. Trade Mark Reg. No. 116696," 3⅛" w., 5" h. (soiling & water stain) **28**

Tire Tube Patch Tin

Tire tube patch, Favorite tin, scene of lady driving early automobile w/"Self Vulcanizing - Tube Patch - Sticks and Stays Stuck" (ILLUS.) **935**

Tobacco, American Blend pocket tin, made for German immigrant market **1,595**

Tobacco, Cameron tin, lithographed gold & black design on red w/green vertical center band, marked "Fine Tobacco Mix,"

hinged lid, Cameron & Cameron Co., Richmond, VA, 3¼" w., 4½ " l., 2" h. (very minor paint chips to edges, scratches & soiling) **83**

Tobacco, Dill's Best Cut Pug tin, 3¼ x 4¼" **45**

Tobacco, Donniford pocket tin **90**

Forest & Stream Tobacco Tin

Tobacco, Forest & Stream tin, two-sided w/hinged lid, illustrated on both sides w/scene of two fishermen & a dog in a canoe, paper label seal on top, by Imperial Tobacco Co. of Canada Limited Factory No. 1 Port 23-D, paint loss & scratches, rust marks on bottom & lid, ¾ x 3", 4¼" h. (ILLUS.) **385**

Tobacco, Hi-Plane (twin engine) pocket tin **225**

Tobacco, Nigger Hair pail, cylindrical, red & black w/bust profile of African native, 6½ " h. . . **275**

Tobacco, Pedro Cut Plug tin, rectangular w/dome lid & bail handle, lithographed on top & sides showing corn cob pipe on one end & peace pipe on other w/"John Q. Adam 1910 U.S. Inter Rev." & "Factory No. 2 District of MD... Patent Applied for," part of original seal on side, 5 x 7¾", 4½" h. (paint chips, denting, edge wear & soiling) **88**

Tobacco, Stanwik pocket tin **450**

Sure Shot Chewing Tobacco Tin

Tobacco, Sure Shot tin, opens at top w/lithographed scene of Native American w/bow & arrow & marked "Sure Shot - Chewing Tobacco - It Touches The Spot," some denting, edge wear, scratches & soiling, 15½ " w., 10¼" l., 7" h. (ILLUS.). **440**

Tucketts Orinoco Tobacco Tin

Tobacco, Tucketts Orinoco tin, round w/lithographed scene of man sitting & leaning against a tree smoking a pipe, holding a fishing pole, his little dog near his feet, marked "Tucketts Orinoco Cut Coarse" w/"MacDonald Mfg. Co. Limited Toronto" on lid & "Manufactured by the Tuckett Tobacco Co. Limited Hamilton Canada" on bottom, remnants of original seal, paint chips, fading surface rust, scratches, soiling & staining, 4¼" d., 3¾" h. (ILLUS.) **121**

Tobacco, Union Leader tin, two-sided, "Series of 1910" stamp on top, front w/"Union Leader Redi Cut" above bust portrait of Uncle Sam smoking a pipe w/"Tobacco" below, text on back, (original paper seal w/pieces missing, scratches, soiling & rust at bottom inside) **66**

Transmission oil, Iso-Vis tin, screw-on top, bail handle, front w/"Net Weight Fifty Pounds" at top & "Standard Oil Company Indiana" in circle around logo, "Iso - Vis Lubricant" in outer border, product information on other sides, 12" w., 11½ " h., 5 gal. (rest spotting, fading & scratches) **77**

Veterinary medicine, Dr. Roberts Dog Remedy tin **1,595**

CASTORS & CASTOR SETS

Castor bottles were made to hold condiments for table use. Some were produced in sets of several bottles housed in silver plated frames. The word also is sometimes spelled "Caster."

Castor set, a silver plated frame w/central handle & pedestal base w/three clear cordial decanters etched w/grapevines, stand marked by Pairpoint, late 19th c., 10½" h. **$374**

Pickle castor, amber pressed glass Daisy & Button patt. insert, ornate silver plate footed holder w/warrior face feet supporting a flaring holder base w/a high arched handle & tongs at the side, holder

Daisy & Button Pickle Castor

marked by Webster & Sons Plating Co., late 19th c., 9¾" h. (ILLUS.) **395**

Bohemian Ruby Pickle Castor

Pickle castor, Bohemian ruby-stained & leaf-etched insert, clear pleated base, in silver plate holder w/plain round foot & tall arched & scroll-pierced handle, tongs at the side, late 19th c. (ILLUS.) **700**

Decorated Cobalt Blue Pickle Castor

Pickle castor, Cobalt blue mold-blown glass insert, squatty bulbous shape w/Inverted Thumbprint patt. & dotted blossom enameling, in a footed silver plate holder w/high arched handle & tongs at the side, late 19th c. (ILLUS.) **800**

Cranberry Glass Pickle Castor

Pickle castor, cranberry Inverted
Thumbprint waisted cylindrical insert,
silver plate holder w/round lacy scalloped
base rim, tall conforming arched handle
w/scrolled top & cover w/tall flame-form
finial, tongs at the side, late 19th c. (ILLUS.) . . **525**

Pickle castor, cranberry pear-shaped
Inverted Thumbprint patt. insert
decorated w/a cluster of blue & white
blossoms, in an ornate silver plate frame
w/high arched handle, silver plate lid
added, 9½ " h. **460**

Mother-of-Pearl Satin Pickle Castor

Pickle castor, mother-of-pearl satin glass
Raindrop patt. cylindrical insert, ornate
silver plate holder w/square base raised
on four pierced tab feet, tall squared
handle w/a pointed pierced arch finial, a
pair of tongs on each side, late 19th c.,
overall 13½ " h. (ILLUS.) **750**

Pickle castor, Rubina mold-blown glass
Inverted Thumbprint waisted cylindrical
inset decorated w/ornate enameled blue
flowering vines w/green leaves, in an
ornate silver plate domed & footed frame
w/arched overhead handle decorated w/a
pierced design of a round fan & small
owl, w/pickle fork, Derby marked frame,
11¾ " h. **546**

Vaseline Glass Pickle Castor

Pickle castor, vaseline mold-blown squatty
flaring glass insert, silver plate holder
w/high scrolled legs, high incurved
handles w/an angled finial, tongs at the
side, late 19th c. (ILLUS.). **625**

Pickle castor, Rubina glass insert w/swelled
base tapering to tall cylindrical sides
decorated w/enameled blue daisies &
white & orange florals, in an ornate silver
plate Rockford Silver Plate Co. frame
w/pierced bow-form finial on the arched
handle, swelled cylindrical base & original
tongs at the side, overall 11½ " h. **625**

CAT COLLECTIBLES

BOTTLES

Advertising, clear glass embossed "Black
Cat Stove Enamel New York NY," 6¼" h. **$15**

FIGURAL ITEMS

Bisque, contemporary black cat w/textured
aqua paint finish, Hagen Renaker paper
label, ca. 1950-60, 3¾" h. **55**

Siamese Cat Figure

Ceramic, bisque, Seal Point Siamese group,
three cats w/turquoise rhinestone eyes,
one w/pink rhinestone collar, ca. 1950s,
4¾" h. to 7¼" h., the set (ILLUS. of one) **55**

Ceramic, three pink kittens on a Victorian-style sofa stamped "©1950 Bradley Ormico & Bradley," Japan paper label, 4" h. . . . **25**

Ceramic, Seal Point Siamese, Lefton Japan paper label, ca. 1960s, 5" l., 4½" h. **30**

Ceramic, "Mischief," a black & white striped & an orange & white striped tabby w/a pitcher of spilled milk, by Gaile Ferretti for Franklin Mint, 1986, 6¼" h., the group **85**

Chalkware, Persian cat, 7½" h. **55**

Glass, clear crystal, No. 5165, Fenton paper label, 3¾" h. **18**

Glass, gold under clear, applied black bow & facial details, Murano, Italy, ca. 1950s, 5" h. **145**

Glass, full leaded crystal, Thumbprint patt., Barthmann Cristall W. Germany paper label, 7½" h. **135**

Porcelain, grey & white cat looking to right, probably by J.J. Kaendler, Meissen, Germany, ca. 1750, 2¼" h. **2,800**

Porcelain, white cat w/brown spots, looking to left, probably by J.J. Kaendler, Meissen, Germany, ca. 1750, 2¼" h. **2,500**

Porcelain, cat & dog playing in a black boot, incised & stamped "Japan," 4¼" l. **35**

Porcelain, white w/high glaze cat, laying down w/a flower petal settled on its backside, marked "Heubach Gebr Lichte Thuringia," ca. 1900, 5" l. **110**

Porcelain, figure of a harlequin w/bird & cat alongside, J.F. Eberlein, Meissen, Germany, ca. 1745, 5¼" h. **15,000**

Porcelain, cat resting w/four legs outstretched, probably by J.J. Kaendler, Meissen, Germany, ca. 1750, 5¾" l., 4" h. . . **4,200**

Porcelain, "The Wizard," HN 2877, a black cat sits at the wizard's feet, Royal Doulton, 8¾" h. **320**

Pottery, white Persian cat w/grey specks, plastic eyes, "Sparklers" line, incised "Roselane USA," 1950s, 3½" h. **75**

MISCELLANEOUS

Doorstop, cement, white Persian cat w/green eyes, unmarked, 10" l. **40**

Glasses, frosted glass w/black & gold painted cats, applied rhinestone collars, "L" Libby hallmark, ca. 1940s, 8" h., set of 8 . . . . **125**

Humidor, ceramic figural cat head w/blue hat & collar, majolica, 4¼" h. **415**

Humidor, ceramic, cat-shaped, blue ribbon & bow w/two mice, majolica, 6½" h. **770**

Letter opener, brass cat w/arched back at top, marked "England," 9" l. **54**

Mug, ceramic, white cat face-shaped w/dark blue floral collar & handle, incised "Avon," 3¾" h. (ILLUS.). **18**

Avon Mug

Pitcher, ceramic, decorated w/cartoon cats by Souter & "East West Hames Best," ca. 1905-1914, 7" h. **950**

Pitcher, jug-type, ceramic, Heraldic & Grotesque Animals line, decorated w/ cats rampant & passant & motto "May we kiss whom we please and please whom we kiss," Royal Doulton, ca. 1914, 7½" h. **750**

Purse, wooden w/Siamese cat, gold & clear colored jewel florals, marked "Sophistikit," Enid Collins, © ec, 1964. . . . . **75**

Child's Jigsaw Puzzle

Puzzle, child's jigsaw-type, yellow cat in sailor outfit playing concertina, 10½ x 14" (ILLUS.) **10**

String holder, chalkware, black & cream cat face, blue ball of string, stamped "James [illegible] Chicago, IL.," 6½" h. **65**

Tray, metal, gold w/thin aqua border, center w/h.p. Seal Point Siamese cats, artist-signed, 15 x 21" **65**

Wall plaque, chalkware, pierced to hang, black & white cat face, red ears & bow, green eyes, 6½" h. **45**

PLANTERS

Ceramic, two cats & a basket, Lefton, Japan paper label **25**

Pottery, light green pot w/red rim w/attached curled up sleeping cat in shades of green, American Bisque **30**

Pottery, stylized laughing cat, Cactus line, Weller Pottery script mark, 6" l., 5" h. **75**

Pottery, cat sitting near a sleeping dog, green, unmarked, 7½" l. **38**

Courtesy of Skinner, Inc., Bolton, Massachusetts

Royal Doulton Chocolate Set

CERAMICS

ABINGDON

Abingdon Mark

From about 1934 until 1950, Abingdon Pottery Company, Abingdon, Illinois, manufactured decorative pottery, mainly cookie jars, flowerpots and vases. Decorated with various glazes, these items are becoming popular with collectors who are especially attracted to Abingdon's novelty cookie jars.

Book ends, model of a seagull, No. 305, ivory glaze, 6" h., pr. **$168**
Book ends/planters, figural dolphin, No. 444D, blue glaze, 5¾" h., pr. **65**
Cookie jar, Choo Choo, No. 651D, 7½" h. **100**
Cookie jar, Money Bag, No. 588D, 7½" h. **40**
Cookie jar, Pumpkin, No. 674D, 8" h. **550**
Cookie jar, Three Bears, No. 696D, 8¾" h., (light hairline in lid) **40**
Cookie jar, Pineapple, No. 664D, 10½" h. **100**
Cookie jar, Miss Muffet, No. 662D, 11" h. **350**
Cookie jar, Wigwam, No. 665D, 11" h. **450**
Cookie jar, Bo Peep, No. 694D, 12" h. **425**
Cookie jar, Mother Goose, No. 695D, 12" h. (ILLUS.) **550**

Mother Goose Cookie Jar

Model of a heron, No. 574, tan glaze, 5¼" h. **68**
Model of a peacock, No. 416, turquoise glaze, 7" h. **96**

AMERICAN PAINTED PORCELAIN

During the late Victorian era American artisans produced thousands of hand-painted porcelain items, including tableware, dresser sets, desk sets, and bric-a-brac. These pieces of porcelain were imported, and usually bear the marks of foreign factories and countries. To learn more about identification, evaluation, history, and appraisal, the following books and newsletter by Dorothy Kamm are recommended: American Painted Porcelain: Collector's Identification & Value Guide, Comprehensive Guide to American Painted Porcelain, *and* Dorothy Kamm's Porcelain Collector's Companion.

Ashtray, decorated w/three panels of a conventional-style floral motif on a gradating yellow to brown ground, w/burnished gold rim & lip, signed "E. W. Misner" & marked "Germany," ca. 1891-1914, 1½" h., 3⅞" d. **$35**

Berry bowl & underplate: 2 pcs., embossed scrolled & gilded rims, pierced bowl w/three gilded feet, decorated w/currants on a pompadour & pale green ground, signed "L.B.S." & marked "T & V, Limoges, France," ca. 1892-1907, bowl, 6⅞" d., 3¾" h.; plate, 7¾" d. **135**

Berry spoon holder, w/pierced handles, decorated w/two clusters of blackberries, leaves, & pink blossoms, pale blue border band, ivory center, w/burnished gold rim & handles, marked "Bavaria," ca. 1891-1914, 4⅝" x 10". **45**

Blotter corners, 4 triangular pieces, each decorated w/a cluster of multi-colored flowers, burnished gold rims, signed "AD," ca. 1900-1925, 3 x 3 x 4¼" **50**

Bonbon box, decorated w/yellow roses & greenery on an ivory ground, w/burnished gold rims & bands, signed "R. STMD" & marked "ADK, Limoges, France," ca. 1890s-1910, 4½" h., 8" d. **225**

Bone dish, crescent-shaped, decorated w/seashells & seaweeds in pastel colors, burnished gold border, ca. 1890-1915, 6⅝" w. **25**

Cake plate, w/pierced handles, decorated w/platinum wild carrot design, scrolls, rim, & handles, signed "E.C.B." & marked "Germany," ca. 1891-1914, 9½" d. **55**

Cake plate or cookie tray, individual-size, w/pierced handles, decorated w/conventional-style florals & basket motifs, w/burnished gold rim & handles, signed "Edith Kredell" & marked "UNO-IT, Favorite, Bavaria," ca. 1910-1920, 6¾" d. **30**

Candlestick, w/bands of delicate pale pink roses & leaves, burnished gold top, bottom rim, & banding, signed "C. M. Fritz," ca. 1880-1900, 7" h. **75**

Celery dish, decorated w/posies of pale pink roses & forget-me-nots, pale blue border, ivory center, white enamel embellishments, signed "McKee" & marked with Royal wreath, "O.& E. G., Austria," ca. 1899-1918, 5¼" x 12" **55**

Coffeepot, cov., decorated at the top w/clusters of pink wild roses & leaves, body covered in pale pink, w/burnished gold borders, handle, finial & spout,

Coffeepot with Wild Roses

marked w/"W. G. & Co., Limoges, France," ca. 1900-1932, holds 16 oz, 7" h. (ILLUS.) **75**

Cookie basket, decorated w/border design of daises on a lemon ground, w/burnished gold border & handle, signed "Alice Kiss, Nov. 1920" & marked "Noritake, Nippon," 2½" h. x 5¼ x 7¼ **60**

Cruet w/stopper, decorated w/clusters of forget-me-nots & leaves, upper body pale blue, lower half ivory, w/burnished gold rim, inside lip, handle, & stopper, marked w/Royal wreath, "O. & E. G., Austria," ca. 1899-1918, 6½" h. **80**

Cup & saucer, decorated w/naturalistic-style nasturtiums in yellows & yellow reds on a pale green ground, w/burnished gold rims & handle, marked "Haviland, Limoges, France," ca. 1894-1931 . . . . **35**

Dresser set: tray, puff box, hair receiver, & pair of candlesticks, 5-pc. set, decorated w/border design of yellow primrose on an ivory ground, w/burnished gold rims & feet, signed "Steve" & marked w/various manufacturer's marks, ca. 1905-1925, tray: 7½ x 11, puff box & hair receiver: 3½" h., 5" d, candlesticks: 5⅛" h. **325**

Egg cups, double, decorated w/border design of naturalistic daisies, moss green border rims, ivory body, ca. 1890-1920, 3⅜" h., set of 6 . . . . **125**

Ewer with Dragon Handle

Ewer, dragon-handled, decorated w/pink mountain primrose & leaves, matte ivory ground, burnished gold handle, neck & base, signed "K. B. R.," ca. 1880-1890, 9¼" h. (ILLUS.)............................ **125**

Fruit bowl, decorated w/cherries on a multi-colored pastel ground, w/burnished gold rim, marked w/crowned double-headed bird, "MZ, Austria," ca. 1884-1909, 2⅝" h, 9¼" d. **85**

Gravy boat, w/attached plate, decorated w/clusters of naturalistic pink roses & greenery, light green border bands rimmed w/burnished gold, w/burnished gold monogram, signed "R. G." & marked "Haviland, France," ca. 1894-1931, 3½" x 6 x 8½" **65**

Hair receiver & puff box, 2-pc. set, decorated w/pastel pink roses on a pale blue & yellow ground, w/burnished gold knob & rim, signed "Al" & marked "T & V, Limoges, France," ca. 1892-1907, 3" h., 4¼" d. **175**

Jelly jar, yellow roses on a dark brown & yellow ground, w/burnished gold rims, knob & foot, ca. 1905-1920, 3¼" d., 4⅞" h. **50**

Mayonnaise bowl, w/attached plate, decorated w/geometric border design in dark blues, w/yellow, yellow red & blue enamel accents, ivory ground, burnished gold borders, signed "E. H. Hall" & marked "Haviland, France," ca. 1894-1931, 2¼" h. x 5⅝" d. **30**

Mustard pot w/spoon, decorated w/maidenhair ferns, burnished gold handles on lid & pot, signed "E. M. B. S." & marked w/a wreath & star, "R. S. Germany," ca. 1904-1938, 2½" d., 3" h....... **45**

Nut bowl, bulbous shape w/undulating rim, decorated w/acorns & leaves on a background ranging from yellow to brown, w/yellow luster interior, signed "A. Mueller, '07," 2" h., 5½" d.............. **45**

Perfume bottle, bulbous base, tapered neck, decorated w/pale pink wild roses & leaves on a pale pink ground, w/burnished gold rim, marked "W. G. & Co., Limoges, France," ca. 1900-1932, 2½" d., 4¾" h..................... **75**

Pin tray, decorated w/pastel floral garlands, border design of gilded raised paste scrolls & lattice design, stamped "Leonard" in a circle & marked "Vienna, Austria," ca. 1908, 4¾" sq................. **50**

Pitcher, lemonade, bulbous shape, decorated on upper half w/conventional-style crab apples & leaves on a burnished gold ground, light apple green ground on lower part of body, w/burnished gold beaded handle, ca. 1910-1920, 5¾" h. **225**

Plaque of Lady with White Fur

Plaque, framed, portrait of fashionable lady w/white fur boa, pink coat, & pink ostrich feather plumed hat, signed "A. J. Riley" & marked "W. G. & C., France," ca. 900-1915, 3⅛" w. 3⅞" h. (ILLUS.) **175**

Plaque of Colonial Lady

Plaque, embossed ribbon border pierced for hanging, portrait of colonial lady, w/burnished gold rim, signed "Ella T. Hissrich, 1912" & marked "CFH/GDM, France," 3⅝" w., 4⅞" h. (ILLUS.) **175**

Plate, 6⅜" d., dessert, central design of pastel garden landscape, pale blue border rimmed with pink floral swags, ca. 1910-1920 .... **28**

Plate, 7½" d., decorated w/conventional-style yellow red & yellow tulips & leaves on an ivory ground, w/burnished gold border & outlines, signed "Wight" & marked w/a crown, "H & Co., Selb, Bavaria," ca. 1911-1934 .... **40**

Plate, 8½" d., decorated w/border design of pastel-colored, conventional-style fans & cherry blossoms on a black & burnished gold border ground, signed "Mamie Stuber" & marked "Thomas, Sevres, Bavaria," ca. 1908 .... **50**

Plate with Roses

Plate, 9⅛" d., central design of naturalistic pink roses & greenery on a multi-colored pastel ground, rim bordered w/pink rose swags, w/burnished gold scrollwork, rim, bands, & border designs, signed "Xmas 1903" & marked "H & Co., Limoges, France" (ILLUS.)........................ **65**

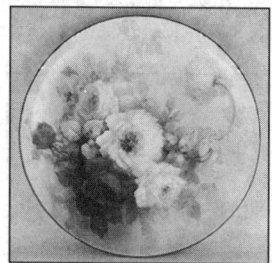

Chop Plate with Large Rose Cluster

Plate, chop (charger), 14¼" d., back pierced for hanging, yellow, pink, & ruby roses & greenery on a pastel blue & yellow ground, signed "L.R.P., Jan. 1900" & marked "D & Co., Limoges, France" (ILLUS.) .. **500**

Punch bowl & stand, decorated w/naturalistic purple grapes & leaves on a pale yellow & green ground, w/burnished gold rim & feet, signed "Sandwich", bowl marked "Favorite, Bavaria," stand marked "D & Co., Limoges, France," ca. 1908-1918, bowl 9½" d., stand 6½" h............. **450**

Ramekin & plate, ruffled edge, decorated w/dainty border design of ruby roses & forget-me-nots, w/bands of burnished gold scrolls & rims, pale green ground, signed "Walters" & marked with a bird, "CT," ca. 1899-1918, ramekin 4⅜" d., 1½" h., plate 5³⁄₁₆" d................ **45**

Ring stand, decorated w/ruby roses on a ground of pastel polychrome colors, w/burnished gold hand & border, marked "T & V, Depose, Limoges, France," ca. 1892-1907, 3¾" d., 2⅞" h. **55**

Salt dip, cauldron-shaped, three-footed, decorated w/border design of naturalistic forget-me-nots on the inside, raised paste scrolled & latticed border covered

w/burnished gold on the outside, ivory ground, marked "T & V, Limoges, France," ca. 1892-1907, 2¾" d. **30**

Salt & pepper shakers, delicate design of oranges & vines, ivory body, yellow-brown top & base rim, w/burnished gold bands; signed "H. B. Hill, Saratoga, N.Y." & marked w/Royal wreath, "O. & E. G., Austria," ca. 1908-1915, 2" d., 3" h. **35**

Sandwich Tray

Sandwich tray, double handled, decorated w/clusters of lilacs & leaves on a pastel polychrome ground, w/burnished gold border, rim & handles, marked w/a crowned double-headed bird, "MZ, Austria," ca. 1884-1909, 6¼" x 19¾" (ILLUS.) **150**

Shaving Mug

Shaving mug, decorated w/Art Nouveau conventional-style border design & monogram in red, green, & burnished gold outlined in black, pale yellow brown ground, w/burnished gold bands, rim, foot, & handle, signed "Oct. 31 '09, Elisabeth" & "JG," 3½" d., 3⅝" h. (ILLUS.)..... **55**

Stein with Geese

Stein, decorated w/a gaggle of geese in a forest landscape, signed "Cora Wright" & marked "T & V," 3½" d., 5⅛" h. (ILLUS.) **95**

Sugar & creamer, decorated w/panels of
conventional-style flowers in pastel-
colored enamels, burnished gold rims,
handle, & beaded borders, marked
"Favorite, Bavaria," ca. 1908-1918 40

Sugar shaker, decorated w/pink roses &
leaves on a pale green & ivory ground,
w/white enamel scrolls & burnished gold
pierced top, signed "E. W. Lawer, B29,"
ca. 1900-1930, 2¾" d., 4½" h. 75

Talcum powder shaker, decorated w/pink
& ruby roses & greenery on an ivory
ground, w/burnished gold top & base,
signed "M. Perl" & marked "Favorite,
Bavaria," ca. 1908-1920, 2" d., 5" h. 95

Teapot stand, decorated w/conventional-
style cherry design, signed "M. H.
WENTE, 1916" & marked w/crown &
shield, "Bavaria," 6¾" d. 45

Tea set: 4 pcs., round tray, sugar, creamer,
& teapot, decorated w/dainty pink roses,
pale blue rim, ivory center on tray & body,
separated by stepped burnished gold
borders, w/burnished gold handles, rims,
& spout, signed "C. E. Tolehard, 1914" &
marked w/crowned double headed bird,
"MZ, Austria," tray 11¼" d., teapot
holds 24 oz. 275

Tobacco jar, decorated w/a geometric
design in browns, pale blue, & pale
yellow, w/burnished gold knob, signed
"Convent, Key West, Fla" & marked "T &
V, Limoges, France," ca. 1892-1907,
5" d., 7½" h. 295

Toothpick Holder

Toothpick holder, decorated w/delicate
clusters of pink roses & leaves on an
ivory ground, mother-of-pearl luster
interior, w/burnished gold center band,
monogram, & rim, signed "V. Ogmeiner"
& marked "HR" in a circle,
"Hutschenreuther, Selb, Bavaria,"
ca. 1891-1920, 1¾" d., 1¾" h. (ILLUS.) 55

Vase, 6⅛" h., double-handled, bulbous
base, tapered sides, decorated
w/naturalistic-style violets on a violet &
ivory ground, w/burnished gold handles &
rim, signed "E. Sprecht," ca. 1880s 55

Vase, 10¾" h., tapered sides, decorated
w/naturalistic wild carrots on a
polychrome ground, burnished gold rim,
signed "M J Leber, 1915" & marked w/a
crown, "H & Co., Selb, Bavaria" 175

Whiskey set: 8 pcs., oval tray, jug, & 6
cups; clusters of corn & leaves on an
ivory & pompadour ground, w/burnished
gold rims & handle, signed "SURQUIST,"
jug marked w/crown & 2 shields, "Vienna,
Austria," cups marked "PP, La Seynie,
Limoges, France," ca. 1903-1917, oval
tray 12 x 8", jug 6½" h., cups 1⅝" d., 2⅛" h. . . . **400**

AUSTRIAN

Austrian Marks

*Numerous potteries in Austria produced
good-quality ceramic wares over many years.
Some factories were established by American
entrepreneurs, particularly in the Carlsbad area,
and other factories made china under special
brand names for American importers. Marks on
various pieces are indicated in many listings.*

Cake plate, open-handled, portrait of
woman w/flowing hair, Imperial, 11" d. **$13**

Cracker jar, cov., Kaufmann scene on
cobalt blue ground, 20th c., beehive mark 165

Dessert set: 8½" plate & four matching 6"
plates; Kaufman transfers, cobalt w/gold
borders, the set (Victoria, Austria) 72

Dish, figural, Art Nouveau style, flaring
oblong shallow form w/a shoulder-length
model of a lady w/flowing hair along one
edge, her arms spread clutching an
applied flower among large waterlilies,
creamy tan & pale green, impressed &
stamped mark, 8" l. (minor rim roughness) . . . 209

Figurine, porcelain figure of a woman
w/raised arms in a black lace evening
gown & cranberry-colored cape, marked
"Victoria - Carlsbad - Austria," 13" h. 460

Fish set: 18" platter & eight 8½" d. plates;
decorated w/different colorful fish centers,
shell & floral raised Rococo borders,
9 pcs. (Imperial - Austria Crown China) 500

Mug, scuttle-shaped, cobalt blue w/floral
decoration. 88

Plate, 8" d., decorated w/sprays of pink
roses (M.Z. Austria) 48

Plate, 8½" d., portrait scene of shepherd &
woman, blue & gold border 17

Vase, 9¾" h., footed, rose painted w/cobalt,
yellow, green & brown background, artist-
signed, marked "Vienna, Austria" **83**

Vase, 12" h., simple cylindrical body, h.p.
w/large pink, red & yellow roses & green
leaves on a shaded ground, artist-signed,
base marked "Vienna Austria" **173**

Vase, 18" h., pedestal base, swan handles,
much openwork, decorated w/purple,
green & yellow flowers ("R.H." Austria) **285**

Austrian Portrait Vase

Vase, 25" h., Art Nouveau style, tall ovoid
body w/slender cylindrical neck & flared
rim w/portrait of young woman in oval
reserve surrounded by floral decoration,
flared foot on square base w/bronze
mounts, artist-signed "Wagner," 20th c.
(ILLUS.) **3,680**

BAUER

Bauer Mark

The Bauer Pottery was moved to Los Angeles, California from Paducah, Kentucky, in 1909, in the hope that the climate would prove beneficial to the principal organizer, John Andrew Bauer, who suffered from severe asthma. Flowerpots, made of California adobe clay, were the first production at the new location, but soon they

were able to resume production of stoneware crocks and jugs, the mainstay of the Kentucky operation. In the early 1930s, Bauer's colorfully glazed earthen dinnerwares, especially the popular Ring-Ware pattern, became an immediate success. Sometimes confused with its imitator, Fiesta Ware (first registered by Homer Laughlin in 1937), Bauer pottery is collectible in its own right and is especially popular with West Coast collectors. Bauer Pottery ceased operation in 1962.

Baby mug, Plainware, yellow, 8 oz. **$60**

Baking dish, cov., Ring-Ware patt.,
orange/red, 4" d. **55**

Bowl, berry, 4" d., Ring-Ware patt., burgundy **50**

Bowl, cereal, 4½" d., Ring-Ware patt., jade
green **55**

Bowl, 12" d., Ring-Ware, yellow **65**

Carafe w/original cap, Plainware, jade glaze **75**

Coffee server, cov., Plain Ware, green **75**

Cookie jar, cov., Ring-Ware patt., yellow **995**

Creamer, Plain Ware, green **65**

Creamer, Ring-Ware patt., jade green **55**

Creamer, Ring-Ware patt., yellow, small **45**

Creamer & cov. sugar bowl, Monterey
patt., white, pr. **75**

Creamer & cov. sugar bowl, Ring-Ware
patt., orange/red, small, pr. **95**

Mixing bowl, Ring-Ware patt., No. 18, jade
green **75**

Model of duck, w/head up, white, 3 x 4½" **45**

Model of hippo, Cal-Art line, white glaze,
ca. 1941 . . . . **375**

Nappy, Ring-Ware, green, No. 8 . . . . **55**

Planter, figural swan, white, 2½ x 6" **110**

Planter, figural swan, white, 3 x 9" **120**

Plate, butter, 4½" d., Plain Ware, yellow **80**

Plate, 9" d., Ring-Ware patt., black **85**

Plate, 9" d., Ring-Ware patt., grey **65**

Plate, chop, 12" d., Ring-Ware patt., green **75**

Plate, chop, 12" d., Ring-Ware patt., yellow **75**

Plate, chop, 13" d., Monterey patt., decorated . . . **175**

Platter, 12" oval, Ring-Ware, green, No. 8 . . . . . . **70**

Pudding cup, No. 3, jade glaze **65**

Pumpkin bowl, No. 513, matte pink w/gold
trim, ca. 1950s, Tracy Irwin, 6½ x 10" **125**

Salt box, w/wooden cover, white
w/strawberry decoration **240**

Salt & pepper shakers, beehive-shaped,
Ring-Ware patt., orange/red, pr. **50**

Soup bowl, lug-handled, Ring-Ware, cobalt
blue, 5½" d. **85**

Teapot, cov., individual size, Plain patt., yellow . . . **85**

Teapot, cov., Ring-Ware patt., yellow **185**

Vegetable bowl, oval w/end handles,
yellow, 5" l. **85**

BAVARIAN

Ceramics have been produced by various potteries in Bavaria, Germany, for many years. Those appearing for sale in greatest frequency today were produced in the 19th and early 20th centuries. Various company marks are indicated with some listings here.

Bowl, 9" d., ribbed mold decorated w/tulips on green & gold ground, marked "R.C. Bavaria, Claire"........................ **$28**

Bowl, 10" d., center portrait of woman on cobalt blue w/gold border, marked "RC Alice Bavaria".......................... **220**

Box, cov., the lid depicting a figural female nude reclining on a sofa, marked "Bavaria," 6" l............................ **66**

Bavarian Cake Plate

Cake plate, slightly scalloped round form w/pierced rim handles, decorated w/h.p. pink roses & green leaves on green tinted center, gold trim on rim & gold scrolls near handles, 11" d. (ILLUS.) .... **70 to 80**

Dinner service: service for 12 including 9½" dinner plates, 7½" salad plates, 6" bread & butter plates, fruit bowls, soup plates, two-handled bouillon cups & saucers, 18 cups & saucers, 12 demitasse sets, cov. coffeepot, cov. teapot, creamer & sugar bowl sets, various platters & serving pieces; "Empress Dresden Flowers" patt., floral borders & a central bouquet & scattered blossoms, marked "Bavaria Schumann, Arzberg, Germany," 20th c., 147 pcs............................... **4,600**

Dresser set: cov. box, cov. powder jar, cov. hair receiver, two hatpin holders, a pair of candlesticks & a pin tray; each w/a simple form & h.p. w/poppies on a peach ground, late 19th - early 20th c., the set...... **316**

Game plates, decorated w/center scene of various ground fowl on burgundy background w/gold scrolled border, marked "S.T.W. Bavaria Germany" & blue beehive mark, 11" d., set of 3............. **110**

Pitcher, tankard, 11" h., decorated w/h.p. strawberries, gold trim **265**

Toothpick holder, figural shell, pearlized finish, marked "Bavaria" **143**

Vase, 14" h., footed ovoid body tapering to tall cylindrical neck w/flared rim, Bird of Paradise decoration, marked "C.T. Hutchenreuther, Bavaria, Germany" **33**

BELLEEK

Irish Belleek Mark

Belleek china has been made in Ireland's County Fermanagh for many years. It is exceedingly thin porcelain. Several marks were used, including a hound and harp (1865-1880), and a hound, harp and castle (1863-1891). A printed hound, harp and castle with the words "Co. Fermanagh Ireland" constitutes the mark from 1891. Belleek-type china also was made in the United States last century by several firms, including Ceramic Art Company, Columbian Art Pottery, Lenox Inc., Ott & Brewer and Willets Manufacturing Co.

IRISH BELLEEK

Bowl, 4¾" d., 4" h., six-scallop rim, Shells & Seaweed patt., lustre interior, green mark **$60**

Bread plate, Shamrock patt., green handles, 3rd green mark, 10⅝" d. **130**

Creamer, Fishscale patt., 4¼" h., green mark **55**

Creamer & open sugar bowl, Shamrock-Basketweave patt., creamer 3" h., sugar 2½" h., green mark, pr.................... **100**

Cup & saucer, demitasse, Shamrock patt., cup 3" d., saucer 4½" d., green mark......... **65**

Cup & saucer, Shell patt., 3rd black mark **85**

Cup & saucer, Tridacna patt., pink-trimmed, 2nd black mark **85**

Dish, leaf-shaped, 5 x 5¼", green mark **30**

Model of a swan, 2nd green mark, 4¾ x 5¾" **80**

Mug, coffee, Shamrock-Basketweave patt., 4" h., green mark **60**

Plate, 5⅞" d., Grass Tea Ware, 1st black mark .. **200**

Plate, 8" d., Shell patt., 3rd black mark.......... **85**

Plate, 10½" d., Shamrock-Basketweave patt., green mark **38**

Spill, Shamrock patt., 3rd black mark, 5¼" h..... **100**

Tea set: cov. teapot, open sugar bowl, creamer, two cups & saucers & undertray; Neptune patt., pink-trimmed, 2nd black mark, the set (tiny chip on rim of teapot spout opening, worn mark on one saucer) **1,700**

Teapot, cov., Limpet patt., 3rd black mark **310**

BENNINGTON

Bennington Marks

Bennington wares, which ranged from stoneware to parian and porcelain, were made in Bennington, Vermont, primarily in two potteries, one in which Captain John Norton and his descendants were principals, and the other in which Christopher Webber Fenton (also once associated with the Nortons) was a principal. Various marks are found on the wares made in the two major potteries, including J. & E. Norton, E. & L. P. Norton, L. Norton & Co., Norton & Fenton, Edward Norton, Lyman Fenton & Co., Fenton's Works, United States Pottery Co., U.S.P. and others. The popular pottery with the mottled brown on yellowware glaze was also produced in Bennington, but such wares should be referred to as "Rockingham" or "Bennington-type" unless they can be specifically attributed to a Bennington, Vermont factory.

Book flask, binding embossed "Life of Kossuth" w/impressed "J," Flint Enamel glaze, 5¾" h. (very minor hairline) **$489**

Bottle, figural, barrel-shaped standing Mr. Toby, mottled Flint Enamel glaze, ca. 1849-58, 10¾" h. (minor chips) **1,610**

Butter churn, stoneware, w/molded rim & eared handles, large slip-quilled stylized floral design, bright Bennington blue, "J. & E. Norton, Bennington, VT," ca. 1859, 3 gal., 15½" h. (restoration to age line but not in blue) **715**

Cake crock, stoneware, cylindrical w/molded rim & eared handles, thick blue & large stylized flower design fills the entire front, "J. Norton & Co., Bennington, VT," ca. 1859, 1½ gal., 7¼" h. (short hairline & rim chip in front & full length tight line on side) **770**

Crock, stoneware, cylindrical w/molded rim & eared handles, slip-quilled stylized floral design, "E & LP Bennington, VT," ca. 1870, 2 gal., 9" h. (surface chip on rim in back) **165**

Crock, stoneware, cylindrical w/molded rim & eared handles, slip-quilled thick blue double flower design, "J. & E. Norton, Bennington, VT," ca. 1859, 3 gal., 10" h. (long J-shaped tight hairline from rim to right of flower) **358**

Crock, stoneware, ovoid w/molded rim & eared handles, brilliant slip-quilled thick cobalt blue flower design, "J. & E.

Norton, Bennington, VT," ca. 1859, 2 gal., 10½" h. (grease stain spot on back) **853**

Crock with Double Flower

Crock, stoneware, ovoid w/molded rim & eared handles, large slip-quilled cobalt blue double flower design, bold cobalt blue, "J. & E. Norton, Bennington, VT," ca. 1855, professional restoration to long j-shaped line in front, through blue & long straight line from rim on back, 4 gal., 13¾" h. (ILLUS) **413**

Cuspidor, squatty waisted paneled form, mottled brown Rockingham glaze, impressed "1849" mark, 9" d. **110**

Jug, stoneware, cobalt decorated jug, impressed mark "L. Norton Co., Bennington, Vermont," double-feather decoration, mid-19th c., 15" h. (minor chip) **230**

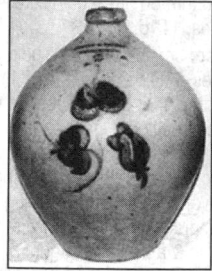

Bennington Jug with Brushed Flowers

Jug, stoneware, ovoid w/brushed cobalt blue triple flower design, "Norton & Fenton, Bennington, VT," ca. 1845, glued chip at spout & some clay discoloration, appears to be in making, 2 gal., 12½" h. (ILLUS.) **385**

Jug, stoneware, semi-ovoid w/bright blue stylized floral design, "J. & E. Norton, Bennington, VT," ca. 1859, 3 gal., 15" h. (some stains from use) **385**

Jug, stoneware, semi-ovoid w/slip-quilled large cobalt blue dotted peacock on stump, "J. & E. Norton, Bennington, VT," ca. 1859, 3 gal., 15" h. (professional restoration to handle) **2,970**

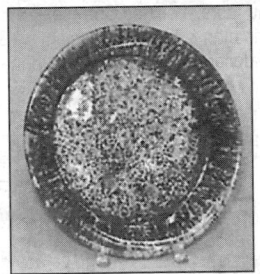

Bennington Pie Plate

Pie plate, wide flat bottom w/flaring rim,
mottled brown Rockingham glaze,
impressed "1849," 11⅞" d. (ILLUS.) 963

Pitcher, 9¾" h., Parian, Wild Rose patt.,
applied molded label "Fenton's Works,
Bennington, Vermont" 605

Toby bottle, overall mottled brown
Rockingham glaze, marked on base, 10½" h. . . . 460

Toby jar, seated Mr. Toby w/an overall light
green sponging w/brownish amber
interior, impressed "1849" mark, 4½" h.
(hat has chips on inner flange) 660

BERLIN (KPM)

*The mark, KPM, was used at Meissen from
1724 to 1725, and was later adopted by the
Royal Factory, Konigliche Porzellan
Manufaktur, in Berlin. At various periods it has
been incorporated with the Brandenburg sceptre,
the Prussian eagle or the crowned globe. The
same letters were also adopted by other factories
in Germany in the late 19th and early 20th
centuries. With the end of the German monarchy
in 1918, the name of the firm was changed to
Staatliche Porzellan Manufaktur and though
production was halted during World War II, the
factory was rebuilt and is still in business. The
exquisite paintings on porcelain were produced
at the close of the 19th century and are eagerly
sought by collectors today.*

Basket, fruit, pierced flaring rim w/enameled
floral design on pink ground, late 19th c.,
Germany, 7¾" h. $288

Charger, round, enameled floral decoration
w/a scrolled gilt rim, "K.P.M." back mark,
late 19th c., 15¾" d. 1,725

Coffee service: 10½" h. cov. coffeepot, cov.
sugar bowl, creamer & six 6 cups &
saucers; each decorated w/an armorial
crest & gilt details, late 19th c., printed
marks, the set 920

Cup & saucer, gilt banded borders & foliate
trim w/h.p. center panel depicting a
stately home, titled under base "Blieniche
bei Potsdam," 19th c., Germany, gilt
wear, KPM marks (ILLUS.) 403

Berlin Topographical Cup & Saucer

Figure group, white-glazed, two scantily-
clad children, mounted on a scrolled oval
base, underglaze-blue "K.P.M." mark,
ca. 1900, 5¼" h. **489**

Lamp, figural, tripod base formed as
three winged griffins, the cone shaped
shade w/pierced circular motifs, printed
marks, 19" h. **1,725**

Plaque, oval, three-quarter length portrait of
the Madonna & Child, back impressed
w/"KPM" & sceptre marks, 19th c., 17" h. **5,462**

Plaque, rectangular, a group portrait in
three-quarters length, two young ladies in
Renaissance dress in the foreground w/a
gentleman centered behind them, after
Titian, impressed "KPM" & sceptre marks,
19th c., 10 x 12½" **4,312**

Plaque, rectangular, decorated in color w/a
scene of the Three Muses of Time,
impressed "K.P.M." mark, early 20th c.,
framed, 7½ x 9⅞" **3,220**

Plaque, square, decorated w/an Art Deco
style grove of trees w/a blue cloudy sky in
the background, ca. 1930, 14" w. **1,495**

Plaque, oval, h.p. bust portrait of a lovely
young lady w/long blonde hair wearing a
pink gown, mounted in an ornate pierced
& scroll-carved giltwood frame, plaque
signed "Wagner," back w/"KPM" &
sceptre mark, plaque 5 x 7" **3,450**

Plaque, rectangular, a colorful scene of a
lovely winged angel & infant w/cherubs
descending on a village, mounted in an
ornate hand-carved giltwood frame,
German inscription on the back & a
"KPM" & sceptre mark, plaque 6¼ x 9¼" . . . **4,600**

Berlin Plaque of the Virgin Mary

Plaque, oval, three-quarter length portrait of
the Virgin Mary flanked by the heads of
angels, after Murrillo, framed, 17" (ILLUS.) . . **6,160**

BISQUE

Bisque is biscuit china, fired a single time but not glazed. Some bisque is decorated with colors. Most abundant from the Victorian era are figures and groups, but other pieces from busts to vases were made by numerous potteries in the U.S. and abroad. Reproductions have been produced for many years so care must be taken when seeking antique originals

Bisque Bust of Young Boy

Bust of a young boy, on a cobalt blue base, after Houdon, France, 16" h. (ILLUS.) **$173**

Candlesticks, two-light, figural, each w/a tan & white tree trunk-form shaft w/a pair of curved arms near the top each ending in a candlecup, one w/a figure of a young girl in a long blue & white dress & bonnet standing to one side of the base, , the other w/a figure of a young boy in a blue & white hat, jacket & kneebreeches, gilt trim, tops separate from base, overall 8½" h., facing pr. **325**

Figure group, a late Victorian gentleman & lady each wearing a bicycle club uniform & riding their safety bicycles, fine hand-decoration, probably France or Germany, late 19th c., 9¼" h. **303**

Figure group, a young lady & gentleman in early 19th c. country-style costume walking under a large greyish blue umbrella, naturalistic coloring, 3⅜" d., 6" h. **145**

Figure of moon-headed man, a seated figure w/his legs straight out to the sides, the large crescent moon head w/a smiling expression & pale yellow tint, his arms holding a tan mandolin, wearing a white suit w/black collar & brown shoes, probably Schafer & Vater, Germany, late 19th - early 20th c., 4" w., 4½" h. **145**

Figures, nodders, a seated Chinese Mandarin man & matching woman, gilt & enamel-decorated, Germany, late 19th - early 20th c., 6¾" h., pr. **633**

Figures, man w/grapes & woman w/rake, 8¾" h., pr. **49**

Seated Bisque Figures

Figures of a boy & girl, seated in cream, tan & green chairs & each dressed in green & white attire w/large green hats, gold shoes & raised gold dot trim on dress, pants & vest, 6¼" h., pr. (ILLUS.) **145**

From left: Bisque Victorian Figures
Bisque Steinbach Dog

Figures of a boy & girl, each dressed in Victorian attire w/yellow hats & jackets w/white floral-decorated skirt or vest, trimmed in gold, blue & brown, each holding a badminton racket, on a round base, facing pr., 2¾" d., 9¼" h., pr. (ILLUS.) **218**

Model of a dog, seated small white Spitz-like dog w/curly coat & a bit of tan around the eyes, orange tongue, marked "Steinbach," 5½" h. (ILLUS.) **135**

Model of dog, Dachshund, 7 x 9½" **300**

Piano baby, crawling, 9½" l., 6¼" h. **425**

Snow baby, seated atop red airplane, Germany. **225**

Vase, 6½" h., fan-form leafy background behind the figures of a Victorian man in a bicycle outfit helping a lady wearing a similar outfit & carrying a basket of flowers who is climbing onto a safety-style bicycle, finely colored, Germany, ca. 1890s **193**

BLUE RIDGE DINNERWARES

Blue Ridge Dinnerwares Mark

The small town of Erwin, Tennessee was the home of the Southern Potteries, Inc., originally founded by E.J. Owen in 1917 and first called the Clinchfield Pottery. In the early 1920s Charles W. Foreman purchased the plant and he revolutionized the company's output, developing the popular line of hand-painted wares sold as "Blue Ridge" dinnerwares. Free-hand painted by women from the surrounding hills, these colorful dishes in many patterns, continued in production until the plant's closing in 1957.

Ashtray, individual, Tralee Rose patt. **$15**

Bonbon, shell-shaped, flat, Nove Rose patt. 65

Bowl, berry, Bountiful patt., large 17

Butter pat/coaster, Lyonnaise patt., 4" d. 45

Cake tray, French Peasant patt., Maple Leaf shape 135

Cake tray, Verna patt., Maple Leaf shape 61

Candy box, cov., Rose Marie patt. 185

Character jug, American Indian 525

Cigarette box, cov., French Peasant patt. 150

Creamer, Mardi Gras patt. 10

Creamer & cov. sugar bowl, Ridge Daisy patt., pr. 19

Cup, Crab Apple patt. 9

Cup, Square Dance patt. 69

Cup & saucer, demitasse, china, Rose Marie patt. 75

Mug, child's, Chanticleer patt. 150

Pie plate, Cassandra patt., wine-colored border 25

Pie plate & server, Cross Stitch patt., 2 pcs 45

Pie server, blue & white lattice design 24

Pitcher, china, decorated w/grapes, Helen shape 80

Pitcher, 5" h., china, Annett's Wild Rose patt., Antique shape 75

Pitcher, 6¼" h., earthenware, Fairmede Fruits patt., Alice shape (small smear on red line trim) 90

Pitcher, 7" h., Sculptured Fruit patt., ... 75

Pitcher, Milady patt. 195

Plate, 6" d., Bluebell Bouquet patt. 4

Plate, 6" sq., "Milkmaid," Provincial Farm Scene, Candlewick shape 50

Plate, dinner, Chanticleer patt. 30

Relish dish, deep shell-shaped, French Peasant patt. 150

Salt & pepper shakers, Dogtooth Violet patt., pr. 65

Salt & pepper shakers, figural Mallard hen & drake, pr. 450

Sugar bowl, cov., Nocturne patt. 12

Teapot, cov., Ball shape, Bluebelle Bouquet patt. 200

Tray, Trellis shape, Daffodil patt. 149

Vase, 5½" h., china, Hampton patt. Hibiscus shape 80

Vase, 9¼" h., ruffle-top style, Delphine patt. 95

Vegetable bowl, cov., Mardi Gras patt. 95

Vegetable bowl, open, round, Ridge Daisy patt. . . . 19

Wall sconce, Rose Marie patt. 250

BLUE & WHITE POTTERY

The category of blue and white or blue and grey pottery includes a wide variety of pottery, earthenware and stoneware items widely produced in this country in the late 19th century right through the 1930s. Originally marketed as inexpensive wares, most pieces featured a white or grey body molded with a fruit, flower or geometric design and then trimmed with bands or splashes of blue to highlight the molded pattern. Pitchers, butter crocks and salt boxes are among the numerous items produced but other kitchenwares and chamber sets are also found. Values vary depending on the rarity of the embossed pattern and the depth of color of the blue trim; the darker the blue, the better. Some entries refer to several different books on Blue and White Pottery. These books are: Blue & White Stoneware, Pottery & Crockery by Edith Harbin (1977, Collector Books, Paducah, KY); Stoneware in the Blue and White by M.H. Alexander (1993 reprint, Image Graphics, Inc., Paducah, KY); and Blue & White Stoneware by Kathryn McNerney (1995, Collector Books, Paducah, KY).

Peacock Baking Dish

Baking dish, round w/heavy egg-and-dart-molded rim over gently curved sides, embossed Peacock patt., 9" d. (ILLUS.) . . . **$800+**

Basin, embossed Apple Blossom patt., 9" d. 185

Batter jar, cov., printed Wildflower patt., 7" d., 8" h. . . . . 300+

Bean pot, cov., marked "Boston Bean Pot,"
10" d., 9" h. **450**

Beer cooler, cov., embossed Elves patt.,
includes spigot, 14" d., 18" h. **725**

Bowl, 3" d., miniature, heavy dark blue rim
band .... **40+**

Bowl, 4" d., 2" h., berry/cereal, pale blue rim
band .... **55+**

Bowl, 4" d., 2" h., embossed Flying Bird
patt., w/advertising .... **300+**

Bowl, 4" d., 2" h., miniature, heavy blue rim
band .... **50+**

Bowl, 4½" to 14" d., embossed Pineapple
patt., ten sizes, price ranges .... **174 up**

Bowl, 4½" d., 2½" h., embossed Reverse
Pyramids patt. .... **65 to 75+**

Bowl, 6" to 12" d., embossed Greek Key
patt., ranges .... **100 to 170+**

Bowl, 7" d., embossed Beaded Rose patt. ..... **150+**

Bowl, 7½" d., 2¾" h., embossed Apricot with
Honeycomb patt. .... **135+**

Bowl, 7½" d., 5" h., embossed Reverse
Pyramids patt. .... **90 to 100+**

Bowl, 9" d., 4" h., embossed Daisy Roaster.... **250+**

Bowl, 9½" d., 3¾" h., embossed Apricot with
Honeycomb patt. .... **185+**

Bowl, 9½" d., 4½" h., embossed Gadroon
Arches or Pedal Panels patt. .... **175+**

Bowl, 10" d., 5" h., embossed Heart Banded
patt. .... **135+**

Bowl, 10½" d., 5½" h., embossed Diamond
Point patt. .... **170+**

Bowls, embossed Cosmos patt., nesting-
type, the set .... **200 to 275**

Bowls, embossed Ringsaround (Wedding
Ring) patt., six sizes, ranges .... **85 to 225+**

Bowls, embossed Scallop patt.,
6" d., 3½" h., 8" d., 3½" h., 9½" d.,
5" h., nesting type, the set .... **85 to 125+**

Bowls, printed Wildflower patt., 4" to 14" d.,
nesting-type, the set .... **350+**

Brush vase, embossed Bow Tie (Our
Lucile) patt., w/rose decal, 5½" h. **115**

Butter crock, cov., embossed Cow and
Fence patt., 7¼" d., 5" h. .... **625+**

Butter crock, cov., embossed Cows and
Columns patt., 2 lbs. to 10 lbs.,
ranges .... **425 to 650+**

Butter crock, cov., embossed Daisy and
Trellis patt., 6½" d., 4½" h. **225**

Butter crock, cov., embossed Daisy &
Basketweave patt., 7" d., 6¾" h. .... **300+**

Butter crock, cov., embossed Diffused Blue
with Blocks patt., 7½" d., 5½" h. **125**

Butter crock, cov., embossed Diffused
Blueb with Inverted Pyramid Bands patt.,
6" d., 4" h. .... **125+**

Butter crock, cov., embossed Dragonfly
and Flower patt., large, 8" d., 5" h.
(ILLUS. right) .... **345+**

Dragonfly & Flower Butter Crocks

Butter crock, cov., embossed Dragonfly
and Flower patt., small, rare (ILLUS. left).... **500+**

Butter crock, cov., embossed Grape and
Leaves Low patt., 6" d., 5" h. **250**

Butter crock, cov., embossed Greek
Column or Draped Window patt.,
available in 2 lb., 3 lb., 4 lb. or 5 lb.
sizes, range. .... **225 to 295**

Butter crock, cov., embossed Indian patt.,
2 lb. .... **650+**

Lovebird Butter Crock

Butter crock, cov., embossed Lovebird
patt., 6" d., 5" h. (ILLUS.) .... **700+**

Butter crock, cov., embossed Peacock
patt., w/bail handle, 1 lb., 4" h. .... **1,000+**

Butter crock, cov., embossed Peacock
patt., w/bail handle, 3 lb., 5" h. .... **800+**

Butter crock, cov., embossed Rose and
Waffle patt., 5" d., 4½" h. .... **300+**

Butter crock, cov., plain. **125**

Butter crock, cov., printed Cows patt.,
6½" d., 5" h. .... **195+**

Butter crock, cov., stenciled, 2 lb. .... **245+**

Butter crock, cov., stenciled, 5 lb. **258**

Butter crock, no cover, embossed Indian
patt., 2 lb. .... **600+**

Butter crock, no cover, embossed Indian
patt., 3 lb. .... **650+**

Butter pot, cov., printed Wildflower patt.,
four sizes, each .... **150+**

Canister, cov., Basketweave & Morning
Glory (Willow) patt., "Coffee," average 5½
to 6½" h. (ILLUS. top left) .... **325+**

Basketweave & Morning Glory Canisters

Canister, cov., Basketweave & Morning Glory (Willow) patt., "Crackers" or "Raisins," average 5½ to 6½" h., each. . . . . . **625+**

Canister, cov., Basketweave & Morning Glory (Willow) patt., "Salt," "Rice," or "Cereal," average 5½ to 6½" h., each (ILLUS. of Salt, upper right w/Coffee) . . . . . . **475+**

Canister, cov., Basketweave & Morning Glory (Willow) patt., "Sugar," average 5½ to 6½" h. (ILLUS. bottom with Coffee & Salt). . . . . **325+**

Canister, cov., Basketweave & Morning Glory (Willow) patt., "Tea," average 5½ to 6½" h. . . . . **325+**

Canister, cov., embossed Basketweave & Morning Glory (Willow) patt., "Beans," average 5½" to 6½" h. . . . . **325+**

Canister, cov., wooden cover, printed Snowflake patt., six various in set, 5¾" d., 6½" h., each **235**

Chamber pot, cov., embossed Open Rose and Spear Point Panels patt., 9½" d., 6" h. . . **300+**

Chamber pot, cov., printed Wildflower patt., 11" d., 6" h. . . . . **250+**

Bead & Rose Chamber Pot

Chamber pot, open, embossed Bead & Rose patt., 9½" d., 6" h. (ILLUS.) . . . . **250+**

Cider cooler, cov., w/spigot, 13" d., 15" h. . . . . . **425+**

Coffeepot, cov., Diffused Blue patt., oval body, 11" h. (ILLUS.). . . . . **1,700+**

Coffeepot, cov., embossed Bull's-eye patt. (ILLUS.). . . . . **2,000+**

Cold fudge crock, w/tin lid & ladle, marked "Johnson Cold Fudge Crock," 12" d., 13" h. . . . . **300+**

Diffused Blue Coffeepot

Bull's-eye Pattern Coffeepot

Cookie jar, cov., embossed Basketweave & Morning Glory (Willow) patt., marked "Put Your Fist In," 7½" h. . . . . **625+**

Flying Bird Cookie Jar

Cookie jar, cov., embossed Flying Bird patt., 6¾" d., 9" h. (ILLUS.) . . . . **1,250+**

Cuspidor, embossed Sunflowers patt., 9¾" d., 9" h. . . . . **200+**

Custard cup, embossed Fishscale patt., 2½" d., 5" h. . . . . **100+**

Peacock Pattern Custard Cup

Custard cup, embossed Peacock patt., $2^7/8$" h. (ILLUS.) . . . . **245+**

Blue & White Ewer & Pitchers

Ewer, embossed Apple Blossom patt.,
    12" h. (ILLUS. lower right) . . . . **450+**
Ewer, embossed Banded Scroll patt., 7" h. . . . . **275+**
Ewer, embossed Bow Tie (Our Lucile) patt.,
    w/rose decal, 11" h. **175**
Ewer, Small Floral Decal (Memphis patt.), 7" h. . . **365+**
Ewer & basin, embossed Apple Blossom
    patt., the set . . . . **700+`**
Ewer & basin, embossed Feather & Swirl
    patt., ewer 8½" d., 12" h., basin 14" d.,
    5" h., the set . . . . **550+`**
Foot warmer, signed by Logan Pottery Co. . . . **250+**
Iced tea cooler, cov., w/spigot, Maxwell
    House, 13" d., 15" h. . . . . **325+**
Jardiniere, embossed Apple Blossom patt.,
    6" h. . . . . **425+**

Tulip Pattern Jardiniere & Pedestal

Jardiniere & pedestal base, embossed
    Tulip patt., jardiniere 7½" h., pedestal
    7" h., the set (ILLUS.) . . . . **1,500+**
Match holder, model of a duck, 5½" d., 5" h. . . . **250+**

Measuring Cup & Pitchers

Measuring cup, embossed Spear Point and
    Flower Panels patt., 6¾" d., 6" h.
    (ILLUS. top) **450**
Meat tenderizer, printed Wildflower patt.,
    3½" d. at face . . . . **370+**
Milk crock, cov., w/bail handle, embossed
    Lovebird patt., 9" d., 5½" h. . . . . **600+**
Mixing bowl, embossed Flying Bird.
    patt.,8" d. . . . . **340+**
Mouth ewer, embossed Bow Tie (Our
    Lucile) patt., 8" h. . . . . **275+**
Mug, Diffused Blue patt., banded design,
    w/advertising . . . . **300+**
Mug, embossed Cattail patt., 3" d., 4" h. . . . **130+**
Mug, embossed Columns and Arches patt.,
    rare, 4½" h.. . . . . **350+**
Mug, embossed Flying Bird patt., 3" d., 5" h. . . . **225+**
Mug, embossed Grape Cluster in Shield
    patt., 12 oz.. . . . . **225+**
Mug, printed Wildflower patt., 4½" h. . . . . **200+**
Mustard jar, cov., 3" d., 4" h. . . . . **200+**

American Beauty Rose & Cosmos Pieces

Pitcher, embossed American Beauty Rose
    patt., 7" d., 10" h. (ILLUS. right) . . . . **425+**

*From left: Apricot Pattern Pitcher
Basketweave & Morning Glory Pitcher*

Pitcher, embossed Apricot patt., 8" h., 5 pt.
    (ILLUS.) . . . . **265+**
Pitcher, embossed Bands and Rivets patt.,
    1 gal.. . . . . **275+**
Pitcher, embossed Bands and Rivets patt..
    1 pt. . . . . **285+**
Pitcher, embossed Basketweave & Morning
    Glory (Willow) patt., tankard-type,
    6½" d., 9" h. (ILLUS.) . . . . **255+**

Capt. John Smith & Other Pitchers

Pitcher, embossed Capt. John Smith &
Pocahontas patt., 6¾" d., 6¼" h. (ILLUS.
bottom right) . . . . **350+**

Pitcher, embossed Castle patt.,
8" h. (ILLUS. bottom left w/Capt. John
Smith pitcher) . . . . **325+**

Pitcher, embossed Cherry Band patt.,
w/advertising, various sizes, ranges . . . **375 to 475**

Pitcher, embossed Cherry Cluster with
Basketweave patt., 8½" d., 10" h. . . . . **325+**

Pitcher, embossed Cosmos patt., 6½" d.,
9" h. (ILLUS. left w/American Beauty
Rose pitcher) . . . . **415+**

Daisy Cluster Pattern Pitcher

Pitcher, embossed Daisy Cluster patt.,
8" d., 8" h. (ILLUS.) . . . . **700+**

Eagle Pattern Pitcher

Pitcher, embossed Eagle patt., 8" h. (ILLUS.) . . **650+**

Pitcher, embossed Grape Cluster in Shield
patt., 4 pt. . . . . **450+**

Pitcher, embossed Grape Cluster in Shield
patt., 5 pt. . . . . **475+**

Pitcher, embossed Grape Cluster on Trellis
patt., squat body, 7" h. . . . . **200+**

Pitcher, embossed Grape with Leaf Band
patt., 9½" h. . . . . **250+**

Pitcher, embossed Grape with Rickrack
patt., large size . . . . **195+**

Pitcher, embossed Grape with Rickrack
patt., middle size . . . . **235+**

Pitcher, embossed Grape with Rickrack
patt., small size. . . . . **325+**

Pitcher, embossed Iris patt., 5½" d., 9" h.
(ILLUS. right w/measuring cup) . . . . **400+**

Leaping & Standing Deer Pitchers

Pitcher, embossed Leaping Deer patt.,
6" d., 8½" h. (ILLUS. left) . . . . **400+**

*From left: Lovebirds Pattern Pitcher
Old Fashioned Garden Rose Pitcher*

Pitcher, embossed Lovebirds patt.,
5½" d., 8½" h. (ILLUS.) . . . . **450+**

Pitcher, embossed Old Fashioned Garden
Rose patt., 7" d., 7" h. (ILLUS.) . . . . **400+**

Pine Cone Pattern Pitcher

Pitcher, embossed Pine Cone patt.,
5¾" d., 9½" h. (ILLUS.) . . . . **625+**

Pitcher, embossed Plume patt. (ILLUS. left
w/Apple Blossom ewer) . . . . **350+**

Pitcher, embossed Shield patt., 6" d., 8½" h.
(ILLUS. center w/Capt. John Smith pitcher). . **475+**
Pitcher, embossed Standing Deer patt.,
6" d., 8½" h (ILLUS. right w/Leaping
Deer Pitcher). . . . . **275+**
Pitcher, embossed Tulip patt., 4" d., 8" h.
(ILLUS. left w/measuring cup & Iris pitcher). . **350+**
Pitcher, embossed Windmill & Bush patt.,9" h. . . **400+**
Pitcher, printed Acorn patt., 8" h. (ILLUS.
top w/Apple Blossom ewer) **300**
Pitcher, printed Dutch Farm patt., 8" d., 9" h. . . **250+**
Pitcher, printed Wildflower patt., 4" d., 7½" h. . . **275+**
Pitcher, 9" h., embossed Columns & Arches
patt. . . . . **600+**
Rolling pin, printed Wildflower patt., large . . . . **300+**

Small Wildflower Rolling Pin

Rolling pin, printed Wildflower patt., small
(ILLUS.) . . . . **375+**
Salt box, cov., Blue Band patt., 5" d., 6" h. . . . . **130+**
Salt box, cov., Diffused Blue patt., 6" d., 4" h. . . **130+**
Salt box, cov., embossed Daisy patt.,
6" d., 6½" h. . . . . **235+**
Salt box, cov., embossed Flying Bird patt.,
6½" d., 6" h. . . . . **550+**
Salt box, cov., embossed Raspberry patt.,
5½" d., 5½" h. . . . . **200+**
Salt box, cov., embossed Waffleweave patt. . . . **230+**
Salt box, cov., plain . . . . **100+**
Salt box, cov., printed Wildflower patt.,
hinged wooden cover, 6" d., 4½" h. . . . . **170+**
Salt jar, embossed Polar patt., 11" d., 13½" h. . . **750+**
Soap dish, printed Wildflower patt., 3" w.,
5¼" l. . . . . **275+**
Stein, embossed Grape with Leaf Band
patt., 5" h. . . . . **125+**
Stewer, cov., embossed Basketweave &
Morning Glory (Willow) patt., 4 qt. . . . . **275+**
Stewer, cov., printed Wildflower patt., 4 qt. . . . . **285+**

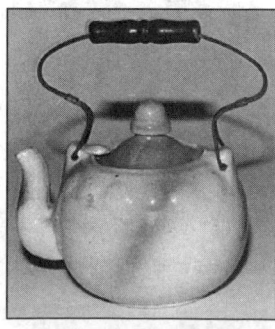

Rare Blue Swirl Teapot

Teapot, cov., spherical body w/row of relief-
molded knobs around the shoulder, inset
cover w/knob finial, swan's-neck spout,
shoulder loop brackets for wire bail
handle w/turned wood grip, blue Swirl
patt., 6" d., 6" h. (ILLUS.) . . . . **800+**
Tobacco jar, cov., embossed Berry Scrolls
patt., 5" d., 6½" h. . . . . **300+**
Umbrella stand, embossed Two Stags
patt., solid blue, 21" h. . . . . **1,000+**
Waste jar, cov., embossed Basketweave &
Morning Glory (Willow) patt. 9½" d., 12½" h. . . **350+**

Apple Blossom Water Cooler

Water cooler, cov., embossed Apple
Blossom patt., w/spigot, 13" h. (ILLUS.) . . . **1,000+**

BRAYTON LAGUNA POTTERY

Brayton Laguna Marks

*In 1927 Durlin Brayton began an operation
in Laguna Beach, California that would prove
highly successful. However, it was not until he
married Ellen (Webb) Webster Grieve and she
became his partner that they were able to realize
the fruits of their labor. The Braytons created
numerous lines over the forty-one years the
company operated. Among them were the very
earliest hand-turned items; the African-*

American series; the Childrens' series; white crackle that stood solely on its own merit or in combination with a high glaze green or a dark brown stain; Calasia, which was basically an art line of pots and vases; Gay Nineties figures; Circus series; and some kitchen items such as creamers and sugars, cookie jars and canisters. Brown-stained items were also made by Treasure Craft and sometimes their pieces are mistaken for Brayton. Treasure Craft items in most cases are a darker brown with a heavier stain application. Various Brayton marks were used over the years making identification easier than with some other California companies. The items found without a mark can be readily identified with a little knowledge about the lines created. Durlin Brayton died in 1951 and Webb Brayton had died two years earlier. The business managed to survive until the late 1960s.

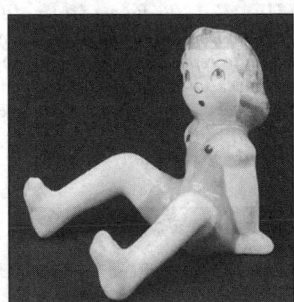

Children's Series "Ann" Figure

Candlesticks, figural Blackamoor, pr. $125
Figure, Chinese Mandarin Man, oxblood
    glaze, large 125
Figure, Children's Series, "John," boy w/horn . . . 95
Figure, Children's Series, "Ann," girl
    seated w/legs apart, knees bent,
    4" h. (ILLUS.) 95
Figure, Children's Series, "Miranda," girl
    standing holding flowers, wearing coat &
    hat, decorations on shoes, 6½" h. 95
Figure, Children's Series, "Ellen," girl
    standing w/pigtails & a hat tied at neck,
    arms bent & palms forward, one leg
    slightly twisted, 7¼" h. 95
Figure, Children's Series, "Jon," boy
    standing & carrying a basket in one hand,
    rooster in other, 8¼" h. 95
Figure group, Chinese mother standing w/a
    baby on her back 90
Figure group, Hillbilly Shotgun Wedding,
    8 pcs. 1,250
Figure group, man & woman seated in a
    horse-drawn carriage, each piece
    w/inscribed mark, the set 250

Figure group, Bridge & Groom, the bride
    standing on the left w/white dress & pink
    flowers w/green leaves & pink hat,
    bouquet in left hand, her right hand on
    the groom's shoulder, he seated wearing
    striped trousers, black jacket, brown
    shoes & brown hat, black hair &
    mustache, stamp mark, 4¾" l., 8½" h. 125
Figure of a baby on all fours 95
Figure of a baby sitting up 95
Figure of a girl sitting w/head between legs . . . 125
Figure of a sailor boy holding a gun 295
Figure of a woman wearing bonnet &
    holding a book, blue dress 135
Figures, Children's Series, "Eric" & "Inger,"
    Swedish boy & girl, pr. 225
Figures of dice players, black boys
    on hands & knees w/original die,
    4¾" l., 3½" h., 3 pcs. 195
Model of a Purple Cow, original sticker. 95
Pencil holder, figural, Gingham Dog 75
Salt & pepper shakers, figural, Gingham
    Dog & Calico Cat, pr. 65
Salt & pepper shakers, figural peasant
    couple, Provincial patt., pr. 65
Teapot & cover on stand, Provincial patt.,
    tulip stand, the set 125
Wall plaque, pierced to hang, model of a
    large zebra, black & gold 95

BUFFALO POTTERY

Buffalo Pottery Mark

Buffalo Pottery was established in 1902 in Buffalo, New York, to supply pottery for the Larkin Company. Most desirable today in Deldare Ware, introduced in 1908 in two patterns, "The Fallowfield Hunt" and "Ye Olden Days," which featured central English scenes and a continuous border. Emerald Deldare, introduced in 1911, was banded with stylized flowers and geometric designs and had varied central scenes, the most popular being from "The Tours of Dr. Syntax." Reorganized in 1940, the company now specializes in hotel china.

DELDARE

Chamberstick, Arlington Lodge, Lake
    Arrowhead, CA, ca. 1923 . . . . $595

Pitcher, 9" h., octagonal, 18th c. scene, "With a cane Superier air," from "The Vicar of Wakefield" 495

Plate, 10" d., "Fallowfield Hunt," signed "H. Sheehan" 220

EMERALD DELDARE

Charger, the Fallowfield Hunt, M. Snea, 13¾" d. 374

Mugs, the Fallowfield Hunt, black stamp, 5" d., 4¼" h., set of 4 489

Pitcher, black stamp, decorated by Newman, 6½" d., 7" h. 316

MISCELLANEOUS

Pitcher, 6" h., jug-type, Cinderella scenes, dated 1909 615

CANTON

This ware has been decorated for nearly two centuries in factories near Canton, China. Intended for export sale, much of it was originally inexpensive blue-and-white hand-decorated ware. Late 18th and early 19th century pieces are superior to later ones and fetch higher prices.

Bowl, 9¼" d., 4¾" h., round w/notched corners, 19th c. (minor area of restoration, hairline) $431

Pitcher, 4¼" h. 220

Platter, 11¼" l. 303

Platter, 13¾" l., oval w/deep sides, 19th c. (very minor chips) 374

Platter, 15⅞" l., oval, typical blue landscape design, 19th c. (very minor rim chips) 259

Platter, 17" l., 19th c. (very minor rim chips) 518

Canton Platter

Platter, 17½" l., octagonal (ILLUS.) 550

Platter, 18" l., oval w/well-and-tree in bottom, 19th c. (very minor rim chips) 690

Punch bowl, painted in underglaze blue, the interior & exterior w/pavilions, pagodas & figures in an island landscape, the inner trelliswork border w/pendant band of arrowheads, outer border reserved w/panels of precious objects, 19th c., 14¾" d. 1,610

Syllabub cups, footed, 19th c., set of 8 (two w/minor chips, two w/hairlines) 863

Teapot, cov., barrel-shaped, cover w/figural foo dog finial, 19th c., 6½" h. (mismatched cover, chips) 690

Tray, oval, 10" l. 165

Vegetable bowl, cov., w/pine cone finial, 9" l. . . . 275

Vegetable bowl, cov., w/pine cone finial, 9½" l. . . . 193

Vegetable bowl, cov., w/pine cone finial, orange peel glaze, 10" l. 330

Warming dish, oval, 19th c., 15⅞" l. 403

CAPO-DI-MONTE

Production of porcelain and faience began in 1736 at the Capo-di-Monte factory in Naples. In 1743 King Charles of Naples established a factory there that made wares with relief decoration. In 1759 the factory was moved to Buen Retiro near Madrid, operating until 1808. Another Naples pottery was opened in 1771 and operated until 1806 when its molds were acquired by the Doccia factory of Florence, which has since made reproductions of original Capo-di-Monte pieces with the "N" mark beneath a crown. Some very early pieces are valued in the thousands of dollars but the subsequent productions are considerably lower.

Ornate Capo-di-Monte Dish

Dishes, oval, each molded in high-relief w/a large group of nude & semi-nude classical figures along the lower half & a wide upper flanged border w/further, small relief-molded classical figures, all w/colorful enamel decoration, late 19th c., 18" l., pr. (ILLUS. of one) $1,955

Capo-di-Monte Stein & Urn

Stein, cov., tapering cylindrical body
decorated w/relief-molded bacchanalian
figures, figural female nude handle,
domed hinged cover w/figural finial of
young bacchante on a goat, late 19th c.,
17½" h. (ILLUS. right) **1,725**

Urns, cov., painted porcelain, each w/lion
finial, body decorated w/a band of
classical sea-gods & nymphs, 19th c.,
16½" h.,. **2,300**

Urns, cov., tall slender trumpet-form body
w/domed flaring foot & cover w/crown
finial, decorated w/relief-molded
baccanalian figures in colored enamel,
19½" h., pr. (ILLUS. of one, left) **1,725**

Vases, cov., 9⅝" h., scrolled handles
terminating at female masks, the sides
decorated w/a frieze band of classical
figures in relief, 20th c., pr. **489**

Vases, cov., bulbous baluster-form body
w/a wide shoulder to the small, short
flaring neck w/a pierced rim supporting
a low domed cover w/a pair of semi-nude
figures, large C-scroll scroll-molded
handles from neck to mid-body, the
mid-body molded in high-relief w/a
continuous band of color classical
mermaids, tridents & hippocampus,
a lobed lower ring over the pedestal
molded w/figural fish over a round
socle molded w/seaweed on a square
gilt-trimmed foot, 19th c., 18" h., pr. **2,875**

CERAMIC ARTS STUDIO OF MADISON

Ceramic Arts Studio Marks

Founded in Madison, Wisconsin in 1941 by
two young men, Lawrence Rabbitt and Reuben
Sand, this company began as a "studio" pottery.
In early 1942 they met an amateur clay sculptor,
Betty Harrington and, recognizing her talent for
modeling in clay, they eventually hired her as
their chief designer. Over the next few years
Betty designed over 460 different pieces for their
production. Charming figurines of children and
animals were a main focus of their output in
addition to models of adults in varied costumes
and poses, wall plaques, vases and figural salt
and pepper shakers.

Business boomed during the years of World
War II when foreign imports were cut off and, at
its peak, the company employed some 100 people
to produce the carefully hand-decorated pieces.

After World War II many poor-quality copies
of Ceramic Arts Studio figurines appeared and
when, in the early 1950s, foreign imported
figurines began flooding the market, the
company found they could no longer compete.
They finally closed their doors in 1955.

Since not all Ceramic Arts Studio pieces are
marked, it takes careful study to determine
which items are from their production.

Bo Peep Figurine

Figurine, Berty w/ball, 4½" h. **$650**
Figurine, Betty, sleeping, 5½" l. **650**
Figurine, Bo Peep, 5¼" h. (ILLUS.) **30**
Figurine, Bobby, sitting, 3¼" h. **750**
Figurine, Chinese boy, Ting-A-Ling, yellow
hat & coat, 5½" h. **45**
Figurine, Cinderella, blonde hair, 6⅜" h. **75**
Figurine, Katrinka, 6¼" h. **35**
Figurine, Little Boy Blue, reclining, 5⅜" l. **25**
Figurine, Mary, 6" h. **65**
Figurine, Pioneer Susie, 5⅛" h. **30**
Figurine, Prince Charming, 6¾" h. **50**
Figurine, Spring Sue, 5⅛" h. **65**
Figurine, Summer Sally, 3⅜" h. **75**
Figurine, "Toadstool Pixie," elf on
mushroom, 3⅞" h. **40**
Figurine, Sung-Tu, 4" h. **35**
Figurine, Pepita, 4½" h. **40**
Figurine, Polish Girl, 6¼" h. **60**
Figurine, Colonel Jackson, 7¼" h. **60**
Figurine, shelf-sitter, Jill, 4¾" h. **45**
Figurine, shelf-sitter, Su-Lin, 5½" h. **60**
Figurine, shelf-sitter, girl w/banjo **60**
Figurines, Aphrodite & Adonis, 7¾" h. &
9" h., pr. **895**
Figurines, Cinderella & Prince, 6⅜" h. &
6¾" h., pr. **185**
Figurines, Mary & her lamb, Mary 6" h., pr. **85**
Figurines, Mop-Pi & Smi-Li, 6" h. & 6¼" h., pr. . . **120**
Figurines, Pioneer Sam & Pioneer Susie,
5⅛" h. & 5⅝" h., pr. **95**

Figurines, Rhumba Dancers, Man & Lady,
7¼" h., & 7⅛" h., pr. 130
Figurines, Ting-A-Ling & Sung-Tu, 5½" h.,
4" h., pr. 85
Figurines, shelf-sitters, Grace & Greg, 6¼"
& 7", pr. 80
Figurines, shelf-sitters, Nip & Tuck, pr. 82
Figurines, shelf-sitters, Young Love Couple,
4⅞" h., pr. 50
Head vase, Becky, 5⅛" h. 125
Lamp, table model, Zorina, original tags 285
Model of Archibald the Dragon, 6¼" h. 193
Model of baby bear, brown, 1¾" h. 50
Model of Baby Boy Skunk, Dinky, 2" h. 45
Model of birds, Lovebirds, 2½" h. 35
Model of Budgie, parrot, turquoise 95
Model of chipmunk, 2" h. 40
Model of Daisy Donkey. 150
Model of dog, Collie pup 35
Model of dog, Scottie, Sooty, black, 3" h. 129
Model of dog, Scottie, Taffy, brown, 3" h. 129
Model of dog, shelf-sitter, Collie Dog, 5⅛" h. 76
Model of elephant, trunk down, "Tembino,"
2½" h. 150
Model of Elsie Elephant, 4¾" h. 136
Model of goat, standing, w/horns, 4⅛" h. 69
Model of leopard, upright 125
Model of Little Lamb, 3⅝" h. 30
Model of Mr. Skunk, 2⅞" h. 55
Model of Tom Cat, standing 125
Models of elephant, Tembo w/trunk up &
Tembino w/trunk down, 6¾" h & 2½" h., pr. . . . 750
Models of fighting leopards, pr. 235
Models of fox & goose, 2" & 3¼" h., pr. 250
Models of Mother Bear & Baby Bear,
nesting-type, white glaze, pr. 50
Models of Mr. & Mrs. Monkey, pr. 200
Models of Pete & Polly Parrot, shelf-
sitters, mauve, pr. 175
Models of skunk family, Mr. & Mrs. Skunk,
2⅞" h., Baby Boy Skunk (Dinkey), 2⅜" h.
& Baby Girl Skunk (Inkey), 2" h.,
unmarked, the set 185
Models of stylized lions, 1¾ x 5¼ & 3¼ x
7¼, pr. 550
Pitcher, 3" h., miniature, Adam & Eve design 55
Planters, models of heads, Manchu &
Lotus, pr. 225
Salt & pepper shakers, figural Chinese Boy
& Girl, 4¼" h. & 4" h., pr. 40
Salt & pepper shakers, figural Clown &
Dog, nesting-type, 3¾" h. & 2½" h., pr 135
Salt & pepper shakers, figural Fighting
Leopards, 2¾ x 6" & 3¼ x 4", pr. (large
leopard repaired) 210
Salt & pepper shakers, figural frog &
toadstool, 2" & 2⅜" h. pr. 63

Salt & pepper shakers, figural Native
Riding Alligator, 2⅝" h., 4¼" l., pr. 45
Salt & pepper shakers, figural ox &
covered wagon, 2⅜" & 3½" h., pr. 90
Salt & pepper shakers, figural Paul Bunyan
& tree, 3⅞" h., 2⅛" h., pr. 250
Salt & pepper shakers, figural Pete & Polly
Parrot, red 7⅞" h. & 8½" h., pr. (small
chip on one wing) 100
Salt & pepper shakers, figural Sambo &
Tiger, tiger 2⅝ x 5¼", Sambo 3¼" h., pr. 750
Salt & pepper shakers, figural stylized
Mother & Baby Cat, brown, 4¼" h. &
2⅝" h., pr. 250
Salt & pepper shakers, figural Thai & Thai-
Thai, 2⅛ x 4⅜" & 2 x 5¼", pr. 115
Wall plaque, pierced to hang, Grace, 8¾" h. 60
Wall plaque, pierced to hang, Greg, 9¼" h. 60

CHINESE EXPORT

Large quantities of porcelain have been made in China for export to America from the 1780s, much of it shipped from the ports of Canton and Nanking. A major source of this porcelain was Ching-te-Chen in the Kiangsi province but the wares were also made elsewhere. The largest quantities were blue and white. Prices fluctuate considerably depending on age, condition, decoration, etc.

CANTON and ROSE MEDALLION export wares are listed separately

Bowl, 10" d., 5" h., blue "Nanking" patt., cut
corners, 19th c. (minute rim chips) **$978**
Figures of hawks, each bird perched on
open blue rockwork & looking slightly to
its right & left respectively, covered in a
rich apple green glaze & w/iron-red beaks
& black eyes, late 19th c., 8½" h. 460
Platter & pierced insert, blue & gilt vintage
border decoration, monogrammed,
17½" l. (glaze & gilt wear) 1,265

Chinese Export Punch Bowl

Punch bowl, exterior decorated w/scene
of court figures on a dragon boat
surrounded by warriors, interior
w/geometric border, rust & gilt scenic
motifs, 19th c., glaze wear, 15⅝" d.
(ILLUS.) 2,645

Salt & pepper shakers, on trumpet foot base w/stylized flat leaf engraving, cylindrical bodies chased & embossed w/figures in foliate landscape, each w/pierced lid, mid-late 19th c., 4" h. (restorations) 575

Teapot, cov., blue "Nanking" patt., lobed form w/reeded strap handles, gilt trim, late 18th - early 19th c., 5½" h. (minor chips, gilt wear) 518

Vases, 24" h., floor-type Famille Rose palette, decorated w/applied kylins & foo dogs, on hardwood stands, 19th c., pr. (minor gilt & glaze wear)......... 633

Warming dish, cov., orange peel glaze, oval dish decorated in a Fitzhugh manner w/Mandarin & floral motifs, black & gilt highlights on white ground, in the French taste, ca. 1820-30, 15½ x 10¼" (minor glaze wear, lid w/minor interior edge chips) 1,840

Warming dishes, orange peel glaze, round dish decorated in a Fitzhugh manner w/Mandarin & floral motifs, black & gilt highlights on white ground, in the French taste, ca. 1820-30, 10¾" d. (one w/handle damage)................. 1,150

Wash bowl, Famille Rose palette, rim decorated w/floral devices, interior sides w/children surrounding the bowl, a seated court lady in the bottom, 11½" d. 173

CHINTZ CHINA

There are over fifty flower patterns and myriad colors from which Chintz collectors can choose. That is not surprising considering companies in England began producing these showy, yet sometimes muted, patterns in the early part of this century. Public reception was so great that this production trend continued until the 1960s.

Ashtray, Peony patt., Royal Winton $45

Ashtray, Paisley patt., Wade Heath, 3¾"........ 40

Cake stand w/chrome base, Lorna Doone patt., W. R. Midwinter Ltd., 3¼ x 9" 95

Candy dish, Peony patt., Royal Winton 50

Coffeepot, cov., Hazel patt., Grecian shape, Royal Winton....................... 1,350

Compote, 6½" h., Marguerite patt., scalloped top,...................... 275

Creamer & cov. sugar bowl, Hazel patt., Royal Winton 110

Creamer & open sugar bowl, Hazel patt., Grecian shape, Royal Winton, pr.......... 160

Creamer & open sugar bowl, Summertime patt., Royal Winton, pr................... 169

Cup & saucer, Black Beauty patt., Lord Nelson.. 145

Cup & saucer, Blossom patt., Oleander shape, pale green exterior, Shelley China 145

Cup & saucer, Hazel patt., Royal Winton 95

Cup & saucer, Heather patt., Lord Nelson....... 65

Cup & saucer, Old Cottage patt., Royal Winton 89

Cup & saucer, Petunia patt., Royal Winton 175

Cup & saucer, Primrose patt., Oleander shape, black matte exterior, Shelley China ... 175

Cup & saucer, Rosebud shape, yellow, Royal Winton 35

Cup & saucer, Summertime patt., Royal Winton 101

Dish, Primrose patt., 4½" l.................. 100

Dish, Spring patt., canoe-shaped, Royal Winton 200

Dish, Sweet Pea patt., rare shape, 4½ x 6½".... 225

Dish, center-handled, Chimarita (blue paisley), James Kent, 8¼" 85

Hair receiver, Paisley patt., Wade Heath........ 75

Jam jar, cov., Lorna Doone patt., W. R. Midwinter Ltd........................ 100

Mustard jar, cover & underplate, Beeston patt., Royal Winton, the set 275

Nut dish, Summertime patt., Royal Winton 40

Nut scoop, Floral Feast patt., Royal Winton 200

Pitcher, jug-type, 5" h., Marguerite patt., Royal Winton 200

Plate, 5" d., Beeston patt., Royal Winton 110

Plate, 5" sq., Welbeck patt., Royal Winton 100

Plate, 6" d., Marion patt., Royal Winton 95

Plate, 6" sq., Summertime patt., Royal Winton.... 79

Plate, 8" sq., Old Cottage patt., Royal Winton 99

Plate, 8" sq., Summertime patt., Royal Winton 95

Plate, 9" d., Lorna Doone patt., Broadhurst 80

Plate, 9¼" sq., green, Royal Winton............ 50

Plate, 10" sq., Summertime patt., Royal Winton 139

Roll tray, ruffled edge, Rapture patt., James Kent, 7 x 13".......................... 275

Salt & pepper shakers, Summertime patt., Royal Winton, pr. 90

Salt & pepper shakers on tray, June Festival patt., Royal Winton, the set........ 100

Server, center-handled, Sunnydale patt., Soho Pottery Ltd., 8" 80

Sugar bowl, open, Old Cottage patt., Royal Winton 69

Sugar bowl, open, round, Old Cottage patt., Royal Winton 59

Teapot, cov., Paisley patt., six-cup, Wade Heath .. 285

Teapot, cov., Summertime patt., Ascot shape, Royal Winton 750

Teapot, cov., Tiger Lily patt., green, Royal Winton 295

Tray, rectangular, Summertime patt., Royal Winton, 6¾ x 12" 220

Tray, rectangular, DuBarry patt., James Kent, 5¾ x 12½"........................ 200

CLEWELL WARES

Clewell Wares Mark

Though Charles W. Clewell of Canton, Ohio, didn't operate a pottery, he is responsible for a category of fine art pottery through his development of a unique metal coating placed on pottery blanks obtained from Owens, Weller and others. By encasing objects in a thin metal shell, he produced copper- and bronze-finished ceramics. Later experiments led him to chemically treat the metal coating to attain the bluish green patinated effect associated with copper and bronze. Although he produced metal-coated pottery from 1902 until the mid-1950s, Clewell's production was quite limited for he felt no one else could competently recreate his artwork and, therefore, operated a small shop with little help.

Vase, 5½" h., 7½" d., footed squatty bulbous body, the wide shoulder tapering to a cylindrical neck w/slightly flaring rim flanked by loop handles, rich deep orange to verdigris patina, etched mark **$880**

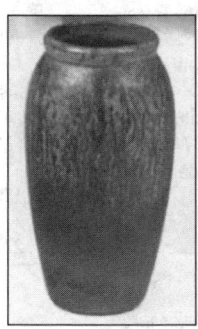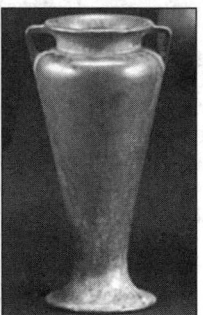

From left: Small Clewell Vase
Rare Clewell Vase

Vase, 6" h., simple ovoid body w/molded rim, original green, blue & orange patina, signed "Clewell 320-24" (ILLUS.) **2,200**

Vase, 7" h., footed bulbous ovoid body w/a narrow shoulder & wide flaring rim, verdigris & dark bronze patina, incised "Clewell" **1,760**

Vase, 9" h., urn-shaped body w/flaring rim flanked by small angled handles from shoulder to rim, rich verdigris patina, etched mark (ILLUS.) **1,210**

Vase, 9½" h., 4" d., tapering cylindrical body raised on a flaring footed pedestal base, decorated w/embossed Egyptian

Unusual Clewell Vase

designs under a rich brown patina, probably on an Owens Pottery blank, unmarked (ILLUS.) **495**

Vase, 11" h., simple tall ovoid body w/a rounded shoulder centered by a short rolled neck, original orange to green to blue patina, incised "Clewell 272-2-6" **1,430**

Vase, 11½" h., slender ovoid body w/a short flaring neck, original drippy orange, green & blue patina, signed "Clewell 302-2-6" **1,430**

Vase, 14½" h., footed ovoid body tapering to a cylindrical neck w/flat rim, covered in a rich orange to green patina, etched mark ... **1,980**

Vase, 17" h., floor-type, shouldered ovoid body tapering to a short wide cylindrical neck, deep green patina, etched mark **1,540**

Vase, 17" h., wide bulbous ovoid body w/a narrow shoulder to the wide, short cylindrical neck w/flaring rim, original orange, brown, green & blue patina, signed "Clewell 460-26" **9,350**

Vase, 19" h., tall footed baluster-form body w/widely flared rim, original orange, green & blue patina, signed "Clewell 430-2-6" **6,600**

COPELAND & SPODE

Copeland & Spode Mark

W. T. Copeland & Sons, Ltd., have operated the Spode Works at Stoke, England, from 1847 to the present. The name Spode was used on some of its productions. Its predecessor, Spode, was founded by Josiah Spode about 1784 and became Copeland & Garrett in 1843, continuing under that name until 1847. Listings dated prior to 1843 should be attributed to Spode.

Copeland & Spode Compote

Compotes, reticulated dish on figural putti form standard, late 19th c., one w/damage to rim, 10" h., pr. (ILLUS. of one) **$1,265**

Cups & saucers, demitasse, gilt-trimmed enamel floral design on pink ground, ca. 1900, six sets **690**

Pitcher, 9" h., ironstone, underglaze blue transfer-printed floral design w/polychrome enamel, impressed "Greek 12," Spode (minor wear & crazing, tip of spout is broken off at hinge & needs to be reattached) **110**

Indian Tree Pattern Plate

Plate, 8½" octagon, Indian Tree patt., ca. 1890, England (ILLUS.) **140**

Plates, dinner, 9¾" d., h.p. in iron-red underglaze blue & gilt w/a central urn brimming w/flowers within a border of dense floral scrolls, fans & arched panels within a shaped brown-edged rim, ca. 1815-30, "2283" pattern number in iron-red, set of 12 (one w/minor hairline to center, small rim chips & surface wear) **1,150**

COWAN

Cowan Mark

R. Guy Cowan first opened a studio pottery in 1913 in Cleveland, Ohio. The pottery continued to operate almost continuously, at various locations in the Cleveland area, until it was forced to close in 1931 due to financial problems. This fine art pottery, which was gradually expanded into a full line of commercial productions, is now sought out by collectors.

Book ends, figural, a nude kneeling boy & nude kneeling girl, each on oblong bases, creamy white glaze, designed by Frank N. Wilcox, Shape No. 519, marks 8 & 9, ca. 1925, 6½" h., pr. **$770**

Book ends, figural, a little girl standing wearing a sunbonnet & full ruffled dress, on a thick rectangular base, ivory semi-matte glaze, Shape No. 521, impressed mark & "Z," ca. 1925, 4" w., 7¼" h., pr. **550**

Candlestick, two-light, large figural nude standing w/head tilted & holding a swirling drapery, flanked by blossom-form candle sockets supported by scrolled leaves at the base, matte ivory glaze, mark No. 8, Shape No. 745, 3 x 7½", 9¾" h. (small black glaze spot to base) **1,320**

Charger, "Polo" plate, incised scene w/polo players & flowers under a blazing sun, covered in a rare glossy brown & cafe-au-lait glaze, designed by Victor Schreckengost, mark Nos. 8 & 9, Shape No. X-48, impressed "V.S. - Cowan," 11¼" d. (grinding chips to retaining ring) **770**

Cigarette/match holder, seahorse decoration, pink, No. 726, 3½ x 4" **65**

Decanter w/stopper, figural King of Clubs, a seated robed & bearded man w/a large crown on his head & holding a scepter covered in Old Ivory glaze, designed by Waylande Gregory, impressed "Waylande Gregory" & "Cowen," 5" d., 10" h. **495**

Figurine, "Nautch Dancer," female w/a flaring pleated skirt on rectangular base, semi-matte ivory glaze w/silver accents, incised "Waylande Gregory," impressed mark, 6¾ x 9¼", 17¾" h. **10,450**

Figurines, "Spanish Dancer," male & female figures h.p. in polychrome glazes, the male mark No. 9, Shape No. 794-D, 8¼" h. & the female, mark No. 8, Shape No. 793-D, 8½" h., designed by Elizabeth Anderson, impressed marks, pr. **2,530**

Flower frog, figural, an Art Deco lady draped in a flowing scarf standing & leaning backward w/her arms bent & her hands touching her shoulders, on a flower-form pedestal base, overall white glaze, impressed mark, 1930s, 9" h. **546**

Flower frog, figural, Art Deco style nude dancing lady in a curved pose standing on one leg & trailing a long scarf, white glaze, No. 698, 6½" h. **325**

Flower frog, figural, Art Deco nude scarf dancer, No. 35, ivory glaze, signed, 7¼" h. . . . **400**

Flower frog, figural, an Art Deco dancing nude lady leaning back w/one leg raised & the ends of a long scarf held in her outstretched hands, overall white glaze, impressed mark, 7½" h. **201**

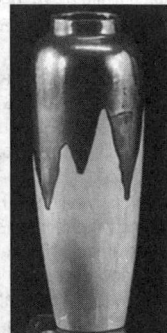

From left: Cowan Figural Flower Frog
Tall Cowan Vase

Flower frog, figural, Art Deco, a nude female dancer standing & leaning to the side, w/one hand on hip & the other holding a scarf which swirls about her, on a round lobed base w/flower holes, glossy white glaze, impressed mark, 4¼" d., 9½" h. (ILLUS.) **1,100**

Flower frog, figural, modeled as a slender, leaping female dancer w/long flowing dress, curved backwards above open scrolls on a molded plinth base, ivory semi-matte glaze, stamped mark, 6½" d., 10" h. (glazed over very tight crazing line to base). **2,200**

Flower frog, model of a leaping stag, relief-molded ribbed leaves in center & around base, designed by Waylande Gregory, mark Nos. 8 & 9, Shape No. 905, 1929, 8½" h. **413**

Lamp, candlestick-form, a disk foot & spiral-twist standard w/a flaring molded socket fitted w/an electric bulb socket, overall marigold lustre glaze, impressed mark, 11" h. . . **52**

Vase, 8" h., 8" d., wide bulbous body w/narrow molded rim, embossed w/a band of stylized leaves and covered in a Persian blue crackled glaze, Shape No. V-61, impressed mark **880**

Vase, 13" h., swelled cylindrical body w/a narrow shoulder to the short cylindrical wide neck covered in a lustered grey & yellow dripping glaze, mark No. 7, Shape No. 552, stamped ink mark (ILLUS.) **825**

CUP PLATES (EARTHENWARE)

Like their glass counterparts, these small plates were designed to hold a cup while the tea or coffee was allowed to cool in a saucer before it was sipped from the saucer, a practice that would now be considered in poor taste. The forerunner of the glass cup plates, those listed below are produced in various Staffordshire potteries in England. Their popularity waned after the introduction of the glass cup plate in the 1820s.

Staffordshire, Cottage in the Woods, impressed "Wood" & "A" under glaze on back, dark blue, unmarked, 3⅝" d. **$165**

Staffordshire, scene of English brick bridge, impressed "Wood," dark blue, 3⅝" d. **149**

Staffordshire, Cadmus patt., ship scene in center, dark blue, impressed "Wood," unmarked, 3¾" d. (chips on table ring) **330**

Staffordshire, Castle Garden Battery, New York, dark blue, impressed "Wood," unmarked, 3¾" d. (wear & stains) **385**

Staffordshire, Jackson w/"New Orleans," red transfer w/red rim, 3¾" d. **138**

Staffordshire, "LaFayette," black transfer, 3¾" d. (chip on rim & table ring) **633**

Staffordshire, scene of three men, dark blue, 3⅞" d. (hairline) **110**

Staffordshire, Winter view of Pittsfield, Massachusetts, dark blue, impressed "Clews," 4⅝" d. (chips & hairline) **193**

DEDHAM & CHELSEA KERAMIC ART WORKS

CHELSEA KERAMIC
ART WORKS
ROBERTSON & SONS.

Dedham & Chelsea Keramic Art Works Marks

This pottery was organized in 1866 by Alexander W. Robertson in Chelsea, Massachusetts, and became A. W. & H. Robertson in 1868. In 1872, the name was changed to Chelsea Keramic Art Works and in 1891 to Chelsea Pottery, U.S.A. About 1895, the pottery was moved to Dedham, Massachusetts, and was renamed Dedham Pottery. Production ceased in 1943. High-fired colored wares and crackle ware were specialties. The rabbit is said to have been the most popular decoration on crackle ware in blue. Since 1977, the Potting

Shed, Concord, Massachusetts, has produced quality reproductions of early Dedham wares. These pieces are carefully marked to avoid confusion with original examples.

Boot, swan design, blue stamp, 4" w., 5" h. . . . **$1,093**

Bowl, 4½" d., swan design, blue registered stamp **460**

Bowl, square, swan design, blue registered stamp, 8¼ x 8¼" sq., 2¾" h. **920**

Candlesticks, elephant design, blue stamp, initials "A.R.," 2" h., the pair **978**

Creamer, elephant design, blue registered stamp, 3" w., 3" h. **1,265**

Cup & saucer, 6" d., snow tree design, blue registered stamp **173**

Cup & saucer, grape design, blue registered stamp, 6" d., 2¾" h. **173**

Cup & saucer, owl design, blue registered stamp, 6¼" d., 2½" h. **1,955**

Dish, 7¼" d., rabbit design, star-shaped, blue registered stamp, two impressed rabbits. **374**

Egg cup, elephant design, blue stamp, 3½" d., 3" h. **1,380**

Flower holder, standing bunny, hint of blue stamp, 4¼" d., 6¼" h. **1,150**

Paperweight, model of turtle, blue registered stamp, 2¼" w., 3¼" l. **1,035**

Pitcher, 4¾" h., 6¼" d., grape design, blue registered stamp. **259**

Pitcher, 6¼" w., 6" h., Oak Block, blue registered stamp, ... **978**

Pitcher, 6¼" h., 7" d., rabbit design, blue registered stamp. **575**

Plate, 6" d., dolphin design, blue registered stamp, two impressed rabbits, blue numbers. . **518**

Plate, 6¼" d., chick design, blue stamp, one impressed rabbit **2,415**

Plate, 6½" d., strawberry raised design, signed Jacob **2,415**

Plate, 8½" d., day lily design, blue stamp **1,093**

Plate, 8¾" d., grouse design, blue stamp, one impressed rabbit (glaze pitting to edge surface) **2,875**

Plate, 10" d., crab design, blue stamp, one impressed rabbit. **1,093**

Plate, 12" d., wolves & owl design, blue stamp (three tight hairlines, peppering). **2,300**

Platter, 12" d., round dished form w/wide flanged rim, Grape patt., marked **201**

Platter, 13" oval, dolphin design, blue registered mark, one impressed rabbit **2,760**

Teapot, rabbit design, blue registered stamp, 7" w., 5½" h. **920**

Toothpick holder, floral design, obscured blue stamp, 2¾" d., 2¾" h. **1,150**

Tureen, cov., rabbit design, blue stamp, 11" w., 8" h. **2,645**

Tureen, cov., turkey design, blue stamp, 9" d., 5¾" h. **2,300**

Vase, 6¼" h., iris design, cylindrical form, blue stamp, impressed "C.K.A.W." **1,840**

Vase, 8½" h., 5" d., tapering cylindrical form, incised "Dedham Pottery," initialed "B.W." . . **3,105**

Vase, 8½" h., 9½" d., spherical form w/extended raised rim & tapered base, glossy mottled sea green glaze, modeled by Hugh Robertson, incised "Dedham Pottery 10.11.96 H.C.R. 3016B" (in-the-making glaze chips near base) **2,070**

DELFT

In the early 17th century Italian potters settled in Holland and began producing tin-glazed earthenwares, often decorated with pseudo-Oriental designs based on Chinese porcelain wares. The city of Delft became the center of this pottery production and several firms produced the wares throughout the 17th and early 18th century. A majority of the pieces featured blue on white designs, but polychrome wares were also made. The Dutch Delftwares were also shipped to England and eventually the English copied them at potteries in such cities as Bristol, Lambeth and Liverpool. Although still produced today, Delft peaked in popularity by the mid-18th century.

Delft Charger

Charger, round, decorated in blue, green & yellow w/the two figures on either side of a blue-sponged tree heavily laden w/yellow fruit & w/the serpent's head appearing in the lower branches, yellow & blue border & blue-dash rim, ca 1700-10, Bristol, England, 11¾" d. (crack) **$4,600**

Charger, round w/center decoration of three stylized tulips amidst other flowers & foliage in blue, green, yellow & ochre, blue & yellow border w/blue-dash rim, ca. 1720, Bristol, England, 11⅞" d. (some glaze flaking to rim & underside, old rim chip). **4,887**

Charger, round w/wide flanged rim, painted in blue w/continuous border of oriental plants & a building, inscribed "B S*E - 1742" in center, the underside w/geometric motifs, minor glaze wear to rim, 12¾" d. (ILLUS.) **2,587**

Charger, round w/wide flanged rim, polychrome full-length portrait of King William standing in a sparse landscape & flanked by initials "W R" within a double line manganese border, ca. 1690, London, 13¼" d. (repaired) **5,750**

Polychromed Dutch Delft Cat Figures

Models of cats, each seated on a grassy mound base, wearing a yellow collar w/red spots, their white coats decorated w/red & blue markings, blue whiskers & eyes, ca. 1700, Holland, 4" h., facing pr. (ILLUS.) **3,450**

Pill slab, canted rectangular form, painted in blue w/arms of the Apothecary's Guild of London above a ribbon inscribed "Opiferque, Per; Orbem, Dicor," ca. 1760-80, England, 12" h. (small rim chips & glaze flaking) **9,200**

Plate, 8½" d., half-length portraits of King William & Queen Mary in blue & yellow flanked by initials "W M R" in center surrounded by two narrow blue bands, ca. 1690, England (restoration to rim, cracks) **6,325**

Plate, 8¾" d., painted in blue w/initials "N G H" within a scrolled cartouche flanked by griffins & surmounted by a crown, dated "1693" (restored chip & small glaze flakes to rim) **977**

Plate, 8⅝" d., polychrome, probably Bristol, inscribed in center w/initials "N*L*M" above date "1736" within a band of stylized plants, paneled border rim, England, 1736, (areas of glaze lost to back rim) **2,300**

Plates, England, 9" d., polychrome, of Ann Gomm type, stylized plants in green, yellow, pink & blue, each inscribed within a central medallion "Mary Johnson" & dated "1793", pr. (ILLUS.) **4,312**

Posset pot, cov., bulbous body w/loop handles, domed cover, painted in red, green & blue w/dense pattern of flowers & foliage, interior & cover both inscribed "R E," ca. 1710, 9¼" h. (minor glaze chips to rims) **5,750**

Lambeth Delftware Polychrome Plates

Punch bowl, polychrome, painted in orange & blue w/stylized vases of flowers within laurel wreath borders, Holland, mid-18th c., 12¾" d., 5½" h. (restored crack) **2,012**

Punch bowl, exterior densely painted in red, green & blue w/stylized flower sprigs & florets within a sawtooth border, interior painted in blue w/stylized tulips, all between narrow blue bands at rim & foot, ca. 1740, possibly England, 12¼" d. (restored crack to side, chips to foot) **4,887**

Tobacco jar, cov., 10¾" h., ovoid form, inscribed "Rappe de St. Vincent No. 7" within a shaped cartouche flanked by tobacco smoking native figures, with brass 'beehive' lid, 18th c. (restored) **2,587**

Water bottle, bulbous body tapering to slender cylindrical neck w/everted rim, decorated in blue w/a bird in a tree above peonies & rockwork below a diaper border, ca. 1770, probably Liverpool, England, 9⅛" h. (restoration to neck & rim) **1,035**

DOULTON & ROYAL DOULTON

Royal Doulton Mark

Doulton & Co., Ltd., was founded in Lambeth, London, about 1858. It was operated there till 1956 and often incorporated the words "Doulton" and "Lambeth" in its marks. Pinder Bourne & Co., Burslem was purchased by the Doultons in 1878 and in 1882 became Doulton & Co., Ltd. It added porcelain to its earthenware production in 1884. The "Royal Doulton" mark has been used since 1902 by this factory, which is still in production. Character jugs and figurines are commanding great attention from collectors at the present time.

ANIMALS & BIRDS

Cat, Persian Cat, seated, black & white,
HN 999, 5" h. **$185**
Dog, Bulldog, HN 1044, small, 3¼" h. **350**
Dog, Cocker Spaniel, large, HN 1002. .... **325**
Dog, Dalmation Ch. 'Goworth Victor,'
HN 1114, 4¼" h. **175**
Dog, French Poodle, HN 2631, white w/pink,
grey & black markings, 5¼" h. **125**
Dogs, Terrier Puppies in a Basket, three
white puppies w/light & dark brown
markings, brown basket, HN 2588,
1941-85, 3" h. **145**
Penguin, K 23, 1½" h., grey, white & black,
green patches under eyes **170**

CHARACTER JUGS

Large Drake

'Arriet, large, D 6208, 6½" h. **250**
Captain Henry Morgan, miniature, 2¼" h. **65**
Dick Whittington, large, D 6375, 6½" h. **500**
Don Quixote, large, D 6455, 7¼" h. **95**
Drake, large, D 6115, 5¾" h. (ILLUS.) **175**
Fortune Teller, miniature, D 6523, 2½" h. **475**
Gaoler, large, D6570, 7½" h. **99**
Gladiator, large, D 6650, 7¾" h. **410**
Gondolier, large, D 6589, 8" h. **665**
Groucho Marx, large, No. D 6710, 7" h. **140**
London Bobby, large, D 6744, 7" h. **100**
Long John Silver, large, D 6335, 7" h. **135**
Night Watchman, large, D 6569, 7" h. **135**
Porthos, large, D 440, 7¼" h. **110**
Robin Hood, 2nd version, large, D 6527, 7½" h. ... **75**
Sairey Gamp, large, No. 5451, 6¼" h. **100**
Witch (The), large, D 6893, 7" h. **245**

DICKENSWARE

Bowl, 9" d., 4⅛" h., Coaching Days street
scenes **127**

Coaching Days Series Jardiniere

Jardiniere, Coaching Days street scene,
signed "NOKE," 10" w., 8½" h. (ILLUS.) **330**

FIGURINES

Autumn Breezes

Abdullah, HN 2104, 1953-62 .... **480**
Anna, HN 2802, purple & white, Kate
Greenaway Series, 1976-82. .... **125**
Autumn Breezes, HN 1911, green & pink,
1939-76 (ILLUS.) **170**
Balloon Man (The), HN 1954, 1940- **225**
Belle O' the Ball, HN 1997, 1947-79 .... **275**
Blithe Morning HN 2021, mauve & pink
dress, 1949-71 .... **185**
Blithe Morning, HN 2065, blue & pink
dress, 1949-71 .... **195**
Blithe Morning, HN 2065, red dress, 1950-73. ... **225**

Bonnie Lassie

Bonnie Lassie, HN 1626, red dress,
1934-53 (ILLUS.) **350**

Boy from Williamsburg, HN 2183, 1969-83 150
Bridesmaid (The Little), HN 2196, white
dress, pink trim, 1960-76 90
Bridget, HN 2070, green, brown & lavender,
1951-73 275
Carolyn, HN 2112, standing, 1953-65 325
Country Lass (A), HN 1991A, blue, brown
& white, 1975-81 95
Diana, HN 1716, pink & blue, 1935-49 350
Ermine Coat (The), HN 1981, 1945-67 230
Fair Lady, HN 2193, green, 1963- 160
Fatboy (The), HN 2096, 1952-67 360
Flora, HN 2349, 1966-73 425
Friar Tuck, HN 2143, brown, 1954-65 450

From left: Genevieve
Her Ladyship

Genevieve, HN 1962, 1941-75 (ILLUS.) 250
Her Ladyship, HN 1977, red & cream,
1945-59 (ILLUS.) 275
Invitation, HN 2170, pink, 1956-75 110
Judith, HN 2089, red & blue, 1952-59 295
Lady Charmian, HN 1948, green dress, red
shawl, 1940-73 185
Lady Charmian, HN 1949, red dress
w/green shawl, 1940-75 195
Lobster Man (The), HN 2317, 1964- 125

From left: Maureen
Roseanna

Maureen, HN 1770, pink dress, 1936-59
(ILLUS.) 250
Midinette, HN 2090, blue dress, 1952-65 258

Miss Muffet, HN 1936, red, 1940-67 165
Noelle, HN 2179, orange, white & black,
1957-67 375
Old Meg, HN 2494, matte finish, 1974-76 250
Omar Khayyam, HN 2247, brown, 6¼" h. 140
Owd Willum, HN 2042, green & brown,
1949-73 210
Parson's Daughter (The), HN 564, red,
yellow & green, 1923-49. 465
Pensive Moments, HN 2704, blue dress,
1975-81 200
Prized Possessions, HN 2942, cream,
purple & green, 1982 400
Professor (The), HN 2281, brown &
black,1965-81 155
Roseanna, HN 1926, rose shading to blue
dress, 1940-59 (ILLUS.) 300
Rosemary, HN 2091, red & blue, 1952-59 350
Silks and Ribbons, HN 2017, 1949 - 200
Skater (The), HN 2117, red & white dress,
1953-71 358
Stop Press, HN 2683, brown, blue & white,
1977-81 155
Suzette, HN 2026, 1949-59 373
Tootles, HN 1680, pink, 1935-75 75
Town Crier, HN 2119, 1953-76 285
Toymaker (The), HN 2250, brown & red,
1959-73 350
Tuppence a Bag, HN 2320, 1968-........... 245
Uriah Heep, HN 2101, 1952-67 335
Winsome, HN 2220, 1960-85................ 220

MISCELLANEOUS

Royal Doulton Chocolate Set

Bowl, 8" d., The Gleaners series 185
Bowl, 8½" h., Gallent Fishers series.......... 245
Charger, Shakespeare Series, scene from
"A Midsummers Night Dream," 12⅝" d. 55
Chocolate set: 8" h. cov. chocolate pot,
6½" h. cov. water pot, creamer, sugar
bowl & eight cups & saucers; bone china,
each enamel decorated w/relief-molded
fox in various poses, crop-form handles,
20th c., England, the set (ILLUS.) 748
Cracker jar, cov., Isaac Walton Ware,
signed "NOKE" 251
Dish, oval, Old English scene "The
Gleaners," 9 x 11¼, 2⅛" h.................. 44

Humidor, cov., Sung Ware, flambé glaze, figural elephant finial, artist-initialed **2,400**

Loving cup, stoneware, three-handled cylindrical form w/a sterling silver rim band, a dark brown glaze band below the rim, most of the body w/a tan glaze, molded around the sides w/three white relief groups of bicycle riders, each titled either "Path," "Military," or "Road," late 19th c., base incised "8238," 5½" h. **330**

Mug, stoneware, tall slender & slightly tapering sides w/a sterling silver rim band, the upper third w/a dark brown glaze, the lower section w/a tan glaze, the upper band molded in relief w/a large scrolling ribbon band reading "Speed Wheel," the lower sides w/three white relief groups of bicycle racers each titled either "Path," "Military," or "Road," base incised "1957," late 19th c., 6" h. **275**

Pitcher, jug-form, Kingsware, "Memories" design w/twelve faces shown, ca. 1920 . . . . . . **600**

Plate, 9½" d., Izaac Walton Ware, signed"NOKE" . . **72**

Plate, 10¼" d., Bradley Golfers, "All Fools Are Not Knaves........," **175**

Plate, 10¼" d., Old English scenes, "The Gleaners" **44**

Plate, 10¼" d., "The Gypsies". **38**

Plate, 10½" d., blue transfer w/center portrait of Shakespeare, border w/twelve characters from his plays **77**

Plate, 10½" d., blue transfer w/central portrait of Dickens, border w/eleven of the Doulton characters used on various wares, unmarked **61**

Plate, 10½" d., overall decoration of Aesthetic Movement florals in green & blue, marked w/lion & crown "Royal Doulton, England, Cyprus" **39**

Plate, 10¾" d., blue transfer w/Burns portrait in center, border shows characters such as Tam-O-Shanter, Highland Mary & others . . . **49**

Teapot, cov., Queen Elizabeth at Moreton Hall series. **195**

Vase, 9" h., Welsh Ladies decoration **295**

DRESDEN

Dresden-type porcelain evolved from wares made at the nearby Meissen Porcelain Works early in the 18th century. "Dresden" and "Meissen" are often used interchangeably for later wares. "Dresden" has become a generic name for the kind of porcelains produced in Dresden and certain other areas of Germany but perhaps should be confined to the wares made in the city of Dresden.

Dish, openwork sides, floral interior, 2 x 6½" **$77**

Figural groups, allegorical of summer & winter, summer modeled w/a young girl draped w/a floral garland & playing a lute, standing beside a young boy seated on a sheaf of wheat, winter modeled w/a young boy wearing a fur hat & fur-lined jacket seated on a sled, a young girl standing to one side warming her hands over a flaming brazier, each on an oval base w/gilt scroll border, blue printed factory marks, early 20th c., after Meissen originals, 5½" h. (minor chips & losses), the pair. **517**

Figure of lady, standing in Victorian dress w/a feathered bonnet & a three-tiered porcelain lace dress which she holds up & out to the sides, on an oblong base, polychrome decoration, late 19th c., 7" h. (minor losses). **173**

Figures, figures of a male & female, enamel & gilt decorated, modeled standing on a scrolled square base, late 19th c., 20" h., pr. . . **920**

Figures of a Monkey Band, various costumed monkey musicians decorated w/bright enameled decoration & gilt trim, underglaze-blue marks, early 20th c., each 5 to 6½" h., set of 12. . . . . **3,450**

Jars, cov., each of compressed ovoid form, painted on front & back w/colorful panels depicting musicians & lovers in a landscape, flanked by lilac ground panels reserved w/colorful floral spray decoration around a gilt baluster finial, each w/"AR" monogram in underglaze-blue, c. 1900, 12¼" h. (one cover restored, very minor wear to gilding), the pair **920**

Plaques, oval, the first w/a bust-length portrait of a courtly lady wearing a grey wig, the second depicting a young woman emerging from a cloud & in an embrace w/a cupid, each mounted within a gilt bronze foliate scroll frame, 5¾" h. **460**

Dresden Potpourri Urns

Potpourri urns, cov., square stepped base below flaring foot, bulbous ovoid body w/openwork incurved neck, scrolled shoulder handles & domed openwork cover w/bud-shaped finial, each decorated on both sides w/harbor scenes, foliate sprigs & figures, 20th c., 16½" h., pr. (ILLUS.) **2,300**

Dresden Covered Punch Bowl & Undertray

Punch bowl, cover & undertray, cov.,
enamel decoration of titled figures
depicting the "Punch Club," around
bowl, undertray & domed cover w/sliced
lemon finial, 19th c., tray 15¼" d., bowl
11¾" d.,the set (ILLUS.) **27,600**

Vase, cov., 10½" h., gilt & enamel decorated
paneled sides alternating in figural
landscapes & blue ground w/floral
sprays, in the manner of Augustus
Rex, late 19th c. **230**

FIESTA

Fiesta Mark

Fiesta dinnerware was made by the Homer Laughlin China Company of Newell, West Virginia, from the 1930s until the early 1970s. The brilliant colors of this inexpensive pottery have attracted numerous collectors. On February 28, 1986, Laughlin reintroduced the popular Fiesta line with minor changes in the shapes of a few pieces and a contemporary color range. The effect of this new production on the Fiesta collecting market is yet to be determined.

Ashtray
  chartreuse **$93**
  forest green **79**
  red **55**
  yellow **44**
Bowl, cream soup
  cobalt blue **58**
  forest green **85**
Bowl, individual fruit, 5½" d.
  chartreuse **35**
  light green **28**
  medium green **71**
  turquoise **26**
  red **30**
  yellow **25**
Bowl, nappy, 8½" d.
  forest green **68**
  grey **54**

  medium green **164**
  turquoise **40**
Bowl, salad, large, footed
  light green **505**
  red **476**
  yellow **331**
Cake plate, 10" d.
  cobalt blue **1,260**
  light green **1,950**
  turquoise **605**

Fiesta Carafe

Carafe, cov.
  cobalt blue **341**
  ivory **405**
  red **384**
  turquoise **323**
  yellow (ILLUS.) **280**
Coffeepot, cov.
  cobalt blue **286**
  forest green **749**
  grey **680**
  ivory **261**
  red **273**
  yellow **168**
Creamer
  cobalt blue **32**
  forest green **33**
  grey **37**
  ivory **29**
Cup & saucer, ring handle
  chartreuse **38**
  cobalt blue **27**
  medium green **67**
  red **32**
  rose **42**
  yellow **25**
Gravy boat
  chartreuse **73**
  cobalt blue **69**
  forest green **87**
  grey **66**
  ivory **58**
  medium green **206**
  red **63**

Marmalade jar, cov.
cobalt blue 408
ivory 337
light green 355
red 383
turquoise 367
yellow 384

Mug,
forest green 87
ivory 92
light green 67
medium green 128
red 80
rose 85
yellow 57

Mustard jar, cov.
ivory 292
light green 293
red 339
turquoise 283
yellow 255

Pitcher, jug-type, 2 pt.
cobalt blue 105
ivory 121
light green 78
turquoise 71

Pitcher, juice, disc-type, 30 oz.
chartreuse 242
ivory 142
medium green 1,550
red 644
turquoise 102
yellow 50

Two Quart Pitcher with Ice Lip

Pitcher, w/ice lip, globular, 2 qt.
ivory 163
red 161
yellow (ILLUS.) 130

Pitcher, water, disc-type
chartreuse 270
forest green 296
grey 280
light green 123
medium green 1,552
red 152
turquoise 107
yellow 116

Plate, 9" d.
chartreuse 22
grey 17
rose 23
yellow 16
ivory 16

Plate, 10" d.
cobalt blue 34
grey 57
light green 35
medium green 150
red 44

Plate, chop, 15" d.
light green 57
yellow 62
ivory 54

Plate, grill, 10½" d.
chartreuse 64
cobalt blue 47
light green 30
rose 74
yellow 31
ivory 49

Platter, 12" oval
grey 58
red 52
rose 58
yellow 42
ivory 34

Salt & pepper shakers, pr.
light green 26
medium green 194
rose 36
turquoise 135

Fiesta Sugar Bowl

Sugar bowl, cov.
grey 75
ivory 59
medium green 217
red 68
turquoise (ILLUS.) 46

Syrup pitcher w/original lid
cobalt blue 440
light green 438
red 527
turquoise 571

Teapot, cov., medium size (6 cup)

ivory 190
medium green 1,198
rose. 332
turquoise. 196
yellow 141

Tumbler, juice, 5 oz.

cobalt blue 43
red. 50
rose. 75
turquoise. 33
yellow 39

Vase, 8" h.

ivory 743
light green 585
cobalt blue 667
red. 762
yellow 507

FLORENCE CERAMICS

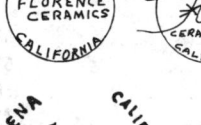  

Florence Marks

Florence Ward began her successful enterprise in 1939. By 1946 she had moved her home workshop into a small plant in Pasadena, California. About three years later it was again necessary to move to larger facilities in the area. Semi-porcelain figurines, some with actual lace dipped in slip, were made. Figurines, such as fictional characters and historical couples, were the backbone of her business. To date, almost two hundred figurines have been documented. For about two years, in the mid-1950s, Betty D. Ford created what the company called "stylized sculptures from the Florence wonderland of birds and animals." Included were about a half dozen assorted doves, several cats, foxes, dogs and rabbits. Several marks were used over the years with the most common being the circle with 'semi-porcelain' outside the circle. The name of the figurine was almost always included with a mark. A "Floraline" mark was used on floral containers and related items. There was also a script mark and a block lettered mark as well as paper labels. The company was sold to Scripto Corporation in 1964 but only advertising pieces were made such as mugs for the Tournament of Roses in Pasadena, California. The company ceased all operations in 1977.

Clock, mantel-type, figural, an ornate scroll-footed & scroll-cast base w/applied roses supporting a rounded embossed case enclosing the round clock dial w/Roman numerals, the scroll-molded high top decorated w/applied rose blossoms & a figural cherub finial, 11½" h. $799
Figure of a girl, "Rose Marie," holding skirts out, 7" h. 189
Figure of a girl, "Tess," wearing large hat, holding up one side of skirt, 7¼" h. 429
Figure of a woman, "Ann," pink w/white hat 95
Figure of a woman, "Ann," yellow w/green hat . . 135
Figure of a woman, "Bea," teal w/white hat. 95
Figures of choir boys, 6½" h., set of 3 300
Flower holder, figure of "Bee," girl wearing hat & carrying a basket, 6¼" h. 50
Flower holder, figure of "Emily," lady standing holding hat on head w/one hand, closed parousel in other hand, 8" h. 50
Flower holder, figure of "June," girl in front of pleated-edge block, 7" h. 50
Flower holder, figure of "Kay," girl standing wearing large hat, holding skirts out to sides, 7" h. 50
Flower holder, figure of "Rita," ivory, 9½" h. 250

FLOW BLUE

Flow Blue ironstone and semi-porcelain was manufactured mainly in England during the second half of the 19th century. The early ironstone was produced by many of the well known English potters and was either transfer-printed or hand-painted (Brush stroke). The bulk of the ware was exported to the United States or Canada. The "flow" or running quality of the cobalt blue designs was the result of introducing certain chemicals into the kiln during the final firing. Some patterns are so "flown" that it is difficult to ascertain the design. The transfers were of several types: Asian, Scenic, Marble or Floral. The earliest Flow Blue ironstone patterns were produced during the period between about 1840 and 1860. After the Civil War Flow Blue went out of style for some years but was again manufactured and exported to the United States beginning about the 1880s and continuing through the turn-of-the-century. These later Flow Blue designs are on a semi-porcelain body rather than heavier ironstone and the designs are mainly florals.

AMERILLIA (Podmore Walker & Co., ca. 1840s-50s)

Plate, 10½" d. $165
Plate, 7½" d. 70
Platter, 16" 600
Teapot, cov., oval body style 850
Vegetable bowl, cov., oval, 10" l. 800

AMOY (Davenport, dated 1844)

Amoy Water Pitcher

Creamer, 6½" h. 300
Cup & saucer, handled 195
Pitcher, water, 12" h., rare body style(ILLUS.) . . 1,500
Plate, 10½" d. 165
Plate, 7½" d. 75
Plate, 8½" d. 85
Plate, 9½" d. 120
Platter, 12" 250
Platter, 16" 450
Platter, 18" 650
Soup plate w/flanged rim, 10" d. 200
Sugar bowl, cov. 375
Teapot, cov. 700
Vegetable bowl, open, 8" l. 595
Waste bowl, "double bulge" style. 325

ANEMONE (Minton, ca. 1860)

Anemone Covered Vegetable Bowl

Plate, 8½" d. 95
Plate, 9½" d. 125
Platter, 14", oval 400
Vegetable bowl, cov., footed (ILLUS.) 400

ARABESQUE (T.J. & J. Mayer, ca. 1845)

Creamer, Classic Gothic style, 6" h. 500
Plate, 10½" d. 195
Plate, 7½" d. 150
Soup plate w/flanged rim, 10" d. 185
Sugar bowl, cov., Classic Gothic style. 595
Teapot, cov., Classic Gothic style 800

ARGYLE (W.H. Grindley & Co., ca. 1896)

Butter dish, cov., w/drainer 600
Cup & saucer, handled 110
Gravy boat 200
Pitcher, 1½ pt. 425
Plate, 10" d. 95
Plate, 7" d. 65
Plate, 8" d. 75
Plate, 9" d. 85
Platter, 14" l. 275
Sauce dish 50
Vegetable bowl, open, medium 185

ATHENS (C. Meigh, ca. 1845)

Athens Punch Cup

Cup & saucer, handleless 225
Gravy boat 350
Plate, 10½" d. 125
Plate, 7½" d. 95
Punch cup (ILLUS.) 145

CARLTON (S. Alcock, ca. 1850)

Carlton Vegetable Bowl

Plate, 8½" d. 130
Plate, 9½" d. 140
Platter, 14" 300
Soup plate w/flanged rim, 10" 150
Vegetable bowl, cov., ca. 1850 (ILLUS.) 400

CASHMERE (Francis Morley, ca. 1845)

Cup & saucer, handleless 300
Mug, 3½" h. 400
Plate, 10½" d. 200
Plate, 7½" d. 100
Plate, 9½" d. 175
Soup plate w/flanged rim, 10" d. 235

CHAPOO (John Wedgwood, ca. 1850)

Creamer, 6½" h. 350
Cup & saucer, handleless 135
Plate, 10½" d. 155
Soup plate w/flanged rim, 10" d. 165

CHINESE (Dimmock, ca. 1845)

Chinese Platter

Platter, 18", well & tree-type (ILLUS.). 700

CHUSAN (J. Clementson, ca. 1840)

Creamer, 6" h. 250
Plate, 7½" d. 125
Plate, 9½" d. 145
Platter, 14" l. 350
Vegetable bowl, open, 8" l. 200

COBURG (J. Edwards, ca. 1850)

Cup & saucer, handleless 150
Plate, 10½" d. 155
Plate, 8½" d. 135
Platter, 16" 300
Soup plate w/flanged rim, 10" 150
Sugar bowl, cov. 450

CONWAY (New Wharf Pottery, ca. 1891)

Cup & saucer, handled 95
Plate, 8½" d. 75
Platter, 12" l. 150
Sauce dish 50
Sugar bowl, cov. 200
Vegetable bowl, open, oval 150

DOROTHY (Johnson Bros., ca. 1900)

Bone dish. 65
Plate, 8" d. 65
Plate, 9" d. 75

DUNDEE (Ridgways, ca. 1910)

Cup & saucer, handled 100
Plate, 8" d. 65
Plate, 9" d. 75
Platter, 10½", oval 95

FESTOON (W.H. Grindley, ca. 1891)

Wash bowl & pitcher, the set 1,200

FLORAL (Laughlin Art China Co., ca. 1900)

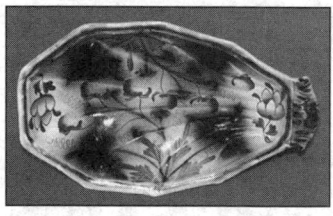

Floral Tyg

Tyg, three-handled (ILLUS.) 350

FLORIDA (W.H. Grindley, ca. 1891)

Cup & saucer, handled 170
Plate, 7" d. 100
Plate, 8" d. 125
Plate, 9" d. 135
Vegetable bowl, open, medium 150

GAUDY (Brushstroke, ca. 1850)

Gaudy Relish Dish

Relish dish, w/polychrome (ILLUS.) 195

GAUDY (Mellor Venables & Co., ca. 1840)

Gaudy Teapot

Creamer, Classic Gothic shape 250
Sugar bowl, cov., Classic Gothic shape 450
Teapot, cov., Classic Gothic shape (ILLUS.) 900

GINGHAM FLOWERS (Brushstroke, ca. 1845)

Gingham Flowers Plate

Cup & saucer, handleless 220
Plate, 7½" d. 175
Plate, 9½" d. (ILLUS.) 200
Platter, 14" l. 350

GOTHIC (J. Furnival, ca. 1850)

Plate, 8½" d. 145
Plate, 9½" d. 165
Soup plate w/flanged rim, 10" 175

GRAPE & BLUEBELL (Brushstroke, ca. 1850)

Plate, 8" d. 150
Soup plate w/flanged rim, 10½" 175

HONG KONG (C. Meigh, ca. 1845)

Cup & saucer, handleless 165
Gravy boat 310
Plate, 10½" d. 175
Plate, 7½" d. 100
Vegetable bowl, open 200
Waste bowl 250

IRIS (Arthur Wilkinson - Royal Staffordshire Potteries, ca. 1907)

Gravy boat 80
Plate, 5¾" d. 15
Plate, 9" d. 30
Platter, 13" l. 90
Vegetable bowl, cov., 7½" d. 180

JAPAN (T. Fell & Co., ca. 1860)

Cup & saucer, handled 150
Pitcher, 8" h. 400
Platter, 16" l. 350

LA BELLE (Wheeling Pottery, ca. 1900)

Bowl, large, helmet-shaped 375
Cake plate 175

Celery dish 235
Cracker jar, cov., 7½" h. 600
Cup & saucer, handled 195
Dessert dish, fancy 155
Mug, chocolate 400
Pitcher, 7½" h. 450

LORNE (W.H. Grindley, ca. 1900)

Lorne Plate

Cup & saucer, handled 125
Plate, 10" d. (ILLUS.) 100
Plate, 7" d. 75
Platter, 12", oval 150

LUCERNE (New Wharf Pottery, ca. 1891)

Cup & saucer 95
Plate, 9" d. 85
Vegetable bowl, cov. 150

MANHATTAN (Johnson Bros., ca. 1895)

Creamer 195
Plate, 9" d. 90
Sugar bowl, cov. 245
Waste bowl 100

MANILLA (Podmore, Walker & Co., ca. 1845)

Manilla Pitcher

Creamer, Primary shape, 6" h. 350
Gravy boat 250
Mug 300
Pitcher, 7½" h., rare body style (ILLUS.) 1,000

Plate, 10½" d. 200
Soup plate w/flanged rim, 10" d. 195

MARGUERITE (W.H. Grindley, ca. 1891)

Bone dish. 65
Plate, 7" d. 60
Plate, 9" d. 85
Sauce dish 55

MELBOURNE (W.H. Grindley, ca. 1891)

Plate, 9" d. 95
Platter, 16" l. 200

MENTONE (Johnson Bros., ca. 1900)

Mentone Teapot

Teapot, cov. (ILLUS.) 600

NANKIN (Davenport, ca. 1850)

Cup & saucer, handleless 200
Plate, 10½" d. 195
Vegetable bowl, open, rectangular, 8" l. 250

NON PARIEL (Burgess & Leigh, ca. 1891)

Bone dish. 90
Cup & saucer, handled 150
Plate, 7" d. 80
Plate, 9" d. 100
Soup plate, 8" d. 130

NORMANDY (Johnson Bros., ca. 1900)

Cup & saucer, handled 150
Gravy boat 95
Plate, 7" d. 90
Plate, 8" d. 100
Plate, 9" d. 120
Soup plate, 8" d. 135

OREGON (T.J. and J. Mayer, ca. 1845)

Creamer, pumpkin shape 350
Cup plate 150
Plate, 10½" d. 195
Plate, 7½" d. 130

Platter, 12" l. 350
Platter, 14" l. 400
Sugar bowl, cov., pumpkin shape 450
Teapot, cov., pumpkin shape 650

OSBORNE (Ridgways, ca. 1905)

Egg cup, large 130
Gravy boat 150
Plate, 7" d. 65
Plate, 9" d. 85

PELEW (E. Challinor, ca. 1850)

Pitcher, water, 9" h. 800
Plate, 10½" d. 175
Plate, 7½" d. 130
Punch cup 150
Teapot, cov., pumpkin shape 650

ROSE (W.H. Grindley, ca. 1893)

Bone dish. 65
Plate, 7" d. 55
Plate, 9" d. 75

ROXBURY (Ridgway, ca. 1910)

Bone dish. 60
Bowl, berry 50
Gravy boat 125
Vegetable bowl, open 150

SCINDE (J&G Alcock, 1839-46)

Scinde Gravy Boat

Cup & saucer, handleless 225
Gravy boat, w/undertray, Full Panel Gothic
style (ILLUS.) 375
Plate, 10½" d. 225
Plate, 7½" d. 160

Scinde Punch Cup

Punch cup (ILLUS.) 175

Scinde Relish Dish

Relish dish, shell-shaped (ILLUS.) 175

Scinde Sugar Bowl

Sugar bowl, cov., Full Panel Gothic style
   (ILLUS.) 450
Waste bowl 300

SCINDE (T. Walker, ca. 1847)

Cup & saucer, handleless 190
Plate, 10½" d. 185
Plate, 7½" d. 150
Plate, 9½" d. 175
Soup plate w/flanged rim, 10" 200
Teapot, cov., Primary shape. 650
Waste bowl 250

SPINACH (Libertas, Brush Stroke, ca. 1900)

Spinach Bowl

Bowl, 5" d. (ILLUS.) 95
Plate, 7" d. 75
Plate, 9" d. 85

STRAWBERRY (J. Furnival, Brush Stroke, ca. 1850)

Cup & saucer, handleless 200
Plate, 7½" d. 150

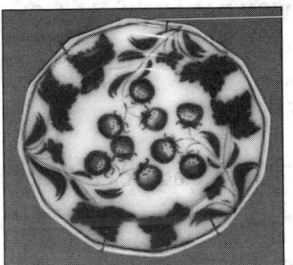

Strawberry Plate

Plate, 9½" d. (ILLUS.) 175
Platter, 14" l. 450
Waste bowl 225

TEMPLE (Podmore, Walker & Co.)

Creamer, Classic Gothic shape, 6" h.. 300
Cup plate 135
Cup & saucer, handleless 175
Relish dish, shell-shaped. 300
Soup plate w/flanged rim, 10" d. 165

TONQUIN (J. Heath, ca. 1850)

Creamer, Full Panel Gothic style, 6" h.. 300
Cup plate 150
Cup & saucer, handleless 195
Plate, 9½" d. 145
Soup plate, 10" d.. 165
Sugar bowl, cov., Full Panel Gothic style 450

TOURAINE (H. Alcock & Co., ca. 1898 or Stanley Pottery, ca. 1898)

Touraine Waste Bowl

Cup & saucer, handled 85
Plate, 7" d. 70
Plate, 8" d. 75
Plate, 9" d. 80
Waste bowl, (ILLUS.) 200

TROY (C. Meigh, ca. 1840)

Cup plate 195
Cup & saucer, handleless 200
Gravy boat 250
Plate, 10½" d. 195
Plate, 8½" d. 175
Soup plate w/flanged rim, 10" 200

WARWICK PANSY (Warwick China Co., ca. 1900)

Cup, chocolate 300
Pitcher, 6½" h. 250
Plate, 8" d. 100

WAVERLY (J. Maddock & Son, ca. 1891)

Butter pat 55
Cup & saucer, handled 125
Gravy boat 130
Plate, 7" d. 65
Plate, 8" d. 75
Vegetable bowl, open 110

WHAMPOA (Mellor Venables, ca. 1840)

Basin & ewer. 1,000
Cup plate 185
Teapot, cov., Primary shape. 795

FRANCISCAN WARE

Franciscan Mark

A product of Gladding, McBean & Company of Glendale and Los Angeles, California, Franciscan Ware was one of a number of lines produced by that firm over its long history. Introduced in 1934 as a pottery dinnerware, Franciscan Ware was produced in many patterns, including "Desert Rose," introduced in 1941 and reportedly the most popular dinnerware pattern ever made in this country. Beginning in 1942 some vitrified china patterns were also produced under the Franciscan name. After a merger in 1963 the company name was changed to Interpace Corporation and in 1979 Josiah Wedgwood & Sons purchased the Gladding, McBean & Co. plant from Interpace. American production ceased in 1984.

Baker, ½ apple-shaped, Apple patt., 4¾" w.,
  5¼" l., 1¾" h. $225
Baking dish, Apple patt., 1 qt. 275
Baking dish, Desert Rose patt., 1 qt. 223
Baking dish, October patt., 1 qt. 100
Batter bowl, pitcher-form, Apple patt., 7" l. 425
Bowl, fruit, 5¼" d., Desert Rose patt., ca. 1941 7
Bowl, fruit, 5½" d., Ivy patt. 15
Bowl, fruit, 5½" d., Wildflower patt. 125
Bowl, soup, footed, 5½", Apple patt. 32
Bowl, soup, footed, 5½" d., Desert Rose patt. . . . 32

Bowl, soup, footed, 5½" d., Ivy patt. 25
Bowl, cereal or soup, 6" d., Desert Rose patt. . . . 11
Bowl, cereal or soup, 6" d., Fresh Fruit patt. 18
Bowl, cereal or soup, 6" d., Ivy patt. 25
Bowl, cereal or soup, 6" d., Meadow Rose patt. . . 10
Bowl, cereal or soup, 6" d., Wildflower patt. 145
Bowl, salad, 10" d., Apple patt. 90
Bowl, salad, 10" d., Wildflower patt. 975
Bowl, salad, 10½" d., Desert Rose patt. 93
Butter dish, cov., California Poppy patt. 175
Butter dish, cov., Ivy patt. 67
Butter dish, cov., October patt. 65
Butter dish, cov., Twilight Rose patt. 125
Casserole, cov., Apple patt., in metal holder. . . 1,500
Casserole, cov., Apple patt., 1½ qt. 90
Casserole, cov., Wildflower patt., 1½ qt. 1,195
Casserole, cov., Desert Rose patt., 2½ qt. 573
Cookie jar, cov., Apple patt. 281
Cookie jar, cov., Desert Rose patt. 330
Creamer & cov. sugar bowl, Apple patt., pr. 55
Creamer & cov. sugar bowl, El Patio
  tableware, Mexican blue glossy glaze, pr. 25
Creamer & cov. sugar bowl, Ivy patt., pr. 90
Creamer & cov. sugar bowl, Meadow Rose
  patt., pr. 38

Apple Pattern Plate, Cup & Saucer

Cup & saucer, Apple patt. (ILLUS.) 10
Cup & saucer, Apple patt., jumbo size 78
Cup & saucer, Coronado Table Ware, coral
  satin glaze 10
Cup & saucer, Desert Rose patt. 10
Cup & saucer, Desert Rose patt., jumbo size 53
Cup & saucer, El Patio tableware, glossy
  yellow glaze 6
Cup & saucer, Ivy patt. 20
Cup & saucer, October patt. 25
Cup & saucer, Starburst patt. 12
Cup & saucer, Twilight Rose patt. 19
Dinner service: 6 each dinner plates, soup
  plates, berry bowls, cups & saucers, 3
  salad plates, one each open sugar bowl,
  creamer, oval platter & vegetable bowl;
  Coronado patt., matte coral, the set 135
Ginger jar, cov., Desert Rose patt. 325
Gravy boat, Arden patt. 65
Gravy boat, California Poppy patt. 95

Gravy boat, Tiempo patt., lime green. 20
Gravy boat w/attached undertray, Desert
    Rose patt. 40
Gravy boat w/attached undertray, Ivy patt. 62
Mixing bowl, Apple patt., 6" d. 135
Mixing bowl, Desert Rose patt., 6" d. 150
Mixing bowl, Desert Rose patt., 7½" d. 150
Mixing bowl, Apple patt., 9" d. 185
Mixing bowl, Desert Rose patt., 9" d. 158
Mug, Meadow Rose patt. 25
Mug, Apple patt., 7 oz. 38
Mug, Desert Rose patt., 7 oz. 26
Mug, Desert Rose patt., 10 oz. 28
Mug, Desert Rose patt., 12 oz. 39
Mug, Apple patt., 17 oz., rare 110
Piggy bank, figural pig, Desert Rose patt. 175
Pitcher, 4" h., Desert Rose patt. 395
Pitcher, milk, 6¼" h., Apple patt., 1 qt. 88
Pitcher, milk, 6½" h., Desert Rose patt., 1 qt. 83
Pitcher, water, 8¾" h., Desert Rose patt.,
    2½ qt. 112

Apple Pattern 2 Qt. Pitcher

Pitcher, water, 8¾" h., Apple patt., 2 qt.
    (ILLUS.) 85
Pitcher w/ice lip, El Patio tableware,
    turquoise glossy glaze, 2½ qt. 125
Plate, bread & butter, 6½" d., Apple patt., ca.
    1940 (ILLUS. w/cup & saucer) 7
Plate, coupe dessert, 7¼" d., Meadow Rose patt. . . 29
Plate, coupe dessert, 7½" d., Apple patt. 65
Plate, coupe dessert, 7½" d., Desert Rose patt. . . . 95
Plate, snack, 8" sq., Apple patt. 195
Plate, snack, 8" sq., Desert Rose patt. 226
Plate, salad, 8½" d., Apple patt., ca. 1940 16
Plate, salad, 8½" d., Desert Rose patt. 11
Plate, salad, 8½" d., Ivy patt. 28
Plate, salad, 8½" d., Meadow Rose patt. 15
Plate, salad, 8½" d., October patt. 18
Plate, salad, 8½" d., Picnic patt. 8
Plate, salad, 8½" d., Wildflower patt. 120
Plate, luncheon, 9¼" d., Ivy patt. 19
Plate, luncheon, 9½" d., Apple patt. 20
Plate, luncheon, 9½" d., Coronado Table
    Ware, coral satin glaze (ILLUS.) 10

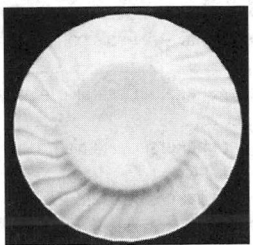

Coronado Table Ware Plate

Plate, luncheon, 9½" d., Coronado Table
    Ware, glossy coral glaze 10
Plate, luncheon, 9½" d., Desert Rose patt. 14
Plate, luncheon, 9½" d., Wildflower patt. 125
Plate, dinner, 10½" d., Desert Rose patt. 10
Plate, dinner, 10½" d., October patt. 28
Plate, chop, 12" d., Apple patt. 60
Plate, chop, 12" d., California Poppy patt. 123
Plate, chop, 12" d., Wildflower patt. 450
Plate, chop, 14" d., Apple patt. 95
Plate, chop, 14" d., Desert Rose patt. 112
Plate, chop, 14" d., Ivy patt. 184
Plate, chop, 14" d., Wildflower patt. 625
Plate, dinner, 10¼" d., Ivy patt. 25
Plate, dinner, 10½" d., Apple patt., ca. 1940 . . . 15
Plate, dinner, 10½" d., California Poppy patt. . . . 37
Plate, dinner, 10½" d., Coronado Table
    Ware, coral satin glaze 10

Dessert Rose Dinner Plate

Plate, dinner, 10½" d., Desert Rose patt.
    (ILLUS.) 15
Plate, dinner, 10½" d., Meadow Rose patt. 13
Plate, dinner, 10½" d., Picnic patt. 10
Plate, dinner, 10½" d., Wildflower patt. 145
Platter, 13" l., oval, Ivy patt. 67
Platter, 14" l., Meadow Rose patt. 29
Platter, 14" l., October patt. 65
Platter, 14" oval, Wildflower patt. 500
Platter, 19" l., oval, Apple patt. 223
Platter, 19" l., oval, Ivy patt., green rim band . . . 300
Platter, 19" l., turkey-size, Desert Rose patt., . . 266
Platter, 19" l., turkey-size, Meadow Rose patt. . . 195
Relish dish, three-part, Apple patt., 11¾" l. 70
Relish dish, three-part, oval, Desert Rose
    patt., 12" l. 67

Salt & pepper shakers, October patt., pr. 35
Salt & pepper shakers, Apple patt.,
2¼" h., pr. 24
Salt & pepper shakers, Desert Rose patt.,
2¼" h., pr. 17
Salt & pepper shakers, California Poppy
patt., 2¾" h., pr. 88
Salt & pepper shakers, Ivy patt., 2¾" h., pr. 35
Salt & pepper shakers, Desert Rose patt.,
6¼" h., pr. 53
Salt & pepper shakers, Meadow Rose
patt., 6¼" h., pr. 38
Salt shaker & pepper mill, Desert Rose
patt., 6" h., pr. 245
Salt shaker & pepper mill, Meadow Rose
patt., 6" h., pr. 145
Soup plate w/flanged rim, Apple patt., 8½" d. 22
Soup plate w/flanged rim, Desert Rose
patt., 8½" d. 20
Soup plate w/flanged rim, Ivy patt., 8½" d. 32
Sugar bowl, cov., Ivy patt. 35
Sugar bowl, cov., October patt. 25
Syrup pitcher, Apple patt., 1 pt., 6¼" h. 82
Syrup pitcher, Desert Rose patt., 1 pt., 6½" h. ... 86
Tea set: cov. teapot, creamer & sugar bowl;
Coronado Table Ware, white, the set. 85
Teapot, cov., Arden patt. 125
Teapot, cov., Desert Rose patt., 6½" h. 102
Teapot, cov., individual, Desert Rose patt.,
6¼" h. 295
Tidbit tray, two-tier, center handle, Ivy patt. 145
Tile, Desert Rose patt., 6" sq. 48
Toast cover, Desert Rose patt., 5½" d., 3" h. ... 204
Trivet, Apple patt., 6" d. 280
Tumbler, El Patio tableware, coral glaze 50
Tumbler, El Patio tableware, Mexican blue
glossy glaze 12
Tumbler, El Patio tableware, redwood
glossy glaze 50
Tumbler, El Patio tableware, turquoise
glossy glaze 50
Tumbler, Apple patt., juice, 6 oz., 3¼" h. 29
Tumbler, Ivy patt., 10 oz., 5" h. 40
Tumbler, California Poppy patt., water,
10 oz., 5¼" h. 145
Tumbler, Desert Rose patt., 10 oz., 5¼" h. 27
Tumbler, Wildflower patt., water, 10 oz.,
5½" h. 250
Tumbler, Ivy patt., 12 oz., 3" h. 43
Vegetable bowl, open, round, Ivy patt., 7¼" d. ... 45
Vegetable bowl, open, round, Apple patt.,
7¾" d. 38
Vegetable bowl, open, round, Desert Rose
patt., 8" d. 24
Vegetable bowl, open, round, Apple patt., 8¼" d. ... 45
Vegetable bowl, open, round, Apple patt., 9" d. ... 50
Vegetable bowl, open, round, California
Poppy patt., 9" d. 125

Vegetable bowl, open, round, Desert Rose
patt., 9" d. 31
Vegetable bowl, open, round, Ivy patt., 8¼" d. ... 47
Vegetable bowl, open, round, Wildflower
patt., 9" d. 250
Vegetable bowl, divided, Apple patt.,
7 x 10¾" 45
Vegetable bowl, divided, Desert Rose patt.,
7 x 10¾" 34
Vegetable bowl, divided, Ivy patt., 8 x 12¼" 40

FULPER

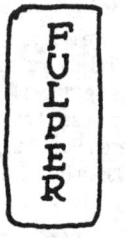

Fulper Marks

The Fulper Pottery was founded in Flemington, New Jersey, in 1805 and operated until 1935, although operations were curtailed in 1929 when its main plant was destroyed by fire. The name was changed in 1929 to Stangl Pottery, which continued in operation until July of 1978, when Pfaltzgraff, a division of Susquehanna Broadcasting Company of York, Pennsylvania, purchased the assets of the Stangl Pottery, including the name.

Book ends, square base w/figural Egyptian
"Rameses" covered in a matte green
glaze, ink marks, 8" h., 4" sq., pr. $770
Bowl-vase, squatty bulbous body raised on
three tiny feet, the wide shoulder tapering
to a short cylindrical neck, smooth matte
green glaze, professional chip restoration
to two feet, mark obscured by glaze,
6¾" d., 3½" h. 413
Candlesticks, flaring socket on a simple
four-sided columnar standard above the
flaring, stepped round foot, top w/a glossy
ivory shading down to a streaked French
blue flambé glaze, ink racetrack mark,
10½" h., pr. 550
Center bowl, Effigy-type, a wide flat-
bottomed shallow bowl w/incurved sides
raised on three crouching figures resting
on a molded thick disc base, cat's-eye
flambé, blue crystalline & speckled brown
matte glaze, ink racetrack mark,
13" d., 4½" h. 715
Flagon, footed bulbous ovoid body w/three
ribbed bands & upright curved neck
w/square cut-out above applied

From left: Fulper Flagon
Fulper "Mushroom" Lamp

braided handle, Chinese blue flambé
glaze, incised racetrack mark, 11" h.,
7" d. (ILLUS.) 440

Flagon, footed bulbous ovoid body w/three
ribbed bands & upright curved neck
w/square cut-out above applied braided
handle, Chinese blue flambé glaze,
incised racetrack mark, 11" h., 7" d.
(ILLUS.) 440

Lamp, table model, a wide low domed
mushroom-shaped pottery shade, inset
around the sides w/textured amber slag
glass & iridescent green jewels, raised
on a tall slender waisted cylindrical base
w/a widely flaring foot, two electric
sockets, grey & light blue flambé glaze
over mirrored lustre gunmetal, base
stamped w/vertical "FULPER" in a box,
circular "VASECRAFT" stamp, also
stamped "Patent Pending U.S. and
Canada" & "6," shade stamped "17-17-8,"
unobtrusive crazing, 20½" h., shade
17" d. (ILLUS.) 21,850

Vase, 3" h., miniature, a squatty bulbous
base w/an angled shoulder below the
conical neck flanked by arched handles
from the rim to shoulder, gunmetal
crystalline glaze over a caramel
crystalline flambé glaze, stamped
vertical mark 220

Fulper Miniature Vases

Vase, miniature, 3½" h., 3" d., footed
squatty bulbous base tapering to
a rounded stepped neck w/molded
rim, Copperdust crystalline glaze,
ink racetrack mark (ILLUS. left) 358

Vase, 4½" h., swelled cylindrical body w/a
sharply angled shoulder to the wide, short
cylindrical neck, fine brown, blue &
caramel drippy flambé glaze, stamped
vertical mark 319

Vase, miniature, 4¾" h., 3¼" d., bulbous
ovoid body w/closed mouth, covered in a
fine ivory to cat's-eye flambé glaze, ink
racetrack mark (ILLUS. right) 165

Vase, 5½" h., bulbous ovoid body
tapering to a wide heavy molded rim,
overall copperdust glaze, embossed
vertical mark 319

Vase, miniature, 5¾" h., 2¼" d., slender
cylindrical form covered in cat's-eye
flambé glaze, interior line does not
go through, rectangular ink mark
(ILLUS. center) 275

Vase, 6½" h., ovoid body w/an angled
shoulder at the short, widely flaring
neck, three flat pierced short handles
from the rim to the shoulder, green
to blue to charcoal semi-gloss drip
glaze over a red matte ground, vertical
stamp mark 253

Vase, 7" h., simple ovoid body w/heavy
molded rim, blue, brown & gunmetal
flambé glaze, embossed vertical mark 231

Vase, 8" h., footed baluster-form w/a gently
flaring neck, outswept & upturned loop
shoulder handles, a creamy drip over a
rust flambé glaze, stamped vertical mark 523

Vase, 8" h., 6" d., bulbous nearly spherical
body w/a short cylindrical closed neck
flanked by angled handles w/small
round openings from rim to shoulder,
fine green crystalline glaze, vertical mark
under glaze 440

Vase, 8" h., 7" d., seven-sided gently
tapering ovoid body, flowing matte olive
flambé glaze, incised racetrack mark 495

Vase, 9½" h., large bulbous nearly spherical
body w/a short cylindrical neck & thick rim
flanked by five small oval ring shoulder
handles, overall streaky bluish green
crystalline glaze, paper label, grinding
flakes on base 770

Vase, 10" h., slender baluster-form w/flared
rim, overall dark matte green glaze,
incised oval vertical mark 489

Vase, 11" h., tall slender slightly waisted
cylindrical body w/rectangular narrow
buttress handles halfway down the sides,
each w/a narrow rectangular opening,
unusual blue & green flambé over red
matte glaze, incised vertical mark 1,100

Vase, 12" h., large classic baluster-form body w/flaring rim, overall two-tone light green crystalline glaze, stamped vertical mark **440**

Vase, 12½" h., bulbous ovoid horizontally ribbed body tapering to a tall smooth flaring neck, small arched shoulder handles, cream flambé drip glaze over orange & brown w/a gunmetal crystalline glaze at the bottom, incised vertical mark . . . **1,210**

Vase, 13" h., tall cylindrical form w/flat rim, overall relief-molded cattails & long slender leaves, covered in a Matte green & Leopard Skin crystalline glaze, the brown clay showing through, rectangular ink mark (restoration to lines from rim) **1,760**

Vase, 13¼" h., squatty bulbous base w/tall trumpet-form neck, gunmetal & Chinese blue flambé glaze, incised racetrack mark & remnant of paper label **1,650**

Vase, 17" h., tall swelled cylindrical body tapering slightly to a short cylindrical neck, leopard skin glaze w/large crystals in green & tan, impressed vertical mark **2,530**

GAUDY DUTCH

This name is applied to English earthenware with designs copied from Oriental patterns. Production began in the 18th century. These copies flooded into this country in the early 19th century. The incorporation of the word "Dutch" derives from the fact that it was the Dutch who first brought the Oriental wares into Europe. The ware was not, as often erroneously reported, made specifically for the Pennsylvania Dutch.

Gaudy Dutch Plates & Teapot

Cup & saucer, handleless, Double Rose patt. (wear, enamel flaking, slight color variation). **$440**

Plate, 7" d., War Bonnet patt. (ILLUS. left) **825**

Plate, 8⅜" d., Sunflowers patt. (minor wear & stains) **715**

Plate, 8" d., War Bonnet patt., minor wear, green enamel flaked (ILLUS. right) **770**

Teapot, cov., War Bonnet patt., some enamel wear, yellowed repairs, 6" h. (ILLUS. center) **605**

Waste bowl, Double Rose patt., 5½" d., 2¾" h. (wear, enamel flaking, slight hairline) . . **550**

GAUDY WELSH

This is a name for wares made in England for the American market about 1830 to 1860, with some examples dating much later. Decorated with Imari-style flower patterns, often highlighted with copper lustre, it should not be confused with Gaudy Dutch wares whose colors differ somewhat.

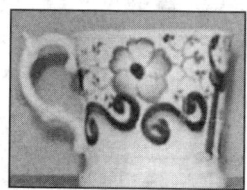

Gaudy Welsh Dogwood Mug

Mug, cylindrical w/ornate C-scroll handle, Dogwood (Shanghai) patt., 3⅛" h. (ILLUS.) . . **$358**

Gaudy Welsh Gwent Pattern Pitcher

Pitcher, 6½" h., hexagonal wide lower body below the waisted neck w/a high arched spout & angled handle, Gwent patt., rim chips (ILLUS.) **413**

Pitcher, 9" h., baluster-form w/wide squatty center, scalloped rim w/wide arched spout & ornate C-scroll handle, Centerpiece patt. w/large six-petal blossom on vine w/dark blue leaves, molded background, blue, red & green w/lustre trim, mid-19th c. (firing flaw near handle, flaking to green) **468**

Washbowl & pitcher, miniature, Tulip patt., footed 4⅜" d. bowl w/flaring sides, baluster form 3⅞" h. pitcher w/arched spout & ornate scrolled handle, minor wear, the set **330**

GOLDSCHEIDER

Goldscheider Marks

The Goldscheider firm, manufacturers of porcelain and faience in Austria between 1885 and the present, was founded by Freidrich Goldscheider and carried on by his widow. The firm came under the control of his sons, Walter and Marcell, in 1920. Fleeing their native Austria at the time of World War II, the Goldscheiders set up an operation in the United States. They were listed in the Trenton, New Jersey, City Directory from 1943 through 1950 and their main production seems to have been art pottery figurines.

While tin-enameled earthenware has been made in Gouda, Holland since the early 1600s, the productions of modern factories are attracting increasing collector attention. The art pottery of Gouda is easily recognized by its brightly colored peasant-style decoration with some types having achieved a "cloisonne" effect. Pottery workshops located in, or near, Gouda include Regina, Zenith, Plazuid, Schoonhoven, Arnhem and others. Their wide range of production included utilitarian wares, as well as vases, miniatures and large outdoor garden ornaments.

Two Goldscheider Figures

Figure group, tall svelte Art Deco lady wearing a long flowered dress & wide-brimmed hat, one hand on her hip, the other holding her hat, striding beside her sleek wolf hound, printed & impressed marks, 15" h. (ILLUS. left) **$575**

Figure of ballerina, wearing a lace skirt, printed marks, 17" h. **862**

Figure of dancer, the tall slender young lady w/long hair posed wearing a halter top & long flowered skirt which she holds out to the sides, on a plinth base, printed marks, 17¾" h. (ILLUS. right) **747**

Figure of nude lady, an Art Deco style lady standing nude except for stockings & a floral-decorated drapery, wearing a high upswept hat, on a paneled plinth, impressed, printed & painted marks, 19" h. . . **2,875**

Lamp base, finely detailed figure of a woman decorated in colors of green, yellow, purple & blue, on a bluish white ground & a black base, signed "Goldscheider, Wien, Made in Austria, XXVII," 32" h. overall **1,610**

Plaque, molded in relief w/the head of a young woman, stamped mark, 12¼" h. **460**

GOUDA

Gouda Marks

Unusual Gouda Clock

Clock, wall-type, a large flattened disk centered by a small round dial w/Arabic numerals, the front decorated in dark blue w/stylized irises & foliage in shades of green, blue, mauve, rust & yellow, glossy glaze, clock works marked "J. Unghans," crazing, clock not working, ca. 1900, 9" d. (ILLUS.) **$805**

Toothpick holder, floral decoration on black ground, side medallion KLM logo silhouette, 208 Zenith, Gouda Fleer, 1¾" h. **80**

Vase, 4" h., decorated w/glossy multicolor florals on mottled grey ground, green interior, Royal Areo 2841 House mark **125**

Vase, 9" h., footed bulbous nearly spherical body centered by a tall slender neck w/flared rim, high slender loop handles from rim to shoulder, decorated in rust & moss & grass green w/stylized tulip blossoms & leaves swirling against a dark green ground, glossy glaze, painted marks . . . **413**

Floral-Decorated Gouda Vase

Vase, 9" h., ovoid shouldered body w/a
slender swelled neck, decorated
w/stylized flowers & leaves in shades of
dark green, rust, brown, pale green &
white, matte glaze, signed "Made in
Holland" (ILLUS.) **176**

Vase, 11" h., shouldered ovoid body,
decorated w/butterflies & foliage, signed.... **1,092**

Vase, 12½" h., tall baluster-form w/a short
small cylindrical neck, a black ground
decorated w/stylized florals in shades of
green, cobalt blue, mustard yellow, rust,
mauve & purple, glossy glaze, marked
"304 - Gouda - Holland - J.B." w/a house
(minor glaze imperfections) **575**

Vase, 12½" h., 4¾" d., footed tall slender
tapering cylindrical form w/a short
cylindrical neck, dark green ground
decorated w/a standing profile portrait of
a Dutch peasant woman w/white cap,
green neckerchief & purple blouse, dark
blue apron & orange dress, marked
"#7052 RR Holland Gouda - #1852R"
(flake on bottom) **385**

Vase, 22" h., tall slender ovoid body,
decorated in colors w/an exotic bird &
foliage, signed **2,760**

GRUEBY

GRUEBY
Grueby Pottery Mark

*Some fine art pottery was produced by the
Grueby Faience and Tile Company, established
in Boston in 1891. Choice pieces were created
with molded designs on a semi-porcelain body.
The ware is marked and often bears the initials
of the decorators. The pottery closed in 1907.*

Rare Grueby Covered Humidor

Bowl, 8" d., 2" h., wide shallow rounded
flaring sides w/a closed rim, interior
w/streaky light green glossy glaze, the
exterior w/a dark green matte glaze,
paper label, impressed mark (minute
inside rim flake) **$495**

Humidor, cov., tapering cylindrical form
w/waisted neck & fitted disk shape lid
w/knob finial, decorated w/repeating floral
band on rim, curdled matte sea-green
glaze, impressed mark & incised "ER,
3 -14," glaze bursts, 8" h. (ILLUS.) **1,093**

Paperweight, figural, model of a scarab
beetle, covered in a leathery mustard
matte enamel, impressed "Grueby
Faience Co. - Boston USA" & paper label,
3" l., 2" h. **770**

Tile, square, cuenca, sea gulls diving in high
waves, browns, green & French blue
enamels, unframed, unmarked, 4" sq. **770**

Fine Grueby Cuenca Tile

Tile, square, cuenca, decorated w/a three-
masted ship & rolling waves against a
blue sky, browns, ivory & French blue
matte enamels, "MM" in glaze, unframed,
6" sq. (ILLUS.) **660**

Tile, square, depicting the cupid Eros in red
bisque clay w/a matte mustard glaze
background, unmarked, unframed, 6" sq. **330**

Tile, square, sculpted & painted design of
tulips in blue & green w/green stems &
leaves against darker green matte
ground, unframed, 6" sq. (minor flakes) **990**

Tile, rectangular, sculpted candle &
chamberstick in yellow, black & green
against a darker green matte ground,
unframed, 4½ x 6" **2,860**

Vase, 4½" h., bulbous ovoid body w/a wide
rounded shoulder centered by a short
flaring neck w/flattened rim, the sides
sculpted & applied w/wide vertical leaves,
dark green matte glaze, impressed mark,
artist-signed **1,210**

Vase, 5½" h., 4" d., ovoid body w/a
short flaring neck, incised vertical
ridges, matte green enamel, impressed
circular mark **1,540**

Vase, 6¼" h., 3½" d., ovoid body w/wide flat
rim, tooled & applied full-height leaves
alternating w/large white crocus buds,
matte French blue ground, stamped
mark, two paper labels (ILLUS.) **19,800**

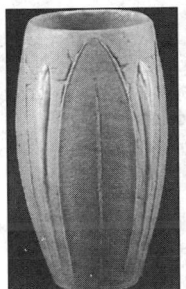

From left: Grueby Vase with Crocus Buds
Grueby Vase with Buds & Leaves

Vase, 7½" h., 8½" d., wide bulbous ovoid body w/a deep rounded shoulder centered by a large cylindrical neck w/rolled rim, the body carved & applied w/a continuous band of wide, pointed overlapping leaves, two-tone green matte glaze, signed "W. Post," impressed mark (neatly restored drill hole in base) **2,860**

Vase, 9" h., slender waisted cylindrical form w/a small molded mouth, sculpted & applied vertical leaves under a thick suspended green matte glaze, signed by Ruth Erickson, impressed mark **2,640**

Vase, 9" h., 3½" d., cylindrical body slightly rounded at base & shoulder w/rolled rim, covered in a matte leathery bluish grey enamel, impressed mark (small chips to rim).. **825**

Vase, 9⅞" h., 4¼" d., cylindrical body swollen at base, decorated w/matte yellow glazed buds on elongated stems alternating w/elongated leaf blades under matte green glaze, designed by Wilhelmina Post, impressed marks & incised artist's initials (ILLUS.) **4,888**

Vase, 11" h., simple ovoid body w/a five-sided pinched & flared rim, the sides sculpted & applied w/tall pointed leaves divided by carved stems & tiny buds, overall dark green matte glaze, impressed mark (repaired chips).......... **2,310**

Large Grueby Vase

Vase, 11¾" h., 8" d., wide cylindrical body w/round shoulder & short molded rim, decorated w/two tiers of overlapping leaf blades & alternating bud on stem, thin

matte green glaze trailing & gathering at decoration edges & base, pale matte yellow glaze on buds, designed by Wilhelmina Post, No. 36, tight spider hairline in base, impressed marks & incised artist's initials (ILLUS.) **5,750**

Vase, 16" h., 8½" d., squatty bulbous base w/the shoulder tapering to very tall slender cylindrical neck w/flat rim, tooled & applied leaves on the base, leathery matte green glaze, spherical pottery mark, "133A" & paper label **1870**

HALL CHINA

 **HALL CHINA**

Hall Marks

Founded in 1903 in East Liverpool, Ohio, this still-operating company at first produced mostly utilitarian wares. It was in 1911 that Robert T. Hall, son of the company founder, developed a special single-fire, lead-free glaze which proved to be strong, hard and non-porous. In the 1920s the firm became well known for their extensive line of teapots (still a major product) and in 1932 they introduced kitchen-wares followed by dinnerwares in 1936 and refrigerator wares in 1938.

The imaginative designs and wide range of glaze colors and decal decorations have led to the growing appeal of Hall wares with collectors, especially people who like Art Deco and Art Moderne design. One of the firm's most famous patterns was the "Autumn Leaf" line, produced as premiums for the Jewel Tea Company. For listings of this ware see "Jewel Tea Autumn Leaf." Helpful books on Hall include The Collector's Guide to Hall China *by Margaret & Kenn Whitmyer, and* Superior Quality Hall China—A Guide for Collectors *by Harvey Duke (An ELO Book, 1977).*

Bean pot, cov., New England shape, No. 4, Crocus patt. **$325**
Bowl, 6" d., Thick Rim shape, Blue Blossom patt. **80**
Bowl, 9" d., salad, Rose Parade patt. **44**
Butter dish, cov., Crocus patt., Zephyr shape, 1 lb. **1,200**
Casserole, cov., Rose Parade patt. **48**
Casserole w/inverted pie dish lid, Radiance shape, No. 488, silver ring trim on casserole lip, pie dish edge & below tab handles, orange, red & purple flowers w/light & dark green leaves, marked in

Casserole with Inverted Pie Dish Lid

gold "Hall's Superior Quality Kitchenware" in a square w/"Made in U.S.A." below the square, 6½" d., 4" h. (ILLUS.). 38
Coffeepot, cov., Coffee Queen, Chinese Red 95
Coffeepot, cov., Waverly patt., Minuet decal. . . . 65
Cookie jar, cov., Five Band shape, Blue Blossom patt. 300
Cookie jar, cov., Flareware, Gold Lace design . . . 65
Cookie jar, cov., Game Birds decal 250

Irish Coffee Mug

Mug, Irish coffee, footed, high gloss yellow exterior w/white interior, marked "Hall" in a circle & "Made in U.S.A. 1273" outside the circle & an incised " B27," 6" h. (ILLUS.) 15
Pitcher, ball-shape, Royal Rose patt.. 95
Pitcher, jug-type, 7½" h., Pert shape, Rose Parade patt. 85
Pretzel jar, cov., Crocus patt.. 195
Salt & pepper shakers, handled, range type, Blue Blossom patt., pr. 90
Salt & pepper shakers, Pert shape, Rose Parade patt., pr. 45

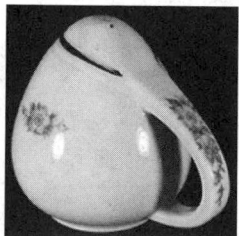

Rose White Salt Shaker

Salt & pepper shakers, Rose White patt., holes form letters "S" & "P," pr. (ILLUS. of one) 29

Syrup pitcher, cov., Five Band shape, Blue Blossom patt.. 165
Teapot, cov., Airflow shape, Chinese red. 100
Teapot, cov., Aladdin shape, Blue Bouquet patt. . . 135
Teapot, cov., Albany shape, mahogany w/gold trim, 6-cup. 95
Teapot, cov., Automobile shape, turquoise w/platinum 650
Teapot, cov., Baltimore shape, green w/gold . . . 195
Teapot, cov., Basketball shape, emerald green w/gold trim 450
Teapot, cov., Birdcage shape, burgundy w/gold trim, 6-cup. 335
Teapot, cov., Boston shape, Crocus patt. 225
Teapot, cov., Connie shape, celadon green, 6-cup 49
Teapot, cov., Coverlet shape, white w/gold cover, 6-cup 40
Teapot, cov., French shape, Chinese red & white, 2-cup 90
Teapot, cov., Globe shape, emerald green w/gold 95
Teapot, cov., Hook Cover shape, turquoise w/gold. 55
Teapot, cov., Illinois shape, Stock Brown w/gold. 250
Teapot, cov., Indiana shape, warm yellow w/gold, 6-cup 308
Teapot, cov., Manhattan shape, Chinese red, 8-cup 500
Teapot, cov., McCormick shape, mahogany w/gold trim, 6-cup. 85
Teapot, cov., Medallion shape, Crocus patt. 65
Teapot, cov., Melody shape, Orange Poppy patt.. 370
Teapot, cov., Nautilus shape, turquoise blue & gold 225
Teapot, cov., New York shape, Wild Poppy patt., 4-cup 295
Teapot, cov., Ohio shape, brown w/gold 200
Teapot, cov., Parade shape, warm yellow w/gold. 45
Teapot, cov., Pert shape, Chinese red, 6-cup 75
Teapot, cov., Rhythm shape, yellow w/gold trim, 6-cup 125

Star Shape Teapot

Teapot, cov., Star shape, cobalt blue w/gold (ILLUS.). 125

Teapot, cov., Streamline shape, Orange
Poppy patt. **343**

Teapot, cov., Sundial shape, yellow w/gold
trim, 6-cup **95**

Teapot, cov., Surfside shape, Cadet blue **275**

Teapot, cov., T-Ball round, black w/gold
label, 6-cup. **195**

Teapot, cov., Thorley series, white
w/rhinestone decoration **295**

Teapot, cov., Tip-pot w/holder, cadet blue **155**

Teapot, cov., Windshield shape, gamebird
decoration. **250**

Water server w/hinged cover,
Westinghouse refrigerator ware, Hercules
shape, cobalt blue **125**

HAMPSHIRE POTTERY

 **HAMPSHIRE**

Hampshire Marks

Hampshire Pottery was made in Keene, New Hampshire, where several potteries operated as far back as the late 18th century. The pottery now known as Hampshire Pottery was established by J. S. Taft shortly after 1870. Various types of wares, including Art Pottery, were produced through the years. Taft's brother-in-law, Cadmon Robertson, joined the firm in 1904 and was responsible for developing over 900 glaze formulas while in charge of all manufacturing. His death in 1914 created problems for the firm and Taft sold out to George Morton in 1916. Closed during part of World War I, the pottery was later reopened by Morton for a short time and manufactured white hotel china. From 1919 to 1921, mosaic floor tiles became the main production. All production ceased in 1923.

Hampshire Ewer

Bowl-vase, squatty bulbous form w/a wide
rounded & flattened shoulder centered by
a low, wide mouth, molded w/wide leaves
up around the sides, overall dark blue
matte glaze, embossed mark, 6" d., 4" h.. . . . **$550**

Ewer, the wide squatty bulbous footed base
w/a wide shoulder tapering to a cylindrical
neck flaring to a long arched spout &
incurved tab attached to the top of the
slender C-scroll handle, matte green
glaze, impressed mark, 9¾" h. (ILLUS.). **440**

Lamp, table model, a wide squatty lobed
bulbous base w/wide vertical ribs & a
wide shoulder tapering up to a flat rim
supporting a domed metal burner,
shoulder & burner fitted w/a widely flaring
conical leaded glass shade composed of
a stylized geometric design of green slag
glass & small bands of blue & red
diamonds, pink blossoms & purple top
segments, base w/impressed mark,
overall 22" h. **2,200**

Vase, 6¼" h., 3½" d., incised foliate design
under a matte green glaze w/frothy
white highlights, incised "Hampshire
Pottery 52/2". **403**

Vase, 7" h., simple ovoid form w/a wide flat
mouth, the sides molded w/stylized three-
petal blossoms above pairs of leaves
atop tall slender stems down the sides,
good medium green matte glaze,
impressed mark **715**

Vase, 9" h., 13" d., lobed circular body,
matte green glaze, designed by Cadmon
Robertson, impressed "Hampshire - M
(in a circle) - 900," ca. 1908 (hairline). **863**

HARLEQUIN

The Homer Laughlin China Company, makers of the popular "Fiesta" pottery line, also introduced in 1938 a less expensive and thinner ware which was sold under the "Harlequin" name. It did not carry the maker's trade-mark and was marketed exclusively through F. W. Woolworth Company. It was produced in a wide range of dinnerwares in assorted colors until 1964. Out of production for a number of years, in 1979 Woolworth requested the line be reintroduced using an ironstone body and with a limited range of pieces and colors offered. Collectors also seek out a series of miniature animal figures produced in the Harlequin line in the 1930s and 1940s.

Creamer, novelty, turquoise **$38**

Creamer, novelty, yellow **45**

Cup & saucer, yellow. **7**

Pitcher, 9" h., ball-shaped w/ice lip, mauve blue . . **95**

Pitcher, jug-type, mauve blue, 22 oz. **85**

Pitcher, jug-type, yellow, 22 oz. **63**

Plate, 6" d., medium green	10
Plate, 7" d., grey	3
Plate, 9" d., chartreuse	13
Plate, 9" d., rose	13
Plate, 9" d., yellow	11
Plate, 10"d., chartreuse	35
Soup plate w/flanged rim, grey	25
Soup plate w/flanged rim, mauve blue	25

HAVILAND

Haviland Marks

Haviland porcelain was originated by Americans in Limoges, France, shortly before the mid-19th century and continues in production. Some Haviland was made by Theodore Haviland in the United States during the last World War. Numerous other factories also made china in Limoges. Also see LIMOGES.

Broth bowl & underplate, No. 448, 2 pcs.	$110
Cake plate, No. 1 Ranson blank, patt. No. 228, 10¾" d.	33
Candleholders, Swirl patt., decorated w/dainty roses, pr.	135
Chocolate cup & saucer, No. 72A	35
Chocolate pot, cov., scallop & scroll mold w/floral decoration & gold trim, marked "Haviland Limoges, France," 9" h.	132
Cup & saucer, Moss Rose patt., "Haviland & Co. - Limoges - France," pr.	20
Cup & saucer, Rosalinde patt.	50
Gravy boat, No. 761	35
Pin box, cov., oblong, ornate scrolled base & rim, loop finial on h.p. floral decorated lid, marked "H & Co. L. France," 4" l.	39
Pitcher, Art Deco stylized figural 'Farewell' cat of yellow & white persuasion, base inscribed "Theodore Haviland Limoges/France Copyright Depose" & "E.M. San Doz sc," 8⅝" h.	690
Plate, dinner, No. 72	38
Plate, dinner, Rosalinde patt.	40
Platter, 17" l., No. 72	85
Serving plate, blue & burgundy Art Deco decoration, black ground, "Haviland & Co.- Limoges - France," 10½" d.	15
Soup plate w/flanged rim, No. 761	10

HISTORICAL & COMMEMORATIVE WARES

Numerous potteries, especially in England and the United States, made various porcelain and earthenware pieces to commemorate people, places and events. Scarce English historical wares with American views command highest prices. Objects are listed here alphabetically by title of view.

Most pieces listed here will date between about 1820 and 1850. The maker's name is noted in parentheses at the end of each entry.

Albany, New York platter, long-stemmed roses border, 16¾ x 20", Jackson (glaze wear)	$690
American Views, Boston and Bunker Hill platter, flowers, moss & leaves border, purple, 16" l., Thomas Godwin (crazing, glaze imperfections, minor staining)	374
Boston Harbor sugar bowl, flowers, foliage & scrolls border, spread-winged eagle w/shield in foreground w/Boston harbor in background, 5 7/8" h., Rogers (some exterior edge wear & pinpoints, inner flange of bowl & lid chipped, chip on finial, lid is slightly undersize)	1,155
Boston Mails...Ladies Cabin platter, border medallions of steamships & two views of "Acadia" & "Columbia," light blue, 16" l., Edwards (minor staining, knife marks)	259
Boston State House dinner service: 29 dinner plates, 19 luncheon plates, 11 soup plates, four bread & butter plates, 10 platters (one w/a pierced inset), a cov. soup tureen, ladle & undertray, four cov. sauce tureens & three undertrays, four cov. serving dishes, a square center bowl; dark blue, Rogers, the set (some w/staple & other repairs, minor cracks, chips & staining)	14,950
Boston State House plate, floral border, dark blue, unmarked, 8½" d. (minor wear)	193
Castle Garden, Battery, New York platter, trefoil separated by knobs border, dark blue, 18½" l., Wood (minor wear & shallow glaze flakes, stains)	3,080
Exchange, Baltimore plate, fruit & flowers border, dark blue, 10" d. (Henshall, Williamson & Co.)	440
Great Fire, City of New York, Burning of Coenties Slip plate, fire engines & eagles border, light blue, unknown maker, 8" d. (wear & small edge flakes)	385
Harvard College plate, acorn & oak leaves border, dark blue, minor roughness on table ring, 10" d., (Stevenson & Williams)	275
Hospital, Boston plate, vine border, dark blue, 8½" d., Stevenson & Williams (wear & scratches)	248
Landing of the Fathers at Plymouth, Dec. 22, 1620 plate, pairs of birds & scrolls & four medallions w/ships & inscriptions border, dark blue, 6½" d. (E. Wood)	173

Landing of the Fathers at Plymouth pitcher, pairs of birds & scrolls & four medallions w/ships & inscriptions border, medium blue, 6½" h., Wood (minor chips, star crack, glaze wear) **345**

Mount Vernon, The Seat of the Late Gen'l. Washington sugar bowl, large white flowers border, dark blue, 5 7/8" h., unknown maker (chips & rim hairlines, lid may be mismatched) **1,155**

Near Fishkill, Hudson River plate, flowers & birds border, black, 10¼" d., Clews (minor glaze rubs) **99**

Near Fishkill plate, flowers & scrolls border, dark blue, 7¾" d. (Clews) **248**

New York From Brooklyn Heights plate, flowers between leafy scrolls border, dark blue, 10¼" d., Stevenson (minor wear & chip on table ring) **1,485**

Octagon Church, Boston fruit bowl, footed & handled, reverse w/"Bank, Savannah" & "Exchange, Charleston," dark blue, Beauties of America series, J. & W. Ridgway, 10" d., 5" h. (minute glaze chips, very minor firing crack on one handle) **1,495**

Park Theatre, New York soup plate, acorn & oak leaves border, dark blue, 10" d., Stevenson & Williams (pinpoint flakes on table ring) **385**

Pass in the Catskill Mountains plate, shell border, circular center, dark blue, 7½" d., E. Wood (minor wear) **193**

Shepherd Boy Rescued platter, six-point star w/birds & flowers border, dark blue,12⅝" l., Clews (staining, knife marks, glaze chips) **115**

Oval States Series Dish

States series oval dish, border w/names of fifteen states in festoons separated by five or eight-point stars, center scene of castle w/flag, boats in foreground, dark blue, crazing & light stains, 11¾" l., Clews (ILLUS.) **1,540**

States series pitcher, border w/names of fifteen states in festoons separated by five-point stars, center scene of castle

w/flag, boats in foreground, dark blue, unmarked, 9¾" h. (small edge flakes on rim, handle & spout, minor wear & shallow flake on bottom) **2,530**

Rare Texian Campaigne Compote

Texian Campaigne - Battle of Palo Alto compote, battle scene center, symbols of war & a "goddess-type" seated border, light blue, 5½" h., 10¼" d., Shaw (ILLUS.) . . . . **2,800 to 3,000**

View of Governor's Island

View of Governor's Island soup plate, floral & scroll border, dark blue, minor wear & small flakes w/crow's foot hairline, 10⅜" d., Stevenson (ILLUS.) **2,475**

Washington plate, flowers & scrolls border, dark blue, 7¾" d. (Clews) **385**

Washington Standing at Tomb, scroll in hand cup & saucer, dark blue, saucer 6½" d., E. Wood (minor chips, staining, transfer imperfections) **403**

Water Works, Philadelphia plate, acorn & oak leaves border, dark blue, 10⅛" d. (Stevenson & Williams) **605**

Winter View of Pittsfield, Massachusetts open vegetable dish, vignette views & flowers border, dark blue, 12½" l., Clews (minor wear w/some glaze wear on edges) **1,870**

Winter View of Pittsfield, Massachusetts plate, vignette views & flowers border, dark blue, 6" d. (Clews) **230**

HULL

Hull Marks

This pottery was made by the Hull Pottery Company, Crooksville, Ohio, beginning in 1905. Art Pottery was made until 1950 when the company was converted to utilitarian wares. All production ceased in 1986.

Reference books for collectors include Roberts' Ultimate Encyclopedia of Hull Pottery by Brenda Roberts (Walsworth Publishing Company, 1992), and Collector's Guide to Hull Pottery - The Dinnerware Lines by Barbara Loveless Gick-Burke (Collector Books, 1993).

Basket, Dogwood patt., center handle, No. 501-7½", 7½" h. **$313**

Basket, hanging-type, Woodland Matte patt., cream & blue **400**

Basket, Blossom Flite patt., No. T2, 6" h. **48**

Basket, Tokay patt., No. 6, overhead branch handle, white ground, 8" h. **55**

Basket, Serenade patt., pink ground, ruffled sides, No. S14, 12" h. **275**

Candleholders, Magnolia Matte patt., upright ovoid socket on an oval base w/small open legs from the bottom to the base, No. 27-4", 4" h., pr. **69**

Candleholders, Orchid patt., No. 315, 4" h., pr. . . **200**

Candleholders, Parchment and Pine patt., No. S-10, 5" h., pr. **50**

Candleholders, Woodland Matte patt., pink ground, No. W30, 3½" h., pr. **105**

Canister, cov., Little Red Riding Hood patt., "Cereal" **1,400**

Console bowl, Butterfly patt., wide-shouldered disk-form w/closed rim, raised on long curved tab feet, pebbled white ground, No. B21, 10" d. **150**

Console bowl, model of a long conch shell w/double-snail handle at one end, pink & gold, No. E-12, 9 X 15¾" **120**

Console bowl, Blossom Flite patt., pink ground, 16½" l. **75**

Consolette, Tokay patt., footed oblong form w/end branch handles, No. 14, 15¾" l. **95**

Cookie jar, cov., figural Ginger Bread Man, grey Flint Ridge line, 1980s, 12" h. **425**

Cornucopia-vase, Butterfly patt., No. B2, 6½" h. . . **40**

Cornucopia-vase, Ebb Tide patt., No. E3, 7½" h. **110**

Cornucopia-vase, Wildflower patt., pink, yellow & green, No. W7, 7½" **95**

Cornucopia-vase, Blossom Flite, No. T-6, 10½" h. **40**

Cornucopia-vase, Woodland Gloss patt., No. W10-11", 11" h. **85**

Cornucopia-vase, Woodland Matte patt., pink ground, No. W10-11", 11" h. **198**

Cracker jar, cov., Little Red Riding Hood patt. . . . **645**

Creamer, Bow-Knot patt., turquoise & blue, No. B-21-4", 4" h. **150**

Creamer & open sugar bowl, Open Rose (Camellia) patt., pink & blue, No. 111-5" & No. 112-5", 5" l., pr. **150**

Ewer, Butterfly patt., No. B15 . . . . **175**

Ewer, Woodland Gloss patt., No. W6-6½", 6½" h. . . **70**

Ewer, Parchment & Pine patt., 13½" **170**

Ewer, Ebb Tide patt., No. E-10, figural fish handle, 14" h. **175**

Flowerpot w/attached saucer, Water Lily patt., pink ground, No. L-25-5¼", 6" h. **58**

Fruit bowl, Serenade patt., No. S15-7", 7" h. **150**

Honey pot, Blossom Flite patt., No. T-1, 6" h. **30**

Jardiniere, Sueno Tulip patt., No. 115-33-9", 9" h. **450**

Jardiniere, Water Lily patt., No. 23-5½", 5½". **95**

Jardiniere, Bow-Knot patt., wide bulbous body w/short & wide molded neck w/small bows at each side, B-19-9⅜", 9⅜" d. **975**

Lavabo & base, Butterfly patt., Nos. B24 & B25, cream & blue, overall 16" h., 2 pcs. **120**

Mustard jar & spoon, Little Red Riding Hood patt., 2 pcs. **425**

Planter, Serenade patt., pink, No. S-9 . . . . **40**

Sandwich tray, Gingerbread Man patt. **150**

Sugar bowl, cov., Blossom Flite patt., No.T-16 . . . **40**

Tea set: cov. teapot, creamer & cov. sugar bowl; Bow-Knot patt., 3 pcs. **850**

Vase, 4¾" h., Magnolia Matte patt., No. 13-4¾" . . . **58**

Vase, 5½" h., Water Lily patt., footed baluster shaped w/scroll shoulder handles, pink ground, No. L-1-5½". **46**

Vase, bud, 6" h., Sueno Tulip patt., blue ground, No. 104-33-6". **75**

Vase, 6¼" h., Wildflower patt., footed baluster-form w/flaring rim & long loop handles down the sides, No. 61-6¼" **150**

Vase, 6½" h., Dogwood patt., ovoid body suspended within a rectangular framework w/an oval foot, No. 502-6½" **250**

Vase, 6½" h., Thistle patt., blue ground **125**

Vase, 6½" h., Wildflower patt., footed flaring ovoid lobed body flanked by double-loop handles, No. W-5-6½" **73**

Vase, 8½" h., Bow-Knot patt., No. B7-8½" **275**

Vase, 8½" h., double-bud, Woodland Matte. patt., pink ground, No. W15-8½" **165**

Vase, 8½" h., Magnolia Matte patt., the baluster-form body w/slender scroll handles from the mid-body to the foot, pink & blue, No. 2-8½" **115**

Vase, 9" h., Granada patt., No. 48-9" 50

Vase, 9" h., Mardi Gras patt., pink & blue,
No. 47-9" 40

Vase, 9¼" h., model of an Angel fish, pink
w/gold, No. E-6. 120

Vase, 10½" h., Iris patt., No. 403-10½",
peach & rose 255

Vase, 10½" h., Magnolia Matte patt., dusty
rose & yellow, footed tiered & flaring body
w/double split rim, loop handles at base,
No. 9-10½" 95

Vase, 12" h., handled, Tokay patt. 90

Vase, 12½" h., Woodland Matte patt., tall
footed trumpet-form body w/double twig
handles on each side, pink ground,
No. W25-12½" 395

Wall pocket, Bow-Knot patt., model of a
whisk broom, No. B27-8", 8" h.. 295

Wall pocket, Open Rose (Camellia) patt.,
fan-shaped, No. 125-8½", 8½" l. 300

Wall pocket, Bow-Knot patt., model of a cup
& saucer, No. B-24-6", 6" h.. 200

IRONSTONE

*The first successful ironstone was patented in
1813 by C. J. Mason in England. The body
contains iron slag incorporated with the clay.
Other potters imitated Mason's ware and today
much hard, thick ware is lumped under the term
ironstone. Earlier it was called by various
names, including graniteware. Both plain white
and decorated wares were made throughout the
19th century. Tea Leaf Lustre ironstone was
made by several firms.*

GENERAL

Bowl, scalloped rim, all-white, ca. 1870,
H. Burgess **$95**

Bowl, 7½"d., 4"h., "gaudy" Amherst Japan
patt., pedestaled bowl, orange flowers,
blue & green leaves, lots of gold, garden
scene 185

Bowl, 12⅝" d., 4¾" h., Imari-style colorful
decoration, England, 19th c. (spider crack
in base, gilt & enamel wear) 201

Bread plate, Fuchsia shape, all-white 18

Chamberpot, cov., Prairie shape, all-white,
J. Clementson 125

Chamberpot, cov., Cable & Ring shape,
all-white, 9½" d. 22

Coffeepot, cov., Fuchsia shape, all-white,
J. & G. Meakin 300

Creamer, Britannia shape, all-white, Powell
& Bishop 115

Creamer, Senate shape, all-white, Maddock
& Gater. 65

Creamer, Shamrock, Thistle & Rose shape,
all-white, ca. 1870s, Powell & Bishop. 135

Creamer, Staffordshire, all-white, Maddock
& Son 110

Cup, handleless, coffee, Ceres shape,
all-white, Elsmore & Forster 50

Cup, handleless, Columbia shape, all-white. 27

Cup, handleless, octagonal, all-white 28

Cup, handleless, tea, Ceres shape,
all-white, Elsmore & Forster 34

Cup plate, all-white, G. Phillips 18

Cup plate, all-white, Longport 18

Cup & saucer, Ceres shape, all-white,
Elsmore & Forster 55

Cup & saucer, handleless, all-white, H. Alcock . . . 48

Cup & saucer, handleless, Boote's 1851
Octagon shape, all-white 65

Cup & saucer, handleless, "gaudy" free-
hand Seaweed patt. in underglaze blue
w/red & green enamel 83

Cup & saucer, handleless, "gaudy" free-
hand Urn patt. in underglaze blue w/red,
pink & green enamel 275

Cups, Fuchsia shape, handled, all-white,
very small, set of 4 120

Cups & saucers, handleless, red transfer
scene, impressed "Pearl China W.R. &
Co.," five sets (minor wear & stains) 204

Cups & Saucers, Stylized Tulip shape,
handleless, all-white, E. Challinor, 5 sets
(one saucer crazed) 245

Ironstone Sauce Tureens with Underplates

Dessert service: pr. of two-handled sauce
tureens, covers & underplates, one
scallop-edged rectangular compote, pr. of
scallop-edged rectangular serving dishes,
pr. of scallop-edged oval serving dishes,
pr. of oval serving dishes & twelve 9⅛" d.
dessert plates; hand-colored decoration
of vase issuing flowers on a stand
opposite a pierced rock issuing flowers
on a blue plateau, framed with a border of
floral & trelliswork panels & a shaped gilt-
edged rim, impressed "Mason's Patent
Ironstone China," factory marks, one
sauce tureen cover w/large rim chip, one
dessert plate w/central crack & two
w/large rim chips, minor wear to gilding,
the set (ILLUS. of part) **3,220**

Dinner service: oval platter, eighteen
10¼" d. dinner plates; each printed &
colored in the center w/large vase of

Mason's Ironstone Dinner Plate

w/iron-red & green lappets, pale yellow ground border reserved w/flowers & foliate scrolls within a lustrous brown edged rim, aubergine printed factory marks & red painted pattern number 2240, ca. 1840-60 (ILLUS. of part) **2,587**

Dish, oval, Tracery shape, all-white, Johnson Bros., 6¼" l. 20

Ewer, Ceres shape, all-white, Turner & Goddard 175

Ewer, Hawthorne's Fern shape, all-white, John Hawthorne 125

Ewer, Panelled Pod shape, all-white, J. & G. Meakin, 11½" h. 175

Ewer, Hyacinth shape, all-white, Hope & Carter, 12½" h. 225

Ewer, Lily of the Valley shape, all-white, J. Hughes, 12¾" h. 225

Honey dish, Girard shape, all-white, Ridgway Bates & Co. 25

Honey dish, Sharon Arch shape, all-white, ca. 1861 18

Mold, Grape Clusters shape, all-white, Davenport, large. 78

Mold, Pineapple shape, all-white, oval, medium size 75

Mold, Sheaf of Wheat shape, all-white, unmarked . . 88

Partial dinner service: four nested platters, well & tree platter, cov. soup tureen w/undertray, twenty-two dinner plates, twenty-four soup plates, fifteen 7¾" d. luncheon plates; Imari-style floral decoration, 77 pcs. (some staple repairs, minor cracks, chips, staining) **2,300**

Pitcher, milk, Senate shape, all-white, T. & R. Boote 60

Pitcher, milk, 5¼" h., Oriental transfer-printed design w/polychrome enamel & snake handle, marked "Mason's" 248

Pitcher, 7" h., Gothic shape, all-white 68

Pitcher, 9¾" h., "gaudy" blue transfer floral design w/red & green enamel, snake handle, marked "Mason's Patent Ironstone China" 275

Pitcher, 10" h., all-white, J. Maddock & Son 175

Pitcher, 10" h., Aurora patt, blue transfer-printed w/polychrome enameling (minor edge wear) 248

Pitcher, 11½" h., Memnon shape, all-white, J. Meir & Son 235

Plate, 7½" decagonal, dessert, Baltic shape, all-white, registered in 1855 18

Plate, 8¾" d., Ceres shape, all-white, Elsmore & Forster 35

Plate, Balanced Vine shape, all-white, J. Clementson 26

Plate, Ceres shape, miniature, all-white, Elsmore & Forster 55

Plate, 7" d., Boote's 1851 Octagon shape, all-white 29

Plate 7¾" d., Ceres shape, all-white, Elsmore & Forster 29

Plate, 8¼" d., "gaudy" free-hand Bittersweet patt. in underglaze blue w/red & green enamel w/luster, impressed "Real Ironstone". . 165

Plate, 8⅝" d., "gaudy" free-hand Strawberry patt. in underglaze blue w/red, pink & green enamel, impressed "Elsmore Forster and Co." (minor wear) 220

Plate, 8¾" d., Portland shape, all-white, Elsmore & Forster 36

Plate, 9⅛" d., Boote's 1851 Octagon shape, all-white 48

Plate, 9¼" d., "gaudy" center decoration of floral wreath in red, blue & green surrounded by black transfer-printed & polychrome enamel rabbits, frogs & cabbages (small rim repair) 275

Plate, 9½" d., Boote's 1851 Octagon shape, all-white 35

Plate 9⅝" d., Ceres shape, all-white, Edward Pearson. 30

Plate, 9⅝" d., Chinese shape, all-white 34

Plate, 9¾" d., "gaudy" center floral decoration in underglaze blue w/red, pink & green enamel w/luster (stains & some wear). 275

Plate, 9¾" d., Paris shape, all-white, John Alcock . . 26

Plate, 10" d., center scene of chick & butterfly w/motto around rim, black transfer-printed w/polychrome enamel, marked "Staffordshire England" 138

Plate, 10¼" d., True Scallop shape, 14 sides, all-white, Edwards. 36

Plate, 10¼" octagonal, all-white 55

Platter, Columbia shape, all-white, Wooliscroft . . . 75

Platter, oval, 16" l., Ceres shape, all-white, Elsmore & Forster 85

Platter, President shape, all-white 95

Platter, oval, 11" l., Tracery shape, all-white, Johnson Bros. 50

Platter, 15¾" l., Wheat in the Meadow shape, all-white, Powell & Bishop 112

Platter, 16" l., Boote's 1851 Octagon shape (good condition) 150

Platter, 16" l., Oriental black transfer-printed scene w/red enamel & worn gilt, marked "Mason's". 50

Gaudy Ironstone Platter

Platter, 16½" l., "gaudy" blue transfer floral decoration w/red & yellow enameling, "Amherst Japan" patt., impressed "Improved Stone China" (ILLUS.) **358**

Platter, 18¼" l., Leaf & Crossed Ribbon shape, all-white, Livesley, Powell & Co....... **145**

Platter, 18¼" l., Scalloped Decagon shape, all-white, registered in 1858, Davenport (light bull's eye on edge of rim) **165**

Platter, 13¼ x 18¼", Tiny Oak & Acorn shape, all-white, J. W. Pankhurst........... **135**

Platter, 13½ x 18¼", Bordered Hyacinth shape, all-white, W. Baker & Co. **135**

Platter, 21⅛" l., decorated w/a central scene of a pavilion & pagoda in a garden of large floral blooms, iron-red & underglaze blue, framed within a border of angular panels & pendant flowers within a shaped rim, mid-19th c., crown & ribbon factory mark printed in brown, Mason (small rim chips & fritting to underside)............. **575**

Platter, 22¼" l., "gaudy" polychrome floral enameling w/underglaze blue, Staffordshire (minor flaking) **770**

Large Ironstone Platter

Platter, 24" l, wide oblong form w/angled corners, well-&-tree-type, "gaudy" style, transfer-printed dark blue Imari-style floral decoration in center w/stylized floral border decorated in polychrome enamel (ILLUS.) **633**

Punch bowl, dark blue transfer-printed decoration w/lattice & scroll work, scalloped rim, RN 298859, England, 19¼" d., 9½" h........................... **605**

Sauce dish, Boote's 1851 shape, round, all-white.. **6**

Saucer, Atlantic "A" shape, all-white, registered in 1858, T. & R. Boote........... **28**

Saucer, Boote's 1851 Octagon shape, round, all-white..................... **35**

Shaving mug, all-white **48**

Soap slab, all-white, A. Shaw................ **35**

Soup ladle, all-white, line design around handle, unmarked...................... **150**

Soup plate, Mocho shape, all-white, T. & R. Boote, 8½" d **14**

Soup plate, Boote's 1851 shape, all-white, 9¼" octagonal.......................... **55**

Soup plate all-white, 9⅜" d., Pankhurst......... **36**

Soup plate, Paris shape, all-white, John Alcock, 9¾" d....................... **45**

Soup plate, President shape, all-white, 9¾" d. **45**

Soup plate, Bellflower shape, all-white, John Edward, 10" d. (some wear) **46**

Soup plate w/flanged rim, "gaudy" free-hand Blackberry patt. in underglaze-blue w/red & yellow enamel w/luster, impressed "Walley Paris White Ironstone," 9⅝" d...................... **220**

Soup plate w/shields, all white, J. W. Pankhurst .. **36**

Soup tureen, cov., Berlin Swirl shape, all-white, 8¾ x 12" **110**

Sugar bowl, cov., Athens patt., black transfer w/some blue, Wm. Adams & Sons, 7¾" h. (stains & crazing) **193**

Sugar bowl, cov., Athens shape, all-white, Wedgwood **135**

Sugar bowl, cov., Wheat & Clover shape, all-white, Tomkinson Bros. & Co........... **110**

Sugar bowl, cov., Wheat (J. F.'s), all white **95**

Syrup pitcher, cov., all-white, small, J. & G. Meakin **48**

Syrup pitcher, grape molding at top, gold line decoration, unmarked, 9" h............. **88**

Tea set: cov. teapot, creamer & cov. sugar bowl; Gothic Paneled shape w/black transfer-printed floral design, teapot 8¾" h., the set (minor chips & hairline in lid of sugar) **248**

Teapot, cov., octagonal, all-white, ring handle (lid has no breathing hole) **115**

Teapot, cov., Wheat shape, all-white, W. & E. Corn **115**

Toddy cup, all-white, three notches on handle ... **25**

Toddy cup Bellflower shape, all-white, John Edwards....................... **35**

Toddy cup, Boote's 1851 shape, all-white....... **38**

Toddy cup, Fuchsia shape, all-white **36**

Toddy cup, Pearl Sydenham shape, all-white **40**

Toddy cup, Quartered Rose shape, all-white, Jacob Furnival **38**

Toddy plate, "gaudy" free-hand Blackberry patt. in underglaze-blue & black w/red & yellow enamel w/luster, impressed "E. Walley Niagara Shape" w/registry mark, 6¾" d. (enamel on base may be retouched)........................... **55**

Toothbrush holder w/underplate, vertical,
all-white, unmarked **58**
Underplate, for sauce tureen, Panelled
Berry shape, all-white **38**
Undertray, for gravy boat, oval, all-white,
Clementson **36**
Undertray, for sauce tureen, Bordered
Gothic shape, all-white, Samuel Alcock **45**
Undertray, for soup tureen, Many Panelled
Gothic shape, all-white, "Reg. September
21, 1850," Mellor, Venables & Co.,
12½ x 15½" octagonal **150**
Vegetable dish, cov., Ceres shape,
all-white, Elsmore & Forster, 8⅝" oval **170**
Vegetable dish, cov., Plain Uplift shape,
all-white, Ed. Clarke, 6½ x 9" oval **68**
Vegetable dish, cov., Plain Uplift shape,
all-white, J. Edwards, 7½ x 9¼" oval **78**
Vegetable dish, cov., Star Flower shape,
all-white, J. W. Pankhurst, 7 x 9½" oval **110**
Vegetable dish, cov., Sevres shape,
all-white, Dean & Stokes, 7½ x 10¼" oval **95**
Wash bowl, transfer-printed Imari-style
decoration in underglaze blue & red
enamel, impressed "Mason's Patent
Ironstone China," 12" d. (glazed-over chip
back edge of lip) **110**
Wash bowl, Boote's 1851 Octagon
shape, all-white, 13" d. **200**
Wash bowl, Athenia shape, all-white,
J. T. Close & Co., Stoke Upon Trent, 14" d. . . . **145**
Wash bowl & pitcher, President shape,
all-white, 2 pcs. **375**
Wash bowl & pitcher, Sydenham patt.,
all-white, the set **395**
Washbowl, Many Panelled shape, 12 sides,
all-white, J. Alcock **125**
Washbowl, Fig shape, 14 sides, all white,
14½" d. **145**

JEWEL TEA AUTUMN LEAF

*Though not antique this ware has a devoted
following. The Hall China Company of East
Liverpool, Ohio, made the first pieces of Autumn
Leaf pattern ware to be given as premiums by
the Jewel Tea Company in 1933. The premiums
were an immediate success and thousands of
new customers, all eager to acquire a piece of the
durable Autumn Leaf pattern ware, began
purchasing Jewel Tea products. Though the
pattern was eventually used to decorate linens,
glasswares and tinware, we include only the
Hall China Company items in our listing.*

Baker, Fort Pitt, 12 oz. **$175**
Bean pot, one-handled, 2¼ qt. (ILLUS.) **1,075**
Bowl, berry **9**
Bowl, cream soup, two-handled **45**

Autumn Leaf Bean Pot

Bowl, 6¼" d. **25**
Bowl, salad, 9" d. **75**

Jewel Tea Butter Dish

Butter dish, cov., square top w/straight
finial, ¼ lb. (ILLUS.) **1,650**
Cake plate **21**
Cake plate, footed metal base **258**
Candy dish, footed metal base **463**
Casserole, round, 2 qt. **35**
Coffee server, cov., 9-cup, 8½" h. **55**
Coffeepot, cov., all-china, electric, percolator . . . **250**

Autumn Leaf Electric Percolator

Coffeepot, cov., electric, percolator (ILLUS.) **437**
Cookie jar, cov. **160**
Cookie jar, cov., large eared handles,
Ziesel, 1957-69. . . . . **275**
Cookie jar, cov., "Tootsie" **285**
Creamer & cov. sugar bowl, 1930s **70**
Custard cup **12**
Custard cup, "Radiance," 3½ oz. **7**
Drip jar, cov. **25**
French baker, 4½" **68**
Gravy boat **28**
Mixing bowls, nesting-type, set of 3 . . . . **100**
Mug, conical **70**

JUGTOWN POTTERY

Jugtown Mark

This pottery was established by Jacques and Juliana Busbee in Jugtown, North Carolina, in the early 1920s in an attempt to revive the skills of the diminishing North Carolina potter's art as Prohibition ended the need for locally crafted stoneware whiskey jugs. During the early years, Juliana Busbee opened a shop in Greenwich Village in New York City to promote the North Carolina wares that her husband, Jacques, was designing and a local youth, Ben Owen, was producing under his direction. Owen continued to work with Busbee from 1922 until Busbee's death in 1947 at which time Juliana took over management of the pottery for the next decade until her illness (or mental fatigue) caused the pottery to be closed in 1958. At that time, Owen opened his own pottery a few miles away, marking his wares "Ben Owen - Master Potter." The pottery begun by the Busbees was reopened in 1960, under new management, and still operates today using the identical impressed mark of the early Jugtown pottery the Busbees managed from 1922 until 1958.

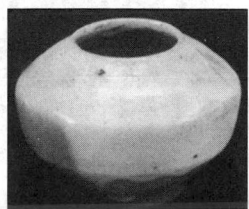

Jugtown Hexagonal Vase

Bowl, 4½" d., 1½" h., a small raised footring supporting a wide rounded bowl w/a flat rim, Chinese blue glaze, impressed mark **$55**

Pitcher, 10½" h., redware, bulbous ovoid body tapering to a flared rim w/rim spout, small C-form shoulder handle, pumpkin orange glaze, impressed mark **303**
Vase, 3½" h., hexagonal body w/wide shoulder tapering to wide flat rim, semi-matte white glaze, impressed mark (ILLUS.) . . **248**
Vase, 4¼" h., ovoid body w/closed rim, covered in a frothy semi-matte white glaze, impressed mark **165**
Vase, 5¼" h., 6¼" d., wide bulbous body w/a wide shoulder tapering to a short rolled neck, mottled turquoise, red & purple Chinese blue glaze, impressed circular mark. . **825**
Vase, 5½" h., 4½" d., pear-shaped body tapering to flat in-curved rim, covered in a flowing red & turquoise Chinese blue glaze, impressed circular mark. **660**
Vase, 6" h., ovoid body tapering to a closed mouth, covered in rich Chinese blue glaze w/red veining, impressed mark **495**

LEFTON

The Lefton China Company was the creation of Mr. George Zoltan Lefton who migrated to the United States from Hungary in 1939. In 1941 he embarked on a new career and began shaping a business that sprang from his passion for collecting fine china and porcelains. Though his funds were very limited, his vision was to develop a source from which to obtain fine porcelains by reviving the postwar Japanese ceramic industry, which dated back to antiquity. As a trailblazer, George Zoltan Lefton soon earned the reputation as "The China King".

Counted among the most desirable and sought after collectibles of today, Lefton items such as Bluebirds, Miss Priss, Angels, all types of dinnerware and tea-related items are eagerly acquired by collectors. As is true with any antique or collectible, prices may vary, depending on location, condition and availability. For additional information on the history of Lefton China, its factories, marks, products and values, readers should consult the Collector's Encyclopedia of Lefton China, Books I and II and the Lefton Price by Loretta DeLozier.

Lefton Large Shell Bowl with Cherub

Bowl, 7" l., large shell w/cherub & applied roses, No. 926, rare (ILLUS.) **$600**

Large Lefton Bowl with Roses

Bowl, 9¼" l., oval footed form, green bisque w/applied pink roses, No. 773, rare (ILLUS.) . . **335**

Lefton Figural Cherub Candleholders

Candleholders, two-light, figural cherub w/musical instrument, pastel green & applied pink flowers, No. 965, each 7" l., pr., rare (ILLUS.) **175**

Casserole, cov., Americana patt., No. 978. . . . . . **145**

Cheese dish, cov., Honey Bee, No. 1285 . . . . **60**

Cookie Jar, cov., Santa Claus, No. 2097, 7¼". . . **110**

Cookie Jar, cov., White Holly patt., No. 6054 . . . **115**

Lefton Black Chintz Sugar & Creamer

Creamer & sugar bowl, Black Chintz patt., No. 1934, pr. (ILLUS.) **95**

Creamer & sugar bowl, Dutch girl, No. 2698, pr. **85**

Lefton Green Holly Creamer & Sugar Bowl

Creamer & sugar bowl, Green Holly, No. 1355 , pr. (ILLUS.) . . . . **45 to 55**

Creamer & sugar bowl, Rose Chintz patt., No. 912, pr. **75**

Cup & saucer, Americana patt., No. 963 . . . . **38**

Cup & saucer, green w/pink roses, No. 801 . . . . . **38**

Cup & saucer, Rose Heirloom patt. **32**

Dessert set: cake plate & 6 serving plates; fruit decoration, No. 1133, 7 pcs. **175**

Dish, lemon, Magnolia patt., No 2618 . . . . **20**

Egg cup, Elegant Rose patt., No. 2048 . . . . **40**

Egg cup, figural bluebird, No. 286 . . . . **60**

Figurine, cherub riding on horse, rare, No. 590 . . **500**

Figurine, Gay Nineties, No. 8574, 8" h. **175**

Figurine, Infant of Prague, No. 718, 8" h. **150**

From left: Lefton Lady Figurine
Lefton Angel - March

Figurine, lady, standing wearing blue gown w/applied flowers, No. 4494, 8" h. (ILLUS.) **80**

Figurine, March, Angel, No. 1978J (ILLUS.) **55**

Figurine, Old Mother Hubbard, No. 1105. . . . . **165**

Figurine, Russian lady, No. 752, 11" h. **225**

Figurine, Sing a Song of Six Pence, nursery rhyme, No. 1254, 6" h. **150**

From left: Victorian Lady with Umbrella
Lefton Waitress Bloomer Girl

Figurine, Victorian lady w/umbrella, creamy yellow, white & gold gown, No. 585, 7½" h. (ILLUS.) . . . . **150 to 250**

Figurine, Waitress Bloomer Girl, No. 10532 (ILLUS.) **95**

Figurine, clown, three kinds, No. 02146, 6¼", each **55**

Figurine, bisque, standing figure, wearing
   h.p. uniform, one hand on sword near hip,
   the other at his side & holding hat, square
   stand marked "Robert E. Lee," 8½" h. **77**
Figurine group, girls on candy cane,
   No. 626, 4" h. **70**
Figurine group, Rock A Bye Baby in
   Treetop, No. 1104, 8" h. **200**
Figurine group, white bisque horses
   w/cherub, No. 772, 7½", rare **950**
Figurines, angels, tumbling, No. 80159,
   2¾" h., 4 pcs. **140**

Lefton Candy Cane Kids

Figurines, Candy Cane Kids, No. 8745,
   4½", 3 pcs. (ILLUS.) **60**

Lefton Cherub Figurines

Figurines, cherub on tree, grey green
   bisque, No. 952, rare, 5", pr. (ILLUS.) **175**
Figurines, Colonial couple, Brian &
   Hildegard, No. 337, 10", pr. **350**

Lefton Miss Priss Jam Jar

Jam jar, cov., Miss Priss, No. 1515 (ILLUS.) **110**
Jam jar, cov., orange, teapot-shaped, No. 6973 . . **35**
Jam jar, cov., Pennsylvania Dutch, No. 3612. . . . . **55**
Jar, cov., Coffee Girl w/hot coffee, No. 4804 . . . . . **85**

*From left: Lefton Hurricane Lamp
Lefton Green Holly Lantern*

Lamp, hurricane-type, Green Holly,
   No. 4229, 5½" h. (ILLUS.) **45**
Lantern, Green Holly, No. 2694, 8½" h. (ILLUS.). . **125**

Lefton Duck

Model of a duck, No. 7555, 11½" (ILLUS.) **125**
Model of a horse, white w/wooden base,
   No. 352, 5¼". **55**

Lefton Leopard

Model of a leopard, No. 6703, 6½" (ILLUS.) **65**
Model of a quetzal, No. 1054, 9" **180**

Lefton Red Fox

Model of a red fox, No. 5058, 5" (ILLUS.) **50**
Model of a sea gull, No. 02715, 7" **70**
Model of a spaniel, No. 80521 . . . . **50**

Lefton White Poodle with Lilacs

Models of a poodle, white w/lilacs, No. 157,
5" h., each (ILLUS.) **40**
Paperweight, glass, figural green apple,
No. 2390 . . . . **40**
Pitcher & bowl, miniature, Paisley Fantazia,
No. 6806, 3½", pr. **22**
Planter, figural Dutch shoe w/boy, No. 5260 . . . . . **36**
Planter, girl w/ponytail, standing in long
floral dress & holding large picture hat,
No. 6094, 6¾" h. **30**
Planter, Valentine w/hearts & Cupid,
No. 2995, 4" **22**
Plate, Old Green Heritage patt., No. 514, 7½" d. . . **22**
Plate, Elegant Rose patt. , No. 2854, 8" d. **32**
Salt & pepper shakers, stein-shaped,
shamrock design, No. 2219. 5" h., pr. **12**
Snack set, Brown Heritage floral patt., No. 1864 . . **32**
Snack set, Elegant Rose patt., No. 2124 . . . . **30**
Snack set, Misty Rose patt., No. 5690 . . . . **18**
Snack set, modern design, decal,
No. 2121, 8" l. **22**
Snack set, Violet Chintz patt., No. 638. . . . . **30**
Teapot, cov., Dresden shape, Elegant Rose
patt., No. 2032 . . . . **225**

Lefton Dutch Girl Teapot

Teapot, cov., figural Dutch Girl, No. 2699
(ILLUS.) **225**
Teapot, cov., figural Miss Priss, No. 1516 . . . . . . **195**
Teapot, cov., Pink Cotillion patt., No. 3186 . . . . . **110**
Teapot, cov., Yellow Tulip patt., No. 6735 . . . . **95**
Toothpick holder, Petites Fleurs patt.,
No. 6436, 4¼" h. **20**
Wall plaque, china, violin w/pink roses,
No. 704, 7" d. **55**

Wall plaque, diamond-shaped apple, No. 921 . . . . **15**
Wall plaque, three mermaids, No. 3107 . . . . **125**

Fish with Babies Wall Plaques

Wall plaques, fish w/two babies,
No. 60419, largest 7" l., the set (ILLUS.) **75**

Wall Plaques with Boy & Girl

Wall plaques, oval, relief-molded w/Colonial
boy & girl figures, No. 1753, 11",
pr. (ILLUS.) **150**
Wall plaques, oval w/Colonial figures,
No. 5826, 10" d., pr. **135**

Lefton Wall Pocket Girl with basket

Wall pocket, girl w/basket, pink, No. 50264,
7" h. (ILLUS.) **135**

LIMOGES

Numerous factories produced china in Limoges, France, with major production in the 19th century. Some pieces listed below are identified by the name of the maker or the mark of the factory. Although the famed Haviland

Company was located in Limoges, wares bearing their marks are not included in this listing. Also see HAVILAND.

An excellent reference is The Collector's Encyclopedia of Limoges Porcelain, Second Edition, *by Mary Frank Gaston (Collector Books, 1992).*

Cabinet plate, central printed scene of lovers in a wooded setting, scrolled gilt trim w/enameled floral cartouches, giltwood frame, ca. 1900, 9½" d. **$173**

Chocolate pot, cov., cream, pink & green ground finely decorated w/birds & holly sprigs, 9¼" h. **110**

Chocolate pot, cov., swelled base below the wide cylindrical body w/an angled rim w/spout, domed cover w/gold loop handle, long gold C-scroll handle down the back, decorated below the spout w/a narrow panel of small florals, the rest of the body studio-decorated w/long stems of colorful blossoms,10½" h. **173**

Dessert set: 9½" d. plate & six matching 6" plates; fancy blanks w/gold & floral decoration, 7 pcs. **121**

Limoges Dessert Set

Dessert set: rectangular tray & eight dessert plates; decorated w/pairs of cherubs in different poses against a background sky, heavy gold-trimmed scalloped border, the set (ILLUS. of part) . . . **1,100**

Dresser tray, decorated w/h.p. yellow flowers, pale pink raised Rococo border, 12" d. **100**

Fish set: 17½" oval platter & 12 small plates; each w/a different fish & shells & sea life, two different manufacturers of the blanks, ca. 1900, the set **1,035**

Limoges Game Plate

Game plates, one w/center h.p. decoration of pheasant, the other w/a quail, both just above water & near yellow flowers & grasses, pastel pink, blue & cream background & heavy gold irregular & beaded rim, artist-signed, 9½" d., pr. (ILLUS. of one) **225**

Luncheon plates, 7¾" d., each h.p. w/different exotic flower, gold border, set of 12, T & V - Limoges - France **182**

Oyster plates, crescent-shaped w/gilt foliate designs, blue, pink, green & yellow ground, six wells, ca. 1900, set of 18 . . . . . . **2,070**

Plaque, pierced for hanging, decorated w/scene of courting couple & sheep, artist-signed, cobalt & gold border, 10½" d. **100**

Limoges Portrait Plaque

Plaques, rectangular, Art Nouveau style enamel bust portrait of female surrounded by large flowers in center circle w/square border decorated w/flowers & scrolling leaves, each set in floral decorated brass frame w/velvet liner, artist-signed "Dorval," ca. 1900, France, 9½ x 12", pr. (ILLUS. of one) **8,050**

Plate, 10" d., pierced to hang, bust portrait of a Cavalier smoking against a shaded ground (Coronet) **100**

Limoges Plate with Fruit

Plate, 12¼" d., pierced to hang, scalloped & scroll-molded gold edge, h.p. center decoration of purple plums, a large orange seed pod & green leaves on a pastel ground, artist-signed (ILLUS.) **225**

Limoges Punch Bowl & Underplate

Punch bowl & underplate, footed flaring bowl w/serpentine gilt rim, interior & exterior decorated w/h.p. grape clusters & leaves, matching round underplate w/gold rim, ca. 1900, bowl 15" d., underplate 18" d., the set (ILLUS.) **1,495**

Tea set: cov. teapot, cov. sugar bowl, creamer & six cups & saucers; each w/black-printed landscapes within blue enamel medallions & w/blue & gilt trim, late 19th c., teapot 7¾" h., the set **173**

Vase, 15" h., two-handled, enamel-decorated scene of a female picking flowers, gilt-trimmed, ca. 1900 . . . . **633**

LIVERPOOL

Liverpool is most often used as a generic term for fine earthenware products, usually of creamware or pearlware, produced at numerous potteries in this English city during the late 18th and early 19th centuries. Many examples, especially pitchers, were decorated with transfer-printed patriotic designs aimed specifically at the American buying public.

Liverpool Mug and Pitcher

Mug, tall cylindrical form, transfer-printed outdoor scene of uniformed soldier on horseback above "George Washington, Esq. General and Commander in Chief of the Continental Army in America," early 19th c., cracks, chips on base & handle, staining, 4⅝" h. (ILLUS. left) **$2,185**

Pitcher, 10⅝" h., jug-type, black transfer-printed decoration, one side w/a frame of entwined ribbon enclosing the names of

fifteen states, signed at the base "F. Morris Shelton," the reverse w/an American three-masted ship under sail & a spread-winged eagle, polychrome highlights, early 19th c. (cracks, minor chips, staining) **805**

Pitcher, 6⅞" h., jug-type, black transfer-printed decoration, one side w/a three-masted ship under full sail, the other side w/the verse "Poor Jack," early 19th c. (staining, cracks, wear) **460**

Pitcher, 7½" h., jug-type, black transfer-printed design w/one side showing the seasons of spring & autumn, the reverse decorated w/a scenic oval reserve above a related verse, framed by floral swags, scrolls & various devices, spout damage, staining, edge roughness, early 19th c. (ILLUS. right) **633**

Pitcher, 8" h., jug-type, transfer-decorated w/a reserve of Masons congregating & "Veritas Prevalerus," & a reserve of various Masonic & regalia designs w/"Holiness to the Lord, it is found," early 19th c. (cracks, staining, crazing, minor glaze wear) **431**

Pitcher, 9¾" h., jug-type, one side decorated w/a black transfer-printed reserve w/a portrait of Washington surrounded by Justice, Liberty & Victory encircled by fifteen stars & the names of the fifteen states, the reverse w/a reserve of "Peace, Plenty and Independence," inscribed under the spout "Philip & Jane Gilkey," early 19th c. (base chip, minor staining, minute rim chip, rim roughness) . . . **1,725**

Liverpool "Patriot" Pitcher

Pitcher, 9¾" h., jug-type, large oval reserve w/transfer-printed decoration of a three-masted ship flying the American flag & a spread eagle w/American shield & "The Memory of Washington and the Proscribed Patriots of America" around border, polychrome highlights, restoration, minor abrasions to transfers, early 19th c. (ILLUS.) **1,725**

Pitcher, 10⅛" h., jug-type, one side decorated w/a black transfer-printed reserve of a three-masted sailing ship under sail flying the American flag, a reserve of Masonic designs & "United for the Benefit of Mankind," & a spread-winged eagle w/shield, polychrome highlights, shadows of gilt trim, early 19th c. (spout chips, minor cracks, staining, transfer wear) **1,150**

Pitcher, 11⅜" h., jug-type, decorated w/three black transfer-printed Masonic reserves w/"United for the Benefit of Mankind," a reserve of a woman w/three children & "To judge with candor...," & under the spout a reserve of various Masonic emblems & "EW," polychrome & gilt trim, early 19th c. (gilt enamel wear) **1,380**

LUSTRE WARES

Lustred wares in imitation of copper, gold, silver and other colors were produced in England in the early 19th century and onward. Gold, copper or platinum oxides were painted on glazed objects which were then fired, giving them a lustred effect. Various forms of lustre wares include plain lustre with the entire object coated to obtain a metallic effect, bands of lustre decoration and painted lustre designs. Particularly appealing is the pink or purple "splash lustre" sometimes referred to as "Sunderland" lustre in the mistaken belief it was confined to the production of Sunderland area potteries. Objects decorated in silver lustre by the "resist" process, wherein parts of the objects to be left free from lustre decoration were treated with wax, are referred to as "silver resist."

Wares formerly called "Canary Yellow Lustre" are now referred to as "Yellow-Glazed Earthenwares."

COPPER

Copper Pitcher with Badminton Players

Creamer, yellow band w/white reserves w/purple transfer-printed scene of woman & child in classical attire, polychrome enamel, 4⅛" h. (repairs) **$182**

Pitcher, 7" h., yellow band w/white reserves & brown transfer-printed scenes of woman & children in garden, yellow & blue enamel (minor wear). **193**

Pitcher, 5¾" h., yellow band w/white reserves w/red transfer-printed scene of badminton players w/blue, yellow & green enamel, minor wear (ILLUS.) **341**

SILVER & SILVER RESIST

Creamer, jug-type, decorated w/silver resist bands of stylized scrolling florals, 3¾" h. (damage & repair) **121**

Mug, cylindrical, pearlware w/relief-molded decoration, wide silver-resist band w/leaf sprigs & red stripes, 3½" h. (small flakes) **110**

SUNDERLAND PINK & OTHERS

Jug-type Pitchers

Pitcher, jug-type, footed wide bulbous squatty body tapering to a short cylindrical neck w/arched spout, decorated w/black transfer-printed scenes & inscribed "Country Lad and Lass" & "Sailor's Farewell," pink luster & polychrome enamel (wear). **550**

Pitcher, 7⅛" h, jug-type, white reserves w/black transfer-printed & polychrome enamel decoration of ship, maiden & seaman & appropriate verses, wear & minor enamel flaking, crow's foot hairlines in bottom (ILLUS. left) **715**

Pitcher, 7⅜" h., jug-type, pink lustre w/grape clusters & green enamel leaves & scrolling vines (some wear & scratches). ... **468**

Pitcher, 7¾" h., jug-type, pearlware, relief-molded basketweave design w/flowers & vintage, double satyr head at spout, polychrome enamel & pink lustre, minor wear & small chip on spout (ILLUS. right) **660**

Sailor's bowl, interior sides decorated w/two verses & a sailing ship enclosed in wreath borders w/"Lady Liberty" in the center, color enhanced w/green & red highlights, pink lustre bands on the interior & exterior rims, England, 19th c., 10" d. (glaze losses, rim & base chip) **489**

MAJOLICA

Majolica, a tin-enameled glazed pottery, has been produced for centuries. It originally took its name from the island of Majorca, a source of figuline (potter's clay). Subsequently it was widely produced in England, Europe and the

United States. Etruscan majolica, now avidly sought, was made by Griffen, Smith & Hill, Phoenixville, Pa., in the last quarter of the 19th century. Most majolica advertised today is 19th or 20th century. Once scorned by most collectors, interest in this colorful ware so popular during the Victorian era has now revived and prices have risen dramatically in the past few years. Also see WEDGWOOD.

GENERAL

Bowl, 12" l., footed, simple oval form w/upright end handles modeled as poodles peering over the bowl rim, George Jones, England, indistinct painted design number, ca. 1870 . . . . **$2,070**

Candlesticks, baroque-style w/a scroll- and lobed-molded cylindrical socket above a disk drip pan above the tall shaft composed of two graduated scroll-molded or lobed knobs separated by disk rings all on a dome-topped waisted base w/S-scroll feet, in the style of Bernard Palissy, modeled by Pierre-Emile Jeannest, impressed "Minton," date code for 1876 & design number "765," 16¼" h., pr. **2,875**

Center bowl, figural, modeled as three figural wood nymphs supporting a free-form bowl, Europe, 19th c., 16" h. **633**

From left: Figural Majolica Centerpiece
Majolica Ewer

Centerpiece, figural, modeled as a cherub riding a dolphin on a base of shell-form dishes & feet joined by coral & supporting a naturalistic shell, George Jones, England, molded "Copyright Reserved," old restorations throughout, ca. 1880, 16" h. (ILLUS.) **690**

Cheese keeper, cov., brown basketweave design w/circlet of pink flowers & green leaves around center, mottled brown & green base, decorated knob finial, 6½" h. (small chip underside of base edge) **350**

Chestnut serving dish, a round footed dish applied w/a half-cover formed as chestnut leafage & ripe fruit, the interior glazed robin's egg blue, impressed "Minton" & date code for 1868, 11" d. **1,380**

Compote, 7¾" h., open, the shaped oval bowl supported by a naturalistically molded oak tree on an oval base applied w/a recumbent hound & a grouse, George Jones, impressed registry mark & indistinct painted design number, ca. 1875 . . **4,887**

Creamer, leaf-form patterned w/primroses & raised on shell feet, impressed "Minton" & dated code for 1868 & "642," 5¼" h. **517**

Creamer, Corn patt., 4½" h. **75**

Ewer, modeled as a shallow barrel w/flaring neck & pedestal base strewn w/grapes, shoulders applied w/four nude putti at play w/grapes, a tambourine & a goblet, the handle in the form of a crown glazed vine stem, ca. 1875, possibly Minton, some traces of restoration to upper rim & pedestal base,14⅞" h. (ILLUS.) **805**

Garden seat, a tall waisted tapering cylindrical form w/round seat above sides molded w/relief florettes & strapwork alternating w/large cartouche-form openings, on three large tab feet, impressed Minton marks & date code for 1873, 17¼" h. (restorations). **1,150**

Minton Majolica Barrel-Form Garden Seat

Garden seat, cylindrical form molded in relief w/birds & dragonflies perched on & flying between reeds & lily pads in colors on pale blue ground between brown straw molded top & borders, interior covered in a mottled brown & green glaze, Minton, impressed year code for 1873 & registration diamond, minor chips & abrasions, 18" h. (ILLUS.) **4,600**

Jardiniere, bulbous baluster-form w/round flat rim, modeled as a Neoclassical urn applied w/lion's mask bail handles on six raised ribs ending in paw feet, decorated in yellow, white, pink & green on a robin's-egg blue ground, pink interior, Minton, England, restorations, ca. 1860, 17½" h. (ILLUS.) **3,162**

Minton Majolica Jardiniere

Jardiniere, figural, modeled as a seated Bedouin w/pipe beside a recumbent camel & jardiniere formed as a mud brick structure, all on a circular base glazed in sand color, impressed "Brown Westhead Moore & Co." w/a painted design number, ca. 1870, base 14½" d. **2,875**

Jardiniere, compressed spherical form w/pink interior, exterior molded in relief w/insects & colorful flowers on a turquoise ground between brown glazed stalk-form borders & hooped feet, impressed "GJ" & circle factory mark, molded patent registration diamond & black painted pattern number 3393, George Jones, England, ca. 1870, 12" h. **2,645**

Jardiniere, hanging-type, modeled as a shallow bowl molded w/Neoclassical portrait medallions & scrolling foliage in Renaissance taste, in mottled glazes on a cobalt blue ground, impressed "WEDGWOOD" & letters "HM," ca. 1870, 12½" d. **1,150**

Jardiniere, squatty bulbous footed base below the wide cylindrical body w/a very wide squatty bulbous shoulder tapering to a short wide flaring neck, the shoulder mounted w/winged sphinx handles in cream & yellow w/green fruited swags around the shoulder, a grotesque mask below the figural handles all on a dark cobalt blue ground, impressed Minton mark, late 19th c., 22" h. (minor glaze flaws, chip repair, firing line) **1,430**

From left: Ornate Minton Majolica Pedestal
Unusual Majolica Covered Pitcher

Pedestal, columnar-form w/molded garlands, florettes, acanthus leaves & an oak leaf & acorn frieze on a cobalt blue ground, Minton mark & date code for 1876, design number 891, small repair to rim, 38" h. (ILLUS.) **5,175**

Pitcher, cov., 13" h., tankard-type, modeled as a band of medieval merrymakers dancing around a castellated tower, the hinged cover w/a jester head knop, Minton mark & date code for 1873, design number 1231, old cracks, loss of thumbpiece (ILLUS.) **1,380**

Pitcher, 7" h., Water Lily patt., cream pebbly ground, turquoise top w/yellow rope design . . . **265**

Pitcher, 9½" h., center decoration of flowers, leaves & buds on aqua ground, large butterfly spout, cobalt rim & band at lower part of body, mauve interior **400**

Plate, 8" l., Begonia Leaf patt. **75**

Sardine box, cover & undertray, oval basket-molded box w/seaweed & rope borders, the cover molded as realistic fish, the interior glazed robin's egg blue, matching undertray, George Jones, painted design number "3517" & date letter for 1876, 9" l., the set (minor cover restoration) **3,450**

Vase, 36" h., floor-type, figural, modeled as a heron holding a fish in its beak & standing against a clump of leafy reeds forming a vase, impressed double fish in oval mark, Hugo Lonitz, ca. 1890 (old cracks, repair to beak tip) **9,200**

Ornate Majolica Vase

Vase, large bulbous baluster-form, a flaring pedestal base supporting a wide squatty bulbous body tapering to a short neck w/wide incurved rim band, ornate figural scrolled dragon handles from rim to shoulder, decorated w/colorful leafy scrolls, masks & a Bacchanalian scene, Italy, late 19th - early 20th c. (ILLUS.) **1,725**

Wine cooler, figural, modeled as a spirally-fluted footed urn w/a rolled, scalloped rim & large leafy swags on each side, supported by two tritons above the

round foot, impressed "Minton" & date
code for 1872, design number 526,
16" h. (restorations) **4,600**

MARBLEHEAD

Marblehead Mark

This pottery was organized in 1904 by Dr. Herbert J. Hall as a therapeutic aid to patients in a sanitarium he ran in Marblehead, Massachusetts. It was later separated from the sanitarium and directed by Arthur E. Baggs, a fine artist and designer, who bought out the factory in 1916 and operated it until its closing in 1936. Most wares were hand-thrown and decorated and carry the company mark of a stylized sailing vessel flanked by the letters "M" and "P."

Bowl, 6" d., 3" h., tapering wide squatty
bulbous form w/a short wide rolled
neck, overall brick red metallic glaze,
impressed mark **$385**
Bowl, 6¼" d., 2¼" h., compressed bulbous
incurved sides, smooth dark blue glaze
w/light blue interior, impressed ship mark **220**
Bowl-vase, miniature, a squatty bulbous
form tapering to a flat rim, overall brown
matte glaze, paper label, impressed
mark, 3½" d. (burst bubble on side) **198**
Bowl-vase, deep slightly tapering cylindrical
sides w/a closed rim, overall yellow matte
glaze, impressed mark, 5½" d., 3½" h. **660**
Bowl-vase, deep wide cylindrical form
w/wide flaring rim covered in matte
mauve glaze, lavender interior,
impressed ship mark, 7½" d., 3¾" h. **385**
Bowl-vase, wide bulbous body tapering
slightly to a wide flat mouth covered in a
smooth speckled brown glaze, impressed
ship mark, 5¼" d., 2¾" h. **358**
Match safe, cov., octagonal, w/striker inside
lid, covered in a fine smooth matte green
glaze, impressed ship mark, 2 x 3" (glaze
abrasion around rim) **385**

Marblehead Pitcher

Pitcher, 5" h., wide bulbous body w/arched
spout & C-form handle, incised
decoration of ship at sea, glossy blue
glaze, impressed mark (ILLUS.) **330**

Rare Marblehead Plate

Plate, 7½" d., border decorated w/a frieze of
camels and nomads in blue & yellow on
white ground, impressed ship mark
(ILLUS.) **1,045**
Tile, square, decorated w/a landscape of
trees in dark green reflected in a lake,
impressed ship mark & paper label,
4¼" sq. (small chip to front & back) **770**
Tile, square, depicting a cluster of trees in
dark green under a blue overcast sky,
impressed ship mark & paper label, 4¼" sq. . . . **880**
Vase, 2¾" h., decorated in a teal blue matte
glaze, black underglaze visible near rim,
narrow mouth on a flared bulbous form,
marked on base, ca. 1910 . . . . **374**
Vase, 3⅝" h., short flared rim on a squat
bulbous body, decorated w/repeating
stylized trees, black trunks & blue leaves
over a grey ground, impressed mark &
initials of Hannah Tutt, ca. 1905 . . . . **2,415**
Vase, 3½" h., simple swelled cylindrical form
w/a closed rim, overall unusual pink
matte glaze, impressed mark **275**
Vase, 3½" h., simple swelled cylindrical form
w/a closed rim, overall dark blue matte
glaze, impressed mark **286**
Vase, 4" h., 5" d., wide ovoid body w/wide
flat mouth, matte blue exterior & light blue
interior, impressed ship mark **440**

Unusual Marblehead Covered Vase

Vase, cov., 4¼" h., 4¾" d., wide bulbous
ovoid body tapering to a wide flaring rim
w/bobeche lid, covered in a smooth matte
grey glaze, paper label (ILLUS.) **660**

Vase, 6" h., cylindrical, carved & painted around the rim w/alternating blue & brown dragonflies against the medium matte green ground, artist-signed "Hanna Tutt" & impressed mark (small base flake) **1,760**

Vase, 6¼" h., 3¾" d., bulbous base below a wide cylindrical body w/flat rim, repeated design around rim of brown stylized flowers on long stems, green ground, early ship mark (repair to minor glaze flaking to rim)........................ **2,860**

Vase, 7¾" h., gently tapering rounded cylindrical body w/a short flared rim, dark blue matte glaze, impressed mark **805**

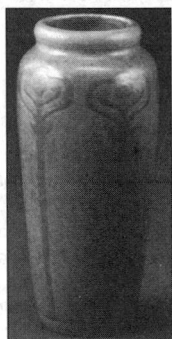

Marblehead Vase with Peacock Feathers

Vase, 8½" h., 4" d., tapering cylindrical body w/molded rim, decorated in wax-resist w/stylized peacock feathers in brown on a mottled green ground, impressed ship mark & "W" (ILLUS.) **4,400**

MARTIN BROTHERS

R.W. Martin & Brothers
London & Southall

Martin Brothers Mark

 Martinware, the term used for this pottery, dates from 1873 and is the product of the Martin brothers–Robert, Wallace, Edwin, Walter and Charles–often considered the first British studio potters. From first to final stages, their hand-thrown pottery was completely the work of the team. The early wares may be simple and conventional, but the Martin brothers built up their reputation by producing ornately engraved, incised or carved designs as well as rather bizarre figural wares. The amusing face-jugs are considered some of their finest work. After 1910, the work of the pottery declined and can be considered finished by 1915, though some attempts were made to fire pottery as late as the 1920s.

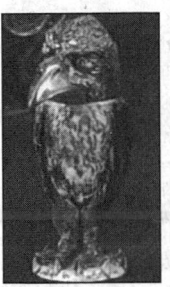 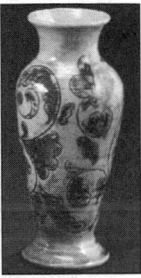

From left: Martin Brothers Humidor
Martin Brothers Floral Vase

Humidor, cov., grotesque bird-shaped body on round base, the cover formed by the head, glazed in brown & black tones, both parts incised "R.W.Martin Bros. London & Southall - 1903," repair to tip of beak, 7¾" h., 3¼" d. (ILLUS.) **$2,530**

Spoon warmer, stoneware, modeled as an open-mouthed caninesque face, glazed in green, brown & cobalt blue, applied loop handle, incised "R.W. Martin - London & Southall - 4-3-80," 5½" h. **2,185**

Vase, 4¼" h., 3½" d., stoneware, flaring foot supporting a baluster-shaped body w/tall wide neck & flaring rim, incised rings near base & at shoulder, decorated overall w/plumes & blossoms in blue & brown on a greyish green ground, incised "R.W.Martin - 680" (ILLUS.) **220**

Vase, 9" h., 4" d., tall squared ovoid form tapering to short square neck w/molded rim, upturned loop handles at the shoulder, decorated in sgraffito w/a veined pattern on an amber ground, incised "N5-7-1903 - Martin Bros. - London & Southall" **1,100**

Vase, 9¼" h., 6¼" d., footed bulbous ovoid body tapering to a wide flaring neck, covered in vivid incised & modeled swirls, brown & black matte glaze, incised "1 - 1 - 1903 - Martin Bros. - London Southall" ... **1,870**

Vases, 9" h., simple ovoid body tapering to a slightly flaring cylindrical neck, decorated w/a large crab on one side & a lobster on the opposite side w/assorted sea creatures in brown against "1903," pr. ... **1,870**

MCCOY

McCoy

McCoy Mark

 Collectors are now seeking the art wares of two McCoy potteries. One was founded in Roseville, Ohio, in the late 19th century as the J.W. McCoy Pottery, subsequently becoming

Brush-McCoy Pottery Co., later Brush Pottery. The other was also founded in Roseville in 1910 as Nelson McCoy Sanitary Stoneware Co., later becoming Nelson McCoy Pottery. In 1967 the pottery was sold to D.T. Chase of the Mount Clemens Pottery Co. who sold his interest to the Lancaster Colony Corp. in 1974. The pottery shop closed in 1985. Cookie jars are especially collectible today. A helpful reference book is The Collector's Encyclopedia of McCoy Pottery, *by the Huxfords (Collector Books), and* McCoy Cookie Jars From the First to the Latest, *by Harold Nichols (Nichols Publishing, 1987).*

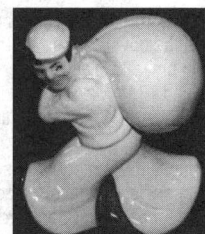

McCoy Seaman's Bank

Bank, figural seaman w/sack over shoulder, white, blue & black, 5¾" h. (ILLUS.).......... **$65**

Coffee serving set: cov. server, stand & eight mugs; El Rancho Bar-B-Que line, 1960, the set........................... 325

Cookie jar, Bean pot......................... 55

Cookie jar, Bobby Baker 53

Cookie jar, Boy on Baseball, 1978............ 310

Cookie jar, Bugs Bunny cylinder, 1971-72...... 185

Cookie jar, Burlap Sack 65

Cookie jar, Cauliflower Mammy.............. 900

Cookie jar, Chairman of the Board, 1985....... 750

Cookie jar, Chef (Bust), w/"Cookies" on hat band .. 70

Cookie jar, Christmas Tree 825

Cookie jar, Clown bust..................... 220

Cookie jar, Clown in Barrel 60

Cookie jar, Coffee Grinder.................. 50

Cookie jar, Covered Wagon (Cookie Wagon), 1959-62 105

Cookie jar, Eagle Basket 40

Cookie jar, Engine, black................... 175

Cookie jar, Friendship 7.................... 70

Cookie jar, Hamm's Bear.................. 350

McCoy Jack-O-Lantern Cookie Jar

Cookie jar, Jack-O-Lantern, orange w/green cover.................................. 600

Cookie jar, Kittens (Three) on Ball of Yarn, green 100

Cookie jar, Leprechaun, red 1,250

Cookie jar, Liberty Bell..................... 55

Cookie jar, Mammy 60

Cookie jar, Mammy, red polka dot dress, ca. 1930s 375

Cookie jar, Midge, without freckles (rare) 600

Cookie jar, Mr. & Mrs. Owl.................. 123

Cookie Jar, Old Fashioned Auto (Touring Car) ... 75

Cookie jar, Pineapple....................... 60

Cookie jar, Pot Belly Stove 55

Cookie jar, Quaker Oats canister............. 695

Cookie jar, Thinking Puppy 40

Cookie jar, Touring Car 130

Cookie jar, W.C. Fields, 1972-74............. 275

Cookie jar, Windmill....................... 60

Creamer & open sugar bowl, Sunburst Gold glaze, ca. 1957, original paper inventory tags, pr.......................... 125

Mug, Irish Setter decoration 35

Planter, figural, flying ducks, green glaze, No. 760................................ 175

Planter, figural, frog w/umbrella, dark glaze, 1954................................. 125

Vase, 8" h., Blossomtime line, pink & green molded florals on creamy yellow ground 45

Wall pocket, figural, model of an owl........... 75

Wall pocket, model of a cluster of grapes, white .. 180

MEISSEN

Meissen Mark

The secret of true hard paste porcelain, known long before to the Chinese, was "discovered" accidentally in Meissen, Germany, by J.F. Bottger, an alchemist working with E.W. Tschirnhausen. The first European true porcelain was made in the Meissen Porcelain Works, organized about 1709. Meissen marks have been widely copied by other factories. Some pieces listed here are recent.

Centerpiece, figural, Blue Onion patt., modeled as a boy & girl figure w/a goat atop a pedestal base, a pierced basket on either side, blue crossed swords mark, No. 1074, late 19th - early 20th c., 18" l., 8¾" h. (damages)..................... **$978**

Ewer, flattened ovoid body, allegorical decoration w/figures & scenes representing the element Water, painted & incised marks, drilled, 19th c., 24" h. **4,600**

Figure group, a shepherdess in 18th c. dress standing & grooming a lamb atop a tree trunk, polychrome decoration, blue crossed swords marks & incised inventory number "F68" & pattern number "61," late 18th c., 5" h. (some early repairs) . . . **518**

Figure group, a tailor in 18th c. dress riding astride a horned goat, one hand aloft holding scissors, finely decorated, incised "73011," on thin rectangular base, early 20th c., 9¼" h. . . . . (ILLUS.) **1,840**

Meissen 20th Century Figure Group

Figure group, an 18th c. maiden seated beside a fruit tree & smelling a flower w/a basket of blossoms beside her, a young suitor standing beside the tree, blue crossed swords mark, No. D94, early 20th c., 10" h. (ILLUS.) **1,265**

Meissen Figure of Exotic Dancer

Figure of a dancer, exotic nude female posed holding her arms out to the sides grasping the sides of a draped cape decorated w/gilt vines, stepping forward on a circular base, her brown hair pulled up into a coiled bun w/gilt head band, early 20th c., underglaze-blue crossed swords mark, incised on base "B256-85" & painted "74," 10¾" h. (ILLUS.) **2,185**

Figure of a lady, dressed in 18th c. attire, seated beside a small table w/cabriole legs which supports a table-top spinning wheel, she holding a religious book, finely decorated, 19th c., 6⅜" h. **1,093**

Figure of a young girl w/mandolin, dressed in 18th c. attire w/a floral-decorated skirt & lavender hat, on a square gilt-trimmed base, blue crossed swords mark, incised "G11" & "106H," late 18th c., 4" h. **403**

Figures, allegorical, representing "Day" & "Night," each a figure of a scantily clad child floating above a gilt hemisphere on an octagonal base, Night in a dark blue flowing cloak & crowned in a tiara w/alternating gilt & platinum stars, Day w/gilt rays emerging from his hair & draped in pale pink & holding a flaming torch & a sprig of roses, blue crossed swords mark, incised numbers "L135" & "L134," late 19th - early 20th c., 20¾" h., pr. (minor chips & restorations) **12,075**

Tea set: breakfast-sized cov. teapot, cov. creamer, cov. sugar bowl & two cups & saucers; Art Nouveau style, each piece of stylized floriform decorated w/pendent green & grey-shaded leaves on a pale grey ground, canceled crossed-swords underglaze-blue mark, incised & painted numbers, early 20th c., teapot 5" h., the set (some minute rim chips) **2,415**

Teapot, cov., figural, model of a rooster, enamel decoration, late 19th - early 20th c., 6" l. **575**

Lovely Large Meissen Vase

Vase, 15½" h., classic baluster-form, a fluted flaring base & pedestal w/rings supporting the ovoid body w/a band of flutes below the wide cobalt blue body band decorated w/large gilt & silver florals, ringed shoulder & short flaring neck w/incurved molded rim flanked by long looped snake handles from rim to shoulder, gilt trim on base & body & new gilt trim on handles, late 19th c. (ILLUS.) . . . **2,300**

METTLACH

Mettlach Mark

Ceramics with the name Mettlach were produced by Villeroy & Boch and other potteries in the Mettlach area of Germany. Villeroy and Boch's finest years of production are thought to be from about 1890 to 1910.

Plaque, round, blue-decorated village landscape on a white ground, titled on the back "Hannover," No. 5036, 17⅜" d. **$259**

Mettlach Plaque with Cavalier

Plaque, round, etched in center w/scene of cavalier seated at table raising a glass of beer in one hand, browns & white on a blue ground w/brown border band, No. 2622, dated 1910, artist-initialed, 7¾" d. (ILLUS.) **235**

Plaque, etched cavalier & bar maid, blue background, castle marked, dated 1900, pierced to hang, No. 2322, 14½"d. **795**

Mettlach Punch Bowl Set

Punch bowl, cover & undertray, bulbous urn-form footed body w/molded double-C scroll handles, flaring foot, low domed cover w/ladle hole & upright scrolled ring handle, printed under glaze w/a decoration of scenes of gnomes

working at a wine press & drinking, No. 2339/1028, early 20th c., 7½ liter, 16" h., the set (ILLUS.) **748**

Vase, 9½" h., large ovoid body w/a short slightly tapering neck, the body in dark blue w/an overall latticework design, each diamond segment w/a small molded red dot or florette, the neck in brick red w/a gold zigzag band & white florettes, impressed marks **330**

Vase, 10" h., tall square tapering form swelled near the base, incised & painted w/a geometric design w/vertical bands down the sides connecting to a group of graduated squares all in dark green & red on a creamy ground, impressed marks **550**

MINTON

Minton Marks

The Minton factory in England was established by Thomas Minton in 1793. The factory made earthenware, especially the blue-printed variety and Thomas Minton is sometimes credited with invention of the blue "Willow" pattern. For a time majolica and tiles were also an important part of production, but bone china soon became the principal ware. Mintons, Ltd., continues in operation today. Also see MAJOLICA in Ceramics.

Dinner service: 21" l. oval well-and-tree platter, five oval platters graduating from 13" to 19½" l., 14" l. cov. soup tureen & undertray, four 11¼" l. oval vegetable dishes & three covers, 10⅝" d. two-handled fruit bowl, 11⅞" d. plateau dish, 11¼" l. oval serving bowl, seventeen 10¼" d. soup plates, nineteen 10¼" d. plates & twenty-five 9" d. plates; fine earthenware, Italian patt., decorated w/border bands w/leafy scroll bands alternating w/round portrait medallions & palmettes, ca. 1865, the set **$1,725**

Plates, 9¼" d., each w/gilt-decorated embossed floral banding on the turquoise rim band, central scenes of animals in landscapes, ca. 1870, set of 6 . . . . **489**

Plates, 10½" d., each w/a scalloped rim, banded, scrolled & festooned foliate designs within a wide ivory-ground border, printed & impressed marks, 1929, set of 12 . . . . **2,070**

MOCHA

Mocha decoration is found on basically utilitarian creamware or yellowware articles and is achieved by a simple chemical reaction. A color pigment of brown, blue, green or black is given an acid nature by infusion of tobacco or hops. When this acid nature colorant is applied in blobs to an alkaline ground color, it reacts by spreading in feathery seaweed designs. This type of decoration is usually accompanied by horizontal bands of light color slip. Produced in numerous Staffordshire potteries from the late 18th until the late 19th centuries, its name is derived from the similar markings found on mocha quartz. In addition to the seaweed decoration, mocha wares are also seen with Earthworm and Cat's Eye patterns or a marbleized effect.

Mug, cylindrical w/C-form handle, Earthworm patt., impressed geometric border in dark brown, blue & cream on a pumpkin ground, 19th c., 5½" h. (hairlines, glaze wear, minute rim chips) **$518**

Pepper pot, footed cylindrical form w/domed top, decorated w/blue & white stripes & dark brown band w/white leaves & dots, blue top, chips, 4¾" h. 715

Pitcher, 8⅛" h., jug-form, wide ovoid body w/a rim spout & C-form handle, white ground banded w/brown & blue wide bands w/the Cat's Eye patt. outlined in thin dark brown pinstripes, early 19th c. (spider crack, minor crazing, wear) 1,210

MOORCROFT

MOORCROFT

Moorcroft Marks

William Moorcroft became a designer for James Macintyre & Co. in 1897 and was put in charge of their art pottery production. Moorcroft developed a number of popular designs, including Florian Ware while with Macintyre and continued with that firm until 1913 when they discontinued the production of art pottery. After leaving Macintyre in 1913, Moorcroft set up his own pottery in Burslem and continued producing the art wares he had designed earlier as well as introducing new patterns. After William's death in 1945, the pottery was operated by his son, Walter.

Bowl, 8" d., 'Poppy' patt., the interior tube-lined w/a garland of large & small blooms in tones of puce & purple, joined by scrolling green foliage, the exterior w/three spiraling stems, all reserved on a watery cobalt blue ground, impressed "MOORCROFT" & painted signature, ca. 1928 . . . . **$747**

Jar, cov., wide ovoid body w/a rounded shoulder to the short cylindrical neck fitted w/a domed cover, Eventide patt., decorated w/a landscape scene w/a band of large mushroom-shaped trees in brown, yellow & greenish brown against a shaded yellow & red sunset background w/brown mountains, ink artist-signature & die-stamped "Made in England - 760," 8½" d., 11" h. 6,600

Lamp bases, 'Poppy' patt., baluster-form, tube-lined w/a continuous band of flowers & foliage colored in tones of yellow, red, cobalt blue & green on a graduated mottled blue ground, all washed in a thin red flambé glaze, ca. 1950, 12¼" h., pr. 1,035

Vase, 3½" h., miniature, tapering cylindrical body w/a rounded shoulder centering a short flaring neck, dark blue ground w/multi-colored Orchid patt., original label 413

*From left: Moorcroft Landscape Vase
Moorcroft Claremont Vase*

Vase, 6" h., 5¼" d., Landscape patt., footed bulbous ovoid body w/flaring rim, scene of blue trees on a mottled blue & yellow ground, script mark (ILLUS.) 2,200

Vase, 6¼" h., 4½" d., Cornflower patt., ovoid body w/cylindrical molded rim, impressed "MOORCROFT - MADE IN ENGLAND - 210" 1,320

Vase, 6½" h., footed baluster-form, large red six-petaled blossoms & green leaves on a shaded pale green to dark blue ground, impressed & painted marks 358

Vase, 8½" h., Claremont patt., ovoid body decorated w/large mushrooms in red, green & yellow against a blue ground, impressed & painted marks (ILLUS.) 2,640

Vase, 10" h., Poppy patt., wide ovoid body w/slightly flaring rim, red & black ground, die-stamped mark & artist-signed 4,400

Vase, 12" h., bottle-form, 'Eventide Landscape' patt., the lower body tube-lined w/trees in an undulating landscape, glazed in watery tones of green, ochre & blue against a deep red sky, impressed "MOORCROFT - 156" & painted signature, ca. 1925 (hairline in upper rim) **862**

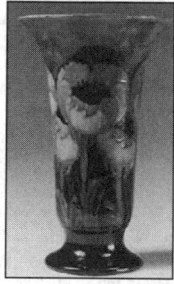

Moorcroft Trumpet-Form Vase

Vase, 17⅛" h., trumpet-form, gently flaring cylindrical body tube-lined w/big poppy pattern, reserved on mottled blue & green ground, interior w/mottled dark cobalt blue glaze, impressed "Moorcroft," Cobridge factory mark, W. Moorcroft signature in blue script, applied paper label "Potter to H.M. the Queen," ca. 1920, upper rim w/traces of restoration (ILLUS.) **2,070**

MULBERRY

Mulberry or Flow Mulberry ironstone wares were produced in the Staffordshire district of England in the period between 1840 and 1870 at many of the same factories which produced its close "cousin," Flow Blue china. In fact, some of the early Flow Blue patterns were also decorated with the dark blackish or brownish purple mulberry coloration and feature the same heavy smearing or "flown" effect. Produced on sturdy ironstone bodies, the designs were either transfer-printed or hand-painted (Brush stroke) with an Asian, Scenic, Floral or Marble design. Some patterns were also decorated with additional colors over or under the glaze; these are designated in the following listings as "w/polychrome." Quite a bit of this ware is still to be found and it is becoming increasingly sought-after by collectors although presently its values lag somewhat behind similar Flow Blue pieces. The standard references to Mulberry wares is Petra Williams' book, Flow Blue China and Mulberry Ware, Similarity and Value Guide *and* Mulberry Ironstone - Flow Blue's Best Kept Little Secret, *by Ellen R. Hill.*

ACADIA (Maker unknown, ca. 1850)

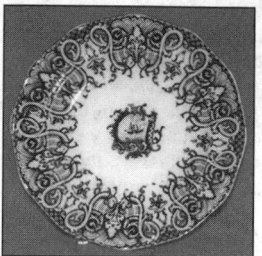

Acadia Plate

Creamer, 6" h., Classic Gothic shape......... $250
Plate, 8" d. (ILLUS.) 100

AMERILLIA (Podmore, Walker & Co., ca. 1850)

Egg cup 200
Plate, 9½" 85
Vegetable dish, cov. 350

ATHENS (Charles Meigh, ca. 1845)

Athens Pitcher

Creamer, 6", vertical-paneled Gothic shape..... 150
Cup plate 100
Pitcher, 6 paneled, 10" h. (ILLUS.)........... 300
Punch cup 125
Sugar, cov., vertical-paneled Gothic shape 200

ATHENS (Wm. Adams & Son, ca. 1849)

Cup plate 95
Plate, 8½" d........................... 55
Soup plate, w/flanged rim, 9".............. 90
Sugar, cov., full-paneled Gothic shape........ 225
Teapot, cov., full-paneled Gothic shape........ 310

AVA (T. J. & J. Mayer, ca. 1850)

Cup & saucer, handleless, w/polychrome 80
Plate, 9½" d., w/polychrome................. 75
Plate, 10½" d., w/polychrome................ 85
Platter, 16" l., w/polychrome............... 250
Sauce tureen, cover & undertray,
    w/polychrome, 3 pcs. 500

BEAUTIES OF CHINA (Mellor Venables & Co., ca. 1845)

Cup plate 95
Plate, 7½" d., w/polychrome 65
Platter, 14" l., w/polychrome 225
Sauce tureen, cover, ladle & undertray,
    long octagon, 4 pcs. 675

BOCHARA (James Edwards, ca. 1850)

Bochara Teapot

Creamer, 6" h., full-paneled Gothic shape 150
Pitcher, 7½" h., full-paneled Gothic shape 170
Plate, 10½" d. 75
Teapot, cov., pedestaled Gothic style (ILLUS.) . . 350

BRUNSWICK (Mellor Venables & Co., ca. 1845)

Plate, 7½" d., w/polychrome 65
Platter, 16" l., w/polychrome 275
Relish dish, stubby mitten-shape,
    w/polychrome 125
Sugar, cov., Classic Gothic shape,
    w/polychrome 225

BRYONIA (Paul Utzchneider & Co., ca. 1880)

Bryonia Plate

Cup & saucer, handled 60
Gravy boat 150
Plate, 7½" d. 50
Plate, 9½" d. (ILLUS.) 65

CEYLON (Charles Meigh, ca. 1840)

Plate, 9½" d. 65
Plate, 10½" d., w/polychrome 85

Platter, 14" l., w/polychrome 175
Vegetable bowl, open, small 125

CHUSAN (P. Holdcroft, ca. 1850)

Plate, 9½" d. 80
Potato bowl, 11" d. 250

CLEOPATRA (F. Morley & Co., ca. 1850)

Basin & ewer, w/polychrome 750
Plate, 9½" d. 70
Soap box, cover & drainer, 3 pcs. 250
Soup plate, w/flanged rim, 9" d. 90

COREA (Joseph Clementson, ca. 1850)

Cup & saucer, handleless 75
Sugar, covered, long hexagon 250
Teapot, covered, long hexagon 350

COREAN (Podmore, Walker & Co., ca. 1850)

Corean Sauce Tureen

Cup plate 75
Cup & saucer, handled, large 125
Relish, mitten-shape. 135
Sauce tureen, cover & undertray, 3 pcs.
    (ILLUS.) 475
Sugar, cov., oval bulbous style. 350

COTTON PLANT (J. Furnival, ca. 1850)

Cotton Plant Teapot

Creamer, 6⅝" h., paneled grape shape,
   w/polychrome **200**
Teapot, cov., cockscomb handle,
   w/polychrome (ILLUS.) **650**

CYPRUS (Wm. Davenport, ca. 1845)

Cyprus Gravy

Cup plate **85**
Gravy boat, unusual handle (ILLUS.) **150**
Pitcher, 11" h., 6-sided **250**

DORA (E. Challinor, ca. 1850)

Plate, 9½" d. **65**
Teapot, cov., Baltic shape, brush stroke **650**

FERN & VINE (Maker unknown, ca. 1850)

Fern & Vine Creamer

Creamer, 6" h., Classic Gothic style (ILLUS.) **225**
Plate, 7½" d. **75**

FLORA (Hulme & Booth, ca. 1850)

Creamer, 6" h., w/polychrome, grand loop
   shape **150**

FLORA (T. Walker, ca. 1847)

Cup & saucer, handleless **65**
Plate, 7½" d. **75**
Plate, 9½" d. **85**
Sugar, cov., Classic Gothic shape **250**

FLOWER VASE (T. J. & J. Mayer, ca. 1850)

Teapot, cov., w/polychrome, Prize Bloom
   shape **560**

FOLIAGE (J. Edwards, ca. 1850)

Foliage Plate

Gravy boat **150**
Plate, 8" d. (ILLUS.) **75**

GERANIUM (Podmore, Walker & Co., ca. 1850)

Geranium Plate

Plate, 8" d. (ILLUS.) **65**
Waste bowl **135**

JARDINERE (Villeroy & Boch, ca. 1880)

Gravy boat **125**
Plate, 7½" d. **55**
Plate, 9½" d. **75**
Vegetable bowl, open, round **150**

JEDDO (Wm. Adams, ca. 1849)

Jeddo Sugar Bowl

Cup plate **95**
Cup & saucer, handleless **75**
Relish dish, octagonal **125**

Sugar, cov., full-paneled Gothic shape (ILLUS.) . . **195**
Teapot, cov., full-paneled Gothic shape **300**

KAN-SU (Thomas Walker, ca. 1847)

Cup & saucer, handleless **75**
Plate, 7½" d. **60**
Platter, 14" l. **250**
Vegetable dish, cov., octagonal. **375**

MARBLE (A. Shaw, ca. 1850)

From left: Marble Creamer
Mellor Venables Marble Teapot

Creamer, 6" h., 10 panel Gothic shape (ILLUS.) . . **200**
Invalid feeder, large **500**
Waste bowl **150**

MARBLE (Mellor Venables & Co., ca. 1845)

Plate, 9½" d. **75**
Teapot, cov., child's, vertical paneled Gothic **350**
Teapot, cov., vertical paneled Gothic shape
   (ILLUS.) **450**

MEDINA (J. Furnival, ca. 1850)

Cup & saucer, handleless **65**
Gravy boat **155**
Sugar, cov., Cockscomb handle **350**

NANKIN (Davenport, ca. 1845)

Nankin Pitcher

Pitcher, 8" h., mask spout jug w/polychrome
   (ILLUS.) **300**
Plate, 8½" d., w/polychrome **75**

NING PO (R. Hall, ca. 1840)

Cup & saucer, handleless **65**

Plate, 10½" d. **85**
Soup plate, w/flanged rim, 10" d. **90**

PARISIAN GROUPS (J. Clementson, ca. 1850)

Plate, 7½" d., w/polychrome **60**
Plate, 8½" d., w/polychrome **70**
Sauce dish, w/polychrome **65**
Sauce tureen, cover & undertray,
   w/polychrome, 3 pcs. **450**

PELEW (Edward Challinor, ca. 1850)

Pelew Teapot

Cup & saucer, handleless, pedestalled **95**
Plate, 7½" d. **60**
Plate, 10½" d. **90**
Punch cup, ring handle **100**
Teapot, cov., pumpkin shape (ILLUS.) **395**

PERUVIAN (John Wedge Wood, ca. 1850)

Peruvian Cup & Saucer

Cup & saucer, handleless, "double bulge"
   (ILLUS.) **85**
Gravy boat **145**
Teapot, cov., 16 paneled **400**
Waste bowl, "double bulge" **150**

PHANTASIA (J. Furnival, ca. 1850)

Creamer, 6" h., w/polychrome, cockscomb
   handle. **325**
Cup plate, w/polychrome **95**
Plate, 9½" d., w/polychrome **85**
Sugar, cov., w/polychrome, cockscomb
   handle. **400**
Teapot, cov., w/polychrome, cockscomb
   handle. **650**

RHONE SCENERY (T. J. & J. Mayer, ca. 1850)

Gravy boat 150
Plate, 7½" d. 45
Plate, 10½" d. 65
Sauce tureen, cover & undertray, 3 pcs. 500
Sugar, cov., full-paneled Gothic shape 200

SCINDE (T. Walker, ca. 1847)

Creamer, 6" h., Classic Gothic shape 150
Plate, 9½" d. 80
Soup plate, 9" d., flanged rim. 90
Teapot, cov., Classic Gothic shape 350

SHAPOO (T. & R. Boote, ca. 1850)

Plate, 8½" d. 75
Sugar, cov., Primary shape 300
Teapot, cov., Primary shape. 450
Vegetable dish, cov., flame finial 350

TEMPLE (Podmore, Walker & Co., ca. 1850)

Cup plate 75
Cup & saucer, handled, large 95
Plate, 8½" d. 55
Sugar, cov., Classic Gothic shape 200
Teapot, cov., Classic Gothic shape 350

VINCENNES (J. Alcock, ca. 1840)

Vincennes Punch Cup

Compote, Gothic Cameo shape. 500
Cup & saucer, handleless, thumbprint. 85
Plate, 7½" d. 60
Plate, 10½" d. 80
Punch cup (ILLUS.) 125
Soup tureen, cover & undertray, 10-sided,
    3 pcs. 2,000

WASHINGTON VASE (Podmore, Walker & Co., ca. 1850)

Creamer, 6" h., Classic Gothic shape. 225
Cup & saucer, handleless 85
Plate, 10½" d. 75
Soup plate, w/flanged rim, 9" d. 85
Teapot, cov., bulbous shape 495

WHAMPOA (Mellor Venables, ca. 1845)

Gravy boat 165
Plate, 10½" d. 95
Sauce tureen, cov., long octagon shape, 2 pcs. . . . 300

WREATH (Thomas Furnival, ca. 1850)

Wreath Ewer

Ewer (ILLUS.) 295
Plate, 9½" d. 85

NEWCOMB COLLEGE POTTERY

Newcomb Mark

This pottery was established in the art department of Newcomb College, New Orleans, Louisiana, in 1897. Each piece was hand-thrown and bore the potter's mark & decorator's monogram on the base. It was always a studio business and never operated as a factory and its pieces are therefore scarce, with the early wares being eagerly sought. The pottery closed in 1940.

Bowl, 6½" d., 3" h., a shallow flaring bottom
    below upright wide sides, the sides
    incised & divided into rectangular panels
    decorated w/stylized painted florals
    outlined in dark blue w/a dark green &
    ivory glossy ground, incised marks
    "C. Payne - J.M." $2,750
Bowl, 7" d., wide squatty bulbous form w/a
    wide three-sided low rim, glossy green &
    blue glaze, impressed marks, w/a flower
    frog, 2 pcs. 660
Bowl, 8½" d., wide shallow rounded sides
    w/a narrow incurved rim, carved &
    painted around the rim w/violets in red
    w/yellow centers & green leaves on a
    greenish blue matte ground, impressed
    mark, "#IC21 - #269 - J.M. - C. Littlejohn" 990

Bowl, 9½" d., low & wide squatty bulbous form w/wide narrow rim, carved & painted florals w/yellow-centered pink blossoms & long green leaves on a dark blue matte ground, impressed marks, "A.F. Simpson - J.M. - #NF31 - 313" (tight line) **990**

Newcomb Bowl-Vase with Crocus

Bowl-vase, decorated w/cobalt blue rim over incised band of repeating crocus above a band of leaves, cream, yellow, pale blue, blue & bluish green over light blue body, interior gloss glazed cream, by Marie H. LeBlanc, 1905, impressed "NC, W - JM - CB54" & artist's cipher, 5½" d., 4¼" h. (ILLUS.) **4,025**

Cup & saucer, tall tapering cylindrical cup & wide dished saucer, each incised & painted w/stylized flowers in dark blue against a light blue ground, glossy glaze, impressed marks, "C. Luria - J.M. - #DO10," saucer 5½" d., cup 3" h. **2,090**

Inkwell, squatty bulbous base tapering to wide cylindrical neck w/flat rim, incised w/bell-shaped green & white flowers on a blue & yellow ground, by Mary Butler, 1908, impressed "NC - MWB - Q - CG79 - JM." 3 x 3¾" (missing lid & liner) **1,430**

From left: Early Newcomb College Jar
Rare Newcomb College Plaque

Jar, cov., ovoid body w/flat inset cover, button finial, blue band around base w/long blue stems & leaves rising to incised blue dogwood blossoms w/yellow centers around upper body & cover, light blue ground, by Marie De Hoa LeBlanc, 1904, incised "NC - JM - PP32 - MHLB," remnant of paper label, touch-up to nick inside lid, 4¼" d., 7" h. (ILLUS.) **13,200**

Pitcher, 3½" h., wide ovoid body tapering to a flat mouth w/pinched spout, C-form handle, carved & painted w/a continuous band of leafy trees in blue & green on a yellow ground, glossy glaze, impressed mark, "J.M. - L. Nicholson - #BP94" **3,850**

Pitcher, 8" h., large ovoid body w/a deep shoulder to the cylindrical neck & pinched spout, angled handle from rim to shoulder, painted w/large dark green leafy stems up the sides topped by green berries against an ivory & dark blue ground, glossy glaze, impressed mark, "R. Kennon - J.M. - #0050" **7,150**

Plaque, tall rectangular form, carved & painted w/a scene of a statue at Newcomb College in shades of blue w/green foliage behind & the white Chapel in the background, pre-1918, matte glaze, impressed mark, "S. Irvine - #SM63," in a wide wood frame, 6 x 10" (ILLUS.) **17,600**

Plate w/flanged rim, 7" d., light blue glossy glaze center encircled by a bluish green band w/incised intertwined white flowers & green stems, dark blue rim band, by Sadie Irvine, 1910, impressed "NC - SI - JM - BP - EC26" **2,640**

Trivet, square, w/an incised & painted border of leaves in dark blue on a light blue matte ground, probably by Henrietta Bailey, incised "NC - HB - K." & painted "EB-72," 4" sq. **825**

Vase, 3" h., miniature, a spherical body w/a short cylindrical neck, painted w/flowers & leaves in green & blue against a light blue & dark blue ground, glossy glaze, impressed mark, "#0011 - Alice Rosalie Urquhart" **2,970**

Vase, 3½" h., bulbous ovoid body w/a wide rounded shoulder centered by a short cylindrical neck, overall dark blue & streaked red glossy glaze, incised marks, "L. Nicholson" **550**

Vase, 5" h., simple ovoid form w/a wide flat mouth, carved & painted w/a continuous landscape of moss-laden oaks w/a soft pink sky, matte glaze, impressed marks, "S. Irvine - J.M. - #JO56" **2,640**

Vase, 5½" h., pear-shaped body, decorated w/incised swirling branches of pussy-willows in pink on a purple ground, by Sadie Irvine, 1929, impressed "NC - SI -RT8" **2,310**

Vase, 6" h., bulbous ovoid body tapering to a tiny neck flanked by wide flat angled wing handles w/round openings, multi-toned overall green crystalline glaze w/gunmetal highlights, overall iridescence, impressed "JM - FR" **935**

Vase, 6" h., wide ovoid body tapering to a short cylindrical neck, carved & painted around the shoulder w/large pink rose blossoms on green stems down the sides against a dark blue matte ground, impressed mark, "#RI28 - #181 - JH - Sadie Irvine" **2,860**

Vase, 6½" h., footed wide squatty bulbous body tapering to short cylindrical neck w/flat rim, decorated w/a carved scene of bluish green Spanish moss over dark blue live oak trees, under a full moon, shaded blue ground, decorated by Anna Frances Simpson, 1920, impressed "NC - AFS - LE27 - 49" (short tight line to rim) **5,225**

Vase, 6½" h., 6½" d., bulbous ovoid body tapering to a short wide neck, carved & painted w/a continuous landscape of moss-laden oaks in dark blue w/a pale blue sky & yellow moon, matte glaze, impressed marks, "S. Irvine - J. Hunt - #500 - SV444" **3,575**

Vase, 9" h., a narrow footring supports a bulbous base tapering gently to a tall cylindrical neck, decorated w/incised light blue irises on dark bluish green leaves, blue ground, decorated by Sadie Irvine, 1912, impressed "NC - SI - JM - B - FA92" . . **3,300**

Vase, 14" h., wide ovoid body w/short cylindrical neck & flat rim, carved w/palm trees in a matte blue & green glaze, by Sadie Irvine, 1913, impressed "NC - SI - B - GC70 - JM - 24S" (restored drill hole at base) **2,750**

NILOAK POTTERY

ΝΙLOΑΚ

Niloak Pottery Mark

This pottery was made in Benton, Arkansas and featured hand-thrown varicolored swirled clay decoration in objects of classic forms. Designated Mission Ware, this line is the most desirable of Niloak's production which was begun early in this century. Less expensive to produce, the cast Hywood Line, finished with either high gloss or semi-matte glazes, was introduced during the economic depression of the 1930s. The pottery ceased operation about 1946.

Candlestick, Mission Ware, swirled colored clays, 10¼" h. **$250**

Pitcher, tankard, 10½" h., corsetted, Mission Ware **495**

Vase, 3" h., Mission Ware, heavy short cylindrical form w/closed rim, swirling cream, brown, blue & red clays, impressed mark **154**

Vase, 4" d., Mission Ware, bulbous ovoid body w/a thick molded rim, swirled grey, tan, rust & blue clays, first art mark **69**

Vase, 4¼" h., Mission Ware, waisted cylindrical form, swirled brown, cream, tan & blue clays **52**

Vase, 5" h., Mission Ware, simple slender ovoid body tapering to a small neck w/widely flaring flattened rim, swirled tan, blue, rust, purple & brown clays **81**

Vase, 5½" h., Mission Ware, simple cylindrical form, sharply contrasting swirled cream, brown, tan & blue clays, first art mark **104**

Vase, 6" h., Mission Ware, bulbous lower body tapering to a tall waisted neck, swirled blue, brown & cream clays **92**

Vase, 10" h., Mission Ware, bulbous body tapering to a large wide trumpet neck, swirled blue, red, brown & cream glazes, impressed mark **275**

NIPPON

"Nippon" is a term which is used to describe a wide range of porcelain wares produced in Japan from the late 19th century until about 1921. It was in 1891 that the U.S. implemented the McKinley Tariff Act which required that all wares exported to the United States carry a marking indicating the country of origin. The Japanese chose to use "Nippon," their name for Japan. In 1921 the import laws were revised and the words "Made in" had to be added to the markings. Japan was also required to replace the "Nippon" with the English name "Japan" on all wares sent to the U.S.

Many Japanese factories produced Nippon porcelains and much of it was hand-painted with ornate floral or landscape decoration and heavy gold decoration, applied beading and slip-trailed designs referred to as "moriage." We indicate the specific marking used on a piece, when known, at the end of each listing below. Be aware that a number of Nippon markings have been reproduced and used on new porcelain wares.

Important reference books on Nippon include: The Collector's Encyclopedia of Nippon Porcelain, Series One through Three, by Joan F. Van Patten (Collector Books, Paducah, Kentucky) and The Wonderful World of Nippon Porcelain, 1891-1921 by Kathy Wojciechowski (Schiffer Publishing, Ltd., Atglen, Pennsylvania).

Ashtray, round flat-bottomed form w/upright low sides & attached rest on rim, the interior painted w/a colorful hand of cards showing a 'full house' of aces & kings against a shaded orangish yellow ground, 4" d. (green "M" in Wreath mark) **$35**

Basket, boat-shaped w/a high arched spout at each end, an arched gold handle across the center, the sides painted w/a lakeside scene w/sailboat & beaded trim, 5½" l. (blue "Rising Sun" mark) **58**

Candlesticks, squared baluster-form w/flaring base, the sides w/a h.p. sunset scene w/house in meadow, gold socket rim, 5½" h., pr. (green "Kinso Nippon" mark) **81**

Celery dish, oblong w/incurved rim, h.p. decoration of house in meadow scene, 12" l. (green "M" in Wreath mark) **66**

Center bowl, squatty rounded oval form w/incurved scalloped rim & upright pointed loop end handles, decorated w/large pink blossoms w/yellow centers & green leaves on a moss green ground, moriage trim, 9" l. (blue "Maple Leaf" mark) . . . **173**

Chocolate pot, cov., tall lobed & waisted body w/a pointed rim spout, forked S-scroll handle & domed cover w/pierced finial, white bands at base & on neck trimmed w/green buttons, the side lobes each w/an oval lavender panel, white on dark green bands on the neck, overall ornate moriage decoration, unmarked, 9" h. . . **201**

Condiment set: salt & pepper shakers, cov. mustard jar w/ladle, toothpick holder & tray; each of hexagonal form & decorated w/ornate gold scrolling & cobalt bands on white, gold handles, rectangular tray w/angled corners, the set ("RC Nippon" mark) **161**

Cracker jar, cov., wide cylindrical form on tiny gold ball feet, gently rounded shoulder supporting a domed cover w/pointed gold finial, h.p. overall w/large purple iris & green leaves on a stippled greenish yellow ground, acanthus leaf brackets molded in relief, 7½" h. (blue "Maple Leaf" mark) **518**

Fernery, footed bulbous form w/deeply scalloped rim, decorated w/h.p. florals & moriage scrolling w/a center scenic transfer of the World Exposition Building, unmarked, 5" h. **286**

Hair receiver, squatty lobed form, decorated w/h.p. florals in gold scrolled medallions on cobalt blue ground, 5" d. (blue "Maple Leaf" mark) **110**

Humidor, cov., squatty bulbous base w/wide cylindrical sides & flared rim, inset slightly domed lid w/large knob finial, h.p. scene of moose head w/large antlers, 5½" h. (green "M" in Wreath mark) **385**

Mug, cylindrical w/gently incurved rim & angled dark gold handle, decorated w/a continuous lakeside landscape w/tall tree & pink cherry blossoms, 5" h. (green "M" in Wreath mark) **58**

Nappy, shallow round form w/ring handle & widely flaring rim w/h.p. ornate gold scroll decorated border, 7" d. (blue "Maple Leaf" mark) **28**

Nut dish, oblong, relief-molded acorns at one end w/large h.p. brown leaves down the center, 8" l. (green "M" in Wreath mark) **69**

Nut dish, octagonal w/two tab handles, h.p. interior decoration of hazel nuts, 8" (green "M" in Wreath mark) **83**

Pitcher, 5½" h., tankard-type, h.p. w/a stylized Dutch landscape w/windmill & lake in background & a man stealing geese being chased by other geese in foreground, enameled jewel trim (green "Wreath Studio Handpainted" mark) **115**

Plaque, pierced to hang, round, stylized scene of a girl w/horn chasing a flock of geese, in color against a shaded brown to mustard yellow ground, enameled rim, 7½" d. . . **81**

Nippon Plaque with Monk Portrait

Plaque, pierced to hang, h.p. center portrait of a monk in red surrounded by a stippled gold border w/scrolled medallions, 9½" d., green "M" in Wreath mark (ILLUS.) **660**

Soap dish, cover & insert, oval, deep sided, the slightly domed cover w/pink-trimmed arched center handle & decorated w/a landscape w/windmill scene, the border of the cover & bottom decorated w/a narrow band of enameling w/jewels, 5" l. (blue "Maple Leaf" mark) **173**

Toothpick holder, footed slightly tapering cylindrical form w/angled rim handles, h.p. landscape scene of a cottage & apple tree, 2¼" h. (green "M" in Wreath mark) **69**

Tray, h.p. w/lovely gold-outlined yellow & red primroses w/heavy gold border & rim, marked, 5½ x 12½" **125**

Urn, cov., large baluster-form w/domed & scroll-molded bolted-on foot, the large ovoid body tapering to a trumpet neck & molded rim w/a high domed small cover w/gold knob finial, upright winged scroll gold shoulder handles, the whole w/a dark cobalt blue ground ornately decorated overall w/delicate gold scrolling centering an oval & banded lakeside

landscape scene in full color, highlighted
w/green jewels, 17½" h. (green "Maple
Leaf" mark) **5,520**

Vase, 5" h., footed wide cylindrical body
w/short neck, angled handles from
shoulder to rim, h.p. cartoon-type outdoor
scene w/cottage (green "M" in wreath mark) . . . **77**

Vase, 6" h., flattened ovoid body tapering to
four small tab feet, small angular
shoulder handles & a flaring rectangular
neck, h.p. lake shore sunset scene,
enameled beading (green "M" in
Wreath mark) **63**

Vase, 7" h., four-footed spherical body w/a
narrow short neck flaring into a four-lobed
upturned rim, large C-scroll round
handles from rim to shoulder, decorated
overall w/ornate moriage beading w/white
& purple florals & green leaves & rim
(blue "Maple Leaf" mark) **350**

Vase, 11½" h., flaring oblong foot tapering to
a slender pedestal continuing to the wide
bulbous ovoid shouldered body centered
by a short narrow neck w/a widely flaring
lobed rim, ring handles on the shoulder,
burgundy ground w/a large central yellow
& white reserve w/delicate blue & green
vining florals in moriage around the sides,
green neck & handles w/further moriage
beading, unmarked (minor losses) **345**

Vase, 12" h., slender tall slightly waisted
hexagonal form, decorated around the
sides w/vining yellow & pink roses &
green leaves on a dusted gold ground
w/gold rim & base bands (blue "M" in
Wreath mark) **715**

Vase, 15" h., tall slender swelled cylindrical
body w/a rounded shoulder to a small
cylindrical gold neck flanked by small
gold loop shoulder handles, the wide
center band h.p. w/large clusters of
purple & green grapes against a shaded
yellow ground, the shoulder & base w/gilt-
bordered & trimmed bands of large h.p.
pink roses, blue blossoms & green leaf
(blue "Maple Leaf" mark) **1,380**

Wine jug w/bulbous stopper, footed
bulbous ovoid body w/a small flared neck
w/rim spout, small arched handle from
rim to shoulder, decorated w/a European
sunset landscape scene w/figures
walking by a large, trees & a large
cottage in the background, 9½" h.
(green "M" in Wreath mark) **600**

NORITAKE

*Noritake china, still in production in Japan,
has been exported in large quantities to this
country since early in this century. Though the
Noritake Company first registered in 1904, it did
not use "Noritake" as part of its backstamp until*
*1918. Interest in Noritake has escalated as
collectors now seek out pieces made between the
"Nippon" era and World War II (1921-41). The
Azalea pattern is also popular with collectors.*

Noritake Mark

Ashtray, figural polar bear, blue ground,
4¼" d., 2½" h. **$52**

Bowl, 7" w., interior w/relief-molded
filbert nuts in brown trimmed w/h.p.
autumn leaves **79**

Bowl, 10" d., gold handles, decorated on the
interior w/a blue, gold, orange & black
peacock feather design **95**

Bowl, 10" sq., open handles, h.p. center
scene of house & large tree by pond,
ornate scalloped border decorated
w/trailing vines & gold trim, ... **121**

Nut set: 6" d. bowl shaped like open
chestnut & six 2" d. nut dishes; earthtone
ground w/h.p. nuts & leaves, the set **150**

Plate, 7⅝" w., fruit or salad, Azalea patt.,
square w/notched corners, No.315 . . . . **85**

Powder box, cov., figural, an Art Deco style
female figure on a chair in colors of
orange, black, green, white & brown w/a
lustre finish, 1930s, 4¼ x 5", 7" h. **2,070**

Vase, 8½" h., bulbous body, Tree in the
Meadow patt. **98**

Wall pocket, double, conical two-part form
w/arched backplate, decorated w/an exotic
blue & yellow bird among branches of red
& blue stylized blossoms against a cream
ground, purple lustre rim band, 8" l. **110**

Wall pocket, trumpet-form, wide upper band
decorated w/an autumn sunset scene,
lavender lustre rim band & base, 8¼" l. **72**

NORTH DAKOTA SCHOOL OF MINES

North Dakota School of Mines Mark

*All pottery produced at the University of
North Dakota School of Mines was made from
North Dakota clay. In 1910, the University hired
Margaret Kelly Cable to teach pottery making
and she remained at the school until her
retirement. Julia Mattson and Margaret Pachl
were other instructors between 1923 and 1970.*

Designs and glazes varied through the years ranging from the Art Nouveau to modern styles. Pieces were marked "University of North Dakota - Grand Forks, N.D. - Made at School of Mines, N.D." within a circle and also signed by the students until 1963. Since that time, the pieces bear only the students' signatures. Items signed "Huck" are by the artist Flora Huckfield and were made between 1923 and 1949. Pieces were marked with the University name until 1963.

North Dakota School of Mines Bowl

Bowl, 6½" d., 2" h., round straight sides decorated w/a h.p. & lightly tooled scene of oxen & cov. wagons on the prairie against a blue sky, brown ground, decorated by Julia Mattson, circular ink mark & incised "JM#6 - 121 - Huck." (ILLUS.) **$1,045**

Bowl-Vase with Coyotes

Bowl-vase, squatty bulbous body decorated w/an embossed band of medium matte green coyotes silhouetted against a darker matte green ground, by Julia Mattson, 1925, circular ink stamp & incised "JM25," stilt pull to base, 3 x 4¼" (ILLUS.) **660**

Figure of cowboy, bentonite, standing, wearing chaps & large hat, neckerchief & gun & holster, brown & black, by Julia Mattson, incised "JM 13 UND," 3 x 4¾" **605**

Model of a hawk, bentonite, wings & back decorated w/yellow & black stripes, rectangular base, by Julia Mattson, incised signature, 5" h., 3¾" l. **880**

Pitcher, 5½" h., bulbous body w/flaring neck, pinched spout & loop handle, incised decoration of children at play & stylized florals, polychrome matte glaze, decorated by Franc Freeman, ink stamp & incised signature, 1947 . . . . **605**

Trivet, round, decorated w/large stylized polychrome bird standing on long branch beneath a stylized flower, by

North Dakota School of Mines Trivet

Julia Mattson, ink mark & incised "JMattson," couple of small burst bubbles, 6" d. (ILLUS.) **440**

Vase, miniature, 3¼" h., squatty bulbous ovoid body w/green stripes on a mustard ground, by Julia Mattson, ink stamp & "M." . . . **358**

Vase, 3½" h., bentonite, bulbous body w/wide narrow rim, decorated w/a band of black wolves in silhouette on a brick red ground, ink stamp & "ML" **1,100**

Vase, 5" h., 6" d., round sharply angled sides w/wide sloping shoulder tapering to short cylindrical neck w/flat rim, decorated w/a repeating incised frieze of bison in matte brown & green on dark brown ground w/dark brown band at mid-body & brown ground on lower body, carved by Margaret Cable, ink stamp & "M. Cable" **5,225**

Vase, 6" h., swelled cylindrical body tapering to wide flaring rim, decorated near the shoulder w/red & white daisies on long green stems, caramel ground, by Hildegarde Fried, 1924, ink stamp & "H.F." . . **3,300**

North Dakota School of Mines Vase

Vase, 7¼" h., wide bulbous body tapering to short slightly flaring cylindrical neck, decorated w/large stylized purple flowers w/orange centers & green leaves on a brown ground, hand-carved by Julia Mattson, 1925, ink stamp & incised "M." (ILLUS.) **7,150**

Vase, 8½" h., simple ovoid body tapering to a short cylindrical neck, deeply molded around the shoulder w/a stylized blossom band, the red clay covered w/a pale cream & lightly tinted blue matte glaze, stamped mark & incised "Cable" & "Prairie Rose" **605**

Vase, 14" h., shouldered ovoid body tapering to a wide flaring neck, decorated w/large trees silhouetted against an orange sky, decorated by Margaret Cable, w/ink stamp mark & "M. Cable 1917" **9,350**

OHR (GEORGE) POTTERY

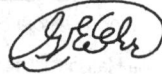

GEO. E. OHR
BILOXI, MISS.

Ohr Pottery Marks

George Ohr, the eccentric potter of Biloxi, Mississippi, worked from about 1883 to 1906. Some think him to be one of the most expert throwers the craft will ever see. The majority of his works were hand-thrown, exceedingly thin-walled items, some of which have a crushed or folded appearance. He considered himself the foremost potter in the world and declined to sell much of his production, instead accumulating a great horde to leave as a legacy to his children. In 1972 this collection was purchased for resale by an antiques dealer.

*From left: George Ohr Ewer
George Ohr Pitcher*

Bowl, 4½" d., 2¼" h., a wide flaring foot supports the squatty rounded body w/a flaring crimped rim, covered in a gunmetal volcanic glaze, die-stamped "G.E. OHR - Biloxi, Miss.". **$990**

Bowl-vase, a short wide cylindrical neck above a squatty bulbous body w/a band of thumbprints around the sides, mottled brown glaze on red, impressed "GEO E OHR Biloxi, Miss.," 2½" h. **1,150**

Ewer, a short flaring pedestal foot supports a ringed spherical base tapering from the round shoulder to a tall cylindrical neck w/wide incurved rim w/small pinched spout, angled handle from below rim to shoulder, covered in a mottled umber & mirrored black glaze, impressed marks "G.E. OHR - Biloxi, Miss." 7¾" h., 4½" d. (ILLUS.) **2,750**

Model of a cabin on slats, pitch-roofed structure w/a diamond lattice roof design & a short round chimney, taupe-

brown clay, signed "GEO. E OHR Biloxi, Miss.," 3" h. (in-the-making imperfections) **518**

Pitcher, 3½" h., 4¾" d., footed bulbous body w/flaring rim, pinched spout & C-scroll handle, covered in gunmetal volcanic glaze, die-stamped "G.E. OHR - Biloxi, Miss." (ILLUS.). **1,430**

Puzzle mug, cylindrical w/large pierced holes around the molded rim above double bands of smaller holes, a pinched & twisted base band, stylized rabbit-form squared handle, mottled brown glaze, impressed "G. E. Ohr Biloxi, Miss.," 3½" h. . . **1,150**

Vase, 2½" h., 3¾" d., wide squatty bulbous base w/flared & ruffled rim, covered in a dark bottle green & gunmetal glaze w/melt fissures, die-stamped "G.E. OHR - Biloxi, Miss." **825**

Vase, 3½" h., 3½" d., wide waisted cylindrical body w/torn & pinched rim, covered in dark olive green & black mottled glaze, die-stamped "G. E. OHR - Biloxi, Miss." (fleck to rim) **2,090**

Vase, 4¼" h., slightly waisted cylindrical body w/upright pinched & scalloped rim & ribbon handles, covered in a rare cobalt blue, green & raspberry mottled glaze, die-stamped "G. E. OHR - Biloxi, Miss." **4,675**

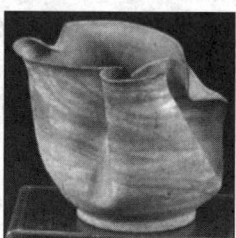

Ohr Free-Form Bisque-Fired Vase

Vase, 4¼" h., 6" w., footed free-form folded & pinched upright sides w/flared & pinched rim, bisque-fired red & ivory marbleized clays, inscribed "XMAS FOR MASAbTLER - FROM EDNA - DEC 18/06," script signature (ILLUS.) **4,675**

Vase, 4¾" h., a crimped rim on a cylindrical body w/thumbprints around the base, mottled black glaze, impressed "G.E. Ohr Biloxi, Miss." **1,380**

Vase, 5" h., bulbous bottom tapering to a tall, wide cylindrical upper body w/long angled handles from the upper neck to the center base, gunmetal to brown glaze, impressed mark **1,980**

Vase, 6" h., bottle-shaped w/flaring rim, covered in an unusual sponged cobalt & green glaze on a pink & white matte glaze, die-stamped "G.E. OHR - Biloxi, Miss." **1,760**

OVERBECK

The four Overbeck sisters, Margaret, Hannah B., Elizabeth G. and Mary F., established their pottery in their old family home in Cambridge City, Indiana in 1911. Different areas of the house and yard were used for the varied production needs.

Their early production consisted mainly of artware before 1937 with most pieces being hand-thrown or hand-built in such forms as vase, bowls, candlesticks, flower frogs, tea sets and tiles. Pieces during this era were decorated generally either with glaze inlay or carving and several colors of subtle matte glazes were used first with brighter glazes added later.

After the death of Elizabeth G. in 1937 Mary F. became the driving force behind the pottery. The output became less varied, until mainly small molded figures of various sorts of humans, some humorous or grotesque, and animals and birds were the main products. Work was carried on alone by Mary F. until her death in 1955.

Marked pieces of Overbeck usually carry the "OBK" cipher and early wares may carry the initial or initials of the sister(s) who produced it.

Overbeck Elephant

Figure group, ceramic tableau, "The Family," depicting a polychrome kitchen scene of stylized figures consisting of two children doing homework by lamp light at the dining table w/other family members sitting nearby, sewing & reading, a wood stove in the background, large rectangular tile floor base in red & blue, signed "Mary Overbeck " & impressed "OBK," base, 6 x 8½", 12 pcs. . . . **$5,225**

Figurine, stylized figure of a postman in brown uniform & cap w/mail bag over one shoulder, marked "OBK," 5½" h. **193**

Figurine, stylized portly bald gentleman standing, wearing blue striped trousers, a white shirt, pink bow tie & holding eyeglasses, marked "OBK," 5¾" h. (nick to foot) **660**

Model of a goose, a stylized large-footed bird, wings up & neck stretched forward, white w/black eyes, brown bill & feet, marked "OBK," 5" l. (roughness to feet) **880**

Model of an elephant, standing, head raised w/trunk curved down, white w/pink highlights & blue eyes, marked "OBK," glaze nick to tip of one tusk, 4 x 7" (ILLUS.). . **1,430**

Vase, 5" h., 6" d., flat-bottomed wide bulbous ovoid body tapering to a flat mouth flanked by heavy angled strap handles, carved & painted design of sixteen hummingbirds in brown & green matte amid delicately carved branches & blossoms, incised mark & initials "EF". **6,050**

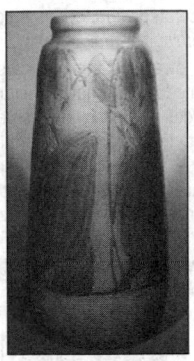

Overbeck Vase with Hostas

Vase, 14" h., slender ovoid body w/short cylindrical neck, decorated w/carved & painted hosta blossoms & large leaves, by Elizabeth G. & Mary F. Overbeck (ILLUS.). **22,000**

PARIS & OLD PARIS

China known by the generic name of Paris and Old Paris was made by several Parisian factories from the 18th through the 19th century; some of it is marked and some is not. Much of it was handsomely decorated.

Old Paris Decorated Desk Set

Desk set: graduated cylindrical pots & covers, 2¾" h., 3¼" h. & 3½" h., on a 7⅜ x 9½" oval tray; each piece w/heavy gilt borders & covers, each decorated w/early 19th c. figures in landscapes, 19th c., the set (ILLUS.) **$2,070**

Fruit compotes, figural, gilt & green
  enamel-decorated openwork bowls
  supported by three cherub figures
  standing on a triangular base, 10⅝" h.,
  the pair **10,925**
Luncheon set: 11⅝" l. cov. oval soup
  tureen & undertray, 8" d. cov. vegetable
  bowl, a sauceboat w/attached undertray,
  cov. sauce tureen w/attached undertray,
  4⅜" h. tazza, 9" h. cov. coffeepot, seven
  8⅜" d. plates, 9½" d. cake plate & 11" l.,
  13¼" l. & 22¼" l. oval platters; each
  enamel-decorated w/butterflies & floral
  sprays, overall gilt trim, late 19th c., the set . . . **978**
Vase, 10½" h., swelled cylindrical lower
  body tapering to a tall ringed cylindrical
  neck, the sides w/large oval reserves,
  one decorated w/the Eiffel Tower, the
  other w/a bust portrait of a Turkish prince,
  the neck decorated w/stylized leafy
  flowering vines, late 19th c. **518**
Vases, 13" h., scrolled handles, pink ground
  decorated w/colored & gilt-trimmed
  florals, late 19th c., pr. **288**

Ornate Paris Porcelain Vase

Vases, 14½" h., footed baluster-form
  w/flaring ringed neck, a dark blue ground
  decorated on the front w/a large oval
  panel of a couple in 18th c. attire in a
  garden, the back w/a floral cartouche, a
  band of gilt florals around the neck & gilt
  bands at top & base, late 19th c., pr.
  (ILLUS. of one) **2,645**
Vases, 17" h., each slender ovoid body
  painted in bold colors w/a continuous
  scene of various birds in a landscape
  w/trees, buildings & mountains beyond,
  all between pale blue everted rims gilt
  w/banded & Greek key borders, faint
  incised factory mark, drilled & fitted as a
  table lamp, second half 19th c., pr. (tiny
  rim chips & wear to gilding) **1,495**
Vases, 17½" h., footed squatty bulbous wide
  lower body w/a wide shoulder tapering to
  a tall slender trumpet neck, each w/a
  colorful continuous landscape painted

around the body & lower neck, one w/a
  view of the Bospherus, the other a view
  of the Grand Canal, each w/a gilt beaded
  ring around the neck below a pink upper
  section w/ornate white scrolling, gilt trim,
  late 19th c., pr. **6,325**

PAUL REVERE POTTERY

Paul Revere Marks

  *This pottery was established in Boston,
  Massachusetts, in 1906, by a group of
  philanthropists seeking to establish better
  conditions for underprivileged young girls of the
  area. Edith Brown served as supervisor of the
  small "Saturday Evening Girls Club" pottery
  operation which was moved, in 1912, to a house
  close to the Old North Church where Paul
  Revere's signal lanterns had been placed. The
  wares were mostly hand decorated in mineral
  colors and both sgraffito and molded decorations
  were employed. Although it became popular, it
  was never a profitable operation and always
  depended on financial contributions to operate.
  After the death of Edith Brown in 1932, the
  pottery foundered and finally closed in 1942.*

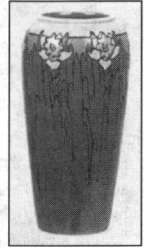

From left: Paul Revere Landscape Bowl
Paul Revere Vase with Daffodils

Bowl, 4½" d., 3⅜" h., swollen form w/glossy
  green glaze & red-tinted rim, signed
  "S.E.G. 3.23 - SJM" **$173**
Bowl, 5½" d., 2½" h., squatty rounded sides
  w/a closed wide rim, the upper half
  decorated w/a continuous landscape
  scene w/brown trees outlined in black on
  a yellow ground & white sky, yellow on
  the lower half (repaired chips) **495**
Bowl, 6" d., center medallion design of a
  stylized landscape scene in cuerda seca,
  w/brown tree outlined in black, against a
  blue sky, surrounded by dark blue band,
  light blue border (ILLUS.) **990**

Charger, round, a narrow rim band
decorated w/green trees against a blue
sky on an ivory ground, ivory center,
signed "S.E.G. - E.T. - 5-17," 1917,
12½" d. (minor inside footring chips) **660**

Creamer, decorated w/incised windmills
in matte shades of green & cream,
marked "SEG" & faint artist's initials,
3¼" h. (hairline) **403**

Plate, 6½" d., the border band w/a
decoration of white hens & chicks
spaced around the rim on a wide
yellow band, white center, artist-signed,
dated "9-13" **715**

Vase, 3⅞" h., cylindrical w/flared rim,
glossy cobalt blue glaze, impressed mark **144**

Vase, 7½" h., wide bulbous ovoid body
tapering sharply to a flat mouth w/closed-
in rim, covered in mottled flowing medium
green microcrystalline glaze, ink mark &
paper label **385**

Vase, 10" h., slightly swelled tapering
cylindrical body w/a wide mouth,
decorated around the shoulder w/incised
& painted daffodils in cream & yellow
w/green stems & leaves, light blue sky
beneath cream band at top, impressed
mark, paper label, artist initialed & dated
"4-24" (ILLUS.) **3,575**

Vase, 10" h., swelled cylindrical body w/wide
flat mouth, medium blue semi-matte
glaze, die-stamped mark & ink-marked
"GM -7.25" **330**

Wall pocket, pocket-form w/slightly flared
rim tapering to base, dark sage green
glaze, marked "S.E.G." & Paul Revere
Pottery paper label, 4" w., 6" l. **288**

PETERS & REED

Peters & Reed Mark

*In 1897 John D. Peters and Adam Reed
formed a partnership to produce flowerpots in
Zanesville, Ohio. Formally incorporated as
Peters and Reed in 1901, this type of production
was the mainstay until after 1907 when they
gradually expanded into the art pottery field.
Frank Ferrell, a former designer at the Weller
Pottery, developed the "Moss Aztec" line while
associated with Peters and Reed and other art
lines followed. Though unmarked, attribution is
not difficult once familiar with the various lines.
In 1921, Peters and Reed became Zane Pottery
which continued in production until 1941.*

Ewer, decorated w/lion's head w/grapevine,
11" h. **$160**

Pitcher, cavalier decoration **125**

Planter, hanging-type, Moss Aztec
line,signed "Ferrell," 9 x 13" **325**

Vase, 6" h., tripod base, glossy brown glaze **160**

Vase, 8" h., Moss Aztec line **95**

Vase, 10" h., Moss Aztec line, tall slender
waisted cylindrical form w/large heavily
embossed triangular Art Nouveau-style
blossoms around the top w/vines & leafy
vines down the sides & around the
bottom, greenish brown overall glaze. **385**

Wall pocket, Egyptian line, matte green glaze. . . **225**

Wall pocket, sprigged-on floral trim, glossy
brown glaze **135**

PEWABIC

Pewabic Pottery Mark

*Mary Chase Perry (Stratton) and Horace J.
Caulkins were partners in this Detroit, Michigan
pottery. Established in 1903, Pewabic Pottery
evolved from their Revelation Pottery, "Pewabic"
meaning "clay with copper color" in the language
of Michigan's Chippewa Indians. Caulkins
attended to the clay formulas and Mary Perry
Stratton was artistic creator of forms & glaze
formulas, eventually developing a wide range of
colors for her finely textured glazes. The pottery's
reputation for fine wares and architectural tiles
enabled it to survive the depression years of the
1930s. After Caulkins died in 1923, Mrs.
Stratton continued to be active in the pottery
until her death, at age ninety-four, in 1961.
Her contributions to the art pottery field
are numerous.*

Bowl, 8½" d., 2½" h., low canted sides
w/incurved rim, the sides covered
w/embossed lily pads, centered at the
shoulder w/ring handles under a flowing
matte green glaze, impressed mark **$3,300**

Vase, miniature, 3¾" h., 2½" d., ovoid base
sharply tapering to wide cylindrical neck,
iridescent cobalt glaze, impressed mark **385**

Vase, 3¾" h., 4" d., baluster-form body
w/wide cylindrical neck covered in a
lustered striated glaze in purple &
green, unmarked **825**

Vase, 5" h., 3¾" d., bottle-shaped, covered
in a lustered celadon & blush glaze,
circular die-stamped mark **495**

Vase, 5" h., 4½" d., footed w/angular ovoid
sides, tapering shoulder w/flaring neck,
covered w/an excellent red metallic luster
glaze w/light green lowlights, unmarked...... **550**

Vase, 6½" h., 4¼" d., footed bulbous ovoid
body w/a rounded shoulder to the wide,
short cylindrical neck w/flaring rim
covered in a mirrored purple, lavender &
green glaze, circular die-stamped mark...... **880**

Vase, 8" h., footed spherical lower body
below a wide trumpet neck, metallic blue,
green & gunmetal overall lustre glaze,
impressed mark........................ **605**

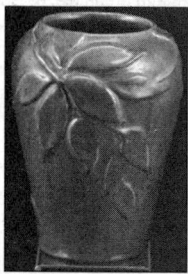 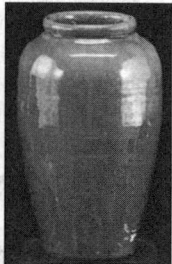

From left: Large Pewabic Vase
Ovoid Pewabic Vase

Vase, 8" h., wide baluster-form body w/a
wide flat rim, embossed w/large flowers &
leaves under a flowing matte green glaze,
impressed mark (ILLUS.) **6,325**

Vase, 8½" h., 4½" d., bulbous ovoid body
w/short molded rim, lustered burgundy &
celadon glaze over a ridged body, circular
die-stamped mark, paper label (ILLUS.) **1,650**

PHOENIX BIRD & FLYING TURKEY PORCELAIN

*The phoenix bird, a symbol of immortality
and spiritual rebirth, has been handed down
through Egyptian mythology as a bird that
consumed itself by fire after 500 years and then
rose again, renewed, from its ashes. This bird
has been used to decorate Japanese porcelain
designed for export for more than 100 years. The
pattern incorporates a blue design of the bird,
variously known as the "Flying Phoenix," the
"Flying Turkey" or the "Ho-o," stamped on a
white ground. It became popular with collectors
because there was an abundant supply since the
ware was produced for a long period of time.
Pieces can be found marked with Japanese
characters, with a "Nippon" mark or a "Made in
Japan" or "Occupied Japan" mark. Though there
are several variations to the pattern and border,
we have lumped them together since values seem
to be quite comparable. A word of caution to
the collectors, Phoenix Bird pattern is still
being produced.*

Phoenix Bird Cup & Saucer

Bowl, 4¾" d. $5
Chocolate pot, cov., scalloped shape 125
Creamer & cov. sugar, 2¾" h., pr. 20
Cup & saucer, demitasse 12
Cup & saucer (ILLUS.)..................... 15
Egg cup, double 8
Plate, 6" d. 4

Phoenix Bird Plate

Plate, 7¼" d. (ILLUS.)...................... 6
Plate, 8½" d. 10
Plate, dinner, 9½" d. 45
Platter, 15" l., oval, dark blue, Nippon mark 110
Salt & pepper shakers, pr. 11
Teapot, cov., individual size 24
Tumbler, 2⅝" h........................... 12

PICKARD

Pickard Mark

*Pickard, Inc., making fine decorated china
today in Antioch, Illinois, was founded in
Chicago in 1894 by Wilder A. Pickard. The
company now makes its own blanks but once
only decorated those bought from other potteries,
primarily from the Havilands and others in
Limoges, France.*

Bowl, 10" d., h.p. blackberries, raspberries,
grapes & blossoms, artist-signed **$495**
Cake plate w/open handles, Classic Ruins
by Moonlight patt., 10½" d. 275
Candlesticks, overall engraved gold florals,
9" h., pr. 250

Chocolate cup & saucer, Haviland blank, "Raised Gold Daisy," artist-signed, ca. 1905 . . . 60

Coffeepot, cov., tankard-type, tall tapering cylindrical body w/a long gold swan's-neck spout & gold long C-scroll handle, small domed cover w/gold knob finial, the cream body decorated around the top w/two wide gold bands overlapped by long looping green tendrils & small purple blossoms, pearlized finish, signed under spout, ca. 1903-05, 8¾" h. 330

Dish, leaf-shaped, overall gold w/etched gold design, 3½ x 5½" 125

Lemonade set: pitcher & eight tumblers; the wide waisted cylindrical tankard pitcher w/a rim spout & C-scroll handle, plain cylindrical tumblers, all decorated overall w/the gold Encrusted Honeysuckle patt., unsigned, the set 1,650

Two Pickard Lemonade Pitchers

Pitcher, lemonade, 6¼" h., bulbous ovoid body tapering to a flat rim, gilt interior band & gold angled handled, h.p. Classic Ruins by Moonlight patt., artist-signed, 1912-18 mark (ILLUS. left) 550

Pitcher, lemonade, 6¼" h., bulbous ovoid body tapering to a flat ring, gold angled handle, large pink carnations on golden stems around the sides on a white ground w/gold bands at the rim & bottom, artist-signed, 1905-10 mark (ILLUS. right) 450

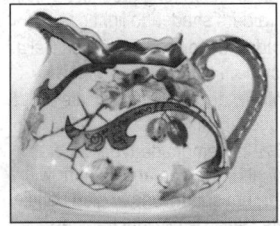

Fine Early Pickard Lemonade Pitcher

Pitcher, lemonade, 6½" h., squatty bulbous ovoid body tapering to a scalloped rim w/wide arched spout, C-form gold handle, wide gold scrolls & red gooseberries w/green leaves on a white ground, Gooseberries Conventional patt., artist-signed, 1903-05 mark (ILLUS.) 700

Vase, 7½" h., floral-decorated in the Art Nouveau style w/enamels & gilt trim, printed mark, ca. 1900 288

PISGAH FOREST POTTERY

Pisgah Forest Marks

Walter Stephen experimented with making pottery shortly after 1900 with his parents in Tennessee. After their deaths in 1910, he eventually moved to the foot of Mt. Pisgah in North Carolina where he became a partner of C.P. Ryman. Together they built a kiln and a shop but this partnership was dissolved in 1916. During 1920 Stephen again began to experiment with pottery and by 1926 had his own pottery and equipment. Pieces are usually marked and may also be signed "W. Stephen" and dated. Walter Stephen died in 1961 but work at the pottery still continues, although on a part-time basis.

From left: Pisgah Forest Bowl-Vase Pisgah Forest Cameo Mug

Bowl-vase, wide squatty bulbous body w/a wide shoulder tapering to a wide rolled rim, covered in white & umber glaze w/white & blue crystals, embossed mark & dated 1941, 6" d., 4½" h. (ILLUS.) $440

Mug, Cameo ware, white relief landscape scene of trees & a cabin in the mountains against a teal blue ground, ca. 1949, embossed "Stephen," 3½ x 4" (ILLUS.) 303

Pisgah Forest Vase

Vase, 5½" h., 5½" d., wide bulbous body w/short cylindrical neck, celadon & pink glaze w/large blooming crystals, embossed mark, 1949 (ILLUS.) 990

Pisgah Forest Vase

Vase, 6" h., 4½" d., trumpet-shaped body,
   covered w/French blue & bone crystalline
   glaze, firing line, raised potter's mark &
   dated 1944 (ILLUS.) **330**
Vase, 6¼" h., trumpet form body, grey &
   beige glaze w/densely-packed crystals,
   pink interior, embossed mark (some
   bubbles to glaze) **385**
Vase, 8" h., wide baluster-form body
   tapering to a wide cylindrical neck
   w/flaring rim, celadon & caramel
   crystalline glaze, mark partially obscured. **825**
Vase, 8¾" h., 5½" d., baluster-form w/short
   cylindrical neck & flaring rim, cream
   & celadon flambé glaze w/blue &
   white crystals near base, pink interior,
   shaved mark. **715**
Vase, 9" h., baluster-form w/short cylindrical
   neck & flaring rim, white, celadon & blue
   crystalline glaze, pink interior, embossed
   mark & dated 1949 . . . . **1,100**

R.S. PRUSSIA & RELATED WARES

R.S. Prussia & Related Marks

*Ornately decorated china marked "R.S.
Prussia" and "R.S. Germany" continues to grow
in popularity. According to the Third Series of
Mary Frank Gaston's Encyclopedia of R.S.
Prussia (Collector Books, Paducah, Kentucky),
these marks were used by the Reinhold
Schlegelmilch porcelain factories located in Suhl
in the Germanic regions known as "Prussia"
prior to World War I, and in Tillowitz, Silesia,
which became part of Poland after World War II.
Other marks sought by collectors include "R.S.
Suhl," "R.S." steeple or church marks, and "R.S.
Poland."*

*The Suhl factory was founded by Reinhold
Schlegelmilch in 1869 and closed in 1917. The
Tillowitz factory was established in 1895 by
Erhard Schlegelmilch, Reinhold's son. This
china customarily bears the phrase "R.S.
Germany" and "R.S. Tillowitz." The Tillowitz
factory closed in 1945, but it was re-opened for a
few years under Polish administration. The
"R.S. Poland" mark is attributed to that later
time period.*

*Prices are high and collectors should beware
of the forgeries that sometimes find their way
onto the market. Mold names and numbers are
taken from Mary Frank Gaston's books on R.S.
Prussia. We illustrate typical markings. The
"R.S. Prussia" and "R.S. Suhl" marks have been
reproduced so buy with care. Collectors are also
interested in the porcelain products made by the
Erdmann Schlegelmilch factory. This factory
was founded by three brothers in Suhl in 1861.
They named the factory in honor of their father,
Erdmann Schlegelmilch. A variety of marks
incorporating the "E.S." initials were used. The
factory closed circa 1935. The Erdmann
Schlegelmilch factory was an earlier and entirely
separate business from the Reinhold
Schlegelmilch factory. The two were not related
to each other.*

R.S. GERMANY

Bowl, 8½" d., decorated w/poppies **$44**
Cake plate, open-handled, leaf-molded
   border, pink roses & green leaves in the
   center, lustre finish, unmarked, 11" d. **58**
Cheese dish, white floral decoration on
   green ground **120**
Chocolate pot, cov., simple cylindrical body
   w/a long plain handle, white shading to
   pale pink roses on long green leafy stems
   against a dark shaded to light ground, 9" h. . . . **160**
Hatpin holder, decorated w/a green Calla
   Lily design **120**
Hatpin holder, decorated w/delicate pink &
   white roses, 5" h. **125**
Pitcher, 6½" h., lemonade-type, wide
   hexagonal body w/an angled narrow
   shoulder, rim spout, long angled handle,
   decorated w/large colorful transfer-
   printed poppy-like flowers & leaves
   on a shaded ground **81**
Plate, 6" d., decorated w/scene of cottage **95**
Plate, 6" d., decorated w/scene of mill **95**
Plate, 8" d., embossed cabbage leaf
   decoration, shaded green. **12**
Plate, 8¾" d., acorn & leaf decoration **39**
Salt & pepper shakers, Cotton Plant
   decoration, pr. **55**
Shaving mug, w/soap holder, scalloped
   base, poppy decoration **95**

R.S. PRUSSIA

Bowl, 10" d., Iris mold (Mold 25), poppies decoration **275**

Bowl, 10" d., Mold 55, peaches & clusters of yellow & purple grapes on shaded pink ground **300**

Bowl, 10¼" d., Hidden Image mold (Mold 4), decorated w/purple & white pansies, yellow flowers & leaves on pink ground, unmarked **413**

Bowl, 10½" d., Carnation mold (Mold 28), pink roses on a lavender & peach ground w/satin finish **595**

Bowl, 10½" d., Mold 329, decorated w/colorful flowers around the inner rim & extending into the bottom, blue lustre finish **92**

Bowl, 11" d., Mold 34, "Honeycomb," decorated w/basket of pink roses on a green background **248**

Cake plate, Iris mold (Mold 25), open handles, shades of lavender w/overall poppies, satin finish, 10" d. **500**

Cake plate, open handles, Mold 341, satin ground decorated w/white flowers & green leaves, 10" d. **110**

Celery tray, Carnation mold, decorated w/pink & yellow flowers on lavender satin finish, large **350**

Celery tray, decorated w/pink roses on white satin finish ground **255**

Coffeepot, cov., Stippled Floral mold (Mold 23), multicolored florals in pastel shades w/raised gilt trim, satin finish **823**

Cracker jar, cov., Mold 529A, decorated w/roses **275**

Cracker jar, cov., Mold 643, decorated w/roses & snowballs, green trim (small chip, upper rim & finial) **275**

Creamer, Carnation mold, Tiffany carnations & pink roses decoration, white satin finish **125**

Creamer, Grape mold, fruit decoration, 4" h. **55**

Dessert set: open-handled cake plate & 6 individual plates; Carnation mold, decorated w/pink & white roses, satin finish, 7 pcs. **995**

Pin dish, cov., Medallion mold, Man in the Mountain decoration on cover, swans on base, 5" w., 3¾" h. **1,018**

Plate, 8" d., Mold 207, decorated w/large pink roses on a shaded ground **80**

Plate, 8¾" d., Mold 152, portrait of "Spring" **880**

Sweetmeat stand, two Shell (Mold 20) fluted bowls decorated w/colorful floral clusters resting on a matching silver plate stand w/upright central scrolled loop handle & two scalloped trays resting on knob feet, unmarked, 12" l. **805**

Teapot, cov., Mold 601, floral decoration, small, unmarked **200**

OTHER MARKS

Bowl, 9¾" d., center portrait of young woman w/fancy jewelled accessories & holding a flower (Prove Saxe) **303**

Bowl, 10½" d., decorated w/sprays of apple blossoms flanked by a narrow gold border w/another narrow gold border on rim (Prov. Saxe, E.S. Germany) **28**

Cake plate, open handled, decorated w/pink flowers, 10" d. (E.S. Germany) **85**

Sauceboat, ivory w/dark red roses w/a pearlized finish (R.S. Poland) **150**

Vase, bud, 7½" h., figural decoration based on scene from Rembrandt's "Night Watch" (R.S. Suhl) **350**

RED WING

Red Wing Marks

Various potteries operated in Red Wing, Minnesota from 1868, the most successful being the Red Wing Stoneware Co., organized in 1878. Merged with other local potteries through the years, it became known as Red Wing Union Stoneware Co. in 1894, and was one of the largest producers of utilitarian stoneware items in the United States. After a decline in the popularity of stoneware products, an art pottery line was introduced to compensate for the loss and this was reflected in a new name for the company, Red Wing Potteries, Inc., in 1930. Stoneware production ceased entirely in 1947, but vases, planters, cookie jars and dinnerwares of art pottery quality continued in production until 1967 when the pottery ceased operation altogether.

CONVENTION COMMEMORATIVES

Red Wing Commemorative Acid Pitcher

Acid pitcher, 1986 Red Wing Collectors
  Society Commemorative, maker
  produced 1,982 (ILLUS.) **$225**
Bowl, 1980 Red Wing Collectors Society
  Commemorative, maker produced 400 . . . . . . **995**
Crock, 1977 Red Wing Collectors Society
  Commemorative, maker produced 250 . . . . . **2,595**
Jug, 1978 Red Wing Collectors Society
  Commemorative, maker produced 350 . . . . . **2,195**
Jug, miniature, 1981 Red Wing Collectors
  Society Commemorative, maker
  produced 750 . . . . **445**
Mug, 1982 Red Wing Collectors Society
  Commemorative, maker produced 697 . . . . . . **695**
Planter, giraffe, 1995 Red Wing Collectors
  Society Commemorative, maker
  produced 8,186 . . . . **85**

DINNERWARES & NOVELTIES

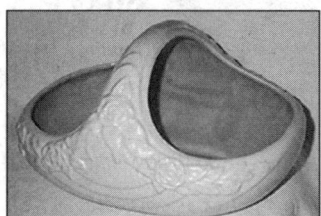

Red Wing Basket

Ashtray, wing-shaped, marked "Red Wing
  Potteries 75th Anniversary, 1878-1953," 7⅜". . . **95**
Basket, white & green, marked "Red Wing
  USA #1275," 9¾" l. (ILLUS.) **80**
Beverage server, cov., Tampico patt. **85**
Bowl, cereal, Provincial patt. **8**
Casserole, cov., French-style w/handle,
  Town & Country patt., rust glaze, ca. 1946 . . . **165**
Console bowl, Magnolia patt., 12" l. **115**
Cookie jar, cov., Bob White patt. **95**
Cookie jar, cov., French Chef, blue on blue,
  Red Wing Pottery stamp (ILLUS.) **135**
Creamer, Provincial patt. **12**

*From left: French Chef Cookie Jar
Red Wing Figurine*

Figurine, brown beaver w/football, signed
  "Red Wing Potteries, Red Wing, Minn.,"
  dated 1939, very rare, 2⅝" h. (ILLUS.) **175**

Figurine, green & yellow sitting deer,
  marked "Red Wing USA #1338," 6" h. **110**
Marmite, Village Green patt.. . . . . **9**
Planter, model of a Dachshund dog, blue
  glaze, No. 1342 . . . . **95**
Planter, green stove, marked "Red Wing
  #765," 7¾" h. **75**

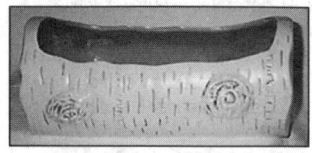

Log Shaped Planter

Planter, log-shaped, white birch pottery,
  unmarked, 11" l. (ILLUS.) **85**
Plate, 10" d., dinner, Provincial patt. **10**
Salt & pepper shakers, Village Green patt., pr. . . **14**

Red Wing Trivet

Trivet, Minnesota Centennial 1858-1958,
  back signed "Red Wing Potteries," 6½" d.
  (ILLUS.) **95**
Vase, brushed ware w/cattails, stamped
  "Red Wing Union Stoneware," rare, 7⅜" h. . . . **105**

STONEWARE & UTILITY WARES

Bean pot, cov., white & brown glaze,
  w/advertising "Christmas Greetings from
  Christel's Cash Store, Brillion, Wisc." **105**
Bean pot, cov., white & brown glaze,
  w/advertising "Peterson Department
  Store, Clintonville, Wisc." **95**
Beater jar, spongeband, w/advertising "It
  Pays to Mix with Allen, Herman, Minn." **850**

Beater Jar with Advertising

Beater jar, white glaze w/blue band, w/advertising "Klatt & Stueber, Clyman, Wisc." (ILLUS.) **150**

Bowl, 5" d., paneled spongeware, ... **280**

Bowl, 6" d., paneled spongeware, w/advertising "Muscoda, Spring Green, Boscobel, Wisc.". **325**

Bowl, 8" d., paneled sides, sponged blue & red decoration **100**

Bowl, 12" d., white & blue glaze, Greek Key patt. **240**

Butter Crock, white glazed stoneware, bottom signed "Minnesota Stoneware Co.," 10 lbs. **75**

Christmas tree holder, green glaze **425**

Churn, white glazed stoneware, large wing, upside down oval stamp, 2 gal. **475**

Stoneware Churn

Churn, white glazed stoneware, large wing, oval stamp below wing, 5 gal. (ILLUS.) **350**

Churn, white glazed stoneware, large wing, oval stamp below wing, 8 gal. **1,550**

Crock, white glazed stoneware, bottom signed "Minnesota Stoneware, Red Wing, Minn.," 8¾" d., 1 gal. **45**

4 Gallon Stoneware Crock

Crock, white glazed stoneware, two birch leaves, w/Union oval stamp mark, 11" d., 4 gal. (ILLUS.) **115**

Crock, white glazed stoneware, two "elephant ears," Union Oval Stamp, earred handles, 12" d., 6 gal. **130**

Crock, white glazed stoneware, 6" wing, Red Wing oval stamp, bail handles, 15¼" d., 10 gal. **135**

Fruit jar, screw-on metal lid, "Stone Mason Fruit Jar," black mark, 1 qt., ... **225**

Fruit jar, cov., Stone Mason, black label, patent date Jan. 24, 1899, "Union Stoneware" stamp, 1 qt. **275**

Fruit jar, cov., Stone Mason, black label, patent date Jan. 24, 1899, "Union Stoneware" stamp, 1 gal. **750**

Pure Leaf Lard Jar

Jar, cov., Hazel Pure Food Co., white glazed stoneware, stamped "Pure Leaf Lard," wire handle, complete with lid, 5 lbs. (ILLUS.) **245**

Jug, beehive-shaped, Albany slip, North Star stoneware, star on base, rare, 1 qt. **285**

Jug, beehive-shaped, salt glazed stoneware, signed "Minnesota Stoneware Company," 2 gal. **1,175**

Jug, shouldered, white glazed stoneware, 4" wing, Red Wing oval stamp, 3 gal. **165**

Jug, shouldered, white glazed stoneware, 4" wing, Red Wing oval stamp, 4 gal. **155**

"Koverwate," (crock cover-weight designed to keep the contents submerged under preserving liquid; bottom & side holes allowed brine to come to the top), white glazed stoneware, stamped "Koverwate, Red Wing, Minn.," 6 gal. size **245**

"Koverwate," white glazed stoneware, stamped "Koverwate, Red Wing, Minn.," 25 gal. size **350**

Stoneware Pie Plate

Plate, pie, white glazed stoneware, signed
"Minnesota Stoneware Co., Red Wing,
Minn.," rare, 9¾" d. (ILLUS.) **145**

Poultry feeder jar, cov., white glazed
stoneware poultry drinking font &
buttermilk feeder, bell-shaped, marked
"Red Wing," complete with base, 1 gal. **145**

Water cooler, cov., white glazed stoneware,
bailed handles, small wing, 3 gal. **450**

Water cooler, cov., white glazed stoneware,
bailed handles, small wing, 8 gal. **475**

REDWARE

*Red earthenware pottery was made in the
American colonies from the late 1600s. Bowls,
crocks and all types of utilitarian wares were
turned out in great abundance to supplement the
pewter and handmade treenware. The ready
availability of the clay, the same used in making
bricks and roof tiles, accounted for the vast
production. The lead-glazed redware retained its
reddish color though a variety of colors could be
obtained by adding various metals to the glaze.
Interesting effects occurred accidentally through
unsuspected impurities in the clay or uneven
temperatures in the firing kiln which sometimes
resulted in streaks or mottled splotches.*

*Redware pottery was seldom marked by the
maker.*

Bowl, 6¾" d., 3" h., wide shallow sides
w/molded edge, a band of white slip
squiggle design below rim, mottled
greenish glaze w/brown flecks &
amber spots **$275**

Slip-Decorated Redware Bread Tray

Bread tray, glazed oblong dish w/notched
rim, decorated w/abstract patterns in
yellow slip on red ground, 19th c., 11½ x
18½" (ILLUS.) **2,070**

Bust, sculpted unglazed gentleman
wearing shirt, bow tie & jacket, on
shaped pedestal, 19th c., 5" h. (some
chips & losses) **287**

Butter churn, wooden lid & plunger, 19th c.,
28" d., 26" h. (ILLUS.) . . . . **300 to 350**

Jar, ovoid w/shoulder handles, clear reddish
brown w/black splotches, chips, 9½" h. **220**

Redware Butter Churn

Jug, globular w/strap handle, brown
w/orange spots, 18th c., America, 27" d.,
11" h. (ILLUS.) . . . . **50 to 75**

Redware Jug

Model of poodle, the seated animal in the
form of a Staffordshire Spaniel covered in
a brown glaze, inscribed on reverse
"H. McD.," 19th c., 7¾" l., 7¼" h. (minor
losses, kiln imperfections) **173**

Pitcher, cov., 9" h., wide ovoid body
w/ribbed strap handle, clear glaze
w/brown sponging on a red ground (lid is
good fit but color varies) **523**

Pitcher, 10¾" h., wide ovoid body tapering
to a flared rim w/pinched spout, ribbed
strap handle, old wooden lid, clear
mottled green glaze w/running daubs of
yellow slip highlighted w/brown & green,
brown glazed interior (minor chips) **9,900**

Pot, cov., squatty bulbous body w/flared rim,
strap handle & pouring spout, dark brown
sponged glaze, 5" h. (small chips &
mismatched lid) **110**

ROCKINGHAM WARES

*The Marquis of Rockingham first established
an earthenware pottery in the Yorkshire district
of England around 1745 and it was occupied
afterwards by various potters. The well-known*

mottled brown Rockingham glaze was introduced about 1788 by the Brameld Brothers and became immediately popular. It was during the 1820s that the production of true porcelain began at the factory and continued to be made until the firm closed in 1842. Since that time the so-called Rockingham glaze has been used by various potters in England and the United States, including some famous wares produced in Bennington, Vermont. However, very similar glazes were also used by potteries in other areas of the United States including Ohio and Indiana and only wares specifically attributed to Bennington should use that name. The following listings will include mainly wares featuring the dark brown mottled glaze produced at various sites here and abroad.

Loving cup, large cylindrical form on a molded base w/large C-form branch handle on each side, one side relief-molded w/a drinking scene, the other side w/a dog fight, molded vintage rim band, overall dark brown mottled glaze, 6⅞" h. (bottom rim chips) **$248**

Model of a bull, overall mottled brown glaze, 19th c., 16" l., 12⅝" h. (minor losses, restoration) **7,475**

Model of a dog, seated on thick irregular-shaped base, freestanding front legs, mottled dark brown glaze, 10¾" h. (painted in edge chips on base) **330**

Mugs, mottled brown & cream, ca. 1890, 3½" d., 4¼" h., set of 6 .... **200**

Pitcher, 9½" h., footed bulbous body w/arched spout & C-form handle, mottled brown glaze w/detailed relief-molded vintage & foliage pinwheels (small chips on spout) **413**

Pitcher, 9⅝" h., bulbous ovoid body tapering to slightly flaring rim, pinched spout, relief-molded hanging game, mottled brown glaze, figural hound handle..................... **275**

Snuff jar, figural, Mr. Toby, mottled dark brown glaze, 19th c., 4⅛" h. (minor glaze wear on rim)................ **374**

Rockingham Teapot

Teapot, cov., footed ovoid body w/swan's-neck spout & C-form handle, domed cover w/bud-form finial, mottled brown glaze w/relief-molded scene of Rebecca at the well, early 20th c., Ohio, 8½" h. (ILLUS.) **200**

ROOKWOOD

Rookwood Mark

Considered America's foremost art pottery, the Rookwood Pottery Company was established in Cincinnati, Ohio in 1880, by Mrs. Maria Nichols Longworth Storer. To accurately record its development, each piece carried the Rookwood insignia, or mark, was dated, and, if individually decorated, was usually signed by the artist. The pottery remained in Cincinnati until 1959 when it was sold to Herschede Hall Clock Company and moved to Starkville, Mississippi, where it continued in operation until 1967. A private company is now producing a limited variety of pieces using original Rookwood molds.

Basket, footed, oval w/rounded sides, crimped & ruffled rim w/deep indentation front & back w/curved loop handles, decorated w/brown, orange & yellow mums & green leaves, stems & yellow bud, green to yellow to orange ground, Standard glaze, No. 45, 1892, Sallie Toohey, 8" l., 4" h. (repaired top) **$209**

Book ends, figural, model of a collie, standing w/face looking front, cream Matte glaze, No. 2778, 1933, 6" h., pr.` **715**

Book ends, figural seated lady in long dress w/ruffled skirt & off-the-shoulder top, holding a fan in one hand, purple, brown & yellow Matte glaze, No. 6252, 1926, 7" h., pr. (minor flakes) **440**

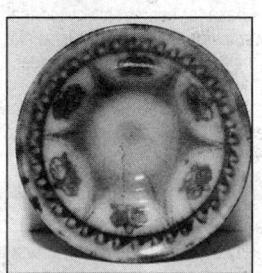
Rookwood Bowl

Bowl, 6½" d., porcelain, flared sides w/center decoration of six-pointed star design w/pink, white & red roses painted between star points, blue scroll design border w/gold trim, No. 2239, 1920, W.E. Hentschel (ILLUS.) **495**

Bowl, 8" d., 3" h., porcelain, flared sides w/flat rim, decorated w/multicolored bouquets at rim, center decorated w/large brown tree covered w/multicolored flowers, No. 2725, 1925, Lorinda Epply **358**

Bowl w/flower frog, 13" d., sharply canted sides w/rolled rim, interior decorated w/multicolored flowers in red, blue, green & orange w/a figural light yellow kingfisher w/blue, orange & brown highlights perched on flower holder, black & brown exterior, both pieces artist-signed, No. 2268B, 1927, Lorinda Epply **990**

Box, cov., octagonal, decorated w/primitive yellow flowers on a red, blue & pink ground, Wax Matte glaze, No. 2796V, 1925, Elizabeth Barrett, 5½" w., 2¾" h. **1,540**

Candlesticks, flat four-footed base w/slender ovoid form decorated w/molded leaves, supporting open flower form surrounding a round candle socket, pink Matte glaze, No. 1248, 1921, 7" h., pr. **275**

Unusual Rookwood Chalice

Chalice, cone-shaped body supported by three large loop handles from rim extending into feet w/relief-molded gargoyle heads, body decorated w/orange & yellow flowers & green foliage under a tiger eye glaze, early Standard glaze, No. 350, 1888, artist's signature illegible, 8" h. (ILLUS.) **605**

Coffeepot,cov., Turkish style, footed bulbous base tapering to tall cylindrical neck w/small domed lid w/pointed finial, ornate molded design on long slender swan's-neck spout & applied C-form handle, Limoges-style decoration w/flock of seventeen fluffy white ducks outlined in black w/body of water surrounded by grasses & reeds, raised anchor mark, impressed "MLN" near handle, 1882, M.L. Nichols, 11½" h. **2,200**

Ewer, squatty bulbous base tapering to a tall slender cylindrical flaring neck w/a rolled tricorner rim, applied S-scroll handle from

Rookwood Standard Glaze Ewer

rim to top of body, the body decorated w/large yellow & orange mums w/green leaves & stems, Standard glaze, No. 495, 1893, A.B. Sprague, 8½" h. (ILLUS.) **715**

Flower frog, figural, two kneeling nudes embracing, yellow Matte glaze, impressed mark & shape number illegible, 1920, Chester Beech, 6" h. **413**

Inkwell, cov., compressed spherical form w/round shoulder tapering to narrow rolled neck, small button finial, incised & painted w/three peacock feathers in blue against a light green matte ground, No. 1073A, 1905, 6" w. (repaired liner & finial) **468**

Jar, cov., squatty bulbous body w/round collared lid, decorated w/yellow & brown flowers on brown & green stems & leaves, Standard glaze, No. 622C, 1892, C.J. Dibowski, 4" d. **660**

Jug, wide waisted cylindrical body, the wide shoulder centered by a short cylindrical neck w/loop handle from rim to shoulder, decorated w/ an orange & brown ear of corn w/green husks, Standard glaze, No. 674, 1899, Sally Coyne, 7" h. (slip crawling & heavy craze line). **220**

Letter rack, consisting of two rectangular stepped holders, green Matte glaze, No. 6271, 1931, 4¼" w., 3½" h. **220**

Model of a deer, standing & facing front, white Matte glaze, No. 6170, 1934, artist-signed "Abel," 6" h. **209**

Native American Portrait Mug

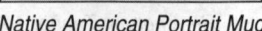

Mug, ovoid body w/wide flat rim, C-form handle, decorated w/bust portrait of Native American brave w/one feather in head band & elaborate bead work on chest, blue & yellow, Standard glaze, incised "Big Mane," No. 837, 1898, Sadie Markland, 5" h. (ILLUS.) **1,870**

Paperweight, figural, model of an elephant, green & brown Matte glaze, No. 2797, 1928, 4" l. **275**

Pitcher, 7" h., tapering cylindrical body w/pinched spout & D-form handle, decorated w/painted horse chestnuts in orange & green w/leaves, stems & berries, the shell on nuts opening to reveal lightly incised interior covered in a gold tiger eye, Standard glaze, No. 251, 1888, Artus Van Briggle **880**

Elaborate Silver Overlay Pitcher

Pitcher, 8" h., wide expanding cylindrical body decorated w/scene of two men in period clothing smoking pipes & drinking, trimmed overall w/elaborate silver overlay of various flowers & leaves, scroll & lattice work w/a silver-overlaid rim, large angled handle & base, Standard glaze, No. 259B, 1891, silver marked by Gorham Co., No. S1346, Harriet Wilcox (ILLUS.). **5,225**

Plaque, rectangular, a nocturnal scene w/white moon over blue lake surrounded by evergreens, 1914, painted signature, K. Van Horne, incised inscription on edge "Saranac Lake, Adirondac Mts., N.Y.," in wide oak frame, 9¼" w., 5¼" h. **2,640**

Unusual Rookwood Scent Jar

Scent jar, cov., bulbous body w/molded rim, slightly domed inset lid w/button finial, decorated w/wild roses in yellow & peach w/incised centers, green & brown stems

& leaves w/similar decoration on lid, which is reversible to allow fragrance to be released, shaded tan & yellow ground, Standard glaze, No. 282D, 1889, Anna M. Valentien, 5" h. (ILLUS.) **880**

Stein w/hinged pewter cover, tapering cylindrical body ringed at the base, C-form handle w/figural eagle thumb lift which holds ceramic insert in lid, decorated w/a portrait of a gentleman in 17th c. pilgrim attire, Standard glaze, No. 775, 1896, Matt Daly, 9½" h. (restoration to ceramic insert) **1,760**

Tea set: 8" h. cov. teapot, creamer & cov. sugar bowl; porcelain, all w/bulbous paneled bodies, decorated w/blue flowers & stylized leaves on each panel, white ground, lids outlined in blue, the creamer w/angled handle & pinched spout, the teapot w/original rattan-wrapped swing bail handle, No. S1844, 1910, Sara Sax, the set **1,100**

Rookwood Standard Glaze Teapot

Teapot, cov., cylindrical w/domed lid & knob finial, swan's-neck spout & C-scroll handle, decorated w/yellow & orange carnations w/green stems & buds on paneled body, Standard glaze, No. 552, 1894, L.N. Lincoln, 7½" h. (ILLUS.) **770**

Tile, square, cloisonné-style landscape decoration w/large blue, brown & green trees in the foreground w/two-tone green grass, a mottled blue lake in the center ground & purplish brown mountains & pale blue sky in the background, early 20th c., in a wide flat Arts & Crafts oak frame, 12" w. **2,530**

Tile, molded stylized design of bird in glossy gunmetal and brown Matte glaze w/pink tulips & green leaves, all on tan ground, No. 442, framed, 6" sq. **308**

Tile, faience, relief-molded center design of two satyrs carrying a bar on their shoulders which holds a basket of grapes, a tree in the background, tan glaze on dark blue ground, the surrounding hexagonal border decorated w/relief-molded intricate multicolor design of vines, leaves, fruits & flowers, Nos. 417, 3246Y, G414, 27" w. (minor chips) **1,650**

Trivet, square, decorated w/a parrot among flowers & branches, ivory, yellow & shades of pink, No. 3077, 1930, 6" sq. **330**

Urn, cov., hand-thrown ovoid body w/domed lid w/flared rim & knob finial, lightly mottled glossy aqua glaze, No. 2300, 1920, 11½" h. **825**

Vase, 2½" h, 4½" d., very wide spherical body w/closed rim, decorated near rim w/red & pink maple leaves on a painted green Matte ground, No. 3163, 1904, Olga G. Reed **1,100**

Vase, 4" h., bulbous ovoid body tapering to a wide flat molded mouth, decorated w/purple flowers on green stems w/green & brown leaves, ivory ground, Glossy glaze, No. 6432, 1945, artist-signed. **358**

Vase, 5½" h., 3¼" d., bulbous ovoid body tapering to a wide cylindrical neck, decorated w/white bachelor's buttons on a shaded grey & pink ground, Iris glaze, No. 906F, 1908, Irene Bishop **660**

Vase, 7" h., slightly tapering cylindrical body decorated w/holly in green & rose on a pink, green & blue ground, Vellum glaze, No. 2041E, 1913, Margaret McDonald (insignificant bruise to top) **440**

Vase, 7½" h., ovoid body w/flared rim, decorated w/painted yellow roses & green leaves, trimmed w/silver overlay stems w/Art Nouveau strap & floral work, w/a silver over-laid rim & base, Standard glaze, No. 568C, 1902, Laura E. Lindeman . . **4,400**

Vase, 8¼" h., ovoid body tapering to a short flaring neck, decorated w/lilies-of-the-valley w/green leaves on a shaded pink ground, Iris glaze, No. 614E, 1909, Carl Schmidt **3,080**

From left: Rookwood Animal Portrait Vase
Standard Glaze Vase with Daylilies

Vase, 9" h., footed urn-form body w/narrow shoulder tapering to cylindrical neck w/wide flaring rim, decorated w/animal portrait of a growling leopard, Standard glaze, No. 410, 1893, overall crazing, Bruce Horsfall (ILLUS.) **4,888**

Vase, 10" h., footed trumpet form w/flaring rim & handles at the base, decorated w/stylized floral & leaf squeezebag design in brown against a green ground w/brown streaks & blue highlights, No. 6115, 1929, Elizabeth Barrett **715**

Vase, 24½" h., tall tapering cylindrical form, streak effect decoration of finely detailed daylilies & leaves, Standard glaze, No. 865, 1889, crazing, glaze bursts, firing cracks to base & body, Albert R. Valentien (ILLUS.). **1,725**

Wall sconce, rectangular, deeply embossed w/pair of owls perched on branches, under a green & brown Matte glaze, square candle holder centered below, No. 1688, 1910, 6 x 11¼". **990**

Wall pocket, conical, molded vertical leaves in pink & green Matte glaze, No. 2008, 1927, 7½" l. **297**

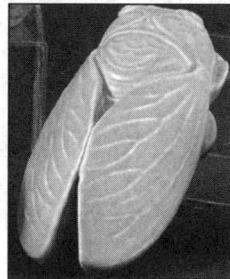

Rookwood Cicada Wall Pocket

Wall pocket, model of a cicada, green Matte glaze, No. 1636, 1908, short glazed-over firing line, 4½ x 9" (ILLUS.) **3,080**

ROSE MEDALLION & ROSE CANTON

The lovely Chinese ware known as Rose Medallion was made through the past century and into the present one. It features alternating panels of people and flowers or insects with most pieces having four medallions with a central rose or peony medallion. The ware is called Rose Canton if florals and birds or insects fill all the panels. Unless otherwise noted, our listing is for Rose Medallion ware.

Basket & undertray, oval reticulated sides on a matching solid undertray, 19th c., basket 9⅜" l., undertray 9⅞" l., 2 pcs. (very minor chips, minor gilt & enamel wear) . . **$920**

Rose Medallion Bough Pot

Bough pots, square waisted upright form w/slightly domed top pieces w/holes, figural panels, foliate gilded side handles, minor glaze wear, 19th c., 9" h., pr. (ILLUS. of one) **4,313**

Bowl, 10½" d., cut-corner bowl, 19th c. (glaze wear) **1,093**

Brush box, cov., rectangular, interior divided into two compartments, 19th c., 2½ x 3½ x 7" (glaze wear) **316**

Chamber pot, usual paneled decoration, 19th c., 9⅝" d. (minute rim chips) **633**

Compotes, 7⅝" d., 3⅝" h., open, wide shallow reticulated bowls raised on funnel bases, 19th c., pr. **633**

Fruit tazza, Rose Mandarin variant, diamond-shaped, 19th c., 12¼" d. (minor glaze wear) . . . **748**

Garden seats, Rose Mandarin variant, 19th c., 19" h., pr. (minor glaze wear) **4,600**

Pitcher, 7¾" h. to top of handle, Rose Mandarin variant, paneled form w/scal-loped rim, 19th c. (minor glaze chips, wear) . . **1,380**

Plate set: six 8½" to 9¾" d. dinner plates & four 9⅛" d. soup plates; 19th c., set of 10 (minor chips, two w/hairlines, minor gilt & enamel wear) **374**

Platter, 14¾" oval, Rose Mandarin variant, 19th c. (gilt & enamel wear, minute rim chips, knife marks) **633**

Punch bowl, enameled w/figural & floral, bird & insect reserves on the interior & exterior, late 19th c., 15¾" d. (very minor losses) **1,890**

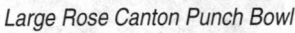

Large Rose Canton Punch Bowl

Punch bowl, Rose Canton variant, large floral panels around the exterior & interior, very minor gilt & enamel wear, 19th c., 21" d. (ILLUS.) **3,450**

Sauce tureens, cov., gilt finials & handles, 19th c., 6 d., pr. (minor chips to handles, glaze wear) **1,093**

Serving dish, cov., footed squatty round form w/upturned end loop handles, low domed reversible pierced cover, 19th c., 7⅛" d. (minute chip to handle, minor gilt & enamel wear) **633**

Shrimp dish, 19th c., 9½" d. (minor glaze chips, wear) **345**

Shrimp dish, Rose Mandarin variant, 19th c., 10⅝" l. (enamel loss, gilt wear) **431**

Tea cups & saucers, similar decoration, 19th c., set of 12 (minor chips, restoration, glaze losses) **978**

Teapot, cov., 19th c., 9½" h. (restoration to handle, glaze wear) **1,035**

Vase, 9⅞" h., Rose Mandarin variant, bottle-form, w/applied kylins & foo dogs, 19th c. (minor gilt & enamel wear) **374**

Wash bowl, wide round form w/paneled decoration, on a hardwood stand, 19th c., 16⅛" d., 4⅞" h. (minor gilt & enamel wear) . . **1,265**

ROSEVILLE

Roseville

Roseville Mark

Roseville Pottery Company operated in Zanesville, Ohio, from 1898 to 1954 after having been in business for six years in Muskingum County, Ohio. Art wares similar to those of Owens and Weller Potteries were produced. Items listed here are by patterns or lines.

BANEDA (1933)

Band of embossed pods, blossoms and leaves on green or raspberry pink ground.

Candleholders, raspberry pink ground, No. 1088-4", 4½" h., pr. **$575**

Candlesticks, raspberry pink ground, No. 1087-5", 5" h., pr. **750**

Console bowl, raspberry pink ground, No. 233-8", 10" l. **395**

Console bowl, six-sided, w/handles from base to rim, green ground, No. 234-10", 11" l. **523**

Jardiniere, two-handled, green ground, 4" h., No. 626-4" **385**

Jardiniere, two-handled, green ground, No. 626-7", 7" h. **1,540**

Jardiniere, two-handled, raspberry pink ground, No. 626-10", 10" h. **1,800**

Jardiniere & pedestal base, green ground, No. 626-10", jardiniere marked "1 spot" & "9," pedestal unmarked, overall 28" h., 2 pcs. (two tight, short lines at rim of jardiniere) **4,290**

Urn, small rim handles, bulbous, green ground, No. 235-5", 5" h. **555**

Vase, 4" h., footed bulbous body w/incurved flat rim, flat shoulder handles, raspberry pink ground, No. 587-4" 220

Vase, 6" h., two-handled, footed, bulbous base w/wide cylindrical neck, raspberry pink ground, No. 589-6" 550

Vase, 6" h., two-handled, footed, bulbous base w/wide cylindrical neck, green ground, No. 589-6" 605

Vase, 6" h., bulbous body w/slightly flaring rim, small loop shoulder handles, raspberry pink ground, No. 591-6" 550

Vase, 6" h., bulbous body w/slightly flaring rim, small loop shoulder handles, green ground, No. 591-6" 660

Vase, 6" h., footed, slender ovoid body w/short collared neck, loop handles from shoulder to rim, green ground, No. 602-6", original black paper label . . 450 to 500

Vase, 6" h., footed, slender ovoid body w/short collared neck, loop handles from shoulder to rim, raspberry pink ground, No. 602-6" . . . . 400 to 450

Vase, 6" h., raspberry pink ground, No. 605-6", original label 523

Vase, 7" h., trumpet-shaped w/handles from base to mid-section, raspberry pink ground, No. 604-7" 700

Vase, 8" h., footed, globular w/shoulder handles, raspberry pink ground, No. 595-8" 880

Vase, 9" h., cylindrical w/short collared neck, handles rising from shoulder to beneath rim, green ground, No. 594-9" 795

Vase, 9" h., cylindrical w/short collared neck, handles rising from shoulder to beneath rim, raspberry pink ground, No. 594-9" 825

Vase, 10" h., footed bulbous body tapering to closed rim, two handles rising from shoulder to beneath rim, raspberry pink ground, No. 597-10" . . . . 860 to 875

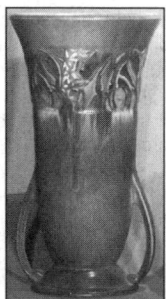

Baneda Vase

Vase, 12" h., trumpet-form on flaring foot, base handles, green ground, No. 598-12" (ILLUS.) 880

Vase, 12" h., expanding cylinder w/small rim handles, green ground, No. 599-12" 1,540

Vase, 15" h., floor-type, bulbous ovoid body w/flat rim, shoulder handles, green ground, No. 600-15" 4,400

BLACKBERRY (1933)

Band of relief clusters of blackberies with vines and ivory leaves accented in green and terra cotta on a green textured ground.

Jardiniere, two-handled, No. 623-4", 4" h. 235
Jardiniere, two-handled, No. 623-9", 9" h. 800
Jardiniere & pedestal base, 28" h., 2 pcs. . . . 3,400
Vase, 4" h., two-handled, bulbous 350

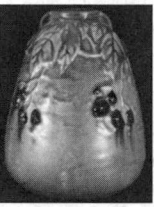

Blackberry Vases

Vase, 5" h., tiny rim handles, canted sides, No. 565-5" (ILLUS., left) 445

Vase, 6" h., bulbous ovoid w/wide rim, small shoulder handles, No. 571-6" . . . 550 to 600

Vase, 6" h., two handles at midsection, No. 573-6" 605

Vase, 6" h., globular w/tiny rim handles, No. 574-6" (ILLUS., right) 660

Vase, 8" h., handles at mid-section, slightly globular base & wide neck, No. 575-8" 880

Vase, 12½" h., ovoid w/loop handles from shoulder to rim, No. 578-12" (minor chip to bottom) 1,320

Wall pocket, basket-shaped w/narrow base & flaring rim, No. 1267-8", 6¾" w. at rim, 8 ½" h. . . . . 925 to 975

BLEEDING HEART (1938)

Pink blossoms and green leaves on shaded blue, green or pink ground.

Basket, pink ground, No. 359-8", 8" h. 325
Basket w/circular handle, blue ground, No. 360-10", 10" h. 250

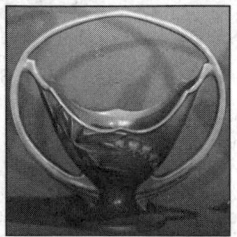

Bleeding Heart Basket

Basket w/circular handle, pink ground,
360-10", 10" h., w/gold foil label (ILLUS.). **413**
Bowl, 8" w., hexagonal, pink ground,
No. 380-8" **110**
Candleholders, pink ground, No. 1140-2", pr. . . . **165**
Console bowl, blue ground, No. 382-10", 10" l. . . **295**
Cornucopia-vase, pink ground, No. 141-6",
6" h. **165**
Ewer, green ground, No. 963-6", 6" h. . . . **200 to 225**
Ewer, pink ground, No. 972-10", 10" h. **275**
Flower frog, pink ground, No. 40 . . . . **110**
Jardiniere & pedestal base, blue ground,
jardiniere 10" h., 2 pcs. **3,500**

Bleeding Heart Pitcher

Pitcher, 8" h., asymmetrical w/high arched
handle, pink ground, No. 1323 (ILLUS.) **440**
Plate, 10½" w., hexagonal, pink ground,
No. 381-10" **110**
Urn-vase, pink ground, No. 377-4", 4" h. **135**
Vase, 5" h., blue ground, No. 962-5" **115**
Vase, 6½" h., base handles, blue ground,
No. 964-6" **175**
Vase, 6½" h., base handles, pink ground,
No. 964-6" **150**
Vase, 8" h., green ground, No. 139-8" **325**
Vase, 8" h., pillow-type, pink ground,
No. 968-8" **275**
Vase, 9" h., pillow-type, blue ground,
No. 970-9" **300**
Vase, 12" h., expanding cylinder w/small
handles at shoulder, pink ground,
No. 974-12" (tiny glaze nick off one handle). . . **248**
Vase, 15" h., two-handled, flaring hexagonal
mouth, pink ground, No. 976-15" **775**
Vase, 18" h., floor-type, blue ground,
No. 977-18" **1,200**

BURMESE (1950s)

*Oriental faces featured on pieces such as wall
plaques, book ends, candleholders and console
bowls. Some plain pieces also included. Comes
in green, black and white.*

Book ends, green ground, pr. **250**
Wall pocket, bust of a woman, white glaze,
No. 72-B, 7½" h. (ILLUS.). **165**

Burmese Wall Pocket

BUSHBERRY (1948)

*Berries and leaves on blue, green or russet
bark-textured ground; brown or green branch
handles.*

Ashtray, blue ground, No. 26 . . . . **195**
Basket, hanging-type w/original chains, blue
ground, No. 465-5", 7" **375**
Basket, hanging-type w/original chains,
green ground, No. 465-5", 7" **275**
Basket, blue ground, No. 370-8", 8" h. **265**
Basket w/asymmetrical overhead handle,
blue ground, No. 369-6 ½", 6 ½" h. **195**
Basket w/asymmetrical overhead handle,
russet ground, No. 369-6 ½", 6 ½" h. **180**
Basket w/low overhead handle, russet
ground, No. 357-10", 10" h. **280**
Basket w/low overhead handle,
asymmetric rim, blue ground, No. 372-
12", 12" h. **400**
Beverage set: 8¾" h. pitcher w/ice lip & six
3½" h. mugs; blue ground, pitcher
No. 1325, mugs No. 1-3½", 7 pcs. **1,500**
Beverage set: 8¾" h. pitcher w/ice lip & six
3½" h. mugs; russet ground, pitcher
No. 1325, mugs No. 1-3½", 7 pcs. **1,100**
Bowl, 4" d., two-handled, russet ground,
No. 411-4" **110**
Bowl, 6" d., russet ground, No. 412-6" **195**
Bowl, 10" d., russet ground, No. 1-10" . . . **100 to 150**
Console bowl, two-handled, blue ground,
No. 414-10", 10" d. **180**
Cornucopia-vase, blue ground, No. 153-6" **135**
Cornucopia-vase, double, green ground,
No. 155-8", 6" h. **100**

*From left: Bushberry Cornucopia-vase
Bushberry Vase*

Cornucopia-vase, double, russet ground,
No. 155-8", 6" h. (ILLUS.) . . . . **100 to 150**
Cornucopia-vase, double, blue ground,
No. 155-8" **215**
Ewer, green ground, No. 1-6, 6" h. **150**
Ewer, russet ground, No. 1-6, 6" h. **185**
Ewer, blue ground, No. 2-10", 10" h. **300**
Ewer, green ground, No. 2-10", 10" h. **275**
Jardiniere, two-handled, No. 657-3" **100**
Jardiniere, two-handled, russet ground,
No. 657-4", 4" h. **100**
Jardiniere & pedestal base, two-handled,
russet ground, No. 657-8", 2 pcs. . . . . . **500 to 600**
Jardiniere & pedestal base, two-handled,
blue ground, No. 657-8", overall 24" h.,
chips off base of jardiniere, 2 pcs. **550**
Mug, green ground, No. 1-3½", 3½" h. **135**
Pitcher, 8¾" h., blue w/green branch
handle, No. 1325 . . . . **413**
Sand jar, green ground, No. 778-14", 14" h. . . **1,400**
Tea set: cov. teapot, creamer & sugar
bowl; blue ground, No. 2, No. 2C,
No. 2S, 3 pcs. . . . . **550 to 575**
Tea set: cov. teapot, open creamer & sugar;
russet ground, No. 2, No. 2C & No. 2S, 3 pcs. . . **650**
Umbrella stand, double handles, blue
ground, No. 779-20", 20½" h. **985**
Vase, 6" h., two-handled, green ground,
No. 30-6" . . . . **90 to 100**
Vase, 6" h., angular side handles, low foot,
globular w/wide neck, blue ground,
No. 156-6" **165**
Vase, 6" h., angular side handles, low foot,
globular w/wide neck, russet ground,
No. 156-6" **95**
Vase, bud, 7" h., asymmetrical base
handles, cylindrical body, blue ground,
No. 152-7" **160**
Vase, 8" h., footed tapering squared body
w/flaring rim flanked by down-turned
forked branch handles, green ground,
No. 33-8" (ILLUS.) **295**
Vase, 9" h., two-handled, ovoid, blue
ground, No. 35-9" **225**
Vase, 9" h., two-handled, ovoid, green
ground, No. 35-9" **175**
Vase, 9" h., two-handled, ovoid, russet
ground, No. 35-9" . . . . **200 to 225**
Vase, 12½" h., large asymmetrical side
handles, bulging cylinder w/flaring foot,
blue ground, No. 38-12" **375**

CARNELIAN I (1910-15)

*Matte glaze with a combination of two colors
or two shades of the same color with the darker
dripping over the lighter tone or heavy and
textured glaze with intermingled colors and
some running.*

Bowl, 8" d., 3" h., deep green & light green,
No. 163-8" **88**

Bowl, 9½" d., wide squatty bulbous sides
tapering sharply to a wide molded rim,
deep green & light green **69**
Candleholder, green ground,
No. 1059-2½", 2½" h. **75**
Candleholders, simple disc base w/incised
rings at base of candle nozzle, deep
green & light green, No. 1063-3", 2½" h., pr. . . **110**
Console bowl, footed low oval form
w/canted sides & ornate scrolled end
handles, light & dark green,
No. 152-8", 10¾" l., 4" h. **165**
Console bowl, hexagonal, blue & green,
No. 170-14", 14" l., 4" h. **83**
Console bowl, footed shallow oval form
w/angled end handles, light & dark green,
No. 157-14", 16" l., 2¾" h. **248**

Carnelian I Console Set

Console set: 9½" l., 3½" h. octagonal bowl
& pair of 3" h. candleholders; pink & blue,
Nos. 164-3" & 1064-3", 3 pcs. (ILLUS.) **103**
Ewer, footed wide compressed globular
body w/wide shoulder to the pointed &
arched spout, scrolled C-form handle
from the neck to lower base, dark & light
blue, No. 1314-8", 8" h. **220**
Flower frog, blue & grey ground, 6¼" w.,
2½" h. **120**
Flower frog, green ground, 4½" h. **175**
Vase, pillow-type, green & turquoise **160**

Carnelian I Double Bud Vase

Vase, double bud, 5" h., gate-form, olive
green & mustard yellow, No. 56-5" (ILLUS.) . . . **83**
Vase, 6" h., pillow-type, light blue &
dark blue . . . . **75 to 100**
Vase, 6" h., footed fan-shaped body,
mustard yellow over light green,
No. 52-6" **83**

Vase, 7" h., footed wide ovoid base w/wide
shoulder to short collared neck, ornate
handles from mid-section to rim, light &
dark blue, No. 271-7" 110

Vase, 7" h., double gourd-form w/wide neck
& flaring rim, ornate pointed & scrolled
handles from mid-section of base to
below rim, light & dark green, No. 310-7"..... 138

Vase, 7" h., bulbous base w/wide collared
neck, ornate handles from shoulder to
beneath rim, light & dark green,
No. 311-7" 110

Vase, 8" h., base handles, fan-shaped, aqua 95

Vase, 8" h., two-handled, ovoid base &
ringed neck, turquoise blue & aqua,
No. 317-8" 110

Vase, 8" h., footed wide compressed
bulbous body w/wide collared neck,
ornate scroll handles from center of base
to rim, light & dark green & mustard
yellow, No. 318-8" 138

Vase, 9" h., cylindrical w/wide collared neck,
dark blue & light blue, No. 313-9"............ 250

Vase, 9" h., wide ovoid w/collared neck &
rolled rim, mustard yellow over light
green, No. 314-9" 110

Vase, 10" h., semi-ovoid base & long wide
neck w/rolled rim, ornate handles, dark
blue & light blue, No. 337-10" .... **125 to 175**

CARNELIAN II (1915)

Intermingled colors, some with a drip effect.

Bowl, footed, six-sided, w/drip glaze in
shades of rose, grey, green & tan,
unmarked, small separation at the rim,
4 x 15" 330

Bowl, 10½ x 3½", footed w/curved end
handles, semi-matte drip glazes in purple
& green intermingled w/maroon 468

Candleholders, aqua & lilac glaze,
No. 1059-2½", 2½" h., pr. 150

Console set: 9¾" d., bowl & pair of 3⅝" h.
candleholders; shades of green over blue
textured glaze, the set 413

Ewer, pink, mauve, green & black mottled
matte glaze, unmarked, 15" h............. **1,760**

Vase, large bulbous handled form,
pink & purple ground 550

Carnelian II Vase

Vase, 5" h., fan-shaped body on round disc
foot, scrolled handles from base to mid-
section, intermingled green & pink glaze,
unmarked (ILLUS.) 138

Vase, bud, 6" h., footed trumpet-
form w/ornate handles from base
to mid-section, blue ground 90

Vase, bud, 6" h., footed trumpet-
form w/ornate handles from base to
mid-section, intermingled shades of
raspberry pink.......................... 135

Vase, 7" h., compressed globular base
w/short wide neck, large handles, purple
& rose.................................... 225

Vase, 7" h., footed baluster-form w/small low
loop handles from shoulder to rim,
shades of green 240

Vase, 8" h., intermingled shades of blue....... 185

Vase, 8" h., intermingled shades of
raspberry pink .... **250 to 300**

Vase, 10" h., compressed globular form
w/angled handles from mid-section
to rim, intermingled blue & green
glaze, unmarked (small glaze flake
off one handle) 193

Wall pocket, slender fanned body flanked
by double-scroll handles, shaded green
ground, 8" h........................... 250

CHERRY BLOSSOM (1933)

*Sprigs of cherry blossoms, green leaves and
twigs with pink fence against a combed blue-
green ground or creamy ivory fence against a
terra cotta ground shading to dark brown.*

Candlesticks, brown ground, pr. 400

Jardiniere, squatty bulbous body, two-
handled, terra cotta ground, 4" h........... 450

Lamp base, footed globular base tapering to
short cylindrical neck flanked by small
loop handles, terra cotta ground, shape
No. 625-8", overall 9" h.................. 770

Vase, ball-shaped, blue ground 535

Vase, 4" h., compressed squatty bulbous
body w/a short slightly flared neck flanked
by small loop handles, terra cotta ground,
No. 617-3½" 220

Vase, 4" h., compressed squatty bulbous
body w/a short slightly flared neck flanked
by small loop handles, blue-green
ground, No. 617-3½" 468

Vase, 5" h., two-handled, globular w/wide
mouth, blue-green ground, No. 627-5"....... 275

Vase, 7" h., pink ground, No. 622-7".......... 525

Vase, 8" h., handles at midsection, terra
cotta ground, No. 624-8" 468

Vase, 8" h., two-handled, globular, terra
cotta ground, No. 625-8" (ILLUS.)..... **600 to 700**

Vase, 10" h., slender ovoid body w/wide
cylindrical neck, loop handles from
shoulder to middle of neck, terra cotta
ground, No. 626-10".................... 595

Cherry Blossom Vase

CHLORON (1907)

Molded in high-relief in the manner of early Roman and Greek artifacts. Solid matte green glaze, sometimes combined with ivory. Very similar in form to Egypto.

Vase, 6½" h., two-handled, expanding
cylinder, green ground, No. 750-6". **300**
Vase, 9" h., squatty bulbous body tapering
to a wide flat mouth, small loop handle on
shoulder w/molded double curved branch
handle on opposite side rising from base
to neck, molded flower decoration, signed **525**
Vase, 12" h., three heavy feet rising to form
base for tapering body w/flared rim, green
matte finish **990**

CORINTHIAN (1923)

Deeply fluted ivory and green body below a continuous band of molded grapevine, fruit, foliage and florals in naturalistic colors, narrow ivory and green molded border at the rim.

Basket, hanging-type w/chains, 8" d. **260**
Bowl, 7" d. **75**
Flower frog, No. 14-3½", 3½" h. **50**
Jardiniere, 8" h., No. 601-8". **325**
Vase, double bud, 4 ½" h., 7" w., gate-form,
No. 37-7" **150**
Vase, bud, 6¼" h., green & ivory ground **195**

Corinthian Vase

Vase, 7" h., footed, baluster-form tapering to
wide cylindrical neck, No. 215-7" (ILLUS.) **138**
Vase, 7" h., waisted cylindrical body, No. 235-7 . . **138**
Wall pocket, conical base tapering to wide
neck w/flaring rim, No. 1228-10", 10" h. **325**

COSMOS (1940)

Embossed blossoms against a wavy horizontal ridged band on a textured ground— ivory band with yellow and orchid blossoms on blue, blue band with white and orchid blossoms on green or tan.

Basket, blue ground, No. 357-10", 10" h. **395**
Bowl, 4" d., blue ground, No. 375-4" **185**
Bowl, 4" d., tan ground, No. 375-4" **165**
Bowl, 8" d., blue ground, No. 370-8" **195**
Bowl, 8" d., tan ground, No. 370-8" **110**

Cosmos Candleholder

Candleholders, loop handles above flat disc
base, slender candle nozzle, blue ground,
No. 1136-2", 2½" h., pr. (ILLUS. of one) **220**
Console bowl, green ground, No. 370-8", 8" l. . . . **150**
Flower frog, pierced globular body
w/asymmetrical overhead handle, blue
ground, No. 39, 3½" h. **145**
Flower frog, pierced globular body
w/asymmetrical overhead handle, tan
shaded to green ground, No. 39, 3½" h. **125**
Jardiniere, two-handled, blue ground,
No. 649-3" **100**
Jardiniere, two-handled, tan ground,
No. 649-4", 4" h. . . . . **100 to 125**
Jardiniere, two-handled, blue ground,
No. 649-6", 6" h. . . . . **150 to 225**
Planter, rectangular w/shaped rim, blue
ground, No. 381-9", 9" l. **320**
Rose bowl, two-handled, blue ground,
No. 375-4", 4" h. **175**
Rose bowl, two-handled, green ground,
No. 375-4", 4" h. **135**
Urn-vase, green ground, No. 135-8", 8" h. **250**
Vase, 7" h., globular base w/long slender
neck w/cut-out rim, large loop handles
rising from midsection of base to middle
of neck, green ground, No. 948-7" **193**
Vase, 8" h., two-handled, cut-out top edge,
tan ground, No. 950-8" **225**
Vase, 10" h., trumpet-shaped w/slender
curved handles from base to midsection,
brown ground, No. 954-10" **245**
Vase, 10" h., trumpet-shaped w/slender
curved handles from base to midsection,
green ground, No. 954-10" **385**
Wall pocket, fanned conical shape w/high
arched handle across the top, blue
ground, No. 1285-6", 6½" h. **595**

Wall pocket, double, tan ground,
No. 1286-8", 8½" h. **400**

CREMONA (1927)

Relief-molded floral motifs including a tall stem with small blossoms and arrowhead leaves, wreathed with leaves similar to Velmoss or a web of delicate vines against a background of light green mottled with pale blue or pink with creamy ivory.

Console bowl w/flower frog, green ground,
No. 178-8", 8" l. **200**

Vase, 4" h., rectangular mouth w/pointed ends, slightly canted sides, stepped foot, pink ground, No. 72-4" **95**

Vase, 5" h., fan-shaped, green ground, No. 73-5 . . **83**

Vase, 5" h., bulbous ovoid w/flaring mouth, green ground, No. 352-5" **110**

Vase, 7" h., round foot below squared flaring baluster-form body w/a wide rolled square rim, No. 354-7" **160**

Cremona Vase

Vase, 8" h., footed, wide cylindrical body tapering to wide flat mouth, No. 355-8", black paper label (ILLUS.) **220**

DAHLROSE (1924-28)

Band of ivory daisy-like blossoms and green leaves against a mottled tan ground.

Basket, hanging-type w/original chain, No. 343-6", 7½" d. **325**

Bowl, 8" d., footed squatty bulbous body tapering to a wide flared rim, angular end handles from rim to shoulder, No. 180-8" **210**

Bowl, 10" l., oval, footed sharply canted sides w/a low molded rim w/angular end handles from rim to shoulder, No. 179-8" **150**

Bowl, 10" d., 3½" h., spherical w/incurved sides & molded rim, unmarked **275**

Candleholders, angular handles rising fromlow slightly domed base, No. 1069-3", 3" h., pr. **135**

Jardiniere, No. 614-4", 4" h. . . . . **250 to 350**

Jardiniere, tiny rim handles, No. 614-7", 7" d., 4" h. **135**

Jardiniere, squatty bulbous form w/tiny rim handles, No. 614-6", 6" h. **165**

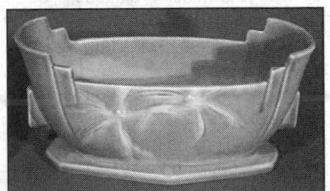

Dahlrose Triple Bud Vase

Vase, triple bud, 6" h., a domed round base w/a swelled cylindrical central shaft joined by floral panels to outcurved squared side holders, No. 76-6" (ILLUS.) . . . . **200 to 350**

Vase, double bud, 6" h., gate-form, No. 79-6", black paper label . . . . **145 to 175**

Vase, 6" h., squatty bulbous body tapering to wide rolled rim, tiny angled handles from shoulder to rim, No. 364-6" **198**

Vase, bud, 7" h., a ringed oblong domed base supports at one side a slender swelled cylindrical vase w/a flaring rim, a long, high arched handle runs from one side of vase down to a forked juncture w/the base, a smaller down-curved angular handle joins the vase to the opposite side of the vase, No. 77-7 . . . . **330**

Vase, bud, 8" h., slender swelled body w/flaring base & rolled rim, angled buttress side handles w/blossoms, No. 78-8" **235**

Vase, 8" h., footed bulbous ovoid, No. 365 8" . . . **413**

Vase, 8" h., footed ovoid body w/flared rim, angled handles from shoulder to rim, No. 366-8" **275**

Vase, 10" h., two-handled, ovoid w/wide flaring rim, No. 369-10" **385**

DAWN (1937)

Incised spidery flowers on green ground with blue-violet tinted blossoms, pink or yellow ground with blue-green blossoms, all with yellow centers.

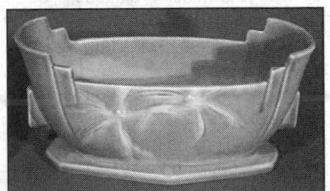

Dawn Console Bowl

Console bowl, long angular foot supporting a deep boat-shaped bowl w/high stepped end panels, green ground, No. 317-10", 10" l. (ILLUS.) **440**

Vase, 8" h., angled squatty base tapering to a tall cylindrical neck w/small tab handles, raised on a square foot, yellow ground, No. 829-8" . . . . **175 to 250**

DOGWOOD II (1928)

White dogwood blossoms & black branches against a smooth green ground.

Jardiniere, No. 590-7", 7" h. **210**
Jardiniere, No. 590-8", 8" h. **385**
Jardiniere, No. 490-10", 10" h. **575**
Jardiniere & pedestal base, No. 590-12", 12" h., 2 pcs. **1,700**
Vase, bud, 8" h., tusk-form w/single handle rising from base to midsection **135**
Wall pocket, double, 9" h. **423**
Wall pocket, two handles in the form of blossoming branches, No. 1218-10", 10" h. **350**

FERELLA (1931)

Impressed shell design alternating with small cut-outs at top and base; mottled brown or turquoise and red glaze.

Ferella Bowl

Bowl, 12" d., canted sides, low foot, mottled brown glaze, No. 212-12" (ILLUS.). **523**
Candleholders, chalice-form w/a low pedestal base supporting a wide deep pierced rounded cup centered by a cylindrical candle socket, mottled brown glaze, No. 1078-4", 4½" h., pr. (professional repair to one) **413**
Console bowl w/attached flower frog, deep flaring sides, brown glaze, No. 87-8", 8" d. **500**
Vase, 4" h., angular handles, short narrow neck, terra cotta glaze, No. 497-4" **429**
Vase, 4" h., angular handles, bulbous, turquoise & red glaze, No. 498-4" . . . . . **300 to 350**
Vase, 5" h., two-handled, flaring rim, brown glaze, No. 503-5" **400**
Vase, 6" h., large semi-circular handles, turquoise & red glaze, No. 499-6" **575**
Vase, 6" h., handles rising from shoulder of compressed globular base to beneath the rim of the long tapering neck, mottled brown glaze, No. 502-6" (ILLUS.). **550**

Ferella Vase

Vase, 6" h., bulbous base w/canted shoulder flanked by small angular handles, wide cylindrical neck, & turquoise & red glaze, No. 505-6" **700**
Vase, 8" h., slightly ovoid, turquoise & red glaze, No. 508-8" . . . . **650 to 700**
Vase, 8" h., spherical body on low foot w/wide slightly flared cylindrical neck, arched handles from mid-section to shoulder, turquoise & red glaze, No. 509-8" **1,100**
Vase, 9¼" h., 5¼" d., footed slender ovoid body tapering to a short flaring neck, low arched handles down the sides, stylized green & yellow blossoms on reticulated bands, brown glaze, No. 507-9" . . . . . . **550 to 600**
Wall pocket, half-round basket-form w/widely flaring rim & high shaped & arched backplate w/hanging hole, turquoise & red glaze, No. 1266-6½", 6½" h. . . . **1,200**

FLORANE I (1920s)

Terra cotta shading to either dark brown or deep olive green on simple shapes, often from the Rosecraft line.

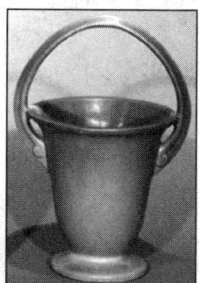

Florane I Basket

Basket, footed, ovoid body w/flaring rim, overhead handle, terra cotta shading to olive green, 8¼" h. (ILLUS.) **358**
Bowl, 8" d., low, dark brown **110**
Bowl, 8" d., rounded w/upright sides & slightly scalloped rim, No. 62-8" **50**
Vase, double-bud, 5" h., gate-form **125**
Vase, 5⅝" h., footed swelled cylindrical body w/short collared neck, terra cotta shading to olive green **110**

Vase, 6" h., cylindrical body w/short squared
handles rising from shoulders to mouth,
dark brown **165**

Vase, 6⅝" h., footed, wide ovoid body w/flat
flared rim, terra cotta shading to olive green . . **193**

Vase, 8" h., footed, cylindrical body w/wide
flaring rim, squared handles, terra cotta
shading to olive green **165**

Vase, bud, 8" h., dark brown. **80**

Vase, 12" h., slender ovoid form, green
ground, No. 64-12" **100**

Wall pocket, two-handled, ovoid w/fan-
shaped top, olive green, 9¾" h. **330**

FLORENTINE (1924-28)

*Bark-textured panels alternating with
embossed garlands of cascading fruit and
florals; ivory with tan and green, beige with
brown and green or brown with beige and green
glaze.*

Bowl, 5¼" d., tan ground **140**

Bowl, 7½" d., brown ground **99**

Candlesticks, flaring base, expanding
cylindrical stem, No. 1049-8", 8" h., pr. **125**

Jardiniere, bulbous footed body w/a wide
molded mouth flanked by tiny angled rim
handles, pastel decoration on a pink
ground, early mark, No. 602-7", 9½" d., 7" h. . . **61**

Jardiniere & pedestal base, 2 pcs. **1,350**

Urn, brown ground, 4½" h. **125**

Vase, 8" h., squared handles rising above
rim, ovoid w/collared neck, ivory, No. 255-8" . . **155**

Vase, 8½" h., squared handles at rim, ovoid,
beige, No. 231-8" **143**

Wall pocket, conical, No. 1239-7", 7" h. **229**

Wall pocket, overhead handle, brown
ground, No. 1238-8", 8½" h. **165**

Wall pocket, brown ground, 9½" h. **325**

FLORENTINE II (after 1937)

*Similar to the ivory Florentine, but with
lighter backgrounds, less decoration and without
cascades on the dividing panels.*

Florentine II Vase

Basket w/pointed overhead handle,
footed, bulbous body w/flared rim,
No. 321-7", 7" h. **138**

Vase, 12" h., ovoid body tapering to wide
cylindrical neck w/flaring rim, angled
handles from shoulder to rim,
No. 234-12" (ILLUS.) **303**

FUCHSIA (1939)

*Coral pink fuchsia blossoms and green leaves
against a background of blue shading to yellow,
green shading to terra cotta or terra cotta
shading to gold.*

Basket, hanging-type, green ground,
No. 359-5", 5" h. . . . . **350 to 450**

Basket, hanging-type, terra cotta
ground, No. 359-5", 5" h. . . . . **375 to 450**

Basket w/flower frog, green ground,
No. 350-8" **695**

Basket wflower frog, blue ground,
No. 350-8", 8" h. **600**

Bowl, urn-form, two-handled, green ground,
No. 346-4" **140**

Bowl, 5" d., two-handled, squatty bulbous
body w/incurved rim, blue ground,
No. 348-5" **150**

Bowl, 6" d., footed bulbous body w/wide flat
rim, loop shoulder handles, blue ground,
No. 347-6" (w/sticker) **275**

Bowl, 6" d., footed bulbous body w/wide flat
rim, loop shoulder handles, terra cotta
ground, No. 347-6" **275**

Bowl, 8" d., two-handled, blue ground,
No. 349-8" **250**

Candlesticks, conical body supported by
two handles rising from domed base,
terra cotta ground, No. 1133-5", 5" h., pr. **275**

Console bowl, footed oval w/shaped rim &
small loop end handles, blue ground,
No. 352-12", 12" l. **335**

Console bowl, two-handled oval w/shaped
rim, green ground, No. 351-10", 12½" l.,
3½" h. **240**

Fuchsia Console Bowl

Console bowl, two-handled oval w/shaped
rim, terra cotta ground, No. 351-10",
12½" l., 3 ½" h. (ILLUS.) **193**

Console bowl, footed low oblong boat-
shaped w/under-rim end loop handles,
terra cotta ground, No. 353-14", 15½" l. **375**

Console set: 10" bowl & pair of 5" h.
candleholders, blue ground,
Nos. 351-10" & 1133-5", the set **750**

Cornucopia-vase, green ground,
No. 129-6", 6" h. **175**

Ewer, terra cotta ground, No. 902-10", 10" h. . . . **300**

Flower frog, green ground, No. 37. . . . . **225**

Flower frog, terra cotta ground, No. 37 . . . . **125**

Flowerpot, terra cotta ground, No. 646-5",
5" h. **155**

Jardiniere, two-handled, blue ground,
No. 645-3", 3" h. **120**

Jardiniere, two-handled, green ground,
No. 645-3", 3" h. **85**

Jardiniere, two-handled, green ground,
No. 645-4", 4" h. **135**

Jardiniere & pedestal, green ground,
No. 645-10", 2 pcs. **2,400**

Pitcher w/ice lip, 8" h., green ground,
No. 1322-8" **395**

Vase, 6" h., ovoid w/handles rising from
shoulder to rim, blue ground, No. 892-6" **125**

Vase, 6" h., ovoid w/handles rising from
shoulder to rim, green ground, No. 892-6" **200**

Vase, 6" h., footed swelled cylindrical body
w/long loop handles, blue ground,
No. 893-6" **200**

Vase, 7" h., ovoid body w/cut-out rim & large
loop handles, blue ground, No. 894-7" **250**

Vase, 7" h., ovoid body w/cut-out rim & large
loop handles, terra cotta ground,
No. 894-7" **220**

Vase, 7" h., bulbous base tapering to flaring
rim, large loop handles from shoulder to
below rim, green ground, No. 895-7" . . **250 to 275**

Vase, 7" h., bulbous base tapering to flaring
rim, large loop handles from shoulder to
below rim, terra cotta ground, No. 895-7"
(ILLUS.). . . . . **150 to 225**

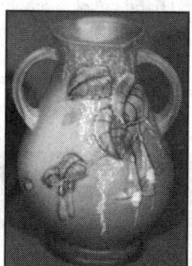

Fuchsia Vase

Vase, 8½" h., pillow-type w/handles rising
from base to midsection, blue ground,
No. 896-8" . . . . **450 to 500**

Vase, 8" h., handles rising from flat base to
shoulder, terra cotta ground, No. 897-8" **225**

Vase, 8" h., wide ovoid body w/handles
rising from flat base to shoulder, green
ground, No. 897-8" **237**

Vase, 9" h., footed ovoid body w/flared rim &
large C-form handles, blue ground,
No. 899-9" **495**

Vase, 9" h., footed ovoid body w/flared rim &
large C-form handles, green ground,
No. 899-9" **285**

Vase, 9" h., footed cylindrical w/wide flaring
rim & large C-form handles, blue ground,
No. 900-9" **350**

Vase, 10" h., footed swelled ovoid body
w/wide shaped rim & large C-form
handles, terra cotta ground, No. 901-10" **325**

Vase, 10" h., footed swelled ovoid body
w/wide shaped rim & large C-form
handles, blue ground, No. 901-10" **475**

Vase, 12" h., cylindrical body w/slightly
flared neck, two handles rising from
above base to neck, blue ground,
No. 903-12" . . . . **750 to 800**

Vase, 15" h., slender ovoid body w/wide
cylindrical neck & large C-form
handles, blue ground, No. 904-15" . . . . **650 to 700**

Vase, 15" h., slender ovoid body w/wide
cylindrical neck & large C-form handles,
terra cotta ground, No. 904-15" . . . . **550 to 600**

Vase, 15" h., slender ovoid body w/wide
cylindrical neck & large C-form handles,
green ground, No. 904-15" **840**

Vase, 18" h., 10" d., floor-type, a disc foot
supports a tall baluster-form body w/long
low C-form handles down the sides, blue
ground, No. 905-18" **1,650**

Wall pocket, two-handled, green ground,
No. 1282-8", 8½" h. **475**

FUTURA (1928)

Varied line with shapes ranging from Art Deco geometrics to futuristic. Matte glaze is typical although an occasional piece may be high gloss.

Futura Basket

Basket, hanging-type, wide sloping
shoulders, sharply canted sides, terra
cotta & brown w/embossed stylized
pastel foliage, No. 344-5", 5" h. (ILLUS.) **248**

Bowl, 5" h., square w/flared rim, raised on
four feet, tan, green & blue glaze,
No. 198-5" **990**

Bowl, 6" d., 5" h., raised on squared feet,
slightly canted sides, yellow & green
glaze, No. 197-6" **660**

Bowl, 8" d., collared base, shaped flaring
sides w/relief decoration, rose glaze,
No. 187-8" **275**

Bowl, 8" w., 4" h., five flaring sides on
square base, orange & green glaze,
No. 188-8" **413**

Bowl-planter, 5½" h., square w/flared rim,
raised on four feet, mottled green glaze,
No. 190-3½ - 6" **303**

Bowl w/flower frog, 8" d., collared base,
shaped flaring sides w/relief decoration,
rose glaze, Nos. 187-8" & 15-3½", 2 pcs.
(professional repair to rim) **138**

Candleholders, shaped square base rising
to square candle nozzle, relief-molded
stylized green vine & foliage on sandy
beige ground, No. 1073-4", 4" h., pr. **385**

Candleholders, stepped tapering cylindrical
base w/wide flaring foot & flaring shallow
socket, mottled green glaze, No. 1075-4",
4" h., black paper label on one, pr.
(professional repair to one) **990**

Console bowl, w/flower frog, cut-out base,
sharply canted sides w/embossed
stylized design, No. 196, 3½ x 5 x 12" **358**

Console bowl w/flower frog, footed
shallow flaring form, shaded green glaze,
No. 195-10", 10" d., 2½" h., 2 pcs. **1,045**

Jardiniere, angular handles rising from wide
sloping shoulders to rim, sharply canted
sides, pink & grey ground, No. 616-6", 6" h.. . . **248**

Jardiniere, angular handles rising from wide
sloping shoulders to rim, sharply canted
sides, terra cotta ground, No. 616-6", 6" h. . . . **275**

Jardiniere & pedestal base, angular
handles rising from wide sloping
shoulders to rim, sharply canted sides,
brown ground, No. 616-10", 10" h.,
unmarked, 2 pcs. **1,100**

Planter, square w/low flat base, sides
decorated w/relief stylized tree w/sparse
foliage, cream w/green highlights,
No. 191-8", 7" sq. **330**

Vase, 4" h., square mounted cone-shaped
body w/four vertical supports extending
down from mid-point of sides to corners
of square disc base, striated blue, green
& yellow, No. 430-9" . . . . **450 to 500**

Vase, 5" h., 5" w., 1½" d., stepped base,
incised fan effect, light & darker blue
glaze, No. 81-5" . . . . **300 to 350**

Vase, 6" h., squared buttressed form, terra
cotta & gold, No. 423-6", unmarked **275**

Vase, 6½" h., a tall squared & gently twisted
slightly tapering form w/molded stylized
foliage in yellow & green, No. 398-6½" **330**

Vase, 7" h., sharply canted base, handles
rising from shoulder to below rim of long
cylindrical stepped neck, grey-green &
tan, No. 382-7" . . . . **425 to 450**

Vase, 7" h., spherical top w/large pointed
dark blue & green leaves curving up the
sides, resting on a gently sloped
rectangular foot, light blue ground,
No. 387-7" . . . . **750 to 800**

Vase, 7" h., square shape tapering to round
foot w/green trim, green "V" design on
pink ground, No. 399-7" (professional
repair to base) **220**

Vase, 7" h., egg-shaped body supported by
small tabbed feet on a square flaring
base, mottled tan & green, No. 400-7" **220**

Vase, 8" h., footed, wide ovoid body w/short
collared neck, buttressed sides,
embossed design of thistles on front &
back, green, lavender & brown (minor
bruise to base) **358**

Vase, 8" h., bottle-shaped w/stepped back
bands, green & pink, No. 384-8" **550**

Vase, 8" h., upright rectangular form on
rectangular foot, stepped neck, long
square handles, grey & pink ground,
No. 386-8", unmarked . . . . **550 to 650**

Vase, 8¼" h., 5" d., conical body on flat disc
base, buttressed sides, orange w/green
buttresses & blue base, No. 401-8" **523**

Vase, 9" h., triangular shaped body tapering
to stepped round base, leafy branch
design, light & dark blue, No. 388-9" **732**

Vase, 9" h., "Emerald Urn," angular handles
rising from bulbous base to rim, sharply
stepped neck shaded dark to light green
high gloss glaze, No. 389-9", unmarked **605**

Futura Vase

Vase, 9" h., footed bulbous base w/canted
sides to wide sloping shoulder w/tapering
stepped cylindrical neck, angled handles
from shoulder to neck, green ribbed leaf
design on shaded tan to brown ground,
No. 409-9" (ILLUS.) **715**

Vase, 10" h., wide nearly spherical body
raised on a small cylindrical foot, the
steeply stepped round neck w/narrow
mouth, swirled black flame-like design
around the lower half, green,
No. 391-10" . . . . **1,000 to 1,200**

Vase, 10" h., compressed globular base supporting long flaring squared neck, elongated triangular design on each side, blue & green, No. 392-10", black paper label **770**

Vase, 10" h., cylindrical, embossed stylized sea gulls decoration, charcoal shading to terra cotta, No. 408-10" (some staining from use) **990**

Vase, 10" h., four flat vertical handles at flaring collared neck, cylindrical body, brown & yellow, No. 432-10" **880**

Vase, 10" h., large spherical body on a small footring, the neck composed of stepped bands, flame-form molded design around the lower half, No. 391-10". **900**

Vase, 12¼" h., 5½" d., tall flaring column rising from four spheres & resting on a square base, grey & peach, No. 393-12" . . . **1,210**

Vase, 14" h., 5½" d., two large handles at lower half, squat stacked base & faceted squared neck, matte glaze in three shades of brown, No. 411-14", old illegible paper label **2,530**

Vase, 15" h., footed tapering cylindrical body w/wide flaring neck, long slender handles, thistle decoration in green on terra cotta & gold ground, No. 438-15" (professional repair of base chip) . . . . . **495 to 525**

Wall pocket, canted sides, angular rim handles, geometric design in blue, yellow, green & lavender on brown ground, No. 1261-8", 6" w., 8¼" h. . . . . **550 to 650**

Wall pocket, canted sides, angular rim handles, geometric design in blue, yellow, green & lavender on brown ground, No. 1261-8", 6" w., 8¼" h. **400**

Window box, rectangular, Art Deco-type shaped rectangular strapwork on sides & ends, grey-blue shading to tan, No. 376-15, 15½" x 5" (small flat base chip) . . **825**

IMPERIAL I (1916)

Pretzel-twisted vine & stylized grape leaves decorate rough-textured background in green and brown. Style of modeling is rather crude.

Basket, tall tapering cylindrical form w/circular overhead handle, 12½" h., unmarked **495**

Bowl, 7" d., No. 71-7" **85**

Bowl, 8" d., No. 71-8" **125**

Bowl, 8" d., No. 71-8" **95**

Bowl, 9" d., two-handled **80**

Jardiniere & pedestal, 2 pcs. **1,300**

Vase, 8" h., bulbous w/pierced handles at shoulder **145**

Vase, triple bud, 8" h., No. 25-8" **140**

Vase, bud, 9" h., cylindrical w/flaring base, long pierced side handles, No. 31-9" **165**

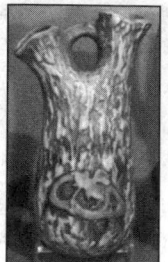

Imperial I Wall Pocket

Wall pocket, double, the two openings joined by slender bridge, No. 1222-9", 10" h. (ILLUS.) . . . . **250 to 300**

IMPERIAL II (1924)

Much variation within the line. There is no common characteristic, although many pieces are heavily glazed, and colors tend to run and blend.

Imperial II Vase

Bowl, 4½" d., ivory ground **75**

Vase, 4½" h., hemispherical w/flat shoulders & short neck, mauve & turquoise glaze, No. 200-4½", wblack paper label (ILLUS.) **413**

Vase, 5" h., wide squatty bulbous body w/a wide shoulder to the short rolled neck, embossed designs around the rim, blue flambé ground, marked w/gold foil label & incised "9" **220**

Vase, 5" h., tapering ovoid ringed body, tan shading to green, No. 467-5" . . . . **200 to 225**

Vase, 5" h., tapering ovoid ringed body, yellow ground, No. 467-5" **275**

Vase, 5½" h., tapering cylinder w/horizontal ribbing above base, mottled green ground, No. 468-5" . . . . **185 to 200**

Vase, 6" h., purple & yellow ground, No. 469-6". . . **250**

Vase, 7" h., globular w/horizontal ribbing at neck, mottled rose glaze, No. 471-7" . . **650 to 750**

Vase, 7" h., No. 472-7" **175**

Vase, 7" h., hemispherical w/sloping shoulder & short collared neck, No. 474-7" . . . **425**

Vase, 8" h., fan-shaped, two handles from base to midsection, intermingled shades of blue & green **150**

Vase, 7" h., 8" d., turquoise & yellow **425**

Vase, 11" h., tapering ovoid body with short
wide rim, blue ground **795**

IXIA (1930s)

*Embossed spray of tiny bell-shaped flowers
and slender leaves—white blossoms on pink
ground; lavender blossoms on green or yellow
ground.*

Bowl, 4" d., pointed closed handles at rim,
pink ground, No. 326-4" **115**
Bowl, 6" d., pink ground, No. 387-6" **225**
Bowl, 6" d., yellow ground, No. 387-6" **125**
Console bowl, pink ground, No. 330-9", 9" l. **140**
Jardiniere, green ground, No. 640-7", 7" h. **300**
Vase, 6" h., elongated closed handles at
shoulders, ovoid body, pink ground,
No. 853-6" **85**
Vase, 6" h., elongated closed handles at
shoulders, ovoid body, yellow & purple,
No. 853-6" **165**
Vase, 7" h., footed ovoid body w/small tab
handles flanking the short neck, pink
ground, No. 855-7" **138**
Vase, 7" h., footed ovoid body w/small tab
handles flanking the short neck, green
ground, No. 855-7" **150**
Vase, 8" h., pillow-form, green ground,
No. 858-8" **265**

Ixia Vase

Vase, 8½" h., closed handles at midsection,
globular w/long wide neck, green ground,
No. 857-8" (ILLUS.) **165**
Vase, 10" h., green ground, No. 863-10" **231**
Vase, 12" h., closed handles, cylindrical,
yellow ground, No. 864-12" **350**

JONQUIL (1931)

*White jonquil blossoms and green leaves in
relief against textured tan ground; green lining.*

Bowl, 3" h., large down-turned handles,
No. 523-3" . . . . **200 to 250**
Bowl-vase, bulbous nearly spherical body
w/downward looped shoulder handles, 4" h. . . **115**
Candleholders, No. 1082-4", 4" h., pr. **400**

Crocus pot w/attached saucer, No. 96-7", 7" h. . . **475**
Jardiniere, No. 621-4", 4" h. **220**
Jardiniere, two-handled, No. 621-8", 8" h. **450**
Jardiniere, No. 621-10", 10" h. **1,200**
Strawberry jar, No. 95-6½", 6½" h. **495**
Vase, 4" h., bulbous spherical form, loop
handles from mid-section to rim **165**
Vase, 5" h., No. 525-5" **231**

Jonquil Vase

Vase, 6½" h., wide bulbous body tapering to
flat rim, C-form handles, No. 543-6½"
(ILLUS.) **365**
Vase, 7⅛" h., two-handled, trumpet form,
handles from foot to mid-section,
No. 541-7" . . . . **300 to 325**
Vase, 8" h., tapering cylinder w/elongated
side handles, No. 528-8" . . . . **350 to 400**
Vase, 8" h., bulbous ovoid body w/short
collared neck, closed handles from
shoulder to rim, terra cotta ground,
No. 672-8" **413**
Vase, 10½" h., cylindrical w/narrow
shoulder, asymmetrical, branch handles,
white ground, No. 583-10" **225**

JUVENILE (1916 ON)

*Transfer-printed and painted on creamware
with nursery rhyme characters, cute animals
and other motifs appealing to children.*

Cup & saucer, Sunbonnet Girl, cup 2" h.,
saucer 3" d., pr. **125**
Feeding dish w/rolled edge, "Baby's Plate"
around rim, five chicks around interior, 7" d. . . **195**

Rabbits "Baby's Plate"

Feeding dish w/rolled edge, "Baby's Plate"
around rim, four rabbits around interior, 7" d.
(ILLUS.) **195**

Feeding dish w/rolled edge, sitting rabbits, 7" d.. . 145
Feeding dish w/rolled edge, chicks
  decoration, 8" d. 121
Feeding dish w/rolled edge, nursery rhyme,
  "Bye Baby Bunting," w/cat, 8" d. 110
Feeding dish w/rolled edge, nursery rhyme,
  "Little Bo Peep," 8" d. 265
Feeding dish w/rolled edge, Santa Claus, 8" d. . . 750
Feeding dish w/rolled edge, Sunbonnet
  girl, 8" d. 165
Feeding dish w/rolled edge, three ducks, 8" d. . . 195
Mug, chicks, 3" h. 95
Mug, duck w/hat, 3" h. 150
Mug, standing rabbit, 3" h.. . . . . 75 to 175
Mug, two-handled, rabbits, 3" h. 195
Pitcher, 3" h., chicks. 115
Pitcher, 3" h. rabbits. 175
Pitcher, 3½" h., duck w/hat. 145
Pitcher, 3½" h., fat puppy 85
Pitcher, 3½" h., side pour, chicks . . . . . . 110 to 125
Pitcher, 3½" h., side pour, rabbits 145
Plate, 8" d., Sunbonnet girl 200

LAUREL (1934)

Laurel branch and berries in low relief with reeded panels at the sides. Glazed in deep yellow, green shading to cream or terra cotta.

Bowl, 6" d., 3½" h., green ground. 193
Bowl, 7" d., shallow, green ground. 121
Candlestick, green ground, 4½" h. 895

Laurel Vase

Urn, bulbous base w/ringed neck, closed
  shoulder handles, green ground,
  No. 250-6¼", 6½" h. (ILLUS.). 468
Urn, deep yellow, No. 250-6½", 6½" h. 265
Vase, 6" h., No. 239-6" 130
Vase, 6" h., tapering cylinder w/wide mouth,
  closed angular handles at shoulder, deep
  yellow, No. 667-6" 231
Vase, 6¼" h., green ground, No. 250-6¼" 450
Vase, 6½" h., green, No. 669-6½" 185
Vase, 7¼" h., green, No. 670-7¼" 358
Vase, 7½" h., tapering cylinder w/pierced
  angular handles at midsection, terra
  cotta, No. 671-7¼" 295

Vase, 8" h., bulbous ovoid body w/short
  collared neck, closed handles from
  shoulder to rim, yellow ground, No. 672-8" . . . 325
Vase, 9" h., deep yellow 195
Vase, 9" h., short cylindrical bottom w/wide
  slightly flaring neck, closed handles at
  midsection, deep yellow or terra cotta,
  No. 675-9", each. 385
Vase, 9¼" h., angular side handles, globular
  base w/wide mouth, green ground,
  No. 674-9¼" 475
Vase, 9¼" h., angular side handles, globular
  base w/wide stepped mouth, deep yellow,
  No. 674-9¼" 358

LUFFA (1934)

Relief-molded ivy leaves and blossoms on shaded brown or green wavy horizontal ridges.

Bowl, 7" d., bulbous w/small pointed rim
  handles, green ground, No. 257-7" 220
Console bowl, green ground, 13" l. 345
Jardiniere & pedestal base, brown ground,
  jardinere 8" h., 2 pcs.. 1,500
Vase, 6" h., two-handled, cylindrical, green
  ground 145
Vase, 6" h., tapering cylindrical body
  w/angled handles from shoulder to rim,
  brown ground, No. 683-6" 118
Vase, 6" h., two-handled, cylindrical body,
  brown ground, No. 684-6" 193
Vase, 6" h., two-handled, cylindrical body,
  green ground, No. 684-6" 180
Vase, 7" h., brown ground. 300

Luffa Vase

Vase, 7" h., ovoid body w/small angled
  handles from shoulder to rim, green
  ground, No. 685-7" (ILLUS.). 220
Vase, 7" h., brown ground, No. 686-7" . . . 250 to 300
Vase, 8" h., shaded brown ground,
  No. 688-8", original label 303
Vase, 9" h., bulbous body tapering to wide
  flat rim flanked by small angled handles,
  brown ground, No. 690-9" 468
Vase, 12" h., brown ground, No. 691-12" 650

MAGNOLIA (1943)

Large white blossoms with rose centers and black stems in relief against a blue, green or tan textured ground.

Bowl, 8" d., two-handled, No. 448-8" 80
Bowl, 10" l., two-handled, blue ground,
    No. 450-10" 425
Candlesticks, angular handles rising from
    flat base to midsection of stem, green
    ground, No. 1157-4½", 5" h., pr. 165
Console bowl, green ground, No. 5-10", 10" l. . . 245
Cookie jar, cov., shoulder handles, blue
    ground, No. 2-8", overall 10" h. 457

Magnolia Ewer

Ewer, blue ground, No. 14-10", 10" h. (ILLUS.) . . 165
Ewer, brown ground, No. 15-15", 15" h. 750
Planter, green ground, No. 183-6" 125
Vase, 7" h., bud, green ground, No. 179-7" 155
Vase, 8" h., blue ground, No. 92-8" 165

MODERNE (1930s)

Art Deco-style rounded and angular shapes trimmed with an embossed panel of vertical lines and modified swirls and circles, white trimmed with terra cotta, medium blue with white and turquoise with a burnished antique gold.

Bowl, 7 x 11", 4" h., pleated body, blue
    ground, No. 301-10" 83

Moderne Vase

Vase, 6" h., a round foot tapering to a narrow
    short stem supporting a tall conical body,
    two small curved handles from foot to lower
    body, white ground, No. 788-6" (ILLUS.) 165
Vase, 8" h., expanding cylinder, small loop
    handles at shoulder, white ground, No. 797-8" . . 193

MONTACELLO (1931)

White stylized trumpet flowers with black accents on a terra cotta band, light terra cotta mottled in blue, or light green mottled and blended with blue backgrounds.

Basket w/pointed overhead handle, tall
    collared neck, green ground, No. 332-6", 6½" . . 605

Montacello Basket

Basket w/pointed overhead handle, tall
    collared neck, terra cotta ground,
    No. 332-6", 6" h. (ILLUS.) 605
Console bowl, brown ground 450
Console bowl, low squatty bulbous oblong
    form w/flat rim & small round end
    handles, rust, camel & tan ground
    w/'small fan-like black & white designs
    scattered around the shoulder, 13" l., 3" h. . . . 413
Vase, 5" h., two-handled, conical, terra
    cotta, black paper label 413
Vase, 7" h., two-handled, slightly ovoid, wide
    mouth, blue ground, No. 561-7" (very
    minor glaze flaws) 413
Vase, 7" h., spherical base tapering to wide
    collared neck w/flat rim, loop handles
    from shoulder to mid-neck, terra cotta
    ground, No. 562-7" 715
Vase, 9" h., bulbous ovoid w/flat rim, loop
    handles, blue ground, No. 564-9" 880

MOSS (1930s)

Green moss hanging over brown branch with green leaves; backgrounds are pink, ivory or tan, shading to blue.

Bowl, 6" d., footed w/rounded sides, small
    angled side handles, pink ground,
    No. 291-6" 165
Console bowl, oval w/shaped rim & angled
    end handles, tan shading to blue ground,
    No. 293-10", 10½" l., 3" h. (ILLUS.) 193

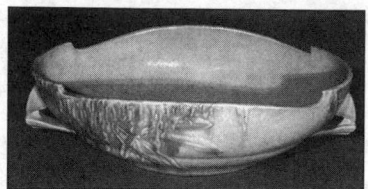

Moss Console Bowl

Rose bowl, footed spherical body w/angled
side handles, pink shading to blue
ground, No. 289-4", 4" h. **248**

Vase, 7" h., stepped bulbous base tapering
to slightly flaring cylindrical neck, angular
side handles, pink ground, No. 777-7" **275**

Vase, 8" h., ovoid w/slightly flaring rim,
ornate angular side handles, blue ground,
No. 780-8" (pin-head size glaze nick on
one handle) **220**

Vase, 12" h., ivory ground, ... **750**

Vase, 12" h., pink ground, No. 785-12"
(minor bruises) **523**

ORIAN (1935)

*Characterized by handles formed on blade-
like leaves with suggestion of berries at base of
handle, high gloss glaze; blue or tan with darker
drip glaze forming delicate band around rim, or
in plain yellow with no over drip.*

Console bowl, pedestal footed, tan & blue
ground, No. 275-5", 5" l. **275**

Vase, 6" h., flared foot below a cylindrical
body w/a spherical top & short cylindrical
neck, long & low loop handles down the
sides, white ground, No. 733-6" **250**

Vase, 7" h., slender handles rising from
shoulder of squatty ringed base to rim of
short wide neck, glossy tan w/turquoise
lining, No. 735-7" **165**

Vase, 9" h., slender handles rising from
compressed ringed base to middle of
long wide neck, rose/magenta ground,
No. 739-9" **275**

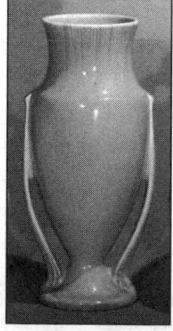

Orian Vase

Vase, 10½" h., baluster form w/slender
handles rising from low foot to shoulder,
glossy turquoise blue w/orange lining,
No. 740-10", gold foil label (ILLUS.) **193**

Vase, 14½" h. **475**

PANEL (1920)

*Background colors are dark green or dark
brown; decorations embossed within the recessed
panels are of natural or stylized floral
arrangements or female nudes.*

Panel Vase

Vase, 7" h., brown ground w/ dandelions,
crisp mold. **200**

Vase, 8" h., footed, wide, slightly expanding
cylindrical body w/short rolled rim, floral
panels, dark green ground, No. 191-8"
(ILLUS.) **413**

Vase, 8¼" h., 5¼" w., flattened fan-shaped
bowl on a short knob pedestal on flaring
round foot, light green on dark green **715**

Wall pocket, nude, brown ground **675**

PAULEO (1914)

*Prestige line of 222 color combinations and
two glaze types, lustre or marbleized.*

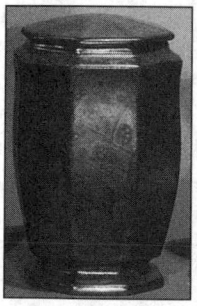

*From left: Pauleo Covered Jar
Large Pauleo Vase*

Jar, cov., hexagonal, red, blue, purple &
black glaze, marked w/impressed "B" &
"322" in black slip, 6¾" h. (ILLUS.) **1,320**

Vase, 16½" h., pearl grey to orange lustre
glaze w/yellow & red fruit w/pale green
leaves decoration bordered by green
bands around shoulder, impressed mark. **605**

Vase, 17⅜" h., slightly swelled cylindrical tapering to wide neck w/flaring rim, decorated w/evenly spaced black streaks descending from the rim, mottled blue-green lustre glaze (ILLUS.) **1,760**

PINE CONE (1931)

Realistic embossed brown pine cones and green pine needles on shaded blue, brown or green ground. (Pink is extremely rare.)

Ashtray, green ground, No. 499, 4½" l. (repaired glaze nick on rim) **55**

Basket, w/overhead branch handle, disc base, flaring rim, blue ground, No. 338-10", 10" h. . . . . **550 to 650**

Basket, brown ground, No. 353-11", 11" h. **475**

Bowl, 4" d., bulbous spherical body w/incurved rim, blue ground, No. 278-4" **270**

Bowl, 4" d., bulbous spherical body w/incurved rim, brown ground, No. 278-4" (pin prick glaze nick at mid-body) **138**

Bowl, 6" d., blue ground, No. 261-6" (tight hairline) **176**

Bowl, 9" d., 4" h., two-handled, footed with rounded sides & pleated & shaped rim, brown ground, No. 355-8" (small repair to rim) **330**

Bowl, 11" l., green ground **325**

Bowl-vase, two handles, green ground, No. 400-4" **176**

Candleholders, green ground, No. 451-4", 4" h., pr. **185**

Candlesticks, green ground, No. 1099-4½", 4½" h., pr. **200**

Console bowl, green ground, No. 322-12", 12" l. **268**

Cornucopia-vase, brown ground, No. 128-8", 8" h. **165**

Dish, footed, sweeping boat-shaped, one end handle in the form of pine needles & cone, brown ground, No. 432-12", 12¾" l. **289**

Ewer, blue ground, No. 851-15", 15" h., ... **2,200**

Jardiniere, blue ground, No. 632-3", 3" h. **222**

Jardiniere, brown ground, No. 632-4", 4" h. **240**

Jardiniere, green ground, No. 632-5", 5" h. **265**

Jardiniere, brown ground, No. 839-6", 6" h. **175**

Jardiniere, blue ground, No. 632-8", 8" h. **1,450**

Jardiniere, green ground, No. 403-10", 10" h. **600**

Jardiniere, brown ground, No. 632-12", 12" h. . . **1,760**

Jardiniere & pedestal base, blue ground, large spherical form w/slightly flared rim, applied branch handles, unmarked, 34" overall **4,025**

Match holder, green ground, No. 498, 3" h. **220**

Pitcher, 9" h., blue ground, No. 415-9". **823**

Planter, brown ground, No. 457-7", 4½" h. **225**

Planter, boat-shaped, blue ground, No. 455-6", 6" l., 3" h., ... **220**

Rose bowl, brown ground, No. 261-6", 6" d. **385**

Vase, 5" h., a deep cup-shaped bowl set off-center on an oval foot w/a pine cone & pine needle handle extending from base to rim, another sprig on pine needles molded into the lower body, No. 124-5". . . . . **175 to 225**

Vase, 6" h., fan-shaped, brown, No. 427-6" **325**

Pine Cone Fan Vase

Vase, 6" h., fan-shaped w/single handle, green ground, No. 472-6" (ILLUS.). **303**

Vase, 6" h., footed tapering cylindrical body w/asymmetric handles, green ground, No. 748-6" **303**

Vase, 6" h., wide cylindrical body w/flaring rim, asymmetrical handles, brown ground, No. 838-6" **178**

Vase, 7" h., footed bulbous ovoid tapering to slightly flaring rim, asymmetric handles, green ground, No. 840-7". **171**

Vase, 8" h., green ground, No. 841-7" **198**

Vase, triple bud, 8" h., brown ground, No. 113-8" **275**

Vase, 8" h., compressed bulbous base tapering to wide cylindrical neck, handles from base to mid-section of neck, brown ground, No. 842-8", 8" h. **270**

Vase, 8" h., blue ground, No. 844-8" **650**

Vase, 8" h., brown ground, No. 908-8" **335**

Vase, 8½" h., horn-shaped w/fanned & pleated rim, pine needles & cone-form handle from base of oval foot to mid-section, brown ground, No. 490-8". **248**

Vase, 9" h., blue ground, No. 846-9" **395**

Vase, 9" h., brown ground, No. 846-9" **475**

Vase, 10" h., expanding cylinder, blue ground, No. 709-10". **509**

Vase, 10" h., brown ground, No. 910-10" **500**

Vase, 12" h., brown ground, No. 492-12" **1,500**

Vase, 15" h., two-handled, ovoid w/waisted neck & flaring mouth, brown ground, No. 807-15" **800**

Wall shelf, brown ground, No. 1-5 x 8", 5" w., 8" h. (1/8" no show chip at back edge) . . **432**

Window box, brown ground, No. 488-8" **225**

Window box, rectangular w/shaped rim & low center handle, brown ground, No. 468-8", 8¾" l., 3¾" h. **193**

Window box, brown ground, No. 516-10", 10" l. **250**

POPPY (1930s)

Shaded backgrounds of blue or pink with decoration of poppy flower and green leaves.

Console bowl, oval, pink ground, No. 138-10",
  10" l. **148**
Jardiniere, 5" h., tiny handles at rim,
  globular, pink ground, No. 642-5", 5" h. **110**
Urn, green handled, 6" h. **200**

Poppy Vase

Vase, 8" h., footed, wide cylindrical form
  w/C-form handles, green ground,
  No. 871-8" (ILLUS.) **165**

ROSECRAFT - PANEL (1920)

A line of common shapes decorated with panels of nudes, florals, fruit and vines in orange, green, ivory, pink or lavender. Matte finish of dark green or brown.

Bowl, 8" d., 2⅜" h., shallow round form
  w/rolled rim, orange floral decoration on
  brown ground **138**
Candleholders, decorated w/purple flowers
  on dark green ground, 2" h., pr. **165**
Vase, 6" h., cylindrical, decorated w/purple
  flowers on dark green ground. **248**
Vase, 8" h., fan-shaped w/nudes decoration
  in orange, brown ground **1,100**
Vase, 8" h., wide bulbous body w/a round
  shoulder to the molded neck, decorated
  w/vines, leaves & fruit in orange on brown
  ground, No. 293-8" **358**

Rosecraft Panel Vase

Vase, 9" h., baluster-form body w/trumpet-
  form neck, orange floral decoration on
  dark brown ground, No. 294-8" (ILLUS.) **248**
Wall pocket, conical form w/ruffled
  rim flanked by cut-out panels, nude
  decoration in orange, dark brown
  ground, 7" h. **825**

ROZANE (1900)

Dark blended backgrounds; slip decorated underglaze artware.

Rozane Vase with Silver Overlay

Vase, 4" h., bulbous base tapering to wide
  cylindrical neck w/flaring neck, yellow
  daisy decoration, No. 844-4" **193**
Vase, 4⅝" h., bulbous base w/tall cylindrical
  neck & flared rim, shaded brown ground
  w/Art Nouveau-style silver overlay
  flowers, impressed "Rozane 923
  RPCo," "E" & "4," silver impressed
  "999/1000" (ILLUS.) **523**

RUSSCO (1930s)

Octagonal rim openings, stacked handles, narrow perpendicular panel front and back. One type glaze is solid matte color; another is matte color with lustrous crystalline over glaze, some of which shows actual grown crystals.

Urn-vase, angular handles, crystalline green
  to gold glaze, No. 108-6, 7" h. **220**
Urn-vase, footed, bulbous base w/small
  buttressed handles, wide tapering
  cylindrical neck w/slightly flaring rim, gold
  crystalline glaze, partial paper label,
  No. 109-8", 8½" h. **187**
Vase, 6" h., two-handled, footed globular
  body w/wide shoulder tapering to flared
  rim, turquoise glaze, No. 259-6", silver
  foil label **83**
Vase, 6" h., two-handled, footed globular
  body w/wide shoulder tapering to flared
  rim, snowflake crystalline yellow over
  green glaze, No. 259-6", silver foil label
  (ILLUS.) **220**
Vase, 8½" h., maroon **95**

Russco Snowflake Crystalline Vase

SILHOUETTE (1952)

Recessed area silhouettes nature study or female nudes. Colors are rose, turquoise, tan and white with turquoise.

Basket, flaring cylinder w/pointed overhead
   handle, florals, turquoise blue,
   No. 708-6", 6" h. **83**
Planter, florals, turquoise ground, footed
   long rectangular form, No. 756-5", 5" h........ **75**

Silhouette Urn

Urn, four wing-shaped feet on disc base,
   reclining female nudes, turquoise ground,
   No. 763-8", 8" h. (ILLUS.)................ **440**
Vase, 5" h., florals, white ground, No. 779-5" **125**
Vase, 7" h., fan-shaped, female nudes, rose,
   No. 783-7" **385**
Vase, 14" h., globular base w/expanding
   cylindrical neck w/fluted rim, foliage, rose,
   No. 789-14", each...................... **460**

SNOWBERRY (1946)

Brown branch with small white berries and green leaves embossed over spider-web design in various background colors (blue, green and rose).

Console bowl, shaded rose ground,
   No. 1BL1-10", 10" l. **138**
Ewer, shaded green ground, No. 1TK-6", 6" h. ... **125**
Jardiniere, two-handled, shaded green
   ground, No. 1J-4", 4" h. **150**
Jardiniere, two-handled, shaded rose
   ground, No. 1J-4", 4" h. **104**
Tray, long leaf-shaped, shaded rose ground,
   No. 1BL1-12", 14" l. **104**
Vase, 6" h., shaded rose ground, No. 1V-6" **125**

Vase, 7" h., two-handled, shaded blue
   ground, No. 1V1-7"..................... **145**

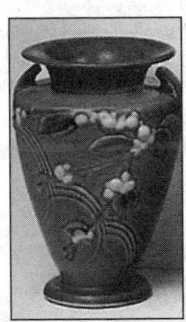

Snowberry Vase

Vase, 8" h., ovoid w/flat shoulder & flaring
   rim, small pointed shoulder handles,
   shaded green ground, No. 1V2-8" (ILLUS.) ... **176**
Vase, 9" h., shaded green ground, No. 1V2 9"... **235**
Vase, 15" h., floor-type, shaded green
   ground, 1V1-15"...................... **450**

SUNFLOWER (1930)

Tall stems support yellow sunflowers whose blooms form a repetitive band. Textured background shades from tan to dark green at base.

Bowl, 3⅝" h., flaring sides, slender loop
   handles............................ **715**
Umbrella stand, footed cylindrical form,
   No. 770-20", unmarked, 20" h. **7,425**
Urn-vase, nearly spherical w/tiny rim
   handles, 4" h. **491**
Vase, 5" h............................. **600**
Vase, 6" h., swelled cylindrical body w/short
   cylindrical neck flanked by small loop
   handles, No. 485-6" **674**

Sunflower Vase

Vase, 8" h., bulbous base, wide tapering
   cylindrical neck, unmarked, No. 491-8"
   (ILLUS.)........................... **1,288**

Vase, 9" h., bulbous base w/wide cylindrical
neck, small loop handles, No. 493-9"
(repair to top) **770**
Vase, 10" h., tall swelled cylindrical body
tapering slightly to a wide flat mouth
flanked by tiny loop handles, No. 494-10"
(nearly invisible flat chip off base) **1,650**
Window box, 3½ x 11" **1,500**

THORN APPLE (1930s)

*White trumpet flower with leaves reverses to
thorny pod with leaves. Colors are shaded blue,
brown and pink.*

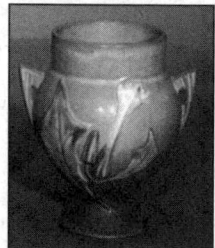

Thorn Apple Vase

Book ends, shaded brown ground, No. 3, pr. . . . **308**
Centerpiece, brown ground, No. 313-11", 11" l. . . **358**
Ewer, shaded pink & green ground,
No. 816-8", 8" h. **265**
Urn, stepped handles, disc foot, shaded pink
ground, No. 304-4" **110**
Vase, 4" h., squatty body w/short narrow
neck, angular pierced handles rising from
midsection, shaded blue ground,
No. 308-4" **138**
Vase, 6" h., bulbous ovoid body w/sharply
angled shoulder handles, short cylindrical
neck, shaded pink ground, No. 811-6"
(ILLUS.) **193**
Vase, bud, 7" h., shaded brown ground,
No. 813-7" **163**
Vase, 15" h., shaded pink & green ground,
No. 824-15" **525**

TOPEO (1934)

*Simple forms decorated with four vertical
evenly spaced cascades of leaves in high relief at
their origin, tapering downward to a point. A
light green crystalline glaze shades to a mottled
medium blue, with cascades in alternating green
and pink. A second type is done completely in a
high-gloss dark red.*

Console bowl, glossy dark red glaze, paper
label, 11½" l., 3" h. **215**

Topeo Vase

Vase, 6½" h., ovoid w/flaring mouth, glossy
deep red glaze, No. 656-6" (ILLUS.) **193**
Vase, 6¾" h., ovoid body w/short wide
cylindrical neck w/flat rim, green
crystalline shading to blue, No. 657-6¾" **248**

VELMOSS (1935)

*Characterized by three horizontal wavy lines
around the top from which long, blade-like
leaves extend downward. Colors are green, blue,
tan and pink.*

Velmoss Bud Vase

Vase, double bud, 8" h., triangular base
w/tall conical form joined to shorter
cylindrical form by figural leaf cluster,
mottled blue, No. 116-8" (ILLUS.) **248**
Vase, 12" h., ovoid body tapering to wide
cylindrical neck w/wide flat rim, angled
handles, mottled raspberry red,
No. 721-12", gold foil label **468**

VISTA (1920s)

*Embossed green coconut palm trees &
lavender blue pool against grey ground.*

Vista Bowl

Bowl, 7" d., 3½" h., deep, few minor flakes **300**

Bowl, 8⅜" d., 4" h., cylindrical form w/flat rim, unmarked (ILLUS.) **220**

Vase, 9¾" h., cylindrical body tapering to flared base, round shoulder w/flat molded mouth, unmarked **660**

WHITE ROSE (1940)

White roses and green leaves against a vertically combed ground of blended blue, brown shading to green or pink shading to green.

Console bowl, blended blue ground, No. 391-10", 10" l. **175**

Ewer, semi-ovoid w/high pointed handle at shoulder, blended blue ground, No. 990-10", 10" h. **295**

Urn-vase, spherical body on footring w/small loop handles flanking the flat mouth, blended blue ground, No. 388-7", 7" h. **248**

Urn-vase, pink & blue ground, No. 147-8", 8" h. . . **175**

Vase, 4" h., footed ovoid body w/lobed rim, pink ground, No. 978-4" **95**

Vase, 6" h., footed swelled cylindrical body w/a short notched neck flanked by pointed angled handles, pink shading to green ground, No. 979-6" **130**

Vase, 6" h., No. 979-6" h. **100**

Vase, 15½" h., footed baluster-form w/flaring split rim, long low side handles, blended blue ground, No. 992-15" **550**

WINDSOR (1931)

Brown or blue mottled glaze, some with leaves, vines and ferns, some with a repetitive band arrangement of small squares and rectangles in yellow and green.

Windsor Bowl

Bowl, 10⅝" l., 3½" h., angular end handles, slightly canted sides, geometric design against mottled terra cotta ground (ILLUS.) . . . **413**

Vase, 5" h., No. 545-5" **535**

Vase, 8" h., two-handled cylindrical body, decorated w/floral sprays in green on terra cotta ground, No. 552-8", black paper label & old sales room label w/price. . . . **660**

ZEPHYR LILY (1946)

Tall lilies and slender leaves adorn swirl-textured backgrounds of Bermuda Blue, Evergreen and Sienna Tan.

Basket, hanging-type, terra cotta ground, No. 472-5", 5" h. **175**

Basket, hanging-type, terra cotta ground, No. 472-5", 7½" h. **175**

Book ends, terra cotta ground, No. 16, 5½" h., pr. **231**

Bowl, 6" d., brown ground, No. 472-6" **95**

Console bowl, end handles, terra cotta ground, No. 479-14", 16½" **99**

Ewer, footed flaring lower body w/angled shoulder tapering to a tall forked neck w/upright tall spout, long low arched handle, blue ground, No. 23-10", 10" h. **200**

Flowerpot w/saucer, blue ground, No. 672-5", 5" h. **225**

Vase, 7" h., blue ground, No. 132-7" **160**

Vase, 8" h., two-handled, terra cotta ground **195**

Vase, 8½" h., a disc foot & short pedestal support a tall slightly swelled cylindrical body w/a thin-rolled rim, low curved handles from mid-body to the base of the pedestal, green ground, No. 133-8" **175**

Vase, 12½" h., handles rising from shoulder of compressed globular base to middle of slender neck w/flaring mouth, blended blue ground, No. 140-12" (ILLUS.) **220**

Vase, 12½" h., handles rising from shoulder of compressed globular base to middle of slender neck w/flaring mouth, green ground, No. 140-12" **295**

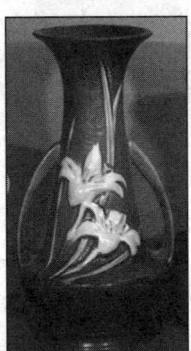

Zephyr Lily Vase

ROYAL BAYREUTH

Royal Bayreuth Mark

Good china in numerous patterns and designs has been made at the Royal Bayreuth factory in Tettau, Germany since 1794. Listings below are by the company's lines, plus miscellaneous pieces. Interest in this china remains at a peak and prices continue to rise. Pieces listed carry the company's blue mark except where noted otherwise.

CORINTHIAN

Corinthian Candlestick

Candlestick, classical figures on black
   ground, tall (ILLUS.) **$195**
Loving cup, three-handled, 4½" h. 150
Plate, 8" d., classical figures on black ground . . . 135
Sugar bowl, open, handled, classical
   figures on black ground 65

DEVIL & CARDS

Beverage set, 5" pitcher & four 4" h. mugs,
   5 pcs. 1,800

MOTHER-OF-PEARL

Creamer & cov. sugar bowl, paneled
   Oyster & Pearl mold, pearlized finish, pr. 475
Creamer & open sugar bowl, Grape mold,
   pearlized finish, pr. 155

ROSE TAPESTRY

Rose Tapestry Basket

Basket, yellow roses, 3¾ x 4¼" (ILLUS.) 350
Basket, double pink roses, 5 x 5" 450
Basket, white roses, 5 x 5" 425
Creamer, two-color roses (tiny glaze nick) 295
Creamer, red roses, 2½" h. 250
Hatpin holder, 4½" h. 395
Model of a shoe, low, two-color roses 495

Planter, squatty bulbous base below wide
   gently flaring sides w/a ruffled rim, small
   loop handles near the base, pink roses,
   2¾" h. (gold wear on rim) 250

SUNBONNET BABIES

Bell, babies fishing 450
Candleholder, shield-back style, Babies
   fishing scene 495
Candlestick, Babies ironing scene. 325
Candlesticks, 4¼" h., pr. 435
Chamberstick 350
Cup & saucer 225

Sunbonnet Babies Hair Receiver

Hair receiver, cov., babies washing, 2¾" h.
   (ILLUS.) 400
Model of a lady's shoe 450
Relish dish, 4 x 8" 300
Stamp box, cov. 235

TOMATO ITEMS

Tomato Creamer & Sugar Bowl

Tomato box, cov., large 45
Tomato creamer & cov. sugar bowl,
   pr. (ILLUS.) 138
Tomato mustard jar, cov. w/leaf-shaped
   underplate, the set 75

Tomato Water Pitcher

Tomato pitcher, water, 6" (ILLUS.) 600
Tomato salt & pepper shakers, pr. 110
Tomato sugar bowl, cov. 110

MISCELLANEOUS

Basket, tapestry, scene of prince & his lady. 575
Candlestick, Brittany Women decoration, 5¼" h. . . . 75
Center bowl, embossed leaf & floral mold
  decorated w/grape clusters & leaves on
  green ground, lion mark in blue, 11" d. 121
Chamberstick, figural gorilla 700
Chamberstick, girl w/dog scene 235
Chargers, "Mirror Image" peacock
  decoration, 12½" d., pr. 950
Covered box, 2"h., 3½" x 2", w/ship scene,
  background colors of blue, peach & yellow 70
Creamer, figural bellringer 400
Creamer, figural bull, brown 265
Creamer, figural bull, grey 250
Creamer, figural clown, red suit 450
Creamer, figural crow, black. 165
Creamer, figural duck 315
Creamer, figural elk 175
Creamer, figural frog. 100
Creamer, figural Milk Maid, red dress, 4¾" h. . . . 950
Creamer, figural orange 150
Creamer, figural pansy, purple 288
Creamer, figural pelican 275
Creamer, figural perch 650

Figural Poppy Creamer

Creamer, figural poppy (ILLUS.). 245
Creamer, figural red parrot handle 700
Creamer, figural robin. 280
Creamer, figural rose, pink 325
Creamer, figural St. Bernard. 285
Creamer, figural water buffalo 225
Creamer, pinched spout-style, "tapestry,"
  hounds & stags decoration, 4" h. 350
Creamer, pinched spout-style, "tapestry,"
  Portrait Lady decoration, 3¾" h. 350
Creamer & cov. sugar bowl, Brittany
  Women color decoration, pr. 265
Creamer & cov. sugar bowl, figural apple, pr. . . 435
Creamer & open sugar bowl, figural Grape
  Cluster, pr. (ILLUS. of creamer) 320
Dish, maple leaf-shaped, "tapestry," scene
  of a courting Colonial couple 225

Figural Grape Cluster Creamer

Hair receiver, cov., ruffled, Mountain Goat
  scenic decoration, large 145
Humidor, cov., figural man w/pipe,
  green, 5½" h. 585
Mug, child's, Dutch Children decoration, 3¼" h. . . . 85
Mustard jar, cov., figural lobster. 125
Mustard jar, cov., figural poppy, red 229
Pitcher, milk, figural alligator 850
Pitcher, milk, tankard, pastoral cow scene. 195
Pitcher, 3" h., decorated w/hunting scene 70
Pitcher, 3¼" h., Highland Goats scene 165
Pitcher, 4" h., nursery rhyme, "Little Jack
  Horner" scene. 165
Pitcher, milk, 4¾" h., figural lemon. 350
Pitcher, milk, 5" h., figural rooster, white 425
Pitcher, milk, 5" h., figural watermelon 523
Pitcher, water, 6" h., figural apple 748
Pitcher, water, 6" h., figural pelican. 1,400
Pitcher, water, 6½" h., pinched spout,
  scenic decoration of three Arab horsemen. . . . 115
Pitcher, 6¾" h., wide ovoid body w/a flaring
  lightly scalloped base & a long pinched
  spout, "tapestry" finish w/a color
  landscape "Don Quixote" scene 523
Pitcher, 7" h., water, figural coachman, ... 2,200
Pitcher, 7" h., water, figural elk, ... 1,050
Planter, Little Jack Horner scene 350
Plate, scene of girl w/dog 325
Plate, 8" d., figural strawberry. 165
Plate, 8½" d., decorated w/h.p. white, pink &
  lavender roses, ivory ground 185
Powder jar, cov., Jack & the Beanstalk scene. . . 285
Relish dish, handled, "tapestry," colored
  chrysanthemums decoration, 8" l. 375
Salt & pepper shakers, decorated w/scene
  of boy w/donkey, pr. 95
Salt & pepper shakers, figural radish, pr. 350
Salt & pepper shakers, figural robin, pr. 280
Salt shaker, tapestry, Highland goats
  decoration. 135
Shaving mug, figural elk head 500
Toothpick holder, figural elk head. 230
Toothpick holder, figural lobster claw &
  lettuce leaf 77
Toothpick holder, Mold 643, decorated
  w/roses & other flowers in pink & cream
  w/green leaves 210

Toothpick holder, ovoid w/side handle,
scene of Dutch boy & goose **195**

Toothpick holder, scuttle-shaped, Dutch
boy & girl scene **195**

Toothpick holder, three-handled, decorated
w/scene of female horse rider & dogs **143**

Toothpick holder, triangular w/overhead
handle, three section decorated w/house,
bird & woman w/baskets **110**

Toothpick holder, tub-shaped, decorated
w/Dutch girl pulling wagon **77**

Vase, 7½" h., 5" d., sheep grazing
color decoration **345**

Vase, miniature, 2¾" h., 2¼" d., nearly
spherical body on three tiny feet,
small cylindrical gold mouth, blue,
yellow & green ground decorated w/a
color scene of an Arab horseback rider
in the foreground & another horse in
the background. **75**

Vase, miniature, 3¼" h., 2" d., ovoid body
w/a low silver neck band, decorated w/a
landscape w/sheep against a shaded
brown to green background **75**

Vase, miniature, 3¼" h., 2" d., tall tapering
cylindrical body below a bulbous
spherical shoulder & flat mouth, a light
blue & pink shading to green, yellow &
brown ground decorated w/a large
colorful peacock near a tree, unmarked **75**

Vase, miniature, 3⅝" h., 1½" d., slender
ovoid body w/a tiny neck, shaded blue,
pink & brown ground decorated w/a color
scene of four foxhunters on horseback
w/a pack of hounds, unmarked **50**

Vase, miniature, 4" h., 3" d., "tapestry,"
ovoid body tapering to a tiny neck,
decorated w/a color landscape of a castle
& village by a lake below mountains **275**

Vase, 7½" h., "tapestry," gold handles,
pheasant scene **425**

Vase, 8" h., bulbous w/stick spout, decorated
w/scene of two fishermen in boat **400**

ROYAL DUX

Royal Dux Marks

  This factory in Bohemia was noted for the
figural porcelain wares in the Art Nouveau style
which were exported around the turn of the
century. Other notable figural pieces were
produced through the 1930s and the factory was
nationalized after World War II.

Centerpiece, figural, modeled in high-relief
as branches & foliage in a buff glaze, the
heads of four maidens incorporated into
the upwardly flowing form ending in
large leaves forming a bowl, marked
"Royal Dux Bohemia" & w/a large "E"
in a triangle, impressed "333 13,"
18½" h. (restoration). **$748**

Figure group, a young boy w/a Setter dog,
enameled & gilt-trimmed, Czechoslovakia
mark, early 20th c., 13¼" h. **288**

Detailed Royal Dux Figure Groups

Figure groups, one w/a shepherd playing
pipes w/sheep around his feet & standing
next to an Ionic column, the other w/a
shepherdess w/a staff standing w/goats
at her feet, also beside an Ionic column,
fine enameled decoration, late 19th -
early 20th c., 16½" h., pr. (ILLUS.) **748**

Serving dish, figural, a maiden & a pair of
lovebirds on an open shell dish, ca. 1900,
8½" h. **230**

Vases, 19" h., Art Nouveau design w/an
ivory ground decorated w/stylized leaves
& berries in relief, raised "Czechoslovakia"
mark, early 20th c., pr. **978**

ROYAL VIENNA

Royal Vienna Mark

  The second factory in Europe to make hard
paste porcelain was established in Vienna in
1719 by Claud Innocentius de Paquier. The
factory underwent various changes of
administration through the years and finally
closed in 1865. Since then, however, the
porcelain has been reproduced by various

factories in Austria and Germany, many of which have also reproduced the early beehive mark. Early pieces, naturally, bring far higher prices than the later ones or the reproductions.

Royal Vienna Cabinet Plate

Cabinet plate, 9½" d., finely painted in the center w/the birth of Venus, the young beauty nude & recumbent on the waves w/five cupids hovering above her, staring down or blowing conch shells, within an elaborately gilt foliate scroll & trelliswork border reserved on a cream ground within a gilt edged rim, shield mark painted in blue, impressed factory marks & letters, title painted in red script, ca. 1900 (ILLUS.) **$1,495**

Cabinet plate, 9⅝" d., finely painted in the center w/portrait of Bianca, the young maiden w/long curly brown hair, wearing a pearl necklace & white chemise, within a gilt foliate frame & cobalt ground border gilt w/interlinking arched panels, shield factory mark in underglaze blue, faint impressed numeral & title in black script, signed Hamer, ca. 1900 .... **747**

Charger, round, the center decorated w/a large colorful scene of Roman soldiers under canopy in the forest being served by a kneeling maiden, gilt scrolled & floral border w/red & blue panels, titled on the reverse "Vortigern and Rovena," overglaze blue beehive mark on back, 16" d. **1,725**

Figural group, modeled as an amorous man wearing a pale yellow hat, buff jacket & breeches, seated beside a fashionable lady wearing a floral decorated dress, accompanied by a young boy seated on the grass behind them, all beneath a tree on a domed shaped base, shield factory mark in underglaze blue, impressed letter "P", 19th c., 9" h. **287**

Plate, 9½" d., cabinet-type, the decorated cobalt blue border around a central h.p. figural scene, titled on back "Soll ich?," underglaze-blue beehive mark, ca. 1900 ..... **518**

Urn, cov., cylindrical body painted w/continuous scene of classical figures on stippled gilt ground, raised on three fluted column supports w/paw feet on stepped circular base, all decorated in gilding on a cobalt ground, removable waisted neck & cover w/similar decoration, pseudo shield factory mark in underglaze blue, titles in blue script, 17½" h. **3,220**

ROYAL WORCESTER

Royal Worcester Marks

This porcelain has been made by the Royal Worcester Porcelain Co. at Worcester, England, from 1862 to the present. Royal Worcester is distinguished from wares made at Worcester between 1751 and 1862 that are referred to as only Worcester by collectors.

Basket, scrolled sides, ivory ground w/yellow & orange tinting & gilt trim, No. 1483, 1892, 10⅜" l., 9¼" h. **$489**

Equestrian group, George Washington on horseback, modeled by Bernard Winskill, number 80 from a limited edition of 750, black printed, painted & incised factory marks, w/wooden base, ca. 1975, overall 17⅞" h. **402**

Equestrian group, Napoleon Bonaparte on horseback crossing the Alps, modeled by Bernard Winskill, from a limited edition of 750, black printed, painted & incised factory marks, w/wooden base, ca. 1969, 15½" h. overall **402**

Royal Worcester Ewer & Covered Vase

Ewer, bottle-form, Patent Metallic-type, bulbous body tapering to a tall cylindrical neck w/a pointed rim spout, a long curling gilt figural lizard handle, decorated in color w/a large sprig of blossoms against a creamy ground, ca. 1886, chip, 8¾" h. (ILLUS. left) 230

Ewer, compressed spherical body beneath attenuated gently flaring cylindrical neck w/gently curving gilt spout, decorated in colored enamels & gilt w/floral sprays on cream ground, upper rim & C-scroll handle pierced w/foliate scrollwork, puce printed factory mark w/year letter, impressed factory marks & numerals, painted letters & numerals, ca. 1887, 14¾" h. 468

Figure, "June," barefoot boy playing harmonica, his dog by his side, No. 3456, designed by F. Doughty, 1949 125

Figure, Sabrina, terra cotta & turquoise glazed figure, finely modeled as a classical maiden partly covered by a voluminous billowing drape, tied around her middle w/a belt, holding an inverted vase & standing barefoot on a manganese glazed drum-shaped base, all on a turquoise glazed cylindrical column molded w/foliate borders heightened in gilding, impressed factory mark, ca. 1880, 25⅜" h. (small chips to headdress & fingers on left hand) 1,610

Figure group, Parian, allegorical group of Peace blessing the Arts, colored & glazed figures modeled as three classical maidens, each wearing a long flowing robe, center maiden w/laurel wreath in her right hand, standing w/arms outstretched & hands on the heads of the other two maidens sitting flanking her, all surrounded by discarded mallet, sword, shield & anvil on an oblong base, impressed factory mark & clay mark "R," ca. 1880, 11½" h. 632

Plate with Scene of Tewkesbury

Plate, 10¾" d., round w/irregular border, decorated overall w/a landscape of the village of Tewkesbury done in natural colors, gilt rim band, artist-signed, dated 1953 (ILLUS.). 225

Vase, cov., 9¼" h., bulbous ovoid body tapering to a short flared neck, fitted domed cover w/molded gilt scroll band & gilt pointed finial, the base & neck molded w/gilt foliate designs & pierced lattice panels around the neck, ornate gilt scrolled shoulder handles, ca. 1892 (ILLUS. right with ewer) 403

Lovely Royal Worcester Vases

Vases, 9" h., gilt-trimmed scroll feet supporting tall swelled cylindrical body w/a short wide reticulated cylindrical neck, each decorated w/a scene of a bird perched on a thistle, a butterfly nearby, in natural colors on a shaded tan ground, gilt rim bands, pr. (ILLUS.) 2,016

RUSSEL WRIGHT DESIGNS

IROQUOIS
CASUAL CHINA
Russel Wright

Russel
Wright
MFG. BY
STEUBENVILLE

Russel Wright Marks

The innovative dinnerwares designed by Russel Wright and produced by various companies beginning in the late 1930s were an immediate success with a society that was turning to a more casual and informal lifestyle. His designs, with their flowing lines and unconventional shapes, were produced in many different colors which allowed the hostess to arrange a creative table. Although not antique, these designs, which we list below by line and manufacturer, are highly collectible. In addition to dinnerwares, Wright was also known as a trend-setter in the design of furniture, glassware, lamps, fabric and a multitude of other household goods.

AMERICAN MODERN (Steubenville Pottery Co.)

Coffeepot, cov., black chutney. $265

Coffeepot, cov., demitasse, granite grey 235
Cup & saucer, cantaloupe 35
Hostess plate, chartreuse 75
Pitcher, water, 12" h., granite grey 110

CASUAL CHINA (Iroquois China Company)

Butter dish, cov., pink sherbet 95
Coffeepot, cov., demitasse, avocado yellow 135
Cup & saucer, sugar white 40
Gumbo soup bowl, handled, cantaloupe, 21 oz.. . 20
Mug, sugar white 95
Vegetable dish, open, cantaloupe, 10" d. 14

SATSUMA

These decorated wares have been produced in Japan since the end of the 18th century. The early pieces are scarce and high-priced. Later Satsuma wares are plentiful and, with prices rising, as highly collectible as earlier pieces.

Large Satsuma Vase

Charger, round, Thousand Flowers patt., Satsum mon in gold on brown, signed, early 20th c. $403
Tea bowl, deep rounded sides, finely decorated on the interior w/a clamshell-shaped reserves enclosing landscapes, courtiers & a central panel of the underwater palace of the dragon king, the exterior decorated w/room interiors & landscapes, the above entirely enclosed in brocade grounds, late 19th c., 4¾" d. 1,840
Urn, cov., wide baluster-form body, domed cover w/gilded foo dog finial, decorated w/pastel enameled scenes w/flowers & butterflies, late 19th c., 18¾" h. 83
Vase, 18" h., domed foot below tall square-shaped body, the narrow shoulder tapering to a short wide cylindrical neck w/slightly flared rim, overall design of Buddist Immortals, highlighted w/heavy gilt trim, late 19th c. (ILLUS.) 575

SCHAFER & VATER

Founded in Rudolstadt, Thuringia, Germany in 1890, the Schafer and Vater Porcelain Factory specialized in decorative

pieces of porcelain usually in white or colored bisque. They produced many novelty figural items such as creamers, toothpick holders, boxes and hatpin holders and also produced a line of jasper ware with white relief decoration in imitation of the famous Wedgwood jasper wares. The firm also decorated whiteware blanks. The company ceased production in 1962 and collectors now seek out their charming pieces which may be marked with a crown over a starburst containing the script letter "R."

Schafer & Vater Mark

Ashtray, figural, jasper ware, grotesque man's head, open mouth w/small holes above simulated whiskers, reads "I Want To Be Shaved" & illegible writing below mouth, 3½" $95
Dresser box, cov., jasper ware, egg-shaped, cameo medallion top w/double silhouettes, lavender, 3 x 3 x 4" 95
Flask, figural Santa in white coat, 6" h. 265
Pitcher, 3" h., jasper ware, Victorian cameo side medallion, light green w/gold trim 45
Toothpick holder, figural, model of a human skull 25

SÈVRES & SÈVRES-STYLE

Sèvres Marks

Some of the most desirable porcelain ever produced was made at the Sèvres factory, originally established at Vincennes, France, and transferred, through permissioin of Madame de Pompadour, to Sèvres as the Royal Manufactory about the middle of the 18th century. King Louis XV took sole responsibility for the works in 1759 when production of hard paste wares began. Between 1850 and 1900, many biscuit and soft-paste pieces were made again. Fine early pieces are scarce and high-priced. Many of those available today are late productions. The various Sèvres marks have been copied and pieces listed as "Sèvres-Style" are similar to actual Sèvres wares, but not necessarily from that factory. Three of the many Sèvres marks are illustrated.

Box, cov., Sevres-style, rectangular w/fluted corners, enamel & gilt-decorated w/floral sides & a landscape w/dogs & cats on the cover, late 19th c., 3⅜" l. **$230**

Dresser box w/hinged cover, oval cartouche-shaped, the low domed cover h.p. w/a large reserve in color of two lovers in a floral garden, framed by gilt scrolling on the cobalt blue ground, cobalt ground base w/further gilt trim, gilt-metal hinged mounts at the rim, the cover opening to reveal an interior h.p. w/florals, artist-signed, base marked "Chateau de Touceneies" w/a blue overglaze ribbon mark, late 19th c., 12" l. **1,150**

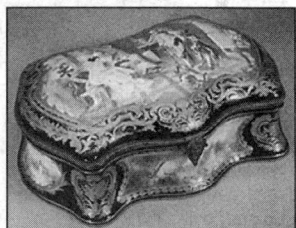

Ornate Sèvres Jewelry Box

Jewelry box, cov., rectangular w/serpentine sides, the slightly domed cover painted w/a large figural scene titled "L'Accord des Violons" framed by ornate gilt scrolling on a cobalt blue ground, the sides w/various color landscape vignettes within gilt scroll borders on a cobalt blue ground, signed illegibly, mid-19th c., 10½ x 15", 5" h. (ILLUS.) **5,175**

Platter, 19" l., oval, mounted in a narrow gilt-metal frame w/pierced scroll end handles & supported on pierced scroll legs, the center of the platter h.p. w/an oval reserve w/a colorful 18th c. courtship scene w/a couple in a landscape, the wide border band in cobalt blue w/ornate gilt scrolling, artist-signed, marked on base w/overglaze blue ribbon mark, late 19th c. **2,300**

Potpourri vases, cov., two-handled w/oval shield-shape, on pedestal stem & oval section cylindrical base, finely painted on either side w/panels of flowers within gilt cartouches on a turquoise ground gilt w/leaves & foliate scrollwork, waisted neck pierced w/single row of ovals beneath a domed cover, mounted as a table lamp, signed "K. Pirkner," late 19th c., vase 13", pr. **4,600**

Urns, a short wide cylindrical neck w/leaf-cast ormolu rim above a wide rounded shoulder above a sharply tapering body resting on an ormolu leaf-tip bracket above a slender porcelain pedestal & round foot fitted onto a thick ormolu trophy- and scroll-cast foot, outswept upright ormolu shoulder handles w/classical lady face terminals, the body in cobalt blue trimmed around the neck & down the body & pedestal w/ornate gilt scrolling, the center side of each h.p. w/a colorful 18th c. interior scene w/figures, artist-signed, porcelain marked w/overglaze blue ribbon mark, late 19th c., 24½" h., pr. **7,820**

Vases, cov., tall urn-form bodies, a slender pedestal base on a scrolled ormolu foot tapering to a ormolu connector ring to the tall tapering urn-form body, ormolu scroll rim mount continuing to ornate scrolled & arched handles, the tapering domed cover w/a gilt pineapple finial, a soft green ground, the body decorated w/a large full-length color portrait of an Art Nouveau maiden between large flowers all trimmed w/ornate gilt highlights, further gilt trim on the cover & base, ca. 1900, pr. **6,875**

Vases, 36" h., tall classical ovoid body w/a trumpet neck & raised on a ringed trumpet foot, cobalt blue ground decorated around the body w/gilt flowers, gilt bands at rim, base of neck, top & rim of pedestal base, marked "Décoré À Sèvres 85," late 19th c., pr. **4,600**

SHAWNEE

Shawnee
U.S.A.

Shawnee Mark

    The Shawnee Pottery operated in Zanesville, Ohio, from 1937 until 1961. Much of the early production was sold to chain stores and mail-order houses including Sears, Roebuck, Woolworth and others. Planters, cookie jars and vases, along with the popular "Corn King" oven ware line, are among the collectible items which are plentiful and still reasonably priced. Reference numbers used here are taken from Mark E. Supnick's book, Collecting Shawnee Pottery, The Collector's Guide to Shawnee Pottery *by Duane and Janice Vanderbilt, or* Shawnee Pottery - An Identification & Value Guide *by Jim and Bev Mangus.*

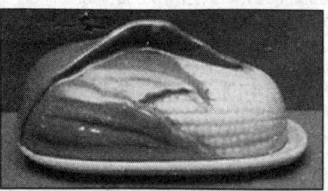

Corn King Quarter-pound Butter

Bank - cookie jar, figural Winnie Pig,
    orange trim **$350**
Butter dish, cov., Corn King line, No. 72,
    ¼ lb. (ILLUS.) 60
Casserole, cov., Corn King line, No. 74, 1½ qt. . . . 55
Cookie jar, Corn King line, No. 66, 10½" h. 90
Cookie jar, embossed Little Chef patt. 70
Cookie jar, figural Dutch Boy (Jack) 225
Cookie jar, figural Dutch Girl (Jill) 50
Cookie jar, figural Dutch Girl, tulip decoration
    & gold trim 298
Cookie jar, figural elephant, pink 50
Cookie jar, figural Fruit Basket 88
Cookie jar, figural Jumbo (Lucky) Elephant,
    decal decoration & gold trim 750
Cookie jar, figural Owl 108
Cookie jar, figural Owl, gold trim & hand-
    decoration 150
Cookie jar, figural Smiley Pig, blue collar 140
Cookie jar, figural Smiley Pig w/tulip
    decoration 200
Cookie jar, figural Winnie Pig, blue collar 200
Cookie jar, figural Winnie Pig, blue collar,
    gold trim 400
Creamer, figural Smiley Pig, yellow & blue
    decoration 95
Cup & saucer, Corn King line, Nos. 90 & 91 65
Figurine, model of Puppy Dog 80
Figurine, model of rabbit, sitting 80
Figurine, model of raccoon 80
Figurine, model of squirrel 80
Pitcher, ball-type, Dutch Tulip patt. 105
Pitcher, figural Smiley Pig w/red & blue flowers. . 165
Planter, model of a globe 40
Planter, model of chick pulling egg on
    wheels, No. 730 35
Platter, 12" l., oval, Corn King line, No. 96 55
Relish or corn ear holder, Corn King line,
    No. 79 40

Large Corn King Salt & Peppers

Salt & pepper shakers, figural, Corn King
    line, No. 77, large range size, 5¼" h.,
    pr. (ILLUS.) 40
Salt & pepper shakers, figural Owl, white
    w/green eyes, pr. 50
Salt & pepper shakers, figural Puss 'n
    Boots, gold trim, small, pr. 85

Salt & pepper shakers, figural Smiley Pig,
    color trim, small, pr. 45
Salt & pepper shakers, figural Watering
    Can, small, pr. 30
Sock darner, stylized standing figure,
    painted trim in pink or blue, each 85
Sugar bowl, cov., Corn King line, No. 78 40
Teapot, cov., figural Granny Ann, green
    apron w/gold trim & gold lace on shoulders . . . 235
Teapot, cov., figural Granny Ann, lavender
    apron w/gold trim & decals 225
Wall pocket, bust of girl w/doll, No. 810 65
Wall pocket, model of a birdhouse, No. 830,
    brown & tan w/gold trim 30
Wall pocket, model of a clock, No. 530 40
Wall pocket, model of a grandfather clock,
    No. 1261 50

SPATTERWARE

This ceramic ware takes its name from the "spattered" decoration, in various colors, generally used to trim pieces hand-painted with rustic center designs of flowers, birds, houses, etc. Popular in the early 19th century, most was imported from England.

Related wares, called "stick spatter," had free-hand designs applied with pieces of cut sponge attached to sticks, hence the name. Examples date from the 19th and early 20th century and were produced in England, Europe and America. Some early spatter-decorated wares were marked by the manufacturers, but not many. 20th century reproductions are also sometimes marked, including those produced by Boleslaw Cybis.

Creamer, bulbous body w/C-form handle &
    arched spout, Rose patt., free-hand
    flower in red, green & black in center
    w/blue spatter ground, 3⅝" h. (stains
    flakes on table ring & chips on rim) **$303**
Creamer, footed bulbous paneled body
    w/scrolled C-form handle & high arched
    spout, Peafowl patt., free-hand red, blue,
    green & black bird w/red spatter, 5½" h. 1,375
Cup, handleless, free-hand Gooney bird in
    blue, teal green, red & black, blue spatter
    ground (flakes on table ring) 220
Cup & saucer, handleless, miniature, Fort
    patt., green, black & red (stains, chip on
    rim of saucer & cup w/hairline) 187
Cup & saucer, handleless, Peafowl patt.,
    free-hand red, blue, yellow & black bird
    w/red spatter border (minor roughness &
    small flakes w/chips on table rings) 413
Cup & saucer, handleless, Peafowl patt.,
    free-hand red, blue, yellow & black bird
    w/blue spatter border (minor edge flakes) 605

Pitcher, water, 10⅝" h., tall tapering paneled body w/high arched spout & D-form handle, overall light blue spatter on white ground (chips & hairline on spout) **220**

Plate, 7¾" d., Peafowl patt., free-hand red, green, blue & black bird, red spatter border (wear, scratches & stains, blue on bird's breast flaked) **413**

Plate, 8¼" d., Peafowl patt., blue, yellow, red & black w/purple spatter over bird's head & border (blue on breast flaked) **440**

Plate, 8¼" d., Rose patt. w/flower in red, blue, teal green & black, blue spatter ground **330**

Platter, 14¼" l., octagonal, w/blue transfer-printed eagle w/shield in center, blue spatter border (minor stains & fain hairlines). **880**

Teapot, cov., Gothic style paneled design w/angled handle, swan's-neck spout & domed cover w/blossom finial, Peafowl patt., free-hand blue, yellow, green & black bird w/red spatter ground, 7⅛" h. (stains & small flakes, lid w/old edge repair) **880**

Teapot, Gothic style paneled tapering body w/angled handle, swan's neck spout & domed cover w/blossom finial, overall blue spatter on white, 9½" h. (chips) **341**

Waste bowl, Fort patt. in red, green, black & yellow, blue spatter border, 5⅜" d., 3⅛"h. (wear & stains w/pinpoint edge flakes) **1,155**

STICK & CUT SPONGE

From left: Stick Spatter Shallow Bowl Gaudy Stick Spatter Chop Plate

Bowl, 14½" d., 3" h., border decorated w/stick spatter floral design in red, blue, green, yellow & purple, marked "Maastricht" (ILLUS.) **88**

Plate, 8¾" d., ironstone w/blue design stick spatter border & purple transfer-printed eagle w/shield, English registry mark w/"Gem, R. Hammersley". **165**

Plate, 9½" d., Rabbit patt., black transfer-printed border band w/six rabbits & three frogs trimmed in yellow & green, free-hand decorated center w/ring of cut-sponge flowers & red striping **633**

Plate, chop, 16¼" d., decorated w/free-hand blue flowers & red & green cut-sponge blossoms & leaves, "Villeroy & Boch" (ILLUS.) **413**

Wash bowl & pitcher, 10¾" h. pitcher, ovoid body w/arched spout & C-form handle, center design of large stylized four-petal flower in red & green, overall blue sponging, 12⅝" d. bowl w/same center design & bordered by blue sponging, the set (chip on back edge of bowl rim) **1,375**

SPONGEWARE

Spongeware's designs were spattered, sponged or daubed on in colors, sometimes with a piece of cloth. Blue on white was the most common type, but mottled tans, browns and greens on yellowware were also popular. Spongeware generally has an overall pattern with a coarser look than Spatterwares, to which it is loosely related. These wares were extensively produced in England and America well into the 20th century.

Spongeware Pig Bank

Bank, figural pig, teal green & tan sponging on cream ground, glaze wear on ears & shallow flake on one foot, 6" l. (ILLUS.) **$275**

Bean pot, bulbous flat-bottomed body tapering to a flat mouth, small loop handle at shoulder, wide spiral bands of blue sponging on white, marked "3 qt.," 6½" h. (lid missing) **165**

Bowl, 3¼" d., cov., miniature, flaring sides w/domed cover & button finial, wire bail w/wooden handle, blue sponging on white (hairline & chips) **468**

Bowl, 10¼" d., 5" h., blue & white w/two blue accent bands, ca. 1880 (two minor exterior rim chips). **143**

Jar, bulbous ovoid body tapering slightly to flared rim, blue on white, 4¼" h. (pinpoint rim flakes) **798**

Jar, cov., ovoid w/molded rim, brown, blue & green sponging on white w/black transfer-printed label reading "Spaulding's Pure Fresh Cookies," 9¼" h. (chip on bottom edge). **220**

Jug, semi-ovoid body w/wire bail & wooden handle, labeled "Grandmother's Maple Syrup of 50 Years Ago" & "Mfg'd by F.H. Weeks, Akron, O" on bottom, blue sponging on white, 8" h. (chips) **1,375**

Mixing bowl, footed, deep slightly flared sides, blue sponging on white, 10" d., 5" h. (glaze wear on rim & internal hairline) . . . **220**

Spongeware Mixing Bowl

Mixing bowl, footed, deep flaring sides, bold repeating bands of blue sponging on white at base & below rim w/blue strips around center, chips on foot, 11¼" d., 5" h. (ILLUS.) **275**

Mug, cylindrical w/molded C-form handle, blue sponging on white, 3⅝" h. (slight crow's foot in bottom) **138**

Pitcher, 6" h., ovoid body w/C-form handle & pinched spout, blue on white w/brown slip interior (chips on lip & wear) **330**

Pitcher, 6½" h., cylindrical w/rim spout & D-form handle, olive green & white w/blue edge band (shallow chip on base) **275**

Pitcher, 6¾" h., cylindrical w/D-form handle, blue sponging on white w/center horizontal stripe (minor flake on table ring) . . . **605**

Pitcher, 6⅞" h., slightly tapering cylindrical body w/rim spout & D-form handle, yellowware w/sponging in brown, green & black (wear & minor chips) **165**

From left: Blue & White Spongeware Pitcher
Blue & White Bulbous Water Pitcher

Pitcher, 7" h., blue & white, ca. 1880, few minor glaze flecks at interior rim (ILLUS.) **330**

Pitcher, 9" h., tall slightly tapering cylindrical body w/pinched spout & C-form handle, relief-molded rose decoration, blue sponging on white **495**

Pitcher, water, 12" h., bulbous, blue & white w/three blue accent bands, ca. 1880, one minor glaze fleck at spout (ILLUS.) **358**

Pot, cylindrical w/pouring spout, wire bail & wooden handle, blue on white, 5¼" d., 4" h. (small rim chips) **385**

Ramekins/custard cups, blue on white, 3¼" d., 2¼" h. set of 6 (pieces are similar) **385**

Soap dish, rectangular w/rounded corners, blue w/a bit of red sponging on white, 4 x 6½" (small chips) **72**

Teapot, cov., miniature, squatty bulbous body w/C-form handle, swan's-neck spout & inset cover w/blossom finial, blue on white, 4⅛" h. (minor chips) **853**

STAFFORDSHIRE FIGURES

Small figures and groups made of pottery were produced by the majority of the Staffordshire, England potters in the 19th century and were used as mantel decorations or "chimney ornaments," as they were sometimes called. Pairs of dogs were favorites and were turned out by the carload, and 19th century pieces are still available. Well-painted reproductions also abound and collectors are urged to exercise caution before investing.

Cat, seated upright animal playing a bass viol, polychrome trim & spotted fur, 19th c., 4" h. (some minor glaze wear) **$86**

Dog, pearlware, hollow-molded, stylized creature w/head turned to the right & painted w/random patches of brown, blue & ocher, lying on a domed naturalistic base, ca. 1790-1810, 4⅛" h. (hair crack to hind quarters) **460**

From left: Staffordshire Spaniel Figure
Staffordshire Figure of Pug

Dog, Spaniel in seated position, molded fur & chain, large copper lustre spots & trim w/painted facial details, embossed numbers on bottom, 19th c., 10" h. (ILLUS.) **225**

Dogs, Pug in seated position w/ears erect, yellow eyes, black & red painted facial details, wearing black collar w/gilt padlock, second half 19th c., 10¼" h., pr. (ILLUS. of one) **1,265**

Dogs, Spaniel seated on his haunches, looking to his right & left respectively & wearing a collar w/lock, glazed in white w/gilt highlights, w/black & pink face markings, mounted as table lamps, late 19th c., 12½" h., pr. (one glass eye missing) **402**

Figure group, Scottish couple standing on oval base, polychrome trim, 19th c., 7⅞" h. (very minor chip & losses) **230**

Figure group, 'The Death of Nelson,' showing the dying admiral seated between two officers, the back modeled as his ship the Victory, polychrome decoration, rectangular base, mid-19th c. **518**

Figure of a hunter, standing on a rounded base, polychrome decoration, 19th c., 7⅛" h. (restoration to gun) **173**

Figure of a lute player, standing on a rounded base, polychrome decoration, 19th c., 5⅛" h. (restoration to lute, very minor chip) **115**

Figure of Dan O'Connell, minister wearing a green scarf & black coat w/gilt trim, standing beside a column covered w/blue & orange drape on a grassy oval base w/gilt title, ca. 1900, 17½" h. **575**

Staffordshire Pearlware Figure of Hercules

Figure of Hercules, pearlware, muscular bearded male wearing red, yellow & black loin cloth, resting on one knee on a black marbled square base w/his head lowered as he supports a pierced pale yellow globe representing the world on his shoulders, early 19th c., possibly by Obadiah Sherrat, minute chips, 11⅜" h. (ILLUS.) **575**

Figure of "The Lion Slayer," standing bearded man wearing a Scottish kilt & feathered hat, a dead lion beside him, polychrome trim, 19th c., 15¾" h. (some worn gilt) **220**

Horses, modeled w/right or left front leg raised & looking straight ahead, supported on an oval bright green base,

the animals in cream w/black spots, mane & facial markings, mid-19th c., 5¼" l., pr. **1,035**

STAFFORDSHIRE TRANSFER WARES

The process of transfer-printing designs on earthenwares developed in England in the late 18th century and by the mid-19th century most common ceramic wares were decorated in this manner, most often with romantic European or Oriental landscape scenes, animals or flowers. The earliest such wares were printed in dark blue but a little later light blue, pink, purple, red, black, green and brown were used. A majority of these wares were produced at various English potteries right up till the turn of the century but French and other European firms also made similar pieces and all are quite collectible. The best reference on this area is Petra Williams' book Staffordshire Romantic Transfer Patterns - Cup Plates and Early Victorian China *(Fountain House East, 1978). Also see other makers and HISTORICAL & COMMEMORATIVE WARES.*

Early Dark Blue Transfer Coffeepot

Coffeepot, cov., footed bulbous baluster-form body w/domed cover, long angled handle & swan's-neck spout, overall design of large roses & other flowers, dark blue, small chips, ca. 1830, 11" h. (ILLUS.) **$825**

Coffeepot, cov., footed bulbous ovoid body w/ringed & waisted neck w/molded rim & inset domed cover w/knob finial, swan's-neck spout & C-scroll handle, dark blue transfer of an English farmyard scene, ca. 1830, 11¼" h. (chips, spider crack, finial reglued) **523**

Cup & saucer, handleless, dark blue transfer of a boy fishing w/an English country house in the background, ca. 1830 (chip on foot) **165**

Gravy boat, Winter patt., pink, 6" l. **55**

Plate, 6" d., Palestine patt., pink **33**

Plate, 8" d., Canova patt., pink, T. Mayer **50**

Plate, 8" d., Carolin patt., purple, B. Hall **22**

Plate, 8¼" d., Palestine patt., pink **39**

Plate, 8½" d., Asiatic View patt., pink, marked "FD" **28**

Plate, 9" d., Asiatic Scenery patt., pink, marked "Jacksons" 50

Plate, 9" d., Lozere patt., light blue, Challinor..... 44

Plate, 9¼" d., Canova patt., pink, T. Mayer 66

Plate, 9½" d., Greek Statue patt., black 44

Plate, 10" d., California patt., light blue, J. Wedgwood 83

Plate, 10" d., Italy patt., light blue, marked "C.M. & S" 39

Plate, 10" d., lightly scalloped flanged rim, the center w/a black transfer scene of Victorian men & women riding safety-style bicycles, titled around scene "Les Sports No. 11 - Bicyclettes," dark blue floral & stem band border trim, back marked "Terre de Fer France," ca. 1900 44

Plates, 7½" d., Tyrolean patt., pink, WR & Co., pr. 66

Platter, 14⅝" l., oval, scrolling foliate border w/reserves of manor houses, a center reserve of game birds, dark blue, ca. 1840 (very minor rim chips & knife marks) 633

Platter, 15½" l., red floral border w/blue central reserve depicting a rural scene of an early train crossing an aqueduct w/a hillside village in the distance, England, late 19th c., (glaze crazing) 374

Early Staffordshire Platter

Platter, 16½" l., oval, scrolling foliate border w/reserves of manor houses, a center reserve of game birds, dark blue, ca. 1840, wear & crazing (ILLUS.) 935

Platter, 17½" l., Wild Rose patt., light blue (wear & minor stains, surface flakes on back) 275

Platter, 16¼ x 19", decorated w/central reserve depicting an American eagle carrying a patriotic banner in flight above a distant group of sailing vessels w/rays of the rising sun in the background, scrolled foliate border, teal green, England, mid-19th c., (minor staining, glaze wear) 460

Platter, 22" l., Chinese Views patt., light blue, R & W 83

Shaving mug, Asiatic Scenery patt., light blue, 3" h.................................. 55

Undertray, round, Italian Flower Garden patt., embossed rim & handles, 9" d. 77

STANGL POTTERY

Stangl Mark

Johann Martin Stangl, who first came to work for the Fulper Pottery in 1910 as a ceramic chemist and plant superintendent, acquired a financial interest and became president of the company in 1926. The name of the firm was changed to Stangl Pottery in 1929 and at that time much of the production was devoted to a high grade dinnerware to enable the company to survive the Depression years. One of the earliest solid-color dinnerware patterns was their Colonial line, introduced in 1926. In the 1930s it was joined by their Americana pattern. After 1942 these early patterns were followed by a wide range of hand-decorated patterns featuring flowers and fruits with a few decorated with animals or human figures.

Around 1940 a very limited edition of porcelain birds, patterned after the illustrations in John James Audubon's "Birds of America," was issued. Stangl subsequently began production of less expensive ceramic birds and these proved to be popular during the war years, 1940-46. Each bird was handpainted and each was well marked with impressed, painted or stamped numerals which indicated the species and the size.

All operations ceased at the Trenton, New Jersey plant in 1978.

Two reference books which collectors will find helpful are The Collectors Handbook of Stangl Pottery by Norma Rehl (The Democrat Press, 1979), and Stangl Pottery by Harvey Duke (Wallace-Homestead, 1994).

BIRDS

Stangl Broadbill Hummingbird

Bird of Paradise, No. 3408, 5½" h. $125

Broadbill Hummingbird, No. 3629, 4½" h. (ILLUS.) 165

Cardinal, revised, No. 3444, 6½" h. 220

Cockatoo, No. 3405, 6" h. 54
Cockatoo, medium, No. 3580, multi-colored,
  8⅞" h. 120
Cockatoo, No. 3584, 11⅜" h. 325
Cockatoos, double, No. 3405-D, 9½" h. 167
Duck, standing, No. 3431, 8" h. 385
Evening Grosbeak, No. 3813, 5" h. 100
Gray Cardinal, (Pyrrhuloxia), No. 3596, 4¾" h. . . . 65
Parrot, No. 2449 169
Rieffers Humming Bird, No. 3628, 4½" h. 150
Yellow Warbler, (Prothonatary), No. 3447, 5" h. . . . 65

DINNERWARES & ARTWARES

Ashtray, Caribbean patt. 50
Bowl, Caribbean patt. 6
Candleholders, Caribbean patt., pr. 30
Coaster, Country Life patt. 25
Cup, Country Life patt. 30
Cup & saucer, Country Life patt. 40
Cup & saucer, demitasse, Ranger patt. 125
Cup & three-part dish, Mealtime Special
  patt., Kiddieware line 145
Dish, fruit, 5½", Country Life, Rooster decoration . . 35
Lamp base, Fruit patt. 250
Mug, Golden Blossom patt. 12
Plate, 11" d., Country Life patt., farmer
  baling hay decoration 200
Plate, "Pony Trail" patt., h.p. boy on pony,
  Kiddieware line 225
Plate, 6" d., bread & butter, Country Life patt. 15
Plate, 8" d., Country Life patt., pig at
  fence decoration 100
Plate, 12½" d., chop, Country Life patt.,
  farmhouse decoration 275
Plate, 14½" d., chop, Country Life patt. 300
Salt & pepper shakers, Star Flower patt., pr. 20
Vase, 13" h., model of a horse head, No. 3611 . . 475

STONEWARE

Stoneware is essentially a vitreous pottery, impervious to water even in its unglazed state, that has been produced by potteries all over the world for centuries. Utilitarian wares such as crocks, jugs, churns and the like, were the most common productions in the numerous potteries that sprang into existence in the United States during the 19th century. These items were often enhanced by the application of a cobalt blue oxide decoration. In addition to the coarse, primarily salt-glazed stonewares, there are other categories of stoneware known by such special names as basalt, jasper and others.

Batter pail, w/bail handle, unusual cobalt
  blue slip-quilled tree stump design,
  "6" in blue script, probably Whites Utica,
  unsigned, ca. 1860, 6 qt., 11¾" h. (chips
  at spout & two through lines extending
  from rim) $660

Bowl, ovoid w/molded rim & eared handles,
  brushed cobalt blue plume design front &
  back, blue accents on ears, attributed to
  Hudson Valley region of NY, ca. 1840,
  3 gal., 11" h. (professional restoration to
  age cracks throughout & just touching the
  blue, some interior lime staining) 275
Butter churn, w/eared handles, thick
  brushed cobalt blue paddletail design,
  "N.A. White & Son, Utica, NY," ca. 1885,
  5 gal., 16½" h. (thick blue w/silvery
  black cast, in making & minor surface
  chip at rim) 1,705
Butter churn, swelled cylindrical form
  w/eared handles & short cylindrical neck,
  cobalt blue stenciled decorated bands
  curved down around the front above the
  label "A.P. Donagho, Parkersbug,
  W. Va.," late 19th c., 17½" h. 303

*From left: Butter Churn w/Double Flower Design
5 Gallon Cake Crock w/Dog*

Butter churn, swelled cylindrical form, slip-
  quilled cobalt blue top to bottom double
  flower, double "6" gal. designation in blue
  slip-quill, includes original dasher guide,
  "A.O. Wittemore Havana, NY," ca. 1870,
  through line on back extending from rim &
  small line at right ear, 18" h. (ILLUS.) 2,750
Cake crock, cov., cylindrical, slip-quilled
  cobalt blue large standing dog amid
  extensive ground cover, rare form &
  design, "West Troy Pottery," 5 gal.,
  ca. 1880, short tight line on back &
  few minor interior surface chips, ½" h.,
  13" d. (ILLUS.) 2,750
Crock, cylindrical w/molded rim & eared
  handles, slip-quilled cobalt blue single
  flower design w/signature & "2"
  designation inside flower, unusual,
  ca. 1870, "C.W. Braun, Buffalo, NY,"
  2 gal., 9½" h. (line up from base on side
  & a few minor chips) 132
Crock, ovoid w/applied & open handles,
  impressed & tooled design around rim,
  incised & blue accented double scalloped
  design in front, blue accents at name
  & handles, "S. Amboy, New Jersey,"
  ca. 1805, almost invisible through line in
  front, 9½" h. (ILLUS.) 2,530

From left: Crock with Double Scalloped Design
"S. Hart Fulton" 3 Gallon Crock

Crock, w/molded rim & eared handles, brushed cobalt blue floral spray top to bottom, "F.B. Norton, Worcester, Mass.," ca. 1870, 1 gal., 7½" h (very minor design fry & stone ping on back) **198**

Crock, ovoid w/molded rim, blue accent stripes & gallon designation in blue brush strokes, "R.T. Williams, New Geneva, PA," ca. 1860, 1½ gal., 9" h. **303**

Crock, cylindrical w/molded rim & eared handles, slip-quilled cobalt blue bird & stylized "3" design, "S. Hart Fulton," ca. 1877, glaze spider on back, 3 gal., 10½" h. (ILLUS) **578**

Crock, cylindrical w/molded rim & eared handles, thick brushed cobalt blue hops vine design, "J. Fisher & Co., Lyons, NY," ca. 1880, 4 gal., 11½" h. **440**

Crock, cylindrical w/molded rim & eared handles, slip-quilled cobalt blue large bird on plume design, "Reidinger & Caire, Pokeepsie, NY," ca. 1870, 5 gal., 12" h. **908**

Jar, cov., swelled cylindrical form w/eared handles, unique cobalt blue eyedropper application to form petals on this flower design, "Clark & Co., Rochester, NY," ca. 1850, 1 gal., 9½" h. (rim chip in front) **413**

Jar, cov., swelled cylindrical form w/eared handles, slip-quilled cobalt blue dancing flower design, "John Burger, Rochester," ca. 1865, 2 gal., 11" h. (stone ping on back) . . **468**

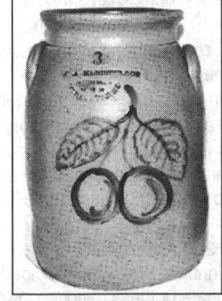

3 Gallon Jar with Brushed Cherries

Jar, swelled cylindrical form w/eared handles, brushed cobalt blue cherries w/two large leaves & stem design & "3," marked "W.A. MacQuoid & Co. Pottery

Works Little W. 12th St. NY," ca. 1870, age spiders on back, 3 gal., 14" h. (ILLUS.) **1,375**

Jug, semi-ovoid w/blue slip-quilled cobalt blue inscription "S.F. Eagan 141 Seneca St. Buffalo N.Y.," J. Fisher, Lyons, NY, ca. 1880, 1 gal., 10 ½" h. (glaze drip in front in making & large rust color stain on back) **132**

Jug, semi-ovoid, slip-quilled cobalt blue "2" & "Lyons," marked "J. Fisher, Lyons, NY," ca. 1880, 2 gal., 13½" h. (surface chip at spout) **715**

Jug, semi-ovoid w/brushed cobalt blue hops design, blue accents at handles, "Cowden & Wilcox, Harrisburg," ca. 1870, 3 gal., 14" h. (small spider on side in making) **220**

Jug, ovoid, brushed light blue plume design, "T. Harrington, Lyons," ca. 1860, 2 gal., 15" h. **157**

Jug, ovoid, incised & blue-trimmed flower at top, blue accents at name & handle, extremely rare mark, "P. Cross, Hartford," ca. 1805, 2 gal., 16" h. (professional restoration to age lines throughout & surface chips at the spout) **990**

Unsigned 1 Gallon Milk Pan

Milk pan, brushed cobalt blue three-leaf decoration, rim pouring lip, ca. 1850, two minor glaze separations in making & small surface chip at rim, unsigned, 1 gal., 4" h. (ILLUS.) **275**

Model of a lamb, unsigned extremely rare molded stoneware reclining lamb, blue accents highlight the ears, also blue accent at the front foot, hand-incised detailed facial features, found in & attributed to Lyons, NY, ca. 1860, 2" h., 2½" l., ... **825**

Pitcher, 10" h., brushed cobalt blue tulip decoration, "Burger & Lang, Rochester, NY," 1 gal., ca. 1870 (some surface wear & chips along the rim from use) **605**

Preserving jar, swelled cylindrical form, brushed thick cobalt blue flower design & blue accents at ears, "Penn Yan," ca. 1860, 1 gal., 9½" h. (very minor surface chip at rim) **198**

Preserving jar, swelled cylindrical form w/eared handles, slip-quilled cobalt blue curlicues, "Nichols & Boynton, Burlington, VT," ca. 1855, 2 gal., 10½" h. **176**

Preserving Jar with Wreath Design

Preserving jar, cov., swelled cylindrical form w/eared handles, thick brushed cobalt blue wreath design & "2," marked "T. Harrington, Lyons," ca. 1860, 2 gal., 11½" h. (ILLUS.) **633**

Ornate Salt Glazed Filter

Water filter, cov., marked "Perfection Filter Manufactured by the Central NY Pottery Utica NY," in relief & blue accented, opposite side w/embossed leaf design accented in blue, relief-molded cupids holding banner around the name, gargoyle handles, age line throughout base & one very tight 3" through line at rim, 10" h. (ILLUS.) **688**

TECO

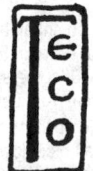

Teco Mark

Teco Pottery was actually the line of art pottery introduced by the American Terra Cotta and Ceramic Company of Terra Cotta (Crystal Lake), Illinois in 1902. Founded by William D.

Gates in 1881, American Terra Cotta originally produced only bricks and drain tile. Because of superior facilities for experimentation, including a chemical laboratory, the company was able to develop an art pottery line, favoring a matte green glaze in the earlier years but eventually achieving a wide range of colors including a metallic lustre glaze and a crystalline glaze. Though some hand-thrown pottery was made, Gates favored a molded ware because it was less expensive to produce. By 1923, Teco Pottery was no longer being made and in 1930 American Terra Cotta and Ceramic Company was sold. A book on the topic is Teco: Art Pottery of the Prairie School, by Sharon S. Darling (Erie Art Museum, 1990).

Bowl, 4½" d., 2½" h., low squatty wide bulbous sides w/throwing ridges, a wide shoulder curving up to a closed rim, deep raspberry matte finish, impressed mark (short hairline) **$220**

Bowl, 8½" d., 2½" h., a wide flat-bottomed squatty bulbous lower body curving upward to a wide flat mouth, upper portion w/a green matte glaze shading into a heavy charcoal glaze, impressed mark **385**

Bowl, 9" d., 2" h., wide flat bottom w/shallow rounded sides & closed molded wide mouth, overall green matte glaze, impressed marks **605**

Ewer, bulbous tapering ovoid body w/the wide shoulder centered by a short small neck w/a deeply folded tricorner rim & loop handle from rim to shoulder, unusual matte brown glaze, 4" h. (stilt chips) **154**

Jardiniere, wide ovoid body tapering to a short flaring neck, molded around the lower body w/eight lily pads below a row of water lily blossoms alternating w/pointed arrowroot leaf buttress-form open handles attaching to the neck rim, smooth matte green glaze, stamped mark, 9¾ x 10" (some restoration) **12,100**

Pitcher, 9" h., corseted-form w/an organic wishbone handle & an undulating rim, matte green glaze, impressed marks **1,100**

Vase, 5½" h., simple ovoid body w/short flared neck flanked by square pierced buttress handles extending halfway down the sides, overall dark matte green glaze (repaired chips) **385**

Vase, 5½" h., 2¾" d., cylindrical body tapering slightly at the top to a molded rim, thin square buttress handles down the sides, smooth deep blue matte glaze, impressed mark **825**

Vase, 6¼" h., 5" d., bulbous ovoid body, the rounded shoulder tapering to a short cylindrical neck w/slightly

Bulbous Teco Vase

These wares were produced in numerous potteries in the vicinity of Teplitz in the Bohemian area of what is now The Czech Republic during the late 19th and into the 20th century. Vases and figures, of varying quality, were the primary products of such firms as Riessner & Kessel (Amphora), Ernst Wahliss and Alfred Stellmacher. Although originally rather low-priced items, today collectors are searching out the best marked examples and prices are soaring.

flaring rim, matte green glaze, tight hairline from rim, stamped mark (ILLUS.) **303**

Vase, 6½" h., 2¼" d., slender cylindrical body tapering to a flaring rim, buttressed handles down the sides, rich yellow matte finish, impressed mark **1,045**

Vase, 8" h., ovoid body tapering to tall wide slightly flaring cylindrical neck, matte green finish, impressed mark **440**

Vase, 9" h., tall slightly tapering cylindrical body w/flaring rim, two small closed buttress handles at shoulder covered in a matte green glaze w/heavy charcoaling, impressed mark **1,650**

Vase, 9" h., tall swelled cylindrical body tapering slightly to the widely flaring neck, small squared shoulder handles, overall dark green matte glaze w/heavy charcoaling, impressed mark **770**

Vase, 11" h., tall slender swelled cylindrical body tapering at the shoulder to a slender flaring trumpet neck, overall terra cotta-colored matte glaze, impressed mark **495**

Vase, 11¼" h., footed bulbous base tapering to a tall cylindrical neck w/flared rim, four whiplash handles from base to below rim, matte green glaze (restoration to small chip at base & on two handles) **1,870**

Vase, 11¾" h., a large cupped tulip blossom framed by four heavy buttress leaf-molded supports forming the squared body, matte green glaze, designed by Fernand Moreau, stamped "Teco" (invisible repair to small chip at rim) **4,125**

TEPLITZ - AMPHORA

Teplitz-Amphora Marks

Ewer, footed, bulbous squatty lower body below tapering swelled sides to the flaring upright ruffled rim, a full-length gilt handle molded as a bizarre lizard-like creature perched on the base & biting the rim, the lower body painted dark green below gold leaf clusters issuing slender stems w/enameled white blossoms w/yellow centers against a textured speckled green ground, impressed Amphora marks, 9" h. **$605**

Model of owl, the large bird perched on a craggy branch w/wings at its sides & head lowered, glazed in deep blue trimmed w/mossy green, impressed "AMPHORA - 1822/16," green printed mark "AMPHORA - MADE IN CZECHOSLOVAKIA," ca. 1920s, 11¾" h. . . . **1,035**

Vase, 6" h., ovoid molded-rib body tapering to a flaring swelled incurved reticulated rim molded w/four spread-winged gold dragonflies above eight smaller dragonflies, low long arched four-loop pierced handles up the sides, dark green ground w/gold & matte cream trim, impressed Amphora marks (minor flake in top) **1,320**

Vase, 7" h., swelled cylindrical body w/a rounded shoulder tapering to a tiny flared neck, decorated w/an Art Nouveau profile portrait of a young woman w/brown hair wearing a pale blue cap decorated w/yellow blossoms & green leaves, gold trim, impressed & stamped Amphora mark . . . **935**

Vase, 8" h., urn-form w/flaring pedestal foot supporting a tall waisted cylindrical body w/a stepped, molded flaring rim flanked by integral double-loop gold handles from the rim to the lower body, decorated on the side w/a large spread-winged butterfly in blue outlined in gold, elaborate gold trim on the background flowers & green leaves, impressed Amphora mark **715**

Vase, 8½" h., swelled squatty base tapering to a tall cylindrical body molded w/Art Nouveau looping scrolls around the base continuing as straight thin ribs up the sides, the squatty bulbous rim composed of a double row of large dark gilt round "buttons" w/pink centers, creamy matte lower body, designed by Paul Daschel, stamped Teplitz mark.................. **770**

Amphora Sea Horse & Dragon Vases

Vase, 9½" h., figural, a slightly swelled cylindrical form tapering to a short cylindrical neck, molded in relief w/a large gold sea horse from the rim to the bottom, on a grey, teal blue & rose mottled tground, impressed Amphora mark & numbers, ca. 1900 (ILLUS. right) ... **1,380**

Vase, 13" h., Art Nouveau-style, bulbous ovoid body tapering to a swelled neck w/four rim knobs continuing down to narrow neck ribs, the body decorated on one side w/a bust profile of an Art Nouveau maiden w/blowing brown hair filled w/white & yellow daisy blossoms, decorated on the reverse w/a forest landscape, impressed & stamped Amphora marks...................... **1,870**

Vase, 13" h., figural, two addorsed realistic full-length eagles w/closed wings perched on the edges of the squatty swelled & footed base flanking a squared central section w/flared four-lobe rim & sides molded w/tiered tight gold scrolls on a pale purplish blue ground, the eagles w/gold heads & trim w/purplish blue feathers, further molded gold scrolls round the base, impressed Amphora marks .. **880**

Vase, 13" h., ovoid body tapering to a short cylindrical neck w/a molded flat rim, a pebbled turquoise ground sgraffito-decorated bands of lotus blossoms around the base & geometric designs around the neck, the center of the body w/an arched rectangular reserve w/sgraffito decoration of a seated ancient Egyptian man, marked on the base "Made in Czechoslovakia - Amphora" **518**

Vase, 13" h., wide bulbous base centered by a tall 'stick' neck, the base enclosed in a deep, smooth-sided rounded casing that tapers up at each side to form loop handles ending at the neck, the lower body w/a textured & quilted design w/narrow ribs up the neck ending in a band of tiny applied jewels at the rim,

dark blue & gunmetal to black glaze w/gold trim at the rim, designed by Paul Daschel, Amphora mark **4,840**

Vase, 13¼" h., figural, large gently swelled ovoid body molded in high-relief w/a large ferocious dragon around the neck w/the wings & long tail down the sides, glazed in mottled shades of orange, green & brown stamped "Amphora - Made in Czecho-Slovakia," ca. 1920 (ILLUS. left) ... **2,875**

Vase, 16" h., earthenware, ovoid body w/two handles at the neck, incised w/a colorful parrot perched on a branch, reserved on a green sponged ground, between borders of stylized fruit, in perwinkle blue, green, teal, pink, cobalt blue, brown, black & caramel, printed mark "AMPHORA - Made in Czecho-Slovakia," & impressed "11607-1," painted "WB" ca. 1930........................... **1,380**

Vase, 16½" h., tall wide cylindrical body w/a bulbous squatty swelled shoulder centered by a short neck w/flattened rim continuing to form short vine-form loop handle to the shoulder, molded around the base w/a narrow undulating band of stylized green blossoms & w/a band of small berries around the neck, the body covered w/a mottled creamy greenish drip glaze on a red, green & yellow streaked ground, impressed & stamped Amphora marks...................... **2,750**

Vase, 17" h., figural, tall tapering cylindrical body w/closed rim applied w/a large realistic ferocious dragon, its wings & body wrapped around the sides & neck, the dragon w/a bronze gunmetal glaze w/slight iridescence, the body of the vase in green, red, black, brown & gold w/overall iridescence, impressed Amphora mark (minor restoration to dragon, drill hole in base) **5,500**

Vase, 17½" h., tall wide swelled cylindrical body w/tapering shoulder to a flat mouth, the sides deeply incised w/deep wide panels molded in relief w/tall stylized creamy tan trees in a grassy landscape against a brick red sky, the outer surface of the body at the top & side bands in medium brown, impressed Amphora marks (filled base chip) **1,320**

TIFFANY POTTERY

Tiffany Mark

In 1902 Louis C. Tiffany expanded Tiffany Studios to include ceramics, enamels, gold, silver and gemstones. Tiffany pottery was usually molded rather than wheel-thrown, but it was carefully finished by hand. A limited amount was produced until about 1914. It is scarce.

Tiffany Bowl-Vase

Bowl-vase, footed wide bulbous body w/wide molded rim, decorated w/low relief-molded flowers & vines, matte tan glaze, inscribed on base "LCT," 9¼" h. (ILLUS.) **$863**

From left: Rare Tiffany Organic Vase Tiffany Vase with Narcissus

Vase, 9½" h., base w/an Art Nouveau design consisting of four long relief-molded lobes, the body swelling slightly at the top w/an undulating rim, covered in an unusual glossy metallic black & green finish, incised "LCT" (ILLUS.) **7,700**

Vase, 10" h., tall cylindrical form w/scalloped rim, glossy pale green glaze on white clay w/a molded organic design of fiddleback fern heads around the top above full-length stems, center base inscribed w/"LCT" monogram (glaze crazing, some interior water stain) **2,875**

Vase, 12" h., tall slender cylindrical form flaring slightly at base, decorated w/embossed jonquil & carved leaves & stems under a shellac & moss satin matte finish, incised "LCT". **5,500**

Vase, 14½" h., stepped disk foot supporting a bulbous ovoid body tapering to a wide cylindrical neck w/flat rim, decorated w/raised narcissus & leaves swirling around the body under a fading brown, dark blue & khaki matte glaze, chip on base, inscribed "LCT" (ILLUS.) **1,380**

TILES

Tiles have been made by potteries in the United States and abroad for many years. Apart from small tea tiles used on tables, there are also decorative tiles for fireplaces, floors and walls and this is where present collector interest lies, especially in the late 19th century American-made art pottery tiles.

Arts & Crafts style, a pair decorated w/squeezebag decoration of a large stylized Art Nouveau light green blossom & leafy stem on a dark aqua ground, in a wide, flat oak frame, tiles 6 x 12", pr. **$660**

Arts & Crafts style, long rectangular form decorated in an unusual squeezebag decoration of a long-tailed colorful parrot perched on the branch of a leafy tree w/tall bushes below, on a white ground, in a wide flat black oak frame, early 20th c., 4½ x 12½" **770**

Arts & Crafts style, square, a stylized English rose in blue w/a purple center flanked by three-leaf green sprigs w/a third suspended below, all on a caramel ground, in a wide flat oak Arts & Crafts frame, 6" sq. (minor flake & scratches) **330**

Grueby Pottery, Boston, Massachusetts, square, mottled matte green glaze w/mustard yellow blossom, mounted in a footed copper frame, raised undecipherable mark, 6¼" w. **1,093**

Marblehead Pottery, Marblehead, Massachusetts, square enbossed design of a white galleon under full sail on a white sea against a dark blue sky, impressed mark, 4" sq. (minor edge flakes). . . **231**

Mosaic Tile Company, Zanesville, Ohio, a scene of a brown galleon under full sail on rough light & dark blue seas & a pale blue sky, impressed mark, 6" sq. **286**

VAN BRIGGLE

Van Briggle Pottery Mark

The Van Briggle Pottery was established by Artus Van Briggle, who formerly worked for Rookwood Pottery, in Colorado Springs,

Colorado at the turn of the century. He died in 1904 but the pottery was carried on by his widow and others. From 1900 until 1920, the pieces were dated. It remains in production today, specializing in Art Pottery.

Bowl-vase, wide rounded squatty lower body below a wide angled & sloping shoulder to the wide flat mouth, molded w/large, wide pointed leaves around the sides, overall maroon & blue matte glaze, post-1920s, 9½" d., 5" h. **$330**

Bowl-vase, wide bulbous body w/molded rim, covered in a fine matte green glaze, incised "AA - VAN BRIGGLE - Colo. Spgs. - 1910," 1910, 4 x 5½" **440**

Mug, ovoid form w/thick C-form handle from rim to base, matte green glaze, incised "AA - COLO SPRINGS - 1907 - 28B," 4½" d., 5" h. **358**

Plate, 8½" d., heavily embossed w/large grapes & leaves under a deep burgundy & blue matte glaze, incised marks ca. 1907-12 . . . . **231**

Vase, 2½" h., 3" d., small bulbous form w/a closed rim, three spread-winged finely carved dragonflies around the rim, overall mustard yellow matte glaze, ca. 1907-12. . . . . **880**

Vase, 4½" h., wide heavy slightly tapering cylindrical form w/deeply carved upright flowers on stems flanked by pairs of pointed leaves, overall dark green & purple matte glaze, incised marks, ca. 1905 . . **880**

Vase, 5" h., waisted cylindrical body slightly swelled near the top then tapering to a wide flat mouth, decorated w/embossed iris blossoms on swirling vertical stems & leaves under a matte raspberry pink glaze, Shape No. 26, 1907-11 . . . . **660**

Vase, 5½" h., ovoid body molded w/four large leaves, matte green glaze on brown ground, ca. 1910 . . . . **259**

From left: Van Briggle Trefoil Vase
Van Briggle Cylindrical Vase

Vase, 6" h., simple ovoid body tapering to a small mouth flanked by relief-molded blue trefoils & small in-body handles, light matte green ground, Shape No. 165 (ILLUS.). **1,623**

Vase, 7" h., slender ovoid body w/trumpet neck, overall maroon matte glaze, incised marks & dated "1914". **330**

Vase, 7¾" h., bulbous paneled base tapering to a wide cylindrical neck, embossed w/stylized blossoms on four long stems,deep mustard yellow matte glaze 1916 . . . . **990**

Vase, 8" h., ovoid body tapering to base, decorated w/four large molded leaves, matte yellowish green glaze, dated 1902 . . . **2,415**

Vase, 8¾" h., slender ovoid body tapering to a cupped rim w/small D-form handles from rim to sides, molded around the base w/large pointed & veined upright leaves, mulberry glaze w/blue overspray, marked, ca. 1920s **288**

Vase, 9½" h., tapering cylindrical body gently swelled at the top w/a closed rim, loop handles, decorated w/embossed daffodils on swirling stems & leaves, covered in a superior curdled brown matte glaze w/the brown clay showing through, incised "AA VAN BRIGGLE - Colo. Sprgs. 1906," 1906 . . . . **2,970**

Vase, 10" h., tall cylindrical form w/swelled closed rim, embossed near top & on rim w/blossoms & leaves on long stems, burgundy glaze, incised "AA - VAN BRIGGLE - 1903 - III," 1903 (ILLUS.) **2,750**

Vase, 14" h., slightly waisted cylindrical body gently swelled at the top w/a closed rim, embossed w/a design of stylized lilies & leaves atop wide stems, matte dark purple glaze, incised "AA - VAN BRIGGLE - 1903 - III- 3," 1903 (minor grind at base from in-fire stilt pull) **5,225**

VERNON KILNS

Vernon Kilns Mark

The story of Vernon Kilns Pottery begins with the purchase by Mr. Faye Bennison of the Poxon China Company (Vernon Potteries) in July 1931. The Poxon family had run the pottery for a number of years in Vernon, California, but with the founding of Vernon Kilns the product lines were greatly expanded. Many innovative dinnerware lines and patterns were introduced during the 1930s, including designs by such noted American artists as Rockwell Kent and Don Blanding. In the early 1940s items were designed to tie in with Walt Disney's animated features "Fantasia" and "Dumbo." Various commemorative plates, including the popular "Bits" series, were also produced over a long period of time. Vernon Kilns was taken over by Metlox Potteries in 1958 and completely ceased production in 1960.

CITIES SERIES - 10½" d.

Plate, "Fort Worth, Texas" $18
Plate, "Greensboro, North Carolina" 18

DINNERWARES

Bowl, fruit, 5½" d., Organdie patt.............. 5
Bowl, salad, 10½" d., Winchester '73
  (Frontier Days) patt. 325
Creamer & cov. sugar bowl, Organdie patt., pr... 18
Cup & saucer, Organdie patt. 6
Gravy boat, Organdie patt.................. 18
Mixing bowl, Gingham patt., 5" d. 16
Pepper mill, Winchester '73 (Frontier Days) patt. . 145
Pitcher, Organdie patt., jug-type, 1 pt.......... 28
Pitcher, 2 qt., jug-type, Winchester '73
  (Frontier Days) patt..................... 295
Plate, salad, Organdie patt. 4
Plate, dinner, 9½" d., Winchester '73
  (Frontier Days) patt...................... 75
Plate, dinner, 10½" d., Organdie patt............ 6
Plate, chop, 14" d., Winchester '73 (Frontier
  Days) patt. 295
Platter, 12" d., Winchester '73 (Frontier
  Days) patt. 225
Platter, 14" d., round, Winchester '73
  (Frontier Days) patt..................... 325
Salt & pepper shakers, Organdie patt., pr....... 18
Sugar bowl, cov., Organdie patt............... 10

DON BLANDING DINNERWARES

Bowl, 5½" d., individual salad, Lei Lani
  patt., maroon 45
Cup & saucer, Lei Lani patt., maroon 75
Gravy boat, Lei Lani patt., maroon........... 165
Nappy, 9" d., Lei Lani patt., maroon........... 165
Plate, bread & butter, Lei Lani patt., maroon 32
Plate, 9" d., Hawaiian Flowers patt., maroon 50
Plate, 9" d., Lei Lani patt., maroon 50

MISCELLANEOUS COMMEMORATIVES

Plate, "Abraham Lincoln" 18
Plate, "Chicago Fair"....................... 18
Plate, "Fort Riley, Texas" 18
Plate, "United States Map," blue 18
Plate, "University of Chicago" 18

MUSIC MASTERS

Plates, brown transfer-printed, the complete
  set of 8 200

ROCKWELL KENT DESIGNS

Plate, chop, 14" d., Our America patt.,
  "Down on the Levee" 110
Tumbler, Moby Dick patt., brown & white....... 195

STATES SERIES - 10½" d.

Plate, "Illinois".......................... 18
Plate, "Louisiana" 18
Plate, "Texas" 18

VOLKMAR

Volkmar Marks

Charles Volkmar came from an artistic family and was able to study pottery making in Europe where he remained fourteen years before returning home in 1875. At the 1876 Philadelphia Centennial Exposition he was intrigued by the French art pottery exhibited and returned to France for further study. Volkmar returned to the United States in 1879 and opened his first kiln in Greenpoint, Long Island, New York in 1879. By 1882 he had established his own studio, kilns, salesroom and home at Tremont, New York. The early Volkmar wares were decorated with applied and underglaze decoration done by Volkmar or an assistant using his designs. During the following years he worked in several partnerships and finally established the Volkmar Keramic Company in Brooklyn in 1895. His last venture was begun in 1902 when he was joined by his son Leon to establish the Volkmar Kilns in Metuchen, New Jersey in 1903. Charles Volkmar died in 1914 and Leon continued pottery production for some years.

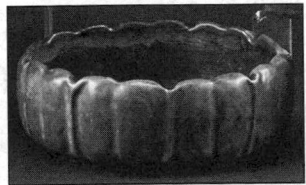

Rare Volkmar Bowl

Bowl, 9¼" d., 3¼" h., low w/sides decorated
  w/overlapping relief-molded broad
  organic leaves under a matte green
  glaze, incised mark (ILLUS.) $495
Bowl-vase, wide squatty bulbous body
  tapering to a short wide rolled neck,
  overall matte brown & dark green glaze,
  incised "VOLKMAR 1910," 6½" d., 4¼" h. 220

Vase, 2¾" h., 4" d., squatty bulbous body tapering to a short neck w/molded rim covered in a smooth matte green glaze, incised "V" **220**

Vase, 7¾" h., bulbous ovoid w/cylindrical neck & flat rim, covered in a leathery bubbled matte green glaze, incised "V" **440**

Vase, 8" h., footed ovoid body tapering to a wide cylindrical neck w/flaring rim, thick matte green glaze, incised "V" mark. **440**

Vase, 10½" h., slender pear-shaped body w/swelling at shoulder & short flat rim, mottled matte green glaze, incised "V" (restoration to hairlines) **220**

WATT

Watt Pottery Mark

    Founded in 1922, in Crooksville, Ohio, this pottery continued in operation until the factory was destroyed by fire in 1965. Although stoneware crocks and jugs were the first wares produced, by 1935 sturdy kitchen items in yellowware were the mainstay of production. Attractive lines like Kitch-N-Queen (banded) wares and the hand-painted Apple, Cherry and Pennsylvania Dutch (tulip) patterns were popular throughout the country. Today these hand-painted utilitarian wares are "hot" with collectors. A good reference book for collectors is Watt Pottery, An Identification and Value Guide, *by Sue and Dave Morris (Collector Books, 1933).*

Bean pot, cov., Rooster patt. **$325**
Bean server, individual, Autumn Foliage patt., No. 75., 3½" d. **70**
Bowl, cov., 7½"d., Apple patt., two-leaf, No. 66 . . . **49**
Bowl, cov., 7½" d., Rooster patt., No. 66 . . . . **200**
Bowl, cov., 8½" d., Apple patt., two-leaf, No. 67 . . . **140**
Bowl, Starflower patt., No. 55, 11¾" d. **110**
Casserole, cov., French handled, Pansy patt. **80**
Casserole, cov., French handled, Raised Pansy patt., No.18 . . . . **135**
Casserole, cov., French handled, Rooster patt., No.18 . . . . **188**
Casserole, cov., four-handled, Old Pansy patt., No. 8, 9½" d., 4¾" h. **50**
Cheese crock, cov., Pennsylvania Dutch Tulip patt., No. 80 . . . . **700**
Creamer, Apple patt., two-leaf, No. 62, w/advertising, 4¼" h. **195**
Creamer, Autumn Foliage patt., No. 62, 4¼" h. . . . **159**

Creamer, Rooster patt., No.62, w/advertising, 4¼" h. **195**
Cup & saucer, Pansy patt. **135**
Ice bucket, cov., Rooster patt. **325**
Mixing bowl, Apple patt., No. 65, 8½" d.,5¾" h. . . **80**
Mixing bowls, nesting-type, Apple patt., Nos. 4, 5, 6, & 7, the set **275**
Pie plate, Pansy patt., cut-leaf, No. 33, 9" d. **90**
Pitcher, American Red Bud (Tear Drop) patt., No. 15 . . . . **85**
Pitcher, Apple patt., No. 15 . . . . **85**
Pitcher, Rooster patt., No. 15 . . . . **100**

Watt Starflower No. 15 Pitcher

Pitcher, Starflower patt., No. 15 (ILLUS.). **85**
Pitcher, Apple patt., No. 16 . . . . **90**
Plate, 10" d., Moonflower patt., pink on green **75**
Platter, Pansy patt., cut-leaf, No.31, 15" d. **90**
Spaghetti bowl, 13" d., Cherry patt., No. 39 . . . . . **85**
Spaghetti bowl, 13" d., Starflower patt., No. 39. . **120**

WEDGWOOD

    Reference here is to the famous pottery established by Josiah Wedgwood in 1759 in England. Numerous types of wares have been produced through the years to the present.

CALENDAR TILES

1911 . . . . **$125**
1915 . . . . **125**
1923 . . . . **125**

JASPER WARE

Urn, three-color two-handled urn on pedestal, of shield shape sprigged in lilac & green on a white ground w/oval portrait medallion reserves w/classical maidens suspended between floral swags beneath an upper border of zodiac symbols, base & pedestal foot w/acanthus lappets, cylindrical pedestal w/a continuous scene of putti at play above a fluted lower section, acanthus & key-fret border, impressed "WEDGWOOD," early 19th c., 18¾" h. **1,150**

QUEENSWARE

Dinner service: eleven dinner plates, eight
bread-and-butter plates, seven teacups,
six bouillon cups, fifteen saucers,
creamer, sugar, oval platter, oval
vegetable dish, pair of compotes,
trumpet-form vase & pair of columnar
candlesticks; each applied w/grapevine
border, impressed & printed factory
marks, ca. 1900, candlesticks 11¼" h.
(chips & repairs), the set **862**

MISCELLANEOUS

Figural Monkey Centerpiece

Centerpiece, Argenta Ware, figural, a wide
rounded bowl patterned w/clambering
monkeys supported by a figure of a
monkey squatting on a round base
molded w/branches, impressed marks,
date letter for 1879, 10" h. (ILLUS.) **1,840**
Cup, "Fairyland Lustre," small footed cup,
decorated w/woodland elves dancing &
at various pursuits on a mottled dark
purple & green ground, the interior
w/birds, butterflies & a bat flying from
a leafy border on a mottled mother-of-
pearl ground, gilt printed factory mark,
ca. 1920, 3" h. **920**

Wedgwood Majolica Fish Set

Fish set: oval plattter & four plates;
majolica, the platter molded w/a large
salmon on a leafy ground, each plate
w/other naturalistically-colored fish on
leafage, date letter for 1879, platter 25" l.,
the set (ILLUS. of part) **2,875**
Plate, 10½" d., 'Ivanhoe' series, dark blue &
white, scene of "Wamba & Cuzch the
swine herd". **69**

WELLER

WELLER   Weller
           Pottery

Weller Marks

This pottery was made from 1872 to 1945 at
a pottery established originally by Samuel A.
Weller at Fultonham, Ohio, and moved in 1882
to Zanesville. Numerous lines were produced.
Listings below are by the pattern or lines.
Reference books on Weller include The Collectors
Encyclopedia of Weller Pottery by Sharon & Bob
Huxford (Collector Books, 1979) and All About
Weller by Ann Gilbert McDonald (Antique
Publications, 1989).

ARDSLEY (1928)

Various shapes molded as cattails among
rushes with water lilies at the bottom. Matte
glaze.

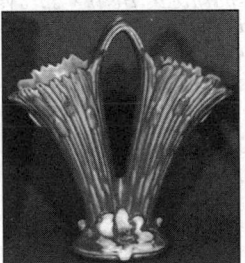

Ardsley Vase

Vase, 7½" h., bud-type, gently flaring
cylindrical form w/molded green & brown
cattails w/white blossoms around the
bottom **$110**
Vase, double, 9½" h., connected by a
pointed branch handle, marked w/half kiln
ink stamp logo (ILLUS.) **138**
Vase, 11" h., tall slightly flaring cylindrical
form w/flaring base molded w/large
blossoms **121**

BALDIN (about 1915-20)

Rustic designs with relief-molded apples and
leaves on branches wrapped around each piece.

Bowl, 4" d., brown ground (unusual high
gloss) **175**
Lamp base, footed metal base w/squatty
bulbous body tapering to wide closed rim,
decorated w/red & yellow apples, green
leaves, brown branches on blue ground,
metal fittings, 12½" h. **880**

Pedestal base, twisted tapering cylindrical base w/curved branch handles, decorated w/red apples & green leaves on brown & green ground, 28½" h.......... **286**

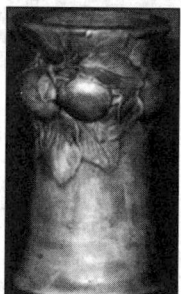

Baldin Vase

Vase, 9½" h., wide cylindrical body flaring at base & rim, apple decoration in rose & yellow, green & yellow ground, marked "Weller" in large block letters (ILLUS.) **248**

BLUE & DECORATED HUDSON (1919)

Hand-painted lifelike sprays of fruit blossoms and flowers in shades of pink and blue on a rich dark blue ground.

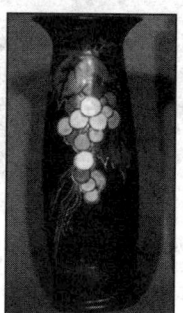

Rare Blue Decorated Vase

Vase, 10" h., bulbous base tapering to wide cylindrical neck w/flat rim, light & dark pink band w/multicolored flowers around base, dark blue ground, impressed mark **286**

Vase, 11½" h., decorated w/two large sprays of blue & white lilacs, impressed "Weller" in large block letters & probable original Weller sales room label (small burst glaze bubble on rim) **660**

Vase, 11⅝" h., deeply incised h.p. grape cluster decoration in shades of pink & blue, green leaves & brown vine, signed "McLaughlin" on side & impressed "Weller" in large block letters, w/probable original Weller paper show room label (ILLUS.) **2,090**

BLUE LOUWELSA (ca. 1905)

A high gloss line shading from medium blue to cobalt blue with underglaze slip decorations of fruits & florals and sometimes portraits. Decorated in shades of white, cobalt and light blue slip. Since few pieces were made, they are rare and sought after today.

Blue Louwelsa Vase with Crocuses

Pitcher, tankard, 12" h., decorated w/white grape cluster & leaves on blue ground, artist-signed "C. Leffler," impressed marks (restoration) **770**

Vase, 6½" h., tapering cylindrical body decorated w/delicate crocus blossoms in cream & blue w/dark & light blue leaves against a shaded blue ground, impressed mark **1,210**

Vase, 10½" cylindrical body w/short rolled rim, unusual decoration of white crocuses against a shaded blue ground, impressed mark (ILLUS.) **1,980**

Vase, 10½" h., tall slender ovoid body tapering to a very slender neck w/flared rim, decorated w/dark & light blue florals under a shaded light to dark blue overall glaze, impressed base mark **1,150**

BONITO (1927-33)

Hand-painted florals and foliage in soft tones on cream ground. Quality of artwork greatly affects price.

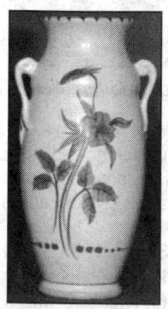

Bonito Vase

Vase, 5½" h., ovoid body tapering to a
ow fanned mouth flanked by small C-
scroll handles, a band of delicate
blossoms around the center on the ivory
ground, marked **144**

Vase, 6" h., footed widely flaring bulbous
ovoid body w/a squared diamond-shaped
wide mouth flanked by two small tab rim
handles, painted w/a leafy swag centered
by blossoms, signed in script **144**

Vase, 11" h., footed ovoid body w/slightly
flaring rim, shoulder handles, decorated
w/orange & lavender flower & bud &
green leaves, incised "Weller Pottery" &
"N" in brown slip, dark craze line at rim
(ILLUS.) **165**

Vase, 11" h., footed wide ovoid body
w/round shoulder & short wide cylindrical
neck, small ornate shoulder handles,
decorated w/stylized floral spray tied w/a
ribbon bow & green lines around foot &
neck, marked & initialed "N. Walsch" **358**

BRIGHTON (1915)

*Various bird or butterfly figurals colorfully
decorated and with glossy glazes.*

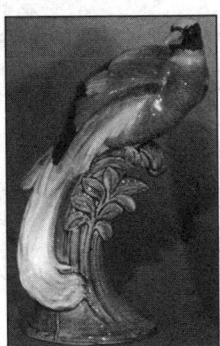

Brighton Bird of Paradise

Flower frog, model of a Flamingo standing
in rushes, head turned facing backward,
marked, 6" h. **288**

Flower frog, model of a Kingfisher, perched
on open arched twig, 6½" h. **173**

Model of bird of paradise, rose, black,
yellow, green, grey, orange, teal & brown
on green & brown stand, impressed
"Weller" in large block letters, 10⅜" h.
(ILLUS.) **2,310**

Model of Kingfisher, blue, brown, black &
white on green & brown stand, impressed
"Weller" in large block letters, 8½" h.
(bubble on bird's back) **248**

Model of "Mad Parrot," blue, lavender,
red & yellow on green & brown stand,
impressed "Weller" in large block letters, 8" h. . . . **715**

BURNT WOOD (1910)

*Molded designs on an unglazed light tan
ground with dark brown trim. Similar to
Claywood but no vertical bands.*

Plate, 9" d., decorated w/birds on branch &
flowers, cream cork-like finish, dark
brown border (minor flakes to back) **187**

Vase, 6½" h., decorated w/scene of children
at play (minor flakes) **495**

Vase, 10½" h., large ovoid body w/a short
cylindrical neck, neck & base band in
dark brown, the body in cream w/a
speckled brown ground & etched vertical
bands of large stylized blossoms
alternating w/bands of leafy branches,
impressed mark **173**

Vase, 11" h., birds decoration **135**

CHASE (late 1920s)

*White relief fox hunt scenes usually on a deep
blue ground.*

Chase Hunting Scene Vase

Vase, 8" h., footed bulbous ovoid body
w/flaring rim, blue ground (ILLUS.) **275**

Vase, 9" h., footed, flattened, rounded
pillow-form body w/three slightly flaring
cylindrical necks at the top, a larger
central one flanked by two smaller angled
ones, matte blue ground, marked **288**

Vase, 12" h., footed baluster-form w/flat rim,
mottled green ground decorated
w/sterling silver deposit hunt scene,
marked on base **288**

CLAYWOOD (ca. 1910)

*Etched designs against a light tan ground,
divided by dark brown bands. Matte glaze.*

Bowl, 6¼" d., wide flat-bottomed form w/low
gently rounded sides, paneled design of
stylized florals in dark brown & creamy
tan **52**

Flower frog, cov., a wide squatty bowl
w/slightly tapering sides fitted w/a pierced
disk cover, a dark brown band around the

top & bottom rims, the sides of the
base in cream etched in dark brown
w/a continuous band of large stylized
blossoms, the cover w/similar blossoms
w/their centers pierced to form the frog, 5" d... **115**

Humidor, cov., etched floral panels **165**

Vase, 8½" h., slender ovoid body w/short
cylindrical rim, pine cone decoration **187**

Vase, 10" h., tall cylindrical body w/a wide
flattened rim, the sides divided into tall
panels by dark brown bands, each panel
etched w/a grape cluster on leafy vines in
creamy white outlined in brown **98**

Vase, 10" h., tall cylindrical form w/a wide
flattened rim, Egyptian design divided by
tall panels, etched border around top
(minor flakes) **413**

COPPERTONE (late 1920s)

*Various shapes with an overall mottled
bright green glaze on a "copper" glaze base. Some
pieces with figural frog or fish handles. Models
of frogs also included.*

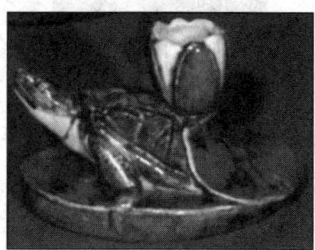

Coppertone Turtle Candleholder

Candleholders, model of a turtle beside
a water lily blossom, 3" h., pr. (ILLUS.
of one) **660**

Jardiniere, large nearly spherical body w/a
closed rim, large arched eared shoulder
handles, covered w/a fine green & rust
mottled matte glaze, incised signature,
8½" d., 7" h. **660**

Vase, 6" h., tapering ovoid body w/a wide
closed flat rim, overall vivid mottled green
over dark brown glaze **230**

Vase, 6½" h., slender gently flaring
cylindrical body, mottled heavy
green over a blackish brown ground,
incised mark **161**

Vase, 7" h., 9" d., spherical body w/closed
handles. **425**

Vase, 8" h., footed, bulbous base w/wide
flaring neck, large C-form handles from
mid-base to just below rim, mottled dark
green glaze, marked w/incised "M" **385**

Vase, 8¼" h., 9" w., fan-shaped top
molded w/reeds above a low squatty
bulbous base composed of lily pads

Coppertone Vase

& molded w/a pair of figural frogs
on the shoulder, stamp mark & artist-
initialed (ILLUS.) **1,045**

Vase, 12½" h., waisted cylinder w/flaring
rim, mottled green & brown glaze,
inscribed "Weller Handmade". **604**

CREAMWARE (about 1915)

Candleholders, square footed base w/tall
cylindrical body & square-shaped rim
above loop handles, 8½" h., pr.
(one w/minor flake). **77**

Vase, 8½" h., tall slender square footed form
w/squared shoulder handles, round
reserve w/classical lady's bust near top **275**

DICKENSWARE 1ST LINE (1897-98)

*Underglaze slip-decorated designs on a
brown, green or blue ground. Glossy glaze.*

Mug, h.p. Virginia creeper decoration by
Sarah Reid McLaughlin, monogrammed
in brown slip on side, impressed "Dickens
Ware Weller" & "327," w/semicircular
logo, 6¾" h. **248**

Mug, decorated w/floral design, impressed
mark, 7" h. **99**

Vase, 17" h., baluster form w/monk
decoration in orange & yellow on shaded
green ground, impressed mark
(restoration) **468**

DICKENSWARE 2ND LINE
(early 1900s)

*Various incised "sgraffito" designs usually
with a matte glaze. Quality of the artwork
greatly affects price.*

Humidor, cov., figural, model of a Chinese
man's head, realistic coloring, 5½" h. **518**

Pitcher, tankard, 12" h., portrait of monk,
orange ground (repaired) **275**

Vase, 8¾" h., 5" d., gourd-shaped body
w/narrow shoulder & short flaring rim,
landscape scene w/children playing,
highlighted w/various colors, shaded tan
& green ground, ca. 1903. . . . . **575**

Dickensware Scenic Vase

Vase, 9¾" h., ovoid body decorated w/forest scene of semi-nude woman holding a bunch of flowers, green trees, dark brown glossy ground, impressed w/"Dickens Ware Weller" semi-circular logo & what appears to be "578" (ILLUS.) **330**

Vase, 15" h., baluster form w/sgrafitto decoration of man w/staff between two trees, impressed mark (restored chips) **468**

Vase, 17½" h., 5½" d., tall slender ovoid form w/incised decoration of a man holding a bird saying "A Bird in the Hand is Worth Two in the Bush," brown, blue, pink, yellow & white, decorated by Edwin L. Pickens, incised "Dickens, Weller, E.L. Pickens" (minute glaze nicks to inside rim). **805**

EOCEAN AND EOCEAN ROSE (1898-1925)

Early art line with various hand-painted flowers on shaded grounds, usually with a clear glossy glaze. Quality of artwork varies greatly.

Candlesticks, widely flaring domed foot supporting a swelled tapering slender standard below the tall socket w/a wide flattened rim, large pink & yellow blossoms around the center of the standard w/dark charcoal above & light lavender below, 10½" h., pr. **316**

Jardiniere, h.p. red roses, leaves & branches decoration on green/grey to white ground, 9" d., 7½" h. **253**

Vase, 5" h., bulbous base tapering to flat rim, decorated w/pink & white floral spray on shaded green ground (minor scratches) . . . **413**

Vase, 5" h., short wide cylinder w/round shoulder tapering to wide neck w/flat rim, h.p. mushroom decoration in burgundy, lavender & white on grey ground, incised & painted mark **1,210**

Vase, 8½" h., waisted cylindrical form decorated w/pink flowers on green to ivory ground **413**

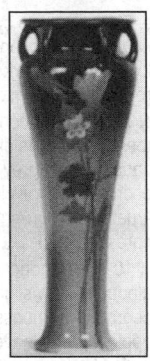

From left: Eocean Vase with Egrets
Eocean Vase with Blossoms

Vase, 11" h., wide tapering cylinder decorated w/two finely detailed fluffy egrets in white, lavender, orange & red on green, cream & lavender ground, incised signature, impressed mark (ILLUS.). **2,750**

Vase, 12" h., tapering cylindrical form w/rolled rim, berry decoration in pink & red on green ground, impressed mark **935**

Vase, 12½" h., expanding cylindrical body w/six open handles rising from narrow shoulder to flared rim, decorated pink & burgundy flowers w/yellow & green leaves, buds & stems against a glossy pale blue to green ground (ILLUS.). **1,650**

Vase, 16" h., cylindrical body w/six loop rim handles, decorated w/h.p. red cherries & green leaves, incised "Weller" in block letters **935**

ETNA (1906)

Colors similar to Early Eocean line but designs are molded in low relief and colored.

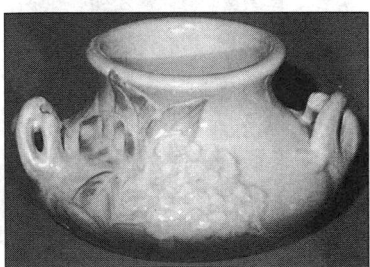

Etna Floral Vase

Vase, 5" h., 9" d., wide squatty lower body w/entwined vine handles tapering to wide flared neck, decorated w/embossed floral decoration in pink & yellow w/green leaves, shaded tan to cream ground, impressed "Weller" in small block letters (ILLUS) **165**

Vase, 5½" h., simple cylindrical form, decorated w/two long-stemmed blossoms on a dark shaded to light grey ground, signed **144**

Vase, 7½" h., wide conical lower body tapering to a wide cylindrical neck, dark shaded to light grey ground slip-decorated w/a tall cluster of pink & red carnations on green leafy stems, impressed mark **173**

Vase, 10" h., cylindrical base tapering to bulbous neck w/slightly flaring rim, decorated w/embossed red & pink poppies, green leaves, bud & stem on shaded brown ground, incised "Weller" **358**

Vase, 10¼" h., ovoid body tapering to a wide cupped rim, dark charcoal shaded to grey ground decorated w/swags of jewel around the shoulder w/an oval reserve w/a white bust profile of a pope, unmarked . . . **316**

FLEMISH (mid-teens to 1928)

Clusters of pink roses and green leaves, often against a molded light brown basketweave ground. Some pieces molded with fruit or small figural birds. Matte glaze.

Jardiniere, wide slightly flaring cylindrical body raised on three small peg feet, molded around the bottom rim w/large lily pad leaves & pink blossoms, marked, 8" d. **69**

Jardiniere & pedestal base, decorated w/bright blue cockatoo, 8" h., 2 pcs. **1,800**

FOREST (mid-teens to 1928)

Realistically molded and painted forest scene.

Forest Vase

Jardiniere, 3¼" h., unmarked. **55**

Planter, tub-shaped w/rim handles, 6½" d., 4¼" h. **83**

Vase, 8" h., cylindrical w/slightly flared rim, marked "12" in black slip (tiny glaze nick off base) **110**

Vase, 8" h., waisted cylinder w/flaring rim, marked "H-" in black slip (ILLUS.) **165**

Vase, 8" h., waisted cylinder w/flaring rim (minute flake to foot). **132**

Vase, 11½" h., tall footed expanding cylindrical body w/flaring rim **358**

GLENDALE (early to late 1920s)

Various relief-molded birds in their natural habitats, lifelike coloring.

Glendale Vase

Console bowl, decorated w/molded sea gulls in yellow, blue, brown & green, 15" d., . . **413**

Vase, 9" h., flaring cylindrical body w/narrow angled shoulder to the flat mouth, molded w/two love birds in color on a leafy tree branch, stamped mark **776**

Vase, 9" h., ovoid body tapering to flat rim, molded forest scene w/two brightly colored parakeets on branch, impressed mark (roughness in glaze on side in marking) **605**

Vase, 10" h., slender ovoid w/short rolled rim, decorated w/red & blue flowers & berries & a blue & yellow bird w/nest in tree, molded McLaughlin signature on reverse, impressed mark **523**

Vase, 11⅞" h., baluster-form w/trumpet neck, decorated w/h.p. scene of a goldfinch on a nest, butterflies, thistles & daisies, artist-signed "Dorothy England" & marked w/the circular "Weller Ware" ink stamp logo (ILLUS.) **1,210**

Vase, 12⅞" h., ovoid body w/short cylindrical neck, w/scene of nesting bird w/eggs in a swampy, cattail-filled area, impressed "Weller" in large block letters **2,310**

GREENBRIAR (early '30s)

Hand-made shapes with green underglaze covered with flowing pink overglaze marbleized with maroon striping.

Vase, 8½" h., an ovoid lower half below a wide trumpet-form upper half, mottled & streaked shades of green on a lavender ground **69**

Vase, 8¾" h., bulbous ovoid body tapering
to wide cylindrical neck w/flared rim,
greenish purple drip glaze **154**
Vase, 15½" h., handled. **525**

GREORA (early 1930s)

*Various shapes with a bicolor orange shaded
to green glaze splashed overall with brighter
green. Semigloss glaze.*

Greora Vase

Strawberry pot, ovoid body w/openings
around the upper half, 5" h. **165**
Vase, 7¼" h., footed, bulbous ovoid w/round
shoulder tapering to short cylindrical
neck, small shoulder handles, incised "E"
(ILLUS.) **220**
Vase, 8¾" h., cylindrical, incised "Weller
Pottery" in script & marked "1B" in black
slip on bottom. **193**
Vase, 9" h., wide cylindrical body w/flat rim **297**
Wall pocket, arrowhead shape w/pointed
overhead handle, marked w/the letter "X"
painted in black slip on the back,
10⅜" h. **358**

HUDSON (1917-34)

*Underglaze slip-painted decoration,
"parchment-vellum" transparent glaze.*

Lamp base, footed, spherical base w/tall
square-form body, molded pink pansy at
top of each panel, white & grey ground,
13" h. (restored original lamp base) **319**

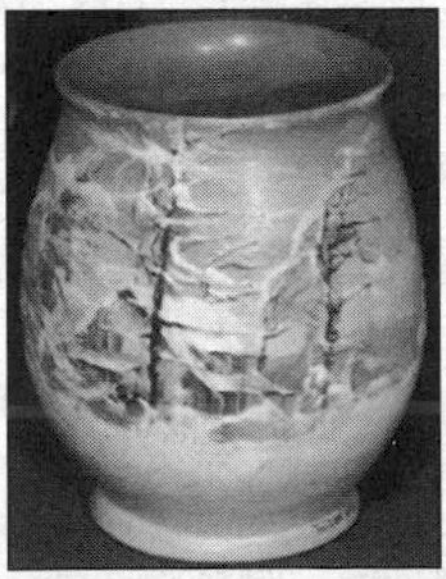

Hudson Winter Scenic Vase

Vase, 6⅜" h., bulbous base on narrow foot
ring, wide cylindrical neck w/slightly
flaring rim, decorated w/detailed scene of
a two-story house in a pine forest, nestled
in deep snow, snow-covered trees blow
in the wind, artist-signed "Timberlake" on
side in black slip, base is incised w/"31" &
"Weller Pottery" (ILLUS.) **6,325**

Hudson Lake Scenic Vase

Vase, 7" h., bulbous ovoid w/narrow footring
& flaring rim, decorated by Hester
Pillsbury w/a scene of trees near a lake &
a blue cloud-filled sky, shades of blue,
green & white (ILLUS.) **3,100**

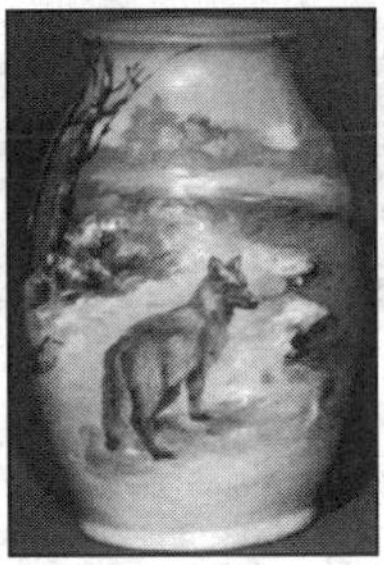

Hudson Winter Landscape Vase

Vase, 8" h., bulbous ovoid body w/rolled
rim, decorated w/a colorful winter
landscape scene w/a fox standing beside
a blue stream & near nicely detailed
snow-covered conifers & deciduous
trees, decorated by Hester Pillsbury
w/"Pillsbury" in black slip, incised "43"
& "Weller Pottery" (ILLUS.) **7,425**
Vase, 8" h., footed bulbous spherical body
w/flaring rim, loop shoulder handles,
decorated w/white flowers & large green
leaves on green to blue ground,
decorated by Hester Pillsbury & marked
w/half kiln "Weller Pottery" ink stamp logo
& "Pillsbury" on side in black slip,
w/original paper label **880**
Vase, 8¾" h., trumpet-form, decorated
w/multicolored daisies & leaves by
Dorothy England, shaded green to pink
ground, half kiln ink stamp Weller logo &
artist-signed "D. England" in black slip **550**

Hudson Vase with Lily of the Valley

Vase, 9" h., ovoid body w/elaborate decoration of lily of the valley in cream w/green leaves on a blue to green ground, signed "Hood," stamp mark (ILLUS.) **1,045**

IVORY (1910 to late 1920s)

Ivory-colored body with various shallow embossed designs with rubbed-on brown highlights.

Ivory Jardiniere

Jardiniere, round squatty bulbous sides w/incurved closed mouth, decorated w/Eskimo & moose designs, unmarked, 11½" d., 7¾" h. (ILLUS.). **413**
Planter, rose trellis design, 5½ x 7½", 7½" h.. . . . . **195**
Vase, 10" h., waisted cylindrical form w/floral & fruit design around the top & ornate design of alternating openings & ram heads around base, unmarked. **176**

JAP BIRDIMAL (1904)

Stylized Japanese-inspired figural bird or animal designs on various solid colored grounds.

Hair receiver, decorated w/four Norse sailing ships, dark blue ground, artist's initials "VH," 4" w., 2" h. **209**
Jardiniere, bulbous body w/wide flat rim, decorated landscape scene of blue trees, yellow moon, grey ground, 8" h. (hairline crack) **275**
Vase, 4½" h., spherical body on three outswept knob feet, tricorner rounded rim, bluish grey ground decorated w/two white geese in flight **265**

Vase, 7" h., ovoid shouldered body tapering to flat mouth, decorated w/geisha girl w/stringed musical instrument, gold, cream, brown, black & green, outlined by slip trailing w/green & yellow leaf decoration around shoulder & green stems around base, impressed "804" & "5" & incised artist's initials "C.M.M." (small line in base, possibly in the making) **1,320**
Vase, 7½" h., decorated w/black cat, back & tail raised, lime green ground **935**
Vase, 10½" h., footed waisted cylindrical body w/tapering shoulder & short slightly flared neck, geisha girl in multicolored robe holding umbrella, trees in background, incised "Weller Rhead Faience," artist-initialed "L.S." **1,980**

JEWELL & CAMEO JEWELL (about 1910-15)

Similar to the Etna line but most pieces molded with a band of raised oval 'jewels' or jewels and cameo portraits in color against a light or dark shaded ground.

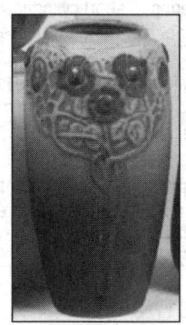

Jewell Vase

Vase, 7½" h., ovoid body, decorated front & back w/incised design of fern fronds w/swirling blue jewels on a blue, green & light pink ground, impressed mark **770**
Vase, 11" h., ovoid, decorated w/relief-molded vine & leaf design w/red flowers & jewels, impressed mark (ILLUS.) **880**

KNIFEWOOD (late teens)

Pieces feature deeply molded designs of dogs, swans, and other birds and animals or flowers in white or cream against dark brown grounds.

Tobacco jar, cov., barrel-shaped w/low domed cover w/button finial, the sides molded in relief w/a continuous scene of a hunting dog & wild fowl in shades of dark & light brown, impressed mark, 6½" h. **920**

Knifewood Vase

Vase, 5" h., squatty bulbous body w/wide
flat rim, decorated w/molded goldfinches
on branches of wisteria, impressed
"Weller" in large block letters (ILLUS.) **770**

Vase, 6" h., squatty bulbous body w/wide
flat rim, decorated w/molded blue &
yellow birds sitting on branches
w/cherries, impressed "Weller" in
large block letters **495**

L'ART NOUVEAU (1903-04)

*Various figural and floral-embossed Art
Nouveau designs.*

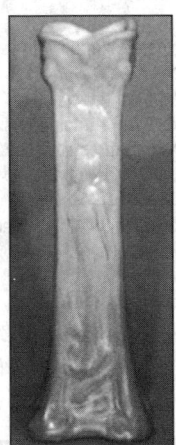

Unusual L'Art Nouveau Vase

Vase, 8" h., slender four-sided body
w/molded florals at the top, decorated on
one side w/embossed figure of young
woman & floral decoration on the other
sides, semi-gloss glaze of rose to blue to
cream, marked "Weller" in small block
letters, unobtrusive stilt pulls on bottom
(ILLUS.) **248**

Vase, 12" h., tall cylindrical body swelled at
the top & tapering to a closed rim, molded
at the top w/large peach & brown irises
against a shaded green & tan ground,
matte glaze, impressed mark **825**

LASA (1920-25)

*Various landscapes on a banded reddish and
gold iridescent ground. Lack of scratches and
abrasions important.*

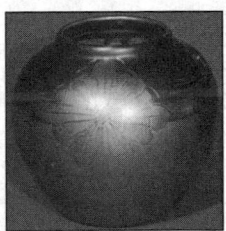

Lasa Stylized Floral Vase

Vase, 3½" h., bulbous body w/short rolled
rim, decorated w/stylized green flowers &
geometric designs on reddish & gold
iridescent ground, unmarked (ILLUS.) **275**

Vase, 3⅝" h., wide bulbous body w/short
rolled rim, decorated w/h.p. yellow
flowers w/green leaves & stems on gold
iridescent ground w/reddish rim **248**

Vase, 10" h., footed, wide ovoid body
tapering to a flat mouth, decorated
w/scene of pine trees & water, gold
iridescent ground **468**

Vase, 12" h., wide flaring foot tapering to
slender cylindrical body & flat rim,
decorated w/a scene of twisted trees on
shoreline, red, green & gold, artist-signed
(worn glaze) **198**

LAVONIA (1927)

*Varied shapes with shaded pale pink and
blue matte glaze.*

Candleholders, ribbed, lavender to green
ground, 5" h., pr. **50**

Console bowl, wide flat bottom w/gently
sloped low sides molded w/leaves &
branches, 11" d. **58**

LOUWELSA (1896-1924)

*Hand-painted underglaze slip decoration on
dark brown shading to yellow ground; glossy
yellow glaze.*

Louwelsa Humidor

Candlestick, squatty bulbous base w/narrow cylindrical neck, spout-shaped candle cup & ornate D-form handle, floral decoration, artist-initialed, impressed mark, 6" h. **286**

Humidor, cov., bulbous body decorated w/h.p. matches & pipes, decorated by Lizabeth Blake, artist-initialed & impressed "Louwelsa Weller" & " X 176 6," lid chips repaired, tiny glaze nicks off rim, 6½" h. (ILLUS.) **550**

Louwelsa Banquet Lamp

Lamp base, banquet-type, trumpet-shaped body w/narrow flat shoulder & short rolled neck, lily decoration done by Minnie Mitchell, artist's name on side & impressed "Louwelsa Weller," "K 617" & half circle logo inside base, metal sleeve for oil font fits inside rim, ca. early 1900s, 26⅝" h. (ILLUS.) **3,300**

Pitcher, 12" h., tankard-type, cavalier decoration, artist-signed, impressed mark (repaired)........................ **385**

Pitcher, 16¾" h., tankard-type, a flaring ringed base below the tall slender & slightly tapering body w/a rim spout & a C-form handle halfway down the side, decorated w/dark yellowish brown clusters of grapes on leafy vines against a dark shaded ground, artist-signed & marked on base **518**

Vase, 6½" h., slightly tapering cylindrical body, carnation decoration, impressed "Louwelsa Weller 525 K" **165**

Vase, 9½" h., pillow-form, footed, hollyhock decoration, artist-initialed, impressed mark (minor scratches). **358**

Vase, 12" h., tall slender ovoid w/loop handles from shoulder to rim, green leaf & berry decoration (minor scratches to rim) **385**

Vase, 19¾" h., squatty bulbous base w/trumpet-form neck, wild rose decoration, base impressed "Weller Louwelsa, 9, 8, X 271," decorated by

Sarah Reid McLaughlin & artist-signed just below flower (scuff marks & glaze flakes off rim) **468**

MARBLEIZED (Bo Marblo, 1915)

Simple shapes with swirled "marbleized" clays, usually in browns and blues.

Bowl, cov., 7" d., 3½" h., wide bulbous shape w/eared handles, knob finial on lid, swirled green & cream high glaze **176**

Compote, 8" h., 5" d., flaring foot tapering to tall cylindrical stand supporting shallow round bowl w/flattened rim, swirled brown & cream, impressed mark **88**

Vase, 7" h., slightly flaring cylindrical sides below a slightly tapering wide neck, swirled colors of dark brown, tan & blue, impressed mark on base **138**

Vase, 9½" h., swelled cylindrical body tapering slightly to a wide flat rim, swirled colors of cream, green & brown, impressed mark **176**

MARVO (mid-1920s-'33)

Molded overall fern and leaf design on various matte background colors.

Vase, 8½" h., baluster-shaped w/trumpet neck, green ground **81**

Vase, 8¾" h., 3" d., slender waisted cylindrical body w/relief-molded foliate decoration under matte butterscotch & green glazes, ca. 1930, impressed "Weller".............................. **173**

Vase, 9½" h., tall slender ovoid w/rolled rim, blue & green matte glaze **358**

MATT GREEN (ca. 1904)

Various shapes with slightly shaded dark green matte glaze and molded with leaves and other natural forms.

Matt Green Planter

Planter, attribution, footed, decorated w/molded landscape w/sheep & flowers, dark green glaze, 6½ x 10½" (ILLUS.) **413**

MUSKOTA (1915-late 1920s)

Figural pieces with human figures, birds, animals or frogs. Matte glaze.

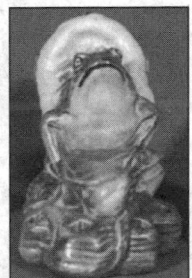

Muskota Flower Frog

Flower frog, figural frog emerging from a
   lotus blossom, unmarked, 4½" h. (ILLUS.).... **220**
Flower frog, figural geese on round footed
   base, 7" h. x 7" d........................ **350**
Model of split rail fence, green & charcoal
   matte glaze, unmarked, 5" h.............. **220**

NOVELTY LINE (1930s)

Various colors. Objects such as ashtrays with figures of monkeys, pigs, dogs, wolves, kangaroos, etc. Also tableware including tumblers with faces. Semigloss glaze. Middle period.

Ashtray, turtle, green, 6" l., 2" h. **90**
Planter, dachshund, 6" l., 3" h................ **75**

PATRA (late 1920s-'33)

Rough orange-peel-like finish with stylized design at the bottom. Matte finish. Middle period.

Patra Jardiniere

Jardiniere, bulbous body, marked "Weller
   Pottery" in script & "3X" in brown slip,
   8½" h. (ILLUS.)........................ **275**
Vase, 4⅞" h., cylindrical lower body below a
   rounded flaring upper body w/a narrow
   molded rim & three-leaf molded designs
   at the rim, the base tapering to three
   short pointed feet, polychrome glaze **50**

ROMA (1912-late '20s)

Cream-colored ground decorated with embossed floral swags, bands or fruit clusters.

Roma Vase

Humidor, cov., octagonal, inset cover
   w/large knob finial, marked, 7" h........... **109**
Vase, 7" h., cylindrical body w/panels of pine
   cone decoration in brown & green **143**
Vase, 9" h., tapering cylinder w/molded ring
   rim, floral decoration, marked "Weller" in
   large block letters **110**
Vase, 10" h., tapering cylindrical body w/a
   wide flattened rim, embossed rings
   around lower body w/paneled decoration
   of pink dogwood blossoms & leaves,
   unmarked (ILLUS.)...................... **110**

SABRINIAN (late '20s)

Seashell body with sea horse handle. Pastel colors. Matte finish. Middle period.

Console bowl, 2½ x 9".................... **195**
Wall pocket, stamp in label **725**

SELMA

Knifewood line with a high-gloss glaze. Occasionally with peacocks, butterflies, and daisies. Middle period.

Selma Vase

Vase, 4" h., squatty bulbous body w/wide
   flat rim, decorated w/molded daisies &
   butterflies, marked "Weller" in large block
   letters & "F" in black slip (ILLUS.).......... **193**

Vase, 5" h., bulbous body w/flat rim, decorated w/goldfinches among wisteria blossoms, impressed "Weller " in large block letters & "C" painted in brown slip **248**

Vase, 5" h., cylindrical w/flat rim, decorated w/white & yellow daisies **110**

SICARDO (1902-07)

Various shapes with iridescent glaze of metallic shadings in greens, blues, crimson, purple or coppertone decorated with vines, flowers, stars or free-form geometric lines.

Sicardo Lobed Vase

Vase, 4" h., three-lobe form, signed "Sicard," impressed mark (ILLUS.) **1,100**

Vase, 4½" h., bell-shaped body decorated w/leaves & berries against a bronze, blue, green, rose & purple iridescent ground, signed "Sicard Weller" **1,380**

Sicardo Vase

Vase, 5" h., bulbous base below gently tapering conical sides, floral decoration in green & gold iridescent glaze, artist-signed (ILLUS.) **413**

Vase, 5" h., tapering four-sided form, floral decoration in iridescent highlights of gold, purple & rose, signed "Weller Sicard" **550**

Vase, 10½" h., tapering ovoid body w/flaring rim, iridescent floral decoration of gold mums w/green highlights against a purple, blue & red ground, signed "Weller Sicard" **1,870**

Vase, 12" h., twisted-form tapering ovoid body w/flat rim, floral decoration in gold, green & blue w/gold, blue purple iridescent highlights, signed "Weller Sicard" **2,090**

SILVERTONE (1928)

Various flowers, fruits or butterflies molded on a pale purple-blue matte pebbled ground.

Silvertone Basket

Basket, fan-shaped w/overhead gnarled branch handle, decorated w/cranberry colored flowers & green leaves, marked w/half kiln ink stamp logo & "3" in black slip, 8½" h. (ILLUS.) **303**

Vase, 6½" h., footed squatty bulbous body w/wide flaring rim, decorated w/pink & lavender poppies & green leaves against a purple ground, ink mark. **413**

Vase, 7" h., gently tapering cylindrical sides w/D-form handles from rim to center of the sides, molded flowers, marked. **320**

Vase, 7½" h., footed ovoid fan-shaped w/widely flaring rim, swirled clusters of flowers **345**

Vase, 10" h., bulbous base w/wide cylindrical neck w/molded rim, D-form handles rising from base to rim, decorated w/red & white embossed flowers on a purple, pink & white ground, original labels **550**

Vase, 11¾" h., slender trumpet-form, calla lily decoration in white w/green leaves, pale purple ground, marked & paper label **605**

Wall pocket, conical w/molded floral decoration on multicolored ground, stamp mark, 10" h. (minute bruise to top) **385**

SOUEVO (1907-10)

Unglazed redware bodies with glossy black interiors. The exterior decorated with black & white American Indian geometric designs.

Basket, hanging-type, w/original chains, 9½" h. . . **198**

Pitcher, tankard, tall tapering cylindrical body w/a flaring cylindrical neck & rim spout, long D-form handle, decorated down the sides w/stripes of graduated triangles. **285**

Souevo Vase

Vase, 7" h., bulbous ovoid body w/short
cylindrical neck, decorated w/Native
American designs under a cranberry
glaze, impressed "Weller" in large block
letters (ILLUS.) **413**

WARWICK (1929)

*Modeled rustic background with trees and
fruit. Matte finish. Middle period.*

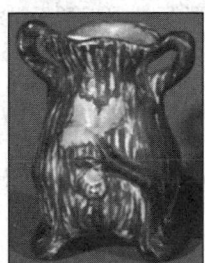

Warwick Vase

Bowl, 3½ x 8½", shallow round form
w/end handles **77**
Planter, log-shaped w/twisted branches
forming end handles, stamp mark,
12" l. (minor flake to base) **88**
Vase, 4½" h., two-handled, footed ovoid
body tapering to a flared rim flanked by
loop handles, half kiln ink stamp logo &
"XII" in black slip (ILLUS.). **55**
Wall pocket, 11½" l., half kiln mark **385**

WHITE & DECORATED HUDSON
(1917-34)

*A version of the Hudson line usually with
dark colored floral designs against a creamy
white ground.*

Vase, 8½" h., tapering cylindrical body,
heavy slip decoration of multicolored
berries & leaves, impressed "Weller" in
large block letters **440**
Vase, 9½" h., ovoid, decorated w/rose &
pink irises w/yellow centers, yellow to
grey ground **264**

White & Decorated Hudson Vase

Vase, 9½" h., ovoid w/short round shoulder
tapering to flat neck, blue band at
shoulder w/multicolored floral decoration,
black band around neck, impressed mark
(ILLUS.) **330**

WOODCRAFT (1917)

*Rustic designs simulating the appearance of
stumps, logs and tree trunks. Some pieces are
adorned with owls, squirrels, dogs and other
animals. Matte finish.*

Woodcraft Basket

Basket, hanging-type, unmarked, 9" d., 4" h. . . . **220**
Basket, figural acorn w/overhead branch
handle, marked "Weller" in large block
letters, 9½" h. (ILLUS.) **358**

Woodcraft Bowl With Squirrel

Bowl, 5½ x 7", shallow bulbous form w/oak
leaves & acorns around the rim & figural
squirrel seated on rim eating a nut, ink
stamp mark "Weller Ware," full kiln logo &
"H" in black slip, two small chips to oak
leaves (ILLUS.). **220**

Candlelamps, footed tree trunk-form w/red berry decoration, branch handles & molded leaves around top, brown & green ground, original candlelamp holder & old bulbs, overall 17" h., pr. (one w/tiny chip to leaf) **825**

Compote, deep rounded & flaring sides supported by figural branches on tree trunk-form pedestal, molded leaves around rim, earth tones w/red berries, impressed mark, 10" h................. **468**

Flower frog, figural crab, 5" l., 1⅜" h. (small nick on left hind leg) **110**

Model of dogs, two brown to yellow hunting dogs in grasses, base in earth tones & green, impressed block mark, 11" l., 7" h. **715**

Planter, log-form w/molded leaf & narrow strap handle at top center, 11" l., 4¼" h. **110**

Woodcraft Double Bud Vase

Vase, double bud, 8" h., cylindrical tree trunk-forms connected by an arch of branches & molded red berries & green leaves (ILLUS.)......................... **165**

Vase, 9" h., chalice shape w/three branch handles rising from base, impressed mark ... **187**

Vase, bud, 10" h., cylindrical tree trunk form w/relief-molded branch, apple & leaves down the front........................... **95**

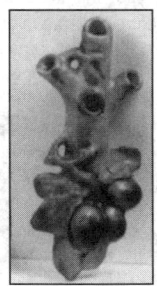

Woodcraft Wall Pocket

Wall pocket, relief-molded purple plums & green leaves against cylindrical tree branch body, openings at ends of branches, 9" l. (ILLUS.) **495**

WOODROSE (before 1920)

Rustic oaken bucket forms with rose clusters or berries near the rim. Matte glaze.

Basket, hanging-type w/hangers, tapering cylinder w/floral design & black banding on earth tone ground, 8" d., 4" h. **143**

Jardiniere, wide tapering cylinder w/panels of leaves & pink roses on green & brown ground, 9" d., 7½" h.................... **132**

Jardiniere, 8" h. **180**

Vase, 7" h., slender slightly flaring cylindrical form .. **63**

Wall pocket, conical, 7" h. **176**

Wall pocket, V-form, lavender w/red floral decoration, 8½" h. **198**

ZONA (about 1920)

Red apples and green leaves on brown branches all on a cream-colored ground; some pieces with molded florals or birds with various glazes. A line of children's dishes was also produced featuring hand-painted or molded animals. This is referred to as the "Zona Baby Line."

Pitcher, 8" h., wide cylindrical form w/flat rim & high arched spout, squared handle, Kingfisher decoration, blue & grey **358**

Plate, 8⅞" d., apple pattern, pairs of red apples & green leaves around the border on brown branches against the ivory ground .. **44**

WHEATLEY POTTERY

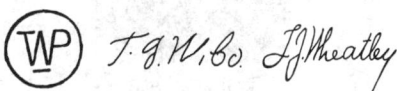

Wheatley Marks

Cincinnati, Ohio in the early 1880s. In 1879 the Cincinnati Art Pottery was formed and after some legal problems it operated under the name T.J. Wheatley & Company. Their production featured Limoges-style hand-painted decorations and most pieces were carefully marked and often dated.In 1882 Wheatley disassociated himself from the Cincinnati Art Pottery and opened another pottery which was destroyed by fire in 1884. Around 1900 Wheatley finally resumed making art pottery in Cincinnati and in 1903 he founded the Wheatley Pottery Company with a new partner, Isaac Kahn.

The new pottery from this company featured colored matte glazes over relief work designs and green, yellow and blue were the most often used colors. There were imitations of the well-known Grueby Pottery wares as well as artware, garden pottery and architectural pieces. Artwork was apparently not made much after 1907. This plant was destroyed by fire in 1910 but was rebuilt and run by Wheatley until his death in 1917. Wheatley artware was generally unmarked except for a paper label.

Wheatley Bowl-Vase

Bowl-vase, wide bulbous body w/short cylindrical neck & flat rim, embossed w/alternating broad pointed & finely ribbed leaves & buds under a matte ochre glaze, impressed "WP - 63," 6¾" d., 5¾" h. (ILLUS.) **$2,750**

Chamberstick, wide round dished base w/heavy molded leaves tapering up the center short shaft molded w/buds under the rolled socket rim, a scrolled loop handle at one side of the base, overall dark green matte glaze, 6" d., 3½" h. (small repaired rim chip) **605**

Jardiniere, wide bulbous base tapering to tall wide cylindrical neck w/incurved-rim, four buttressed handles from rim to base, covered in a leathery matte green glaze, 7¾" d., 7" h. (nearly invisible restoration to drilled base hole) **3,080**

Wheatley Octagonal Planter

Planter, octagonal sharply canted sides to rolled rim, each panel decorated w/relief-molded woven design in a buff terra cotta, impressed mark, minor chips, 24" d., 14" h. (ILLUS.). **770**

Vase, 6 5/8" h., 4" w., rectangular form decorated w/a Limoges-style branch of white apple blossoms on a glossy dark blue ground, incised marks including "T J W Co, Pat. Sep 28," ca. 1880 (minor scratches) **144**

Vase, pillow-type, 9¼" h., 6¾" w., a small rectangular foot supports a wide round flattened body w/a short cylindrical neck, barbotine-painted w/white daisies w/yellow centers & green leaves on a celadon & black ground, incised "T.J. Wheatley - no. 77" (glaze bruise to rim) **110**

Vase, 11" h., 10" d., squatty bulbous base below a bulbous body tapering slightly to a wide, flat mouth, applied w/four leafy

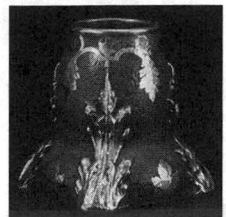

Unusual Large Wheatley Vase

scroll electroplated silver bands up the sides & w/plated leaves & scrolls between each of these, over a matte green glaze, no visible mark, minor losses (ILLUS.) **2,750**

Vase, floor-type, 18½" h., 9½" d., slightly tapering cylindrical body w/rolled rim issuing four long strap handles, covered in a rich green textured flowing glaze, incised "W" in a circle & "616" (drill hole to base) **3,575**

WILLOW WARES

This pseudo-Chinese pattern has been used by numerous firms throughout the years. The original design is attributed to Thomas Minton about 1780 and Thomas Turner is believed to have first produced the ware during his tenure at the Caughley works. The blue underglaze transfer print pattern has never been out of production since that time. An Oriental landscape incorporating a bridge, pagoda, trees, figures and birds, supposedly tells the story of lovers fleeing a cruel father who wished to prevent their marriage. The gods, having pity on them, changed them into birds enabling them to fly away and seek their happiness together.

BLUE

Bowl, berry, Japan **$5**
Bowl, berry, Royal China Co., small **3**
Bowl, cereal, Johnson Bros., England **6**
Bowl, cereal, Royal China Co. **12**
Bowl, soup, Allerton, England **179**
Bowl, soup, 8¼" d., Royal China Co. **10**
Bowl, 9" d., 4" h., Royal Doulton, early 20th c. **225**
Casserole, cov., Japan. **50**
Condiment set insert, Japan. **40**
Creamer, Japan **17**
Creamer, Johnson Bros., England **12**
Creamer, Royal China Co. **6**
Cup & saucer, interior decal decoration, Japan. . . **10**
Cup & saucer, Japan **15**
Cup & saucer, Johnson Bros., England. **10**
Cup & saucer, Royal China Co. **6**
Cup & saucer, Japan, 24 oz. **35**
Ladle, pattern in bowl **120**

Plate, bread & butter, Japan 4
Plate, bread & butter, Royal China Co. 4
Plate, chop, Japan (crazed) 40
Plate, dinner, unmarked, Royal China Co. 6
Plate, grill, Japan 11
Plate, salad, England 13
Plate, child's, 4½" d., Japan 9
Plate, 6" d., Japan. 5
Plate, 6¼" d., England 5
Plate, 6½" d., Johnson Bros., England 4
Plate 9" d. 11
Plate, 9" d., Homer Laughlin 8
Plate, 9¾" d., Ridgway, England 39
Plate, dinner, 10" d., Johnson Bros., England 9
Plate, 10½" d., Royal China Co. 15
Plate, grill, 10¾" d., Wm. Adams, Staffordshire . . . 20
Platter, 11½" l., oval, Homer Laughlin 30
Platter, 8½ x 11½" oval, unmarked 35
Platter, 9½ x 11½" rectangular, England 60
Platter, 12" l., Johnson Bros., England. 20
Platter, 10 x 13" oval, Homer Laughlin 35
Platter, 10 x 13" rectangular, Ridgway, England . . 70
Platter, 11 x 13½" oval, Ridgway, England 135
Sauce tureen, cover & ladle, interior
    pattern, 3 pcs. 225
Soup plate, w/flanged rim, England 18
Sugar bowl, cov., Japan 25
Sugar bowl, cov., Johnson Bros., England 15
Sugar bowl, cov., Royal China Co. 15
Sugar bowl, cov., upswept open handles 40
Teapot, cov. 70
Teapot, cov., Japan, 4" h. 50
Tureen, cov., scalloped footed base,
    unmarked, Japan, 6 x 10". 150
Vegetable bowl, cov. 100
Vegetable bowl, open, Japan, 10½" oval 35
Vegetable bowl, open, oval, Johnson Bros.,
    England 30
Vegetable bowl, open, round, Johnson
    Bros., England, 8" d. 20
Vegetable bowl, open, rectangular, Globe
    Pottery, 7 x 9" 58
Vegetable bowl, open, round, Royal China
    Co., 10" d. 25

Blue Willow Wash Bowl & Pitcher

Wash pitcher & bowl, Doulton - Burslem,
    the set. 990

YELLOWWARE

Yellowware is a form of utilitarian pottery produced in the United States and England from the early 19th century onward. Its body texture is less dense and vitreous (impervious to water) than stoneware. Most, but not all, yellowware is unmarked and its color varies from deep yellow to pale buff. In the late 19th and early 20th centuries bowls in graduated sizes were widely advertised. Still in production, yellowware is plentiful and still reasonably priced.

Yellowware Dog Bank

Bank, model of a seated dog, facing front,
    on a rectangular base w/coin slot, green
    & brown running glaze, chips on base &
    coin slot, 7½" h. (ILLUS.) $1,045

Yellowware Dog Inkwell

Inkwell, figural dog, green & brown running
    glaze, 6⅛" l. (ILLUS.) 440

ZSOLNAY

This pottery was made in Pecs, Hungary, in a factory founded in 1862 by Vilmos Zsolnay. Utilitarian earthenware was originally produced but by the turn of the century ornamental Art Nouveau style wares with bright colors and lustre decoration were produced and these wares are especially sought today. Currently Zsolnay pieces are being made in a new factory.

Basket, egg-shaped, reticulated, yellow,
    blue & pink, 6½ x 8½" $795
Pitcher, cov., the pierced body enamel-
    decorated & molded in relief w/flowers &
    leaves, early 20th c., 12¼" h. 403
Vase, 10¼" h., Art Nouveau style, elongated
    ovoid form w/extended neck & handle,
    the surface in brilliant orangish red, fiery
    purples & gold w/floral & leaf designs &
    a sunset over a tree-lined landscape,
    raised round stamp trademark, impressed
    "5572 M 23," ca. 1900 1,610

CHALKWARE

So-called chalkware available today is actually made of plaster of Paris, much of it decorated in color and primarily in the form of busts, figurines and ornaments. It was produced through most of the 19th century and the majority of pieces were originally quite inexpensive when made. Today even 20th century "carnival" pieces are collectible.

Bank, model of a pear, original red & yellow paint, replaced wooden stem, 5½" h. (minor wear & chips) **$358**

Bank, "Devils Head," early Carnival-type, ca. 1950, 6½" h. **61**

Bank, model of a pig, "Junior Pig Bank," standing w/front legs in begging position, early Carnival-type, ca. 1940-50, 9½" h. **28**

Bank, model of a standing spotted pig, early Carnival-type, ca. 1950, 11" l. **55**

Chalkware Indian Book End

Book ends, figural Indian chief w/headdress, kneeling on one knee, hand resting on other knee, spear by side, ca. 1940, pr. (ILLUS of one) **75**

Figure group, George Washington on horse, early Carnival-type, ca. 1940, 11" h. **39**

Figure of a baby, Kewpie-like, early Carnival-type, ca. 1935-45, 13" h. **50**

Figure of a black baby, Kewpie-like, early Carnival-type, ca. 1935-45, 12" h. (repaired) **110**

Figure of a clown, holding balloons, early Carnival-type w/coin slot, ca. 1950, 13" h. **39**

Figure of a girl, dressed in slacks, sweater & hat, early Carnival-type, ca. 1930-40, 10" h. **39**

Figure of a girl, "Sailor Girl," wearing bell-bottom slacks, top w/sailor collar & sailor hat, one hand in pocket, the other near her face, early Carnival-type, ca. 1930-40, 14" h. **55**

Figure of a girl, "Apache Babe," wearing jacket & slacks w/beret on the side of her head, heavy make-up, standing w/hands in pockets, early Carnival-type, ca. 1936, 15" h. **39**

Figure of a girl, "Tom Boy," dressed in suit & cap, early Carnival-type, ca. 1940, 15½" h. **61**

Figure of a hula girl, early Carnival-type, long dark curly hair, one arm behind her head, the other hand near her face, wearing only short skirt, ca. 1947, 15" h. (repaired) **149**

Figure of an Indian, seated w/drum, head band, early Carnival-type, ca. 1940-50, 12½" h. **72**

Figure of "Uncle Sam," early Carnival-type, white hair & beard, dark pants & light shirt, standing & rolling up one sleeve, ca. 1935, 15" h. **94**

Mantel garniture, compote of fruit in circular bowl on fluted foot & square base, various fruits painted yellow, brown, red, & black, 19th c., 12½" h. **2,300**

Mantel garniture, compote of fruit in circular bowl w/flaring ruffled rim on circular foot, grapes, pears, oranges & bananas painted yellow, green & orange, 19th c., 15" h. (scattered chips & wear to paint). **1,265**

Mantel garniture modeled as a cluster of fruits & leaves on footed base, painted red, green, yellow & black w/indecipherable inscription on verso, 19th c., 14¼" h. (wear to paint) **3,450**

Model of a buffalo, early Carnival-type w/coin slot, ca. 1950, 10½" h. **28**

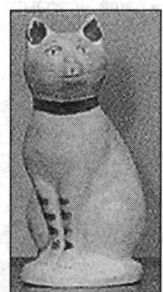

Fine Chalkware Cat

Model of a cat, seated animal, old worn paint in red, black & yellow, 19th c., 9⅞" h. (ILLUS.) **1,430**

Chalkware Sleeping Cat

Model of a cat, large reclining animal
w/head down, original polychrome paint,
wear & some edge damage w/touch-up
repair, 12" l. (ILLUS., previous page) **440**
Model of a dog, standing w/open legs, head
turned to the side, long dark ears, short
tail, on a rectangular base, worn red &
black paint, 7½" h. **193**
Model of a gorilla, "King Kong," early
Carnival-type, ca. 1930-40, 12½" h. **61**
Model of a pig, standing on hind legs, early
Carnival-type, ca. 1935, 6" h. **17**
Model of an elephant, standing on hind
legs, early Carnival-type, ca. 1960,
10½" h. **33**
Model of hand, holding an ear of corn for
Iowa Centennial, 1838-1938, ca. 1938,
12" h. (minor losses) **28**
Model of a deer, recumbent animal, old
worn paint in red, black & yellow, 19th c.,
5½" h., pr. **935**

CHARACTER COLLECTIBLES

*Numerous objects made in the likeness
of or named after comic strip and comic book
personalities or characters abounded from
the 1920s to the present. Scores of these
are now being eagerly collected and prices
still vary widely. Also see LUNCH BOXES,
POP CULTURE COLLECTIBLES, RADIO &
TELEVISION MEMORABILIA, WESTERN
CHARACTER COLLECTIBLES, SPACE AGE
COLLECTIBLES and TOYS.*

Alley Oop child's game, original can,
Royal Toy Co. **$300**

Barnacle Bill Walking Toy

Barnacle Bill toy, windup tin walker,
J. Chein, very good condition, 7½" h.
(ILLUS.) **385**
Barney Google figure, Syroco, marked on
front "Barney G." & "KFS 1944" on back,
4" h. (near mint condition) **135**

Rare Betty Boop Composition Doll

Betty Boop doll, jointed composition,
painted features, black dress w/red heart
decal, near mint, 1930s, 13" h. (ILLUS.) **2,255**
Betty Boop figure, chalkware, early
Carnival-type, ca. 1930-40, 15" h. (repaired) . . **248**

Buck Rogers Space Gun

Buck Rogers space gun, painted tin,
futuristic design, good paint, 1930s (ILLUS.) . . **165**

Buck Rogers Space Ranger Kit

Buck Rogers toy kit, "Buck Rogers Space
Ranger Kit," includes Space Ranger
helmet, space phones, space compass,
flying saucers, disintegrator, Martian
mask, membership card, commission
pendants, space rocket, Martian nodding
head Dynagator target & more, Sylvania
premium, 1952, unopened in box (ILLUS.) . . . **468**
Captain Marvel pinback button, "Captain
Marvel Club - Shazam," lithographed
metal, half-length portrait of Captain
Marvel in the center, wording around
border, in red, white & blue, pristine
condition, ⅞" d. (ILLUS., next page) **99**

Fine Captain Marvel Club Button

Casper the Friendly Ghost toy, "Casper the Talking Ghost," plush w/hard plastic face & talking mechanism, Mattel, 1960s, works, in original box, 14" h. **193**

Dick Tracy Master Detective Game

Dick Tracy game, "Dick Tracy, Master Detective," board-type, Selright, 1960, excellent & complete (ILLUS.) **66**

Dick Tracy police car, windup tin, color lithographed, good condition, w/instructions, Marx **250**

Dick Tracy toy, squad car, friction-type, blue, machine gun in window, 1950s, Marx, 6½" l. **150**

Elmer Fudd planter, ceramic, figural Elmer Fudd w/rifle, ca. 1940, U.S.A.. . . . . **78**

Felix the Cat crayons, colored wood pencils in original box, copyright Pat Sullivan, set of 8. . . . . **75**

Early Felix Jointed Figure

Felix the Cat figure, painted silhouetted cut-out wood w/hinged joints, black & white w/red nose, 1930s, 7" h. (ILLUS.) **550**

Flash Gordon Signal Pistol

Flash Gordon pistol, Signal Pistol, lithographed tin, green w/red fin & tip, decal w/bust of Flash & his name on side, Marx, 1935, 7" l. (ILLUS.) **1,600**

Flash Gordon Rocket Fighter

Flash Gordon toy, windup tin, "Flash Gordon Rocket Fighter," futuristic space ship w/Flash aiming a gun from the cockpit, Marx, ca. 1930s, missing back fin, minor paint loss, 12" l. (ILLUS.) **275**

Harold Lloyd bell toy, tin, litho, German, 6¼" l., excellent **275**

Huckleberry Hound Toy

Huckleberry Hound toy, windup tin, Huckleberry walker w/large feet, blue body w/pink snout & yellow hat, Line Mar, ca. 1960, 3¾" h. (ILLUS.). **303**

Humphreymobile Windup Toy

Humphrey (Joe Palooka) toy, windup tin,
color lithographed, Humphreymobile,
Wyandotte, original box, near mint, 8½" l.
(ILLUS., previous page) 605

Jackie Googan toy, windup tin "The Kid,"
Jackie Googan walker, young boy w/cap,
eyes move from side to side, 7¼" h. 440

James Bond 007 action figure, James
Bond 007, w/complete set of accessories,
all in original packages, excellent, Gilbert . . . 2,933

James Bond 007 action figure, pistol &
manual, w/box, good, Gilbert 135

**James Bond 007 action figures from
"Moon Raker,"** vinyl, lot of 4, all in
original boxes, Mego, 1979 776

James Bond Aston Martin DB5, w/original
box, autographed by Desmond Llewelyn,
Corgi 1965. 1,208

James Bond automobile, lithographed tin,
friction-type, multi-action 711 Aston
Martin Secret Ejector Car, original receipt
of purchase, good w/fair box, United, 11" l. . . . 483

James Bond gun, ricochet-type, James
Bond "Thunderball Secret Agent 007,"
Lone Star Tada, good w/fair box, 23" l. 863

James Bond Moonbuggy, inspired by
"Diamonds Are Forever," excellent
w/good box, Corgi 690

James Bond spy watch, excellent
w/display card & fair case, Gilbert. 1,035

Joe Penner toy, windup tin, color
lithographed, Joe Penner & his duck,
Louis Marx, pristine, 8½" l. 605

Kermit the Frog telephone, mint in original
decorative box, 1970s 225

Li'l Abner & his Dogpatch band, tin, litho,
clockwork w/original box, 1945, Unique
Art, 5¾" x 9" (toy pristine, box very good) 825

Maggie & Jiggs Windup Toy

Maggie & Jiggs (Bringing Up Father) toy,
windup tin, figures of Maggie & Jiggs on
facing wheeled platforms joined by a
slender rod, good paint, Nifty (ILLUS.) 1,100

Maggie & Jiggs Schoenhut dolls,
unmarked, wooden character heads,
intaglio eyes, Maggie w/molded frowning
mouth, Jiggs w/smiling mouth w/hole for
cigar, molded & painted hair, five-piece
wooden jointed bodies, Maggie dressed
in original yellow print blouse, white skirt,

Schoenhut Maggie & Jiggs

pants, Jiggs dressed in original red felt
shirt, black felt pants, suspenders, both
w/facial soil & crazing, minor flaking,
Maggie missing her rolling pin, Jiggs
missing his cigar & sauerkraut pail,
8 & 7½" h., pr. (ILLUS.) 525

Nancy doll, stuffed cloth, marked on wrist
tag "Georgene," Georgene Novelties,
New York, New York, cloth mask face,
painted black eyes, pug nose w/accented
nostrils, closed smiling mouth, applied
ears, cloth body jointed at shoulders &
hips, original black fuzzy hair, black &
white striped cloth lower legs for socks,
beige flannel feet for shoes, wearing
original black, orange & white dress,
nylon panties, w/original marked box,
13" h. (ILLUS. left w/Sluggo) 850

Oddjob (James Bond) action figure, good
w/fair box, Gilbert, 10½" h. 1,035

Gund Olive Oyl Marionette

Olive Oyl marionette, vinyl & cloth, vinyl
head & hands w/cloth costume in red,
green & yellow, Gund, 11" h. (ILLUS.) 165

Popeye bubble blowing set, ca. 1936 58

Popeye Christmas tree light set, eight light
shades in original display box, Mazda,
ca. 1920s, the set. 250

Popeye flicker ring 10

Popeye knockout bank, lithographed tin,
very good, Straits Mfg. Co. 900

Popeye pencil, large metal-type, 1929, in
original box, 8" l. **75**
Popeye pencil sharpener, tin **165**
Popeye pirate pistol, clicker-type gun,
Marx, 1920s **360**
Popeye puzzle, hand-held dexterity-type
pinball style, 1929. **75**
Popeye toy, lithographed tin, drummer,
squeeze-type, Chein, 7" h., very good
(missing drum head) **1,210**

Popeye Carrying Parrot Cages Toy

Popeye toy, windup tin, color lithographed,
Popeye carrying parrot cages, Marx,
1930s, w/damaged box, 8½" h. (ILLUS.) **440**
Popeye toy, windup tin, color lithographed,
Popeye in rowboat, figure in pressed
steel, aluminum rowboat, ca. 1935, Hoge,
pristine condition, 14½" l. **4,620**
Popeye toy, windup tin, color lithographed,
Popeye roller skater, w/cloth pants, Line
Mar, very good condition, 6¾" h. **935**
Popeye toy, windup tin, color lithographed,
Popeye the Pilot in airplane, red, white &
blue, clockwork, excellent condition,
Louis Marx **990**

Popeye with Punching Bag Toy

Popeye toy, windup tin, color lithographed,
Popeye w/punching bag, tin platform
w/overhead suspended celluloid
punching bag, J. Chein, very good,
works, 7" h. (ILLUS.) **770**

Popeye toy, windup tin, "Popeye Express,"
Popeye pushing a wheelbarrow
w/rectangular trunk on top, 1930s, winder
needs repair, some wear **578**
Popeye toy, windup tin, "Popeye Express,"
Popeye pushing a wheelbarrow w/trunk
on it & parrot on trunk, Louis Marx,
excellent, 8½" l. **715**

Popeye on Tricycle Toy

Popeye toy, windup tin, Popeye riding a
tricycle w/bell on the back, Line Mar,
Japan (ILLUS.) **495**
Popeye toy, windup tin, Popeye walking,
w/box, very good, Marx **600**
Porky Pig figure, chalkware, early
Carnival-type, w/coin slot, ca. 1945, 12" h. **33**
Powerful Katrinka toy, windup tin, color
lithographed, Powerful Katrinka lifting
Jimmy in cart, Nifty, very good condition,
6½" l. . . . . **1,350 to 1,650**

Prince Valiant Dime Bank

Prince Valiant dime bank, lithographed tin,
the front printed in red, black & white on
yellow w/title & scene of the Prince
charging on his horse & wielding his
sword, King Features trademark, 1954,
very good condition (ILLUS.) **83**
Shirley Temple chalk figure, gold, "Shirley"
on base, 4" h. **125**
Shirley Temple doll carriage, wooden,
decals on side, all original, 1930s **875**
Sluggo doll, stuffed cloth, marked on wrist
tag "A "Georgene" Doll, Georgene
Novelties, Inc., New York 10, N.Y., Made
in U.S.A.," doll unmarked, cloth mask
face, painted black eyes, pug nose

Georgene Nancy & Sluggo Dolls

w/accented nostrils, closed smiling mouth, applied ears, jointed body, beige flannel feet for shoes, dressed in original blue pants, striped knit shirt, black jacket & brown cap, in original box w/marked label "A Georgene Product, No. 6102," three small dirty smudges, 13" h. (ILLUS. right) **775**

Smokey the Bear record, 45 rpm, w/original folder, ca. 1959 .... **38**

Superman badge, "Superman of America Club," figural, brass **180**

Superman bicycle siren, in original box **75**

Rare Large Superman Doll

Superman doll, jointed composition, painted blue & red outfit w/original cloth cape, Ideal, 1930s, some crazing, 13½" h. (ILLUS.) **1,595**

Superman game, Quoit set, old, in original box... **65**

Superman movie viewer, #800, w/three movies, Acme, very good w/good box,....... **205**

Superman muscle building set, "Superman Golden Muscle Building Set No. 1001," complete w/equipment & progress chart, by Peter Puppet Playthings, original box 11¼ x 18" (ILLUS.) **990**

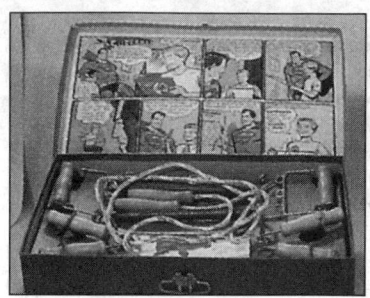

Superman Muscle Building Set

Superman pinback button, "Superman of America Club," ca 1948 .... **60**

Superman puzzle, in cylinder box **45**

Superman raygun, Krypto raygun, pressed steel projector pistol, able to flash pictures on wall, embossed design features Superman, original rolls in box, Daisy, 7½" x 10" (minor pitting on gun) **550**

Toonerville Trolley Windup Toy

Toonerville Trolley toy, windup tin, color lithographed model of the trolley, Fischer, ca. 1922, pristine, 5" l. (ILLUS.) **825**

Georgene Tubby Tom Doll

Tubby Tom doll, stuffed cloth, marked on paper hang tag "Tubby Tom by Marge, © 1951 by Marjorie H. Buell, Tubby Tom by Marge, Georgene Novelties, Inc., New York City, Exclusive Licensed Manufacturers, Made in U.S.A.," large painted black eyes, closed smiling mouth, applied ears, black yarn tuft of hair in front, brown flannel back of head for hair, jointed body, red fabric on ankles for socks, black cloth feet for shoes, dressed in original white shirt, brown pants, black jacket, red ribbon tie, white sailor hat, including marked box, 13", light age discoloration on edge of sailor hat, one bottom edge of box repaired inside (ILLUS., previous page) **900**

Uncle Wiggly toy, windup tin car, 1935, excellent condition, 8" l. **770**

Uncle Wiggly toy, windup tin, color lithographed, Uncle Wiggly Crazy Car, Distler, excellent, 9½" l., ... **3,520**

Woody Woodpecker Costume

Woody Woodpecker costume, one-piece cloth suit w/large red & white Woody on the chest, w/a molded plastic face mask, Collegeville, in original box (ILLUS.) **33**

CHILDREN'S BOOKS

CLASSIC CHILDREN'S BOOKS

The field of children's books is a large and complex one in which sizable price disparities exist. The values given below are average retail prices for first editions (or sometimes the first edition with a particular artist's illustrations) in fine condition. If post-1930, the dust jacket (if published with one) is assumed present. Crayon scribbles, damaged bindings, torn (or torn out) pages and other defects typical of children's books will substantially reduce value.

Some of these classic and desirable titles, notably those by L. Frank Baum and Lewis Carroll, exist in a bewildering variety of editions (as well as different "states" and "points" within an edition and further complications), with varying illustrators, publishers and so on; some also exist in signed, limited editions worth significantly more than the first trade edition.

Determining the correct edition can be particularly challenging with children's books; specialized author bibliographies should be consulted. Keep in mind that only one significant edition is listed here and that other highly desirable editions may also exist.

Alcott, Louisa May, "Little Men," Boston, 1871, first U.S. edition **$200**

Alcott, Louisa May, "Little Women," Boston, 1868-69, two volumes, first U.S. edition **3,500**

Alger, Horatio, Jr. "Ragged Dick or Street Life in New York with the Boot-Blacks," Boston, 1868, first U.S. edition **1,500**

Andersen, Hans Christian, "Fairy Tales," London, 1932, first edition with Arthur Rackham illustrations **300**

Bannerman, Helen, "The Story of Little Black Sambo," New York, 1901, first U.S. edition **450**

Barrie, James M., "Peter Pan in Kensington Gardens," New York, 1906, first U.S. edition **300**

Baum, L. Frank, "The Patchwork Girl of Oz," Chicago, 1913, first U.S. edition **300**

Baum, L. Frank, "The Wonderful Wizard of Oz," Chicago, 1900, first U.S. edition **6,500**

Carroll, Lewis, "Alice's Adventures in Wonderland," Boston, 1869, first U.S. edition **650**

Carroll, Lewis, "Through the Looking Glass, and What Alice Found There," Boston, 1872, first U.S. edition **350**

Cox, Palmer, "The Brownies: Their Book," New York, 1887, first U.S. edition **600**

Dahl, Roald, "Charlie and the Chocolate Factory," New York, 1964, first U.S. edition **125**

Grahame, Kenneth, "The Wind in the Willows," New York, 1908, first U.S. edition **300**

Grimm, Jacob, and Wilhelm, "The Fairy Tales of the Brothers Grimm," London, 1909, first British edition w/Arthur Rackham illustrations **250**

Gruelle, Johnny, "Raggedy Ann Stories," Joliet, Ill., 1920, first U.S. edition **200**

Kipling, Rudyard, "The Jungle Book," New York, 1894, first U.S. edition **200**

Lewis, C.S., "The Lion, the Witch, and the Wardrobe," New York, 1950, first U.S. edition **300**

Milne, A.A., "Winnie-the-Pooh," London, 1926, first British trade edition **750**

Montgomery, L.M., "Anne of Green Gables," New York, 1908, first U.S. edition **450**

Moore, Clement C., "A Visit from St. Nicholas," New York, 1862, first separate appearance, in pamphlet **900**

Potter, Beatrix, "The Tale of Peter Rabbit," London, 1902, first British trade edition **850**

Rey, H.A., "Curious George," Boston, 1941, first U.S. edition **250**

Saint-Exupery, Antoine de, "The Little Prince," New York, 1943, first U.S. edition **250**

Sendak, Maurice, "Where the Wild Things Are," New York, 1963, first U.S. edition **2,000**

Seuss, Dr., "And to Think That I Saw It on Mulberry Street," New York, 1937, first U.S. edition **300**

Seuss, Dr., "The Cat in the Hat," New York, 1957, first U.S. edition **400**

Stevenson, Robert Louis, "A Child's Garden of Verses," New York, 1885, first U.S. edition **300**

Stevenson, Robert Louis, "Treasure Island," Boston, 1884, first U.S. edition **1,500**

Thompson, Ruth Plumly, "The Gnome King of Oz," Chicago, 1927, first U.S. edition **400**

Tolkien, J.R.R., "The Hobbit," Boston, 1938, first U.S. edition **1,500**

White, E.B., "Charlotte's Web," New York, 1952, first U.S. edition **300**

Wilder, Laura Ingalls, "Little House on the Prairie," New York, 1935, first U.S. edition **200**

LITTLE GOLDEN BOOKS

"Alphabet From A-Z (The)," No. 3, 1942, illustrations by Vivienne Leah Blake, 42 pp. **40**

"Bedtime Stories," No. 2, 1942, illustrations by Gustaf Tenggren, 42 pp. **40**

"Betsy McCall," No. 559, 1965, copyright by McCall Corporation, illustrations by Ginnie Hofmann, written by Selma Robinson, 24 pp. **75**

"Bugs Bunny's Birthday"

"Bugs Bunny's Birthday," No. 98, 1950, copyright by Warner Bros. Cartoon, Inc., illustrations & text by Warner Bros., 28 pp. (ILLUS.) **14**

"Color Kittens (The)," No. 86, 1949, 1st edition, illustrations by Alice & Martin Provensen, written by Margaret Wise Brown, 28 pp. **25**

"Day In The Jungle (A)," No. 18, 1943, illustrations by Tibor Gergely, written by Janet Sebring Lowrey, 42 pp. **30**

"Doctor Dan, The Bandage Man," No. 295, 1950, w/Band-Aids, illustrations by Corinne Malvern, written by Helen Gaspard, 24 pp. **90**

"Duck And His Friends"

"Duck And His Friends," No. 81, 1949, illustrations by Richard Scarry, written by Kathryn & Byron Jackson, 28 pp. (ILLUS.) **14**

"Duck And His Friends," No. 81, 1949, puzzle edition, illustrations by Richard Scarry, written by Kathryn & Byron Jackson, 24 pp. **100**

"Frosty The Snowman," No. 142, 1951, illustrations by Corinne Malvern, written by Annie North Bedford, 28 pp. **11**

"Gaston And Josephine"

"Gaston And Josephine," No. 65, 1949, illustrations by Feodor Rojankovsky, written by George Duplaix, 42 pp. (ILLUS.) **25**

"Gene Autry," No. 230, 1955, copyright by Gene Autry, illustrations by Mel Crawford, written by Steffie Fletcher, 28 pp. **22**

"Hopalong Cassidy And The Bar 20 Cowboys," No. 147, 1952, copyright by Doubleday & Co., Inc., illustrations by Sahula-Dycke, written by E.M. Mulford, 28 pp. **25**

"Howdy Doody And The Princess," No. 135, 1952, copyright by Kagran Corp., illustrations by Art Seiden, written by Edward Kean, 28 pp. (ILLUS., next page) **25**

"Howdy Doody And The Princess"

"Mister Dog"

"Little Black Sambo"

"The Night Before Christmas"

"The Saggy Baggy Elephant"

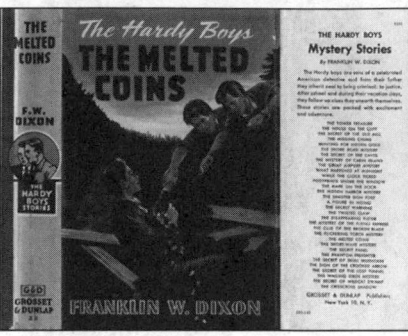

Hardy Boys *"The Melted Coins"*

"Shy Little Kitten (The)," No. 23, 1946, illustrations by Gustaf Tenggren, written by Kathleen Schurr, 42 pp. **25**

"Three Bears (The)," No. 47, 1948, 1st cover (one printing only), illustrations by Feodor Rojankovsky, 42 pp. **60**

"Tom And Jerry," No. 117, 1951, copyright by Leow's Inc., illustrations by Harvey Eisenberg & Don Maclaughlin, written by MGM, 28 pp. **14**

"Where Did The Baby Go?" No. 116, 1974, illustrations by Eloise Wilkin, written by Sheila Hayes, 24 pp. **11**

"Yogi Bear," No. 395, 1960, copyright by Hanna-Barbera Productions, illustrations by M. Kawaguchi, written by S. Quentin Hyatt, 24 pp. **18**

YOUTH BOOKS

HARDY BOYS

"Clue of the Broken Blade (The)," No. 21,1957, by Franklin W. Dixon, Heffelfinger, Grosset & Dunlap, ©1942, beige tweed w/brown multi-picture endpapers, yellow spine dust jacket w/37 Hardy Boys titles on front flap (Fn/Fn) **25**

"Flickering Torch Mystery (The)," No. 22,1960, by Franklin W. Dixon, Heffelfinger, 1st printing, Grosset & Dunlap, ©1943, beige tweed w/brown multi-picture endpapers, yellow spine dust jacket w/39 Hardy Boys titles on front flap (Fn/Fn). **30**

"Ghost of the Hardy Boys," by Leslie McFarlane, 1976, 1st printing, Methuen, Toronto, front free endpaper removed, library copy w/usual library stamps, dust jacket (VG/VG) **75**

"Melted Coins (The)," No. 23, 1953, by Franklin W. Dixon, Heffelfinger, 1st printing, Grosset & Dunlap, ©1944, beige tweed w/orange endpapers, orange spine dust jacket w/32 Hardy Boys titles, (Fn/Fn) (ILLUS.) **25**

"Secret of the Wildcat Swamp (The)," No. 31, by Franklin W. Dixon, Carpentieri, 1st printing, 44th title printing, ca. 1965, Grosset & Dunlap, ©1952, blue spine pictorial cover w/brown multi-picture endpapers, back cover w/44 Hardy Boys titles, original text (Fn) **15**

"Sign of the Crooked Arrow (The)," No. 28, 1959, by Franklin W. Dixon, Heffelfinger, 1st printing, Grosset & Dunlap, ©1949, beige tweed w/brown multi-picture endpapers, wrap-around dust jacket w/38 Hardy Boys titles on front flap (Fn/Fn) **25**

"Twisted Claw (The)," No. 18, 1959, by Franklin W. Dixon, Heffelfinger, 2nd printing, Grosset & Dunlap, ©1939, beige tweed w/brown multi-picture endpapers, yellow spine dust jacket w/38 Hardy Boys titles on front flap, light chipping to dust jacket spine (Fn/Fn-) **15**

NANCY DREW

"Bungalow Mystery (The)," No. 3, 1955, by Carolyn Keene (pseud.), Farah, 1st printing, 52nd title printing, story by Grosset & Dunlap, ©1930, blue tweed w/"digger" endpapers, wrap-around dust jacket w/32 Nancy Drew titles on front flap, closed tear & slight chipping to dust jacket spine (Fn/Fn-). **25**

"Haunted Bridge (The)," No. 15, 1942, by Carolyn Keene, Farah, 1st printing, 12th title printing, story by Grosset & Dunlap, ©1937, thick blue cloth w/orange silhouette on front cover & endpapers, good paper w/glossy frontispiece, white spine dust jacket w/18 Nancy Drew titles on front flap, slightly darkened dust jacket spine (Fn/Fn-). **180**

"Haunted Bridge (The)," No. 15, 1961, by Carolyn Keene, Farah, 2nd printing, 51st title printing, story by Grosset & Dunlap, ©1937, blue tweed w/multi-picture endpapers, white spine dust jacket w/38

Nancy Drew titles on front flap, last dust jacket printing, price clipped & closed tears on dust jacket (Fn/Fn-) 20

"Hidden Staircase (The)," No. 2, 1961, by Carolyn Keene, Farah, 2nd printing, 84th title printing, story by Grosset & Dunlap, ©1959, blue tweed w/multi-picture endpapers, wrap-around dust jacket w/38 Nancy Drew titles on front flap (Fn/Fn) 20

"Secret of the Old Clock (The)," No. 1, 1960, by Carolyn Keene, Farah, 2nd printing, 84th title printing, story by Grosset & Dunlap, NY, ©1959, blue tweed w/multi-picture endpapers, wrap-around dust jacket w/37 Nancy Drew titles on front flap (Fn/Fn) 20

"Whispering Statue (The)," No. 14, 1961, by Carolyn Keene, Farah, 2nd printing, 45th title printing, story by Grosset & Dunlap, ©1937, blue tweed w/multi-picture endpapers, white spine dust jacket w/38 Nancy Drew titles on front flap, slight chipping to top edge of dust jacket on back surface & small hole near foredge (Fn-/Fn-) 35

CHILDREN'S DISHES

During the reign of Queen Victoria, doll-houses and accessories became more popular; as the century progressed, there was greater demand for toys which would subtly train a little girl in the art of homemaking. Also see CHARACTER COLLECTIBLES, DISNEY COLLECTIBLES, under Glass, DEPRESSION GLASS and PATTERN GLASS.

Berry set: master bowl & six sauce dishes; clear pressed glass, Pattee Cross patt., the set............................... **$55**

Butter, cov., pressed glass, Drum patt., clear ... **145**

Butter dish, cov., clear pressed glass, Tulip & Honeycomb patt., large size **66**

Cake stand, pressed glass, Rexford patt., clear .. **35**

Two Children's Castor Sets

Castor set, four-bottle, clear bottles & shaker in the clear pressed glass, American Shield patt., in a silver-plated frame w/flaring openwork foot, ring holder & central handle w/top loop centered by a small figural bird, late 19th c., the set (ILLUS. left) **121**

Castor set, four-bottle, two shakers & two bottles in clear pressed glass, Flute patt., in a silver-plate frame w/high stamped-design foot, ring holder & central handle w/a large top loop centered by a sitting girl, late 19th c., the set (ILLUS. right) **220**

Coffeepot, porcelain, embossed scroll & grape leaf design w/cobalt blue trim, Germany, 5" h.......................... **88**

Children's Creamer

Creamer, pressed glass, Drum patt., clear (ILLUS.) **55**

Creamer, pressed glass, Pennsylvania patt., clear **35**

Pitcher, lemonade, pressed glass, Oval Star patt., clear........................... **65**

Punch bowl, pressed glass, Inverted Strawberry patt., clear **65**

Punch bowl, pressed glass, Oval Star patt., clear w/gold rim **55**

Punch bowl, pressed glass, Wheat Sheaf patt., clear........................... **30**

Punch cup, pressed glass, Wheat Sheaf patt., clear............................ **8**

Punch set: punch bowl & six cups; clear pressed glass, Wheat Sheaf patt., Cambridge, the set..................... **121**

Children's Punch Set

Punch set: punch bowl & six cups; pressed glass, Nursery Rhyme patt., milk glass, the set (ILLUS.) **193**

Sauce dish, pressed glass, Wheat Sheaf patt., clear............................ **9**

Children's Spooner

Spooner, pressed glass, Hawaiian Lei patt.,
Higbee mark, clear (ILLUS.) 35

Sugar bowl, cov., clear pressed glass,
Amazon patt. 33

Sugar bowl, cov., Menagerie patt., figural
sitting bear, clear 149

Sugar bowl, cov., pressed glass, Drum
patt., clear. 150

Sugar bowl, cov., pressed glass, Hawaiian
Lei patt., Higbee mark, clear 40

Sugar bowl, cov., pressed glass, Oval Star
patt., clear. 30

Sugar bowl, cov., pressed glass, Tulip with
Honeycomb patt., clear 25

Table set: cov. butter, cov. sugar bowl,
creamer & spooner; clear pressed glass,
Button Panel No. 44 patt., the set 198

Table set: cov. butter, cov. sugar, creamer
& spooner; clear pressed glass, Rexford
patt., the set 72

Table set: cov. sugar, creamer, cov. butter
dish & spooner; Nursery Rhyme patt.,
clear, the set. 220

Table set: creamer, sugar, cov. butter,
spooner & matching tray; clear pressed
glass, Hobnail w/Thumbprint Base patt.,
5 pcs. 275

Table set, pressed glass, Oval Star patt.,
clear, 4 pcs. 175

Tea set: cov. teapot, creamer & sugar bowl,
waste bowl & 6 cups & saucers;
ironstone, Moss Rose patt., 16 pcs.
(teapot damaged) 220

Tumbler, pressed glass, Oval Star patt., clear 11

Water set: pitcher & five tumblers; clear
pressed glass, Pattee Cross patt., the set 66

Water set: pitcher & seven tumblers;
pressed glass, Nursery Rhyme patt.,
clear, 8 pcs. 198

CHILDREN'S MUGS

The small sized mugs used by children first attempting to drink from a cup appeal to many collectors. Because they were made of such diverse materials as china, glass, pottery, graniteware, plated silver and sterling silver, the collector can assemble a diversified collection or single out a particular type around which to base a collection. Also see CHILDREN'S DISHES and PATTERN GLASS.

Pressed glass, Beaded Column & Panel
patt., clear $15

Pressed glass, Butterfly patt., clear 38

Pressed glass, Diagonal Flowered Band
patt., clear 25

Pressed glass, Grapevine with Ovals patt.,
clear 21

Pressed glass, Little Bo Peep patt., clear 85

Pressed glass, Little Bo Peep patt., clear,
etched 65

Pressed glass, Ribbed Forget-me-not patt.,
clear 23

Pressed glass, Robin patt., amber 25

Pressed glass, Scampering Lamb patt., clear . . . 59

Staffordshire pottery, cylindrical w/molded
base & C-scroll handle, black transfer-
printed design representing the month of
December w/a young girl w/a cart full of
guns, drum, fiddle, doll, a British flag & a
rhyme, 2⅛" h. 61

Staffordshire pottery, cylindrical w/molded
base & C-scroll handle, black transfer-
printed design representing the month of
August, shows men, women & children
hand-harvesting wheat w/a printed
rhyme, 2¼" h. 77

Staffordshire pottery, cylindrical w/molded
base & C-scroll handle, blank transfer-
printed design of a young girl grooming a
large dog, the ground littered w/bones &
a food dish, 2⅜" h. 33

Staffordshire pottery, cylindrical, blue
transfer-printed sheep in front of a
cottage above the words "A PRESENT
FROM WASHINGTON," blue line border,
ca. 1820-30, 2" h. 605

Staffordshire pottery, cylindrical, black
transfer-printed scene titled "Cornwallis
Surrendering His Sword at Yorktown,"
pink lustre border, probably by Wood, first
quarter 19th c., 2¹⁄₁₆" h. (line across the
base, repair to base chip damages part of
the title). 413

Staffordshire pottery, cylindrical,
polychrome decorated "Keep thy Shop &
Thy Shop will Keep Thee," 2½" h. (hairline) . . . 50

CHRISTMAS COLLECTIBLES

Starting in the mid-19th century more and more items began to be manufactured to decorate the home, office or commercial business to celebrate the Christmas season. In the 20th century the trend increased. Companies such as Coca-Cola, Sears and others began to employ specially produced Christmas items. The inexpensive glass, then plastic Christmas tree decoration began to reach into almost every home. With the end of World War II the toy market moved into the picture with annual Santa Claus parades and children's visits to Santa to leave Christmas wish lists. As the 21st century approaches this trend will continue and material from earlier Christmas seasons will climb in value.

CHRISTMAS ORNAMENTS

Acorn

Acorn, silver, ca. 1940s, "Made in the United States," 4" (ILLUS.)............... **$25**

Angel

Angel, small spun fiberglass decoration w/angel figure inside, ca. 1920s, 2" (ILLUS.) 30
Angel w/silver wings, Dresden-type, Germany, ca. 1880-1900s 200
Bicycle, cotton batting 200
Camel, Dresden-type, Germany, ca. 1880-1900s........................ 65
Football, Dresden-type Germany, ca. 1880-1900s........................ 165
Guitar w/applied decorations, Dresden-type, Germany, ca. 1880-1900s............ 225
Peach, w/rough tinsel, made in Germany, 2" 100
Santa beating drum, cotton batting, w/die cut, 4" h. 300

CHRISTMAS TREE LIGHTS

FIGURAL BULBS

Andy Gump, decorated milk glass............. 50
Angel, hard plastic, painted, Japan, ca. 1930-50s, 4¾" h. 12
Aviator, decorated milk glass, Japan, ca. 1930-50s, 3" h......................... 24
Cat w/fiddle, milk glass, painted, Japan, ca. 1930-50s, 3½" h. 28
Clown w/mask, milk glass, painted, Japan, ca. 1930-50s, ½" h. 24
Dog in basket, milk glass, painted, Japan, ca. 1930-50s, 3¼" h. 28
Father Christmas, double-sided, milk glass, painted, Japan, ca. 1930-50s, 3" h. 25
Frog, milk glass, painted, Japan, ca. 1930-50s, 2¾" h. 30
Jiminy Cricket, milk glass, painted, Japan, ca. 1930-50s, Disney, 2¾" h............... 28
King Cole, decorated milk glass.............. 25
Lantern, milk glass, painted, snow-laden, Japan, ca. 1930-50s, 2¼" h............... 6
Little Orphan Annie, milk glass, painted, Japan, ca. 1930-50s, 3" h. 60
Mickey Mouse, milk glass, painted, Disney, Japan, ca. 1930-50s, 2¾" h............... 30
Moon Mullins, milk glass, painted, Japan, ca. 1930-50s, 2" h....................... 50
Owl, milk glass, painted, Japan, ca. 1930-50s, 3¼" h. 40
Parrot, milk glass, painted, Japan, ca. 1930-50s, 3¾" h. 15
Pluto, milk glass, painted, Japan, ca. 1930-50s, Disney, 3" h. 24

From left: Santa Light Bulb & Snowman Light Bulb

Santa, milk glass, painted, Japan, ca. 1930-50s, 3" h. (ILLUS. left)............. 15
Santa w/trees & toys, decorated milk glass, regular socket, Japan, ca. 1930-50s, 5" h........................ 95
Snowman, milk glass, painted, Japan, ca. 1930-50s, 3½" h. (ILLUS. right) 24
St. Nicholas w/staff, milk glass, painted, Japan, ca. 1930-50s, 2¾" h................. 28

HALLMARK KEEPSAKE ORNAMENTS
(1973-1976)

In 1973, Hallmark Cards introduced its new product line of Keepsake Ornaments. Adding color and variety to the present-day standard glass balls, these eighteen Keepsake Ornaments quickly blossomed into a new holiday tradition and collectibles field. The listings below represent pricing for unboxed and unpackaged Keepsake Ornaments from 1973 through 1976. Boxed and packaged ornaments will sell at a higher price.

Adorable Adornments: Betsey Clark, 1975, No. QX 157-1, by artist Donna Lee, 3½" h. **240**

Adorable Adornments: Drummer Boy, 1975, No. QX 161-1, handcrafted, by artist Donna Lee, 3½" h. **150**

Angel, 1974, No. QX 110-1, white glass ball, 3¼" d. **67**

Baby's First Christmas, 1976, No. QX 221-1, white satin ball marked "Baby's First Christmas," dated "1976," 3" d. **100**

Betsey Clark, 1973, No. XHD 100-2, white glass ball, depicts five girls around Christmas tree, 3¼" d. **75**

Betsey Clark series, 1976, No. QX 195-1, white glass ball marked "Christmas 1976," 3¼" d. **75**

Bicentennial Charmers, 1976, No. QX 198-1, marked "Merry Christmas 1976" on white glass ball, 3¼" d. **55**

Blue Girl, 1973, No. XHD 85-2, yarn ornament, 4½" h. **25**

Chickadees, 1976, No. QX 204-1, marked "Christmas 1976" on white glass ball, 2⅝" d. . . . **60**

Colonial Children set: 1976, No. QX 208-1, depicts children making snowman & marked "Christmas 1976" on one, children bringing home Christmas tree & marked "Merry Christmas 1976" on other, white glass balls, set of 2, 2¼" d. **80**

Elf, 1973, No. XHD 79-2, yarn ornament, 4½" h. **28**

Happy Holidays Kissing Ball, 1976, No. QX 225-1, red & green holly surrounding "Happy Holidays" on white satin ball, comes w/mistletoe, 5-6" d. **220**

Little Girl, 1973, No. XHD 82-5, yarn ornament w/pink dress & blond hair, 4½" h. **25**

Manger Scene, 1973, No. XHD 102-2, white glass ball, designed scene on dark red background, 3¼" h. **85**

Mrs. Santa, 1973, No. XHD 75-2, yarn ornament , 4½" h. **25**

Norman Rockwell, 1976, No. QX 196-1, front depicts Santa resting after travels, Santa feeding reindeer on back, marked "Christmas 1976," white glass ball, 3¼" d. **60**

Norman Rockwell series, 1974, No. QX 106-1, white glass ball, dated "1974," depicts "Jolly Postman" & father & son bringing home Christmas tree, marked "Merry Christmas 1974," 3¼" d. **70**

Nostalgia Ornaments: Locomotive, 1975, No. QX 127-1, by artist Linda Sickman, dated "1975," 3¼" d. **180**

Nostalgia Ornaments: Peace On Earth, 1975, No. QX 131-1, snowy village scene, by artist Linda Sickman, dated "1975," 3¼" d. **130**

Raggedy Ann, 1976, No. QX 221-1, depicts Ann hanging stockings on fireplace, marked "Merry Christmas 1976," white satin ball, 2½" d. **50**

Raggedy Ann and Raggedy Andy set: 1974, No. QX 114-1, white glass balls, set of 4, 1¾" d. **70**

Rudolph and Santa, 1976, No. QX 213-1, front marked "Rudolph the Red-Nosed Reindeer" w/"Merry Christmas 1976" on back, white satin ball, 2½" d. **75**

Santa, 1973, No. XHD 74-5, yarn ornament, 4½" h. **25**

Santa With Elves, 1973, No. XHD 101-5, white glass ball, 3¼" d. **70**

Snowgoose, 1974, No. QX 107-1, white glass ball, 3¼" d. **70**

Tree Treats: Santa, 1976, No. QX 177-1, marked "Season's Greetings 1976," 2¾-3⅝" h. **180**

Tree Treats: Shepherd, 1976, No. QX 175-1, marked "Season's Greetings 1976," 2¾-3⅝" h. **100**

Twirl-Abouts: Partridge, 1976, No. QX 174-1, partridge in pear wreath, dated "1976," by artist Linda Sickman, 3½-4" h. **145**

Twirl-Abouts: Santa, 1976, No. QX 172-1, Santa in wreath, dated "1976," by artist Linda Sickman, 3½-4" h. **100**

Yesteryears: Santa, 1976, No. QX 182-1, dated "1976," 2¾"-4" h. **150**

Yesteryears: Train, 1976, No. QX 181-1, dated "1976," 2¾"-4" h. **155**

POSTCARDS

Father Christmas Holding Lantern

Father Christmas, dressed in grey-blue suit, holding lantern up to street sign, reads "A Merry Christmas," Germany, B & W, No. 296 (ILLUS., previous page) **14**

Father Christmas With Children

Father Christmas, dressed in long blue robe, w/children outside house, marked "Christmas Greetings" (ILLUS.) **20**

Father Christmas Ice Skating With Children

Father Christmas, dressed in red robe, skating w/little boy on his back & holding little girl's hand, marked "Wesolych Swiat" (ILLUS.) **15**

Santa, celluloid add-on, polycolor w/fringe **30**

Santa In Sleigh, metal add-on, marked "Merry Christmas," fur trim **35**

Santa With Nimble Nicks

Santa w/Nimble Nicks, Santa in old car w/Nimble Nicks & presents, marked "Merry Christmas From Us All," Whitney Publishing (ILLUS.) **15**

St. Nicholas w/Krampus, standing behind dish of nuts & fruit, Austria, M. M. Vienne (ILLUS.) **45**

St. Nicholas With Krampus

MISCELLANEOUS

Advertising, pictorial die-cut counter card for Ayers Cherry, Lowell, Mass. Co., ca. 1890s **400**

Album, embossed, w/multiple Santas, Victorian .. **75**

Animated elf, rubber-type head, glass eyes, cloth clothing, electric, U.S.A., 18" h. **600**

Belsnickle, white robe covered w/glitter, early, Germany, 7¾" h. **600**

Book, "Night Before Christmas," McLoughlin, ca. 1888 .... **140**

Cake pan, tin, Santa, 9" l. **65**

Candy container, old-fashioned Santa on elephant nodder, 8½" h. (some wear to flocking) **500**

Candy container, Santa in chenille boot, Japan, 8½" h. **100**

Snowman Candy Container

Candy container, snowman, pressed board (ILLUS.) **125**

Child angel, die-cut, Victorian, Germany, 11" h. **175**

Christmas seals booklet, No. 80-935, Dennison Co., set of 48 .... **8**

Christmas tree stand, cast iron, electrified w/pointsetters & sockets for bulbs, painted ... **135**

Christmas tree stand, cast iron, large round stand w/elves, painted **400**

Costume, Santa Claus, in original box,
ca. 1940 (missing beard) 45

Creche & Figures

Creche & figures, the creche made in
Germany, figures made in Japan,
Germany & Italy, value of figures
depends on condition & where
manufactured, ca. 1930s, creche price
only (ILLUS.) . . . . 100+
Die-cut Santa Claus, air-brushed, 9¼" h. 85
Die-cut Santa Claus, in blue suit w/glittery
& gold additions, German, Victorian, 20" h. 600
Doll, Santa Claus, composition, dressed in
brown suit, snow on Santa, Germany,
30" h. 2,800

Santa Bisque Figurine

Figurine, bisque, Santa w/bag of toys,
Hallmark (ILLUS.). 125

"Nightmare Before Christmas" Santa

Figurine, "Nightmare Before Christmas"
Santa Claus, in original box (ILLUS.) 125

Figurine, Santa Claus, celluloid, dressed
in blue, in sleigh w/toys & Teddy
bear 125
Game, "Visit of Santa Claus," McLoughlin 500
Hanging lantern, Santa face w/glass eyes,
molded composition 700
Kugel, figural ball, silver, Germany, 9" d. 200
Kugel, figural grape, bluish purple,
Germany, 12" h. 600
Match cover, Santa on front cover, candle-
shaped matches inside, 3½" 20
Photograph, shows little boy & girl dressed
in nightgowns sitting in front of Christmas
tree w/toys, ca. 1910 60
Russian Santa, white cotton batting,
all-white, 18" h. 800

*Santa Claus & Mrs. Claus
Salt & Pepper Shakers*

Salt & pepper set, ceramic, Santa Claus &
Mrs. Claus, white rough spaghetti texture
to represent fur, ca. 1950s, made in
Japan, 5" (ILLUS.) 50
Tinsel, metallic strand-type, U.S.A.,
mint in box 18
Tray, tin, oval, depicts full-figure Santa in
blue suit w/toys, early tray painted by
artist John Moreno in 1997 350

Coca-Cola Santa Claus Tray

Tray, Coca-Cola Santa Claus, 1973,
10¾ x 13¼" (ILLUS.) 60
Tree, green bristle brush-type, on red base,
simulated snow on end of branches,
ca. 1940s-1950s, 21" h. (ILLUS. left, next
page) 35
Tree, feather-type, turn-of-the-century, on
decorated red base, w/small decorations,
27" h. (ILLUS. right, next page) . . . . 400+

*From left: Green Bristle Brush Tree &
Feather Tree w/Decorations*

CLOCKS

Rosewood Grained Banjo Clock

Banjo clock, E. Howard & Co., Boston,
Massachusetts, rosewood grained No. 5
timepiece, the circular molded bezel
enclosing a white painted metal dial
inscribed "Howard & Co., Boston" &
eight-day weight-driven movement above
the half round moldings framing the throat
& pendulum box églomisé black &
maroon tablets, mid-19th c., very minor
imperfections, 28½" h. (ILLUS.) **$2,415**

Banjo clock, Leonard Noyes, New
Hampshire attribution, mahogany case
w/gilded facade moldings & brass trim,
original reverse-painted glass in the waist
w/flaking & touch-up, replaced glass in
bottom panel, brass works w/weight,
pendulum & key, round dial w/Roman
numerals & traces of maker's label, early
19th c., 31¼" h.(case reinforced w/glue,
early finial replaced) **1,430**

English Georgian Bracket Clock

Bracket clock, Frodsham & Sons, England,
ebonized wood case, the pagoda-form
flattened rectangular top w/inset beveled
glass panel & angled swing loop carrying
handle, the upright beveled glass sides
showing the works & the ornately
engraved brass dial w/Roman numerals,
gadrooned base band over the stepped &
flaring base over a scrolled apron &
bracket feet, signed, England, Georgian
period, ca. 1790 (ILLUS.) **3,250**

Cuckoo clock, wall-type, carved hardwood
Black Forest-style, typical house form,
topped by a carved bird & flanked by
clusters of fruit, the face w/ivory hands,
two-train weight-driven movement,
Germany, late 19th c., 23½ " h.
(restoration) **348**

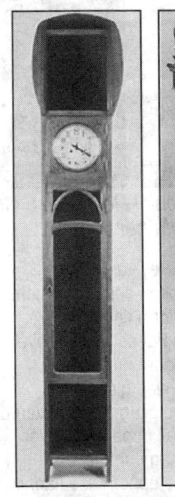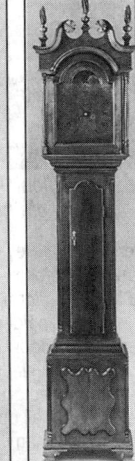

*From left: Arts & Crafts & Chippendale
Cherrywood Grandfather Clocks*

Grandfather, Arts & Crafts style, tall slender
oak case w/an oblong top backboard
behind an open compartment over a
square door w/scroll-carved corners
flanking the round bezel opening to a
round dial w/Arabic numerals above a tall
slender amber glass glazed door
w/arched loop at the top, an open

compartment at the bottom, low arched bootjack feet, applied brasses, Europe, early 20th c., 86¼" h. (ILLUS. left, previous page). **1,265**

Grandfather, Benjamin Rittenhouse, Philadelphia, Pennsylvania, Chippendale carved cherrywood, the broken swan's neck pediment w/pinwheel terminals & urn & flame finials above an arched glazed door opening to an engraved brass dial inscribed "BENJAMIN RITTENHOUSE - FECIT 1790," w/second hand, date hand & moon phase dial flanked by colonettes, the arched door below flanked by fluted quarter-columns above a 'turtle-mounted' base w/similar columns on ogee bracket feet, ca. 1780, 11 x 19¼", 8' 3" h. (ILLUS. right, previous page) **17,250**

From left: Colonial Revival & Gothic Grandfather Clocks

Grandfather, Colonial Revival carved mahogany case, broken-scroll pediment centered by a lotus-form finial & carved w/rosettes & scrolling decoration above the arched glazed door bordered by carved beading, beveled glass door opening to an arched gilt-brass & silvered metal dial w/two small upper dials over the main dial w/Roman numerals & ornate spandrels, the upper case flaring out & bead-carved above the long case fitted w/a long door w/nine small square beveled panes above & below the large beveled central pane showing the large brass pendulum, the stepped-out lower case w/an ornately scroll-carved central panel over a scalloped apron & boldly carved hairy paw feet, Westminster & Whittington chimes, retailed by Bigelow, Kennard & Co., Boston, late 19th - early 20th c., overall 95" h. (ILLUS. left). **4,888**

Grandfather, Elliott, London, England, mahogany Gothic Revival case, the Gothic arch crest topped by a large flame-style finial & flanked by spiked spire corner finials over the arched glass door opening to a moon phase dial over the clock dial w/Arabic numerals, the lower glass panel of the door w/Gothic arch muntin opening to the weights & chimes, the door flanked by blocked pilasters above the paneled platform w/Gothic trefoil carving, molded base band on beveled bun feet, dial labeled "Elliott, London," brass works w/tubular Westminster & Whittington chimes, w/key & pendulum w/its mercury vials removed, England, late 19th - early 20th c., 97" h. (ILLUS. right) **7,700**

Grandfather, Renaissance Revival-style, carved walnut, a male & a female caryatid flanking either side of hood, the face w/painted lunar phases in arch, brass mounts & subsidiary dials, the case w/glass door flanked by carved terms, square base w/winged beast terms to sides, carved paw feet, late 19th c., 97½". **9,775**

Renaissance Revival-style Grandfather Clock

Grandfather, Renaissance Revival-style, walnut case, the hood w/fruit & scroll carving, the round face w/painted stylized sun w/brass hands as stylized rays, weight-driven movement, the case open w/bobbin-turned columns on acanthus bases topped by carved female faces, the columns flanking a carved grotesque, the base w/fruit & scroll carving, ca. 1900, Germany, 79" h. (ILLUS.) **1,955**

Lantern clock, Thomas Wheeler, London, England, brass, the sides w/hinged plates, the top bell w/straps applied to

Early English Lantern Clock

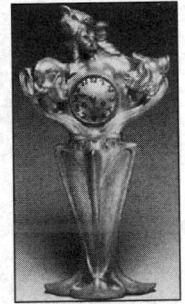

Art Nouveau Mantel Clock

finials centering pierced plates, the silvered chapter ring w/Roman numerals centering an alarm indicator, w/one hand, on bun feet, signed "Thomas Wheeler near ye French Church, London," Charles II period, late 17th c. (ILLUS) **4,889**

Novelty, table model "swinging-arm" type, painted cast-metal, a round foot supporting the figure of a standing classical maiden in flowing gown holding one arm up & supporting the round clock dial & free-swinging pendulum in the other, late 19th c., 14" h. **440**

Novelty, table model "swinging-arm" type, bronzed spelter w/a standing figure of a classical maiden holding aloft a free-swinging torch topped by a brass sphere enclosing the works & w/a band of applied numbers, Ansonia Clock Company, Ansonia, Connecticut, late 19th c., overall 31" h. (loss to the suspension) **1,210**

Shelf or mantel, Aaron Williard, Jr., Boston, Massachusetts, Federal mahogany & mahogany veneer case, the tall upright case w/a pierced fretwork centering a fluted plinth & brass ball finial above the flat half-round molded cornice & glazed door w/half-round molding framing the églomisé tablet w/shield spandrels inscribed "Aaron Willard Jr. Boston," opening to an iron concave white & gilt dial w/Roman numerals & a brass eight-day weight-driven striking movement, the lower mahogany hinged door on rounded base band & small ball feet, refinished, early 19th c., 36¼" h. (restored) **2,990**

Shelf or mantel, Ansonia Clock Company, New York, New York, "Regal" model, gilded metal Louis XV-Style upright case, the footed base, corner posts & top cast overall w/ornate leafy scrolls, rounded top corners centered by a pointed scrolling finial, beveled glass sides & a round enameled dial w/Arabic numerals, late 19th c., 18½" h. **1,870**

Shelf or mantel, Art Nouveau, gilt-metal, the circular clock face w/black Arabic numerals surrounded by three fully sculpted female busts, each w/long hair & smiling, angular tapering base terminating in a quatrefoil foot, works impressed "Medaille d'Argent," ca. 1900, France, 10½" h. (ILLUS.) **977**

Shelf or mantel, Atkins & Downs, Bristol, Connecticut, carved & painted Classical style case, carved eagle crestrail flanked by small turned finials over a long two-pane door opening to a painted dial w/Arabic numerals, door flanked by half-round carved columns, overall black paint w/gilt accents, small carved paw front feet, mirrored lower door, ca. 1830-40, 39¼" h. (loss & restoration to case) **578**

Shelf or mantel, Chelsea Clock Company, Boston, Massachusetts, Classical style gilt-bronze, ivory & marble case, a large round gilt-bronze narrow leaf-cast framework topped by a large fruit & leaf finial & enclosing the large marble dial w/overlaid pierced metal Roman numerals, raised on a double C-scroll & leaf pedestal on a leaf-cast rectangular ring over a rectangular white marble platform w/narrow gilt-bronze & thin marble base, retailed by Caldwell & Co., New York, New York, late 19th c., 12" h. . . . **10,350**

Shelf or mantel, china case, a high arched case front w/molded scroll border & pierced scroll handles, molded leafy scrolls at the bottom sides above the paneled plinth base, a round metal dial w/Arabic numerals, decorated w/large scattered yellow roses & green leaves, late 19th - early 20th c., 15½" h. **403**

Shelf or mantel, Coe & Co., New York, papier-maché, the scrolled front embellished w/gilt, polychrome & mother-of-pearl floral designs, housing the circular enamel dial inscribed "Saml. S. Spencer" & lever spring-driven movement, all mounted on a decorated oval base on brass ball feet under glass

Papier-maché Clock

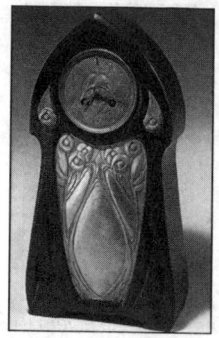

Maurice Dufrêne Mantel Clock

dome, labeled "Botsford's Improved Patent Timepiece manufactured by Coe & Co. 52 Dey Street, New York," 11" h. (ILLUS.) **1,265**

Shelf or mantel, Eli Terry, Jr., Plymouth, Connecticut, carved mahogany Classical style case w/a carved eagle crest above a two-pane long door opening to a painted dial w/Roman numerals flanked by leaf carved half-columns, small paw-carved front feet, label inside, eight-day wooden works, first half 19th c., 37" h. (finials missing). **440**

Shelf or mantel, Eli Terry, Plymouth, Connecticut, miniature pillar-and-scroll mahogany case, the swan's-neck cresting above a two-pane glazed door, the upper pane over the painted dial w/Arabic numerals & decorated spandrels, the lower pane reverse-painted w/a landscape showing a classical building, slender colonettes down the sides, molded base, shaped apron & slender French feet, old refinish, 30-hour movement, minor imperfections, ca. 1822, 22½" h. **7,455**

Shelf or mantel, gilt-bronze, the porcelain face mounted in a drum case, works marked "S. Marti Medaille d'Or Paris 1900," the top w/a large bank of gilt-bronze clouds atop which rests an angel blowing a trumpet (presumably Gabriel), above the dial a putto holding a scroll inscribed "Raphael Poussin, Montesquiew, Michelange," 22¼" h. **1,265**

Shelf or mantel, Maurice Dufrêne, Art Nouveau mahogany & gilt-bronze case, model 218-v, produced by La Maison Moderne, arched molded hood above a gilt-bronze face cast w/numerals flanked by apostrophic gilt-bronze bosses cast w/flowers above a lower gilt-bronze panel cast w/leafage & flowers, ca. 1902 (ILLUS.). **4,025**

Shelf or mantel, Neoclassical-Style, gilt-bronze, cloisonné & porcelain, the top w/a cloisonné-decorated figural urn finial w/scrolled handles & pedestal foot atop a domed cloisonné top above the upright case w/six cloisonné colonettes w/turned metal finials framing porcelain plaques decorated w/scenes of Neoclassical maidens, the beveled glass front & back showing the suspended works & round enameled dial w/Roman numerals centered by a group of cherubs & ornate metal pendulum, compressed knob metal feet, France, ca. 1900, 16" h. **3,105**

Shelf or mantel, New Haven Clock Co., New Haven, Connecticut, mahogany veneer, an upright rectangular ogee case surrounding the tall two-part glazed door, the upper section over the painted dial w/Roman numerals, the lower section w/a reverse-painted scene of a beehive, 30-hour movement, mid-19th c., 26" h. **110**

Shelf or mantel, Norris North, Torrington, Connecticut, Classical mahogany & stenciled style case, the flat cornice above a two-pane glazed tall door w/the larger upper pane over the gilt-trimmed white-painted dial w/Arabic numerals above the lower panel reverse-painted w/a large round central reserve w/a bust portrait of an elegant lady framed by leafy scrolls, engaged black-painted stenciled columns down the sides, flat base, 30-hour movement, ca. 1825, 23¾" h. **4,888**

Shelf or mantel, Richmond Fabi, France, bronze & gilt-bronze, a tall rectangular plinth in bronze w/gilt-bronze scroll feet & applied band & pierced scroll mounts supporting a round gilt-bronze case enclosing the movement topped by a gilt-bronze figure of Cupid leaning on a bow, marked "Richmond Fabri," France, late 19th c., 4½ x 8¼", 15¼" h. **1,430**

Shelf or mantel, Seth Thomas Clock Co., Thomaston, Connecticut, bird's-eye maple & mahogany veneer, upright ogee case w/maple front sides & mahogany banding, a single tall two-pane glazed door, the upper glass over the painted dial w/Roman numerals, the lower pane reverse-painted in color w/a scene of the Baltimore cemetery, 30-hour works, mid-19th c., 26" h. **121**

From left: Federal-style Mahogany Mantel Clock & Louis XV-Style Waterbury Clock

Shelf or mantel, Seth Thomas, Plymouth, Connecticut, Federal-style, mahogany pillar & scroll case, the scrolled cresting joining three plinths & brass urn finials above the glazed door & églomisé tablet showing a town green flanked by free standing columns, the gilt & polychrome dial w/a basket of flowers decoration housing the wooden thirty-hour weight-driven movement, all resting on cut-out bracket feet, old finish, ca. 1825, tablet w/paint loss, 31½" h. (ILLUS. left) **2,415**

Shelf or mantel, Waterbury Clock Co., Waterbury, Connecticut, Louis XV Revival-Style, gilt-metal, the upright domed case w/ornate leafy scrolls & arches & a loop top handle above the round glass door w/bezel opening to a an inset porcelain plaque decorated w/putti, scroll-framed mask at the front bottom, ornate leafy scroll legs, ca. 1900, w/key (ILLUS. right) **200**

Ship's bell clock, Model No. 10, w/twin-train movement striking on gong, Arabic numerals, silvered dial, & lacquered brass case & glazed door in the form of a ship's wheel, patent dated 1910, Waterbury Clock Co., Waterbury, Connecticut, 8¼" d. **288**

Wag-on-wall clock, André Spéth, France, embossed brass, the square upper section w/a sheet steel frame w/an arched stamped brass cornice, the open enameled dial w/Roman numerals signed "André Spéth à la Charité," the large long tapering rounded pendulum of ornate stamped brass w/C-scroll, flowers & a classical urn, the dial w/hairlines & yellowed repair, w/weights & key,

From left: Early French Wag-on-Wall Clock & Large Ornate Cartel-style Wall Clock

wrought-iron shelf a late replacement, Normandy, France, late 18th - early 19th c., overall 56" h. (ILLUS. left) **935**

Wall clock, cartel-style, gilt-bronze Louis XVI-Style case, the lyre-form case flanked by putto terms holding a wreath, the tall neck centered by a sphinx term below a domed canopy & scrolls, the lower case cast also w/delicate floral bands around the round dial w/enameled Roman numerals, probably France, ca. 1900, retailed & signed by J.E. Caldwell & Co., Philadelphia, overall 55" h. (ILLUS. right) **2,875**

Wall clock, Hector Guimard, Paris, France, Art Nouveau style gilt-bronze & copper case, a rounded border frame of gilt-bronze pointed loopings around a copper bezel around the large round dial w/Arabic numerals surrounded w/a band of small leaf & berry sprigs, the center signed "Pardieu - Agen.," designed by Guimard, ca. 1900, 19" h. **23,000**

CLOISONNÉ & RELATED WARES

Cloisonné work features enameled designs on a metal ground. There are several types of this work, the best-known utilizing cells of wire on the body of the object into which the enamel is placed. In the plique-a-jour form of cloisonné, the base is removed leaving translucent enamel windows. The champlevé technique entails filling in, with enamels, a design which is cast or carved in the base. Pigeon Blood" (akasuke) cloisonné includes a type where foil is enclosed within colored enamel walls. Cloisonné is said to have been invented by the Chinese and brought to perfection by the Japanese.

CLOISONNÉ

Early Chinese Cloisonné Bowl

Bowl, round footring supporting a deep bell-form bowl, decorated in color w/dragon Pa Pao Hsiang (eight auspicious emblems), bats for prosperity & double happiness characters, China, possibly late Ch'en Lung, late 18th - early 19th c., 7¼" d., 3¾" h. (ILLUS.)................**$431**

Fine Chinese Cloisonné Censor

Censor, cov., globular body raised on tripod legs w/gilt-bronze animal masks, large squared upright S-scroll handles & the domed cover w/gilt-bronze vents depicting bats & a pierced gilt-bronze dragon finial, the entire piece w/a turquoise blue ground w/multi-colored enamels of scrolling vines & blossoms, Ching Dynasty, China, 18" h. (ILLUS.) **2,013**

Censor, cov., wide squatty bulbous body raised on three curved animal heads & paw legs, upright rectangular keyfret-style shoulder handles, the high domed cover w/a gilt foo lion w/ribbon in its mouth, figural finial, decorated w/rampant dragons around the cover & overall delicate scrolls around the body, China, late 19th c., 39" h. **2,990**

Charger, round, a design of various types of chrysanthemums on a turquoise ground, brocade border, fishscale back, perhaps signed by Hayashi Kihyoe, Japan, 14½" d. **201**

Kogo (incense burner), cov., miniature, hexagonal body covered w/flowers in white, foliage & ground in two shades of blue, Japan, 19th c., 3½" d., 1½" h. **230**

Tray, footed, mustard yellow central medallion of morning glories, chrysanthemums & butterflies w/three different brocade borders, Japan, 9¼ " sq. ...**690**

Tray, square w/rounded corners, dished sides, decorated w/a large colorful rooster & seated hen on a shaded blue ground w/brocade edges, the back entirely in brocade on a brown ground, signed Ota" on bottom seal, Japan, 11" sq. (loss to back)..................**1,495**

Small Japanese Cloisonné Vase

Vase, footed spherical body tapering to a tiny cylindrical neck, dark goldstone ground decorated w/colorful flowers & butterflies, base w/round raised mark depicting crossed flags & the moon & a star, Japan, 6" h. (ILLUS.) **633**

Vase, hexagonal form w/silver wire inlay of birds & chrysanthemum flowers, gin bori ground of flowering chrysanthemums, silver mounts, Japan, 6" h..............**173**

Vase, slender footed octagonal body w/rounded shoulder to the slender trumpet neck, the silver wire panels alternating designs of iris, wisteria & mixed spring flowers, signed Ota" in a koro, Japan, 6" h. **2,415**

Vase, shouldered swelled cylindrical body w/a short flared neck, red foil ground on metal w/circular rose-like designs, decorated w/a large finely detailed green, white & red dragon wrapping around the body, silver base & rim bands, "Suzuki" mark, 4" d., 7½" h. **495**

Vase, wide gently flaring cylindrical body w/a wide rounded shoulder to the short rolled neck, silver wire w/a decoration of a pair of crows on a branch of ripening persimmons, brocade borders, Japan, 10" h........................**1,495**

RELATED WARES

Champlevé center bowl, oval, the deep sides decorated w/colored scrolling designs & mounted w/gilt-bronze leafy

Fine French Champlevé Center Bowl

scrolled footed mounts & rim handles,
w/a brass liner, France, ca. 1885, 16¾" l.
(ILLUS.) **3,738**

*From left: French Champlevé Mantel Clock &
French Champlevé Mantel Vase*

Champlevé clock, mantel-type, in the
Moorish style, rectangular upright gilt-
metal frame w/glass sides, the domed
top, corner finials, column-form supports
& base band all enameled in color
depicting stylized foliage, France, late
19th c., 7¾" w., 15" h. (ILLUS. left) **1,840**

Champlevé vases, mantel-type, squared
tall body w/a narrower square neck
w/flattened square mouth, all sides w/light
borders enclosing fine multicolored
flowers on a blue ground, fitted w/bronze
scroll handles & a bronze scroll-pierced
base, in the Chinese taste, France, late
19th c., 12¼ " h., pr. (ILLUS. of one, right) . . **1,150**

CLOTHING

Recent interest in period clothing, uniforms
and accessories from the 18th, 19th and through
the 20th century compels us to include this
category in our compilation. While style and
fabric play an important role in the values of
older garments of previous centuries, designer
dresses of the 1920s and '30s, especially evening
gowns, are enhanced by the original label of a
noted courtier such as Worth or Adrian. Prices
vary widely for these garments which we list by
type, with infant's and children's apparel
so designated.

Bloomers, lady's, black pleated-style,
ca. 1890s, excellent condition **$83**
Blouse, lady's, black silk, pleated front &
puffed sleeves, ca. 1890s, excellent condition . . **60**
Bonnet, lady's, poke-type, finely woven
poplar splint in natural & black trimmed
w/beige ribbon down the neck & as the
ties, paper label "5," 9½" l. **138**
Christening gown, three piece, tucked &
embroidered (some staining) **110**
Cloak, Sabbath day lake Shaker, red,
fully lined **900**

Cotton Print Dress

Dress, cotton, long sleeves, cream
w/orange & green floral print, early
1820s-30s (ILLUS.) **1,150**

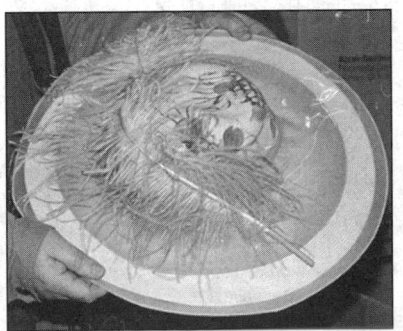

Victorian Bonnet

Hat, lady's, Victorian, cream & lavender
w/large lavender feather & flower trim
(ILLUS.) **250**

Rare Harley Davidson Leather Jacket

Jacket, leather biker-type w/Harley
 Davidson logo on back, drooping & loose
 feathers to indicate depressed period for
 company, ca. 1970s (ILLUS.) **400**
Shawl, paisley, large square, black central
 area surrounded by scrolling floral motifs
 in red, sky blue, gold, aubergine & green,
 borders of similar coloration, Europe,
 20th c., (small hole in black area)
 10' 6" x 5' 6" **288**

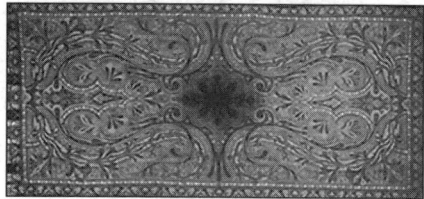

Long Paisley Shawl

Shawl, paisley, black star medallion
 surrounded by scrolling floral motifs in
 red, sky blue, gold, ivory & green, border
 of similar colors, late 19th c., England,
 11' 2" x 5' (ILLUS.) **863**
Shoes, lady's high-button, black, small **160**
Suit, lady's two piece Victorian summer suit,
 linen w/embroidery, cut work & lace on
 the bodice & skirt **55**

NECKTIES

1950s, black w/white fleur de lis, labeled
 "Custom Craft Cravats" **12**
1950s, car motif, Park Lane **20**
1960s, cotton, barber pole striped, hot pink
 & gold, labeled "Made in Hong Kong"
 (ILLUS.) **12**
1960s, cotton, compass motif, labeled
 "Rooster" **15**

*From left: Barber Pole Striped Tie,
Indian Print Tie, Pop Art Motif Tie*

1960s, Indian print, labeled "The Bum Steer
 Ltd." (ILLUS. **15**
1960s, pop art, labeled "Schiaparelli" **25**
1960s, pop art motif, unmarked (ILLUS. **30**
1960s, wool, mod tie, labeled "designed by
 John Stephens, Carnaby Street, London" **45**
Bold Look, abstract art, labeled "Atoms" on
 back, Tina Lesser design **65**

*From left: Bright Lights Tie,
Salvador Dali Designed Tie, Handpainted Tie*

Bold Look, bright lights, Fashion Craft
 Cravats (ILLUS.) **35**
Bold Look, crepe, yellow, labeled "Korry
 Ties of California" . . . . **12 to 18**
Bold Look, designer tie, castle w/bird in
 flight, Salvador Dali (ILLUS.) . . . . **300 to 500**
Bold Look, designer tie, labeled "The Road
 to Toledo," Salvador Dali **300**
Bold Look, girlie-type, peek-a-boo tie,
 popular in 1950s **65**
Bold Look, glitter & screen-printed spider
 web design **30**
Bold Look, Glow-in-the-Dark necktie, "Kiss
 Me in the Dark, Baby" **50**

Bold Look, handpainted, oranges & blossoms (ILLUS., previous page) ...... **20 to 45**

From left: "Highlander" Tie, Floral Tie, Zig-Zag Designed Tie

Bold Look, "Highlander," Countess Mara design (ILLUS.) .... **35 to 75**

Bold Look, horse, handpainted, Penney's Towncraft **25**

Bold Look, "Hunter's Delight," duck hunting scene, the classics, Park Lane **35**

Bold Look, "Proton Streak," w/electric shapes, marked, Atomoderns .... **15 to 25**

Bold Look, rayon, floral, Beau Brummel (ILLUS.) **25**

Bold Look, rayon, Paris motif, labeled "Hyde Park" **25**

Bold Look, stylized plant forms, green & white, Countess Mara design **30**

Bold Look, "Swirl Time," blue w/abstract design, Regal Cravats .... **20 to 30**

Bold Look, zig-zag design, Pilgrim Cravats (ILLUS.) .... **25 to 35**

From left: "Jonathon" Contemporary Tie, "Railroad" Contemporary Tie, Lucy & Gang Novelty Tie

Contemporary, earthy decorative style, blue-green tones, labeled "Jonathon" (ILLUS.) .... **20 to 45**

Contemporary, earthy decorative style, browns & pastels, labeled "Railroad" (ILLUS.) .... **20 to 45**

Contemporary, novelty-type, Lucy & Gang, by Ralph Marlin (ILLUS.) **28**

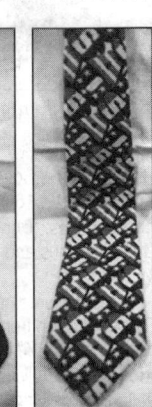

From left: "Starry Night" Novelty Tie , Peace Sign Design Tie, USA Design Tie

Contemporary, novelty-type, "Starry Night," by Ralph Marlin (ILLUS.) **25**

Peacock Look, "By the Bay," labeled "Berkeley Cravats" **25**
labeled "Wembely" **6**

Peacock Look, peace sign design, labeled "Resisto" (ILLUS.) **30**

Peacock Look, polyester, racing flags, labeled "Montgomery Wards" **12**

Peacock Look, polyester, w/playing card design .. **10**

Peacock Look, textured polyester, brown, w/figures crossing bridges, labeled "Adrian," RN 16861 .... **20**

Peacock Look, USA design, labeled "Resisto" (ILLUS.) **30**

COCA-COLA ITEMS

Coca-Cola promotion has been achieved through the issuance of scores of small objects through the years. These, together with trays, signs and other articles bearing the name of this soft drink, are now sought by many collectors. The major reference in this field is Petretti's Coca-Cola Collectibles Price Guide, 10th Edition, *by Allan Petretti (Antique Trader Books). An asterisk (*) indicates a piece which has been reproduced.*

Ashtray, porcelain, marked "50th Anniversary Coca-Cola 1886-1936," w/signature on rim, 1936 (ILLUS., next page) **$700**

50th Anniversary Ashtray

Bag holder, metal w/"For Home Refreshment - Coca-Cola" & the Sprite Boy, ca. 1949, 16 x 40" **650**

Banner, canvas, "Drink A Bottle of Coca-Cola Delicious and Refreshing," 1911, 16" x 11" **2,500**

Bell, brass, pictures cow w/"Our Only Competitor" on front, "Coca-Cola" on back, 1920s, 3¼" h. **425**

Blotter, 1906, "Delicious - Refreshing - Invigorating - Drink Coca-Cola - The Most Refreshing Drink In The World," in rectangle flanked by glasses being filled by a soda fountain dispenser **125**

Blotter, 1923, "Drink Coca-Cola - Delicious and Refreshing" within a shield, flanked by bottles **30**

Blotter, 1929, "One little minute for a big rest," pictures radio announcer holding bottle . . **225**

Blotter, 1940, pictures a clown, "The greatest pause on earth" & "Drink Coca-Cola - Delicious and Refreshing" **65**

Book, "When You Entertain - What To Do And How," 1932, by Ida B. Allen, 124 pp. **8**

Booklet, "Know Your War Planes," w/Coca-Cola advertising, 1943 . . . . **50**

Booklet, "The Truth about Coca-Cola," 1912, 16 pp. **35**

Bookmark, 1898, celluloid, heart-shaped, beautiful woman w/glass in center, "Drink Coca-Cola - Delicious ... - 5¢ - Refreshing" in border, 2 x 2¼" **700**

Hilda Clark 1903 Bookmark

Bookmark, 1903, "Drink Coca-Cola - 5¢" w/Hilda Clark pictured below, 2 x 6" (ILLUS.). . **375**

Bottle, "Christmas Coke" marked "Pat'd Dec. 25, 1923" . . . . **3 to 8**

Bottle carrier, wooden, closed box base, pointed ends joined by a straight wooden handle, "Drink Coca-Cola" on sides, 1940s . . . **150**

Bottle display rack, for six-bottle cartons, holds 24, "Take home a Carton - Coca-Cola - 6 Bottles - 25¢ - Plus Deposit," 1930s . . **400**

Bottle opener, flat brass finish wrench-form, embossed "Drink Coca-Cola in bottles," 1910 . . **75**

Calendar, 1899, picture of Hilda Clark sitting at a table & "Coca-Cola Relieves Mental and Physical Exhaustion" in upper right corner, 7⅜ x 13" **10,000**

1905 Coca-Cola Calendar

Calendar, 1905, picture of Lillian Nordica standing next to pedestal holding a large feather fan, "Coca-Cola At Soda Fountains - 5¢" at top, 7¾ x 15¼" (ILLUS.) **6,000**

From left: 1913 Coca-Cola Calendar & 1929 Coca-Cola Calendar

Calendar, 1913, lovely lady wearing large hat & holding glass marked "Coca-Cola 5¢," w/"Drink Coca-Cola - Delicious and Refreshing" below, by Hamilton King, 13½ x 22½" (ILLUS.) **4,000**

Calendar, 1917, young lady seated by small table holding glass, palm tree in background **3,500**

Calendar, 1929, young woman w/bobbed hair, wearing flapper-style dress & long necklace, holding glass of Coca-Cola (ILLUS., previous page) **1,500**

Calendar, 1933, scene w/boy watching blacksmith at work **800**

Calendar, 1937, N.C. Wyeth's boy w/fishing pole & dog, "It's the Refreshing Thing to Do," full pad **950**

Calendar, 1939, young lady in black dress holding Coca-Cola bottle in one hand & glass in other, lithograph by Forbes of Boston **600**

Calendar, 1941, girl ice skater seated on a snowy log holding a bottle of Coca-Cola & "Thirst knows no season" **450**

Calendar, 1945, snowy scene of pretty girl wearing coat & gloves & tying headscarf under her chin, ice skates hanging over her left shoulder w/"Thirst knows no season" below & a smaller scene of a couple sitting in front of a fireplace, the logo & a bottle of Coca-Cola in the lower left corner **300**

Calendar, 1950, head & shoulders of girl carrying bottles of Coca-Cola on tray, "Hospitality in your hands" **250**

Calendar, 1968, pretty teenaged girl holding phonograph records & a bottle of Coca-Cola, couple dancing in background, "Coke has the taste you never get tired of" **60**

Cigar bands, bottle on one & glass on other, 1930s, each **175**

Cigarette box, oblong, frosted glass, 1936, "50th Anniversary - Coca-Cola - 1886 - 1936" **700**

Cigarette lighter, bottle-shaped, opens at center, tin cap w/"Coca-Cola" logo, 1950s, 2½" h. **25**

Clock, neon-type, octagonal, "Ice Cold Coca-Cola" above silhouette of woman drinking from bottle, 1941 . . . . **2,800**

Clock, wall regulator, Gilbert Clock Co., wooden case, "Drink Coca-Cola" on glass front, 1916-20 . . . . **1,000**

Clock, wall-type, electric, round, wide silver metal outer edge w/numbers, "Drink Coca-Cola" printed in center, 1951, 7½" d. **185**

Cooler, Glascock ice chest-type, double case model, "Drink Coca-Cola" on side panels, 1929-32, 24 x 67" **1,000**

Counter display bottle, "Christmas Coke" style marked "Pat'd Dec. 25, 1923," clear, 20" h. **375**

Coupon, w/magazine ad illustrating Lillian Nordica, 1905, 6½ x 9¾" **275**

Dispenser-bank, battery-operated, tin w/plastic window on front, w/original box, 1950s **700**

Doll, Santa Claus standing holding bottle of Coca-Cola, cloth stuffed body, white boots, ca. 1950-60 . . . . **100**

Door push plate, porcelain, red & white, "Ice Cold Coca-Cola in Bottles," 1950s, 4 x 30" **400**

Fan, cardboard, "Quality Carries On - Drink Coca-Cola," illustrates hand holding Coca-Cola bottle, 1950s **60**

Fan, cardboard, Sprite Boy & large Coca-Cola Bottle, "Have a Coke," 1950s **100**

Festoon, cut-out cardboard, band of colorful maple leaves, girl holding bottle at center, 1927 . . . . **4,000**

Game, cribbage board, wooden, w/pegs, 1940s . . **65**

Game, Dominos, in original box, 1940s **60**

Letter w/envelope, letterhead stationery & envelope w/logo & advertising, signed by Asa G. Chandler, dated 1892 (edge wear on envelope) **1,200**

*Marbles, glass swirls in plastic bag, "Free with every carton! - Drink Coca-Cola in Bottles - Delicious & Refreshing," 1950s **50**

Menu board, tin, Art Deco style, "Drink Coca-Cola" & "Specials To-Day" at top, 1929. . **600**

Menu board, wood & Masonite, Art Deco style, "Drink Coca-Cola" & the silhouette of a girl at the bottom of the frame, 1939 . . . . . **650**

Safe Driving Award Pin

Pin, deliveryman's ten year "Safe Driving Award," gold, winged tire below enameled white cross in green enameled oval w/"Universal Safety" in border, red enameled banner at top w/"Coca-Cola" (ILLUS.) **350**

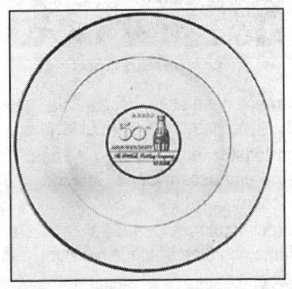

Coca-Cola Anniversary Plate

Plate, circle in center w/"50th Anniversary - the Coca-Cola Company" below five stars, bottle on the side, Lenox China, 1950s, 10½" d. (ILLUS., previous page) **475**

Plate, china, shows bottle & glass & "Drink Coca-Cola - Refresh Yourself " around rim, American Chinaware Corp., 1931, 7⅜" d. **425**

Playing cards, girl holding bottle & glass on each,1939, complete deck **475**

Playing cards, girl wearing cowboy hat & drinking from a bottle of Coca-Cola, 1951, complete deck **85**

Early Coca-Cola Girl Postcard

Postcard, pictures a pretty girl & "The Coca-Cola Girl" in the bottom left-hand corner & "Drink Delicious Coca-Cola" in the bottom right corner, Hamilton King artwork, 1910 (ILLUS.) **700**

Poster, cardboard, colorful scene of bottle of Coca-Cola floating in Arctic waters, "Have a Coke," 1944, framed, 20 x 36". **500**

Coca-Cola Radio

Radio, carrying case-style, "Coca-Cola refreshes you best," 1950s (ILLUS.) **950**

Sandwich toaster, electric, used in soda fountains, embossed "Coca-Cola" on sandwich (no cord) **1,000**

Sign, tin, rectangular, "Coca-Cola" & picture of a woman holding bottle in her right hand all within an oval, 1927, framed, 8½ x 11" (ILLUS.) **2,400**

1927 Coca-Cola Sign

Sign, wooden shield-shaped w/metal leaf-like scrolling at top, pierced for hanging, pictures two Coke glasses above "Drink Coca-Cola," 1930s, 9 x 11" **2,500**

Sign, porcelain, button-type, "Drink Coca-Cola in Bottles," 1950s, 12" d. **350**

1937 Reverse-painted Glass Sign

Sign, reverse-painted glass, foil back & metal frame, "We Serve - Coca-Cola - In Bottles - Ice Cold," 1937, 10 x 12" (ILLUS.) **4,000**

Coca-Cola Counter-top Sign

Sign, counter-top light-up type, an upright glass disc in red w/"Drink Coca-Cola" & a glass in a leaf-molded frame & raised on a platform base w/"Lunch With Us" spelled out, made by Brunhoff Mfg. Co., ca. 1930s, 12 x 14" (ILLUS.) **3,900**

Sign, reverse-painted glass, oval, black & silver, "Drink Coca-Cola," 1932, 12 x 20" ... **3,800**

"The Four Seasons" Trolley Sign

Sign, trolley-type, titled "The Four Seasons," shows four young women w/bottles & glasses of Coca-Cola & "Drink Coca-Cola, delicious and refreshing all the year round," 1923, framed, 11 x 20½" (ILLUS.) .. **2,000**

Sign, neon, "Coca-Cola Cigars," red & green, transformer marked "Property The Coca-Cola Co., 342 Madison Ave., NYC.," 12 x 23" **3,000**

Sign, neon enclosed in chrome case, Art Deco style, "Drug Store - Drink Coca-Cola," red & blue, 1930s, 15 x 24" **5,000**

Sign, tin, rectangular, "Take a case home Today - Quality Refreshment," w/picture of a case of Coca-Cola bottles, 1950, 19 x 28" **325**

Sign, tin die-cut, bottle-shaped, 1960s , 3' h. **425**

Signs, cardboard cut-outs, stand-up type, Coca-Cola girls, each representing a different branch of the armed service, 1944, 25 x 64", set of 5 .... **6,000**

Thermometer, tin, "Drink Coca-Cola - Delicious and Refreshing" on red ground circle above thermometer & black-on-white silhouette of girl drinking from bottle in circle below, 1939, 6½ x 16" **325**

Thermometer, tin, shaped oblong form w/two small bottles flanking thermometer scale above "Drink Coca-Cola," 1941, 7 x 16" **385**

Coca-Cola Bottle-form Thermometer

Thermometer, tin, embossed bottle shape, 1930s, 17" h. (ILLUS.) **385**

Thermometer, metal, oblong, turquoise, white & red, marked "Refresh Yourself" above thermometer scale & "Drink Coca-Cola" in circle below, pierced at top & bottom for hanging, 3¼" w., 17" h. (minor scratches & few very small chips) **650**

Toy, yo-yo, shaped like bottle cap, red & white plastic, "Drink Coca-Cola," 1960s **12**

Toy, cardboard cut-outs of "Toy Town," 1927, 10 x 15" **125**

Toy, cardboard cut-outs, "Uncle Remus Story," 1931, 10 x 15"................... **325**

Coca-Cola Route Truck

Toy truck, route delivery-type, battery-operated, white & yellow metal w/red hood, "Drink Coca-Cola" on side panels, Allen Haddock Co., 1950s-60s, w/original box, 12½" l. (ILLUS.) **330**

1910 Hamilton King Girl Tray

*Tray, 1910, rectangular, Hamilton King Girl above "Drink Delicious Coca-Cola" lower right corner & "The Coca-Cola Girl" in left corner, 10½ x 13¼" (ILLUS.) **1,600**

1920 Coca-Cola Tray

Tray, 1920, oval, Garden Girl, 13¼ x 16½"
(ILLUS.,) 950

Tray, change, 1901, Hilda Clark w/flowers,
6" d............................... 2,800

Tumbler, bell-shaped, pewter, ca. 1930s,
w/leather pouch 550

Tumbler, soda fountain-type, clear glass,
straight sides, marked w/"Coca-Cola"
logo near top, syrup line all around the
base, ca. 1900-04 1,000

Vienna Art plate, tin, titled "Topless," issued
by Western Reserve, original ornate
giltwood frame, ca. 1908 1,800

Watch fob, celluloid, rectangular, 1911,
pretty girl at wheel of early auto on front,
"Drink Coca-Cola in Bottles, 5¢" on back 900

Watch fob, metal, oval w/bulldog on front,
"Drink Coca-Cola Delicious and
Refreshing 5¢" on back, 11¼" w., 1¼" h. 150

Coca-Cola Window Display

Window display, folding cardboard, three-
fold theatre stage design, lithographed in
deep blue, greens & red, the center stage
section w/a cameo illustration of a pretty
lady w/glass, flanked by theatre curtain
side panels each printed w/"Drink Coca-
Cola" in an oval, 1913, some stains,
minor edge wear & separated at folds,
(ILLUS.) 7,000

COMIC BOOKS

*Comics originated at the turn of the century
as "strips" in the newspaper. By the early 1930s,
they had taken on their present day "book" form
and the golden age of comic books had begun,
continuing full-force through the 1940s. Comics
from this era may be hard to find and can be
quite valuable. New story lines and format
changes have evolved since the comic book's
beginning, with style and popularity fluctuating.
The following prices include higher-end copies in
near mint condition unless otherwise noted.*

Action, DC Comics, No. 1 (June 1938),
Superman rescues Evelyn Curry from
electric chair, NM................... $185,000

Action, DC Comics, No. 144, Clark Kent
reporting for Daily Planet, NM 450

Action, DC Comics, No. 268, Hercules, NM 125

Adventure, DC Comics, No. 104, Toy Town
USA, NM 800

Adventure, DC Comics, No. 200, "Superboy
and the Apes," NM 450

Adventure, DC Comics, No. 210, "The
Superdog from Krytpon," NM 3,000

Adventure, DC Comics, No. 48, Hourman,
NM............................... 22,000

All-American, DC Comics, No. 1 (1939-48),
NM............................... 5,500

All-American, DC Comics, No. 16, Green
Lantern, NM........................ 62,000

All-American, DC Comics, No. 56, Elegant
Esmond, NM........................ 700

All-Flash, DC Comics, No. 1 (1941-47),
Flash, The Monocle, NM 13,000

All-Flash, DC Comics, No. 17, Tale of Three
Wishes, NM 500

All-Star, DC Comics, No. 54, Circus issue,
NM 850

Amazing Spider-Man

Amazing Spider-man, Marvel Comics,
No. 1 (March 1963), NM (ILLUS.) 20,000

Amazing Spider-man, Marvel Comics,
No. 14, NM 1,600

Animal, Dell Publishing Co., No. 1 (1942),
Pogo, NM 1,000

Aquaman, DC Comics, No. 7, Sea Beasts
of Atlantis, NM 75

Archie, MLJ Magazines, No. 1 (Winter
1942-43), Jughead & Veronica, NM 10,000

Archie, MLJ Magazines, No. 2, NM......... 2,200

Archie, MLJ Magazines, No. 3, NM......... 1,600

Atom, DC Comics, No. 1 (1962-68), Planet
Master, NM......................... 750

Avengers, Marvel Comics, No. 4, Captain
America, NM 1,500

Avengers, Marvel Comics, No. 53, X-Men,
NM 40

Batman

Batman, DC Comics, No. 1 (Spring 1940),
National Periodical Publications, ½"
surface flaking off lower "red" building
surface & very slight fraying to upper left
corner of top spine, FN- (ILLUS.) **21,850**

Batman, DC Comics, No. 1 (Spring 1940),
NM.. **65,000**

Batman, DC Comics, No. 113, Fatman, NM **300**

Batman, DC Comics, No. 328, Two-Face, NM.... **11**

Brave & the Bold, DC Comics, No. 31,
Cave Carson, NM...................... **350**

Brave & the Bold, DC Comics, No. 47,
Strange Sports, NM **75**

Captain America, Timely/Atlas, No. 1
(May 1941), NM..................... **55,000**

Captain America, Timely/Atlas, No. 15, Den
of Doom, NM........................ **2,800**

Casper, The Friendly Ghost, St. John
Publishing, No. 1 (Sept. 1949), Baby
Huey, NM **1,200**

Daredevil, Marvel Comics, No. 2, Electro,
NM **550**

Daredevil, Marvel Comics, No. 3, The Owl,
NM **375**

Daredevil Battles Hitler

Daredevil Battles Hitler, Lev Gleason
Publications, No. 1 (July 1941), cover
near mint, interior very FN+ (ILLUS.) **4,600**

Daring Mystery, Timely, No. 1 (Jan. 1940),
NM **17,500**

Daring Mystery, Timely, No. 6, NM **3,000**

Detective, DC Comics, No. 1 (March 1937),
NM................................. **65,000**

Detective, DC Comics, No. 14, NM......... **3,500**

Detective

Detective, DC Comics, No. 15, some
restoration, very FN (ILLUS.) **1,955**

Detective, DC Comics, No. 198, Batman in
Scotland, NM **375**

Fantastic Four, Marvel Comics, No. 12,
Hulk, NM **1,100**

Fantastic Four, Marvel Comics, No. 4,
Submariner, NM **2,900**

Flash, DC Comics, No. 1 (Jan. 1940), Flash,
Hawkman, The Whip & Johnny Thunder,
NM............................... **60,000**

Flash, DC Comics, No. 117 (Feb.-March
1959), Capt. Boomerang, NM **300**

Four Color, Dell Publishing Co., No. 108
(2nd Series), Donald Duck in the Terror
of the River, NM **1,600**

Four Color, Dell Publishing Co., No. 1152
(2nd Series), Rocky & His Friends, NM **275**

Four Color, Dell Publishing Co., No. 9
(2nd Series), Donald Duck finds Pirate
Gold!, NM **8,000**

Four Color, Dell Publishing Co., No. 956
(2nd Series), Ricky Nelson, NM **225**

Green Lantern, DC Comics, No. 1 (Fall
1941), Green Lantern, Master of Light,
Arson in the Slums, NM............... **27,000**

Hawkman, DC Comics, No. 14, Chaw, NM **75**

Hawkman, DC Comics, No. 22, Falcon, NM **45**

Hopalong Cassidy, DC Comics, No. 104,
"The Secret of the Surrendering
Outlaws," NM **60**

Hopalong Cassidy, DC Comics, No. 86
(Feb. 1954), "The Secret of the Tattooed
Burro," NM **250**

House of Mystery, DC Comics, No. 1
(Dec.-Jan. 1952), "I Fell in Love With a
Monster," NM......................... **1,700**

Human Torch, Marvel Comics, No. 8, Sub-
   Mariner, NM. **2,500**

Incredible Hulk, Marvel Comics, No. 1 (May
   1962), NM **11,000**

Justice League of America, DC Comics,
   No. 1 (Oct. -Nov. 1960), Despero, NM **3,000**

Looney Tunes & Merry Melodies, Dell
   Publishing Co., No. 1 (1941), Bugs
   Bunny, Elmer Fudd & Daffy Duck, NM **10,000**

Marvel Mystery, Marvel Comics, No. 5,
   Human Torch, NM **16,000**

Master Comics, Fawcett Publications, No. 1
   (March 1940), Master Man, oversized,NM . . **7,000**

Mighty Mouse, Marvel Comics, No. 1 (Fall
   1946, 1st series), NM **900**

Mystery in Space, DC Comics, No. 1 (April-
   May 1951), Knights of the Galaxy, NM **2,800**

Mystery in Space, DC Comics, No. 16,
   Honeymoon in Space, NM **400**

Pep, MJL Magazines/Archie Publications,
   No. 1 (Jan 1940), NM **7,000**

Pep, MJL Magazines/Archie Publications,
   No. 22, Archie, Betty & Jughead, NM **9,200**

Sensation, DC Comics, No. 82, King Lunar,
   NM **200**

Star Spangled, DC Comics , No. 1 (Oct.
   1941), NM **3,500**

Strange Tales, Marvel Comics, No. 1 (June
   1951, 1st regular series), "The Room,"
   NM **2,500**

Strange Tales, Marvel Comics, No. 4,
   "Terror in the Morgue," NM. **650**

Sub-Mariner, Timely, No. 1 (Spring 1941),
   Sub-Mariner, The Angel, NM. **20,000**

Superman, DC Comics, No. 75, Prankster,
   NM **450**

Superman

Superman, National Periodical Publications,
   No. 1 (Summer 1939), good condition
   (ILLUS.) **8,625**

Tales of Suspense, Marvel Comics, No. 1
   (Jan. 1959), "The Unknown Emptiness,"
   NM. **1,500**

Tales of Suspense, Marvel Comics, No. 30,
   "The Haunted Roller Coaster," NM **200**

Tales of Suspense, Marvel Comics, No. 9,
   "Diablo," NM **400**

Tales to Astonish, Marvel Comics, No. 1
   (Jan. 1959), "Ninth Wonder of the World,"
   1st series, NM **1,500**

Tales to Astonish, Marvel Comics, No. 15,
   "The Blip," NM **400**

Tales to Astonish, Marvel Comics, No. 5,
   "The Things on Easter Island," 1st series,
   NM **425**

Tarzan, Dell Publishing Co., 1950s **8**

Tomahawk, DC Comics, No. 1 (1950-72),
   Prisoner Called Tomahawk, NM **1,200**

Tomahawk, DC Comics, No. 29, The
   Conspiracy of Wounded Bear, NM. **175**

Tomahawk, DC Comics, No. 4, Tomahawk
   Wanted: Dead or Alive, NM **325**

Uncle Sam Quarterly, Quality Comics
   Group, No. 1 (Fall 1941), slight sun lines
   to front cover, FN **690**

Uncle Sam Quarterly, Quality Comics
   Group, No. 1, NM **2,800**

World's Best, DC Comics, No. 1 (Spring
   1941), Superman vs. the Rainmaker,
   Batman vs. Wright, NM **14,000**

World's Finest, DC Comics, No. 16, "Music
   for the Masses," NM **1,000**

World's Finest, DC Comics, No. 2
   (1941-86), NM **3,700**

X-Men, Marvel Comics, No. 1 (Sept. 1963),
   NM **5,600**

X-Men, Marvel Comics, No. 12, Juggernaut,
   NM **325**

X-Men, Marvel Comics, No. 2, Vanisher, NM . . **1,750**

X-Men, Marvel Comics, No. 38, Banshee,
   Cyclops, NM. **100**

COMPACTS & VANITY CASES

   A lady's powder compact is a small portable cosmetic make-up box that contains powder, a mirror and puff. Eventually, the more elaborate compact, the "vanity case," evolved, containing a mirror, puffs and compartments for powder, rouge and/or lipstick. Compacts made prior to the 1960s when women opted for the "au natural" look are considered vintage. These vintage compacts were made in a variety of shapes, sizes, combinations, styles and in every conceivable natural or man-made material. Figural, enamel, premium, commemorative, patriotic, Art Deco and souvenir compacts were designed as a reflection of the times and are very desirable. The vintage compacts that are multipurpose, combined with another accessory—the compact/watch, compact/music box, compact/fan, compact/purse, compact/ perfumer, compact/lighter, compact/cane, compact/hatpin—are but a few of the combination compacts that are not only sought after by the compact collector but also appeal to collectors of the secondary accessory. Today vintage compacts and vanity cases are a very desirable collectible. There are compacts and vanities to suit every taste and purse. The "old" compacts are the "new" collectibles. Compacts have come into their own as collectibles. They are listed as a separate category in price guides, sold in prestigious auction houses, displayed in museums, and several books and many articles on the collectible compact have been written. There is also a newsletter, Powder Puff, *written by and for compact collectors. The beauty and intricate workmanship of the vintage compacts make them works of fantasy and art in miniature.*

Bakelite compact, round, yellow, decorated w/pink flowers, Bakelite tube (lipstick or perfume) concealed in tassel, carrying cord, interior reveals mirror & powder well, 1¾" d., tube 2½" . . . . **$150 to 190**

Bakelite compact, oblong, coral colored, sides ivorene, front lid decorated w/black enamel designs & red colored stones, interior contains mirror & powder compartment, carrying cord & tassel, 2 x 2½" . . . . **175 to 225**

Black & silvertone fob compact, lid decorated w/silvertone scene, fob attached by chain to compact contains creme lip/cheek rouge, Vashe, 1½ x 2½", fob 1" d. . . . . **80 to 125**

Brass colored compact, basket-shaped, engine-tooled, satin-finish lid, embossed swinging handle, metal interior, K & K, 1¼ x 2½" . . . . **80 to 120**

Brushed goldtone compact, round, lid decorated w/polished goldtone heart & arrow & "I Love You" printed around lid, Dorset, 2½" d. . . . . **60 to 80**

Brushed goldtone compact, square, thermometer centered on lid, incised polished goldtone figures of women playing tennis, golf, ice skating & horseback riding decorate the four corners of lid, Elgin American, 2¾" . . . . **120 to 150**

Brushed goldtone compact, the endearment "Mother" & leaves in polished goldtone decorate lid, Elgin American, 2¼ x 3" . . . . **60 to 100**

Brushed goldtone compact, designed to resemble artist's palette, lid decorated w/paint tube, paint brushes & colors, interior mirror & powder compartment, Volupte, 2¾ x 3" . . . . **175 to 225**

Brushed goldtone compact, "lip-lock" style, lid decorated with applied framed disc of colored stones, pull-out lipstick

opens compact, interior reveals signed powder well & mirror, Trifari, 1 x 2¼ x 3¼" . . . . **225 to 275**

Brushed goldtone compact, "Lucky Purse With Captive Lipstick," polished goldtone flap opens to reveal opening for picture or rouge, tango chain lipstick tube suspended by two chains, sticker on interior mirror reads "Genuine Collectors Item by Volupte," Volupte, 2¾ x 3½". . . **145 to 175**

Brushed goldtone compact, oval, Savoir Faire, black raised enameled harlequin mask centered on lid, lid enhanced w/rhinestones & incised ribbons, Dorothy Gray, 3 x 3¾". . . . . **100 to 125**

Brushed goldtone compact, hand-shaped, lid decorated w/enameled white lace mitt, multicolored enamel bracelet, Des. Patent #120,347, Volupte, 2 x 4½" . . . . **225 to 275**

Brushed goldtone vanity/watch combination, square, interior reveals powder & rouge compartments, Illinois Watch Case Co., 2¾" . . . . **110 to 145**

Brushed silver tango chain compact, round, lid decorated w/polished goldtone flowers, lipstick attached by chain, Rex, 3½" d. x 8" . . . . **175 to 200**

Campaign compact, round, red, white & blue, designed to resemble telephone dial w/campaign slogan "We Need Stevenson" imprinted on lid, red map of the United States centered on lid, 3½" d. . . . . **200 to 250**

Celluloid compact, designed to resemble a female, exterior sliding beveled mirror incorporated as part of skirt, dress, orange accented w/black dots, "Pat'd Apr. 28-'25" . . . . **125 to 175**

Celluloid vanity case, light green, lid decorated with h.p. Oriental scene, interior reveals compartments w/removable covered lip & cheek rouge containers, mirror & powder compartment, 2¾ x 4" . . . . **125 to 175**

"Christmas Ball" Compact

"Christmas Ball" compact, ball-shaped, green iridescent, exterior highlighted w/red & white stripes, plastic interior, also comes in solid iridescent colors red or green & in a striped red iridescent color, 2" d. (ILLUS.) . . . . **150 to 175**

Compact-bracelet combination, polished satin finish, hinged bracelet, lid decorated w/red & clear crystal stones, K & K, 1½ x 2" . . . . **250 to 300**

Compact & matching comb/case, brushed silvertone, Mercedes Benz logo imprinted on lid of compact, Germany, 2¾" d. . . . . **75 to 150**

Embossed leather vanity, designed to resemble book, multicolored leather lids, interior reveals metal-framed mirror, powder & rouge compartments, Raquel, 2 x 3" . . . . **80 to 125**

Enamel mesh vanity pouch, blue, round, light blue mesh bottom, interior reveals powder well, metal mirror opens to reveal rouge compartment, Evans, 2¼" d. . . . . . . **50 to 75**

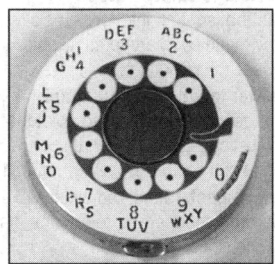

Telephone Dial-style Compact

Enameled compact, pink enamel w/lid designed to resemble telephone dial, goldtone numbers & letters imprinted on pink enamel, 2¾" d. (ILLUS.) . . . . **125 to 150**

Enameled souvenir compact, round, green, w/goldtone "U.S. Zone Germany" map & army insignia on lid, polished goldtone scalloped edges frame lid, reverse side goldtone, 4" d. . . . . **250 to 300**

Enameled vanity, oblong, yellow, enamel lid decorated w/flowers, interior reveals metal mirror separating rouge & powder compartments, 1¾ x 2¼" . . . . **50 to 75**

Gold (14k yellow) compact, script monogram within cartouche, R. Blackington . . **490**

Gold-plate mini-carryall, textured polished goldtone lid decorated w/bands of black enamel & black cartouche, gilded interior reveals powder & rouge compartments & well w/miniature perfume bottle, center mirror flanked by two lipstick tubes, cigarette compartment behind mirror, mesh carrying chain, Dermay, 2¾ x 4" . . . . **175 to 250**

Goldtone "Ball & Chain" compact, goldtone lipstick tube attached by chain to round goldtone compact, plastic interior, Wadsworth, 2" d. . . . . **150 to 175**

Goldtone carryall, dual opening, watch

centered on embossed sunburst lid, interior contains powder compartment, mirror & coin compartment, lipstick, comb holder & cigarette case, mesh carrying chain, Evans, 3¼ x 5½" . . . . **250 to 325**

Goldtone compact, polished finish w/four deeply incised triangles on the top & bottom, Elizabeth Arden, in original sleeve, never used **45**

Karess Goldtone Compact

Goldtone compact, round, goldtone top lid decorated w/profile of woman, a rose & a star on a dark blue & black background framed w/goldtone bars, silvertone lid on reverse side, Karess, 1¾" d. (ILLUS.). . . **80 to 150**

Goldtone compact, round, "Mirador," incised rings around compact, slide-out lipstick, top & bottom exterior beveled mirrors, interior reveals beveled mirror & powder compartment, Paris, Miref, 2" d. . . . . **125 to 175**

Goldtone compact, round, textured silvertone lid decorated w/applied enameled heart, wishbone, cap, duck, heart, suitcase, shoe, saw & organ grinder charms, reverse side black enamel, interior mirror & powder compartment, 2" d. . . . . **150 to 175**

Goldtone compact, miniature, designed to resemble fan, exterior lid decorated w/yellow, pink, silvertone & goldtone flowers, pearl twist lock closure, interior mirror & powder well, 1½ x 2½" . . . . **40 to 60**

Goldtone compact, square, lid designed to resemble gift package, raised gift card & bow decorate lid, Volupte, 3" . . . . **50 to 75**

Goldtone Compact with Travel Stickers

Goldtone compact, designed to resemble suitcase decorated w/B.O.A.C. travel stickers, push-back rigid handle, 2½ x 3" (ILLUS.)........................ **160 to 180**

"Initially Yours" Goldtone Compact

Goldtone compact, round, "Initially Yours" dial-a-monogram, two dials on exterior rim set first and last initials in panels on lid of compact, beautiful clear stones frame panels, lid decorated with incised swirls, interior reveals mirror, puff & powder well, Zell, 3¼" d. (ILLUS.)..... **125 to 175**

Goldtone compact, round, prong-set emerald cut & round rhinestones decorate lid, interior mirror & powder well, Pilcher, 3½" d................. **75 to 150**

French Goldtone Compact/Bracelet

Goldtone compact-bracelet combination, compact lid decorated w/goldtone stars on an onyx disc, cut-outs of stars surround cuff bracelet, signed "Claudine Cereola," Flamand-Fladium, France, 1½" d. (ILLUS.) .... **275 to 325**

English Goldtone Compact/Bracelet

Goldtone compact-bracelet combination, designed to resemble wrist watch, hours on the lid of compact set w/green & clear stones, movable hands, bubble-link

chain, interior reveals mirror & puff, Le Rage, England, 1½" d., 7" l. (ILLUS.)........................ **350 to 400**

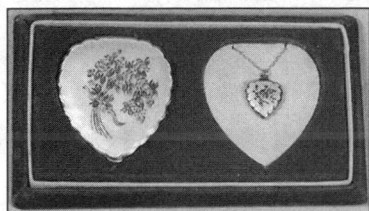

La Mode Compact & Locket Set

Goldtone compact & locket set, matching heart-shaped compact & locket, light blue enamel compact & matching locket decorated w/flowers, interior of compact reveals metal mirror that separates powder & rouge compartments, La Mode, 2 ¼ x 2 ¼" (ILLUS.).............. **200 to 250**

Goldtone compact w/lipstick incorporated in lid, front lid decorated w/troubadour courting transfer scene, Stratton hand logo on interior powder well, label on mirror reads "To open inner door press mirror-lid gently back, door swings open - To shut, bring mirror lid forward & press door down," England, Stratton, 2¾ x 3¼" .... **80 to 120**

Goldtone compact w/matching lipstick, compact lid & lipstick decorated w/green pear-shaped stones, interior reveals powder well, puff & mirror, Flato, 2⅛ x 2½"....................... **150 to 200**

Goldtone compact w/matching lipstick, square, compact lid & lipstick top decorated w/faux pearls, interior mirror & powder well, gold threads decorate black fitted case, signed powder lid, Ciner, 2¾"....................... **175 to 200**

Goldtone compact w/matching lipstick, square, compact lid & lipstick top decorated w/pale orange cabochon stones, interior mirror & powder well, gold threads decorate black fitted case, powder lid signed, Ciner, 2¾" .... **150 to 175**

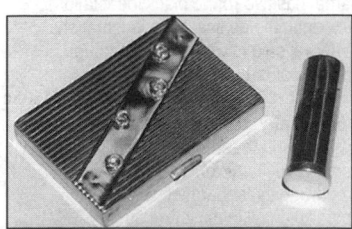

Hattie Carnegie Compact & Lipstick

Goldtone compact w/matching lipstick, oblong, polished strip w/small applied goldtone knots set w/colored stones

decorate deeply incised compact lid;
interior mirror & powder well; powder lid &
lipstick tube signed, Hattie Carnegie,
2¼ x 3¾" (ILLUS.). . . . . **175 to 225**

Goldtone "Dial-A-Date" Compact

Goldtone "Dial-a-Date" compact, points of
interest in Paris printed on lid protected
by clear plastic, two movable dials, one to
set time, one to indicate destination,
beveled mirror, France, 2½ x 3"
(ILLUS.). . . . . **150 to 175**

Goldtone vanity, oblong, lid decorated
w/blue & goldtone Art Deco design,
interior reveals mirror & side-by-side
rouge & powder compartments,
1½ x 2¾" . . . . **75 to 100**

Goldtone "Air Express" Vanity

Goldtone vanity, designed to resemble Air
Express delivery, blue lid decorated
w/"Air Express, RUSH Railway Express
Agency" & destination labels, raised
goldtone cord, interior reveals mirror,
powder & rouge compartments, Patent
#1883793, 2⅛ x 3⅛" (ILLUS.). . . . . . . **125 to 200**

Goldtone vanity, "Seven Come Eleven,"
black & white enamel, designed as pair of
dice, lid divided into two sections, one
white enamel & one black enamel, white
enamel has two round black indentations,
black enamel has five white indentations,
interior reveals mirror, powder & rouge
compartments & puffs, Coty,
2¼ x 3¼". . . . . **150 to 250**

Goldtone vanity, orange, black & goldtone
Art Deco/Art Moderne design on lid,
interior reveals mirror, powder & rouge
compartments, separate lipstick
compartment with miniature gold
lipstick tube, Zanadu, 1½ x 3½" . . . . . . **100 to 125**

Goldtone vanity, lid decorated w/wishbone
& star set w/rhinestone, interior reveals
rouge & powder compartments, Coty,
2¼ x 3¾". . . . . **80 to 120**

**Goldtone vanity cigarette case/compact
combination,** white enamel lids
decorated w/purple enamel orchids, top
interior reveals compartments for powder,
rouge & lipstick tube, lower section for
cigarettes, Richard Hudnut . . . . **150 to 175**

Lucite compact, sunburst medallion molded
& painted separately, hand applied to lid,
two hinged closures on either side of the
front lid, interior reveals mirror & powder
compartment, Roger & Gallet,
4 x 4". . . . . **150 to 225**

**Mother-of-pearl compact/music box
combination,** mother-of-pearl lid
decorated w/notes & G clef, Stratton,
2¾" x ¾ x 3¼". . . . . **150 to 175**

Petite-point compact, lid centered
w/colorful petit-point scene, bordered by
floral petite-point, brushed goldtone back
lid, Elgin American, 3 x 3½" . . . . **80 to 120**

Plastic compact, round, silvertone Scottie
dog centered on top of ivorene lid,
reverse lid black, Astor-Pak, 3½" d. . . . **100 to 125**

Plastic souvenir compact, oval-shaped,
yellow marbleized, Miami, FL & painted
palm trees decorate lid, interior contains
mirror & powder well, 3 x 3½" . . . . **40 to 80**

Polished goldtone compact, harlequin-
shaped, Elizabeth Arden, 1⅝ x 3". . . . . **125 to 175**

Presentation boxed set, matching goldtone
compact & cigarette lighter, round, tan
suede, compact & lighter decorated
w/scenic transfer design, compact tap-sift
model, Evans, 2" d., box 1½ x 5" . . . . . . **60 to 100**

Roll-top vanity, miniature, coppertone roll-
top, red enameled side pieces, interior
mirror, powder & rouge compartments,
2 x 3". . . . . **75 to 125**

Silver-plate compact, heart-shaped,
powder well & mirror, Halston, Elsa
Peretti designed, 3 x ¾" . . . . **150 to 200**

Silvertone compact, round, w/plastic discs
on either side, discs depict musicians in
relief playing instruments, 2¼" d. . . . . . . **50 to 75**

Silvertone compact, round, fashioned as
picture hat, raised dome centered on lid,
decorated w/bow & flowers,
Dorothy Gray, 3⅞" d. . . . . **125 to 175**

Silvertone compact, round, lid decorated
w/light blue, grey & white Art Deco
design, interior reveals mirror & powder
well, signed interior rim, beautiful blue
suede fitted presentation box w/tassel,
Estee Lauder, 4" d. . . . . **175 to 225**

Silvertone vanity, Art Deco-style, step
pyramid-shaped black & red striped,
interior reveals metal mirror which
separates powder & rouge compartments, small triangular fraternal emblem
applied to lid, Fillkwik Co., 1½ x 1¾" . . . **75 to 100**

Snakeskin compact/key chain combin-
ation, miniature, round, snakeskin lids,
interior metal mirror, swans-down puff &
powder compartment, key chain attached
to side rim of compact, Italy, 1½" d. .... **80 to 100**

Sterling silver compact, heart-shaped,
interior reveals heart-shaped puff, screen
& mirror, heart-shaped cartouche on lid
monogrammed with initials R.G.,
Hingeco, 2½ x 2½" .... **145 to 175**

Sterling silver compact/cane combin-
ation, hallmarked, compact in cane
handle, gilded interior contains framed
mirror & powder compartment, blue
cloisonné enameled lid, incised flower on
collar, black wood shaft, metal ferrule
protector at end of stick, 1⅞" d. x ½" .. **350 to 450**

Sterling silver vanity, engine-turned vanity
designed to resemble cigarette lighter,
front opens to beveled mirror, powder &
rouge compartments, top lifts to reveal
sliding lipstick, Patent No. 1639628,
Alfred Dunhill, 1⅛ x 1⅞" .... **225 to 300**

Textured goldtone compact/bank
combination, "Vanity-Bank," square
compact/bank combination, lid
highlighted w/blue enamel accents, logo
"The Broadway National Bank of
Paterson" imprinted on dime bank,
reverse side reads "A. R. Martine Co.
Inc., 2 Wall Street, New York," interior
reveals mirror, bank & powder
compartment, Lucille Buhl,
2¼ x 2¼" .... **150 to 175**

White enameled compact, round, lid
decorated with a red anchor & a blue
rope, Volupte, 2¹⁄₁₆" dia. .... **40 to 80**

COOKIE JARS

All sorts of charming and whimsical cookie jars have been produced in recent decades and these are increasingly collectible today. Many well known American potteries such as McCoy, Hull and Abingdon produced cookie jars and they are included in those listings. Below we are listing cookie jars produced by other companies. Current reference books for collectors include: The Collectors Encyclopedia of Cookie Jars *by Fred and Joyce Roerig (Collector Books, 1991);* Collector's Encyclopedia of Cookie Jars, Book II *by Fred and Joyce Roerig (Collector Books, 1994); and* The Complete Cookie Jar Book *by Mike Schneider (Schiffer, Ltd. 1991). Also see:* CERAMICS, CHARACTER COLLECTIBLES *and* DISNEY COLLECTIBLES

AMERICAN BISQUE

Animal Crackers **$40**

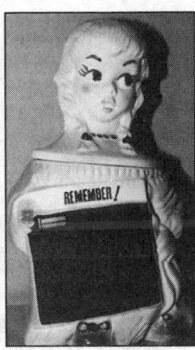

*From left: Blackboard Boy & Blackboard Girl
Cookie Jars*

Blackboard Boy (ILLUS. left)................ **425**
Blackboard Clown........................ **283**
Blackboard Girl (ILLUS. right)............... **288**
Blackboard Hobo **100**
Boots **120**
Bow Bear **50**
Candy Baby **80**
Carousel................................. **50**
Cat in Basket **30**

Cheerleaders Cookie Jar

Cheerleaders, flasher-type (ILLUS.) **300**
Chef **70**
Chick with Tam **40**
Churn Boy **220**
Clown on Stage, flasher, green curtains **375**
Collegiate Owl **40**
Collegiate Owl, gold trim **150**
Cookie Truck **30**
Davy Crockett **290**
Deer, log finial........................... **60**
Dog in Basket **40**
Dutch Boy **70**
Fire Chief **50**
Horse, sitting position **1,095**
Jack in Box **60**
Kitten, on quilted base **145**
Kitten & Beehive **30**
Lady Pig, unmarked....................... **150**
Magic Bunny **80**

Modern Rooster. 30
Mr. Rabbit. 130
Pig Dancer 140
Pirate 50
Poodle 60
Puppy. 50
Rabbit with Hearts. 250
Ring for Cookies, bell in lid 30
Rooster. 60
Sack of Cookies 30
Saddle Blackboard 200
Sandman Cookies, kids watching TV,
    w/flasher. 375
School House 40
Soldier 60
Teddy Roosevelt 80
Toothache Dog 300
Wilma on Telephone. 750

BRAYTON - LAGUNA

Brayton Laguna Plaid Dog Cookie Jar

Dog, white w/yellow trim, yellow & brown
    plaid design, unmarked (ILLUS.) 450
Swedish Maiden 450

BRUSH - MCCOY

Cheerleaders, "Corner Cookie Jar, 802
    USA," flasher 400
Cinderella Pumpkin. 120
Circus Horse, 1950s 875
Clown, blue pants & tie. 220
Clown, brown pants 265
Clown Bust 250
Cookie House 90
Cookie House, blue & grey 65
Crock w/Cat finial 40
Davy Crockett, gold-decorated 850
Dog with Basket 250
Donkey and Cart 250
Elephant, wearing baby hat 275

Formal Pig, green hat, coat & tie 325
Granny, white w/pink apron & yellow trim 120
Happy Bunny, matte finish, white w/pink &
    yellow trim 178
Happy Bunny, white & grey w/blue neck
    scarf 140
Hen on Basket 80
Hillbilly Frog 4,300

Brush Hobby Horse Cookie Jar

Hobby Horse (ILLUS.) 950
Humpty Dumpty, brown trim 130
Lantern. 50

Laughing Hippo Cookie Jar

Laughing Hippo, w/Monkey (ILLUS.) 585
Nite Owl 100
Old Shoe 100
Panda 150
Peter Pan, large 700
Pumpkin with Lock on Door. 375
Siamese Cat. 290
Smiling Bear 215
Squirrel on Log 90
Squirrel with Top Hat 260
Teddy Bear, feet apart 80
Three Bears 70

CALIFORNIA ORIGINALS

"Bambi". 600
Circus Wagon 50
Cookie Crocodile. 90
Cookie Monster. 50
Cookie Time Clock 50

Cupcake 30
Elephant 30
Elf School House 10
Ernie 60
Gum Ball Machine 50

Oscar The Grouch Cookie Jar

Oscar the Grouch (ILLUS.) 80
Pelican 50
Pinocchio (w/flake) 400
Rabbit on Safe 30
Santa Claus 200

California Originals Scarecrow Cookie Jar

Scarecrow with pumpkins, "871 USA"
  (ILLUS.) 50
Sheriff 30
Sitting Turtle 50
Small Squirrel on Stump 20
Superman 250
The Tortoise and the Hare 20
Tigger 190

CARDINAL

French Chef 70
Garage 40

Smart Cookie 50

DORANNE OF CALIFORNIA

Donkey, blue tie 30
Hound Dog, green 30
Snowman 210

ENESCO

Betsy Ross 225
Snow White, Dwarfs around her skirt, Walt
  Disney Productions 1,100
Winking Kitty 295

METLOX

Apple 40

Brownie Scout Cookie Jar

Brownie Scout (ILLUS.) 750
Buelah, cow head 380
Cat head, w/original Poppytrail label 95
Corn 80
Drum 30
Fido Dog 190
Frog (Prince) 90
Jolly Chef 410
Mouse Mobile 150
Parrot 210
Pinocchio head 250
Pretty Ann 200
Santa 525
Scotty Dog, black 60
Spaceship 1,300

REGAL

Churn Boy 140
Davy Crockett 350
Diaper Pin Pig 400

Regal Dutch Girl Cookie Jar

Dutch Girl (ILLUS.) 675
French Chef 375
Hobby Horse 275
Humpty Dumpty 275
Old MacDonald Barn 385

ROBINSON RANSBOTTOM

Chef 70
Dutch Girl 170
Hi Diddle Diddle, gold trimmed 230
Hootie Owl 50
Oscar 40
Peaches, embossed on white ground 30
Sheriff Pig 80

SIERRA VISTA

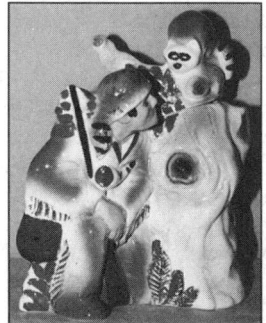

Davy Crockett Cookie Jar

Davy Crockett (ILLUS.) 900
Elephant 90
Squirrel 75

TREASURE CRAFT

Big Al, marked "Walt Disney Productions"
   around base 50
Cookie Trolley 60

Hobby Horse 50
Jackpot 50
Monk 20
Puppy in Basket 40
Sitting Clown 40

TWIN WINTON

Buddha, standing, brown glaze 60

Grandma Cookie Jar

Grandma (ILLUS.) 35
Hotei 45
Jack-in-the-Box 495
Ole King Cole 260

VANDOR

"Cowmen Mooranda" Cookie Jar

"Cowmen Mooranda," 1852 (ILLUS.) 260
Crocagator, head w/sunglasses 95

MISCELLANEOUS

Bear, Gilner 30
Bear on Blocks, unmarked, Starnes of
   California 160
C3PO, original box, Roman Ceramics 550
Cloth Doll, green polka dot dress,
   unmarked, Starnes of California 160

Clown, DeForest of California 40
Dove, Fredericksburg Art Pottery Co........... 30
Eskimo, Starnes........................... 300
Hobby Horse, Gilner 120
Howdy Doody, Purinton................... 365
Little Red Riding Hood, Pottery Guild........ 125

Mammy With Watermelon Cookie Jar

Mammy, w/watermelon, Weller (ILLUS.)...... 1,800
Mammy Look-A-Like National Silver.......... 200
Mickey Mouse on Drum, Roman Ceramics 350
Monk, DeForest of California 80
Monk, William H. Hirsch Mfg. Co.............. 50
Rolls Royce, Fitz & Floyd.................. 175
Tar Baby Shirley Corl's Kiln 320

CURRIER & IVES PRINTS

This lithographic firm was founded in 1835 by Nathaniel Currier with James M. Ives becoming a partner in 1857. Current events of the day were portrayed in the early days and the prints were hand-colored. Landscapes, vessels, sport and hunting scenes of the West all became popular subjects. The firm was in existence until 1906. All prints listed are hand-colored unless otherwise noted. Numbers at the end of the listings refer to those used in Currier & Ives Prints-An Illustrated Checklist, *by Frederick A. Conningham (Crown Publishers).*

American Country Life - October
Afternoon, large folio, N. Currier, 1855, framed, 122, toning, a few scattered fox marks (ILLUS.) $1,495
American Fireman (The) - Rushing to the Conflict, large folio, 1858, No. 155, framed (staining, cockling) 690
American Railroad Scene - "Snowbound," small folio, 1871, framed, 187, (mottled discoloration in margins, small tear in lower edge) 3,335
Battle of Antietam, Md., Sept. 17th, 1862 (The), small folio, undated, framed, 384 (stains)........................... 165
Battle of Chancellorsville, Va., May 3rd, 1863, small folio, undated, framed, 395 (minor edge wear & stains) 286
Battle of Fair Oaks, Va., May 31st, 1862 (The), small folio, 1862, framed, 402 (minor edge damage & stains) 270
Battle of Fredericksburg, Va., Decr. 13th, 1862, small folio, 1862, framed, 405 (stains) .. 286
Battle of Pea Ridge, Arkansas, March 8th, 1862 (The), large folio, framed, 421 (minor stains, wear & top corners glued down) 990
Battle of the Wilderness, Va., May 5th & 6th, 1864 (The), large folio, undated, framed, 435 (stains in margins & edge damage)........................ 1,650
Capture of Andre (The), small folio, N. Currier, undated, framed, 806 (stains & paper damage)......................... 83
Clipper Ship "Lightning," large folio, N. Currier, 1854, framed, 1158 (toning, soiling, unobtrusive cockling, not examined out of frame) 920
Cottage Life - Summer, small folio, undated, framed, 1267 (minor stains & edge damage, top edge glued down, margins trimmed) 193
Darktown Bicycle Race - The Start, small folio, 1895, 1377..................... 523
Ethan Allen and Mate and Dexter, large folio, 1867, framed 1757 (stains, edge damage & margins trimmed slightly) 770
Express Train (The), small folio, 1855, framed, 1790, (faint discoloration & pale water stains in margins) 2,070

American Country Life

The Express Train

Express Train (The), small folio, 1870,
   framed, 1793, few small fox marks at
   upper right (ILLUS., previous page) **2,300**

**Genl. Meagher at the battle of Fair Oaks,
   Va. June 1st, 1862,** small folio, 1862,
   framed, 2289 (stains & repaired tears) **248**

**Great East River Suspension Bridge
   (The),** large folio, 1883, framed, 2597
   (foxing, paper discoloration) **632**

Haunts of the Wild Swan (The), small folio,
   1872, new curly maple frame, 3757
   (foxing & minor edge damage) **303**

Henry Clay - Of Kentucky, small folio, N.
   Currier, 1842, framed, 2786 (minor stains
   & damage) **176**

Lexington of 1861 (The), small folio,
   undated, framed, 3484 (margin stains) **303**

The Life of a Fireman - The Race

Life of a Fireman (The) - The Race, large
   folio, 1854, framed, 3519 (ILLUS.) **1,265**

Lightning Express (The), small folio,
   undated, framed, 3534 (light stain & few
   soft handling creases) **2,760**

On the Owago, small folio, undated, 4608
   (some edge damage, wear & stains) **165**

Riverside (The), medium folio, undated,
   framed, 5164 (edge damage & stains) **330**

Scenery of the Catskills, small folio,
   undated, old gilded frame, 5419
   (minor stains) **385**

**Second Battle of Bull Run, Fought Augt.
   29th, 1862 (The),** small folio, undated,
   framed, 5452 (edge tears, fold lines &
   stains) **262**

**Storming of Fort Donelson, Tenn., Feby,
   15th, 1862 (The),** large folio, 1862,
   framed, 5824 (some damage) **825**

**Surrender of General Lee - At
   Appomattox, C.H. Va., April 9th, 1865,**
   small folio, 1873, framed 5911 (margins
   trimmed & damage to title) **253**

Tomb of Washington (The), small folio,
   undated, framed, 6108 (stains, short
   tears in margin) **138**

Western Farmer's Home (The), small folio,
   1871, framed, 6619 (minor stains &
   edge damage) **341**

Winter in the Country

Winter in the Country - A Cold Morning,
   large folio, 1864, framed, 6736, repaired
   tear at left extending one inch into image,
   rubbed spots along left edge of image,
   staining in margins (ILLUS.) **10,925**

CZECHOSLOVAKIAN COLLECTIBLES

*Czechoslovakia did not exist until the end of
World War I in 1918. The country was put
together with parts of Austria, Bohemia and
Hungary as a reward for the help of the Czechs
and the Slovaks in winning the war. In 1993
Czechoslovakia split and became two countries:
the Czech Republic and the Slovak Republic.
Items are highly collectable because the country
was in existence only 75 years. For a more
thorough study of the subject, refer to the
following books: Made in Czechoslovakia Books
1 and 2 by Ruth A. Forsythe; Czechoslovakian
Glass & Collectibles Books I and II by Dale &
Diane Barta and Helen M. Rose and
Czechoslovakian Perfume Bottles and Boudoir
Accessories by Jacquelyne Y. Jones North.*

GLASS

Basket, yellow w/black rim & handle,
   6½" h. **$200**

Basket, green w/dark green stripes &
   handle, 8" h. **245**

Beverage set, mauve w/coralene bird &
   flowers, egg-shaped, six small glasses &
   bottle inside, 9" h. **150**

Candy dish, cov., green spatter on red
   ground, 6" h. **300**

Candy dish, cov., red spatter w/black
   pedestal base, 7" h. **375**

Charm, rabbit, blue,1" h. **40**

Place card holder, 1¼" cameo, blue
   stone 2¼" h. **65**

Place card holder, pot of flowers, 1½" h. **8**

Three-handled Powolny Vase

Vase, bulbous body w/cylindrical neck
flanked by three angled applied handles,
scarlet w/three blue handles, Powolny,
5½" h. (ILLUS.) **1,200**
Vase, opaque white w/crystal rim top, 5½" h...... **65**
Vase, brown to mottled yellow chip glass, 7" h. ... **180**

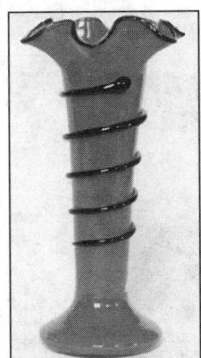

Trumpet-form Vase with Blue Trim

Vase, trumpet-form w/ruffled rim, red w/dark
blue serpentine trim, 7½" h. (ILLUS.) **145**
Vase, bulbous, charcoal w/red flame, 8" h....... **175**

Glass Fan Vase with Mottled Colors

Vase, fan-shaped, mottled turquoise blue &
yellow spatter, 8" h. (ILLUS.) **180**
Vase, satin, painted desert scene, 8½" h........ **300**
Vase, satin glass w/controlled bubbles,
applied cattail leaves, base of iridescent
blue w/darker blue veins, 9" h. **1,400**

Water set, five pieces, orange w/enamelled
tropical bird, the set **625**

JEWELRY

Beads, green opaque, 20" l................... **35**
Brooch, gold w/enamel gent & lady, 2" d. **65**
Buckle, green & orange enamel, 2" l........... **25**
Earrings, crystal w/small crystal drop, pr. **20**
Necklace, graduated sizes black beads
w/small crystals between, 18½" l............. **40**
Necklace, rhinestone, 20" l. w/four drops........ **45**
Pin, butterfly garnet, 2" **70**
Purse, black beads w/V-shaped center of
white beads, zipper closure, 9"............. **45**
Purse, blue, yellow, & white wooden beads, 10" .. **45**

LAMPS

Lamp, dancing lady, blue & white satin
finish, 10" h............................ **245**
Lamp, yellow Art Deco decor, Peasant Art,
Mrazek, 10" h........................... **390**
Lamp, beaded basket w/glass fruit top, 11" h... **1,200**
Lamp, enameled tulips w/cone shade, 11" h..... **285**

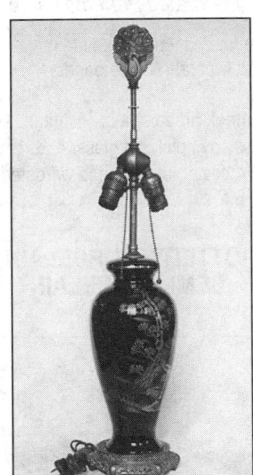

Peacock Lamp & Peacock Finial

Lamp, baluster-form w/peacock decoration
on a black ground & w/peacock finial,
lobed metal base & lamp fittings,
12½" h (ILLUS.) **350**
Lamps, crystal & brass 13" h., pr. **145**

PERFUME ITEMS

Bottle, purse, jeweled filigree, 2" **95**
Bottle, clear w/jeweled screw top, 2½"......... **45**
Bottle, black w/clear stopper, 3"............... **90**
Bottle, clear w/clear frosted stopper, 3" **65**
Bottle, clear w/red stopper, 3¼".............. **125**
Bottle, black w/clear stopper, 4½" **135**

Bottle, clear w/pink stopper, figural nude
applicator, 5½"....................... **2,200**

Bottle, malachite crystal, bluebells, 6½"........ **600**

Bottle, blue w/brass overlay, clear nude
female w/Russian wolfhound stopper,
7½"..................................... **500**

Bottle, blue w/blue stopper, woman holding
flowers, 8"............................. **600**

Bottle, pink w/pink floral stopper, 8"........... **350**

Bottle, clear w/blue stopper, 8½"............. **250**

Bottle, pink w/clear stopper, couple w/sheep
in a garden, 9"......................... **700**

Decorated Perfume Lamp

Lamp, clear frosted, conical shade
decorated w/florals & blue bands, 6"
(ILLUS.)............................... **275**

Perfume funnel, amber glass, Hoffman, 2½"..... **75**

Powder box, cov., pink cut glass, 4" d......... **65**

Powder box, cov., blue cut base w/frosted
floral lid, 6½" d......................... **70**

POTTERY, PORCELAIN,
SEMI-PORCELAIN

Amphora Basket with Cherub

Basket, figural cherub & small roses applied
near rim, gray w/pale green trim,
Amphora, 6½" h. (ILLUS.)............... **400**

Basket, purple majolica, 7½" h............... **165**

Book ends, horse head, white, 6¼" h., pr....... **75**

Bowl, cov., cream w/red & blue flowers
painted underglaze (rare), 5" h............ **250**

Bowl, cov., tan w/figural fox lid, duck &
rooster on side, Amphora, 11" h........... **750**

Box, cov., Peasant Art, blue w/fruits &
flowers, 5½" d., 4½" h................... **185**

Candleholders, tan figural fish, Amphora,
3½" h., pr.............................. **400**

Clock, mantel, airbrushed birds & water, two
figural birds on top, 11½" w., 11½" h....... **750**

Clock, Peasant Art, blue w/fruits & flowers,
10½" h................................. **400**

Cookie jar, cov., white w/black silhouette,
7½" h.................................. **145**

Cow creamer, walking animal, brown
spotted, 6½" l........................... **65**

Creamer, figural moose head, 5¼" h............ **45**

Dish, cov., figural crab, scarlet, 3½"........... **50**

Flower holder, figural parrot, blue
tan, 5" h............................... **40**

Jardiniere, blue w/floral border, 5½" h......... **75**

Kitchen set, slip-decorated w/scarlet ground
& yellow, purple & blue flowers, 15 pcs...... **750**

Models of hen & rooster, 6½" & 7" h., pr...... **110**

Mug, scarlet, black, & white stripes, 4½" h...... **55**

Art Deco Czech Pitcher

Pitcher, Art Deco design w/a yellow ground
& black, purple, orange & blue Peasant
Art decoration, Mrazek 4" (ILLUS.).......... **145**

Pitcher, milk, Peasant Art, blue bird &
flower, Myrazek, 5½"..................... **95**

Pitcher, figural ram, yellow & red, 8½" h....... **450**

Art Deco Majolica Planter

Planter, majolica, pedestal-based oblong Art
Deco design w/oblong bowl w/dark blue &
grey highlighted by pink flower clusters &
green leaves, Eichwald, 7½" l. (ILLUS.)...... **165**

Plate, scarlet w/fruit & flowers, Myrazek,
  8¼" d. **75**
Plate, lobster & crab, scarlet & cream, 9½" d. **45**
Teapot, cov., scarlet w/fruit & flowers,
  Myrazek, 7" h.. . . . . **285**
Teapot, cov., stacking-type w/trivet, blue,
  5½" h. **185**
Teapot, cov., tan w/orange flowers, ring
  handle, knob lid, 5½" h **150**

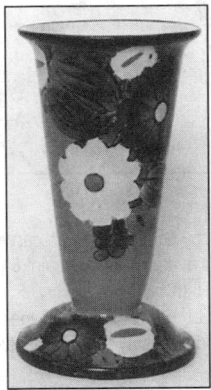

Art Deco Peasant Art Vase

Vase, trumpet-form on domed foot, Art
  Deco-style Peasant Art, stylized yellow,
  dark red, green & blue fruit & flowers on a
  scarlet ground, Mrazek, 8½" h. (ILLUS.) **185**
Vase, handled, pink painted flowers, 5½" h. **25**
Vase, fan-shaped, slip decoration in orange
  & blue, 7½" h **225**

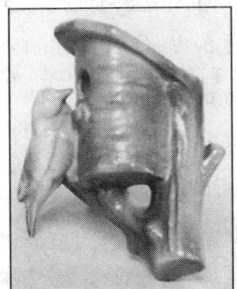

Bird at Birdhouse Wall Pocket

Wall pocket, bird at birdhouse, 5¼" h. (ILLUS.). . . **50**

DECOYS

*Decoys have been utilized for years to lure
flying water fowl into target range. They have
been made of carved and turned wood, papier-
mâché, canvas and metal, and some are in the
category of outstanding folk art and command
high prices.*

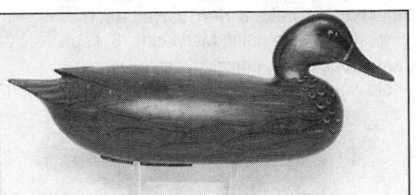

Rare New Jersey English Decoy

Black Duck, Dawson-style by John English,
  New Jersey, carved wood, glass eyes,
  original paint (ILLUS.) **$27,500**
Bluebill Drake & Hen, carved wood
  w/original worn paint, Maryland, 14" l., pr. **220**

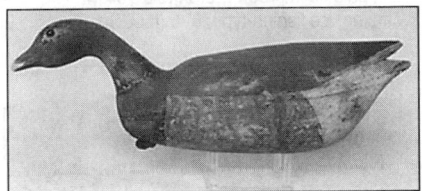

Brant Decoy

Brant, by Nathan Cobb, Jr., carved &
  painted wood, hollow body, ca. 1880
  (ILLUS.). **132,000**
Brant, swimming pose, carved wood w/old
  worn working paint, 20½" l. (some edge
  damage, crack in neck at nailed repair) **253**

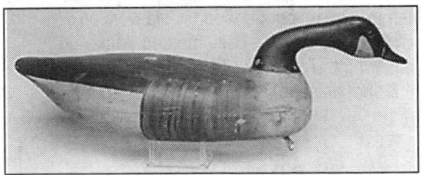

Canada Goose

Canada Goose, by Harry Mitchell Shourds,
  carved wood, swimming position, original
  paint w/some wear (ILLUS.) **63,250**
Canada Goose, by Phinneas Reeves,
  carved wood, original paint, ca. late
  1800s. **10,200**
Canada Goose, swimming position, carved
  wood w/snakey head, original realistic
  paint & good carved detail, signed
  "Canada Goose by Clem Wilding,"
  Missouri, 31" l. (glued break in neck) **165**
Canada Goose, primitive carved wood
  w/white & black repaint, class eyes, 21" l. **88**
Canvasback Drake, carved wood w/old
  working repaint & glass eyes,
  Wisconsin, 15" l. **193**
Canvasback Drake, carved wood, working
  paint & glass eyes, branded "Hall,"
  15½" l. (minor wear & damage on
  bottom edge) **83**

Canvasback Drake & Hen, carved wood w/original worn paint, Maryland, 16" l., pr. **242**
Canvasback Hen, primitive, carved wood, old working repaint, 17¾" l. (some damage) .. **138**

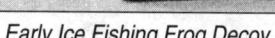

Early Ice Fishing Fish Decoy

Fish, carved & painted wood, wide-pointed fish painted in green w/orange & yellow striping, ice fishing-type, 8" l. (ILLUS.) **99**

Early Ice Fishing Frog Decoy

Frog, carved & painted wood, swimming position, green w/black spots & open red mouth, ice fishing-type, 8" l. (ILLUS.) **88**
Greenwing Teal Hen, by Charles Perdew, Illinois, carved wood, original paint, early version **14,850**
Mallard Drake, cork & wood w/old working repaint, tack eyes, base marked "Maker Enwright, Toledo, O.," 17" l. (some edge & shot damage) **83**

Mallard Drake & Hen

Mallard Drake & Hen, "1924 exhibition" by Charles Perdew, Henry, Illinois, carved wood, original paint & good patina, pr. (ILLUS.)........................... **66,000**
Mallard Hen, by Robert Elliston, carved wood in sleeping pose, original paint **10,450**
Merganser Drake, by Mason Decoy Company, Detroit, Michigan, carved wood, glass eyes, original paint **7,250**

Merganser Drake, carved full-bodied solid figure painted black & white w/orange & yellow eyes & a pale orange bill, retains inset lead weight, probably Maritime provinces, 20th c. (shrinkage cracks down underside)........................ **805**

Pintail Drake

Pintail Drake, by Charles Walker, carved wood, glass eyes, w/original paint & good feather detail (ILLUS.) **44,000**
Pintail Drake, by Elmer Crowell, Cape Cod, carved wood, glass eyes, original paint.... **55,000**

Ward Bros. Pintail Drake

Pintail Drake, by Ward Brothers, Crisfield, Maryland, "pinch breasted," carved wood, glass eyes, original paint, ca. 1932 (ILLUS.)........................... **104,500**

Teal Drake & Hen

Teal Drake & Hen, by Ward Brothers, Crisfield, Maryland, carved wood, glass eyes, original paint, pr. (ILLUS.) **38,400**

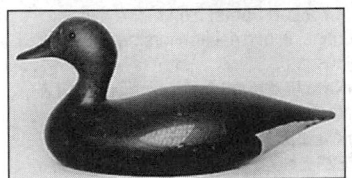

Wigeon Drake

Wigeon Drake, by Joseph Lincoln, Accord,
Massachusetts, carved wood, glass eyes,
original paint (ILLUS.) **12,650**
Yellowlegs, by Elmer Crowell, carved wood,
original paint **22,550**

DISNEY COLLECTIBLES

*Scores of objects ranging from watches to
dolls have been created showing Walt Disney's
copyrighted animated cartoon characters, and
an increasing number of collectors now are
seeking these, made primarily by licensed
manufacturers.*

Abu (Aladdin) movie cel, gouache on
celluloid applied to a matching production
background, Abu steals a melon from a
vendor for breakfast while swinging by his
tail, 1992, 12½ x 17" **$4,600**
Alice in Wonderland figure, ceramic, Alice,
Evan K. Shaw Co., w/label **1,000**
Alice in Wonderland figure, ceramic, The
Mad Hatter, Evan K. Shaw **300**
Alice in Wonderland figure, ceramic, The
White Rabbit, Evan K. Shaw label **300**
Alice in Wonderland movie cel, reclining
Cheshire Cat pointing, 1951, 4¾" x 7". **5,750**
Alice in Wonderland movie cel, gouache
on trimmed celluloid applied to a
prepared background, Alice swings a
paint brush brimming w/red paint, 1951,
10 x 12" **1,610**
Alice in Wonderland paint box. **55**
Aristocats movie cel, "Amelia, Abigail &
Uncle Waldo," Walt Disney Production
seal, 6 x 1½" **377**
Aristocats mug, pottery, gold rim, 1970 . . . . **45**

Bambi Bank by Leeds

Bambi bank, ceramic, marked "Leeds"
(ILLUS.) **68**
Bambi card game, Vol. 4 . . . . **25**
Bambi figure, ceramic, prone position,
American Pottery, Evan K. Shaw , "Lying" **150**
Bambi figure, ceramic, standing w/butterfly
on tail, American Pottery, 1947, 8" h **190**

Bambi & Thumper Movie Cel

Bambi movie cel, gouache on trimmed
celluloid applied to a Courvoisier
background, a scene of Bambi looking
down at Thumper perched on a rock,
stamped "W.D.P." on mat w/Courvoisier
Galleries label on back, 1942, 7 x 7½"
(ILLUS.) **4,025**
Bambi planter, ceramic, depicts Bambi
looking into a pond, 7 x 10" **70**
Bambi record album, three records,
narrated by Shirley Temple, RCA, 1949 . . . . . . **165**
Bambi sheet music, "Love is a Song" **38**

Bambi Steiff Toy

Bambi toy, stuffed plush, standing Bambi
w/tan white-spotted fur, Steiff, button in
ear, ca. 1950s, mint, 6" h. (ILLUS.) **99**
Big Al cookie jar, cov., Walt Disney
Productions **130**
**Big Bad Wolf (from "Three Little Pigs")
doll,** stuffed cloth, colorfully dressed in
blue felt trousers and a tall red felt hat,
standing w/his mouth open & tongue
hanging out, about to devour a sandwich
containing one of the pigs, 20½" h. **1,050**
**Big Bad Wolf (from "Three Little Pigs")
figure,** bisque, 3" h. **105**

Blue Fairy (Pinocchio) movie drawing, graphite & colored pencil on paper, a large full-figure drawing of the Blue Fairy grasping her wand, production numbers stamped in lower right corner, 1940, 12½ x 15½" **1,035**

Disney Bongo the Bear Doll

Bongo the Bear doll, stuffed plush, painted face, red jacket & blue bow tie, small hat, in original box w/small story book, 1948, 15" h. (ILLUS.) **275**

Brer Rabbit (from Song of the South) figure, ceramic, 7" h. **80**

Cinderella alarm clock, Bradley **70**

Cinderella cookie jar, ceramic, Enesco **400**

Cinderella handkerchief, Walt Disney Productions, 8½" square **25**

Cinderella paint set, tin box **85**

Cinderella planter, ceramic, standing in rags w/white apron, Evan K. Shaw Co., sticker **500**

Cinderella sheet music, "So This Is Love," France, 1958 .... **19**

Cinderella & Prince salt & pepper shakers, ceramic, Walt Disney Productions, pr. **105**

Clarabelle Cow book, "Story of Clarabelle Cow," story & picture book w/adventures of Donald Duck & Mickey Mouse & Clarabelle as a secondary character, Whitman Publishing, child's scrawled name & date on cover, 1938, 94 pp., 5 x 5½" (ILLUS. center w/Goofy book) **48**

Cruella De Vil (101 Dalmations) animation cel, gouache on celluloid, Cruella stands & shoots an evil glance over her shoulder, 1961, 9 x 9" **1,840**

Daisy Duck wristwatch, 1948, w/original box **385**

Davy Crockett bank, embossed "Davy Crockett Pony Express," saddle bag-shaped, mint in package **65**

Davy Crockett bedspread & rug, chenille, 2 pcs. **405**

Davy Crockett billfold, vinyl **22**

Davy Crockett binoculars **45**

Davy Crockett boots, high rubber-type w/fringe, in original frontiersman box, 1950s **225**

Davy Crockett breakfast set: mug, bowl & plate, Oxford China, 3 pcs. **55**

Davy Crockett candy dispenser, plastic, "PEZ" **18**

Davy Crockett charm bracelet, mint on original card **95**

Davy Crockett cookie jar, ceramic, standing boy, name on rifle, Brush **500**

Davy Crockett costume & accessories, in original box w/picture of Fess Parker on cover **120**

Davy Crockett figure, w/coonskin hat, rifle, powder horn & canteen, Remco, mint condition **120**

Davy Crockett hobby horse **350**

Davy Crockett knife, "Davy Crockett's own Frontier Knife," Barlow **55**

Davy Crockett lamp, composition, figure of Davy, w/original shade **175**

Davy Crockett lunch box w/thermos, official Walt Disney model, Kruger,1955 ..... **275**

Davy Crockett movie projector, "Magic Picture," in the shape of a gun, battery-operated, unused in original box **140**

Davy Crockett pencil box, "Frontierland" **48**

Davy Crockett play set, "Davy Crockett at the Alamo," Marx **325**

Davy Crockett poster, movie poster, "Davy Crockett And The River Pirates," 27 x 41" **185**

Davy Crockett record, "The Ballad of Davy Crockett," 1955, yellow jacket **350**

Davy Crockett records, "So Dear To My Heart," 78 rpm, set of 3 .... **45**

Davy Crockett revolver, click-gun-type, metal, picture of Davy holding a rifle **120**

Davy Crockett scrapbook, all-wood hinged covers, fine design on the front cover, 9 x 12" **195**

Davy Crockett teaspoon, silver plate **17**

Davy Crockett tumblers, glass, ca. 1955, set of 6 .... **125**

Davy Crockett wallpocket, ceramic, model of a moccasin **100**

Davy Crockett wristwatch, Bradley, 1956 ..... **130**

Davy Crockett wristwatch, U.S. Time, 1954, w/powder horn case, mint in box **385**

Disney characters book, Annual 1937, w/dust jacket, 10½ x 13½" (well worn dust jacket) **360**

Disney characters book, "Disney Peculiar Penguins," 1934 .... **40**

Disney characters book, "Disney's Silly Symphonies," 1930s **27**

Disney characters book, "Previews of Pictures to Come," drawings include 101 Dalmations, etc., Vol. 13 .... **60**

Disney characters book, "Previews of
Pictures to Come," drawings include
Donald Duck & Ludwig Von Drake, Vol. 14 . . . . **60**

Disney characters book, "School Days in
Disneyville," 1939. . . . . **30**

Disney characters book, "Silly Symphony
Book To Color," Whitman No. 660, 1932 . . . . . . **75**

Disney characters book, "The Three
Caballeros," Walt Disney Productions,
1944, excellent condition **60**

Disney characters book, "Walt Disney
Comics & Stories, No. 11, Vol. 3,"
August 1943 . . . . **1,400**

Disney characters book, "Walt Disney's
Forest Friends," 1938, hard cover, w/dust
jacket **78**

Disney characters cartoon drawing,
graphite & colored pencil on paper, a
storyboard drawing of Katharine Hepburn
as Little Bo Peep w/four large sunflowers
behind her, from "Mother Goose Goes
Hollywood," 1931, 6¾ x 8½". **920**

Disneyland record set, "Your Trip To
Disneyland," the set **50**

Donald Duck cartoon cel, gouache on
celluloid applied to a Courvoisier
background w/"W.D.P." stamped on the
mat, shows Donald dressed as a Western
hero twirling a gun on the index finger of
his left hand, Walt Disney's signature on
the lower right hand corner, 8" d. **2,185**

Donald Duck cartoon cel, gouache on
trimmed celluloid applied to a drawing of
a tree branch & nest, Donald, w/out-
stretched arms & a menacing squawk,
approaches the eagle's nest, from "Alpine
Climbers," 1936, 9¾ x 11". **1,035**

Donald Duck cartoon drawing, graphite &
pencil on paper, from "Orphan's Benefit,"
Donald attempts to recite "Little Boy Blue
Come Blow Your Horn," 1935, 9½ x 12" **345**

Donald Duck cartoon drawing, graphite &
colored pencil on paper, an angry Donald
w/hammer & horseshoe in hand, from
"The Village Smithy," production notes
throughout, 1942, 10 x 12". **517**

Donald Duck Advertising Blotter

Donald Duck ink blotter, advertising-type,
"Sunoco," color-printed paper,
rectangular w/a color scene of a laughing,
waving Donald seated in an open auto
racing across a snowy landscape w/a
Billy goat butting the back of the car,

reads "A Quck Start - Blue Sunoco (in
logo) - Peps Up Cold Motors," ca. 1938,
edge wear, scratches, soiling, small tear
at top (ILLUS.) **149**

Donald Duck nodder, celluloid figure on
metal base, Japanese, 6¼" h., very good **880**

Donald Duck pencil sharpener, celluloid,
figure w/sharpener inside, ca. 1930s **185**

Donald Duck toothbrush holder, bisque,
long-billed Donald in typical sailor suit,
Japan, 5¼" h. **390**

Donald Duck Jack-in-the-Box

Donald Duck toy, jack-in-the-box,
composition & cloth Donald in a
lithographed cardboard box, very good
condition (ILLUS.). **138**

Donald Duck wristwatch, round, Donald's
hands indicating the minutes & hours,
three Mickey figures on subsidiary
seconds dial, leather band w/enameled
metal figures of Donald, Ingersoll,
1935-39 . . . . **400**

Donald Duck & Goofy toy, a dancing figure
of Goofy atop a round base lithographed
w/Disney characters, w/a Donald Duck
drummer playing on a smaller attached
drum, Marx, ca. 1946, 10" h. **2,800**

Donald Duck & Goofy toy, windup tin,
Donald & Goofy duet, 1946, Marx,
10¼" h., very good (Goofy missing one ear) . . **462**

Donald Duck & Joe Carioca cookie jar,
ceramic, turnabout-type, Leeds China Co.. . . . **500**

Donald Duck & nephews billfold, plastic,
dressed in Western garb roping a calf,
Disney Productions, 3 x 7½" **88**

**Donald Duck & nephews Huey, Louie &
Dewey candy pail,** Overland Candy Co.,
Chicago, 1949, 3 oz., 3½" h. **65**

Donald Duck & nephews rug, shows the
nephews playing tricks **95**

Donald Duck & Pluto toy, automobile, hard
rubber, Sun Rubber Co., Barberton, Ohio,
1940s, 6½" l. **120**

Dumbo the Elephant book, "Dumbo of the
Circus," 1942 . . . . **60**

Dumbo the Elephant book, "Dumbo the
Flying Elephant," Whitman, 1941 . . . . **28**

Dumbo the Elephant cookie jar, ceramic, "Dumbo's Greatest Cookies on Earth," California Originals **625**

Dwarf Bashful figure, bisque, playing saxaphone, 4½" h. **125**

Dwarf Bashful figure, ceramic, Evan Shaw, 6¼" h. **125**

Dwarf Bashful movie drawing, graphite & colored pencil on paper, a production drawing of Bashful walking forward, 1937, 10 x 12" **460**

Dwarf Bashful Toothbrush Holder

Dwarf Bashful toothbrush holder, porcelain, figural, Bashful standing next to a textured brown container w/a blue rim, h.p. clothing & face, Japan, 1930s, 3½" w., 4" h. (ILLUS.) **110**

Dwarf Doc animation drawing, graphite on paper, outline sketch of Doc smiling & looking to his right, 1937, 10 x 12" **575**

Dwarf Doc doll, stuffed cloth, Knickerbocker Toy Co., 11" h. **98**

Dwarf Doc figure, porcelain, Goebel,1950s **45**

Dwarf Doc figure, bisque, 5" h. **105**

Dwarf Doc lamp, ceramic, Walt Disney Productions, dated 1938, 7" h. **250**

Dwarf Doc toothbrush holder, ceramic, "Doc Says Brush Your Teeth" **280**

Dwarf Dopey bank, composition, 1938 . . . . **180**

Dwarf Dopey cookie jar, ceramic standing figure, Treasure Craft, mint in box, 11" h.. . . . . . **175**

Dwarf Dopey figure, bisque, 5" h. **105**

Dwarf Dopey pencil sharpener, Bakelite, figural, 1930s **95**

Dwarf Grumpy doll, stuffed velvet, Knickerbocker, dated 1938 on original tag, 10" h **450**

Dwarf Grumpy figure, porcelain, Goebel, 1950s **45**

Dwarf Happy figure, porcelain, Goebel, 1950s . . . **45**

Dwarf Happy figure, bisque, 2½" h. **40**

Dwarf Sleepy figure, porcelain, Goebel, 1960s. . . **45**

Dwarf Sleepy figure, bisque, 5" h.. . . . . . . **95 to 105**

Dwarf Sneezy figure, bisque, 4½" h. **85**

Dwarf Sneezy toothpick holder, china, 1937. . . **180**

Dwarfs Happy & Doc toothbrush holder, ceramic, Maw, England, 1938, 4" h.. . . . . **445**

Dwarfs Doc, Dopey, Sleepy, Grumpy, Sneezy, Happy & Bashful movie cel, gouache on one piece of trimmed celluloid, a scene depicting all seven of the Dwarfs dancing jubilantly as Prince Charming's kiss brings Snow White back to life, 1937, 6¼ x 13" **5,750**

Evil Hag (Snow White & the Seven Dwarfs) production drawing, graphite & colored pencil on paper, showing a half-length portrait of the Evil Hag in profile, stamped w/production numbers in lower left corner, 1937, 10 x 12" **977**

Fantasia figure, china, Centaurette, blonde, Vernon Kilns, No. 18 . . . . **1,000**

Fantasia movie cel, gouache on celluloid applied to a Courvoisier background & mat, a centaurette looks down as her attendant grooms her, from the "Pastoral Symphony" segment, w/a skirt airbrushed onto the background & stamped "W.D.P.," 1940, 3¼ x 4½" oval **690**

Fantasia "Sorcerer's Apprentice" Cel

Fantasia movie cel, gouache on trimmed celluloid, Mickey timidly peers up the steps to see if Yen Sid has left, from "The Sorcerer's Apprentice" segment, 1940, 4¾ x 5¼" (ILLUS.). **4,887**

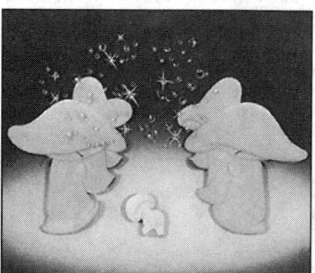

Fantasia Mushroom Dancers Cel

Fantasia movie cel, gouache on celluloid applied to an airbrushed Courvoisier background, scene of The Mushroom Dancers lining up in two rows while Hop Low bows to them, "W.D.P." stamped in lower right corner & Courvoisier Galleries label on back, 1940, 6 x 6¾" (ILLUS.). **2,300**

Fantasia Centaur Movie Cel

Fantasia movie cel, gouache on celluloid, a male centaur spots the approaching centaurettes, from the "Pastoral Symphony" segment, 4½ x 7" (ILLUS.) **920**

Fantasia movie cel, gouache on trimmed celluloid, the ballerina ostriches line up on point in the "Dance of the Hours" sequence, 1940, 7 x 8½" **920**

Fantasia Mickey Production Drawing

Fantasia production drawing, graphite & colored pencil on paper, showing Mickey Mouse directing his new-found magic powers, from "The Sorcerer's Apprentice" segment, 1940, 10 x 12" (ILLUS.) **2,875**

Ferdinand the Bull bracelet, marked "Walt Disney Enterprises" **80**

Ferdinand the Bull cartoon cel, gouache on trimmed celluloid applied to a Courvoisier airbrushed background, Ferdinand charges down a field while astonished men look on, 1938, 9¼ x 9¾" ... **1,725**

Ferdinand the Bull figure, bisque, Japan, 1932-38, 3" h............................ **75**

Ferdinand the Bull hand puppet, cloth w/composition head, w/flower in hand, Walt Disney Enterprises.................. **120**

Rare Ferdinand the Bull Toy

Ferdinand the Bull toy, pull-type, lithographed paper on wood, seated cut-out of Ferdinand on a green wood platform w/red metal wheels, Fisher Price No. 34, 1939, minor wear (ILLUS.).......... **715**

Figaro (Pinocchio's cat) cookie jar, ceramic, featuring two kittens, one on the jar, the other on the cover, ca. 1940s, 11" h........................... **190 to 225**

Figaro (Pinocchio's cat) figure, porcelain, rolling a ball, Goebel w/full Bee mark........ **350**

Flora (good fairy from Sleeping Beauty) movie cel, gouache on celluloid, large cel of Flora w/out-stretched wand, 1959, 11 x 14" **460**

Flower the Skunk (Bambi) figure, ceramic, American Pottery, small **85**

Gideon from Pinocchio Movie Cel

Gideon (from Pinocchio) movie cel, gouache on trimmed celluloid applied to a Courvoisier veneer background, full figure of Gideon sitting, Courvoisier Galleries label on back, 1940, 5¼ x 5¾" (ILLUS.) **1,150**

Goofy, Clarabelle & Minnie Books

Goofy book, "Dippy the Goof," small hardbound story & picture book, Whitman Publishing, 1938, child's scrawled name & date on front, some wear, 94 pp., 5 x 5½" (ILLUS. top)..................... **48**

Goofy figure, bisque, 1930s, 3" h............ **165**

Goofy pencil sharpener, celluloid, Walt
Disney Productions **185**

Goofy toy, windup tin, litho, clockwork,
original box, Line Mar, Japan, 4¼" h.,
near mint **528**

Goofy & Donald Duck cartoon drawing,
graphite on paper, outline sketch showing
a surprised Goofy & Donald, from
"Mickey's Service Station," 1935,
9½ x 12" **690**

Hades (from Hercules) movie cel, half-
length portrait of Hades angered by the
incompetence of his assistants, Pain &
Panic, two-cel set-up, 1997, 12½ x 17" **3,737**

Hercules animation maquette, full-figure
statuette of Hercules in action, hand-
painted, numbered 36 of 40, 20½" h. **4,887**

Hercules movie cel, color scene w/half-
length portraits of Zeus & Hera, Zeus
holding the baby Hercules & the baby
Pegasus hovering behind Hera, two-cell
set-up, 1997, 19½ x 30¾" **2,990**

**Ichabod Crane (Adventures of Ichabod
and Mr. Toad, The) cartoon cel,**
gouache on celluloid, Brom Bones leans
over & beckons w/one finger, from "The
Legend of Sleepy Hollow" sequence,
1949, 7½ x 11½" **575**

**Ichabod Crane (Adventures of Ichabod
and Mr. Toad, The) cartoon cel,**
gouache on trimmed celluloid, scene of
Ichabod bowing to the rich & beautiful
Katrina Van Tassel in "The Legend of
Sleepy Hollow" segment, 1949, 10 x 12" **1,150**

Jiminy Cricket (from Pinocchio) doll,
velvet body, felt jacket & vest, 13½" h.
(hat missing) **105**

**Jiminy Cricket (from Pinocchio) movie
cel,** gouache on celluloid applied to a
prepared background, Jiminy, standing in
front of a large eight ball threatens to
knock Lampwick's block off after having
been sunk in the corner pocket, 1940,
7 x 9" **1,955**

**Jiminy Cricket (from Pinocchio)
wristwatch,** Ingersoll, in box **300**

Johnny Appleseed record album, 1949 . . . . **36**

Mowgli and Kaa Movie Cel

Jungle Book (The) movie cel, gouache on
celluloid applied to a production
background, a matching production set-
up w/Mowgli scolding the snake Kaa,
1967, 12½ x 16" (ILLUS.) **8,050**

Lady and The Tramp movie cel, gouache
on celluloid applied to a printed
background, Lady & Tramp sit side by
side in anticipation of their romantic
dinner, 1955, 8¼ x 10¼" **3,450**

Lady and The Tramp movie cel, gouache
on celluloid applied to a hand-prepared
background, scene of Lady looking back
at Tramp & two of their puppies, 1955,
9½ x 13½" **2,587**

Lady and The Tramp movie cel, Tramp,
gouache on celluloid applied to a printed
background, Tramp smiles & walks
forward, 1955, 12½ x 14" **920**

Lady and The Tramp Movie Cel

Lady and The Tramp movie cel, gouache
on celluloid applied to a printed
background, Joe & Tony look down &
smile at the startled Lady, 1955,
13½ x 17½" (ILLUS.) **3,450**

Little Red Riding Hood figure, bisque,
marked "Walt E. Disney - Borgefeldt -
1934," 3" h. **400**

Ludwig von Drake cookie jar, ceramic,
American Bisque **500**

Mary Poppins Cookie Jar

Mary Poppins cookie jar, ceramic, figural
Mary in a pink dress & parasol
w/penguins dancing in front, unknown
maker, 1960s (ILLUS.) **1,350**

Meg (from Hercules) animation maquette, full-figure statuette of Meg, hand-painted, numbered 25 of 44, 13" h. **2,875**

Mickey Mouse book, "The Sorcerer's Apprentice," 1940 . . . . **38**

Mickey Mouse book set, "The Mickey Mouse Box," #2146, includes "Brave Little Tailor," "Mother Pluto," "The Practical Pig," "Timid Elmer," and "The Ugly Duckling," set, Whitman Co., 1939, set **275**

Mickey Mouse bridge score pad, large illustration of Mickey on cover **95**

Mickey Mouse camera, "Mick-A-Matic," ear-activated. **60**

Mickey Mouse candy container, composition Mickey head & molded cardboard body, w/original paper label, 1940s **305**

Mickey Mouse cartoon cel, gouache on celluloid, large image of Mickey standing smiling & holding an envelope, ca. 1950s, 9 x 10" **1,380**

Mickey Mouse cartoon cel, gouache on trimmed celluloid applied to an airbrushed Courvoisier background, from "Brave Little Tailor," Mickey the Tailor leans out a window, flyswatter in hand, 1938, 7½ x 8¾" **4,025**

Mickey Mouse cartoon drawing, graphite & colored pencil on paper, a production drawing of Mickey in bed reading "The Cry in the Night," ca. 1930s, 9½ x 12" **575**

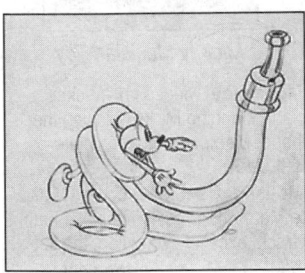

Mickey Mouse Cartoon Drawing

Mickey Mouse cartoon drawing, graphite & colored pencil on paper, a scene of Mickey wrestling w/a huge garden hose, from "Mickey's Garden," 1935, 9½ x 12" (ILLUS.) **805**

Mickey Mouse cartoon drawing, graphite & colored pencil on paper, Mickey recoils in horror at the sight of his new family, from "Mickey's Nightmare," 1932, 9½ x 12" **920**

Mickey Mouse cartoon drawing, graphite & colored pencil on paper, showing Mickey dangling from a vine, in full cowboy attire, from "Two Gun Mickey," full production notes throughout, 1934, 9½ x 12" **690**

Mickey Mouse cartoon production drawing, graphite & colored pencil on paper, large image of Mickey ready to swing a golf club, from "Canine Caddy," 1941, 10 x 12" **1,035**

Mickey Mouse doll, stuffed w/oversized hands, Margarete Steiff, 6¾" h. (missing tail & button) **770**

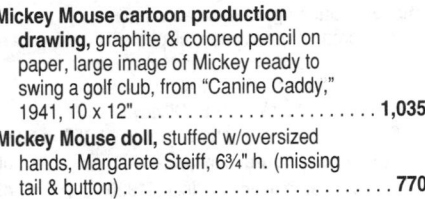

Very Rare Mickey Mouse Cowboy Doll

Mickey Mouse doll, cowboy, jointed composition, character head w/large "pie" eyes, large orange hands w/three fingers & a thumb, original red bandanna, white leather fur chaps w/red belt, two metal guns, made by Knickerbocker Toy Company, paper wrist tag, w/original box missing top flaps, ca. 1936, 9½" h. (ILLUS.) **12,100**

Gund Mickey Mouse Doll

Mickey Mouse doll, plush w/painted face, red felt shorts, white felt gloves & orange felt shoes, red ribbon bow tie, Gund, ca. 1950s-60s, 14" h. (ILLUS.) **77**

Very Early Mickey Mouse Figure

Mickey Mouse figure, painted wood, leatherette & rope, when tail pushed down, his head bobs up, thought to be the very first American Mickey, marked "ca. 1928-30 by Walter E. Disney," 6¼" h. (ILLUS., previous page).... **1,750 to 1,900**

Mickey Mouse figure, chalkware, 10" h. **300**

Mickey Mouse hairbrush, tin, ca.1930s **45**

Mickey Mouse Mug

Mickey Mouse mug, ceramic, swelled cylindrical form w/embossed standing figure of Mickey in long blue pants & yellow shirt, name at bottom, pale blue angled handle, Walt Disney Productions, ca. 1950s (ILLUS.) **38**

Mickey Mouse pencil case, rocket-shaped, ca. 1960, 12" l. **25**

Mickey Mouse Porcelain Tea Set

Mickey Mouse tea set: cov. teapot, cov. sugar bowl, creamer, six cups & saucers in original cardboard box; porcelain, transfer decorations in color of Mickey in different poses, golden lustre trim, Japan, ca. 1930s, the set (ILLUS.).............. **578**

Mickey Mouse toy, battery-operated, "Loop the Loop," mint in box **155**

Mickey Mouse Floor Walker Toy

Mickey Mouse toy, floor walker-type, painted & hinged wood, standing wearing yellow shorts, hands on hips, hinged straight square wooden legs w/green block feet, stick handle at back, ca. 1930s, 13½" h. (ILLUS.).............. **138**

Mickey Mouse Dipsy Car Toy

Mickey Mouse toy, wind-up tin, "Mickey Mouse Dipsy Car," colorful, Marx, Walt Disney Productions, excellent working condition, 6" h. (ILLUS.) **440**

Mickey Musician Toy

Mickey Mouse toy, windup tin, "Mickey Musician," standing Mickey playing the xylophone, Marx, working, complete w/box (ILLUS.) **660**

Mickey Mouse toy set, wind-up tin, "Mickey Mouse Meteor Express," five-piece train set w/track, excellent condition, the set **595**

Mickey & Minnie Mouse cartoon cel, gouache on trimmed celluloid applied to a Courvoisier background, Mickey & Minnie take a dangerous curve in their new "horsecar," from "The Nifty Nineties," 1941, 5¾ x 6¾" **4,887**

Early Mickey & Minnie Drawing

Mickey & Minnie Mouse cartoon drawing,
graphite & colored pencil on paper, a
large drawing of a jubilant Mickey &
Minnie being carried atop the winning
football goal post after Mickey has made
the winning touchdown, from "Touchdown
Mickey," 1932, 9½ x 12" (ILLUS.,
previous page) **2,070**

Mickey & Minnie Mouse Plaques

Mickey & Minnie Mouse plaques, die-cut
cardboard, colorfully printed, one
w/Mickey & the other w/Minnie, each w/a
small sign at the bottom, Mickey's reads
'Lo Mickey," Minnie's reads Hello Folks,"
ca. 1930s, 10½" h., facing pr. (ILLUS.) **165**

Mickey & Minnie Mouse toy, windup
celluloid & tin acrobats, George Borgfeldt,
very good, 13" h. (both faces pushed in) **418**

Mickey Mouse & Pluto figure, bisque,
Mickey riding on Pluto, George Borgfeldt,
ca. 1930s, 2¼" h. **65**

Mickey Mouse Club letter & envelope,
paper, large Disney letterhead &
information on club magazine, dated
1956, the set **45**

Minnie Mouse book, "Story of Minnie
Mouse," story & picture book, Whitman
Publishing, child's scrawled name & date
on cover, 1938, 94 pp., some wear,
5 x 5½" (ILLUS. bottom w/Goofy book) **48**

**Nana (nursemaid dog in Peter Pan) movie
cel,** gouache on trimmed celluloid applied
to a prepared background, an agitated
Nana straightens up blocks in the
children's bedroom, 11¼ x 13½" **920**

Nightmare Before Christmas Bank

Nightmare Before Christmas bank,
ceramic, figural Mayor Schmid, Disney-
authorized (ILLUS.) **75**

Peter Pan game, "Peter Pan Adventure
Game," Transogram **30**

Peter Pan handkerchief, Walt Disney
Productions, 8½" square **20**

Peter Pan movie drawing, graphite &
colored pencil on paper, Peter Pan
stretched out on his hammock holding his
pan flute, 1953, 9 x 11" **575**

"Walt Disney's Pinocchio" Book

Pinocchio book, "Walt Disney's Pinocchio,"
colorful picture of Pinocchio & friends on
the cover, hard cover, full-color, Whitman,
1940, 9¼ x 13" (ILLUS.) **33**

Pinocchio doll, wood-jointed, Ideal, mint in
original box, 12" h. . . . . **400 to 600**

Pinocchio doll, composition, large features,
Steiff, Germany, 1938, 15" h. **700**

Pinocchio doll, composition, Knickerbocker,
16" h. **450**

Pinocchio toy, windup tin, acrobat, Marx,
16½" h. **495**

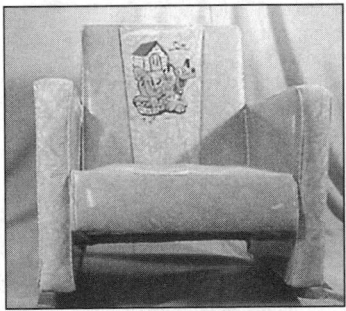

Pluto Child's Rocking Chair

Pluto child's rocking chair w/arms,
covered in white & yellow vinyl w/a color
decal of Pluto by his doghouse on the
back, Walt Disney Productions, ca. 1950s
(ILLUS.) **248**

Pluto mug, ceramic, Salem China **90**

Pluto pencil sharpener, Bakelite,
figural,1940s **45**

Pluto on Tricycle Toy

Pluto toy, windup celluloid & tin, Pluto on
tricycle, celluloid Pluto on tin tricycle
w/rear bell, colorful, Line Mar, Japan
(ILLUS.) **413**

Pluto toy, windup tin, "Drum Major," Line
Mar, Japan, 5½" h....................... **525**

Pluto toy, windup tin, "Roll-Over Pluto,"
when wound the lithographed pooch
bounds forward & rolls over, w/original
ears, Marx, w/original box, 8" l. **308**

**Prince Charming (from Cinderella)
planter,** ceramic, gold sword, w/sticker,
Shaw Pottery **400**

Robin Hood Movie Cel

Robin Hood movie cel, gouache on
celluloid applied to a production
background of three tents, Robin Hood
defends himself w/his sword from the
advances of Prince John's men, gouache
on paper w/a photocopy line-on-cel
overlay, 1973, 5¼ x 11" (ILLUS.) **2,300**

Robin Hood movie cel, gouache on
celluloid applied to a production
background, a key cel set-up of Lady
Cluck charging toward Prince John's men
during the battle/football game, 1973,
12½ x 16" **1,610**

Saludos Amigos cartoon cel, gouache on
trimmed celluloid applied to a Courvoisier
wood veneer background, Donald Duck
smiles & points upward, stamped
"W.D.P." on mat, w/Courvoisier Galleries
label on back, 1943, 5½" sq. **920**

**Scamp & Jock (Lady and The Tramp)
movie cel,** gouache on celluloid applied
to a printed background, Scamp the
puppy pulls at Jock's sweater, 1955,
10 x 12" **1,840**

Si & Am (Lady and The Tramp) movie cel,
gouache on celluloid applied to a key
production background, a key production
set-up of Si and Am destroying the parlor,
1955, 12 x 19½" **4,025**

Sleeping Beauty Movie Cel

Sleeping Beauty movie cel, gouache on
celluloid applied to printed background,
Flora, Merryweather & Fauna
contemplating Princess Aurora's fate,
12¾ x 14 12" (ILLUS.)................... **1,150**

Sleeping Beauty movie cel, gouache on
celluloid applied to a printed background,
King Stefan & King Hubert duel w/a fish,
1959, 12½ x 17" **1,035**

Snow White bank, ceramic, figural, Leeds
China Co. **86**

Snow White book, "Snow White Sketch
Book," coffee table-type, Collins, 1938....... **950**

Snow White Christmas tree lights, Noma,
boxed set **195**

Snow White figure, ceramic, American
Pottery, 9" h........................... **275**

Snow White movie cel, gouache on
celluloid applied to an airbrushed
background, Snow White improvises
while cleaning the Dwarfs' cottage by
using a young deer to hang laundry on,
1937, 5½ x 6" **1,265**

Snow White Movie Cel

Snow White movie cel, gouache on
trimmed celluloid applied to a Courvoisier
airbrushed background, Snow White
sitting under a quilt w/two rabbits in her
lap, 1937, 6¼ x 7" (ILLUS.)............. **6,325**

Snow White movie cel, gouache on trimmed celluloid applied to an airbrush-on-patterned paper Courvoisier background, scene of Snow White preparing a pie w/the help of squirrels & four birds, 1937, 7 x 7½" **4,600**

Snow White wristwatch, "Magic Mirror," U.S. Time, 1950, w/box **350**

Snow White & the Seven Dwarfs animation sketch, graphite & colored pencil on paper, the Evil Hag offers Snow White the poisoned apple, 1937, 7¾ x 9½" **1,150**

Snow White & the Seven Dwarfs child's chair, leather & plush, lithograph of Snow White & the dwarfs on front trim below the seat, lithograph of forest animals on the back, marked by Walt Disney Enterprises, 1938, 12" w., 15" h. **795**

Snow White & the Seven Dwarfs figures, bisque, George Borgfeldt, complete set w/original box, pristine **528**

Snow White & the Seven Dwarfs soap figures, Schultz, original package, the set. **295**

Sword in the Stone animation cel, gouache on celluloid applied to a matching production background, Wart is held spellbound by an enchanted sugar bowl, 1963, 12½ x 16". **2,185**

Three Little Pigs ashtray, ceramic, consisting of the three pigs, all wearing suits, perched on one end of the triangular ashtray, Japan, 4½" w. **145**

Three Little Pigs drum, lithographed tin, Ohio Art Co., 6½" **210**

Three Little Pigs playing cards, "Silly Symphony," Walt Disney Enterprises, 1932 . . . . **95**

Three Little Pigs & Big Bad Wolf pocket watch, w/fob, Ingersoll **1,250**

Three Little Wolves book, Whitman, copyright 1937, 9½ x 13" **65**

Thumper (from Bambi) figure, china, Disney No. 131, Goebel, small. **35**

Thumper Movie Cel

Thumper (from Bambi) movie cel, gouache on trimmed celluloid applied to a Courvoisier background, Thumper stands & wrinkles his nose, stamped "W.D.P." in lower right corner, 5½ x 6½" (ILLUS.) **1,955**

Thumper (from Bambi) planter, ceramic, Leeds China Company. **35**

Thumper's Girlfriend (from Bambi) ashtray, china, Disney No. 8, Goebel **325**

Tinkerbell (from Peter Pan) figure, china, Goebel, Germany, 1959, 8" h. **285**

Tinkerbell Movie Cel

Tinkerbell (from Peter Pan) movie cel, gouache on trimmed celluloid applied to a printed background, Tinkerbell looks to the side, stretches her arms & lifts one leg while standing beside a group of large thread spools, 1953, 8½ x 11" (ILLUS.) **3,162**

Tinkerbell (Peter Pan) movie drawing, graphite & colored pencil on paper, a large drawing of Tinkerbell, 1953, 7½ x 9½" . . **805**

Ugly Duckling animation cel, trimmed celluloid applied to an airbrushed Courvoisier background, the Ugly Duckling ponders a frog in a pond, partial Disney label on back, 1939, 7 x 8" **1,150**

Uncle Remus (from Song of the South) doll, stuffed cloth, 1940s, 14" h. **500**

White Rabbit (from Alice in Wonderland) creamer, ceramic, Regal China **195**

Who Framed Roger Rabbit Movie Cel

Who Framed Roger Rabbit movie cel, gouache on celluloid applied to a photographic background, Jessica's car has been smashed & Benny the Cab offers her a ride, 1988, 10¾ x 16½" (ILLUS.) **4,095**

Winnie the Pooh toy, jack-in-the-box **38**

Winnie the Pooh and Tigger Too production set-up, gouache on celluloid applied to a water-color production background, scene of Tigger asking Roo if he is "ready for some bouncin'," marked on bottom center "2518 VI sc. 212," 1974, 12½ x 16" **1,955**

Zorro figures, Zorro on horse, Marx, 1958, very fine, 2 pcs. **121**

DOLL FURNITURE & ACCESSORIES

Victorian Doll Bed

Bed, Victorian, walnut, turned posts & balusters, 19th c., 21 x 24", 39" h. (ILLUS.) **$121**

China closet, oak, two framed glass doors opening to three shelves, two drawers below, 1930s, 12¾" w., 20½" h. **165**

Cradle, dovetailed pine w/old brownish green sponged repaint, 13½" l. (some damage) **72**

Cradle, poplar w/old red paint & yellow striping, 18¾" l. **209**

Cradle, dovetailed pine w/old dark grained finish, heart cut-out in foot board, 26" l. **165**

Cradle, dovetailed poplar, heart cut-outs in ends, refinished, curly maple rockers replaced, 39" l. **105**

Woven Wicker Doll Carriage

Doll carriage, woven wicker, the deep rounded wicker body w/a hinged wicker hood w/small triangular windows, on bent steel springs & wire wheels w/rubber

rims, long upright curved metal handle w/wood grip, ca. 1920s, 24" l., 24" h. (ILLUS.) **193**

Doll carriage, wood w/steel frame, leatherized cloth top w/worn fringe, original varnish w/dark brown & yellow striping, wooden wheels, interior cushion & wallpaper trim, 36" l., 33" h. (some wear) . . . **385**

Dollhouse, wood & fiberboard two-story bungalow, simulated grey stone & brick w/red tile roof, front, sides & back each have two framed windows w/original curtains, one window on each side second floor, full length front porch w/decorative wooden railings, three wooden steps, both sides open to reveal two small rooms in back, a large living room in front w/fireplace, wallpaper on all walls, wood textured paper on floor, original window glass, celluloid plaque on side of base marked "A. Schoenhut Co., Philadelphia, PA," 16 x 22", 17" h. (light wear on edges of roof & gable) **1,050**

Gottschalk Dollhouse

Dollhouse, elaborate German or Austrian villa-style, lithographed paper on wood, two-story w/blue roof, brick-like exterior & original interior papers, two rooms up & two down, separate front steps to front porch w/baluster-form posts & decorative railings, matching balconies on second floor by two front windows, Gottschalk, ca. 1870s, Saxony, tower roof missing, some paper & wood damage, 18⁵⁄₁₆ x 26½ , 31" h. (ILLUS.) **9,200**

French Carved Oak Dollhouse

Dollhouse, carved oak, two-story
w/mansard roof, hinged shutters, carved
arches above all windows, balconies
outside two second floor windows,
France, on black painted stand, house
27 x 33", 40" h. (ILLUS., previous page) **1,955**

Large Wooden Dollhouse

Dollhouse, wooden two-story, yellow
clapboards, simulated shingle roof w/two
chimneys, porch w/six large turned
pillars, one over one opening glass sash,
interior Christian doors, old wallpapers,
six rooms include parlor, kitchen,
hallways, master bedroom, nursery,
grandfather room in attic, w/family of four
& fine collection of assembled furniture &
accessories in various scales 1¼ to 2" &
materials, electrified, late 19th c.,
modification & some restoration, w/porch
& chimneys, 34 x 75", 52" h. (ILLUS.) **2,300**

Late Victorian Oak Doll Dresser

Dresser, oak, a rectangular mirror frame
w/serpentine edges swiveling between
slender turned uprights above a
serpentine splashboard over the
rectangular top, case w/three long
drawers w/ring pulls, one pull missing,
ca. 1900, 15" w., 24" h. (ILLUS.) **160**
Living room suite: sofa w/matching
upholstered open-arm armchair, coffee
table & two end tables; produced to
accompany Barbie, hand-finished wood
construction, stamped "Mattel - Japan,"
simple rectangular modern style,
ca. 1960s, sofa 3½ x 9½", 3½" h., the set **121**
Step-back wall cupboard, walnut & poplar
w/old finish, Gothic arch door panel
w/reverse-painted glass in red & white

Step-back Wall Cupboard

lattice design above three dovetailed
drawers, cut-out feet w/scrolled trim,
replaced white porcelain pulls, some
renailing, 9 x 13¼", 19½" h. (ILLUS.) **275**
Table, softwood w/old greyish yellow paint
w/brown & red stiping & flouish, drop-leaf
type, 9¼ x 15¼" w/6⅛" leaves, 11¼" h. **303**
Waffle iron, for toy cook stove, metal,
marked "Wagner Mfg. Co.
Sidney, O.," 7½" l. **165**

DOLLS

Also see: STEIFF TOYS & DOLLS

A.B.G. China head Boy & Girl

**A.B.G. (Alt, Beck & Gottschalck) china
head boy,** marked "784 #11," shoulder
head w/painted blue eyes w/dark accent
lines & red lines over eyes, closed mouth
w/accent line, molded & painted blonde
hair w/exposed ears, cloth body w/china
lower arms, nicely redressed in white
shirt, grey wool pants, vest & double-
breasted coat, gold sash, black belt, light
wear, body w/soil & stains, arms new,
right lower leg replaced, 24" (ILLUS. left) **$450**
A.B.G. bisque socket head girl, marked
"ABG, 1362, Made in Germany," brown
sleep eyes w/real lashes, open mouth
w/four upper teeth, original dark h.h.
(human hair) wig, jointed wood &
composition body, dressed in antique
yellow dotted Swiss dress, underclothing,

pale yellow socks, leatherette tie shoes, 20½" (numerous wig pulls under wig cap area, small chip at side of neck opening, light wear & soil, finish "washed" on legs) **240**

A.B.G. china head "Highland Mary" girl, marked "1000 #10," shoulder head w/painted blue eyes w/dark accents, red accent line above, molded & painted blonde hair, closed mouth, cloth body w/china lower arms & legs w/molded & painted black heeled boots, redressed in lavender two-piece gown w/lace trim, underclothing, cloth body old replacement, minor damage to limbs, 23" (ILLUS. right, previous page) **700**

A.M. (Armand Marseille) bisque socket head baby, marked "Made in Germany, Armand Marseille, 560a, A. 10/0 M., DRMR 232, 1," blue sleep eyes, open mouth w/full accented lips & two upper teeth, original blonde h.h. wig, composition bent-limb baby body, dressed in pale pink dotted Swiss dress w/embroidery trim, matching bonnet, underclothing, socks & shoes, 8" (tiny inherent line on cheek, general wear & soil, repairs at shoulders & hips from stringing) **195**

A. M. bisque socket head baby, marked "590, A. 3/0 M., Germany, D.R.G.M.," brown sleep eyes, open-closed mouth, original light mohair wig, five-piece composition bent-limb baby body, dressed in old crocheted romper w/matching hat, 8½" (inherent color flaw on right ear, inherent bubble in bisque on forehead at crown, body finish "washed" and worn, wear on fingers & toes) **275**

A. M. character solid dome bisque socket head boy, marked "500, Germany, A. 3. M., DRGM," blue intaglio eyes, closed smiling mouth, molded & painted hair, jointed wood & composition body, dressed in navy blue sailor suit, old socks & shoes, 15" (color of limbs does not match torso, thighs repainted, thumbs repaired, tip off finger, finish off spot on back) **550**

A.M. "googly" bisque socket head baby, marked "200, A. 3/0 M., Germany, D.R.G.M., 243," set brown eyes to side, closed smiling mouth w/tip of tongue between lips, original blonde mohair wig, bent-limb composition baby body, dressed in antique baby dress, one-piece underwear w/lace trim, 11½" (few minor imperfections in bisque, two tiny wig pulls, head too small for body, finish of body "washed," thumb tips chipped) **1,250**

A. W. Special bisque socket head girl, marked "8, Germany, AWS, II," set brown eyes, open mouth w/four upper teeth, dark h.h. wig, marked jointed wood &

composition body, dressed in red antique dress w/lace trim, slip, replaced socks & shoes, 24" (small chip on neck socket of head, inherent color flaw on back of head) . . . **225**

Alexander (Madame) Dionne Quintuplets composition head girls, marked "Alexander," painted brown eyes to side, closed mouths, molded & painted hair, composition bent-limb baby bodies, dressed in tagged pastel rompers, matching hats, gold name pins, including basket which is not original & book "Dionne Quintuplet Picture Album," 7", the set (Cecile w/minor lip rub, Marie w/finish off tip of big toe, Emilie's bonnet missing, all dolls w/minor craze lines) **1,125**

Madame Alexander "Glamour Girl"

Alexander (Madame) "Glamour Girl" No. 2001C - Picnic Day, marked "Alexander" on back of head, hard plastic head w/blue sleep eyes & real lashes, closed mouth, original synthetic brown wig, hard plastic body w/walking mechanism, wearing original blue print long gown trimmed in lavender & black w/original tag, original slip w/hoop, panties, stockings & black shoes, straw hat w/black net ties, black hat box, clothing lightly faded, "played with" hair, replaced hat box handle, 18" (ILLUS.) **425**

Alexander (Madame) Scarlett O'Hara, composition head w/green sleep eyes, black hair, original white dress w/red roses, ca. 1937, 18" **975**

Alexander (Madame) "Sonja Henie" composition head girl, marked "Alexander," brown sleep eyes w/real lashes, open mouth w/four upper teeth, dimples, original h.h. blonde wig in original set, composition body w/jointed waist, dressed in original tagged skating outfit, panties, replaced socks & skates, 14" . . **450**

Alexander (Madame) "Wendy Ann" composition head girl, marked "Wendy-Ann, Mme. Alexander, New York," brown sleep eyes w/real lashes, closed mouth, original brown h.h. wig, composition body w/jointed waist, dressed in original tagged pink dress, attached slip, panties, original socks & shoes, straw hat w/flower trim, 13" (right eye cloudy, light stain on front of skirt) **190**

All-bisque "Bonnie Babe" character swivel head boy, unmarked, set brown eyes, open mouth w/two lower teeth, well modeled & painted hair, five-piece body w/molded & painted socks & shoes, 5" **600**

All-bisque character baby, marked "#790/92.6," painted blue eyes, open-closed mouth as if child is crying, lightly molded & painted hair, stiff neck, jointed body, dressed in antique white lace-trimmed romper, 6" (chips on hips, arms pink bisque & probably not original) **250**

All-bisque "googly" socket head character girl, marked "292/0," set blue eyes to side, closed "watermelon" mouth, original mohair wig, jointed body, molded & painted blue socks & black shoes, dressed in original regional-type costume, 4½" (only upper back & top of arms inspected as original clothing was not removed) **825**

All-bisque Mibs girl, marked "©, LA & S 1921, Germany," painted blue eyes, closed mouth, molded & painted hair, head turned to right & tilted down slightly, stiff neck, jointed body, molded & painted socks & shoes, dressed in original dress w/green satin bodice trimmed w/ribbon, net skirt, 4½" (end of nose slightly flattened) .. **300**

Early American Character Girl

American Character composition shoulder head Petite Mama girl, marked "Petite, Amer.Char.Dolls," blue tin sleep eyes w/real lashes, open mouth w/four upper teeth & tongue, original brown mohair wig, cloth body w/composition arms & lower legs, dressed in original pink ruffled dress & matching bonnet, one-piece underwear combination, socks & leatherette shoes, including original marked box w/excelsior packing, minor flaking at corners of mouth, top half of cloth body covered,

light wear, minor flaking, coloring of arms & legs faded, box is worn somewhat, lid missing, 24" (ILLUS.) **475**

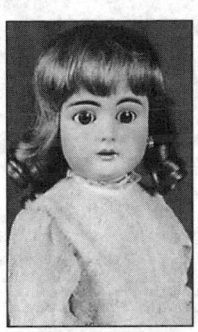

Bahr & Proschild Girl

Bahr & Proschild bisque socket head girl, marked "B& P - ??3 - 13," blue sleep eyes, pierced ears, open mouth w/accented lips, replaced synthetic wig, jointed wood & composition body, wearing antique lace dress, underclothing, knit socks, replaced shoes, teeth replaced, body repainted, 23½" (ILLUS.)......................... **475**

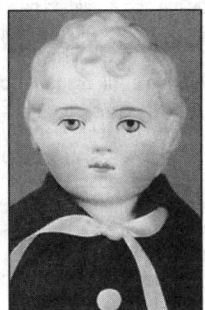

Bisque Shoulder Head Boy

Bisque shoulder head boy, unmarked, painted blue eyes w/red accent line, molded & painted curly blond hair w/exposed ears, closed mouth w/accent line, cloth body w/kid arms, bisque lower arms, printed stockings on cloth lower legs, leather boot feet, wearing a dull green corduroy suit, black stockings, new shoes, slight damages & repair, 19" (ILLUS.) **300**

Buddy Lee all-composition boy, unmarked, composition head w/painted side glancing eyes, closed smiling mouth, molded & painted hair, composition body w/stiff neck, jointed shoulders only, painted black boots, wearing original denim shirt, labeled Lee bib overalls & matching labeled cap, front of left foot broken & reglued, 12" (ILLUS., next page).... **375**

Original Buddy Lee Doll

Bye-Lo Baby, marked "© 1823 by Grace S.
Putnam, Made in Germany, #1372/45,"
bisque flange head, brown sleep eyes,
closed mouth, lightly molded & painted
hair, cloth body w/"frog" legs & non-
working crier, celluloid hands, dressed in
long baby dress w/rosebuds, slip,
crocheted bonnet, 14" (cracks in palms
of hands & one finger) 325

Bye-Lo Baby, marked "6-15," all-bisque
swivel head, blue sleep eyes, closed
mouth, lightly molded & painted hair, five-
piece marked body, 5½" (right arm one
size larger than left, fine hairline) 250

**Catterfelder Puppenfabrik bisque socket
head baby,** marked "(C.P. design), 262.,
made in Germany, 63," blue sleep eyes
w/remnants of real lashes, open mouth
w/accented lips, two upper teeth &
tongue, original light mohair wig,
composition bent-limb baby body,
dressed in antique white baby dress, slip,
knit panties, antique white baby bonnet,
24" (most of real lashes gone, repair at
joints, chipped big toe) 650

China head "high brow" lady, unmarked,
painted blue eyes w/red accent line,
closed mouth, molded & painted hair,
cloth body with china lower arms & legs
w/pink garters & black flat shoes,
redressed in blue plaid dress,
underclothing, 15½" (three specks of kiln
dirt on cheeks) 210

China head "Highland Mary" lady, marked
"1000 #8," painted blue eyes w/red
accent line, closed mouth w/accent line
between lips, molded & painted blonde
hair w/bangs, stamped cloth body
w/china lower arms & legs w/molded &
painted stockings & black heeled shoes,
dressed in probably original red checked
dress, underclothing, 19" (minor kiln
specks, repair on thumb, fingers chipped
on right hand, legs w/patches over holes
from wire in body). 305

China head lady, unmarked, painted blue
eyes w/red accent line, closed smiling
mouth, molded black hair w/molded
ribbon, exposed pierced ears, cloth body
w/leather lower arms, red corset, red
lower legs w/black oilcloth boots, dressed
w/antique fabric, slip, 17" (kiln dust in
china head, lower leather arms damaged,
body reinforced under shoulder plate) 325

China shoulder head girl, unmarked,
wigged solid dome, painted black spot on
top of head, painted blue eyes w/red
accent line, closed mouth w/red accent
line between lips, original brown mohair
wig, cloth body w/leather lower arms,
stitch-jointed at hips & knees, dressed in
possibly original black silk & velvet two-
piece outfit trimmed w/jet, antique
underclothing, socks, red leather
boots, 22½" (inherent flaw on brow,
black spot from wigs, small patch on
left leg, one finger missing & one
mended) 1,500

**Cuno & Otto Dressel bisque shoulder
head girl,** marked "COD 93, DEP," set
brown eyes, open mouth w/four upper
teeth, original dark h.h. wig, kid body
w/bisque lower arms, cloth lower legs,
gussets at hips and knees, dressed in
pink dress trimmed w/lace & ribbons,
antique underclothing, new socks &
shoes, 20" (small inherent black speck on
side of head). 205

**Cuno & Otto Dressel bisque socket head
girl,** marked "1349, Dressel, S & H, 7,"
open mouth w/accented lips & four upper
teeth, pierced ears, original h.h. brown
wig, stamped jointed wood & composition
body, dressed in possibly original white
dress, slip, socks & high button boots,
19½" (minor inherent line, minor wig
pulls, finger missing, finish removed over
COD stamp) 515

**Cuno & Otto Dressel bisque socket head
girl,** marked "1913, Made in Germany, +,
1912-4," blue sleep eyes, open mouth
w/accented lips & four upper teeth,
synthetic dark wig, jointed wood &
composition body, redressed in new
sailor dress, antique underclothing, black
socks & shoes, blue felt hat, 22" (fine kiln
dust in cheeks, sliver off inside edge of
eye, minor flaking) 325

**Dewees Cochran latex character-head
girl,** painted brown eyes, closed mouth
w/hint of a smile, replaced blonde saran-
type hair, marked five-piece latex child
body, dressed in light green dress
w/embroidery trim, underclothing, rayon
socks & white leather replacement shoes,
14½" (overall light soil, cracks & wear on
fingers of both hands 375

Effanbee "Baby Grumpy Soldier" composition shoulder head boy, marked "Effanbee Dolls, Walk - Talk - Sleep," painted blue eyes to side, closed pouty mouth, molded & painted hair, cloth body w/composition arms & legs, molded & painted brown army boots for feet, dressed in original army uniform w/shirt, replaced tie, jacket & pants, imitation leather belt, replaced hat, 12" (minor crazing & flaking, body lightly soiled, repair at crotch area of cloth body) **225**

Effanbee "Patricia Joan" composition head girl, marked "Effanbee, Patsy Joan," green sleep eyes w/real lashes, closed mouth, molded hair painted around edges only, original brown h.h. wig, marked metal heart bracelet, dressed in original mint green silk dress w/matching one-piece undergarment, replaced white socks & green leatherette tie shoes, 16" (tiny line at edge of eye, minor crazing). **300**

Effanbee "Patsy Babyette Twins" composition head babies, marked "Effanbee," blue sleep eyes w/real lashes, closed mouths, molded & painted hair, five-piece composition baby bodies, dressed in original blue & white check rompers tied around necks, 9", pr. (one baby w/cracks above both eyes, two tiny flakes on foot of one baby) **300**

Effanbee "Patsy" composition head girl w/trunk, marked "Effanbee, Patsy, Pat. Pend., Doll," brown painted eyes to side, closed "rosebud" mouth, molded & painted hair, five-piece composition body w/bent right arm, marked metal heart bracelet, dressed in pink & white gingham dress, underclothing, pink flannel coat & matching hat, old socks & shoes, contained in wooden & cardboard trunk w/two drawers, cardboard hangers appear original, travel stickers on outside, metal handle & corner covers, trunk contains red plaid beach pajamas w/matching hat, blue & white print dress w/matching one-piece underclothing, red velvet coat w/fur collar, matching hat, red flannel sunsuit w/net bodice, extra pair old socks, new leather shoes, 14", the set (light wear, finger repairs, repainted hands, trunk w/light fading & wear) **400**

Effanbee "Patsy Joan" composition head girl, marked "Effanbee, Patsy Joan," green sleep eyes w/real lashes, closed "rosebud" mouth, molded & painted hair, five-piece composition child body, dressed in original green & white sailor dress, matching one-piece underwear & hat, old white socks, green leatherette

shoes, 16" (most painted lashes & brows missing, light flaking, coloring somewhat pale, finish off right heel) **375**

Effanbee "Patsyette" "Anne of Green Gables" composition head girl, marked "Effanbee, Patsyette Doll," painted brown eyes to side, closed mouth, molded hair is painted on lower part, unpainted on top, original red mohair in braids, five-piece composition body w/bent right arm, marked metal heart bracelet, dressed in original blue & white check dress w/attached underclothing, blue jacket w/red ribbon trim, original socks & leatherette shoes w/metal buckle trim, braids w/blue ribbons, missing felt hat, 9" (minor crazing & flaking, clothing lightly discolored) **325**

Effanbee "Patsyette" composition head girl, marked "Effanbee Patsyette Doll," painted brown eyes, closed mouth, original brunette mohair wig, composition five-piece body w/bent right arm, dressed in original tagged dress w/matching one-piece underwear, old socks & tie shoes w/metal ornament on "bow," 9" (minor flaking on hand & wrist, one shoe yellowed somewhat). **265**

Effanbee "Patsyette" composition head girl, marked "Effanbee, Patsyette Doll," painted brown eyes to side, closed "rosebud" mouth, molded & painted hair, five-piece composition child body w/bent right arm, dressed in original red & white dress, matching one-piece underclothing, socks & leatherette shoes, 9" (lashes & brows missing, minor crazing, light wear on finger tips) **155**

Effanbee "Skippy" composition socket head boy, marked "Effanbee, Skippy, ©, P.L. Crosby," painted blue eyes to side, peaked brows, closed mouth, molded & painted hair, cloth body w/composition arms & legs, molded & painted black over-the-knee socks & shoes, composition hands have magnets to "hold" metal toys, including harmonica, slingshot & tin soldier, redressed in copy of original outfit w/white shirt, black checked shorts & matching hat, 14" (two small holes in front of cloth torso w/tape mark, minor crazing). **425**

Effanbee "Skippy" soldier, marked "Effanbee - Skippy - © - P.L. Crosby," composition head w/blue side-glancing eyes, peaked brows, closed "rosebud" mouth, molded & painted brown hair, cloth body w/composition arms & legs, molded & painted long brown socks & shoes, small break in hair, light wear, 14" (ILLUS., next page) **450**

Effanbee "Skippy" Soldier

Effanbee "Tinyette" composition head baby, marked "Effanbee," painted blue eyes to side, closed mouth, molded & painted hair, five-piece marked composition toddler body, redressed in copy of original pink organdy dress & matching bonnet, matching lace-trimmed underclothing, pink socks, white leather shoes, outfit won first in Costumed by Owner at 1990 U.F.D.C. national exhibit, 7½" (minor crazing, minor flaking) **230**

Effanbee "Tinyette Twins" composition head babies, marked "Effanbee," painted blue eyes, closed mouths, molded and painted hair, composition marked bent-limb baby body, dressed in original white dress, slip, diaper, one in blue coat & matching bonnet, other in pink coat & matching bonnet, replaced socks & shoes, original marked box w/pillow, one flannel bunting, old handmade sweater and bonnet sets, 7", pr. (light crazing, flaking & wear) **275**

Effanbee "Wee Patsy" composition head girl, marked "Effanbee, Wee Patsy," composition head w/stiff neck, painted blue eyes, closed mouth, molded & painted hair, composition jointed child body, molded & painted socks & shoes, dressed in original blue & white striped one-piece outfit, 5½" (light crazing & wear, some flaking) **155**

Freundlich "General MacArthur" composition head man, unmarked, stiff neck, painted eyes w/molded lids, molded & painted hat w/military insignias, composition body jointed at shoulders & hips, right arm bent to salute, dressed in original military uniform, white shirt, black felt tie, socks & brown tie leatherette shoes, 18" (facial coloring rather faded) **155**

Georgene Averill "Bonnie Babe" bisque flange head baby, marked "Copr. by Georgene Averill, 1005/3652/4, Germany, 1386/47," blue sleep eyes, open mouth w/two lower teeth & molded tongue, cloth body w/composition lower arms & lower legs, dressed in antique white long baby dress, long slip, socks, booties & diaper, 20" (light crazing, wear on fingers, tips off two fingers, minor flaking, coloring & stitch holes look like the body may have had a shoulder head at one time) **825**

Giebeler-Falk metal head girl, marked "20, G (in star), U S P A," blue tin sleep eyes, open-closed mouth w/four painted teeth, replaced blonde h.h. wig, marked jointed wood & composition body w/metal hands & flat wooden feet, dressed in white organdy dress w/ruffle trim, new underclothing, socks & shoes, 18" **205**

Guttmann & Schiffnie bisque socket head girl, marked "G & S 6, Germany," brown sleep eyes w/real lashes, open mouth w/accented lips & five upper teeth, replaced dark synthetic wig, jointed wood & composition body, dressed in white antique dress, underclothing, socks & shoes, 25½" (tiny fleck on lower lip, light inherent discoloration on forehead, inherent circular flaw on back of head, minor touch-up in places, new hands) **450**

Handwerck (Heinrich) bisque socket head girl, marked "69-12x, Germany, Handwerck, 4," brown sleep eyes, open mouth w/accented lips & four upper teeth, pierced ears, replaced light wig, jointed wood & composition body, redressed in green dress trimmed w/flowers, pants, new socks, pale green leatherette shoes, 23" (minor wig pulls, fine flake on rim of eye, body repainted, some new flaking on body) **305**

Handwerck (Heinrich) bisque socket head girl, marked "109 - 1 1 3/4, DEP, Germany, Handwerck," brown sleep eyes, open mouth w/accented lips & four upper teeth, pierced ears, original blonde mohair wig, jointed wood & composition body, redressed in antique-style flowered dress, underclothing & original chemise, original socks & shoes, 23½" (minor flaw corner of mouth, minor flaking & cracking, fine line in finish) **725**

Large Heinrich Handwerck Girl

Handwerck (Heinrich) bisque socket head girl, marked "Germany - Heinrich Handwerck - Simon & Halbig - 6," brown sleep eyes, molded & feathered brows, pierced ears, open mouth w/four upper teeth, original long blonde mohair wig, jointed wood & composition body, wearing antique white dress w/embroidery trim, underclothing, socks & replacement shoes, body neck socket reinforced, 27" (ILLUS., previous page) **2,500**

Handwerck (Heinrich) bisque socket head girl, marked "15. 79. DEP," set blue eyes on well-modeled lids, open mouth w/accented lips & four upper teeth, pierced ears, brown mohair wig, jointed wood & composition body, dressed in possibly original antique maroon dress trimmed w/white, antique underclothing, brown socks, high button boots, star hat trimmed w/red flocked flowers, 28" (wig pulls, imperfections in coloring at opening of neck socket, finish of arms "washed" **825**

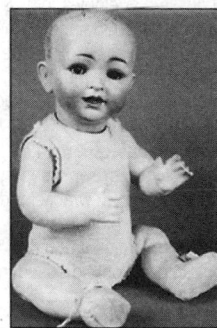

Hertel, Schwab & Co. Baby

Hertel, Schwab & Co. bisque socket head baby, marked "Made in Germany. 151/6," solid dome head w/lightly molded & brush-stroked hair, brown sleep eyes, open mouth w/accented lips & four upper teeth, composition bent-limb baby body, wearing antique ecru knit romper & cloth booties, light wear & small neck chips w/front of neck socket broken loose, 14" (ILLUS.) **300**

Hertel, Schwab & Co. bisque socket head baby, marked "152, 14," brown sleep eyes, open-closed mouth w/two upper teeth, original dark mohair wig, composition bent-limb baby body, dressed in antique white baby dress & lace trimmed bonnet, underclothing & socks, 24"............................. **950**

Heubach (Ernst) bisque shoulder head bride, marked "Germany - 275 - 4/0 - Heubach - Koppelsdorf," blue sleep eyes w/real lashes, open mouth w/four upper teeth, original brown mohair wig, kidette

Ernst Heubach Bride Doll

body w/lower bisque arms & composition lower legs, rivet joints at elbows, hips & knees, wearing white velvet wedding dress trimmed w/lace & beads, original underclothing trimmed w/lace & ribbons, lace stockings w/ribbon garters, oilcloth shoes, long lace veil w/headpiece trimmed w/flocked flowers, 20½" (ILLUS.) **300**

Heubach (Ernst) bisque shoulder head lady, marked "Germany, 275 · 4/0, Heubach · Koppelsdorf," blue sleep eyes w/real lashes, open mouth w/four upper teeth, original brown mohair wig, kidette body w/bisque lower arms, composition lower legs, rivet joints, dressed in very ornate satin & gold dress w/long train, very detailed matching underclothing w/ribbon trim, net stockings w/ribbons, leatherette shoes, gold decoration in hair, 20" (minor darkening on mold lines of head, small break in composition on left knee) **350**

Heubach (Gebruder) bisque socket head boy, marked "(sunburst) DEP, 7622 6, Germany," blue intaglio eyes, closed mouth, molded & lightly tinted hair, five-piece late French-type body, dressed in antique white shirt w/large lace collar, blue velvet pants, replaced socks & lace-up boots, 16" (repair w/circular hairline on neck socket, wear at joints & on fingers, two toes damaged)..................... **425**

Horsman composition flange head baby, marked "A Genuine Horsman Art Doll," on original paper tag, blue tin sleep eyes w/real lashes, eye shadow, closed mouth, molded & painted hair, cloth body w/composition arms & lower legs, dressed in original blue dress w/matching bonnet, underclothing, socks & shoes, 14" (few light age spots on torso).......... **250**

Ideal "Harriet Hubbard Ayer" vinyl head girl, marked "Ideal Doll," blue sleep eyes w/real lashes, synthetic blonde hair in original set, hard plastic body w/vinyl arms, molded & painted fingernails, dressed in original white, blue & red print piqué, attached panties, original socks & shoes, in original marked box w/make-up kit marked "Cleanse-Ayer," eye shadow, rouge, perfume stick, lipstick, eyebrow pencil, face powder & tissue, all contained & unused in original make-up kit made to look like a dressing table, 14" (box somewhat worn w/two tears on cardboard, doll has light wear on lip color) 380

Ideal "Marama," brown composition head girl, unmarked, brown painted eyes to side, open-closed smiling mouth w/four painted upper teeth, original black yarn wig, five-piece brown composition child body, dressed in original "grass" skirt w/gold felt waist, cotton panties, leatherette tie shoes, two original paper leis around her neck, multi-color strings tied around her waist, composition & flocked flowers in her hair, 13" (minor crazing, originality of strings & hair flowers is not determined) 600

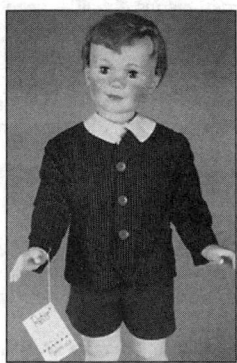

Original Ideal Peter Playpal

Ideal "Peter Playpal" boy, marked "© Ideal Toy Corp. - BE-35-38," vinyl socket head w/blue sleep eyes w/real lashes, freckles, closed smiling mouth, original rooted brown hair, five-piece vinyl child body, wearing original white shirt, grey shorts, red & black striped jacket, red socks, suede shoes, missing cap & bow tie, w/original marked paper hang tag, 38" (ILLUS.) 500

Jumeau (E.) bisque socket head Fashion lady, marked "6, (red artist marks)," blue eyes, closed mouth, pierced ears, kid fashion-type body, no elbow, hip or knee gussets, individually stitched fingers, redressed in two-piece outfit w/antique fabric, underclothing, possibly original socks & high button boots, included is possibly an original handmade two-piece outfit, 17" (inherent dark marks & white area in middle of rear shoulder plate, "soft" waist, seam restitched & glued) 3,000

Jumeau Portrait Fashion Lady

Jumeau (E.) bisque socket head portrait Fashion lady, unmarked, set cobalt blue eyes, painted lashes, closed mouth w/shapely accented lips, pierced ears, original brown mohair wig, kid fashion-type body w/gussets at elbows, hips & knees, individually stitched fingers, finely dressed in short two-piece outfit made w/antique silk & much detail, antique underclothes, stockings & leather three-button shoes, 20½" (ILLUS.) 3,700

Jutta bisque socket head girl, marked "1349, Jutta, S & H, 9," brown sleep eyes w/real lashes, open mouth w/accented lips & four upper teeth, pierced ears, original mohair wig, jointed wood & composition stamped body, dressed in old yellow organdy dress, taffeta underclothing, lace socks & leather shoes, 21" (minor flaw on left forehead, minor wig pull, minor flaking) 675

K * R (Kammer & Reinhardt) bisque socket head baby, marked "K * R, Simon & Halbig, 126, 36," blue sleep eyes, open mouth w/two upper teeth & tongue, dark mohair wig, composition bent-limb baby body, dressed in antique slip, silk gown w/feather stitching, bonnet w/embroidery, ruffles & ribbons, replaced diaper, socks & booties, 16" (tiny wig pulls, general aging & light soil, arms repainted, finger repaired, head sits high in neck socket of body). 350

K * R bisque socket head baby, marked "K * R, Simon & Halbig, 121, 42," blue sleep eyes, open mouth w/accented lips & two upper teeth, original brown mohair wig, bent-limb composition baby body, dressed in old white baby dress w/embroidery & lace trim, underclothing, new booties, 16½" (few minor wig pulls) 800

K * R bisque socket head baby, marked "K * R, Simon & Halbig, 126, 42," blue sleep eyes, open mouth w/two upper teeth &

spring tongue, original brown mohair wig,
five-piece composition baby body,
dressed in white baby dress w/ribbon
trim, underclothing, booties, white wool
baby cape, 17" (worn finish on chest,
fingers & toes) **500**

K * R bisque socket head girl, marked
"Simon & Halbig, K * R, 39," brown sleep
eyes, open mouth w/four upper teeth,
pierced ears, replaced brown h.h. wig,
jointed wood & composition body,
dressed in antique white dress, antique
underclothing, new socks & shoes, 15"
(missing left thumb & right little finger) **525**

K * R bisque socket head girl, marked
"Halbig, K * R, 58," brown sleep eyes,
open mouth w/accented lips & four upper
teeth, pierced ears, replaced dark
synthetic wig, jointed wood & composition
K * R body, dressed in antique pink low-
waisted dress, underclothing, new socks
& shoes, 23" (tiny flake on rim of eye,
aged body w/light wear, finish on lower
arm flaked off w/part reglued) **405**

K * R bisque socket head baby, marked
"X, K * R, 22., Germany, 36," large brown
eyes, open mouth w/two upper teeth &
tongue, blonde h.h. wig, composition
bent-limb baby body, dressed in pink
baby dress, undershirt, pink socks,
sweater & bonnet, 15½" (eyes need
rewaxing, torso repainted, repair at hip
joints, wear on arms & legs) **375**

Rare Kammer & Reinhardt Baby

K * R bisque head character baby, marked
"V - K * R - Simon & Halbig - 115A - 38,"
brown sleep eyes, closed pouty mouth,
original auburn mohair wig, composition
bent-limb baby body, wearing white baby
dress trimmed w/pink, slip & diaper,
normal wear & aging, 15" (ILLUS.) **3,900**

K * R bisque socket head toddler, marked
"K * R - Simon & Halbig - 126 - 28," blue
sleep eyes, feathered brows, open mouth
w/two upper teeth & tongue, brown
mohair wig, jointed wood & composition
toddler body w/diagonal hip joints,

Kammer & Reinhardt Toddler

wearing antique-style blue dress trimmed
in white, underclothing, socks & shoes,
hand & lower legs repainted,
finger repairs & touch-up, 13" (ILLUS.) **575**

Karl Hartman bisque socket head boy,
marked "29, K/1 (inside large H)," set
brown eyes w/real lashes, open mouth
w/accented lips & four upper teeth,
replaced synthetic light wig, jointed wood
& composition body, dressed in brown
two-piece Buster Brown suit, ecru shirt,
brown socks, brown saddle shoes, 22"
(painted lashes are light, darkening from
moisture damage on front of torso, minor
wear, repairs on feet) **275**

Karl Hartman bisque socket head girl,
marked "30, K/3 (inside large H),
Germany" brown sleep eyes, open mouth
w/accented lips & four upper teeth,
replaced dark wig, jointed wood &
composition body, dressed in pink
antique-style dress trimmed w/ribbons,
underclothing, lace stockings & leather
shoes, 24" (minor inherent flaws, wig
pulls, speck of kiln dirt on face, general
aging & soil, repair on right hip, hands
repainted) **325**

Karl Hartman bisque socket head girl,
marked "32, K/7 (inside large ornate H),"
blue sleep eyes w/real lashes, open
mouth w/accented lips & four upper teeth,
original dark h.h. wig, jointed wood &
composition body, dressed in antique
white dress, underclothing, socks,
replaced baby shoes, bonnet, 28" (few
minor wig pulls, general wear & aging,
minor cracking, minor repair on upper
arms & feet) **525**

Kathe Kruse celluloid socket head boy,
marked "(turtle in diamond), T40," blue
set eyes w/real lashes, closed pouty
mouth, original dark h.h. wig, marked
five-piece child body, dressed in original
blue & white shirt, blue shorts, socks &
brown tie shoes, 15" (lightly faded
clothing w/small tear in shorts) **200**

Kathe Kruse celluloid socket head girl,
marked "(turtle in diamond), T40," painted
blue eyes, closed pouty mouth, molded &
painted hair, five-piece child body marked
"(turtle in diamond), Modell, Kathe Kruse,
T40," probably dressed in original dark
green dress w/embroidery & lace trim,
underclothing, replaced socks & black
oilcloth tie shoes, 14" **275**

Kestner (J.D.) bisque shoulder head girl,
marked "10, 148," brown sleep eyes,
open mouth w/accented lips & four upper
teeth, original plaster pate intact, original
light mohair wig, marked & stamped kid
body w/gussets, bisque lower arms, cloth
lower legs, probably dressed in original
pink lace-trimmed dress & wire-rimmed
hat, matching antique underclothing,
socks & newer shoes, 21" (minor inherent
flaw) **500**

Kestner (J.D.) bisque shoulder head girl,
marked "12. 154. Dep., H made in
Germany," brown sleep eyes, open
mouth w/accented lips & four upper teeth,
original dark h.h. wig, marked kid body
w/bisque lower arms, rivet joints, dressed
in gold three-piece outfit trimmed w/white
ruffles, underclothing, socks, replaced
shoes, 24" (minor wig pulls, normal soil
& aging w/several repairs) **375**

**Kestner (J.D.) bisque socket head baby
girl,** marked "K. made in Germany, 14.,
211., J.D.K.," blue sleep eyes, open
mouth w/two lower teeth, original light
mohair wig, composition bent-limb baby
body, dressed in white antique dress,
matching underclothing, blue bed jacket,
bonnet & booties, 17" (wear on lower
arms & hands) **825**

Kestner No. 220 Toddler

**Kestner (J.D.) bisque socket head
toddler,** marked "B. made in Germany 6.
- J.D.K. 220," brown sleep eyes, original
blonde mohair wig, open mouth
w/accented lips & two upper teeth, jointed
composition toddler body w/diagonal hip
joints, separate ball joints at shoulders,

elbows & knees, jointed wrists, wearing
an ecru romper w/pink rosebuds made of
antique fabric, light wear, 11" (ILLUS.) **3,500**

**Kestner (J.D.) bisque turned shoulder
head girl,** marked "L," set blue eyes,
open mouth w/accented lips & four upper
teeth, blonde mohair wig, kid body w/kid
over wood upper arms, bisque lower
arms, rivet joints at elbows and hips,
gussets at knees, dressed in dark green
satin dress w/black lace & net trim,
matching embroidered bonnet,
underclothing, socks & handmade shoes,
23" (tiny wig pulls, repairs on upper arms,
body lightly soiled, upper arms need
tightening). **450**

**Kestner (J.D.) bisque turned shoulder
head lady,** marked "H," blue sleep eyes,
open mouth w/accented lips & four upper
teeth, original brown h.h. wig, kid body
w/bisque lower arms, gussets at elbows,
rivet joints at hips & knees, dressed in
ornate handmade velvet & satin dress
w/black lace trim, gold beads &
decoration, underclothing, new stockings
& leather shoes, 18½" (light aging & soil,
rust marks from stand on torso) **400**

Kestner (J.D.) socket head baby, marked
"J.D.K., made in 10 Germany," solid
dome, blue sleep eyes, open mouth
w/two lower teeth, lightly molded & brush
stroked hair, composition bent-limb baby
body, dressed in lace-trimmed baby
dress, underclothing & socks, 12" (light
wear & soil). **375**

Kling bisque shoulder head girl, marked
"123-4," solid dome, set pale blue
threaded eyes, closed mouth w/accent
line between lips, replaced brown wig, kid
body w/gussets, individually stitched
fingers, dressed in possibly original plum
silk & velvet dress, underclothing, socks,
high button boots, 15" (body shows
general aging & soil, right hand replaced,
repair on right shoulder, left lower leg
mended) **800**

Kling bisque socket head girl, marked
"182, Germany, 13., 62," blue sleep eyes
w/real & painted lashes, open mouth
w/four upper teeth, original dark mohair
wig, jointed wood & composition body,
dressed in gray wool dress, white collar
embroidered "Pet" & trimmed w/eyelet,
underclothing, antique pink socks &
shoes, 26" (minor flaking & cracking,
minor inherent color flaw under chin) **275**

Kling china shoulder head lady, marked
"Germany, 189 K (in bell), 7," painted
blue eyes w/accent line, closed mouth,
molded & painted hair, kid body w/china
lower arms, cloth lower legs, gussets,
dressed in antique blue dress trimmed

w/ruffle, underclothing, black socks, 20"
(few scattered black specks in finish of
china, back of hair touched-up, wear on
scalloped edge of kid on shoulder plate,
china lower arms replaced) **225**

Costumed Lenci Girl

Lenci girl, marked "Bolzano, Tirolo" on
paper hand tag & "Lenci, Torino" on dress
tag, pressed-felt swivel head w/painted
blue eyes, molded single-stroke brows,
two-toned lips, applied felt ears, original
blonde mohair wig pulled to the back,
cloth torso & felt arms & legs, wearing
original regional costume w/white blouse,
green felt vest w/red felt bodice, black felt
skirt w/purple waistband, red & white
waistband, red felt socks, black felt
shoes, light soiling & aging, 14" (ILLUS.) **375**
Lenci girl w/jump rope, unmarked,
pressed-felt swivel head w/painted blue
eyes to side, closed two-tone mouth,
applied felt ears, original blonde mohair
wig in original set, cloth torso w/felt arms
& legs, dressed in original green felt
jumper w/felt flowers trim, white organdy
blouse, original underclothing, white
socks, green felt shoes & bow in hair, doll
holds original jump rope w/blue wooden
handles, 14" (light soil on arms & legs,
clothing lightly aged)..................... **500**
Milliner's Model papier-maché head lady,
unmarked, painted blue eyes, closed
mouth, molded & painted black hair
w/wide curls & braided bun in back, kid
body w/wooden lower arms & legs, red
paper bands where wooden arms & legs
attach, painted blue shoes, dressed in
original lace-trimmed print dress &
underclothing, 6 3/4" (light soil & wear,
dress deteriorating somewhat, body not
inspected as original clothing was not
removed) **300**
**Papier-maché French-type shoulder head
lady,** unmarked, painted blue eyes,
closed mouth, light mohair wig, kid body
w/mitten hands, no gussets, dressed in
original ecru silk wedding dress trimmed
w/lace & ribbon, long train & bustle in

back, underclothing, replaced stockings &
shoes, carries original wax flowers in right
hand, 13" (light wear & soil, body not
completely inspected as original clothing
was not removed)...................... **475**
**Parian "Countess Dagmar," untinted
bisque shoulder head lady,** unmarked,
painted blue eyes w/red accent line,
closed mouth, molded & painted blonde
hair w/curls & bow in front, molded blouse
on shoulder plate, cloth kid body is well
modeled w/large hips and gussets at
joints, dressed in very detailed ornate
dress w/much gold lace, beading & velvet
trim, legs covered w/lace-trimmed pant
legs, gloves, 21" (left side of shoulder
plate broken & reglued, inherent chip on
hair has original factory color, bisque
lower legs are possibly replaced)........... **500**

Fine Parian Lady

Parian shoulder head lady, unmarked,
painted blue eyes w/red accent line,
closed mouth, molded & painted cafe-au-
lait hair, cloth body w/brown kid lower
arms, wearing old navy blue striped two-
piece outfit w/fringe trim, antique
underclothing, knit socks, light wear, 14"
(ILLUS.) **210**
Peg wooden head lady, unmarked, painted
eyes, closed mouth, painted black hair
w/curls around face, molded & painted
tuck comb in hair, peg jointed wooden
jointed, painted lower arms & legs,
painted brown shoes, dressed in probably
original brown silk dress, 4½" (minor
flaking, joints at hips loose & legs will
come out) **365**
"Queen Louise" bisque socket head lady,
marked "30, Germany, Queen Louise, 9,"
brown sleep eyes w/real lashes, open
mouth w/accented lips & four upper teeth,
replaced dark wig, jointed wood &
composition body, dressed in antique
white dress w/embroidery trim, ribbon
belt, antique underclothing, socks &
leatherette tie shoes, 25" (two tiny wig
pulls, arms & lower legs repainted) **550**

Ravca man & woman, marked "Original Ravca, Fabrication Francaise" on paper tags on both dolls, sculptured cloth faces w/painted blue eyes, wrinkle lines painted on face, applied sculptured ears on man, white mohair wigs, bodies of padded wire armature w/excelsior or straw fill, stockinette hands, dressed in original peasant-type clothing, woman wearing molded "wooden" shoes, man wearing marked sandals & seated on wooden chair reading French newspaper dated 1937, pr. (light fading on woman's blouse, newspaper is worn & darkened, chair seat is split) 265

Recknagel bisque socket head girl, marked "1914, DEP, R & A," set blue eyes, open mouth w/accented lips & four upper teeth, dark mohair wig, jointed wood & composition body looks like Kammer & Reinhardt body, dressed in brown plaid sailor dress w/large white collar & cuffs, underclothing, socks, new shoes, 22" (coloring rather uneven, finish of body "washed," minor cracking, finger repair on right hand, toe repaired, touch-up on upper right arm) 275

S.F.B.J. Character Girl

S.F.B.J. (Société Francaise de Frabrication de Bebes & Jouets) bisque head character girl, marked "S.F.B.J. - 246 - Paris - 6," blue sleep eyes w/real lashes, open-closed mouth w/two openings on each side of protruding tongue, original brown h.h. wig, jointed wood & composition French body w/jointed wrists, wearing antique white dress w/eyelet skirt & ribbon trim, some minor flaws & leg repainting, 16½" (ILLUS.) 3,100

S.F.B.J. bisque socket head girl, marked "S.F.B.J., 60, Paris, -4/0-," blue sleep eyes, open mouth w/four upper teeth, original auburn mohair wig, jointed wood & composition body w/jointed wrists, dressed in original regional-type costume w/white blouse, red satin skirt trimmed w/black ribbon, black apron, black velvet vest, blue print scarf, original

underclothing, socks & shoes, black velvet hat w/oversize ribbon, 13½" (tiny flake on eye rim touched-up, fingers touched-up on left hand, rest of body not inspected as original clothing was not removed) 275

S.F.B.J. Walking, Kiss Throwing bisque socket head lady, marked "Depose, S.F.B.J., 9," brown flirty eyes w/real lashes, open mouth w/accented lips & four upper teeth, pierced ears, original brown h.h. wig, jointed wood & composition body, walking mechanism from straight legs to head, string in right arm so her mother can make her "throw" kisses by pulling string coming from lower rear torso, dressed in old rose taffeta dress covered w/lace & ribbon trim, underclothing, socks & old turquoise boots, brown velvet bonnet, 22" (right finger tips worn) 950

Schoenau & Hoffmeister bisque socket head girl, marked "Germany, S PB (in star) H, 1906," blue sleep eyes, open mouth w/accented lips & four upper teeth, replaced dark synthetic wig, jointed wood & composition body, dressed in red & white polka dot long dress w/white eyelet collar & cuffs, underclothing, black net stockings & old replacement shoes, 27" (two inherent cuts in bisque near crown, finish worn on right hand & arms) 325

Schoenau & Hoffmeister "Hanna" painted bisque socket head girl, marked "S PB (in star) H, Hanna, 12/0," brown sleep eyes, open mouth w/two upper teeth, original black mohair wig, five-piece composition body, dressed in original Hawaiian outfit with "grass" skirt, 6½" (paint pulled off back of head by glued-on wig) 105

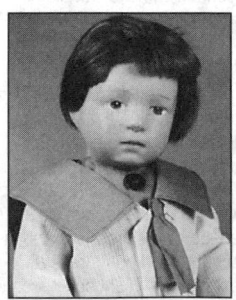

Schoenhut Character Boy

Schoenhut character boy, marked "Schoenhut Doll - Pat. Jan. 17th, 1911, U.S.A.," wooden socket head w/brown intaglio eyes, feathered brows, closed pouty mouth, original brown mohair wig, spring-jointed wooden body, well redressed in white sailor suit w/blue collar

& belt, red tie, cotton socks & red tie
shoes, paint flake on nose, minor crazing,
16" (ILLUS.) **475**

Schoenhut character girl, marked
"Schoenhut Doll, Pat. Jan 17th 1911,
U.S.A." in oval label, wooden socket
head, blue intaglio eyes w/molded lids,
closed pouty mouth, original blonde
mohair wig, spring-jointed wooden body,
dressed in original dress, replaced
underclothing, original socks w/hole in
bottom for Schoenhut stand, replaced
shoes, 14" (original paint & nail color on
fingers) **1,350**

Schoenhut character girl, incised mark
illegible because of repaint, wooden
socket head, brown intaglio eyes, open-
closed mouth w/carved teeth, carved &
painted hair w/blue bow, spring-jointed
wooden body, dressed in factory
chemise, replaced socks, original
Schoenhut shoes w/holes in soles, 16"
(doll has been repainted, chemise is
aged, shoes are worn) **500**

Schoenhut dolly-face girl, marked
"Schoenhut doll, Pat. Jan. 17th 1911,
U.S.A." in oval label, wooden socket
head, painted blue eyes, accented
nostrils, open-closed mouth w/four
painted teeth, original blonde mohair wig,
spring-jointed body, dressed in original
lace-trimmed factory underclothing, 16"
(minor crazing, touch-up on mouth, light
repaint in spots) **220**

Schoenhut Wooden Girl

Schoenhut girl, marked "Schoenhut Doll -
Pat. Jan. 17, '11 U.S.A. & Foreign
Countries," wooden socket head w/blue
intaglio eyes, single stroke brows, closed
mouth, carved brown hair w/braids tied in
back w/blue bow, spring-jointed wooden
body, redressed in white sailor dress
w/blue trim, knit underclothing, cotton
socks, reproduction Schoenhut shoes &
stand, repainted face & touched-up arms
& legs, 14" (ILLUS.) **275**

Fine Shirley Temple Doll

Shirley Temple composition head girl,
marked "Shirley Temple, Cop. Ideal N &
T Co.," hazel sleep eyes w/real lashes,
open mouth w/six upper teeth & molded
tongue, original mohair wig in original set,
five-piece marked composition child
body, dressed in original tagged blue
organdy dress, underclothing, blue socks,
shoes, eyes are cloudy, finish wrinkled
from moisture on legs, clothing has been
washed, indications of pleats remain in
dress, tiny lines around eyes, fine cracks
in finish of left hand, light crazing, 22"
(ILLUS.) **500**

Shirley Temple vinyl head girl, marked
"Ideal Doll, ST-12," hazel sleep eyes
w/molded lashes, open-closed mouth
w/six upper teeth, original blonde rooted
hair in original set w/plastic clips, five-
piece marked vinyl child body, marked
paper wrist tag, dressed in original blue &
white print play suit, Shirley Temple script
pin, red felt coat, original socks & black
plastic shoes, 12" **255**

Simon & Halbig bisque socket head girl,
marked "1299, Simon & Halbig, S & H, 5"
blue sleep eyes, open mouth w/two upper
teeth, dimple on chin, original brown
mohair wig, jointed wood & composition
body, dressed in white lace-trimmed baby
dress, underclothing, old socks & booties,
13½" (minute fleck at corner of eye, few
minor inherent dark spots on bisque) **1,000**

Simon & Halbig bisque socket head girl,
marked "S 8½ H 1009, DEP, St.," set
brown eyes, open mouth w/accented lips
& four upper teeth, pierced ears, replaced
dark wig, jointed wood & composition
body, dressed in antique red sailor dress
trimmed in black, underclothing, black
socks, replaced shoes, 19" (hairline on
head, minor cracking in finish) **300**

Simon & Halbig bisque socket head girl,
marked "550, Germany, Simon & Halbig,"
brown sleep eyes w/remnants of real
lashes, open mouth w/four upper teeth,
dark h.h. wig, marked jointed wood &

composition body, dressed in white eyelet & embroidered low-waisted dress, underclothing, antique socks & shoes, 21½" (paint touch-up, some cracking) **475**

Simon & Halbig bisque socket head girl, marked "550, Germany, Halbig," set blue eyes w/real lashes, open mouth w/four upper teeth, replaced blonde h.h. wig, stamped jointed wood & composition body, redressed in maroon taffeta w/lace & ribbon trim, underclothing, antique socks & maroon leather shoes, 22" (light kiln dust on side of nose, right hip ball reglued, spot of finish off upper right arm) **385**

Simon & Halbig bisque socket head girl, marked "S & H 1249, DEP, Germany, 13," blue sleep eyes, open mouth w/well accented lips & four upper teeth, pierced ears, dark h.h. wig, jointed wood & composition body, dressed in antique blue dress w/white blouse, underclothing, new socks & shoes, 27" **1,700**

Simon & Halbig bisque socket head girl, marked "1079, Halbig, S & H Germany, 13½," brown sleep eyes, open mouth w/accented lips & four upper teeth, pierced ears, original dark h.h. wig, marked jointed wood & composition body, redressed in antique silk child's dress, antique underclothing, socks & shoes, 29" (minor flaking at right earring hole, few fine lines in finish, cracking & chipping around neck socket of body, two fingers glued) **575**

Simon & Halbig bisque socket head girl, marked "S.H. 1079 - 14½, DEP," blue sleep eyes, open mouth w/four upper teeth, pierced ears, original blonde mohair wig, jointed wood & composition body, dressed in original white low-waisted dress, underclothing, long socks & white leather shoes, 30½" (2¾" hairline on right back, minor flaking at earring holes) **800**

Lovely Simon & Halbig Lady

Simon & Halbig bisque socket head lady, marked "1159 - Germany - Simon & Halbig - S&H - 9½," brown sleep eyes

w/real lashes, molded & feathered brows, open mouth w/accented lips & four upper teeth, pierced ears, original brown h.h. wig, jointed wood & composition lady body w/small waist & molded bosom, wearing lovely ecru lace dress, underclothing, new socks & shoes, normal, minor damages, 24" (ILLUS.) **3,200**

Simon & Halbig "Santa" bisque socket head girl, marked "S & H 1249, DEP, Germany, Santa, 11," dark brown sleep eyes, open mouth w/accented lips & four upper teeth, pierced ears, original blonde mohair wig in small curls, jointed wood & composition body, dressed in white factory chemise, antique underclothing, socks, old replacement shoes, 23" (spot of damage on upper left leg, small flake at earring hole) **1,025**

Steiner Figure A bisque socket head girl, marked "J. Steiner, Bte S.G.D.G., Paris, Fre A 15," blue paperweight eyes, closed mouth, pierced ears, original brown h.h. wig, jointed composition body w/straight wrists & long slender fingers, marked "Le Petit Parisien, Bebe J. Steiner, Marque Deposee, Medaille d'Or, Paris, 1889" on paper label w/flag on left hip, dressed in antique two-piece blue & white outfit, antique pants, cotton socks & black oilcloth shoes, 22½" (hairline on forehead has been fused in Germany & virtually undetectable, small chip at right earring hole, general wear w/cracking, touch-up on lower arms & hands) **3,200**

Rare A. Steiner Lady

Steiner Figure A bisque socket head lady, marked "Steiner, Paris, Fre · A · 9," blue paperweight eyes, closed mouth, pierced ears, replaced h.h. wig, jointed marked composition Steiner body w/straight wrists & stubby fingers, redressed in blue china silk dress, white lace-trimmed chemise showing at neckline, slip, socks, antique black shoes, very light color wear on neck socket of head, minor repair or touch-up, 16" (ILLUS.) **5,000**

Vogue Toddles "Mistress Mary" composition head lady, marked "Vogue," blue eyes painted to side, closed mouth, blonde mohair wig over molded hair, five-piece marked composition body, dressed in original tagged flower print dress w/blue bodice, matching hat, blue apron, long white pants, socks & marked blue leatherette snap shoes, 7" (minor crazing)............ **275**

Vogue Toddles "Red Riding Hood" composition head girl, marked "Vogue," painted blue eyes to side, closed mouth, original blonde mohair wig, five-piece marked composition toddler body, dressed in original flowered dress, matching one-piece underwear, red wool cape, original socks, marked red leatherette shoes, 7½" (cape may be faded) .. **275**

Vogue Toddles "Uncle Sam" composition head boy, marked "Vogue," painted blue eyes to side, closed mouth, original blonde mohair wig, five-piece marked composition toddler body, dressed in original labeled patriotic outfit, pressed felt hat, red marked leatherette shoes, 7½" (inherent bubble in finish of left arm, light paint covering on hands & toes, minor flaking on hands, clothing lightly aged) **450**

Poured Wax Head Girl

Wax head girl, unmarked, reinforced poured wax head w/set dark brown eyes, feathered brow, closed mouth, original mohair blonde wig w/original braids, kid body w/gussets at elbows, hips & knees, individually stitched fingers, nicely dressed in possibly original white dress w/lacy collar, antique underclothes, socks & bluish green oilcloth shoes, pale bluish green velvet lacy-trimmed bonnet, light wear, small repaired piece on shoulder plate, minor body repairs, 16" (ILLUS.) **150**

Wax over papier-maché girl, unmarked, shoulder head w/blue sleep eyes, light brows, closed mouth, pierced ears, original long blonde mohair wig w/braids, cloth body w/non-working crier, composition lower arms & legs w/molded

Wax over Papier-maché Girl

& painted boots, wearing new pink silk dress trimmed w/lace & blue velvet ribbons, underclothing, light wear, minor cloth repair to torso, cloth upper arms replaced or recovered, composition wear, 12½" (ILLUS.)......................... **230**

Wax over papier-maché shoulder head lady, unmarked, blue sleep eyes, closed mouth, molded & painted hair w/orange ribbon, cloth body w/composition lower arms & lower legs w/molded & painted boots, dressed in antique-style two-piece outfit w/lace insert & trim, underclothing, 21" (touch-up on cheeks, light scratching on wax finish, back of torso recovered, seam split in upper leg, feet repainted) **180**

DOORSTOPS

All doorstops listed are flat-back cast iron unless otherwise noted. Most names are taken from Doorstops—Identification & Values, *by Jeanne Bertoia (Collector Books, 1985).*

Apple and grapes, heavy base, near mint, 4⅞ x 7¼" **$1,430**

Basket of tulips, brown wicker basket, red & yellow tulips, green base, Hubley, pristine, 9 x 13" **1,980**

Black man, on cotton bale, bale is cast iron & figure is made of pot metal, near mint, 6⅞ x 6⅞" **3,520**

Bobby Blake, holding teddy bear, Hubley, pristine, 5¼ x 9½" **1,100**

Boy, in top hat, w/fruit basket, near mint, 9¼" h... **880**

Castle, polychrome, pristine, 5¼ x 8" **1,210**

Cat, black, on pink rug, pristine, 7¼" l........ **1,430**

Cat, licking paw, rare, Eastern Speciality Mfg. Co., near mint, 7½ x 10¾" **2,750**

Cat, climbing, Art Deco style, near mint, 13¾" h. **1,870**

Cat Scratch Fever, girl scratching herself while cat looks on, signed by A. Diouhy, marked "cJo 1271," very rare, Judd Co., near mint, 8¾" h...................... **1,540**

Child, reaching, very rare, excellent, 17" h..... **3,080**

Cosmos, largest of the floral doorstops,
Hubley, pristine, 17¾" h................ **1,870**

Dog, yawning pup, very rare, pristine, 5 x 7"... **1,540**

Dog, Dachshund, marked "Made in USA,"
Hubley, pristine, 5½ x 9½"............... **1,100**

Dog, Wirehaired Fox Terrier, Hubley,
pristine, 10½ x 12¾" **4,180**

Dog, Pekingese, Hubley, pristine, 9 x 14½" ... **3,300**

Duck, pecking dog, A.M. Greenblatt,
pristine, 8¾ x 9¾" **2,750**

Flowered doorway, includes bench,
illustrated in reference books, pristine,
7½ x 7⅝" **1,430**

Fruit basket, tall woven square lattice
flaring basket holding a tapering tower of
fruit w/a tall center handle topped by a
large looped bow handle, Hubley, old
worn polychrome repaint, 15⅛" h.......... **138**

Girl, seated in canoe, excellent, 9¾" l. **1,320**

Girl, holding dress, rubber knobs intact,
marked "B&H 7798," Bradley & Hubbard,
excellent, 6¾ x 13" **2,090**

Golfer, small, holding golf bag on shoulder,
rare, 3½ x 6" **1,210**

Jester, sitting on trunk, rare, Eastern
Specialties, pristine, 7¼" h.............. **1,320**

Lady, holding carpet bag, rare, signed
"Sarah Symonds," excellent, 12" h........ **1,650**

Lighthouse of Gloucester, MA, depicts
lighthouse keepers home & ocean wave,
A.M. Greenblatt Studios, pristine,
9 x 11½" **4,400**

Little Red Riding Hood and Wolf, rare,
embossed "Little Red Riding Hood,"
NUYDEA, pristine, 7½ x 9½"............ **2,200**

Man With Top Hat Doorstop

Man with Top Hat, wearing tuxedo,
4½" x 8¼" (ILLUS.) **1,760**

Mary Quite Contrary, figure is holding
water can, flowers & rake, rare, excellent,
8 x 15" **1,045**

Mountain top mansion, rare, includes
details of forest & road, Bradley &
Hubbard, excellent, 8¼ x 9⅜" **1,760**

Narcissus, Hubley, near mint, 6¾ x 7¼" **550**

Old doorway with woman, rare, Sarah
Symonds, pristine, 7½ x 8½"............. **6,600**

Owl, rubber knob intact, Bradley & Hubbard,
near mint, 15½" h..................... **2,420**

Peasant girl, holding flowers, blue apron &
red jewelry beads, No. 1277, very rare,
"cJo," excellent, 11⅞" h. **1,760**

Peter Rabbit Doorstop

Peter Rabbit, eating a carrot, Hubley,
pristine, 4¾ x 9½" (ILLUS.) .... **700 to 1,100**

Rabbit, pushing wheelbarrow, very rare,
pristine, 8¼ x 11".................... **4,620**

Rabbit, large, two rubber knobs intact,
marked "B&H 7800," Bradley & Hubbard,
pristine, 15" h....................... **4,400**

Satyr head, bearded head w/tall slender
curled cornucopia cap, scrolled collar, on
stepped rectangular base, 11¼" h.......... **193**

Spanish woman, with fan in hand, marked
"LACS, #760," pristine, 5½ x 9⅞" **1,210**

Turkey, large, rubber knob intact, rare,
Bradley & Hubbard, pristine, 11½ x 12½" ... **4,400**

Windmill, ocean scene painted in
background, near mint, 11½" l........... **2,200**

DRUGSTORE & PHARMACY ITEMS

The old-time corner drugstore, once a familiar part of every American town, has now given way to a modern, efficient pharmacy. With the streamlining and modernization of this trade, many of the early tools and store adjuncts have become outdated and now fall into the realm of "collectibles." Listed here are the variety of tools, bottles, display pieces and other ephemera once closely associated with the druggist's trade.

Apothecary jar w/original ball stopper,
blown glass, spherical body w/tall
tapering neck & rolled lip, deep purple

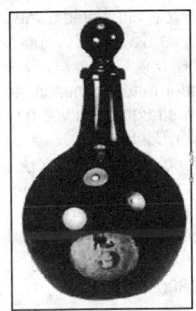

English Apothecary Jar

w/original painted white & black round label w/"5," ground pontil, probably England, ca. 1850-70, 11½" h. (ILLUS.).....**$275**

From left: Old Milk Glass Show Jar & Three-Piece Drugstore Show Jar

Apothecary show jar w/original stopper, blown glass, tall ovoid body raised on a slender pedestal & round foot, the tall cylindrical neck w/a flared rim, tall bulbous ovoid stopper, milk glass, 19th c., 11¾" h. (ILLUS. left)..............**121**

Apothecary show jar w/original stopper, three-piece, mold-blown glass, a bulbous ovoid body above a round stepped foot, a tall cylindrical neck w/a tooled rim, the stopper formed as a miniature jar form w/another small teardrop green glass stopper, two lower tiers in clear, American-made, early 20th c., 11½" h. (ILLUS. right)........................**165**

Bottle, "A. B. Stewart Druggist, Seattle W.T." (below monogram), rectangular w/rounded shoulders & tooled lip, clear, ca. 1880-90 ....**385**

Bottle, "C.W. Snow & Co., Druggists (design of eagle w/shield & mortar & pestle), Syracuse, N.Y.," square w/tooled lip, ca. 1885-95, deep cobalt blue, 8¼" h........**468**

Bottle, "Citrate of Magnesia - H.B. Wakelee - Druggist," cylindrical w/applied mouth & smooth base, cobalt blue, 7⅝" h. (lightly cleaned) **143**

Bottle, "D. Vollmer, Druggist, Ft. Wayne, Ind.," base marked "B.F.G. Co.," square w/beveled corners, ca. 1875-85, medium electric cobalt blue, 7½ " h. **550**

Bottle, "G.W. Merchant - Chemist - Lockport - N.Y.," cylindrical w/applied sloping collar, deep emerald green, ca. 1855-65, 7¼" h..................................**198**

Bottle, "J.D. Morgan - Druggist - Pittsburgh," rectangular w/rolled lip, ca. 1845-55, deep bluish aqua, 5¼" h. **121**

Bottle, "Maguire Druggist, St. Louis Mo.," rectangular w/paneled sides & applied sloping collar, light apple green, ca. 1845-55, 5¾" h. (lightly cleaned, small flake at base) **633**

Bottle, "St. Clairs Hair Lotion," rectangular w/paneled sides & tooled lip, cobalt blue, ca. 1900, 7¼" h. (lightly cleaned) **66**

Bottle, "The Owl Drug Co. (design of owl on mortar & pestle) Trade Mark," rectangular w/tooled lip, clear sun-colored amethyst, ca. 1900, 10" h. **143**

FARM COLLECTIBLES

Asparagus Buncher

Asparagus buncher, metal on wood, came in assorted colors, adjustable to bunch length, ca. 1800-1900s (ILLUS.).........**$35-50**

Barbed wire stretcher, 2-fold metal blocks w/hook, chain & grab, Canton, ca. 1850s, rope pull 3 to 5', self locking **20-25**

Calf Weaner

Calf weaner, metal w/pointed spring units, held on head w/chain, unmarked, ca. late 1800s to 1900s, 6" inside measurement, 6" l. springs (ILLUS.).......**15-50**

Cant hook, commercial, hook w/no point,
ca. 1700-1900, 18" to 6' **50**

Cider press, top grinder w/wood slate sides,
unknown manufacturer, ca. 1900, 4' h. . . **100-200**

Corn husking pegs, wood, hand-carved
w/leather finger loop, ca. 1850s, 3 to 5" **2-5**

Corn Sheller

Corn sheller, excellent metal & wood
construction, similar to Sloane-Stanley
Museum piece, ca. 1800-1900, approx.
3' h. (ILLUS.) **250-300**

Cradle scythe, grain, wooden & wire
collector, fine scythe blade, unknown
manufacturer, usable, ca. 1800-1900 . . . . **100-300**

Planet Junior Cultivator

Cultivator, hand, red or natural handles,
w/assortment of attachments, Planet Jr.,
late 1800s to late 1900s, 36 to 40" h.,
4 to 6' l., 12 to 24" wheels (ILLUS.) **25-100**

Dung hoe, blacksmith, made from
horseshoe, adze-type handle eye, oak
handle, ca. 1700-1900 . . . . **50-100**

Fence wire stretcher, wooden handle,
metal jaws & hook, Neverslip, ca. 1850s,
25" to 30" **20-35**

Flail, grain, local shop or farmer, natural
wood swivel & thong, handle length for
user, flail length & diameter for material,
ca. 1700-1900 . . . . **5-50**

Gate weight, cast iron, model of a dove, full-
bodied figure w/outspread wings, retains
traces of white paint, late 19th c., 9½" l. **1,955**

Grain scoop, wooden, commercially made,
all wood, no sparks, ca. 1800s, 12" w.,
40" l. **25-35**

Hay knife, saw type, unpainted blade, red or
black handle, ca. 1800-1900, approx.
2' l., 4 to 8 teeth. **25-50**

Hay probe, farmer-made, common, apple
tree branch w/straight & curved prong tip,
ca. 1800-1900, 3 x 5'. **5-50**

Hay rake, all-wood, a long slender pole
w/one end formed into four long gently
curved tines joined at their base by two
small arched braces, 64½" l. **275**

Hoe, horse-drawn for tilling, red, marked
"Prout," ca. 1800s **50-250**

Horse Bog Shoe

Horse bog shoes, blacksmith, all steel, ca.
1800-1900, set of four (ILLUS. of one) **50-200**

Ice pike pole, painted red tip, Wm. T. Wood,
ca. 1800-1900s, 2 to 20' (Wm. T. Wood
prior to 1906, Gifford-Wood & other
manufacturers after 1900). **1-25**

Jack With Screw and Rachet Gear

Jack, screw & ratchet gear, black paint, top
hinged to lower 2", Ajax six-ton style, ca.
1900, 12 to 18" (ILLUS.) **25-75**

Ox cart, double axle, blue grey, ca.
1750-1850, 5 x 12' w/pole . . . . **800+**

Peevee, homemade, hook blacksmith, ca.
1800s, 5'. **50**

Pitchfork, common 3-tang, ca. 1700-1900,
4 to 6' handle. **5-25**

Hand Planter

Planter, corn, hand, unmarked, ca.
1700-1800 (ILLUS.). **5-25**

Child's Toy Plow

Plow, child's toy, farmer-made w/scrap wood, ca. 1800-1900s, 2' l., 18" handle (ILLUS.) **50-100**

Plow, wood moldboard w/assorted scrap metal, ca. 1750-1850 (price depending on attached metal) **100-1,200**

Potato digger, two-horse, marked "Champion," usable, ca. 1800s **300-500**

Rake, bull, unpainted, peg teeth w/collector teeth, unreadable manufacturer, 5 to 6' l. . . . **25-75**

Rick fork, 3-tang, farmer-made, ca. 1700-1800, 10 to 12' handle **25-75**

Ropemaker, homemade, wooden frame head & tail, 3-strand, hand-crank style w/connecting rod, usable, 2' w., 4' h.. . . . . . **75-150**

Saw, 2-man, flat back, bellied teeth, Lance Perforated teeth, Atkins-Victory, ca. 1800s, 5' **20-50**

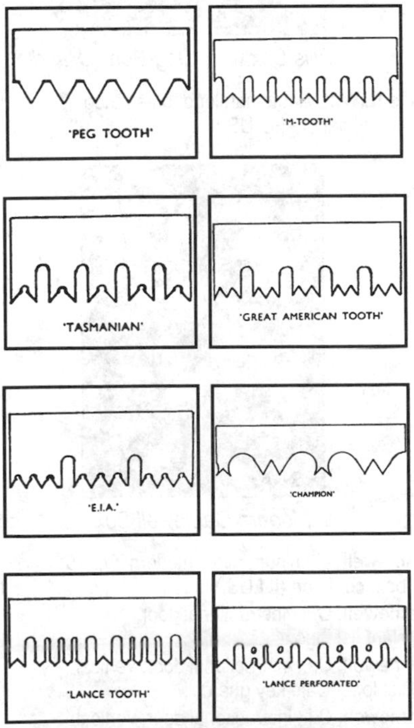

'PEG TOOTH'

'M-TOOTH'

'TASMANIAN'

'GREAT AMERICAN TOOTH'

'E.I.A.'

'CHAMPION'

'LANCE TOOTH'

'LANCE PERFORATED'

Early Saw Teeth Profiles

Saw, 2-man, rust-free metal, Great American Tooth pattern, Disston, usable, ca. 1700-1900, 5'. **25-300**

Saw, buck, varnished, occasionally w/red paint, wood spreader varied from plain bar to unique designs, tensioning rod from simple turnbuckle to extremely fancy device, ca. 1700-1900, in half size for boys, medium or full **25-300**

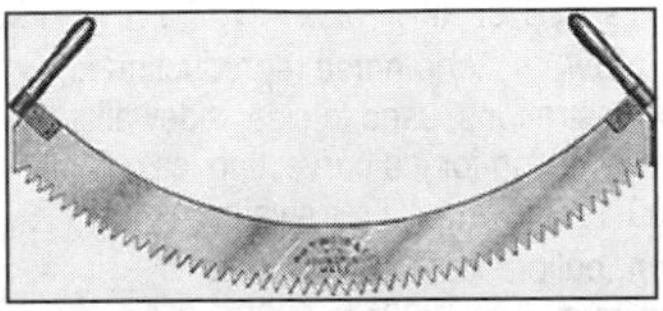

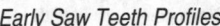

Wm. T. Wood & Co. Crescent Ice Saw

Saw, ice, crescent moon shape, deeply curved w/handles well above cutting blade, Wm. T. Wood & Co., w/no rust, ca. 1800-1900, 6' (ILLUS.). **200-700**

Saw, ice, gasoline-powered, original chain, insert tooth saw blade, Gifford-Wood Model "C," ca. 1920-1930 . . . . **1,000-2,000**

Saw, ice, minimal rust, w/original red wooden case, legible mark of Wm. T. Wood, ca. 1800s, usable condition, 5'. **25-50**

Shaving horse, made of natural wood, many styles including some made of tree forks & others finely crafted, utility item only, ca. 1700-1900, 3 to 8' l. **50-500**

Shovel, scoop, iron w/riveted triangular handle attachment, ca. 1700-1900 . . . . **25-100**

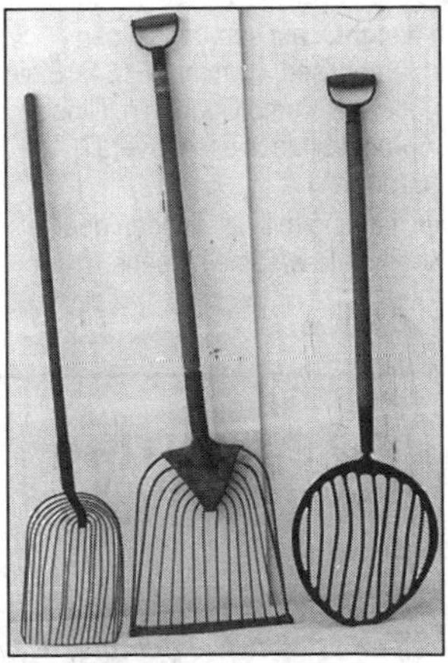

Shovels: Clam, Ice, Potato

Shovel, sieve, clam, fine wire tangs, ca. 1800s (ILLUS. left) **5-25**

Shovel, sieve, ice, short & long handled, heavy, rugged construction for removing harvest ice chunks, Gifford-Wood, ca. 1900s (ILLUS. center) **10-50**

Shovel, sieve, potato, heavy scoop construction w/2" holes, unpainted, Ames, ca. 1800-1900, small enough to place potatoes in tubs or barrels (ILLUS. right, previous page) **15-50**

Sleigh, one-horse style w/single seat, bright red, ca. 1800s, 5 x 7' (repainted)....... **250-500**

Snow plow, "V," farmer-made, one-horse, used to clear sidewalks & windrowing for ice harvesting, ca. 1800-1900, 2' h., 4' l., 3' swath.................... **50-200**

Snow plow, "V," one-horse reproduction for demonstrations, used to clear sidewalks & windrowing for ice harvesting, ca. 1800-1900, 2' h., 4' l., 3' swath **75**

Tendon, puller, cast iron & painted aluminum, late 1800s to 1900s, 25" **40-60**

Tractor license plate, Pennsylvania, 1915, one-sided porcelain, rectangular w/blue ground & "Penna—1915—Tractor" in small white letters at one end & "E1222" in white filling the remainder, "Brilliant Mfg. Co. Philadelphia, Pa." stamped on back, 6 x 14" (chips to mounting holes, manufacturer's defect in white letters) **132**

Wagon, buggy style, black, single seat, high narrow wheels, interchangeable pole or shafts, ca. 1800s **250-1,000**

Wagon wheels, single wood w/metal rim, ca. 1800s........................... **25-100**

Weed cutter, "Dock," cast-iron & steel, narrow rectangular blade on wooden handle, unmarked, ca. 1900s, 40"........ **10-25**

Wheelbarrow, adult, wood, light weight w/wooden wheel, metal shod, removable sides, usable, ca. 1700-1900 .... **100-200**

Windmill weight, cast iron, model of a rooster, embossed "Hummer E184," Elgin Wind, Power & Pump Co., Elgin, Illinois, now on wooden block base, overall 13½" h. (pitted)....................... **330**

Winnower, fanning mill, all wooden gear & crank, complete w/some screens, ca. 1800s......................... **100-300**

FIRE FIGHTING COLLECTIBLES

American fire fighting antiques are considered those items over 100 years old which were directly related to fire fighting, whereas fire fighting collectibles are items less than a century old. Pieces from both eras are very sought-after today. Foreign-made fire fighting antiques and collectibles have a marketplace of their own and, for the most part, are not as expensive and in demand as similar American pieces. H. Thomas Laun was the special consultant for this category.

ALARM - TELEGRAPH STREET BOXES

Street alarm boxes are those used on street corners in cities and villages around the country, whereas auxiliary and other types were used in factories, schools and institutions. This second variety is less collectible unless they were special boxes marked with the original user's name cast on the door or housing. This type would include boxes marked for the Ford Motor Company, Radio Corp. of America (R.C.A. with the Nipper logo) and others that will have cross-over collector appeal. Prototype, patent models and extremely early fire boxes are also very collectible but are rare and seldom found on the market. Most early street "call" boxes are cast iron (C. I.) and should be complete with the mechanism and matching code wheel number plate. Beginning in the 1920s cast aluminum alloy models came into use and continue to be the standard today.

L.W. Bills Box with "Dog-Bone" Handle

Bills (L.W.), Minuteman logo, brass "dog-bone" handle (ILLUS.) **$350**

Modern Gamewell Box

Gamewell, aluminum alloy, modern Type 51 box, common (ILLUS.) **135**

Gamewell, C. I., instructional door, slant fist logo **195**

Gamewell, C.I., instructional door, vertical fist logo, Cole key guard.................. **180**

Gamewell, C.I., instructional door, vertical fist logo, Smith key guard (ILLUS.).......... **190**

Gamewell Box with Smith Key Guard

Gamewell, C.I., quick-acting door w/glass
bull's-eye **165**
Gamewell, C.I., telegraph door, slant fist
logo, trap lock & key **235**
Gamewell, C.I.,Tooker keyless door w/bell **500**

Gamewell Auxiliary Box

Gamewell, early cast-iron auxiliary model
box, quite scarce (ILLUS.) **225**
Gamewell, "Excelsior" size, C.I.,
instructional door, Smith key guard **300**
Gamewell, "Excelsior" size, C.I., telegraph
door, trap lock & key. **360**

Very Rare C.I. Gamewell-Utica Box

Gamewell, full-sized cast-iron Gamewell
case w/a Utica Fire Alarm mechanism &
telegraph door w/a Smith key guard,
extremely rare (ILLUS.) **650**
Moses Crane, C.I. **450**
Star Electric, C.I., produced in Binghamton,
New York **500**

Very Rare Utica "Excelsior" Size Box

Utica Fire Alarm & Telegraph Co., C.I.,
"Excelsior" size, bell logo, Utica,
New York, extremely rare (ILLUS.) **650**
Utica Fire Alarm & Telegraph Co., C.I.,
telegraph door, Utica, New York **450**
Utica Fire Alarm & Telegraph Co., C.I.
w/"quick action" door, Utica, New York ,
very rare **550**

Utica Box with Smith Key Guard

Utica Fire Alarm & Telegraph Co., C.I.
w/Smith key guard (ILLUS.) **450**

FIRE EXTINGUISHERS

Generally these cylindrical containers are brass or sometimes copper and brass. Some early examples were also nickel-plated while later ones were often chrome-plated. Various types were designed for use in buildings, motor vehicles or exclusive use on fire apparatus such as fire trucks. Those listed here are complete with their top, name plate and hanging bracket. Dented pieces or those missing labels generally are considered to have only scrap value. Glass "grenade" types date from the late-19th and early-20th centuries.

GLASS HAND-GRENADE STYLE

Harden's "Diamond Quilted" Grenade

Harden, semi-square w/diamond quilted design & round reverse embossed "Harden's Hand Grenade Fire Extinguisher," w/original contents, deep blue, 6¼" h. (ILLUS.) **121**

Harden, semi-square w/diamond quilted design & round reverse embossed "Harden's Hand Grenade Fire Extinguisher," w/original contents, deep blue, scarce 8 oz. size, one side panel embossed "Patented #2 August 8, 1871 - August 14, 1888," 5" h., pr. **467**

Harden "Star" Grenade Extinguisher

Harden, spherical ribbed form w/large embossed star, w/original contents & wire bell, deep blue (ILLUS.,) **132**

Red Comet, red-stained glass, w/bracket **15**

Shur Stop, clear, w/bracket **18**

Shur Stop, set in red tin box, set of 3 . . . . **65**

METAL EXTINGUISHERS

Brass, carbontetrachloride, marked "American LaFrance," nickel-plated, w/bracket, 1 qt. **65**

Brass, carbontetrachloride, marked "Fire Gun," w/bracket, 1½ qt. **18**

Brass, carbontetrachloride, marked "Ford," nickle-plated, 1 qt. **49**

Brass, carbontetrachloride, marked "Fyr-Fyter," 1 or 1½ qt., each **35**

Brass, carbontetrachloride, marked "Pyrene," chrome-plated, 1 qt. **23**

Brass, carbontetrachloride, marked "Pyrene," heavy vehicle model w/bracket, 1½ qt. **25**

Brass, carbontetrachloride, marked "Randolph," 1 ½ qt. **18**

Brass, soda & acid-type, building model, marks such as "Red Star" or "Kontroc," 2½ gal., each . . . . **20 to 35**

Brass, soda & acid-type, marked "Childs," Utica, New York, riveted back & top, 2 ½ gal. **30**

Brass, soda & acid-type, marked "Ecnarusni" for "Insurance" spelled backwards, 2½ gal. **30**

Brass, soda & acid-type, marked "Pyrene," 2½ gal. **25**

From left: "Standard" Fire Department Model & Elkhart Brass & Copper Extinguisher

Brass, soda & acid-type, "Standard," fire department model carried on fire vehicles, hand wheel-valve on top, finely engraved in large diamond logo, red metal top ring frame (ILLUS. left) **250**

Brass & copper, soda & acid-type, "Elkhart," heart w/stag-head logo, polished, 2½ gal. (ILLUS. right) **80**

Nickel-plated brass, soda & acid-type, "Empire," early patent date of "July 19, 1887," pony-sized **235**

Wilbur Painted Metal Extinguisher

Painted metal, carbontetrachloride, "Wilbur," red-painted ground w/copper labels w/black print, w/bracket, 1 qt. (ILLUS.) **55**

HELMETS

Early fire helmets are very collectible, but much of their value depends on two factors in addition to condition: 1. The type of front piece and its detail. 2. The type of front piece holder, i.e. a figural eagle, which is common. Scarcer figural forms include a sea serpent, lion, fox or a fireman with trumpet. These factors can elevate the value of a multi-coned, high-front helmet to over $1,000. Earlier helmets were most often of leather and featured a "high-eagle" front holder. Later metal "low fronts" usually had a 6" high flat brass front holder. These are common from the World War II era through the 1960s and early 1970s. The later variety must be complete with front shield, liner and good overall condition, although some "service wear" is acceptable.

Leather, early "high eagle" type, working style by Cairns, front shield 8" h., each . . . . **185 to 350**
Leather, "low-front" style, Cairns "New Yorker" 20th c., pre-OSHA, front flat brass shield holder 6" h. . . . . **165 to 235**
Leather, "low-front" style, Cairns "Volunteer," 20th c., pre-OSHA, front flat brass shield holder 6" h. . . . . **135 to 185**
Metal, "low-front" style, Cairns "Senator," 20th c., shield holder of flat stamped brass for 6" h. shield . . . . **65 to 110**

OTHER ITEMS

Bucket, painted leather, cylindrical, decorated w/inscription "Danvers Fire Soc. John Dunn 1826," 19th c., 12¼" h. (repainted, other imperfections) **403**

Bucket, painted leather, slightly tapering cylindrical form w/swing leather handle, decorated w/"Benj. Pitman 1830" on a scrolling banner, painted in black & yellow on a green ground, 12¾" h. (break & losses to handle, paint loss) **460**

Early Fire Engine Bell

Fire engine bell, nickel-plated iron, swings in iron yoke & mount, used on horse-drawn fire engines, early 20th c., 10" d. (ILLUS.) **575**

La France Gas Mask Case

Fire gas mask & case, suitcase-form carrying case of steel-banded board, applied label w/red on white reading "La France Gas Mask - American LaFrance Fire Engine Company, Inc....," case & mask in good condition, the set (ILLUS.) **100**

Rare Early Fire Station Gong

Fire station gong, arched, finely carved walnut case above large 15" d. brass gong, "Gamewell" manufactured model, "Moses Crane" style case, late 19th c., gong 15" d. (ILLUS.) **3,250**

American-LaFrance Fire Truck Bell

Fire truck bell, chrome-plated, figural eagle finial, "American - LaFrance," complete w/bracket, commonly found w/an aluminum eagle finial but also sometimes w/a brass or nickel-plated brass eagle, 12" d. (ILLUS.) . . . . **700 to 800**

Fire wagon lantern, nickel-plated, rounded metal frame w/three oval glass panels above the slender cylindrical drop font, a pierced tiered chimney top, acid-etched & engraved blue, red & clear glass panels depicting fire fighting equipment, a geometric & foliate design & "Prospect 4," w/removable oil font, marked "DeVoursney Bros. makers 389 Broome St. New York," 19th c., 23¼" h. (nickel wear, minor dents) **1,725**

Fire Suction Hose Strainers

Hose strainer, suction-type, fire department model, brass or nickel-plated brass or stainless steel, various sizes, each (ILLUS. of three) . . . . **15 to 60**

Lantern, brass or brass w/nickel plating, "Dietz Fire King," also marked "American La France" on water shield, complete & excellent condition **310**

Lantern, brass or brass w/nickel plating, "Dietz Fire King," also marked "Seagrave" on water shield, complete & excellent condition **385**

Lantern, brass or brass w/nickel plating, "Eclipse," complete & excellent condition **950**

Lantern, brass or brass w/nickel plating, "Ham's," two-piece slide-over cage **300**

Lantern, brass or brass w/nickel plating "Steam Gauge and Lantern Co.," complete & excellent condition **700**

Lantern, steel, "Steam Gauge and Lantern Co.," metal cage, no water shield **350**

"LaFrance" Hose Nozzle

Nozzle for hose, copper, marked "La France," handles at base,1930s-40s, 2½" d. (ILLUS.) **235**

Nozzle for hose, Underwriter's play pipe-type, originally wrapped in red string, many found without string in polished copper & brass, no shut-off valve, used in large factories or institutions w/outside "yard" hydrant w/gate valve, 30" to 32" l., 2½" d., common, each . . . . **65 to 75**

Nozzles for hoses, various 20th c. nickel-plated shut-off nozzles w/leather handles,12" to 14" l., depending on maker & condition, each . . . . **75 to 250**

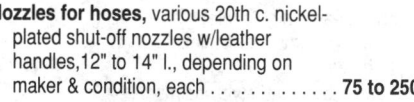

Sterling Model 30 Fire Truck Siren

Truck siren, chrome-plated, "Sterling Model 30" (ILLUS.) **185**

Trumpet, presentation-type, silver-plated
brass or Britannia metal, depending on
provenance, style of engraving (fire
scenes & fire apparatus bring more than
florals) & condition, 19" to 23" tall,
each . . . . **650 to 1,800**

Two Early "Working" Model Trumpets

Trumpet, working model, various metals
including brass, nickel-plated brass or
silver plate over brass, plain vertical side
seam usually not found on reproductions,
19 to 21" tall, depending on condition,
each (ILLUS. of two) . . . . **200 to 475**

FIREARMS

Ball Civil War Carbine

Carbine, Ball Civil War period model, walnut
stock (ILLUS.) **$2,000**
Carbine, Maynard .50 cal. **1,232**
Carbine, Model 1859 Sharps, .52 cal. **1,792**
Carbine, Model 1863 Sharps, .52 cal. **1,904**
Carbine, Sharps, factory conversion to
metallic cartridge, faint cartouche on side
of stock, 22" blued barrel w/faint "New
Model" mark (wear to some stampings,
stock w/some dings) **1,430**
Long rifle, Kentucky-type, cherry stock
w/brass patch box & hardware,
checkered wrist, octagonal barrel, two
small side plates w/simple engraving,
barrel 48" l. (repairs w/some
replacements) **1,100**

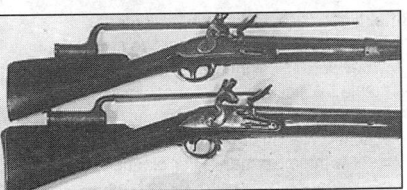

"Brown Bess" & Flintlock Muskets

Musket, "Brown Bess" flintlock, wooden
stock w/refinish & repaired age crack
along barrel channel, boldly marked
"Tower" & "G.R" w/crown, barrel
shortened to 39" l., brass hardware & butt
plate engraved "68," w/bayonet (ILLUS.
bottom) **1,210**
Musket, flintlock, wood stock w/old ark
patina w/iron mountings & light pittings on
lock & breech, three bands & 42" l. round
barrel, early, unmarked, one lock bolt
missing, w/bayonet, overall 57½" l.
(ILLUS. top) **880**
Musket, Parkers Snow & Co. 1861
percussion model, .58 cal., 40" brown
barrel, stock w/inspector's mark &
cleaned dark finish **1,265**
Musket, Pottsdam percussion model,
European walnut stock w/old finish &
stamped "F.W." w/crown, 41" round barrel
w/"1820" stamp, brass hardware (pieced
repair along barrel channel) **495**
Pistol, pepper box percussion model, six-
shot, 3" fluted barrels, one chamber
w/blown-out opening, frame w/simple
scroll engraving & bar hammer, 8" l. **248**
Pistol, S. North flintlock Model 1819,
reconverted flint w/later hammer, brass
pan & friesian, 10" barrel w/bold
inspector's stamps, walnut stock (pieced
repair & age cracks in grip) **550**

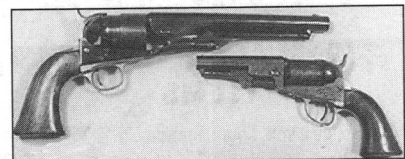

Colt 1849 and 1860 Revolvers

Revolver, Colt 1849 pocket model,
percussion-type, cylinder w/painted
engraved stagecoach scene, all serial
numbers match, few dents, octagonal
barrel 4" l. (ILLUS. bottom) **660**
Revolver, Colt 1860 Army model, .44 cal.,
reblued finish w/all serial numbers &
matching including cylinder, grips w/faint
inspector's stamp, 8" barrel w/New York
address & cylinder engraved w/scene
w/light pitting (ILLUS. top) **715**

Rifle, flintlock Kentucky type w/sighted smoothbore barrel formed in two stages w/beveled lock signed "H. Parker," w/tiger maple full stock, brass mounts including large pierced patchbox engraved w/scrolls & animals, reverse side of butt inset w/three German silver plaques of an eagle, hare & game bird, three brass ramrod pipes & wooden ramrod, 19th c., 56" l. **10,925**

Rifle, Model 1861, percussion-type, .58 cal. **1,000**

Rifle, percussion half-stock, boy's model, curly maple stock w/a poured end cap & nickel silver inlays including dog & deer & escutcheon plates, lock marked "Moore," 24" l. barrel w/brass cap box, overall 39" l. **1,980**

Rifle, Remington Model 6 single-shot, .32 cal., select grade walnut butt stock, case colors on frame, serial number 458793 . . . . . .**248**

Rifle, Stevens-Ideal #44, 25 rimfire cal., blued 24" octagonal to round barrel, some case colors left on receiver. **220**

Rifle, U.S. Whitney Model 1848, percussion-type, .52 cal., a.k.a. "Mississippi Rifle" **1,904**

Rifle, Winchester Golden Spike commemorative, 30 - 30 cal., original box (box sleeve w/end tears) **303**

Rifle, Winchester Model 1892, lever-action, 25-20 cal., octagonal barrel & full-length magazine tube, barrel 24" l. **495**

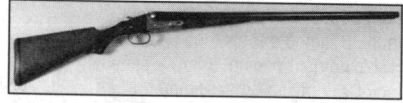

Parker Brothers Shotgun

Shotgun, Parker Brothers double-barrel model, 12 ga., finely engraved, walnut stock (ILLUS.) **1,840**

FIREPLACE & HEARTH ITEMS

Andirons, cast iron, figural standing Hessian soldiers, 19th c., 20½" h., pr. **$230**

Andirons, wrought iron, Arts & Crafts style, a looped spade-shaped top on a pair of canted slender uprights on a flat lower crossbar w/S-scroll end feet, square log bar, similar to Gustav Stickley Model No. 314, original patina, early 20th c., 13 x 21", 21" h., pr. **231**

Andirons, wrought iron & cast-brass knife-blade style, Federal, urn-form finials above a flaring support on arched legs w/penny feet, probably Pernnsylvania, one andiron stamped "IC," 1780-1810, 15½" l., 9½" w., 20½" h., pr. **1,955**

Figural Andirons

Andirons, cast iron, figural, cast in the half-round, cat w/green glass eyes seated on haunches on a flaring pedestal, American-made, 20th c., 16" h., pr. (ILLUS.) **1,495**

Andirons, brass, steeple top finials, angled tubular legs w/ball feet, 21½" h., pr. (damage & old repairs) **275**

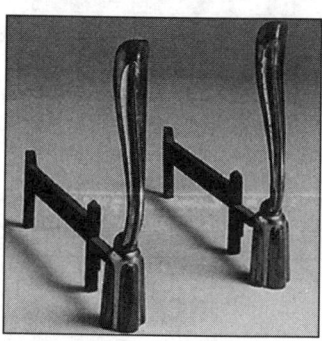

Art Deco Style Andirons

Andirons, bronze & nickeled metal, Art Deco style, flaring feather-form standard on a lobed base w/an iron log support behind, ca. 1930, wear to finish, some oxidation, 23½" h., pr. (ILLUS.) **1,840**

Arts & Crafts Andirons

Andirons, brass, Arts & Crafts style, each formed w/a sinuous standard & flaring foot surmounted by a swirling quatrefoil finial, England, last quarter 19th c., 24" h., pr. (ILLUS.) **1,035**

Andirons, cast brass, Classical style w/gilding & tapering cylindrical red marble columns topped w/small urn-form finials, 28½" h., pr. (restored cracks in marble & one finial bent) **660**

Bellows, painted wood, original red paint w/stenciled & free-hand vintage design in gold, bronze & black, old worn releathering, brass nozzle, 19th c., 18" l. **193**

Bellows, turtle-back type, painted wood, original white paint w/smoked graining & yellowed varnish, stenciled & free-hand flowers & foliage in red, green, black & gold, brass nozzle, professionally releathered, 19th c., 17½" l. **358**

Bellows, turtle-back type, painted wood, small rounded tab handles & tapering rounded sides w/original yellow painted decorated w/stenciled & free-hand fruit & flowers, brass nozzle, old releathering, small size, 19th c., 15¼" l. (wear, especially on handle) **358**

Bellows, turtle-back type, painted wood, decorated w/cornucopia in black, gold & green on worn red ground, brass nozzle, old leather deteriorated, 19th c., 18" l. **193**

Bellows, turtle-back type, painted & decorated wood & leather, old red paint w/polychrome floral decoration, tin nozzle, 17½" l. (old leather is torn & valve missing) **303**

Ornately Carved Bellows

Bellows, turtle-back type, decorated wood w/very ornate relief-carved eagle, lions & scrollwork, Europe, 25" l. (ILLUS.) **385**

Fire screen, metal w/tooled interior scene in high relief, man sitting in front of fireplace w/children & woman working in the background, 27½" w., 18¼" h. (feet have been soldered & are loose) **220**

Fireplace clock jack, brass, slender cylindrical neck above the wide cylindrical casing for the works above a suspended small hook & round iron suspension ring, marked "Geo. Salter & Co. Improved, Warrented," 19th c., 17" h. **193**

Brass & Wire Fire Fender

Fireplace fender, brass & wire, a curved form w/brass top rim & five urn-form finials above a vertical wire screen, 19th c., 48" l, 8" h. (ILLUS.) **575**

Fireplace fender, steel & wire w/brass top rail, above a wire screen w/serpentine design, 57" w., 12" h. (some battering & damage) **1,210**

Fireplace fender, cast brass w/marble inserts & ribbon decoration, 69¾" l., 7½" h. (minor dent in top rail) **385**

Brass Fireplace Andirons

Fireplace tool set, brass, double lemon top design andirons, 19¾" h., signed "Bailey," ca. 1800, New York, New York, together w/a matching pr. of tongs & a shovel, the set (ILLUS. of part) **2,070**

Hearth fork, wrought steel, decorated w/an engraved geometric design, England or America, late 18th - early 19th c., 15¼" l. **115**

FISHING COLLECTIBLES

BOOKS & PAPER ITEMS

Book, "The American Angler's Book," 1865, by Thaddeus Norris, E. H. Butler, green cloth cover, 701 pp. **$149**

Book, "The Book of Fish and Fishing," 1917,
by Louis Rhead, Scribners, NY, 306 pp. **50**
Book, "The Game Fishes of the World,"
1913, by Charles Frederick Holder,
Hodder & Stoughton, London, 411 pp....... **165**
Book, "The Idyl of the Split Bamboo," 1920
first edition, by Dr. George Parker
Holden, Stewart & Kidd, 278 pp. **275**
Catalog, "Edward Vom Hofe," 1938,
177 pp., tackle (minor tears on cover edges) .. **220**
Catalog, "Heddon Catalog," 1929, large
bass below "How to Catch Fish," intact
tear-out centerfold, 32 pp. **935**
Catalog, "S. Allcock & Co.," 1910, Redditch,
England, 42 pp., tackle, 8½ x 11" (some
torn areas on first page attached to spine).... **805**
Catalog, "The Creek Chub Bait Co.," 1919,
marked "Casting and Trolling Nature
Lures, Catch More Fish" above line of
hanging fish, 8 pp. fold-out style folds)....... **770**
Catalog, "The Creek Chub Bait Co.," 1928,
cover depicts couple in canoe, 44 pp.
(minor creases) **1,100**
Ink blotter, C.F. Orvis, Manchester, VT, left
corner depicts trout leaping for fly,
ca. 1880-1890, 3½ x 6½"................. **578**

LURES

Minnow Lures

Creek Chub Bait Co., "Gar Minnow,"
No. 2900 series (ILLUS. bottom) **990**
Creek Chub Bait Co., "Underwater
Minnow," No. 1800 series (ILLUS. top) **990**
Flasher "Pike Flasher," large glass eyes &
extract of fish scales finish, includes
original box & four-panel fold-out
depicting Flasher Lure baits, Long Island
Mfg. Co., 4½" l........................ **99**
Heddon "Artistic Minnow," No. 51, sienna
crackleback finish w/two h.p. gill marks,
glass eyes, rear treble w/red & white
bucktail w/yellow feather accent, original
box w/paper label **440**
Heddon "Dummy Double," No. 1500,
minnow w/"football" hook hangers,
marked props & three dummy-double
hooks, white, red & green decoration,
includes box & rare introductory flyer
(ILLUS., next page) **1,375**

Heddon "Dummy Double"

Heddon "Musky Minnow," No. 700, three-
hook w/heavy duty cup hardware, marked
props, three h.p. gill marks & four belly
weights, green crackleback finish, 5" l...... **2,420**
Heddon "Swimming Minnow," No. 800,
glass eyes, one belly weight, white & red
spots on green finish, one tail treble, two
h.p. gill marks......................... **770**
Outing "Du-Getum," hollow metal, white &
green w/detachable double hooks,
includes box marked "700 WG - white
green" & fold-out flyer................... **330**
Pepper (Joe E.), slim-bodied revolving
minnow, two trebles & adjustable pectoral
fins, Rome, NY, 2¼" l. (shows wear) **220**

Pepper's "Peppy Lure Spinner Special"

Pepper "Peppy Lure Spinner Special,"
bat-wing style on original cardboard,
ca. 1920-30s, The Joe Pepper Bait Co.
(ILLUS.) **248**
Pflueger "Neverfail," three-hook wooden
minnow, includes sliding lid wooden box
w/paper label, mounted w/detachable
hooks, spinners & connections,
ca. 1911, 2¾" l........................ **990**
Rush-Tango, minnow, red head w/white
body, includes original "$50 Gold Prize" box .. **116**
Shakespeare, No. 44GW (old No. 1604),
0/2 size wooden minnow, five-hook style,
/gem clip hook hangers, three h.p. gill
marks, type "B" style props, green back,
salmon side & white belly finish, includes
maroon cardboard box, 3⅝" l. (much
wear to box) **330**
South Bend Bait Co. "Vacuum Bait,"
unused, in original box (ILLUS.) **2,420**

"Vacuum Bait" Lure

REELS

Abbey & Imbrie, trout, German silver & hard rubber, w/characteristics of ca. 1877 Philbrook & Paine reel, 1" w., 1⅜" d. **1,870**

Billinghurst "Birdcage" Reel

Billinghurst, click-type, "Birdcage," unmarked experimental model, ca. 1859, 3" d. (ILLUS.) **990**

Bogdan (Stan), salmon, marked "AF-100-M" on foot, made for Abercrombie & Fitch, 1⅛" w., 3⅜" d. **1,650**

Chubb (Thomas C.), Vt. Henshall-Van Antwerp model, black bass reel, ca. 1887, German silver **6,600**

Fullilove Casting Reel

Fullilove (Frank), click-switch casting type, marked "Frank Fullilove, Owenton, KY - Crown," knurled sliding rim drag control,

fixed bearing caps & fancy turned ivory handle grasp, German silver, ca. 1903, 1⅜" w., 2⅛" d. (ILLUS.) **3,960**

Hall (Allen E.) & Smith (Wm. G.), handle-reel type, nickel plated w/turned wood butt, pump grips & hard rubber spool, marked "Pat. July 14, 1903," 3 pc., 24" l. **1,430**

Hardy, trout, No. C-1900, brass-faced, ⅝" w., 3" d. **930**

Leonard - Mills, salmon, No. 48M, "Pat. No. 1,673,382, Pat. Pending," 1⅜" w., 4" d. **825**

McNeese, "Baby" trout, anti-reverse type, No. 01-2.4N, ¾" w., 2¾"d. **385**

Meek (B.F.) & Sons, casting style w/click switch & thumb rest, Blue Grass No. 33, "Carter's Pat. Jul 5, 04, Nov. 28, 05," Louisville, KY **220**

Meek & Sons (B.F.), trout, No. 44, "Flat Back" model, German silver, Louisville, KY, 1" w., 2¼" d. **4,510**

Orvis (C.F.), trout, riveted construction, pat. May 12, 1874, Manchester, VT, ½" w., 2⅞" d. **385**

Pfluegar "Auto Pla," No. 2479 . . . . **150**

Pflueger "Golden West," trout, No. 5092, German silver w/hard rubber & aluminum plates, black Bulldog medallion, pat. Feb. 10, 1903 & Jan. 23, 1907, ⅞" w., 2⅞" d. **1,210**

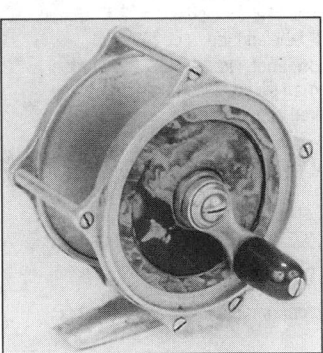

Early Philbrook & Paine Trout Reel

Philbrook & Paine, trout, click-type, German silver & orange & black marbleized hand rubber, ca. 1877, Bangor, ME, 1" w., 2⅝" d. (ILLUS.) **3,850**

Pluegar No. 1893L **50**

Robichand (D.L.), trout, marked "D. L. Robichand, Hudson, N.H. U.S.A.," three-position click switch type w/drag switch on back, ⅞" w., 2¾" d. **303**

Shakespears "Wonder Wheel," No. 1810 . . . . . . **50**

Shakespears "Criterion" **50**

Ustonson, trout, multiplying click-type, engraved "Ustonson Makers to his Majesty Temple Bar Ld'n," ca. 1830-1837, 1¾" w., 1¾" d. **10,450**

Vom Hofe (Edward), multiplying salmon-
type, Model 504, German silver & hard
rubber, pat. May 20, 1902, 2/0 size,
1⅜" w., 3⅜" d. **1,430**

Vom Hofe (Edward), trout, No. 360,
"Perfection," German silver & hard
rubber, pat. Jan. 23, 1883, 2/0 size,
⅞" w., 2¾" d. **4,950**

Vom Hofe (Julius), salmon, click-type, "Pat.
Oct. 8, 89," German silver & hard rubber,
Boston, raised pillar, Dame, Stoddard
Co., Boston, MA, 4/0 size, 1¾" w., 4" d. **660**

Vom Hofe (Julius), trout, nickel plating, pat.
Oct. 8, 1889, 3.5/0 size, ⅝" w., 2¼" d. **770**

Winchester, trout, fly type, No. 1235, raised
pillar-type w/bone handle, 80% original
black finish **110**

Zwarg (Otto), salmon, Model 300, Serial
No. B52, Saguenay, marked "Otto Zwarg,
Brooklyn, N.Y. - Maker," German silver,
aluminum & hard rubber, 4/0 size,
1¾" w., 3⅞" d. **1,100**

Zwarg (Otto), salmon, No. 300, Saguenay,
marked "O. Zwarg Co., Inc. - St.
Petersburg, Fla. - Maker," German silver
& hard rubber, 2/0 size, 1⅜" w., 3⅜" d. **1,265**

RODS

Carlson (Sam), trout, "Carlson's Mount
Carmel #7-5," includes bag & "Thomas
Rod" labeled tube, 2 pc., 7' l. **2,475**

Garrison, trout, No. 212 F-8-11, knurled
German silver slide band, includes
original bag & tube, 1962, 2 pc., 8' l. **3,850**

Gillum (H.S.), fly, "Pinky," No. 1-725,
includes original bag & tube marked "H.S.
Gillum - Finest Custom Built Rods -
Ridgefield, Conn.," 2 pc., 8' l. **3,300**

Orvis (C.F.), trout, No. 380, "Patented June
6, 1882," includes original three tips &
two mid sections, original bag
w/compartments for all sections, 3 pc.,
9' l. **953**

Payne, trout, Model 198, stamped "Made for
Abercrombie & Fitch Co.," includes
original bag w/hanging tag & tube w/red
label, 3 pc., 7⅞' l. **3,300**

Shakespeare steel casting rod **75**

Spalding (A.G.) & Bros., trout, Serial No.
1540, "The Kosmic" w/removable
independent handle, ferrule marked
"Pat'd May 6, 1890, Pat'd May 27, 1890,"
original brass fitted bamboo tip case,
3 pc., 10' l. **385**

Thomas & Thomas, "Amabilis," trout rod,
ca. 1985, Limited Edition No. 9 of 20 rods . . **3,850**

Thomas & Thomas, walnut & bamboo, No.
9 of ten rod Limited Edition, includes
certificate of ownership & signed seal,
tiger-stripe maple fitted case,1979, 2 pc.,
8' l. (ILLUS.). **2,640**

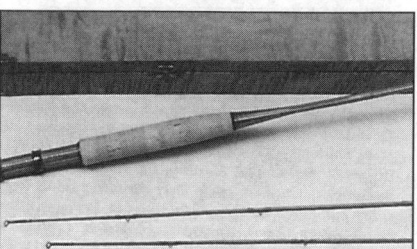

Thomas & Thomas Limited Edition Rod

MISCELLANEOUS

Bait tin, oval, copper hand-soldered bottom,
hinged tin lid ventilated w/screened cut-
out heart in center, two tin belt loops on
back, remnants of painted star & dots on
side & bottom, all handmade,
Pennsylvania, old, 4¼" l. **468**

Split Willow Creel

Creel, marked "Established 1857 - The
George Lawrence Co., Portland, Oregon"
on metal tag, stamped "4-A" on top, split
willow construction, leather strap &
buckle lid latch, full-length leather lid
hinge w/tooled 10" rule, leather hanging
strap & flower-tooled leather harness
(ILLUS.). **2,860**

Creel, marked "Turtle Trade Mark" & "Ilhan
New," bulbous shape w/leather trim &
tight rattan weave & split-reed reinforcing
on bottom **2,200**

Norlund Fish Grabber

Fish grabber, marked "Norlund's Patent,"
spring-loaded early model, 45" l. (ILLUS.) **110**

Flies, salmon, early hand-tied, in tray
w/original dove-tailed walnut case, Hardy
Bros., Ltd., England label on inside cover
(ILLUS.). **2,970**

Salmon Flies in Walnut Case

Fly, realistic mayfly nymph, by Bill Blades, in
glass dome, includes documentation card **165**

Fly, salmon, "Peacock Queen," tied by Kim
Rasmussen, in 7 x 8⅞" burl frame
w/signed back. **138**

Fly box, chest-type, marked "Fye Box
Osceola Mills, PA," four hinged trays
w/lids, three w/divided compartments,
canvas straps, 4 x 5⅞ x 6" **138**

Line drier, marked "Hardy Bros. Makers
Alnwick," four brass arms mounted
w/bone grasp on handle & attached to
iron frame, attached clamp, first produced
by Hardy Brothers, ca. 1897. . . . . **385**

Lure box, top marked "Pflueger's 'Monarch'
Minnow. - We are the original makers of
the Wooden Minnow..., The Enterprise
Mfg. Co., Akron, O., U.S.A.," ends
stamped "Pfluegers Monarch Minnow -
2173 - 35/8," sliding lid, 8" l.
(some light stains) **1,650**

Rare Minnow Bucket

Minnow bucket, galvanized w/lift-out inner
liner, Abbey & Imbre label depicting large
mouth bass (ILLUS.) **396**

Net, collapsible trout net w/"Winchester"
decal, 9" ribbed wooden handle **330**

Net, Leonard (H.L.) Rod Co., limited edition,
cherry wood, hand-knotted, signed by
Guy Rich, ca. 1979. **138**

Brown Trout Oil Painting

Painting, oil, signed "E. Harrington-88,"
depicts brown trout leaping w/fly in jaw &
dropper fly trailing, bold red & black
coloring on trout, deep mahogany frame
w/applied ball trim, slight crazing,
18 x 24" (ILLUS.). **1,210**

Photograph & flies, picture of Charles
DeFro tying flies w/his cat looking over
his shoulder, includes four low water
Atlantic salmon flies by DeFro, letter of
authenticity from his widow mounted on
back of double matted gold frame,
15 x 23" **413**

Pin, salmon fly pin by Reid & Sons, variation
of Tranerne's Wonder, tied w/authentic
Indian Crow, Blue Chatterer & Speckled
Bustard materials, original velvet & silk-
lined box, 19th c. **352**

Salesman's lure sample case, "Paw Paw
Bait Co.," heavy fiberboard w/metal strip
reinforced edges, fold-down front w/ten
shallow 8 x 15" display trays, 9 x 16 x 21" **220**

Tackle box, wood, marked "The Seamaster
Made by J.C. Gilson, Stuart, Florida,"
layered plywood construction w/lift out
divided tray, brass tag on compartment
lid, leather handle, 9 x 9½ x 20" **248**

FRAKTUR

*Fraktur paintings are decorative birth and
marriage certificates of the 18th and 19th
centuries and also include family registers and
similar documents. Illuminated family
documents, birth and baptismal certificates,
religious texts and rewards of merit, in a
particular style, are known as "fraktur" because
of the similarity to the 16th century type-face of
that name. Gay watercolor borders, frequently
incorporating stylized birds, hand-lettered
documents, which were executed by local
ministers, school masters or itinerant penman.
Most are of Pennsylvania Dutch origin.*

**Birth & baptismal fraktur (Geburts und
Taufschein),** pen & ink, watercolor & cut
paper on laid paper by Frederick Krebs,

recording 1804 birth in Northampton County, decorated w/crown, suns, flowers & tulips in black ink w/red, brown & yellow watercolor, cut-outs in gilt paper or w/embossed gilded religious figures, printed format w/"F. Krebs," heavily alligatored frame decorated w/red & yellow stenciled designs on black ground, Pennsylvannia, 15⅞" w., 12⅝" h. (fold lines & taped repairs) **$2,420**

Birth & baptismal fraktur (Geburts und Taufschein), pen & ink & handcolored floral detail w/tulips & hearts in red, green & yellow, recording 1820 birth in Union County, Pennsylvania, framed, 18¾" w., 16¼" h. **743**

Birth & baptismal fraktur (Geburts und Taufschein), rectangular, printed & handcolored, recording 1817 birth in Berks County, printed by "Johann Ritter, Reading," handcolored angels & birds in yellow, red, blue & black, Pennsylvania, framed, 14¾" w., 18¾" h. (wear, tears, stains & fold lines) **55**

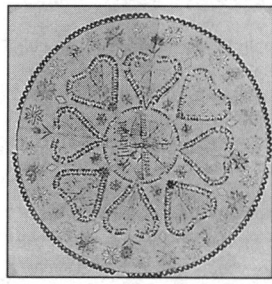

Cutwork 'Scherenschitten' Birth Certificate

Birth record, fine cutwork 'Scherenschitten,' the circular document w/pinked edges & pin-pricked stars, flowers & hearts, the design elements picked out in red, blue, brown & green ink & watercolor, Southeastern Pennsylvania, dated 1782, 11" d. (ILLUS.)....................... **1,380**

Pennsylvania German Fraktur

Birth record, pen & ink & watercolor, records 1845 birth in Union County, stylized floral & heart decoration in red, yellow, blue & black, signed "Martin

Breckall," Pennsylvania, beveled poplar frame w/original red & black paint, minor wear & stains w/creases, 19" w., 13½" h. (ILLUS.)............................ **2,200**

Birth record, pen & ink & watercolor on wove paper, large heart flanked by parrots & tulips, corner fans, crown & birds in red, blue, brownish yellow & green, records 1820 birth in Columbia County, Pennsylvania, framed, 19¾" w., 17" h. (worn & wrinkled w/edge damage, stains & tears, old newspaper backed repair along one tear) **2,530**

Birth record, pen & ink & watercolor on laid paper, recording 1795 birth in Weyenburg township, Northampton county, Pennsylvania, stylized flowers, birds, two angels, heart & center ring w/sawtooth design encircling text, red, green, yellow & black, framed, 22¼" w., 18¾" h. (stains & some damage repaired).............. **3,410**

Early Birth Record

Birth record for Elizabeth Wenger, watercolor & ink on wove paper, floral design on one side & top, "Elizabeth Wenger" in large letters w/date of 1795, red, black & yellow w/reddish brown ink, Pennsylvania, minor stains, framed, 10" w., 7½" h. (ILLUS.) **1,760**

Book plate, watercolor on wove paper, stylized tree w/birds on branches, "S.Z.," red, blue, green, yellow & black, frame covers bird at top of tree & date "1823" in bottom right, framed, 5⅝" w., 6½" h. (minor damage) **165**

Book plate, pen & ink & watercolor on wove paper, a large heart w/pinked edges w/"Maria Christ 1828" in red, green, yellow & black, ink in name is faded brown, framed, 7⅝" w., 6⅞" h. (minor wear & edge damage) **220**

Book plate, pen & ink & watercolor on lined paper, "Benjamin Frailich - and - Mary Frailich," & signed "Israel Gorb, Apr. 29, 1868," red, pink, green & black, framed, 6⅛" w., 8¾" h. (wear, tape stain along one edge & edges glued to backing) **330**

Drawing, watercolor on wove paper, stylized bird on branch in black, green, pink, yellow & orange, pen inscription in upper right reads "Pretty Polle Birde," framed, 7½" w., 5¾" h. **605**

Drawing, pen & ink & watercolor on wove paper, stylized tulip tree w/a bird on each side, yellow border stripe w/blue, salmon red, green yellow & black, framed, 5" w., 6" h. (minor stains w/tape stains) **935**

Drawing, ink & watercolor on wove paper, primitive scene w/bird, flowers & tree in blue, red, yellow & green, back signed "May 15th, 1848 Catrine Gice," framed, 10⅜" w., 12" h. (fly specks & minor stains) . . . **660**

Drawing, pen & ink cut-out on wove paper, farm yard scene w/very good detail & color w/buildings, people, animals, etc., cut-out vignettes of farm activities & cut-out title backed w/black coated paper, Dutch inscriptions & title dated 1848, rebacked on heavy paper, framed, 18" w., 16¾" h. (damage & stains) **1,430**

House blessing (Haus Seegen), printed & hand-colored floral & heart design in red, blue, green & yellow, dated "1785," framed, 18½" w., 21½" h. (damage & portions missing w/old tape stains on repairs in left corner) **385**

"Tauf Zettel," printed & handcolored floral design in red, blue, green & yellow on black & white engraving, framed, 8½" w., 9" h. (stains & some damage at fold lines) **220**

Vorschrift fraktur, pen & ink & watercolor, decorative name w/flowers & border design in red, yellow, green & black, old black molded frame, 14⅜" w., 11⅜" h. (wear, some damage & bits of paper adhering to watercolor surface) **1,210**

Vorschrift fraktur, pen & ink & watercolor, flowers & heart along side of text, red, yellow, green & black, framed, 10⅝" w.,12¾" h. (stains, small holes & tattered edges) **165**

FRATERNAL ORDER COLLECTIBLES

Also see: BARBERIANA

G.A.R. (Grand Army of the Republic) booklet, souvenir-type,43rd National GAR Encampment - Salt Lake City Utah - August 1909" **$45**

G.A.R. cane head, metal figural head of General U.S. Grant, 1897. . . . . **250**

I.O.O.F. ring, gold (10k yellow) w/the standard markings on enameled face & sides **125**

I.O.O.F. trivet, brass, three circles in center, hand w/heart. **85**

Masonic apron, polychrome-decorated silk w/various Masonic emblems, silver braided fringe, American-made, 19th c., 16" sq. (fiber wear) **288**

Page from Early Masonic Scrapbook

Masonic scrapbook, contains Masonic & Knights Templer business cards, invitations & other ephemera dating from 1872 to 1890, original owner's name in front, North Baltimore, Ohio, 60 pp., soil, tears, some rodent damage at back, loose spine, 8 x 9 1/2" (ILLUS) **83**

Shriner badge. 1906, Chicago Imperial Council". . **45**

Shriner pin, enamel, 1910, Cedar Rapids, Iowa . . **75**

Shriner plate, 10¼" d., porcelain, center medallion depicts drunken Shriner w/bandaged head, Shenango China Co. **50**

FRUIT JARS

Almy, base marked "Patented - Dec 25 1877," ground lip, original screw-on glass lid, ca. 1877-80, aqua, qt. **$132**

Bee, smooth base, ground lip, ca. 1875-85, aqua, ½ gal. (closure missing) **440**

Bodine (F. & J.) Manufacturers - Philadelphia PA, smooth base, ground lip, ca. 1870-75, aqua, qt. (reproduction metal & wire closure) **88**

Bodine (F. & J.) - Philada, smooth base, ground lip, reproduction metal & wire closure, ca. 1870-80, aqua, qt. (ILLUS., next page) **94**

Brooks (C.D.) - Boston, smooth base, applied mouth, golden yellow amber, qt. **55**

Champion (The) - Pat. Aug. 31 1869, smooth base, sheared & ground lip, correct glass insert & iron yoke clamp, ca. 1869-75, aqua, ½ gal. (tiny chip on insert) **165**

Common Sense Jar - Gregory's Patent - Aug 17th 1869, smooth base, applied mouth, original glass stopper & metal yoke closure, ca. 1870-80, aqua, qt. (small chip on lid) **825**

F. & J. Bodine Fruit Jar

Eureka 17 - Patd Dec 27th 1864, smooth
    base, ground lip, ca. 1865-70, aqua,
    ½ gal. (missing closure) 66
Globe, original closure, "23" on base, amber, pt. . . 110
Haines's Improved - March 1st 1870,
    smooth base, applied mouth, correct
    glass lid marked "Patented March 1870,"
    aqua, qt. (lid wire probably reproduction,
    some lid stain) 72
Indicator, smooth base, ground lip,
    ca. 1875-85, aqua, qt. (reproduction
    metal lid & neck band, some lip
    chipping) 440
Lafayette (in script), original gasket, aqua, pt. . . 175

Rare Lightning Half Pint Fruit Jar

**Lightning - Putnam 763 - Trade Mark (on
    base)** smooth base, ground lip, original
    glass lid embossed "Lightning Pat. April
    25, 82," wire bail, amber, ½ pt. (ILLUS.) **1,980**
Mason.s S Patent Nov. 30th 1858,
    shoulder seal, aqua, qt. 10
Mason's 2 Patent - Nov 30th 1858, smooth
    base, ground lip, original zinc screw-on
    lid, aqua, midget pt. (some lid
    deterioration, milky bruise on screw thread). . . . 22
**Mason's (keystone) Patent Nov. 30th
    1858,** original lid, good whittle, lime aqua
    variation, qt. 143
Mason's Patent - Nov 30th 1858, smooth
    base, ABM lip, zinc screw-on lid, ca.
    1920-30, deep aqua w/heavy yellowish
    olive striations, ½ gal. 220

**Mason's Patent - Nov 30th 1858 - Dupont
    (in circle)** smooth base, ground lip, zinc
    screw-on lid, light apple green, ½ gal.
    (minor inside lip bruise) 231
Mason's - SGCo - Patent Nov. 30th 1858,
    w/zinc cap, good whittle, lime aqua, ½ gal. . . . 198
**Moore (John M. & Co.) Manufacturers,
    Fislerville, NJ (in script),** also marked
    "Patented Dec. 3d 1861," jar only, aqua, pt. . . 495
Peerless, glass lid, iron yoke clamp, lid
    marked "Patented Feb. 13 1863," aqua,
    qt. (very light haze) 165
**Potter & Bodine - Air Tight - Fruit Jar -
    Philada - Patented - April 15th 1858,**
    cylindrical shouldered bottle w/grooved
    neck w/ring for wax sealer, aqua, ca.
    1860-65, ½ gal. (stress crack in ring) 177
Puritan (The) - L.S. Co. (monogram),
    smooth base, ground lip, original glass lid
    in citron, ca. 1880-90, aqua, pt. (iron ring
    & closure reproductions) 165
Spencer's (C.F.) Patent Rochester, N.Y.,
    different style lip, aqua, qt. (two under
    lip chips) 25
Stone & Co. (A.) - Philada, smooth base,
    applied mouth w/internal screw threads,
    original screw stopper embossed "A.
    Stone & Co. - 2 - Philada," ca. 1860-70,
    aqua, pt. (V-shaped chip on side of
    mouth, chips on stopper edge) 149

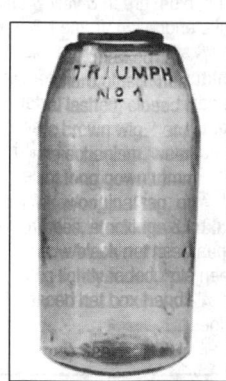

Triumph No. 1 Fruit Jar

Triumph No. 1, smooth base, pressed-down
    wax seal channel, ground lip, remnants of
    original pressed-on tin lid exist on lip,
    ca. 1865-75, bluish aqua, ½ gal. (ILLUS.) 908
Union #4, aqua, qt. (1/4" chip on back) 450
Western Pride - Patented June 22, 1875,
    smooth base, applied mouth, original
    glass lid embossed "Patented June 22,
    1875," metal clamp closure, aqua, ½ gal.
    (small rainbow-type bruise on inside
    applied lip) 77
**Yeoman's Fruit Bottle - Patent Applied
    For,** smooth base, outward rolled lip,
    ca. 1865-75, aqua, ½ gal. 50

Courtesy of Sotheby's, New York, New York

Victorian Renaissance Revival Parlor Suite

FURNITURE

Furniture made in the United States during the 18th and 19th centuries is coveted by collectors. American antique furniture has a European background, primarily English, since the influence of the Continent usually found its way to America by way of England. If the style did not originate in England, it came to America by way of England. For this reason, some American furniture styles carry the name of an English monarch or an English designer. However, we must realize that, until recently, little research has been conducted and even less published on the Spanish and French influences in the area of the California missions and New Orleans.

After the American revolution, cabinetmakers in the United States shunned the prevailing styles in England and chose to bring the French styles of Napoleon's Empire to the United States; thus we have the uniquely named "American Empire" style of furniture in a country that never had an emperor. During the Victorian period, quality furniture began to be mass-produced in this country with its rapidly growing population. So much walnut furniture was manufactured that the vast supply of walnut was virtually depleted and it was of necessity that oak furniture became fashionable as the 19th century drew to a close.

For our purposes, the general guidelines for dating will be:

Pilgrim Century—1620-85
William & Mary—1685-1720
Queen Anne—1720-50
Chippendale—1750-85
Federal—1785-1820
    Hepplewhite—1785-1820
    Sheraton—1800-20

American Empire (Classical)—1815-40
Victorian—1840-1900
    Early Victorian—1840-50
    Gothic Revival—1840-90
    Rococo (Louis XV)—1845-70
    Renaissance—1860-85
    Louis XVI—1865-75
    Eastlake—1870-95
    Jacobean & Turkish Revival—1870-95
    Aesthetic Movement—1880-1900
Art Nouveau—1890-1918
Turn-of-the-Century—1895-1910
Mission (Arts & Crafts movement)—1900-15
Art Deco—1925-40
All furniture included in this listing is American unless otherwise noted.

BEDROOM SUITES

Art Deco Bedroom Suite

Art Deco: stepped vanity, five-drawer chest of drawers, bedside table, double bed & bench; bird's-eye maple, simple classic squared design w/narrow curved metal pulls & large upright round off-center mirror on dressing table, dated & marked "1936—Triangle Brand—Crane & McMahon," the set (ILLUS. of part) **$288**

Jacobean Revival: a tall chest of drawers, a dresser w/mirror, a dressing table w/mirror, a double bed, stool & non-matching side chair; mahogany veneer & burled mahogany veneer, the tall chest w/a rectangular top w/molded edges above a long drawer w/a central raised burl panel flanked by carved scrolls & ring pulls w/quarter-round corner turnings above a stepped-back & inset stack of three long burl veneered drawers flanked by ring- and knob-turned outset posts on a rectangular top w/molded edges over a lower case w/two long burl veneered drawers trimmed w/a continuous raised rectangular banding & w/four ring pulls, half-round ring-turned side colonettes above the apron w/double beaded bands centered by a scroll-carved scalloped central section, raised on ring- and double-knob-turned front legs on casters, other pieces w/similar decoration, by the Continental Furniture Company, ca. 1920s, the set **550**

Chest from Aesthetic Movement Set

Victorian Aesthetic Movement: chest of drawers w/mirror, two-door cupboard, commode, full-size bed; walnut & burl walnut, each piece w/a tall crown-form crest w/a pediment crest above a deeply carved rectangular panel of flowering vines flanked by arched brackets on a paneled rail between incised uprights, the chest of drawers w/a tall rectangular mirror flanked by small handkerchief drawers raised on turned colonettes above the rectangular white marble top

over a cases w/three long paneled & burl veneered drawers w/angular brass pulls & round wood keyhole escutcheons, side stiles w/blocked & incised decoration, commode & cupboard also w/white marble tops, ca. 1870, chest of drawers 24 x 55½", 87¾" h., the set (ILLUS. of chest of drawers) **7,475**

Golden Oak Bedroom Suite

Victorian Golden Oak substyle: dresser, double bed & commode; the dresser w/a large rectangular mirror in a frame w/scroll-carved cresting & rounded corners swiveling between turned uprights & a scrolled crestboard above the molded rectangular serpentine top over a conforming case w/a pair of drawers over two long drawers; the matching medium-height headboard w/a large scroll-carved central cartouche, the commode w/a long bowed drawer over two small drawers beside a single paneled door, all on casters, ca. 1890-1900, the set (ILLUS.) **1,000**

Ornate Moorish Revival Armoire

Victorian Moorish Revival: armoire, single bed & bedside table w/marble top; walnut, burl walnut & parcel-gilt, each piece w/elaborate pierced & carved decoration, the armoire w/an arched & pierced scroll-carved crest above a latticework crestrail between turned corner finials over a plain frieze band on scalloped rounded arched & turned columns above & flanking the set-back paneled doors w/a top rondel, large center panel & ornately parcel-gilt lower panel, a long raised-panel drawer across the bottom, molded base on bun feet, last quarter 19th c., armoire 23 x 51", 76½" h., the set (ILLUS. of armoire) **4,025**

BEDS

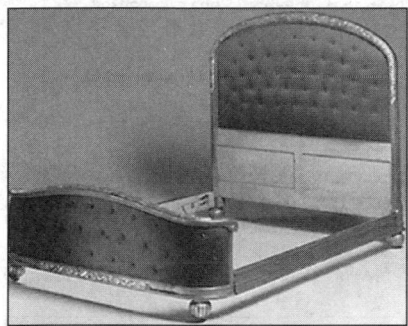

French Art Deco Bed

Art Deco bed, giltwood & upholstery, the high arched headboard & lower footboard carved w/narrow borders of flowerheads enclosing black silk tufted upholstery, joined by molded rails, in the manner of Paul Follot, France, ca. 1925, chips to gilding, 56" w. (ILLUS.) **2,070**

Majorelle Art Nouveau Bed

Art Nouveau bed, Les Lilas patt., carved mahogany, the high headboard w/shaped crestrail w/rounded corners over panels of carved lilacs above a wide veneered panel over a rail & four small veneered panels, the conforming lower footboard w/carved corners & two large veneered panels, shaped low feet, designed by Louis Majorelle, France, ca. 1900, 65 x 85", 61" h. (ILLUS.) **4,600**

Country-style low poster "folding" bed, painted wood, turned headposts flanking a shaped headboard, joined to the footposts by jointed rails fitted for roping & folding, old Spanish brown paint, New England, early 19th c., 52¾ x 77½", 33½" h. (imperfections) **690**

Early Low-Poster Bed

Country-style low-poster bed, painted pine & maple, the pointed headboard between blocked stiles w/flattened knob turned finials & swelled turned & tapering legs, original side rails w/rope holes & low footposts w/flattened knob turned finials over the corner blocks on swelled turned & tapering legs, old red paint, Pennsylvania, early 19th c., 52 x 80", headboard 34½" h. (ILLUS.) **575**

Federal tall poster bed, carved mahogany, the vase- and ring-turned footposts carved w/pineapples above a reeded swelled post w/carved sheaves of wheat continuing to acanthus leaves & carved palmettes on vase- and ring-turned legs, the headposts also vase- and ring-turned but uncarved, all joined by a flat tester frame, 54 x 72", 87" h. **12,650**

Federal tall poster bed, painted, the vase- and ring-turned & reeded footposts joined to the simple turned headposts & shaped pine headboard w/an arched canopy frame, ring- and baluster-turned legs, old red stain, New England, ca. 1820, 48 x 69", 75" h. (minor imperfections) **2,645**

Federal tall-poster bed, carved mahogany, the square tapering tall headposts centering a scroll-cut pine headboard, the footposts w/waterleaf -carved tapering reeded posts on swag- and leaf-carved urn-form supports on square tapering legs, all legs w/spade feet, w/flat tester, headboard possibly replaced, North Shore Massachusetts, ca. 1795, 59 x 80", 92" h. (ILLUS.) **5,750**

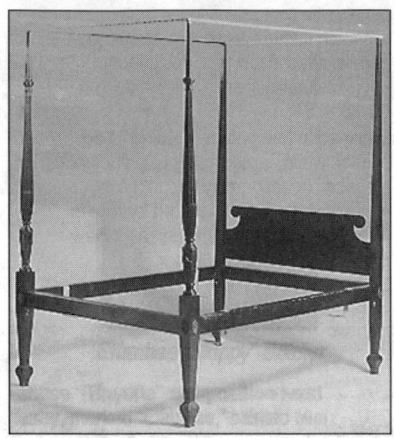

Massachusetts Federal Bed

Federal tall-poster canopy field bed,
maple, a low peaked headboard flanked
by simple slender turned & tapering
posts, the footposts w/ring- and baluster-
turned posts & square tapering legs, w/an
arched serpentine canopy frame, late
18th to early 19th c., 58½" w., 68" h........ **2,000**

**Mission-style (Arts & Crafts movement)
double bed,** oak, tall square corner
posts, the headboard w/rails flanking the
seven slats, matching but slightly lower
footboard, wide side rails, fine original
finish, L. & J.G. Stickley, Model No. 84,
58" w., 54" h.......................... **7,150**

Gustav Stickley Bed

**Mission-style (Arts & Crafts movement)
double bed,** the headboard & slightly
shorter footboard each w/a narrow
inverted V-top crestrail flanked by tall
square tapering posts, five wide slats in
each w/a wide lower rail, original finish,
branded signature mark of Gustav
Stickley, original side rails, 59 x 78"
(ILLUS.)............................. **8,800**

Turn-of-the-century bed, brass, elaborately
scrolled head- and footboards w/foliate
detail, ca. 1900, one small spindle
missing, 61" w., 64" h. (ILLUS.).......... **2,200**

Ornate Early Brass Bed

Victorian double bed, Renaissance Revival
substyle, walnut, highback headboard
w/an arched scroll-pierced & pointed
crestrail on an arched molding over a pair
of large oval panels w/half-round raised
molding across the top & a raised rondel
above, the flattened stiles topped by
spearpoint finials, curved corners, low
arched footboard centered by a large
raised bull's-eye rondel, ca. 1870, original
side rails, refinished, 61 x 72", 83" h.
(repairs to crestrail) **770**

Record-breaking Belter Patented Bed

Victorian Rococo substyle bed, laminated
rosewood, the tall serpentine & arched
headboard crowned by an ornately
pierce-carved crest w/a basket of fruit
crest flanked by leafy scrolls & figures of
putti, the headboard dropping down &
continuing into serpentine deep carved
side rails joining the lower serpentine
footboard w/rounded corners & a
cartouche-carved crest, patented by John
Henry Belter, ca. 1850s, record for
19th c. American furniture (ILLUS.)...... **101,750**

BENCHES

Bucket (or water) bench, painted pine, a low backrail w/notched corners on a long rectangular board top w/chamfered front corners over an apron w/chambered ends, raised on tall inset one-board legs w/low arched cut-outs, old worn & weathered grey paint, 19th c., 15 x 52", 31¾" h. (some edge damage) **363**

Kneeling bench, poplar, a long narrow board top w/a narrow apron raised on three arched bootjack legs, old brown finish, 7 x 76 3/4" **220**

Modern style bench, upholstery & chrome, the wide rectangular upholstered top composed of two reupholstered cushions in green wool raised on a chrome frame w/short square end legs joined by a square stretcher, designed by George Nelson, manufactured by Herman Miller, ca. 1950s, 30 x 60", 15" h.. . . . . **1,320**

Long Wood & Iron Park Bench

Park bench, cast-iron & wood, the long wooden slat back & seat joining the pierced scrolled iron arms above pierced ends of squirrels among leafy vines on short legs of gargoyles ending in paw feet, painted green, George Smith and Co., Glasgow, Scotland, late 19th c., 31 x 98", 33" h. (ILLUS.) **2,070**

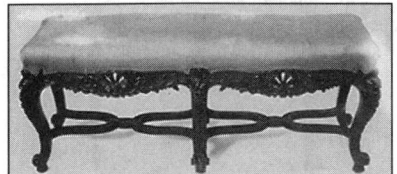

Regency-Style Bench

Regency-Style bench, walnut, a long serpentine-edged upholstered top in green striped silk over a foliage-carved & shell-pierced apron, raised on six cabriole legs ending in scrolled toes, joined by stretchers, Europe, late 19th c., 17 x 45½", 17" h. (ILLUS.). **1,840**

Window bench, Classical style, mahogany veneer, the up-curving seat flanked by scrolled ends above four outscrolled legs, New York, 1815-25, old refinish, some veneer cracking & loss, 14 x 39½", 23⅝" h. (ILLUS.) **3,450**

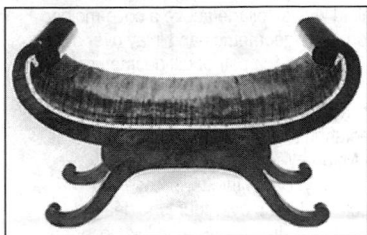

Classical Window Bench

Window bench, Classical style, carved mahogany veneer, upholstered seat above a veneered rail on leaf-carved cyma-curved ends joined by a ring-turned medial stretcher, old surface, Boston, 1835-45, 16¼ x 48", 17½" h. (imperfections). **2,185**

BOOKCASES

Arts & Crafts bookcase, oak, a thin rectangular top overhanging a wide case w/three tall sliding doors each w/a top arched leaded-glass panel w/organic loops & scrolls above a single tall rectangular panel, opening to eight adjustable shelves, slightly shaped apron, original dark finish, metal tag of the Paine Furniture Co., missing backsplash, early 20th c., 14 x 60", 59" h.. . . . . **2,420**

Fine Federal Bookcase

Federal bookcase, inlaid mahogany, two-part construction: the upper section w/a rectangular top & molded swan's-neck crest w/openwork foliate designs centering a turned urn finial on a plinth inlaid w/oval foliage above a cove-molded cornice w/geometric band inlay over a frieze band & a pair of tall geometrically glazed cupboard doors w/incurved inlaid muntins centered by églomisé rectangular portrait medallions of George & Martha Washington, signed "by Kennedy, Balt.," the lower case w/a rectangular top over four long beaded graduated drawers w/string inlay over an inlaid band & scalloped apron continuing to tall French feet, the bookcase section w/a lift-top secret compartment behind the cornice, ca. 1800, 38¼" w., 88" h. (ILLUS.) **9,775**

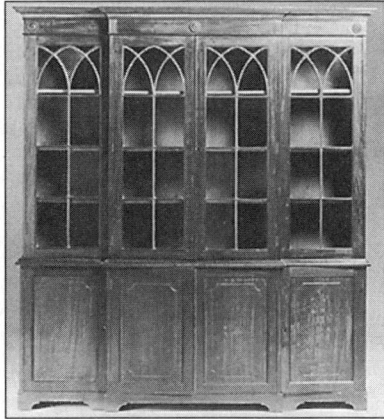

George III Breakfront Bookcase

George III bookcase, mahogany, two-part breakfront-type: the upper section w/a removable paterae-mounted cornice above four tall multi-paned glazed doors w/Gothic arch-top panes opening to three shelves; the lower section w/mid-molding & conforming stepped-out central section w/a pair of paneled cupboard doors flanked by paneled end doors opening to shelves, on low bracket feet, England, ca. 1800, 19 x 77", 86" h. (ILLUS.) **10,350**

Mission-style (Arts & Crafts movement) bookcase, oak, a rectangular narrow top w/a low galleried top w/keyed tenon ends above a case w/three tall 12-pane glazed cupboard doors opening to shelves, flat apron, lower keyed tenons & low arched end openings, original hammered copper hardware, fine original finish, "Handcraft" decal mark, L. & J.G. Stickley, Model No. 647, 12 x 73", 55" h. **17,600**

Mission-style (Arts & Crafts movement) bookcase, oak, a three-quarters galleried top w/gently arched ends & keyed through-tenons on the top above a case w/a pair of tall 8-pane glazed doors opening to shelves, keyed through-

tenons on the base, original iron hardware, cleaned finish, unsigned Gustav Stickley Model No. 718, 13 x 47", 56" h. **6,600**

Gustav Stickley Bookcase

Mission-style (Arts & Crafts movement) bookcase, oak, a rectangular top w/a low three-quarters gallery w/gently arched end board w/flush tenons, the case w/a pair of tall 8-pane glazed cupboard doors opening to shelves, original iron hardware, branded mark & paper label of Gustav Stickley, Model No. 717, recent finish, 13 x 48", 56" h. (ILLUS.) **5,225**

Mission-style (Arts & Crafts movement) bookcase, oak, a low three-quarter gallery top above three inset tall doors, each w/a geometrically leaded-glass top panel above a single long rectangular glass panel opening to shelves, new square hammered-copper pulls, decal mark of the Charles Limbert Furniture Co., 12 x 54", 57½" h. (some touch-ups to original finish) **1,100**

Stickley Brothers Bookcase

Mission-style (Arts & Crafts movement) bookcase, oak, a rectangular long top w/arch-centered backsplash & round-topped corner stiles framing the long case w/three doors, each door w/a narrow panel of two rows of caramel slag-glass squares above pairs of plain glass tall narrow panels opening to adjustable shelves, original copper hardware, fine original finish, unsigned Stickley Brothers, 12 x 59", 60" h. (ILLUS.) **5,225**

Regency-Style "breakfront" bookcase, rosewood, a rectangular top w/a stepped-out wide central section all w/a flaring molded cornice, the narrow stepped-back side sections each w/six open adjustable shelves, the center w/additional open adjustable shelves above & below a reeded medial band, molded plinth base, England, late 19th - early 20th c., 100" w., 100" h. **7,763**

Turn-of-the-century bookcase, oak, the rectangular top w/narrow molded edges above a frieze band w/a half-round horizontal colonette above the tall glazed door opening to four shelves, raised on simple bracket feet, ca. 1910, 13 x 26", 56" h. **316**

Turn-of-the-century bookcase, quarter-sawn oak, lawyer's stacking-type, four-section, each rectangular section w/a rectangular glass lift-front door, curved top edge molding, raised on short cabriole front legs, ca. 1900, marked "Macey," 12 x 34", 59" h. **748**

Lawyer's Stacking-Type Oak Bookcase

Turn-of-the-century bookcase, quarter-sawn oak, lawyer's stacking-type, three sections, the top w/a rectangular top & plain frieze band above the lift-front glazed door above two additional lift-front

sections on a rectangular base w/short square stile legs, labeled "Macey," early 20th c., 11½ x 34", 47" h. (ILLUS.). **330**

Turn-of-the-century bookcase, quarter-sawn oak, lawyer's stacking-type, three sections w/a flat three-quarter gallery on the rectangular top over the three sections w/a glazed lift-front door, raised on an aproned base w/short square legs, marked "Globe-Wernicke," old mellow finish, ca. 1910, 11½ x 34", 53" h. **550**

Golden Oak Bookcase

Victorian bookcase, Golden Oak style, the narrow rectangular top w/a high three-quarter gallery w/a central rolled crest bar above a rounded cornice band over a pair of large single-pane glazed doors opening to eight adjustable shelves, flared molded base on simple bracket feet, ca. 1900-10, 14 x 49", 64" h. (ILLUS.) . . . **633**

Fine Renaissance Revival Bookcase

Victorian bookcase, Renaissance Revival substyle, walnut w/ebonized panels, breakfront-style, two-part construction: the stepped rectangular top fitted w/an ornate scroll-cut crest w/incised scrolls & ebonized panels flanked by turned corner finials, the stepped-out central section w/an ebonized frieze band over the tall arched glazed door w/ebonized banding opening to shelves flanked by two matching shorter set-back doors flanked by chamfered front corners; the lower stepped-out base section w/three conforming drawers w/ebonized panels on a molded plinth base w/chamfered front corners, ca. 1875, originally from important Iowa mansion, 16 x 101", 114" h. (ILLUS.) **11,500**

BUREAUX PLAT

Empire-Style Bureau Plat

Empire-Style bureau plat, gilt-bronze mounted mahogany, the rectangular top w/inset tooled leather writing surface, above an apron w/a center long drawer flanked by two short drawers all w/ormolu mounts including an urn flanked by classic lions & scrolled keyhole escutcheons, each corner block w/an ormolu lyre mount, raised on tapering round legs surmounted by a winged classical bust & terminating in a lion's paw ormolu mount, France, late 19th c., 29½ x 47½", 29" h. (ILLUS.) **11,500**

Louis XV-Style Bureau Plat

Louis XV-Style bureau plat, gilt-bronze mounted fruitwood, the rectangular top inset w/a leather writing surface & w/gilt-bronze rounded corner mounts above the scalloped veneered apron w/a long center drawer flanked by shorter, deeper drawers all w/gilt-bronze bail pulls & shield-form keyhole escutcheons as well as scrolled feather gilt-bronze edge mounts & mask & scroll corner mounts above the simple cabriole legs ending in gilt-bronze lion's paw feet, France, late 19th c., 37 x 74", 32" h. (ILLUS.) **11,500**

Louis XV-Style bureau plat, gilt-bronze mounted tulipwood, the shaped rectangular top w/a gilt-tooled leather inset writing surface within a gilt-bronze band above a shaped apron w/two deep round-edged drawers flanking a long shallower central drawer on one side opposed by matching faux drawers each w/scrolled bronze mounts, on cabriole legs headed by pierced foliate-case chutes & ending in scrolled sabots, France, late 19th c., 48" l., 31" h. **6,900**

Napoleon III-Style Bureau Plat

Napoleon III-Style bureau plat, ebonized & gilt-trimmed wood, the rectangular top w/gilt tooled leather writing surface above a shaped apron w/a narrow long central drawer flanked by shorter, deeper end drawers, all w/gilt banding & gilt-bronze banding, pulls & leafy scroll mounts, on tapering reeded legs headed by gilt leaf clusters & gilt-bronze corner block mounts & terminating in gilt-bronze capped feet, late 19th c., 32 x 60", 30" h. (ILLUS.) **6,900**

CABINETS

China cabinet, turn-of-the-century Golden Oak style, a demi-lune top above a conforming case w/a curved top frieze centered at the front by a straight rounded bar above a long single pane glazed door flanked by carved lions on monopodia over half-round columns, curved glass sides, opening to three wooden shelves, narrow molded apron raised on four short cabriole legs ending in paw feet, lions w/added "jeweled" eyes, ca. 1900, 14 x 39¾", 65" h. **1,073**

Fine Limbert China Cabinet

China cabinet, Mission-style (Arts & Crafts movement), oak, a high gently arched crestrail w/a plate rail above the rectangular top overhanging a tall case w/molded corbels under each corner above a pair of tall glazed doors w/a small rectangular pane over a tall pane w/original copper strap hinges, a long drawer across the bottom w/original copper hardware, original shelves, original finish, branded Limbert company signature, Model No. 1468, 17 x 48", 62" h. (ILLUS.)....................... **4,950**

China cabinet, Mission-style (Arts & Crafts movement), oak, a high rounded crestboard above the trapezoidal top w/a projecting center above a pair of tall doors w/four square panes above a large single pane, glazed sides, arched aprons, five heavy stile legs, original copper pulls, refinished, branded mark of the Charles Limbert Co., Model No. 428, 19 x 40", 63" h. **4,675**

China cabinet, Mission-style (Arts & Crafts movement), oak, a rectangular top w/a low three-quarters gallery w/gently arched ends above a pair of tall 8-pane glazed cupboard doors opening to shelves, 8-pane glazed sides, raised on sides w/arched cut-out feet, original brass hardware, lightly cleaned original finish, branded & paper label marks of Gustav Stickley, Model No. 815, minor distress to the top, 15 x 42", 64" h................ **8,800**

China cabinet, Mission-style (Arts & Crafts style), oak, the rectangular top w/a plate rail above a tall case w/a pair of 8-pane glazed doors opening to shelves, 4-pane side panels, original copper hardware, original finish, Stickley Brothers, illegible model number, 17 x 42", 64" h. **3,575**

Turn-of-the-century China Cabinet

China cabinet, turn-of-the-century, oak, D-form top above deep cornice over conforming case w/long curved glass sides flanking a tall flat glazed door opening to four wooden shelves & a mirror in the upper half, molded base on four bun feet, ca. 1900, 15 x 48", 65" h. (ILLUS.)............................ **1,093**

Ornate Oak China Cabinet

China cabinet, turn-of-the-century, carved oak, D-form serpentine top w/outset half-round projections above a leafy scroll-carved cornice above a conforming case w/the top projections over tall reeded & carved columns headed by carved lions' heads w/"jeweled" eyes, over pilasters on each side of the tall curved glass central door, all flanked by curved glass sides, molded base on two large paw front feet & two plain back feet, four interior shelves, ca. 1900, 20 x 49", 70¾" h. (ILLUS.)............................ **2,090**

China Cabinet with Mirrored Crest

China cabinet, turn-of-the-century, oak, D-form top w/a high mirrored back crest w/a flat top & leafy scroll-carved rounded corners, the front w/a flat crest over a curved glass tall door opening to four shelves & flanked by slender columns headed by narrow carved lion head monopeds w/"jeweled" eyes & ending in short cabriole front legs w/paw feet, curved glass sides, outswept square back legs, original alligatored finish, ca. 1900, 15¾ x 38½", 72⅝" h. (ILLUS.)........... **1,045**

Corner cabinet, Mission-style (Arts & Crafts movement), oak, a low gallery on the top above a pair of two cupboard doors each w/two tall panes of glass opening to shelves above a small central drawer over two paneled cupboard doors w/metal hardware, fine original dark finish, branded mark of Gustav Stickley, early 20th c., 29 x 41", 72¼" h. **27,500**

Display cabinet, Victorian Aesthetic Movement substyle, ebonized wood, the arched top w/gallery above an inset panel over a galleried shelf, a central beveled glass cabinet door enclosing shelves & flanked by shelves, above a drawer, on stylized feet, last quarter 19th c., 11 x 44", 79" h. (lacking inset panel, minor losses) **978**

Filing cabinet, Mission-style (Arts & Crafts movement), oak, stacking-type, four rectangular panel-fronted drawers w/brass name plate holders & loop handles vertically arranged on short square legs, paneled sides, ca. 1910, 15 x 24", 60" h........................ **288**

Turn-of-the-century Filing Cabinet

Filing cabinet, turn-of-the-century, oak, a rectangular flat top above a stack of four deep square drawers w/brass rectangular name tag holders & simple curved pulls, flat base, refinished, ca. 1900-20, 16½ x 25", 51½" h. (ILLUS.).............. **358**

Music cabinet, Victorian, walnut, a rectangular top w/molded cornice above a thin punched design band over the single door w/two recessed panels each w/punched rectangular designs in the panels & small punched panels at top, bottom & sides of the door, two narrow drawers w/further punched detail below, molded base on porcelain casters, door opens to four adjustable shelves, old varnish finish, 16¼ x 22", 37½" h. **440**

Sewing cabinet, Mission-style (Arts & Crafts movememt), oak, a square top flanked by wide drop leaves above the deep apron w/a stack of two short drawers w/original copper ring pulls, square stile legs, cleaned original finish, some restoration to the top, unsigned Gustav Stickley, Model No. 630, 18" sq., 28" h. **1,210**

Art Deco Side Cabinet

Side cabinet, Art Deco style, chrome-mounted rosewood & burlwood, a narrow stepped rectangular black marble top w/wide central section w/a pair of flat cupboard doors in light wood flanked by graduated stacks of four drawers each, all on a high plinth base, repairs, losses to veneer, France, ca. 1930, 19½ x 58", 39½" h. (ILLUS.) **2,070**

Chinese Coromandel Side Cabinet

Side cabinet, Coromandel-type, lacquered, the rectangular top above a pair of tall paneled doors each incised & lacquered w/Chinese figures in interiors, landscapes & pavilions, birds & flowers in side panels & delicated floral border bands, raised on bracket feet, China, 19th c., 16 x 30", 46" h. (ILLUS.) **1,955**

Napoleon III Decorated Side Cabinet

Side cabinet, Napoleon III, gilt-bronze mounted marquetry-inlaid, a rectangular top w/outset rounded corners & a slightly outset central section above a conforming frieze band w/gilt classical banded

designs above a conforming case w/the central cupboard door painted w/a panel depicting 18th-century lovers in a landscape, the narrow painted side panels w/a slender rod trimmed w/a bow & ribbons & leafy vines, gilt-bronze banding & carved & reeded colonettes at each corner, conforming plinth base, some damages, France, late 19th c., 17 x 52", 42½" h. (ILLUS.). **3,220**

Neoclassical Revival Side Cabinet

Side cabinet, Neoclassical Revival style, painted wood, a tall flat rectangular superstructure w/upper painted rectangular panel of 17th c. figures in a landscape above a large nearly square mirror bordered by molded bow & leafy vines both flanked by tall slender panels w/molded clusters of trophies at the top & a classical urn at the bottom, all above the rectangular top w/molded edge above a cupboard w/a pair of flat flush cupboard doors painted w/a continuous oval landscape reserve w/delicate leafy scrolls above & below & flanked by narrow painted side panels, on short square legs, pale green ground w/gilt & polychrome painting, France, superstructure 19th c., base 20th c., wear, edge damage & paint touch-up, 12 x 48", 94½" h. (ILLUS.). **1,650**

Vice cabinet, Mission-style (Arts & Crafts movement), oak, a thick rectangular top above a deep apron w/a long drawer front over a pair of small drawer fronts over another long drawer front, four of the six fronts being false to hide a wine rack & a compartment accessible from a swiveling top, original dark finish, early 20th c., 12 x 20", 29" h. **715**

Vitrine cabinet, Louis VX-Style, ormolu-mounted mahogany & mahogany veneer, a rectangular marble top above a frieze band & raised center panel w/ormolu leaf sprigs flanked at the corners by ormolu cherub head mounts all above a wide single pane glazed door w/ormolu inner banding & an arched bottom rim opening to two glass shelves & a silk-lined back, the lower door w/a burl panel mounted w/a large ormolu leaf cluster, the short curved apron w/a long leafy ormolu mount flanked by cabriole legs w/long leafy scroll ormolu mounts at the knees, glass sides, early 20th c., 14 x 28", 65" h.... **3,410**

Vitrine cabinet, Louis XV-Style "Vernis Martin" style, a D-form top above a glazed center door flanked by curved glass sides all w/lower painted figural panels, short shaped legs, Europe, late 19th c., 15 x 28", 56" h. **977**

One of Two Victorian Vitrine Cabinets

a deep molded base w/bead-trimmed disk-topped peg feet, Europe, late 19th c., 10 x 28", 29½" h., pr. (ILLUS. of one) **5,980**

CHAIRS

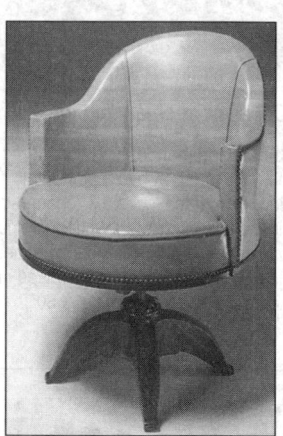

Ruhlmann Art Deco Desk Chair

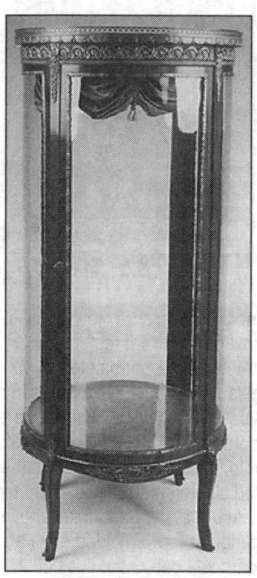

Louis XVI-Style Round Vitrine

Vitrine cabinet, Louis XVI-Style, gilt-metal mounted mahogany, round marble top w/a low pierced gilt-metal gallery above a conforming case w/four curved sides, two forming doors, doors w/thin gilt-metal banded trim w/further trim on the narrow rounded apron, raised on simple cabriole legs ending in sabots, France, late 19th to early 20th c., 25¾" d., 59" h. (ILLUS.).... **3,738**

Vitrine cabinets, Victorian, ormolu-mounted inlaid satinwood, each w/oblong crossbanded molded top w/canted corners above glazed sides & a glazed door, the door w/an arched pane below a delicate inlaid leafy swag band, raised on

Art Deco desk chair, upholstered rosewood, the arched upholstered back sloping down to raised closed arms above a round deep upholstered seat, raised on a round rosewood frame above a central pivoting mechanism, further raised on four arched tapering wide flat legs, mustard yellow leather upholstery, branded "Ruhlmann B.," Emile-Jacques Ruhlmann, France, ca. 1926 (ILLUS.)..... **29,900**

Art Nouveau armchair, carved mahogany, the arched pierced crestrail carved w/clematis blossoms & leaves fanned above a solid center panel flanked by upholstered back panels, the top continuing to molded & carved wing arms flanking the upholstered seat above a serpentine & scroll-carved apron above slightly canted squared legs, modern blue suede upholstery, Louis Majorelle, France, ca. 1900 . . . . **7,475**

Early Campeche Lolling Chair

Campeche armchair, lolling-type, walnut, tall back w/rolled flat crestrail flanked by stiles continuing down to upcurved seat, small truncated wings at top sides, flat S-scroll open arms on shaped arm supports, inverted-U legs joined by squared & shaped cross-stretchers, old webbing, Southern United States, first half 19th c. (ILLUS.) **8,338**

Chippendale Armchair with Wingback

Chippendale armchair w/wingback, upholstered mahogany, the serpentine crest above the curving wings & outwardly scrolling arms flanking a cushioned seat & upholstered apron, on square molded legs joined by square molded stretchers to the raking rear legs, old surface, surface imperfections, New England, 1780-1800, 48½" h. (ILLUS.) **7,475**

Country Chippendale Side Chair

Chippendale country-style side chair, cherry, serpentine crestrail w/flared ears over a loop-pierced splat between raked stiles, upholstered slip seat on square beaded legs, old surface, crewel-worked seat cover in golds & blues, Connecticut, 1770-1800, imperfections, 37¾" h. (ILLUS.) . . **690**

Chippendale country-style side chair, tiger stripe maple, serpentine crestrail w/raked molded ears above a pierced splat, old rush seat & block- and vase-turned front legs joined by a turned stretcher, old refinish, Connecticut River Valley, 39" h. (imperfections) **863**

Chippendale "ladder-back" side chairs, carved mahogany, a serpentine crestrail pierced w/a central circle & scrolls & w/a beaded edge above three matching slats between the raked molded stiles over the trapezoidal upholstered slip seat, on square beaded legs joined by box stretchers, old refinish, probably Philadelphia, ca. 1780, 37½" h., pr. (minor imperfections) **1,725**

Philadelphia Chippendale Chair

Chippendale side chair, carved mahogany, serpentine crestrail w/decorated carved scrolls & flaring ears above a lattice-carved back splat between carved canted stiles over the molded upholstered slip seat accented by pierced brackets & flanked by square molded legs, old refinish, Philadelphia, 1770-85, imperfections (ILLUS.). **2,185**

Carved Mahogany Chippendale Chair

Chippendale side chair, carved mahogany, the serpentine crestrail w/leaf carving & molded ears above the carved pierced scrolled splat flanked by raked stiles joined to the frontal cabriole legs ending in pad feet w/block-turned stretchers, old refinish, missing returns, other imperfections, Massachusetts, ca. 1780, 37½" h. (ILLUS.) **1,380**

Carved Chippendale Side Chair

Chippendale side chair, carved mahogany, the shaped leaf-, scroll- and ruffle-carved crestrail flanked by leaf-carved ears above a pierced strapwork splat, gadrooned shoe & trapezoidal slip

seat flanked by wavy stiles, the shaped molded seat frame below on leaf-, bellflower-, and scroll-carved cabriole legs ending in scroll feet, possibly Southern United States, crack to crest at juncture w/splat, 1740-70, 38½" h. (ILLUS.). **4,025**

Massachusetts Chippendale Chair

Chippendale side chair, carved walnut, serpentine crestrail w/raked ears above the pierced splat w/C-scrolls & lattice over the upholstered compass slip seat over cabriole front legs ending in high pad feet, raking rear legs, old refinish, restoration to stiles, Boston or Salem, Massachusetts, 1760-80, 38½" h. (ILLUS.). . **2,185**

Chippendale "Ladder-back" Side Chair

Chippendale side chair, mahogany, four serpentine pierced horizontal splats above an over-upholstered seat & stop-fluted front legs joined to the raking rear legs by square stretchers, old dark surface, Rhode Island, 1775-1810, minor imperfections, 36½" h. (ILLUS.) **1,150**

Chippendale side chair, mahogany, the serpentine crest w/molded ears above a pierced strapwork splat, the overupholstered seat raised on angular cabriole legs joined by turned stretchers & ending in pad feet, New England, third quarter 18th c. **1,092**

New Hampshire Chippendale Chair

Chippendale side chair, mahogany, the serpentine crestrails w/central piercing & beaded edge above a scrolled pierced splat flanked by gently outswept stiles over the over-upholstered seat, on square molded legs joined by square stretchers, old surface, minor repairs, attributed to Robert Harrold, 1765-75, Portsmouth, New Hampshire, 37" h. (ILLUS.)............................ **1,955**

Chippendale side chair, carved mahogany, the oxyoke crestrail w/upswept molded ears above a scroll-pierced vasiform splat & raked stiles over the trapezoidal slip seat, front cabriole legs ending in pad feet on platforms, raked chamfered rear legs, Massachusetts, ca. 1780, old refinish, 37" h. **1,725**

Chippendale side chair, carved mahogany, a serpentine crestrail w/molded ears above a pierced Gothic design splat, molded seatrails w/upholstered seat, cabriole front legs ending in claw-and-ball feet, baluster- and block-turned stretchers joining front legs to rear chamfered raked legs, old refinish, Massachusetts, 1755-90, 36⅛" h. (minor surface abrasions) . **4,255**

Chippendale side chairs, transitional-style, painted & decorated wood, the serpentine oxbow crestrail w/outswept ears centered by a lunette over the vase-form loop-pierced splat over the upholstered slip seat, on square tapering legs joined by flat stretchers, later black paint w/gilt band trim, Newport, Rhode Island, or Connecticut, 1765-90, 37¾" h., pr. (repair to a foot)...................... **2,645**

Chippendale-Style Armchair

Chippendale transitional-style armchair, mahogany, the simple oxyoke crestrail w/rounded corners continuing into the inward curving stiles flanking the simple solid vasiform splat, shaped open arms w/scroll-carved hand grips on incurved arm supports, wide needlepoint-covered slip seat, plain curved seatrail over cabriole front legs w/acanthus leaf-carved knees & ending in heavy claw-and-ball feet, canted square rear legs joined to front legs w/a block- and reel-turned H-stretcher, old finish, late 19th - early 20th c., minor wear, 43¾" h. (ILLUS.) **275**

Queen Anne Chippendale-Style Chair

Chippendale transitional-style side chair, carved mahogany, the arched crestrail w/rounded corners centered by ornate leafy scroll section centering a flowerhead above the spooned solid vasiform splat, the tapering curved stiles above the upholstered balloon-form slip seat, curved plain seatrail above cabriole front legs ending in claw-and-ball feet, square canted rear legs w/spade feet, old finish, Centennial era, late 19th - early 20th c., 40" h. (ILLUS.) **358**

Chippendale-Style armchair, mahogany, the serpentined crestrail w/carved leafy scrolls above a pierced leafy scroll-carved vasiform splat flanked by molded stiles, serpentine open arms w/scroll-carved handholds on incurved arm supports flanking the wide overupholstered seat w/a thin gadroon-carved seatrail, cabriole front legs w/leafy scroll-carved knees & ending in claw-and-ball feet, canted square rear legs, old dark finish, early 20th c., 37½" h. (repairs, seat reupholstered) **330**

Chippendale-Style corner chair, a back-scrolled crestrail on a U-form even rail ending in shaped arms w/scrolled handholds above two scroll-bordered vase-form splats pierced w/a central spade design & alternating w/three ring-turned columnar spindles above the square upholstered slip seat, cabriole legs w/scrolled returns & ending in claw-and-ball feet joined by a turned cross-stretcher, old dark finish, early 20th c., 33½" h. (one arm w/age crack) **330**

Chippendale-Style side chair, mahogany, the serpentine crestrail w/carved swags above the ornately pierced looping splat flanked by the square slightly flaring stiles above the over-upholstered seat, cabriole front legs w/leafy scroll-carved knees & ending in claw-and-ball feet, square canted rear legs, Centennial-type, old refinishing, late 19th c., 38" h. **440**

Chippendale-Style side chairs, hardwood w/old brown finish, ladder-back style w/four pierced ribbon-form back slats flanked by molded stiles above the upholstered slip seat w/needlepoint upholstery, square molded legs joined by an H-stretcher, early 20th c., 37" h., set of 8............................ **1,144**

Chippendale-Style wing chair, the tall upholstered back w/a serpentine crest flanked by slightly curved upholstered wings above the rolled upholstered arms, cushion seat above the upholstered seatrail, on mahogany cabriole front legs w/leafy scroll-carved returns & ending in claw-and-ball feet, reupholstered, 20th c., 41" h......................... **385**

Classical side chairs, brass-inlaid & carved mahogany, a horizontal reverse-scrolling crest board above a pierced flowerhead- and leaf-carved lower rail, upholstered slip seat, on sabre legs, rich patina, nice old finish, New York City, ca. 1810, 32" h., set of 4 .... **5,175**

Classical side chairs, carved mahogany, gently curving & rolled veneered crestrail above a leaf-carved & pierced splat, upholstered slip-seat over a flat veneered

Baltimore Classical Side Chairs

seatrail between ring-, knob- and reeded rod-turned tapering legs w/pad feet, Baltimore, 1815-20, imperfections, 34½" h., set of 4 (ILLUS. of two) **805**

Classical side chairs, grain-painted, a curved horizontal crestrail atop stiles flanking a flat lower rail above the caned seat, on klysmos-type legs, original graining in imitation of rosewood w/gold accent striping, northern New England, ca. 1825-35, 33" h., set of 6 (imperfections) **1,380**

Classical side chairs, tiger stripe maple, stepped rectangular curved crestrail above angular-cut vase-form splat above the seat w/curving front rail, on flat Grecian legs, refinished, one branded "A.G. Case," Norwich, Connecticut area, 1830-50, 33½" h., set of 6 (caned seats missing, other imperfections) **3,105**

Woven Splint Armchairs

Country-style armchairs, stained maple, the squared back panel of tightly woven splint between projecting backswept stiles w/long shaped open arms on baluster-turned arm supports continuing down to form side braces, tightly woven splint seat, simple turned legs w/plain turned double front & side & rear stretchers, splints partially distressed, minor chips to feet, back of stiles worn, late 19th - early 20th c., 34½" h., pr. (ILLUS.) **805**

Country-style "banister-back" side chair, maple, the high scroll-cut crestrail between ring-, knob-, rod- and block-turned stiles w/mismatched turned finials flanking four split-banisters above a shaped base rail over the woven rush seat, knob- and block-turned front legs joined by a ring- and knob-turned front stretcher & plain side & back stretchers, on front knob feet, old refinish, New England, 18th c., 44½" h. **460**

Early "Ladder-Back" Armchair

Country-style "ladder-back" armchair, maple & ash, four arched slats joining knob- and rod-turned stiles w/knob finials over long scrolled arms on baluster- and knob-turned arm supports continuing into turned front legs, woven splint seat, double knob-turned front stretchers & plain double side stretchers, old painted surface, restored, probably Massachusetts, early 18th c., 45½" h. (ILLUS.) **546**

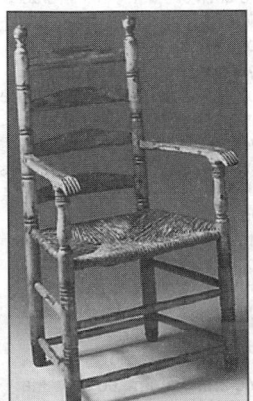

Painted New England "Ladder-back" Armchair

Country-style "ladder-back" armchair, painted birch & hickory, four arched back slats between sausage-turned stiles w/knob finials flanked by shaped arms w/fluted terminals, baluster-turned arm supports above the woven rush seat, ring- and rod-turned front legs joined by two ring-turned stretchers, double plain side stretchers, old yellow & red paint, losses to paint, height reduced, formerly fitted w/rockers, New England, 1700-40, 41¼" h. (ILLUS.). **920**

Danish Modern dining chairs, teak, each w/a swelled arched crestrail curving to form a U-form rail w/slender flattened open arms all supported on four slightly canted turned & swelled supports flanking the caned seat, designed by Hans Wegner, each branded "Johannes Hansen Copenhagen Denmark," ca. 1949, set of 12. . . . . **28,750**

Early American "ladder-back" side chair, maple, tall simple turned back stiles w/pointed knob finials flanking five arched slats, woven rush seat, baluster- and rod-turned front legs w/knob feet joined by a double-knob and ring-turned stretcher, double plain side stretchers & one at the back, found in Bucks County, Pennsylvania, reputed to have belonged to an early Quaker, old refinishing & rush seat, late 18th - early 19th c., 43¾" h. **605**

Federal Leather & Wood Armchair

Federal armchair, mahogany, butternut & leather, the ring-turned slender crestrail above the raking leather-upholstered back, downward scrolling open arms on urn-shaped arm supports on a wide leather-upholstered seat over ring- and baluster-turned tapering front legs on peg feet, square back stile legs, original surface & leather, minor imperfections, possibly Portsmouth, New Hampshire, early 19th c., 40" h. (ILLUS.) **1,150**

Federal "lolling" armchair, mahogany, the tall upholstered back w/a serpentine crest above molded open serpentine arms on slightly molded & incurved arm supports joining an over-upholstered seat on molded square front legs joined by square stretchers to the raking rear legs, muslin under-upholstery, Massachusetts, 1785-1800, 43¼" h. (minor imperfections) .. **4,255**

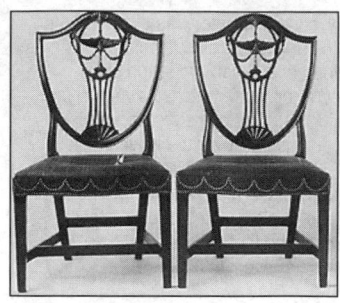

Part of Federal Shield-back Chair Set

Salem, Massachusetts, ca. 1795, four side chairs & matching armchair, armchair w/arm restoration, 37¾" h., the set (ILLUS. of two)................ **23,000**

Salem Federal Side Chair

Federal side chair, carved mahogany, the back w/an arched crestrail centered by a narrow tablet w/carved swags & draping on a star-punched background above thin latticework splats carved w/Neoclassical design, over-upholstered seat w/serpentine front seatrail over molded tapering front legs joined to canted rear legs by square stretchers, old refinish, minor repairs, Salem, Massachusetts, 1790-1800, 35½" h. (ILLUS.) **863**

Federal side chairs, carved mahogany, a gently arched & stepped crestrail on a square back w/Neoclassical carving on the tablet & beaded edges above reeded & carved criss-cross splats on a curved beaded stay rail over the over-upholstered seat w/bowed front seatrail, on square tapering front legs ending in spade feet joined by square stretchers to the raking rear legs, old surface, Salem, Massachusetts, ca. 1800, 35" h., set of 4 (very minor imperfections)............. **6,900**

Federal side chairs, carved mahogany, shield-back style, the arched & molded crestrail & molded stiles above a carved kylix splat w/festoons draped from flanking carved rosettes, above a pierced splat terminating in a carved lunette at its base above the molded rear seatrail & over-upholstered seat w/serpentine front, square tapering front & canted rear legs joined by flat stretchers, seats w/old black horsehair, old surface, Rhode Island or

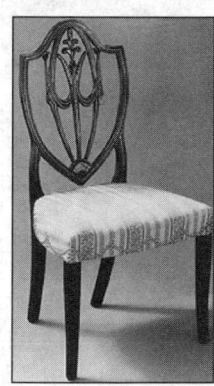

New York Shield-back Federal Chair

Federal side chairs, carved mahogany, shield-back style w/serpentine molded arched crestrail above a pierced splat carved w/swags, plumes & feathers, the over-upholstered seat below on square tapering molded front legs & gently canted rear legs, one w/repair to crest & patches to back of splat, other w/cracks to splat, New York, ca. 1795, 40" h., pr. (ILLUS. of one) **5,175**

Federal-Style armchair, mahogany & mahogany veneer w/inlay, a spiral-turned & leaf-carved straight crestrail atop backcurved stiles flanking a wide lower back rail w/line inlay, S-scroll open arms on reeded arm supports flanking the wide upholstered slip seat, narrow slightly straight seatrail between corner blocks above the front legs w/inverted acanthus-carved tops over tapering spiral-turned section ending in knob & peg feet, square canted rear legs, late 19th - early 20th c., 36¼" h............. **303**

Federal-Style armchair, mahogany, the squared upholstered back w/rounded corners above padded open arms on incurved molded arm supports, overupholstered curved seat, square tapering legs ending in spade feet, old dark finish, early 20th c., 35½" h. **303**

Hitchcock side chair, child's, painted & decorated, a rolled crest above a rectangular splat above the woven rush seat & ring-turned legs, black-painted ground, some of it wood-grained, & gold-leaf decoration, Hitchcocksville, Connecticut, early 19th c., 21" h. (minor surface imperfections) **863**

Hitchcock side chairs, rosewood-grained surface w/the original gilt decoration including an urn centering the cornucopia-form splat, old rush seat, ring-turned legs, original surface, Hitchcocksville, Connecticut, 1830s, 35½" h., set of 4 . . . . **1,265**

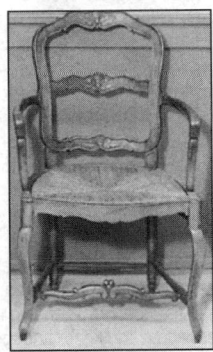

French Provincial-Style Armchair

Louis XV Provincial-Style armchair, carved hardwood, the arched serpentined crestrail w/leaf carving continuing to oblong back frame w/serpentine carved medial rail, slender curved open arms on incurved arm supports over the woven rush seat, curved front seatrail w/scalloped rim, simple cabriole front legs w/scroll-carved stretchers, plain turned side & back stretchers, worn brown finish, France, late 19th - early 20th c., 37¼" h. (ILLUS.) **138**

Louis XV Revival armchair w/wingback, the narrow walnut gently arched crestrail centered by a scroll-carved boss & continuing to form the framing of the rounded, tapering side wings continuing to the padded arms w/carved grips, incurved carved arm supports flank the upholstered back, wings & spring seat, gently serpentine seatrail carved w/a central leafy scroll & border scrolls, simple cabriole legs w/carved knees ending in scroll & peg feet, France, late 19th - early 20th c., reupholstered, 42½" h. (some frame damage). **440**

Mission-style (Arts & Crafts movement) armchair, oak, a wide gently curved upper & lower rail flanking the three wide slats between square stiles above flat shaped arms above front stile legs w/corbels, recovered drop-in leather cushion seat, wide box stretchers, original finish, branded mark of Charles Limbert Co., Model No. 931, 24 x 28", 37" h. **880**

Mission-style (Arts & Crafts movement) armchair, oak, a wide gently curved crestrail w/a square cut-out at each end between the square stiles & a single lower slat, flat curved arms above square stile legs w/top corbels, high flat front stretcher & low flat stretchers at the side & back, original finish, branded mark of the Limbert Furniture Co., 38" h. (torn original woven rush seat) **990**

Mission-style (Arts & Crafts movement) armchair, oak, a wide peaked crestrail above five narrow slats between the narrow stiles, flat shaped arms on slender square front stile legs, drop-in recovered leather cushion seat, "The Work of..." mark of L. & J.G. Stickley, Model No. 810, 39" h. **440**

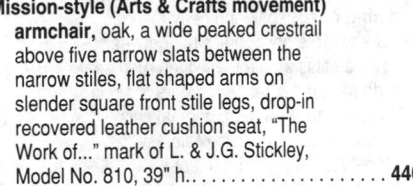

Gustav Stickley Armchair

Mission-style (Arts & Crafts movement) armchair, oak, a top & lower back rail flanking three wide slats between the slender square back stiles over flat shaped arms on square front leg stiles w/corbels under the arms, replaced upholstered seat, recent finish, unsigned Gustav Stickley, Model No. 340, 41" h. (ILLUS.) **605**

Mission-style (Arts & Crafts movement) cube chair, oak, a wide crestrail above two vertical slats flanked by low stiles projecting slightly above the thick rectangular arms each over two slats, through-tenons on apron rails, deep drop-in spring seat, original dark finish, decal mark of Ritter Craft, 25¾ x 27", 32" h. **605**

Mission-style (Arts & Crafts movement) desk chair, oak, the back w/three vertical slats between upper & lower rails & square stiles forming rear legs, single high flat front & rear stretchers & double side stretchers, original finish, branded mark of L. & J.G. Stickley, 36" h. (recovered leather seat) **413**

Mission-style (Arts & Crafts movement) dining chairs, oak, each w/a narrow curved crestrail above a single back splat flanked by slender square stiles & a lower rail raised above the trapezoidal seat w/replaced inset tacked-in seat inserts, square legs w/box stretchers, original dark finish, branded mark of the Charles Limbert Furniture Co., six side chairs Model No. 911 & two armchairs Model No. 613, 37" h., set of 8. . . . . **3,080**

Mission-style (Arts & Crafts movement) dining chairs, oak, the heavy ladder-back w/three horizontal slats between square stiles above the woven rush seat, wide flat front & rear stretchers & small double side stretchers, original finish, faint signature of Gustav Stickley, Model No. 349, 37" h., set of 4 (two seats replaced) **3,300**

Mission-style (Arts & Crafts movement) Morris chair, a slatted adjustable back above wide flat arms on heavy square stile legs w/underarm corbels flanking five slats, wide front apron, new dark finish, paper label of J.M. Young, 37" h. (loose seat & back cushions) **3,300**

Mission-style (Arts & Crafts movement) Morris chair, the adjustable back w/a wide curved top slat above three lower slats between the heavy stiles, wide flat shaped arms above pairs of slats & stile legs w/corbels, wide lower side stretchers, original sling cushion seat, recent finish, unsigned Gustav Stickley, Model No. 2341, 30 x 34", 39" h. **3,575**

Mission-style (Arts & Crafts movement) Morris rocking chair, oak, the adjustable back w/horizontal slats above wide flat shaped arms on front leg supports w/corbels, recovered original back & seat cushions, recoated original finish, unsigned L. & J.G. Stickley, 40" h. **1,045**

Mission-style (Arts & Crafts movement) rocking chair w/arms, oak, the tall back composed of five slats between the square stiles, flat shaped arms above vertical slats & front corbels on the stile legs, deep apron, on rockers, branded signature mark of Gustav Stickley, Model No. 323, 29 x 33", 40" h. (replaced cushions, one rocker replaced) **1,870**

Gustav Stickley Sewing Rocker

Mission-style (Arts & Crafts movement) sewing rocker, oak, an H-style back w/a single wide slat notched at the top & bottom, above a drop-in seat w/original Japan leather, mint original finish, branded Gustav Stickley mark, 34" h. (ILLUS.) **413**

Modern style rocking chair w/arms, fiberglass, metal & wood, the molded fiberglass U-form seat w/arched back & rolled arms in salmon raised on slender black wire struts w/curved birch rockers, designed by Charles Eames, label of Herman Miller Co., ca. 1950, 27" h. **1,540**

Pilgrim Century "Great" chair, turned & painted, the knob- and rod-turned stiles w/knob finials joining three flattened-arch slats & shaped flat open arms ending in a knob handrest above the knob- and rod-turned front legs, simple turned double rungs in from sides & single rung at back, woven rush seat, old red paint, southern New England, late 17th c., 43" h. (imperfections) **4,025**

Queen Anne corner chair, maple, the curved shaped crest continuing to form arms on curved armrests over three ring-turned tapering stiles centered leg twin trapezoidal splats, the trapezoidal slip-seat on front cabriole legs ending in a pad foot, New England, 18th c. **1,500**

Queen Anne Corner Chair

Queen Anne corner chair, walnut, U-form crestrail w/raised center continuing to form flat scrolled arms above two wide scroll-cut vase-form splats & three ring-, rod- and knob-turned spindles, upholstered compass seat, front cabriole leg ending in pad foot & three simple turned legs w/pad feet, block-, rod- and baluster-turned cross-stretchers, old refinish, restored, southern New England, 18th c., 29⅝" h. (ILLUS.) **2,990**

Queen Anne Corner Commode Chair

Queen Anne corner commode chair, maple, U-form back crestrail w/raised center section & continuing to scrolled arms over two slender vase-form splats & three ring- and rod-turned spindles over the upholstered molded seat, deep scalloped aprons, cabriole frontal leg w/deep pad foot, turned & swelled side & back legs, old refinish, minor imperfections, New England, 18th c., 31" h. (ILLUS.) **2,070**

Queen Anne side chair, carved cherry, the bow-form crestrail w/curved & curled ears on slightly canted flat stiles flanking the vasiform splat & shaped upholstered slip seat within arched rails, on cabriole front legs & square canted rear legs joined by baluster- and block-turned stretcher & ending in pad feet, old & possibly original finish, Massachusetts, 1730-50, 39" h. **2,587**

Queen Anne side chair, walnut, the serpentine crestrail w/upturned ears above a vasiform splat, raked stiles, molded seatrails frame the upholstered seat, front cabriole legs ending in pad feet, joined to rear legs w/block- and vase-turned stretchers, old refinish, die-branded under front seatrail "F. Shaw," Massachusetts, 18th c., 37¼" h. (restored, imperfections) **805**

Queen Anne side chairs, carved walnut, shaped crestrail w/volute-carved ears above a pierced beaker-form splat, upholstered slip seat over scalloped front apron & cabriole front legs ending in trifid

Queen Anne Walnut Side Chair

feet, turned & canted rear legs, chocolate brown color, old finish, Mid-Atlantic States, ca. 1740, 40" h., pr. (ILLUS. of one) **10,925**

Queen Anne-Style side chair, mahogany, the tall back w/an oxyoke crestrail w/rounded corners & tall spooned stiles flanking the tall solid vasiform splat, trapezoidal upholstered slip seat, slightly shaped front seatrail on cabriole front legs w/scroll-cut returns & ending in pad feet, canted square rear legs, old worn finish, early 20th c., 44" h. **83**

Queen Anne-Style wing chair, the high upholstered back flanked by rounded tapering wings above outrolled upholstered arms, cushion seat over the upholstered seatrail, simple cabriole front legs ending in pad feet, square canted rear legs, modern reproduction w/striped velvet upholstery, 46" h. **248**

Salem-type rocking chair w/arms, child's, painted & decorated, the flat crestrail w/around corners decorated w/painted flowers & leaves above canted turned stiles flanking four slender spindles, S-shaped arms on canted, turned arm supports & one spindle over the deeply S-shaped seat, turned front legs joined by turned rung above inset rockers, old blue w/striping & polychrome crest, New England, mid-19th c., 24¾" h. (surface imperfections). **316**

Turn-of-the-century armchair, mahogany-finished hardwood, the wide arched crestrail carved w/a grotesque Old Man of the North face over a grouping of five baluster- and knob-turned slender spindles all between slender stiles & shaped open arms ending in scrolled grips over incurved arm supports, the wide shaped seat raised on cabriole front legs ending in claw-and-ball feet & square canted rear legs joined by swelled box stretchers, old dark worn finish, early 20th c., 36½" h. **193**

Victorian Aesthetic Movement Armchair

Gothic Revival Armchair

Victorian Aesthetic Movement corner armchairs, ebonized & parcel-gilt, flat crestrails forming square corner w/each back section centered by a panel of gilt stenciled stylized birds & geometric designs flanked by short ring-turned spindles all raised above the over-upholstered seat on a line-incised gilt-trimmed seatrail on chamfered legs ending in casters, Kimbel and Cabus, New York, New York, ca. 1870s, 27½" h., pr. (ILLUS. of one) **4,485**

Victorian gentleman's armchair, Rococo substyle, rosewood & rosewood veneer, the wide waisted balloon back w/a raised & scroll-carved crest on the finger-molded back frame enclosing the tufted upholstered back raised above the over-upholstered spring seat, curved padded open arms on incurved molded arm supports, serpentine finger-molded seatrail on demi-cabriole front legs w/bead-carved knees, old finish, mid 19th c., 42¼" h. (age cracks, repairs to frame, reupholstered) **330**

Victorian gentleman's armchair, Rococo substyle, walnut, the waisted upholstered balloon back w/a low arched leaf & rose-carved crest above the finger-molded frame, padded curved open arms raised on incurved molded arm supports over the upholstered spring seat, serpentine seatrail w/a carved central medallion, demi-cabriole front legs w/rose & leaf carving at the knees & raised on casters, old worn refinishing, ca. 1860, 43" h. (repairs to frame) **358**

Victorian Gothic Revival hall armchair, walnut, the tall back w/a Gothic arch-pointed crest w/spire finial over carved rails & a panel w/pierced trefoils, a diamond & a raised ring band over the tall arched upholstered back panels flanked by free-standing squared stiles & low

padded three-quarter arms on curved supports, upholstered seat on front seatrail w/raised burl panels, ring-, rod- and knob-turned front legs on casters, 19th c., 70" h. (ILLUS.) **518**

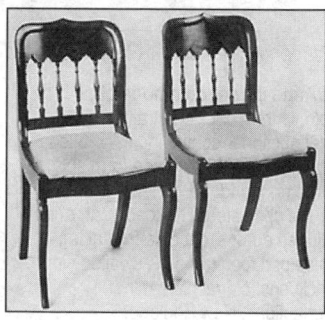

Victorian Gothic Revival Side Chairs

Victorian Gothic Revival side chairs, mahogany & mahogany veneer, rounded & peaked molded crestrail over a veneered panel above four slender ring- and baluster-turned spindles forming five Gothic arches, the lower rail raised above the upholstered slip seat, simple flattened cabriole front legs & canted rear legs, ca. 1850, 32" h., set of 10 (ILLUS. of two) . . . **1,380**

Victorian Gothic Revival substyle side chairs, mahogany veneer, each w/a flat crestrail pierced w/three trefoils above three arch-topped slats between the molded stiles, back frame raised above the over-upholstered seat w/curved, veneered seatrail, simple flattened cabriole front legs, old refinish, New York City, ca. 1850, 33½" h., set of 8 (new upholstery, minor imperfections) **6,900**

Victorian Rococo substyle armchair, laminated carved rosewood, the high balloon back w/a raised arched crestrail w/gadroon-carved border flanking a

"Stanton Hall" Pattern Chairs

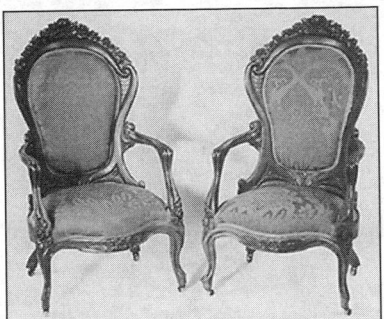

Rococo Carved Rosewood Armchairs

central carved painted crest all above
pierce-carved rail continuing to flaring
pierce-carved back stiles flanking the
waisted oblong upholstered back panels
raised on open arched supports & flanked
by padded open arms on molded
incurved arm supports flanking the deep,
wide upholstered seat w/serpentine front
seatrail carved banding & central
cartouche, demi-cabriole front legs,
curved & canted rear legs, "Stanton Hall"
patt., attributed to J. & J. Meeks, New
York, ca. 1855, old needlepoint
upholstery, minor age cracks, 43¾" h.
(ILLUS. center) **3,410**

Victorian Rococo substyle side chair,
carved laminated rosewood, high arched
crestrail w/gadroon-carved rails flanking a
carved pointed central cartouche all over
a scrolling pierce-carved rail continuing
down to pierce-carved wide side rails
flanking the waisted tufted upholstered
back panel raised on scrolls over the
round deep upholstered seat on a mold-
carved round seatrail w/central carved
cartouche, demi-cabriole front legs on
casters, canted rear legs, slightly worn
velvet upholstery, minor age cracks,
"Stanton Hall" patt., attributed to J. & J.
Meeks, New York, ca. 1855, 41" h.
(ILLUS. left) **1,760**

Victorian Rococo substyle side chair,
carved laminated rosewood, high arched
crestrail w/gadroon-carved rails flanking a
carved pointed central cartouche all over
a scrolling pierce-carved rail continuing
down to pierce-carved wide side rails
flanking the waisted tufted upholstered
back panel raised on scrolls over the
round deep upholstered seat on a mold-
carved round seatrail w/central carved
cartouche, demi-cabriole front legs on
casters, canted rear legs, colorful floral
brocade upholstery, minor age cracks,
"Stanton Hall" patt., attributed to J. & J.
Meeks, New York, ca. 1855, 40½" h.
(ILLUS. right) **1,870**

Victorian Rococo substyle armchairs,
carved laminated rosewood, the tall
balloon back w/an arched crestrail topped
by a carved band of realistic florals, the
crestrail continuing to long S-scroll side
rails flanking the waisted upholstered
back panels raised on leaf-carved panels
over the wide upholstered seat flanked by
open curved & carved arms, serpentine
seatrail w/central carved leaf & flower
band, demi-cabriole front legs w/floral-
carved knees, curved & canted square
rear legs all on casters, rust colored
damask upholstery, probably New York
City, ca. 1850s, 43¼" h., pr. (ILLUS.) **6,038**

Rare Labeled Belter Side Chairs

Victorian Rococo substyle side chairs,
carved laminated rosewood, the high
arched & pierced floral-carved crestrail
w/an arched floral-carved crest, top rail
continuing halfway down the sides to
large carved C-scrolls over S-scroll rails
flanking further pierce-carved florals, oval
upholstered back panel & upholstered
seat w/serpentine seatrail carved
w/ornate floral clusters in the center & at
the corners above the demi-cabriole front
legs on casters, square curved & canted
rear legs on casters, labeled by John
Henry Belter, New York, ca. 1855, pr.
(ILLUS.) **31,900**

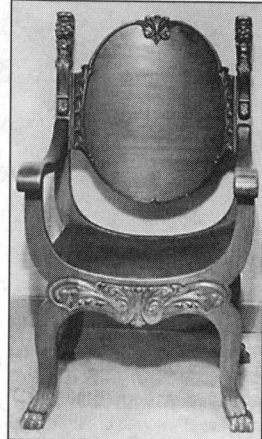

Victorian Roman-style Armchair

Victorian Roman-style chairs, mahogany & mahogany veneer, armchair & matching rocker, each w/a large oval back panel w/delicate scroll-carved borders suspended between heavy carved stiles topped by carved lion's head w/"jeweled" eyes, heavy shaped open arms on U-form supports enclosing the solid curved seat, wide scroll-carved seatrail continuing to flattened cabriole legs ending in large paw feet, old dark finish, one arm support w/glued break, ca. 1900, armchair 42" h., pr. (ILLUS. of armchair) **550**

William & Mary-Style armchair, walnut, the tall back w/an arched & pierced scroll-carved crestrail above a pierced scroll-carved framework centering an oval caned panel, free-standing ropetwist-turned stiles w/knob finials above long shaped open arms ending in scrolled hand grips, wide upholstered seat above a narrow flat carved seatrail on ropetwist- and block-turned front legs joined by an arched, pierced & scroll-carved wide flat stretcher, the front & rear legs joined by a ropetwist-turned H-stretcher, old finish, late 19th - early 20th c., 50" h. (minor edge damage) **275**

William & Mary-Style side chair, walnut, the tall back w/arched & pierced scroll-carved crest rails above a back panel framed w/further scroll carving centered by an oval caned panel, free-standing twist-turned stiles w/knob-turned finials above the wide upholstered seat above a narrow scroll-carved seatrail above twist- and block-turned legs joined by a wide arched & scroll-pierced front stretcher, the four legs joined by a ropetwist-turned H-stretcher, old finish, early 20th c., seat originally caned, 46½" h. (ILLUS.) **248**

William & Mary-Style Side Chair

Windsor "Arrow-back" Highchair

Windsor "arrow-back" highchair, painted, a stepped crestrail raised on backswept tapering stiles flanking three long curved arrow slats over simple turned arms on bamboo-turned spindles over the thick shaped plank seat, tall canted swelled bamboo-turned legs w/a front footrest over a high turned swelled stretcher & matching rear stretcher, lower side stretchers, early red paint, very minor surface imperfections, New England, 1820-30, 36" h. (ILLUS.) **2,875**

Windsor "bamboo-turned" side chairs, painted & decorated, the flat crestrail above four swelled bamboo-turned spindles between bamboo-turned stiles over a shaped saddle seat, canted bamboo-turned legs joined by box stretchers, yellow ground w/green & red stenciled leaf & berry decoration on the crestrail & green accents, New England, ca. 1820-30, some repaint, 33¼" h., set of 4 (ILLUS. of two) **863**

Bamboo-turned Windsor Side Chairs

Windsor "birdcage" side chairs, the back w/two simple turned horizontal crestrails joined by three short spindles above seven simple turned long spindles all flanked by canted bamboo-turned stiles, oblong-shaped plank seat on canted bamboo-turned legs joined by bamboo-turned box stretchers, old refinishing, first half 19th c., 33½" h., pr. **275**

Windsor "bow-back" side chair, painted, slender arched backrail above seven slender turned spindles over the shaped saddle seat, canted bamboo-turned legs joined by a swelled H-stretcher, old worn black paint, late 18th - early 19th c., 38" h. **358**

Windsor Child's Rocking Chair

Windsor child's rocking armchair, painted & decorated, rectangular tablet crestrail decorated w/colored florals & leaves raised on simple turned stiles joined by a narrow medial rail & flanked by simple turned open arms over the thick shaped saddle seat, ring-turned front legs & plain turned rear legs w/simple turned stretchers, mounted on heavy, long rockers, greenish yellow ground w/striping decoration in olive green & black, minor damage, Pennsylvania, mid-19th c., 18" h. (ILLUS.) **3,450**

Windsor "continuous-arm" armchair, painted, the arched slender crestrail continuing down to form flat arms, the back w/seven slender swelled spindles w/two short spindles & a canted baluster- and ring-turned arm support under each arm, a shaped saddle seat on four canted baluster- and ring-turned legs joined by a swelled H-stretcher, green paint, probably Pennsylvania, late 18th - early 19th c., 39" h. (repairs) **978**

Windsor "continuous-arm" brace-back armchair, painted, the slender arched crestrail curving down to form slender arms w/scrolled grips above numerous slender turned spindles & canted baluster- and ring-turned arm supports, shaped saddle seat, on canted baluster-, ring- and rod-turned tapering legs joined by a swelled H-stretcher, old black paint, New York, school of W. MacBride, 18th c. . . . **2,500**

Windsor "Continuous-arm" Armchair

Windsor "continuous-arm" brace-back armchair, painted, the slender molded crestrail continuing down to form narrow arms above six tall slender swelled spindles & two under-arm spindles & canted baluster-turned arm supports, the shaped saddle seat w/a back projection supporting a pair of flared brace spindles, on baluster- and rod-turned tapering canted legs joined by a swelled H-stretcher, old black over early paint, imperfections, underside left arm repair, branded "E. Swan," Elisha Swan, Stonington, Connecticut, 1755-1807, 39" h. (ILLUS.). **2,760**

Windsor "fan-back" armchair, a narrow serpentine crestrail supported by six short spindles on a U-form medial rail continuing to form shaped arms ending in shaped handholds w/canted baluster-turned arm supports & above eleven turned spindles, wide carved saddle seat on four canted baluster- and ring-turned legs joined by a swelled H-stretcher, three old coats of red paint, New England, ca. 1790, 31" h. (minor imperfections). **6,325**

Windsor "fan-back" side chairs, a cupid's-bow shaped crestrail above six swelled spindles flanked by baluster- and ring-turned canted stiles & a pair of projecting back braces, the shaped saddle seat raised on canted baluster-, ring- and rod-turned legs joined by a swelled H-stretcher, 18th c., pr. **3,100**

Windsor "fan-back" side chairs, painted, shaped crest & shaped incised seats above turned, splayed legs joined by medial stretchers, old black paint, New England, early 19th c., 35⅞" h., pr. (imperfections). **1,035**

Windsor "fan-back" writing-arm armchair, painted, a small shaped crestrail above five tall slender spindles above the U-form mid-rail continuing at one side to form a wide writing surface w/two small drawers beneath, numerous slender swelled spindles from mid-rail to wide shaped seat over a small drawer, raised on canted bamboo-turned legs joined by a bamboo-turned H-stretcher, old black paint, New England, early 19th c., 42½" h. (restoration to drawers) **4,025**

Windsor low-back writing-arm armchair, country-style, a curved shaped crestrail continuing to form arms ending in knuckled armrests & a wide teardrop-shaped writing surface at one side above a small bowed drawer all raised on simple bamboo-turned spindles, a wide shaped plank seat on canted bamboo-turned legs joined by turned box stretchers, overall worn black paint, Vermont, late 18th - early 19th c. **5,200**

Windsor "rod-back" child's side chairs, painted, a curved crestrail above seven bamboo-turned spindles & a shaped saddle seat over bamboo-turned canted legs joined by stretchers, painted dark red, New England, ca. 1790, 28" h., pr. (minor imperfections) **633**

Windsor "rod-back" side chairs, painted & grained, double crestrails over raked incised spindles, incised saddle seat on splayed, turned legs, old repaint w/gold striping & brown graining on the seats, New England, early 19th c., 33" h., pr. (surface imperfections). **920**

Windsor "sack-back" armchair, grain-painted, the wide bowed crestrail over seven spindles continuing through the medial rail that extends to form scrolled arms on a spindle & a baluster- and ring-

Grain-painted "Sack-back" Windsor

turned canted arm support, wide oblong-shaped saddle seat, on canted ring- and baluster-turned legs joined by a swelled H-stretcher, later rosewood graining & yellow outlining, old surface, minor repairs, southern New England, late 18th c., 38" h. (ILLUS.) **1,495**

Early "Sack-back" Windsor Armchair

Windsor "sack-back" armchair, painted, the bowed crestrail over seven spindles continuing through the medial rail that extends to form narrow shaped arms over a spindle & baluster- and ring-turned canted arm support, wide oblong saddle seat, on slightly splayed ring- and baluster-turned tapering legs joined by a swelled H-stretcher, old green paint over earlier black, imperfections, southeastern New England, ca. 1780, 38½" h. (ILLUS.). . . **3,335**

Windsor "sack-back" armchair, the bowed crestrail above eight spindles continuing through a curved medial rail ending in shaped arms above a plain spindle & a baluster- and knob-turned canted arm support, wide shaped seat on canted ring-, baluster- and rod-turned legs joined by a knob-turned H-stretcher, painted salmon red & black over earlier green, New England, ca. 1780, 37½" h. (loss to feet). **1,840**

Windsor "step-down" side chairs, the narrow stepped crestrail above backswept & tapering stiles & seven slender spindles above the wide shaped saddle seat, on canted swelled & turned legs joined by box stretchers, decorated w/the original yellow ground paint w/freehand gold & green decoration on the crestrail w/light brown front seatrail & leg decoration, highlighted w/brown striping, original surface, Farmington, Maine, ca. 1820, 35" h., set of 4 (very minor imperfections) **9,200**

Windsor-Style "arrow-back" side chairs, a flat crestrail between tapering rabbit ear stiles flanking the arrow slats above the shaped saddle seat, raised on canted bamboo-turned legs w/an arrow form stretcher & plain turned side & back stretchers, old worn dark brown finish, branded label of L. & J.G. Stickley, "Stickley - Fayetteville - Syracuse," New York, early 20th c., 34¾" h., set of 6 . . . . **825**

CHESTS & CHESTS OF DRAWERS

Apothecary chest, hardwood w/old dark stain, a rectangular top above a tall case w/six rows of three small drawers each, simple bail pulls, a single paneled long drawer at the bottom flanked by two small square panels, molded apron & short square stile legs w/corner brackets, faint Chinese characters on each drawer, China, late 19th to early 20th c., 22 x 32", 40" h. **770**

Apothecary chest, pine & walnut, a rectangular walnut top over a case enclosing 32 small square drawers w/white porcelain knobs over two rows of 12 slightly larger drawers w/large porcelain knobs, wire nail construction, refinished, 14¼ x 36¾", 21¾" h. (top board added) **1,375**

Art Deco chests of drawers, aluminum, rectangular top over a case w/three long drawers w/"porthole" handles & original salmon vinyl drawer facing, ca. 1930s, 19 x 43", 34" h., pr. **1,650**

Blanket chest, Chippendale country-style, painted & decorated pine, a hinged rectangular top w/molded edges & original bright-cut strap hinges opening to a well & till, the case decorated w/tombstone & diamond panels, flowers & dated "1771," the sides similarly painted, the molded base below hung w/a central pendant on straight bracket feet, Pennsylvania, 22 x 51", 20" h. (top decoration worn, feet shortened). **1,265**

Blanket chest, country-style, painted & decorated poplar, a rectangular lid w/molded edges opening to a well w/a lidded till w/secret compartment over a dovetailed case w/two small drawers at the bottom above a base molding & scroll-cut bracket feet, the sides decorated w/original brown graining & green painted trim & stenciled decoration in gold, white & green including fruit, flowers, lyres & foliage w/"D.R. 1857," similar to the Soap Hollow School, Pennsylvania, 20¾ x 46¾", 29½" h. (back feet repaired, other minor repair). **3,025**

Blanket chest, country-style, painted & decorated poplar, rectangular top w/molded edges & wrought-iron strap hinges opening to a well w/lidded till, the dovetailed case w/a molded base & scroll-cut bracket feet, decorated w/original red graining, early 19th c., 19½ x 45", 23" h. (some foot repair) **1,210**

Blanket chest, country-style, painted & decorated, six-board construction, the rectangular molded & hinged top opening to a well w/a till & drawer above a dovetailed case w/a molded base on bracket feet, the exterior painted mustard yellow to resemble tiger stripe or bird's-eye maple, brass keyhole escutcheon, lettered in black on the back "G.H.C.," possibly New England, early 19th c., 14¾ x 32", 16⅛" h. (repairs). **431**

Blanket chest, country-style, painted & decorated six-board style, the rectangular hinges opening to a deep well, solid board ends w/high arched bootjack legs, overall putty-grained finish in quarter-round and half-round designs, New England, 19th c., 39" l. **1,700**

Blanket chest, country-style, painted pine, six-board dovetailed construction, the rectangular top w/molded edge hinged above a deep well above a molded base raised on bracket feet, original red paint, New England, ca. 1780, 19 x 43¾", 26" h. (minor imperfections) **690**

Early Massachusetts Blanket Chest

Blanket chest, painted pine, rectangular hinged top w/molded edges opening to a well w/a lidded, molded till, a single long drawer across the bottom w/old replaced pressed glass pulls, molded base band on shaped bracket feet, old green over old red paint, paint wear on top, western Massachusetts, 18th c., 17 x 45", 31⅝" h. (ILLUS.)............................ **2,645**

Chippendale "block-front" chest of drawers, mahogany, the rectangular thumb-molded top w/a double-blocked front edge above a conforming case of four long blocked drawers on a molded base, raised on scroll-cut bracket feet, old refinish, replaced butterfly brasses, Boston, 1750-90, 19¼ x 33", 29¼" h. (rear foot missing)................. **46,000**

Cherry Chippendale Chest of Drawers

Chippendale chest of drawers, walnut, rectangular top w/molded edges above a pair of molded overlapping drawers above three long overlapping graduated drawers all w/simple bail pulls & brass keyhole escutcheons, molded base on ogee bracket feet w/scroll-cut returns, the front corners w/reeded quarter columns, late 18th c., 20¾ x 37", 37½" h. (old worn finish, feet & brasses replaced, other restoration)............. **3,025**

Chippendale country-style chest of drawers, maple & birch, a rectangular top slightly overhanging a case of four long reverse-graduated drawers w/incised beading & diamond inlaid escutcheons, molded base on tall bracket feet, replaced oval brass pulls, varnish over old red wash, New England, ca. 1790, 17 x 40", 38¾" h. (minor restoration).................... **2,185**

Chippendale "Block-front" Chest

Chippendale "block-front" chest of drawers, mahogany, the rectangular top w/serpentine front w/molded edge overhanging a conforming cockbeaded case w/four graduated block-front drawers, molded base, pointed central apron drop & shaped bracket feet, old but not original brasses, restored, Boston, ca. 1770, 19 x 33", 30" h. (ILLUS.)....... **19,550**

Chippendale "bow-front" chest of drawers, inlaid mahogany, a rectangular molded top w/a bowed front edge above a conforming case w/four long graduated line-inlaid cockbeaded drawers, molded base on short cabriole legs ending in claw-and-ball feet, appears to retain original simple bail pulls, 21 x 41¾", 35¼" h. (losses to beading, feet replaced & chipped)................. **5,750**

Chippendale chest of drawers, cherry, a rectangular top w/molded edge widely overhanging a case w/four long graduated beaded drawers w/simple bail pulls, molded base on scroll-cut bracket feet, appears to retain original brasses, two foot facings replaced, New England, probably Connecticut, ca. 1790, 20¼ x 31", 31½" h. (ILLUS.)............. **4,025**

Connecticut Chippendale Chest

Chippendale "serpentine-top" chest of drawers, cherry, rectangular top w/a molded edge & serpentine front overhanging a case of four long graduated beaded drawers w/oval pulls flanked by fluted quarter-columns, the molded base on heavy ogee scroll-cut bracket feet, repair to front left foot & both rear feet, Connecticut, ca. 1780, 23 x 41", 37¾" h. (ILLUS.) **6,325**

Chippendale tall chest of drawers, tiger stripe maple, rectangular top w/a deep stepped cornice above a case of seven long graduated thumb-molded drawers w/replaced butterfly brasses, refinished, southeastern New England, ca. 1780, 22 x 36", 64" h. (restored) **3,220**

Tall Chippendale Chest over Drawers

Chippendale tall chest over drawers, painted pine, a rectangular molded hinged top opening to a deep well in a case w/two false long drawer fronts over four long working thumb-molded graduated drawers, molded base on tall bracket feet, simple bail brasses appear to be original, minor imperfections, painted red, New England, late 18th c., 18 x 36", 52½" h. (ILLUS.) **4,888**

Classical (American Empire) country-style chest of drawers, birch, a high crestboard w/a flat top & scroll-cut & rounded corners above a pair of small handkerchief drawers w/small replaced round brasses, the rectangular top above an single long, deep stepped-out drawer above ring-, rod- and block-turned columns flanking three long setback drawers, ring-turned tapering legs w/ball feet, replaced butterfly brasses, old mellow refinishing, first half 19th c., 17¾ x 37", overall 48¼" h. **935**

Classical chest of drawers, carved mahogany & mahogany veneer, a flat-topped scroll-ended top backboard above a row of three short drawers stepped back on the rectangular top over a pair of overhanging deep drawers above three long drawers flanked by columns w/a

Classical Mahogany Chest of Drawers

carved pineapple over leaf bands & a spiral-carved section, molded conforming base on heavy knob-, ring- and baluster-turned tapering legs, replaced early glass pulls, refinished, imperfections, North Shore Massachusetts, ca. 1825, 22 x 42¾", 45" h. (ILLUS.) **978**

Paw-footed Classical Chest

Classical chest of drawers, carved mahogany & mahogany veneer, the rectangular top over a long drawer overhanging a case w/three long drawers flanked by carved free-standing columns on a molded base, simple turned wooden knobs, acanthus-carved heavy paw front feet & turned rear feet, old refinish, minor imperfections, possibly Pennsylvania, ca. 1825, 23½ x 45½", 47" h. (ILLUS.) **920**

Classical chest of drawers, child's, carved pine, the scroll-carved splashback centered by a shell crest & reeded corner posts flanking an inset narrow rectangular top w/molded edges over a pair of small handkerchief drawers w/turned wood knobs on the rectangular top above the case w/a deep long projecting drawer over two long narrower drawers flanked by swelled columns, small tapering turned front feet, turned knobs on all the drawers, dark finish, ca. 1840, 19" w., 23" h. **1,200**

Classical country-style chest of drawers, cherry & poplar w/old cherry red finish, a rectangular top above a pair of deep overhanging drawers over ring-turned columns flanking a lower case w/three long graduated drawers, simple turned wood pulls, on ring- and knob-turned feet, ca. 1840, 21 x 43⅛", 47¼" h. **605**

Classical country-style chest of drawers, tiger stripe maple, a scroll-cut crestrail w/block ends on the rectangular top over a case w/three small shallow projecting drawers over a long deep drawer above three long graduated drawers all w/turned wood knobs, short turned legs w/knob feet, paneled ends, old finish, probably Pennsylvania, ca. 1830, 19½ x 46", 49½" h. **2,185**

Curly Maple Classical Tall Chest

Classical country-style tall chest of drawers, curly maple, a rectangular top over a pair of drawers over four long graduated drawers flanked by baluster- and ring-turned free-standing columns, molded base on heavy turned ovoid front feet on casters, first half 19th c. (ILLUS.) **715**

Early Pennsylvania Dower Chest

Dower chest, painted & decorated, a rectangular top w/molded edges opening to a well, the front decorated w/a large arch-topped rectangular panel centered by a large spread-winged eagle w/shield

& banner in its beak, pinwheels, compass stars & tulips around the bird, in dark shades of umber, black, red & yellow within a red & white border, the background w/a finely sponged black & brown ground, black base molding & scroll-cut bracket feet, light surface cleaning, several spurs replaced, Center County, Pennsylvania, ca. 1814 (ILLUS.) . . **12,500**

Fine Federal "Bow-front" Chest

Federal "bow-front" chest of drawers, cherry & bird's-eye maple veneer, a rectangular top w/bowed front over a case of four long graduated cockbeaded drawers outlined in cross-banded mahogany around bird's-eye maple, scalloped apron & tall slender French feet, replaced oval brasses, old surface w/minor veneer patching, attributed to Eliphalet Briggs, Keene, New Hampshire, ca. 1810, 20½ x 39¾", 38½" h. (ILLUS.) **9,775**

Federal "Bow-front" Chest of Drawers

Federal "bow-front" chest of drawers, mahogany, a rectangular top w/molded edges & a bowed front above a conforming case w/four long graduated cockbeaded drawers w/oval pulls, molded base on slightly canted bracket feet, patches & repairs to feet, New England, ca. 1795, 24 x 42", 33½" h. (ILLUS.) **3,737**

Federal "bow-front" chest of drawers, cherry, a rectangular top w/bowed front above a conforming case w/four long cockbeaded graduated drawers w/oval brasses & keyhole escutcheons, veneered cyma-curved front apron, tall French feet, original brasses, old refinish, New England, early 19th c., 21⅜ x 41½", 37" h. (surface imperfections) **2,875**

Federal Bird's-eye Maple Chest

Federal chest of drawers, birch & bird's-eye maple veneer, a rectangular top w/reeded edges above a case w/four long reverse-graduated beaded drawers w/oval pulls & brass keyhole escutcheons, flat base, raised on baluster- and ring-turned legs w/peg feet, brasses appear to be original, old refinish, imperfections, New England, 1815-25, 19 x 40½", 38" h. (ILLUS.) **2,415**

Federal Curly Maple Chest of Drawers

Federal chest of drawers, curly maple & curly maple veneer, a rectangular top above a case of four long graduated cockbeaded drawers w/oval pulls, valanced apron w/center blocked drop, tall slender French feet, brasses appear to be original, old finish, imperfections, southern New England, ca. 1790, 18 x 39¾" h., 37" h. (ILLUS.) **4,888**

Federal chest of drawers, inlaid cherry, rectangular top w/string-inlaid edges slightly overhanging a case w/four long graduated cockbeaded drawers above a double-scallop apron & flaring slender French feet, New England, ca. 1800, 19¾ x 42", 38" h (replaced oval brasses, refinished) **2,990**

Federal chest of drawers, mahogany & figured mahogany veneer, the rectangular top over a case of four cockbeaded long graduated drawers & replaced oval brasses & keyhole escutcheons, deeply scalloped apron & tall flaring French feet, early 19th c., 20 x 42½", 41" h. (age cracks in top & ends, minor veneer repair) **2,750**

Federal country-style chest of drawers, cherry, a rectangular top above a case of four long dovetailed graduated drawers w/simple turned wood knobs, scalloped apron, simple turned feet, paneled ends, refinished, early 19th c., 19¾ x 40¾", 39½" h. **770**

Federal Tall Birch Chest of Drawers

Federal tall chest of drawers, birch, a rectangular top w/a flaring molded cornice above a case of six long thumb-molded drawers w/oval brasses, molded base on simple bracket feet, original brasses, refinished, Concord, New Hampshire, late 18th to early 19th c., 16¼ x 35¾" h., 54¾" h. (ILLUS.) **4,255**

George III-Style "bow-front" chest of drawers, inlaid satinwood, rectangular top w/bowed front over a case w/four long graduated bowed drawers w/inlaid banding over the serpentine apron continuing to tall French feet, oval brass & metal keyhole escutcheons, small veneer losses, England, ca. 1900, 20½ x 33", 33" h. (ILLUS.) **4,600**

George III-Style Chest of Drawers

Georgian-Style Chest on Chest

Georgian-Style chest on chest, mahogany & mahogany veneer, two-part construction: the upper section w/a rectangular top w/cut front corners over a narrow cornice above three long deep drawers flanked by chamfered reeded edges; the lower section w/a mid-molding over two long, deep drawers, all w/butterfly brasses & keyhole escutcheons, molded base & serpentine apron on simple bracket feet, England, late 19th to early 20th c. (ILLUS.)........... **800**

Hardware chest, poplar, a thin rectangular top & sides enclosing stacks of 35 small drawers w/tiny knobs, old brown finish, wire nail construction w/plywood back, some drawers w/worn tape labels, 5¼ x 16⅜", 16⅜" h. **330**

Louis XV-Style chest of drawers, fruitwood, a rectangular top w/serpentine cove-molded border on three front sides, a pair of narrow long drawers in the front of this border above the wide bombé case w/swelled sides & front w/two long drawers carved w/incised oblong panels,

paneled ends & cartouche-carved front corners, serpentine flared apron on molded cabriole legs ending in short peg feet, antique finish, 20th c., 19 x 45½", 33¼" h. **578**

Gustav Stickley Tall Chest of Drawers

Mission-style (Arts & Crafts movement) tall chest of drawers, a low splashboard on the rectangular top overhanging a tall case w/two stacks of three small drawers above three long graduated drawers, hammered copper pulls, bowed side stiles & arched apron, fine original finish, red decal of Gustav Stickley, Model No. 913, minor stains on top, 20¼ x 36", 50½" h. (ILLUS.) **9,350**

Mission-style (Arts & Crafts movement) tall chest of drawers, oak, a low backsplash on the rectangular top overhanging a tall case w/two ranks of three small drawers each over three long graduated drawers, hammered copper pulls, bowed side stiles, arched apron, designed by Harvey Ellis, original finish, red decal mark of Gustav Stickley, Model No. 913, 20¼ x 36", 50½" (minor stains on top) **9,350**

Grain-painted Early Mule Chest

Mule chest (box chest w/one or more drawers below a storage compartment), painted pine, rectangular top w/molded edges opening to a deep well above a single long drawer across the bottom, on high arched & shaped bracket feet, original turned wood knobs, original red & yellow painting simulating tiger stripe maple, old dry surface, minor surface scratches on top, Rhode Island, 1830-40, 20 x 39¾", 36" h. (ILLUS.)............................. **2,070**

Mule chest (box chest w/one or more drawers below a storage compartment), pine, the molded rectangular hinged top opening to a deep well over a single lower drawer below w/small turned wood pulls, bootjack ends, the keyhole escutcheon made from a brass button impressed w/the legend "long live the president GW," old surface, New England, late 18th c., 17¾ x 36¼", 32½" h. (imperfections) **1,265**

Mule chest (box chest w/one or more drawers below a storage compartment), painted pine, rectangular hinged top w/molded edge opening to a deep well above a pair of long drawers below, original grain painting resembling mahogany w/two banded false drawers at the top over the two working drawers, four oval brasses at the top & two each on the working drawers, molded band w/simple bracket feet w/painted banding, old repaint, early 19th c., 17½ x 21½", 44½" h. (repairs to feet, scratches on side) **825**

Pilgrim Century chest of drawers, painted oak, cedar & yellow pine, a rectangular top w/applied molding above a case of four long drawers each w/molded fronts & chamfered mitered borders & separated by applied horizontal moldings, the sides w/two recessed vertical molded panels above a single horizontal panel, deep cove-molded base on turned ball feet, old red paint, southeastern New England, ca. 1700, 20½ x 37¾", 35" h. (minor imperfections)................. **26,450**

Queen Anne chest of drawers, figured walnut, a rectangular molded top w/notched corners overhanging a case w/a pair of short drawers over three long graduated drawers flanked by fluted chamfered corner columns, the molded base on ogee bracket feet, appears to retain original rare openwork brass butterfly pulls & keyhole escutcheons, Pennsylvania, 1750-60, 22 x 36½", 34½" h. (patched to back of top where mirror was fitted, half of front left foot replaced) **13,800**

Queen Anne chest-on-frame, walnut & burl walnut veneer, the rectangular top above a case w/four long graduated dovetailed drawers w/brass teardrop pulls set onto a molded frame w/arched apron & short cabriole front legs ending in duck feet, England, first half 20th c., 19¼ x 33½", 38½" h..................... **825**

Queen Anne chest-on-frame, carved & painted pine & maple, two-part construction: the upper section w/a rectangular top w/a widely flaring & stepped cornice above a band of dentil molding over a case w/two pairs of small drawers flanking a deep fan-carved central drawer w/incised scallops & overlapping lunettes, over a stack of four long graduated drawers, all w/simple bail pulls; the lower section w/a molded top above a deeply scalloped apron raised on short angled cabriole legs ending in pad feet, New Hampshire, 18th c., 36" w., 56" h....................... **2,500**

Queen Anne Mule Chest

Queen Anne mule chest (box chest w/one or more drawers below a storage compartment), painted pine, a rectangular top w/molded edges opening to a deep well w/a case front of three thumb-molded graduated false drawers over two working drawers, molded base on simple high bracket feet centering a small shaped pendant, replaced butterfly pulls, old dark brown paint, minor imperfections, probably Massachusetts, mid 18th c., 17¼ x 36½", 46½" h. (ILLUS.) .. **3,738**

Queen Anne tall chest of drawers, carved & painted, a rectangular top w/a deep stepped projecting cornice above a case of five long graduated drawers w/simple rounded butterfly pulls & oval keyhole escutcheons, molded base w/carved beading & dog-tooth carving, raised on short bandy cabriole legs ending in pad feet, old red paint, New Hampshire, Dunlap School, 18th c., 35¾" w., 48" h. **40,000**

Queen Anne Tall Chest of Drawers

Queen Anne tall chest of drawers, maple, the rectangular top w/flaring stepped cornice over a pair of small drawers over four long graduated drawers, molded base on simple shaped bracket feet, appears to retain most of the original brasses, numerous chips & patches to drawer lips, one inch missing on left rear foot, New England, 1740-60, 19½ x 39", 45¼" h. (ILLUS.) **2,300**

Victorian country-style chest of drawers, Renaissance Revival substyle, walnut, a tall oval mirror swiveling between a pierced "wishbone" frame on a short pedestal above the rectangular top over a case w/long drawer w/a raised panel & curved leaf pulls slightly overhanging three matching long lower drawers, bracket front feet, ca. 1875, 18 x 41", base, 43" h. plus mirror **489**

Victorian country-style chest of drawers, Renaissance Revival substyle, walnut, an arched & scalloped crestboard above a narrow rectangular shelf above a pair of shallow handkerchief drawers w/turned wood knobs & quarter-rounded bobbin turnings at the corners, the rectangular top w/molded edges above a case w/chamfered front corners & half-round bobbin-turned drops at the top corners above four long graduated drawers w/turned wood knobs, half-round bobbin turnings at the bottom front corners flanking the scroll-cut bracket feet, refinished, ca. 1870, 18 x 39½", overall 50¾" h. **605**

Victorian Eastlake Cottage-style chest of drawers, painted & decorated pine, the superstructure w/a notch-cut crestboard

Victorian Eastlake Cottage-style Chest

w/peaked center & incised & gilt-trimmed lines & florettes over a gilt-banded frame enclosing a rectangular swivel mirror over decorated panels & a narrow open shelf flanked by shaped side uprights w/gilt-trimmed line-incised florals & loops, the rectangular top w/molded edge w/further gilt trim over a case of four long graduated drawers painted w/a large round continuous reserve decorated w/a lakeside landscape, the reserve surrounded by a rectangular gilt band frame w/angled corners & further stylized gilt florals, on original brown & orange comb-grained ground accented w/black, the top in olive green w/a rose & gold floral design, original round ring pulls & paint, on casters, ca. 1880-90, height loss, 18¾ x 38", 76" h. (ILLUS.) **978**

Victorian Empire Revival chest of drawers, mahogany veneer, a large rectangular mirror w/rounded wide frame swiveling between S-scroll uprights above the rectangular top w/a pair of long, narrow round-fronted drawers w/small brass ring pulls above a bombé swelled lower case of three long drawers, each w/stamped brass pulls, rounded baseboard on short claw-and-ball front legs on casters, ca. 1890s, 27 x 48", 72" h. **403**

Victorian Golden Oak chest of drawers, the top mounted w/a large squared mirror w/rounded corners within a framework w/a high arched & scroll-carved crestrail & shaped sides & rounded bottom corners swiveling between tall scrolled uprights w/scroll carving across the base, the rectangular top w/a serpentine front over a conforming case w/a pair of

Golden Oak Chest of Drawers

drawers over two long drawers, all w/pierced brass pulls, simple cabriole front legs & square rear legs, on casters, ca. 1900, 20 x 44", 82" h. (ILLUS.) **403**

Golden Oak "Highboy" Chest

Victorian Golden Oak "highboy" chest of drawers, oak, a rectangular top w/molded edges mounted w/a simple wishbone upright support holding an oblong serpentine-framed beveled swiveling mirror, the tall case w/a pair of small serpentine-front drawers over four long drawers, simple turned wood pulls, scalloped apron & short shaped front legs & square rear legs, on casters, ca. 1900, 19 x 34", 66" h. (ILLUS.) **259**

Victorian Golden Oak "highboy" chest of drawers, the rectangular top w/molded edges & incurved sides mounted w/an oblong cartouche-form beveled mirror in

Victorian Golden Oak "Highboy" Chest

conforming scroll-carved frame swiveling between wishbone uprights w/scroll carving along the bottom, the tall case w/a pair of drawers over four long drawers, all w/pierced brass pulls, scroll-carved apron & leaf-carved front cabriole legs & square back legs, excellent condition, ca. 1900 (ILLUS.) **850**

Golden Oak "Side-by-Side" Chest

Victorian Golden Oak "side-by-side" chest of drawers, a tall narrow rectangular beveled mirror on one side swiveling within a framework w/an arched & scroll-carved crestrail, beside a short scroll-carved top crest over a stack of two small drawers over a small paneled cupboard door, all on a rectangular top w/molded edges over two long drawers, stamped brass pulls, ca. 1900, possibly missing feet (ILLUS.) . . . . **150 to 300**

Renaissance Revival Walnut Chest

Victorian Renaissance Revival chest of drawers, walnut & burl walnut, the tall superstructure w/a scroll-carved crowned pediment over angled molded rails over a frieze w/burl raised panels over a tall arch-topped mirror flanked by sides w/raised burl panels, rounded candle shelves & curved base brackets over a stepped white marble top w/two small drawers flanking a marble-topped well over two long drawers each w/two oblong raised burl panels, stamped brass pulls, molded base on casters, ca. 1880, 21 x 43", 88" h. (ILLUS.). **661**

William & Mary chest over drawer, child's, painted pine, a rectangular hinged top w/molded edges opening to a deep well, half-round edge moldings down the corners & above the long base drawer molded to resemble two small drawers, front & sides w/a red painted wash & brown free-hand designs of concentric rings, demilune & meandering vines, the drawer painted salmon, red, & brown, single arch molding in black, possibly coastal Massachusetts, early 18th c., 17⅛ x 28", 19" h. (minor imperfections) **9,200**

CRADLES

Bentwood, the arched bentwood matching head- and footrail above simple turned spindles w/the side composed of seven turned spindles between turned rails, a slat rail bottom, suspending & swinging between simple turned uprights w/knob finials raised on shaped & arched shoe feet w/a central drop w/two long rod stretchers from end to end, ivory fittings, late 19th - early 20th c., 41" l., 39" h.. . . . . . **440.00**

Country-style Painted Cradle

Country-style, painted pine, rectangular deep mortised frame w/paneled side slats w/double almond-shaped cut-outs, hooded end, found in Amish country, old worn black paint, 19th c., 31" l. (ILLUS.) **880**

Rustic style, twig-constructed sides on a rocker base, unsigned, early 20th c., 22 x 33", 22" h.. . . . . **55**

CUPBOARDS

Chippendale Cherry Corner Cupboard

Corner cupboard, Chippendale, carved cherry, two-part construction: the upper section w/a scrolled molded pediment flanking a fluted keystone w/flame finial above a wide arched door w/geometric glazing flanked by reeded columns, opening to three serpentine-shaped painted shelves; the slightly projecting lower section w/a pair of paneled cupboard doors opening to single shelf flanked by reeded columns, scalloped apron on simple bracket feet, old refinish, hardware changes, minor patching, probably Pennsylvania, early 19th c., 17¾ x 41½", 95" h. (ILLUS.) **9,200**

Chippendale Poplar Corner Cupboard

Corner cupboard, Chippendale, poplar, two-part construction: the top section w/a flat top & deep stepped cornice over a wide arched molding w/central keystone above a pair of geometrically glazed cupboard doors opening to two serpentine shelves w/plate rail & spoon cut-outs; the slightly stepped-out lower section w/a pair of raised panel doors w/H-hinges opening to a single shelf, serpentine apron & simple bracket feet, old surface, imperfections, Pennsylvania, late 18th - early 19th c., 25½ x 51", 67" h. (ILLUS.) **3,680**

English Chippendale-Style Cupboard

Corner cupboard, Chippendale-Style, mahogany, two-part construction: the upper section w/a flat top & narrow molded cornice over a lattice-carved

frieze band over a tall single geometrically glazed door opening to three shaped shelves; the stepped-out lower section w/a wide single geometrically glazed door opening to a single shaped shelf, molded base & bracket feet, England, early 20th c., 28" w., 72¼" h. (ILLUS.) **715**

Painted Federal Corner Cupboard

Corner cupboard, Federal country-style, painted poplar, one-piece construction, the flat top over a deep stepped cornice over a pair of tall paneled doors w/double incised vertical bands & cast-iron latch over a pair of shorter matching doors, flat apron & plain bracket feet, worn blue paint, Pennsylvania, ca. 1830, 43" w., 69½" h. (ILLUS.) **5,175**

Federal Tulipwood Corner Cupboard

Corner cupboard, Federal country-style, tulipwood, two-part construction: the upper section w/a flat top over a deep coved cornice over a wide tall 12-pane glazed door w/the three upper panes forming Gothic arches, opening to three shelves; the lower section w/a paneled central drawer flanked by small recessed panels above a pair of paneled cupboard doors w/H-hinges opening to a shelf, serpentine apron continuing to bracket feet, old refinish, some imperfections, probably Pennsylvania, ca. 1830, 19 x 41", 84¾" h. (ILLUS.). **3,910**

Country Federal Corner Cupboard

Corner cupboard, Federal country-style, cherry, one-piece construction, a flat top w/a widely flaring deep coved cornice over a dentil band above a pair of tall double raised-panel doors opening to shelves over a pair of shorter raised panel cupboard doors, deeply scalloped apron & bracket feet, old worn refinishing, repairs, edge damage & wear, early 19th c., 52½" w., 85" h. (ILLUS.) **1,045**

Corner cupboard, Federal country-style, pine, two-piece construction: the upper section w/a deep flaring & stepped cornice above a pair of tall, narrow 8-pane glazed cupboard doors w/molded muntins & wooden knob opening to three shelves; the lower section w/a mid-molding over a single cockbeaded drawer w/two wooden knobs above a pair of cross-form paneled cupboard doors w/brass latch, molded base on scroll-cut ogee bracket feet, Middle Atlantic states, early 19th c., restoration, 21½ x 48½", 87" h. **2,415**

Corner cupboard, Federal country-style, cherry, one-piece construction, a flat top w/cove-molded cornice over a pair of tall

Federal One-piece Corner Cupboard

8-pane cupboard doors opening to three shelves over a pair of small drawers over a pair of wide paneled cupboard doors, curved apron & simple bracket feet, minor edge damage & age cracks, one pane w/corner crack, old refinishing, first quarter 19th c., 53¾" w., 88¾" h. (ILLUS.) . . **2,970**

Federal Cherry Corner Cupboard

Corner cupboard, Federal, cherry & tiger stripe maple inlaid, the flat top w/a coved cornice over a narrow arched band w/center block continuing down to two blocks over narrow inlaid tiger stripe maple bands all flanking the arched open front w/three shaped shelves above a slightly stepped-out lower section w/a single raised double-panel door flanked by narrow tiger stripe bands & opening to a single shelf, flat molded base, Mid-Atlantic States, early 19th c., restored, 20 x 41½", 89" h. (ILLUS.). **1,610**

Large Inlaid Federal Corner Cupboard

Corner cupboard, Federal, cherry, two-part construction: the upper section w/a flat top over a deep coved cornice over a reeded frieze band over a tall 12-pane glazed cupboard door opening to three shelves; the lower section w/mid-molding over a pair of small paneled cupboard doors centered by inlaid rings, molded base on shaped bracket feet, old finish, feet replaced, minor repairs, found in Tennessee, early 19th c., 49½" w., 89¾" h. (ILLUS.) **5,225**

Fine Federal Walnut Corner Cupboard

Corner cupboard, Federal, carved walnut, two-part construction: the upper section w/a flat top & deep coved cornice over a narrow tiger stripe maple frieze band over a raised arched molding w/center keystone & serrated inner edge continuing down to tall pilasters flanking the tall arched geometrically glazed cupboard door opening to three shelves; the lower section w/a mid-molding over a pair of drawers above a pair of paneled cupboard doors w/H-hinges, flat molded apron on scroll-cut bracket feet, old refinish, imperfections, probably New Jersey, early 19th c., 22 x 44", 94¼" h. (ILLUS.) **8,625**

Federal-Style Corner Cupboard

Corner cupboard, Federal-Style corner cupboard, poplar, one-piece construction, the flat top w/a deep stepped cornice above a tall cross-framed four-panel door above a lower shorter double-panel door w/overall thin fluting, scappled apron & simple bracket feet, simple turned wood knobs, wear, late 19th c., 22 x 38", 84" h. (ILLUS.) **1,092**

European Hanging Cupboard

Hanging cupboard, painted, a rectangular top w/a flaring coved cornice over a single paneled door w/scrolled brass keyhole escutcheon, molded base, old dark green paint bordered by red, probably lacks interior drawers, other imperfections, probably Northern Europe, last half 18th c., 8 x 16", 17" h. (ILLUS.) **1,495**

Hanging wall cupboard, country-style, butternut, a rectangular top w/a flat chamfered cornice above a pair of glazed cupboard doors w/recessed panels opening to shelves, on a molded base, refinished, probably New England, 19th c., 11 x 26¾", 29" h. **863**

Hutch cupboard, country-style, painted, a flat rectangular top above slightly sloping front framed by molded boards around the two-shelf open upper section above the stepped-out lower section w/a pair of tall flat cupboard doors w/wooden thumb latches, painted red, New England, late 18th - early 19th c., 35" w., 70" h. **2,800**

Early Pine Hutch Cupboard

Primitive Hutch Cupboard

Slant-back Hutch Cupboard

Hutch cupboard, pine, slant-back style, a flat rectangular overhanging top above a cockbeaded open front w/three shelves above a tall raised panel door w/wrought-iron HL hinges, flat base, old refinish, replaced door, New England, 18th c., 12¾ x 29½", 93" h. (ILLUS.) **1,610**

Hutch cupboard, pine, slant-front style, the flat rectangular top w/a stepped cornice above narrow back-slanting boards framing the open front w/two shelves, the stepped-out lower section w/wide side boards flanking the narrow tall raised panel door w/small wood knob, flat base, old refinish, imperfections, top doors missing, New England, late 18th c., 18 x 37½", 73" h. (ILLUS.). **2,300**

Hutch cupboard, poplar, one-piece construction, the wide flat top above wide flat boards framing the open front w/two shelves above the stepped-out lower section w/wide side boards flanking the narrow crude flat cupboard door, one-board sides w/bootjack feet, old dark reddish brown finish, age cracks, top probably cut down, 19th c., 18 x 42", 71½" h. (ILLUS.) **1,430**

Jelly cupboard, painted & decorated pine, the rectangular top over a deep coved cornice above a tall narrow paneled & molding-trimmed central door w/original brass thumb latch flanked by tall narrow molding-trimmed side panels, wide double-arched apron, original overall red flame graining, minor damage, 19th c., 16½ x 48¼", 63" h. (ILLUS.) **4,620**

Fine Decorated Jelly Cupboard

Pine Jelly Cupboard

Jelly cupboard, pine, a rectangular top w/beaded edges overhanging a case w/a pair of tall raised & molding-trimmed double-paneled doors w/wood turn latch & replaced brass thumb latch, slightly scalloped apron & low bracket feet, refinished, strip between doors added, age cracks in top, 19th c., 18 x 43½",42½" h. (ILLUS.) **605**

Kitchen cupboard, Golden Oak, two-piece construction: the upper section w/a rectangular top w/stepped cornice above a pair of single-pane glazed doors opening to two shelves above a row of drawers w/a long drawer flanked by two small drawers; the lower section w/a cylinder front w/a pull-out work shelf over a tall paneled-front fold-down flour bin beside a square double-paneled door over a drawer, scrolled bracket feet, on casters, ca. 1900, 21 x 37½", 83" h. (ILLUS.) **1,320**

Golden Oak Kitchen Cupboard

Old Glass-doored Kitchen Cupboard

Kitchen cupboard, oak & pine, two-part construction: the upper section w/a rectangular top over two wide square frosted glass doors w/etched geometric designs opening to a shelf over a row of three small drawers, the center w/a curved-down bottom over incurved sides & a narrow shelf; the lower section w/a wide rectangular top overhanging a case w/a central pull-out work shelf over a large paneled door beside a drawer over a smaller paneled door, flat apron, square stile legs, ca. 1910, 26 x 45", 70" h. (ILLUS.) **345**

Linen press, Chippendale, cherry, two-part construction: the upper section w/a rectangular top w/deep flaring cornice over a pair of tall paneled cupboard doors w/serpentine top molding & opening to

Fine Cherry Chippendale Linen Press

three shelves; the lower slightly projecting section includes three long thumb-molded graduated drawers, molded base on scroll-cut bracket feet, old oval brasses, old refinish, repairs, imperfections, probably Pennsylvania, late 18th c., 19½ x 47", 80" h. (ILLUS.). **6,325**

Chippendale Maple Linen Press

Linen press, Chippendale, figured maple, two-part construction: the upper section w/a stepped rectangular top molded above two arched paneled cupboard doors opening to two shelves flanked by fluted stiles; the lower section fitted w/a mid-molding over a pair of drawers over two long drawers, molded base on bracket feet, repairs to feet, right side of cornice repairs, New York or New Jersey, ca. 1780, 23 x 56", 78" h. (ILLUS.) **9,775**

Fine Federal Linen Press

Linen press, Federal, inlaid mahogany, two-part construction: the upper section w/a swan's-neck pediment centering an acorn finial on a conch shell-inlaid support, the field-paneled cupboard doors below each centering a patera inlaid w/a spread-winged eagle clutching a shield beneath two rows of stars; the lower section w/a mid-molding over four long cockbeaded graduated drawers w/oval brass, scalloped apron & slender tall French feet, front left foot restored, rear foot repaired, finial of later date, repairs at upper hinges, partially illegible inscription on the top of the lower section "My — Salyer (?) 1810, 1810," New York, ca. 1810, 21 x 46¼", 93" h. (ILLUS.) **12,650**

Linen press, Victorian, oak, two-part construction: the upper section w/a rectangular top & overhanging cornice above a pair of cupboard doors w/large recessed & gently pointed panels & opening to later shelves, the sides w/knob- and spiral-turned columns; the lower section w/a mid-molding over two pairs of short drawers over a single long drawer at the bottom, molded base on scroll-cut bracket feet, England, mid-19th c., 21 x 53¼", 79" h. **4,600**

Pewter cupboard, Chippendale country-style, pine & poplar, two-part construction: the upper section w/a rectangular top over a deep molded cornice above a pair of 9-pane glazed cupboard doors opening to two shelves over an open pie shelf w/shaped projecting ends; the lower section w/a stepped-out rectangular top over a row of three small drawers w/wooden knobs over a pair of paneled cupboard doors w/wooden turn latches & knobs, molded

Scarce Early Pewter Cupboard

base on short bracket feet, old refinish, imperfections & repairs, probably Pennsylvania, late 18th c., 21 x 56¾", 86" h. (ILLUS.) **5,463**

Pie safe, cherry, a rectangular top w/a low three-quarters gallery above a pair of tall three-panel doors each w/a punched-tin panel decorated w/a central diamond framed by four punched circles, one door w/wood knob, a long drawer w/two wood knobs at the base, raised on ring-, rod- and knob-turned tapering legs, three matching tin panels on each end, refinished, 19th c., 18 x 42", overall 60" h. (considerable foot restoration, gallery replaced) **1,045**

Pie safe, grain-painted wood, a rectangular flat top slightly overhanging the case w/a single screened door flanked by narrow screened panels, pair of narrow screened panels on each side, raised on tall stile legs, overall grain-painted finish, 19th c., 35" w., 48" h. **850**

Painted Poplar Pie Safe

Pie safe, painted poplar, the rectangular top above a pair of tall three-panel cupboard doors, a punched tin in each panel in a circle & star design, one door w/simple wooden knob, a single long drawer across the bottom w/two wooden knobs, three panels on each side w/punched-tin panels, tall stile legs, old blue paint over other colors, 19th c., 17½ x 39¾", 59" h. (ILLUS.) **1,540**

Pie safe, painted wood, a flat rectangular top above a pair of tall three-panel doors each w/a punched tin panel in a tulip & vase design, three matching tin panels down each side, raised on short stile legs, painted white, 19th c., 41½" w., 45" h. **850**

Step-back wall cupboard, butternut w/old dark brown finish, two-part construction: the upper section w/a rectangular top w/a deep flaring cornice above a pair of tall double-paneled cupboard doors opening to shelves, the top one w/cut-out for spoons; the stepped-out lower section w/a pair of flush drawers above a pair of paneled cupboard doors, on short double knob-turned feet, found in Cairo, Ohio, mid 19th c., 13 x 49¼", 80" h. (most hardware removed) **1,980**

Cherry Step-back Wall Cupboard

Step-back wall cupboard, country-style, cherry, two-part construction: the upper section w/a rectangular top w/a wide flat & flaring cornice over a pair of tall 6-pane glazed cupboard doors opening to two shelves over a low open pie shelf; the stepped-out lower section w/a pair of shallow drawers w/wood knobs over a pair of paneled doors w/a keyhole & wooden knob, flat apron & curved bracket feet, original brass latch in top, replaced wooden pulls, old refinishing, 19th c., 15½ x 54¼", 83¾" h. (ILLUS.) **3,960**

Painted Pennsylvania Cupboard

Step-back wall cupboard, country-style, painted pine, two-part construction: the upper section w a/rectangular top over a shallow widely flaring stepped cornice over a deep frieze above a pair of 6-pane glazed cupboard doors opening to two shelves over a low pie shelf w/shaped end brackets; the lower stepped-out section w/a row of three drawers w/turned wood knobs over a pair of double-paneled cupboard doors w/wood knobs & a wooden thumb latch, molded apron on heavy ball feet, yellow paint of later date, chips to cornice, missing right side of mid-molding, Pennsylvania, ca. 1830, 18 x 54", 88" h. (ILLUS.) **7,475**

Early Pine Step-back Wall Cupboard

Step-back wall cupboard, country-style, pine, one-piece construction, the flat rectangular top above a molded edging across the top & down the sides flanking a pair of tall double-paneled doors w/a small square panel over a long rectangular panel over a deep pie shelf, the stepped-out lower section w/further molded edging & a pair of tall paneled doors w/small turned wood knobs, flat base, two shelves in top & three in bottom, old refinish, New England, 1790-1810, 21 x 37½", 86" h. (ILLUS.) **2,990**

Poplar & Curly Maple Wall Cupboard

Step-back wall cupboard, country-style, poplar w/some curly maple, two-part construction: the upper section w/a rectangular top over a deep coved cornice above a pair of tall 3-pane glazed cupboard doors opening to two shelves over a low open pie shelf; the lower stepped-out section w/a pair of drawers w/turned wood knobs over a pair of paneled cupboard doors w/a replaced brass thumb latch, tightly scalloped apron on low bracket feet, pieced cornice repair, 19th c., 14 x 45½", 81" h. (ILLUS.) **1,595**

Step-back wall cupboard, country-style, walnut, one-piece construction, a rectangular top w/a wide flat & flaring cornice above a pair of 6-pane glazed cupboard doors w/original brass latch opening to two shelves, the stepped-out lower section over a pair of shallow drawers w/small wood knobs over a pair of paneled cupboard doors w/a brass latch, gently scalloped apron on bracket feet w/casters, knobs missing on latches, light blue interior repaint, minor foot damage, old varnish finish, mid 19th c., 16¾ x 50½", 81¼" h. (ILLUS.) **1,980**

Nice Walnut Step-back Cupboard

Step-back wall cupboard, Georgian, walnut, two-piece construction: the upper section w/a rectangular top over a narrow flared cornice & a carved dentil band above a pair of 6-pane glazed cupboard doors flanking three central fixed panes all flanked by side rails w/a carved paterae panel above a row of three small raised rectangular panels over an open pie shelf w/scroll-cut brackets; the projecting lower section w/a pair of drawers w/small wood knobs flanked by horizontally incised rectangular panels over a pair of raised panel cupboard doors flanked by long narrow raised panels, molded base on scroll-cut bracket feet, old dark varnish finish, Canada, early 19th c., 12½ x 63", 85¼" h. (restoration to top, back replaced by plywood) **4,400**

Step-back wall cupboard, Neoclassical, inlaid mahogany, two-part construction: the upper section w/a pair of flat-topped rectangular cupboards w/a single-pane glazed door opening to two shelves & mounted at the upper corners w/ormolu bosses flanking the central set-back rectangular tall mirror w/a gently arched top & molded crestrail w/an ormolu shell & leafy branch mount, the lower section w/a light rectangular marble top above a case w/a pair of banded drawers w/simple pulls above a pair of banded cupboard doors w/central oval floral urn inlays, leafy sprig ormolu mounts at each upper corner, flat molded apron on simple baluster-turned legs, France, early 20th c., 20¾ x 55", 75½" h. **1,265**

Step-back wall cupboard, Victorian-Style, mahogany, two-part construction: the upper section w/a rectangular top above

a deep flaring ogee cornice above a pair of tall glazed cupboard doors topped w/a band of applied pierced scroll carving across the top & scroll-carved drops at the front corners; the stepped-out lower section w/a rectangular top over a pair of flush ogee-fronted drawers over a pair of raised panel cupboard doors w/a band of applied pierced scroll carving across the top & flanked by scroll-carved drops at the sides, molded flat plinth base, early 20th c., 12½ x 42½", 86½" h. **935**

European Baroque Revival Cupboard

Wall cupboard, Baroque Revival style, oak, rectangular raised-center top w/wide stepped & flaring cornice over a wide frieze band centered by a wide carved scrolled cartouche over a molding above a pair of tall set-back cupboard doors w/leafy scroll-carved panels over arched tops & three tall narrow panels of beveled glass in each door over a square stepped panel, the doors flanked by bold stepped-out spiral-turned columns w/top & base capitals over a pair of small drawers at the bottom on a molded base w/short bracket feet, old dark finish, repairs, back reinforced w/plywood, Europe, late 19th c., 22½ x 56", 83¼" h. (ILLUS.) **660**

Wall cupboard, country-style, cherry, a flat rectangular top w/no cornice above a pair of tall paneled doors w/original brass thumb latches w/porcelain knobs above a lower pair of shorter paneled doors w/matching latches, flat bottom, refinished, mid-19th c., 16½ x 46½", 83¾" h. (porcelain knobs damaged, minor edge damage) **990**

Wall cupboard, country-style, painted pine, one-piece construction, rectangular flat top over a single wide raised double-paneled door w/latch & simple wood knob

Red-painted Pine Wall Cupboard

opening to three painted shelves over a medial rail & a short two-panel lower door opening to one shelf, shaped apron w/short bracket feet, original red exterior paint, repainted interior, hardware changes, minor height & cornice loss, old scraping to original red, New England, early 19th c., 19¼ x 43½", 81" h. (ILLUS.) .. **1,093**

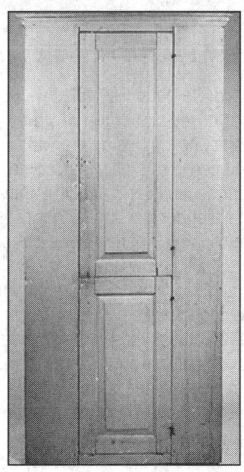

Simple Painted Pine Cupboard

Wall cupboard, country-style, painted pine, one-piece construction, the rectangular top w/a molded cornice over a tall narrow raised panel door opening to three full shelves & one contoured shelf over a similar shorter door opening to a single shelf, tall wide solid board front sides, hardware losses & changes, repainted chrome yellow, restoration, probably New York state, early 19th c., 19 x 36", 81" h. (ILLUS.) **978**

Early Canadian Painted Cupboard

Wall cupboard, country-style, painted pine, rectangular top w/a deep stepped cornice over a pair of wide & tall raised double-paneled doors w/wooden thumb latches at the top, molded base on tall scroll-cut bracket feet, paneled sides, painted blue, restoration, Canada, late 18th c., 21¼ x 53½", 71½" h. (ILLUS.)............**1,725**

Wall cupboard, country-style, painted pine, the rectangular top w/a deep flaring stepped cornice above a tall narrow case w/two double raised-panel cupboard doors opening to six shelves, molded base on bracket feet, remnants of red paint, New England, late 18th c., 18¼ x 38", 79½" h. **4,830**

European Wall Cupboard

Wall cupboard, country-style, painted pine, the rectangular top w/a high arched central section topped by a tall pierced & scrolling crest over flattened side cornices w/turned finials at the front corners, raised panel narrow frieze panels alternating w/rondels over a pair of tall cupboard doors w/single-pane glazed sections w/raised molding borders w/outset corners over matching solid panels in the lower section all opening to wooden shelves, a pair of drawers at the base above a flat apron on heavy ring- and peg-turned legs, old dark painted finish, damage & repairs, Europe, second half 19th c., 16 x 39", 73" h. (ILLUS.). **605**

Early Painted Wall Cupboard

Wall cupboard, country-style, painted, rectangular top w/a narrow stepped molding over a wide frieze board w/wooden thumb latch above a pair of tall paneled doors w/a turned wood knob, flat wide apron on slender baluster-turned legs on knob and peg feet, opens to unpainted interior w/two shelves, bluish green worn paint, all original condition & surfaces, Pennsylvania or Ohio, 1835-45, 14⅛ x 36¼", 59¼" h. (ILLUS.). **4,600**

Unusual Early Pine Wall Cupboard

Wall cupboard, country-style, pine, one-piece construction, the rectangular top w/stepped-out front corners over a deep conforming flaring cornice above a pair of sliding triple-paneled tall doors enclosing three shelves above a gadrooned molding & a single four-panel hinged door, all flanked by paneled pilasters w/molded capitals & bases, old refinish, remnants of bluish green paint, minor imperfections, southeastern New England, 18th c., 19½ x 37½", 78" h. (ILLUS.). **9,775**

Walnut One-piece Wall Cupboard

Wall cupboard, country-style, walnut, one-piece construction, the rectangular top w/a thick slightly overhanging cornice over a single wide double-paneled door w/a brass thumb latch over a medial band & a slightly shorter matching lower door, flat base, old finish, 19th c., 18 x 44", 76¾" h. (ILLUS.) **1,375**

Wall cupboard, pine, a pair of glazed cupboard doors opening to a single shelf above a pair of recessed-panel doors opening to six shelves, refinished, New England, mid 19th c., 17¾ x 39", 81¾" h. (some height loss, one pane missing). **1,840**

Wall cupboard, walnut, rectangular top above a pair of short square ornately pierce-carved doors each w/a central floral- or bird-carved cartouche framed by pierced scroll bands above a pair of tall flat cupboard doors w/flat oval two-part central latch, serpentine apron carved w/slender facing dragons, on slender square stile legs, old finish, China, late 19th - early 20th c., 18 x 38", 60¾" h. **660**

DESKS

McArthur Art Deco Desk

Art Deco desk, aluminum tubing & black lacquered wood, the rectangular black lacquered top w/a central raised support w/a tubular light, raised on anodized tubular framed w/a kneehole opening on the right & an open black lacquered shelf over two yellow lacquered drawers on the left, drawers w/aluminum arched pulls, designed by Warren McArthur, made by McArthur Industries, 1930s, repainted, 24 x 44", 29" h. (ILLUS.) **5,225**

Art Deco pedestal desk, mahogany, the rectangular top w/molded edges overhanging a long flush central drawer over the kneehole opening flanked by two stacks of four short drawers each, raised on stepped square plinths, all trimmed w/ormolu & ormolu bar-form pulls, w/ivory plaque inscribed "J. Leleu," France, ca. 1935, 34½ x 78", 30" h. **17,250**

Art Nouveau writing desk, fruitwood parquetry, the rectangular top inlaid in various woods w/a large butterfly amid blossoms & chestnut leaves, the apron w/a single long drawer, raised on slender buttressed slightly flaring molded legs, signed in marquetry "Gallé," France, ca. 1900, 26 x 41", 31" h. **4,312**

Unique Carved Burmese Desk

Burmese desk, carved hardwood, the superstructure w/a high undulating pierce-carved central crestrail over two openings w/pierced arched crests & center small columns over a rectangular surface fronted by a sloped writing surface, all flanked on each side w/a tall narrow rectangular cupboard w/scallop-carved crest above a pierce-carved door, all on a rectangular top w/carved rim over a central kneehole opening w/pierced arched bracket flanked by two ranks of three ornately carved drawers all on square carved short stile legs joined by a back stretcher, Burma, late 19th c., 28 x 56", 51" h. (ILLUS.) **1,840**

Chippendale slant front desk, curly maple, a narrow rectangular top above a wide hinged slant front opening to an interior fitted w/a row of small drawers above a row w/two drawers centering a pigeonhole above arcaded & plain pigeonholes, the case w/three long thumb-molded graduated drawers w/butterfly brasses, molded base on scroll-cut bracket feet, old refinish, Massachusetts or New Hampshire, late 18th c., replaced brasses, 17½ x 36", 43½" h. (imperfections) **3,335**

Chippendale slant front 'reverse serpentine' desk, carved mahogany, narrow rectangular top above the wide hinged slant front opening to a stepped interior of small drawers, the central one w/shaping on a case w/four long graduated scratch-beaded conforming drawers above a conforming molded base w/central drop & front ball-and-claw feet & shaped bracket rear feet, old refinish, Massachusetts, 18th c., 22 x 42", 44½" h. (repairs) **5,175**

Chippendale Slant-Front Desk

Chippendale slant-front desk, carved maple & cherry, a narrow rectangular top above a hinged molded slant lid opening to an interior fitted w/a central fan-carved drawer flanked by document drawers &

six pigeonholes above four short drawers, the case below w/four long graduated drawers above a central apron pendant, scroll-cut bracket feet, repairs to feet, New England, probably New Hampshire, ca. 1780, 17½ x 35", 41¾" h. (ILLUS.) **6,900**

Chippendale-Style Block-Front Desk

Chippendale-Style block-front slant-front desk, mahogany, a narrow top above a winged slant lid opening to an interior fitted w/three shell-carved arches above stacks of small drawers separated by arched pigeonholes over small drawers, the case w/four long block-front drawers each w/brass butterfly pulls & keyhole escutcheons, labeled "Museum Reproduction, Authorized by Edison Institute, Dearborn, Mich., Colonial Mfg. Co. Zeeland, Mich.," old finish, early 20th c., minor wear & edge damage, 22¼ x 40½", 43¼" h. (ILLUS.) **1,375**

Chippendale-Style slant-front desk, mahogany, a narrow rectangular top above a wide hinged slant front opening to a fitted interior above a double-serpentine fronted case w/four long graduated drawers w/butterfly brass & keyhole escutcheons, molded conforming base on short front cabriole legs w/claw-and-ball feet, marked "Maddow Colonial, Jamestown, NY," ca. 1920s, refinished, 16 x 28½", 40" h. **440**

Classical Butler's Desk

Classical butler's desk, carved mahogany & mahogany veneer, the rectangular top above a drawer opening to a writing surface & a bird's-eye maple interior of eight drawers & six valanced pigeonholes, the case w/three recessed long drawers w/flanking free-standing columns w/acanthus carved Corinthian capitals, on a stepped plinth base & large ball-turned feet on casters, replaced brasses, old feet, possibly New England, ca. 1825, imperfections, 22 x 45", 48" h. (ILLUS.) **920**

Early Cherry Desk on Stand

Country-style desk on stand, cherry, a narrow galleried top shelf above a hinged slanted lift lid w/applied edge molding opening to a compartmented interior set into a base w/a long thumb-molded drawer & flat apron raised on four tall slender square beaded legs joined by box stretchers, original brown paint, central Massachusetts, ca. 1800, 19 x 30¾", 47½" h. (ILLUS.) **3,220**

Country-style fall-front desk, walnut, a rectangular top above a large flat hinged fall-front opening to form a writing surface w/an interior composed of pigeonholes & letter slots w/two small drawers & a secret compartment, the lower case w/the long drawers each w/two turned wood knobs & a keyhole, simple bracket feet, old finish, 19th c., 17 x 37", 44¾" h. **605**

Federal lady's desk, carved mahogany & mahogany veneer, the rectangular box top opening to an interior of three drawers & a writing surface on a base w/a single long drawer w/two round brass pulls raised on ring-, knob- and spiral-turned legs ending in disk & peg feet on casters, old finish, probably Massachusetts, ca. 1825, minor imperfections, 19½ x 29½", 37¾" h. (ILLUS.) **1,093**

Federal Lady's Desk on Turned Legs

Federal Lady's "Tambour-front" Desk

Federal lady's "tambour-front"desk, inlaid mahogany, two-part construction: the upper section w/a rectangular top above a pair of tambour sliding doors opening to four short drawers & two valanced pigeonholes flanking a central door opening to two short drawers & a valanced pigeonhole; the lower projecting section w/a hinged writing flap above two long drawers w/oval brasses & inlaid dies, on square double-tapering line-, bellflower-, dot- and lozenge-inlaid legs ending in crossbanded cuts, appears to retain original brasses, Boston, Massachusetts, ca. 1795, losses to inlay, patches to veneer, repair to one front leg, 20 x 36½", 43" h. (ILLUS.)............. **4,312**

Federal slant-front desk, cherry, a narrow rectangular top above a wide hinged slant-front w/breadboard ends opening to a stepped interior of a central drawer flanked by eight valanced compartments above five short drawers & two shallow drawers, the case w/four long graduated drawers above a valanced apron &

slender French feet, New England, ca. 1800, 15 x 40", 44" h. (replaced butterfly brasses, refinished, imperfections) **4,880**

Federal slant-front desk, inlaid mahogany veneer, a narrow rectangular top above a hinged slant front opening to an interior fitted w/two groups of four small drawers over arcaded pigeonholes flanking a center prospect door, the lower case w/four long drawers w/banded veneer & stringing inlay, oval brasses & keyhole escutcheons, curved apron & French feet, old surface, original brasses, New York state, early 19th c., 21½ x 41½", 44" h. (veneer cracking, loss & patching, other surface imperfections) **2,530**

Federal "tambour" desk, inlaid mahogany, two-part construction: the upper section w/a stepped-back rectangular top above a row of two long drawers flanking a short center drawer all above twin tambour doors flanking a small plain prospect door all opening to an arrangement of drawers & valanced pigeonholes; the lower section stepped-out w/a fold-down writing surface over a case of three long graduated drawers flanked by banded stiles & raised on ring- and rod-turned tapering cylindrical legs w/peg feet, probably Newburyport, Massachusetts, early 19th c., 21½ x 40¾", 52" h......... **4,140**

Federal-Style writing desk, inlaid mahogany, a rectangular top above a pair of long drawers w/inlaid border banding above a central arched kneehole opening w/applied fans at corner brackets flanked by two smaller inlaid drawers, round brass pulls, worn blonde finish, 20th c., 30 x 48", 28¾" h. **220**

George III-Style pedestal desk, mahogany, the rectangular molded top inset w/gilt-tooled green leather, above a long center drawer over the kneehole flanked by two stacks of four small drawers each, deep molded plinth base on casters, England, ca. 1900, 28½ x 54", 29½" h. (wear, lower drawers loose within case) **1,610**

Georgian-Style "kidney-shaped" desk, mahogany veneer, the oblong gently curved top w/a long central drawer over the kneehole opening flanked by stacks of five graduated drawers all w/banded veneer trim & oval brasses, the back of the case w/open book shelves, refinished, probably England, early 20th c., 23 x 48", 29½" h. **605**

Louis XV-Style "bonheur du jour" desk, gilt-bronze mounted marquetry, the upper section w/a central tall solid door set w/an oval "Sevres" porcelain plaque surrounded by gilt-metal banding &

Louis XV-Style "Bonheur du Jour"

crossbanded veneer & a gilt-lattice crest, flanked by two lower sections each w/three small drawers above the projecting serpentine base w/gilt-metal banding above a serpentine veneered apron w/long drawer w/a writing surface all raised on slender veneered cabriole legs w/gilt-metal knee mounts & "sabots," France, late 19th c., 22 x 36", 44" h. (ILLUS.)........................... **4,312**

Louis XV-Style Cylinder-front Desk

Louis XV-Style 'cylinder-front' desk, gilt-bronze mounted mahogany, a rectangular top w/a low gilt-metal gallery above three narrow drawers w/gilt-bronze pulls & mounts above the wide cylinder front w/gilt-bronze scroll banding opening to a slide-out inset leather writing surface, all above a heavy gilt-bronze border over the apron w/a long central drawer w/gilt-bronze mounts flanked on one side by two small drawers & on the other by a single deep drawer each w/scrolling gilt-bronze mounts, on simple cabriole legs w/long gilt-bronze scroll mounts down the legs ending in feet w/"sabots," France, late 19th c., 30 x 64", 48" h. (ILLUS.) **13,800**

Louis XV-Style desk, mahogany, the rectangular top w/a superstructure containing drawers & pigeonholes, the apron w/three drawers, raised on twisted columnar legs, France, 19th c., 24 x 49", 36" h......................... **862**

Louis XVI-Style desk, gilt bronze-mounted mahogany, the rectangular top w/inset tooled leather writing surface above a conforming case w/a single center drawer over a kneehole opening flanked by two stacks of three drawers each, France, late 19th c., 34½ x 72", 31" h............ **3,162**

Mission-style (Arts & Crafts movement) desk, a rectangular top slightly overhanging an apron w/a long flush central drawer over the kneehole opening flanked on each side by a stack of two deep drawers w/original copper hardware, through-tenon construction & paneled sides & back, square legs, original finish, branded mark of L. & J.G. Stickley, Model No. 501, 30 x 48", 30" h. **2,090**

Mission-style (Arts & Crafts movement) desk, a rectangular top above a case w/a long flush drawer over the central kneehole opening flanked on one side by a stack of three small drawers & on the other side w/a single small drawer over a false-double-fronted file drawer, pull-out writing shelves, original dry finish, "Handcraft" decal of L. & J.G. Stickley, Model No. 615, 32 x 60", 30" h. (some refinishing on the top) **4,400**

Mission-style (Arts & Crafts movement) desk, oak, a narrow rectangular raised shelf above an open compartment of pigeonholes, slots & small drawers on the rectangular top overhanging the apron w/a pair of small drawers w/original iron hardware, square stile legs, recent finish, paper label mark of Gustav Stickley, Model No. 720, 23 x 38", 37" h........... **1,375**

Mission-style (Arts & Crafts movement) partner's desk, oak, a wide rectangular top supported by eight square legs inset into the top, four on each side of the central kneehole opening, each side w/a pair of small deep drawers flanking the kneehole opening & each w/a square, pointed pull, applied X-design on the ends, the legs ending in shaped Mackmurdo feet, original dark finish, attributed to McHugh, 37 x 56", 29" h. (one knob replaced) **1,430**

Mission-style (Arts & Crafts movement) slant front desk, oak, a low crestrail on a narrow top shelf over the wide hinged slant front opening to a fitted interior including drawers above a deep apron w/a pair of small, deep drawers flanking a small, arched central kneehole drawer,

Lifetime Mission Slant Front Desk

square legs extending above the top of the front edge, low side stretchers joined by a narrow medial shelf stretcher, new dark finish, foil decal of the Lifetime Furniture Company, 16 x 31½", 44½" h. (ILLUS.). **1,045**

Stickley Brothers Slant Front Desk

Mission-style (Arts & Crafts movement) slant front desk, a narrow rectangular top w/pointed rear stiles above a wide hinged slant top w/long copper strap hinges, opening to a fitted interior above a long drawer above the kneehole opening, slender square legs joined by short double end stretchers & a single rear stretcher, on slightly arched shoe feet, cleaned original finish, unsigned Stickley Brothers, Model No. 6516, 15 x 30", 47" h. (ILLUS.) **2,090**

Mission-style (Arts & Crafts movement) slant front desk, oak, a narrow top w/a high three-quarters gallery above the wide hinged slant front w/original pointed copper strap hinges opening to a fitted

interior above a pair of short drawers over a long drawer above a pair of flat cupboard doors w/long pointed copper strap hinges, original hardware, flush tenons at sides, fine original finish, early red decal mark of Gustav Stickley, Model No. 550, ca. 1902, minor separation on one side, 14 x 33", 48" h. **12,100**

Queen Anne slant front desk, maple, a narrow top above a wide hinged slant front opening to an interior of valanced compartments above small drawers, the end drawers separated by scrolled dividers, above a case of three long thumb-molded drawers on a molded base w/bracket feet & central drop pendant, old darkened surface, probably northern Maine, 18th c., 17½ x 35½", 40¼" h. (imperfections). **5,175**

Queen Anne-Style Child's Desk

Queen Anne-Style child's desk on frame, curly maple, two-part construction: the upper section w/a narrow rectangular top over a hinged slant-lid opening to a block-and fan-carved interior w/three graduated drawers below; the lower section w/a mid-molding over one long drawer above a scroll-cut apron on cabriole legs ending in pad feet, butterfly pulls, probably 19th c., 15 x 25¾", 38½" h. (ILLUS.). **6,900**

Queen Anne-Style desk on stand, parcel-gilt red-japanned wood, two part construction: the upper section w/a narrow rectangular top over a hinged slant-lid opening to an interior w/pigeonholes & three small drawers over two long cockbeaded drawers w/teardrop pulls; on a base w/a mid-molding above a narrow apron w/central drop all raised on tall cabriole legs ending in pad feet, decorated overall w/chinoiserie scenes & designs, probably 19th c., chips, 16¼ x 21½", 37" h. (ILLUS.). . **2,300**

Queen Anne-Style Desk on Stand

Queen Anne-Style Library Desk

Queen Anne-Style library desk, oak, a wide rectangular top w/molded edge above a deep bowed band w/a long conforming drawer w/bail pulls at the front above the kneehole opening, above an incurved band w/a small drawer on each side of the kneehole, raised on heavy cabriole legs ending in paw feet, ca. 1900, 28 x 45", 30" h. (ILLUS.) **863**

Dutch Rococo-Style Lady's Desk

Rococo-Style lady's slant-lid desk, mahogany & floral marquetry, a narrow rectangular top above a wide hinged slant-lid opening to a fitted writing compartment above a slightly inset small central drawer over the kneehole opening flanked by double small square drawers on each side, simple cabriole legs ending in "sabots," Holland, third quarter 19th c., together w/a Neoclassical-style mahogany & floral marquetry side chair, desk 18½ x 29½", 37½" h., 2 pcs. (ILLUS. of desk) **1,840**

Victorian "Cylinder-front" Desk

Victorian "cylinder-front" desk, Renaissance Revival substyle, walnut, a narrow molded top above the high cylinder-front w/recessed burl panels opening to an interior fitted w/large pigeonholes over small drawers above a mid-molding over the lower case w/an arched central long drawer over a paneled kneehole opening flanked by a pair of projecting drawers w/recessed burl panels above stacks of three drawers w/recessed burl panels flanked by molded & shaped blocks, paneled base ends, plinth base, right side w/side-lock false drawer, kneehole w/false privacy panel w/locking door, ca. 1880, 31 x 48", 56" h. (ILLUS.) **2,588**

Victorian "Davenport" desk, mahogany, the upper section w/a leather-lined slanted writing surface opening to three drawers & one false drawer front releasing one at the right, above the lower case fitted w/five drawers on one side opposing false drawers, raised on carved turned feet on casters, second quarter 19th c., England, 20 x 22", 30" h. (wear) **805**

Victorian plantation desk, walnut & mahogany veneer, two-part construction: the upper section w/a rectangular top w/flaring stepped cornice above a wide veneered frieze band over a full-width two-panel fall-front hinged lid opening to a fitted interior; the lower stepped-out section w/a rectangular top over a single long veneered drawer w/replaced brasses, raised on four ring-, knob- and block-turned legs w/ball feet, mid-19th c., 21½ x 34", 59¼" h. (restoration). **770**

William & Mary Desk on Frame

William & Mary desk on frame, tulipwood & oak, two-part construction: the upper section w/a narrow rectangular top over a hinged raised-panel fall-front opening to an interior of four compartments, three drawers & a well w/sliding closure above a double arched deep molded front; the lower section w/a mid-molding above a wide molded rectangular top overhanging a deep apron w/a long drawer w/brass teardrop pulls & a diamond-form keyhole escutcheon over the valanced apron, knob- and trumpet-turned legs on shaped flat cross stretchers over turned 'turnip' feet, replaced brasses, old refinish, minor imperfections, probably Connecticut, early 18th c., 15 x 24¾", 42½" h. (ILLUS.). **17,250**

William & Mary-Style writing desk, oak, rectangular top w/molded edges above a case w/a central long drawer w/angular border molding forming a long panel over the kneehole opening flanked by two stacks of three drawers each decorated w/similar molding & panels, each drawer w/a brass teardrop pull, raised on eight baluster-, ring- and block-turned legs joined by low ball-turned stretchers, on ball feet, old finish, early 20th c., 27¾ x 59", 31" h. (one piece of drawer molding missing) **495**

DRY SINKS

Grain-painted Country Dry Sink

Painted & decorated poplar, rectangular well top w/a raised backboard w/curved ends above a pair of drawers w/turned wood knobs over a pair of paneled doors w/the original cast-iron thumb latch w/porcelain knob, one-board ends, cut-out feet, original dark brown graining, 19th c., 17¼ x 41", 34" h. plus crest (ILLUS.). **1,045**

Painted pine & birch, rectangular well top projecting over a case w/a single cupboard door, old salmon-colored paint, 19th c., 34" l. **1,500**

HALL RACKS & TREES

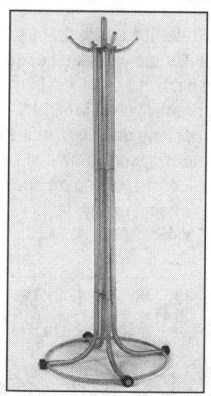

Early Aluminum Hall Rack

Hall rack, Modern style, anodized tubular aluminum frame w/rubber "doughnut" feet, multi-tube shaft & upturned hooks at top, manufactured by Warren McArthur Industries, ca. 1930s, 24" d., 67" h. (ILLUS.). **3,575**

Hall rack, Victorian Golden Oak, the tall superstructure w/a high arched & scroll-carved crest flanked by high scroll-carved ears above a rectangular mirror flanked by flat stiles mounted w/forked bronzed

metal coat hooks w/the wide lower back
panel w/bands of raised scroll carving,
low open arms flanking the rectangular lift
seat & boxed base w/scalloped apron &
scrolled front feet, ca. 1900, 15 x 36", 83" h. . . . **690**

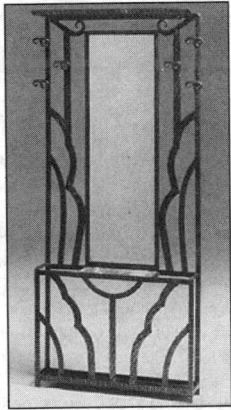

French Art Deco Hall Tree

Hall tree, Art Deco style, marble-inset
wrought iron, the rectangular upright
framework composed of hammered
bands, the rectangular hat rack above a
beveled long mirror flanked by hooks
above an inset marble shelf & umbrella
stand w/a drip pan, wear, small dents,
France, ca. 1925, 6 x 32", 74" h. (ILLUS.). . . **5,750**

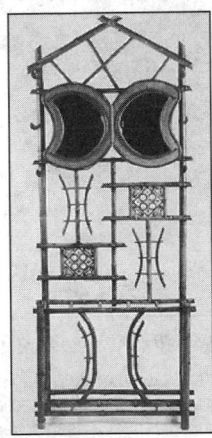

Victorian Bamboo Mirrored Hall Tree

Hall tree, Victorian bamboo, rattan & tile-
inset tree, an openwork design of
bamboo twigs above a pair of back-to-
back wide crescent-form beveled mirrors
over further curved & square bamboo
w/tiles & woven rattan sections above the
umbrella rack bottom framework,
probably England, late 19th c., 9½ x 32",
84" h. (ILLUS.) **978**

Two Late Victorian Hall Trees

Hall tree, Victorian Eastlake substyle,
walnut, a tall slender form w/a scroll-cut
crestrail on three small spindles between
narrow stiles w/a projecting bar w/hooks
at the left side & hooks down the right
stile all flanking a small rectangular mirror
over fanned spindles beside a tall row of
short horizontal spindles above the
backed rectangular seat flanked by
slender turned open arms & spindled
apron on turned legs joined by flat
stretchers, ca. 1890, 14 x 20", 77" h.
(ILLUS. right) **633**

Hall tree, Victorian Golden Oak, the tall
back w/an arched scroll- and shell-carved
crestrail over a wide oval frame mounted
w/bronzed metal hooks surrounding the
oval beveled mirror over flat stiles
flanking a waisted & scroll-carved splat
over the curved open arms on curved
supports flanking the lift-top deep seat
w/a scroll-carved apron & curved stile
front legs, ca. 1900, 16 x 29", 82" h.
(ILLUS. left) **661**

Hall rack, Victorian Aesthetic Movement
substyle, walnut, the tall superstructure
w/an arched crestrail pierced w/leafy
rondels & side arches above a molded
rail over a panel of raised scrolling
molding above a tall rectangular mirror
flanked by wide pierced side panels
w/metal coat hooks above a lower wide
panel w/four rondel-carved corner panels
alternating w/pierced spindled panels all
centering a larger central panel, shaped
arms w/an umbrella bracket above a drip
pan at one side, wide lift seat above a
deep paneled base on turned feet,
15 x 33", 82" h. **886**

HIGHBOYS & LOWBOYS

HIGHBOYS

Queen Anne "Flat-top" Highboy

Queen Anne "flat-top" highboy, carved maple, two-part construction: the upper section w/a flat rectangular top w/a flaring stepped cornice over a row of three drawers w/two larger flanking a small fan-carved center drawer over a stack of four long graduated drawers; the lower section w/a mid-molding over two long drawers over a long drawer disguised as three deep drawers, the center one fan-carved, scalloped apron, cabriole legs ending in pad feet, replaced mid-moldings, New Hampshire, 1740-60, 20½ x 39½", 77" h. (ILLUS.) **8,200**

Queen Anne "flat-top" highboy, figured maple, two-part construction: the upper section w/a rectangular flat top w/a deep widely flaring stepped cornice over a pair of thumb-molded drawers over a stack of four long graduated thumb-molded drawers; the lower section w/a medial band above a single long, narrow drawer over a pair of deep square drawers flanking a central short drawer all above a deeply scalloped apron w/two turned acorn drops, on cabriole legs ending in pad feet, appears to retain original butterfly brasses & keyhole escutcheons, Rhode Island, ca. 1740, 18½ x 37", 70½" h. (some drawer lip patches, replaced drops) **10,925**

Queen Anne "flat-top" highboy, figured maple, two-part construction: upper section w/a rectangular top w/deep molded cornice above a row of three small drawers over a stack of four long graduated drawers; the lower section w/a mid-molding over two long drawers above a row of three deep drawers, the central one fan-carved, scalloped & scroll-cut apron above cabriole legs ending in pad feet, appears to retain original butterfly brasses & keyhole escutcheons, attributed to Major John Dunlap, New Hampshire, ca. 1760, 19½ x 38½", 77" h. (bottom drawer discolored) **9,775**

Queen Anne "flat-top" highboy, maple, two-part construction: the upper section w/a rectangular flat top w/a deep coved cornice above a pair of small drawers over a stack of four long thumb-molded drawers all w/butterfly brasses & keyhole escutcheons; the lower section w/a molded edge over a long drawer over a row of three drawers w/two small square drawers flanking a long center drawer, arched apron w/two drops, simple cabriole legs ending in pad feet, probably Massachusetts, ca. 1760, 21 x 38", 72" h. (imperfections). **9,775**

Fine Queen Anne Maple Highboy

Queen Anne "flat-top" highboy, maple, two-part construction: the upper section w/a rectangular top over a deep coved cornice over a row of three drawers w/the center one fan-carved over a stack of four long graduated thumb-molded drawers; the lower section w/a mid-molding over a long drawer over three deep drawers w/the center one fan-carved, scalloped apron & cabriole legs ending in pad feet on platforms, the butterfly brasses appear to be original, old refinish, minor imperfections, Massachusetts, ca. 1760, 20¼ x 38½", 74½" h. (ILLUS.). **27,600**

Fine Veneered Queen Anne Highboy

Queen Anne "flat-top" highboy, walnut &
walnut veneer, two-part construction: the
upper section w/a rectangular top over a
deep stepped & flaring cornice w/a
concealed linen drawer above a pair of
small drawers over three long graduated
drawers all w/veneering & crossbanding;
the lower section w/a deep flaring mid-
molding over a pair of shallow drawers
over a pair of deep drawers flanking a
shallow central drawer above the highly
arched & scalloped apron w/two acorn
drips, on simple cabriole legs ending in
raised pad feet, old engraved butterfly
pulls & keyhole escutcheons, old refinish,
minor restorations, probably Boston or
Essex County, ca. 1730-50, 22½ x 38½",
72¼" h. (ILLUS.) **33,350**
Queen Anne "flat-top" highboy, cherry &
maple, two-part construction: the upper
section w/a rectangular flat top w/a deep
coved cornice over two pairs of small
drawers flanking a deep fan-carved
center drawer over a stack of four long
graduated drawers; the lower section w/a
mid-molding over a single long drawer
over a row of three drawers w/plain
smaller square drawers flanking a central
longer fan-carved drawer, scalloped
apron, cabriole legs ending in pad feet,
refinished, 18th c., Massachusetts, 21½ x
29", 79¾" h. (replaced Ball & Ball
butterfly brasses, repairs & some
replacements) **8,525**
William & Mary "flat-top" highboy, painted
pine, two-part construction: the upper
section w/a rectangular top w/a shallow
flaring cornice over a pair of short
drawers over three long graduated

Early William & Mary Highboy

drawers; the lower section w/a widely
flaring stepped mid-molding over a pair of
deep drawers flanking a shallow central
drawer above the deeply arched apron on
trumpet-turned legs joined by flat
stretchers & bun feet, teardrop brasses
may be original, painted dark brown,
restoration, southeastern New England,
early 18th c., 18 x 33", 55" h. (ILLUS.) **16,100**

LOWBOYS

Queen Anne Lowboy

Queen Anne lowboy, mahogany, a
rectangular top w/molded edges above a
single long drawer w/three large butterfly
brasses over a row of three drawers
w/the central one fan-carved, scalloped
apron w/two teardrop drops, cabriole legs
ending in pad feet, New England, 18th c.,
20 x 30", 30" h. (ILLUS.) **4,600**

LOVE SEATS, SOFAS & SETTEES

French Art Deco Daybed

Daybed, Art Deco, rosewood, upright slightly scrolled ends enclosing an upholstered seat above a shaped front apron trimmed w/ormolu, on heavy blocked canted short legs w/ormolu mounts, Jules LeLeu, France, ca. 1935, 85" l., 35" h. (ILLUS.).................. **8,050**

Daybed, Mission-style (Arts & Crafts movement), oak, the even ends w/heavy square posts flanking a wide top rail over four vertical slats at each end, chamfered side rails & narrow lower stretchers, reupholstered drop-in spring seat, original medium dark finish, branded L. & J. G. Stickley mark, 29 x 80", 28" h............. **3,300**

French Art Deco Love Seat

Love seat, Art Deco, stained beech, a narrow U-form crestrail over the conforming tightly upholstered back & deep upholstered seat flanked by reeded tapering front stile legs, spots on fabric, restorations, France, ca. 1925, 48" l. (ILLUS.)............................. **2,300**

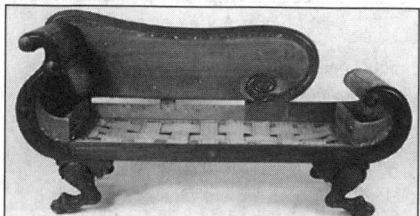

Finely Carved Classical Recamier

Recamier, Classical, mahogany, the molded & shaped back rail continuing to a leaf-carved scroll above the scrolled paneled arms w/concentric ringed bosses, above a paneled seat rail & carved paw feet on casters, Boston, old finish, ca. 1825, 65⅛" l. (ILLUS.)..................... **8,625**

Recamier, Federal, mahogany, a narrow reeded downward curving crestrail above the upholstered back & joining a high & low scrolled end arm w/reeded scrolled framing continuing down to the reeded seat rail, on reeded sabre legs ending in brass paw feet w/casters, probably Boston, early 19th c., 76" l.............. **7,475**

Federal-Style Decorated Recamier

Recamiers, Federal-Style, parcel-gilt & ebonized wood, the outscrolled open back rest formed w/turned & paneled slats above a long shaped arm over the narrow rectangular caned seat on slender knob- and ring-turned splayed legs joined by turned stretchers, decorated overall w/Classical designs in gold on black, some wear, ca. 1900, 76" l., pr. (ILLUS. of one) **2,875**

Settee, Chippendale-Style, mahogany, the delicately carved slender triple-arch crestrail above delicate scroll- and swag-carved pierced splats, slender curved open end arms on incurved arm supports, upholstered spring seat w/a thin serpentine seat rail, slender carved cabriole front legs & square canted rear legs, old finish, early 20th c., 42" l. (one back leg repaired) **770**

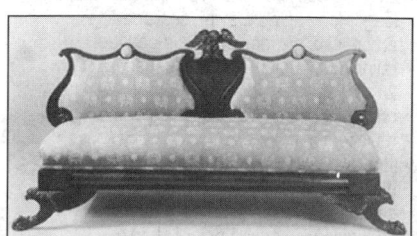

Finely Carved Classical Settee

Settee, Classical, carved mahogany, the upholstered double-shield-form back centered by a carved spread-winged eagle above a veneer panel, scrolled back stiles above the deep semi-overupholstered seat on a bolection-molded plinth & eagle-carved legs ending in paw feet, formerly fitted w/casters, probably New York City, ca. 1825, 72" l. (ILLUS.). **6,325**

Settee, William & Mary-Style, mahogany, triple-back style, the back section w/a high arched & pierced scroll-carved crestrail above a scroll-carved frame enclosing an oval caned panel between free-standing rope-twist stiles w/knob finial, long shaped open-end arms w/scroll-carved hand grips on rope-twist supports above the long upholstered seat on new plywood over the original caning, narrow carved seat rail raised on four rope-twist- and block-turned front legs joined by three wide arched & scroll-carved flat stretchers, long rope-twist H-stretcher joining front & rear legs, early 20th c., old dark finish, 66" l., 50" h. **715**

Settee, William & Mary-Style, oak, the high double-arched upholstered back flanked by shaped upholstered wings above the rolled upholstered arms, long cushion seat above the scalloped upholstered seat rail, raised on onion- and block-turned front legs & square canted rear legs joined by two sets of flattened double-arch stretchers, old worn finish, early 20th c., Europe, 60" l. **935**

Settee, Windsor "arrow-back" style, painted & decorated, the long flat crestrail divided into three sections w/four tapering stiles, seven arrow slats in each section, scrolled end arms above slender turned spindles & canted turned arm supports, long plank seat raised on eight ring-turned tapering legs joined by stretchers w/three central tablets & plain side & back stretchers, the crestrail w/gilt floral sprig decoration & banding on a dark ground, overall dark ground w/gold banding on slats & leaf bands on stretcher tablets, Pennsylvania, 1820-30, 78" l., 36" h. (some old repaint, minor imperfections). **1,093**

Settee, Windsor country-style, bamboo-turned hickory & poplar, a long flat crestrail between turned & flattened stiles w/two other stiles dividing the back into three sections filled w/slender turned tapering spindles, scrolled end arms over turned, canted arm supports & four spindles, long thick plank seat raised on eight canted bamboo-turned legs joined by flattened front stretchers & turned rear stretchers, refinished, first half 19th c., 84" l. (age cracks in seat). **935**

Windsor Country-style Settee

Settee, Windsor country-style, painted & decorated, the shaped triple-back crestrail raised on three stiles over a pair of long lower rails over numerous knob-turned short spindles, scrolled arms on two spindles & a canted turned arm support over the wide plank seat, raised on eight ring-turned tapering legs joined by turned box stretchers, worn original brown paint w/light green & cream-colored striping & h.p. rose decoration on the crest sections, stenciled label "E.D. Jeffries... Philadelphia, PA," plank seat worn, repaired break in one arm at post, first half 19th c., 73½" l. (ILLUS.). **1,430**

Gustav Stickley Signed Settee

Settee, Mission-style (Arts & Crafts movement), oak, a wide V-back top rail above twelve vertical slats between the square stiles, flat shaped arms on square front stile legs w/corbels under the arms, recovered leather seat, wide flat front & rear stretchers & narrow double side stretchers, large red decal mark of Gustav Stickley, Model No.212, 24 x 48", 36" h. (ILLUS.). **3,300**

Settle, Mission-style (Arts & Crafts movement), oak, the tall solid paneled back w/rounded side wings w/oval cut-out continuing to form low side arms flanking the wide lift-seat w/a deep apron, cut-out low feet, through-tenon construction, recoated original finish, some distress to the sides, red decal mark of Gustav Stickley, Model No. 224, 22 x 48", 45" h. (ILLUS.). **4,400**

Unusual Gustav Stickley Settle

Sofa, Art Deco, bent bamboo, the rectangular back & seat w/loose cushions flanked by arms formed w/concentric bands of bundled bamboo, ca. 1940s, 78" l. (small losses) **2,070**

Sofa, Baroque-Style, carved walnut, the simple rectangular back w/an elaborate surmounted crest in the form of a grotesque mask surrounded by foliate scrolls, flanked by winged female figures, Europe, late 19th c., 85" l. **3,737**

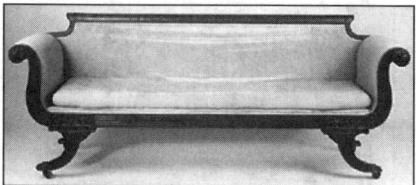

Duncan Phyfe-attributed Sofa

Sofa, Classical, carved mahogany, the long narrow rolled single paneled crestrail above out-scrolled arms w/reeded arm supports punctuated w/carved rosettes, upholstered back, arms & cushion seat, reeded seat rail w/flanking panels of foliate & leaf carving above reeded sabre legs on brass paw feet on casters, old surface, minor imperfections, attributed to the workship of Duncan Phyfe, New York City, 1815 25, 85" l. (ILLUS.) **4,600**

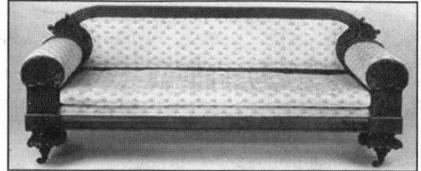

Classical Sofa

Sofa, Classical, carved & veneered mahogany, a gently arched reeded crestrail w/scroll-carved terminals over

the upholstered back & flanked by rolled arms w/applied carved frontal shells over the cushion seat & seat rail w/gadrooning on front egg-and-dart-carved feet on casters w/ring-turned rear feet, Baltimore or Philadelphia, ca. 1825-35, imperfections, 84" l. (ILLUS.) **690**

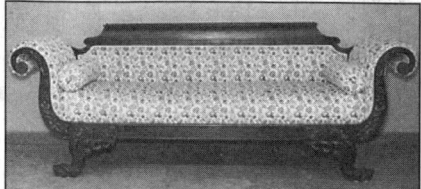

Dolphin-footed Classical Sofa

Sofa, Classical, mahogany & mahogany veneer, the raised crestrail w/rope-carved top & incurved ends above the upholstered back flanked by out-scrolling arms w/floral & cornucopia-carved arm supports continuing to carved panels & a flat molded seat rail raised on figural dolphin-carved front legs & turned back legs, refinished, reupholstered, first quarter 19th c., 107" l. (ILLUS.) **3,850**

Classical-Victorian Transitional Sofa

Sofa, Classical-Victorian transitional style, carved mahogany & mahogany veneer, the triple-arch crestrail w/high arched end sections centered by a shell & leafy scroll crest w/each end topped by a pierce-carved scroll crest, crestrail curved down around the upholstered back & arms & terminates in heavy scroll-carved arms on heavy scrolled front legs, molded serpentine seat rail, reupholstered, some frame damage, ca. 1840, 92" l. (ILLUS.) **743**

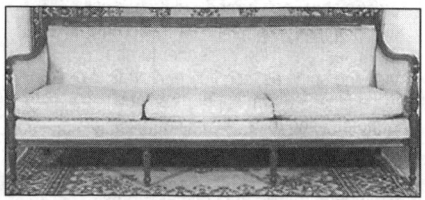

Federal-Style Mahogany Sofa

Sofa, Federal-Style, mahogany, long narrow crestrail carved w/three drapery- and floral-carved panels over the upholstered back flanked by scrolled closed arms on reeded turned & tapering arm supports & paneled corner blocks, flat seat rail on four reeded, turned & tapering legs w/peg feet, labeled "Hickory, N.C.," 20th c., 80" l. (ILLUS.) **468**

Sofa, Queen Anne-Style, walnut, rectangular-framed upholstered back over outscrolled arms, three loose cushions in seat, raised on cabriole front legs ending in pad feet, floral upholstery, England, early 20th c., 76½" l., 39" h. **1,840**

World Record Belter Sofa

Sofa, Victorian Rococo substyle, carved laminated rosewood, the long triple-arch back w/a high, ornately pierce-carved crestrail centered by a very high arched flower- and scroll-carved crest over scrolling grapevines continuing to arched corners w/carved baskets of flowers w/vines continuing down to the padded closed arms all flanking the tufted upholstered back, double-serpentine seatrail carved w/fruit and flower clusters alternating w/twist-carved & reeded sections, on three front demi-cabriole legs on casters & two rear legs, by John Henry Belter, New York City, ca. 1855, record price, 93½" l. (ILLUS.) **77,000**

Meeks' "Stanton Hall" Sofa

Sofa, Victorian Rococo substyle, carved & laminated rosewood, the ornate arched & pierce-carved crestrail centered by a

pointed rose crest over gadrooned bands & open scrolls continuing to curved pierce-carved corners continuing down & flanking the high tufted upholstered back, closed arms w/incurved carved arm supports continuing to the serpentine finger-carved seat rail & demi-cabriole front legs on casters, "Stanton Hall" patt. attributed to J. & J. Meeks, ca. 1855, age cracks, some edge damage, 65½" l. (ILLUS.) **5,500**

Meeks "Henry Ford" Pattern Sofa

Sofa, Victorian Rococo substyle, carved & laminated rosewood, the ornate arched & pierce-carved crestrail centered by a pointed rose crest over gadrooned bands & open scrolls continuing to curved pierce-carved corners continuing down & flanking the high tufted upholstered back, closed arms w/incurved carved arm supports continuing to the serpentine finger-carved seat rail & demi-cabriole front legs on casters, "Henry Ford" patt. attributed to J. & J. Meeks, ca. 1855 (ILLUS.) **13,200**

Sofa, Mission-style (Arts & Crafts movement), oak, even-arm style, wide top rails above the low back & sides w/numerous wide slats, recovered seat cushions, through-tenon construction, original finish, faint red decal mark of Gustav Stickley, Model No. 208, 32 x 76", 29" h. **8,800**

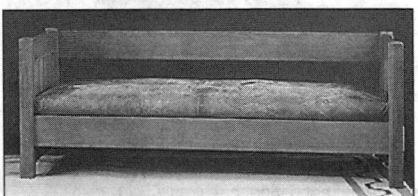

Gustav Stickley Model 225 Sofa

Sofa, Mission-style (Arts & Crafts movement), oak, a single wide back rail & even end arms w/five slats at each end flanking the original leather-covered drop-in spring seat w/some tears, original light finish, paper label & decal of Gustav Stickley, Model No. 225, 31 x 78", 29" h. (ILLUS.) **4,950**

Sofa, Mission-style (Arts & Crafts movement), oak, a wide flat crestrail above twelve wide vertical slats between the square stiles, flat tapering arms raised on front leg supports w/corbels, wide flat apron, original drop-in spring cushion seat recovered in brown leather, refinished, unsigned L. & J. G. Stickley, 25 x 65", 36" h. **1,980**

Sofa, Mission-style (Arts & Crafts movement), oak, even-arm style w/wide flat top rails joined by heavy square corner leg stiles w/tapering tops, the back composed of 22 narrow & wider slats & each end w/seven slats, wide seat rail, two large recovered cushions, recent finish, unsigned L. & J.G. Stickley, probably the Onondaga Shop, 31 x 77", 39" h. **6,600**

Wagon seat, painted & turned wood, two pairs of arched slats joining three simple turned back stiles, double woven rush seat flanked by turned arms & turned handholds atop the turned, tapering front end legs, shorter center legs all joined by simple turned rungs, old brown paint over earlier grey, New England, late 18th c., 30" l., 15" h. **1,093**

MIRRORS

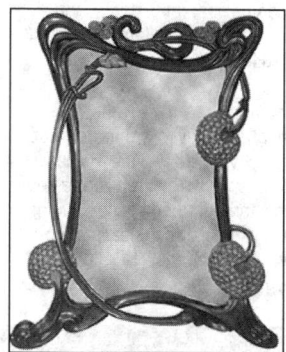

Art Nouveau-Style Mirror

Art Nouveau-Style wall mirror, carved mahogany, the rectilinear form of pierced whiplashes w/gilded blossom clusters surrounding the conforming mirror, some age but not period, age cracks, old finish, 38 x 47½" (ILLUS.) **715**

Chippendale wall mirror, mahogany & gilt gesso, the high arched & scroll-carved crestrail centered by a gilded round foliate device & ending in curved ears

Chippendale Wall Mirror

over the molded gilt-incised liner & gilt-incised scrolled base pendant, old refinish & regilding, England, late 18th c., 20½ x 36" (ILLUS.) **1,265**

Chippendale wall mirror, parcel-gilt mahogany, the high arched & scroll-cut crest centered by a gilt-incised concave round shell above upward scrolled ears over the narrow rectangular molded frame & mirror plate w/gilt-incised liner, downward scrolled ears & arched & scroll-cut base apron, probably England, ca. 1790, 14¾ x 27" (old refinish) **633**

Classical overmantel mirror, gilt gesso, the molded cornice above a horizontal split baluster joined to the vertical split balusters by corner blocks & rosettes enclosing the three-part mirror, New England, ca. 1830, 59¾" l., 21¾" h. (some imperfections) **920**

Classical wall mirror, mahogany & mahogany veneer, the flaring stepped cornice w/blocked ends above lyre-inlaid blocks flanking a wide veneer panel over the double mirror plate flanked by half-round ring-turned, leaf-carved & rope-twist columns above small bottom corner blocks w/rondels flanking a narrow veneer panel, ca. 1815-30, 25¼" w., 50½" h... **715**

Finely Decorated Federal Mirror

Federal wall mirror, giltwood & églomisé, stepped pedimented top suspending spherules over a tapering cornice above the rectangular églomisé panel painted white w/a gilt spread-winged eagle within a wreath & floral swags & bows, finely beaded side & bottom rails, attributed to Barnard Cermenati, probably Newburyport, Massachusetts, 1807-19, 19½ x 36" (ILLUS.) **3,335**

Federal Mirror with Rustic Panel

Federal wall mirror, giltwood & églomisé, stepped rectangular pediment crest suspending spherules above a conforming frieze band w/molded rosettes at each side over the églomisé panel painted w/a rustic landscape over the rectangular mirror plate all flanked by slender half-round reeded colonettes, molded flat base, probably Boston, early 19th c., original gilt, one spherule missing, restoration, 22¾ x 41½" (ILLUS.) . . **1,265**

Federal wall mirror, giltwood, the flaring flat pediment w/stepped-out ends above a band of acorn drops over a frieze band molded w/panels of paterae centering a floral basket panel above the two-part rectangular mirror flanked by ring- and baluster-turned pilasters w/molded classical scrolls w/a long central rope-twist section, ring- and rope-twist-turned lower rail, first quarter 19th c., 31 x 53" **4,313**

Federal wall mirror, inlaid mahogany & giltwood, the delicate swan's-neck cresting centered by a low giltwood urn issuing slender stemmed plants above a frieze panel w/a central eagle-inlaid oval above the molded rectangular mirror frame w/slender carved filets suspended from the upper corners, ornate scroll-cut lower corners & apron centered by an inlaid oval panel w/a seashell, late 18th to early 19th c., 59" h. **3,000**

Mahogany Federal Wall Mirror

Federal wall mirror, mahogany & églomisé, a stepped pediment crest w/coved cornice over a plain conforming frieze band over the rectangular églomisé panel painted w/a landscape w/a Native American & tiger over the rectangular mirror plate all flanked by half-round reeded colonettes, stepped-out base molding w/corner blocks & rondels, early 19th c., 38" h. (ILLUS.) **3,335**

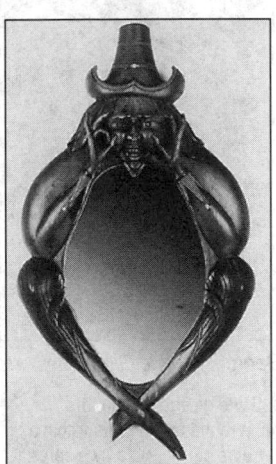

Folk Art Court Jester Wall Mirror

Folk art wall mirror, polychrome decorated carved pine, figural, the body of a court jester-like man w/tall hat, long hair & pointed chin wrapping around the oval mirror plate as the frame, finely carved facial detail & delicately carved hands framing his face, legs crossed at the bottom, late 19th c., repair to right foot, minor losses, 12 x 21" (ILLUS.) **3,738**

George II Mahogany Mirror

George II wall mirror, parcel-gilt mahogany, the high arched & scroll-cut crest centered by a gilded spread-winged phoenix above a molded narrow frame & gilt liner w/scroll-cut apron below, patches to veneer, replacements, England, mid-18th c., 22¼ x 39½" (ILLUS.) **1,380**

George III-Style Girandole Mirror

George III-Style girandole mirrors, giltwood, a round mirror plate within a molded frame surmounted by a spread-winged eagle & scrolling leafy vines, the similar apron fitted w/a pair of candlearms, chips & losses, England, late 19th c., 20 x 34½", pr. (ILLUS. of one) . . **4,312**

Queen Anne country-style wall mirror, figured walnut veneer, a high scroll-cut arched crest w/inwardly curled ears above a rectangular narrow molded frame enclosing the old mirror replacement, old refinishing, 18th c., 11 x 20½" (age cracks in veneer) **583**

Victorian pier mirror, Aesthetic Movement substyle, walnut, the tall superstructure w/a crown crestrail w/an arched & pierced center crest flanked by pierced stylized carved bands over a raised burl frieze band & shaped corner blocks above the tall rectangular mirror flanked by turned half-round colonettes, a narrow white marble shelf below the mirror supported on a stepped-out shelved bracket w/a small drawer above bobbin spindles & curved bracket supports on slender turned front legs, solid backboard w/molded base, 11 x 23", 87" h. **633**

Victorian Eastlake Pier Mirror

Victorian pier mirror, Eastlake substyle, carved walnut, the arched crest w/applied stepped molding over a leafy vine panel flanked by brackets w/turned finials above the slender side rails w/half-round colonettes halfway down above line-incised bands & blocked brackets on a rectangular marble shelf below the tall mirror plate, the base w/a central leaf cluster-carved panel flanked by curved brackets & turned spindles fronting the back panel & resting on a rectangular molded flat base, old finish, ca. 1880, 28" w., 92" h. (ILLUS.) **1,155**

Victorian pier mirror, Rococo substyle, giltwood, the high pointed arch crest ornately pierce-carved w/rococo scrolls & a central trefoil above the tall rectangular mirror plate w/rounded top, narrow molded side & base framed w/carved scrolls at the bottom corners, ca. 1850, 36½" w., 94" h. (well done repairs & some regilding) **1,155**

PARLOR SUITES

Art Deco: sofa & pair of club chairs; silvered & carved wood, each w/lobed upholstered back & seat flanked by uprights boldly carved w/curling feathers, American-made, ca. 1930s, sofa 84" l., 3 pcs. (chips) **1,380**

Art Deco: sofa & two armchairs; fully upholstered, each w/a flared, squared back & outswept squared arms, raised on short sycamore legs w/bronze sabots, Jules Leleu, France, ca. 1930, the set **10,925**

Art Nouveau Armchair & Side Chair

Art Nouveau: two armchairs & two side chairs; carved mahogany, "Les Pins" patt., tall slightly tapering back frames carved at the crest w/pinecones & needles above upholstered back panels, the armchairs w/curved closed arms over curved carved seat rails, gently outswept square legs, upholstered in tan leather, Louis Majorelle, France, ca. 1900, the set (ILLUS. of part) **10,350**

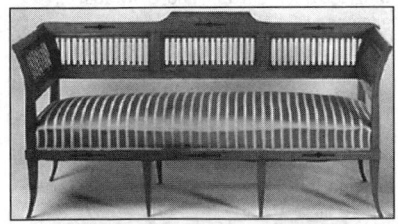

Biedermeier-Style Fruitwood Settee

Biedermeier-Style: settee & two armchairs; inlaid fruitwood, each w/a shaped crestrail w/raised center & small inlaid bands over back stiles flanking numerous tiny short turned slender spindles raised on a lower rail, the settee w/outswept matching arms, deep upholstered seats over a flat seat rail w/small inlaid bands, on square tapering legs w/end sabre legs on the settee, Europe, late 19th c., settee 67" l. (ILLUS. of settee) **3,738**

Empire-Style Parlor Suite

Empire-Style: settee & two armchairs; gilt-bronze mounted mahogany, each piece w/a square upholstered back within a conforming frame, the wide crestrail centered by gilt-bronze swans & scrolls continuing to padded arms w/round hand grips & further mounts raised on gilded swan-form supports enclosing the deep upholstered seat, flat seat rail w/long fern leaf mounts on turned front legs ending in gilt leaftips, heavy square rear legs, France, late 19th c., the set (ILLUS.) **14,950**

Louis XVI-Style: settee & two open-arm armchairs; each w/a square upholstered back within a ribbon-tied & bead-carved frame continuing to leaf-carved scrolled padded arms flanking the upholstered seat, gently curved seat rail w/bead carving & round fluted foliate-carved legs headed by rosettes, upholstered in floral Aubusson tapestry panels, France, late 19th c., settee 50¾" l., the set **6,900**

Renaissance Revival Suite

Victorian Renaissance Revival substyle: sofa, armchair, two "demi" side chairs & center table; the center table w/a shaped oval marble-inset top w/marquetry panel all within a bronze figural-cast band above an apron centered by marquetry panels, raised on scrolled incurved supports headed by gilt-bronze Egyptian heads ending in stylized hoof feet, the seating pieces w/squared upholstered backs, the sofa w/three tufted sections centered by a carved bust medial finial, outswept upholstered arms, the sofa w/gilded child mask arm supports, ring- and rod-turned tapering legs on casters, possibly by Pottier and Stymus, New York City, third quarter 19th c., the set (ILLUS. of part) **20,700**

SCREENS

Fire screen, Art Deco, iron & mesh, in three parts, the arched central panel flanked by pivoting sloping side panels, each cast w/slender stylized hounds, the whole painted black, designed by William Hunt Diederich, ca. 1920s, 41" l., 26½" h. **6,325**

Classical Mahogany Firescreen

Firescreen, Classical, mahogany, tiger stripe maple & mahogany veneer, the high rolled crestrail above the silk textile screen flanked by veneered columns w/brass capitals & bases above arched feet, repairs, Mid-Atlantic States, 1815-25, 13 x 26¼", 40¾" h. (ILLUS.). **1,610**

Fine Aesthetic Movement Firescreen

Firescreen, Victorian Aesthetic Movement, brass & colored glass, the rectangular screen frame inset w/amber & topaz colored glass square tiles within a leaftip cast frame raised on foliate-scrolled supports joined by an arched pierced leafy vine stretcher, American-made, ca. 1890, 30 x 38" (ILLUS.) **12,650**

Carved Aesthetic Movement Firescreen

Firescreen, Victorian Aesthetic Movement, ebonized wood, the high arched frame crestrail pierce-carved as leafy cattails flanked by the wings & heads of herons at the upper corners of the rectangular frame enclosing a needlepoint & beaded panel featuring a guardian angel carrying a child above a bouquet of roses, the lower rail also pierce-carved w/cattails flanked by arched animal-form legs w/paw feet, last quarter 19th c., probably English, 51" h. (ILLUS.). **1,265**

Folding screen, two-fold, lacquer & carved ivory, each panel decorated w/ivory birds, Japan, late 19th to early 20th c., each panel 30½" w., 70" h. **575**

Folding screen, three-fold, Edwardian style, painted satinwood, each panel decorated w/foliage & flowers, England, early 20th c., each panel 24" w., 70" h. **2,875**

Green-japanned European Screen

Folding screen, four-fold, green-japanned & gilt-decorated wood, each panel w/three inset panels decorated w/Chinese figures or birds & foliage, Europe, 19th c., losses, retouching, splits to some panels., each panel 23" w., 90" h. (ILLUS.) **2,587**

Folding screen, four-fold, lacquered wood, each panel screen-printed in black & colors to resemble continuous open book shelves filled w/books & "objets d'art" on the obverse, each reverse panel w/a clustered trophy printed *en grisaille* against a mottled grey ground, Piero Fornasetti, unsigned, ca. 1960, 55" w., 52" h. **8,625**

Chinese Lacquer Folding Screen

Folding screen, four-fold, lacquered wood, the four panels decorated w/a continuous battle scene w/horses, riders, warriors & trees in colored hardstone, bone & ivory inlaid on the black lacquer ground, China, 72" h. (ILLUS.) **403**

Folding screen, five-fold, gilt & black lacquer, each fold decorated on both sides w/a border above & below, centering a Chinese landscape including figures, raised on shallow feet, Chinese Export, 19th c., each panel 17⅝" w., 70¾" h. (chips & repairs, missing hinges, now mounted w/hanging brackets) **2,530**

Folding screen, six-fold, molded ash plywood, the undulating panels joined by canvas hinges, designed by Charles Eames, manufactured by Herman Miller, ca. 1950, 60" w., 68" h. (some minor chips) **4,675**

Pole screen, Louis XVI-Style, gilt bronze-mounted mahogany, the standard set w/an oval pastel portrait of an 18th c. woman, mounted as a lamp, France, late 19th c., overall 54" h. **1,840**

SECRETARIES

Chippendale Secretary-Bookcase

Chippendale secretary-bookcase, cherry, two-part construction: the upper section w/a rectangular top w/a deep coved cornice over a pair of tall paneled cupboard doors; the projecting lower section w/a rectangular top over a hinged slant-lid opening to a central prospect door flanked by valanced compartments & shallow drawers, the lower case w/four long graduated thumb-molded drawers w/butterfly pulls & keyhole escutcheons, molded base w/scroll-cut bracket feet, replaced brasses, refinished, New England, ca. 1780, restored, 20⅛ x 39¼", 86" h. (ILLUS.). **4,140**

Fine Classical "Secretaire à Abattant"

Classical *secretaire à abattant,* mahogany & mahogany veneer, the rectangular white marble top above a coved cornice over a wide frieze band over two veneered side columns w/Corinthian capitals & ending in large ebonized ball feet flanking the recessed central section w/a wide hinged fall-front opening to a writing surface & fitted interior over a pair of plain cupboard doors at the bottom, paneled sides, old refinish, imperfections, Boston, Massachusetts, 1820-25, 17½ x 35", 57½" h. (ILLUS.) **16,100**

Classical *secretaire à abattant,* marquetry, a rectangular top above a tall case w/a long narrow slightly projecting top drawer w/two knobs & a band of marquetry inlaid leafy blossoms & light banding flanked by light inlaid banded corner blocks above a wide rectangular flat hinged fall-front decorated w/a light wood central design of a compote of fruit framed by leafy scrolls & butterflies within an oval band framed by butterflies & a series of thin rectangular bands enclosed by leafy scroll corner designs & floral vines, the fall-front opening to a fitted interior above the lower case of three long drawers each w/matching marquetry designs of pairs of cornucopias issuing flora vines, the front sides w/light band inlaid columns on blocked feet, Holland, 19th c., 19½ x 39", 56½" h. **2,070**

Classical Mahogany Secretary

Classical secretary-bookcase, figured mahogany veneer, two-part construction: the upper section w/a rectangular top & deep ogee cornice above a pair of Gothic arched glazed doors w/pairs of trefoil cut-outs opening to shelves & w/a pair of narrow drawers below; the stepped-out lower section w/a fold-out writing surface above a case w/a slightly projecting long top drawer over two long drawers all w/simple wooden knobs, scalloped apron & bracket feet on casters, some edge & veneer damage, ca. 1840, 14¼ x 43¾", 82" h. (ILLUS.). **1,540**

Classical Rosewood Secretary

Classical secretary-bookcase, rosewood veneer, two-part construction: the rectangular top w/rounded front corners & a deep coved cornice above a beaded band over a pair of tall Gothic-arch glazed cupboard doors opening to three adjustable shelves over a row of three smaller drawers, the stepped-out lower case w/a hinged narrow fold-down writing surface opening to small satinwood-veneered drawers & valanced compartments over a pair of Gothic arch paneled & beaded cupboard doors on a molded base w/scroll-cut bracket feet, ivory escutcheons & tapered wooden pulls, old refinish, minor losses, New York City, ca. 1840s, 20⅝ x 44", 94¼" h. (ILLUS.). **5,175**

Inscribed Federal Secretary

Federal secretary-bookcase, mahogany & mahogany veneer; two-part construction: the top section w/a shallow shaped gallery above a flat molded cornice & two diamond-glazed square doors opening to a small drawer & compartments flanking a square flat central door over a small drawer; the projecting lower section w/a fold-down writing surface above a pair of cockbeaded drawers over two long cockbeaded drawers all w/round brass pulls w/rings, square tapering legs w/inlaid cross-banding, old refinish, imperfections & some restoration, New England, inscribed "22 Geo. L. Deblois September 12th 1810," 20 x 37⅛", 51½" h. (ILLUS.) **2,990**

Federal Secretary-Bookcase

Federal secretary-bookcase, rosewood & birch-inlaid mahogany, two-part construction: the upper section w/a rectangular top w/narrow molded cornice & veneered frieze band over a pair of Gothic arch-glazed cupboard doors opening to two shelves, four short drawers & ten pigeonholes; the stepped-out lower section w/a cross-banded hinged writing flap opening to a tooled leather surface above four cockbeaded long graduated drawers w/oval brasses, band-inlaid apron w/central squared pendant, tall slender French feet, North Shore, Massachusetts, ca. 1810, 20 x 39¾", 65" h. (ILLUS.) **14,950**

Federal "tambour" secretary-bookcase, mahogany & mahogany veneer, two-part construction: the tall upper section w/a rectangular top w/a deep flared cornice over a carved dentil band above a pair of geometrically glazed cupboard doors opening to shelves over a pair of sliding tambour doors opening to a figured maple interior; the lower stepped-out section w/a hinged writing surface over a

Rare Federal "Tambour" Secretary

case w/two long cockbeaded drawers w/oval pulls raised on tall square tapering legs joined by recessed box stretchers, probably New England, early 19th c., 40" w., 73" h. (ILLUS.) **5,750**

Queen Anne secretary on frame, cherry, three-part construction: the upper section w/a rectangular top w/a deep stepped molded cornice above a pair of tall raised paneled doors opening to shelves; the lower section w/a mid-molding over a hinged slant top opening to eight small drawers & twelve pigeonholes above four long graduated drawers on the separate molded stand w/short cabriole legs ending in pad feet w/peaked toes, New England, 18th c. & later, 19 x 36½", 91" h. . . . **4,600**

Queen Anne Secretary

Queen Anne secretary-bookcase, carved & figured maple, two-part construction: the upper section w/a broken swan's-neck pediment w/pinwheel terminals surmounted by three turned finials over a pinwheel-carved scrollboard above a pair of tall raised-panel cupboard doors w/tiny knobs & brass keyhole escutcheons opening to an interior fitted w/thirteen pigeonholes; the lower section w/a hinged slant front opening to an interior w/eight valanced pigeonholes & fifteen short drawers, the case w/four long cockbeaded graduated drawers w/butterfly pulls & keyhole escutcheons, molded base on scroll-cut bracket feet, repairs, eastern Connecticut, 1740-60, 18 x 36", 84" h. (ILLUS.) **43,125**

Victorian Aesthetic Fall-front Secretary

hinged fall-front opening to a fitted writing compartment; the stepped-out lower section w/a rectangular top & rounded front corners over a conforming dentil-carved cornice over a long drawer & raised panel cupboard door flanked by side panels topped by boldly carved putto heads, molded base on scroll-cut bracket feet, possibly Boston, last quarter 19th c., 19½ x 39¾", 68¼" h. (ILLUS.) **2,300**

Victorian "Cylinder-front" Secretary

Victorian "cylinder-front" secretary-bookcase, walnut & burl walnut, two-part construction: the upper section w/a rectangular top w/deep flaring cornice over frieze band w/narrow raised burl panels & a rondel above a pair of tall arched & glazed cupboard doors opening to shelves; the lower section w/a curved "cylinder front" w/burl panels opening to a fitted interior & writing surface above a long slightly projecting drawer w/two raised burl panels above two further long drawers w/burl panels & flanked by carved blocks, plinth base, ca. 1875, 13¾ x 43¾", 92" h. (ILLUS.) **1,870**

Victorian fall-front secretary, Aesthetic Movement substyle, mahogany, two-part construction: the upper section w/a rectangular top w/a widely flaring stepped cornice over a dentil-carved band above pairs of reeded & carved flat pilasters at the sides flanking the paneled & mirrored

Golden Oak Secretary-Bookcase

Victorian secretary-bookcase, Golden Oak substyle, the superstructure w/a rounded squared mirror frame w/scroll carving enclosing a matching beveled mirror beside w/scroll-carved cornice over two shallow drawers all on a rectangular top above a hinged fall-front w/applied carving opening to a fitted interior above

A CENTURY OF COLLECTING

THE OLD AND THE NEW

by Emyl Jenkins

Things changed from throw-aways to treasures mighty fast," my 90-year-old father remarked not long ago. Then he told me about how, as a boy in Massachusetts, he had found an old wooden coffee grinder in perfect condition that had been discarded, thrown away, in a vacant lot. "Sure wish I had kept it," he sighed.

That mind-set keeps you and me from throwing out lots of things these days. In fact, a hundred years from now, anyone looking back at the late 1990s will surmise that antique collecting was a popular national pastime.

Antique malls, antique shows, and antiquing publications are everywhere. On TV there are collecting shows, tours of historic homes and museums, and

discovery hours—all designed to help the unfortunate, unknowledgeable soul identify the objects that his ancestors bought and treasured years ago.

Need more proof? At the end of the century, one of Wall Street's darlings is eBay—the Internet site where anyone can buy, or sell, antiques and collectibles to his heart's content.

As the 20th century comes to a close, antiquers and collectors rank right up there with avid gardeners and food aficionados. But it hasn't always been that way. The present-day passion for collecting antiques is actually a fairly recent phenomenon that can be traced back to the turn of the last century.

Looking at the 20th century as a whole, two epochs emerge as being

Out with the old—in with the new. Around 1900 early Historical Staffordshire (platter left) was being packed away as finely decorated Haviland porcelain (dessert set below) became fashionable and affordable.

1906 Country Life in America: The Home Builder's Supplement *living room (right) with eagle over mantel, blue and white Staffordshire plates, simple (but period) Queen Anne chairs in a Connecticut circa 1750 house. Dining room (above) fitted with plates and pewter, from the same house.*

particularly significant: 1900-1929, when antique collecting truly began in America, and the 1970s to the present when the collectibles market took off.

According to the accounts at the turn of the last century—the end of the 19th century and beginning of the 20th century—the attic steps were a mighty busy place.

While movers were bringing one of the new mass-manufactured oak side-by-sides in the front door, Dad and the boys were hauling the deeply-patinated, 18th-century cherry secretary/bookcase up the attic steps. While Mother was unpacking her new set of mail-order Haviland china, Grandmother was carefully packing away her mother's old English Staffordshire plates for safe-keeping alongside the old secretary.

Unless, that is, you were one of the new breed in 1900—a collector. In that case, you were the one climbing the steps and digging around in every accessible attic—your own, your grandparents, and even the one in the deserted farmhouse at the end of the dirt road—in hopes of finding an 18th-century secretary and some lovely early 19th-century Staffordshire.

In other words, while some families were putting away their heirlooms, others were bringing down their own (and others) treasures from the past to proudly display in their homes.

However, it should be made clear from the outset that at the turn of the century, the majority of Americans were much more fascinated with the remarkable technological and industrial developments going on right in front of them, than they were with foraging out relics from the past.

The story of how and why antique collecting became so popular in the 20th century is really fascinating. It isn't just about who was collecting what, though. It is the story of how Americans saw themselves, their homes, and their pasts. It is the story of technology and nostalgia.

Today, the very technology that was so new and fascinating to our ancestors has become commonplace and is taken for granted. Today, the "old" is mysterious and alluring to us. That's why so many more of us have the collecting bug.

How it all happened follows.

LAYING THE FOUNDATION FOR THE FUTURE
1900-1929

At the turn of the century, the man in the street, as well as the man in the mansion, had fairly well-defined ideas about how he wanted his home furnished.

Then, just as now, newspapers and magazines were filled with lifestyle stories and features. In fact, it wasn't unusual for editorials to expound on the importance of the home in building moral character in the new generation.

At the same time, the new technological breakthroughs of the last quarter of the 19th century were changing 20th century home life considerably.

Electricity and telephones and sewing machines were becoming commonplace in houses on Main Street, U.S.A.—along with Colgate's dental powder and Heinz's 57 varieties. In a word, the world had entered the modern age. (What a bonanza all those now old-fashioned early 20th-century objects would provide for 21st-century collectors!)

Technological marvels that excited the fancy of early 20th century Americans included treadle sewing machines, typewriters in nearly every office, the arrival of the "horseless carriage," phonographs for entertainment and the telephone for rapid communication.

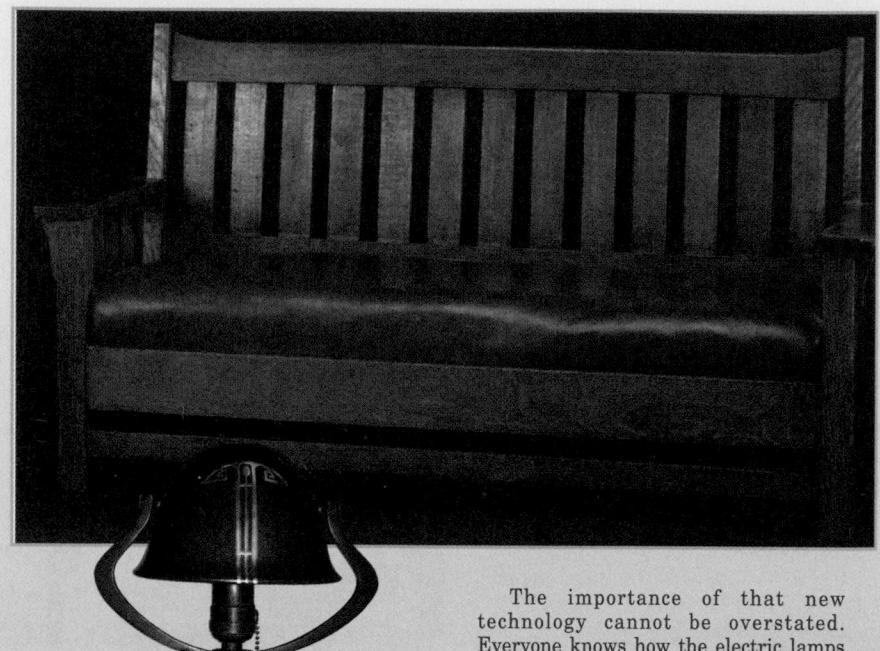

The importance of that new technology cannot be overstated. Everyone knows how the electric lamps and ice boxes of the early 1900s eventually changed our lives and lifestyles. But there was another much more subtle change taking place. For the first time in history the middle class had choices.

During earlier eras, people had to settle for whatever was available. Now, thanks to the new machinery and widespread technology, it was as simple to turn out a four-legged table as a three-legged one. It was as easy to print a floral drapery pattern as to make stripped upholstery fabric.

Add to that the availability of having these new goods in every city, town, and hamlet across the country, thanks to ribbons of rails spanning the continent! Amid all those changes, shopping, as we know it today, was born.

Once railroad trains could deliver manufactured goods almost anywhere,

Competing in popularity in the early years of the 20th century were furniture styles such as the fussy "Golden Oak" and the new, austere "Mission" style in oak where straight lines predominated and fussy details were eliminated. This was part of the Arts & Crafts movement of that era which included other decorative pieces such as hand-worked copper pieces (Heintz Art Metal Shop lamp), art pottery and textiles.

stores—from department stores to specialty shops—sprung up overnight. If you couldn't find what you liked there, then you'd order the goods the same way we often do today—by mail-order through catalogues and advertisements.

Suddenly, people in Massachusetts found soap shipped in from Chicago less expensive than that made locally, and people in Virginia realized that furniture ordered from Michigan would be delivered more quickly than that commissioned from the local craftsman's shop.

If money was tight in those early years of the 20th century—no problem. Families saved coupons that came with the necessary everyday products, especially Larkin Soap and various chewing gums. When they had saved enough coupons, they ordered the premium they once had only dreamed of having—a bedroom suite or a dining room table—pieces that looked just like the ones displayed on the showroom floors.

The "new" look during the early 1900s is one familiar to us today—large quarter-sawn oak pieces built for utility,

The "Early American" style was also getting much recognition and if you couldn't afford the fine originals, furniture makers were producing inexpensive "copies" such as dining room suites and 'highboys.'

A Colonial Revival living room as shown in American taste-maker Clarence Cook's 1878 volume—"The House Beautiful." The scene is titled "Things New and Old."

function, and endurance. (When these pieces once again became all the rage in the 1970s they were called "golden oak.") The family's picture-book-perfect scene was made complete by adding hand-forged copper candlesticks and a floppy, leather-bound book by Elbert Hubbard.

But while some early 20th-century Americans were busy acquiring the most up-to-date furnishings and accessories, an ever-growing segment of the population was longingly looking backward to the beautiful furniture, china, silver, and objets d'art of by-gone years. To satisfy their wants, American furniture companies manufactured copies of the old styles.

Herein lies one of the great ironies in the history of the decorative arts. Much of what was being made new in the first years of the 20th century looked remarkably like the old.

There are several reasons why this happened. It started with the 1876 American Centennial celebration.

The years between 1776 and 1876, particularly the destructive Civil War years, had been pretty tumultuous for this young country. So it was only natural that when visitors to the great Centennial Exhibition of 1876 in Philadelphia saw such quaint exhibits as "A New England Kitchen," and "Log Cabin in 'Ye Olden Times,'" they longed to recapture the simpler, more "idyllic" life of Colonial America in their own homes.

For many people living in Victorian homes with knick-knacks on every shelf,

This turn-of-the-century, ca. 1900, china cabinet recalls the Classical (Empire) style of the 1830s with its mahogany veneer, heavy columns and paw feet.

Wallace Nutting's hand-tinted photographs were all the rage in the early years of this century. Some of his most popular were interior scenes recreating the "Colonial" look of years gone by such as 'A Stitch In Time,' shown here.

opulent flowered draperies held back with braided roping, and an array of fern stands, floor-to-ceiling mirrors, and heavily carved picture frames everywhere they turned, the change was welcomed.

Simple 18th-century Windsor chairs; graceful, unadorned Chippendale desks; the always nostalgic spinning wheel— these surely must have seemed like a breath of fresh air.

Even those who couldn't see these exhibits first-hand, read about them in such widely-circulated periodicals as *Harper's, Scribner's,* and *Every Saturday.* These newsworthy, yet heart-warming, scenes sparked a nostalgic longing among the masses. People now wanted what "grandmother" had had.

Even if you were living in a Victorian house, you could show how up-to-date you were by replacing some of furniture your family had purchased in the 1860s or 1880s with pieces reminiscent of the 1760s or 1780s. Soon the demand for the 18th century look became so popular that in the mid-1880s, a furniture trade journal reported, "The manufacture of antiques has become a modern industry."

Actually, looking backward was part of the Victorian tradition. Think about it.

The names given to the various Victorian decorative arts styles all harkened back to an earlier time. There was the "Renaissance Revival," the "Gothic Revival," the "Egyptian Revival,"

even the "Rococo Revival." So why not a "Colonial Revival?" That is exactly what happened.

The April, 1895, issue of *Vogue* described the fervor of this end-of-the-century trend this way:

"Farmers' wives were startled by visits from richly dressed ladies in search of spinning wheels, brass andirons and coal-scuttles, and much admiration was lavished upon the antique writing desks and chests of drawers.

"Since then the demand for these things has increased so enormously year by year that all modern furniture is manufactured in imitation of them, though the imitations are sadly inferior to the originals."

By 1900, the mainstream taste of the times was definitely moving toward a revival of the Colonial.

Helping the movement along was Wallace Nutting. His turn-of-the-century "cottage industry" equaled Martha Stewart's efforts today.

Nutting, a Congregational minister turned antiques guru, wrote books— *Connecticut Beautiful, Massachusetts Beautiful, Virginia Beautiful,* etc.— expounding the beauty and serenity, as well as virtues, of old American houses and her untouched countryside.

To make his point, he photographed what he saw and started yet another venue: hand-colored photographs of "Colonial" scenes.

For the very wealthy with baronial tastes and deep pockets, highly ornate, heavily-carved and expensive pieces were available, either brought over from Europe or carefully crafted in America.

Nutting produced untold numbers of romanticized pictures of costumed ladies and children participating in "Colonial" activities set in appropriate proper "Colonial" settings—tea parties, flower gathering, letter writing.

He also put his skills as a furniture maker to work. A quick glance at Nutting's furniture catalogues shows exactly what people wanted for their homes—copies of American furniture from the late 17th, 18th, and early 19th centuries. In other words, anything "old"—as long as it wasn't Victorian.

Why, we might wonder today, was it necessary to make "new" objects that looked like the "old" ones when the genuine pieces were still around?

A clever ad by the Stickley Furniture Company of Fayetteville, N. Y., (not to be confused with the L. & J. G. Stickley Company, also of Fayetteville which specialized in the competing Arts and Crafts style) said it all. "Old family trees have countless branches....but the forefathers' furniture did not multiply."

By the dawn of the 20th century, there simply wasn't enough of the old remaining to meet the new demand. Anyway,

some people always want the look of the old, without the marks of age.

Popular books on antiques were also beginning to appear. Such wonderful, provocative titles as *The Quest of the Colonial* and *The Lure of the Antique* made the hunt sound irresistible.

Alice Morse Earle had begun the trend in 1898 with her publication, *Home Life in Colonial Days.* The illustrations in her book catalogue the decorative items early 20th-century collectors were looking for to go with their furniture: warming pans, upright churns, tinder boxes, door knockers, candle boxes and molds, Betty lamps, fire buckets, old gourd dishes, and "old-time Bandboxes."

It would be erroneous, however, to think that the only antiques attracting attention at this time were American Colonial antiques.

Just as improved transportation made it easier to ship goods anywhere, so it also made travel much easier for all who could afford it. With the fortunes being made from the new technology—manufacturing, steel, railroads, electricity, oil, rubber, tobacco, etc.—there were new fortunes galore.

When America's newly wealthy class came home from their European travels they brought souvenirs with them. For some, "souvenirs" meant jewelry and knick-knacks. For others, "souvenirs" meant containers full of opulent period furniture, as well as new reproductions of the old European styles, and Old Master paintings.

Such American "castles" as Biltmore, The Breakers, and San Simeon were built based on the combination of new wealth and greater international exposure. Contributing to this lifestyle was Edith Wharton's 1897 book, *The Decoration of Houses,* co-authored by Ogden Codman, Jr., an architect/decorator.

In general, however, during the 1900s and 1910s, Colonial simplicity was much preferred over European grandeur. In fact, the general public could identify with neither the wealth, life-style, nor the tastes of this very small, elite group.

All the while the new technology was spreading and the "quest for the Colonial" was becoming popular, the Chatauqua movement was touching American lives.

Chatauqua was a combination Sunday School, Summer School, and cultural enrichment program held on the shores of the lake by the same name in upper New York State.

Though the fine and decorative arts were never part of the Chatauqua program, as small towns across the United Sates began modeling "study groups" after Chatauqua, an increased awareness of art and culture and history spread quickly.

Following this example, grass-roots women's clubs and art societies quickly formed with the express purpose of raising the burgeoning middle class's level of awareness of "fine things."

Thus, in its own way, Chatauqua paved the way for museum lectures, traveling exhibits, and even antique shows with accompanying educational lectures that we enjoy to this day.

Technological innovations, choices, greater cultural awareness, swifter communications, a sweet nostalgic longing for the past...these were the dominating socio-economic forces affecting middle America's homelife in early years of the 1900s. It was in this environment that serious antique collecting began—so serious that some of our country's finest museums eventually sprang from the core private collections amassed during this era.

Collectors of Early Americana were inspired by writers like Alice Morse Earle to search out vintage items such as bandboxes, Jacquard coverlets, splint woven baskets and even early leather fire buckets like those shown here and on the previous page.

ANTIQUE COLLECTING COMES INTO ITS OWN
LATE 1910s AND '20s

Surrounded by newly-built factories and whirling machines, an elite group of well-to-do, well-educated men looked around, took stock of the new that looked like the old, and despaired.

They saw poorly-designed, shoddily crafted objects when compared to the originals. These are the men, and in a few instances, women, (remember this was the 1920s) who began collecting antiques with a vengeance. (Elizabeth Stillinger's landmark 1980 book, *The Antiquers,* chronicles the lives, motivations, and adventures of America's pioneering antique collectors.)

Of course, collectors have always been around. Half a century earlier, when educated Americans became fascinated by natural history, large collections of shells and butterflies were proudly displayed in well-to-do homes. Now the focus was on American furniture and the appropriate accessories.

By the mid-1910s, dissatisfaction with new, mass-manufactured goods, combined with a deep intellectual curiosity about early American life, had ignited an interest among certain wealthy highbrows (as the intellectual wealthy were often called). Their deep pockets and intellectual approach to the subject exceeded the middle class's financial capability and mostly

sentimental yearning to recapture the aura of the past.

The majority of early serious antique collectors lived in New England. They were inspired, in part, by *The Colonial Furniture of New England,* written in 1891 by Dr. Irving W. Lyon. This scholarly and remarkably accurate volume sent out many enthusiastic and curious collectors in pursuit of the best of the past.

But there are other reasons why so many of the most famous collectors during the 1910-1920s era were centered in the North. First, the people there were, by nature, frugal. They saved old things.

Hand in hand with their frugal nature, New Englanders tended to "stay at home." Cleveland Amory, the great social historian, delighted in telling the story of "The Beacon Hill lady who, when chided for her lack of travel, asked simply, 'Why should I travel when I'm already here?'"

In contrast to their New England counterparts, wealthy and geographically widespread Southerners had looked across the Atlantic for their finest goods from their earliest Colonial days.

Just recall pictures of English-influenced Williamsburg, French-influenced New Orleans, and Spanish-influenced St. Augustine in your mind

In the 1910s, when the Kroehler Manufacturing Company was selling the "living room" concept to take the place of the 19th century "parlor," their inspiration was clearly updated Jacobean.

In the "fireside" group the candlestand is 18th century syle, the mantel clock and pictures are mid-19th century-type, and the chairs and side-tables are early 20th century adaptations of "Colonial" styles.

Beginning In 1900 Stickley of Fayetteville, N.Y., produced reproductions suitable for the "ideal" 20th century Early American home. Their early brochure featured a late 17th or early 18th century "Pilgrim" type breakfast room group.

and it all begins to make sense. Not only was the South much larger than the North, the Southern people were more diverse in their origins than the homogeneous Northerners.

These days scholars and historians like to dismiss the effect the devastation of the War Between the States had on Southern property. Even if the battles themselves are ignored, the poverty that racked the region during Reconstruction must be taken into account.

Robert and Elizabeth Shackleton, in their 1921 publication, *The Quest for the Colonial,* put it this way: "In the ever delightful Old Dominion, there are many fascinating and romantic houses which have withstood time and war. Some of them are shattered, unrestored, still in disrepair, waiting for happier days..."

Of course Southern homes had wonderful pieces, but just not as many American "Colonial" pieces as did the North. Nor were there so many people with the ways and means to begin serious antique collections at this point in history.

By the 1920s, when the Shackletons and others were on their "quest for the Colonial," Henry Ford's sweeping contribution to the 20th-century, the automobile, was changing every aspect of

American life. If trains had made it possible to furnish the home with new, stylish goods, cars now made it possible for families to move to new, stylish homes in the suburbs.

On the surface, the importance of this option would appear to be mostly socio-economic. In truth, the move to the suburbs by the middle class greatly affected America's taste in antiques and their collecting habits. With wheels at their disposal, they were ready to embark on shopping adventures....but for what?

As long as people lived in Victorian houses, they tended to buy large furniture to take up space in the rooms.

Granted, in their attempt to achieve a "Colonial" look many people had discarded the earmarks of the Victorian—heavy draperies, robustly-carved étagères, and over-stuffed tête-à-têtes. But the two most popular "antique" furniture styles during the early 1900s were Jacobean (or William and Mary) and Empire.

On the surface, the square, boxy lines of these styles were in stark contrast to the curvy mid-Victorian styles. Still, the furniture was sufficiently large-scaled to look good in high-ceilinged 19th-century rooms.

These color images from the 1928-29 "Furniture Dealers' Reference Book" clearly illustrate the 'lighter' Colonial look popular in the 1920s. The upper view of a small living room shows revival examples of Hepplewhite, Sheraton and Queen Anne. The "Bedroom of the Early American Type" shown below features Empire (Classical) Revival pieces.

When, in the early- and mid-1920s, the middle-American built his scaled-down dream house on a postage-stamp sized lot in the suburbs, he needed smaller-scaled furniture.

Suddenly the most popular "Colonial" styles became the daintier Hepplewhite and Sheraton styles, followed by Queen Anne and Chippendale. For those few preferring a more sophisticated look, the lighter gilt and painted Louis XV and XVI styles gradually began to catch on.

American furniture manufacturers responded by turning out copies of the original styles in every grade and quality for every pocketbook. Reproduction furniture was in its heyday.

In these post-World War I years, new houses in any variety of styles sprung up along suburban newly-paved, electric-lighted streets with bucolic, sonorous names like Maple Lane, Elm Street, and Virginia Avenue. Floor plans and blueprints were taken straight out of *Ladies' Home Journal* and local newspapers. The standard three-bedroom, one-and-a-half-bath house was charmingly "antique" and named accordingly—Dutch Colonial, English County, Spanish Hacienda, French Provincial.

But don't be misled by those "foreign"-named house plans. The "Colonial" craze begun by the Centennial Celebration some 50 years earlier had never stalled. National pride was stronger than ever in these post-World War I years.

Now, with World War I behind them, more people had more, but smaller, houses.

Ten, fifteen years earlier, back in the 1900s and 1910s, darker wood, larger, 17th-century furniture was the rage. But in truth, there had only been so many period court cupboards and trestle tables and settles in America originally.

Jump ahead to 1920 and 1925. The nation's high spirits and smaller homes now called for a lighter look and more delicate furniture.

There had been many more maple Sheraton fancy chairs and cherry candle stands made originally in America's later "Colonial" days—in the late 18th and early 19th centuries—than in the 17th century. Further, the furniture made in those years (also called American Federal), was generally smaller and lighter than that built by America's Pilgrim forefathers.

What could be more appropriate for these new houses? Not only were these later smaller antique pieces plentiful, they were more affordable for the ever-growing middle-class.

Likewise, the accessories of the late 18th and early 19th centuries—especially glass and china—were plentiful and inexpensive. Quilts, rugs, handicrafts, andirons, Currier and Ives prints—anything that was old—became coveted and collected.

Suddenly, antique shops were immensely popular. But so also, every deserted, or occupied, farmhouse and storage barn became the antiquer's hunting ground.

In the throes of this 1920s collecting boom, even old structures became fodder for the passionate antiquer. Whole rooms, and sometimes dwellings, were purchased by wealthy collectors who incorporated them in their "Colonial Revival" homes. For the more modest collector, cobblers' benches were turned into coffee tables. Worn wagon wheels and spinning wheels became chandeliers.

And... many a "fake" was made out of old wood for the unknowledgeable, unsuspecting, and gullible antiquer. If the 1920s were bonanza years for collectors, they were equally good for the charlatans who were muddying the antiques waters for collectors.

Books of the era were already warning readers about pieces that were being made of old wood and sold as "antiques," and of semi-old pieces that had been "antiqued" by darkening the wood to give them an aged patina or spotted with old-looking worm-holes made with a very fine drill or even bird-shot!

In a climate where fabulously wealthy collectors were purchasing entire shops and housefulls of antiques, and the man on the street was suddenly

Early American glass became a collecting rage during the 1920s and 1930s. Lacy glass (1825-40s), blown-three-mold (circa 1830) and early decorative vases (circa 1845), such as these examples, became especially popular.

Photos courtesy of Collector's Sales & Service. Middletown, Rhode Island.

These fine 19th century paperweights have long been choice collector treasures. Cheap imitations, especially from China, have flooded the market since the 1930s, but skilled artists have revived this artform today. Condition, design and origin are as important as age when buying.

a "serious" buyer, faking antiques became a profitable business.

One observer, seeing how calculating dealers played on the innocent for all they were worth, wrote: "The selling campaign of the bogus antique was remarkably well managed through skillful publicity and propaganda, by those who were first to see its commercial possibilities...."

In truth, fakes became so commonplace in the 1920s that in the early 1930s, Ruth Webb Lee published her book *Antique Fakes & Reproductions.*

In the following excerpt, Lee describes the dark side of the antiques business. At the same time, the passage gives the present-day reader a first-hand look at those objects the public was collecting in the 1920s—and a subtle warning that later collectors should proceed cautiously.

She shows us the items that made it worth someone's time to forge and reproduce. She tells us what pieces led her to write the treatise:

"Thousands of dollars have been lost by credulous buyers who have paid for reproductions the high prices that only genuine antiques should bring....blown glass, pattern glass, cup plates, paper weights, Bohemian glass, hats, historical flasks, milk-white glass, lamps and globes, iron work, ceramics, and silver fakes and forgeries."

Nonetheless, antiques were given a resounding vote of confidence when, in 1924, the American Wing of the Metropolitan Museum of Art opened. Here, for all to see, were period rooms filled with American antiques—America's historical treasures.

Following the Met's example, museums in Brooklyn, Boston, and Philadelphia opened period rooms. American antiques were also the drawing card for the famous fund-raiser, The Girl Scouts Loan Exhibition held in New York City in 1929.

More and more, the public could step back in time by stepping into a museum, or an old building.

Henry Ford had recently saved the Wayside Inn in Massachusetts and in 1929 John D. Rockefeller would begin restoring and rebuilding Colonial Williamsburg in Virginia.

Equally significant was the start-up of America's longest-running antiques publication, *The Magazine, Antiques.* Begun in 1922, *Antiques* was responding to the public's interest in the subject. Its commitment to the history and scholarship of America's decorative arts is what has given this publication staying power through the century, while other antiques-related newspapers and magazines have come and gone.

Coinciding with all these activities— museum openings, books and magazines

Cover of the first issue of The Magazine, Antiques.

Early 20th Century collectors were inspired by the 1876 Centennial celebration to seek all things "Pilgrim." The rare, 17th Century pieces assembled and preserved during that time later became the basis of many period rooms in American museums. Shown—The Criss Cross Great Hall courtesy of the Museum of Early Southern Decorative Arts.

on the subject, antique hunting expeditions—were news-making auctions. Henry Francis Du Pont, who is generally considered America's most important collector of antiques began his lifelong quest for the best in 1923. Du Pont, who chronicled every step of his collecting life, attended his first auction in June, 1924, and made a few modest purchases.

In April, 1929, when the first of two record-breaking auctions was held—the famed Reifsynder sale—Du Pont was there. He outbid William Randolph Hearst for the Van Pelt highboy. When the bidding stopped at $44,000, Henry Francis Du Pont had set the record for the most money ever paid for an American antique.

The following January, only a few short months after the Crash of '29, Mr. Du Pont bought a labeled secretary by John Seymour & Sons for $30,000 and a Rhode Island tea table for $29,000. These would go in his private collection which would eventually become the basis for Winterthur Museum which opened to the public in 1951.

As the early decades of the 20th century drew to an end it was obvious: antiques from the past were well on their way to becoming the wave of the future.

SEEKING COMFORT IN TROUBLED TIMES
1930-1945

Say 1930 and most people think, "the Great Depression."

In the world of antiques, collecting, and the decorative arts of the 20th century, another, equally seminal word was to be reckoned with—Modernism.

The Colonial Revival was so strongly in place by the mid-1920s that the United States declined an invitation to exhibit at the 1925 Paris Exposition des Arts Decoratifs et Industriels Modernes because there were no "modern decorative arts in America." Ironically, four years later, in 1929, the Metropolitan Museum of Art unveiled a landmark "modern" exhibit, "The Architect and the Industrial Arts."

Shortly before the Wall Street Crash, Art Deco, which already was immensely popular in Europe, began to take a strong foothold here. Soon, stunning Deco buildings with matching interior designs, such as Radio City Music Hall, caught the public's imagination.

Once Wall Street crashed, however, a longing for the quality, beauty, and yes, serenity, of the past became even more important than ever. In these turbulent times, once again, antiques provided the perferred "homey" look.

Emily Post's book, *The Personality of the House,* was published in 1930. Throughout the pages, Post provided in-depth looks at classical architecture and furniture styles. Only at the end did she give lip-service to the new look in the chapter, "The Style We Know As Modern."

About the kindest thing Post had to say about modernism was, there might be possible value in an occasional "modern accent." For, she concludes, "Having throughout several thousand years accepted as permanent nothing less than beauty, it is not likely that we are beginning a permanent esthetic decline that will ultimately accept plaids and cubes and prisms on the walls, plaids and cubes and prisms under foot, a tiger skin flung across a sloppily made up bed, coffin sideboards, crypts built into the walls, furniture made in the image of vegetables with the legs of insects, or sausages skewered on bent lengths of gas pipe—simply because it has not been done before."

And so, for the man on the street, and the wealthy tycoon who had seen his fortune disappear, alike, tradition was symbolic of permanence.

In retrospect, the Great Depression more directly affected new production than it did the collecting habits of most Americans. In fact, if anything, these lean years made the public more aware of its "old things."

Hobbies magazine, begun in 1931, became immensely popular. Not only were adults urged to delve into the history and craftsmanship of 18th- and 19th-century antiques, children were encouraged to spend their idle hours pursuing the handicrafts and pastimes their ancestors had enjoyed rather than purchasing new, expensive toys.

This 1938 special Christmas supplement to House & Garden proves that a picture is worth a thousand words. For the New England saltbox house Santa has traditional "Colonial" pieces. For the ultra-modern Art Deco home he has all the latest contemporary fashions. And the houses are right next door to one another!

Other, more scholarly, popular collecting pub-lications of the decade were *American Collector, The Antiquarian,* and *Interna-tional Studio,* and, of course, *The Magazine, Antiques. Avocations: A Magazine of Hobbies and Leisure,* began publication in October, 1937.

The demand to learn more and more about cherished objects led to more and more books on the subject. There was F. C. Morse's *Furniture of the Olden Times,* Ruth Webb Lee's numerous glass books, and even a reissuing in a new edition of N. Hudson Moore's 1905 volume, *The Collector's Manual.*

Representative of the rebirth of interest in things "Victorian," this Fenton glass cranberry opalescent Hobnail cruet was part of their extensive Hobnail line.

On the other hand, the popular "ladies'" magazines of the day, *The American Home, Ladies' Home Journal, House and Garden,* pushed the new look of the era—the very same modern look that Emily Post had so vehemently demeaned. They had to. The manufacturers of these pieces were their advertisers.

But every issue also included nostalgic, collecting, and antiques related articles ranging from "Furniture for an Elizabethan House," to "Recreating a dinner table at which George Washington might have played the host."

Of course some extraordinarily wealthy collectors—Henry Francis Du Pont, Henry Ford, and Francis Garvin among them—continued as they had in the 1920s—buying everything in sight. (As Elizabeth Stillinger wrote in the Epilogue of *The Antiquers,* when she ended her story of the century's great collectors at 1930, the collections assembled in the 1920s "have influenced our thinking about the American past and its artifacts ever since.")

But in the economically difficult 1930s, small, easily portable items definitely dominated the antiques scene, particularly glass and china. The number of articles on paperweights and dolls, cup plates and lustre ware, ladies' fans and standing salts begin to outnumber treatises on furniture.

For most collectors it was glass, glass, glass..... For, as the advertisement for Mary Harrod Northend's book, *American Glass* read: "America has reason to be proud of her glass industry, one of the very first industries in this country, established in Colonial days in the face of difficulties almost insurmountable."

Remembering those "insurmountable difficulties" seemed to put the troubles of the 1930s in perspective. If our American ancestors could turn out beautiful, breakable glass in the pioneering days, it was now the collector's bountiful duty to cherish and preserve it.

Wistarberg, Stiegel, and Sandwich became the buzz words of the antiques industry. Cup plates, salt cellars, flasks, lamps, candlesticks, decanters, tumbler, jars—literally every item made of glass became collected—so passionately so, that after the success of Minnie Watson Kamm's book, *Two Hundred Pattern Glass Pitchers,* in 1940 she wrote *A Second Two Hundred Pattern Glass Pitchers.* She then followed these with volumes three through eight.

Going hand-in-hand with the American collector's fascination with glass, was a growing interest in everything Victorian. A decade earlier, after hungry collectors had gobbled up all things 18th century, early 19th century Empire and Victorian objects slowly became more appealing.

The best barometer of the man in the street's taste are the reproductions of the time. By the later 1920s, copies of 1860s Victorian furniture were rolling off the production lines.

By 1932, the floral-carved Victorian look had gained so much momentum that in February, *House & Garden* ran a feature on "Victorian chintzes that suit today's revival."

Not just Victorian glass and furniture, but the dolls, fans, mourning jewelry, and crazy quilts of the era returned to a visible place in the American home.

It should also be noted that by the last years of the decade, the word "investment," combined with the joy of the hunt, begins to creep into the antiquers vocabulary.

No one said it better than Alice Carrick when she titled her 1937 volume, *Collector's Luck: Or, A Repository of Pleasant and Profitable Discourses Descriptive of the Household Furniture and Ornaments of Olden Time.*

Still, "modernism" had not entirely faded from the home furnishing scene.

As the 1930s progressed, Art Deco became more accepted by the general public and many wonderfully designed, fine quality items were made.

Then, as often happens, once the general public took to the new look, the market became flooded with poorly designed, cheaply made, and poor quality Art Deco knock-offs. When the 1939 New York's World Fair became a showplace for Deco souvenirs, its eventual demise began.

Art Deco would hold on through the war years, but by the late 1940s it was definitely passé....until it was rediscovered about a quarter of a century later.

By and large, people were seeking a comfortable, simple life, especially after the belt-tightening depression era. Rural life was idealized and Marion Nicholl Rawson's 1940 publication, *The Antiquer's Picture Book,* included yokes, cranberry scoops, and mailboxes among pictures of hand-crafted hobby horses, silver tea strainers, and Bennington pottery jugs.

And so, another phase of American 20th century life was nearing its end. Art Deco had threatened; but its influence was passing.

Those who were so inclined bought the "real thing." A few were misled and talked into buying "fakes." Others chose

the "reproductions" being offered everywhere—furniture showrooms, the local craftsman's shop, even in Colonial Williamsburg, which, of course, gave an air of respectability to "museum-quality reproductions."

World War II disrupted every aspect of American life. New home furnishings all but disappeared from the scene when the nation turned its attention to the war effort. After it was over, the war only reinforced America's love affair with her past.

In 1944, Carl W. Drepperd published *The Primer of American Antiques.* The name of this perennially popular book was most apt. A whole new generation of antiquers would soon tuck it under their arms when, after the war, they began their foraging into the countryside in their new cars with a full tank of gasoline.

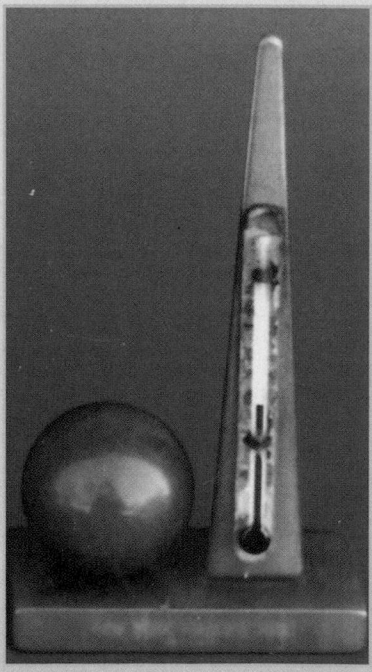

The Trylon and Perisphere, symbols of the 1939-40 New York World's Fair, represented the Art Deco theme on a grand scale. This little Bakelite souvenir thermometer illustrates the final commercialized phrase of the Art Deco design movement. Photo courtesy of Kevin McConnell.

COLLECTING AT MID-CENTURY
1946-1969

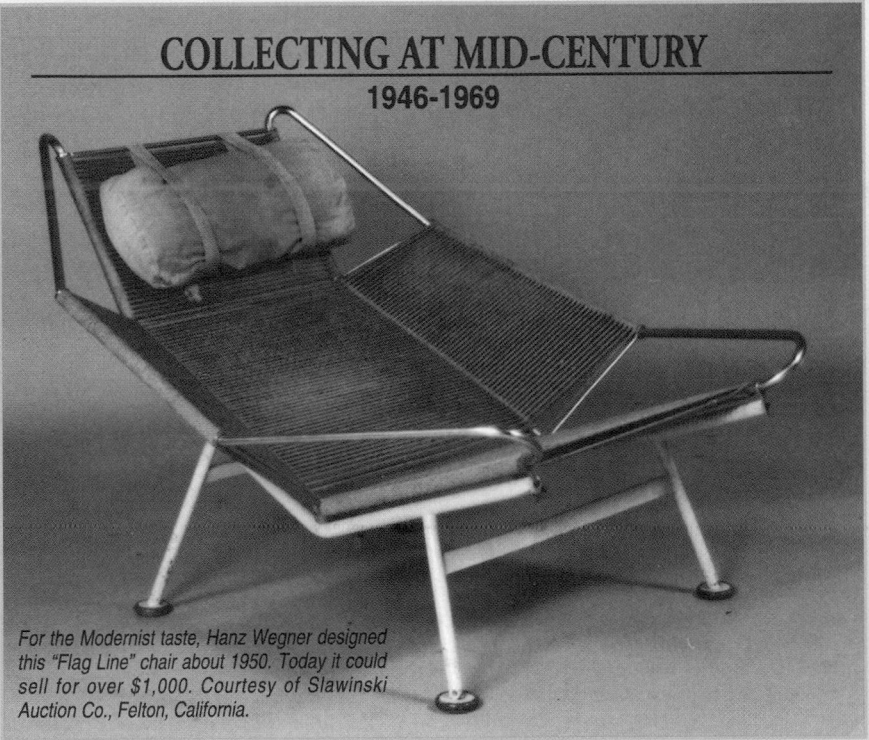

For the Modernist taste, Hanz Wegner designed this "Flag Line" chair about 1950. Today it could sell for over $1,000. Courtesy of Slawinski Auction Co., Felton, California.

The face of America had changed radically over the past 50 years, yet her heart was much the same. Needlepoint plaques proclaiming "Home, Sweet Home" no longer hung in the parlor. In fact, new homes had no parlors. Rather, they had a "rumpus" room.

The 1910s had had its "Main Street." The 1920s had had its "Virginia Avenues." The 1950s introduced ranch-style and split-level homes to everyday America.

But despite these modern exteriors and rooms designed for post World War II life-styles, sentiment was not forgotten.

Two design styles dominated the 1950s magazines—Early American and, that catch-all phrase, "modern."

But "modern" was a throw-back to the past, declared Russell Lynes in his 1955 book, *The Tastemakers:* "For the nostalgic pleasures of exhuming the early American past, this generation has substituted the romantic dream of the prairie. The enchantment of Paul Revere, hero and silversmith, has been displayed by Hopalong...."

In this atmosphere, Americans once again set about collecting anything and everything in sight. Their enthusiasm resembled that of the 1920s boom. There were some differences, though, this go-round.

First, in these now more upwardly-mobile days, regionalism no longer dominated the antiques scene. The collector living in New England might as easily be a transplanted Midwesterner interested in American Indian artifact as a Bostonian with a collection of inherited family pieces.

Further, widely-circulated magazines like *Antique Trader* (launched in 1957), *Spinning Wheel,* and *The Antiques Journal* (both begun in 1945) kept the interested public up-to-date with the new collecting trends. Anyone with "old things" could learn about them—what they were, how old they were, where to buy them, and where to sell them.

Next, the value—the pure monetary value of antiques—was more important than ever before. This decade saw the birth of the annual price guide.

Ruth Webb Lee again was on the cutting edge of the antiques world with her early 1950s books, *Price Guide to Pattern Glass,* and *Current Values of Antique Glass,* which she wrote "by popular demand."

In fact, old glass was still so wildly popular that even the first 125 pages of Edwin G. Warman's 1959 *Fifth Antiques and Their Current Prices* were devoted to pattern glass. The other categories, beginning with ABC plates and ending with Wooden Wares, were covered in 197 pages.

Still, though, the technological and manufacturing changes brought about by first, World War II, and then, the Korean War, greatly affected American tastes and buying habits during the 1950s.

The pages of the home magazines of the day were filled with new homes and new furnishings made of new materials all intended to create a new look.

One home magazine described the "new look" of the day this way: "All the beauty that is contained in the broad surfaces of 20th-century plywood, combined with the translucence of plastics, is here revealed in the soaring, singing spaces that they have made possible in our time."

Interestingly, though, this very look brought back memories of, and tributes to, the past.

In its 60th anniversary issue, the January, 1957, *House Beautiful* opened with an editorial entitled, "To know where you are going, you need to know where you have been."

The following pages celebrated the 20th-century's "ever-flowing fountain-head, Frank Lloyd Wright," and gave the fabled 1907 Green and Green designed David P. Gamble Pasadena, California, house a seven-page spread.

Ironically, a whole new realm for collectors had been opened up.

Equally ironic, anytime the world begins moving too quickly, technology introduces too many new concepts, and the "contemporary" becomes too prominent, human nature steps in and to slow it all down, looks backward.

Colorful Coca-Cola serving trays such as these were becoming "hot" collectibles as the decade of the 1960s drew to a close. Photos courtesy of Allan Petretti.

An American Icon: Mickey Mouse was an ingrained part of American culture by the 1930s when these little Japanese bisque figures were made. By the 1960s such pieces were becoming choice "collector's items."

That's what happened the first time Frank Lloyd Wright rose to national prominence. It also happened the second time.

A 1959 movie, *Pillow Talk,* perfectly summed up the changing attitude toward the contemporary. When Doris Day, an interior decorator, decides to get even with Rock Hudson, she redecorates his apartment with those same "plaids and cubes and prisms" that Emily Post has decried 30 years earlier—in spades.

By the mid-1960s, antiques were once again so firmly entrenched that American Queen Anne chairs and English Chippendale slant-front desks, even Spanish mirrors and German kas were adorning the pages of both antiques publications and mainstream American magazines.

But not all was as lovely and serene as it appeared in the movies and glossies of the early 1960s.

Globally, Americans had faced the Cuban crisis. Vietnam lay ahead.

At home there was the unrest surrounding the Civil Rights Movement.

And in cities and villages throughout the country, people were beginning to look around and see the errors of their ways.

You see, in the 1950s, at the height of the post-war building enthusiasm, many a beautiful, perfectly fine home or building had been demolished to make way for parking lots, flat-roofed apartment buildings, and singularly unattractive low-slung office buildings.

To right these wrongs, the National Historic Preservation Act was passed in 1966. Once some of the endangered buildings were out of immediate danger, attention turned to the antiques needed to furnish "old buildings."

But just as before, when the demand for "old things" outnumbered the available supply, collectors began gathering up more recently-made items.

By the late 1960s collectibles—not antiques (which by definition, must be 100-years-old to earn the hallowed title)—but items with no more than a couple or more decades of age, Coca-Cola trays, Jim Beam bottles, Al Smith buttons, Hummel figurines, vintage Mickey Mouse toys...even newly-manufactured plates and figures bearing those magical, but often meaningless adjectives "limited edition"—were claiming shelf space in antiques shops alongside Chinese Export china, coin silver tea services, and 18th century hand-seamed candlesticks.

Connoisseurs of truly hand-crafted pieces, be they furniture, silver, porcelain, rugs, textiles—anything–

By the late 1960s, the pioneering reference books by Hazel Marie Weatherman had established inexpensive colored glassware of the Depression era as a "hot" collecting field. Green "Georgian" (Lovebirds) and pink "Adam" were two popular 1930s designs still widely collected today.

looked on these Johnny-come-lately pieces with askance, even horror. However, a glance back in history shows that "collectibles" were nothing new.

In 19th century England, the middle class had clamored over barge wares, fairings and pot lids. Bing & Grondahl, the famous Danish factory introduced their Christmas plates in 1895. Their rival, Royal Copenhagen, followed suit in 1905.

In the December, 1965, *Antiques Journal,* the lead article was about A. Michelsen's line of silver commemorative Christmas spoons, "the collector's items of tomorrow."

Concurrent with the new, 1960s "collectibles" craze came a flood of specialized books advising the public exactly which items within every category of collectible was rare, valuable, and of course, collected.

On the heels of their instantly successful first book, *Know Your Antiques,* Ralph and Terry Kovel brought out *Kovels' Antiques & Collectibles Price List* in 1968. Specialized books by the Kovels followed on any variety of subjects—silver, Depression glass, pottery, bottles, even labels, and of course, "plates, figurines, paperweights, and other limited editions." Their industry was only one of several that feed the public's desire for knowledge.

Soon, for every collecting area there were specialized experts—for Hummels there was Carl F. Luckey, for Depression glass there was Gene Florence.

In a word, the 1960s had seen a collectibles trend begin that would snowball over the remaining years of the century.

For a while it appeared that antiques were taking a back seat in the market. But the grass-roots ground swell of historic preservation, combined with skyrocketing auction prices for period antiques, the great silver meltdown, and inflation would quickly marry the antiques and collectibles in the investor's, and the public's mind.

THE LAST TWENTY-NINE YEARS
1970-1999

Antiques and collectibles literally exploded on the marketplace in the 1970s. At the time, it seemed to just happen. Now we know why.

For the first time in history, America lost a war.

For the first time, a President resigned.

For the first time, there was a peacetime gasoline shortage.

To top it all off, with every year inflation soared, until, by the mid-'70s it reached double-digits....and mostly stayed there.

Out-the-roof interest rates made a lot of people stop and think. If I can't take it with me, they reasoned, I might as well spend it on things that I will enjoy.

And so, antiques prices soared too. And so did theft. After all, the numbers were there.

When Monet's *La Terasse à Saint-Adresse* sold in 1926, it fetched $11,000. In 1967, its selling price was $1.4 million.

By 1973, art theft was so rampant that Interpol published a "most wanted paintings" list, and in 1974 *Art Cop,* the story of NYPD's Robert Volpe's recoveries of stolen art works, was published.

For the man on the street, these were such terribly disruptive times that anything that provided a distraction and a sense of permanence was precious.

In this climate the expressions, "getting on" and "getting ahead" also meant having material possessions—and it wasn't just calculators, Ataris, and digital electronics that people wanted.

They clamored for Nippon and Noritake china, Bakelite and Golden Oak—the very items no one could "give away" just a few years earlier.

So what if these objects had been mass-manufactured when they were made originally? When they were seen side-by-side with plastic dinnerwares, Formica, plastic tops fused on to "solid hard rock maple," naugahyde and Vectar upholstery...even on Chippendale- and Queen Anne-style chairs....well, the products of the early 20th century looked pretty darn good.

While part of the world was consumed with space travel and microchip technology, many young people of the day were speaking out for the environment. Ironically this movement led to a greater and more widely-spread awareness of both conservation and craftsmanship.

1950s revisited–vinyl-covered chairs with maple legs around a formica-covered cafe table.

This played right into the antiques dealers' hands. They were the ones selling hand-crafted solid mahogany chests and finely figured walnut corner cupboards. And they hadn't cut down one single tree to do so!

At the same time, the world was becoming much more sophis-ticated, worldly-wise. Air travel became common-place. Every summer, increasing numbers of American adults were embarking on their own "grand tours." When they arrived in those foreign lands they had to compete with well-heeled "hippie" American college kids for tickets to Versailles and Windsor Castle.

This trend also played right into the antiques dealers hands. Continental antiques—everything from Spanish vargueño to French Sevres—caught the American public's attention and interest.

Then, when Christie's opened its New York office in 1977, antiquing in America took on a new face. Suddenly not only was there a flurry of new activity on the auction front, it had an international flavor.

Sotheby's had already acquired Parke-Bernet in 1964. Now two English-based, international auction houses joined the ranks of such noted American auction houses as Sloan's, Weschlers, and Butterfield. The wares were irresistible and the bidders were there.

Even the changing food industry was putting a new spin on the antiques world. *Gourmet* magazine had been introduced in 1967. By 1971, its circulation had doubled. Gourmet food stores were opening everywhere. Suddenly there was great talk about how food looked on the table.

Collecting china had been quite a fad in the 1920s and '30s, but historical blue and white Staffordshire had dominated.

Ornate Nippon hand-painted sugar bowl.

Now the search was on in antique shops for more colorful, Oriental-influenced Mason's ironstone tureens and platters, Derby reticulated baskets, and Minton dessert sets. The antiques world was simply reflecting changes that were happening in every sector of American life.

All this fascination with everything old, and semi-old, wasn't just for the elite. When Time-Life Books brought out *The Encyclopedia of Collectibles* it was obvious that beer cans, Roseville pottery, rock and roll memorabilia, and even framed Cream of Wheat advertisements were in the running for the public's money.

Interestingly, this multi-volume set, and several other voluminous antiques books published in the 1970s, attempted to cover all the fronts. It was not unusual to find rare 18th century brass candle boxes discussed in the same pages with 1920s collectible cigar boxes.

Pop culture memorabilia left over from the recent 1950s decade caught on...again. The call went out for

Golden oak china cabinet—note Chippendale-style cabriole legs. This turn-of-the-century furniture found widespread appeal with collectors by the 1970s.

Hall teapots are big on today's market. Here's an Aladdin shape example with the popular "Autumn Leaf" pattern.

Watt pottery pieces, ca. 1950s, are hot collectibles in the 1990s.

Hull Wildflower vase. Such pieces have soared in value in recent years.

"original" Corning Ware items (introduced in 1950), the first issues of MAD comic books (1952), original KFC advertising items (1955), even Arthur Godfrey-inspired Hawaiian shirts and old preppy-schoolgirl-type madras blouses.

In the 1970s, the Arts and Crafts and Art Deco revivals began for real. Art historians gave them their blessing when, in 1972, the Metropolitan Museum of Art installed a 1914 Frank Lloyd Wright living room. Magazines were filled with articles on expensive Art Glass: Tiffany, Lalique, Daum Nancy, Gallé, Loetz, and Steuben.

And not to be forgotten was the less-pricey Collectible Pottery: Roseville, Hall, Shawnee, Hull, Watt, and Weller.

In this collecting climate, it seemed that if it had been made, there was someone to buy it. And someone else standing in line to get the next one.

A hundred years earlier, widespread centennial celebrations had brought hope and a sense of unity to the country. They had set off a string of celebrations that would continue for years.

In contrast, in the 20th century, the Bicentennial seemed to just come and go within a year's time. Nor did it have as great an impact on the public in general. Still, the Bicentennial did create renewed and increased interest in 18th century material culture.

Museums across the country were researching and publishing scholarly treatises on the era, especially *Winterthur's Portfolio*. In addition, the presence of both Sotheby's and Christie's raised the American public's perception of antiques, especially fine furniture. Specialized books on American furniture included Bob Bishop's *How to Know American Antique Furniture,* Dean Fales' *American Painted Furniture: 1660-1880,* E. H. Bjerkoe's *The Cabinetmakers of America,* and the reissuing of Moreton Marsh's 1959 classic, *The Easy Expert in American Antiques.*

American folk and native art were also finding new audiences and greater appreciation.

During the early 1970s, several American Indian art shows were

Fine folk art: Slip-decorated redware plate. The collector who purchased this circa 1800 plate in rural North Carolina in early 1926, probably paid no more than $1 or $2 for it and saved it for future generations.

(Courtesy of the Museum of Early Southern Decorative Arts)

mounted. In 1975 the Whitney Museum featured "The Flowering of American Folk Art."

Additionally, thanks to the ground swell begun by the previous decade's National Preservation Act, more and more house museums celebrating the craftsmen and tastes of the country's various regions were opening. Navaho rugs, redware, whirligigs, and weathervanes had now become respectable, desirable, and pricey.

As the 1970s wound down, antiques and collectibles had never been hotter.

Money was flowing into every segment of the antiques world—auction houses, antiques shops, that new phenomenon "discovery days," even the mail-order business.

Yep. In 1978 Nelson Rockefeller invested some $4 million in a mail-order business of reproductions from his private collection.

To keep everyone well informed, *Antique Trader* joined Warman and the Kovels by introducing its *Antiques & Collectibles Price Guide,* and Sam Pennington started *The Maine Antiques Digest.*

If the '70s saw an explosion of available goods for the collector, the 1980s saw a publishing explosion in the antiques world.

At home, Wallace-Homestead and Schiffer Publishing Company, were among the various publishing companies covering every category of collectibles. In light of America's new role in the international antiques scene, England's Antique Collectors' Club publications became the darling of the serious collector. In addition, reprints of turn-of-the-century companies became valuable research tools and provided amusing pricing comparisons.

On the antique and collecting scene, the 1980s were little different from the preceding decade. Everything was on an upward spiral...including the problems that come when prices soar upward.

If you were selling, all was great. And with lots of money in most everyone's pocket, even buying seemed easy.

Nickel and dime pieces were selling for twenty-five and fifty cents. Hundred dollar pieces were selling for five and ten times their value of just a few years earlier. House and garage sale lines began forming the day before. Competition was rife. Novices and long-established shop owners were vying for anything antique and collectible.

If there was one loud and clear advice given in the early 1980s it was to invest. Invest in gold, in silver, in antiques, in collectibles. Flea markets, antique shops, and auction galleries sprang up as quickly as investment advisers. Price lists and price guides could be found in the glove compartment of every car....just in case you happened upon an unexpected yard sale.

Wall Street wasn't about to let this financial boom go unnoticed. Of course antiques and collectibles weren't suitable for big board trading. After all, personal taste is the primary motivator behind a collector's purchases.

But when major Wall Street players like Dick Jenrette and Eddy Nicholson paid record prices for antiques, and national publications publicized their very valuable collections, the word spread. When the mouthpiece of "the Street," the *Wall Street Journal,* ran articles and profiles about their successful antique investments, the everyday American was even more eager to follow suit.

But there were downsides, too.

The knowledgeable antiquer expected that fakes and hard-to-distinguish reproductions would flood the market. They were on the lookout for them.

What was not anticipated was the rash of thievery that came along during this boom time.

Suddenly newspapers were full of accounts of moving trucks backing up to homes and crafty burglars taking the family's Oriental rugs, oil paintings, easily-portable antiques, and, of course, silver.

Gold and other precious metals began escalating in the late 1970s as a hedge against inflation. But when the Texas Hunt family manipulated the silver market by buying and holding, and thus forcing up the value of raw silver, the antiques world paid the price.

Somehow, even street gangs now could tell the difference between sterling and plated silver. And if it were sterling, it was at risk.

Rare and important 18th-century (and earlier) silver in private collections, along with the family's 1950s or 1970s silver flatware was often stolen and melted down in the burglars' frenzy to

In the early 1980s, silver thieves showed no regard for age, quality, rarity, design, or family sentiment as they stole and melted down every piece of sterling silver they could find. Fortunately, this Tiffany sterling tea set escaped destruction.

Another "traditional" look that's popular in the 1990s is Arts & Crafts—the early 20th century movement which was a reaction against ornate, cheaply made wares. Gustav Stickley was a leading proponent and manufacturer of this style. This setting he would have approved of, with simple Mission Oak furniture, a Prairie-style slag glass lamp and an elegant art pottery vase. Photo courtesy of Dave Rago, Lambertville, New Jersey.

reap $35, $40, even $50 for an ounce of raw silver.

Prices dropped back, as quickly as they had risen, but the damage had been done.

Out of others' misfortunes came a new face in the antiques world at the end of the century—the appraiser. Of course there had always been a few appraisers around, but the new economics required more of them. Insurance companies, bank estate officers, tax assessors, and just plain people awakening to the value of all those objects now needed to know, "What's it worth?"

The appraiser could tell them.

The result? More savvy sellers. More savvy buyers.

All the while antiques and collectibles were capturing the minds and money of the fabulously rich and the man on the street alike, the work-a-day world was hurling even faster into a life dictated and directed by the new technology—lasers, fiber optics, PCs, and eventually the Internet.

Inflation eventually calmed down. So did art crime. But the world didn't. By now, you know what happened next...

Just as they had when technological and industrial developments took major leaps ahead in the 1920s and the 1950s, people in the 1980s and the 1990s looked for an escape from the ever-more impersonal real-world.

In 1989, *House Beautiful*, that main-stay magazine of the home, published its 90th anniversary issue. "Three Looks That Last" was the title given its Design Focus feature. Those three looks were, in a word, conservative and traditional. Chinzes and toiles, lolling chairs and comfortable sofas, Chippendale-style mirrors and floral still-life paintings dominated the room.

Even in the most contemporary room, there were Biedermeier and Adams-type chairs, a Neo-classical center table, and a Romanesque bust. Other than the leopard-print valences and contemporary sunburst mirror, there wasn't a single thing that would have offended Emily Post fifty-nine years earlier.

In fact, as we wind down this century-long overview of some of the major events and happenings that have shaped the ups and downs of the antiques and collectible world for the past hundred years, one thing becomes ever more evident.

There truly is nothing new under the sun. So, in the 1980s, when Martha Stewart burst onto the scene as a major tastemaker, she was just following in the footsteps of Wallace Nutting and Emily Post and multiple others who had taken their personal tastes into the American home over the past hundred years.

Still a player in the 1990s, Stewart, like those before her, can make or break a collecting trend by what she says about it on TV or in the pages of her magazine, *Martha Stewart Lives*.

Bill Cosby, a major collector of fine American furniture, had attempted to raise the public's consciousness of early craftsmanship when the set of his TV series featured 18th century furniture, but not many of his watchers could afford to pay tens of thousands of dollars for an antique chest or table.

When Oprah Winfrey brought attention to Shaker goods, that market soared, but small Shaker accessories—boxes, lemon squeezers and rug beaters, for example—were only going to sell for so much and just having one Shaker piece could add interest and conversation to home decor. Anyway, not everyone loves or understands the Shaker design.

Then there is the legendary story of Andy Warhol's cookie jar collection. Bidders paid hundreds of dollars, even thousands, for the very same, mass-

The cookie jar market skyrocketed after the sale of Andy Warhol's collection. This Brayton Laguna Pottery Mammy jar has the double appeal of being a good example of Black Americana, another important area of collecting today. The original sold for a few dollars, in top condition this lady could new sell for thousands. Vintage figural cookie jars from numerous American potteries are in demand today.

Once Martha Stewart featured Depression-era jadeite kitchen glass on her program, the demand boomed. This set of leftover jars was made by the Jeannette Glass Company. Courtesy of Kate Trabue.

manufactured pieces they could find on dusty shelves in that new shopping arena, the antiques mall, priced at $35, $75, or $100. Why? Because Andy Warhol, that 20th century pop culture celebrity and icon, had owned them.

On the auction front, the late 1980s and 1990s rocked along just as they had in the 1920s and early 1930s...knocking down old records, setting new ones— even after inflation grew under control. And, just like always, the new prices made headlines.

To most people, million-dollar record-breaking prices paid for rare antiques are beyond comprehension. Ending the 1980s there was the sale of the shell-carved John Goddard secretary/bookcase for $12.1 million at Christie's. In 1996 there was the $1.1 million Tiffany Virginia Creeper lamp sold at Sotheby's.

But even more amazing have been the prices paid for 20th century pieces that once were kitchen and playroom and sports arena items—a grantineware

An icon for collectors of the 1990s—this No. 1 Ponytail Barbie of 1959 sold for over $4,000 a few years ago. Courtesy of McMasters Auctions, Cambridge, Ohio.

Battery-operated tin robots of the 1950s are big sellers today. This one sold for over $1,000. Courtesy DeFina Auction, Austinburg, Ohio.

Toys and character collectibles from the 1950-1970 era are among the biggest areas of collecting as this century draws to a close.

Emerald ware coffeepot, $500,000; Robby Space Patrol Robot, $24,200; and $7,087 for a Mickey Mantle 1952 Topps baseball card.

But while much hoopla surrounds the "new antiques" and the mind-boggling prices being paid for not-so-old collectibles, still all you have to do to find the dominating taste of times is to open the pages of the slick home magazines appearing in the very last months of 1999.

Just as *House Beautiful* had predicted in 1986, the century is leaving on a traditional note.

So, is there anything new under the sun?

Not really, but trends and fashions do come and go. And throughout time, antiques have both led and followed trends.

In the 1990s gardening has captured everyone's imagination. Elite antique dealers have responded to this new craze by offering 18th, 19th, and early 20th century garden accessories—chairs, benches, statuary, urns, sun dials. In less-expensive shops rusty trowels and dented watering cans, bent rakes and well-worn picks are being displayed in the shop windows.

This Emerald Swirl graniteware cream can in top condition could sell today in the $850 range. Courtesy J. Allers.

One of the "hottest" areas of collecting today is kitchen glasswares. These Fire King sapphire blue mugs, ca. 1942-48, rate high with collectors. The "thin" and "heavy" version, both in the Philbe design, are valued in the $30 to $50 range. Photo courtesy of Kate Trabue.

Then, quite in contrast, there is the high-tech sector.

Everyone is asking: Should I keep the Commodore computer? How much is my old hi-fi turntable worth? Wonder where the kids' first transistor radio is?

The market for these objects lies years in the future.

But how far in the future?

That's another unknown, but probably a lot closer than most of us who love "the old things" will feel good about.

What is known is that when all is said and done, though tastes are always quixotic, human desires inspire and motivate the antiques and collectibles collector.

Mankind never stops dreaming of the good old days, no matter when they might have been. For, just like the 100-

year rule required for an item to be an antique, the good old days are on a sliding scale.

Now, as we in 1999 bid goodbye to the 20th century and gaze toward the millennium, changes are already looming on the antiques and collectibles horizon.

Thanks to 21st-century communications, our shrinking world is inspiring greater interest in international cultures. People everywhere are discovering that there are wonderful treasures that they never before knew existed. As has always happened down through the ages, the demand for fine objects from the past will continue to greatly surpass the supply.

A world of treasures await harvesting over the Internet. Yet, Internet auctions pose challenges, maybe even threats, to Mom and Pop antiques shops...and possibly to auctions as we have known them since the 18th century.

Could we possibly be moving toward becoming a generation of virtual collectors whereby we are content to stare at objects on a computer monitor, rather than touching and feeling them, possessing them, and reveling in our pride of ownership?

No, it is highly unlikely any virtual experience will ever take the place of touching, feeling, and enjoying fascinating objects.

Even with all the recent technological changes, man still yearns for permanence and beauty. Such experiences complement the human spirit and soul. This will continue into future generations.

Happy New Year. Happy New Millennium. Happy Antiquing!

Once state-of-the-art in technology, today typewriters have nearly been replaced by computer terminals. Even this early Blickensderfer Model No. 7, though a classic, can still be bought for under $100.

a pair of single-pane glazed cupboard doors opening to shelves over a long drawer at the bottom, scalloped apron & bracket feet on casters, ca. 1900, 14 x 32", 66" h. (ILLUS.).................. **633**

Country Renaissance Secretary

Victorian secretary-bookcase,
Renaissance Revival substyle, country-style, walnut, two-part construction: the upper section w/a rectangular top w/a stepped cornice above a plain frieze band over a pair of arched glazed cupboard doors opening to shelves; the lower section w/a wide flat hinged fall-front opening to a deep compartment w/pigeonholes, drawers & letter slots above a lower case w/three long drawers w/leaf- and nut-carved pulls, molded base on casters, ca. 1875, 13½ x 43¼", 88¾" h. (ILLUS.) **1,513**

Renaissance Revival Secretary

Victorian secretary-bookcase,
Renaissance Revival substyle, parcel-gilt walnut & burl walnut, a rectangular top w/a coved border above a deep cornice above a shallow paneled long drawer w/two large turned wood knobs above a wide paneled hinged fall-front enclosing a writing compartment above three long paneled lower drawers w/knobs all flanked by ring-, knob- and reeded side columns w/top & bottom end blocks, plinth base, third quarter 19th c., 20¼ x 38¾", 62" h. (ILLUS.) **1,840**

Renaissance Revival Secretary-Bookcase

Victorian secretary-bookcase,
Renaissance Revival substyle, walnut & burl walnut, two-part construction: the upper section w/a rectangular top w/wide stepped-out corners above a deep flaring conforming cornice over a pair of round-topped glazed cupboard doors w/raised burl panels at the top & thin reeded side pilasters; the lower section w/a hinged fall-front opening to pigeonholes & flanked by curved sides above a pair of shallow drawers projecting above a pair of double-paneled lower doors flanked by blocked pilasters, molded plinth base, repairs, ca. 1875, 25¼ x 52", 91¾" h. (ILLUS.)............................ **1,650**

Victorian "side-by-side" secretary-bookcase, Golden Oak substyle, one side w/a tall single glazed-door bookcase opening to four shelves below a flat crestboard w/scrolled crest all beside w/an arched & scroll-carved crest & frame enclosing an oval beveled mirror over a small half-round shelf over a narrow rectangular shelf above the wide

Oak "Side-by-Side" Secretary

scroll-carved hinged flat fall-front opening to a fitted interior over three long drawers w/pierced brass bail pulls, an egg-and-dart-carved apron on bracket feet w/casters, ca. 1900, 13 x 40", 71" h. (ILLUS.) **604**

SHELVES

Floor shelves, country-style, painted pine, a rectangular board top above board sides on arched cut-out feet, a board back enclosing two shelves, old grey paint, square nail construction, 19th c., 35" w., 35½" h. **523**

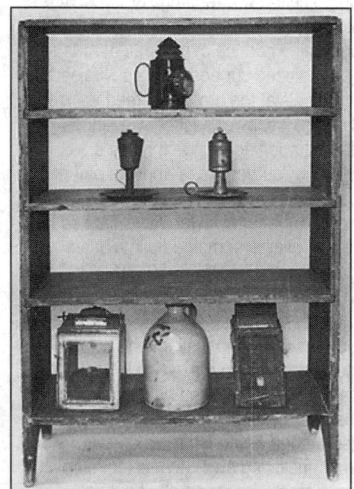

Painted Pine Floor Shelves

Floor shelves, country-style, painted pine, a rectangular top above single-board sides w/arched cut-out feet framing four open mortised shelves, wooden peg construction, old green paint, some old renailing, a bit shaky, open knot holes in one end, 14¾ x 33½", 49¼" h. (ILLUS.) **550**

Floor shelves, painted pine, tall one-board ends tapering sharply toward the top & w/arched base cut-outs, three staggered open shelves, old red finish, 19th c., 12½ x 43", 46" h. **935**

Floor shelves, painted poplar, tall one-board ends w/rounded cut-out feet & curved top front corners, four open shelves, brass braces added to the back, old worn red, 9½ x 26", 50" h. **880**

Hanging shelves, Federal country-style, mahogany, whale-side shaped sides supporting four open shelves, the lower shelf above a pair of short drawers, New England, early 19th c., 24" w., 34" h........ **1,000**

Painted Pine Hanging Shelves

Hanging shelves, painted pine, four open graduated shelves between deeply scalloped side boards, square nail construction, old black paint, mid 19th c., some edge damage on back, 8 x 29", 34½" h. (ILLUS.) **1,100**

Hanging shelves, walnut, four graduated rectangular boards w/rounded front corners joined to each other w/two simple turned corner posts & a flat stick at the back projecting at the top w/a hanging hole, old worn dark patina, possibly Shaker, 7 x 24", 19½" h. (repairs, back post replaced). **495**

Wall shelf, walnut, a narrow rectangular shelf above a pair of shallow nailed drawers w/tiny pulls above a lower backboard all joined by scalloped tapering bracket ends, old worn reddish finish, 19th c., 32" l. **550**

SIDEBOARDS

Art Deco sideboard, mahogany, the long rectangular top w/gently curved front & angled corners above a conforming case w/a pair of large curved doors opening to an interior fitted w/a drawer & shelves, outset blocked corner bands above short curved front legs w/bronze "sabots," France, in the manner of Jules Leleu, ca. 1930, 21 x 63", 33¾" h. **5,462**

Virginia Classical Sideboard

Classical country-style sideboard, cherry, rectangular top above a projecting row of drawers w/a long drawer flanked by shorter drawers over tall end doors flanking a pair of central doors each w/double punched-tin panels decorated w/pinwheels in ovals within a looped border, the doors separated by four baluster-, rod- and ring-turned columns on a conforming plinth base raised on ring-turned tapering short legs w/knob & peg feet, further tin panels at the ends, Virginia, ca. 1840 (ILLUS.) **6,250**

Classical Mahogany Server

Classical server, carved mahogany & cherry veneer, rectangular top w/molded edges over a long veneered drawer w/turned wood knobs over a beaded band & a pair of beaded panel recessed tall cupboard doors opening to a shelf, all flanked by veneered squared ogee

pilasters on block feet, old refinish, hardware changes, missing top splashboard, minor surface imperfections, Mid-Atlantic States, 1840-45, 18¾ x 40", 40⅛" h. (ILLUS.). **2,530**

Fine New York Classical Sideboard

Classical sideboard, carved mahogany, the pedimented splashboard w/three urn- and pineapple-carved finials over the rectangular top w/a molded edge over a long drawer flanked by short drawers all projecting over a series of four paneled cupboard doors separated by four free-standing columns resting on blocks above heavy paw feet, round brass drawer pulls, Duncan Phyfe or a contemporary, New York City, ca. 1830, 26 x 79", 58" h. (ILLUS.) **6,038**

Federal country-style huntboard, walnut, rectangular top above a deep apron w/a pair of deep beaded-edge dovetailed drawers flanking a narrow matching center drawer, turned wood knobs, on knob-, ring- and rod-turned legs w/ball-and-peg feet, refinished, Southern, first half 19th c., 22¼ x 49", 43¾" h. (repairs, top replaced) **2,475**

Delicate Federal Server

Federal server, brass-mounted figured mahogany, the rectangular top above two short drawers w/lion head & ring pulls on turned swelled supports joined by a

platform stretcher over tapering ring-
turned legs ending in brass ball feet, pulls
appear original, New York City, ca. 1800,
18 x 32", 35" h. (ILLUS.) **4,600**

Mahogany Inlaid Federal Server

Federal server, inlaid mahogany, the
rectangular top w/a border of lunette inlay
above a single long line-inlaid drawer
above a pair of central cupboard doors
flanked by tall narrow bottle drawers all
flanked by reeded stiles & above another
border of lunette inlay, a scalloped apron
above the square tapering legs, New
England, early 19th c., 22 x 38", 41" h.
(ILLUS.) **4,025**

Federal sideboard, inlaid mahogany, the
rectangular top w/square corners &
banded center above a conforming case
w/an inlaid long central drawer flanked by
a shorter drawer at each end above
single end cupboard doors flanking a pair
of central cupboard doors, raised on short
inlaid square double tapering legs,
replaced butterfly brasses, old finish,
Massachusetts, ca. 1790-1800,
27½ x 64", 41" h. (imperfections) **2,990**

Federal Virginia Walnut Sideboard

Federal sideboard, walnut & yellow pine,
rectangular top w/molded edges above
cockbeaded case w/end drawers, the
right drawer visually divided into two
drawers & the left w/two working drawers,
flanking a central cupboard door

w/cockbeading, raised on four tall slender
square tapering legs, old oval brass pulls,
old refinish, repairs, Virginia, 1790-1810,
22 x 56", 39" h. (ILLUS.) **5,520**

**Federal-Style "serpentine-front"
sideboard,** mahogany veneer, the
rectangular top w/a serpentine front
above a conforming case w/two long
bowed central drawers above an arched
opening w/fan-applied corner brackets all
flanked by two ranks of three short
concaved drawers, oval brasses, pairs of
incised bands down stiles, square
tapering legs w/pairs of incised grooves &
ending in spade feet, first half 20th c.,
23½ x 68", 38½" h. **825**

George III Inlaid Sideboard

George III sideboard, satinwood-inlaid
mahogany, the rectangular top
w/serpentine sides & front above a
conforming case fitted w/a central drawer
above the shaped skirt & flanked by two
doors, all w/crossbanding & line inlay, on
square tapering legs ending in spade
feet, veneer losses, England, late 18th c.,
26½ x 65½", 37" h. (ILLUS.) **5,462**

**Mission-style (Arts & Crafts movement)
server,** oak, rectangular top w/narrow
backsplash overhanging a narrow apron
on four tall slender square legs joined by
a framed medial shelf, unsigned Stickley
Brothers, 20 x 36", 36" h. (recoated
original finish) **880**

**Mission-style (Arts & Crafts movement)
server,** oak, a low backsplash above the
rectangular top w/inset legs above a
single long apron drawer w/hammered
brass hardware, the legs joined by a
lower medial shelf & back stretcher, fine
original finish, branded Stickley Brothers
mark, 19 x 36", 37" h. **1,760**

**Mission-style (Arts & Crafts movement)
server,** a double-rail plate rack on the
rectangular top overhanging a case w/a
row of three small drawers above a single
long drawer, all w/cast copper oval pulls,
square stile legs & rectangular medial
shelf, fine new reddish brown finish,
branded Gustav Stickley mark, Model No.
819, 20 x 48", 43" h. (small veneer
patches on side) **1,870**

Gustav Stickley Sideboard

**Mission-style (Arts & Crafts movement)
sideboard,** oak, a high closed plate rack
above the rectangular top overhanging a
case w/a pair of tall flat cupboard doors
w/long pointed strap hinges flanking a
central stack of four long drawers w/bail
pulls, on eight square stile legs, new
medium finish, paper label of Gustav
Stickley, 25½ x 70", 41" h. (ILLUS.) **6,050**

**Mission-style (Arts & Crafts movement)
sideboard,** oak, a high replaced plate rail
above the rectangular top overhanging a
case w/a paneled cupboard door w/long
strap hinges at each end flanking a
central stack of four small drawers
w/copper pulls all above a single long
drawer across the bottom, square stile
legs, cleaned original finish on base,
unsigned L. & J.G. Stickley, Model No.
745, 24 x 54", 48" h. (stains on the top) **2,090**

**Mission-style (Arts & Crafts movement)
sideboard,** oak, a high two-bar plate
rack at the back of the rectangular top
overhanging a case w/three small central
drawers flanked by flat cupboard doors
w/long strap hinges above a long drawer,
original copper hardware, recent finish,
red decal mark of Gustav Stickley, Model
No. 814½, 22 x 54", 48" h. (height
slightly reduced) **3,190**

Charles Limbert Sideboard

**Mission-style (Arts & Crafts movement)
sideboard,** oak, the superstructure w/a
tiered & arched top rail over a setback
rectangular mirror on the rectangular top,
the case w/a pair of small drawers
flanking a long central drawer over an
arch-topped central section w/four
paneled doors over a single long drawer
across the bottom, original copper strap
hinges & hardware, arched aprons &
paneled ends, through-tenon
construction, fine original finish, Charles
Limbert Co., Model No. 362, 21 x 51",
52" h. (ILLUS.) **2,970**

**Mission-style (Arts & Crafts movement)
sideboard,** oak, a high rectangular
superstructure w/a single open shelf
supported on curved brackets above the
rectangular top w/rounded front corners
above a case w/long front corbels
flanking a case w/a pair of drawers over
a pair of square paneled cupboard doors
over a single long bottom drawer, on
casters, overcoat on original reddish
brown finish, Limbert Furniture Co.,
no visible mark, 20 x 48", 58" h.
(some stain on top, one pull replaced
w/another early pull) **3,850**

Unique Carved Aesthetic Sideboard

Victorian sideboard, Aesthetic Movement
substyle, carved mahogany, the
superstructure w/a tall rectangular mirror
w/a crestrail of short bobbin-turned
spindles flanked by corner blocks
w/turned finials over bamboo-turned stiles
joining the flanking small open shelves
w/further spindled crestrails above curved
brackets & leaf- and berry-carved panels
over a long open shelf w/carved edge
supported on two central curved brackets
& turned end spindles all backed by
floral- or vining leaf-carved panels over a

stepped top w/carved edging, the raised central section w/a boldly carved fern leaf panel above a pair of tall cupboard doors carved w/flying birds, the lower side sections w/two open galleried shelves supported by turned corner spindles & the lower w/a spindled front gallery, short notch-cut arched aprons on tapering block feet, by the Cincinnati Women's Wood Carving Movement, 1870s, 16¼ x 58", 97" h. (ILLUS.)............ **10,925**

Ornate Victorian Baroque Sideboard

Victorian sideboard, Baroque-Style, oak, the superstructure w/a high wide crestboard w/a gadroon-carved rail centered by a grotesque mask above a long open shelf raised on scroll-trimmed lions' heads over heavy ring- and urn-turned & leaf-carved posts on heavy open scroll brackets & backed by a long rectangular beveled mirror, the rectangular top w/molded edges over a pair of long ornate scroll-carved drawers w/shell-form pulls over a long paneled cupboard door flanked by shorter doors all w/ornate scroll carving, a long deep drawer across the bottom w/further scroll carving, the back section flanked at each corner by carved & reeded blocks & bulbous turnings, on heavy paw feet, late 19th c. (ILLUS.) **2,300**

Victorian sideboard, Eastlake substyle, oak, the superstructure w/a pierced & scroll-carved crestrail over a narrow carved band & two raised-panel sections centered by a round beveled mirror flanked by small open shelves w/lattice-carved brackets on slender bobbin-turned spindles all backed by panels w/overall incised leafy vine carving, the rectangular stepped-out top w/molded edge over a pair of line-incised drawers over a long line-incised drawer above a pair of paneled cupboard doors w/a carved band above the recessed panel w/an S-scroll

Ornate Eastlake Carved Sideboard

line-incised leafy vine centered by a florette, incised side stiles ending in block feet & a flat plinth base, on casters, ca. 1890, 20 x 43", 68" h. (ILLUS.).......... **920**

Victorian sideboard, Renaissance Revival substyle, walnut & burl walnut, the long rectangular white marble top w/molded edges & rounded front corners above a conforming case w/a row of three drawers across the top, two longer w/recessed oval burl panels & cartouche-carved pulls & round keyhole escutcheons flanking a shorter central drawer w/recessed oval burl panel & round keyhole escutcheon all above a pair of large cupboard doors w/recessed large oval burl panels w/raised molding, one w/a relief-carved pair of hanging fish & the other w/a hanging gamebird, a narrow central door w/a plain oval burl panel w/raised molding, on a conforming molded flat plinth base, ca. 1870, 21½ x 59½", 36¾" h................... **2,310**

Renaissance-Style Walnut Sideboard

Victorian sideboard, Renaissance-Style, walnut, the superstructure w/a narrow rectangular top over a deep flaring cornice supported on tall ring-, rod- and bulbous knob-turned front columns flanking the large rectangular beveled mirror w/curved bottom corner brackets over the stepped-out bow-fronted rectangular top, the bowed center section over a pair of large projecting drawers w/rectangular brasses over a pair of set-back square paneled cupboard doors w/ornate carving & notched panel corners, wide front side stiles, paneled ends, deep plinth base, late 19th c., 20 x 59", 79" h. (ILLUS.). **834**

STANDS

Fine Chippendale Candlestand

Book stand, Mission-style (Arts & Crafts movement), ash, rectangular board sides w/half-round hand holes near the top flanking the V-shaped top trough over a lower open shelf, keyed through-tenon construction, original green finish, attributed to Gustav Stickley, Model No. 74, 10 x 30", 31" h. **770**

Candlestand, Chippendale, carved & figured mahogany & walnut, the round top tilting above a slender flaring standard & urn-form support on a tripod base w/cabriole legs ending in claw-and-ball feet, chips to feet, New York City, ca. 1770, 20½" d., 27½" h. (ILLUS.) **5,175**

Candlestand, country-style, cherry & maple, a rounded top on a ringed columnar-turned pedestal on a tripod base w/three tapering flat canted legs ending in button feet, remnants of old dark green paint, southeastern New England, late 18th c., 12" d., 25" h. (imperfections) **1,035**

Candlestand, Federal country-style, birch, the square top above a slender slightly flaring standard on an urn-form support

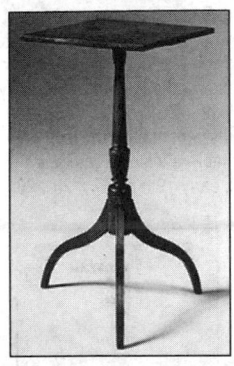

Federal Country-style Candlestand

on a tripod base w/spider legs, top stained, slightly warped, northern New England, ca. 1800, 14½ x 15¼", 28¼" h. (ILLUS.). **1,150**

Fine Federal Candlestand

Candlestand, Federal, inlaid cherry, the long octagonal cockbeaded top w/a central oval inlaid in mahogany veneer panel framed by stringing & set in bird's-eye maple w/crossbanded mahogany border, on a slender vase- and ring-turned post on a tripod base w/widely canted simple cabriole legs w/pad feet, refinished, minor imperfections, possibly New Hampshire, ca. 1810-20, 13 x 18⅛", 28" h. (ILLUS.). **1,955**

Candlestand, Federal, mahogany, the oval top tilting above a vase- and ring-turned pedestal on a tripod base w/cabriole legs ending in arris pad feet on platforms, old refinish, Massachusetts, ca. 1790, 17 x 17", 28½" h. **2,415**

Candlestand, Federal, maple, a rectangular top w/rounded corners on a vase- and ring-turned pedestal on a tripod base w/spider legs, old red finish, New England, ca. 1825, 16½ x 19¾", 28¾" h. **431**

Candlestand, Federal country-style, mahogany & curly maple, the oblong top w/notched corners in mahogany & tilting above a ring- and baluster-turned curly maple column raised on a tripod base w/three outswept mahogany legs on small ball feet, refinished, attributed to New York, early 19th c., 17 x 23", 26" h. **715**

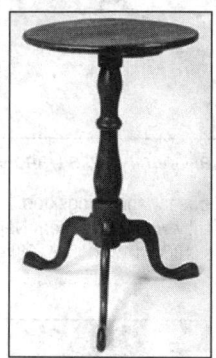

Queen Anne Candlestand

Candlestand, Queen Anne, cherry, the round top on a baluster- and ring-turned standard on a tripod base w/flattened cabriole legs ending in arris pad feet on platforms, old refinish, possibly Vermont, 18th c., 15¼" d., 25¾" h. (ILLUS.) **1,035**

Candlestand, Queen Anne country-style, painted, the small square top on a vase- and ring-turned pedestal on a tripod base w/cabriole legs ending in pad feet, old dark brown paint, New England, second half 18th c., 11¾ x 11⅞", 27¼" h. (imperfections) **748**

Early Windsor Candlestand

Candlestand, Windsor, a central candlearm w/a socket at each end adjusting on a screw-turned central post above a round

dished platform on a simple turned post on a small thick disk on three tall canted turned legs, old dark finish, candle cups later, New Hampshire, late 18th c., 13" d., 36" h. (ILLUS.) **1,840**

Crock stand, painted pine, four rectangular tiers, the three upper tiers w/open fronts & backed by an angled frame board, the bottom tier w/a deep apron & raised on heavy square chamfered legs on porcelain casters, old worn green paint, 24 x 48", 35¼" h. **578**

Drink stand, Mission-style (Arts & Crafts movement), oak, a round top above cross braces on four tall square legs joined by lower cross stretchers & a small round shelf, new finish on top, original finish on the base, "Handcraft" label of L. & J.G. Stickley, 18" d., 29" h.. .... **990**

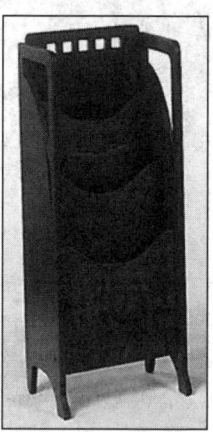

Arts & Crafts Magazine Stand

Magazine stand, Arts & Crafts style, oak, narrow upright form w/three vertical slots under a back containing five small square cut-outs w/arched & cut-out sides, recent finish, unsigned Lakeside Craftshop, early 20th c., 10 x 14", 38" h. (ILLUS.) **1,210**

Magazine stand, Mission-style (Arts & Crafts movement), oak, a thin square top overhanging a front & back apron above four open rectangular shelves flanked by slender square legs & applied double slats on each side, keyed through-tenons on bottom shelf, tops of shelves refinished, Lifetime Furniture Co., Model No. 6002, 16½" sq., 33" h. **825**

Magazine stand, Mission-style (Arts & Crafts movement), oak, a square top above paneled solid sides w/cut-out feet flanking three deep open shelves w/a narrow apron at the bottom, flush tenon construction, good recent finish, retailer's tag, box mark of Gustav Stickley, Model No. 547, 15" sq., 36" h. (ILLUS.) **4,675**

Gustav Stickley Magazine Stand

Magazine stand, Mission-style (Arts & Crafts movement), oak, rectangular tapering sides w/cut-out half-spheres at the base, four graduated open shelves, original dark finish, five missing screw plugs, branded Charles Limbert Furniture Co. mark, 14 x 20¼", 36¾" h.. . . . . **880**

Magazine stand, Mission-style (Arts & Crafts movement), oak, four open shelves above a narrow arched toe board between four square stiles & crestrails over three vertical slats on each side, refinished, minor repair to top, unsigned L. & J.G. Stickley, Model No. 46, 13 x 21", 42" h. **1,320**

Night stands, Danish Modern, walnut & cherry, a rectangular top w/concave front above a conforming case w/two drawers within a framework raised on four outset ovoid tapering legs w/incurved rails between the drawers, retailer's metal tag, Scandinavia, ca. 1960, 17½ x 26½", 23" h., pr. **575**

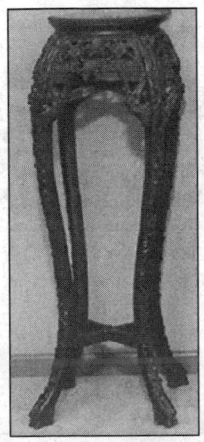

Chinese Carved Teak Plant Stand

Plant stand, carved teak, the round top inset w/red soapstone above a rounded apron ornately pierce-carved w/flowering vines & continuing down to four carved cabriole legs joined near the bottom by a small cross-stretcher, old finish, China, late 19th to early 20th c., some damage, 36¼" h. (ILLUS.). **300**

Painted Country Plant Stand

Plant stand, country-style, painted wood, three graduated demi-lune shelves on baluster- and ring-turned supports joined by square rail, old green paint, on casters, probably New England, 19th c., 20 x 40", 39" h. (ILLUS.) **1,610**

Ornate Victorian Plant Stand

Plant stand, Victorian, gilded brass & onyx, a square white onyx top set onto an ornately pierced flaring apron raised on ornately pierced & leaf-cast slender cabriole legs w/scroll feet all joined by a pierced brass lower medial shelf w/a turned onyx & brass finial, ca. 1890, 18" w., 30½" h. (ILLUS.). **633**

Plant stand, Victorian Renaissance Revival substyle, cherry, square top w/cut corners on the molded edges above crenulated apron edges & fanned leaf carving at each corner at the top of a molded & incurved flat leg joining at a central post w/reeded pointed finial & a bottom ball drop, the lower legs curving outward & each carved along the top w/a long stylized fish, ca. 1880, refinished, 16¾" sq., 31¾" h. (top replaced) **413**

Plant stand, Mission-style (Arts & Crafts movement), oak, a small square top raised on a heavy tapering pedestal on a square base raised on four faceted square low blocks, original finish, branded mark of the Stickley Brothers, 13" sq., 34" h. **1,100**

Plant stand, Mission-style (Arts & Crafts movement), oak, a square top overhanging a deep flaring apron w/rectangular caned panels & arched bottoms, shaped brackets at each corner under the top, slender square canted legs joined by a cross stretcher supporting a square medial shelf, Ebon Oak line, recent finish, branded signature of the Charles Limbert Furniture Co., 14" sq., 34" h. **2,310**

Plant stand, Mission-style (Arts & Crafts movement), oak, a square top raised on a square slightly tapering tall pedestal w/four corbel brackets, cross-form shoe feet, cleaned original reddish brown finish, minor top edge roughness, branded "The Work of..." mark of L. & J.G. Stickley, 13¼" sq., 42" h. **2,860**

Federal Reading Stand & Canterbury

Reading stand w/canterbury, Federal, mahogany, the rectangular lattice stand above a baluster- and ring-turnd post on a rectangular canterbury base w/pairs of slender turned spindles forming six slots, on casters, labeled "Blanchard and Parson No. 294 North Market Street, Albany," Albany, New York, early 19th c., 14 x 22¼", 47½" h. (ILLUS.) **3,105**

Smoking stand, Mission-style (Arts & Crafts movement), oak, a rectangular top above a small drawer over a tall paneled door opening to short shelves, rounded wood knobs, added varnish to dark finish, one shelf missing, possibly by J.M. Young, 7 x 14¾", 29" h............. **1,430**

Telephone stand, Louis XV Revival, walnut, the rectangular top w/serpentined molded edges centered by an upright compartment w/an arched scroll-carved crest over the molded arched cornice & a conforming door w/ornate leafy scroll carving centered by a cupid face, door opens to telephone compartment, the stand top above a conforming apron w/a single drawer carved w/a latticework design flanking a central scroll-carved cartouche, on tall slender cabriole legs w/leaf-carved knees & ending in scroll-and-peg feet, old finish ca. 1920s, overall 48¾" h. **550**

Umbrella stand, Mission-style (Arts & Crafts movement), oak, a slightly tapering cylindrical container w/slatted sides riveted to interior iron hoops, cleaned original finish, drip-pan missing, unsigned Gustav Stickley, Model No. 100, 12" d., 24" h. **1,760**

Victorian washstand, Renaissance Revival substyle, walnut & burl walnut, a high scroll-carved & molded backsplash on the rectangular top w/molded edges & rounded front corners over a case of three long drawers w/burl walnut & raised oval banding, carved leaf- & fruit-carved pulls, pull-out towel bar on side, chamfered front corners w/short knob-turned quarter drops at the top, scalloped apron & bracket feet, old worn finish, ca. 1870, 16¼ x 30¼", 29" h. plus crest (some edge damage) **248**

English Classical Washstand

Washstand, Classical country-style, painted & decorated, the high arched splashback w/lower scroll-cut sides over a rectangular top over an apron w/two drawers w/simple turned wood knobs, on ring-, knob- & rod-turned tapering legs w/peg feet, grain-painted to simulate mahogany except the top which simulates grey marble, minor imperfections, England, ca. 1830, 19 x 36", 40" h. (ILLUS.). **863**

Tiger Stripe & Bird's-eye Maple Stand

Washstand, Classical country-style, tiger stripe & bird's-eye maple, the high scrolled backsplash & scrolled lower sides on the rectangular top over a single long drawer w/a simple turned wood knob raised on rod- and ring-turned supports to the rectangular medial shelf w/block corners on ring-turned short legs w/knob feet, refinished, imperfections, probably Pennsylvania, ca. 1825, 17 x 21¾", 29" h. (ILLUS.). **1,150**

Washstand, Federal, carved mahogany veneer, a three-quarters shaped low splashboard on the rectangular top above a veneered cabinet door flanked by ovolo top corners & carved columns of leaves & grapes on a punchwork ground continuing to slender ring-turned tapering legs ending in brass casters, paneled sides, narrow cockbeaded drawer below the door w/round pulls, North Shore Massachusetts, ca. 1815-25, 16 x 21½", 35⅝" h. (old replaced brasses, old refinish, minor imperfections) **2,300**

Washstand, Federal, inlaid mahogany, corner-style, the pointed arch & shaped splashboard centered by a quarter-round shelf above a round-fronted top w/a pierced basin hole, the edge w/square string inlay, raised on three square supports continuing to an open shelf over

Fine Portsmouth Area Washstand

a satinwood veneered apron centered by a small drawer, string inlay on the supports & the three outswept lower legs joined by three slender tapering stretchers centered by an inlaid patera, patterned inlay trim, old finish, minor imperfections, Portsmouth, New Hampshire, area, ca. 1800, 16½ x 23", 41" h. (ILLUS.). **5,750**

Washstand, Federal, mahogany, a tall shaped splashboard w/a narrow shelf above the rectangular top w/a round cut-out basin hole raised on ring-turned & reeded supports to a medial shelf over a shallow drawer w/wooden pulls raised on ring-turned & reeded tapering legs ending in knob feet, school of John & Thomas Seymour, Boston, early 19th c., 22" w., 41" h. **2,070**

Federal Rectangular Washstand

Washstand, Federal, mahogany, a tall three-quarters gallery w/sloping sides & a small quarter-round shelf in each corner above the rectangular top w/a central large pierced basin hole flanked by two small cup holes over a scalloped front apron, raised on four ring-turned posts on a medial shelf over a single long cockbeaded drawer w/a round brass knob all raised on slender ring-, knob- & baluster-turned tapering legs w/peg feet, old finish, replaced brass, minor imperfections, probably Massachusetts, ca. 1815, 14½ x 20", 41½" h. (ILLUS.) **690**

Federal Mahogany & Tiger Stripe Stand

Early Federal Corner Washstand

Washstand, Federal, mahogany & mahogany veneer, corner-style, the high arched & shaped splashboard centered by a small quarter-round shelf over the conforming top w/a cut-out round basin hole over the conforming case w/a pair of cockbeaded cupboard doors over a narrow central drawer w/oval brass flanked by two small cockbeaded panels, on square outward flaring legs joined by the loop-pierced stretchers centered by a molded round medallion, replaced brass, old finish, minor imperfections, probably Massachusetts, ca. 1810, 15¾ x 22¾", 40¾" h. (ILLUS.) **690**

Washstand, Federal, mahogany & tiger stripe maple, corner-style, the high pointed arch & serpentine-sided splashboard above a quarter-round top w/a round basin cut-out & scalloped shallow apron raised on three square supports to the medial shelf above a row of three small tiger stripe maple-veneered drawers over the three square tapering legs & a central turned & reeded front leg, Massachusetts, early 19th c., 23" w., 39" h. (ILLUS.) **1,840**

Federal "Tambour-front" Washstand

Washstand, Federal "tambour-front" style, mahogany, the top arched & reeded sides centering a retracting tambour top on paneled dies centering a drawer over a cupboard door on turned & reeded legs w/baluster-turned legs on casters, appears to retain original cast-brass hardware, losses to veneer, missing fitted interior, New York City, ca. 1810, 20" sq., 36½" h. (ILLUS.) **1,495**

Washstand, Victorian cottage-style, painted & decorated pine, the tall splashback w/beveled corners fitted w/two small shelves w/brackets above the rectangular top over a case w/a long drawer w/two narrow oblong brass pulls over a pair of cupboard doors on a molded base, original decoration w/painted decoration of outlined panels & stylized florals w/brown & grey flowers, black striping, etc., wear, some edge damage, ca. 1880, 14¾ x 29¼", 35½" h. (ILLUS.) **248**

Painted Victorian Cottage Washstand

Washstand, Victorian Renaissance Revival substyle, walnut, a high double-arched splashboard w/two half-round candle shelves above the rectangular top over a long drawer w/an incised long band & two round wood pulls over a pair of paneled cupboard doors each w/an incised rectangular panel, thin block feet, ca. 1870, 18 x 41", 30" h. **403**

Classical two-drawer stand, curly maple, a rectangular two-board drop above a deep apron w/two round-fronted drawers each w/two small turned wood knobs, raised on heavy rope-twist-turned legs w/ring-turned top & bottom segments & baluster-turned feet, refinished, ca. 1840, 18¼ x 23", 28½" h. (top replaced) **825**

Federal country-style one-drawer stand, cherry, a rectangular one-board top over an apron w/a single drawer w/turned wood knob, raised on slender ring- and rod-turned tapering legs ending in baluster- and knob-turned feet, first half 19th c., 20½ x 22½", 30" h. (top reattached & w/plugged holes) **523**

Federal country-style two-drawer stand, cherry & bird's-eye maple, the rectangular top above a deep case w/two graduated drawers w/bird's-eye maple fronts, on spiraled leaf-carved round legs on baluster-form feet on casters, clear lacy glass pulls on one drawer, pressed ribbed knobs on others, refinished, first half 19th c., 17⅝ x 22", 28" h. **1,100**

Federal country-style two-drawer stand, walnut, a rectangular top flanked by two wide hinged drop leaves over the deep case w/two drawers w/Rockingham-glazed pottery knobs, raised on simple sausage-turned legs, old soft finish, mid 19th c., 18 x 24" plus 11¾" w. leaves, 28¾" h. **330**

Federal Grain-painted Stand

Federal one-drawer stand, country-style, painted & decorated pine, the nearly square top w/shaped corners overhanging an apron w/a single drawer w/a small turned knob, raised on tall square tapering legs, grain-painted in old burnt sienna & ochre, heavy graining wear to top, replaced pull, New England, early 19th c., 18 x 18½", 27" h. (ILLUS.) **1,725**

Pine & Butternut Country Stand

Federal one-drawer stand, country-style, pine & butternut, rectangular two-board pine top above an apron w/a single drawer, on turned & tapering legs w/bulbous ankles & tall peg feet, imperfections, early 19th c., 19 x 20½", 30" h. (ILLUS.) **805**

Federal Inlaid-Cherry Stand

Federal one-drawer stand, inlaid cherry, the nearly square top w/line inlay including a center diamond enclosing a pinwheel design & edge banding overhanging the apron w/a single line-inlaid drawer w/round brass pulls, line-inlaid apron & slender tall tapering square legs, crack repair under top, appears to retain original drawer pull, Connecticut, ca. 1800, 19¾ x 20¼", 28" h. (ILLUS.) **2,300**

Federal one-drawer stand, mahogany, diminutive size w/an oval top above a small drawer w/turned pull, raised on slender square tapering legs, New England, early 19th c., 13¼ x 19½", 27" h. **4,250**

Federal Country Two-drawer Stand

Federal two-drawer stand, country-style, tiger stripe maple & mahogany veneer, rectangular top flanked by two wide drop leaves w/rounded corners over a deep apron w/two mahogany-veneered drawers w/simple turned wood knobs, raised on ring- and baluster-turned

tapering legs w/knob feet, imperfections, New England, ca. 1825, 17 x 20", 28½" h. (ILLUS.) **2,990**

Federal two-drawer stand, painted birch & bird's-eye maple, the rectangular top overhanging a deep apron w/two cockbeaded graduated drawers w/bird's-eye maple fronts, the borders stained to imitate inlay, on slender square tapering legs, simple bail pulls & oval keyhole escutcheon appear to be original, New England, ca. 1810, 13½ x 17⅛", 28¾" h. (minor imperfections). **2,990**

STOOLS

Frank Lloyd Wright Bank Stools

Bank teller stools, Modern style, oak, a rectangular top raised on four pair of slender square supports joined by a narrow medial rail above the squared outswept lower legs w/square feet, one w/paper label "First National Bank of Dwight," designed by Frank Lloyd Wright for Frank L. Smith Bank, Dwight, Illinois, 1908, 12¼ x 18½", 27 & 28" h., pr. (ILLUS.) **7,475**

Classical Carved Footstool

Classical footstool, carved mahogany, the deep rectangular upholstered top above a deep cove-molded & bead-trimmed apron on a half-round band centered by a carved spread-winged eagle w/shield, leafy scroll-carved paw feet, ca. 1830, 24" l. (ILLUS.) **2,185**

Classical footstool, mahogany veneer, the high square rounded floral needlepoint top above a deep serpentine apron w/a scalloped & scroll-bordered apron on round bracket feet on casters, ca. 1840, 18½" sq., 16" h. (some edge damage) **220**

Classical footstools, painted & decorated, pillar & scroll style w/pierced seatrails, grain-painted in raw & burnt umber, possibly New York or Pennsylvania, ca. 1830-40, 15½" l., 6" h., pr. (imperfections) **230**

Classical piano stool, mahogany & mahogany veneer, the circular overupholstered top on a conforming veneered base bordered in brass beading on a baluster-turned shaft & three scrolled brass-inlaid legs, resting on brass ball feet, possibly Boston, ca. 1825, 11½" d., 20½" h. (imperfections) **633**

Federal footstools, mahogany, the upholstered rectangular seat on horizontally reeded rails joining swelled ring-turned legs on ball feet, old finish, possibly New York City, ca. 1815-25, 9 x 13" l., 8½" h., pr. (minor imperfections) . . . **920**

Gout stool, Victorian, mahogany, a rectangular upholstered top, adjustable ratchet base, on turned feet, England, mid 19th c., 12 x 19" **173**

Jacobean-Style stool, oak, a rectangular expanding top & cubbyhole above a deep canted apron w/panels carved w/double S-scrolls, one side forming a hinged door, on short baluster-, ring- and block-turned legs joined by box stretchers, metal label for Kittinger, 20th c., 14½ x 22½", 20" h. **110**

Modern style stool, wire & upholstery, the tall waisted cylindrical base w/flaring top composed of fine vertical bronze wires w/a round upholstered seat & cushion in peach fabric, designed by Warren Platner, manufactured by Knoll, ca. 1950s, 17" d., 21" h. **358**

Modern style stools, molded birch, four flat tall legs curved at the top supporting a round seat frame w/laminate seats in red, blue or yellow, a low open square back & low footrest near front base, designed by Alvar Aalto, manufactured by Artek, ca. 1950s, 15" d., 29" h., set of 4 . . . . **413**

Windsor Painted Footstool

Windsor footstool, painted pine, the oval top w/incised edge raised on widely splayed bamboo-turned legs joined by turned box stretchers, painted white w/red trim, early 19th c., 9½ x 15", 10¼" h. (ILLUS.) **287**

TABLES

Art Deco Bedside Table

Art Deco bedside tables, pale maple w/mirrors, each of cylindrical form w/a flattened back & mounted w/two projecting rounded mirrored shelves, raised on a conforming plinth, losses to veneer, England, probably by Hille, ca. 1930, 14½" d., 35" h., pr. (ILLUS. of one) **1,092**

Fine Art Deco Dining Table

Art Deco dining table, figured mahogany, the round top w/a rayed mahogany design raised on a heavy wood column on a nickel band raised on three low arched splayed legs w/nickeled feet, attributed to Jules Leleu, France, ca. 1930, 42" d., 22" h. (ILLUS.) **14,950**

Art Deco dining table, mahogany, the oval divided top above a square standard w/chamfered corners raised on a conforming stepped plinth base, France, ca. 1930, 39½ x 47", 29½" h. (repairs, no leaves) **1,380**

Art Deco dining table, walnut, the round top w/a sunburst pattern overhanging a narrow apron raised on five slender turned & tapering legs w/wide disks near the top, France, ca. 1935, 63" d., 30" h. 5,750

American Art Deco Dressing Table

Art Deco dressing table, burled walnut, the large circular mirror plate suspended within the case above a lower shelf on the right & a projecting rounded section w/four drawers on the left, American-made, chips & losses, ca. 1930, 27 x 70", 54" h. (ILLUS.) 345

Art Deco side table, black lacquer, thick round top widely overhanging a cylindrical accordian-pleat standard & spreading round foot, France, ca. 1925, 29½" d., 22" h. (wear) 2,185

Majorelle Art Nouveau Dressing Table

Art Nouveau dressing table, carved mahogany, "les Lilas" patt., the large squared upright mirror within a foliate-carved frame flanked by flaring stained side panels, above a central plateau

w/raised ends over two pairs of small drawers flanking an arched kneehole, gilt-bronze mounts, raised on slender & slightly curved foliate-carved legs, Louis Majorelle, France, ca. 1900, 22½ x 49", 62½" h. (ILLUS.) 4,140

Arts & Crafts library table, quarter-sawn oak, a rectangular top slightly overhanging an apron w/a long flush drawer, raised on two square end posts w/scroll-ended flat shoe feet joined by a flat medial stretcher, ca. 1910,. 26¼ x 44", 30" h. 248

Baroque Revival Parlor Table

Baroque Revival parlor table, walnut veneer, the octagonal top w/fanned veneering centered by an inlaid floral medallion over a deep carved apron raised on four legs w/ornate scroll carving at the top & feet & joined by a quatrefoil-form stretcher w/central rosette, early 20th c., 30" d., 29" h. (ILLUS.) 345

Early Bentwood Library Table

Bentwood library table, mahogany, rectangular w/reeded edges above a bentwood double-loop trestle base w/top scrolls & flaring leg bases on arched stretchers on bun feet, by J. & J. Kohn, Austria, ca. 1910, wear, 24 x 40", 29½" h. (ILLUS.) **690**

Chippendale card table, carved mahogany, the rectangular hinged top w/rounded corners above a deep apron w/a pair of cockbeaded drawers w/butterfly brasses, cabriole legs w/leaf-carved knees & ending in claw-and-ball feet, New York or Philadelphia, 18th c., 36" l. **3,500**

Fine Chippendale Pembroke Table

Chippendale Pembroke table, figured mahogany, the rectangular top w/rounded ends flanked by serpentine-edged drop leaves, a cockbeaded apron drawer at one end w/simple bail pull, on square tapering stop-fluted legs ending in spade feet, appears to retain original brass, minor patches to veneer, sunbleached, Mid-Atlantic States, ca. 1780, closed 20½ x 32", 27½" h. (ILLUS.) **8,050**

Chippendale Pembroke table, mahogany, a rectangular top flanked by two rectangular drop leaves above an apron w/one end drawer w/replaced brass, raised on four square tapering legs w/inside chamfer joined by a cross-stretcher, old finish, late 18th to early 19th c., 20 x 33" w/9½" leaves, 29" h. (repair to stretcher) **1,540**

Chippendale tea table, carved & figured mahogany, round dished top tilting on a birdcage mechanism above a ring-, rod- and ball-turned pedestal on a tripod base w/cabriole legs ending in claw-and-ball feet, Philadelphia, ca. 1770, 33" d., 28½" h... **14,950**

Chippendale tea table, figured mahogany, a round top tilting above a birdcage support & ring- and baluster-turned pedestal on a tripod base w/three cabriole legs ending in claw-and-ball feet, New York City, ca. 1780, 31½" d., 27½" h. (feet worn & chewed) **3,450**

Chippendale-Style tea table, mahogany, tne scalloped round top w/carved fans & rings for plates, raised on a turned columnar support above a spiral-twist knob over the tripod base w/cabriole legs leaf-carved at the knees & ending in elongated claw-and-ball feet, old finish, England, late 19th c., 31½" d., 28½" h...... **1,045**

Chippendale-Style tea table, mahogany, wide round top tilting on a birdcage mechanism above a ring- and knob-turned column w/gadrooned & reeded sections above the squatty tripod base w/cabriole legs ending in snake feet, refinished, 20th c., 35 " d., 27¾" h. (two-board top & birdcage old replacements, top wobbles) **275**

Classical Mahogany Breakfast Table

Classical breakfast table, carved & inlaid mahogany, the rectangular top w/brass inlay in outline & stamped brass on the edges of the flanking, shaped drop leaves above one working & one faux end apron drawer, drop pendants at the corners, raised on four ring-turned columns on a rectangular curve-edged platform raised on outswept leaf-carved legs ending in paw feet on casters, replaced pulls, old refinish, repairs, losses, New York City, ca. 1820-30, 24 x 39", 28" h. (ILLUS.)...... **2,415**

Classical card table, carved mahogany & mahogany veneer, the fold-over rectangular top w/rounded front corners above a paneled veneered apron flanked by scrolled end panels, raised on a square molded tapering pedestal resting on a quadripartite platform on four scroll- and acanthus-carved feet, attributed to Isaac Vose & Son, Boston, ca. 1825, 18 x 36½", 30" h. (refinished) **3,105**

Classical card table, carved mahogany, the rectangular hinged top w/rounded corners above a conforming apron w/horizontally reeded corners above a leaf-turned & leaf-carved & reeded pedestal on outswept beaded legs ending in brass

Classical Mahogany Card Table

paw feet on casters, old refinish, imperfections, New England, 1825, 17¾ x 36", 29⅝" h. (ILLUS.) **805**

Grain-painted Classical Card Table

Classical card table, grain-painted, rectangular hinged top w/rounded corners opening above a simple ogee apron raised on a heavy slightly tapering square pedestal on a cross-form platform base above flattened ball feet, original red & gold graining simulates mahogany, imperfections, Maine, 1830s, 18 x 36", 28¾" h. (ILLUS.) **1,093**

Classical Center Table on Ball Feet

Classical center table, carved mahogany veneer, the round top w/rounded edge on a conforming veneered apron w/banded lower edge, raised on a heavy ring- and knob-turned & acanthus-carved pedestal on a tripartite platform on incised ball feet, imperfections, possibly Boston, ca. 1840, 40½" d., 30¾" h. (ILLUS.) **1,955**

Classical Center Table on Casters

Classical center table, carved & veneered mahogany, the round top w/rounded edge above a conforming apron w/applied panels & cast-brass beaded edge, raised on a ring-turned & acanthus leaf-carved post on four outswept scrolled & acanthus-carved legs ending in cast-brass cap caster feet, refinished, minor imperfections, probably Massachusetts, ca. 1825, 36" d., 27½" h. (ILLUS.) **8,050**

Mid-Atlantic Classical Center Table

Classical center table, carved & veneered mahogany, round top w/a flat veneered edge over a cockbeaded veneered apron raised on a heavy ring- and knob-turned pedestal set on a concave-shaped platform on acanthus- and scroll-carved paw feet, w/an additional leaf, refinished, minor imperfections, Mid-Atlantic States, ca. 1825, closed 44" d., 28¾" h. (ILLUS.) . . . **1,035**

Classical center table, parcel-gilt & carved mahogany, the round white marble top on a conforming apron w/brass & mother-of-pearl-inlaid edge raised on three white marble columns w/gilt carved scroll capitals on gilt carved winged paw feet joined by a tripartite platform w/central rondel, New York City, ca. 1830, 39" d., 31½" h. (ILLUS.) **8,338**

Fine Classical Center Table

Rare Small Classical Center Table

Classical center table, part-ebonized mahogany, figured round top above a conforming apron fitted w/a drawer, the turned flaring heavy pedestal on a tripartite platform on leaf-carved scrolling feet on casters, patches & veneer losses, Boston, Massachusetts, possibly by Vose or one of its comtemporaries, ca. 1825, rare small size, 24" d., 26¼" h. (ILLUS.) **3,737**

Classical Country Dressing Table

Classical country-style dressing table, painted & decorated, the scroll-cut crestboard behind a small rectangular drawer on the rectangular top overhanging an apron w/a single long drawer, raised on slender ring- and rod-turned tapering legs w/peg feet, original red & brown graining simulating rosewood w/yellow foliate designs on the leg corner blocks & overall yellow-painted bordering to simulate inlay, Maine, early 19th c., 17¾ x 34", 34½" h. (ILLUS.) **1,150**

Classical Country Work Table

Classical country-style work table, tiger stripe maple, a nearly square top flanked by hinged drop leaves w/rounded corners above a case w/two round-fronted drawers w/pairs of turned wood knobs, raised on a heavy square tapering pedestal on a stepped square base on four belted bun feet on thick short pegs, old finish, minor imperfections, New England, ca. 1820-30, 16½ x 17", 30½" h. (ILLUS.) **1,495**

Fine Classical Dining Table

Classical dining table, carved & veneered mahogany, extension-type, round top w/molded edge over a smooth apron w/thin gadrooned base band raised on a clustered column-form split pedestal ending in four downswept foliate-carved legs ending in paw feet on casters, together w/seven leaves, New York City, ca. 1840, closed 48" d., 29½" h. (ILLUS.) **7,475**

Classical library table, mahogany, the wide rectangular top flanked by two hinged drop leaves w/notched & rounded corners above an apron w/a single long drawer w/round brass pulls & turned corner drops, raised on a short bulbous pedestal over four outswept leaf-carved legs ending in brass eagle caps on casters, appears to retain original hardware, New York City, ca. 1830, 39 x 52", 28¼" h. **2,875**

Classical Marble-topped Pier Table

Classical pier table, mahogany & mahogany veneer, a rectangular white marble top w/molded edges above the ogee molded apron on two heavy S-scroll supports & a shaped concave platform w/scrolled front feet & turned rear feet, a recessed molded base panel flanked by tapering pilasters, old refinish, imperfections, probably Boston, ca. 1825, 19¼ x 40¼", 37" h. (ILLUS.) **2,070**

Classical side table, decorated pine & poplar, a rectangular top w/cut corners decorated w/a grey marbleized decoration w/brown glazing over the grey base color, molded apron, square molded & tapering pedestal centered on a square platform base w/slightly scalloped apron, mid 19th c., 19¼ x 25¾", 28¼" h. (wear, top braced but loose) **495**

Classical work table, carved & veneered mahogany, the rectangular top flanked by wide drop leaves w/rounded corners over an apron w/two round-fronted veneered drawers w/early pressed-glass pulls raised on a leaf- and floral-carved lyre-form pedestal on a square platform w/beveled top edge all raised on S-scroll carved feet on casters, probably Massachusetts, ca. 1825, 18 x 19", 28½" h. (ILLUS.) **1,610**

Classical Lyre-based Work Table

Classical-Style games table, mahogany, the demi-lune top w/hinged leaf & beaded edge above a conforming apron w/three blocks above the three front legs w/a ring- and compressed knob-turned section above a reeded tapering section ending in a brass claw w/glass ball foot, fourth matching swing-out support leg, old finish, early 20th c., closed 18¼ x 36", 29¼" h. **633**

Edwardian center table, satinwood-inlaid rosewood, the shield-shaped top raised on scrolling legs joined by a shelf stretcher, England, early 20th c., 23½" w., 28" h. **1,092**

Federal card table, inlaid mahogany, rectangular fold-over top w/ovolo corners & inlaid edges above a conformingly shaped apron centering an inlaid shaped contrasting panel, bordered by stringing w/geometric banding on the lower edge joining four square double tapering legs, the dies inlaid w/panels & stringing continuing to banded cuffs, old finish, probably Massachusetts, ca. 1790, 17 x 35¾", 30¾" h. (minor imperfections) . . . **5,175**

Massachusetts Federal Card Table

Federal card table, mahogany & flame birch veneer inlay, the rectangular serpentine-edged hinged top w/banded inlay edges & ovolo corners above a conforming top & apron centered by an inlaid birch veneer oval reserve in a rectangular panel, raised on ring-turned & reeded tapering legs w/knobbed ankles & peg feet, imperfections, North Shore, Massachusetts, early 19th c., 17½ x 34¾", 29⅜" h. (ILLUS.) **4,600**

Federal card table, tiger stripe maple, birch & bird's-eye maple veneer, the rectangular fold-over top w/a serpentine front & half-serpentine sides & ovolo corners above a conforming apron w/bird's-eye maple veneer joining quarter engaged ring-turned legs ending in swelled peg feet, old refinish, New Hampshire or Massachusetts, ca. 1820, 18 x 36", 28½" h. (imperfections) **1,495**

Federal country-style dining table, birch, a rectangular two-board top flanked by deep hinged drop leaves w/rounded corners, the apron raised on swelled turned round legs ending in ring-turned ankles & peg & ball feet, first half 19th c., old red finish, 16½ x 41½" plus 11¾" w. leaves, 29¼" h. (age crack & edge repair in top, age crack & repair to one leg) **330**

Federal country-style dining table, cherry, a rectangular top flanked by wide hinged drop leaf w/rounded cut corners, one dovetailed drawer in the apron at one end, raised on turned cylindrical legs w/double-knob feet, refinished, first half 19th c., 20 x 42" plus 16¾" leaves, 28½" h. (age cracks in top). **550**

Country Federal Dining Table

Federal country-style dining table, tiger stripe maple, the rectangular top flanked by wide hinged drop leaves over a plain apron & six ring- and rod-turned legs w/small bun feet, old refinish, no casters, New England, ca. 1825, 29 x 56½", 28" h. (ILLUS.) **3,335**

Federal country-style dressing table, painted & decorated, the scroll-cut backsplash w/shaped ends above the rectangular top over a long narrow drawer in the apron, raised on ring-, knob- and tapering rod-turned legs w/knob feet, the backsplash painted w/a stylized stenciled fruit & leaf cluster in gold & green, the table w/a green & mustard gold grained surface & banding, old replaced opalescent glass drawer pulls, New England, early 19th c., 15 x 32¼", 34" h. (some old repaint) **1,380**

Federal dining table, mahogany, two-part, each half of demilune form w/a molded edge & a wide hinged drop leaf, wide plain conforming apron, each half w/four reeded & ring-turned legs w/ball feet, one leg a swing-out support for the leaf, Massachusetts, probably Newburyport, late 18th to early 19th c., open 48 x 90", 30" h. **7,188**

Federal games table, carved mahogany, the rectangular top w/serpentine sides & front w/a hinged leaf over a conforming apron w/flowerhead-carved corner dies on waterleaf-carved reeded tapering legs ending in peg feet, appears to retain old & possibly original finish, attributed to the Haines-Connelly School, Philadelphia, ca. 1810, closed 18 x 35¾", 29½" h. (top warp repairs, repairs to top left rear leg) **2,587**

Federal Pembroke Table

Federal Pembroke table, cherry, rectangular top flanked by rectangular drop leaves above an apron w/a single end drawer w/wooden knob, raised on slender square tapering legs joined by arched cross-stretchers, old refinish, New England, ca. 1810, open 34 x 38", 29" h. (ILLUS.). **1,495**

Federal Pembroke table, inlaid mahogany, a rectangular top flanked by hinged drop leaves w/notched & rounded corners bordered by inlaid stringing, the apron w/a working drawer at one end & a false drawer at the other, each w/stringed inlay & flanked by shaped satinwood corner panels above the square tapering legs, old oval brasses, old finish, probably New York, 1790-1800, closed 19 x 32", 28½" h. (imperfections) **2,990**

Federal Pembroke table, inlaid mahogany, a rectangular top w/gently bowed ends flanked by D-form drop leaves above a conforming apron w/a single line-inlaid drawer at one end, on square tapering legs w/inlaid cuffs, New York, early 19th c., 32" l., 28" h. **5,175**

Federal side table, inlaid cherry, a rectangular top w/tiger maple inlaid edging above an apron w/a single long drawer w/line inlay above a serpentine front apron, raised on square tapering legs w/arched line & geometric inlay, Newburyport, Massachusetts, early 19th c., 21 x 33", 30½" h. **8,050**

Federal side table, mahogany, a rectangular top w/molded edges flanked by D-form drop leaves flanking an apron w/a single long drawer w/replaced lion head brass pulls, raised on a tapering octagonal column over four outswept sabre legs ending in brass paw feet on casters, refinished, early 19th c., 29¼ x 79¼" plus 9½" leaves, 27½" h. **605**

Unusual Federal Sofa Table

Federal sofa table, figured maple, the rectangular long top w/reeded edges flanked by D-form drop leaves above an apron w/a long cockbeaded drawer w/two oval brass pulls, on slender ring- and rod-turned legs w/knob ankles & peg feet, appears to retain original hardware, probably New England, early 19th c., 29¾ x 44¾", 29" h. (ILLUS.) **4,887**

Federal work table, birch & mahogany veneer, rectangular top flanked by D-form drop leaves over an apron w/two drawers each w/two large round brass pulls,

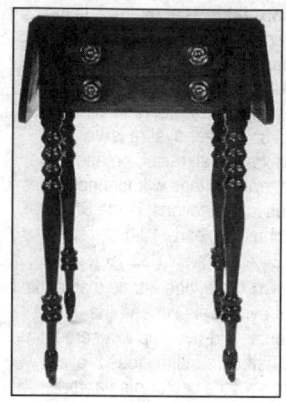

Federal New England Work Table

raised on bobbin-, baluster- and ring-turned tapering legs w/knob feet on casters, old finish, imperfections, New England, ca. 1830, 16¾ x 19¾", 28¾" h. (ILLUS.) **748**

Fine Federal Work Table

Federal work table, figured mahogany, the hinged rectangular top opening to a fitted interior w/adjustable writing surface flanked by compartments, the deep case w/two flush drawers w/pairs of round brass pulls raised on slender ring- and baluster-turned supports to a medial shelf w/concave front over short ring- and baluster-turned legs on casters, appears to retain original drawer pulls, patches to veneer, New York City, ca. 1810, 16¾ x 20½", 31" h. (ILLUS.) **4,312**

Federal work table, mahogany & figured mahogany veneer, a rectangular top above a deep case w/figured veneer on the front including two drawers w/original florette & ring gilded brasses, a shallow small writing drawer under the top to the right side, raised on turned reeded legs w/ring-turned sections at the top & bottom w/peg feet on casters, refinished, ca. 1810-20, 16½ x 21", 30" h. (minor veneer repair, writing drawer missing hinged shelf, age cracks) **1,540**

George II-Style Console Table

George II-Style console table, carved giltwood, the rectangular thick marble top above a carved frieze band centering a large scroll-carved cartouche, raised on fully carved spread-winged giltwood eagles on rockwork raised on a conforming plinth base, England, 19th c., 27 x 73", 35" h. (ILLUS.) **8,625**

Rectangular Hutch Table

Hutch (or chair) table, painted pine, the rectangular cleated top w/old red paint tilting above wide sides & closed back over seat w/narrow apron, low cut-out feet, original red surface, minor surface imperfections, New England, early 19th c., 36 x 43", 27½" h. (ILLUS.) **3,220**

Early Painted Pine Hutch Table

Hutch (or chair) table, painted pine, the round top tilting on two cut-out ends joined by a beaded frontal panel continuing to molded shoe feet, red paint over earlier paint, probably New England, 18th c., 31" d., 26¼" h. (ILLUS.) **6,900**

Hutch (or chair) table, painted wood, a wide rectangular four-board top lifting above one-board sides w/bootjack feet flanking a lift-top seat compartment, greenish grey paint, early 19th c., 37 x 57" . . **2,250**

Jacobean Revival side table, oak, the rectangular top composed of two caned panels within a scroll-carved narrow frame & apron w/floret-carved corner blocks above the slender rope-twist-turned legs w/bottom floret blocks on ovoid feet, rope-twist- and block-turned H-stretcher, old finish, early 20th c., 24 x 30", 24" h. **176**

Jacobean-Style Dining Table

Jacobean-Style dining table, inlaid walnut, draw-leaf extension-type, the rectangular top w/draw-leaf extensions above an S-scroll-carved apron w/scroll-carved brackets above the bulbous carved cup-and-cover design legs on shaped shoe feet joined by a half-round stretcher, some wear, ca. 1900, 35 x 71½", 31" h. (ILLUS.) **8,625**

Fine Louis XV-Style Side Table

Louis XV-Style bouilllotte side table, bronze-mounted veneer, the rounded shaped inset marble top w/gilt-bronze edge banding over a veneered apron w/gilt-bronze banding & simple slender cabriole legs w/long leafy scroll gilt-bronze mounts & banding ending in leaf-form "sabots," France, late 19th c., 23" d., 29¾" h. (ILLUS.) **5,175**

Louis XVI-Style center table, carved giltwood, the shaped rectangular top above an apron w/floral sprays, raised on fluted tapering round legs joined by an H-stretcher, France, late 19th c., 27 x 35", 31" h **632**

Mission-style (Arts & Crafts movement) dining table, oak, the wide rectangular top w/rounded ends flanked by narrow D-form drop leaves, over a round split apron supported on a heavy square central post issuing cross stretchers to the four heavy square outside legs, new reddish brown finish, red decal mark of Gustav Stickley, open 54" d., 28½" h **4,675**

Mission-style (Arts & Crafts movement) dining table, oak, divided round top w/molded edge above a square pedestal w/four square extended feet, fine original finish, branded marks of the Charles Limbert Furniture Co., w/two original leaves, veneer chip to apron, 48" d., 30" h **2,090**

Mission-style (Arts & Crafts movement) lamp table, oak, a round top over a narrow conforming apron w/four inset square slender legs joined by a round medial shelf, refinished top, remnant of Gustav Stickley paper label, 24" d., 29" h. **2,310**

Mission-style (Arts & Crafts movement) library table, oak, spindle-style, the rectangular top above a narrow apron on slender square legs joined by end stretchers w/13 small slender close spindles joining them to the top at each end, medial shelf below, fine new finish, unsigned Gustav Stickley, Model No. 655, 24 x 36", 29" h. **4,125**

Mission-style (Arts & Crafts movement) library table, oak, rectangular top over an apron w/a single drawer w/original brass pulls flanked by book shelves opening at the sides, fine original reddish brown finish, branded mark of Charles Limbert Co., Model No. 132, 28 x 45", 29" h. . . . **935**

Mission-style (Arts & Crafts movement) library table, rectangular top overhanging an apron w/two drawers w/original copper hardware, double-keyed lower stretcher, refinished, unsigned L. & J.G. Stickley, Model No. 531, 30 x 48", 29" h. (extensive restoration). . . **413**

Lifetime Mission-style Library Table

Mission-style (Arts & Crafts movement) library table, oak, rectangular top above a deep apron w/gently arched ends & two long drawers w/original hardware along one side, long corbels at the outside top of the four square legs, six wide slats on the lower ends on rails joined by a narrow medial stretcher shelf, original finish, some veneer restoration, paper label of the Lifetime Furniture Co., Model No. 999, 30 x 54", 30" h. (ILLUS.) **990**

Lifetime Company Library Table

Mission-style (Arts & Crafts movement) library table, oak, a thick wide rectangular top overhanging a deep apron w/two long drawers on the long sides w/original copper hardware, on heavy square legs w/through-tenon end stretchers & a medial shelf stretcher, recent finish, paper label of the Lifetime Furniture Company, Model No. 911, 32 x 54", 30" h. (ILLUS.) **1,870**

Mission-style (Arts & Crafts movement) library table, oak, a wide rectangular top overhanging an apron w/a pair of drawers w/original copper bail pulls, heavy square legs w/upper corbels & through-tenon end stretchers joined by a wide medial shelf, fine original reddish brown finish w/some color added to stretcher, branded signature of Gustav Stickley, Model No. 617, 32 x 54", 30" h. **3,850**

Mission-style (Arts & Crafts movement) parlor table, round top overhanging an apron w/inset square legs joined by cross stretchers below a round medial shelf, original finish w/some stains, "Handcraft" decal of L. & J.G. Stickley, Model No. 541, 30" d., 29" h. **1,760**

Mission-style (Arts & Crafts movement) parlor table, oak, round top above a deep apron w/molded rim, four inset square legs joined by a cross stretcher, fine original finish, orb mark of The Roycroft Shop, Model No. 073, 36" d., 30" h. **7,700**

Mission-style (Arts & Crafts movement) side table, oak, a round top raised on heavy square legs joined by an arched cross-stretcher w/through-tenon construction, cleaned original finish, signed w/faint box mark of Gustav Stickley, Model No. 603, 18" d., 20" h. (minor splits) **1,440**

Mission-style (Arts & Crafts movement) side table, oak, octagonal top w/through-tenon square legs joined by arched cross stretchers, top w/a recent finish, base w/original finish, branded mark of L. & J.G. Stickley, Model No. 558, 18" w., 20" h. **1,320**

Mission-style (Arts & Crafts movement) side table, oak, a rectangular top raised on four slender square legs joined by a rectangular medial shelf, legs mortised through the top w/flush tenons, some wear to top otherwise good original finish, L. & J.G. Stickley, Model No. 509, 17 x 26", 24" h. **2,420**

Mission-style (Arts & Crafts movement) side table, round top w/inset heavy square legs joined by a flared cross-stretcher base, cleaned original finish, unsigned Gustav Stickley, Model No. 440, 30" d., 29" h. **2,200**

Stickley Brothers "Quaint" Side Table

Mission-style (Arts & Crafts movement) side table, oak, a round top above a square narrow apron on four slender

square legs w/through-tenon cross stretchers, original finish, Quaint metal tag of the Stickley Brothers, Model No. 2500, 24" d., 30" h. (ILLUS.). **990**

Mission-style (Arts & Crafts movement) trestle table, oak, a rectangular top widely overhanging end aprons w/incurved ends above pairs of wide slats joined by a medial shelf w/through-tenons, flat wide shoe feet below, recoated original finish, branded Gustav Stickley mark, 29 x 48", 30" h. **1,980**

Modern style dinette table, laminate & aluminum, the round white laminate top w/rubber edge raised on a white enamel slender pedestal & case aluminum cross-form base, designed by Charles Eames, manufactured by Herman Miller, ca. 1950s, 48" d., 29" h. **176**

Modern style 'dish' table, ash plywood & metal, the wide round dished plywood top raised on four slender black metal legs w/rubber boot feet, designed by Charles Eames, manufactured by Herman Miller, ca. 1950s, 34" d., 16" h. (minor stains in top). . **990**

Fine Napolean III Side Table

Napolean III side table, marquetry & burl, square top w/ornate central marquetry squared panel framed by ornate scrolling above four D-form burl-banded & marquetry scroll-decorated drop leaves, on gilt-metal-mounted turned & tapering legs w/ring-turned peg feet joined by a curved cross stretcher centered by an urn-form finial, France, late 19th c., 21" sq., 30" h. (ILLUS.) **2,300**

Queen Anne dining table, carved & figured walnut, the rectangular top flanked by deep rectangular drop leaves, arched end aprons on cabriole legs ending in paneled trifid feet, appears to retain an old & possibly original finish, warm nut-brown color, Pennsylvania, ca. 1750, closed 17½ x 50½", 28" h. (ILLUS.) **4,887**

Early Queen Anne Dining Table

Quality Queen Anne Tavern Table

Queen Anne Dressing Table

Queen Anne dressing table, maple & pine, rectangular top w/molded edges above an apron w/a pair of deep drawers flanking a small shallow central drawer above a deeply scalloped apron w/two urn-turned drops, simple cabriole legs ending in pad feet, rear knee return missing, formerly painted white, New England, 1740-60, 18½ x 34½", 29½" h. (ILLUS.) **3,737**

Queen Anne mixing table, painted, a rectangular top w/a projecting molded edge enclosing a black marble slab above a deep openwork apron carved w/overlapping circles & diamonds, raised on angular cabriole legs w/scrolled returns & ending in stylized hairy paw feet, painted black, 18th c., 20 x 32½", 28" h. **7,000**

Queen Anne tavern table, painted pine, oval top widely overhangs a deep apron on splayed ring- and rod-turned tapering legs ending in turned feet, scrubbed top, original red paint on base, minor imperfections, New England, 18th c., 26⅜ x 35", 26¼" h. (ILLUS.) **14,950**

Queen Anne Small Tavern Table

Queen Anne tavern table, poplar & turned maple, rectangular top w/rounded corners above a deep apron on tapering turned legs ending in pad feet, repair to top, top possibly reshaped, New England, 1740-60, 14 x 19½", 25½" h. (ILLUS.) **2,875**

Queen Anne Tilt-top Tea Table

Queen Anne tea table, mahogany, wide round top tilting on a vase- and ring-turned pedestal on a tripod base w/cabriole legs ending in pad feet on platforms, refinished, minor imperfections, probably Massachusetts, ca. 1760, 33⅛" d., 27¾" h. (ILLUS.) **1,840**

Pennsylvania Queen Anne Tea Table

Queen Anne tea table, turned walnut, the large round dished top hinged & tilting & revolving above a birdcage support, the tapering columnar pedestal w/urn-form compressed-ball bottom on a tripod base w/squatty cabriole legs ending in snake feet, small section of stem at top of pedestal replaced, Pennsylvania, ca. 1750, 25½" d., 26½" h. (ILLUS.) **6,900**

Queen Anne work table, painted black walnut, the removable rectangular plank three-board pine top supported by cleats w/four dowels widely overhanging a deep apron w/a long & shorter drawer on one side each w/a simple turned wood knob, on beaded-edge straight cabriole legs ending in pad feet, original apple green paint, old replaced wood pulls, Pennsylvania, 1760-1800, 32 x 48½", 27" h. (surface imperfections, cracked foot) **2,415**

Regency-Style center table, mahogany, round top above a frieze raised on three monopodia supports carved w/lion's heads at the top & terminating in hairy paw feet joined by a tripartite concave-sided plinth centering a foliate finial, England, late 19th c., 64" d., 30¼" h. (wear) **6,325**

Renaissance-Style refectory table, mahogany, the simple rectangular top raised on a scrolling standard carved w/an armorial medallion, Europe, late 19th c., 39 x 101", 30" h. **2,760**

Early "Sawbuck" Table

"Sawbuck" table, painted pine, the rectangular overhanging top on a nail-constructed rectangular skirt & chamfered crossed legs joined by a turned medial stretcher w/keyed exposed tenon, old reddish brown paint, New England, mid-19th c., 28 x 50", 30" h. (ILLUS.) **2,070**

"Sawbuck" table, pine & painted pine, the rectangular top w/a natural finish raised on a black-painted base w/end cross-legs joined by a flat chamfered stretcher, each section of legs w/chamfered edges, late 19th c. copy of earlier style, 23 x 48¾", 30" h. **880**

Tavern table, country-style, painted pine, a rectangular top widely overhanging a beaded apron on four square chamfered legs w/molded edges, painted red, early, 27 x 38½", 26½" h. **2,000**

Early Country Tavern Table

Tavern table, country-style, pine & cherry, rectangular overhanging top on four square tapering beaded splayed legs joined by a deep beaded skirt, old refinish, imperfections, top stains, some surface loss, two interior 19th c. braces, New England, ca. 1790, 32 x 34¼", 25½" h. (ILLUS.) **1,265**

Tavern table, painted birch, rectangular top widely overhanging a deep apron raised on simple turned & tapering legs, later blue paint, northern New England, early 19th c., 22 x 38", 27½" h. (ILLUS.) **920**

Painted Country Tavern Table

Turn-of-the-century Oak Dining Table

Turn-of-the-century dining table, oak & oak veneer, extension-type, square top w/rounded corners & center split over a conforming apron, raised on an octagonal split pedestal w/four angled block legs on casters, w/leaves, ca. 1900, closed 45" w. (ILLUS.) **345**

Old Physician's Examination Table

Turn-of-the-century physician's examination table, quarter-sawn oak, the upholstered rectangular top above a deep apron w/applied leaf carving & hinged fold-down extensions at each end, the lower case w/a small & two larger drawers beside a large cupboard door w/applied wreath carving, all flanked by fluted corner columns, molded base, drawers fitted w/instrument trays (one missing), cast-steel foot rests labeled "The Allison. W.D. Allison Co. Indianpolis, Ind.," top recovered, ca. 1900, 22 x 40", 29" h. (ILLUS.) **550**

Baroque Revival Library Table

Victorian Baroque Revival library table, carved mahogany, rectangular top w/beveled & carved edges above a deep gadroon-carved front apron centered by carved cherub panels, end aprons supported on central round columns flanked by figural scroll-carved winged seated griffins on blocks joined by flat medial rails, on low beaded bun feet, late 19th to early 20th c. (ILLUS.) **3,100**

Victorian center table, Renaissance Revival substyle, walnut marquetry, part-ebonized & parcel-gilt, the rectangular top w/rounded ends & blocked corners decorated w/inlay above a deep conforming apron w/raised burl panels w/incised gilt line decoration, on four square legs w/large square knobby blocks above the reeded tapering lower legs ending in tapering knob feet & joined by a pierced scroll-carved fan-end H-stretcher w/a turned central urn finial, ca. 1865-75, 28½ x 54", 28½" h. (shrinkage) **3,738**

Victorian Golden Oak dining table, rounded divided top slighly overhanging the apron, raised on a heavy round pedestal above four large outstretched downcurved legs w/pleat-carved knees & ending in large paw feet on casters, ca. 1900, 42" d., 29½" h. **413**

Victorian parlor center table, Rococo substyle, walnut, a white marble "turtle" top above a narrow conforming molded apron w/scalloped center panels, raised on four heavy molded & scroll-carved S-scroll legs joined by a lower platform stretcher topped by the carved figure of a small reclining dog, old dark finish, ca. 1860, 23 x 37", 29" h. (marble cracked & repaired) **770**

Victorian Renaissance Revival parlor table, walnut, rectangular white marble top w/molded serpentine edges on a conforming molded apron w/central arched panels, raised on a scroll-carved & molded four-leg base centered by a ring-turned column & drop, on casters, refinished, ca. 1870, 20 x 28¼", 29" h. (ILLUS.) **578**

Renaissance Revival Parlor Table

Victorian Rococo substyle card table,
walnut, serpentine hinged molded top
over a carved apron, raised on foliate-
carved cabriole legs ending in scrolled
toes on casters, third quarter 19th c.,
19¼ x 35½", 31⅜" **546**

Rococo Ornate "Turtle-top" Table

Victorian Rococo substyle parlor table,
carved rosewood, the long white marble
"turtle-top" above a deep scroll-carved
conforming apron, raised on four slender
ring-turned posts over outswept pierce-
carved figural griffin legs centered by an
ornately carved central post, on casters,
attributed to George Henkel, ca. 1850s
(ILLUS.) **11,550**

Rare & Fine Meeks Parlor Table

Victorian Rococo substyle parlor table,
laminated carved rosewood, white marble
"turtle-top" on a molded conforming frame

w/a deep arched floral- and fruit-carved
pierced apron raised on four flower- and
leaf-carved cabriole legs w/scroll & peg
feet on brass casters, arched pierced-
carved cross stretcher centered by a
large carved urn of fruit over gadroon-
carved bands & pierced scroll carving,
J.&J.W. Meeks, New York City, ca. 1855
(ILLUS.) **31,350**

Rococo Parlor Table with Carved Dog

Victorian Rococo substyle parlor table,
walnut, white marble "turtle-top" above a
molded conforming apron w/central
arched panels w/scrolls, raised on four
bold tapering S-scroll supports tapering to
an oblong platform centered by a carved
reclining dog, raised on outswept scroll-
carved legs on casters, 22 x 36", 28" h.
(ILLUS.) **805**

Victorian side table, Eastlake substyle,
walnut & burl walnut, the rectangular
pinkish brown marble top w/cut corners
above a line-incised apron w/rectangular
burl panels at the centers w/fan-scalloped
designs, raised on four flat rectangular
supports joined by line-incised & pierced-
cut stretchers joined to a central turned
post w/knob drop, raised on downswept
legs w/rondels above long burl panels &
scroll-incised feet raised on casters,
ca. 1880, 20 x 30", 30" h. **358**

Round Wicker Table with Shelf

Wicker side table, round oak top w/wicker banding on four tightly woven wicker panels framing a lower oak shelf over a tightly woven conforming apron, pointed flaring woven legs, painted white, ca. 1910, 30" d. (ILLUS.) **201**

Rare William & Mary Dining Table

William & Mary dining table, figured walnut, a rectangular top w/rounded molded ends flanked by D-form matching drop leaves over an apron w/a deep drawer at each end, on square chamfered legs & swing-out gate-leg supports, joined by box stretchers, repairs to drawer fronts, possibly Southern U.S., 1700-30, closed 16 x 44", 31½" h. (ILLUS.) **10,925**

Early William & Mary Dining Table

William & Mary dining table, turned & figured maple, the rectangular top w/gently rounded ends flanked by two wide D-form drop leaves above an apron w/a drawer at one end, swing-out gate-leg supports, baluster- and ring-turned legs joined by block-, ring- and baluster-turned stretchers, on ball feet, restoration, New England, 1730-50, closed 19 x 49", 28" h. (ILLUS.) **3,737**

William & Mary "hutch" or chair table, painted maple & pine, the oval two-board top tilting on a base of two horizontal supports ending in scrolled handholds joining four block- and baluster-turned legs w/a medial seat & box stretchers all resting on turned feet, original Spanish brown paint, southeastern New England, early 18th c., 47¼ x 51¼", 26" h. (minor imperfections)................. **20,700**

William & Mary tavern table, maple & pine, the wide rectangular breadboard top overhanging the apron w/a single long drawer w/wooden knob, on ring-, baluster- and block-turned legs joined by square stretchers & ending in button feet, old refinish, New England, 18th c., 21 x 33", 27" h. (minor imperfections) **1,610**

William & Mary tavern table, painted, a wide rectangular top w/breadboard ends above an apron w/a single long drawer w/simple turned pull, on baluster-, ring- and block-turned legs joined by box stretchers, worn red paint, Massachusetts, 18th c., 28 x 38", 28½" h. .. **3,000**

Small William & Mary Tavern Table

William & Mary tavern table, pine & birch, the oval top above a deep canted apron w/a single drawer raised on canted baluster- and ring-turned legs ending in blocks joined by box stretchers & raised on waisted knob feet, retains traces of red wash, New England, 1700-30, diminutive size, 17¼ x 25½", 25" h. (ILLUS.)............................ **12,650**

William & Mary-Style games table, inlaid wood, the shaped rectangular top w/bone & ebony geometric designs, above an apron w/a single drawer, raised on turned legs joined by a cross stretcher, England, late 19th c., 32 x 45", 29" h. **3,737**

WARDROBES & ARMOIRES

Early Biedermeier Armoire

Armoire, Biedermeier, mahogany, the stepped rectangular top over a flaring graduated cornice over a pair of tall three-panel cupboard doors opening to later shelves, restoration, Europe, early 19th c., 21 x 49", 76" h. (ILLUS.) **3,450**

Provincial Louis XVI Armoire

Armoire, Lous XVI Provincial-style, oak, the rectangular top w/a widely flaring curved cornice w/round corners over a pair of tall cupboard doors each w/three matching molded serpentine panels, rounded paneled front stiles, on plain feet, France, late 18th to early 19th c., 22 x 44½", 86½" h. (ILLUS.) **4,025**

Early William & Mary Kas

Kas (American version of the Netherlands Kast or wardrobe), William & Mary style, cherry, pine & poplar, the rectangular top w/a high flaring architectural cornice molding over a pair of two arch-paneled cupboard doors flanked by reeded pilasters over applied mid-molding over a single long bottom drawer flanked by reeded panels, molded base on painted detachable disc & stretcher turnip-form feet, replaced hardware, refinished, restored, Long Island, New York area, 1730-80, 26¼ x 65½", 77¼" h. (ILLUS.) **4,025**

Fine Classical Wardrobe

Wardrobe, Classical, mahogany veneer, the wide rectangular top w/a deep stepped & flaring cornice above a pair of large, tall two-panel doors opening to an interior w/veneered drawers, molded base on simple bracket feet, paneled sides, some small interior drawers added, other minor imperfections, Mid-Atlantic States, ca. 1840, 26 x 65", 79½" h. (ILLUS.) **3,105**

Early Canadian Wardrobe

Wardrobe, country-style, painted pine, rectangular top w/low cornice overhanging a pair of tall six-panel cupboard doors & paneled sides opening to an interior of four shelves, molded scroll-cut apron & simple bracket feet, old green paint, some hardware loss & changes, shelves added later, some paint retouched, Canada, 19th c., 16 x 57", 87½" h. (ILLUS.) **1,495**

Wardrobe, Victorian country-style, painted pine, five-board construction, a flat rectangular top above a tall case w/wide front side boards flanking the central beaded board tall door w/wooden thumb latch & white porcelain knob, original blue paint, late 19th c., 17 x 41", 71" h. **518**

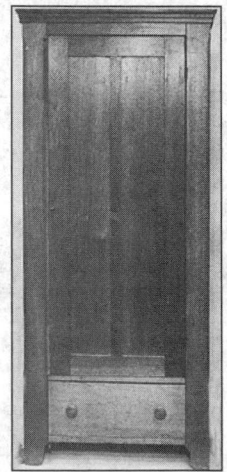

Simple Country Victorian Wardrobe

Wardrobe, Victorian country-style, walnut, a rectangular top w/a narrow molded cornice over a single tall double-panel door opening to a fitted rod above a single deep bottom drawer, simple bracket feet, one-board sides, door edge strip w/pieced repairs, found in Missouri, mid-19th c., 17¾ x 32", 73" h. (ILLUS.) **1,650**

Victorian Gothic Revival Wardrobe

Wardrobe, Victorian Gothic Revival substyle, walnut, the rectangular top w/a deep flaring cornice over a pair of tall cupboard doors w/Gothic Arch panels over a single long drawer at the bottom, scalloped front apron, ca. 1865, 16 x 42", 73" h. (ILLUS.) **690**

L. & J.G. Stickley Wardrobe

Wardrobe, Mission-style (Arts & Crafts movement), oak, a low arched crestrail above the rectangular top over a pair of tall paneled doors opening to a group of four small drawers w/copper pulls above four long drawers, flat apron, square stile legs, fine original finish, "The Work of..." decal of L. & J. G. Stickley, Model No. 111, 19 x 40", 48" h. (ILLUS.) **8,250**

WHATNOTS & ETAGERES

Rare Gallé Etagere

Etagere, Art Nouveau, fruitwood marquetry, ombellière patt., the pierce-carved gallery top w/leafage above a flat door w/foliate-cast hinges inlaid on one side w/a tableau of thistles beneath rays of sun & on the other w/a scrolling ribbon inlaid "L'INSTANTEST SI BLAU LUMIERE DE NOTRE COEUR AUX FUND DE NOUS," opening to storage, above a center support carved as an open blossom & molded supports, above open shelving & back panel inlaid w/thistles, crown & stars w/a pierce-cut crest, all raised on molded gently outswept legs joined by a pierce-carved blossom apron, inlaid in marquetry "Gallé," ca. 1900, 18 x 26", 59" h. (ILLUS.). **23,000**

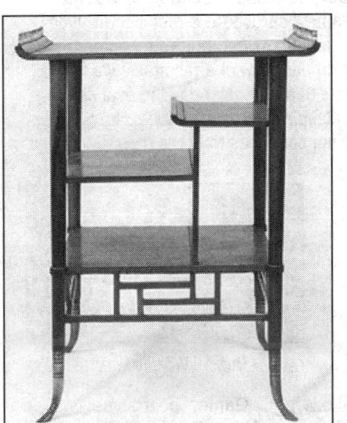

Aesthetic Movement Etagere

Etagere, Victorian Aesthetic Movement substyle, brass-mounted rosewood, rectangular top w/upturned ends w/pierced metal rails raised on four simple round tapering legs joined by three staggered open shelves over a fretwork front apron, splayed brass feet, possibly by Lejambe, Philadelphia, last quarter 19th c., 19 x 24¼", 23" h. (ILLUS.) . . **1,265**

Victorian Walnut Whatnot Shelf

Whatnot, Victorian corner-style, walnut, six graduated quarter-round open shelves each backed w/pierced scrollwork & joined by three ring- and baluster-turned spindles w/finials, some damage to scrollwork & some missing, refinished, joints loose, ca. 1870, 67½" h. (ILLUS.) **160**

Whatnot, Victorian Rococo substyle, walnut, six-shelf, the upper three open shelves w/molded serpentine front & joined by slender baluster- and ring-turned spindles & turned pointed corner finials, the upper three shelves stepped back from top of the conforming lower section w/a shallow drawer at the top & bottom shelf, each shelf backed by an arched & scroll-pierced backrail, on short double-knob feet on casters, refinished, mid 19th c., 12½ x 34", 66" h. **440**

GAMES & GAME BOARDS

Also see: CHARACTER COLLECTIBLES, DISNEY ITEMS and RADIO & TELEVISION COLLECTIBLES.

Neck & Neck Horse Race Game

"Bicycle - The Race," board-type, published by JWS&S, New York, designed in England by "JAP," box cover shows highwheel racers, w/game box & box, late 19th c. **$358**

Checkerboard, painted poplar, rectangular w/applied low gallery edges & narrow divided end compartments, the center painted in old dark red & black w/the checkerboard, the narrow end sections painted each w/three stars, 19th c., 19 x 27½" (wear) **545**

Dominos set, laminated bone & ivory, each piece apparently hand-cut & w/a brass pin through it, w/original dove-tailed wood box, turn-of-the-century, box 2¼ x 7", the set. **193**

Game board, marquetry inlay, nearly square form w/the top inlaid w/an intricate design, the center large square filled w/bands of alternating light & dark squares, the dark squares each w/inlaid wheels, a wide outer border band w/inlaid fans at the corners of the inner square & scattered small inlaid stars & chevrons, the reverse inlaid w/a horse & "F.C.B." along w/the pencil inscription "2000 pieces Jan. 17, 1911," old alligatored varnish finish, 16⅝ x 17¼" **688**

Game board, painted wood, bean bag toss board w/square opening, decorated in greens, orange, pink & yellow, stenciled w/the name "Bessie," along w/two bean bags, hinged support on the back, 19th c., 15 x 30" (minor surface abrasion, areas of repaint) **575**

Game board, painted wood, hinged in the center, decorated in each corner w/a large round hex-style design w/painted bars between each & a large square w/half-circles of color in the center,

painted green w/red, yellow, blue & black, late 19th - early 20th c., 19¼" sq. (minor paint loss) **2,645**

"Neck & Neck Horse Race," lithographed tin, a long narrow rectangular low platform w/racing lanes, small cast metal horses & riders, w/original box, Wolverine, Model 142, very good condition (ILLUS.). **100**

"Six Day Bike Race," board-type, by Lindstrom Tool & Toy Co., Bridgeport, Connecticut, late 19th - early 20th c., boxed, 9½ x 15¼". **303**

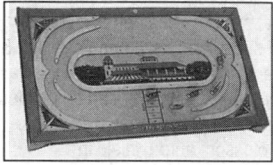

Sunray DX Getaway Chase Game

"Sunray DX Getaway Chase Game," board-type, cardboard & plastic, two auto play pieces, board & accessory sheets, w/original box, created by AMF for Sunray DX Oil Company, ca. 1940s, new in box, soiling & tears to box, 20 x 24½", 3½" h. (ILLUS.). **110**

Tudor Tru-Action Horse Race Game

"Tudor Tru-Action Electric Horse Race Game," cardboard & metal board-type, rectangular w/red border & center printed overhead view of a racetrack w/a front view of a grandstand in the oval center, metal playing pieces, Model No. 525, minor scratches to board (ILLUS.) **303**

Uncle Wiggily Game

"Uncle Wiggily Game," board-type, color-printed box, Milton Bradley, little use, ca. 1950s (ILLUS.). **22**

Grouping of Steuben Aurene

GLASS

AGATA

Agata was patented by Joseph Locke of the New England Glass Company in 1887. The application of mineral stain left a mottled effect on the surface of the article. It was applied chiefly to the Wild Rose (Peach Blow) line but sometimes was applied as a border on a pale opaque green. In production for a short time, it is scarce. Items listed below are of the Wild Rose line unless otherwise noted.

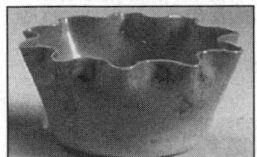

Fine Agata Bowl

Bowl, 5¼" d., 2½" h., deep gently flaring sides w/a ten-ruffle rim, good color & spotting (ILLUS.) **$546**

Vase, 4⅝" h., ovoid body w/four deeply dimpled sides tapering to an upright flaring crimped four-point rim, New England....................... **1,380**

Vase, 8" h., bottle-form, bulbous ovoid body tapering to a tall slender "stick" neck, excellent gold & blue spotting, New England....................... **1,955**

AMBERINA

Amberina Mark

Amberina was developed in the late 1880s by the New England Glass Company; a pressed version was made by Hobbs, Brockunier & Company (under license from the former). A similar ware, called Rose Amber, was made by the Mt. Washington Glass Works. Amberina-Rose Amber shades from amber to deep red or fuchsia; cut and plated (lined with creamy white) examples were also made. The Libbey Glass Company briefly revived blown Amberina, using modern shapes, in 1917.

Bowl, 8" d., 3½" h., Plated Amberina, wide squatty form w/five-lobed pinched & ruffled rim, twelve-rib design, New England........................... **$4,313**

Celery vase, slightly waisted cylindrical body w/a lightly scalloped rim, Diamond Quilted patt., 6⅛" h. **248**

Creamer, ovoid body tapering to a short cylindrical neck w/arched spout, applied amber handle, Inverted Thumbprint patt., 5½" h. **187**

Cruet w/original stopper, Swirl mold **245**

Cuspidor, lady's, round squatty bulbous form w/a widely flaring gently ruffled rim, rich colors, 5" d., 2⅞" h................... **330**

Finger bowl, rounded w/deep upright sides, nearly all deep red w/narrow band of amber at base, 4⅜" d., 2⅞" h. **330**

Lemonade set: 7" h. pitcher w/square rim & applied reeded handle & five matching 2¼" h. punch cups w/applied handles; Inverted Thumbprint patt., 6 pcs. **600**

Pitcher, 7⅞" h., bulbous ovoid body tapering to a flared square mouth, inverted Thumbprint patt., applied ribbed amber handle, late 19th c. **253**

Pitcher, 7¾" h., bulbous ovoid Diamond Quilted patt. body w/a tall, wide cylindrical neck w/pinched spout, applied angled reeded amber handle (ILLUS., next page).... **380**

Pitcher, 9" h., bulbous swirl-molded body w/applied reeded amber handle **259**

From left: Amberina Diamond Quilted Pitcher, Amberina Shakers in Ornate Frame

Salt & pepper shakers, cylindrical optic-ribbed salt & pepper shakers w/original silver-plate tops set in an ornate silver-plate Victorian frame centered by a napkin ring below a tiny trumpet-form bud vase, bead & leaf brackets & pierced scroll feet on stand, the set (ILLUS.) **900**

Sugar shaker w/original lid, footed squatty bulbous plain body tapering to a swelled neck, Reverse Amberina, 4½" h. **385**

Toothpick holder, ringed base below the bulbous ovoid body tapering slightly to a tightly crimped rim, Inverted Thumbprint patt., 2¼" h. **220**

Tumbler, tall slightly waisted cylindrical form, optic paneled design, 4⅛" h. **165**

Tumblers, juice, slightly flaring cylindrical form w/a small applied ribbed ring handle near the base, 3½-3¾" h., set of 10 . . . . **690**

Vase, 6¼" h., Plated Amberina, waisted cylindrical form w/gently flaring flat rim, New England **4,025**

Vase, 9½" h., lily-form w/tricorner rim, disk foot, optic ribbed design **403**

Vase, 10" h., scalloped & ruffled 6" d. flared rim **210**

Decorated Amberina Vase

Vase, 11" h., baluster-form body on a stepped cushion foot, flaring cylindrical neck w/a deeply crimped & flaring rim, decorated in white enamel in the Mary Gregory style w/a boy & bird in a landscape (ILLUS.). **875**

Tall Amberina Vases

Vases, 12¼" h., 3¼" d., lily-form, tall slender tapering scroll-form Optic Ribbed patt. body on a ball knob stem applied to a disk foot, applied amber spiral trim around the lower half, rim coming to a point at the back, pr. (ILLUS.) **295**

ANIMALS

Americans evidently like to collect glass animals, and for the past sixty years American glass manufacturers have turned out a wide variety of animals to please the buying public. Some were produced for long periods and some were later reproduced by other companies, while others were made for only a short period of time and are rare. We have not included late productions in our listings and have attempted to date the productions where possible. Evelyn Zemel's book, American Glass Animals A to Z, *will be helpful to the novice collector. Another helpful book is* Glass Animals of the Depression Era *by Lee Garmon and Dick Spencer (Collector Books, 1993).*

Asiatic Pheasant, clear, Heisey Glass Co., 7½" l., 10½" h. **$280**

Borzoi, clear, large, New Martinsville Glass Mfg. Co. **50**

Boxer dog, lying down, clear, American Glass Co., 3⅞" h. **65**

Boxer dog, sitting, clear, American Glass Co., 4¾" h. **65**

Cat, light blue, Fostoria Glass Co., 3¼" h. **30**

Cat, dark medium blue, No. 1322, 1960s, Viking Glass Co., 8" h. **45**

Chanticleer, clear, Fostoria Glass Co., 10¼" h. **215**

Dog, dark medium blue, No. 1323, 1960s, Viking Glass Co., 8" h. **50**

Dragon Swan, clear, Paden City Glass Co., 9¾" h. **175**

Dragon Swan, pale blue, Paden City Glass Co., 9¾" h. **650**

Elephant book end, clear, No. 237, New Martinsville Glass Co., 5½" h. **75**

Fawn, w/flower floater & sockets for three candles, citron green, Tiffin Glass Co., ca. late 1940s, 14½" l., fawn 10" h., ... **325**

Fawn, w/flower floater & sockets for three candles, copen blue, Tiffin Glass Co., ca. late 1940s, 14½" l., fawn 10" h. **500**

Fish candleholder, clear, A.H. Heisey & Co., 1941-58, 5" h. **135**

Frog, covered dish, green, 1969, Erskine Glass Co. **130**

Goose, pale blue, Paden City Glass Co., ca. 1940, 5" h. **125**

Goose, wings up, clear, A.H. Heisey & Co., 1942-53, 7½" l., 6½" h. **75**

Goose (The Fat Goose), clear & frosted, Duncan & Miller Glass Co., 6" l., 6½" h. **195**

Horse, Plug (Sparky), clear, A.H. Heisey & Co., 1941-46, 3½" l., 4¼" h. **115**

Horse, Colt, standing, clear, A.H. Heisey & Co., 1942-52, 5" h. **75**

Mama Pig, w/three nursing piglets attached on each side, clear, No. 1, limited edition of approximately 200, New Martinsville Glass Co., 6" l., 3" h. **325**

Marmota Sentinel (Woodchuck), caramel slag, Imperial Glass Co., 4" h. **55**

"Oscar," 1991 Heisey Club souvenir, sapphire blue opalescent frosted, Fenton Art Glass Co. **45**

"Oscar," 1994 Heisey Club souvenir, frosted green, Fenton Art Glass Co. **40**

Pelican, clear, No. 761, New Martinsville Glass Co., 8" h. **95**

Penguin, amber, No. 1319, 1960s, Viking Glass Co., 7" h. **20**

Polar Bear, clear, Fostoria Glass Co., 4⅝" h. **65**

Polar Bear on ice, clear, No. 611, Paden City Glass Co., 4½" h. **60**

Porpoise on wave, clear, No. 766, New Martinsville Glass Co., 6" h. **475**

Rabbit, large mama, clear, No. 764, New Martinsville Glass Co., 2½" h. **325**

Ringneck Pheasant, clear, A.H. Heisey & Co., 1942-53, 11" l., 4¾" h. **115**

Scottie Dog book ends, Cambridge Glass Co., 6½" h., pr. **195**

Squirrel on curved log, clear, No. 677, Paden City Glass Co., 5½" h. **50**

Swordfish, blue opalescent, Duncan & Miller Glass Co., 5" h. **425**

Swordfish, clear, Duncan & Miller Glass Co., 5" h. **275**

Wolfhound, clear, No. 716, New Martinsville Glass Co., 7" h. **90**

APPLIQUED

Simply stated, this is an art glass form with applied decoration. Sometimes master glass craftsmen applied stems or branches to an art glass object and then added molded glass flowers or fruit specimens to these branches or stems. At other times a button of molten glass was daubed on the object and a tool pressed over

it to form a prunt in the form of a raspberry, rosette or other shape. Always the work of a skilled glassmaker, applied decoration can be found on both cased (two-layer) and single layer glass. The English firm of Stevens and Williams was renowned for the appliqued glass they produced.

Appliqued & Overshot Bowl

Bowl, 6" d., 3⅞" h., wide cylindrical form w/a swelled bottom, pale blue opaque w/an overshot background & applied amber rigaree around the rim & applied green leaaves on purple stems w/blue & red & white & red applied blossoms (ILLUS.) **$195**

Box w/hinged lid, rounded base in yellowish opalescent fitted w/gilt brass scroll feet & hinged collar fittings w/a wide domed cover applied w/amethyst branches & green leaves w/a red flower & bud, 5⅝" d., 4¼" h. **450**

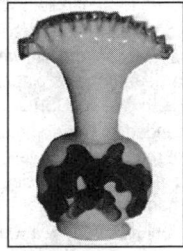

Fan-topped Vase with Acorns

Vase, 7" h., 4½" d., opaque white w/a fanned & crimped rim w/applied amber edging, the spherical footed base applied w/a large amber leaf & acorn cluster (ILLUS.) **135**

Vase, 7" h., 5" d., baluster-form w/a bulbous body tapering to a widely flaring ruffled & crimped rim, white opaque body w/ applied crimped amber foot band & rim band & a large amber leaf & bellflower around the body **135**

ART GLASS BASKETS

Popular novelties in the late Victorian era, these ornate baskets of glass were usually hand-crafted of free-blown or mold-blown glass. They were made in a wide spectrum of colors and shapes. Pieces were highlighted with tall applied handles and often applied feet; however, fancier ones might also carry additional appliqued trim.

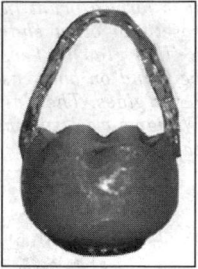

From left: Rubina Honeycomb Basket
Spangled Art Glass Basket

Rubina, bulbous nearly spherical form in the Honeycomb patt., the wide ruffled & crimped rim applied w/a high clear angular thorn handle, 5½" d., 9" h. (ILLUS.) **$175**

Rubina verde, footed rounded body w/a wide deeply rolled & crimped rim w/two sides pulled up & joined by a high applied light green twisted thorn handle, the body w/applied green leaves & red & white blossoms, 8½" h. **253**

Sapphire blue, squatty round bowl w/swirl-molded design continuing to the deeply rolled & crimped rim w/the back edge pulled up, applied clear handle, 5½" d., 6" h... **145**

Spangled, footed spherical body in blue w/a coral-like silver mica decoration, white lining, applied clear arched & pinched handle, 5¾" d., 9¼" h. (ILLUS.) **295**

Spatter, wide rounded bowl w/star-crimped upright rim, maroon, orange & yellow spatter cased in white, applied clear angled thorn handle, 5⅞" d., 5½" h.......... **175**

Spatter, squatty bulbous body w/a wide upright crimped rim, the exterior in yellow, gold & pink spatter, white lining, applied high clear knobby handle, 5" d., 6½" h. **165**

BLOWN THREE MOLD

This type of glass was entirely or partially blown in a mold and was popular from about 1820 to 1840. The object was formed and the decoration impressed upon it by blowing the glass into a metal mold, usually of three—but sometimes more—sections hinged together. Mold-blown glass actually dates back to ancient times. Recent research reveals that certain geometric patterns were reproduced in the 1920s; some new pieces, usually sold through museum gift shops, are still available. Collectors are urged to read all recent information available. Reference numbers are from George L. and Helen McKearin's book, American Glass.

Decanter w/bar lip, Baroque, pontiled base, rare applied bar lip, clear, 7¼" h. (GV-8) **$495**

Decanter w/flattened unpatterned stopper, geometric, miniature, ovoid body tapering to a plain neck w/flared rim, clear, 3½" h. (GIII-12)................... **495**

Blown Three Mold Decanters

Decanter w/pressed wheel stopper, geometric, ovoid body tapering to double-ringed neck w/flattened flared rim, slightly oversized stopper, clear, ½ pt., 7½" h., GII-33 (ILLUS. right)................... **209**

Decanter w/stopper, Baroque patt., probably original hollow blown ribbed stopper, clear, 11½" h., GV-9 (some light interior residue)............... **209**

Decanter w/stopper, geometric, flared mouth, rayed base, possibly original hollow blown stopper, clear, 10½" h., GIII-24 (slight light mold impression) **142**

Decanter w/stopper, geometric, large star in ring design around sides w/rows of short ribs above & below, flared folded lip & original hollow blown stopper, clear, 11¼" h. (GV-10)...................... **550**

Decanter w/stopper, geometric, ovoid body tapering to a plain neck w/flattened flared rim, original hollow patterned ball stopper, clear, 10½" h., GIII-5 (ILLUS. left) **176**

Decanter w/stopper, Gothic arch design, bands of Gothic arches above & below a central reserve molded w/"RUM," flared rim w/original compressed hollow blown stopper, clear, 10¾" h., GIV-7 (some light amber residue) **220**

Dish, geometric, shallow round form w/folded rim, clear, 5⁵⁄₁₆" d., 1⅛" h. (GII-22).... **99**

Dish, geometric, shallow round form w/rolled rim, rough pontil, clear, 6" d. (GIII-5) **187**

Model of a top hat, geometric, folded rim, deep sapphire-violet blue, unlisted, 2¾" h. (GI-6) **1,320**

Pitcher, 3⅛", miniature, geometric, squatty bulbous body w/widely flaring rim & pinched spout, applied handle, clear, GII-18 (hard to see line in handle) **132**

Salt dip, geometric, cushion foot & flaring squatty body w/low flared rim, clear, 2½" d., 2⅛" h. (GIII-25).................. **143**

Salt dip, geometric, wide bell-form top
w/flared rim raised on a short flaring
pedestal foot, clear, unseen pontil chip,
2¼" h. (GII-21) **468**

Shakers w/original brass lids, geometric,
cylindrical body tapering slightly toward
top, ringed base w/pontil, loose lids,
clear, 4½" h., GIII-27 (one w/chip
under lid), pr. **143**

Tumbler, geometric, cylindrical w/fine
ribbing around lower half, clear, McKearin
Collection sticker, 3¼" h. (GI-?) **303**

Tumbler, miniature, geometric, cylindrical,
ringed base, clear, 1¾" h. (GII-16) **275**

Wine, geometric, flaring cylindrical bowl
w/applied bladed stem & pontiled foot,
clear, 4" h. (GII-19) **330**

BOHEMIAN

*Numerous types of glass were made in the
once-independent country of Bohemia, and fine
colored, cut and engraved glass was turned out.
Flashed and other inexpensive wares also were
made; many of these, including amber- and
ruby-shaded glass, were exported to the United
States during the last century and during the
present one. One favorite pattern in the late 19th
and early 20th centuries was Deer & Castle.
Another was Deer and Pine Tree.*

Console set: 10" d. console bowl & pair of
candlesticks; ruby-flashed & cut to clear,
the bowl w/a small footring supporting
wide deep rounded sides w/a flat rim
engraved w/large scrolled cartouches
alternating w/leaping stags, a narrow
band of scrolls around the rim, the footed
baluster-form candlesticks w/flaring
sockets w/similar engraving, late 19th to
early 20th c., the set **$259**

Cruet w/stopper, ruby-flashed, footed
bulbous body tapering to a curved rim
spout & hollow knop stopper, ruby
engraved w/a leaping stag design, clear
applied smooth handle, late 19th to early
20th c., 5½" h. **110**

Cup & saucer, deep ruby blown widely
flaring rounded cup w/applied handle
decorated w/an enameled portrait of a
woman framed by gilt scrolling & floral
swags, dished matched saucer, late 19th c. **75**

Goblet, a trumpet-form bowl w/a flared rim
set on a thick short stem on a round disk
foot, clear w/an engraved body w/a layer
of vaseline & black stain, the sides
w/engraved oval panels w/wheat design
borders, one panel showing a girl w/a
watering can in a garden, one showing a
house w/trees & a third showing a church
& trees, black stain w/clear cut panels

around the base of the bowl above the
black-stained stem w/an engraved
diamond design above the black-stained
foot cut w/clear rounded petals,
ca. 1880-90, 7" h. **1,475**

*From left: Rare Bohemian Flashed & Cut Goblet
Amber-flashed Etched Vase*

Goblet, cov., chalice-form, ruby-flashed, the
tall flaring panel-cut bowl etched to clear
w/a continuous hunt scene, the heavy
double-knop facet-cut stem on a deeply
cut & paneled round foot, the panel-cut &
domed cover w/a notch-cut rim & tall
paneled & pointed finial, late 19th c.,
20" h. (ILLUS.) **6,325**

Goblets, paneled octagonal body, ruby-
flashed cut w/panels & enameled in color
w/florals & scrolled foliate designs,
19th c., 6⅜" h. (gilt wear), pr. **690**

Jars, cov., tall chalice-form, cut-overlay in
yellow cut to clear, late 19th to early
20th c., 13¼" h., pr. **288**

Vase, 4¾" h., ruby red, thick disk foot w/a
short knob stem supporting the flaring
waisted bowl finely enameled w/a bust
portrait of a woman within a gold scrolled
cartouche & gilt florals, probably Moser,
late 19th c. **77**

Vase, 5¼" h., crackle glass, mold-blown
pinched fishbowl sphere of faint opal
w/cracked finish, enamel-painted w/fish,
water lilies & aquatic plants, late 19th c. **345**

Vase, 6¼" h., amber-flashed, the widely
flaring trumpet-form body w/a pointed
scallop rim cut to clear w/a continuous
deer in forest scene, the lower bulbous
body facet-cut above a short pedestal &
thick round foot (ILLUS.) **145**

Vase, 7" h., classic urn form w/a short funnel
foot supports the large ovoid shouldered
body w/a slightly flaring ringed cylindrical
neck flanked by applied clear handles,
Islamic-style enameled decoration
w/panels of Arabic lettering & geometric
design, on a gilt-decorated floral ground,
the neck in green, white & orange w/floral
designs, painted Lohmeyr mark,
late 19th c. (ILLUS.) **6,325**

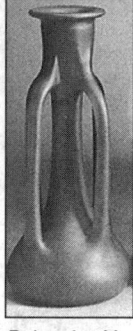

From left: Islamic-style Bohemian Vase
Unusual Bohemian Iridescent Vase

Vase, 8¾" h., tapered ovoid body, clear green ground w/interior texture giving a glitter effect, etched & enameled to depict mauve & yellow iris, gilt trim **518**

Vase, 9½" h., ovoid body w/short flaring neck, burgundy red cased w/opal white, the exterior elaborately decorated in gilded scroll & swag designs trimmed w/glass beads of opal, green & turquoise, late 19th c. **431**

Vase, 9¾" h., 4¾" d., trumpet-form body w/an eight-scallop rim & a flaring eight-scallop foot, cranberry cut to clear w/eight elongated arches up the sides to below a wide rim band enameled in ivory & gold w/intertwined scrolls, each scallop of the foot w/similar decoration, ca. 1840 . . . . **1,275**

Vase, 10½" h., a squatty bulbous base issuing four solid slender open buttress handles around the slender waisted center body, short cylindrical neck w/a flattened rim, rose red iridescent finish, polished pontil, late 19th to early 20th c. (ILLUS.) **489**

Vase, 15" h., bulbous ovoid body tapering to a tall cylindrical neck, deep ruby decorated overall w/silver leaf designs & enameled bird & flower in blue sharkskin, early 20th c. **413**

Vase, 17" h., tall cylindrical form w/wide base & flared ruffled rim, frosted lightly iridized ground shading from blue to green w/gilt & enameled entwining roses, large polished pontil, late 19th c. **374**

Vases, mantel-type, 14½" h., ruby cut to clear overlay, a ruby flute-cut cushion foot centered by a tall trumpet-form body w/a large rectangular front panel decorated in color w/a garden setting showing three Victorian maidens, one holding a white dove, another a garland of flowers, alternating side panels w/three ruby cut to clear rose blossoms & clear wheat-cut panels, clear wheat-cut rim & base bands (chip on each rim), pr. **880**

Wine set: decanter w/large bubble stopper & six stemmed wine glasses; dark ruby cut to clear, the decanter w/a small cushion foot below the wide round compressed body centered by a tall slender waisted neck, the edges of the body cut w/oval reserves alternating w/crossed leafy branches & a flowerhead, a panel-cut neck & stopper, matching design on the wines, early 20th c., decanter 11" h., the set **275**

BRIDE'S BASKETS & BOWLS

These berry or fruit bowls were popular late Victorian wedding gifts, hence the name. They were produced in a variety of quality art glasswares and sometimes were fitted in ornate silver-plate holders.

Cased Rich Pink Bride's Bowl

Cased bowl, rich shaded pink interior w/crimped rim applied w/clear band & the front edge turned down, decorated around the interior w/gold & silver sanded flowers & leafy branch decoration, white exterior, 8" d., 3⅛" h. (ILLUS.) **$165**

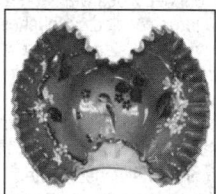

Cased Bowl with Bird & Flower Decor

Cased bowl, pink interior w/crimped rim & applied amber band, two sides turned up, the interior's rim boldly enameled w/white blossoms on green leafy branches, a small bird on twig in the center, white exterior, 6½ x 8½", 3" h. (ILLUS.). **165**

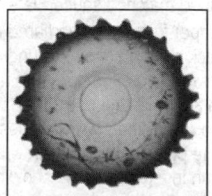

Shaded Purple Satin Bowl

Cased bowl, purple shaded to white satin, tightly scalloped rim, wide inner rim decorated w/delicate enameled flowers & leafy stems, white exterior, 10¾" d., 3½" h. (ILLUS.)........................ 210

Cased bowl, cranberry shading to white w/ruffled rim & enameled decoration, 4 x 11" 135

Cased bowl, shaded dark green satin interior relief-molded in a lattice design, ruffled rim, white exterior, 11½" d., 3⅝" h. 150

Orangish red, deep round ribbed sides w/deeply ruffled flaring rim, set on an ornate silver-plate stand w/fanned, outswept upright side handles w/large bird perched at the top of each, the waisted disc platform base raised on four pierced, angular curved tall legs, late 19th c., 8⅞" d., 9½" h. 385

Pink shading to cream, 12" d., 11½" h. overall, bowl decorated w/pink & white bunches of flowers & sprays of small blue flowers, lovely resilvered frame embossed w/flowers & leaves across handle & around the base 525

BURMESE

Burmese is a single-layer glass that shades from pink to pale yellow. It was patented by Frederick S. Shirley and made by the Mt. Washington Glass Co. A license to produce the glass in England was granted to Thomas Webb & Sons, which called its articles Queen's Burmese. Gundersen Burmese was made briefly about the middle of this century, and the Pairpoint Crystal Company is making limited quantities at the present time.

From left: Fine Webb Burmese Lamp
Burmese Lamp with Guba Ducks

Dish, short waisted cylindrical form w/crimped flared rim pulled into points, applied leaf on each side, small **$413**

Lamp, kerosene-type, a footed tapering cylindrical base w/a ringed shoulder supporting the burner & shade ring w/a spherical shade w/a crimped rim, shade & base each enameled w/large bands of leafy oak branches w/acorns in browns, greens & yellows, Thomas Webb & Sons Queen's Burmese, late 19th c., 17" h. (ILLUS.)........................ 11,200

Lamp, kerosene-type, a scroll-cast gilt-metal foot supporting a squatty bulbous tapering glass font topped w/a gilt-metal ribbed shoulder & kerosene burner w/spider support for the domed glass shade w/top opening, w/chimney, the base & shade each decorated w/conventionalized flying ducks in bright natural colors painted by Frank Guba, Mount Washington, late 19th c., electrified, shade 10" d., overall 19½" h. (ILLUS.)........................ 11,500

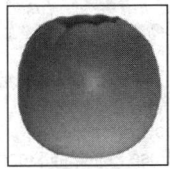

Burmese Rose Bowl

Rose bowl, spherical body w/eight-crimp rim, plain undercorated satin finish, unsigned Thomas Webb, 3" d., 3⅜" h. (ILLUS.) 210

Vase, 4⅛" h., tapering cylindrical slightly rounded form w/narrow short neck below the widely flaring crimped rim, the body decorated w/colored enamel florals 358

Vase, 5¾" h., footed spherical body w/a tall slender "stick" neck, decorated w/yellow-centered white blossoms & green leaves around the body & up the next, attributed to Mount Washington 546

Vase, 7¾" h., lily-form on round foot.......... 303

Vase, 9¼" h., trumpet-form w/jack-in-the-pulpit crimped rim, Mt. Washington 316

Vase, 10" h., lily-form, footed w/tricorner rim, Mount Washington 230

Burmese Vase with Egyptian Scene

Vase, 11½" h., a tiny round foot supporting a tall ovoid body tapering to a small mouth, enamel-decorated w/an Egyptian desert scene w/pyramids & ibis in flight, gilt trim, Mount Washington, satin finish, late 19th c. (ILLUS.) **2,530**

CAMBRIDGE

NEAR CUT

TUSCAN

C

Cambridge Marks

The Cambridge Glass Company was founded in Ohio in 1901. Numerous pieces are now sought, especially those designed by Arthur J. Bennett, including Crown Tuscan. Other productions included crystal animals, "Black Amethyst," "blanc opaque," and other types of colored glass. The firm was finally closed in 1954. It should not be confused with the New England Glass Co., Cambridge, Massachusets.

Ashtray, etched Minerva patt., Crystal **$55**

Ashtray, Silhouette line, Royal Blue bowl on clear Nude Lady stem **325**

Basket, etched Rose Point patt., reeded handle, No. 3500/52, Crystal, 6" h.. . . . . **550**

Bowl, 10" d., etched Chantilly patt., three-part, on silvered metal base, Crystal **89**

Bowl, 10½" d., etched Rose Point patt., No. 1359, Crystal **125**

Bowl, 11" d., etched Apple Blossom patt., low footed, gold-encrusted, Mandarin Gold **125**

Bowl, 12" d., etched Wildflower patt., four-footed, flared, gold-encrusted Crystal, No. 3400/4 . . . . **175**

Bowl, 12" l., etched Rose Point patt., four-footed, oblong, fancy rim, No. 3400/160, Crystal **150**

Bowl, 12½" d., 5½" h., crimped rim, footed, pressed Caprice patt., Moonlight (light blue), No. 61 . . . . **139**

Butter dish, cov., etched Rose Point patt., round, Crystal **200**

Candelabra, etched Rose Point patt., three-light, No. 1338, Crystal, pr.. . . . . **200**

Candleholder, Martha Washington line, Ebony (black), 4" h. **20**

Candlesticks, etched Apple Blossom patt., one-light, yellow, pr. **48**

Candlesticks, etched Diane patt., Martha line blank, No. 497, Crystal, pr. **375**

Candlesticks, etched Portia patt., two-light, cornucopia-stem, Mandarin Gold, pr.. . . . . . . **229**

Candlesticks, etched Rose Point patt., Martha line blank, No. 497, w/prisms, Crystal, 7½" h., pr. **550**

Candlesticks, figural dolphin stem, domed base, Crystal, 8¼" h., pr. **125**

Candlesticks, Gadroon (No. 3500) line, molded ram's heads on the socket, Amber, 4½" h., pr. **149**

Candlesticks, pressed Caprice patt., three-light, No. 1338, Mandarin Gold, 6" h., pr.. . . . . **135**

Candy box, cov., etched Chantilly patt., footed, Crystal **135**

Candy box, cov., etched Wildflower patt., No. 3900/165, Crystal. **100**

Center bowl, Gadroon (No. 3400) line, footed, scalloped rim, ram's head handles, Amber, 9" d.. . . . . **129**

Claret, pressed Caprice patt., Moonlight, No. 5, 4½ oz. **195**

Claret, Statuesque line, Carmen bowl, clear Nude Lady stem, 7⅝" h.. . . . . **275**

Cocktail, Mt. Vernon line, footed, Crystal, No. 26, 3½ oz. **6**

From left: Statuesque Line Cocktail Compote on Chrome Nude Lady Base

Cocktail, Statuesque line, Mandarin Gold bowl, clear Nude Lady stem (ILLUS.). **80**

Cocktail, Statuesque (No. 3011) line, Emerald (light green) bowl, clear Nude Lady stem, 4½ oz., 6½" h. **110**

Cocktail & icer, etched Rose Point patt., No. 3600, Crystal, 2 pcs. **110**

Compote, etched Rose Point patt., blown, No. 3121 stem, Crystal, 5⅜" h.. . . . . **175**

Compote, open, chrome Farberware Nude Lady stem w/Amethyst bowl insert (ILLUS.) **68**

Cordial, etched Chantilly patt., No. 3625, Crystal, 1 oz. **65**

Cordial, etched Diane patt., Crystal **42**

Cordial, Line 1341, mushroom-style, Amber **7**

Cordial, Line 1341, mushroom-style, Carmen (bright red) **25**

Cordial, etched Portia patt., No. 3130, Crystal, 1 oz. **60**

Crown Tuscan candy dish, cov., shell-shaped, gold decoration, 6" w.. . . . . **70**

Crown Tuscan cigarette box, cov. **55**

Crown Tuscan compote, 6" d., Nude Lady stem, gold-encrusted 200

Crown Tuscan urn, cov., 8" h. 140

Crown Tuscan vase, 10" h., Sea Shell patt., pedestal base 43

Cruet w/original stopper, pressed Caprice patt., oil, No. 101, Crystal, 3 oz. 50

Cup & saucer, pressed Caprice patt., Moonlight . . 40

Decanter w/stopper, etched Portia patt., No. 1321, Crystal, 28 oz. 350

Decanter w/stopper, etched Portia patt., No. 3400/92, Crystal, 32 oz. 375

Figure flower holder, "Draped Lady," Emerald, 8½" h. 295

Figure flower holder, "Draped Lady," Ritz blue, 8½" h. 325

Goblet, etched Apple Blossom patt., Crystal, 9 oz. 20

Goblet, etched Diane patt., No. 3122, Crystal, 9 oz. 30

Goblet, etched Elaine patt., water, Crystal 25

Goblet, Statuesque line, banquet-size, Emerald bowl, clear Nude Lady stem, 10" h. 375

Lamp, table model, etched Diane patt., gold-encrusted, slender ovoid body, metal fittings, Carmen, 14½" h. 585

Mayonnaise bowl & ladle, etched Portia patt., Crystal, 2 pcs. 40

Mayonnaise set: bowl, underplate & ladle; etched Wildflower patt., No. 3900/129, gold-encrusted Crystal, the set 125

Model of a swan, Emerald, No. 1040, 3" l. 50

Mug, Mt. Vernon line, stein-type, No. 84, Amber, 14 oz. 38

Nut dish, low, divided, pressed Caprice patt., Moonlight, No. 94, 7½" d. 52

Pitcher, etched Apple Blossom patt., ball-shaped, Crystal, 80 oz. 175

Pitcher, etched Cleo patt., No. 955, Amber, 62 oz. 260

Pitcher, etched Portia patt., ball-shaped, gold-encrusted, Mandarin Gold (light yellow) . . 179

Pitcher, pressed Caprice patt., ball-shaped, No. 183, Crystal, 80 oz. 150

Plate, 7" w., etched Cleo patt., Decagon line, Moonlight 20

Plate, 14" d., four-footed, pressed Caprice patt., Moonlight, No. 28 98

Platter, 13½" l., etched Apple Blossom patt., rectangular w/tab handles, Mandarin Gold 110

Relish dish, etched Rose Point patt., three-part, gold-encrusted, Crystal 69

Relish dish, pressed Caprice patt., three-part, No. 124, Crystal, 8" l. 30

Rose bowl & flower frog, pressed Caprice patt., footed, No. 235, Moonlight, 6" d., 2 pcs. 450

Salt & pepper shakers w/glass tops, etched Gloria patt., tall, Mandarin Gold, pr. 120

Salt shaker w/original top, etched Wildflower patt., No. 3900/1177, Crystal 20

Salt shaker w/original top, pressed Caprice patt., Moonlight, No. 96. 50

Sherbet, blown Caprice patt., tall, No. 300, Crystal, 6 oz. 16

Sherbet, etched Apple Blossom patt., Mandarin Gold, tall, No. 3130, 6 oz. 20

Smoke set, pressed Caprice patt., Moonlight, shell-footed, six pieces in original box, the set 110

Sugar sifter w/lid, etched Cleo patt., footed, Moonlight, 6¾" h. 1,500

Tumbler, etched Apple Blossom patt., No. 3130, footed, Mandarin Gold, 12 oz. 40

Tumbler, etched Elaine patt., iced tea, Crystal, 12 oz. 25

Tumbler, pressed Caprice patt., footed, No. 184, Moonlight, 12 oz. 60

Tumbler, pressed Caprice patt., old fashion, Moonlight, No. 310, 7 oz. 130

Vase, 6½" h., etched Wildflower patt., globe-shaped, No. 3400/103, Mandarin Gold 375

Water set: Doulton-style 80 oz. pitcher & five flat tumblers; No. 3400, Cobalt (dark blue), the set 275

Water set: pitcher & four tumblers; Gyro Optic line, Amber, the set 68

Water tray, etched Cleo patt., Amber. 225

CARNIVAL

Earlier called Taffeta glass, the Carnival glass now being collected was introduced early in this century. Its producers gave it an iridescence that attempted to imitate that of some Tiffany glass. Collectors will find available books by leading authorities Donald E. Moore, Sherman Hand, Marion T. Hartung, Rose M. Presznick and Bill Edwards. For a more extensive listing of Carnival Glass, please refer to Antique Trader Books' American Pressed Glass & Bottles Price Guide.

ACORN BURRS (Northwood)

Acorn Burrs Creamer

Berry set: master bowl & 4 sauce dishes; purple, 5 pcs. . . . . **$395 to 425**

Berry set: master bowl & 6 sauce dishes; marigold, 7 pcs.. . . . . **250 to 260**

Butter dish, cov., green **750**

Butter dish, cov., marigold. **150**

Butter dish, cov., purple . . . . **200 to 325**

Creamer, purple (ILLUS.) **150**

Pitcher, water, green **400**

Pitcher, water, marigold **425**

Pitcher, water, purple . . . . **425 to 500**

Punch bowl base, green **125**

Punch cup, marigold **27**

Punch cup, purple . . . . **35 to 40**

Sauce dish, green **60**

Sauce dish, marigold **30**

Sauce dish, purple . . . . **40 to 50**

Spooner, green. . . . . **170 to 180**

Spooner, marigold **100**

Spooner, purple **223**

Sugar bowl, open, purple. **220**

Tumbler, green. **58**

Tumbler, marigold. . . . . **45 to 50**

Tumbler, purple **80**

Water set: pitcher & 6 tumblers; purple, 7 pcs. . . . . **955 to 975**

ADVERTISING & SOUVENIR ITEMS

"Great House of Isaac Benesch" Bowl

Basket, "Miller's Furniture," marigold **88**

Bell, souvenir, BPOE Elks, "Atlantic City, 1911," blue **2,200**

Bowl, "Isaac Benesch," 6¼" d., purple, Millersburg (ILLUS.) . . . . **400 to 450**

Bowl, "Dreibus Parfait Sweets," smoky lavender, ruffled **567**

Bowl, souvenir, BPOE Elks, "Atlantic City, 1911," blue, one-eyed Elk **1,298**

Bowl, souvenir, BPOE Elks, "Detroit, 1910," blue, one-eyed Elk **900**

Bowl, souvenir, BPOE Elks, "Detroit, 1910," green, one-eyed Elk **850**

Bowl, souvenir, BPOE Elks, "Detroit, 1910," purple, two-eyed Elk (Millersburg) **2,700**

Bowl, souvenir, "Brooklyn Bridge," marigold **258**

Bowl, souvenir, "Millersburg Courthouse," purple **720**

Bowl, souvenir, Millersburg Courthouse, purple, unlettered . . . . **2,000 to 2,500**

Card tray, "Fern Brand Chocolates," turned-up sides, purple, 6¼" d. **600**

Paperweight, souvenir, BPOE Elks, green **3,500**

Plate, "Dreibus Parfait Sweets," 6¼" d., purple . . . . **385 to 400**

Plate, "Fern Brand Chocolates," 6" d., purple. . . . **775**

Plate, "Old Rose Distillery," green, Grape & Cable patt., stippled, 9" d. **614**

Plate, "Spector's Department Store," marigold, Heart & Vine patt., 9" d. **988**

Vase, "Howard Furniture," green, Four Pillars patt., green **65**

BASKET (Fenton's Open Edge)

Amber . . . . **200 to 250**

Aqua **125**

Aqua, two sides turned up **110**

Aqua, w/two rows, jack-in-the-pulpit shape . . . . **100 to 125**

Aqua, w/two rows, two sides turned up **110**

Black amethyst, two sides turned up . . . . **175 to 185**

Blue **70**

Blue, jack-in-the-pulpit shape **78**

Blue, w/two rows. **45**

Celeste blue **250**

Green, four sides turned up **225**

Green, jack-in-the-pulpit shape . . . . **200 to 300**

Green, low sides . . . . **125 to 175**

Ice blue. **195**

Ice blue, w/three rows . . . . **560 to 575**

Ice blue, w/two rows, open edge, six ruffled. **270**

Ice green . . . . **200 to 225**

Ice green, w/three rows. . . . . **300 to 325**

Lavender **118**

Marigold . . . . **35 to 40**

Marigold, hat-shaped **30**

Marigold, jack-in-the-pulpit shape **31**

Marigold, w/two rows . . . . **30 to 35**

Marigold, 5" h., w/applied crystal handle **75**

Purple. **93**

Red **428**

Red, hat shape . . . . **265 to 285**

Red, jack-in-the-pulpit shape. . . . . **450 to 500**

Red, w/two rows, small . . . . **300 to 350**

Reverse Amberina. **650**

Vaseline **85**

Vaseline, jack-in-the-pulpit shape, small **115**

Vaseline, plain interior **95**

Vaseline, w/marigold overlay, small **95**

Vaseline, w/two rows, large . . . . **65 to 75**

White, 6" . . . . **220 to 230**

White, 9" **95**

White, square **125**

White, w/two rows. **175**

White, w/two rows, four sides turned up . . **100 to 110**

BLACKBERRY (Fenton)

Basket, blue . . . . 65 to 75
Basket, clambroth. 45
Basket, green . . . . 145 to 160
Basket, marigold. 45
Basket, purple. . . . . 95 to 120
Basket, red . . . . 250 to 375
Bowl, 7" d., purple 80
Bowl, 8" to 9" d., green, ruffled. 93
Bowl, 8" to 9" d., marigold, ruffled 50
Plate, marigold, openwork rim. . . . . 500 to 525

BUTTERFLY & FERN (Fenton)

Pitcher, water, blue 538
Pitcher, water, green 510
Pitcher, water, marigold . . . . 275 to 300
Pitcher, water, purple . . . . 350 to 400
Tumbler, blue . . . . 55 to 60
Tumbler, green . . . . 65 to 75
Tumbler, marigold 38
Tumbler, pastel marigold 35
Tumbler, purple. 45 to 50
Water set: pitcher & 6 tumblers;
   purple, 7 pcs. 620

CAROLINA DOGWOOD

Bowl, 8½ " d., blue opalescent . . . . 250 to 375
Bowl, 8½ " d., marigold. 103
Bowl, 8½ " d., milk white w/marigold
   overlay . . . . 200 to 250
Bowl, 8½ " d., peach opalescent. . . . . . . 110 to 125
Bowl, peach opalescent, tricornered,
   dome-footed. 130
Bowl, ruffled, peach opalescent 70
Bride's bowl, peach opalescent. 325

CHERRY (Dugan)

Bowl, 5" d., purple, Jeweled Heart exterior 63
Bowl, 6" d., purple. . . . . 85 to 100
Bowl, 6" d., purple, Jeweled Heart exterior 75
Bowl, 7" d., peach opalescent,
   three-footed, crimped rim . . . . 185 to 200
Bowl, 8" d., purple, ruffled 173
Bowl, 8" to 9" d., marigold, three-footed. 75
Bowl, 8" to 9" d., peach opalescent,
   three-footed. 175
Bowl, 8" to 9" d., purple, three-footed . . . . 160 to 175
Bowl, 10" d., purple, Jeweled Heart
   exterior . . . . 220 to 250
Plate, 6" d., purple, ruffled 275
Plate, 6½ " d., purple, candy ribbon edge. 330
Plate, 6½ " d., purple, ruffled, Jeweled
   Heart exterior 225
Sauce dish, purple. 75
Sauce dish, purple, Jeweled Heart exterior 60

COIN DOT

Coin Dot Bowl

Bowl, 6" d., green. 48
Bowl, 6" d., red, ice cream shape . . . . 1,000 to 1,500
Bowl, 6½ " d., purple, stippled 50
Bowl, 7" d., green, candy ribbon edge 50
Bowl, 7" d., green (ILLUS.). 50
Bowl, 7" d., purple, candy ribbon edge. 35
Bowl, 7" d., red 1,450
Bowl, 7½ " d., blue 55
Bowl, 8" d., purple, pie crust rim. 20
Bowl, 8" to 9" d., green . . . . 45 to 50
Bowl, 8" to 9" d., green, stippled 25
Bowl, 8" to 9" d., marigold. . . . . 35 to 40
Bowl, 8" to 9" d., peach opalescent 149
Bowl, 8" to 9" d., purple 43
Bowl, 9" d., purple, three-in-one edge 97
Bowl, 9½ " d., purple, ruffled. . . . . 60 to 65
Bowl 10" d., peach opalescent, ruffled. 158
Bowl, green 70
Bowl, marigold, ruffled 15
Bowl, purple. 77
Compote, celeste blue opalescent. 850
Compote, purple. 60
Rose bowl, green . . . . 70 to 75
Rose bowl, marigold 45
Rose bowl, marigold, stippled 60
Rose bowl, purple, stippled . . . . 65 to 70
Rose bowl, vaseline. 100

CORN VASE (Northwood)

Corn Vase

Black amethyst. 3,000
Green, emerald 2,700
Green (ILLUS.). 746

Ice blue 1,750
Ice green . . . . 375 to 400
Marigold 956
Purple . . . . 500 to 575
Purple, electric 1,850
White . . . . 290 to 300

COSMOS

Bowl, 5" d., green, ice cream shape 59
Bowl, 8" d., ruffled, blue 125
Bowl, 9" d., blue 80
Bowl, 9" d., marigold . . . . 50 to 60
Bowl, 10" d., ruffled, marigold 47
Bowl, 10½" d., blue, ice cream shape . . . . . 80 to 100
Bowl, 10½" d., green, ice cream shape 80
Plate, 6" d., green 62
Plate, chop, 10½ " d., marigold . . . . 165 to 175

DAISIES & DRAPE VASE (Northwood)

Aqua opalescent . . . . 575 to 600
Cobalt blue 900
Ice blue 2,500
Marigold 613
Purple 1,100
White 287

DAISY CUT BELL

Daisy Cut Bell

Marigold (ILLUS.) 425

DAISY & PLUME

Bowl, 8" to 9" d., marigold, three-footed 75
Candy dish, green, footed 70
Candy dish, ice blue, footed 875
Candy dish, ice green, footed 750
Candy dish, lime green, footed 700
Candy dish, marigold, footed 85
Candy dish, purple, footed . . . . 100 to 110
Compote, green 60
Compote, purple 73
Rose bowl, blue, three-footed, Blackberry
    interior 475
Rose bowl, green, three-footed 93
Rose bowl, green, three-footed, Blackberry
    interior . . . . 375 to 400

Rose bowl, green, three-footed, Stippled
    Rays interior 95
Rose bowl, ice blue, three-footed,
    Blackberry interior 1,100
Rose bowl, ice green, three-footed 950
Rose bowl, marigold, three-footed 55
Rose bowl, marigold, three-footed,
    Blackberry interior 110
Rose bowl, purple, three-footed . . . . 90 to 95
Rose bowl, white, three-footed . . . . 850 to 900
Rose bowl, white, three-footed, Blackberry
    interior 750

DANDELION (Northwood)

Dandelion Pitcher

Mug, aqua 365
Mug, aqua opalescent . . . . 475 to 500
Mug, blue . . . . 500 to 550
Mug, ice blue opalescent 750
Mug, marigold 375
Mug, purple . . . . 225 to 275
Mug, Knights Templar, marigold 513
Pitcher, water, tankard, green . . . . 1,000 to 1,200
Pitcher, water, tankard, marigold
    (ILLUS.) . . . . 350 to 400
Tumbler, green 150
Tumbler, ice blue . . . . 100 to 150
Tumbler, marigold 80
Tumbler, purple 100
Tumbler, white 100
Water set: pitcher & 6 tumblers; marigold,
    7 pcs. 1,110

DIAMOND RING (Imperial)

Diamond Ring Bowl

Bowl, 8" to 9" d., marigold . . . . 40 to 45
Bowl, 8" to 9" d., purple 200
Bowl, 8" to 9" d., smoky (ILLUS.) . . . . 40 to 45
Rose bowl, marigold 400

DIAMOND & SUNBURST

Decanter w/stopper, purple. 295
Wine, lavender 70
Wine, marigold 30
Wine, purple 65

DOLPHINS COMPOTE (Millersburg)

Blue, Rosalind interior 5,250
Green, Rosalind interior. 4,500
Purple, Rosalind interior 1,900

FASHION (Imperial)

Fashion Pitcher

Bowl, 9" d., clambroth. 40
Bowl, 9" d., marigold. 25
Bowl, 9" d., smoky, ruffled 175
Breakfast set: small size creamer & sugar
   bowl: smoky, pr. 175
Creamer, purple, breakfast size 225
Creamer, smoky 85
Pitcher, water, marigold (ILLUS.) . . . . 100 to 125
Pitcher, water, purple. . . . . 900 to 1,000
Punch bowl & base, marigold, 12" d.,
   2 pcs. . . . . 125 to 150
Punch cup, marigold 23
Punch cup, smoky 40
Rose bowl, purple, large 2,050
Sugar bowl, smoky 90
Tumbler, marigold 25
Tumbler, purple 200
Tumbler, smoky . . . . 95 to 115

FINECUT & ROSES (Northwood)

Candy dish, amber, three-footed 55
Candy dish, aqua opalescent, three-footed 425
Candy dish, blue w/electric iridescence,
   three-footed 150
Candy dish, green, three-footed . . . . 130 to 150
Candy dish, ice blue, three-footed . . . . . . 275 to 300
Candy dish, marigold, three-footed 75
Candy dish, pastel marigold, three-footed 95

Candy dish, purple, three-footed . . . . 70 to 85
Rose bowl, aqua opalescent. 1,650
Rose bowl/whimsey, lavender, straight top 650

FISHSCALE & BEADS

Banana boat, peach opalescent, 7" l. 75
Bonbon, marigold, 6" 30
Bowl, 6½" d., purple, ruffled & crimped edge 88
Bowl, 7" d., marigold . . . . 25 to 40
Bowl, 7" d., purple, candy ribbon edge 40
Card tray, peach opalescent, 4 x 7" 70
Plate, 6" d., peach opalescent. . . . . 125 to 150
Plate, 7" d., marigold . . . . 95 to 125
Plate, 7" d., peach opalescent, ruffled
   rim. . . . . 125 to 150
Plate, 7" d., purple 375
Plate, 7" d., white 125
Plate, 7½ " d., marigold. 75

FLORAL & GRAPE (Dugan or Diamond Glass Co.)

Pitcher, water, blue. . . . . 300 to 350
Pitcher, water, dark marigold 250
Pitcher, water, marigold 180
Pitcher, water, purple 233
Pitcher, water, white. 475
Tumbler, blue . . . . 35 to 40
Tumbler, purple. 35 to 45
Tumbler, white 80
Tumblers, purple, set of 4 180
Water set: pitcher & 4 tumblers; blue, 5 pcs. 450

FLUTE (Imperial)

Flute Match Holder

Celery vase, purple, 5½ " 400
Compote, marigold, 11" d., 7" h. 100
Creamer, green, breakfast size 50
Creamer, marigold, breakfast size 50
Creamer, purple, breakfast size . . . . 65 to 70
Creamer & open sugar bowl, purple,
   breakfast size, pr. . . . . 100 to 115
Match holder, purple (ILLUS.) 900
Pitcher, water, marigold 275

Pitcher, water, purple 575
Punch cup, marigold 37
Punch set: bowl, base & 5 cups; marigold,
 7 pcs. 495
Toothpick holder, marigold . . . . 65 to 75
Toothpick holder, purple 58
Toothpick holder, vaseline . . . . 200 to 250
Tumbler, marigold 40
Tumbler, purple 90

FOUR SEVENTY FOUR (Imperial)

Goblet, water, marigold . . . . 50 to 55
Pitcher, milk, green . . . . 365 to 400
Pitcher, water, green . . . . 400 to 450
Pitcher, water, marigold . . . . 175 to 225
Punch bowl & base, marigold, 2 pcs. 168
Punch cup, green 40
Punch cup, marigold . . . . 20 to 25
Punch set: bowl, base & 6 cups; marigold,
 8 pcs. 375
Tumbler, green 125

GOLDEN HARVEST OR HARVEST TIME (U.S. Glass)

Golden Harvest Wine Set

Decanter w/stopper, marigold . . . . 125 to 140
Wine, marigold . . . . 15 to 20
Wine, purple 75
Wine set: decanter & 6 wines; marigold,
 7 pcs. (ILLUS.) . . . . 225 to 250

GRAPE & CABLE

Banana boat, banded rim, stippled, aqua 575
Banana boat, blue, banded rim . . . . 550 to 600
Banana boat, green 400
Banana boat, ice blue 700
Banana boat, ice green 750
Banana boat, marigold, stippled . . . . 200 to 250
Banana boat, purple . . . . 200 to 250
Berry set: master bowl & 4 sauce dishes;
 purple, 5 pcs. 375
Bonbon, two-handled, blue 133

Bonbon, two-handled, blue w/electric
 iridescence . . . . 225 to 275
Bonbon, two-handled, green . . . . 75 to 100
Bonbon, two-handled, horehound 375
Bonbon, two-handled, marigold . . . . (75)
Bonbon, two-handled, purple . . . . 75 to 100
Bonbon, two-handled, stippled, blue . . . . 175 to 200
Bonbon, two-handled, stippled, green 165
Bonbon, two-handled, stippled, marigold . . . 50 to 75
Bowl, 5" d., blue (Fenton) 60
Bowl, 5" d., green 60
Bowl, 5" d., marigold 30
Bowl, 5" d., purple 60
Bowl, 6" d., three-in-one edge, marigold
 variant 160
Bowl, 6½" d., Amberina (Fenton) 650
Bowl, 7" d., ice cream shape, marigold
 (Fenton) 35
Bowl, 7" d., ice cream shape, milk white
 w/marigold overlay (Fenton) 250
Bowl, 7" d., ice cream shape, purple
 (Fenton) 55
Bowl, 7" d., ice cream shape, vaseline
 (Fenton) 45
Bowl, 7" d., ruffled, marigold 25
Bowl, 7½" d., ball-footed, aqua (Fenton) . . . . 80 to 85
Bowl, 7½" d., ball-footed, red (Fenton) 575
Bowl, 7½" d., ruffled, green 85
Bowl, 7½" d., ruffled, red . . . . 800 to 825
Bowl, 7½" d., ruffled, vaseline, ... 100
Bowl, 7½" d., spatula-footed, green
 (Northwood) 100
Bowl, 7½" d., spatula-footed, purple
 (Northwood) 63
Bowl, 8" d., ice cream shape, footed, blue
 (Fenton) . . . . 60 to 65
Bowl, 8" d., ruffled, green . . . . 65 to 70
Bowl, 8" d., ruffled, red (Fenton) 800
Bowl, 8" to 9" d., ball-footed, celeste
 blue (Fenton) 1,200
Bowl, 8" to 9" d., piecrust rim, aqua
 opalescent (Northwood) 3,900
Bowl, 8" to 9" d., piecrust rim,
 blue, stippled . . . . 375 to 425
Bowl, 8" to 9" d., piecrust rim, blue
 w/electric iridescence . . . . 300 to 350
Bowl, 8" to 9" d., piecrust rim, green . . . . . 100 to 110
Bowl, 8" to 9" d., piecrust rim, green,
 Basketweave exterior . . . . 250 to 300
Bowl, 8" to 9" d., piecrust rim, ice blue 1,300
Bowl, 8" to 9" d., piecrust rim, marigold 85
Bowl, 8" to 9" d., piecrust rim, marigold,
 Basketweave exterior . . . . 40 to 45
Bowl, 8" to 9" d., piecrust rim, marigold,
 stippled 185
Bowl, 8" to 9" d., piecrust rim, pastel marigold 90
Bowl, 8" to 9" d., piecrust rim, purple . . . . 135 to 150

Bowl, 8" to 9" d., piecrust rim, purple,
Basketweave exterior . . . . 150 to 175

Bowl, 8" to 9" d., spatula-footed, blue
(Northwood) 250

Bowl, 8" to 9" d., spatula-footed, green
(Northwood) 90

Bowl, 8" to 9" d., spatula-footed, lavender 250

Bowl, 8" to 9" d., spatula-footed, marigold
(Northwood) 65

Bowl, 8" to 9" d., spatula-footed, ruffled,
purple (Northwood) . . . . 85 to 90

Bowl, 8" to 9" d., stippled, blue 388

Bowl, 8" to 9" d., stippled, green, ruffled 275

Bowl, 8" to 9" d., stippled, marigold, ruffled,
Basketweave exterior 300

Bowl, 8½" d., scalloped, marigold 85

Bowl, 8½" d., scalloped, purple (Northwood) 95

Bowl, 8½" d., ruffled, stippled, green 270

Bowl, 9" d., Basketweave exterior, green 78

Bowl, 9" d., ruffled, Basketweave exterior,
marigold 40

Bowl, berry, 9" d., green 188

Bowl, berry, 9" d., marigold 135

Bowl, 10" d., ruffled, stippled, Basketweave
exterior, marigold 225

Bowl, 10½" d., ruffled, Basketweave
exterior, marigold 70

Bowl, 10½" d., ruffled, Basketweave
exterior, purple 125

Bowl, 10½" d., ruffled, white 150

Bowl, orange, 10½" d., blue, footed 475

Bowl, orange, 10½" d., blue, footed,
Persian Medallion interior (Fenton) 350

Bowl, orange, 10½" d., blue w/electric
iridescence, footed, stippled
(Northwood) . . . . 825 to 850

Bowl, orange, 10½" d., green, footed 325

Bowl, orange, 10½" d., green, footed,
Persian Medallion interior (Fenton) . . . . 225 to 250

Bowl, orange, 10½" d., ice green, footed 1,050

Bowl, orange, 10½" d., marigold, banded 413

Bowl, orange, 10½" d., marigold, footed 188

Bowl, orange, 10½" d., marigold, footed,
Persian Medallion interior (Fenton) . . . . 125 to 150

Bowl, orange, 10½" d., purple, footed 325

Bowl, orange, 10½" d., purple, footed,
Persian Medallion interior (Fenton) 500

Bowl, orange, 10½" d., white, footed 1,538

Bowl, 11" d., ice cream shape, blue 1,200

Bowl, 11" d., ice cream shape, green,
Basketweave exterior 750

Bowl, 11" d., ice cream shape, ice blue 2,425

Bowl, 11" d., ice cream shape, purple . . . . 350 to 400

Bowl, 11" d., ice cream shape, purple,
Basketweave exterior 400

Bowl, 11" d., ice cream shape, white 375

Bowl, 11" d., ice cream shape, white,
Basketweave exterior . . . . 300 to 325

Bowl, 11" d., ruffled, green 195

Butter dish, cov., blue 350

Butter dish, cov., green . . . . 200 to 250

Butter dish, cov., marigold . . . . 125 to 150

Butter dish, cov., purple . . . . 150 to 225

Candle lamp, marigold . . . . 650 to 700

Candle lamp, purple . . . . 650 to 700

Cologne bottle w/stopper, green . . . . . . 250 to 275

Cologne bottle w/stopper, ice blue . . . . . 725 to 775

Cologne bottle w/stopper, marigold . . . . 200 to 275

Cologne bottle w/stopper, purple . . . . . . 250 to 300

Cologne bottle w/stopper, white . . . . 625 to 650

Compote, open, green, large . . . . 925 to 1,100

Compote open, marigold, large 425

Compote, open, purple, large . . . . 550 to 600

Creamer, green 125

Creamer, marigold . . . . 75 to 80

Creamer, purple 86

Cup & saucer, purple . . . . 250 to 300

Grape & Cable Whiskey Decanter

Decanter w/stopper, whiskey, marigold
(ILLUS.) 618

Dresser set, purple, 7 pcs. 1,500

Dresser tray, green . . . . 250 to 275

Dresser tray, marigold 200

Dresser tray, purple 250

Hatpin holder, marigold . . . . 300 to 375

Hatpin holder, purple . . . . 350 to 375

Humidor, cov., marigold . . . . 300 to 375

Humidor, cov., purple . . . . 550 to 600

Pin tray, green 350

Pin tray, ice blue . . . . 900 to 950

Pin tray, marigold . . . . 125 to 175

Pitcher, water, 8¼" h., green 475

Pitcher, water, 8¼" h., marigold 275

Pitcher, water, 8¼" h., purple . . . . 185 to 275

Pitcher, tankard, 9¾" h., ice green 8,000

Plate, 5" to 6" d., marigold, two sides up 125

Plate, 5" to 6" d., purple (Northwood) 125

Plate, 8" d., clambroth . . . . 125 to 150

Plate, 8" d., marigold, flat, spatula-footed 175

Plate, 8" d., marigold, footed 95

Plate, 8" d., purple . . . . 200 to 225

Plate, 9" d., purple 195
Plate, 9" d., stippled, marigold 700
Plate, 9" d., stippled, marigold, variant . . . 175 to 300
Powder jar, cov., green 335
Powder jar, cov., marigold . . . . 150 to 175
Punch cup, purple . . . . 25 to 30
Sherbet or individual ice cream dish,
   marigold 30
Sherbet or individual ice cream dish,
   purple . . . . 55 to 65
Sherbet or individual ice cream dish,
   white . . . . 160 to 170
Spooner green 100
Spooner marigold 68
Spooner purple 85
Tumbler, green . . . . 55 to 65
Tumbler, marigold . . . . 50 to 75
Water set: pitcher & 6 tumblers; purple,
   7 pcs. . . . . 500 to 600
Whiskey shot glass, marigold . . . . 125 to 150
Whiskey shot glass, purple 155

GRAPE LEAVES (Northwood)

Bowl, 8" d., green . . . . 75 to 85
Bowl, 8" d., green, ribbon candy rim . . . . . 200 to 250
Bowl, 9" d., green, ruffled 125
Bowl, 9" d., marigold . . . . 50 to 75
Bowl, 9" d., purple . . . . 125 to 150
Bride's basket, w/handle & silver exterior,
   purple 250

HEART & VINE (Fenton)

Bowl, 8" to 9" d., blue . . . . 90 to 100
Bowl, 8" to 9" d., blue, candy ribbon
   edge . . . . 100 to 125
Bowl, 8" to 9" d., green 83
Bowl, 8" to 9" d., green, candy ribbon edge 80
Bowl, 8" to 9" d., marigold, candy ribbon edge 70
Bowl, 8" to 9" d., purple . . . . 90 to 100
Bowl, 8½" d., purple, candy ribbon
   edge . . . . 100 to 120
Plate, 9" d., blue 725
Plate, 9" d., marigold 250
Plate, 9" d., purple . . . . 395 to 425

HEAVY GRAPE (Imperial)

Bowl, 4" d., purple 45
Bowl, 5" d., 2" h., marigold 30
Bowl, 7" d., green, fluted 40
Bowl, 7" d., purple . . . . 60 to 70
Bowl, 8" to 9" d., green 54
Bowl, 8" to 9" d., marigold 45
Bowl, 8" to 9" d., purple . . . . 75 to 85
Bowl, 9" d., aqua 150
Plate, 7" to 8" d., amber . . . . 175 to 200
Plate, 7" to 8" d., marigold . . . . 50 to 60
Plate, 7" to 8" d., purple 200

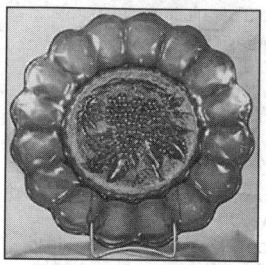
Imperial Heavy Grape Chop Plate

Plate, chop, 11" d., amber (ILLUS.) . . . . . . 245 to 275
Plate, chop, 11" d., lavender 410
Plate, chop, 11" d., smoky 500
Punch bowl & base, marigold, 2 pcs. 400

HEAVY IRIS (Dugan or Diamond Glass)

Pitcher, water, marigold . . . . 300 to 350
Pitcher, water, peach opalescent 1,000
Pitcher, water, white 1,250
Tumbler, purple . . . . 100 to 125
Tumbler, white 225

HOBNAIL SWIRL - See SWIRL HOBNAIL

HOLLY, HOLLY BERRIES & CARNIVAL HOLLY (Fenton)

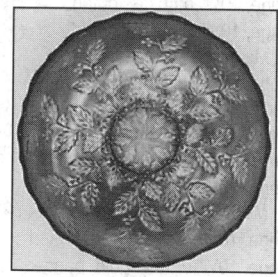
Holly Bowl

Bowl, 5" d., marigold 28
Bowl, 8" d., black amethyst 225
Bowl, 8" to 9" d., amber 150
Bowl, 8" to 9" d., aqua 550
Bowl, 8" to 9" d., blue . . . . 75 to 100
Bowl, 8" to 9" d., green 70
Bowl, 8" to 9" d., marigold (ILLUS.) . . . . 70 to 80
Bowl, 8" to 9" d., purple 130
Bowl, 8" to 9" d., candy ribbon edge,
   green . . . . 150 to 175
Bowl, 8" to 9" d., candy ribbon edge,
   purple . . . . 100 to 125
Bowl, 8" to 9" d., ice cream shape, blue . . . 75 to 100
Bowl, 8" to 9" d., ice cream shape, celeste
   blue . . . . 1,500 to 2,000

Bowl, 8" to 9" d., ice cream shape,
ice green 2,700
Bowl, 8" to 9" d., ice cream shape,
marigold . . . . 55 to 75
Bowl, 8" to 9" d., ice cream shape,
red . . . . 2,000 to 2,500
Bowl, 8" to 9" d., ruffled, blue 113
Bowl, 8" to 9" d., ruffled, blue opalescent 1,350
Bowl, 8" to 9" d., ruffled, green 135
Bowl, 8" to 9" d., ruffled, marigold 63
Bowl, 8" to 9" d., ruffled, purple . . . . 100 to 120
Bowl, 8" to 9" d., ruffled, vaseline . . . . 250 to 300
Compote, small, red . . . . 800 to 1,000
Compote, small, vaseline 95
Dish, hat-shaped, Amberina . . . . 400 to 425
Dish, hat-shaped, aqua, 5¾" . . . . 75 to 85
Dish, hat-shaped, marigold, 5¾" . . . . 35 to 40
Dish, hat-shaped, purple, 5¾" . . . . 40 to 45
Dish, hat-shaped, red, 5¾" . . . . 450 to 500
Dish, hat-shaped, vaseline, 5¾" . . . . 80 to 90
Plate, 9" to 10" d., marigold . . . . 225 to 300
Plate, 9" to 10" d., purple . . . . 700 to 1,000

INVERTED STRAWBERRY (Cambridge)

Bowl, master berry, 10" d., purple . . . . 235 to 300
Celery, blue 1,200
Compote, souvenir, marigold (minor
roughness on edge) 295
Compote, open, green, 5" d., 6" h. 525
Creamer, blue . . . . 300 to 400
Creamer, marigold . . . . 150 to 200
Creamer, purple 270
Cuspidor, green . . . . 1,000 to 1,200
Cuspidor, marigold 900
Spooner, purple . . . . 200 to 250
Sugar bowl, cov., green . . . . 250 to 300
Tumbler, green 275

LEAF & BEADS (Northwood)

Leaf & Beads Rose Bowl

Candy bowl, footed, aqua opalescent 500
Nut bowl, green, handled, w/interior pattern 175
Rose bowl, aqua opalescent (ILLUS.) . . . 450 to 525
Rose bowl, blue 205
Rose bowl, blue w/electric iridescence . . . 300 to 500
Rose bowl, green . . . . 130 to 150
Rose bowl, ice blue 1,400

Rose bowl, ice green opalescent 3,000
Rose bowl, marigold . . . . 95 to 100
Rose bowl, marigold, souvenir 125

LION (Fenton)

Bowl, 6" d., blue . . . . 250 to 350
Bowl, 6" d., marigold . . . . 100 to 125
Bowl, 7" d., blue 335
Bowl, 7" d., ice cream shape, blue . . . . . . 300 to 315
Bowl, 7" d., ice cream shape, marigold 175
Bowl, 7" d., ruffled, blue . . . . 275 to 300
Bowl, 7" d., ruffled, marigold 150

LITTLE STARS BOWL (Millersburg)

Bowl, 7" d., green . . . . 200 to 250
Bowl, 7" d., marigold . . . . 135 to 140
Bowl, 7" d., purple 164
Bowl, 7½" d., marigold, three-in-one edge 425
Bowl, 7½" d., purple, ruffled 200
Bowl, 8" d., ice cream, green 450
Bowl, 8" d., ruffled, green 265
Bowl, 8" d., ruffled, marigold 90
Bowl, 8" d., ruffled, purple 200

LOUISA (Westmoreland)

Louisa Rose Bowl

Bowl, 7" d., footed, green 43
Bowl, 7" d., ice cream shape, blue 250
Bowl, 8" to 9" d., three-footed, green 50
Bowl, 8" to 9" d., three-footed, marigold 46
Plate, 9½" d., footed, aqua . . . . 140 to 150
Plate, 9½" d., footed, marigold 105
Plate, 9½" d., footed, purple 110
Rose bowl, footed, green (ILLUS.) 57
Rose bowl, footed, lavender 110
Rose bowl, footed, purple 69

LUSTRE ROSE (Imperial)

Bowl, 7" d., three-footed, amber 35
Bowl, 7" d., three-footed, green 40
Bowl, 7" d., three-footed, marigold . . . . 40 to 45
Bowl, 8" to 9" d., three-footed, amber 83
Bowl, 8" to 9" d., three-footed, clambroth 56
Bowl, 8" to 9" d., three-footed, green 45
Bowl, 8" to 9" d., three-footed, marigold 38
Bowl, 8" to 9" d., three-footed, olive green 75

Bowl, 8" to 9" d., three-footed, purple......... 110
Bowl, 11" d., ruffled, collared base, green 75
Bowl, 11" d., ruffled, footed, marigold.......... 43
Bowl, 11" d., ruffled, footed, smoky 95
Bowl, fruit, red................. 2,500 to 3,000
Bowl, whimsey, centerpiece, amber ..... 150 to 175
Butter dish, cov., marigold .... 75 to 100
Butter dish, cov., purple.................... 250
Fernery, blue 110
Fernery, marigold......................... 35
Fernery, olive 85
Fernery, purple.......................... 110
Pitcher, water, marigold 65
Rose bowl, clambroth 50
Rose bowl, green........................... 45
Rose bowl, marigold 43
Sauce dish, clambroth 30
Sauce dish, green 24
Sauce dish, smoky......................... 50
Spooner, amber 50
Spooner, green 40
Spooner, marigold 35
Sugar bowl, cov., marigold 40
Tumbler, marigold 24

MANY FRUITS (Dugan)

Many Fruits Punch Bowl & Base

Punch bowl & base, purple, 2 pcs.
  (ILLUS.)....................... 775 to 800
Punch bowl & base, white, 2 pcs............. 765
Punch cup, blue .... 30 to 40
Punch cup, marigold 35
Punch cup, purple .... 30 to 40
Punch cup, white........................... 70
Punch set: bowl, base & 6 cups; purple,
  8 pcs......................... 900 to 1,000

MEMPHIS (Northwood)

Bowl, master berry, marigold 175
Fruit bowl & base, purple, 2 pcs.............. 400
Punch bowl & base, ice green,
  2 pcs. .... 5,000 to 7,000
Punch bowl & base, purple, 2 pcs............ 625
Punch cup, green..................... 35 to 55
Punch cup, ice green...................... 135
Punch cup, marigold 20
Punch cup, purple 36

Punch cup, smoky 60
Punch cup, white 45
Punch set: bowl, base & 10 cups; purple,
  12 pcs......................... 950 to 1,000
Sauce dish, marigold 75

MILLERSBURG COURTHOUSE BOWL
See Advertising & Souvenir Items

MORNING GLORY
(Millersburg & Imperial)

Morning Glory Pitcher

Pitcher, tankard, purple (ILLUS.)........... 10,000
Tumbler, purple......................... 1,200
Vase, 4" to 10" h., green.................... 88
Vase, 4" to 10" h., marigold............. 50 to 75
Vase, 4" to 10" h., purple............. 125 to 150
Vase, 4" to 10" h., smoky 110
Vase, 4" to 10" h., white 150
Vase, 10 x 12", marigold, funeral 195
Vase 12½" h., funeral, purple 795
Vase, 9½ x 13", purple 345
Vase, 16" h., funeral, green 210
Vase, 18" h., marigold..................... 200
Vase, smoky, miniature..................... 55

MULTI-FRUITS - See Many Fruits Patt.

NIPPON (Northwood)

Bowl, ruffled, Basketweave exterior, purple 225
Bowl, 8" d., piecrust rim, ice blue 400
Bowl, 8" d., piecrust rim, ice green ...... 600 to 900
Bowl, 8" d., piecrust rim, marigold 250
Bowl, 8" d., piecrust rim, pastel lime green
  w/opal tips........................ 2,950
Bowl, 8" d., piecrust rim, purple ...... 300 to 325
Bowl, 8" d., piecrust rim, white 270
Bowl, 8" to 9" d., 2¼" h., ice blue .... 300 to 350
Bowl, 8" to 9" d., 3" h., green .... 275 to 325
Bowl, ruffled, purple 500
Plate, 9" d., green .... 1,500 to 2,000
Plate, 9" d., marigold..................... 750
Plate, 9" d., purple............... 1,700 to 2,000

OCTAGON (Imperial)

Octagon Wine Decanter

Compote, jelly, marigold. 85
Creamer, marigold 60
Creamer, purple . . . . 180 to 200
Creamer & sugar bowl, marigold variant, pr. 110
Decanter w/stopper, green 500
Decanter w/stopper, marigold
   (ILLUS.). . . . . 100 to 125
Goblet, water, marigold 45
Pitcher, milk, marigold 85
Pitcher, milk, purple . . . . 250 to 275
Pitcher, water, 8" h., purple. . . . . 550 to 600
Spooner, marigold 45
Sugar bowl, cov., marigold 50
Toothpick holder, marigold 130
Tumbler, purple 125
Vase, 8" h., marigold . . . . 80 to 90
Wine, marigold 28
Wine set: decanter & 6 wines; marigold,
   7 pcs. . . . . 260 to 270

ORANGE TREE (Fenton)

Orange Tree Loving Cup

Bowl, 8" to 9" d., green . . . . 225 to 275
Bowl, 8" to 9" d., marigold. . . . . 55 to 60
Bowl, 8" to 9" d., purple 195
Bowl, 10" d., three-footed, blue. . . . . 250 to 325
Bowl, 10" d., three-footed, marigold 135
Bowl, ice cream shape, blue, w/trunk center 230
Bowl, ice cream shape, green 250
Bowl, ice cream shape, marigold 85

Bowl, ice cream shape, purple . . . . 250 to 300
Bowl, ice cream shape, red. . . . . 2,050 to 3,000
Bowl, milk white w/marigold overlay . . 1,150 to 1,250
Centerpiece bowl, footed, purple,
   12" d., 4" h. . . . . 1,000 to 1,500
Compote, 5" d., green 85
Creamer, footed, white . . . . 125 to 175
Creamer, marigold, individual size 37
Creamer, purple, individual size 45
Dish, blue, ice cream, footed 38
Dish, marigold, ice cream, footed . . . . 30 to 40
Goblet, blue 55
Goblet, marigold. 57
Hatpin holder, blue. . . . . 300 to 350
Hatpin holder, marigold . . . . 300 to 325
Loving cup, blue. . . . . 325 to 375
Loving cup, green . . . . 400 to 475
Loving cup, marigold (ILLUS.) . . . . 200 to 225
Mug, amber. 89
Mug, Amberina 385
Mug, blue . . . . 65 to 75
Mug, green . . . . 875 to 900
Mug, lavender. 180
Mug, lime green 500
Mug, marigold . . . . 35 to 45
Mug, purple . . . . 80 to 100
Mug, red 500
Pitcher, water, blue 325
Pitcher, water, marigold 275
Plate, 9" d., flat, blue . . . . 475 to 500
Plate, 9" d., flat, teal blue. . . . . 1,000 to 1,500
Plate, 9½" d., trunk center, Beaded Berry
   exterior, clambroth 250
Plate, 9" d., trunk center, flat, Beaded Berry
   exterior, marigold 200
Plate, 9" d., trunk center, white. 275
Plate, 9" d., Blackberry exterior, "Souvenir of
   Hershey," blue 335
Powder jar, cov., blue. . . . . 150 to 175
Powder jar, cov., green. . . . . 400 to 500
Powder jar, cov., marigold 75
Rose bowl, blue . . . . 75 to 85
Rose bowl, clambroth 90
Rose bowl, green . . . . 100 to 125
Rose bowl, purple . . . . 100 to 125
Rose bowl, white . . . . 200 to 225
Sauce dish, footed, white . . . . 100 to 125
Shaving mug, green 875
Shaving mug, marigold 50
Shaving mug, marigold, large . . . . 100 to 125
Shaving mug, olive green 975
Shaving mug, purple 195
Shaving mug, red. . . . . 600 to 650
Tumbler, blue . . . . 50 to 55
Tumbler, marigold 40
Tumbler, white 100
Wine, green 225

PEACOCK AT FOUNTAIN (Northwood)

Bowl, fruit, blue 1,450
Bowl, fruit, blue w/electric iridescence. 2,000
Bowl, master berry, green 625
Bowl, master berry, marigold 200
Bowl, master berry, purple . . . . 225 to 250
Bowl, master berry, white . . . . 400 to 450
Bowl, orange, three-footed, blue 1,080
Bowl, orange, three-footed, marigold . . . . 275 to 300
Bowl, orange, three-footed, purple 800
Compote, ice blue 1,325
Compote, ice green . . . . 1,750 to 1,850
Compote, purple. 750
Compote, white. . . . . 650 to 700
Creamer, purple . . . . 100 to 125
Pitcher, water, marigold 375
Pitcher, water, white . . . . 1,000 to 1,025
Punch bowl & base, blue, 2 pcs. 2,700
Punch bowl & base, ice green, 2 pcs. 9,500
Punch bowl & base, purple, 2 pcs. . . 1,400 to 1,425
Punch cup, ice green 525
Punch cup, marigold 35
Punch cup, purple . . . . 40 to 45
Punch set: bowl, base & 8 cups; purple,
    10 pcs. 1,825
Sauce dish, ice blue . . . . 100 to 110
Sauce dish, teal blue 75
Spooner, ice blue 280
Spooner, purple . . . . 100 to 120
Sugar bowl, cov., ice blue . . . . 375 to 400
Tumbler, blue. 80
Tumbler, ice blue 325
Tumbler, marigold. . . . . 40 to 50
Tumbler, purple. 65 to 70
Tumbler, teal blue 139
Tumbler, white . . . . 225 to 250

PEACOCK & GRAPE (Fenton)

Bowl, 8" d., collared base, blue. . . . . 70 to 90
Bowl, 8" d., collared base, marigold. 40
Bowl, 8" d., collared base, peach
    opalescent. . . . . 575 to 600
Bowl, 8" d., collared base, red, ruffled. 1,250
Bowl, 8" d., ice cream shape, green . . . . . 100 to 125
Bowl, 8" d., ice cream shape, marigold. . . . 100 to 125
Bowl, 8" d., ice cream shape, red . . . . 1,000 to 1,125
Bowl, 8" d.,spatula-footed, green . . . . 125 to 150
Bowl, 8" d., spatula-footed, ice green
    opalescent. . . . . 450 to 500
Bowl, 8" d., spatula-footed, marigold 55
Bowl, 8" d., spatula-footed, purple . . . . 95 to 125
Bowl, 9" d., ruffled, collared base, blue. . . 125 to 150
Bowl, 9" d., ruffled, green. 85
Bowl, 9" d., ruffled, marigold. . . . . 60 to 75
Bowl, 9" d., ruffled, purple 110
Bowl, 9" d., ruffled, red. 300

Bowl, Bearded Berry exterior, blue. 165
Bowl, ruffled, spatula-footed, lime green
    opalescent 245
Bowl, footed, ice cream shape, purple 175
Bowl, ice cream shape, blue 125
Plate, 9" d., collared base, green 250
Plate, 9" d., collared base, pastel marigold. 750
Plate, 9" d., dark marigold, berry exterior 875
Plate, 9" d., flat base, marigold. 500
Plate, 9" d., spatula-footed, emerald green 1,250
Plate, 9" d., spatula-footed,
    green. . . . . 175 to 200
Plate, 9" d., spatula-footed,marigold . . . . . 300 to 325
Plate, 9" d., spatula-footed, purple . . . . . . 375 to 400
Plate, footed, green 700

PEACOCKS ON FENCE
(Northwood Peacocks)

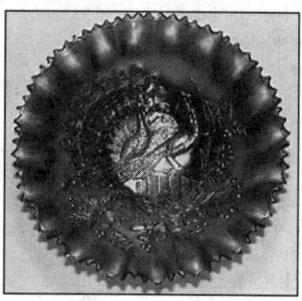

Peacocks on Fence Bowl

Bowl, 8" to 9" d., piecrust rim, aqua
    opalescent. . . . . 4,000 to 5,000
Bowl, 8" to 9" d., piecrust rim, blue. 485
Bowl, 8" to 9" d., piecrust rim, blue, stippled,
    w/ribbed back. 600
Bowl, 8" to 9" d., piecrust rim, green
    (ILLUS.). . . . . 1,850 to 1,950
Bowl, 8" to 9" d., piecrust rim, ice
    blue. . . . . 1,400 to 1,450
Bowl, 8" to 9" d., piecrust rim, marigold . . 300 to 325
Bowl, 8" to 9" d., piecrust rim, pastel
    marigold . . . . 320 to 350
Bowl, 8" to 9" d., piecrust rim, purple 425
Bowl, 8" to 9" d., piecrust rim, Renniger
    blue, stippled. 1,000
Bowl, 8" to 9" d., piecrust rim,
    white. 1,025
Bowl, 8" to 9" d., ruffled rim, blue 700
Bowl, 8" to 9" d., ruffled rim, green . . . 1,500 to 2,000
Bowl, 8" to 9" d., ruffled rim, purple. . . . . . 400 to 450
Bowl, 8" to 9" d., ruffled rim, smoky. 1,750
Bowl, 8" to 9" d., ruffled rim, white . . . . . . 900 to 975
Plate, Renniger blue, stippled 2,600
Plate, w/ribbed exterior, white . . . . 450 to 500
Plate, 9" d., blue w/electric iridescence 1,200
Plate, 9" d., cobalt blue, stippled 2,300

Plate, 9" d., green 1,535
Plate, 9" d., ice blue. . . . . 1,750 to 2,500
Plate, 9" d., ice green . . . . 550 to 600
Plate, 9" d., lavender . . . . 700 to 1,000
Plate, 9" d., marigold. . . . . 450 to 500
Plate, 9" d., marigold, dark 550
Plate, 9" d., marigold, stippled 600
Plate, 9" d., pastel marigold. 2,100
Plate, 9" d., purple. . . . . 800 to 825
Plate, 9" d., white. . . . . 650 to 750

PETAL & FAN (Dugan)

Bowl, 5" d., purple. . . . . 95 to 125
Bowl, 6" d., ruffled, peach opalescent 70
Bowl, 6" d., ruffled, purple 80
Bowl, 10" d., ruffled, peach opalescent. . . 200 to 250
Bowl, 10½" d., purple, Jeweled Heart exterior . . . 625
Bowl, 11" d., fluted, white . . . . 450 to 500
Bowl, 11" d., peach opalescent 365
Bowl, 11" d., purple, ruffled 300
Bowl, 11" d., star-shaped, stippled, Jeweled
    Heart exterior, purple 300
Bowl, 12" d., Jeweled Heart exterior, white 325
Plate, 6" d., candy ribbon rim, green. 225

QUESTION MARKS

Bonbon, two-handled, white, 5½" sq. 94
Bonbon, footed, peach opalescent, 6" d., 3¾" h. . . 65
Bonbon, footed, purple, 6" d., ¾" h. . . . . 55 to 65
Bonbon, footed, purple, Georgia Belle
    exterior, 6" d., 3¾" h. 155
Bonbon, stemmed, marigold 50
Bonbon, stemmed, peach opalescent 48
Bonbon, stemmed, purple . . . . 90 to 125
Bonbon, stemmed, white . . . . 65 to 75
Compote, crimped edge, marigold. 55
Compote, crimped edge, peach opalescent. 92
Plate, candy ribbon edge, footed, peach
    opalescent 150
Plate, dome-footed, white. 225
Plate, stemmed, marigold. 110
Plate, stemmed, white 280

RASPBERRY (Northwood)

Pitcher, milk, green. . . . . 350 to 400
Pitcher, milk, marigold . . . . 150 to 200
Pitcher, milk, purple. 350
Pitcher, milk, white 1,000
Pitcher, water, green 325
Pitcher, water, ice blue 2,100
Pitcher, water, ice green. . . . . 2,000 to 2,150
Pitcher, water, marigold . . . . 160 to 175
Pitcher, water, white. 685
Sauceboat, purple . . . . 100 to 125
Tumbler, green w/marigold overlay 125
Tumbler, ice blue . . . . 275 to 300

Tumbler, ice green . . . . 550 to 650
Tumbler, marigold 45
Tumbler, purple 75
Water set: pitcher & 6 tumblers; marigold,
    7 pcs. . . . . 450 to 500

RIPPLE VASE

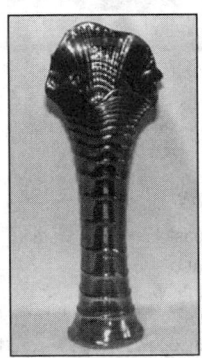

Ripple Vase

Amber, 6" h. 95
Amber, 7½" h. 77
Amber, 9" h. 175
Amber, 10" h. 95 to 100
Amber, 11½" h. 125
Aqua, 10" h. 125
Aqua, 11" h. 225 to 275
Aqua, ... 145 to 150
Blue, 9" h. 350
Clambroth, 10" h. 75
Clambroth, funeral, 15½" h. 225
Green, 8¼" h. 55
Green, 9½" h. 85
Green, 10" h. . . . . 40 to 50
Green, 11" h. 38
Green, 12½" h. 95
Green, 13" h. 93
Green, 15½" h. . . . . 100 to 125
Green, funeral, mid-size 175
Ice green, 14½" h. . . . . 200 to 245
Lavender, 7½" h. 115
Lavender, 14" h. 135
Marigold, 5" h. . . . . 150 to 155
Marigold, 6" h. . . . . 100 to 150
Marigold, 6½" h. . . . . 45 to 55
Marigold, 8" h. 30
Marigold, 9½" h. . . . . 25 to 30
Marigold, 10½" h. 40
Marigold, 12" h. 78
Marigold, 16½" h., funeral 58
Marigold, 17" h. 65
Marigold, funeral, 17½" h. 248
Marigold, funeral, 19" h. 175
Marigold, 20" h. (ILLUS.) . . . . 150 to 200

Purple, 8" h. 75
Purple, 8½" h. 153
Purple, 10" h. 100
Purple, 11" h. 250
Purple, 11½" h. 175
Purple, 12" h. 100 to 125
Purple, 13" h. 208
Smoky, 12" h. 86
Smoky, 15½" h. 250
Teal blue, 11½" h. 350
White, 8" h. 155
White, 9" h. . . . . 100 to 125
White, 9½" h. 175 to 200

ROSE SHOW

Bowl, ruffled, pastel marigold, variant 1,400
Bowl, 9" d., aqua. . . . . 750 to 850
Bowl, 9" d., aqua opalescent. 1,255
Bowl, 9" d., blue 900
Bowl, 9" d., blue opalescent . . . . 1,450 to 1,500
Bowl, 9" d., green . . . . 2,775 to 2,875
Bowl, 9" d., ice blue. 1,225
Bowl, 9" d., ice green . . . . 1,500 to 2,000
Bowl, 9" d., marigold. . . . . 550 to 600
Bowl, 9" d., purple 895
Bowl, 9" d., sapphire blue 3,150
Bowl, 9" d., white 400
Bowl, Renniger blue, variant 1,000
Plate, 9" d., blue . . . . 1,300 to 1,400
Plate, 9" d., blue, variant 2,700
Plate, 9" d., cobalt blue 2,100
Plate, 9" d., dark marigold 2,000
Plate, 9" d., green 3,200
Plate, 9" d., ice blue. . . . . 1,800 to 2,000
Plate, 9" d., ice green . . . . 3,000 to 3,500
Plate, 9" d., lime green . . . . 3,500 to 3,700
Plate, 9" d., marigold. 900
Plate, 9" d., pastel marigold. . . . . 1,000 to 1,500
Plate, 9" d., purple. . . . . 1,250 to 1,300
Plate, 9" d., white. . . . . 425 to 475
Plate, emerald green 7,500

RUSTIC VASE

Blue, 7" to 12" h. . . . . 35 to 55
Blue, 15" h. 105
Blue, 16" h. . . . . 100 to 125
Blue, funeral, 18" h., 5" base . . . . 900 to 1,000
Blue, 19" h. 165
Blue, funeral, 19½" h. . . . . 900 to 1,000
Blue, funeral, 23½" h., w/plunger base, blue . . . 1,300
Green 6" h. to 10½" h. 75
Green 16" h. . . . . 100 to 125
Green funeral, 19" h. . . . . 1,400 to 2,000
Marigold, 6" to 10½" h. 35
Marigold, 11" h. 35
Marigold, 15" h. . . . . 100 to 125

Marigold, funeral, 16" h., ... 385
Marigold, 16" to 21½" h., 5½" base . . . . . 100 to 125
Marigold, funeral, 19" h., marigold . . . . . . 650 to 675
Purple, 6" to 10½" h. 50
Purple, 11" h. 44
Purple funeral, 12" h. 175
Purple, 15" h. 160
Purple, 16" h. 255
Purple, 16¾" h. 88
Purple, 18½" h. . . . . 750 to 1,000
Purple funeral, 19" h. 1,050
Purple funeral, 20" h. 1,250
Purple funeral, 5" base 1,350
Red, 6" to 10½" h., crimped top 2,900
Vaseline, funeral 3,500
White 6" to 12½" h. 75
White, funeral, 15" h., ... 250
White funeral, 18" h. 850

SKI STAR (Dugan)

Ski Star Bowl

Banana bowl, peach opalescent 170
Basket, peach opalescent 520
Bowl, 5" d., ruffled, purple. . . . . 75 to 95
Bowl, 6" d., ruffled, peach opalescent. . . . . . 55 to 65
Bowl, 10" d., marigold. 62
Bowl, 10" d., peach opalescent. . . . . 95 to 100
Bowl, 10" d., purple. . . . . 300 to 375
Bowl, 11" d., peach opalescent. . . . . 125 to 150
Bowl, 11" d., purple. . . . . 225 to 275
Bowl, tricornered, dome-footed, peach
    opalescent (ILLUS.) . . . . 100 to 125
Plate, 7" d., deep, candy ribbon edge,
    peach opalescent 65
Plate, 8½" d., dome-footed, w/handgrip,
    peach opalescent 194

SPRINGTIME (Northwood)

Bowl, master berry, marigold 125
Butter dish, cov., green 400
Butter dish, cov., marigold (ILLUS.) . . . . . 250 to 275
Butter dish, cov., purple. 300
Creamer, marigold 125

Springtime Butter Dish

Pitcher, green	950 to 1,000
Sauce dish, 5" d., green	53
Sauce dish, 5" d., purple	55
Spooner, green	255 to 275
Spooner, marigold	125
Spooner, purple	300
Sugar bowl, cov., marigold	235
Sugar bowl, open, green	165
Tumbler, green	170 to 175
Tumbler, marigold	65
Tumbler, purple	70 to 75

STAR & FILE (Imperial)

Bowl, 8" to 9" d., marigold	35
Bowl, two-handled, marigold	35
Compote, large, marigold	45 to 50
Creamer, marigold	30
Plate, 6" d., marigold	105
Rose bowl, marigold	40 to 50
Sherbet, marigold, w/underplate, tall	125
Wine decanter w/stopper, marigold	138

STIPPLED RAYS

Stippled Rays Bowl

Bonbon, two-handled, celeste blue	275 to 300
Bonbon, two-handled, green	35 to 45
Bonbon, two-handled, ice green	250
Bonbon, two-handled, purple	40 to 50
Bowl, 5" d., Amberina	300 to 400
Bowl, 5" d., blue	50
Bowl, 5" d., green	20 to 30
Bowl, 5" d., marigold	25
Bowl, 5" d., red	400 to 450

Bowl, 6½" d., blue, stippled, Scale Band exterior	75 to 100
Bowl, 6½" d., red, ruffled	395
Bowl, 6¾" d., dome-footed, aqua	100 to 150
Bowl, 7" d., red	250 to 450
Bowl, 8" to 9" d., purple	40 to 45
Bowl, 8" to 9" d., teal blue	50
Bowl, 10" d., amber	42
Bowl, 10" d., lavender, ruffled	75
Bowl, 10" d., marigold, ruffled	80
Bowl, 10" d., purple, piecrust rim(ILLUS.)	75 to 85
Bowl, 10" d., white	175
Creamer & sugar bowl, blue, pr.	75 to 100
Creamer & sugar bowl, individual size, blue, pr.	55
Creamer & sugar bowl, marigold, pr.	50
Plate, 6" to 7" d., marigold	50
Rose bowl, purple	70
Sugar bowl, open, green	35
Sugar bowl, open, marigold	24

SWAN PASTEL NOVELTIES (Dugan)

Salt dip, amber	250
Salt dip, celeste blue	40 to 45
Salt dip, ice blue	33
Salt dip, ice green	45 to 50
Salt dip, peach opalescent	375 to 450
Salt dip, purple	250 to 275
Salt dip, teal	350

SWIRL HOBNAIL (Millersburg)

Swirl Hobnail Cuspidor

Cuspidor, marigold	1,000
Cuspidor, purple (ILLUS.)	725
Rose bowl, marigold	200 to 225
Rose bowl, purple	350 to 400
Vase, green	700
Vase, marigold	350
Vase, purple	250
Vase, 10" h., green	395
Vase, 16" h., marigold, variant	450

TWO FLOWERS (Fenton)

Bowl, 6" d., footed, aqua	175
Bowl, 6" d., footed, blue	75 to 80
Bowl, 6" d., footed, lime green	175
Bowl, 6" d., footed, vaseline	100 to 125
Bowl, 7" to 8" d., footed, blue	85 to 100

Bowl, 7" to 8" d., footed, green 90
Bowl, 7" to 8" d., footed, marigold . . . . 60 to 65
Bowl, 7" to 8" d., footed, purple, fluted . . . . . 50 to 60
Bowl, 8" d., marigold, collared base . . . . . 100 to 125
Bowl, 8" d., marigold, collared base, ice
   cream shape 133
Bowl, 8½" d., blue, footed . . . . 275 to 300
Bowl, 9" d., footed, black amethyst,
   ice cream shape 375
Bowl, 9" d., footed, blue, ice cream shape 195
Bowl, 9" d., footed, purple, ice cream shape 65
Bowl, 10" d., footed, aqua . . . . 350 to 375
Bowl, 10" d., footed, blue . . . . 125 to 150
Bowl, 10" d., footed, blue, scalloped rim . . . 95 to 100
Bowl, 10" d., footed, green, scalloped rim 95
Bowl, 10" d., footed, marigold 85
Bowl, 10" d., footed, marigold, scalloped rim 60
Bowl, 10" d., footed, purple 525
Bowl, 10½" d., blue, ruffled . . . . 125 to 150
Bowl, 10½" d., marigold, footed, ruffled . . . . 65 to 70
Bowl, 11" d., blue . . . . 225 to 250
Bowl, 11" d., blue, ice cream shape . . . . . 140 to 150
Bowl, 11" d., lime green/marigold,
   ice cream shape 175
Bowl, 11" d., marigold 115
Bowl, 11" d., purple, footed, ruffled 750
Bowl, 13" d., footed, marigold 75
Plate, 9" d., footed, marigold . . . . 600 to 650
Plate, chop, 11½" d., three-foot, marigold 1,600
Rose bowl, three-footed, blue 180
Rose bowl, three-footed, giant, marigold . . 250 to 300
Rose bowl, three-footed, marigold 70
Rose bowl, three-footed, vaseline 150

WINDMILL OR WINDMILL MEDALLION (Imperial)

Windmill Tumbler

Bowl, 7" d., marigold 38
Bowl, 8" to 9" d., ruffled, purple . . . . 90 to 100
Bowl, 8" to 9" d., ruffled, smoky 127
Bowl, 9" d., purple, footed . . . . 95 to 100
Bowl, 10" d., purple 150
Dresser tray, oval, purple 370
Pickle dish, green 125
Pickle dish, marigold 37

Pickle dish, purple 58
Pitcher, milk, ice green . . . . 95 to 100
Pitcher, milk, marigold 80
Pitcher, milk, purple . . . . 675 to 750
Pitcher, milk, smoky . . . . 200 to 225
Pitcher, water, marigold 94
Pitcher, water, purple 900
Tumbler, marigold (ILLUS.) 36
Tumbler, purple 150

CHOCOLATE

This glass is often called Caramel Slag. It was made by the Indiana Tumbler and Goblet Company of Greentown, Indiana, and other glasshouses, beginning at the turn of this century. Various patterns were produced, highly popular among them being Cactus and Leaf Bracket.

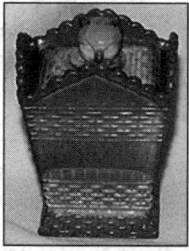 

From left: Greentown Cat on Hamper Dish · Cactus Pattern Jelly Compote

Animal covered dish, Cat on Hamper,
   Greentown (ILLUS.) $425
Animal covered dish, Hen on Nest,
   Greentown 725
Bowl, three-footed, Vintage patt., Fenton 250
Compote, jelly, Cactus patt., Greentown
   (ILLUS.) 225
Cruet w/original stopper, Geneva patt.,
   Greentown 850

From left: Outdoor Drinking Scene Mug Tall Cactus Pattern Tumbler

Mug, Outdoor Drinking Scene, Greentown
   (ILLUS.) 155
Sauce dish, Leaf Bracket patt., Greentown 50

Syrup pitcher w/original lid, Cord Drapery
  patt. 325
Tumbler, iced tea or lemonade, Cactus
  patt., Greentown (ILLUS.) 60
Tumbler, Leaf Bracket patt., Greentown 75

CONSOLIDATED

Consolidated Martelé Label

The Consolidated Lamp and Glass Company of Coraopolis, Pennsylvania was founded in 1894 and for a number of years was noted for its lighting wares but also produced popular lines of pressed and blown tablewares. Highly collectible glass patterns of this early era include the Cone, Cosmos, Florette and Guttate lines.

Lamps and shades continued to be good sellers but in 1926 a new "art" line of molded decorative wares was introduced. This "Martelé" line was developed as a direct imitation of the fine glasswares being produced by René Lalique of France and many Consolidated patterns resembled their French counterparts. Other popular lines produced during the 1920s and 1930s were "Dancing Nymph," the delightfully Art Deco "Ruba Rombic," introduced in 1928, and the "Catalonian" line, imitating 17th century Spanish glass, which debuted in 1927.

Although the factory closed in 1933, it was reopened under new management in 1936 and prospered through the 1940s. It finally closed in 1967. Collectors should note that many later Consolidated patterns closely resemble wares of other competing firms, especially the Phoenix Glass Company. Careful study is needed to determine the maker of pieces from the 1920-40 era.

A recent book which will be of help to collectors is Phoenix & Consolidated Art Glass, 1926-1980, by Jack D. Wilson (Antique Publications, 1989).

CONE

Cone Syrup Pitcher

Cruet w/original stopper, yellow satin $250
Sugar shaker w/original lid, green opaque 165
Syrup pitcher w/original top, cased pink
  (ILLUS.) 375

COSMOS

Cosmos Butter Dish

Butter dish, cov., blue band decoration
  (ILLUS.). .... **225 to 250**
Syrup pitcher w/original top, pink band
  decoration. 248
Tumbler, pink band decoration. 65

FLORETTE
Syrup pitcher w/original top, pink satin 450
Toothpick holder, blue opaque satin. 110

GUTTATE

Guttate Cased Pink Pitcher

Pitcher, 9½" h., cased pink, glossy finish
  (ILLUS.) 325
Salt & pepper shakers, green & blue, pr. 40
Syrup pitcher w/original lid, pink cased,
  applied clear handle, tall. 285

LATER LINES

Ruba Rombic Bowl

Bowl, 8 x 9", 3½" h., Ruba Rombic patt., oblong w/closed rim, jade green w/slight opalescence, minor rim nick, ca. 1928 (ILLUS.). . . . . **800 to 900**

Candlesticks, Ruba Rombic patt., smoky topaz, pr. **595**

Creamer & open sugar bowl, Ruba Rombic patt., topaz, 2⅛" & 3½" h., pr. (minor neck on both rims) **1,265**

Dinner set: six each of goblets, sherbets, 8½" d. plates & one 12" d. plate; Five Fruits patt.each w/molded fruit design & overall purple wash, ca. 1930, the set (mold imperfections, slight wear to wash) **230**

Ruba Rombic Dresser Set

Dresser set: multifaceted oblong tray, a large toilet bottle w/stopper & smaller perfume bottle w/stopper; Ruba Rombic patt., lavender finish cased over colorless, tray 10½ x 11½", toilet bottle 7¾" h., the set (ILLUS.). **5,750**

Lamp, table model, Dogwood patt., Martelé line, brass fittings, baluster-form, tan **125**

Vase, 6" h., Screech Owls patt., Martelé line, brown decoration on a milk white ground **90**

Vase, 6" h., Screech Owls patt., Martelé line, brown owls on green reeds against a custard satin ground. **115**

Vase, 6" h., 4" d., Dragonfly patt., Martelé line, ovoid w/wide mouth, blue on white satin ground **115**

Vase, 6" h., 4" d., Dragonfly patt., Martelé line, ovoid w/wide mouth, green & brown on white satin ground **80**

Vase, 6¼" h., Peonies patt., Martelé line, pink, green & brown on milk white ground **80**

Vase, 6½" h., Chickadee patt., wide flattened ovoid form w/rectangular mouth, brick red birds on green leafy branches against a custard ground **144**

Vase, 6½" h., Jonquil patt., slender ovoid body w/flaring mouth, deep rose peach blossoms w/green stems on a creamy custard satin ground (ILLUS.) **115**

Vase, 10" h., Poppy patt., wide ovoid body w/wide low flared rim, decorated w/red poppies on custard ground. **275**

 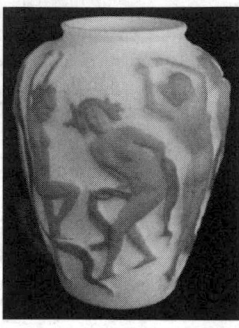

*From left: Consolidated "Jonquil" Vase
Consolidated "Dancing Girls" Vase*

Vase, 11" h., Dogwood patt., dark rosy peach petals on greenish tan stems on a creamy custard ground **403**

Vase, 11" h., pillow-type, Sea Gulls patt., blue ground **595**

Vase, 11½" h., Dancing Girls patt., tall ovoid body, girls & Pan relief-molded & colored in deep rose & tan on a creamy custard ground (ILLUS.) **518**

CORALENE

Coralene is a method of decorating glass, usually satin glass, with the use of beaded-type decoration customarily applied to the glass with the use of enamels, which were melted. Coralene decoration has been faked with the use of glue.

Basket, cased pink mother-of-pearl satin Diamond Quilted patt. w/fine yellow coralene beading, applied frosted clear loop thorn handle (small heat check under one foot) **$650**

Bowl, 8¼" d., footed deep rolled sides, cased satin w/a deep rose shading to white interior w/an applied crimped amber rim & interior decoration of a band of coralene beaded blue flowers & green leaves, white exterior, signed by Thomas Webb **385**

Ewer, bulbous body tapering to a tall slender cylindrical neck w/an upright arched spout, shaded lavender satin body & applied frosted lavender handle, body decorated overall w/yellow "seaweed" coralene beading, 8½" h. **248**

Ewer, ovoid body w/a thin neck & tricorner rim, decorated w/coralene beaded leaves & flowers, white enamel trim, round applied foot, applied strap crystal handle, 16¼" h. **920**

Pitcher, 6½" h., bulbous body w/tricorner mouth, pink & white "seaweed" coralene beading, rose interior, applied amber handle **495**

Powder box, cov., decorated overall w/coralene beaded green leaves w/gold & white water lilies 165

Rose bowl, squatty bulbous shaded pink mother-of-pearl satin Snowflake patt. bowl w/8-crimp rim, decorated w/yellow "wheat" design coralene beading, raised on applied frosted clear slender feet, 5" d., 3¾" h. 695

Tumbler, shaded deep pink to white satin ground decorated w/yellow "seaweed" coralene beading, 3¾" h. 358

Tumbler, cylindrical, pink shaded satin Diamond Quilted patt. decorated w/yellow "seaweed" coralene beading, 3⅞" h. 143

Tumbler, swelled cylindrical body on a foot, amber w/applied rigaree band above the foot & decorated w/a colored coralene floral design, base marked "Patent," Thomas Webb & Son, England, 5" h. 66

From left: Small Amber Coralene Vase Satin Glass Coralene Vase

Vase, 3½" h., 2¼" d., flaring cylindrical body w/angled shoulder to a cupped rim, honey amber w/green & white coralene leaves around the neck & multicolored coralene flowers & leaves around the body (ILLUS.) 135

Vase, 3⅞" h., footed spherical body w/a short, wide cylindrical neck, shaded blue to white satin ground decorated overall w/yellow "seaweed" coralene beading, 19th c. 193

Vase, 4" h., footed spherical body w/a wide short cylindrical neck, shaded red to white mother-of-pearl satin Diamond Quilted patt., decorated overall w/yellow "seaweed" coralene beading, 19th c. 320

Vase, 4¼" h., ovoid body tapering to a short, slightly flared cylindrical neck, shaded orange to white mother-of-pearl Diamond Quilted patt., decorated overall w/scattered blue florette coralene decoration, signed "Webb," late 19th c. 358

Vase, 5½" h., wide cylindrical body w/rounded edges & a short neck w/a widely flaring flattened & crimped rim, shaded blue mother-of-pearl satin Diamond Quilted patt., overall orange "seaweed" coralene beading, 19th c. 275

Vase, 6" h., 7" w., large spherical fiery opalescent body w/wide flat mouth, decorated w/a wide swirled red band & overall colored coralene beaded decoration of a large pear on twigs w/green leaves, on four curved applied amber branch legs, two continuing up the sides to form thorn bands, 19th c. **1,265**

Vase, 7½" h., bulbous ovoid body w/a short flaring flat neck, yellow mother-of-pearl satin Herringbone patt. decorated w/an overall beaded fern leaf decoration, white lining (ILLUS.) **1,055**

Vase, 8½" h., simple ovoid body w/a small mouth, yellow shaded to pale pink cased satin exterior decorated w/an overall diamond & cross yellow beaded coralene design, gold rim, opal white lining (slight bead loss) 173

CRANBERRY

Gold was added to glass batches to give this glass its color on reheating. It has been made by numerous glasshouses for years and is currently being reproduced. Both blown and molded articles were produced. A less expensive type of cranberry was made with the substitution of copper for gold.

Cranberry Glass Box

Bowl, 8" d., 4½" h., deep flaring four-lobed form w/clear applied wishbone feet & clear applied drops around the rim, the interior enameled w/blue, pink, yellow & white flowers......................... $175

Box, cov., round optic-ribbed base w/wide neck ring w/applied clear shell rigaree, the inset domed cover w/applied clear flame finial, 6" d., 6" h. (ILLUS.) 210

Celery vase, w/floral enamel decoration, attributed to Mt. Washington 250

Claret jug, cov., tall tapering cylindrical body w/overall fine exterior threading, wide brass collar w/rim spout & flat hinged cover, long pointed angled handle down the side, 5" d., 9½" h. 225

From left: Decorated Cranberry Decanter
Cranberry-flashed Decorated Perfume

Decanter w/clear facet-cut stopper, flared
cylindrical body w/rounded shoulder &
slender cylindrical neck w/flattened, flared
rim, wide optic rib design, the shoulder
decorated w/a wide gold band & white
enamel dots, 2⅞" d., 8⅝" h. (ILLUS.). 135

Dresser box w/hinged cover, cylindrical
w/flat top & brass fittings, ring handles &
footed ring base, the top decorated w/an
ornate white enamel floral cluster & bird,
a delicate band of white enamel florals
around the sides, late 19th c., 4" h. 242

Perfume bottle w/clear teardrop stopper,
cranberry flashed on clear, footed wide
ovoid body tapering to a tiny cylindrical
neck, ornate gilt & white panels & scrolls
around the shoulder, Europe, ca. 1940s,
6¼" h. (ILLUS.). 95

From left: Gilt-decorated Cranberry Perfume
Cranberry Optic-Ribbed Pitcher

Perfume bottle w/facet-cut clear stopper,
cylindrical body w/rounded shoulder &
short cylindrical neck w/flared rim, the
body decorated w/a wide band of
squiggle-work between lines, gold
trimmed rim, 1¾" d., 4½" h. (ILLUS.) 135

Pitcher, footed wide ovoid optic-ribbed body
w/a wide cylindrical neck & pinched
spout, applied clear reeded handle,
4½" d., 7½" h. (ILLUS.). 135

Sugar shaker w/metal lid, bulbous base. 195
Sugar shaker w/metal lid, Parian mold. 295
Sugar shaker w/metal lid, ring neck, mold,
optic rib design 195
Sugar shaker w/metal lid, Venetian
Diamond patt.. 195

CROWN MILANO

Printed Crown Milano Mark

This glass, produced by Mt. Washington
Glass Company late last century, is opal glass
decorated by painting and enameling. It appears
identical to a ware termed Albertine, also made
by Mt. Washington.

Cracker jar, cov., squatty bulbous tapering
body in opal w/a mottled peach & yellow
ground ornately decorated w/gilt
enameled florals, silver plate ruffled rim,
inset domed cover & twisted bail handle,
cover marked "M.W. 441 9/c". **$863**

Cracker jar, cov., barrel-shaped creamy
white body decorated w/ornate florals &
gold enamel scroll band, base w/"CM"
mark, silver plate rim, cover & bail handle
marked "MW 4404," late 19th c., 6¾" h. 748

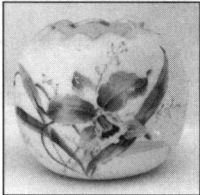

From left: Crown Milano Rose Bowl with Orchid
Crown Milano Rose Bowl with Asters

Rose bowl, eight-crimp rim, pale blue
shaded to white satin ground, h.p.
shaded maroon orchid w/long green &
yellow leaves, unsigned, 4" d.
(ILLUS.). . . . . 250 to 300

Rose bowl, eight-crimp rim, shaded soft
yellow ground enameled w/large yellow
& small white asters on pale green &
brown leafy stems, unsigned, 5" d.
(ILLUS.). . . . . 300 to 350

Vase, 9½" h., bulbed satin white body
w/flared elongated neck split at rim in four
decorative points, delicate pink blossoms
w/gold leaves & tracery overall, base
marked "(Crown)CM" in purple. 863

Rare "Albertine" Crown Milino Vase

Vase, 12¼" h., bulbous ovoid body tapering to a short flared neck flanked by three small loop handles, decorated w/Egyptian landscape scenes w/an Arab man w/camel & on the reverse a scene of riders & camels in front of pyramids, elaborate gilt borders of Mideastern scroll designs, marked "Albertine" on base, gilt wear (ILLUS.) **6,900**

Vase, 12¼" h., satin finish on creamy white bulbous body w/graceful elongated neck, decorated by beaded gold & bronze shaded rose blossoms, buds, & thorny branches, purple crown "CM" mark over "565" on base **920**

CRUETS

From left: Decorated Amber Cruet
Cobalt Blue Decorated Cruet

Amber, mold-blown footed paneled barrel-form w/short neck & arched spout, applied amber handle & ovoid ringed stopper, decorated w/enameled flowers & leaves in white, pink, yellow & green, 3½" d., 8¾" h. (ILLUS.) **$165**

Blue, mold-blown optic ribbed bulbous ovoid body tapering to a slender neck w/tricorner rim, the sides enameled w/clusters of small white dotted blossoms, original clear facet-cut stopper, 7½" h **86**

Blue, pressed glass, Bellaire patt. **95**

Cobalt blue, footed mold-blown form w/swirled rib design on the bulbous tapering body & tall cupped rim, applied blue handle, the sides boldly decorated w/large white flowers w/yellow centers & white leaves, all w/a beaded finish, late 19th c., 5" h., pr. (ILLUS. of one) **290**

Green Cruet with Gold Flowers

Lime green, mold-blown ovoid body tapering to a tall cylindrical neck w/curved spout, applied green handle & large green bubble stopper, the sides decorated w/large gold blossoms & leaves trimmed in black & white, 3¼" d., 8¾" h. (ILLUS.) **135**

CUP PLATES

Produced in numerous patterns beginning over 170 years ago, these little plates were designed to hold a cup while the tea or coffee was allowed to cool in a saucer. Cup plates were also made of ceramics. Where numbers are listed below, they refer to numbers assigned these plates in the book, American Glass Cup Plates, *by Ruth Webb Lee and James H. Rose. Plates are of clear glass unless otherwise noted. A number of cup plates have been reproduced. Also see* CUP PLATES *under Ceramics.*

L & R-128, round, central large eight-point star w/bull's-eyes alternating w/diamonds, band of half-round shells within rope border, clear, 3⁵⁄₁₆" d. (three scallops missing) **$55**

L & R-130, round, four pointed leaf cluster in center on diamond point ground, small pointed leaves rayed around the border within small knob rim band, clear, 3⁷⁄₁₆" d. (mold roughness, two scallops tipped) **121**

L & R-167B, round, plain concentric rings, smooth rim, clear, 3" d. (light mold roughness) **132**

L & R-197C, round, central blossomhead surrounded by delicate band of blossoms & leaves, looped arch border band, violet blue (very shallow large rim chip & underfill) .. **132**

L & R-250A, round, central six-point diamond point star surrounded by panels of criss-cross design, outer border of rounded pod-like devices (three tipped scallops) 33

L & R-253, round. Roman Rosette patt., bluish green, 3½" d. 77

L & R-253, round, Roman Rosette patt., light bluish green (few scallops missing or tipped) 138

L & R-262, round, four-point central cross alternating w/four heart-form double scrolls, outer border of alternating quatrefoils & fleur-de-lis, dark blue, 3¼" d. (tiny rim spall, few tipped scallops) 330

Scrolls & Quatrefoils Cup Plates

L & R-262, round, four-point central star alternating w/heart-form double scrolls, border of alternating quatrefoils & fleur-de-lis, dark cobalt blue, eight scallops tipped (ILLUS. right) 143

L & R-262, round, four-point central star alternating w/heart-form double scrolls, border of alternating quatrefoils & fleur-de-lis, greyish blue, few scallops tipped (ILLUS. left) 715

L & R-277, round, large central three-arm cross alternating w/diamonds, leaf sprig & scroll border, peacock blue (small refracting line, light mold roughness) 770

L & R-279, round, large multi-petaled central blossomhead, narrow border bands, lavender (usual mold roughness).......... 413

L & R-279, round w/scalloped rim, a large multi-petaled central blossom, simple outer band decor, light green, 2⅞" d. (light mold roughness) 176

L & R-311, round, simple six-petal star surrounded by bull's-eyes in the center, band of diamonds in the border, deep opal opaque (mold roughness, few tipped scallops) 176

L & R-37, round, large eight pointed-petal central blossom alternating w/tiny blossoms in center, diamond point inner band & palmette scalloped outer border, opaque white (mold roughness)........... 990

L & R-37 round w/scalloped rim, center eight-petal large blossom alternating w/tiny blossoms, inner diamond point band & palmette outer border, fiery opalescent, 3¼" d. (moderately heavy mold roughness, chip on back rim) 154

L & R-388, round, simple eight-petal central blossom, diamond point outer border, opaque white w/amber flashing (mold roughness) 418

L & R-390 variant, round, smooth rim, Sunburst patt. center, diamond point border band, medium blue (light mold roughness)....................... 165

L & R-412, ten-sided, open five-point star in center, plain rim, peacock green (several chips & flakes on rim)................... 715

L & R-440B, round, Valentine patt., lyre border, deep blue, 3½" d. (two scalloped tipped, mold roughness)................. 165

L & R-440b, round, Valentine patt., lyre border, greyish blue, 3½" d. (small rim spall, few scallops tipped) 110

L & R-440B, round, Valentine patt., lyre border, medium blue, few scallops tipped, mold roughness (ILLUS. with L & R-522)..... 176

Heart Pattern Cup Plate

L & R-459D, round, Heart patt., loop & dart center, brilliant emerald green, one & one-half scallops chipped, some others tipped (ILLUS.) 605

L & R-502, round, Sunburst center patt., plain border, light green 138

L & R-508, round, starburst center, plain border, peacock blue, 3" d. (mold roughness, one scallop tipped) 176

Two Scarce Colored Cup Plates

L & R-522, round, Sunburst patt., plain border, deep reddish amber, two scallops tipped (ILLUS. left) 275

L & R-523, round, Sunburst center patt., plain rim, light olive green (one scallop missing, six tipped).................... 121

L & R-524, round, Sunburst center design, plain border, blue (light mold roughness)..... 198

L & R-530, round, Sunburst patt., amethyst (four scallops missing, few tipped) 154

L & R-531, round, bull's-eye & sunburst center design, plain border, knobby rim, light green (few tipped scallops) **132**

L & R-571, round, Queen Victoria design, central small bust of queen w/"Victoria" above, outer border w/a crown at the top & flowering vines around the sides (mold roughness) **44**

L & R-610A, round, sailing ship center scene framed by rope band within lacy scrolls, looping scroll outer border, deep blue, 3½" d. (three scallops tipped, mold roughness) **198**

L & R-612A, octagonal, steamship center design, scroll & shield border, clear, 3½" d. (mold roughness, few scallops chipped) **110**

L & R-686, round, Harp patt., harp. long leafy branches & a star in center, delicate meandering vine outer border, clear (mold roughness) **66**

L & R-80, round, tight ring of hearts in center, leafy undulating vine band & other swirled leaf sprig band, plain rim, light opal, 3¾" d. **358**

L & R-88, round, small florals around border band, concentric rings in center, opal, 3¾" d. (area of underfill, few minor rim flakes) **385**

CUSTARD

Northwood

Northwood Script Mark

This ware takes its name from its color and is a variant of milk white glass. It was produced largely between 1890 and 1915 by the Northwood Glass Co., Heisey Glass Company, Fenton Art Glass Co., Jefferson Glass Co., and a few others. There are 21 major patterns and a number of minor ones. The prime patterns are considered Argonaut Shell, Chrysanthemum Sprig, Inverted Fan and Feather, Louis XV and Winged Scroll. Most custard glass patterns are enhanced with gold and some have additional enameled decoration or stained highlights. Unless otherwise noted, items in this listing are fully decorated.

For an expanded listing of Custard Glass see Antique Trader Books American & European Decorative & Art Glass.

ARGONAUT SHELL (Northwood)

Berry set, master bowl & 6 sauce dishes, 7 pcs. **$575**
Butter dish, cov., decorated **395**
Compote, jelly, 5" d., 5" h. **132**
Cruet w/original stopper . . . . **850 to 895**

Argonaut Shell Pitcher

Pitcher, water (ILLUS.) . . . . **400 to 495**
Salt & pepper shakers w/original tops, pr . . . . **325 to 350**
Sauce dish, gold trim, decorated **65**
Sugar bowl, cov. **204**
Table set: cov. butter dish, cov. sugar bowl, creamer & spooner; 4 pcs. **550**
Toothpick holder **365**
Tumbler **110**
Water set, pitcher & 6 tumblers, 7 pcs. **900**

BEADED CIRCLE (Northwood)

Beaded Circle Jelly Compote

Berry set, master bowl & 5 sauce dishes, 6 pcs. **495**
Bowl, master berry or fruit **185**
Compote, jelly (ILLUS.) **350**
Salt & pepper shakers w/original tops, pr. **255**
Sauce dish **55**
Water set, pitcher & 4 tumblers, 5 pcs. **850**

BEADED SWAG (Heisey)

Beaded Swag Pickle Dish

Pickle dish (ILLUS.) **250**
Spooner . . . . **40 to 60**
Toothpick holder, ruby-stained **45**
Wine, w/advertising **75**

CHERRY & SCALE OR FENTONIA (Fenton)

Cherry & Scale Sugar Bowl

Berry set, master bowl & 4 sauce dishes,
  5 pcs. 280
Butter dish, cov.. 235
Creamer 95
Cruet w/original stopper, decorated. 120
Pitcher, water 325
Sugar bowl, cov. (ILLUS.) 125
Tumbler 75
Water set, pitcher & 6 tumblers, 7 pcs. 600

CHRYSANTHEMUM SPRIG (Northwood's Pagoda)

Chrysanthemum Sprig Celery Vase

Berry set, master bowl & 4 sauce dishes,
  5 pcs. 375
Bowl, master berry or fruit, 10½" oval,
  decorated . . . . 200 to 225
Celery vase (ILLUS.) 755
Compote, jelly 40
Condiment set, four-footed tray, salt &
  pepper shakers w/original tops, &
  toothpick holder, 4 pcs. 945
Pitcher, water, decorated 476
Pitcher, water, undecorated 225
Sauce dishes, oval, gold trim & paint,
  set of 6 250
Sugar bowl, cov., decorated 220
Sugar bowl, cov., undecorated. . . . . 150 to 180
Table set, cov. sugar bowl, creamer, cov.
  butter dish & spooner, 4 pcs. 705
Toothpick holder, gold trim & paint, signed 283
Tumbler 91
Water set, pitcher & 6 tumblers, 7 pcs. 725

DIAMOND WITH PEG (Jefferson)

Diamond with Peg Master Berry Bowl

Berry set, master bowl & 6 sauce dishes,
  7 pcs. 600
Bowl, master berry or fruit (ILLUS.) 225
Butter dish, cov.. 265
Creamer, individual size, souvenir 45
Mug, rose decoration 45
Napkin ring,. souvenir 145
Pitcher, tankard 375
Pitcher, tankard (wear on gold) 200
Punch cup 60
Salt & pepper shakers w/original tops,
  souvenir, pr. 90
Sauce dish 35
Sugar bowl, cov., souvenir. 105
Sugar bowl, open. 95
Tunbler, souvenir 39
Vase, 6" h., souvenir. 50
Vase, 8" h.. 85
Water set, pitcher & 6 tumblers, 7 pcs.. . . 475 to 525
Whiskey shot glass. 45
Wine 38

EVERGLADES OR CARNELIAN (Northwood)

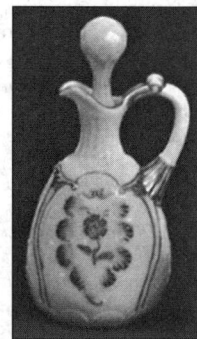

Everglades Cruet

Berry set, master bowl & 6 sauce dishes,
  7 pcs. 725
Butter dish, cov.. 370
Cruet w/original stopper (ILLUS.) 275
Pitcher, water 650
Salt & pepper shakers w/original tops, pr. 450
Salt shaker w/original top. 150

FAN (Dugan)

Fan Sugar Bowl

Berry set, master bowl & 6 sauce dishes,
7 pcs. 395
Butter dish, cov. 215
Ice cream set, master bowl & 6 individual
ice cream dishes, 7 pcs. 500
Sugar bowl, cov. (ILLUS.) 95
Table set, cov. butter dish, cov. sugar bowl
& spooner, 3 pcs. .... 350 to 450
Tumblers, set of 6 400
Water set, pitcher & 6 tumblers, 7 pcs.... 550 to 650

FLUTED SCROLLS OR KLONDYKE (Northwood)

Pitcher, water, footed 250
Salt & pepper shakers w/original tops, pr. 95
Salt shaker w/original top 40
Sauce dish 43
Sugar bowl, cov. 135
Tumbler 35
Water set, pitcher & 6 tumblers, 7 pcs. 475

GENEVA

Geneva Syrup Pitcher

Banana boat, four-footed, 11" oval .... 95 to 125
Berry set, oval master bowl & 6 sauce
dishes, 7 pcs. 318
Bowl, master berry or fruit, 8½" d.,
three-footed 135
Compote, jelly 75
Compote, jelly, green stain 45
Creamer .... 80 to 100
Cruet w/original stopper .... 250 to 350

Pitcher, water 223
Salt & pepper shakers w/original tops, pr. 241
Sauce dish, oval .... 38 to 47.50
Sauce dish, round 40
Sugar bowl, cov. .... 125 to 150
Syrup pitcher w/original top (ILLUS.) 275
Toothpick holder, decorated 125
Tumbler, decorated 38
Tumbler, w/green 38
Water set, pitcher & 6 tumblers, 7 pcs. 425

GEORGIA GEM OR LITTLE GEM (Tarentum)

Georgia Gem Tumbler

Berry set, master bowl & 6 sauce dishes,
7 pcs. 275
Bowl, master berry or fruit, decorated.... 100 to 125
Celery vase 132
Creamer & cov. sugar bowl, pr. 60
Pitcher, water, decorated 310
Salt & pepper shakers w/original tops, pr. 75
Tumbler (ILLUS.) 50
Water set, pitcher & 4 tumbler, 5 pcs. 435

GRAPE & GOTHIC ARCHES (Northwood)

Grape & Gothic Arches Spooner

Berry set, master bowl & 6 sauce dishes,
7 pcs. 550
Bowl, master berry or fruit 125
Creamer 90
Pitcher, water 285
Sauce dish 38
Spooner (ILLUS.) .... 50 to 75
Sugar bowl, cov. 195
Water set, pitcher & 6 tumblers, 7 pcs.... 550 to 650

INTAGLIO (Northwood)

Intaglio Large Fruit Compote

Bowl, fruit, 9" d., footed compote (ILLUS.) 325
Butter dish, gold & blue decor 196
Creamer & cov. sugar bowl, pr. 275
Cruet w/original stopper. 310
Pitcher, water 373
Salt & pepper shakers w/original tops, pr. 203
Sauce dish, green decoration 60
Spooner 105
Tumblers, blue & gold trim, set of 4 225
Water set, pitcher & 6 tumblers, blue & gold
    trim, 7 pcs. 475

INVERTED FAN & FEATHER (Northwood)

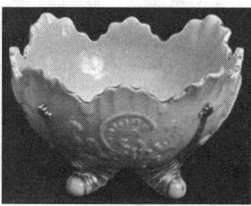

Inverted Fan & Feather Master Berry Bowl

Berry set, master bowl & 4 sauce dishes,
    5 pcs. 570
Bowl, master berry (ILLUS.) 303
Cruet w/original stopper. 865
Punch bowl, footed 2,500
Salt shaker w/original top. 168
Table set, cov. butter dish, creamer &
    spooner, 3 pcs. 695
Water set, pitcher & 6 tumblers, 7 pcs. 895

JACKSON OR FLUTED SCROLLS WITH FLOWER BAND (Northwood)

Jackson Creamer

Bowl, master berry or fruit 85
Creamer (ILLUS.) 85
Pitcher, water, undecorated 275
Salt & pepper shakers w/original tops, pr. 135
Salt shaker w/original top, undecorated. 58
Tumbler 44
Water set, pitcher & 4 tumblers, 5 pcs. . . . 365 to 385

LOUIS XV (Northwood)

Louis XV Sugar Bowl

Berry set, master bowl & 6 sauce dishes,
    7 pcs. . . . . 500 to 525
Bowl, master berry w/gold 295
Butter dish, cov.. 145
Creamer 78
Cruet w/original stopper. 450
Glove box, cov. 110
Pitcher, water 223
Salt shaker w/original top. 80
Sauce dish, 5" oval, w/gold trim. 35
Spooner 80
Sugar bowl, cov. (ILLUS.) 123
Table set, cov. butter, sugar, creamer,
    spooner, 4 pcs. 300
Tumbler 65
Water set, pitcher & 6 tumblers, 7 pcs. 800

MAPLE LEAF (Northwood)

Maple Leaf Cruet

Berry set, master bowl & 6 sauce dishes,
  7 pcs. 800
Bowl, master berry or fruit 265
Cruet w/original stopper (ILLUS.) 1,100
Salt & pepper shakers w/original tops, pr. 500
Table set, creamer, cov. buter dish &
  spooner, 3 pcs. 485
Water set, pitcher & 6 tumblers, 7 pcs. 750

NORTHWOOD GRAPE, GRAPE & CABLE OR GRAPE & THUMBPRINT

Northwood Grape Cracker Jar

Banana boat. 325
Berry set, master bowl & 6 sauce dishes,
  7 pcs. 300
Butter dish, cov. 250
Cologne bottle w/original stopper 538
Cracker jar, cov., two-handled (ILLUS.) 600
Creamer, nutmeg trim. 100
Dresser tray 300
Fernery, footed, 7½" d., 4½" h. 150
Hatpin holder 450
Nappy, two-handled 48
Pin dish 165
Pitcher, water. 385
Plate, 8" d. 55
Plate, 8" w., six-sided 65
Punch bowl & base, 2 pcs. 800
Spooner 135
Sugar bowl, cov. 150
Table set, cov. butter dish, cov. sugar bowl
  & creamer, 3 pcs. 475
Tumbler 47
Water set, pitcher & 6 tumblers, 7 pcs. 1,250

PRAYER RUG (Imperial)

Nappy, two-handled, ruffled, 6" d. 55
Plate, 7½" d. 60
Tumbler 80
Tumbler, nutmeg stain 70
Vase 50

PUNTY BAND (Heisey)

Salt & pepper shaker w/original tops,
  souvenir, pr. 80
Vase, 5½" h., souvenir 75
Wine, souvenir 50

RIBBED DRAPE (Jefferson)

Ribbed Drape Butter Dish

Butter dish, cov. (ILLUS.) 265
Cruet w/original stopper. 250
Salt & pepper shakers w/original tops, pr. 110
Table set, 4 pcs. (open sugar) 575
Toothpick holder. 95
Toothpick holder, rose decoration 273

RING BAND (Heisey)

Ring Band Creamer

Bowl, master berry or fruit, decorated 278
Celery Vase 300
Condiment set, condiment tray, jelly
  compote, toothpick holder & salt &
  pepper shakers, 5 pcs. 429
Creamer (ILLUS.) 80
Creamer & cov. sugar bowl, pr. 235
Cruet w/original stopper. 300
Pitcher, water, enameled floral decoration. 450
Salt & pepper shakers w/original tops, pr. 100
Salt & pepper shakers w/original tops,
  souvenir, pr. 115
Table set, 4 pcs. 523
Water set, pitcher & 6 tumblers, 7 pcs. 550
Whimsey, hat shape (from tumbler mold) 295

VICTORIA (Tarentum)

Victoria Water Pitcher

Berry set, master bowl & 6 sauce dishes,
    undecorated, 7 pcs. **275**
Berry set, master bowl & 6 sauce dishes,
    undecorated, green, 7 pcs.. . . . . **395**
Bowl, master berry or fruit **165**
Creamer **85**
Pitcher, water (ILLUS.). **275**
Sauce dish **50**
Sugar bowl, cov. **165**
Tumbler **60**

WINGED SCROLL (Heisey)

Winged Scroll Sugar Bowl

Berry set, master bowl & 6 sauce dishes,
    decorated, 7 pcs. **320**
Bowl, master berry **165**
Butter dish, cov. **167**
Creamer **91**
Pitcher, water, 9" h., bulbous **230**
Salt & pepper shakers w/original tops, pr. . . . **150**
Sugar bowl, cov., decorated (ILLUS.) **195**
Toothpick holder **129**
Tumbler **69**
Water set, tankard pitcher & 6 tumblers,
    7 pcs. **725**

MISCELLANEOUS PATTERNS

DELAWARE

Delaware Sauce Dish

Bowl, 5½" (hat-shaped) **45**
Sauce dish, w/blue decoration **45**
Sauce dish, w/rose stain (ILLUS.) . . . . **40 to 65**

HEART WITH THUMBPRINT

Creamer **40**
Creamer & sugar bowl, individual size, pr. **125**
Finger lamp, w/green decoration **263**

Heart with Thumbprint Wine

Sugar bowl, open, individual size, w/green
    decoration. **55**
Wine (ILLUS.) **125**

VERMONT

Vermont Card Basket

Card basket, 7½" d. (ILLUS.) **95**
Pickle tray **30**
Pitcher, w/blue trim & enameled decoration. **373**
Table set, cov. butter, creamer & spooner,
    3 pcs. **195**
Tumbler. . . . . **75 to 100**
Vase **25**

WILD BOUQUET

Cruet w/original stopper, undecorated. **300**
Sauce dish **50**

OTHER MISCELLANEOUS PIECES

Three Fruits Bowl

Bowl, master berry, Tiny Thumbprint patt. **259**
Bowl, 7¼" d., Three Fruits patt., ruffled rim,
    nutmeg stain (ILLUS.) **40**
Lamp, kerosene-type, Sunset patt. **270**

Lamp, kerosene, finger-type, greenish color w/embossed tulip design, applied handle complete w/burner & chimney, 3¾" to top of collar. **185**

Pitcher, tankard, Tiny Thumbprint patt. **369**

Salt & pepper shakers w/original tops, Tiny Thumbprint patt., pr. **225**

Sauce dish, Tiny Thumbprint patt. **59**

Spooner , Tiny Thumbprint patt. **129**

Sugar bowl, cov., Tiny Thumbprint patt. **165**

Tumbler, Royal Oak, patt. w/green stain **45**

CUT

Hawkes, Hoare, Libbey & Strauss Marks

Cut glass most eagerly sought by collectors is American glass produced during the so-called "Brilliant Period" from 1880 to about 1915. Pieces listed below are by type of article in alphabetical order.

BOTTLES

From left: Hawkes' Venetian Pattern Cologne Cologne with Hobstars & Prism Cuts

Cologne, Hawkes' Venetian patt., cut diamonds, fans & vesicas, facet-cut stopper, 3½" d., 6½" h. (ILLUS.). **345**

Cologne, hobstars alternating w/notched prisms, facet-cut stopper (ILLUS.) **350**

BOWLS

Clark's Jubilee Pattern Bowl

Clark's Jubilee patt., large hobstars alternating w/fans & diamonds around the rim above plain panels & almond cuts, 9½" d. (ILLUS.). **375**

Large Bowl Attributed to Dorflinger

Dorflinger-attributed, wide form w/pointed & arched notched rim, four large hobstars alternating w/small hobstars above fan-cut panels, hobstar in bottom,12" d. (ILLUS.) **575**

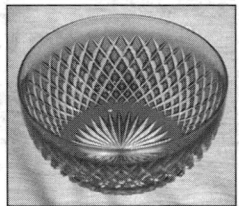

Dorflinger Ruby to Clear Finger Bowl

Finger bowl, Dorflinger, ruby cut to clear w/overall small diamonds, star-cut bottom, 5" d., 2½" h. (ILLUS.). **345**

Handled Long Hawkes' Centauri Bowl

Hawkes' Centauri patt., wide shallow flaring form w/notched loop end hanadles, cut across the center w/hobstars & fans w/large central hobstar, 12¾" l. (ILLUS.). **1,250**

Fine Hawkes' Kensington Bowl

Hawkes' Kensington patt., large hobstars above triangular panels w/smaller hobstars & buttons, scalloped & notched rims, 9" d. (ILLUS.) **1,000**

Rare Hawkes' Nautilus Bowl

Hawkes' Nautilus patt., three large zipper-cut shell forms alternating w/pointed arches & hobstars at the rim, 10" d. (ILLUS.) **3,250**

Footed Bowl with Hobstars

Hobstars, three large hobstars separated w/heavy cross banding w/smaller hobs & buttons, shallow wide bowl on three feet, 8" (ILLUS.) **175**

Cut Bowl with Sterling Silver Rim

Hobstars & diamonds, wide deep sides cut w/large hobstars alternating w/diamond & hobstar vesica panels, rolled & pierced applied Gorham sterling silver rim, 11" d., 4" h. (ILLUS.) **1,350**

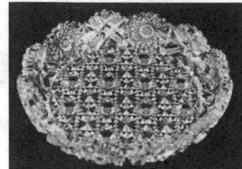

Hunt's Royal Pattern Bowl

Hunt's Royal patt., wide shallow form w/notched & scalloped rim, 8" d. (ILLUS.) **395**

Libbey's Florence Pattern Serving Bowl

Libbey's Florence patt., serving-type w/wide shallow unusual form w/upturned sides, two sides w/points & fans rims, large flashed hobstar in bottom, w., 3¼" h. (ILLUS.) **485**

BOXES

C.F. Monroe Cut Dresser Box

Dresser box, hinged cover, Hawkes signed, hobstars, crosshatching & fans, 6½" d. **395**

Dresser box, hinged glass cover, round flattened top & tapering cylindrical low sides cut w/hobstars alternating w/zipper cutting, C.F. Monroe Co., 6½" d., 4¼" h. (ILLUS.) **585**

Finely Cut Jewelry Box

Jewelry box, rectangular w/rounded corners, hinged flat top w/silver plate mountings, cut overall w/large hobstars alternating w/zipper-cut panels & fans (ILLUS.) **2,450**

CANDLESTICKS & CANDLEHOLDERS

*From left: Bergen's Colonial Pattern Candlestick
Hawkes-signed Candlesticks*

Bergen's Colonial patt., tall standard cut
w/paneled central stem flanked by facet-
cut knobs, hexagonal foot, paneled tulip-
form socket, 10¾" h., each (ILLUS.) **310**

Hawkes-signed, round disk foot w/a swelled
stem resting on a knob & cut w/plain
panels below bold diamond cuts, paneled
socket w/flattened rim, 10" h., pr. (ILLUS.). . . . **595**

Unusual Cut Glass Chamberstick

Hobstars, strawberry diamonds & fans,
chamberstick w/a round shallow dished
cut base w/scalloped & notched rim &
applied loop handle, plain tulip-form
socket w/metal insert, 5" d. (ILLUS.) **875**

CHAMPAGNES, CORDIALS, GOBLETS & WINES

*From left: Two Cut Glass Goblets
Dorflinger's No. 28 Champagne*

Clark's San Mateo patt., goblet, deep bowl
cut w/hobstars alternating w/blocked
diamonds, paneled zipper-cut stem,
5⅞" h. (ILLUS. left) **75**

Cross-cut diamonds, deep bowl w/overall
cutting, paneled zipper-cut stem, 6" h.
(ILLUS. right) **60**

Dorflinger's No. 28 patt., continental-style
flute champagne, tall tapering bowl cut
overall w/strawberry diamonds &
crosshatched diamonds w/fans around
the top, facet-cut knobbed stem on thick
cut disk foot (ILLUS.) **195**

*From left: Flutes & Diamonds Cut Wine
Russian Cut Goblet*

Hawkes' Flutes & Diamonds patt., wine,
ruby-flashed bowl cut w/rounded flutes
above overall diamonds, tapering
paneled & zipper-cut stem, 2¾" d., 4¾" h.
(ILLUS.) **320**

Russian cut, gobelts, knopped facet-cut
stem, Russian cut foot, set of 12
(ILLUS. of one) **2,200**

CREAMERS & SUGAR BOWLS

Hobstar-cut Creamer & Sugar Bowl

Hobstars & fans, low pedestal foot, notched
applied handles, 3¼" h., pr. (ILLUS.) **320**

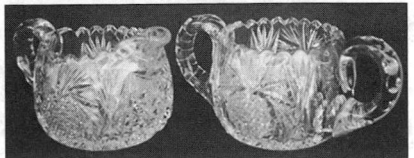

Heart Pattern Creamer & Sugar

Parsche's Heart patt., sides cut w/blaze-cut
heart, large hobstars under creamer
spout, notched applied handles, 3¼" h.,
pr. (ILLUS.) **350**

DECANTERS

From left: Columbia & Wheat Pattern Decanters
Clark's Orloff Pattern Decanter

Bergen's Columbia patt., applied foot, ovoid body w/diamond blocks & vesicas below the paneled zipper-cut neck w/flattened rim, facet-cut ball stopper, 12¼" h. (ILLUS. right) **895**

Clark's Orloff patt., squatty bulbous body w/large cut rings framed by ornate cutting, tall paneled neck & flattened rim, facet-cut ball stopper, 6¼" d., 11" h. (ILLUS.) **2,175**

Hoare's Wheat patt., spherical body w/swirled alternating cut panels below the tall facet-cut neck w/flaring flattened rim, facet-cut ball stopper, 12¼" h. (ILLUS. left) **1,450**

From left: Nicely Cut Handled Decanter
Ornately Cut Straus Decanter

Hobstars, cane, fans & strawberry diamonds, wide tapering shouldered body w/a short paneled & ringed neck, applied angled handle, facet-cut knob stopper, 9¼" h. (ILLUS.) **595**

Straus-signed, wide rounded body deeply cut w/hobstars in squares & cross-cut squares alternating w/rib-cut panels & fans, stepped shoulder & heavy cut ring below ring-cut neck w/silver rim & bulbous floral-embossed silver knob stopper, 11½" h. (ILLUS.) **1,610**

DISHES, MISCELLANEOUS

Straus-signed Cheese Dish

Cheese, cov., Straus-signed, tall octagonal cover cut w/diamonds & fans, flat top w/facet-cut knob, comforming dished base (ILLUS.) **895**

Cut Glass Mint Dish

Mint, shallow bowl on short pedestal base, hobstars alternating w/cane-cut almond-form panels, star-cut foot, 6" d., 4" h. (ILLUS.) **225**

Cut Individual Nut Dish

Nut, rectangular w/shallow upright sides, hobstar cut in the bottom, diamond-cut deeply notched sides, 2½ x 3¼" (ILLUS.) **25**

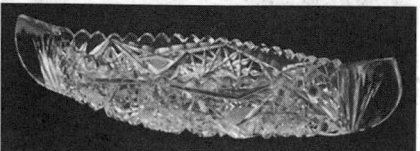

Canoe-shaped Cut Relish Dish

Relish, Pitkin & Brooks' Plaza patt., model of a canoe w/hobstars, triangles & fans around the sides, 3½ x 9" (ILLUS.) **240**

ICE TUBS & BUCKETS

Diamond-cut Ice Bucket

Diamonds & fans, footed swelled cylindrical
form cut w/large diamonds alternating
w/fans around the scalloped & notched
rim, facet-cut applied handles, 5" h.
(ILLUS.) **385**

Hawkes' Chrysanthemum Ice Bucket

Hawkes' Chrysanthemum patt., deep
rounded form cut w/large hobstars &
cane & cross-hatch cut petals, silver rim
band & bail handle, 6½" d. (ILLUS.) **545**

Straus Cut Ice Bucket

Straus-signed, widely flaring bowl w/tab
handles & scalloped fan-cut rim above
diamonds w/hobstars alternating
w/zipper-cut bands, 10¾" d. (ILLUS.) **795**

KNIFE RESTS

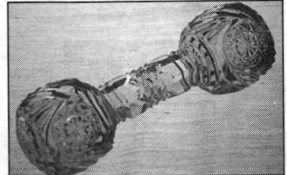

Hobstar & Fan-cut Knife Rest

Barbell-shaped, cut w/hobstar rings &
swirled fans, 5¼" l. (ILLUS.) **115**

Prism & Strawberry Diamond Rest

Barbell-shaped, notched center ring,
notched prism & strawberry diamond
cutting, 5" l. (ILLUS.) **170**

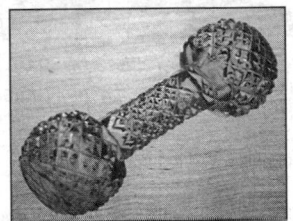

Strawberry Diamond-cut Knife Rest

Barbell-shaped, overall strawberry diamond
cutting, 4¼" l. (ILLUS.) **80**

LAMPS

Boudoir lamp, a clear domed shade cut
w/strawberry diamond & an outer
vertically ribbed band, a large domed
hobstar at the top center, raised on a
slender waisted faceted standard on a
domed foot w/a strawberry diamond band
around an outer vertically ribbed band, in
the Hawkes - Sinclaire manner, silvered
metal two-socket electrical fittings, early
20th c., overall 13½" h. **690**

Table, 11½" d. domed & pointed shade cut
w/large Hobstars alternating w/fan-cut
panels, on a ring suspending cut prisms,
raised on a tall slender baluster-form
base cut around the top w/Hobstars
alternating w/fan cutting over long cut
panels & a domed foot w/further bands of
Hobstar & fan cutting, electrified, overall
29½" h. (minor chips) **3,680**

Table, a 12" d. pointed deep domical
shaped cut & etched w/swirled leaves &
daises on a shade ring hung w/spearpoint
prisms, raised on a baluster-form base
w/a matching design & scalloped
sawtooth rim, overall 25" h. **1,150**

Table, Clark's El Tova patt., mushroom
shade cut w/large hobstars & narrow
almond panels, shade ring suspending
facet-cut prisms, baluster-form matching
base w/domed foot, two-light electric
fitting, 20" h. (ILLUS.) **4,850**

From left: El Tova Pattern Lamp by Clark
Lamp with Pointed Domed Shade

Table, pointed domical shade cut w/wide cane panels & diamond point vesicas, panel-cut lower rim on metal ring, raised on a trumpet-form matching base, chips to base, w/prisms, 27" h. (ILLUS.) **1,150**

Tall Cut Lamp with Hobstars

Table, teardrop-form shade cut w/zipper bands at the top above large hobstars alternating w/spearpoint panels, fitted into matching all-glass electrified base, 16" h. (ILLUS.) **3,450**

MISCELLANEOUS

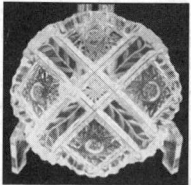

From left: Hobstar & Vine Butter Pat
Unusual Cut Glass Door Knob

Bell, panel-cut shoulder, emerald green w/clear facet-cut stem & knob, probably Hawkes. **295**
Butter pat, round w/scalloped & notched rim, four hobstars divided by a wide cross engraved w/leafy vines, 2¼" d. (ILLUS.) **35**
Door knobs, round, florette-style cut design w/small center hobstars & pointed fans, on brass shank, ca. 1900, pr. (ILLUS. of one) **880**

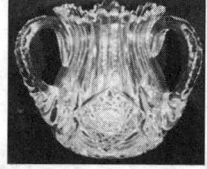

Loving Cup Cut with Hobstars

Loving cup, ovoid body tapering to flaring notched & scalloped rim, three applied facet-cut handles, large hobstars below the zipper-cut neck, 5" h. (ILLUS.) **495**

Mercedes Pattern Rose Bowl by Clark

Rose bowl, Clark's Mercedes patt., wide squatty bulbous form tapering to scalloped & notched mouth, cut w/large hobstars below swags of small hobstars & fans (ILLUS.) **1,850**

Cut Glass Salt Dip

Salt dip, deep round form cut w/diamond panels, 1¼" d. (ILLUS.) **35**

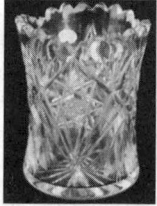

Cut Glass Spooner with Hobstars

Spooner, slightly waisted cylindrical form
w/notched & lightly scalloped rim, cut
w/hobstars, fans & single stars,
3¼" d., 4¼" h. (ILLUS.)................... **70**

Sugar shaker, breakfast, Strawberry &
Diamond patt........................ **165**

NAPPIES

Prism Pattern by Bergen Nappy

Bergen's Prism patt., low cylindrical sides
& wide flat bottom, large hobstar in
bottom, notched applied ring handle,
5¾" d. (ILLUS.)....................... **145**

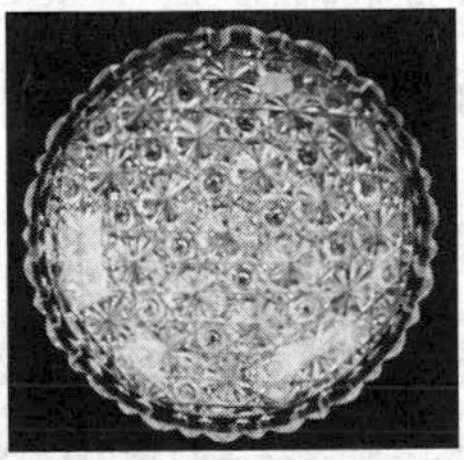

Russian Pattern Nappy

Russian patt., shallow round form
w/upturned notched rim, 6" d. (ILLUS.) **115**

PITCHERS

*From left: Easter Pattern Pitcher by Hawkes
Pitcher Cut with Hobstar Bands*

Tankard, cut w/large hobstars alternating
w/fanned rays, applied notched handle,
9½" h................................ **144**

Tankard, Hawkes' Easter patt., tall tapering
cylindrical form w/small rim spout, applied
notched handle, cut w/narrow stripes of
small hobstars & starbursts alternating
wstripes of small diamonds & plain
bands, 12" h. (ILLUS.)................. **1,150**

Tankard, slightly tapering body gently flared
at the notched rim, cut w/large hobstars
in diamond reserverse altnerating w/large
fan-cut panels, applied notched handle,
11½" h................................ **805**

Tankard, tall tapering cylindrical form w/a
high arched spout, applied notched
handle, cut w/long graduated bands of
hobstars alternating w/almond-shaped
cane & starburst panels, 14" h. (ILLUS.).... **1,350**

PLATES

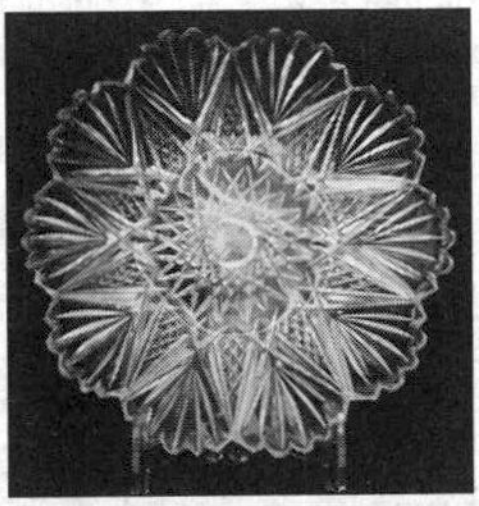

Fans & Hobstar Plate

Fans & hobstar, scalloped & notched rim
w/large fans surrounding spearpoints & a
central large hobstar, 7" d. (ILLUS.)......... **175**

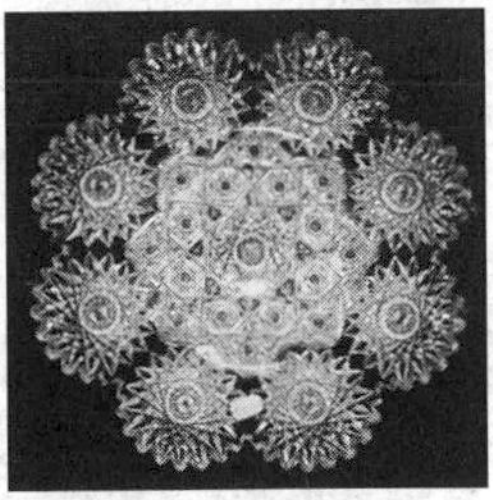

Festoon Variation Plate

Festoon Variantion patt., eight large
hobstar scallops around the border
centering clusters of small hobstars w/a
larger center hobstar, 7" d. (ILLUS.)........ **450**

New Panel Pattern Plate by Hawkes

Hawkes' New Panel patt., a narrow border
band of small stars, ring of cut bars
around central starburst, signed, 7" d.
(ILLUS.) **125**

Colonna Pattern Plate by Libbey

Libbey's Colonna patt., squared notched rim, florette design w/panels of hobstars, signed, 7" d. (ILLUS.) **185**

Middlesex Variation Pattern Plate

Middlesex Variation patt., notched rim w/fans alternating w/notched diamonds enclosing hobstars, large starburst in center, 7" d. (ILLUS.) **125**

TRAYS

Ice Cream Tray with Hobstars

Ice cream, rectangular w/scalloped & notched rim, large hobstars at ends w/panels of hobstars & fans cut around the center, 14" l. (ILLUS.) **950**

Rex Variation Ice Cream Tray

Ice cream, Rex Variation patt., almond-shaped w/pointed ends, scalloped & notched rim w/outer border of hobstars around large central blossom-form starburst, 18" l. (ILLUS.) **2,950**

Large Tray with Hobstars & Cane

Serving, round w/notched rim w/scallops & points, large hobstars alternating w/six points & panels of fine cane cutting, six point star in center, 14" d. (ILLUS.) **2,850**

TUMBLERS

*From left: Star & Diamond Tumbler by Clark
Double-Shot Tumbler with Hobstars*

Clark's Star & Diamond patt., large block-cut diamonds w/fan-cut borders, 3" d., 4" h. (ILLUS.). **65**
Hobstars & fans, double-shot size, cylindrical, 2¼" d., 2½" h. (ILLUS.). **45**

*From left: Jewel Pattern Tumbler by Libbey
New Brilliant Pattern Shot Glass*

Libbey's Jewel patt., slightly flared cylindrical form cut w/hobstars below fans alternating w/cut spearpoints, signed, 3" d., 3¾" h. (ILLUS.) **60**

Libbey's New Brilliant patt., shot-size, slightly flaring cylindrical form w/arched fans over hobstars alternating w/zipper-cut bands, 2" d., 2¼" h. (ILLUS.) **55**

VASES

From left: No. 50 Pattern Vase by Dorflinger Brazilian Pattern Vase by Hawkes

Dorflinger's No. 50 patt., tapering ovoid body on a paneled stem w/star-cut notched round foot, the upper body cut w/hobstars & strawberry diamond above plain cut swirled ribs, 10½" h. (ILLUS.) **895**

Hawkes' Brunswick patt., trumpet-form, 14" h. **550**

Hawkes' Brazilian patt., tall waisted cylindrical form w/notched & scalloped rim, cut w/hobstars, bands of strawberry diamond & fans, 5¾" d., 11" h. (ILLUS.). **550**

Hawkes-signed, tall cylindrical body w/iridized clear finish cut & etched w/flowers, swags & tassels, topped by an applied band of sterling silver w/a repeating swag & oval design, glass stamped "Hawkes" on base, silver marked "Hawkes Sterling 2262," 3¾" d., 9¾" h. **460**

From left: Ellsmere Variation Pattern Vase C.F. Monroe Sylph Pattern Vase

Libbey's Ellsmere Variation patt., tall baluster-form w/flaring notched rim, large zipper-cut bars around the neck above hobstars & starbursts over further panels of zipper cutting & large hobstars around the base, signed, 6" d., 12" h. (ILLUS.) **1,585**

Monroe's Sylph patt., footed squatty bulbous lower body below a tall gently flaring neck, scalloped & notched fan-cut rim, cut rings & zipper-cut panels down the neck, a band of hobstars & strawberry diamond above the heavy zipper-cut ribs around the bottom, 7½" d., 9¾" h. (ILLUS.) ... **685**

Pairpoint-signed, Buckingham patt., tall slender baluster-form body w/a widely flaring trumpet neck mounted on a patinated metal pedestal foot on a square white onyx base raised on a metal rim w/paw feet, impressed "Pairpoint C1517," 15¼" h., pr. (abrasions to stone base) **1,840**

Trophy-form, flattened ovoid tapering sides w/wide flared mouth, slender stem on wide round star-cut foot, long D-form applied notch-cut handles, the sides cut w/large starbursts in diamond panels w/fan-cutting at corners, 10¼" h. **1,380**

Trumpet-shaped, tall slender cylindrical body w/flared & ruffled rim w/notch-cut rim, diamond panels over large Buzzstars above zipper-cut panels & fan- and star-cutting down to the flaring panel-cut foot w/zipper-cut edge, 14¼" h. (rim chips) **460**

Finely Cut Urn-form Vase

Urn-form, wide flaring bowl w/plain scalloped rim, ring-cut sides above squatty bulbous lower body cut w/hobstars, raised on a panel-cut pedestal on a square foot, 9½" d., 7½" h. (ILLUS.) **1,825**

WATER SETS

Water set: 10½" h. waisted tankard pitcher w/high arched spout & applied notched handle & five matching tumblers; Hawkes signed, the pitcher w/a wide center band w/large hobstars within diamonds alternating w/fan over geometric cutting, wide bands of strawberry diamond cutting at the base & rim, each piece signed, tumblers, 3⅝" h., the set. **550**

D'ARGENTAL

D'Argental Mark

Glass known by this name is co-called after its producer, who fashioned fine cameo pieces in St. Louis, France late last century and up to 1918.

From left: *D'Argental Egg-shaped Box*

Cameo box, cov., egg-shaped, yellow overlaid w/crimson, the base carved w/azaleas, the cover w/butterflies, signed in cameo, ca. 1910, 6" h. (ILLUS.) **$1,150**

Cameo lamp, table model, a 10½" d. pointed wide mushroom shade & matching tall slender ovoid body on a wide disk foot, both in grey infused w/ochre-yellow & overlaid in deep crimson, cut w/an overall pattern of ripe blackberries, leafage & thorny branches, w/a three-arm bronze mount, base signed in cameo "D'Argental," ca. 1915, overall 22" h. **6,325**

D'Argental Cameo Powder Box

Cameo powder jar, cov., squatty bulbous form w/applied knob finial, yellow overlaid w/russet & dark purple, the cover cut w/flowers, buds & leaves on thorny stems, the base w/a border of leaves on short stems, signed in cameo, ca. 1900, 6¾" d. (ILLUS.) **1,150**

Cameo vase, 9¾" h., tall ovoid body tapering to a flat rim, fiery amber overlaid in maroon brown & cameo-cut

w/blossoming trumpet vine pendent after signature "D'Argental" at the lower side (some interior bubbles) **1,035**

Cameo vase, 6¼" h., tall slender ovoid form w/a small flared rim, yellow overlaid w/orange & cameo-cut w/a continuous river landscape w/tall trees in the foreground, signed **460**

Cameo vase, 8" h., simple ovoid body tapering to a tiny neck, lime green overlaid w/dark brown & cut overall w/large clusters of berries on leafy vines, cameo signature **990**

Cameo vase, 13" h., tall very slender swelled cylindrical body w/a flared rim & cushion foot, frosted shaded dark to light purple ground overlaid in dark purple & cut w/detailed wisteria blossoms down the sides, cameo signature **1,320**

D'Argental Tropical Scene Vase

Cameo vase, 13¾" h., tall slender ovoid body w/a rounded shoulder to a short flaring neck, amber overlaid w/brown & cut w/a continuous scene of palm trees & mountains by water, ca. 1910, signed in cameo (ILLUS.) **1,495**

DAUM NANCY

Daum Nancy Marks

This fine glass, much of it cameo, was made by Auguste and Antonin Daum, who founded a factory in 1875 in Nancy, France. Most of their cameo and enameled glass was made from the 1890s into the early 20th century.

Daum Cut & Enameled Small Bowl

Bowl, 4¼" h., pointed cup-form bowl raised on three deep purple loop feet, the bowl in grey mottled w/white shading to deep purple, cut w/violets & leaves & finely enameled in purple & green trimmed w/gilt, signed, ca. 1900 (ILLUS.) **$5,570**

Box, cov., three short pad feet below a swelled ring base below the short cylindrical sides, fitted nearly flat cover, grey shading to rich violet at the base, internally streaked w/frosty white cut w/stalks of wheat, leafage & pinwheels, enameled in green, amber & cream, the whole trimmed in gilt, all reserved against a textured ground, unsigned, ca. 1900, 7" d. **6,900**

Daum Nancy Cameo Bowl

Cameo bowl, 8½" d., wide disk foot supporting a deep rounded bowl w/flat rim, clear overlaid w/green & cut w/a morning glory vine w/gilt trim, reserved on an acid-textured ground, mounted w/a silver gadrooned foot rim & a floral vine rim at the lip possibly added later & damaged, faintly inscribed, ca. 1900 (ILLUS.) **2,300**

Cameo lamp, table model, a pair of thistle-shaped cameo glass shades in grey overlaid in mottled pink shading to mint green & cut as stylized thistle blossoms, fitted into a branched wrought-iron standard w/serrated curved leaves under each shade at the bottom flanking the round domed foot, iron designed by Louis Majorelle, shades signed "DAUM - NANCY" w/cross of Lorraine, ca. 1900, 20¾" h. **11,500**

Cameo pitcher, 7½" h., flattened round form w/applied handle, grey cased & internally decorated w/yellow & orange powders, inscribed "DAUM NANCY" w/cross of Lorraine, ca. 1920s **345**

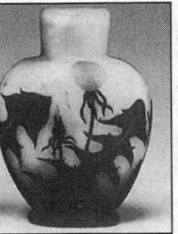

From left: Daum Nancy Dandelions Cameo Vase Miniature Daum Nancy Pitcher

Cameo vase, 7⅝" h., tapering shouldered body w/a flat front & back & w/a short cylindrical neck, grey overlaid in turquoise & green, cut w/dandelions, signed in cameo & w/retailer's label, ca. 1900 (ILLUS.) **1,840**

Cameo vase, 9¼" h., slender baluster-form w/flat mouth, grey overlaid in crimson & deep forest green, cut w/poppy blossoms & undulating leafage & fire-polished, the ground in "martelé," inscribed & trimmed in gilt "DAUM - NANCY" w/cross of Lorraine, ca. 1900 . . . . **3,450**

Cameo vase, 11¼" h., bottle-form, nearly spherical base below a very tall slender 'stick' neck w/flared rim, pale aquamarine blue overlaid in deep crimson red, cut w/cyclamen blossoms & undulating leafage, all finely wheel-carved, signed in gilt intaglio "DAUM - NANCY" w/cross of Lorraine, ca. 1900 . . . . **6,900**

Cameo vase, 15¾" h., tall slender ovoid body w/flared rim raised on a double knop stem on a disk foot, grey internally mottled w/pale lavender, shading to ochre yellow & deepest purple at the base, overlaid in mottled olive green & cut w/poppy leafage, the blossoms w/applied burnt orange & purple finely delineated w/wheel carving, signed in intaglio "DAUM - NANCY" w/a cross of Lorraine, ca. 1900. . . . . **11,500**

Cameo vase, 31" h., flaring base tapering to a very tall slender body, grey streaked w/lemon & tangerine, overlaid in orange & red & cut w/stems of foxgloves & leaves, signed "Daum - NANCY - FRANCE," w/cross of Lorraine, ca. 1900 . . . **6,900**

Ewer, bulbous ovoid body w/a short slightly flaring neck w/small pinched spout, applied C-form handle, grey cut w/delicate bell-form flowers w/long narrow leaves, a dragonfly & a butterfly, inscribed signature in gilt, ca. 1900, 4¼" h. **862**

Pitcher, 3½" h., miniature, footed spherical body flattened on the front & back, short flaring neck & applied loop handle, opalescent grey cut w/clover blossoms & leaves on an acid-textured ground, the neck w/a beaded gilt band & scrolling vine, enameled in pink, grey, black & gold, signed, some wear to rim gilt, ca. 1900 (ILLUS.) **2,415**

Miniature Daum Landscape Vases

Vase, 1⅝" h., miniature, flattened ovoid form, grey tinted w/yellow shading to amber, cut w/leafless brown trees in a snowy field, signed, ca. 1900 (ILLUS. left) . . **1,265**

Vase, 2⅝" h., miniature, footed bulbous baluster-form, grey mottled w/white & specks of blue, cut w/a river landscape w/pine trees & trees w/falling leaves, enameled in yellow, red, green & brown, signed, ca. 1900 (ILLUS. right) **1,265**

Vase, 5" h., slightly swelled cylindrical form, grey shaded w/purple at the base, cut w/branches of bleeding heart blossoms & enameled in pink, purple & green, incised signature, ca. 1900 . . . . **1,610**

Vase, 5½" h., ovoid w/slightly flattened front & back, pale apricot mottled w/yellow, cut w/leafless trees & a snow-covered ground, enameled decoration, faintly inscribed "Daum - Nancy" w/cross of Lorraine, ca. 1900 . . . . **1,150**

Daum Vases with Molded Designs

Vase, 10½" h., footed wide campana-form w/wide flared rim, mottled cranberry, molded w/a circle & wave design, signed (ILLUS. right) **2,415**

Vase, 10½" h., gently swelled cylindrical form tapering slightly at the shoulder to a short neck w/a closed rim, grey mottled w/tangerine & raspberry, cut w/branches of apple blossoms & enameled w/white, pink & yellow flowers on brown stems w/green leaves, incised & enameled signature, ca. 1900 . . . . **3,737**

Vase, 11½" h., flat-bottomed ovoid body w/a short neck & flattened rim, aquamarine, the lower half molded w/overlapping pointed stylized leaves below a textured upper ground, signed (ILLUS. left) **1,840**

From left: Daum Vase in Majorelle Iron Frame Tall Daum Nancy Vase

Vase, 12½" h., ovoid teardrop form w/flared rim, mottled amber to dark orange blown into a Majorelle-designed wrought-iron framework, incised "Daum (cross) Nancy-L. Majorelle" (ILLUS.). **1,610**

Vase, 14½" h., small thick flaring foot supporting a tall, large trumpet-form ribbed acid-etched body in deep purplish blue, inscribed "Daum Nancy France" w/a cross of Lorraine, ca. 1925 . . . . **5,175**

Vase, 16⅝" h., a tall slender cylindrical body w/a small bulb above the wide cushion foot, a large bulbed top tapering to a small flared mouth, grey mottled w/ochre yellow shading to crimson & moss green, cut w/a pattern of prunus blossoms & leafage enameled in shades of white, grey, brown & green, signed in enameled cameo "DAUM - NANCY FRANCE," w/a cross of Lorraine, ca. 1900 . . . . **4,025**

Vase, 17¼" h., a swelled top w/a closed rim over sharply tapering sides to a slender bottom on a knopped cushion foot, grey mottled w/white shading to deep purple, finely cut w/violets & leaves, enameled in shades of purple & deep forest green, trimmed w/gilt, signed in cameo, ca. 1900 (ILLUS.) **11,500**

DE LATTE

Andre de Latte of Nancy, France, produced a range of opaque and cameo glass after 1921. His company also produced light fixtures but his cameo wares are most collectible today.

Cameo vase, 8" h., ovoid double-gourd form, orange overlaid in dark amethyst & cut w/a continuous design of leaves & berries, signed in cameo "Delatte Nancy" . . . **$600**

De Latte Cameo Landscape Vase

Cameo vase, 15" h., very slender ovoid body w/a short neck & wide flattened rim, raised on a round cushion foot, light blue overlaid w/green & dark blue, w/peacocks & trees in the foreground, a lake in the middle ground & architectural ruins & trees in the distance, inscribed "ADELATTTE - NANCY," ca. 1925 (ILLUS.)..........................**1,150**

Vase, 6⅛" h., flared cylindrical form, frosted colorless enameled in brown & etched w/a tree-lined shore & rocky outcropping & distant hills, raised on a gilt-metal pedestal w/raised leaf design, signed "A. Delatte Nancy," on lower side, ca. 1920......**518**

DEPRESSION

The phrase "Depression glass" is used by collectors to denote a specific kind of transparent glass produced primarily as tablewares, in crystal, amber, blue, green, pink, milky-white, etc., during the late 1920s and 1930s when this country was in the midst of a financial depression. Made to sell inexpensively, it was turned out by such producers as Jeannette, Hocking, Westmoreland, Indiana and other glass companies. We compile prices on all the major Depression glass patterns. Collectors should consult Depression glass references for information on those patterns and pieces which have been reproduced. For a more extensive listing of Depression glass, please refer to Antique Trader Books' American Pressed Glass & Bottles Price Guide.

ADAM, Jeanette Glass Co., 1932-34 (Process-etched)

Bowl, 4¾" sq., dessert, green................$19
Bowl, 4¾" sq., dessert, pink..................20
Bowl, 5¾" sq., cereal, green..................44
Bowl, 5¾" sq., cereal, pink...................49

Bowl, 7¾" sq., dessert, green................26
Bowl, 7¾" sq., nappy, pink...................27
Bowl, 10" oval, vegetable, green.............32
Bowl, 10" oval, vegetable, pink..............33
Butter dish, cov., green....................354
Butter dish, cov., pink.....................100
Cake plate, footed, green, 10" sq.............29
Cake plate, footed, pink, 10" sq.............27
Candlesticks, green, 4" h., pr................91
Candlesticks, pink, 4" h., pr.................91
Candy jar, cov., green......................111

Adam Candy Jar with Cover

Candy jar, cov., pink (ILLUS.).............102
Creamer, green..............................23
Creamer, pink...............................22
Cup & saucer, green.........................29
Cup & saucer, pink..........................32
Pitcher, 8" h., 32 oz., cone-shaped, green.......43
Pitcher, 8" h., 32 oz., cone-shaped, pink........40
Plate, 6" sq., sherbet, green..................9
Plate, 6" sq., sherbet, pink...................9
Plate, 7¾" sq., salad, green..................16
Plate, 7¾" sq., salad, pink...................16
Plate, 9" sq., dinner, green..................30
Plate, 9" sq., dinner, pink...................37
Plate, 9" sq., grill, green...................20
Plate, 9" sq., grill, pink....................28
Plate, salad, round, pink....................60
Plate, salad, round, yellow..................110
Platter, 11¾" l., green......................31
Platter, 11¾" l., pink.......................32
Relish dish, two-part, green, 8" sq............25
Relish dish, two-part, pink, 8" sq.............25
Salt & pepper shakers, footed, green, 4" h., pr. ...88
Salt & pepper shakers, footed, pink, 4" h., pr. ...80
Sherbet, green, 3" h........................38
Sherbet, pink, 3" h.........................31
Sugar bowl, cov., pink......................43
Tumbler, cone-shaped, green, 4½" h., 7 oz. 29
Tumbler, cone-shaped, pink, 4½" h., 7 oz........31
Tumbler, iced tea, green, 5½" h., 9 oz. 60
Tumbler, iced tea, pink 5½" h., 9 oz. 78
Vase, 7½" h., green.........................81
Vase, 7½" h., pink.........................413

AMERICAN SWEETHEART, MacBeth-Evans Glass Co., 1930-38 (Process-etched)

Bowl, 4½" d., cream soup, Monax ...... **125 to 150**
Bowl, 4½" d., cream soup, pink 87
Bowl, 9" d., berry, Monax 65
Bowl, 9" d., berry, pink 57
Bowl, 9½" d., soup w/flanged rim, Monax 83
Bowl, 9½" d., soup w/flanged rim, pink. 73
Bowl, 11" oval vegetable, Monax 81
Bowl, 11" oval vegetable, pink 76
Console bowl, blue, 18" d. 1,525
Console bowl, Monax, 18" d. 574
Console bowl, ruby red, 18" d. 2,125
Creamer, footed, Monax. 13
Creamer, footed, pink. 15
Creamer, footed, ruby red 106
Cup & saucer, blue 151
Cup & saucer, Monax 13
Cup & saucer, pink 23
Cup & saucer, ruby red 121
Lamp shade, Monax 703
Pitcher, 7½" h., 60 oz., jug-type, pink. 615
Pitcher, 8" h., 80 oz., pink 749
Plate, 8" d., salad, blue. 130
Plate, 8" d., salad, Monax. 9
Plate, 8" d., salad, pink. 13
Plate, 8" d., salad, ruby red. 102
Plate, 9" d., luncheon, Monax. 14
Plate, 9¾" d., dinner, Monax. 27
Plate, 9¾" d., dinner, pink. 39
Plate, 10¼" d., dinner, Monax. 27
Plate, 10¼" d., dinner, pink. 40
Plate, 11" d., chop, Monax 20
Plate, 12" d., salver, blue 235
Plate, 12" d., salver, Monax 21
Plate, 12" d., salver, pink 24
Plate, 12" d., salver, ruby red 215
Plate, 15½" d., w/center handle, blue 725
Plate, 15½" d., w/center handle, Monax 223
Platter, 13" oval, Monax 86
Platter, 13" oval, pink 61
Salt & pepper shakers, footed, Monax, pr. 395
Salt & pepper shakers, footed, pink, pr. 384
Sugar bowl, cov., Monax (only) 355
Sugar bowl, open, Monax 9
Sugar bowl, open, pink 15
Sugar bowl, open, ruby red 90
Tidbit server, three-tier, Monax 241
Tidbit server, two-tier, Monax 99
Tidbit server, two-tier, pink 56
Tidbit server, two-tier, ruby red 220
Tumbler, pink, 3½" h., 5 oz. 101
Tumbler, pink, 4¼" h., 9 oz. 86
Tumbler, pink, 4¾" h., 10 oz. 138

AUNT POLLY, U.S. Glass Co., late 1920s (Press-mold)

Bowl, 4¾" d., berry, blue 18
Bowl, 4¾" d., berry, green 7
Bowl, 7¼" d., oval, handled pickle, blue. 35
Bowl, 7¼" d., oval, handled pickle, green. 10
Bowl, 7⅞" d., large berry, blue 40
Bowl, 7⅞" d., large berry, green. 16
Butter dish, cov., blue 213
Butter dish, cov., green 240
Candy dish, footed, two-handled, blue 50
Candy dish, footed, two-handled, green 22
Creamer, blue. 50
Pitcher, 8" h., 48 oz., blue 200
Plate, 6" d., sherbet, blue 16
Plate, 6" d., sherbet, iridescent. 13
Sherbet, blue 14
Sherbet, green 11
Sherbet, iridescent 6
Sugar bowl, cov., blue 210
Sugar bowl, cov., iridescent. 65
Tumbler, water, blue, 3⅝" h., 8 oz. 35
Vase, 6½" h., blue. 61

BLOCK or Block Optic, Hocking Glass Co., 1919-33 (Press-mold)

Block Creamer & Sugar Bowl

Bowl, 4¼" d., berry, green 9
Bowl, 4½" d., berry, green 29
Bowl, 5¼" d., cereal, green 15
Bowl, 5¼" d., cereal, pink. 32
Bowl, 8½" d., large berry, green. 30
Butter dish, cov., rectangular, green
 clambroth, 3 x 5". 350
Candlesticks, amber, 1¾" h., pr. 89
Candlesticks, green, 1¾" h., pr. 112
Candlesticks, pink, 1¾" h., pr. 79
Candy jar, cov., green, 2¼" h. 62
Candy jar, cov., pink, 2¼" h. 51
Candy jar, cov., yellow, 2¼" h. 66
Candy jar, cov., green, 6¼" h. 61
Candy jar, cov., pink, 6¼" h. 128
Compote, 4" d., cone-shaped, green 27
Compote, 4" d., cone-shaped, pink 17
Console bowl, rolled edge, pink, 11¾" d. 143
Creamer, various styles, green (ILLUS. right) 14

Creamer, various styles, pink 14
Creamer, various styles, yellow 12
Cup & saucer, green 16
Cup & saucer, pink 11
Cup & saucer, yellow. 13
Goblet, wine, clear, 4½" h. 9
Goblet, wine, green, 4½" h. 32
Goblet, wine, pink, 4½" h.. 32
Goblet, clear, 5¾" h., 9 oz.. 12
Goblet, green, 5¾" h., 9 oz. 29
Goblet, pink, 5¾" h., 9 oz. 31
Goblet, clear, 7¼" h., 9 oz. 12
Goblet, yellow, 7¼" h., 9 oz.. 36
Pitcher, 7⅝" h., 54 oz., bulbous, green 66
Plate, 6" d., sherbet, green. 4
Plate, 6" d., sherbet, pink 4
Plate, 6" d., sherbet, yellow 3
Plate, 8" d., luncheon, clear 3
Plate, 8" d., luncheon, green. 6
Plate, 8" d., luncheon, pink. 5
Plate, 8" d., luncheon, yellow 7
Plate, 9" d., dinner, green. 25
Plate, 9" d., grill, yellow. 45
Plate, 10¼" d., sandwich, clear. 22
Plate, 10¼" d., sandwich, green 38
Plate, 10¼" d., sandwich, pink 26
Salt & pepper shakers, footed, clear, pr. 22
Salt & pepper shakers, footed, green, pr. 39
Salt & pepper shakers, footed, pink, pr. 81
Salt & pepper shakers, footed, yellow, pr. 77
Sherbet, stemmed, clear, 4¾" h., 6 oz. 6
Sherbet, stemmed, green, 4¾" h., 6 oz.. 14
Sherbet, stemmed, pink, 4¾" h., 6 oz. 16
Sherbet, stemmed, yellow, 4¾" h., 6 oz. 18
Sugar bowl, open, various styles, clear 9
Sugar bowl, open, various styles, green
  (ILLUS. left) 13
Sugar bowl, open, various styles, pink 15
Sugar bowl, open, various styles, yellow. 13
Tumbler, footed, green, 9 oz.. 23
Tumbler, footed, pink, 9 oz. 16
Tumbler, footed, yellow, 9 oz. 21
Tumbler, iced tea, footed, green, 6" h., 10 oz. . . . 32
Tumbler, iced tea, footed, pink, 6" h., 10 oz. 25
Tumbler, green, 4⅞" h., 12 oz.. 23
Tumbler, pink, 4⅞" h., 12 oz.. 28

CAMEO or Ballerina or Dancing Girl, Hocking Glass Co., 1930-34 (Process-etched)

Bowl, 4¼" d., sauce, clear 5
Bowl, 4¾" d., cream soup, green 177
Bowl, 5½" d., cereal, clear 6
Bowl, 5½" d., cereal, green 36
Bowl, 5½" d., cereal, yellow 37
Bowl, 8¼" d., large berry, green. 39

Bowl, 8¼" d., large berry, pink 125
Bowl, 9" d., soup w/flange rim, green. 78
Butter dish, cov., green 258
Cake plate, three-footed, green, 10" d. 26
Candlesticks, green, 4" h., pr. 123
Candy jar, cov., green, 4" h.. 91
Candy jar, cov., yellow, 4" h. 98
Candy jar, cov., green, 6½" h. 215
Console bowl, three-footed, green, 11" d. 86
Console bowl, three-footed, pink, 11" d. 65
Console bowl, three-footed, yellow, 11" d. 95
Creamer, green, 3¼" h. 22
Creamer, yellow, 3¼" h. 22
Creamer, green, 4¼" h. 28
Cup & saucer, green 23
Cup & saucer, yellow. 11
Decanter w/stopper, green, 10" h. 170
Decanter w/stopper, green frosted, 10" h. 36
Goblet, water, green, 6" h.. 62
Goblet, water, pink, 6" h. 164
Ice bowl, tab handles, green, 5½" d., 3½" h. 222
Tumbler, juice, green, 3¾" h., 5 oz. 33
Tumbler, water, clear, 4" h., 9 oz. 10
Tumbler, water, green, 4" h., 9 oz. 29
Tumbler, water, pink, 4" h., 9 oz. 95
Tumbler, footed, green, 5" h., 9 oz. 30
Tumbler, footed, yellow, 5" h., 9 oz.. 16
Tumbler, green, 4¾" h., 10 oz.. 28
Tumbler, green, 5" h., 11 oz. 32
Tumbler, yellow, 5" h., 11 oz. 58
Tumbler, footed, green, 5¾" h., 11 oz.. 73
Tumbler, green, 5¼" h., 15 oz.. 75
Vase, 5¾" h., green 257
Water set: pitcher & 6 tumblers; green, 7 pcs.. . . 250

CHERRY BLOSSOM, Jeannette Glass Co., 1930-38 (Process-etched)

Cherry Blossom Pieces

Bowl, 4¾" d., berry, Delphite 16
Bowl, 4¾" d., berry, green 18
Bowl, 4¾" d., berry, pink. 17

Bowl, 5¾" d., cereal, green 48
Bowl, 5¾" d., cereal, pink. 46
Bowl, 7¾" d., soup, green 84
Bowl, 9" d., two-handled, Delphite 34
Bowl, 9" d., two-handled, green 65
Bowl, 9" d., two-handled, pink 50
Bowl, 9" oval vegetable, green. 45
Bowl, 9" oval vegetable, pink 52
Bowl, 10½" d., fruit, three-footed, green. 92
Bowl, 10½" d., fruit, three-footed, pink 107
Butter dish, cov., green 105
Butter dish, cov., pink 92
Creamer, Delphite 23
Creamer, green 19
Creamer, pink. 22
Cup & saucer, Delphite 24
Cup & saucer, green 25
Cup & saucer, pink (ILLUS.) 32
Mug, green, 7 oz. 254
Mug, pink, 7 oz. 180
Pitcher, 6¾" h., 36 oz., overall patt., Delphite 92
Pitcher, 6¾" h., 36 oz., overall patt., green 59
Pitcher, 6¾" h., 36 oz., overall patt., pink. 66
Pitcher, 8" h., 36 oz., footed, cone-shaped,
    patt. top, green. 77
Pitcher, 8" h., 36 oz., footed, cone-shaped,
    patt. top, pink. 56
Pitcher, 8" h., 42 oz., patt. top, green. 68
Pitcher, 8" h., 42 oz., patt. top, pink 55
Plate, 6" d., sherbet, Delphite 8
Plate, 6" d., sherbet, green. 8
Plate, 6" d., sherbet, pink 9
Plate, 7" d., salad, green. 21
Plate, 7" d., salad, pink. 24
Plate, 9" d., dinner, Delphite 22
Plate, 9" d., dinner, green. 24
Plate, 9" d., dinner, pink (ILLUS. w/cup &
    saucer) 24
Plate, 9" d., grill, green 26
Plate, 9" d., grill, pink 30
Platter, 11" oval, Delphite. 42
Platter, 11" oval, green. 47
Platter, 11" oval, pink 49
Platter, 13" oval, green. 63
Platter, 13" oval, divided, pink 70
Salt & pepper shakers, green, pr. 1,085
Sandwich tray, handled, Delphite, 10½" d. 24
Sandwich tray, handled, green, 10½" d. 30
Sandwich tray, handled, pink, 10½" d. 30
Sherbet, Delphite 12
Sherbet, green 19
Sherbet, pink 18
Sugar bowl, cov., clear 18
Sugar bowl, cov., Delphite. 35
Sugar bowl, cov., green. 39
Sugar bowl, cov., pink 37
Tumbler, patt. top, green, 3½" h., 4 oz. 25

Tumbler, juice, footed, overall patt.,
    Delphite, 3¾" h., 4 oz. 20
Tumbler, juice, footed, overall patt., green,
    3¾" h., 4 oz. 22
Tumbler, juice, footed, overall patt., pink,
    3¾" h., 4 oz. 20
Tumbler, footed, overall patt., Delphite,
    4½" h., 8 oz. 21
Tumbler, footed, overall patt., green, 4½" h.,
    8 oz. 38
Tumbler, patt. top, green, 4¼" h., 9 oz. 25
Tumbler, patt. top, pink, 4¼" h., 9 oz. 24
Tumbler, footed, overall patt., Delphite,
    4½" h., 9 oz. 23
Tumbler, footed, overall patt., green, 4½" h.,
    9 oz. 32
Tumbler, footed, overall patt., pink, 4½" h., 9 oz.. . 35
Tumbler, patt. top, pink, 5" h., 12 oz. 76

JUNIOR SET:
CHERRY BLOSSOM, Jeannette Glass Co., 1930-38 (Process-etched)

Creamer, Delphite 51
Creamer, pink. 48
Cup & saucer, Delphite 47
Cup & saucer, pink 45
Plate, 6" d., Delphite. 14
Plate, 6" d., pink 13
Set, Delphite, 14 pcs. 350
Set, pink, 14 pcs. 322
Sugar bowl, Delphite 46
Sugar bowl, pink 45

CLOVERLEAF, Hazel Atlas Glass Co., 1931-35 (Process-etched)

Bowl, 5" d., cereal, green 27
Bowl, 7" d., salad, deep, green. 42
Bowl, 7" d., salad, deep, yellow 47
Candy dish, cov., green. 69
Candy dish, cov., yellow 124
Creamer, footed, black, 3⅝" h. 18
Creamer, footed, green, 3⅝" h. 10
Creamer, footed, yellow, 3⅝" h. 16
Cup & saucer, black. 26
Cup & saucer, green 11
Cup & saucer, pink 11
Cup & saucer, yellow. 14
Plate, 6" d., sherbet, black 38
Plate, 6" d., sherbet, yellow 8
Plate, 8" d., luncheon, black 15
Plate, 8" d., luncheon, clear 5
Plate, 8" d., luncheon, green. 8
Plate, 8" d., luncheon, pink 10
Plate, 8" d., luncheon, yellow 14
Plate, 10¼" d., grill, green. 23
Plate, 10¼" d., grill, yellow 25
Salt & pepper shakers, black, pr. 90

Salt & pepper shakers, green, pr. 36
Salt & pepper shakers, yellow, pr. 100
Sherbet, footed, black, 3" h. 21
Sherbet, footed, green, 3" h. 9
Sherbet, footed, pink, 3" h. 8
Sherbet, footed, yellow, 3" h. 11
Sugar bowl, open, footed, black, 3⅝" h. 20
Sugar bowl, open, footed, green, 3⅝" h. 10
Sugar bowl, open, footed, yellow, 3⅝" h. 15
Tumbler, flared, green, 3¾" h., 10 oz. 40
Tumbler, flared, pink, 3¾" h., 10 oz. 27
Tumbler, footed, green, 5¾" h., 10 oz. 28
Tumbler, footed, yellow, 5¾" h., 10 oz. 34

CUBE or Cubist, Jeannette Glass Co., 1929-33 (Press-mold)

Bowl, 4½" d., deep, pink. 5
Bowl, 4½" d., dessert, green 9
Bowl, 4½" d., dessert, pink. 5
Butter dish, cov., green 65
Butter dish, cov., pink 62
Candy jar, cov., green, 6½" h. 34
Candy jar, cov., pink, 6½" h. 33
Creamer, clear, 2⅝" h. 2
Creamer, pink, 2⅝" h. 6
Creamer, clear, 3½" h. 1
Creamer, green, 3½" h. 8
Creamer, pink, 3½" h. 7
Cup & saucer, green 12
Cup & saucer, pink 11
Pitcher, 8¾" h., 45 oz., green. 238
Pitcher, 8¾" h., 45 oz., pink 230
Plate, 6" d., sherbet, clear. 1
Plate, 6" d., sherbet, green 4
Plate, 6" d., sherbet, pink 4
Plate, 8" d., luncheon, green. 9
Plate, 8" d., luncheon, pink 7
Powder jar, cov., three-footed, green. 31
Powder jar, cov., three-footed, pink 32
Salt & pepper shakers, green, pr. 32
Salt & pepper shakers, pink, pr. 34
Sherbet, footed, green 9
Sherbet, footed, pink 7
Sugar bowl, cov., green, 3" h. 20
Sugar bowl, cov., pink, 3" h. 20
Sugar bowl, open, clear, 2⅜" h. 2
Sugar bowl, open, pink, 2⅜" h. 4
Tumbler, green, 4" h., 9 oz. 73
Tumbler, pink, 4" h., 9 oz. 65

DAISY or Number 620, Indiana Glass Company, 1933-40 (Press-mold)

Bowl, 4½" d., cream soup, amber 12
Bowl, 6" d., cereal, amber 25
Bowl, 6" d., cereal, clear. 9
Bowl, 7⅜" d., berry, amber. 14

Bowl, 7⅜" d., berry, clear 6
Bowl, 9⅜" d., berry, amber. 28
Bowl, 9⅜" d., berry, clear 13
Bowl, 10" oval vegetable, amber 18
Creamer, footed, amber 8
Cup & saucer, amber. 7
Cup & saucer, clear 6
Plate, 6" d., sherbet, amber 3
Plate, 6" d., sherbet, clear. 2
Plate, 7⅜" d., salad, amber. 11
Plate, 7⅜" d., salad, clear. 5
Plate, 8⅜" d., luncheon, amber. 5
Plate, 8⅜" d., luncheon, clear. 3
Plate, 9⅜" d., dinner, amber 8
Plate, 9⅜" d., dinner, clear 4
Plate, 11½" d., amber (cake or sandwich) 14
Plate, 11½" d., clear (cake or sandwich) 7
Platter, 10¾" l., amber 15
Relish dish, three-part, amber, 8⅜". 30
Relish dish, three-part, clear, 8⅜" 10
Sugar bowl, open, footed, amber. 7
Sugar bowl, open, footed, clear. 4
Tumbler, footed, amber, 9 oz. 17
Tumbler, footed, amber, 12 oz. 42
Tumbler, footed, clear, 12 oz. 20

DOGWOOD or Apple Blossom or Wild Rose, MacBeth-Evans, 1929-32 (Process-etched)

Dogwood Cup & Saucer

Bowl, 5½" d., cereal, green 37
Bowl, 5½" d., cereal, pink. 32
Bowl, 8½" d., berry, Monax 44
Bowl, 8½" d., berry, pink. 62
Bowl, 10¼" d., fruit, green 279
Bowl, 10¼" d., fruit, pink. 548
Cake plate, heavy solid foot, green, 13" d. 133
Cake plate, heavy solid foot, pink, 13" d. 143
Creamer, thin, green, 2½" h. 46
Creamer, thin, pink, 2½" h. 19
Creamer, thick, footed, pink, 3¼" h. 19
Cup & saucer, green (ILLUS.) 47
Cup & saucer, Monax 39
Cup & saucer, pink 23
Pitcher, 8" h., 80 oz., American Sweetheart
 style, pink 560

Pitcher, 8" h., 80 oz., decorated, pink 214
Plate, 6" d., bread & butter, green 9
Plate, 6" d., bread & butter, pink. 9
Plate, 8" d., luncheon, clear 4
Plate, 8" d., luncheon, green. 8
Plate, 8" d., luncheon, pink. 8
Plate, 9¼" d., dinner, pink. 44
Plate, 10½" d., grill, border design, pink 24
Plate, 10½" d., grill, overall patt., pink. 25
Sherbet, low foot, pink 37
Sugar bowl, open, thin, green, 2½" h. 31
Sugar bowl, open, thin, pink, 2½" h. 18
Sugar bowl, open, thick, footed, pink, 3¼" h. 19
Tumbler, decorated, pink, 3½" h., 5 oz. 274
Tumbler, decorated, green, 4" h., 10 oz. 83
Tumbler, decorated, pink, 4" h., 10 oz. 42
Tumbler, decorated, green, 4¾" h., 11 oz. 116
Tumbler, decorated, pink, 4¾" h., 11 oz. 49
Tumbler, decorated, pink, 5" h., 12 oz. 69
Tumbler, molded band, pink. 22

FLORENTINE or Poppy No. 2, Hazel Atlas Glass Co., 1932-35 (Process-etched)

Bowl, 4½" d., berry, clear 11
Bowl, 4½" d., berry, green 12
Bowl, 4½" d., berry, pink. 17
Bowl, 4½" d., berry, yellow 22
Bowl, 4¾" d., cream soup, plain rim, clear 12
Bowl, 4¾" d., cream soup, plain rim, green 13
Bowl, 4¾" d., cream soup, plain rim, pink 17
Bowl, 4¾" d., cream soup, plain rim, yellow 22
Bowl, 8" d., clear. 19
Bowl, 8" d., green 27
Bowl, 8" d., pink 31
Bowl, 8" d., yellow 36
Bowl, 9" oval, cov., vegetable, yellow. 72
Butter dish, cov., clear. 93
Butter dish, cov., green 99
Butter dish, cov., yellow. 151
Candlesticks, green, 2¾" h., pr. 53
Candlesticks, yellow, 2¾" h., pr. 70
Candy dish, cov., clear 117
Candy dish, cov., green. 105
Candy dish, cov., pink 165
Candy dish, cov., yellow 162
Coaster-ashtray, clear, 3¾" d. 18
Coaster-ashtray, green, 3¾" d. 18
Coaster-ashtray, yellow, 3¾" d. 30
Coaster-ashtray, green, 5½" d. 22
Coaster-ashtray, yellow, 5½" d. 38
Compote, 3½", ruffled, cobalt blue 50
Compote, 3½", ruffled, pink 21
Creamer, clear 8
Creamer, green 10
Creamer, yellow 12

Cup & saucer, clear 10
Cup & saucer, green 13
Cup & saucer, yellow 14
Gravy boat w/platter, yellow, 11½" oval 115
Pitcher, 6¼" h., 24 oz., cone-shaped, yellow. . . . 168
Pitcher, 7½" h., 28 oz., cone-shaped, clear 30
Pitcher, 7½" h., 28 oz., cone-shaped, green 46
Pitcher, 7½" h., 28 oz., cone-shaped, yellow. 34
Pitcher, 7½" h., 48 oz., straight sides, green 79
Pitcher, 7½" h., 48 oz., straight sides, pink 133
Plate, 6" d., sherbet, clear. 5
Plate, 6" d., sherbet, green 5
Plate, 6" d., sherbet, yellow 6
Plate, 8½" d., salad, clear. 9
Plate, 8½" d., salad, green 9
Plate, 8½" d., salad, pink 6
Plate, 8½" d., salad, yellow. 11
Plate, 10" d., dinner, clear. 12
Plate, 10" d., dinner, green 15
Plate, 10" d., dinner, yellow 17
Plate, 10¼" d., grill, clear 12
Plate, 10¼" d., grill, green. 14
Plate, 10¼" d., grill, yellow 15
Platter, 11" oval, clear 8
Platter, 11" oval, green. 18
Platter, 11" oval, yellow 21
Platter, 11½", for gravy boat, yellow. 37
Relish dish, three-part or plain, clear, 10" 13
Relish dish, three-part or plain, green, 10" 22
Relish dish, three-part or plain, pink, 10". 24
Relish dish, three-part or plain, yellow, 10" 33
Salt & pepper shakers, clear, pr. 40
Salt & pepper shakers, green, pr.. 46
Salt & pepper shakers, yellow, pr. 50
Sherbet, clear. 9
Sherbet, green 11
Sherbet, yellow. 12
Sugar bowl, cov., clear 25
Sugar bowl, cov., yellow 35
Sugar bowl, open, clear. 9
Sugar bowl, open, green 9
Sugar bowl, open, yellow. 11
Tumbler, footed, clear, 3¼" h., 5 oz. 13
Tumbler, footed, green, 3¼" h., 5 oz.. 13
Tumbler, footed, yellow, 3¼" h., 5 oz. 16
Tumbler, juice, yellow, 3½" h., 5 oz.. 20
Tumbler, footed, clear, 4" h., 5 oz. 14
Tumbler, footed, green, 4" h., 5 oz. 15
Tumbler, footed, yellow, 4" h., 5 oz. 18
Tumbler, water, clear, 4" h., 9 oz. 10
Tumbler, water, green, 4" h., 9 oz. 14
Tumbler, water, pink, 4" h., 9 oz. 16
Tumbler, water, yellow, 4" h., 9 oz. 24
Tumbler, footed, green, 4½" h. 9 oz. 30
Tumbler, footed, yellow, 4½" h. 9 oz. 38
Tumbler, blown, clear, 5" h., 12 oz. 20

Tumbler, blown, green, 5" h., 12 oz. 16
Tumbler, iced tea, clear, 5" h., 12 oz.. 24
Tumbler, iced tea, green, 5" h., 12 oz.. 33
Tumbler, iced tea, yellow, 5" h., 12 oz. 49
Vase (or parfait), 6" h., clear 28
Vase (or parfait), 6" h., green 33
Vase (or parfait), 6" h., yellow 60

GEORGIAN or Lovebirds, Federal Glass Co., 1931-36 (Process-etched)

Bowl, 4½" d., berry 10
Bowl, 5¾" d., cereal 23
Butter dish, cov.. 75
Creamer, footed, 3" h. 12
Creamer, footed, 4" h. 15
Cup & saucer 13
Hot plate, center design, 5" d. 69
Plate, 6" d., sherbet 6
Plate, 8" d., luncheon 12
Plate, 9¼" d., dinner 24
Plate, 9¼" d., center design only 22
Platter, 11½" oval, closed handles 62
Sherbet. 13
Sugar bowl, cov., footed, 3" h.. 53
Sugar bowl, open, footed, 3" h. 9
Sugar bowl, open, footed, 4" h. 12
Tumbler, 4" h., 9 oz.. 59
Tumbler, 5¼" h., 12 oz. 142

HOLIDAY or Buttons and Bows, Jeannette Glass Co., 1947-mid '50s (Press-mold)

Holiday Milk Pitcher

Bowl, 5⅛" d., berry 14
Bowl, 7¾" d., flat soup 59
Bowl, berry, 8½" d.. 30
Bowl, 9½" oval vegetable 26
Butter dish, cov.. 41
Cake plate, three-footed, 10½" d.. 98
Candlesticks, 3" h., pr.. 115
Console bowl, 10¾" d.. 116
Creamer, footed 12
Cup & saucer, plain or rayed base 13
Pitcher, milk, 4¾" h., 16 oz., iridescent 29
Pitcher, milk, 4¾" h., 16 oz., pink (ILLUS.). 64

Pitcher, 6¾" h., 52 oz. 38
Plate, 9" d., dinner 22
Platter, 8 x 11⅜" oval, pink. 21
Platter, 8 x 11¾" oval, iridescent 12
Sandwich tray, 10½" d. 22
Sugar bowl, cov. 32
Sugar bowl, open. 10
Tumbler, footed, pink, 4" h., 5 oz. 48
Tumbler, footed, 6" h., 9 oz.. 172
Tumbler, 4" h., 10 oz.. 23

LACE EDGE or Open Lace, Hocking Glass Co., 1935-38 (Press-mold)

Lace Edge Butter Dish

Bowl, 6½" d., cereal, pink. 23
Bowl, 7¾" d., salad or butter dish bottom, pink . . . 26
Bowl, 9½" d., plain or ribbed, pink 28
Butter dish or bonbon, cov., pink (ILLUS.). 69
Candy jar, cov., ribbed, pink, 4" h. 55
Compote, open, 7" d., footed, pink. 27
Creamer, pink. 23
Cup & saucer, pink 37
Flower bowl w/crystal block, pink 34
Plate, 8¼" d., luncheon, clear. 4
Plate, 8¼" d., luncheon, pink 23
Plate, 10½" d., dinner, pink. 34
Plate, 10½" d., grill, pink 25
Platter, 12¾" oval, clear 10
Platter, 12¾" oval, pink. 38
Platter, 12¾" oval, five-part, clear 17
Platter, 12¾" oval, five-part, pink 35
Relish dish, three-part, deep, pink, 7½" d. 67
Relish plate, three-part, pink, 10½" d. 25
Relish plate, four-part, solid lace, pink, 13" d. 64
Sugar bowl, open, pink 21
Tumbler, pink, 4½" h., 9 oz. 22
Tumbler, footed, pink, 5" h., 10½ oz. 76

LORAIN or Basket or Number 615, Indiana Glass Co., 1929-32 (Process-etched)

Bowl, 9¾" oval vegetable, green 44
Bowl, 9¾" oval vegetable, yellow 48
Creamer, footed, green 16
Creamer, footed, yellow 24

Cup & saucer, clear 15
Cup & saucer, yellow 25
Plate, 5½", sherbet, green 7
Plate, 5½", sherbet, yellow 12
Plate, 7¾", salad, clear 10
Plate, 7¾", salad, green 12
Plate, 7¾", salad, yellow 14
Plate, 8⅜", luncheon, green 17
Plate, 8⅜", luncheon, yellow 28
Plate, 10¼", dinner, clear 36
Plate, 10¼", dinner, green 48
Plate, 10¼", dinner, yellow 62
Platter, 11½", green 33
Platter, 11½", yellow 47
Relish, four-part, clear, 8" 16
Relish, four-part, green, 8" 20
Relish, four-part, yellow, 8" 39
Sherbet, footed, green 21
Sherbet, footed, yellow 34
Sugar bowl, open, footed, green 15
Sugar bowl, open, footed, yellow 22
Tumbler, footed, green, 4¾" h., 9 oz 22
Tumbler, footed, yellow, 4¾" h., 9 oz. 33

MADRID, Federal Glass Co., 1932-39 (Process-etched)

Bowl, 4¾" d., cream soup, amber 16
Bowl, 5" d., sauce, amber 6
Bowl, 5" d., sauce, blue 35
Bowl, 5" d., sauce, green 9
Bowl, 7" d., soup, amber 16
Bowl, 7" d., soup, green 18
Bowl, 9½" d., salad, deep, amber 32
Bowl, 10" oval vegetable, amber 21
Bowl, 10" oval vegetable, green 21
Butter dish, cov., amber 69
Butter dish, cov., green 90
Cake plate, amber, 11¼" d. 16
Cake plate, clear, 11¼" d. 15
Cake plate, pink, 11¼" d. 12
Candlesticks, amber, 2¼" h., pr. 21
Console bowl, flared, iridescent, 11" d. 16
Creamer, amber 8
Cup & saucer, amber 9
Cup & saucer, green 15
Cup & saucer, pink 14
Gelatin mold, amber, 2⅛" h. 14
Pitcher, juice, 5½" h., 36 oz. amber 40
Pitcher, 8" h., 60 oz., square, amber 49
Pitcher, 8" h., 60 oz., square, blue 167
Pitcher, 8" h., 60 oz., square, clear 22
Pitcher, 8" h., 60 oz., square, green 141
Plate, 6" d., sherbet, amber 4
Plate, 6" d., sherbet, green 7
Plate, 7½" d., salad, amber 10
Plate, 7½" d., salad, green 9

Plate, 8⅞" d., luncheon, amber 7
Plate, 8⅞" d., luncheon, green 11
Plate, 10½" d., grill, amber 9
Plate, 10½" d., grill, green 19
Platter, 11½" oval, amber 17
Platter, 11½" oval, green 19
Relish plate, amber, 10½" d. 15
Relish plate, clear, 10½" d. 7
Salt & pepper shakers, amber, 3½" h., flat, pr. . . 42
Salt & pepper shakers, green, 3½" h., flat, pr. . . 63
Sherbet, amber 7
Sherbet, blue 15
Sherbet, green 12
Sugar bowl, cov., green 58
Sugar bowl, open, amber 6
Sugar bowl, open, green 11
Tumbler, juice, amber, 3⅞" h., 5 oz. 14
Tumbler, juice, clear, 3⅞" h., 5 oz. 14
Tumbler, footed, amber, 4" h., 5 oz. 27
Tumbler, footed, green, 4" h., 5 oz. 38
Tumbler, amber, 4½" h., 9 oz. 15
Tumbler, clear, 4½" h., 9 oz. 10
Tumbler, green, 4½" h., 9 oz. 25
Tumbler, pink, 4½" h., 9 oz. 22
Tumbler, footed, clear, 5¼" h., 10 oz. 11
Tumbler, amber, 5½" h., 12 oz. 23

MANHATTAN or Horizontal Ribbed, Anchor Hocking Glass Co., 1938-43 (Press-mold)

Ashtray, clear, 4" d. 14
Ashtray, clear, 4½" sq. 22
Bowl, 4½" d., sauce, two-handled, clear 9
Bowl, 5⅜" d., berry, two-handled, clear 18
Bowl, 5⅜" d., berry, two-handled, pink 16
Bowl, 5½" d., cereal, clear 69
Bowl, 7½" d., large berry, clear 16
Bowl, 8" d., two-handled, clear 23
Bowl, 9" d., salad, clear 20
Candleholders, clear, 4½" sq., pr. 18
Candy dish, open, three-footed, pink 12
Coaster, clear, 3½" d. 13
Compote, 5¾" h., pink 34
Creamer, oval, clear 9
Creamer, oval, pink 10
Cup & saucer, clear 25
Pitcher, juice, 24 oz., ball tilt-type, clear 31
Pitcher w/ice lip, 80 oz., ball tilt-type, clear 43
Pitcher w/ice lip, 80 oz., ball tilt-type, pink 73
Plate, 6" d., sherbet or saucer, clear 7
Plate, 8½" d., salad, clear 16
Plate, 10¼" d., dinner, clear 20
Relish tray, four-part, clear, 14" d. 18
Relish tray insert, pink 6
Relish tray insert, ruby 5
Salt & pepper shakers, square, clear, 2" h., pr. . . 28

Salt & pepper shakers, square, pink, 2" h., pr.... 50
Sherbet, clear............................... 11
Sherbet, pink 14
Sugar bowl, open, oval, clear 11
Sugar bowl, open, oval, pink 11
Tumbler, footed, clear, 10 oz. 18
Tumbler, footed, green, 10 oz. 17
Vase, 8" h., clear........................... 19
Wine, clear, 3½" h. 7

MAYFAIR or Open Rose, Hocking Glass Co., 1931-37 (Process-etched)

Bowl, 5", cream soup, pink.................... 63
Bowl, 5½", cereal, blue....................... 49
Bowl, 5½", cereal, pink....................... 26
Bowl, 7", vegetable, blue 61
Bowl, 7", vegetable, pink 26
Bowl, 9½" oval vegetable, blue 71
Bowl, 9½" oval vegetable, pink................ 36
Bowl, 10", cov. vegetable, blue 140
Bowl, 10", cov. vegetable, pink.............. 150
Bowl, 10", open vegetable, blue.............. 73
Bowl, 10", open vegetable, pink 29
Bowl, 11¾" d., low, blue..................... 74
Bowl, 11¾" d., low, pink 62
Bowl, 12" d., fruit, deep, scalloped, blue 110
Bowl, 12" d., fruit, deep, scalloped, green 39
Bowl, 12" d., fruit, deep, scalloped, pink......... 62
Butter dish, cov., blue 327
Butter dish, cov., pink 73
Cake plate, footed, blue, 10" 76
Cake plate, footed, pink, 10" 31
Cake plate, handled, blue, 12" 73
Cake plate, handled, pink, 12" 47
Candy jar, cov., blue 331
Candy jar, cov., pink........................ 62
Celery dish, pink, 10" l. 42
Celery dish, two-part, blue, 10" l............. 69
Celery dish, two-part, pink, 10" l............ 254
Cookie jar, cov., blue 298
Cookie jar, cov., pink 54
Creamer, footed, blue....................... 97
Creamer, footed, pink....................... 29
Cup, blue 56
Cup, pink.................................. 19
Cup & 5¾" underplate, blue 76
Cup & 5¾" underplate, pink 34
Cup & saucer w/cup ring pink 50
Decanter w/stopper, pink, 10" h., 32 oz........ 213
Goblet, cocktail, pink, 4" h., 3 oz............. 118
Goblet, water, pink, 5¾" h., 9 oz............. 71
Pitcher, juice, 6" h., 37 oz., blue............ 188
Pitcher, juice, 6" h., 37 oz., clear 19
Pitcher, juice, 6" h., 37 oz., pink............. 60
Pitcher, 8" h., 60 oz., jug-type, blue 195
Pitcher, 8" h., 60 oz., jug-type, pink 61

Pitcher, 8½" h., 80 oz., jug-type, pink......... 108
Plate (or saucer), 5¾", blue 25
Plate (or saucer), 5¾", pink 14
Plate, 6½" d., sherbet, off-center indentation,
  blue 30
Plate, 6½" d., sherbet, pink.................. 14
Plate, 8½", luncheon, blue 59
Plate, 8½", luncheon, pink 29
Plate, 9½", dinner, pink..................... 56
Plate, 9½", grill, blue....................... 59
Plate, 9½", grill, pink....................... 42
Platter, 12" oval, open handles, blue 73
Platter, 12" oval, open handles, pink 33
Relish, four-part, blue, 8⅜"................. 83
Relish, four-part, pink, 8⅜"................. 36
Salt & pepper shakers, flat, blue, pr.......... 319
Sandwich server w/center handle, green, 12"... 42
Sandwich server w/center handle, pink, 12"... 54
Saucer w/cup ring, pink..................... 35
Sherbet, flat, blue, 2¼" h................... 129
Sherbet, footed, pink, 3" h.................. 17
Sugar bowl, open, footed, blue 93
Sugar bowl, open, footed, pink 31
Tumbler, whiskey, pink, 2¼" h., 1½ oz.......... 73
Tumbler, juice, footed, pink, 3¼" h., 3 oz. 103
Tumbler, juice, blue, 3½" h., 5 oz............ 150
Tumbler, water, blue, 4¼" h., 9 oz. 136
Tumbler, water, pink, 4¼" h., 9 oz........... 35
Tumbler, footed, blue, 5¼" h., 10 oz......... 130
Tumbler, footed, pink, 5¼" h., 10 oz......... 43
Tumbler, iced tea, pink, 5¼"h., 13½ oz........ 64
Tumbler, iced tea, footed, pink, 6½" h., 15 oz..... 44
Vase, 5½" x 8½", sweetpea, hat-shaped, blue ... 118

MISS AMERICA, Hocking Glass Co., 1935-38 (Press-mold)

Miss America Candy Jar

Bowl, 6¼" d., berry, clear 10
Bowl, 6¼" d., berry, pink.................... 27
Bowl, 8" d., fruit, curved in at top, pink......... 90

Bowl, 8¾" d., fruit, deep, pink. 79
Bowl, 10" oval vegetable, pink 33
Butter dish, cov., pink 598
Cake plate, footed, clear, 12" d. 30
Cake plate, footed, pink, 12" d. 49
Candy jar, cov., clear, 11½" h. 54
Candy jar, cov., pink, 11½" h. (ILLUS.) 181
Celery tray, clear, 10½" oblong 15
Celery tray, pink, 10½" oblong. 33
Coaster, clear, 5¾" d.. 16
Coaster, pink, 5¾" d. 33
Compote, 5" d., clear 15
Compote 5" d., pink 28
Creamer, footed, clear 13
Creamer, footed, pink 21
Cup, clear 11
Cup, green 14
Cup, pink. 25
Cup & saucer, clear 17
Cup & saucer, pink 33
Goblet, wine, clear, 3¾" h., 3 oz. 23
Goblet, wine, pink, 3¾" h., 3 oz.. 98
Goblet, juice, clear, 4¾" h., 5 oz. 24
Goblet, juice, pink, 4¾" h., 5 oz.. 103
Goblet, water, clear, 5½" h., 10 oz. 25
Goblet, water, pink, 5½" h., 10 oz. 54
Pitcher, 8" h., 65 oz., clear. 60
Pitcher, 8" h., 65 oz., pink 166
Pitcher w/ice lip, 8½" h., 65 oz., pink 188
Plate, 5¾" d., sherbet, clear 6
Plate, 5¾" sherbet, pink 10
Plate, 6¾" d., green 9
Plate, 8½" d., salad, clear. 15
Plate, 8½" d., salad, pink 25
Plate, 10¼" d., dinner, clear 17
Plate, 10¼" d., dinner, pink. 38
Plate, 10¼" d., grill, clear 14
Plate, 10¼" d., grill, pink. 28
Platter, 12¼" oval, clear 14
Platter, 12¼" oval, pink. 34
Relish, four-part, clear, 8¾" d. 11
Relish, four-part, pink, 8¾" d 26
Relish, divided, clear, 11¾" d. 21
Salt & pepper shakers, pink, pr.. 60
Saucer, clear 5
Saucer, pink 7
Sherbet, clear. 9
Sherbet, pink 17
Sugar bowl, open, footed, clear 7
Sugar bowl, open, footed, pink 21
Tumbler, juice, clear, 4" h., 5 oz. 18
Tumbler, juice, pink, 4" h., 5 oz.. 53
Tumbler, water, clear, 4½" h., 10 oz.. 18
Tumbler, water, green, 4½" h., 10 oz. 18
Tumbler, water, pink, 4½" h., 10 oz.. 36
Tumbler, iced tea, pink, 6¾" h., 14 oz.. 93

MOONSTONE, Anchor Hocking Glass Corp., 1941-46 (Press-mold)

Moonstone Puff Box

Bonbon, heart-shaped, w/handle, 6½" w. 13
Bowl, 5½" d., dessert, crimped rim. 10
Bowl, 6" w., three-part, cloverleaf-shaped 11
Bowl, 6½" d., two-handled, crimped rim. 12
Bowl, 7¾" d., flat. 13
Bowl, 9½" d., crimped rim. 23
Candleholders, pr.. 17
Candy dish, cov., two-handled, 6" d. 27
Cigarette box, cov., rectangular. 23
Creamer, footed 9
Cup & saucer. 13
Goblet, 10 oz. 21
Plate, 6¼" d., sherbet 7
Plate, 8⅜" d., luncheon. 14
Puff box, cov., 4¾" d. (ILLUS.). 24
Relish bowl, divided, 7¾" d.. 11
Sherbet, footed. 7
Sugar bowl, footed. 8

NORMANDIE or Bouquet & Lattice, Federal Glass Co., 1933-40 (Process-etched)

Bowl, 5" d., berry, Sunburst iridescent 4
Bowl, 6½" d., cereal, Sunburst iridescent. 7
Bowl, 10" oval vegetable, amber 15
Bowl, 10" oval vegetable, Sunburst iridescent . . . 17
Creamer, footed, pink. 9
Cup & saucer, amber. 10
Cup & saucer, pink 11
Cup & saucer, Sunburst iridescent 8
Pitcher, 8" h., 80 oz., pink 152
Plate, 6" d., sherbet, pink 7
Plate, 8" d., salad, amber 9
Plate, 8" d., salad, pink 12
Plate, 11" d., dinner, amber 27
Plate, 11" d., dinner, pink 111
Plate, 11" d., grill, pink 20
Plate, 11" d., grill, Sunburst iridescent 9
Platter, 11¾" oval, Sunburst iridescent 14
Salt & pepper shakers, amber, pr. 49
Salt & pepper shakers, pink, pr. 99
Sherbet, pink 10

Sherbet, Sunburst iridescent 7
Sugar bowl, open, Sunburst iridescent 7
Tumbler, juice, amber, 4" h., 5 oz. 30
Tumbler, water, amber, 4½" h., 9 oz. 21
Tumbler, iced tea, pink, 5" h., 12 oz. 142

NUMBER 612 or Horseshoe, Indiana Glass Co., 1930-33 (Process-etched)

Bowl, 6½" d., cereal, yellow 35
Bowl, 7½" d., salad, yellow. 26
Bowl, 9½" d., large berry, green. 48
Bowl, 9½" d., large berry, yellow 50
Cup, green 13
Cup & saucer, green 18
Cup & saucer, yellow. 15
Pitcher, 8½" h., 64 oz., yellow 367
Plate, 6" d., sherbet, green. 9
Plate, 6" d., sherbet, yellow 8
Plate, 8⅜" d., salad, yellow. 11
Plate, 9⅜" d., luncheon, green 14
Plate, 11½" d., sandwich, green. 23
Plate, 11½" d., sandwich, yellow 24
Platter, 10¾" oval, green 28
Platter, 10¾" oval, yellow. 28
Relish, three-part, footed, yellow 38
Saucer, green. 4
Sherbet, green 15
Sherbet, yellow. 16
Sugar bowl, open, footed, green 16
Tumbler, footed, green, 9 oz. 27
Tumbler, footed, yellow, 9 oz. 24

PARROT or Sylvan, Federal Glass Co., 1931-32 (Process-etched)

Bowl, 5" sq., berry, amber 21
Bowl, 5" sq., berry, green. 27
Bowl, 7" sq., soup, amber. 33
Bowl, 7" sq., soup, green 45
Bowl, 10" oval vegetable, green. 61
Butter dish, cov., green 403
Creamer, footed, green 49
Cup & saucer, green 60
Hot plate, green, scalloped edge 888
Jam dish, amber, 7" sq. 34
Plate, 5¾" sq., sherbet, amber 25
Plate, 5¾" sq., sherbet, green 28
Plate, 7½" sq., salad, green 37
Plate, 9" sq., dinner, amber 40
Plate, 9" sq., dinner, green 54
Plate, 10½" d., grill, green. 36
Plate, 10½" sq., grill, amber 30
Platter, 11¼" oblong, green 54
Salt & pepper shakers, green, pr. 298
Sherbet, footed, cone-shaped, amber 23
Sugar bowl, cov., green. 191
Sugar bowl, open, green 31

PATRICIAN or Spoke, Federal Glass Co., 1933-37 (Process-etched)

Patrician Grill Plate

Bowl, 4¾" d., cream soup, amber 16
Bowl, 4¾" d., cream soup, clear. 13
Bowl, 4¾" d., cream soup, green 23
Bowl, 4¾" d., cream soup, pink 19
Bowl, 5" d., berry, amber 11
Bowl, 5" d., berry, clear 12
Bowl, 5" d., berry, green. 14
Bowl, 5" d., berry, pink 14
Bowl, 8½" d., large berry, amber 47
Bowl, 8½" d., large berry, green. 39
Bowl, 8½" d., large berry, pink 29
Bowl, 10" oval vegetable, amber 32
Bowl, 10" oval vegetable, clear 30
Bowl, 10" oval vegetable, green. 31
Bowl, 10" oval vegetable, pink 19
Butter dish, cov., amber 89
Butter dish, cov., clear. 91
Butter dish, cov., green 104
Butter dish, cov., pink 282
Cookie jar, cov., amber 85
Cookie jar, cov., green. 478
Creamer, footed, amber 8
Creamer, footed, green 14
Cup & saucer, amber. 18
Cup & saucer, clear 16
Cup & saucer, green 20
Jam dish, amber, 6". 32
Pitcher, 8" h., 75 oz., molded handle, amber 110
Pitcher, 8" h., 75 oz., molded handle, clear 107
Pitcher, 8" h., 75 oz., molded handle, green 148
Pitcher, 8" h., 75 oz., molded handle, pink. 119
Pitcher, 8¼" h., 75 oz., applied handle, clear. . . . 128
Pitcher, 8¼" h., 75 oz., applied handle, green . . . 110
Plate, 6" d., sherbet, amber 10
Plate, 6" d., sherbet, green. 9
Plate, 6" d., sherbet, pink 8
Plate, 7½" d., salad, amber. 17
Plate, 7½" d., salad, green 15
Plate, 9" d., luncheon, amber 11
Plate, 9" d., luncheon, green. 14

Plate, 10½" d., dinner, amber 7
Plate, 10½" d., dinner, pink. 42
Plate, 10½" d., grill, amber 13
Plate, 10½" d., grill, green (ILLUS.) 19
Platter, 11½" oval, amber. 30
Salt & pepper shakers, amber, pr. 56
Salt & pepper shakers, green, pr. 62
Sherbet, amber. 12
Sherbet, green 14
Sugar bowl, cov., amber 63
Sugar bowl, cov., clear 54
Sugar bowl, open, amber. 8
Sugar bowl, open, green 12
Tumbler, amber, 4" h., 5 oz. 34
Tumbler, clear, 4" h., 5 oz. 20
Tumbler, green, 4" h., 5 oz. 26
Tumbler, pink, 4" h., 5 oz. 33
Tumbler, footed, amber, 5¼" h., 8 oz. 50
Tumbler, amber, 4½" h., 9 oz. 29
Tumbler, iced tea, amber, 5½" h., 14 oz. 46
Tumbler, iced tea, green, 5½" h., 14 oz. 48

PRINCESS, HOCKING GLASS CO., 1931-35 (Process-etched)

Bowl, 4½", berry, green 26
Bowl, 4½", berry, pink. 30
Bowl, 5", cereal, green 40
Bowl, 5", cereal, pink 36
Bowl, 9" octagon, salad, green. 43
Bowl, 9" octagon, salad, pink 44
Bowl, 9½" hat shape, green 50
Bowl, 10" oval vegetable, green. 29
Bowl, 10" oval vegetable, pink 40
Butter dish, cov., green 110
Butter dish, cov., pink 113
Cake stand, green, 10". 32
Cake stand, pink, 10". 37
Candy jar, cov., green 67
Candy jar, cov., pink. 75
Coaster, green, 4" 38
Cookie jar, cov., green. 59
Creamer, oval, amber. 14
Cup & saucer, green 24
Cup & saucer, pink 23
Cup & saucer, yellow 12
Pitcher, 6" h., 37 oz., jug-type, green. 60
Pitcher, 6" h., 37 oz., jug-type, pink 68
Pitcher, 8" h., 60 oz., jug-type, green. 56
Pitcher, 8" h., 60 oz., jug-type, pink 71
Plate, 5½", sherbet, amber 4
Plate, 5½", sherbet, green 10
Plate, 5½", sherbet, pink. 11
Plate, 8" d., salad, green. 16
Plate, 8", salad, amber 15
Plate, 8", salad, pink. 15
Plate, 9½", dinner, amber. 12

Plate, 9½", dinner, green 30
Plate, 9½", dinner, pink. 27
Plate, 9½", dinner, yellow 15
Plate, 9½", grill, amber 7
Plate, 9½", grill, green. 10
Plate, 9½", grill, pink. 14
Plate, 9½", grill, yellow 9
Platter, 12" oval, closed handles, green. 30
Platter, 12" oval, closed handles, yellow 52
Relish, divided, pink, 7½" 32
Salt & pepper (or spice) shakers, green,
   5½" h., pr. 53
Salt & pepper shakers, yellow, 4½" h., pr. 78
Sherbet, footed, green 23
Sherbet, footed, pink 24
Sugar bowl, cov., yellow 27
Tumbler, juice, pink, 3" h., 5 oz. 32
Tumbler, water, green, 4" h., 9 oz. 31
Tumbler, water, pink, 4" h., 9 oz. 28
Tumbler, water, yellow, 4" h., 9 oz. 24
Tumbler, footed, green, 5¼" h., 10 oz. 33
Tumbler, footed, pink, 5¼" h. 10 oz. 29
Tumbler, footed, yellow, 5¼" h., 10 oz. 22
Tumbler, footed, green, 6½" h., 12½ oz. 104
Tumbler, footed, pink, 6½" h., 12½ oz. 98
Tumbler, iced tea, pink, 5¼" h., 13 oz. 36
Tumbler, iced tea, yellow, 5¼" h., 13 oz. 28
Vase, 8" h., green 36
Vase, 8" h., pink 44

SHARON OR CABBAGE ROSE, FEDERAL GLASS CO., 1935-39 (Chip-mold)

Bowl, 5" d., berry, amber 8
Bowl, 5" d., berry, green. 17
Bowl, 5" d., berry, pink 13
Bowl, 5" d., cream soup, amber 23
Bowl, 5" d., cream soup, green 56
Bowl, 5" d., cream soup, pink 49
Bowl, 6" d., cereal, amber 17
Bowl, 6" d., cereal, green 27
Bowl, 6" d., cereal, pink 29
Bowl, 7½" d., soup, amber 45
Bowl, 7½" d., soup, pink. 55
Bowl, 8½" d., berry, amber 7
Bowl, 8½" d., berry, green 33
Bowl, 8½" d., berry, pink. 33
Bowl, 9½" oval vegetable, amber 18
Bowl, 9½" oval vegetable, green 35
Bowl, 9½" oval vegetable, pink. 34
Bowl, 10½" d., fruit, amber 19
Bowl, 10½" d., fruit, pink. 39
Butter dish, cov., green 90
Butter dish, cov., pink 58
Cake plate, footed, amber, 11½" d. 23
Cake plate, footed, clear, 11½" d. 14

Cake plate, footed, green, 11½" d. **66**
Cake plate, footed, pink, 11½" d. **42**
Candy jar, cov., amber **43**
Candy jar, cov., green **174**
Candy jar, cov., pink. **62**
Creamer, amber **14**
Creamer, green **25**
Creamer, pink **18**
Cup, amber. **9**
Cup, green **20**
Cup, pink. **14**
Cup & saucer, green **32**
Cup & saucer, pink **26**
Jam dish, green, 7½" d., 1½" h. **43**
Pitcher, 9" h., 80 oz., green **448**
Pitcher, 9" h., 80 oz., pink **139**
Pitcher w/ice lip, 9" h., 80 oz., amber **120**
Pitcher w/ice lip, 9"h., 80 oz., pink **180**
Plate, 6" d., bread & butter, amber **5**
Plate, 6" d., bread & butter, green **9**
Plate, 6" d., bread & butter, pink. **8**
Plate, 7½" d., salad, amber. **14**
Plate, 7½" d., salad, pink **31**
Plate, 9½" d., dinner, amber **9**
Plate, 9½" d., dinner, green **25**
Plate, 9½" d., dinner, pink. **23**
Platter, 12½" oval, amber. **17**
Platter, 12½" oval, green **33**
Platter, 12½" oval, pink. **32**
Salt & pepper shakers, green, pr. **76**
Salt & pepper shakers, pink, pr. **50**
Sherbet, footed, amber. **13**
Sherbet, footed, green **38**
Sherbet, footed, pink **16**
Sugar bowl, cov., amber **31**
Sugar bowl, cov., pink **41**
Sugar bowl, open, amber. **7**
Sugar bowl, open, pink **14**
Tumbler, amber, 4" h., 9 oz. **24**
Tumbler, pink, 4" h., 9 oz. **45**
Tumbler, amber, 5¼" h., 12 oz. **59**
Tumbler, green, 5¼" h., 12 oz. **107**
Tumbler, pink, 5¼" h., 12 oz. **51**
Tumbler, footed, amber, 6½" h., 15 oz. **135**
Tumbler, footed, pink, 6½" h., 15 oz. **57**

SIERRA OR PINWHEEL, JEANNETTE GLASS CO., 1931-33 (Press-mold)

Bowl, 5½" d., cereal, green **18**
Bowl, 5½" d., cereal, pink. **15**
Bowl, 8½" d., berry, green **32**
Bowl, 8½" d., berry, pink. **32**
Butter dish, cov., pink **52**
Creamer, pink. **20**
Cup, pink. **14**
Cup & saucer, green **23**

Cup & saucer, pink **19**
Pitcher, 6½" h., 32 oz., green. **140**
Pitcher, 6½" h., 32 oz., pink **106**
Plate, 9" d., dinner, green **21**
Plate, 9" d., dinner, pink **21**
Platter, 11" oval, pink **45**
Salt & pepper shakers, green, pr. **38**
Serving tray, two-handled, green. **19**
Serving tray, two-handled, pink **21**
Sugar bowl, cov., green. **32**
Sugar bowl, cov., pink **21**
Tumbler, footed, pink, 4½" h., 9 oz. **77**

SWIRL OR PETAL SWIRL, JEANNETTE GLASS CO., 1937-38 (Press-mold)

Swirl Salad Bowl

Bowl, 5¼" d., cereal, Delphite **14**
Bowl, 5¼" d., cereal, pink. **11**
Bowl, 5¼" d., cereal, ultramarine **17**
Bowl, 9" d., salad, Delphite. **30**
Bowl, 9" d., salad, pink **21**
Bowl, 9" d., salad, ultramarine (ILLUS.) **30**
Bowl, 10" d., fruit, closed handles, footed,
   ultramarine **30**
Butter dish, cov., pink **227**
Candleholders, double, ultramarine, pr. **49**
Candy dish, cov., ultramarine **163**
Candy dish, open, three-footed, pink, 5½" d. **14**
Candy dish, open, three-footed,
   ultramarine, 5½" d. **20**
Coaster, ultramarine, 3¼" d., 1" h. **13**
Console bowl, footed, ultramarine, 10½" d. **33**
Creamer, ultramarine **16**
Cup & saucer, ultramarine **20**
Plate, 6½" d., sherbet, Delphite **8**
Plate, 6½" d., sherbet, ultramarine **7**
Plate, 7¼" d., ultramarine **14**
Plate, 8" d., salad, ultramarine **19**
Plate, 9¼" d., dinner, Delphite **16**
Plate, 9¼" d., dinner, ultramarine **19**
Plate, 12½" d., sandwich, ultramarine **30**
Salt & pepper shakers, ultramarine, pr. **46**
Sherbet, pink **15**
Sherbet, ultramarine. **23**

Soup bowl w/lug handles, ultramarine 44
Sugar bowl, open, ultramarine 15
Tumbler, footed, ultramarine, 9 oz. 45
Tumbler, ultramarine, 4" h., 9 oz 38
Tumbler, ultramarine, 5⅛" h., 13 oz. 133
Vase, 8½" h., ultramarine 28

TEA ROOM, Indiana Glass Co., 1926-31 (Press-mold)

Tea Room Creamer & Sugar Bowl on Tray

Bowl, 8¾" d., salad, green 115
Bowl, 8¾" d., salad, pink 91
Bowl, 9½" oval vegetable, pink. 71
Creamer, footed, pink, 4½" h 20
Creamer & open sugar bowl on center-
handled tray, pink (ILLUS.) 93
Creamer & open sugar bowl on
rectangular tray, green 96
Lamp, electric, green, 9" 152
Lamp, electric, pink, 9" 127
Pitcher, 64 oz., green 140
Plate, 8¼" d., luncheon, green 32
Plate, 8¼" d., luncheon, pink 31
Sherbet, low, flared edge, pink. 26
Tray, rectangular, for creamer & sugar bowl,
pink. 59
Tray w/center handle, for creamer & sugar
bowl, green 200
Tray w/center handle, for creamer & sugar
bowl, pink 194

Tea Room Vase

Vase, 11" h., straight, pink (ILLUS.) 165

WATERFORD or Waffle, Hocking Glass Co., 1938-44 (Press-mold)

Ashtray, clear, 4" 8
Bowl, 4¾" d., berry, pink. 19
Bowl, 5¼" d., cereal, pink. 35
Bowl, 8¼" d., berry, clear 15
Butter dish, cov., clear. 26
Butter dish, cov., pink 220
Cake plate, handled, clear, 10¼" d. 11
Pitcher, juice, 42 oz., tilt-type, clear 25
Pitcher w/ice lip, 80 oz., clear 34
Pitcher w/ice lip, 80 oz., pink. 173
Plate, 6" d., sherbet, pink 7
Plate, 7½" d., salad, clear. 7
Plate, 9⅝" d., dinner, clear 11
Plate, 13¾" d., sandwich, clear. 11
Plate, 13¾" d., sandwich, pink 26
Salt & pepper shakers, clear, short, pr. 9
Sherbet, footed, clear. 4
Sherbet, footed, pink 14
Sugar bowl, cov., oval, clear 15
Tumbler, footed, clear, 5" h., 10 oz. 13
Tumbler, footed, pink, 5" h., 10 oz. 24

WINDSOR DIAMOND or Windsor, Jeannette Glass Co., 1936-46 (Press-mold)

Windsor Diamond Pitcher

Ashtray, Delphite, 5¾" d. 43
Ashtray, green, 5¾" d. 45
Ashtray, pink, 5¾" d. 36
Bowl, 4¾" d., berry, clear 6
Bowl, 4¾" d., berry, green 11
Bowl, 4¾" d., berry, pink. 10
Bowl, 5" d., cream soup, green 26
Bowl, 5" d., cream soup, pink. 21
Bowl, 5" d., pointed edge, clear 7
Bowl, 5" d., pointed edge, pink. 27
Bowl, 5⅛" or 5⅜" d., cereal, green 25
Bowl, 5⅛" or 5⅜" d., cereal, pink 24

Bowl, 7" d., three-footed, pink **28**
Bowl, 8" d., pointed edge, clear **15**
Bowl, 8½" d., berry, pink. **23**
Bowl, 7 x 11¾" boat shape, clear. **20**
Bowl, 7 x 11¾" boat shape, green **37**
Bowl, 7 x 11¾" boat shape, pink **38**
Bowl, 12½" d., fruit, clear **28**
Bowl, 12½" d., fruit, pink. **115**
Butter dish, cov., clear. **26**
Butter dish, cov., green **87**
Butter dish, pink. **48**
Cake plate, footed, pink, 10¾" d. **22**
Candlestick, clear, 3" h. **14**
Candlestick, pink, 3" h. **47**
Candlesticks, clear, 3" h., pr. **20**
Candlesticks, pink, 3" h., pr. **95**
Coaster, green, 3¼" d. **13**
Creamer, flat, green **17**
Creamer, flat, pink **12**
Cup & saucer, clear **7**
Cup & saucer, green **19**
Cup & saucer, pink **17**
Pitcher, 4½" h., 16 oz., clear (ILLUS.) **25**
Pitcher, 4½" h., 16 oz., pink **117**
Pitcher, 6¾" h., 52 oz., clear **12**
Pitcher, 6¾" h., 52 oz., green. **64**
Pitcher, 6¾" h., 52 oz., pink **31**
Plate, 6" d., sherbet, green. **7**
Plate, 6" d., sherbet, pink **6**
Plate, 7" d., salad, green. **21**
Plate, 9" d., dinner, clear. **7**
Plate, 9" d., dinner, green **25**
Plate, 9" d., dinner, pink **24**
Plate, 10¼", sandwich, handled, green **24**
Plate, 10¼", sandwich, handled, pink. **18**
Plate, 13⅝" d., chop, green **41**
Plate, 13⅝" d., chop, pink. **41**
Platter, 11½" oval, pink. **20**
Salt & pepper shakers, green, pr. **46**
Salt & pepper shakers, pink, pr. **37**
Sherbet, footed, clear. **5**
Sherbet, footed, green **15**
Sherbet, footed, pink **13**
Sugar bowl, cov., flat, clear **9**
Sugar bowl, cov., flat, green **33**
Sugar bowl, cov., flat, pink. **30**
Tray, pink, 4⅛ x 9", w/handles **17**
Tray, green, 8½ x 9¾", w/handles **25**
Tumbler, clear, 3¼" h., 5 oz. **10**
Tumbler, green, 3¼" h., 5 oz.. . . . . **33**
Tumbler, pink, 3¼" h., 5 oz. **25**
Tumbler, clear, 4" h., 9 oz. **6**
Tumbler, green, 4" h., 9 oz. **34**
Tumbler, pink, 4" h., 9 oz. **19**
Tumbler, green, 5" h., 12 oz. **47**
Tumbler, pink, 5" h., 12 oz. **29**

DEVEZ & DEGUÉ

The Saint-Hilaire, Touvier, de Varreaux and Company of Pantin, France used the name De Vez on their cameo glass earlier this century. Some of their examples were marked "Degué," after one of their master glassmakers. Officially the company was named "Cristallerie de Pantin."

Scenic DeVez Cameo Vase

Cameo vase, 5" h., 2½" d., deeply waisted ovoid form tapering to a small flat mouth, frosted clear overlaid in dark blue & gold & cut w/a landscape of an island, house, trees & water w/mountains in the background & leafy branches in the foreground, signed "DeVez" (ILLUS.). **$645**

Cameo vase, 6¼" h., footed ovoid body tapering to a slender trumpet neck, opaque cream overlaid in rose red & maroon & cameo-cut w/detailed poppy blossoms, seed pods & leafy stems, signed "DeVez" on lower edge **1,380**

Cameo vase, 8¼" h., slender ovoid body tapering to a tall slender neck, pale lavender overlaid in dark purple & cut w/a lakeside scene w/leafy branches & grasses in the foreground & a sailboat in the background, signed in cameo "de Vez" . . . **805**

Cameo vase, 10" h., elongated ovoid form, frosted colorless cased in amber, olive & deep blue, cameo-etched silhouetted trees overlooking water w/distant village & mountains, signed "de Vez" on lower side **1,150**

Degué Cameo Vases

Cameo vase, 13¼" h., ovoid body w/a short flaring rim, grey mottled w/traces of ochre, overlaid w/purple shading to reddish orange & cut w/morning glory vines, signed "Degué," ca. 1925 (ILLUS. left) **2,300**

Cameo vase, 13½" h., thick disk foot below the slender ovoid body w/a heavy molded ring mouth, grey overlaid w/orange powdered glass cut w/a long zig-zag design against an acid-treated ground, signed in cameo "Degué," ca. 1920s **805**

Cameo vase, 15½" h., double-gourd form w/flaring neck, blue & grey mottled ground overlaid w/tangerine shading to dark purple & cut w/stylized bellflowers on thin stems w/spade-form leaves, signed "Degué - France," ca. 1925 (ILLUS. right) **1,610**

Cameo vase, 18" h., tall gently swelled ovoid form w/a flaring rim, acid-etched clear overlaid in mottled green & cameo-etched w/large barred Art Deco-style triangles, signed on side "Degué" (interior stain) **920**

Vase, 6" h., ovoid body in maroon & fiery amber, etched w/cottages & a mother & child under tall trees, polished rim, signed "deVez" at side **863**

DUNCAN & MILLER

Duncan & Miller Glass Company, a successor firm to George A. Duncan & Sons Company, produced a wide range of pressed wares and novelty pieces during the late 19th century and into the early 20th century. During the Depression era and after, it continued making a wide variety of more modern patterns, including mold-blown types, and also introduced a number of etched and engraved patterns. Many colors, including opalescent hues, were produced during this era. Especially popular today are the graceful swan dishes produced in the Pall Mall and Sylvan patterns.

The numbers after the pattern name indicate the original factory pattern number. The Duncan factory was closed in 1955. Also see ANIMALS and PATTERN GLASS in the Glass section.

Ashtray, Canterbury patt. (No. 115), clear, 3" ... **$12**

Ashtray, Early American Sandwich patt. (No. 41), clear, 3" sq. **8**

Basket w/loop handle, Early American Sandwich patt., amber, 6" h. **150**

Basket w/loop handle, Early American Sandwich patt., clear, 12". **295**

Bonbon, heart-shaped, handled, Early American Sandwich patt., clear, 5". **15**

Bowl, cream soup, Spiral Flutes patt., amber..... **25**

Bowl, fruit, Canterbury patt. (No. 115), clear **8**

Bowl, 5" d., Early American Sandwich patt., clear **10**

Bowl, 9" d., Canterbury patt. (No. 115), clear..... **30**

Bowl, 9" d., tab-handled, Caribbean patt., clear... **35**

Bowl, 10½" d., 5" h., crimped rim, etched First Love patt., clear **60**

Candlestick, three-light, Canterbury patt. (No. 115), clear, 6" h. **35**

Candlesticks, Canterbury patt. (No. 115), pink opalescent, 3" h., pr. **65**

Candy dish, cov., Early American Sandwich patt., clear, 6" sq. **425**

Candy dish, cov., Canterbury patt. (No. 115), clear, 7" h. **33**

Candy dish, cov., footed, Early American Sandwich patt., green, 8" h. **75**

Celery dish, etched Beverly patt., amber, 11" l.... **15**

Champagne, Early American Sandwich patt., clear, 5¼" h. **17**

Teardrop Champagne

Champagne, Teardrop patt. (No. 301), clear, 5" h., 5 oz. (ILLUS.) **10**

Coaster, Early American Sandwich patt., clear, 5" d. **11**

Cocktail, Teardrop patt., clear, 4½" h., 3½ oz..... **14**

Cocktail, Caribbean patt., blue, 4¾" h., 3 oz...... **45**

Compote 5" h., 7" w., Puritan patt., green **40**

Cordial, etched First Love patt., clear, 3¾" h., 1 oz. **60**

Cordial, Teardrop patt., clear, 4" h., 1 oz. **30**

Cornucopia vase, footed, Three Feathers patt. (No. 117), clear, 8" h. **21**

Creamer, Early American Sandwich patt., clear.... **8**

Creamer, Festive patt. (No. 155), aqua **25**

Creamer & cov. sugar bowl on tray, Festive patt. (No. 155), aqua, 3 pcs. **85**

Creamer & sugar bowl, individual-size, Early American Sandwich patt., clear, pr. **18**

Cup & saucer, Canterbury patt. (No. 115), clear .. **13**

Cup & saucer, Early American Sandwich patt., clear. **18**

Cup & saucer, demitasse, Puritan patt., pink..... **21**

Deviled egg plate, Early American Sandwich patt., clear, 12" d. **73**

Epergne, Early American Sandwich patt., clear.. **250**

Finger bowl & liner, Spiral Flutes patt.,
   amber, 2 pcs. 25
Goblet, Caribbean patt., clear, 4" h., 3 oz. 25
Goblet, etched Buttercup patt., low 20
Goblet, water, Spiral Flutes patt., green. 15
Goblet, juice, footed, etched First Love patt.,
   clear, 4½" h., 5 oz. 24
Goblet, Teardrop patt., clear, 5¾" h., 9 oz. 14
Ice tub, handled, Spiral Flutes patt., pink 52
Lamp, oil-type, Mardi Gras patt. (No. 42), clear . . 195
Lamp shade, Mardi Gras patt. (No. 42), clear 39
Model of a swan, Pall Mall patt. (No. 30),
   clear, 5" l. 15
Model of a swan, Sylvan patt. (No. 122),
   pink opalescent, 5½" l. 95
Model of a swan, Pall Mall patt. (No. 30),
   cranberry stained, 8" l. 29
Model of a swan, Pall Mall patt. (No. 30½),
   clear, 10" l. 40
Nut cup, Spiral Flutes patt., amber. 12
Oyster cocktail, Early American Sandwich
   patt., clear. 18
Parfait, Spiral Flutes patt., amber. 25
Pitcher, Caribbean patt., blue, 16 oz. 275
Pitcher, Iris patt., clear 35
Pitcher w/ice lip, Early American Sandwich
   patt., clear, ½ gal., 8" h. 110
Plate, 7" d., Early American Sandwich patt.,
   clear 24
Plate, 7" d., Puritan patt., green 7
Plate, 7" d., Spiral Flutes patt., amber 4
Plate, salad, 8½" d., etched First Love patt.,
   clear 20
Plate, dinner, 9½"d., Early American
   Sandwich patt., clear 40
Plate, dinner, 10½" d., Puritan patt., clear 25
Plate, sandwich, 11" d., two-handled,
   Canterbury patt. (No. 115), clear 22
Plate, cracker, 13" d., Early American
   Sandwich patt., clear 30
Plate, 14" d., Teardrop patt., clear 35
Plate, chop, 14" d., etched Beverly patt., amber. . . 28
Plate, torte, 14" d., Canterbury patt.
   (No. 115), clear. 25
Plate, Lazy Susan, 18" d., Teardrop patt.,
   w/leaf cutting, clear. 125
Punch bowl & ladle, Festive patt.
   (No. 155), clear, 2 pcs. 50
Relish dish, three-part, Canterbury patt.,
   chartreuse, 8" 25
Relish dish, three-part, etched First Love
   patt., clear, 6 x 10½". 45
Relish dish, five-part, Caribbean patt., clear 40
Relish dish, six-part, Teardrop patt., clear. 30
Salt & pepper shakers, etched First Love
   patt., clear, pr. 35
Sauce ladle, Festive patt. aqua 40
Sherbet, Early American Sandwich patt., clear ... 10

Soup plate w/flanged rim, Puritan patt.,
   pink, 8" d. 35
Sugar bowl, Early American Sandwich patt.,
   clear. 8
Sugar bowl, etched First Love patt., clear 18
Tumbler, etched Buttercup patt., footed, 12 oz.... 25
Tumbler, iced tea, Early American
   Sandwich patt., clear, 12 oz. 18
Tumbler, iced tea, flat, Spiral Flutes patt., green . . 65
Tumbler, juice, for ice dish, etched Shirley
   patt, pink. 10
Tumbler, Spiral Flutes patt., green, 2½ oz. 10
Vase, 8¾" h., Spiral Flutes patt., green 25
Vase, 5" h., 6" d., Hobnail patt., pink opalescent . . 65
Vase, 9½" h., ruffled rim, Caribbean patt., blue . . 175
Vase/flower arranger, 8" h., Canterbury
   patt. (No. 115), clear. 35
Violet vase, 3" h., Canterbury patt.
   (No. 115), clear. 15
Wine, Caribbean patt., blue, 3 oz. 35
Wine, Early American Sandwich patt., clear...... 19
Wine, etched First Love patt., clear,
   5¼" h., 3 oz. 26

DURAND

*Fine decorative glass similar to that made by
Tiffany and other outstanding glasshouses of its
day was made by the Vineland Flint Glass
Works Co. in Vineland, New Jersey, first headed
by Victor Durand, Sr., and subsequently by his
son Victor Durand, Jr., in the 1920s.*

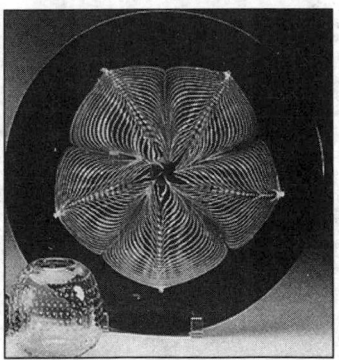

Durand Charger & Small Vase

Box, cov., footed squatty round form
   w/flattened round fitted cover, King Tut
   patt., Lady Gay Rose color w/gold
   interior, applied ambergris disk foot,
   cover star-cut at center top pontil mark,
   unsigned, 4½" d., 3¼" h., ... **$1,610**
Charger, large transparent blue disk
   centered by five colorless & lighter blue &
   grey pulled feathers, numerous bubbles,
   14¼" d. (ILLUS. right). **747**

Unusual Durand Jar

Jar, cov., wide sharply tapering ovoid body
w/a domed fitted cover, green w/iridized
"King Tut" decoration, applied amber
button on cover, 7¼" h. (ILLUS.) **3,105**

Lamp base, Spanish Lace design, the glass
shaft w/a flared ruffled rim on the slender
ovoid body of transparent amber w/blue
pulled feathers & cut in the "Bridgeton
Rose" patt., mounted on a gilt-metal short
pedestal & domed ringed foot & w/a
socket rod issuing from the top, glass
8½" h. (metal worn, sockets replaced) **230**

Vase, 4" h., nearly spherical form, colorless
w/controlled bubble interior decoration,
base signed "V. Durand 1995-4"
(ILLUS. left) **288**

Vase, 5¾" h., footed squatty bulbous base
center by a tall trumpet neck, overall gold
iridescent interior & exterior, signed
"V. Durand 1990 6" **518**

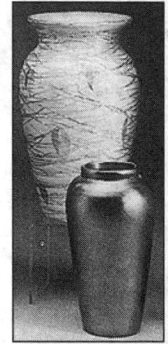

*From left: Threaded & Plain Durand Vases
Large Decorated Durand Vase*

Vase, 6" h., large ovoid body tapering to a
widely flaring short neck, opal ground
w/greenish gold leaves & silvery gold
threading, gold iridescent interior, signed
"V Durand 1812-6," some thread loss
(ILLUS. left) **633**

Vase, 6" h., slender ovoid body w/a short
cylindrical neck, overall blue iridescence,
signed "Durand 1722½-6" (ILLUS. right) **431**

Vase, 8" h., wide cylindrical form rounded at
the base & shoulder w/a short, wide rim,
overall strong blue iridescence, polished
pontil signed "Durand 1968-8" **805**

Vase, 10" h., green on gold "King Tut" vase,
broad shouldered cased glass oval body
w/strong green pulled & coiled decoration
on lustrous iridescent gold surface, gold
interior over opal, base inscribed
"Durand 1964-10" **2,415**

Vase, 12½" h., cushion foot below the wide
squatty bulbous body w/a wide rounded
shoulder tapering to a tall cylindrical neck
w/flared rim, rose pink w/coiled
iridescence, yellowish white interior, silver
enameled mark on pontil "Durand"
(ILLUS.) **2,875**

Vase, 15½" h., genie-shaped, bulbous
cobalt ribbed body w/elongated slender
neck, lustrous blue-silver iridescent
surface overall, mirror bright near base **2,415**

FENTON

Fenton Mark

Fenton Art Glass Company began producing
glass at Williamstown, West Virginia, in
January 1907. Organized by Frank L. and John
W. Fenton, the company began operations in a
newly built glass factory with an experienced
master glass craftsman, Jacob Rosenthal, as its
factory manager. Fenton has produced a wide
variety of collectible glassware through the
years, including Carnival. Still in production
today, its current productions may be found at
finer gift shops across the country.

William Heacock's three-volume set on
Fenton, published by Antique Publications, is
the standard reference in this field.

Basket, Rose Burmese, No. 7731 . . . . **$80**
Basket, Hobnail patt., French
Opalescent, 7½" **35**
Bowl, 9¾" d., fruit, Mandarin Red on black
glass stand, No.846, 2 pcs. **85**
Bowl, 10" d., low sides, Wisteria, stretch finish . . . **80**
Bowl, 10" d., Silver Crest, No. 7221, yellow
jonquil decoration w/gold trim on crest edge . . . **46**
Bowl, 12" d., Silver Crest **28**
Bowl, 14" d., Peach Crest **60**
Cocktail glass, Historic America patt., clear **22**
Cookie jar, cov., Big Cookies patt., black,
handled. **125**

Cruet w/original stopper, Coin Dot patt.,
  No. 418, pink opalescent 75
Cruet w/original stopper, Dot Optic patt.,
  cobalt blue opalescent 75
Cruet w/original stopper, Drape patt.,
  cranberry opalescent 75
Cruet w/original stopper, Drape patt.,
  mulberry opalescent 75
Cruet w/original stopper, Fern patt.,
  No. 815, Persian blue opalescent 75

Pink Opalescent Fenton Cruet

Cruet w/original stopper, Hobnail patt.,
  pink opalescent (ILLUS.) 80
Cruet w/original stopper, Rose Burmese 100
Cruet w/original stopper, Swirl patt.,
  French Opalescent 75
Epergne, one-lily, Rose Burmese,
  No. 7202. 125
Epergne, three-lily, Diamond Lace patt.,
  white opalescent. 115
Goblet, Historical America patt., clear 30
Lamp, Gone-with-the-Wind type, Poppy
  patt., custard, 24" h. 250

Cranberry Opalescent Hobnail Pitcher

Pitcher, footed spherical form, cranberry
  opalescent Hobnail patt., applied clear
  handle (ILLUS.) 35
Plates, 8" d., Silver Crest, set of 8 155
Rose bowl, No. 857, Periwinkle blue 48
Vase, fan-type, dolphin base, Jade green 35
Vase, 8" h., double crimped rim, Hobnail
  patt., No.3958, milk glass 25

FOSTORIA

Fostoria Mark

Fostoria Glass Company, founded in 1887, produced numerous types of fine glassware over the years. Its factory in Moundsville, West Virginia, closed in 1986.

Ashtray, American patt., clear, 2⅞" sq. $5
Ashtray, American patt., clear, 5" sq.. 100
Basket, w/reed handle, American patt.,
  clear, 7 x 9". 110
Beer mug, American patt., clear, 12 oz., 4½" h. . . . 75
Bell, American patt., clear. 650
Bottle w/original stopper, cordial,
  American patt., clear, 9 oz., 7¼" h. 75
Bowl, 11" d., footed, rolled edge, Century
  patt., clear. 40
Bowl, cream soup, Colony patt., clear 59
Bowl, 8½" d., two-handled, Chintz etching, clear . . 45
Bowl, 9" d., Century patt., clear 30
Bowl, 12½" oval, 2⅞" h., Flame patt.,
  Navarre etching, clear 115
Bowl, toddler's, American patt., No. 150, clear . . . 25
Cake plate, handled, Chintz etching, clear,
  10" d. 40
Candlestick, Coronet patt., clear, 4½" h. 20
Candlestick, Chintz etching, clear 5½" h. 30
Candlesticks, triple-light, Navarre etching,
  clear, 6¾" h., pr. 150
Candlesticks, Colony patt., w/eight prisms,
  clear, 7½" h., pr. 195
Candy dish, cov., three-part, Royal etching,
  amber 60
Celery tray, American patt., clear, 10" l.. 17
Champagne, Holly cutting, clear 10
Cigarette box, cov., American patt., clear 30
Claret, American patt., clear, 7 oz., 4⅞" h. 75
Cocktail, Chintz patt., clear, 5" h. 20
Compote, 4⅜" h., open, Century patt., clear 20
Compote, 4½" h., open, Navarre etching, clear . . . 35
Compote, 6½" h., cov., Colony patt., clear. 30
Console set: No. 2402 Art Deco-style bowl
  & pair of candleholders, Ebony, the set 70
Cordial, Navarre etching, clear, 1 oz., 3⅞" h.. . . . 65
Creamer & open sugar bowl, Colony patt.,
  clear, pr. 12
Creamer & open sugar bowl, Jamestown
  patt., pink, pr. 50
Creamer, open sugar bowl & undertray,
  individual size, Century patt., clear, the set 35
Creamer & sugar bowl, footed, Navarre
  etching, clear, 4¼" h., pr. 45

Creamer & sugar bowl, Romance etching,
clear, pr. 30
Cruet w/original stopper, American patt.,
clear, 5 oz. 28
Cup & saucer, Century patt., clear. 14
Decanter w/original stopper, American
patt., clear, 24 oz., 9¼" h.. 83
Finger bowl, Colony patt., clear 75
Finger bowl, American patt., clear, 4½" d. 90
Goblet, American patt., water, clear 16
Goblet, Holly cutting, water, clear. 12
Goblet, Jamestown patt., clear. 8
Goblet, Navarre etching, water, blue, 10 oz. 45
Goblet, Century patt., water, clear, 10½ oz.,
5¾" h. 16
Hurricane lamp, American patt.,
clear, 8½" h. 325
Ice bucket, Century patt., clear (no handle) 50
Ice bucket, Chintz etching, clear 140
Ice bucket, Colony patt., clear 200
Ice dish, American patt., clear 35
Ice dish w/juice tumbler, Hermitage patt.,
Topaz 22
Ice tub, American patt., clear, 6½" d., 4½" h. 55
Ice tub liner, American patt., clear, large 95
Marmalade, cover & spoon, American
patt., clear. 118
Mayonnaise bowl & underplate, Romance
etching, clear, 2 pcs. 36
Mayonnaise bowl, undertray & spoon,
Century patt., clear, 3 pcs. 40
Muffin tray, American patt., clear, 10" 36
Nappy, Century patt., clear, 4½" d.. 7
Nappy, American patt., deep, clear, 8" d. 125
Oyster cocktail, American patt.,
clear, 4½ oz. 17
Pin tray, American patt., clear,
4½ x 5½" oval 125
Pitcher, Vesper etching, amber 295
Pitcher w/ice lip, American patt., clear 45
Plate, Holly cutting, clear 8
Plate, Meadow Rose etching, clear 12
Plate, salad, 7½" d., American patt., clear 12
Plate, salad, 7½" l., crescent-shaped,
Century patt., clear, ... 30
Plate, 8¼" d., Jamestown patt., pink. 18
Plate, dinner, 9½" d., American patt., clear 26
Plate, dinner, 9½" d., Trojan etching, topaz 20
Plate, 12" d., footed, Colony patt., clear 125
Platter, 10½" l., American patt., clear 40
Platter, 12" l., American patt., clear 50
Punch bowl, Tom & Jerry-type, pedestal
footed, American patt., clear, 12" d. 235
Relish dish, three-part, Romance
etching, clear 35
Relish dish, two-part, Century patt.,
clear, 7⅜" l.. 16
Ring holder, American patt., clear 700

Rose bowl, Baroque patt., topaz 50
Rose bowl, American patt., clear, 5" d. 20
Salt dip w/spoon, American patt.,
clear, 2 pcs. 20
Salt & pepper shakers, Navarre etching,
clear, 3¼" h., pr.. 65
Salt & pepper shakers, Colony patt., clear,
3⅝" h., pr.
Salt shakers, individual, American patt.,
clear, 3" h., set of 3. 37
Sherbet, Chintz patt., clear. 17
Sherbet, Jamestown patt., amber 11
Spooner, American patt., clear, 3¾" h. 65
Sundae, American patt., clear, 6 oz., 3⅛" h. 8
Toothpick holder, American patt., clear 24
Tray, center-handled, Chintz etching, clear,
11" d. 40
Tumbler, footed, iced tea, Jamestown patt.,
blue. 20
Tumbler, juice, Jamestown patt., blue 15
Tumbler, water, Jamestown patt., amber. 16
Tumbler, whiskey, American patt., clear,
2 oz., 2½" h. 10
Tumbler, old-fashioned, American patt.,
clear, 6 oz., 3⅜" h. 12

American Pattern Iced Tea Tumbler

Tumbler, iced tea, American patt., clear,
12 oz., 5¾" h. (ILLUS.) 19
Vase, 5" h., Navarre etching, No. 4128, clear. . . . 125
Vase, 6½" h., footed, American patt., amber 80
Vase, 9½" h., flared rim, American patt., clear . . . 100
Vase, 10" h., cupped-in top, American patt.,
clear 250
Vase, 10" h., straight sides, American patt.,
clear 80
Vegetable bowl, Century patt., clear, 9½" oval . . . 25
Water carafe, Carmen patt., ca. 1900 95
Water set: pitcher w/ice lip & six flared
tumblers; American patt., clear, 7 pcs. 100
Wedding bowl, American patt., clear, large . . . 1,000
Wine, Century patt., clear. 24
Wine, Jamestown patt., pink. 20
Wine, Century patt., clear, 3½ oz., 4½" h. 24

GALLÉ

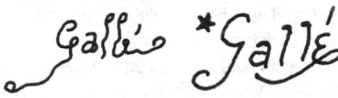

Gallé Marks

Gallé glass was made in Nancy, France, by Emile Gallé, a founder of the Nancy School and a leader in the Art Nouveau movement in France. Much of his glass, both enameled and cameo, is decorated with naturalistic motifs. The finest pieces were made in the last two decades of the 19th century and the opening years of the 20th.

Pieces marked with a star preceding the name were made between 1904, the year of Gallé's death, and 1914.

Silver-mounted Gallé Box

Bottle w/stopper, footed bulbous squared ovoid lobed body w/a tiny cylindrical neck w/mushroom stopper, clear enameled in mauve, maroon, teal, chartreuse, black, white & gilt w/a dragonfly among delicate sprigs of flowers, inscribed "E. Gallé - à Nancy," ca. 1895, 5½" h., ... **$1,092**

Box, cov., upright square form in mottled burnt orange, ochre, white & lemon yellow, lightly acid-etched & enameled w/a design of wildflowers & grasses, the hinged cover matching, w/foilate pierced leafy & berry silver mounts around the rim & forming the footed base, glass inscribed "Emile Gallé - à Nancy-Modéle et décors déposés," silver hallmarked, ca. 1900, 6¼" h. (ILLUS.) **7,475**

Cameo atomizer, bulbous spherical base tapering to a tall, slender trumpet neck fitted w/an atomizer, frosted & shaded yellow to pale purple to green ground overlaid in dark purple & cut w/a continuous landscape w/large trees in the foreground & mountains in the distance, cameo signature, 7" h. **880**

Cameo box, cov., flattened diamond form in opalescent grey infused w/pale pink & overlaid w/purplish red, the cover cut w/a rowboat by a wooded shore, the base w/falling leaves, cover & base signed, ca. 1900, 7¾" l. **2,300**

Gallé Cameo Ceiling Fixture

Cameo ceiling fixture, a 14" d. domical shade in frosted white overlaid in dark brown & cameo cut w/an overall design of berried leafy vines, suspended on three straight brass arms issuing from a central shaft & domed ceiling plate (ILLUS.) **4,480**

Cameo vase, 3¼" h., miniature, shoulder ovoid form, yellow overlaid w/purple & cameo-cut w/flowers, signed **431**

Cameo vase, 6" h., slender baluster-form w/short flared neck, frosted pale pink overlaid in purplish amethyst, acid-etched w/a flower & leaf design around the lower half, signed above border "Gallé" **805**

Cameo vase, 6¾" h., bottle-form, bulbous ovoid base tapering to a tall, slightly flaring stick neck, frosted grey overlaid in brown, cut w/stylized flowers & leaves, signed in cameo **575**

From left: Gallé Cameo Vase with Bellflowers Gallé Cameo Apple Blossom Vase

Cameo vase, 7" h., wide ovoid body w/a wide flaring rim, yellow overlaid in blue & cut w/a design of large bellflowers, signed (ILLUS.) **3,162**

Cameo vase, 7½" h., footed shaped & tapering cylindrical form w/flat rim, rose ground overlaid in amber & cameo-etched w/flowers & foliage, signed **977**

Cameo vase, 8½" h., wide bulbous ovoid form w/a deep shoulder centering a short rolled neck, grey shaded w/lemon yellow, overlaid in crimson & red & cut w/pendent hibiscus blossoms & leafage, signed in cameo, ca. 1900 . . . . **3,737**

Cameo vase, 10½" h., bulbous ovoid body tapering to a small flared neck, grey infused w/pale blue, overlaid in bubblegum pink, spring green & amber & cameo cut w/clusters of applied blossoms & leaves, cameo-signed "Gallé," acid-stamped "FABRICATION FRANCAIS," ca. 1900 (ILLUS.) **5,462**

Cameo vase, 11¼" h., tall slender barbell-form on a cushion foot, grey shaded w/green, overlaid w/brown & cut w/ferns, signed in cameo, ca. 1900 . . . . **1,265**

Cameo vase, 13⅝" h., slender ovoid body w/a spreading round foot, grey overlaid w/white & caramel, cut w/flowering blossoms on long stems, incised on bottom "Galle deposé" w/leaf, "EG" & a cross of Lorraine, partial original paper label, ca. 1900. . . . . **2,300**

Cameo vase, 14" h., slender ovoid body tapering to a short trumpet neck, grey shaded lemon yellow overlaid in red, amber & green & cut w/hibiscus blossoms & leafage, signed in cameo, ca. 1900. . . . . **11,500**

Gallé Cameo Vase with Clematis

Cameo vase, 14¼" h., footed large spherical body w/a short cylindrical neck, grey opalescent mottled w/lemon yellow & overlaid in blue & purple, cut w/clematis blossoms, buds & trailing foliage, signed in cameo (ILLUS.) **12,650**

Cameo vase, 17¾" h., wide flattened round moon flask form w/a short small neck tapering to a widely flaring cupped rim, grey opalescent mottled w/pale lemon yellow, overlaid in pale blue & purple & finely cut w/upright iris blossoms, buds & leaves, signed in cameo, ca. 1900 . . . . **9,200**

Cameo vase, 19¾" h., baluster-form, thick waisted foot below the slender ovoid body tapering to a tall slender neck w/flared rim, opalescent grey infused w/pale pink, overlaid in white, lavender & moss green & cut w/hydrangea blossoms & leafage, signed in cameo, ca. 1900 . . . . . . **4,600**

Cameo vase, 23¼" h., thick cushion foot tapering to a tall slender cylindrical neck, grey infused w/peach, overlaid in pale amber & dark brown & cut w/a pattern of ripe grape clusters & tendrilled leafage, signed in cameo, ca. 1900 . . . . **4,312**

Cameo veilleuse (night light), footed squatty bulbous form w/a short neck supporting a metal umbrella-form cover cast w/ferns & a berry finial, the body in grey overlaid w/russet & cut w/ferns, signed in cameo, ca. 1900, 4" h. **2,415**

Scent bottle w/stopper, footed ovoid form w/a tiny cylindrical neck w/mushroom stopper, pale lavender w/each side applied w/oval bosses, one showing a landscape, the body cut w/leaves & berries enameled in shades of yellow, ochre, pale blue & orange, the whole trimmed w/gilt, signed in gilt cameo, w/original retailer's paper label, ca. 1880, 6¼" h. **6,900**

Vase, 9¾" h., round applied silver foot & pierced leaf band support for the ovoid body tapering to a squared mouth, pale green cut w/stylized fuchsia blossoms enameled in lime green, pink, white & brown, trimmed in gilt, enameled w/phrase "J'avais cent raisons de toujours aimer," signed in gilt cameo, mount w/French export mark, ca. 1900. . . . . **5,175**

Vase, 13⅜" h., thick wide disk foot below the gently tapering tall cylindrical body, grey shaded pale aubergine & cut w/squash, blossoms & leaves & enameled in shades of grass & lime green, mustard yellow, cream, rust & pink, the whole trimmed w/gilt, signed in enameled cameo, ca. 1900 (signature worn) **5,175**

HEISEY

Heisey Diamond "H" Mark

Numerous types of fine glass were made by A.H. Heisey & Co., Newark, Ohio, from 1895. The company's trademark, an H enclosed within a diamond, has become known to most glass collectors. The company's name and molds were acquired by Imperial Glass Co., Bellaire, Ohio, in 1958, and some pieces have been reissued. The glass listed below consists of miscellaneous pieces and types. Also see Animals and Pattern Glass under "glass."

Ridgeleigh Floral Bowl

Bowl, cream soup, two-handled, Yeoman patt., Sahara (yellow) **$25**

Bowl, jelly, 6½" d., footed, Orchid etching, clear **62**

Bowl, 8" d., Twist patt., nasturtium-type, Moongleam (light green) **109**

Bowl, 9" d., Twist patt., floral-type, Moongleam (green) **69**

Bowl, 10" d., Orchid etching, crimped rim, Queen Anne blank, clear **68**

Bowl, 11" d., Minuet etching, floral-type, clear **95**

Bowl, 11" d., New Era patt., floral-style, clear **85**

Bowl, 11½" d., Ridgeleigh patt., floral-type, clear (ILLUS.) . . . . **30 to 40**

Bowl, 13" d., Rose etching, shallow floral-type, clear **70**

Bowl, 13" l., Ipswich patt., oval, floral-type, clear **36**

Butter dish, cov., Orchid etching, clear **145**

Butter dish, cov., Rose etching, clear **145**

Cake plate, Rose etching, footed, clear, 15" d. . . . **325**

Candlesticks, Empress patt., three-light, No. 301, Sahara w/clear bobeches, pr. **950**

Candlesticks, Empress patt., two-light, No. 301, amber arms, pr. **485**

Candlesticks, Orchid etching, one-light, clear, 3" h., pr. **50**

Candlesticks, Waverly patt., two-light, Orchid etching, clear, pr. **120**

Candy box, cov., Stanhope patt., round, clear w/black knob stem on round foot **350**

Candy dish, cov., Plantation patt., footed, tall, clear, 8" h. **185**

Catsup bottle w/stopper, Old Sandwich patt., clear **70**

Celery dish, Plantation patt., clear, 13" l. **50**

Celery tray, Rose etching, Waverly blank, clear, 12" l. **48**

Celery tray, New Era patt., clear, 13" l. **35**

Celery vase, Fandango patt., clear **85**

Champagne, Albermarle patt., saucer-type, clear **25**

Champagne, Lariat patt., clear **12**

Champagne, Minuet etching, saucer-type, No. 5010, clear, 6 oz. **30**

Champagne, Orchid etching, saucer-type, clear, 6 oz. **29**

Champagne, Pied Piper etching, saucer-type, clear **28**

Cheese dish, cov., Lariat patt., footed, clear, 5" d. **40**

Cigarette box, cov., Lariat patt., clear **48**

Claret, New Era patt., clear, 4 oz. **22**

Coaster, Plantation patt., clear, 4" d. **45**

Cocktail, figural rooster stem, clear **40**

Cocktail, figural sea horse stem, clear **150**

Cocktail, Minuet etching, No. 5010, clear, 3½ oz. **35**

Cocktail, New Era patt., high stem, clear, 3½ oz. **18**

Cocktail, Orchid etching, clear, 4 oz. **40**

Cocktail, Rosalie etching, Kenilworth (No. 4092) blank, clear, 3 oz. **10**

Cocktail, Stanhope patt., clear, 3½ oz. **35**

Cocktail, Orchid etching, No. 5025, clear, 4 oz. **36**

Cocktail shaker, cov., Orchid etching, No. 4225, clear, 1 pt. **295**

Compote, Charter Oak etching, pink **65**

Compote, 6½" d., Rose etching, Waverly blank, low footed, clear. **50**

Compote, 7" h., Empress patt., oval, Sahara **110**

Compote, 7" h., Twist patt., Flamingo (pink) **65**

Cordial, New Era patt., clear, 1 oz. **45**

Cordial, Rose etching, clear, 1 oz. **100**

Creamer, miniature, Sawtooth Band patt., floral etching, ca. 1900 . . . . **55**

Creamer & open sugar bowl, Plantation patt., footed, clear, pr. **72**

Creamer & open sugar bowl, individual size, Rose etching, clear, pr. **85**

Heisey Twist Pattern Cruet

Cruet w/original stopper, Twist patt., Moongleam (ILLUS.) **79**

Cup & saucer, Crystolite patt., clear **22**

Cup & saucer, Empress patt., Sahara **32**

Cup & saucer, New Era patt., clear 65
Cup & saucer, Orchid etching, footed, clear 40
Cup & saucer, Rose etching, clear 90
Decanter w/stopper, Old Sandwich patt.,
  cobalt blue, No. 98, 1 pt. 550
Decanters w/stoppers, Ridgeleigh patt.,
  clear, 1 pt., pr. 325
Goblet, Albemarle patt., clear 30
Goblet, Graceful patt., No. 5022, clear 40
Goblet, Minuet etching, water, clear 45
Goblet, Old Dominion patt., water, Marigold
  (dark yellow), 8¾" h. 55
Goblet, Orchid etching, water, low stem,
  No. 5025, clear, 10 oz. 38
Goblet, Rose etching, water, clear, 9 oz. 42
Goblet, Twist patt., Flamingo, 9 oz. 39
Ice tub, Twist patt., Moongleam 95
Jelly dish, Plantation patt., Ivy etching,
  two-handled, 6½" h. 60
Lemon dish, cov., Yeoman patt., round,
  Moongleam, 5" d. 45
Nut dish or ashtray, New Era patt.,
  individual size, clear 60
Oil cruet w/original stopper, Victorian
  patt., clear, 3 oz. 68
Oyster cocktail, Ipswich patt., footed, clear. 22
Pilsner glass, New Era patt., clear, 12 oz. 60
Pitcher, Orchid etching, Donna blank
  (No. 3484), clear, ½ gal. 625
Pitcher, Plantation patt., blown, w/ice lip,
  clear, ½ gal. 450

Heisey Puritan Pitcher

Pitcher, water, Puritan patt., clear, 3 qt.
  (ILLUS.). . . . . 125 to 150
Plate, 8" d., Fandango patt., clear 45
Plate, Acorn patt., dinner, clear 59
Plate, 4¾" d., Colonial patt., clear. 5
Plate, 6" d., Empress patt., round, Sahara 13
Plate, 6" w., New Era patt., clear 35
Plate, 7" d., Orchid etching, salad, clear. 18
Plate, 8" d., Empress patt., salad, round,
  Sahara 15
Plate, 8" d., Minuet etching, luncheon, clear. 21
Punch bowl, Ridgeleigh patt., clear, 11" d. 169
Punch cup, Locket & Chain patt., ca. 1900,
  clear 35

Punch set: 9 qt. Dr. Johnson punch bowl,
  six cups & ladle; Plantation patt., clear,
  8 pcs. 1,100
Punch set: 14" d. punch bowl, 21" d.
  underplate & eight punch cups; Lariat
  patt., original hooks, clear, 10 pcs. 225
Relish dish, New Era patt., three-part, clear,
  13" l. 40
Relish dish, Orchid etching, Waverly blank,
  three-part, clear, 11" l. 65
Relish dish, Plantation patt., three-part,
  clear, 11" l. 45
Relish dish, Rose etching, Waverly blank,
  four-part, round, clear, 9" d. 70
Relish tray, Crystolite patt., three-part,
  clear, 12" l. 32
Rose bowl, Mermaid etching, clear, 5" d. 500

Heisey Pillows Rose Bowl

Rose bowl, pedestal foot, Pillows patt.
  (No. 325), clear (ILLUS.). . . . . 225 to 250
Salt dip, Fandango patt., No. 1201, clear. 22
Sandwich server, Rose etching, Waverly
  blank, center-handled, clear, 14" d. 175
Sherbet, Orchid etching, No. 5025, clear 22
Sherbet, Pied Piper etching, clear 25
Sherbet, Rose etching, clear, 6 oz. 22
Spooner, Greek Key patt., clear, large. 89
Stem, Saturn patt., Zircon (blue green),
  10 oz. 125
Syrup bottle w/top, Plantation patt., clear. 150
Toothpick holder, Continental patt., clear. 125
Toothpick holder, Pineapple & Fan patt.,
  green 185
Tray, Ridgeleigh patt., oval, clear, 10½" l. 39
Tumbler, Ipswich patt., juice, Sahara. 42
Tumbler, Ipswich patt., soda-type, clear, 5 oz. . . . 30
Tumbler, Ipswich patt., soda-type, clear, 8 oz. . . . 30
Tumbler, Ipswich patt., water, Sahara 52
Tumbler, Minuet etching, tea, No. 5010, 12 oz. . . . 60
Tumbler, Old Sandwich patt., toddy-type,
  clear, 6½ oz. 9
Tumbler, Orchid etching, iced tea, clear, 12 oz. . . . 65

Tumbler, Orchid etching, No. 5025, iced
    tea, clear, 9½ oz. **60**
Tumbler, Plantation patt., footed pressed
    juice, clear, 5 oz. **50**
Tumbler, Saturn patt., flat bottom, Zircon,
    10 oz. **75**
Tumbler, Twist patt., juice, footed,
    Flamingo, 5 oz. **29**
Tumblers, Lariat patt., Moonglo etching,
    blown iced tea, footed, 12 oz., set of six **195**
Wine, Albermarle patt., clear, 2½ oz. **20**
Wine, Orchid etching, No. 5025, clear, 3 oz. **70**

HISTORICAL & COMMEMORATIVE

*Reference numbers refer to Bessie M.
Lindsey's book,* American Historical Glass.

Admiral Dewey Pitcher

Dewey (Admiral) pitcher, bust portrait of
    Dewey & flagship Olympia reverse,
    w/mounted cannons, crossed rifles, U.S.
    & Cuban flags & stacks of cannon balls
    toward base, clear, 9½" h., No. 400 (ILLUS.). . **$75**
Dewey (Admiral) plate, bust portrait of
    Dewey, clear, 5½" d., No. 392 . . . . **15**
Egyptian Pattern bread tray, Cleopatra
    center, inscribed w/daily bread motto,
    clear, 8½ x 13¼", No. 504 . . . . **80**
Garfield Drape pitcher, clear w/applied
    handle, three swags around the body of
    floral & foliage festoons against a lightly
    stippled ground, clear, 8¾" h., No. 305 . . . . . . **135**
Garfield Drape plate, 11¼" d., center
    portrait bust of Garfield surrounded by a
    circle of stars & inscribed "We Mourn our
    Nation's Loss....," Garfield Drape border,
    scalloped rim, clear **75**
Liberty Bell Signer's platter, clear,
    9½ x 13", No. 42. . . . . **125**
Lincoln Drape with Tassel Pattern goblet,
    clear, 6" h., No. 280 . . . . **135**
Martyr's mug, Lincoln & Garfield bust
    portraits & inscription, clear, 2⅝" h.,
    No. 272 (ILLUS.) **295**

Lincoln-Garfield Martyr's Mug

McCormick Reaper platter, clear, 8 x 13",
    No. 119. . . . . **145**
Old Statehouse tray, shows Independence
    Hall above "Old Statehouse, Philadelphia,
    Erected 1735," clear, round, No. 32 . . . . **55**
Rock of Ages bread tray, clear w/milk
    white center, No. 236 . . . . **350**
Three Graces plate, "Faith, Hope &
    Charity," clear, 10" d., No. 230 . . . . **135**

IMPERIAL

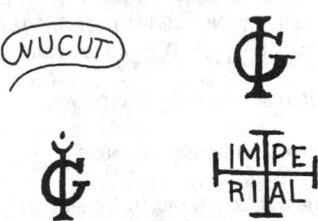

Imperial Marks

Imperial Glass Company, Bellaire, Ohio, was
organized in 1901 and was in continuous
production, except for very brief periods, until its
closing in June 1984. It had been a major
producer of Carnival glass earlier in this century
and also produced other types of glass, including
an art glass line called "Free-Hand Ware"
during the 1920s and "Jewels" about 1916. The
company acquired a number of molds of other
earlier factories, including the Cambridge and
A.H. Heisey Companies, and reissued numerous
items through the years. Also see CARNIVAL
GLASS under Glass.

CANDLEWICK

Candlewick Bell

Ashtray, w/embossed eagle center,
No. 1776/1, clear, 6½" $70
Bell, No. 400/108, clear, 5" h. (ILLUS.) 59
Bonbon bowl, handled, No. 400/51H, clear, 6" . . . 31
Bonbon bowl, heart-shaped, No. 400/174,
clear, 6½" 22
Bowl, 8½" d., handled, No. 400/72B. 39
Bowl w/underplate, 8" d., two-handled
w/10" underplate, bowl No. 400/4272B,
underplate No. 400/4272D, the set 55

Candlewick Butter Dish

Butter dish, cov., w/beaded top,
No. 400/161, clear, ¼ lb. (ILLUS.) 34
Butter dish, cov., No. 400/144, clear, 5½" d. 30
Cake stand, No. 400/67D, low-footed, clear,
10" d. 95
Candle/flower holder, No. 400/40C, clear,
5" h. 44
Celery tray, oval, handled, No. 400/105,
clear, 13½" l. 40
Cigarette box, cov., No.400/134, clear 35
Coaster, No. 400/78, clear, 4" d. 7
Compote, No. 400/63B, clear, 10½" 33
Console bowl, clear, three-toed,
No. 400/205, 10" l. 33
Cordial decanter, applied handle,
No. 400/82, clear etched (top chip) 495
Creamer & sugar bowl, beaded handle,
No. 400/30, clear, pr. 15
Cup & saucer, No. 400/35, clear 12
Cup & saucer, No. 400/37, clear, pr. 13
Mint bowl, ring-handled, No. 400/51F, clear, 6" . . . 30
Nappy, handled, No. 400/51, clear, 6" 17
Pastry tray, No. 400/68D, clear, 11½" d. 83
Pickle/celery dish, No. 400/57, clear, 7½" 27
Plate, 4½" d., No. 400/34, clear 7
Plate, bread & butter, 6" d., two-handled,
No. 400/1D, clear 8
Plate, canapé, 6" d., w/off-center
indentation, No. 400/36, clear 14
Plate, salad, 7" d., No. 400/3D, clear 9
Plate, torte, 17" d., cupped edge,
No. 400/20V, clear 72
Platter, 16" l., oval, two-handled,
No. 400/131D, clear 193
Relish dish, two-part, No. 400/84, clear, 6½" 22
Relish dish, four-part, No.400/112, clear,
10½" l. 33
Salad fork & spoon, No. 400/75, clear, pr. 36
Salt & pepper shakers, individual,
No. 400/109, clear, pr. 20

Candlewick No. 400/247 Shakers

Salt & pepper shakers w/chrome tops,
No. 400/247, clear, pr. (ILLUS.) 45
Tray, lemon, center-handled, No. 400/221,
clear, 5½" 50
Tray, pastry, center-handled, No. 400/68D,
clear, 11½" 40
Tumblers, footed, No. 400/19, clear, 12 oz.,
set of 6 77
Vase, 8" h., fan-shaped w/beaded handles,
No. 400/87F, blue 121
Vase, 8" h., fluted rim w/beaded handles,
No. 400/87C, clear 44

CAPE COD PATTERN

*From left: Cape Cod Cocktail
Cape Cod Dinner Plate*

Ashtray, clear 10
Cocktail, No. 1602, clear, 3½ oz. (ILLUS.) 10
Creamer, clear 15
Egg cup, No. 160/225, clear. 25
Plate, dinner, 10" d., No. 160/10D, clear
(ILLUS.) 15
Sherbet, No. 1600, clear, 6 oz.. 7
Wine, clear, 3 oz. 10

MISCELLANEOUS PATTERNS & LINES

Vase, 6½" h., Free-Hand ware, "Mosaic"
design, deep cobalt blue body shaded &
swirled w/opal & lined in iridescent orange . . . 489
Vase, 8¾" h., Free-Hand ware, green heart
& vine decoration on opaque white body
w/iridescent lustre overall 690
Vase, 8" h., Free-Hand ware, small swelled
base below the tall slightly flaring
cylindrical body w/a widely flaring

flattened & deeply ruffled rim, iridescent
metallic hues of purple, green & blue in a
wavy random design **121**

Vase, 8½" h., Free-Hand ware, simple
cylindrical form, orange iridescent ground
decorated w/blue hanging heart design,
cased over white, rim possibly ground **575**

Vase, 9½" h., Free-Hand ware, bulbous
base w/a wide flared neck, white cased to
a cobalt blue exterior, interior of rim
flashed in brilliant iridescent orange,
polished pontil, early 20th c. **575**

Vase, 10¾" h., Free-Hand ware, very
slender baluster-form body w/flaring short
neck, overall orange iridescence w/a blue
pulled drapery design cased on milk glass. . . . **748**

Vase, 11" h., Free-Hand ware, slender
swelled cylindrical body w/short rolled
neck, overall orange lustre over a milk
glass body, ground pontil **98**

Wine, Old Williamsburg patt., amber **18**

Wine, Old Williamsburg patt., Azalea **18**

JACK-IN-THE-PULPIT VASES

*Glass vases in varying sizes and resembling
in appearance the flower of this name have been
popular with collectors since the 19th century.
They were produced in various solid colors and
in shaded wares.*

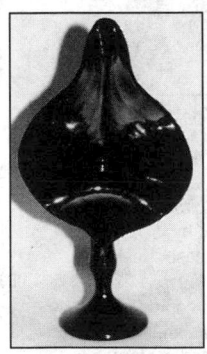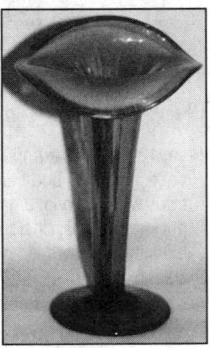

From left: Black Amethyst Vase
Blue Opalescent Jack-in-the-Pulpit

Black amethyst, widely flaring oversized
top w/shallow opening, raised on a
slender baluster-form stem on a round
foot, 6" h. (ILLUS.) **$40**

Blue opalescent, round blue foot below
slender body & widely flaring opalescent
rim, probably English, ca. 1880, 7" h.
(ILLUS.). . . . . **65 to 75**

Blue, white & clear, swirled stripes of blue
& white in clear, Gingham patt., attributed
to Stevens & Williams, England, 12" h.
(ILLUS.) **250**

From left: Stevens & Williams "Gingham" Vase
Cased Jack-in-the-Pulpit Vase

Cased, satin white exterior, yellow interior,
spherical body w/a short neck to the
widely flaring & scalloped rim, 19th c.,
7" h. (ILLUS.) . . . . **50 to 75**

Cranberry shaded to pink, the squatty
bulbous base in pink centered by a wide
tall cylindrical neck shading to deep
cranberry scattered w/bits of goldstone,
flaring rolled & ruffled rim w/applied clear
edge band & upturned back, 4½" d., 7¾" h.. . . . **165**

Green Decorated Jack-in-the-Pulpit

Green, cushion foot w/a slender flaring body
below the wide rolled rim, satiny ground
decorated w/bold gold flowers & leaves
trimmed w/white, Bohemia, ca. 1900,
9" h. (ILLUS.) **150**

Westmoreland Jack-in-the-Pulpits

Green satin, hexagonal foot below the plain
flaring sides & wide gently scalloped rim,
original Westmoreland Glass Company
sticker on the foot, 7" h. (ILLUS. left) . . . . **25 to 50**

Iridescent, squatty bulbous base tapering to a cylindrical body w/wide rolled rim, purple & green streaked iridescent highlights w/stretched effect at rim, Glasform, Blackpool, England, designed by John Ditchfield, modern, 9" h. . . . . . **175 to 200**

Pigeon blood, hexagonal foot below the plain flaring sides & wide gently scalloped rim, Westmoreland Glass Company, 7" h. (ILLUS. right). . . . . **25 to 50**

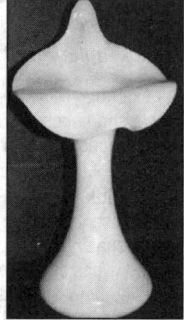

Fenton White Jack-in-the-Pulpit

White opaque, flared base tapering to a tall slender waisted body below the widely flaring & ruffled rim, marked w/Fenton logo, post-1970, 15" h. (ILLUS.) . . . . **25 to 50**

KOSTA

The Kosta Glassworks was founded in the Smaland region of Sweden in 1742 and has grown over the past two centuries to become one of that country's leading makers of fine glassware. Originally its products were utilitarian, but by the 19th century it was producing decorative wares and tablewares. In the 20th century it produced fine crystal wares in modern designs by noted glass artists. In 1970 it merged with several other Swedish glasshouses and continues to produce high quality cut glass and tableware.

Bowl, 5⅜" d., swirled glass-type, colorless half-round internally decorated with opaque white horizontal threading, base inscribed "LH 1004," stamped "Kosta/Lind/Strand" **$230**

Paperweight, mushroom-shaped crystal w/bubbled core, bluish green looping inclusions in base, by Ann or Goran Warff, base signed "Kosta 97070 Warff," 5½" h. **259**

Paperweight, mushroom-type, colorless cap revealing internal bubbles above amber-colored stem, base inscribed "Kosta 97323/Warff," designed by Ann Warff, 3¾" h. **288**

Sculpture, aquamarine glass iceberg w/etched elk at center, base edge inscribed "Kosta V. Lindstrand W.L. 90002," 6" h. **201**

Vase, 6¾" h., Trad I-type, heavy walled flattened colorless oval internally decorated with dark tree forms w/multicolored leaves around base & falling above, labeled at side & inscribed "Kosta 41753 Lindstrand," designed by Vicke Lindstrand **1,265**

Vase, 7" h., "Trad I Autumn," thick-walled simple ovoid body w/flat rim in colorless crystal internally decorated w/stylized blackish brown trees w/multicolored leaves falling & below in yellow, red & orange, designed by Vicke Lindstrand, signed on the base "Kosta LU 2011" (shallow scratch on side). **2,645**

Vase, 7⅛" h., crystal thick cylinder internally decorated with teal blue amorphous element enhanced by cut & polished surface ovals, designed by Vicke Lindstrand, signed "Kosta 46693 V. Lindstrand" **518**

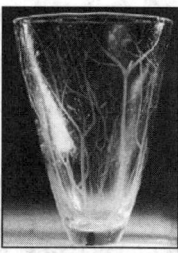

Engraved Kosta Vase

Vase, 12¼" h., tall trumpet-form on a small base, colorless body engraved w/stylized trees w/occasional small birds among the polished leaves, designed by Vicke Lindstrand, engraved on base "Kosta LG2268" (ILLUS.) **1,093**

Vase, 13" h., slender double-gourd form, tall swelled & waisted form w/a sheared angled mouth, clear w/slender internal canes of alternating white & black, designed by V. Lindstrand, engraved "Kosta LH 1258," ca. 1950s (scratches). **330**

LACY

Lacy glass is a general term developed by collectors many years ago to cover the earliest type of pressed glass produced in this country. "Lacy" refers to the fact that most of these early patterns consisted of scrolls and geometric designs against a finely stippled background, which gives the glass the look of fine lace. Formerly this glass was often referred to as "Sandwich" for the Boston & Sandwich Glass

Company of Sandwich, Massachusetts, which produced a great deal of this ware. Today, however, collectors realize that many other factories on the East Coast and in the Pittsburgh, Pennsylvania, and Wheeling, West Virginia, areas also made lacy glass from the 1820s into the 1840s.

All pieces listed are clear unless otherwise noted. Numbers after salt dips refer to listings in Pressed Glass Salt Dishes of the Lacy Period, 1825-1850, *by Logan W. and Dorothy B. Neal. Also see CUP PLATES.*

Large Heart & Lyre Lacy Plate

Bowl, 6¼" w., hexagonal, the center w/six long diamond point diamonds alternating w/small scrolls, the wide border composed of leafy scrolls alternating w/scroll cartouches, New England (mold roughness) **$55**

Compote, 4¾" d., 3½" h., open, round Heart patt. bowl, on an double-knob applied pedestal & round foot w/pontil, two chips, mold roughness **440**

Compote, 6" d., 4" h., open, deep curved Roman Rosette patt. bowl on an applied baluster stem resting on a cup plate foot (mold roughness on cup plate base) **2,475**

Creamer, Heart & Scale patt., clambroth, 4½" h. **385**

Dish, cov., oblong w/undulating flanged rim, base w/central pointed cartouche reserve framed by a border in the Princess Feather patt., matching stepped & domed cover w/arched loop handle, very rare, 5½ x 10½" (few base scallops chipped) **8,250**

Dish, rectangular w/cut corners, the bottom w/a central star framed by C- and S-scrolls, the border w/cartouche panels, Midwestern, 7¼" l. (mold roughness, two scallops chipped, two tipped) **209**

Dish, round, Roman Rosette patt., fiery opalescent, probably Boston & Sandwich, 5½" d. (light mold roughness) **198**

Plate, 9½" d., flanged rim, large four-point star in bottom framed by a band w/small swirled panels, outer wide zigzag border band & scalloped rim, probably Boston & Sandwich (few scallops tipped, light mold roughness) **55**

Plate, 5⅝" d., the wide outer border w/wide arched fern-like leaves alternating w/narrowing diamond point arches, undocumented (two scallops chipped, two tipped) **308**

Plate, 7¼" w., paneled edges, the round center w/large pairs of acanthus leaves alternating w/small palmettes within a ring of scrolled small acanthus leaves & an outer border of palmettes & fans, very rare, New England (few minor chips, three scallops tipped) **303**

Plate, 9¼" d., Heart & Lyre (Harp) patt., wide border band of alternating hearts & lyres, bands of strawberry diamond design around the central eight-point star, attributed to the Boston & Sandwich Glass Co., mold roughness, three scallops damaged (ILLUS.) **330**

Salt dip, Classical sofa-form, Eagle patt., the outscrolled corners formed by perched American eagles looking back over their shoulders, looped rope border above a shield on each side, probably Boston & Sandwich Glass Co., opaque white (EE-3b) **1,430**

Salt dip, Classical sofa-form w/S-scroll ends & scalloped rim, lyre design on each side, medium blue, probably Boston & Sandwich Glass Co., LE-2 (some mold roughness on one foot) **935**

Salt dip, cov., Classical sofa-form w/high scrolled ends & legs, the high domed cover w/a berry finial, rare (CD-2A) **2,090**

Salt dip, footed rectangular form w/slightly flaring patterned sides, central divider on interior, attributed to Pittsburgh area, cobalt blue, DI-12 variant (several small chips, mold roughness) **550**

Salt dip, oval, Peacock Eye patt., scalloped rim of round "eyes," PO2A (light mold roughness) **121**

Salt dip, paddle side-wheeler boat shape, "Lafayet" molded on sides, company marking on stern, opalescent purplish blue, Boston & Sandwich Glass Co. (BT-3) **1,650**

Salt dip, rectangular, post corners on peg feet, overall strawberry diamond design on sides, deep purplish blue, Boston & Sandwich Glass Co., SD-15 (mold roughness, few small chips) **413**

Salt dip, rounded footed form, the curved sides composed of pointed Gothic arches, octagonal foot, cobalt blue, unlisted, 3" d. **248**

Strainer, round, a border of circles & swags around a plain interior pierced w/five small holes, 4⅛" d. (mold roughness) **132**

Sugar bowl, cov., Gothic Arch patt., round foot & octagonal finely detailed Gothic arch side panels w/flaring, flanged rim, matching domed cover w/button finial, light bluish fiery opalescent, 5¼" h. (in-the-making line on foot). **935**

Sugar bowl, cov., Gothic Arch patt., round foot & octagonal finely detailed Gothic arch side panels w/flaring, flanged rim, matching domed cover w/button finial, electric blue, 5¼" h. **1,320**

Toddy plate, round, Lyre patt., leafy scroll border band & scalloped rim, probably Boston & Sandwich Glass Co., medium blue, 4¾" d. **468**

Toddy plate, round, multi-paneled sides each panel w/graduated rows of facing C-scrolls, scalloped rim, bright light amethyst, unlisted, 5" d. (light mold roughness) **550**

LALIQUE

R. Lalique France N° 3752

R LALIQUE
FRANCE

R.LALIQUE

FRANCE

Lalique Marks

Fine glass, which includes numerous extraordinary molded articles, has been made by the glasshouse established by René Lalique early in this century in France. The firm was carried on by his son, Marc, until his death in 1977 and is now headed by Marc's daughter, Marie-Claude. All Lalique glass is marked, usually on or near the bottom, with either an engraved or molded signature. Unless otherwise noted, we list only those pieces marked "R. Lalique" produced before the death of René Lalique in 1945.

Bowl, 8" d., "Ondes," round opalescent form w/deep sides molded in low-relief w/diminishing elliptical disks, introduced in 1935 . . . . **$488**

Bowl, 11½" d., "Poisson No. 1," opalescent wide round shallow form molded w/a gently spiraling band of sardines, the center w/a cluster of bubbles, molded "R. LALIQUE," ca. 1931 . . . . **690**

Bowl, 12" d., "Plumes de Paon," wide shallow form w/a serpentine rim, molded in medium-relief w/overlapping peacock feathers, acid-stamped "R. LALIQUE - FRANCE," introduced in 1932. . . . . **1,265**

Box, cov., "Enfants," cylindrical base in grey molded in relief w/a continuous band of infants supporting tiers of roses on the domed cover, coral patina, acid-stamped "R. LALIQUE - FRANCE," introduced in 1931, 3¼" h. **1,265**

Box, cov., "Hirondelles," upright flat silhouetted grey sculpture molded in medium-relief as a pair of birds in flight, the bronze base mount w/floral decoration in relief, glass molded "R. LALIQUE," introduced in 1922, 16¼" h. low round disk-form in opalescent, the top molded in medium-relief w/three dragonflies, molded "R. LALIQUE," introduced in 1921, 6¾" d. **805**

From left: Lalique "Roger" Box
Lalique Sainte-Odile Carafe

Box, cov., "Roger," No. 75, spherical grey glass w/black patina, the cover molded w/bosses on a ground of scrolling grapevines & pheasants, introduced in 1926, inscribed "Lalique - France," 5¼" d. (ILLUS.) **805**

Carafe w/original stopper, "Sainte-Odile," No. P.736, rectilinear body w/chamfered edges, ring-molded neck, raspberry-form stopper & decorated w/molded profile medallion of Ste. Odile, traces of sepia patina, introduced in 1927, "R. LALIQUE" molded under medallion, bottom molded "CLOS STE. ODILE - OBERNAI - PIERRE WEISSENBURGER," 7½" h. (ILLUS.) **805**

Clock, desk-type, "Papillons," large round frosted disk molded around the face in low-relief w/overlapping butterflies, upright on a round disk foot, the Arabic numerals enameled in black, pale blue patina, acid-stamped "R.LALIQUE - FRANCE," introduced in 1931, 9⅛" h.. . . . . . **6,325**

Clock, "Inséparables," No. 765, square grey & frosted glass molded in medium relief w/two pairs of love birds perched on flowering branches flanking the circular clock face, introduced in 1926, molded "R. LALIQUE" & inscribed "Lalique France," 4⅜" h. (ILLUS.) **1,725**

Lalique "Inséparables" Clock

Cruet set: flaring cylindrical pair of bottles w/tall stoppers all fitted in an oval holder; "Bourgueil," clear, the lower half molded w/tiered bands of triangles, introduced in 1933, 5½" h., the set **230**

Figure group, two dancing female nudes in frosted clear standing close together on a textured clear round base, inscribed "Lalique France," 10" h. **546**

Figure of a woman, "Thais," opalescent form of a nude female shown dancing & holding up a large diaphanous drapery, inscribed "R. Lalique - France," introduced in 1925, 8¼" h. (right hand re-carved) **5,175**

Hood ornament, "Libellule," grey molded full-relief stylized dragonfly, mounted on a chrome radiator cap, glass molded "LALIQUE," & inscribed "R. Lalique," mount cast "The Stant Mfg. Co. Connersville, Ind.," introduced in 1928, 9" h. (chip to tail) **4,600**

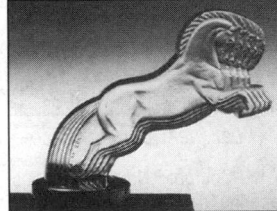

Lalique Hood Ornament

Hood ornament, "Cinq Chevaux," No. 1122, grey glass molded in high-relief w/five rearing steeds, set within a chromed-metal mount, introduced in 1925, molded "R. LALIQUE," 5⅛" h. (ILLUS.) **9,200**

Luminiere, "Hirondelles," upright flat silhouetted grey sculpture molded in medium-relief as a pair of birds in flight, the bronze base mount w/floral decoration in relief, glass molded "R. LALIQUE," introduced in 1922, 16¼" h. **1,380**

Model of a cat, "Chat Assis," No. 1208, molded clear & frosted seated cat, introduced in 1932, inscribed "Lalique - France," 8⅛" h. (ILLUS.) **1,725**

From left: Lalique Model of a Cat
Lalique Elephant

Model of an elephant, "Matcho Gros Eléphant," No. 1216, molded clear & frosted high relief pachyderm w/upraised curled trunk, introduced in 1932, acid-stamped "R, LALIQUE FRANCE," 13¼" h. (ILLUS.) **14,950**

Oil lamp, "Artichaut," small bulbous body in grey molded in full-relief w/bands of artichoke leaves, pierced conical metal cap, molded "R. LALIQUE - LAMP HYGIENIQUE BERGER - MADE IN FRANCE," introduced in 1927, 3½" h. **1,380**

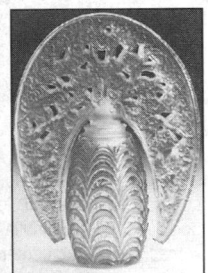

From left: Lalique Rooster Paperweight
Lalique Perfume Flacon

Paperweight, "Coq Nain," No. 1135, molded clear chicken, head lowered & tall tail raised, square base, introduced in 1928, molded "R. LALIQUE - FRANCE," inconspicuous chip to tail, 7¾" h. (ILLUS.) . . **1,380**

Pendant, "Guepes," oval green disk molded w/rows of wasps & two apertures for hanging cord & tassel, inscribed "Lalique," hung w/a green silk tassel, introduced in 1920, 2¼" l. **1,035**

Perfume bottle w/stopper, "Ambre D'Orsay," upright slender tapering rectangular dark purple form w/the corners molded w/draped female figures holding flowers, the square stopper molded w/flowers & vines, molded "AMBRE D'ORSAY - LALIQUE," inscribed "698" introduced in 1911, 5⅛" h. . . **1,725**

Perfume bottle w/stopper, "La Belle Saison," upright rectangular frosted form w/rectangular stopper, molded w/radiating leafy branches centered by the profile of a maiden, coral patina, molded "R. LALIQUE" introduced in 1925, 3⅞" h. **747**

Perfume flacon w/stopper, "Bouchon Fleurs de Pommier," clear barrel-shaped body w/green patina in scalloped ridges, molded tiara stopper w/matching patina on blossom motif, base inscribed "R. Lalique France No. 493," 5½" h. (ILLUS.). **10,063**

Plate, 11" d., "Ondines," round opalescent form molded in medium-relief w/floating female nudes, inscribed "R. LALIQUE - FRANCE," introduced in 1929. . . . . **1,725**

Powder box, cov., round, the flattened cover molded w/an outer band of elongated running rabbits surrounding an inner design of tiny birds & leafy vines, clear w/brown patina, molded "R. Lalique," 3½" d., 1½" h. **633**

Lalique Dahlias Vase

Vase, 4⅞" h., "Dahlias," No. 938, compressed spherical clear & frosted body decorated w/dahlia blossoms w/black enameled centers, brown patina, introduced in 1923, inscribed "R. Lalique - France No. 938" (ILLUS.) **1,295**

Vase, 5" h., "Moissac," short widely flaring inverted conical form in opalescent molded in high-relief w/overlapping leaves, traces of blue patina, molded "R. LALIQUE - FRANCE," introduced in 1927. . . . . **1,380**

Lalique "Fontaines" Vase

Vase, 5¾" h., "Fontaines," No. 906, ovoid body w/short narrow cylindrical neck, blue frosted molded in low relief w/an abstract

pattern resembling flames or water, introduced in 1912, inscribed "Lalique" (ILLUS.) **1,092**

Vase, 6¼" h., cire perdue type, "Poivre Graines en Relief, Feuilles en Creux," simple ovoid body w/a wide, flat rim, grey molded in low- and medium-relief w/pendent clusters of peppercorns interspersed w/rows of leafage, inscribed "R. LALIQUE 194-20," dated 1920 . . . . **36,800**

Vase, 6½" h., "Courlis," bulbous ovoid body tapering toward base, wide & low cylindrical neck, frosted deep amber molded overall in low-relief w/a flock of terns amid clouds, w/original white patina, acid-stamped "R. LALIQUE - FRANCE," introduced in 1931. **5,175**

Vase, 6½" h., "Nivernais," smoky grey bulbous body molded w/three tiers of rounded ribs separated w/zigzag borders, acid-etched "R. Lalique - France," ca. 1927. . . . . **1,265**

Vase, 7" h., "Danaides," footed swelled cylindrical body w/a wide flat rim, smokey grey frosted molded in low relief w/female nudes emptying urns of water, molded "R. LALIQUE - France," introduced in 1926. . . . . **2,415**

Lalique "Courges" Vase

Vase, 7½" h., "Courges," No. 900, bulbous base tapering to short narrow cylindrical neck, molded & frosted deep turquoise blue w/low relief-molded pear-shaped gourds pendent from swirling vines, introduced in 1914 & molded "LALIQUE" (ILLUS.). **13,800**

Vase, 9" h., "Malesherbes," bulbous ovoid body tapering to a small neck w/flattened flared rim, opalescent molded in medium relief w/overlapping pointed leaves, inscribed "R. LALIQUE". **1,495**

Vase, 9⅛" h., "Damiers," footed wide & gently flaring cylindrical form in grey molded in low and medium relief w/concentric rows of dashes enameled in black & reserved against a textured ground, introduced in 1936, acid-stamped "R. LALIQUE - FRANCE" **6,900**

Vase, 9⅝" h., "Farandole," a wide cylindrical lower body in frosted clear molded in high-relief w/a band of putti below the clear flat flaring upper half, inscribed "R. LALIQUE," ca. 1930 . . . . **2,415**

Vase, 10½" h., "Tortues," footed bulbous ovoid body w/a short cylindrical neck & flattened rim, deep amber molded overall in medium relief w/overlapping tortoiseshells, molded "R. LALIQUE," inscribed "France," introduced in 1926 . . . . **20,700**

Lalique "Acanthes" Vase

Vase, 11⅛" h., "Acanthes," No. 902, shouldered bulbous ovoid body w/narrow molded rim, molded in low-relief w/acanthus leaves, frosted red, original white patina, introduced in 1921, inscribed "Lalique," 11⅛" h. (ILLUS.) **16,100**

Vase, 13¾" h., "Grande Boule Lierre," footed spherical form w/a small, short clear neck, the body in grey molded in low relief overall w/trailing ivy vines & leaves, inscribed "R. LALIQUE" & acid-etched "R.LALIQUE - FRANCE," introduced in 1919 . . . . **14,375**

Wine rinser, "Ricquewihr," slightly flaring wide cylindrical body w/three thick bands decorated w/delicate trailing grapevines, clear w/teal patina, inscribed "R. LALIQUE - FRANCE," ca. 1938, 5" h. **517**

LE VERRE FRANCAIS

Various Le Verre Francais Marks

Glassware carrying this marking was produced at the French glass factory founded by Charles Schneider in 1908. A great deal of cameo glass was exported to the United States early in this century; much of it was marketed through Ovingtons in New York City.

Le Verre Francais Cameo Ewer

Cameo ewer, bulbous cylindrical lower body tapering to a tall slender neck w/bulbed top & upright pointed spout, D-form applied purple handle from rim to center of neck, mottled yellow & flame orange overlaid w/brown & cut w/a frieze of cats in various positions, abstract brickwork cut around the neck & shoulder, signed in intaglio "Le Verre Francais," ca. 1920-22, 11½" h. **$3,737**

Cameo ewer, ovoid body tapering to a bulbed neck w/a tall upright pointed spout, applied pointed angular handle, shaded pink overlaid in lavender & cut w/stylized flowers & leaves, signed, 12½" h. (ILLUS.) **1,150**

Le Verre Francais Jar & Lamp

Cameo jar, cov., bulbous ovoid ginger jar-form w/fitted domed cover, mottled pink overlaid w/purple & cut w/five stylized dahlias alternating w/spade-form leaves, signed, 14" h. (ILLUS. left) **3,737**

Cameo lamp table model, the tapering cylindrical base w/a cushion foot mounted w/three wrought-iron arms ending in leaves supporting the mushroom-form shade, all in grey internally shaded w/light blue & yellow, overlaid in purple mottled w/orange & cut w/stylized thistles & leaves, signed, ca. 1925-27, 19" h. (ILLUS. right) **4,025**

Cameo vase, 5½" h., cushion foot on a wide swelled cylindrical body w/a wide flared rim flanked by tiny loop handles, yellow overlaid w/mottled & shaded purple to orange & cut w/a geometric Art Deco design w/vines & berries around the top & stepped rectangular blocks down the center, signed on the boot "Le Verre Francais" **690**

Cameo vase, 9½" h., 9" d., bulbous body of mottled orange & yellow overlaid in tango red shaded to aubergine & cameo-etched w/stylized Art Deco flowering trees, inscribed "Le Verre Francais" at the base . . . **1,610**

Cameo vase, 11½" h., a cushion foot below a slender stem flaring to a large bulbous top w/a closed rim, grey mottled w/yellow & light blue, overlaid w/reddish orange shading to purple, cut w/three orchids on leafy stems, inscribed "Le Verre Francais," ca. 1925-27 . . . . **1,840**

From left: Cylindrical Le Verre Francais Vase
Three Le Verre Francais Vases

Cameo vase, 14" h., disk foot & short knop stem supporting a tall cylindrical body w/beveled base & rim, mottled orange & white ground overlaid in orange & cut w/stylized flowers & leaves, signed (ILLUS.) **1,265**

Cameo vase, 15¼" h., large ovoid body w/a wide closed rim, supported on a short knop stem & disk foot, white & grey mottled w/touches of purple, overlaid w/brown shading to orange & cut w/pendent twisted ribbons & floating spots above a honeycomb border, signed, ca. 1925-26 . . . . **2,300**

Cameo vase, 15½" h., cushion foot w/small pedestal supporting a tall cylindrical body rounded at the bottom & w/a swelled cupped lip, orange mottled w/grey overlaid w/purple shading to rust, cut w/five-petal stylized flowers on straight

slender stems growing from a border of grass around the foot, a border of flowers & beads around the lip, inscribed "Le Verre Francais," ca. 1925 . . . . **1,380**

Cameo vase, 15¾" h., tall slender inverted pear-form body w/a wide flat rim, raised on a thick cushion foot, mottled orange, red & yellow, overlaid in glossy maroon cameo-etched w/trailing vines of stylized grape clusters, foot signed (ILLUS. left) **1,495**

Cameo vase, 17" h., cushion foot w/narrow short stem supporting the bulbous ovoid body tapering to a tall slender neck w/flaring top, mottled white overlaid in tortoiseshell amber & browns shaded to orange, cameo etched w/an abstract design of twisting ribbons & dots, signed on the foot (ILLUS. right) **920**

Cameo vase, 19" h., 13½" d., very large trumpet-form body on a thick cushion foot, yellow overlaid in deep cobalt blue w/a variegated orange band cameo etched w/stylized hollyhocks, signed (ILLUS. center) **3,738**

Cameo vase, 24¾" h., tall cylindrical body w/a slightly flaring lip & cushion foot, mottled light blue overlaid w/royal blue & cut w/stylized berried branches & a lower border of brickwork, inscribed "Le Verre Francais - France," ca. 1925 . . . . **1,840**

Veilleuse (night light), a mushroom-shaped glass shade in grey mottled w/white & blue, overlaid w/mottled brick red & cobalt blue & cut w/stylized fuchsia blossoms, on a round metal base w/three arched leaf-form feet, shade inscribed "Le Verre Francais," ca. 1925, 6" h. **920**

LIBBEY

In 1878, William L. Libbey obtained a lease on the New England Glass Company of Cambridge, Massachusetts, changing the name to the New England Glass Works, W.L. Libbey and Son, Proprietors. After his death in 1883, his son, Edward D. Libbey, continued to operate the company at Cambridge until 1888 when the factory was closed. Edward Libbey moved to Toledo, Ohio, and set up the company subsequently known as Libbey Glass Co. During the 1880s, the firm's master technician, Joseph Locke, developed the now much desired colored art glass lines of Agata, Amberina, Peach Blow and Pomona. Renowned for its cut glass of the Brilliant Period (see CUT GLASS), the company continues in operation today as Libbey Glassware, a division of Owens-Illinois, Inc.

Bowl, 9" d., experimental, clear w/internal bubble design & pale green powders, designed by Nash, stamped on base "Libbey" **$86**

Stemware set: two champagnes, nine red
wines, a water goblet, eight white wines,
seven highballs & one liqueur; Art Deco
design, clear w/a drawn ovoid bowl, fluted
rectangular stem & circular foot, etched
Libbey mark, the group **2,645**

Table service: six wine goblets w/polar bear
stems, four candlesticks w/camel stems,
one compote w/giraffe stem; opalescent
stems on colorless glassware, each piece
stamped "Libbey," designed by Nash,
compote 7" h., the group **2,300**

Vase, 14" h., "Talisman" patt., optic ribbed
flared oval of colorless glass w/spiraled
green internal thread, raised on applied
colorless foot, base marked "Libbey,"
designed by Nash. **230**

Libbey-Nash "Zipper" Vase

Vase, 12" h., cushion base tapering to a tall
trumpet-form body, colorless crystal
w/seafoam green "zipper" decoration,
designed by Nash, catalog No. K523
(ILLUS.) **345**

LOETZ

*Loetz,
Austria*

Loetz Mark

*Iridescent glass, some of it somewhat
resembling that of Tiffany and other
contemporary glasshouses, was produced by the
Bohemian firm of J. Loetz Witwe of Klostermule
and is referred to as Loetz. Some cameo pieces
were also made. Not all pieces are marked.*

Loetz Bowl-Vase

Bowl-vase, globular body w/four large
dimples around the sides below the wide
flattened mouth, green w/gold-striped
iridescent pink pulled feather design,
bears partial paper label, ca. 1900, 5" d.
(ILLUS.). **$1,265**

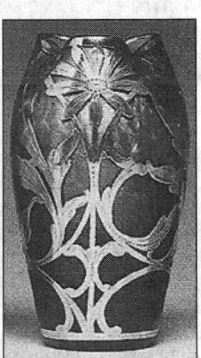

*From left: Loetz Signed Ewer
Loetz Vase with Ornate Silver Overlay*

Ewer, tall hexagonal baluster-form body w/a
cylindrical neck, cupped riim & long
angled rim spout, applied loop handle
from rim to shoulder, opalescent ground
w/amber feathering & silvery blue
iridescence, signed, ca. 1900, 10¼" h.
(ILLUS.). **1,955**

Vase, 3¾" h., wide squatty bulbous body
raised on a tapering base, the wide
shoulder centering a short flaring neck,
rich amber shaded w/bands of salmon at
the neck & purple around the base,
decorated w/iridescent silvery blue
waves, designed by Franz Hofstatter,
signed "Loetz - Austria," ca. 1900 . . . . **4,887**

Vase, 4¾" h., bulbous ovoid body tapering
to a wide upright scrolled & crimped rim,
golden amber decorated w/swirling
trailings in silvery blue & pink iridescence,
signed "Loetz - Austria" **2,300**

Vase, 5" h., simple ovoid body w/three-lobed
rim, orange ground decorated
w/iridescent green & blue & cased in
clear, overlaid w/overall pierced silver
scrolling leafy vine decoration, small chip
to base, ca. 1900, unsigned (ILLUS.) **1,380**

Vase, 6" h., bulbous ovoid body tapering to
a short neck w/a wide flat rim, amber
decorated w/irregular green leafage at
the bottom & silvery blue iridescent
waves, signed, ca. 1900 . . . . **3,162**

Vase, 7⅛" h., bulbous ovoid body tapering
to a small foot, the wide flat shoulder
centered by a short cylindrical flared
neck, deep red decorated w/overall
silvery blue wavy concentric trailings,
signed, ca. 1900 . . . . **2,875**

Vase, 8" h., squatty bulbous base tapering sharply to a tall slender cylindrical neck w/a widely flaring & flattened rim, pale green ground w/a band of heavy blue threading wrapped around the neck & blue applied disks around the lower body, overall pale purple & green iridescence **358**

Vase, 9¼" h., ovoid double-gourd form w/a tapering neck, amber w/silvery blue iridescence & oil spotting, overlaid w/silver flowering whiplash decoration, ca. 1900. . . . . **2,070**

Vase, 10" h., squatty bulbous body tapering to a wide cylindrical neck flanked by four applied & loop-pulled handles from the center neck to the shoulder, grey decorated w/iridescent silvery blue & copper oil spots, signed, early 1900s **1,380**

Vase, 10½" h., ovoid bottle-form w/deeply dimpled bottom & tall neck w/rounded knob below the flattened, flared rim, pale amber opalescent decorated w/pulled trailings in silvery iridescence, signed, ca. 1900. . . . . **2,875**

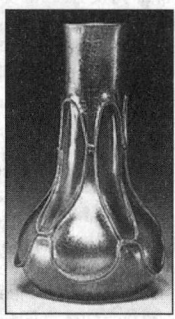

Loetz Vase with Looped Trailings

Vase, 11⅜" h., squatty bulbous base tapering to a tall cylindrical neck w/applied chain of looping trailings, colorless shaded w/amber & finished w/pink & blue iridescence, erroneously signed "LCT," ca. 1901 (ILLUS.) **1,725**

Vase, 18½" h., bottle-form, spherical dimpled bottom tapering to a tall slender & slightly tapering neck w/flattened flaring rim, grey cased in peach & decorated overall w/concentric trailings of golden iridescence, further decorated w/four applied prunts around the lower body w/slender straight tails running up the neck, ca. 1901, signed "Loetz - Austria" . . . **11,500**

MARY GREGORY

Glass enameled in white with silhouette-type figures, primarily of children, is now termed "Mary Gergory" and was attributed to the Boston and Sandwich Glass Company. However, recent
research has proven conclusively that this was not decorated by Mary Gregory, nor was it made at the Sandwich plant. Miss Gregory was employed by Boston and Sandwich Glass Company as a decorator; however, records show her assignment was the painting of naturalistic landscape scenes on larger items such as lamps and shades, never the charming children for which her name has become synonymous. Further, in the inspection of fragments from the factory site, no paintings of children were found. It is now known that all wares collectors call "Mary Gregory" originated in Bohemia beginning in the late 19th century and were extensively exported to England and the United States well into this century.*

For further information, see The Glass Industry in Sandwich, Volume #4, *by Raymond E. Barlow and Joan E. Kaiser, and the book* Mary Gregory Glassware, 1880-1900, *by R. & D. Truitt.*

From left: Cranberry Mary Gregory Decanter Blue Mary Gregory Decanter

Cake basket, a silver-plate frame w/tall tapering legs supporting a round dished bowl w/a wide reeded border framing a central round blue glass disk enameled in white w/a figure of a girl feeding a bird, an overhead swing strap handle, frame by the Middletown Silver Co., late 19th c., 9½" d., 10" h. **$550**

Decanter w/original clear facet-cut stopper, cranberry, the footed tapering cylindrical & ring-molded body w/an optic rib design & wide shoulder, tall cylindrical neck w/flared rim, decorated w/white enameled winged cupid batting at a heart, white lily-of-the-valley trim, gilt banding, 4" d., 10" h. (ILLUS.) **185**

Decanter w/tall ringed & tapering blown stopper, sapphire blue, the footed flaring cylindrical body w/a stepped shoulder & tall cylindrical neck, optic rib design, white enamel decoration of a young boy in a garden, 3¼" d., 10¼" h. (ILLUS.) **195**

Mary Gregory Lemonade Set

Lemonade set: tall waisted tankard pitcher w/applied handle & two tall tapering cylindrical tumblers; lime green w/optic ribbing, the pitcher w/a white enameled scene of a man on a bicycle w/color-painted face & hands, one tumbler w/a man on a bicycle, the other w/a lady on a bicycle, late 19th to early 20th c., pitcher 13" h., the set (ILLUS.) 435

Mary Gregory Cranberry Mug

Mug, cranberry, cylindrical w/an applied clear handle, white enameled young girl walking on tiptoes through a garden, engraved "Dora" on one side, 2⅜" d., 3⅝" h. (ILLUS.) 95

Perfume atomizer, white enameled scene of little girl 345

Plates, 9⅜" d., cobalt blue, one w/a white enameled figure of a young woman in long dress holding a fan in a garden, the other w/a young man in armour & shield, pr. . . 350

Pocket watch-ring tray, a brass round ring around a shallow light blue glass dish flanked by decorated upright tall legs joined by a top arch & braces to a round metal pocket watch holder, the dish decorated w/a white enameled figure of a young boy holding a balloon on a string, 5¼" w., 6¼" h. 297

Tumbler, sapphire blue, white enameled girl in garden 50

Vase, 7" h., 2⅞" d., cobalt blue, footed tall slender waisted cylindrical body w/clear applied shell rigaree trim down each side, white enamel young boy standing among lily-of-othe-valley blossoms & leaves (ILLUS.) 145

From left: Slender Mary Gregory Vase with Trim Large Mary Gregory Vase with Figures

Vase, 8" h., 4" d., amber baluster-form w/an optic ribbed design & cylindrical neck w/wide ruffled & crimped rim, white enameled figure of a girl standing in a garden w/her arms stretched out 175

Vase, 11⅛" h., 4" d., baluster-form, green opaque Bristol glass body w/cushion foot, ringed stem, tall swelled cylindrical body w/a multiple ring shoulder below the wide cylindrical neck w/a crimped rim, white enamel figure of a boy carrying a tray of flowers 225

Vase, 13½" h., 5¾" d., olive green, wide baluster-form body w/cushion foot & white ringed & cupped rim, optic ribbing, decorated w/white enamel figures of a woman & man in 18th c. costume standing near a rail fence (ILLUS.) 395

Vases, 8¾" h., footed simple slender ovoid body w/a short cylindrical neck, dark lavender blue, one decorated w/a white enameled girl holding a flower, the other w/a boy holding a basket of flowers, pr. 231

Vases, 10¼" h., baluster-form w/cushion foot & short cylindrical neck w/deeply ruffled & crimped rolled rim, dark blue, one w/a white enameled figure of a girl, another w/a facing figure of a boy, pr. 523

MCKEE

The McKee name has been associated with glass production since 1834, first producing window glass and later bottles. In the 1850s a new factory was established in Pittsburgh, Pennsylvania, for production of flint and pressed glass. The plant was relocated to Jeanette, Pennsylvania, in 1888 and operated there as an independent company almost continuously until 1951, when it sold out to Thatcher Glass Manufacturing Company. Many types of collectible glass were produced by McKee through the years including Depression, Pattern, Milk White and a variety of utility kitchenwares. See these categories for additional listings.

KITCHENWARES

From left: Red Ships Pattern Butter Dish
Roman Arch Pepper Shaker

Batter pitcher, Red Polka Dots patt. **$175**
Bowl, 8" d., Red Polka Dots patt. **18**
Bowl, 9" d., 5" h., flared, Red Ships patt. on
   white opal **37**
Bowl, 9½" d., Tulips patt. on white opal **40**
Butter dish, cov., Red Ships patt. on white
   opal, 1 lb. (ILLUS.) **60**
Canister, cov., French Ivory, 40 oz. **90**
Canister, cov., Green Polka Dots patt. on
   French Ivory, 48 oz. **75**
Canister, cov., round, "Flour," Skokie
   Green, 5" h. **145**
Canister, cov., round, Skokie Green, no
   lettering, 5" h. **90**
Custard cup, marked "Sunkist," Skokie
   Green **75**
Custard cup, Skokie Green **28**
Egg beater bowl w/spout, French Ivory **60**
Egg beater bowl w/spout, Skokie Green **18**
Egg cup, Chalaine Blue **25**
Flour shaker w/original metal top, large
   box, French Ivory **45**
Flour shaker w/original metal top, Roman
   Arch style, Chalaine blue **140**
Flour shaker w/original metal top, Roman
   Arch style, French Ivory, 4¼" h. **35**
Flour shaker w/original metal top, Roman
   Arch style, Red Polka Dot patt. on French
   Ivory, 4¼" h. **45**
Flour shaker w/original metal top, small
   box, French Ivory **40**
Measuring cup, two pour spouts, Seville
   Yellow. **275**
Pepper shaker w/original metal top,
   Roman Arch patt., Chalaine blue **22**
Pepper shaker w/original metal top,
   Roman Arch patt., white opal **25**
Pepper shaker w/original metal top,
   Roman Arch style, French Ivory, 4¼" h.
   (ILLUS.) **30**
Pepper shaker w/original metal top, small
   box, French Ivory **30**
Reamer, marked "Sunkist," Skokie Green **60**
Refrigerator dish, cov., triangular,
   French Ivory **75**
Refrigerator dish, cov., French Ivory, 4 x 5" **40**

Refrigerator dish, cov., rectangular, Red
   Ship patt. on white opal, 4 x 5" **35**
Refrigerator dish, cov., Skokie Green, 4 x 5" **52**
Refrigerator dish, cov., rectangular, Red
   Ships patt. on white opal, 4 x 8" **38**

McKee Water Dispenser

Refrigerator water dispenser, cov., oblong,
   Skokie Green, faucet is stuck (ILLUS.) **145**
Sugar shaker, Roman Arch style, French
   Ivory, 4¼" h. **35**
Sugar shaker w/original metal top, black
   w/white lettering **35**
Sugar shaker w/original metal top,
   Chalaine Blue **190**
Sugar shaker w/original metal top, large
   box, French Ivory **45**
Sugar shaker w/original metal top, small
   box, French Ivory **35**
Tom & Jerry cup, Skokie Green **28**

PRES-CUT LINES

Compote, open, 9⅛" h., Puritan patt., wide
   shallow bowl w/a scalloped rim, slender
   swelled pedestal on a round foot, Skokie
   Green, early 20th c. **110**
Compote, 11½" d, Rock Crystal patt.,
   footed, amber **65**
Pitcher, "Eclipse," line, Yutec patt., clear **45**
Pitcher, tankard, 8½" h., Toltec patt., clear **100**
Pitcher, water, cov., Rock Crystal patt., pink **350**
Sundae, Rock Crystal patt., ruby **35**
Tumbler, Rock Crystal patt., footed, pink, 7 oz. . . . **25**

MISCELLANEOUS PATTERNS & PIECES

Bottoms-Up Whiskey Tumbler & Base

Bowl, berry, French Ivory 10
Bowl, w/pour spout, French Ivory 26
Bowl, 8" d., Laurel patt., Skokie Green. 45
Bowl, berry, 9" d., Laurel patt., French Ivory 25
Tumbler, French Ivory 12
Vase, 8" h., Sarah patt., Skokie Green 48
Whiskey tumbler & base, Buttoms-Up
patt., Seville Yellow, 2 pcs. (ILLUS.) 275
Whiskey tumbler & base, Buttoms-Up
patt., Skokie Green, satin finish, 2 pcs. 138

MILK GLASS

Opaque white glass, or "opal," has been called "milk-white glass" perhaps to distinguish it from transparent or "clear-white glass." Resembling fine white porcelain, it was viewed as an inexpensive substitute. Opacity is obtained by adding bone ash or oxide of tin to clear molten glass. By the addition of various coloring agents, the opaque mixture can be turned into blue milk glass, or pink, yellow, green, caramel, even black milk glass. Collectors of milk glass now accept not only the white variety but virtually any opaque colors and color mixtures, including slag or marbled glass. It has been made in numerous forms and shapes in this country and abroad from about the first quarter of the 19th century. It is still being produced, and there are many reproductions of earlier pieces. Pieces are all-white unless otherwise noted. Also see HISTORICAL, PATTERN GLASS and WESTMORELAND.

Cat on Split-Ribbed Base Dish

Animal covered dish, "American Hen,"
eagle w/eggs inscribed "Porto Rico,"
"Cuba," & "Philippines," 6" l., 4" h. $55
Animal covered dish, Bull's Head mustard
jar, w/separate tongue spoon, original
paint, Atterbury 250
Animal covered dish, Cat on Drum,
Porteaux, France, 4⅝" d. 110
Animal covered dish, Cat on lattice base,
blue glass eyes, Westmoreland Specialty
Company, early 20th c. 110
Animal covered dish, Cat on split-ribbed
base, signed "McKee," 5½" l. (ILLUS.) 375
Animal covered dish, Cow on oval paneled
base, maker unknown, 6¼" l. . . . . 400 to 450

Animal covered dish, Crawfish on two-
handled oblong base, overall 7½" l. . . . 200 to 250
Animal covered dish, Deer on fallen tree
base, Flaccus, 6¾" l. . . . . 250 to 275
Animal covered dish, Dog on oval wide rib
base, blue head, Westmoreland Specialty
Company, early 20th c., 5½" l. . . . . 55 to 60

Setter Dog on Square Base Dish

Animal covered dish, Dog, Setter Dog on
square base, Vallerysthal (ILLUS.) . . . . 200 to 250
Animal covered dish, Dove on split-ribbed
base, signed "McKee" 275
Animal covered dish, Duck w/amethyst
head, Atterbury, 11" l., 5" h. . . . . 350 to 400
Animal covered dish, Duck w/wavy base,
glass eyes, Challinor, Taylor & Co.,
5¼" h. . . . . 125 to 150

Entwined Fish Covered Dish

Animal covered dish, Fish, Entwined Fish
on lacy-edge base, shell finial, Atterbury,
7½" d. (ILLUS.) . . . . 200 to 225
Animal covered dish, Fish, Vallerysthal,
7" l. . . . . 225 to 250
Animal covered dish, Fox on ribbed top &
lacy-edge base, Atterbury, 7¾" l. 175
Animal covered dish, Frog sitting, mouth
slightly open, signed "Vallerysthal" . . . . 225 to 250
Animal covered dish, Hen on Basketweave
base, all-white, Challinor, Taylor & Co., 7" l. . . . 70
Animal covered dish, Hen w/amethyst
head, lacy base, Atterbury . . . . 200 to 225
Animal covered dish, Horse on split-ribbed
base, McKee . . . . 275 to 300
Animal covered dish, Lion, Majestic Lion,
molded bird & foliage base, 6¾" h. 2,600
Animal covered dish, Lion on scroll base,
5¾" l. (ILLUS.) 75

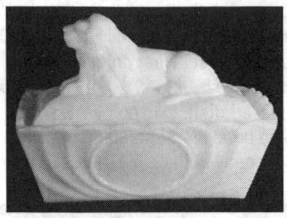

Lion on Scroll Base Dish

Animal covered dish, Owl Head on split-ribbed base, McKee . . . . **800 to 1,000**

Animal covered dish, Rabbit, Flat-Eared Rabbit on split-ribbed base, McKee, 5½" l. . . . **300**

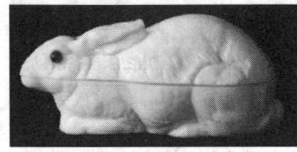

Atterbury Rabbit Dish

Animal covered dish, Rabbit, original red glass eyes, patent date stamped on bottom, Atterbury, 9" l. (ILLUS.) . . . . . . **250 to 275**

Animal covered dish, Robin on pedestal Nest, signed "Vallerysthal" **275**

Animal covered dish, Rooster on wide rib base, Westmoreland Specialty Company, 5½" l. **45**

Animal covered dish, Squirrel on acorn-shaped base, Vallerysthal, 7¼" l **255**

Animal covered dish, Swan w/raised wings & glass eyes on lacy-edged base, Atterbury, 9½" l. . . . . **150 to 175**

Animal covered dish, Turkey on ribbed base, McKee, 5½" l. **85**

Animal covered dish, Turkey on split-ribbed base, McKee . . . . **250 to 275**

Animal covered dish, Turtle on two-handled oblong base, overall 7½" l. . . . . **225 to 250**

Basket, two-handled, chick emerging from egg on cover **75**

Bowl, 7" d., 5" h., Chain & Petal Edge patt. **35**

Bowl, 8" d., footed Wide Weave Basket design, Atterbury, open **60**

Bowl, 8¾" d., 3½" h., Crinkled Lacy Edge patt. **38**

Rectangular Open Edge Bowl

Bowl, 8¾ x 9¼", rectangular w/open edge loop border (ILLUS.) . . . . **55 to 60**

Bowl, 10" d., 4½" h., Acanthus Leaf patt., all-white **75**

Bowl, 10" l., 5¾" h., oblong, Shell patt., two ribbed & two petal feet **55**

Box, cov., heart-shaped, embossed floral design highlighted w/touches of blue & gold, McKee **35**

Bread tray, Basketweave patt., Atterbury, patent-dated 1874, 9¾ x 12" **65**

Butter dish, cov., Blackberry patt. **75**

Butter dish, cov., Daisy & Tree of Life patt. **175**

Cake stand, Lacy Edge patt., Atterbury, 12" d., 2¾" h. **55**

Compote, cov., Melon with Leaf & Net patt., small size . . . . **75 to 90**

Compote, open, 7½" h., Jenny Lind figural bust pedestal, ribbed bowl **85**

Goddess of Liberty Compote

Compote, open, 7⅝" h., Goddess of Liberty patt., figural stem (ILLUS.) . . . . **125 to 150**

Covered dish, Admiral Dewey on round basket base, "Dewey" on cover, 5½" h. . . . . **300 to 350**

Covered dish, Automobile, signed "Portieux," France **175**

Covered dish, Battleship "Maine," 7½" l., 3½" h. **53**

Covered dish, Hand & Dove on lacy-edged base, Atterbury, 8¾" l., 4¾" h. . . . . . **125 to 150**

Covered dish, Santa Claus, Santa on Sleigh base, large head, Westmoreland Specialty Company, early 20th c., 5½" l. . . . . **90 to 125**

Covered dish, Snare Drum w/Cannon finial, 4½" d., 4" h. . . . . **70 to 90**

Creamer, Apple Blossom patt., decorated & w/yellow band **25**

Creamer, Paneled Flower patt. **85**

Creamer, Swan patt., 5" h. . . . . **50 to 60**

Creamer, miniature, Owl w/glass eyes, 3½" h. **40**

Dresser bottles w/stoppers, Leaf patt., green & gold decoration, 10" h., pr. **50**

Dresser jar, cov., Versailles patt., 3 x 3½" **65**

Dresser tray, Actress patt., Fostoria Glass Co. . . . . **55 to 65**

Inkwell, model of a Minstrel boy . . . . **125 to 135**

Jar, cov., embossed British royal arms on sides, figural bust portrait of Queen Victoria on cover.......................... **95**

Match holder, model of bulldog head w/striker on back of head, possibly McKee, 2¼" h..................... **125 to 150**

Match holder, pierced for hanging, basket-shaped w/scrolls & relief-molded painted rabbit & chick, attributed to Eagle Glass Co. ... **125**

Mug, Swan & Cattails patt.................... **45**

Pickle dish, model of a fish, Atterbury, 5¼ x 8" ... **32**

Challinor, Taylor Fish Pickle Dish

Pickle dish, model of a fish on base, waffle pattern on sides, glass or molded eyes, Challinor, Taylor & Company, all-white, 9" l., 3" h. (ILLUS.) **125**

Pitcher, tankard-type, Opaque Scroll patt....... **125**

Pitcher, water, Wild Iris patt. **75**

Pitcher, 7" h., milk, Block Daisy patt. **70**

Plate, 4⅜" d., Rising Sun patt. **50**

Plate, 6" d., Three Puppies patt., open leaf border, Westmoreland Specialty Company, early 20th c. **100**

Plate, 6¾" d., Easter Rabbits, in cabbage patch, old paint......................... **45**

Plate, 7" d., Challinor's Forget-Me-Not patt....... **40**

Plate, 7" d., Roger Williams Memorial, flag, fleur-de-lis & eagles border.......... **150 to 160**

Three Bears Plate

Plate, 7" d., Three Bears patt., traces of original brown, green & gilt paint (ILLUS.).......................... **45 to 55**

Plate, 7¼" d., "Easter," rabbits & eggs, scroll border **38**

Plate, 7¼" d., Lacy-Edge Indian patt., good paint......................... **50 to 75**

Plate, 7¼" d., Pansy patt., molded openwork border .... **50 to 75**

Plate, 7½" d., Crown Border patt............... **30**

Plate, 7½" d., Hare & Cloverleaf patt., scalloped & beaded border........... **70 to 90**

Plate, 7½" d., Yoked Slatted Border patt. .... **30 to 40**

Plate, 6½ x 7¾", Horseshoe & Anchor patt., patent-dated on back "December 10, 1901".... **45**

Plate, 8" d., Fan & Circle Border patt., Atterbury................................ **30**

Plate, 8" d., Single Forget-Me-Not patt., openwork border **20**

Plate, 8" sq., Backward-C Border patt.......... **45**

Plate, 8¼" d., Three Puppies patt., open leaf border, Westmoreland Specialty Company, early 20th c............. **125 to 150**

Lattice Edge Plate with Decoration
Roman Cross Sugar Bowl

Plate, 9" d., Lattice Edge Border patt., painted trumpet vine center decoration (ILLUS.)........................... **45 to 65**

Plate, 11" d., Pinwheel Border patt., shallow pedestal, h.p. center.................... **50**

Platter, 10½ x 13¾", model of a fish, flattened form w/scale details, Atterbury, patent-dated "June 4, 1872" .... **125 to 150**

Relish dish, model of a bird, flattened form w/oval dished center, attributed to Hemingray Glass Company, ca. 1876, 5 x 10¾", 2" h. **75**

Salt dip, footed, Strawberry patt. **40**

Salt dip, model of a basket w/handle, Atterbury, patent-dated .... **45 to 50**

Salt & pepper shakers w/original tops, Heron & Lighthouse patt., pr................ **95**

Salt & pepper shakers w/original tops, Scroll patt., pr. **50**

Salt shaker w/original top, Twisted Scroll patt. ... **20**

Smoke bell, cranberry trim on fluted rim, w/original brass chain, 7" h................. **55**

Spooner, Acanthus Leaf patt., base marked "Pat'd Apr. 23, '78," 4⅝" h................. **55**

Spooner, Blackberry patt...................... **50**

Spooner, Flower & Panel patt................. **40**

Sugar bowl, cov., Melon with Leaf patt., patent-dated 1878................... **90 to 110**

Sugar bowl, cov., model of a beehive, Vallerysthal............................ **85**

Sugar bowl, cov., Roman Cross patt. (ILLUS.) ... **65**

Sugar bowl, cov., Versailles patt., pink decoration, 6" h........................ **45**

Sugar shaker w/original top, Challinor's
Forget-Me-Not patt. **110**
Sugar shaker w/original top, Little Shrimp patt. . . **75**
Syrup pitcher w/original top, Challinor's
Banded Shells patt., h.p. apple blossoms
& green shells. **95**
Syrup pitcher w/original top, Heavy
Scroll patt. **75**
Syrup pitcher w/original top, Torquay
patt., h.p. yellow stripes **150**
Toothpick holder, Horseshoe & Clover
patt. . . . . **40 to 50**
Tray, Dahlia (in corners) patt., 8 x 10¼" **50**
Tray, Diamond Grill patt. center, "Give Us
This Day" border, 10 x 12" **25**

Scroll Pattern Water Set

Water set: tankard pitcher & four tumblers;
Scroll patt., Challinor, Taylor & Company,
1880s, 5 pcs. (ILLUS.) **245**
Whimsey, model of a canoe, enameled
flowers & gold trim, 6" l. **15**
Whimsey, model of a Straw Hat (College
Hat), w/old paint, McKee, 4" d. **55**
Whimsey, model of Uncle Sam's Hat, color
decoration, w/coin bank closure inside brim. . . . **75**
Whimsey vase, model of a hand holding a
cornucopia, ruffled rim, 8½" h. **90**

MORGANTOWN (OLD MORGANTOWN)

Morgantown, West Virginia, was the site where a glass firm named the Morgantown Glass Works began in the late 19th century, but the company reorganized in 1903 to become the Economy Tumbler Company, a name it retained until 1929. By the 1920s the firm was producing a wider range of better quality and colorful glass tablewares; to reflect this fact, it reassumed its earlier name, Morgantown Glass Works, in 1929. Today its many quality wares of the Depression era are growing in collector demand.

Bowl, dessert, Krinkle patt., yellow **$30**
Bowl, finger, footed Sunrise Medallion
(Dancing Girl) etching, clear **45**

Bowl, individual salad, Krinkle patt.,
moss green. **22**
Bowl, 5" d., Krinkle patt., moss green. **25**
Champagne, American Beauty etching,
No. 7668 . . . . **25**
Champagne, Art Moderne patt., green. **50**
Champagne, Art Moderne patt., transparent
green **50**
Champagne, Georgian patt., No. 7667,
Alexandrite **50**
Champagne, Golf Ball patt., cobalt bowl
w/clear golf ball stem **44**
Champagne, Golf Ball patt., red bowl
w/clear golf ball stem, large **25**
Champagne, Golf Ball patt., ruby bowl
w/clear golf ball stem **25**
Champagne, Monroe patt., No. 7690,
red & crystal **35**
Champagne, Plantation patt., No 8445,
cobalt blue **120**
Champagne, Plantation patt., ruby. **40**
Champagne, saucer type, No. 7692 . . . . **50**
Champagne, Sunrise Medallion (Dancing
Girl) etching, No. 7664, clear **95**
Champagne, Yale patt., No. 7684, ruby red **50**
Champagne-sherbet, Button patt., ruby red. **18**
Champagnes, Hampton No. 7614, green
Palm Optic bowl, crystal stem, set of 4 . . . . . . **100**
Claret, Button patt., ruby red **24**
Claret, Golf Ball patt., ruby bowl w/clear golf
ball stem. **22**
Claret, Old English patt., Stiegel green, 5 oz. . . . **30**
Cocktail, Carlton No. 7606-1/2 stem, 3½ oz. **20**
Cocktail, flat, Krinkle patt., ruby red **10**
Cocktail, Golf Ball patt., cobalt bowl w/clear
golf ball stem **34**
Cocktail, Golf Ball patt., red bowl w/clear
golf ball stem **31**
Cocktail, Golf Ball patt., Steigel green bowl
w/clear golf ball stem **35**
Cocktail, Old Fashion, Krinkle patt., amethyst **13**
Cocktail, Plantation patt., No. 8445, cobalt
blue. **110**
Cocktail, Polynesian Bis (aka Mai Tai),
amber stem **25**
Cocktail, Superba etching, Legacy patt.,
No. 7654-1/2, clear **30**
Cocktail, American Beauty etching, pink,
3¼ oz. **60**
Cocktail, American Beauty etching, pink, 3¼ oz. . . **60**
Cocktail, Carlton etching, platinum Marco
decoration, No. 7653, 3½ oz. **45**
Cocktail, twist, Elizabeth etching, blue, 5½". **55**
Cordial, Golf Ball patt., cobalt blue bowl
w/clear golf ball stem **50**
Cordial, Golf Ball patt., ruby bowl w/clear
golf ball stem
Cordial, Golf Ball patt., ruby bowl w/clear
golf ball stem **50**

Cordial, Golf Ball patt., smoke bowl w/clear
golf ball stem **39**

Cordial, Golf Ball patt., Stiegel green bowl
w/clear golf ball stem **39**

Cordial, Plantation patt., No.8445, cobalt blue . . . **175**

Cordial, Sunrise Medallion patt., crystal **110**

Dinner service: ten 8" plates, 5 water
goblets, 4 champagnes, 3 footed water
tumblers; Mikado patt., 22 pcs. **120**

Goblet, American Beauty etching, No. 7668 . . . . . **32**

Goblet, Fontinelle patt., ebony filament
stem, 7½", 9 oz. **160**

Goblet, Golf Ball patt., emerald green bowl
w/clear golf ball stem **53**

Goblet, Majesty patt., Spanish Red **30**

Goblet, Sunrise Medallion (Dancing Girl)
etching, No. 7630, Azure blue **50**

Goblet, water, Art Moderne patt., green **65**

Goblet, water, Button patt., Cobalt blue **35**

Goblet, water, Button patt., ruby red **22**

Goblet, water, Carlton etching, ebony
filament stem **120**

Goblet, water, Churchill, No. 7692, cobalt **90**

Goblet, water, Golf Ball patt., cobalt blue
bowl w/clear golf ball stem **42**

Goblet, water, Golf Ball patt., ruby bowl
w/clear golf ball stem **30**

Goblet, water, Golf Ball patt., smoke bowl
w/clear golf ball stem **26**

Goblet, water, Old English patt., No. 7678,
ruby red **35**

Goblet, water, Plantation patt., No. 8445,
cobalt blue **135**

Goblet, water, tulip-shaped, Golf Ball patt.,
ruby bowl w/clear golf ball stem **56**

Goblet, juice, Golf Ball patt., Ritz Blue bowl
w/clear golf ball stem, 5" h. **50**

Goblet, iced tea, Golf Ball patt., Ritz Blue
bowl w/clear golf ball stem, 6¾" h. **60**

Goblet, Golf Ball patt., cobalt blue bowl
w/clear golf ball stem, 9 oz. **60**

Goblet, water, Golf Ball patt., Crystal w/clear
golf ball stem, No. 7643, 9 oz. **30**

Goblet, water, Krinkle patt., pink, 10 oz. **14**

Goblet in pierced metal stem holder,
cupped, amber **4**

Goblet in pierced metal stem holder,
cupped, amethyst **8**

Goblet in pierced metal stem holder,
cupped, emerald **4**

Goblet in pierced metal stem holder,
cupped, heliotrope **7**

Goblet in pierced metal stem holder,
flared, amethyst **7**

Highball, Krinkle patt., Amethyst, 12 oz. **14**

Ivy ball vase, Peacock Optic patt.,
No. 7643, meadow green w/golf ball
stem, 4" d. **89**

Pitcher, juice, Krinkle patt., Amethyst **45**

Pitcher, Krinkle patt., red w/crystal handle,
50 oz. **150**

Plate, 7½" d., Sunrise Medallion (Dancing
Girl) etching, clear **18**

Plate, 7½" sq., Bridge Set, ebony **12**

Sherbet, Fontinelle patt., ebony filament
stem, tall **120**

Sherbet, footed, Krinkle patt., emerald green **16**

Sherbet, footed, Krinkle patt., moss green **14**

Sherbet, Golf Ball patt., amber bowl w/clear
golf ball stem **20**

Sherbet, Golf Ball patt., amethyst bowl
w/clear golf ball stem **20**

Sherbet, Golf Ball patt., cobalt blue bowl
w/clear golf ball stem **33**

Sherbet, Golf Ball patt., smoke bowl w/clear
golf ball stem **22**

Sherbet, Golf Ball patt., topaz bowl w/clear
golf ball stem **22**

Sherbet, low, Golf Ball patt., red bowl
w/clear golf ball stem **19**

Sherbet, Sunrise Medallion patt., Crystal **25**

Sherbet, footed, Krinkle patt, amethyst, 6 oz. **14**

Sherbet, Golf Ball patt., No. 7643, teal bowl
w/clear golf ball stem, 7 oz. **20**

Tumbler, iced tea, footed, Krinkle patt.,
moss green **21**

Tumbler, iced tea, footed, Krinkle patt., pink **25**

Tumbler, iced tea, footed, Krinkle patt.,
round, pink **25**

Tumbler, iced tea, Golf Ball patt., green
bowl w/clear golf ball stem **28**

Tumbler, iced tea, footed, Krinkle patt.,
emerald green, 5½" h. **20**

Tumbler, juice, flat, Krinkle patt., amber **8**

Tumbler, juice, flat, Krinkle patt., pastel **10**

Tumbler, juice, footed, Golf Ball patt., red
bowl w/clear golf ball stem **25**

Tumbler, Sunrise Medallion patt., blue,
3¼" h., 3 oz. **150**

Tumbler, water, footed, Mayfair (Sears
Florentine) patt. **14**

Tumbler, water, Mayfair patt. **30**

Tumbler, water, Sunrise Medallion patt.,
crystal **35**

Tumbler, American Beauty etching, clear,
10 oz., 3¾" h. **45**

Tumbler, Queen Mary patt., pink, 5" h. **65**

Tumbler, juice, Krinkle patt., amethyst, 6 oz. **8**

Tumbler, Sunrise Medallion, crystal, footed,
6⅛" h. **40**

Tumbler, Palm Optic patt., No. 9715, 9 oz. **10**

Tumbler, footed, Krinkle patt., amethyst, 10 oz. . . . **10**

Tumbler, American Beauty etching., clear,
10 oz., 3¾" h. **45**

Tumbler, footed, Krinkle patt., amethyst, 13 oz. . . **20**

Tumbler, Krinkle patt., amethyst, 14 oz. **13**

Vase, 4" w., Kimble Ivy Ball, No. 7643, red
w/clear base & golf ball stem **95**

Vase, 6" h., squat, Palm Optic patt., No. 59,
 aquamarine **135**

Vase, bud, 6" h., petite, Palm Optic patt.,
 No. 46, Venetian green w/clear foot **35**

Whiskey, footed, Art Moderne patt., clear &
 black **85**

Whiskey, footed, Krinkle patt., yellow **30**

Wine, Button patt., ruby red **22**

Wine, Golf Ball patt., cobalt blue bowl
 w/clear golf ball stem **48**

Wine, Golf Club patt., red bowl w/clear golf
 ball stem. **32**

Wine, low, Golf Club patt., ruby bowl w/clear
 golf ball stem **50**

Wine, Majesty patt., Spanish red **35**

Wine, Old English patt., No. 7678, cobalt blue . . . **65**

Wine, Old English patt., ruby bowl w/clear
 gold ball stem. **55**

Wine, Plantation patt., No.8445, cobalt blue. **165**

Wine, American Beauty etching, No. 7565,
 clear, 2 oz. **65**

Wine, American Beauty etching, No. 7565,
 clear, 2 oz. **65**

Wine, Sunrise Medallion patt., crystal, 2½ oz. **45**

Wine, Golf Ball patt., No. 7643, crystal
 w/clear golf ball stem. **20**

Wine, Russel Wright, smoke, 4 oz. **20**

MOSER

Ludwig Moser opened his first glass shop in 1857 in Karlsbad, Bohemia (now Karlovy Vary, in the former Czechoslovakia). Here he engraved and decorated fine glasswares especially to appeal to rich visitors to the local health spa. Later other shops were opened in various cities; throughout the 19th and early 20th centuries lovely, colorful glasswares, many beautifully enameled, were produced by Moser's shops and reached a wide market in Europe and America. Ludwig died in 1916 and the firm continued under his sons. They were forced to merge with the Meyer's Nephews glass factory after World War I. The glassworks was sold out of the Moser family in 1933.

Acid-etched Moser Rose Bowl

Rose bowl, spherical, Art Deco design in
 smoky ground heavily acid-etched w/a
 design of stylized deer in a garden,
 signed on the polished pontil, ca. 1920s,
 5½" d., 4¼" h. (ILLUS.). **$403**

Vase, 8" h., wide bulbous tapering cylinder
 w/a widely flaring rim, amber acid-cut w/a
 continuous frieze of elephants under
 palm trees on a grassy plain w/birds in
 the sky, three fluted bands around the
 base, highlighted overall w/gilt, incised
 mark "Moser - Karlsbad," the base -
 nscribed "Made in - Czecho-Slovakia -
 Moser - Karlsbad," ca. 1925 . . . . **1,725**

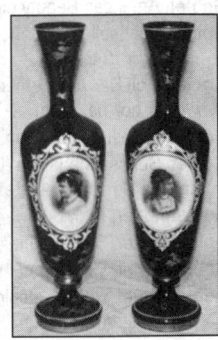

*From left: Moser Portrait Vase
Moser Portrait Vases*

Vase, 14" h., urn-form, wide ovoid body w/a
 short wide cylindrical neck & flanged rim,
 raised on a small short pedestal & thick
 disk foot, emerald green ground
 decorated w/a large round reserve w/a
 bust portrait of a woman wearing a lacy
 shawl, outllined in scrolling gold &
 w/overall lacy gilt vines (ILLUS.) **2,800**

Vases, tall slender baluster-form w/a
 cushion foot & short ringed stem
 supporting the long ovoid body w/a tall
 trumpet neck, emerald green, each
 decorated w/a large oval medallion
 enclosing a bust portrait in color of a
 Victorian woman, scrolling white
 medallion border & leafy gold vine
 background decoration, late 19th c.,
 unsigned, pr. (ILLUS.) **500**

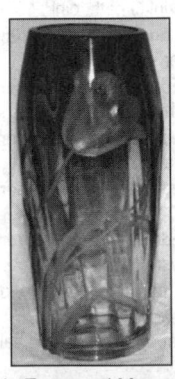

Finely Engraved Moser Vase

Vases, tall swelled cylindrical & optic-ribbed body in dark purple shading to clear, deeply engraved w/large tulip blossoms on leafy stems, signed, early 20th c., pr. (ILLUS. of one) **1,800**

MULLER FRERES

Muller Freres Mark

The Muller Brothers made acid-etched cameo and other fine glass at Luneville, France, starting in 1910 and until the outbreak of World War II in Europe.

Muller Fres. Blue Cameo Vase

Cameo lamp, table model, 19" d. wide domed umbrella-form shade on a bulbous nearly spherical matching base, both in grey overlaid in amber & forest green & cut w/a landscape of birch trees, simple four-arm iron mount, signed in cameo "MULLER FRES - LUNEVILLE," overall 19" h. **$25,300**

Cameo lamp, table model, a large 8" d. pointed mushroom shade on a three-arm wrought-iron mount above the slightly tapering cylindrical base w/a thick cushion foot, shade & base in creamy opalescent internally mottled w/ochre-yellow & blue, overlaid in deep crimson & midnight red & cut w/poppy blossoms & leafage, both signed "MULLER FRES - LUNEVILLE," ca. 1925, overall 14½" h. **10,925**

Cameo vase, 9½" h., simple ovoid body tapering to a flared mouth, shaded peach, azure & grey ground overlaid in dark purple & cut w/a mountainous landscape w/a lake & large fir trees in the foreground, signed in cameo "Muller Fres. Luneville" **3,910**

Cameo vase, 11" h., bulbous ovoid body w/a short cylindrical neck, grey internally decorated w/silver foil inclusions, overlaid

in turquoise & deep cobalt blue & cut w/stylized large blossoms & leaves, signed in cameo, ca. 1925 (ILLUS.) **3,450**

Cameo vase, 13½" h., wide cylindrical form rounded at the base & shoulder & tapering to a low flat rim, grey shaded lemon yellow & overlaid in orange & brown & cut w/a continuous river landscape of leafy trees, signed in cameo "MULLER FRES. - LUNEVILLE," pontil label stamped "MADE IN FRANCE," & vendor's label stamped "FORTUNATOR A. FASCE - Florida 425 - BUENOS AIRES," ca. 1900. . . . . **3,450**

From left: Large Muller Fres. Floral Cameo Vase Rare Muller Frères Ewer

Cameo vase, 18½" h., ovoid body tapering to a flattened flaring rim, creamy opalescent ground mottled w/ochre-yellow & blue, overlaid in crimson red & deep umber & cut w/undulating poppy blossoms & leaves, signed in cameo, ca. 1925 (ILLUS.) **5,462**

Ewer, squatty wide base w/an angled shoulder sharply tapering to a tall neck w/upright pointed & scallop-edged rim, applied pale amber handle down the neck, the sides w/a continuous carved & enameled frieze in "fluogravure" of an evening scene w/a deep red owl perched on a branch before an impressionistic wooded landscape in shades of ochre, umber, chocolate brown, sapphire blue & opalescent olive green, signed in cameo "Muller Croismare," ca. 1900, 10⅝" h. (ILLUS.) **11,500**

Lamp, table model, bullet-form shade of grey glass molded w/a textured surface, molded "Muller Fres - Luneville," on a wrought-iron base composed of seven scrolls on a square foot & surmounted by four arms to support the shade, ca. 1925, overall 16" h. **1,725**

Vase, 11¼" h., tapering ovoid body w/frosted surface in mottled cobalt blue, orange & yellow, acid-stamped on lower side "Muller Fres - Luneville" (annealing fracture at rim) **633**

NAILSEA

Nailsea was another glassmaking center in England where a variety of wares similar to those from Bristol, England were produced between 1788 and 1873. Today most collectors think of Nailsea primarily as a glass featuring swirls and loopings, usually white, on a clear or colored ground. This style of glass decoration, however, was not restricted to Nailsea and was produced in many other glasshouses, including some in America.

Two Nailsea Rolling Pins

Rolling pin, cylindrical w/end knob handles, ruby ground w/fine bands of white loopings, 19th c., 12" l. (ILLUS. top) **$385**

Rolling pin, cylindrical w/knob end handles, clear w/elongated cranberry & white looping, 16¼" l. (ILLUS. bottom) **330**

Sugar bowl w/witch ball cover, bowl w/applied clear foot supporting the nearly spherical body w/wide galleried rim, clear w/heavy white looping, fitted w/a large clear white ball w/white loopings, overall 8½" h. **660**

Vase, 11½" h., bulbous lower body w/a tall cylindrical neck w/a widely rolled rim, clear w/heavy white looping down the sides, on an applied clear short pedestal foot w/pontil, probably Pittsburgh (some interior residue & cloudiness) **605**

Vase & witch ball, 11¼" h., free-blown vase of trumpet form w/cushion foot, clear w/white loopings, supporting a round clear ball w/white loopings, 2 pcs. **660**

Nailsea Vase & Witch Ball

Vase & witch ball, white loopings in clear vase w/a tall cylindrical bowl w/a wide rolled rim & a swelled, ringed base raised on an applied clear stem & disk foot, topped by a large 5" d. witch ball in clear w/white loopings, overall 14" h., 2 pcs. (ILLUS.) **2,640**

NEW MARTINSVILLE

The New Martinsville Glass Mfg. Co. opened in New Martinsville, West Virginia in 1901 and during its first period of production came out with a number of colored opaque pressed glass patterns. They also developed an art glass line they named "Muranese," which collectors refer to as "New Martinsville Peach Blow." The factory burned in 1907 but reopened later that year and began focusing on production of various clear pressed glass patterns, many of which were then decorated with gold or ruby staining or enameled decoration. After going through receivership in 1937, the factory again changed the focus of its production to more contemporary glass lines and figural animals. The firm was purchased in 1944 by The Viking Glass Company (later Dalzell-Viking).

Book ends, Ship patt., No. 499, clear, 5¾" h., pr. **$60**

Bowl, cream soup, Moondrops patt., amber. **70**

Bowl, 8" d., three-footed, Moondrops patt., amber. **22**

Cup & saucer, Moondrops patt., amber. **10**

Cup & saucer, Moondrops patt., red **20**

Plate, 6⅛" d., Moondrops patt., amber. **4**

Plate, 8½" d., Moondrops patt., amber. **8**

Sherbet, Moondrops patt., red, 4½" h. **27**

Soup bowl, Moondrops patt., red. **115**

Sugar bowl, individual, Moondrops patt., red **13**

Sugar bowl, Moondrops patt., amber. **10**

Swan dish, Sweetheart shape, emerald green, 5" l. **20**

Swan dish, Janice patt., crystal body, cobalt blue head, 12" l. **76**

Sweetmeat w/holder, Muranese (Sun Glow Peach Blow) **250**

Tumbler, Muranese (Peach Blow) **250**

Tumbler, whiskey, Moondrops patt., red, 1¾" h. **14**

Tumbler, Moondrops patt., red, 3¼" h., 3 oz. **14**

Tumbler, Moondrops patt., pink, 4⅞" h., 9 oz. **13**

Tumbler, Moondrops patt., handled, green, 9 oz. **27**

Wine, Moondrops patt., red, 4" h. **20**

NORTHWOOD

Northwood (N)®

Northwood Script & Circle Marks

Harry Northwood (1860-1919) was born in England, the son of noted glass artist John Northwood. Brought up in the glass business, Harry immigrated to the United States in 1881 and shortly thereafter became manager of the La Belle Glass Company, Bridgeport, Ohio. Here he was responsible for many innovations in colored and blown glass. After leaving La Belle in 1887 he opened The Northwood Glass Company in Martins Ferry, Ohio in 1888. The company moved to Ellwood City, Pennsylvania in 1892 and Northwood moved again to take over a glass plant in Indiana, Pennsylvania in 1896. One of his major lines made at the Indiana, Pennsylvania plant was Custard glass (which he called "ivory"). It was made in several patterns and some pieces were marked on the base with "Northwood" in script. Harry and his family moved back to England in 1899 but returned to the U.S. in 1902 at which time he opened another glass factory in Wheeling, West Virginia. Here he was able to put his full talents to work and under his guidance the firm manufactured many notable glass lines including opalescent wares, colored and clear pressed tablewares, various novelties and probably best known of all, Carnival glass. Around 1906 Harry introduced his famous "N" in circle trade-mark which can be found on the base of many, but not all, pieces made at his factory. The factory closed in 1925. In this listing we are including only the clear and colored tablewares produced at Northwood factories. Specialized lines such as Custard glass, Carnival and Opalescent wares are listed under their own headings in our Glass category.

Berry set: master bowl & 6 sauce dishes; Leaf Umbrella patt., cranberry, 7 pcs. $600
Butter dish, cov., Apple Blossom patt., decorated milk glass.................... 60
Cologne bottle w/original stopper, Leaf Mold patt., vaseline w/cranberry spatter...... 450
Creamer, Netted Oak patt., decorated milk glass 60
Creamer & cov. sugar bowl, Netted Oak patt., decorated milk glass, pr............. 195
Pitcher, water, Netted Oak patt., decorated milk glass .... 175 to 200
Salt & pepper shakers w/original lids, Paneled Sprig patt., white opalescent w/lattice design, 3¼" h., pr. 85

Salt & pepper shakers w/original tops, Apple Blossom patt., decorated milk glass, pr................................ 60
Salt shaker w/original lid, Leaf Mold patt., pink & white cased spatter 143
Sauce dish, Leaf Medallion patt., purple w/gold trim 40
Spooner, Netted Oak patt., decorated milk glass................................. 45
Sugar shaker w/original lid, Leaf Mold patt., pink & white cased spangle.......... 358
Sugar shaker w/original lid, Parian Swirl, grey satin 325
Sugar shaker w/original top, Flower Mold patt., blue 395
Sugar shaker w/original top, Netted Oak patt., decorated milk glass 130
Sugar shaker w/original top, Paneled Sprig patt., decorated milk glass....... 50 to 100
Sugar shaker w/original top, Parian Swirl patt., decorated milk glass 130
Sugar shaker w/original top, Quilted Phlox patt., milk glass decorated w/blue flowers 195
Sugar shaker w/original top, Quilted Phlox patt., undecorated milk glass 140
Syrup pitcher w/original hinged lid, Apple Blossom patt., undecorated milk glass........ 80
Syrup pitcher w/original hinged lid, Netted Oak patt., milk glass w/green & gold decoration....................... 90
Syrup pitcher w/original lid, Leaf Mold patt., opal-cased red spatter w/silver mica flakes 695
Tumbler, Apple Blossom patt., decorated milk glass 45
Tumbler, Crystal Queen patt.................. 45
Tumbler, Netted Oak patt., decorated milk glass................................. 40
Tumbler, Paneled Holly patt., blue opalescent 100
Water set: pitcher & four tumblers; Apple Blossom patt., decorated milk glass, the set........................ 350 to 400

OPALESCENT

Presently, this is one of the most popular areas of glass collecting. The opalescent effect was attained by adding bone ash chemicals to areas of an item while still hot and refiring the object at tremendous heat. Both pressed and mold-blown patterns are available to collectors and we distinguish the types in our listing below. Opalescent Glass from A to Z by the late William Heacock is the definitive reference book for collectors. For an expanded listing of Opalescent Glass see Antique Trader Books American & European Decorative & Art Glass Price Guide.

MOLD-BLOWN OPALESCENT PATTERNS

BIG WINDOWS

Lamp, kerosene finger-type, Swirl mold,
   cranberry **$995**
Lamp, Stand, No. 1, Eason (rare)............. **635**

CHRYSANTHEMUM SWIRL

Chrysanthemum Swirl Sugar Shaker

Creamer, cranberry **385**
Sugar shaker w/original lid, blue (ILLUS.)..... **340**
Sugar shaker w/original lid, cranberry **495**
Table set: butter dish, creamer & spooner;
   cranberry, 3 pcs...................... **2,195**

COIN SPOT

 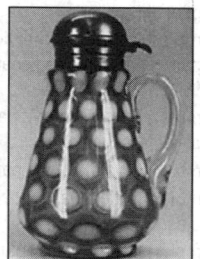

*From left: Coin Spot Sugar Shaker
Coin Spot Syrup Pitcher*

Lemonade set, ruffled pitcher & 4 tumblers,
   white, 5 pcs........................ **295**
Pitcher, clover leaf-crimp rim, cranberry **325**
Pitcher, tankard, three-tiered, cranberry **1,375**
Pitcher, triangular crimped rim, Windows
   mold, cranberry **395**
Sugar shaker w/original lid, nine-panel,
   Jefferson variant, cranberry **295**
Sugar shaker w/original lid, ring-neck
   mold, blue (ILLUS.) **148**
Syrup pitcher w/original metal lid, blue
   (ILLUS.)........................ **175 to 200**

CRISS CROSS

Creamer, white **318**
Spooner, white satin...................... **185**

DAISY & FERN

Daisy & Fern Cruet

Cruet w/original stopper, Apple Blossom
   mold, blue **295**
Cruet w/original stopper, Parian Swirl
   mold, cranberry (ILLUS.) **723**
Spooner, Parian Swirl mold, cranberry **175**
Sugar shaker w/original lid, blue **295**
Sugar shaker w/original lid, Parian Swirl
   mold, cranberry **355**
Tumbler, cranberry........................ **85**

FERN

Cruet w/original stopper, blue **343**
Salt shaker w/original top, cranberry **195**

HOBNAIL, HOBB'S

Hobb's Hobnail Celery Vase

Celery vase, 9" h., bulbous cylindrical body
   w/a crimped & ruffled rim, cranberry
   (ILLUS.) **248**

REVERSE SWIRL

Reverse Swirl Sugar Shaker

Cruet w/original stopper, cranberry 375
Sugar shaker w/original lid, cranberry
   (ILLUS.) 490
Syrup pitcher w/original lid, blue 345
Tumbler, cranberry 105
Water bottle, cranberry satin 545

RIBBED OPAL LATTICE

Ribbed Opal Lattice Toothpick Holder

Cruet w/original stopper, cranberry 595
Spooner, cranberry 185
Toothpick holder, blue (ILLUS.) 140
Tumbler, cranberry 135

SPANISH LACE

Spanish Lace Bowl

Bowl, w/upturned rim, canary, 7" d.
   (ILLUS.) . . . . 100 to 125
Butter dish, cov., canary 445
Pitcher, water, 9½" h., ruffled rim, blue . . . 300 to 325
Tumbler, canary 50

STARS & STRIPES

Stars & Stripes Tumbler

Cruet w/original stopper, cranberry 575
Tumbler, cranberry (ILLUS.) . . . . 450 to 475

STRIPE

Stripe Pitcher

Celery vase, blue 145
Pitcher, ring-neck mold, cranberry (ILLUS.) . . . 1,500
Tumbler, cranberry 60

SWIRL

Swirl Sugar Shaker

Celery vase, blue 135
Sugar shaker, blue (ILLUS.) . . . . 300 to 400
Sugar shaker w/original lid, cranberry 488

SWIRLING MAIZE

Tumbler, cranberry 105

TWIST, BLOWN

Sugar shaker w/original lid, blue 295

WIDE STRIPE

Cruet w/original stopper, blue 395

WINDOWS, SWIRL

Sugar shaker w/original lid, cranberry 635

PRESSED OPALESCENT PATTERNS

ARGONAUT SHELL

Butter dish, cov., white 243
Creamer & cov. sugar bowl, undecorated,
   white, no gold, pr. 225
Jelly compote, canary, enamel decorated 145
Sauce dish, canary 90

Argonaut Shell Spooner

Spooner, blue (ILLUS.)............... 150 to 175
Spooner, white........................... 169
Toothpick holder, canary 465

BEATTY HONEYCOMB
Sugar shaker w/original lid, blue 260
Tumbler, blue........................... 275

BEATTY RIB

Beatty Rib Celery Vase

Celery vase, blue (ILLUS.) .... 250 to 275
Salt dip, white........................... 42
Spooner, white........................... 43
Toothpick holder, blue................ 75 to 100
Toothpick holder, white.................... 30

CIRCLED SCROLL
Cruet w/original stopper, blue 575
Sauce dish, blue 50

DIAMOND SPEARHEAD

Diamond Spearhead Butter Dish

Butter dish, cov., blue 235
Butter dish, cov., green (ILLUS.) .... 225 to 250
Celery dish, green 275
Creamer, miniature, cobalt blue 68
Jelly compote, canary 150
Pitcher, 5⅜" h........................... 145
Pitcher, 6" h............................ 159
Sugar bowl, cov., canary 235
Syrup pitcher w/original top, canary 775
Toothpick holder, canary 95
Toothpick holder, green 63

EVERGLADES

Everglades Spooner & Butter Dish

Butter dish, cov., canary 345
Salt shaker w/original top, canary 195
Table set, blue, 4 pcs. (ILLUS. of part)... 550 to 600
Tumbler 25

FLORA
Spooner, blue............................ 100
Syrup pitcher w/original lid, white w/gold trim .. 285

FLUTED SCROLLS

Fluted Scrolls Creamer

Creamer, blue w/enameled florals (ILLUS.) 75
Creamer, canary......................... 145
Pitcher, water, blue 350
Rose bowl, canary 105
Sugar bowl, cov., blue 130
Water set: pitcher & 5 tumblers, blue, the set ... 645

INVERTED FAN & FEATHER
Card tray, canary 255
Creamer, blue...................... 125 to 150
Spooner, blue...................... 150 to 175

IRIS WITH MEANDER

Iris with Meander Creamer

Bowl, 9" d., footed, green 40
Creamer, blue (ILLUS.) 125
Sauce dish, canary 25
Sauce dishes, blue, set of 5 380
Toothpick holder, blue 115

JEWEL & FLOWER

Jewel & Flower Creamer & Sugar Bowl

Cruet w/original stopper, canary 750
Table set, canary w/gold trim, 4 pcs.
   (ILLUS. of part) . . . . 775 to 800
Tumbler, blue 82

REGAL, NORTHWOOD'S

Butter dish, cov., green 250
Sugar bowl, cov., green 85

RIBBED SPIRAL

Compote, blue 67
Spooner, blue 105

SWAG WITH BRACKETS

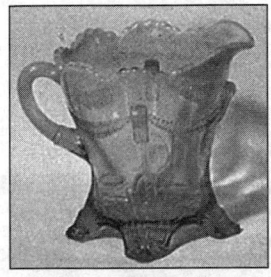

Swag with Brackets Creamer

Creamer, blue (ILLUS.) . . . . 105 to 115
Cruet, green 350
Sauce dishes, green, set of 6 275
Sugar bowl, cov., canary . . . . 115 to 125
Toothpick holder, white 50
Tumbler, canary 55

TOKYO

Tokyo Compote

Bowl, master berry, green 75
Compote, jelly, blue (ILLUS.) 60
Creamer 79
Creamer, blue . . . . 70 to 80
Plate, footed 69

WATER LILY & CATTAILS

Water Lily & Cattails Pitcher

Bowl, master berry, blue 65
Bowl, six-sided, purple 65
Butter dish, cov., white 230
Pitcher, water, purple (ILLUS.) . . . . 225 to 250
Plate, purple 85
Vase, purple 79

WILD BOUQUET

Wild Bouquet Jelly Compote

Berry set, enameled, 5 pcs. 375
Compote, jelly, blue (ILLUS.) 160
Creamer, green 140
Pitcher, water, blue 300

WREATH & SHELL

Wreath & Shell Sugar Bowl

Bowl, master berry, 8½" d., canary 110
Bowl, master berry, 8½" d., clear 45
Creamer, decorated, canary 135
Spooner, white 72
Sugar bowl, cov., blue (ILLUS.) 200
Table set, blue, 4 pcs. 695
Table set, canary, 4 pcs. 650
Tumbler, footed, canary 375

MISCELLANEOUS PRESSED NOVELTIES

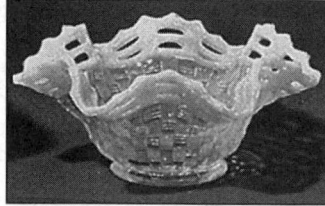

Basketweave Base Bowl

Basketweave Base bowl, open-edge,
   canary (ILLUS.) . . . . 25 to 30

Beaded Drapes rose bowl, blue 57
Bushel Basket, blue. 140
Corn vase, blue 180
Dahlia vase, blue 60
Northwood's Block celery vase, blue 55
Peacocks on a Fence bowl, blue 300
Piasa Bird bowl, whimsey-type, blue. 85
Piasa Bird rose bowl, blue 98
Ruffles & Rings bowl, 9½" d., green. 38

ORREFORS

Orrefors

Orrefors Mark

This Swedish glasshouse, founded in 1898 for production of tablewares, has made decorative wares as well since 1915. By 1925, Orrefors had achieved an international reputation for its Graal glass, an engraved art glass developed by master glassblower Knut Berquist and artist-designers Simon Gate and Edward Hald. Ariel glass, recognized by a design of controlled air traps and the heavy Ravenna glass, usually tinted, were both developed in the 1930s. While all Orrrefors glass is collectible, pieces signed by early designers and artists are now bringing high prices.

Cut Crystal Leopard Centerbowl

Bottle w/stopper, funnel-footed ovoid body
   tapering to a very tall slender 'stick' neck
   fitted w/a leaf-form stopper, pale smoky
   amber, designed by Simon Gate,
   ca. 1925, unsigned, 15⅜" h. **$230**
Bowl, 5" l., "Ravenna," small boat-form in
   clear cased over dark blue tesserae
   w/green interstices, inscribed
   "ORREFORS -Ravenna 5115 -
   Sven Palmqvist," designed ca. 1948,
   executed 1971 862
Bowl, 11¾" l., "Kanterra," oblong form
   w/upright pulled & ruffled sides, deep
   burgundy cased over pale amber,
   designed by Sven Palmqvist, designed
   ca. 1945, inscribed "ORREFORS - pu
   3023 - 1". 460

Centerbowl, cut crystal, caged animals achieved by cut & faceted 'bars' w/frosted spotted leopards behind peering through, raised upon applied dark blue disk base inscribed "Orrefors 4688-13 Gunnar Cyren," designed by Gunnar Cyren, 8" d. (ILLUS.) **1,380**

Charger, "Aqua Graal," broad round colorless crystal form w/folded rim, internally decorated w/concentric rings of aubergine windows & golden yellow swirls all around a central dark core, designed by Edward Hald, base signed "Aqua Graal No. 481P - Edward Hald - Orrefors '58," ca. 1958, 14¼" d. **805**

Decanter, squared crystal bottle engraved w/Romeo serenading on observe, Juliet on balcony on reverse, optically as one, case engraved "Orrefors No. 880," 12½" h. **345**

Decanter w/stopper, domed rectangular crystal form engraved on one side w/a sailor playing accordion & on the other w/a vignette of sailors on shore leave, designed by Nils Landberg, signed on the base "Orrefors Landberg 1938 C IAD " 6" w., 10¼" h. (slight stopper nick) **1,150**

Vase, 5" h., 8½" l.,"Ravenna," small clear round pedestal foot supporting a large oblong boat-shaped bowl in clear w/an internal layer of red over a layer of blue containing windows w/a heavy blue rim band, engraved "Orrefors Ravenna nr1033 Sven Palmqvist" **2,200**

Vase, 5½" h., "Ariel," bubbled heavy flattened oval colorless vessel internally decorated w/aubergine-amber spots in symmetrically arranged progression, base inscribed "Orrefors Ariel No. 341L/Ingeborg Lundin" **1,840**

Vase, 5½" h., "Edvin," heavy cylindrical form in turquoise blue overlaid in purple, cut w/a stylized gypsy palmist amid an open palm w/life lines, w/linear devices & stars in the background, designed by Edvin Ohrstrom, signed "Orrefors Sweden 944 - Edvin - nr:89 - Edvin Ohrstrom," dated 1944 . . . . **20,700**

Vase, 5¾" h., fish "Graal," oval colorless body w/brown & green fish & water weeds in reflective illusion, base inscribed "Orrefors Sweden Graal No. 2770D Edward Hald," designed by Edward Hald. **805**

Vase, 6" h., "Ariel," thick ovoid form enclosing a pair of stylized reclining odalisques within an interior, deep cobalt blue & aubergine, inscribed "ORREFORS - Sweden - ARIEL - 573 E - E. OHRSTROM," designed by Edvin Ohrstrom, ca. 1950 . . . . **17,250**

From left: "Ariel" Scenic Portrait Vase
Tall Engraved Orrefors Vase

Vase, 6⅛" h., "Ariel," scenic, cylindrical heavy walled colorless body w/internal cobalt blue & amber air trap decoration of boat & gondolier w/guitar/mandolin serenading woman under moonlit sky, base inscribed "Orrefors/Ariel No. 637.E.4/Edvin Ohrstrom," 1974 (ILLUS.) . . . **5,175**

Vase, 6⅛," h., exposition-type, flaring slightly squared cylindrical form in clear decorated w/engraved vertical stripes, inscribed "Of. Expo 1035. C 1," w/engraver's monogram, designed by Ingeborg Lundin, ca. 1960 . . . . **460**

Vase, 7" h., clear flared cylindrical form, copper-wheel engraved decoration of a dancing female nude & a snake, designed by Simon Gate, incised "Orrefors Gate 128J. 03. XR" (scratches) **374**

Vase, 7⅜" h., "Ariel," bottle-type, raised rim on oval colorless body internally decorated by alternating vertical aubergine & clear bubble stripes, inscribed on base "Orrefors Ariel Sweden 1851E/Edvin Ohrstrom" **316**

Vase, 8½" h., "Kraka," flattened teardrop form in deep cobalt blue shading to amber encompassing a fine network of tiny bubbles, further encased in a thick layer of clear glass, designed by Sven Palmqvist, designed ca. 1954, inscribed "ORREFORS - KRAKA - nr. 349 - Sven Palmqvist," retains retailer's label "A. B. SCHOU - NY OSTERGADE 1" **1,150**

Vase, 9" h., slender ovoid form w/a short ringed neck & flared rim flanked by pairs of small S-scroll applied handles, the clear body engraved w/a Bacchanalian tableaux of nude female dancers & musicians within fringed borders, signed by Simon Gate, Model G 234, dated 1925, engraved "Orrefors - Gate - 234.25. A.D." **2,070**

Vase, 11⅞" h., tall clear cylindrical form slightly incurved at the base, thick walls etched on the exterior w/a nude young woman standing in a garden & holding aloft a bunch of flowers, butterflies flitting around her, signed "Orrefors . Landberg. Expo. 3521...C3," early 20th c. (ILLUS.) **1,150**

Vase, 14¼" h., "Slipgraal," thick tall teardrop-form, clear enclosing deep burgundy spiraling threads, signed "ORREFORS - Sweden - S. Graal nr. 1218 L - Edward Hald," designed by Edward Hald, ca. 1953 . . . . **920**

Large Orrefors "Apple" Vase

Vase, 15⅛" h., "The Apple," very large spherical form w/stem neck, overall rich green, designed by Ingeborg Lundin, inscribed "ORRESFORS - Expo. Nr. 32-57 - Ingeborg Lundin," ca. 1957 (ILLUS.) . . . **6,037**

Vases, 10" h., each colorless oval engraved w/two exotic angelfish, bubbles overall, base engraved "Orrefors LA 1916," the pair **345**

PADEN CITY

The Paden City Glass Manufacturing Company began operations in Paden City, West Virginia in 1916, primarily as a supplier of blanks to other companies. All wares were hand-made, that is, either hand-pressed or mold-blown. The early products were not particularly noteworthy but by the early 1930s the quality had improved considerably. The firm continued to turn out high quality glassware in a variety of beautiful colors until financial difficulties nessitated its closing in 1951. Over the years the firm produced, in addition to tablewares, items for hotel and restaurant use, light shades, shaving mugs, perfume bottles and lamps.

Bowl, 11" d., footed, Mrs. "B" line, yellow **$57**

Bowl, 13¼" d., rolled edge, Black Forest etching, green **300**

Bowl, 11¾" d., rolled edge, Black Forest etching, pink **250**

Cake plate, Ardith patt., No. 300, footed, topaz, 11" d. **145**

Cup, Black Forest etching, red **120**

Gravy boat, Ardith patt., green **80**

Water set: pitcher & six tumblers; Ardith patt., green, 7 pcs. **550**

PAIRPOINT

Originally organized in New Bedford, Massachusetts in 1880, as the Pairpoint Manufacturing Company, on land adjacent to the famed Mount Washington Glass Company, this company first manufactured silver and plated wares. In 1894, the two famous factories merged as the Pairpoint Corporation and enjoyed great success for more than forty years. The company was sold in 1939 to a group of local businessmen and eventually bought out by one of the group who turned the management over to Robert M. Gundersen. Subsequently, it operated as the Gundersen Glass Works until 1952 when, after Gundersen's death, the name was changed to Gundersen-Pairpoint. The factory closed in 1956. Subsequently, Robert Bryden took charge of this glassworks, at first producing glass for Pairpoint abroad and eventually, in 1970, beginning glass production in Sagamore, Massachusetts. Today the Pairpoint Crystal Glass Company is owned by Robert and June Bancroft. They continue to manufacture fine quality blown and pressed glass.

Pairoint Ruby Ewer

Candlestick lamps, gold finish base w/pale green cut crystal standard, eight 6" clear crystal hanging prisms, 10" h., pr. **$1,400**

Compote, 12" d., 6½" h., open, widely flaring bell-form bowl in black amethyst raised on a clear bubble ball stem on a round black amethyst foot, unsigned **115**

Console set: candlesticks & vase; the disk-footed ovoid bulbous vase tapering to a short waisted neck w/a widely flaring flattened rim, the slender baluster-form disk-footed candlesticks w/a cylindrical socket w/flattened rim, all in cobalt blue cut & etched overall w/a grapevine design, ca. 1930, candlesticks 10¾" h., the set **1,495**

Console set: console bowl & pr. of candleholders; Vintage cut, green, 3 pcs. **750**

Ewers, classic baluster-form w/clear applied ring foot supporting an ovoid ruby body tapering to a tall tricorner flaring neck, high arched applied clear handle, unsigned, 13½" h., pr. (ILLUS. of one) **374**

PATE DE VERRE

Pate De Verre Marks

Pate de Verre, or "paste of glass," was molded by very few artisans. In the pate de verre technique, powdered glass is mixed with a liquid to make a paste which is then placed in a mold and baked at a high temperature. These articles have a finely-pitted or matte finish and are easily distinguished from blown glass. Duplicate pieces are possible with this technique.

Book ends, figural, each upright back molded in full-relief w/two nude female musicians standing on either side of a fruit-filled bower, in shades of green, blue, beige, ochre & mauve, modeled by Henri Mercier, molded "AWALTER NANCY," & "h. mercier," ca. 1920s, 6" h., pr. **$5,175**

Bowl, 5⅜" d., lobed vessel w/short foot & lappet decoration around rim, in emerald green w/dark purple interior mottling, impressed "DECORCHEMENT," ca. 1910 (imperfections) **1,380**

Bowl, 9¾" w., hexagonal, flat bottom & low angled sides, molded around the rim in low-relief w/festoons, the center molded w/a crab & sea weeds, shades of brown, yellow, ochre & bluish green, molded "A. WALTER - NANCY" & "Bergé - scp.," ca. 1920s **4,025**

Pate de Verre Bowl-Vase

Bowl-vase, deep rounded & gently flaring body in grey mottled & streaked w/green & turquoise, molded around the sides in low-relief w/a stylized wave design, the side handles molded as two leaping fish in full relief, molded "Décorchemont" w/a horseshoe, inscribed "D 69 H," 1903-09, 5¼" h. (ILLUS.) **11,500**

Dish, shallow rounded form in yellow, green & brown, molded in medium-relief w/a butterfly & in low-relief w/pine needles, signed in intaglio "AWALTER - NANCY," ca. 1920, 6⅞" d. **2,070**

Inkstand, figural, double, a long rectangular platform w/wide rounded projecting central section, each end w/a raised buttressed square turret w/cross-molded lids on the inkwells, the center section molded w/a large model of a stag beetle, in shades of lemon yellow, ochre, brown & black, molded "A. Walter - Nancy" & "Bergé - SC," modeled by Henri Bergé, ca. 1920, 6" l. **5,175**

Lamp, the ovoid base in grey mottled w/purple & deep crimson, molded in in low-relief w/large crimson flowers w/cascading stamens resembling tassels, high domed & pointed molded shade on an iron ring & three-arm support & the base on an iron round disk w/small ball feet, shade & base signed "G. Argy-Rousseau," ca, 1925, shade 7⅛"d., 15½" h. **40,250**

Lamp bases, bulbous ovoid form, each molded in low- and medium-relief w/a frieze of ancient dancers in orange & black on a mottled greenish ground between upper & lower black foliate bands, gilt-metal stepped base & electric fittings, each molded "G. ARGY-ROUSSEAU," ca. 1923, overall 30" h., pr. (cracks to one base) **14,950**

Paperweight, figural, molded in high-relief w/a beetle in cinnamon & black on a domed oval base in lime green speckled w/yellow, signed "A WALTER - NANCY" & "BERGÉ - SC.," modeled by Henri Bergé, ca. 1925, 3¼" l. **1,610**

Pendant, butterfly design, pierced square w/blue, green, reddish orange wings against colorless & clear ground, inscribed "GAR" in design, G. Argy-Rousseau, 2⅛ x 2¼" **2,415**

Pendant, round disk in yellow, orange, brown & black, molded in relief w/a scarab, signed in intaglio "AWALTER," ca. 1920, 1¾" d. **2,012**

Vase, 4" h., 4½" d., molded inverted bell-form of muted amber-tan decorated w/a band of raised stylized flowers in maroon & supported by a dark green disk foot, impressed "A.Walter Nancy" **1,495**

Vase, 4½" h., footed swelled cylindrical form w/a wide molded rim, upper section molded in low-relief w/a frieze of ovals above a ribbed lower portion, in olive green swirled w/brown, molded "DECORCHEMONT," France, ca. 1925 .... **2,875**

Pate de Verre Vase with Figures

Vase, 9⅜" h., wide ovoid body w/a short flared rim, molded in medium-relief w/a frieze of classical ladies picking apples above a lower border of square scrolls, in shades of grey, brown, russet, black & yellow, incised "G. Argy-Rousseau" & impressed "France," base drilled & cracked, 1926 (ILLUS.) **6,325**

Vase, 10⅛" h., "Papyrus," simple ovoid form w/a flared rim, grey molded in low-relief w/papyrus fronds in turquoise & blue w/charcoal stems, between scalloped upper & lower borders in deep aubergine, molded "G. ARGY-ROUSEAU" & "GA085," ca. 1924 .... **11,500**

Veilleuse (night lamp), a domed grey glass shade molded in low-relief w/three butterflies w/out-stretched wings, in rich shades of orange, crimson, white, purple & black, on a round iron disc base w/three small ball feet, shade molded "G. ARGY-ROUSSEAU - FRANCE," ca. 1924, 5½" h. **10,350**

Veilleuse (night light), "La Coupe Fleurie," a high bulbous domed shade molded in low-relief w/a pattern of large flowerheads in shades of royal blue, teal green, plum & black, on a simple round iron dished base on small knob feet, molded "G.ARGY - ROUSSEAU - FRANCE," ca. 1923, 5" h. **14,950**

Vide poche (figural dish), oblong shallow dished form modeled in full-relief on one edge w/a lizard, in shades of lemon yellow, green, orange & black, modeled by Henri Bergé, molded "A. WALTER - NANCY" & "Bergé - SC," ca. 1920, 6¾" l. **6,900**

PATTERN

Though it has never been ascertained whether glass was first pressed in the United States or abroad, the development of the glass pressing machine revolutionized the glass industry in the United States, and this country receives the credit for improving the method to make this process feasible. The first wares pressed were probably small flat plates of the type now referred to as "lacy," the intricacy of the design concealing flaws.

In 1827, both the New England Glass Co., Cambridge, Massachusetts, and Bakewell & Co., Pittsburgh, took out patents for pressing glass furniture knobs; soon other pieces followed. This early pressed glass contained red lead which made it clear and resonant when tapped (flint). Made primarily in clear, it is rarer in blue, amethyst, olive green and yellow.

By the 1840s, early simple patterns such as Ashburton, Argus and Excelsior appeared. Ribbed Bellflower seems to have been one of the earliest patterns to have had complete sets. By the 1860s, a wide range of patterns was available.

In 1864, William Leighton of Hobbs, Brockunier & Co., Wheeling, West Virginia, developed a formula for "soda lime" glass, which did not require the expensive red lead for clarity. Although "soda lime" glass did not have the brilliance of the earlier flint glass, the formula came into widespread use because the glass could be produced cheaply.

An asterisk (*) indicates a piece which has been reproduced. For an expanded listing of Pattern Glass, see Antique Trader Books' American Pressed Glass & Bottles Price Guide.

ACTRESS

Actress Cheese Dish

Bowl, 8" d., Adelaide Neilson **$65**
Bread tray, Miss Neilson, 12½" l. 45
Celery vase, Pinafore scene 160
Celery vase, frosted rim, stem & foot, 9" h. 220
Cheese dish, cov., "Lone Fisherman" on cover, "The Two Dromios" on underplate (ILLUS.). .... **225 to 250**
Cologne bottle w/original stopper, 11" h. 90
Compote, cov., 6" d., 10" h. 95

Compote, cov., 10" d., 14½" h., Fanny
Davenport & Maggie Mitchell 200
Compote, open, 6" d., 3" h. 55
Compote, open, 8" d., 5" h. . . . . 65 to 70
Creamer, clear 75
Creamer, frosted. 100
Creamer, Miss Neilson & Fanny Davenport 110
Dresser box, cov., 3½" d. 60
Dresser box, cov., footed, 2½ x 6" oval 75
Egg cup 70
Goblet, clear bowl, frosted stem 135
Goblet, frosted bowl 125
Mug, Pinafore scene. 50
Pitcher, water, 9" h., Miss Neilson & Maggie
Mitchell 350
Platter, 7 x 11½", Pinafore scene. 125
Relish, Maude Granger, 5 x 9" 63
Salt & pepper shakers w/original tops, pr. 100
Salt shaker w/original pewter top 60
Sauce dish, Maggie Mitchell & Fanny
Davenport, 4½" d., 2¼" h. 20
Sauce dish, clear, footed 16
Spooner 50
Sugar bowl, cov., Lotta Crabtree & Kate
Claxton 130
Table set, creamer, cov. sugar bowl, cov.
butter dish, spooner, 4 pcs. 275

ANIMALS & BIRDS ON GOBLETS & PITCHERS

GOBLETS

Alligator, acid-etched . . . . 100 to 120
Bear climber, acid-etched 95
Bird in Swamp . . . . 75 to 85
Bird & Roses, acid-etched . . . . 55 to 75
Birds at Fountain, pressed . . . . 50 to 55
Camels, acid-etched. 70
Deer & Castle, acid-etched. . . . . 25 to 35
Deer & Doe, acid-etched 25
Deer & Doe w/lily-of-the-valley, pressed 135
Dog w/rabbit in mouth, acid-etched . . . . . . 65 to 75
Dragon, pressed 1,900
Elephant, acid-etched 26
Elk & Doe, pressed . . . . 140 to 150
Falcon Strawberry, pressed 35
Flamingo Habitat, acid-etched 35
Flying Birds, pressed. 95
Flying Storks, pressed, pr. 120
Frog & Spider, pressed 350
Giraffe, acid-etched 54
Horse, acid-etched 76
Horse, Cat & Rabbit, pressed . . . . . . 1,050 to 1,075
Hummingbirds w/Frog, acid-etched 70
Ibex, acid-etched 81
Leopard, acid-etched . . . . 90 to 100

Lion in the Jungle, acid-etched . . . . 100 to 125
Monkey Climber, acid-etched 110
Monkey Swinging, acid-etched 70
Nestlings, acid-etched . . . . 45 to 50
Ostrich Looking at Moon, pressed . . . . 60 to 75
Owl in Horseshoe, pressed. 110
Owl & Possum, pressed. . . . . 100 to 125
Pigs in Corn, pressed 475
Pigs in Corn, tassel at right 600
Reversed Elephant, acid-etched 75
Rooster, acid-etched 225
Rooster & Hen, acid-etched . . . . 135 to 155
Scarab 93
Snake Stalking Monkey, acid-etched 50
Squirrel, pressed, non-Greentown. 725
Stag, acid-etched 70
Stork Eating, acid-etched 96
Stork & Flowers, acid-etched 65
Stork Walking, acid-etched 15
Three Deer 225
Tiger, acid-etched. 60
Two Giraffes, acid-etched . . . . 55 to 75
Two Herons, acid-etched . . . . 90 to 100
Whippet, acid-etched 15

PITCHERS

Squirrel Pitcher

Bird & Castle, acid-etched. 60
Bringing Home Cows, pressed. 600
Crane, tankard, acid-etched 45
Deer & Oak Tree, pressed . . . . 160 to 170
Deer Racing, pressed 110
Dog & Cat, pressed. . . . . 275 to 300
Dog w/Rabbit in Hole 155
Flamingo Habitat, acid-etched . . . . 120 to 125
Fox & Crow, pressed . . . . 375 to 400
Heron, pressed . . . . 175 to 200
Heron w/Fish, acid-etched. 75
Heron w/Snake, tankard, acid-etched 65
Heron wading, pressed 375
Kingfisher, tankard, acid-etched 60
Oasis Camel Caravan, acid-etched. 100
Pointer, pressed. 200

Racing Deer, pressed 150
Squirrel, pressed, non-Greentown
    (ILLUS.). . . . . 275 to 325
Stag in Brambles, 11" h., tankard,
    acid-etched . . . . 55 to 65
Two Swans in Rushes, acid-etched 55

BAMBOO—See Broken Column Pattern

BASKETWEAVE

Bread plate, amber 30
Bread plate, blue 40
Creamer, amber 35
Cup, blue 30
Cup & saucer, amber. 28
Cup & saucer, canary yellow 45
*Goblet, amber . . . . 20 to 25
*Goblet, blue. 35
*Goblet, canary yellow . . . . 30 to 35
*Goblet, clear 20
Pitcher, milk, blue. 80
*Pitcher, water, amber 50
*Pitcher, water, blue. 90
*Pitcher, water, canary yellow 85
Pitcher, water, clear 55
Plate, 8¾" d., handled, amber 24
Plate, 8¾" d., handled, blue 20
Plate, 8¾" d., handled, clear. 11
Sauce dish 10
*Tray, water, scenic center, amber, 12" 47
*Tray, water, scenic center, blue, 12" . . . . . 90 to 100
*Tray, water, scenic center, canary yellow, 12" . . . 70
*Tray, water, scenic center, clear, 12" 50
*Tray, water, scenic center & six goblets,
    amber, 7 pcs. 125
Tray, water, 12" d., w/scenic center, pitcher
    & 6 stemmed goblets, amber, 8 pcs. 125
Vase, 8½" h. 20
Wine . . . . 25 to 30

BEADED DEWDROP—See Wisconsin Pattern

BEADED LOOP (Oregon, U.S. Glass Co.)

Bowl, berry, 7" d. 17
Bowl, 8¼" d. 20
Bowl, berry, 9½" l., 6¾" w. oval, clear 25
Bowl, berry, 9½" l., 6¾" w. oval, ruby-stained 35
Bread platter 35
Bread tray 35
Butter dish, cov., clear. 70
Butter dish, cov., ruby-stained. 125
Cake stand, 8" d., 5" h. 50
Cake stand, 9" to 10½" d. 56

Carafe, individual size. 30
Celery vase, clear, 7" h. 30
Compote, cov., 6" d., 10" h. 95
Compote, cov., 7" d. 80
Compote, cov., 11". 125
Compote, open, jelly, clear. 31
Compote, open, 5¼" d., 4½" h., clear 20
Compote, open, 6½" d., clear. 20
Compote, open, 7" d., clear 27
Compote, open, 7½" d., low stand, clear 38
Creamer, clear 40
Creamer, ruby-stained 70
Cruet w/faceted stopper, clear 35
Cruet w/faceted stopper, ruby-stained 75
Goblet, clear w/gold trim. 50

Beaded Loop Goblet

*Goblet (ILLUS.). 49
Mug, footed, clear. 40
Mug, ruby-stained. 55
Pitcher, pint, 7" h. 44
Pitcher, milk, 8½" h. 55
Pitcher, water, tankard 60
Salt & pepper shakers w/original tops, pr. 43
Sauce dish, flat or footed, each 13
Spooner, clear 28
Spooner, ruby-stained 55
*Sugar bowl, cov., clear. 39
Sugar bowl, cov., ruby-stained 55
Toothpick holder 48
Tumbler, clear 49
Tumbler, ruby-stained 35
Vase, small 43
Wine . . . . 65 to 70

BEARDED HEAD—See Viking Pattern

BELLFLOWER

Bowl, 6" d., 1¾" h., single vine. 150
Bowl, 8" d., 2" h., round, single vine, scallop
    & point rim, plain polished base 180
Butter dish, cov. 150
Castor set, 4-bottle, w/pewter stand 400
Castor set, 5-bottle, single vine, w/pewter stand . . 675

Celery vase, w/cut bellflowers 325
Champagne, barrel-shaped, fine rib, single
    vine, knob stem, rayed base 85
Champagne, fine rib, double vine, w/cut
    bellflowers, 5" h. 450
Cologne bottle w/stopper, clambroth 500
Compote, open, 7" d., 5" h., fine rib, double
    vine . . . . 90 to 100
Compote, open, 8" d. 85
Compote, open, 8" d., high stand. 190
Compote, open, coarse rib, single vine, low
    foot w/scallop rim, 8" d., 5" h. 250
Cordial, barrel-shaped, knob stem, rayed base . . 165
Cordial, fine rib, single vine, knob stem 150
Cordial, fine rib, single vine, plain stem . . 120 to 125
Creamer, fine rib, single vine, applied handle . . . 275

Bellflower Decanter

Decanter, double vine, flint, qt., no stopper
    (ILLUS.) 110
Decanter w/bar lip, cut shoulder, single
    vine, w/stopper 550
Decanter w/bar lip, double vine, qt. 140
Decanter w/bar lip, single vine, qt. 188
Egg cup, coarse rib 28
Egg cup, double vine, w/cut bellflowers 75
Egg cup, fine rib, single vine 44
Goblet, barrel-shaped, fine rib, single vine,
    knob stem, rayed base 75
*Goblet, barrel-shaped, fine rib, single vine,
    plain stem 35
Goblet, coarse rib, flared top 90
Goblet, fine rib, double vine, w/cut bellflowers . . . 425
Goblet, fine rib, single vine, w/cut
    bellflowers, 5½" h. 2,050
Goblet, single vine w/cut bellflowers, 6¼" h. 400
Honey dish, scalloped rim, star base, 3" d. 100
Lamp, whale oil, pattern on inside of font,
    top of ribs scalloped, scalloped base, 9"
    h. (replaced collar, hard to see internal
    line under collar, probably factory flaw) 650
Lamp, whale oil, brass stem, marble base 300
Pitcher, double vine, straight sides, 1 pt.,
    6¼" h. 1,800

Pitcher, milk, double vine, 7" h. . . . . 550 to 575
Pitcher, milk, single vine, 7½" h. 1,800
Pitcher, water, 8¾" h., coarse rib, double vine. . . 450
Sauce dish, single vine 16
Spooner, low foot, double vine. 90
Spooner, scalloped rim, single vine 65
Sugar bowl, cov., double vine . . . . 150 to 200
Sugar bowl, cov., single vine . . . . 80 to 100
Sugar bowl, cov., octagonal, domed lid, 8" h. . . 1,325
Syrup pitcher w/original top, applied
    handle, fine rib, single vine, clear 625
Syrup pitcher w/original top, applied
    handle, milk white 1,100
Tumbler, bar, fine rib, single vine 105
Tumbler, whiskey, single vine, 2⅞" h. 230
Tumbler, double vine, w/cut bellflowers, 3½" h. . . 400
Tumbler, fine rib, double vine, 4⅞" h. 275
Wine, barrel-shaped, knob stem, fine rib,
    single vine 50
Wine, barrel-shaped, knob stem, fine rib,
    single vine, rayed base. 115
Wine, fine-rib, single vine, straight sides 40
Wine, double vine w/cut bellflowers, 4" h. 250

BROKEN COLUMN (Irish Column, Notched Rib or Bamboo)

Broken Column Goblet

Banana stand. 195
Bowl, 7" d. 40
Bowl, 9" d. 32
Bowl, cov., vegetable 95
Butter dish, cov. 115
Celery tray, 5 x 10", w/red notches 65
Celery vase, clear 55
Celery vase, ruby-stained 155
Compote, cov., 5" d., high stand, clear 70
Compote, cov., 5" d., high stand w/red notches. . 225
Compote, cov., 7" d., high stand. . . . . 175 to 200
Compote, cov., 8" d., high stand 175
Compote, cov., 8" d., high stand w/red notches. . 525
Compote, open, 6" d., high stand. 35
Compote, open, 7" d., low stand 50
Compote, open, 8" d., high stand, ruby-stained. . 250
Compote, open, 8" d., low stand 63

Compote, open, 9" d., 7½" h., clear 75
Compote, open, 9" d., 7½" h. w/red notches 175
*Creamer, clear . . . . 35 to 40
Creamer, w/red notches 250
Cruet w/original stopper, w/red notches 525
Decanter w/original stopper, 10½" h. 85
*Goblet, clear (ILLUS.) 60
Pickle castor, cov., clear, original ornate frame. . 238
Pickle castor, ruby-stained, w/frame & tongs . . . 413
*Pitcher, water, clear 100
Pitcher, water, w/red notches. 450
Relish, 3¾ x 5" 13
Relish, 6½" l. 18
Relish, clear, 9" l., 5" w. . . . . 25 to 30
Relish, w/red notches, 9" l., 5" w. 78
Salt & pepper shakers w/original tops, pr. 85
Salt shaker w/original top, w/red notches 75
Sauce dish, w/red notches. 32
*Spooner, clear 32
Spooner, w/red notches 125
*Sugar bowl, cov., clear. 72
Sugar bowl, cov., w/red notches 150
Sugar bowl open, clear 30
Sugar bowl, open, w/red notches 73
Sugar shaker w/metal top. 110
Sugar shaker w/metal top, w/red
    notches . . . . 450 to 500
Syrup pitcher w/metal top, clear . . . . 175 to 200
Syrup pitcher w/metal top, w/red notches 405
Tumbler, clear 48
Tumbler, w/red notches . . . . 75 to 100
*Wine 85

CARDINAL BIRD

Cardinal Bird Goblet

Butter dish, cov. 95
Butter dish, cov., three unidentified birds 98
Creamer 48
*Goblet (ILLUS.) . . . . 35 to 40
Honey dish, cov., 3½" h. 35
Honey dish, open. 19
Sauce dish, flat or footed, each 14
Spooner . . . . 25 to 35
Sugar bowl, cov. 55

CHAIN WITH STAR

Bread plate, handled 29
Butter dish, cov. 33
Cake stand, 8¾" to 10" d. 33
Compote, open, jelly 17
Compote, open, 8" d., 4" h. 19
Compote, open, 8" d., 6½" h. 20
Compote, open, 9½" d. 25
Creamer . . . . 25 to 35

Chain With Star Goblet

Goblet (ILLUS.) 23
Pickle dish, oval. 13
Pitcher, water 50
Plate, 7" d. 28
Plate, two-handled 25
Relish 14
Sauce dish 13
Spooner 30
Sugar bowl, cov. 38
Sugar bowl, open. 27
Tumbler 18
Water set: water pitcher & 6 goblets; clear,
    7 pcs. 150
Wine 30

COLLINS—See Crystal Wedding Pattern

COLORADO (Lacy Medallion)

Berry set: master bowl & 6 sauce dishes;
    clear w/gold, 7 pcs. 125
Bowl, 4" d., blue 39
Bowl, 4" d., green w/gold 20
Bowl, 5" d., blue, ruffled rim 35
Bowl, 5" d., clear, flared edge. 20
Bowl, 5" d., green w/gold 45
Bowl, 7" d., blue, footed, scalloped rim 25
Bowl, 7" d., clear, footed. 25
Bowl, 7" d., green, flat 23
Bowl, 8" d., blue, turned-up sides. 65
Bowl, 8" d., green w/gold, turned-up sides 63
Bowl, 9" d., clear, footed, three turned-up sides. . . 32
Bowl, 9" d., green, footed, crimped edge 40

Bowl, 9" d., green w/gold 43
Butter dish, cov., blue w/gold 260
Butter dish, cov., clear. 63
Butter dish, cov., green 125
Cake plate, handled, blue, 12" d. 180
Cake stand, clear. 65
Card tray, blue 40
Card tray, blue w/gold 120
Card tray, clear. 20
Card tray, green 33
Celery vase, clear 35
Celery vase, green 48
Celery vase, green w/gold 70
Cheese dish, cov., blue w/gold 70
Compote, open, 8" d., 7" h., beaded rim,
    green. . . . . 100 to 125
Compote, open, 10½" d., high stand, blue. 215
Compote, open, 10½" d., 7" h., green w/gold . . . 135
Creamer, blue. 80
Creamer, clear 34
Creamer, green 55
Creamer, green, souvenir. 65
Cup & saucer green. 45
Match holder, green. 35

Colorado Mug

Mug, clear, 2½" h. (ILLUS.) 25
Mug, green 30
Mug, ruby-stained. 55
Nappy, tricornered, blue w/gold 48
Nappy, tricornered, clear 20
Nappy, tricornered, green w/gold 30
Pitcher, 6" d., blue w/gold. 115
Pitcher, 6" d., green w/gold 42
Pitcher, water, blue w/gold. 400
Pitcher, water, clear w/gold 116
Pitcher, water, green w/gold. . . . . 250 to 300
Salt shaker w/original top, green w/gold 45
Sauce dish, clear 13
Sauce dish, green w/gold. 25
Spooner, blue w/gold 55
Spooner, clear 40
Spooner, green w/gold . . . . 60 to 70
Sugar bowl, cov., clear, large 42
Sugar bowl, cov., green, large . . . . 85 to 100
Sugar bowl, cov., green w/gold, large 110
*Toothpick holder, clear w/gold 30

Tumbler, clear 35
Tumbler, green w/gold 40
Tumbler, green w/gold, souvenir 30
Tumbler, ruby-stained, souvenir. 40
Vase, 12" h., trumpet-shaped, green 275
Vase, 14" h., trumpet-shaped, clear 60
Water set: pitcher & 6 tumblers; green
    w/gold, 7 pcs. 450
Wine, clear 30
Wine, green w/gold. 35
Wine, ruby-stained w/gold 40

CRYSTAL WEDDING (Collins)

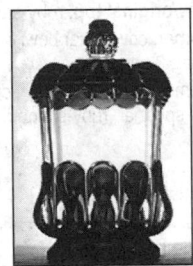

Crystal Wedding Sugar Bowl

Banana stand, 10" h. 125
Bowl, cov., 7" sq. 95
Bowl, 7" d., scalloped edge 65
Butter dish, cov., amber-stained 100
Butter dish, cov., clear. 75
Butter dish, cov., ruby-stained. 130
Cake stand, 10" sq. 95
Celery vase 50
Compote, cov., 6" sq., high stand 65
Compote, open, 5" sq., low stand 45
Compote, open, 6" sq. 47
Compote, open, 6" sq., high stand,
    scalloped rim 50
Compote, open, 7" sq., high stand. 50
Compote, open, 8" sq., low stand 55
Creamer, clear 65
Creamer, ruby-stained 125
Creamer & cov. sugar bowl,
    amber-stained, pr. . . . . 180 to 195
Cruet w/original stopper, amber-stained 225
Cruet w/original stopper, canary 225
Cruet w/original stopper, clear. 175
*Goblet, clear 40
*Goblet, ruby-stained 65
Goblet w/fern etching 45
Honey dish, cov., 6" sq. 80
Honey dish, cov., 7". 90
Humidor, w/resilvered top, 5" h. 125
Lamp, kerosene-type, 8" h. 145
Lamp, kerosene-type, banquet-style, blue
    base, clear font. 280
Lamp base, kerosene-type, square font, 10" h. . . . 225

Pitcher, 12" h., tankard, water......... 165 to 185
Pitcher, milk, square......................... 150
Plate, 10" sq., engraved 45
Plate, 10" sq., plain.......................... 35
Relish...................................... 20
Salt dip, individual 30
Salt dip, master size......................... 55
Spooner, canary............................. 45
Spooner, clear 40
Sugar bowl, cov., amber-stained 135
Sugar bowl, cov., clear 60
Sugar bowl, cov., ruby-stained (ILLUS.) 125
Syrup pitcher w/original top................. 185
Syrup pitcher w/original top, ruby-stained..... 250
Table set: creamer, cov. sugar bowl &
   spooner; clear, 3 pcs..................... 175
Table set: creamer, cov. sugar bowl, cov.
   butter dish & spooner; ruby-stained,
   4 pcs............................... 450-475
Tumbler, clear 45
Tumbler, ruby-stained 65
Wine 75
Wine, ruby-stained 39

CURRIER & IVES

Bread plate, children sawing felled log,
   frosted center 75
Cake stand, blue 125
Cake stand, clear 65
Celery..................................... 50
Cordial, 3½" h............................... 50
Cup & saucer, clear.......................... 40
*Goblet, canary............................. 85
*Goblet, clear .... 25 to 30
Lamp, kerosene-type, 8" h.................... 80
Mug, clear.................................. 25
Pitcher, milk 65
Pitcher, water, amber....................... 135
Pitcher, water, blue 165
Pitcher, water, clear 85
Salt & pepper shakers w/original tops,
   amber, pr............................... 165
Salt & pepper shakers w/original tops,
   blue, pr. 190
Syrup jug w/original top, amber............. 210
Syrup jug w/original top, blue 162
Syrup jug w/original top, clear 50
Tray, water, amber, Balky Mule on Railroad
   Tracks, 9½" d. 85
Tray, water, blue, Balky Mule on Railroad
   Tracks, 9½" d. 165
Tray, water, clear, Balky Mule on Railroad
   Tracks, 9½" d. 65
Tray, water, canary, Balky Mule on Railroad
   Tracks, 10½" d. 175
Tray, water, clear, Balky Mule on Railroad
   Tracks, 10½" d. 88

Tumbler, amber 48
Tumbler, clear 40
Wine, blue................................. 55
Wine, clear 30
Wine, ruby-stained 85
Wine set, decanter w/original stopper &
   6 wines, 7 pcs.......................... 150

DAKOTA (Baby Thumbprint)

Dakota Celery Vase

Butter dish, cov., ruby-stained w/flared
   edge on base 250
Cake stand, 8" d., plain 175
Cake stand, 9" d., engraved................. 250
Cake stand, 9½" d.......................... 180
Cake stand, 10½" d., engraved 295
Cake stand, 10½" d., plain................. 250
Cake stand, w/high domed cover............ 375
Castor set: salt shaker, oil & vinegar cruets
   w/original stoppers & tray, 4 pcs........... 300
Celery vase, flat base, clear, engraved (ILLUS.) .. 50
Celery vase, pedestal base, ruby-stained 110
Compote, open, jelly, 5" d., 5½" h., plain 45
Compote, open, 9" d., high stand, engraved 45
Compote, open, 10" d., high stand............ 45
Creamer, hotel 65
Cruet w/original stopper, engraved 150
Cruet w/original stopper, plain.............. 95
Doughnut stand, cov. 300
Goblet, clear, engraved 55
Goblet, clear, plain 60
Goblet, ruby-stained, engraved 95
Goblet, ruby-stained, plain 85
Honey dish................................ 25
Mug, clear................................. 45
Mug, ruby-stained, 3½" h.................... 65
Pitcher, milk, jug-type, engraved, pt. .... 120 to 130
Pitcher, milk, tankard, engraved, pt.......... 120
Pitcher, milk, tankard, engraved, qt.......... 125
Pitcher, milk, tankard, ruby-stained, pt. 135
*Pitcher, water, tankard, engraved leaves,
   ½ gal. .... 140 to 150
Pitcher, tankard, 12" h., souvenir engraving 120
Plate or water tray, 10" d. 90

Plate or water tray, 10½" d., ruffled **120**

Salt & pepper shakers w/original tops,
  ruby-stained, pr. **165**

Salt shaker w/original top, ruby-stained **85**

Sauce dish, flat or footed, clear, engraved, each. . **18**

Sauce dish, flat or footed, clear, plain, each **15**

Sauce dish, flat or footed, cobalt blue, each **95**

Sugar bowl, cov., engraved **75**

Sugar bowl, cov., plain **50**

Waste bowl, engraved **75**

Waste bowl, plain **58**

Wine, clear, engraved . . . . **30 to 40**

Wine, clear, plain **25**

Wine, ruby-stained **55**

DORIC—See Feather Pattern

ESTHER

Esther Sauce Dish

Berry set: master bowl & 6 sauce dishes;
  green, 7 pcs. . . . . **245 to 255**

Bowl, 8" d., clear **35**

Bowl, 9" d., green, footed **25**

Cake stand, 10½" d., 6" h., amber-stained **95**

Cake stand, 10½" d., 6" h., clear **75**

Cake stand, 10½" d., 6" h., ruby-stained **110**

Celery vase, green w/gold **95**

Cheese dish, cov., amber-stained, high dome. . . **140**

Cheese dish, cov., clear, high dome **90**

Cheese dish, cov., green, high dome . . . . **175 to 200**

Cheese dish, cov., ruby-stained, high dome **140**

Compote, open, 8" d., high stand . . . . **40 to 50**

Cracker jar, cov., clear . . . . **100 to 120**

Cracker jar, cov., green . . . . **250 to 275**

Cracker jar, cov., ruby-stained **250**

Creamer, amber-stained **70**

Creamer, clear **60**

Creamer, ruby-stained **75**

Creamer & cov. sugar bowl, amber-
  stained, pr. **175**

Cruet w/original stopper, green, small **195**

Doughnut stand w/turned edge . . . . **60 to 75**

Goblet, clear **80**

Goblet, green **100**

Pickle dish, clear **25**

Pickle dish, ruby-stained **45**

Pitcher, water, clear . . . . **75 to 100**

Pitcher, water, green . . . . **275 to 300**

Plate, 5½" d., green, footed **75**

Sauce dish, clear **30**

Sauce dish, clear, engraved (ILLUS.) **25**

Sauce dish, green **35**

Sauce dish, green w/gold . . . . **35 to 40**

Sugar bowl, cov., green **135**

Toothpick holder, green . . . . **100 to 125**

Toothpick holder, green w/gold . . . . **140 to 160**

EXCELSIOR

Bar bottle, flint, pt. **75 to 90**

Bar bottle, flint, qt. . . . . **100 to 115**

Bowl, 4½" h., footed, scalloped rim **45**

Candlestick, flint, 8¼" h. . . . . **150 to 165**

Claret, flint **45**

Cologne bottle w/faceted stopper **145**

Cordial **110**

Creamer, applied handle . . . . **100 to 125**

Egg cup, double, clear **75**

Goblet, "barrel", flint **75**

Lamp, kerosene, flint font, brass collar,
  black iron stem & base **195**

Lamps, whale oil, 9¾" h. to collar, 11¼" h.
  to burner, pr. **295 to 300**

Mug **45**

Pickle jar, cov. **60**

Pitcher, milk, flint **250**

Salt dip, master size **40**

Shaving mug, dated Sept. 20, 1870, gold trim . . **170**

Spooner **65**

Sugar bowl, cov. . . . . **125 to 160**

Sweetmeat compote, cov., flint, 9¾" h. . . **125 to 150**

Syrup pitcher, applied handle **125**

Syrup pitcher w/original top, green **750**

Tray, wine **60**

Tumbler, bar, flint, 3½" h. . . . . **75 to 85**

Tumbler, footed, flat . . . . **75 to 100**

Tumbler, footed, flint . . . . **75 to 90**

Wine, flint . . . . **60 to 65**

FEATHER (Doric, Indiana Swirl or Finecut & Feather)

Banana boat, footed, clear **120**

Banana boat, footed, green **200**

Bowl, 6½" d. **20**

Bowl, 7" oval **25**

Cake stand, 8½" d. . . . . **45 to 55**

Cake stand, clear, 9½" h. . . . . **55 to 65**

Cake stand, clear, 11" d. **75**

Compote, cov., 6¼" d., low stand . . . . **50 to 55**

Compote, cov., 7" d., high stand . . . . **100 to 110**

Compote, cov., 8½" d., high stand . . . . . . **100 to 125**

Compote, open, jelly, 4½" d., 4¾" h.,
  amber-stained **150**

Cordial . . . . **100 to 120**

Creamer, amber-stained. 175
Cruet w/original stopper, clear. 60
Doughnut stand, 8" w., 4½" h. . . . . 60 to 65
Honey dish, 3½" d. 15
Marmalade jar, cov. . . . . 90 to 100
Pickle dish 25
Pitcher, water, clear . . . . 60 to 65
Pitcher, water, green . . . . 125 to 150
Plate, 10" d., clear. . . . . 35 to 40
Plate, 10" d., green . . . . 45 to 55
Relish, 8¼" oval, green 40
Salt & pepper shakers w/original tops,
    clear, pr. . . . . 65 to 75
Salt & pepper shakers w/original tops,
    green, pr. . . . . 150 to 180
Salt shaker w/original top, clear. 35
Salt shaker w/original top, green . . . . 75 to 85
Sauce dish, amber-stained, flat or footed, each . . 25
Sauce dish, clear, flat or footed, each 10
Spooner, amber 195
Spooner, amber-stained. 60
Spooner, clear . . . . 25 to 30
Sugar bowl, cov., clear. . . . . 50 to 55
Sugar bowl, cov., green . . . . 110 to 130
Sugar bowl, cov., child's 25
Syrup pitcher w/original top, clear . . . . . 100 to 125
Syrup pitcher w/original top, green . . . . 200 to 250
Table set, cov. butter dish, cov. sugar bowl,
    creamer & spooner, 4 pcs. 155
Tumbler, green. 95
Vase, 10" h., green 25
Wine, amber-stained. 95

FINECUT & FEATHER—See Feather Pattern

FISHSCALE

Fishscale Compote

Bone dish, 4 x 5½". 25
Bowl, 12" d. 25
Bowl, cov., 12" d. . . . . 40 to 45
Compote, open, 7" d., high stand (ILLUS.) 31
Condiment tray 35

Lamp base, kerosene-type, pedestal base,
    original burner. . . . . 75 to 85
Mug . . . . 40 to 45
Plate, 7" d. 21
Shoe w/attached sq. underplate, amber 150
Shoe w/attached sq. underplate, blue 150
Shoe w/attached sq. underplate, clear 125
Shoe w/attached sq. underplate, vaseline. 160

FROSTED WAFFLE—See Hidalgo Pattern

GONTERMAN

Gonterman Compote

Bowl, cov., 7" d., high stand, frosted clear
    w/amber stain. 90
Bowl, cov., 8" d., high stand, frosted clear
    w/amber stain. 95
Bowl, 7" d., low stand, frosted clear
    w/amber stain. 80
Bowl, 8" d., low stand, frosted clear
    w/amber stain. 85
Butter dish, cov., frosted clear w/amber
    stain . . . . 135 to 150
Cake stand, high stand, frosted clear
    w/amber stain, 10" d. . . . . 125 to 135
Celery vase, pedestaled, smooth rim,
    frosted clear w/amber stain. . . . . 100 to 110
Compote, cov., 5" d., high stand, frosted
    clear w/amber stain. . . . . 110 to 120
Compote, cov., 7" d., high stand, frosted
    clear w/amber stain. . . . . 115 to 125
Compote, cov., 8" d., high stand, frosted
    clear w/amber stain. . . . . 125 to 140
Compote, open, 5" d., high stand, frosted
    clear w/amber stain. . . . . 65 to 75
Compote, open, 7" d., high stand, frosted
    clear w/amber stain (ILLUS.) . . . . 75 to 85
Compote, open, 8" d., high stand, frosted
    clear w/amber stain. . . . . 80 to 90
Creamer, frosted clear w/amber stain. . . . 125 to 150
Goblet, frosted clear w/amber stain 550
Honey, flat, frosted clear w/amber stain, 3½" d. . . . 30
Honey, footed, frosted clear w/amber stain,
    3½" d. 30
Pitcher, milk, frosted clear w/amber stain,
    1 qt. . . . . 165 to 175

Pitcher, water, frosted clear w/amber stain,
½ gal. . . . . **180 to 195**

Salt shaker w/original top, frosted clear
w/amber stain . . . . **75 to 80**

Sauce dish, footed, frosted clear w/amber
stain, 4" d. . . . . **30 to 35**

Sauce dish, frosted clear w/amber stain,
4" d. . . . . **30 to 35**

Sauce dish, footed, frosted clear w/amber
stain, 4½" d. . . . . **30 to 35**

Sauce dish, frosted clear w/amber stain,
4½" d. . . . . **30 to 35**

Spooner, frosted clear w/amber stain. . . . **175 to 200**

Sugar bowl, cov., frosted clear w/amber
stain . . . . **120 to 130**

GREEK KEY (Heisey's Greek Key)

Champagne . . . . **90 to 100**
Goblet. **70**
Pickle dish, 8" l. **25**
Plate, 5½" d. **25**
Plate, 6¾" d. **30**
Plate, 9" d. **30**
Sugar bowl, open . . . . **25 to 30**
Vase, 6½" h., footed . . . . **65 to 70**
Wine . . . . **75 to 85**

HIDALGO (Frosted Waffle)

Hidalgo Goblet

Bowl, 5½" sq., 2½" h. **20**
Bowl, 7½" sq., footed **25**
Bowl, 9" sq., clear & frosted **35**
Bowl, 9½" sq. **35**
Bowl, salad, 11" sq. **35**
Bread plate . . . . **60 to 65**
Goblet, amber-stained **40**
Goblet, clear. **30**
Goblet, engraved **35**
Goblet, ruby-stained (ILLUS.) . . . . **45 to 50**
Pitcher, water. **50**

INDIANA SWIRL—See Feather Pattern

IOWA (Paneled Zipper or Zippered Block)

Iowa Goblet

Bowl, 9" d., 5½" h., ruby-stained **135**
Carafe, water, clear **35**
Carafe, water, ruby-stained **60**
Compote, jelly **24**
Compote, 8½" d., high stand **95**
Creamer, ruby-stained **65**
Cruet w/original stopper. **50**
Finger bowl, ruby-stained **55**
Goblet, clear w/ruby stain. **110**
Goblet (ILLUS.) **20**
Lamp, kerosene-type **105**
Olive dish, handled **23**
Salt & pepper shakers w/original tops,
clear, pr. **45**
Salt & pepper shakers w/original tops,
ruby-stained, pr. . . . . **85 to 100**
Salt shaker w/original top, clear . . . . **25 to 30**
Sauce dish, flat **15**
Spooner **17**
Sugar bowl, cov., ruby-stained **75**
Sugar bowl, cov., small **20**
Toothpick holder, clear **21**
Toothpick holder, ruby-stained **60**
Tumbler, clear **20**
Tumbler, ruby-stained **41**
Wine **30**
Wine, w/gold trim **32**

JUMBO AND JUMBO & BARNUM

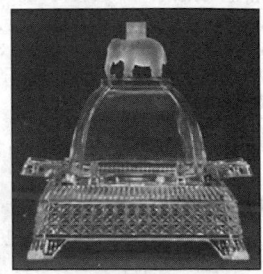

Jumbo Butter Dish

Butter dish & cover w/frosted elephant finial, oblong (ILLUS.) . . . . 675 to 700

Butter dish & cover w/frosted elephant finial, round . . . . 375 to 400

Castor set, w/four original bottles & metal tops, amber. 450 to 500

Castor set, w/four original bottles & metal tops, clear. 275

Celery vase, etched . . . . 175 to 200

Creamer . . . . 235 to 250

Creamer w/Barnum head at handle . . . . 250 to 275

Goblet . . . . 1,000 to 1,200

Pitcher, water, w/elephant in base 695

Spoon rack, blue . . . . 700 to 775

Spoon rack, clear w/frosted elephant. . . . 425 to 500

Spoon rack, clear . . . . 275 to 300

Sugar bowl, w/Barnum head handles & cover w/frosted elephant finial . . . . . . 450 to 475

LACY MEDALLION—See Colorado Pattern

LOG CABIN

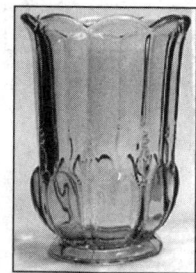

Log Cabin Sugar Bowl

Bowl, cov., 5¼ x 3⅝" 125

Butter dish, cov. . . . . 345 to 375

Compote, cov. . . . .

*Creamer, 4¼" h.. . . . . 125 to 175

Honey dish, cov. 190

Lamp, dated 1875. 200

Marmalade jar, cov. . . . . 175 to 225

Pickle jar, cov., 6¾" h. . . . . 95 to 100

Pitcher, water. 325

Salt dip, master size. 110

Sauce dish, flat oblong. 85

*Spooner, clear 145

*Sugar bowl, cov., clear, 8" h. (ILLUS.) . . 375 to 450

Sugar bowl, cov., canary 675

Sugar bowl, open. 75

LOOP & PILLAR—See Michigan Pattern

LOUISIANA

Bowl, cov., round, 6" d.. 40

Bowl, cov., round, 7" d.. 40

Bowl, cov., round, 8" d.. 45

Bowl, open, round, 6" d.. 45

Bowl, open, round, 7" d.. 35

Bowl, open, round, 8" d.. 40

Bowl, open, square, 6" w.. 30

Bowl, open, square, 7" w.. 30

Bowl, open, square, 8" d.. 35

Bowl, open, square, 9" w.. 40

Butter dish, cov. . . . . 80 to 85

Cake stand, high stand, 7" d. 55

Cake stand, high stand, 10" d. 75

Celery vase 35

Compote, cov., high stand, 6" d. 50

Compote, cov., high stand, 7" d. 50

Compote, cov., high stand, 8" d. 55

Compote, open, deep bowl, 7" d.. 22

Compote, open, deep bowl, 8" d.. 28

Compote, open, flared bowl, 6" d. 28

Compote, open, shallow bowl, 8" d.. 30

Compote, open, shallow bowl, 10" d.. 30

Creamer . . . . 40 to 45

Dish, cov., handled, 6" d. 35

Dish, open, handled, 6" d. 20

Match holder on attached saucer base . . . 35 to 40

Mustard jar, cover & underplate . . . . 45 to 50

Pickle dish, boat-shaped 20

Pitcher, milk, pressed handle. 40

Relish tray 15

Salt & pepper shakers w/original tops, pr.. 45

Salt shaker w/original top. 20

Sauce dish, round, 4" d. 10

Sauce dish, round, 4½" d. 10

Sauce dish, square, 4½" w. 7

Spooner 30

Sugar bowl, cov.. . . . . 45 to 50

Tumbler, water . . . . 25 to 30

Wine . . . . 40 to 45

MICHIGAN (Paneled Jewel or Loop & Pillar)

Michigan Celery Vase

Bowl, 8" d., pink-stained w/gold trim . . . . 65 to 70

Butter dish, cov., clear. 60

Butter dish, cov., pink-stained . . . . 150 to 175

Butter dish, cov., yellow-stained, enameled florals . . . . 150 to 175

Celery vase, clear (ILLUS.) 35
Celery vase, pink-stained, gold rim 75
Compote, open, 6½" d., scalloped rim . . . . . 40 to 45
Compote, open, 8½" d., pink-stained . . . . . 60 to 65
Compote, open, flared, 9¾" d., pink-stained,
  enameled florals . . . . 250 to 275
Creamer, 4" h., clear. 30
Creamer & sugar bowl, pink-stained, gold
  trim, pr. 95
Cruet w/original stopper. 125
Egg cup 25
Goblet, clear . . . . 35 to 40
Honey dish, 3½" d. 8
Mug, clear . . . . 30 to 35
Mug, pink-stained, gold trim 38
Mug, yellow-stained, enameled florals . . . . . 45 to 55
Parfait. 30
Pitcher, miniature, clear . . . . 35 to 40
Pitcher, miniature, pink-stained 58
Pitcher, water, 8" h. 50
Pitcher, water, tankard, 12" h.,
  pink-stained. . . . . 175 to 185
Platters, 8½ x 12½", 7¼ x 10¼", 6½ x 9½",
  nested set of 3 125
Relish, clear 18
Relish, pink-stained 24
Salt & pepper shakers w/original tops,
  clear, pr. . . . . 70 to 75
Salt & pepper shakers w/original tops,
  pink-stained, pr. 80 to 85
Salt & pepper shakers w/original tops,
  individual size, pr. . . . . 70 to 75
Salt shaker w/original top, yellow-stained,
  enameled florals . . . . 35 to 40
Spooner, clear, child's 60
Sugar bowl, cov., pink-stained, gold trim . . . 75 to 80
Syrup jug w/pewter top. 165
Toddy mug, clear, tall 45
Toddy mug, pink-stained, gold trim, tall. 37
Toothpick holder, blue-stained 75
Toothpick holder, pink-stained, gold
  trim . . . . 175 to 180
Toothpick holder, yellow-stained. . . . . . . 160 to 165
Toothpick holder, yellow-stained,
  enameled florals . . . . 175 to 190
Tumbler, clear. . . . . 25 to 30
Tumbler, clear w/gold trim 36
Waste bowl 68
Wine, blue-stained. . . . . 50 to 55
Wine, clear 40
Wine, yellow-stained. 55

NEW ENGLAND PINEAPPLE

Bar bottle, qt. 275
Cake stand . . . . 150 to 160
Castor set, 2 castor bottles & 2 mustard jars
  in frame, set . . . . 175 to 220

Champagne . . . . 175 to 210
Compote, open, 8" d., 5" h. . . . . 150 to 200
Compote, open, 8" d., 7" h. 140
Compote, open, 9" d. 145
*Cordial, 4" h. 119
Creamer, applied handle. . . . . 150 to 175
Decanter w/original stopper, qt. . . . . . . 250 to 275
Egg cup. . . . . 50 to 55
*Goblet . . . . 85 to 90
Goblet, lady's . . . . 125 to 130
Goblets, set of 5 . . . . 425 to 450
Pitcher, milk, 1 qt. 650
Pitcher, water 400
Spooner . . . . 65 to 70
Sugar bowl, cov. . . . . 140 to 145
Sugar bowl, open . . . . 25 to 30
Tumbler, water . . . . 95 to 100
Tumbler, water, extra large. . . . . 125 to 130
Tumbler, whiskey, applied handle . . . . . . 180 to 190
*Wine. . . . . 160 to 170
Wines, set of 3 . . . . 480 to 500

OLD MAN OF THE MOUNTAIN—See Viking Pattern

OREGON NO. 1—See Beaded Loop Pattern

PANELED 44—See Reverse 44 Pattern

PANELED JEWEL—See Michigan Pattern

PANELED ZIPPER—See Iowa Pattern

REVERSE 44 (Paneled 44, U.S. Glass "Athenia")

Berry set: master bowl & 6 sauce dishes;
  clear w/gold or platinum stain, 7 pcs. . . 195 to 225
Bowl, flat, 8" d., deep straight sides, clear 45
Bowl, 8" d., shallow sides, clear w/gold or
  platinum stain 75
Butter dish, cov., clear w/gold or platinum
  stain 150
Compote, jelly, clear w/gold or platinum stain 69
Compote, open, 6½" d., flared rim, high
  standard, clear 125
Creamer, berry, clear w/gold or platinum stain. . . . 95
Creamer, table size, clear w/gold or
  platinum stain. 55
Creamer, tankard, clear w/gold or platinum stain . . 30
Cruet w/original stopper, clear w/gold or
  platinum stain. 175
Goblet, clear. 65
Goblet, clear w/gold or platinum stain 145

Pitcher, jug-type, clear w/gold or platinum
    stain, ½ gal.................... **170 to 180**
Pitcher, tankard-type, footed, clear **225**
Punch cup, plain rim, clear w/gold or
    platinum stain........................... **75**
Sauce dish, 4" d., straight sides, clear
    w/gold or platinum stain................... **20**
Spoonholder, handled, clear w/gold or
    platinum stain........................... **80**
Sugar bowl, cov., table size, clear w/gold or
    platinum stain.................... **75 to 100**
Syrup jug w/original top, clear w/gold or
    platinum stain.......................... **275**
Toothpick holder, footed, handled, clear
    w/gold or platinum stain .... **85 to 90**
Tumbler, flat, clear w/gold or platinum stain....... **70**
Vase, 11" h., handled, clear **145**

ROSE IN SNOW

Rose in Snow Creamer

Berry set, 8¼" sq. footed bowl & 4 footed
    sauce dishes, 5 pcs........................ **75**
Bitters bottle w/original stopper **100**
Bowl, 8½ x 11½" oval...................... **48**
Butter dish, cov., round **60**
Butter dish, cov., square **50**
Cake plate, handled, amber, 10" d. **50**
Cake stand, clear, 9" d.................. **90 to 100**
Compote, cov., 7" d., low stand **125**
Compote, cov., 8" d., 10" h., clear .... **90 to 95**
Compote, open, 6" d., canary................. **42**
Compote, open, 8" d., high stand............. **70**
Creamer, round, clear.................. **40 to 45**
Creamer, square, canary **60**
Creamer, square, clear (ILLUS.) **32**
*Goblet, blue............................ **85**
*Goblet, canary....................... **35 to 45**
*Goblet, clear .... **40 to 45**
Marmalade jar, cov., 5¾" d.................. **55**
Mug, blue, large **105**
Pitcher, water, applied handle, blue........... **225**
Pitcher, water, applied handle, canary......... **160**
Pitcher, water, applied handle, clear..... **125 to 135**
Plate, 5" d. **26**
Plate, 6" d. **30**
Plate, 6½" d., handled, clear................ **19**

*Plate, 9" d., amber....................... **40**
*Plate, 9" d., clear .... **25 to 30**
Relish, 6¼ x 9¼" **18**
Spooner, round **25**
Tumbler **41**

S-REPEAT

S-Repeat Condiment Set

Butter dish, cov., apple green .... **125 to 150**
Butter dish, cov., clear.................... **125**
Butter dish, cov., sapphire blue w/gold **150**
Condiment set, apple green (ILLUS.) ... **250 to 275**
Condiment tray, apple green................. **55**
Cruet, amethyst **195**
*Cruet, apple green **110**
Decanter w/stopper, wine, amethyst.......... **155**
Decanter w/stopper, wine, apple green w/gold.. **138**
Decanter w/stopper, wine, sapphire blue
    w/gold................................ **158**
Pitcher, green............................ **85**
Salt & pepper shakers, apple green, pr........ **103**
*Toothpick holder, apple green............... **50**
*Wine, apple green........................ **45**
*Wine, sapphire blue....................... **50**

SHELL & JEWEL (Victor)

Shell & Jewel Pitcher

Bowl, 8" d. **30**
Butter dish, cov............................ **85**
Cake stand, 10" d., 5" h. **40**
Compote, cov., 8½" d., high stand............. **75**
Compote, open, 7" d., 7½" h.................. **55**
Creamer **45**

Pitcher, water, clear (ILLUS.) . . . . 55 to 65
Pitcher, water, green. . . . . 90 to 95
Sauce dish, clear 8
Spooner 30
Sugar bowl, cov. 43
Tumbler, amber 24
Tumbler, blue . . . . 35 to 40
Tumbler, clear 19
Tumbler, green. 44
Water set: pitcher & 6 tumblers; clear,
  7 pcs. . . . . 170 to 190

SQUIRREL—See Animals & Birds on Goblets & Pitchers

TREE OF LIFE WITH HAND (Tree of Life-Wheeling)

Tree of Life with Hand Creamer

Cake stand, 8¾" d. 80
Cake stand, frosted base, 11½" d. . . . . . . 115 to 125
Celery vase 56
Compote, open, 8" d., clear hand & ball
  stem . . . . 50 to 55
Compote, open, 9" d., frosted hand & ball stem. . . 83
Compote, open, 10" d., 10" h., frosted hand
  & ball stem 95
Creamer, w/hand & ball handle (ILLUS.) 75
Spooner 42

VICTOR—See Shell & Jewel Pattern

VIKING (Bearded Head or Old Man of the Mountain)

Viking Sugar Bowl

Apothecary jar w/original stopper . . . . . 120 to 125
Bowl, cov., 8" oval 100
Bowl, 8" sq. 45
Butter dish, cov., clear. 115
Celery vase . . . . 50 to 55
Compote, cov., 9" d., low stand 170
Compote, cov., 12" h. . . . . 135 to 145
Compote, open, 8" d., high stand. 63
Creamer 65
Mug, applied handle 63
Pickle dish, 7" l. 45
Pitcher, water, 8¾" h., clear . . . . 110 to 115
Pitcher, water, 8¾" h., clear & frosted . . . 240 to 250
Salt dip, master size . . . . 40 to 45
Sauce dish, footed 17
Sugar bowl, cov. (ILLUS.) 70

WISCONSIN (Beaded Dewdrop)

Banana stand, turned-up sides, 7½" w., 4" h. 72
Bonbon, handled, 4". 24
Bowl, 6½" d. 35
Bowl, 8" d. 36
Bowl, 8½" oblong 35
Butter dish, cov. 79
Cake stand, 8¼" d., 4¾" h. 36
Cake stand, 9¾" d. 85
Celery tray, flat, 5 x 10" 36
Celery vase. . . . . 35 to 40
Compote, open, 6½" d., 3½" h. 30
Compote, open, 6½" d., 6½" h. 45
Compote, open, 7½" d., 5½" h. 50
Creamer, individual size 35
Cruet w/original stopper. 45
Cup & saucer. 40
Dish, cov., oval 36
Goblet. 80
Mug, 3½" h. . . . . 50 to 55
Mustard jar, cov., bulbous 60
Nappy, handled, 4" d. 34
Pitcher, milk . . . . 55 to 60
Plate, 5" sq. 20
Plate, 6½" sq. 26
Salt shaker w/original top. 55
Sauce dish. 12
Spooner 33
Sugar bowl, cov., 5" h. 95
Sugar shaker w/original top. 126
Tumbler 45
Vase, 6" h. 58
Wine 75

WYOMING

Bowl, 7" d., footed 43
Cake stand, 9" d., high stand . . . . 55 to 60
Cake stand, 10" d., high stand. 55
Compote, open, 6" d., scalloped rim, deep bowl . . 38

Compote, open, 8" d., shallow bowl 40
Creamer, open, individual, tankard shape 30
Goblet 175
Mug . . . . 70 to 75
Pitcher, water, pressed handle, 3 pt. 65
Relish tray 19
Sauce dish, flat, round, 4" d. 18
Sugar bowl, cov. 95
Wine 160

ZIPPERED BLOCK—See Iowa Pattern

PEACH BLOW

Several types of glass lumped together by collectors as Peach Blow were produced by half a dozen glasshouses. Hobbs, Brockunier & Co., Wheeling, West Virginia, made Peach Blow as a plated ware that shaded from red at the top to yellow at the bottom and is referred to as Wheeling Peach Blow. Mt. Washington Glass Works produced an homogeneous Peach Blow shading from a rose color at the top to pale blue in the lower portion. The New England Glass Works' Peach Blow, called Wild Rose, shaded from rose at the top to white. Gunderson-Pairpoint Co. also reproduced some of the Mt. Washington Peach Blow in the early 1950s and some glass of a somewhat similar type was made by Steuben Glass Works, Thomas Webb & Sons and Stevens & Williams of England. New England Peach Blow is one-layered glass and the English is two-layered.

Another single layered shaded art glass was produced early in this century by the New Martinsville Glass Mfg. Co. Originally called "Muranese," collectors today refer to it as "New Martinsville Peach Blow."

GUNDERSON

Gunderson Peach Blow Decanters

Compote, 5⅝" d., 2¾" h., open, the wide shallow flaring bowl raised on a short applied stem & wide disk foot, satin finish . . . **$143**
Decanters w/original stoppers, footed tall ovoid body tapering to a small flared neck, tall oval stoppers, satin finish, mid-20th c., 12" h., pr. (ILLUS.) 575

MT. WASHINGTON

Pitcher, 6" h., applied reed handle 400

NEW ENGLAND

Tumbler, cylindrical 209
Vase, 7¾" h., jack-in-the-pulpit form w/very slender stem & round disk foot 495

WHEELING

Wheeling Peach Blow Sugar Shaker

Salt & pepper shakers w/original lids, footed spherical bodies, cased w/exterior shading from deep fuchsia to amber, 2¾" h., pr. 690
Sugar bowl, open 445
Sugar shaker w/original metal lid, cylindrical body tapering to neck fitted w/metal screw cap, glossy finish, 5½" h. (ILLUS.) 316

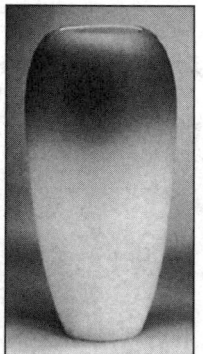

Wheeling Peach Blow Vase

Vase, 13¾" h., tall slender ovoid body w/a closed rim, satin finish, pinhead-size interior bubble (ILLUS.) 546

PHOENIX

This ware was made by the Phoenix Glass Co. of Beaver County, Pennsylvania, which produced various types of glass from the 1880s. One special type that attracts collectors now is a molded ware with a vague resemblance to cameo in its "sculptured" decoration. Similar peices with relief-molded designs were produced by the Consolidated Lamp & Glass Co. (which see) and care must be taken to differentiate between the two companies' wares. Some Consolidated molds were moved to the Phoenix plant in the mid 1930s but later returned and used again at Consolidated. These pieces we will list under "Consolidated."

Cosmos Vase in White on Brown

Cake tray, Jewel & Dewdrop patt., blue on white ground, 11½" d. **$145**

Candlesticks, milk glass, Early American line, Sawtooth patt., 6¾" h., pr. **38**

Cigarette box, cov., Phlox patt., floral design on front, back & cover w/raised bands on sides, white on blue ground, 4½" . . . **125**

Cigarette box, cov., Phlox patt., floral design on front, back & cover w/raised bands on sides, white on brown ground, 4½" **140**

Vase, 4¾" h., globular w/flaring rim, Jewel patt., white design on pearlized burgundy ground **75**

Vase, 4¾" h., globular w/flaring rim, Jewel patt., white design on pearlized powder blue ground **80**

Vase, 6" h., wide ovoid body w/slightly flaring rim, Figured patt., stylized florals, satin finish over milk glass, labeled **90**

Vase, 7" h., baluster-form, Fern patt., white leaves on brown ground **100**

Vase, 7" h., bulbous base w/trumpet-form sides, Bluebell patt., pearlized burgundy finish **95**

Vase, 7" h., bulbous base w/trumpet-form sides, Bluebell patt., white on brown ground . . **110**

Vase, 7" h., Starflower patt., spherical w/raised bands alternating w/panels of sculptured flowers, white on blue ground **140**

Vase, 7" h., Starflower patt., spherical w/raised bands alternating w/panels of sculptured flowers, white on brown ground . . . **140**

Vase, 7½" h., rounded rectangular form, Cosmos patt., white blossoms & foliage centered by raised bands, brown ground (ILLUS.) **125**

Vase, 7½" h., rounded rectangular form, Cosmos patt., white blossoms & foliage centered by raised bands, blue ground **150**

Vase, 8¼" h., fan-shaped, Freesia patt., white blossoms & leaves on brown ground . . . **125**

Vase, 9½" h., 11½" w., pillow-shaped, Wild Geese patt., white birds on brown ground **220**

Vase, 9½" h., 11½" w., pillow-shaped, Wild Geese patt., white birds on blue ground, original paper label **230**

Vase, 9½" h., 11½" w., pillow-shaped, Wild Geese patt., white birds on tan ground w/pearlized finish **259**

Vase, 10" h., Madonna patt., relief-molded bust on brown ground. **220**

Vase, 10" h., Madonna patt., relief-molded pearlized bust on burgundy ground **177**

Vase, 10½" h., baluster-form, Wild Rosepatt., white florals & stems on brown ground **125**

Vase, 10½" h., baluster-form, Wild Rose patt., white florals & stems on slate blue ground **489**

Vase, 11½" h., bulbous base tapering to wide cylindrical neck, Philodendron patt., white leaves on blue ground. **160**

Vase, 11½" h., bulbous base tapering to wide cylindrical neck, Philodendron patt., white leaves on brown ground **160**

Vase, 18" h., tall ovoid body, Thistle patt., pearlized powder blue ground **520**

PILLAR-MOLDED

This heavily ribbed glassware was produced by blowing glass into full-sized ribbed molds and then finishing it by hand. The technique evolved from earlier "pattern moulding" used on glass since ancient times but in pillar-molded glass the ribs are very heavy and prominent. Most examples found in this country were produced in the Pittsburgh, Pennsylvania area from around 1850 to 1870, but similar English-made wares made before and after this period are also available. Most American items were made from clear flint glass and colored examples or pieces with colored strands in the ribs are rare and highly prized. Some collectors refer to this as "steamboat" glass believing that it was made to be used on American riverboats, but most likely it was used anywhere that a sturdy, relatively inexpensive glassware was needed, such as taverns and hotels.

Rare Pillar-Molded Candlestick

Candlestick, eight-rib, bulbous tapering ribbed stem topped by a thick applied wafer & a ringed & tooled tall cylindrical socket w/flattened rim, on a short applied stem & wide disk foot, rough pontil, clear, 10⅛" h. (ILLUS.) **$2,200**

Celery vase, eight-rib, tall waisted tulip-shaped bowl w/ferns, grapes & leaves engraved between ribs, applied knob stem & disk foot, clear, probably Pittsburgh, 10¾" h. **209**

Celery vase, eight-rib, very tall waisted tulip-form bowl w/scalloped rim, on an applied knop stem & round foot, ground pontil, clear, 10⅞" h. **193**

Creamer & open sugar bowl, eight-rib, each w/squatty thick heavy ribs forming the body, the creamer w/a high plain neck w/wide spout, applied handle w/curled end, raised on three-wafer pedestal & applied foot w/polished pontil, matching sugar w/wide plain upper sides w/folded rim, matching stem & foot, clear, 19th c., each 4" h., pr. **2,750**

Cruet w/original hollow blown stopper, eight-rib, bulbous ovoid body tapering to a tall slender neck w/arched spout, applied long strap handle w/end curl, rough pontil, clear, Pittsburgh, 9½" h. **275**

Decanter w/bar lip, miniature, eight-rib, tapering conical sides below triple applied rings at the base of the tall neck w/bar lip, polished pontil, clear, 6" h. **330**

Decanter w/pewter jigger top, eight-rib, tapering conical form w/applied rim & hollow strap handle w/curled end, clear, Pittsburgh, 9¼" h. **303**

QUEZAL

Quezal

Quezal Mark

In 1901, Martin Bach and Thomas Johnson, who had worked for Louis Tiffany, opened a competing glassworks in Brooklyn, New York. The Quezal Art Glass and Decorating Co. produced wares closely resembling those of Tiffany until the plant's closing in 1925.

Cup & saucer, the cup in opalescent & amber iridescence w/a band of scrolled feathering, the saucer in overall amber iridescence, both signed, ca. 1900, saucer 4⅛" d. **$805**

Lamp base, footed wide baluster-form w/trumpet neck, elaborate pulled & hooked gold feather design on a dark green body & creamy ground at the shoulder & neck, pulled gold feather design around the neck, good iridescence, lined in gold iridescence, 12" h. . . . **825**

Vase, 8" h., gold iridescent flared oval cased glass body w/interior & exterior golden orange lustre, base inscribed "Quezal" **460**

Vase, 3" h., miniature, slightly ribbed form w/a bulbous base & flared neck, amber w/strong overall gold iridescence, signed in polished pontil "Quezal 866". **690**

Vase, 5" h., a round cushion foot below a short, slender pedestal continuing to the bell-form bowl w/a flattened & flaring ruffled rim, the exterior w/a green pulled-feather design w/gold border against a white ground, the interior in gold iridescence, inscribed mark "#838" **1,100**

Vase, 5" h., bulbous squared form w/a flattened shoulder pulled & pinched into four incurved points, overall gold iridescence, inscribed mark **605**

Vase, 5½" h., a thin cushion foot centered by a tall very slender cylindrical body below the wide, shallow cupped rim, overall gold iridescence w/rose & blue highlights, inscribed mark. **413**

Vase, 5½" h., bulbous teardrop-form tapering to a tiny cylindrical neck, deep cobalt blue decorated w/silver iridescent vines of heart-shaped leaves, base inscribed "Quezal N.Y." **3,335**

Vase, 6" h., cushion foot w/a slender stem on the trumpet-form body w/a 'jack-in-the-pulpit' flattened rim, the back side only slightly curved up, green body w/overall iridescent blue exterior, signed on the base. . . **690**

Vase, 7" h., trumpet-form body w/deeply ruffled rim raised on a cushion foot, opalescent decorated w/green & amber iridescent striated feathering & trailings, amber iridescent interior, inscribed "Quezal R 922," ca. 1920 . . . . **1,840**

Vase, 8¼" h., gently flaring cylindrical shouldered body w/a tapering neck & swelled closed mouth, ambergris w/blue iridescence, signed on base (ILLUS. right) . . . **690**

Two Signed Quezal Vases

Vase, 8¾" h., lily-type w/jack-in-the-pulpit upturned rim on a slender stem & cushion foot, stretched overall gold iridescence, signed "Quezal 176" (ILLUS. left) **1,150**

Vase, 9⅞" h., squatty bulbous base tapering to a tall slender trumpet neck w/widely flared rim, overall gold iridescence, signed . . **1,045**

Vase, 11¾" h., baluster-form, a short ringed stem on a round disk foot supporting a bulbous ovoid body tapering to a tall trumpet neck, deep tomato red iridescence decorated w/deep amber iridescent striated feathering bordered in blue iridescence, stem & foot decorated w/amber & caramel iridescent swirls, signed "Quezal," ca. 1920 . . . . **4,887**

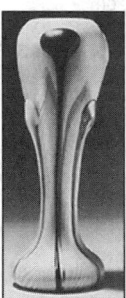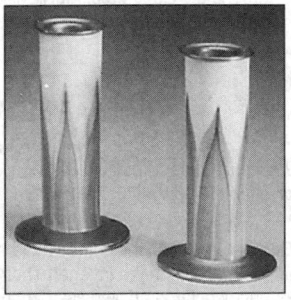

From left: Fine Tall Quezal Vase
Quezal Candlestick-form Vases

Vase, 12" h., slender baluster-form body w/a cushion foot & closed rim, rich opalescent cased over amber decorated w/pulled green leafage reserved against gold, applied w/six large iridescent drips in white, amber & blue, signed (ILLUS.) **6,325**

Vases, 4¾" h., slender opal cylinder on an applied disk foot, green & gold pulled feather design, gold iridescent interiors, each signed on base, accompanied by gold metal candlecup bobeche, pr. (ILLUS.) . . **690**

ROSE BOWLS

These decorative small bowls were widely popular in the late 19th and early 20th centuries. Produced in various types of glass, they are most common in satin glass or spatter glass. They are generally a spherical shape with an incurved crimped rim, but ovoid or egg-shaped examples were also popular. Their name derives from their reported use, to hold dried rose petal potpourri or small fresh-cut roses.

From left: Blue Stevens & Williams Rose Bowl
Herringbone Satin Rose Bowl

Blue, spherical w/six-crimp rim, box pleat style w/zipper bands on ribs, Stevens & Williams' "Jewell" line, etched English registry number on the bottom, 4" h. (ILLUS.) . . . . **$125 to 165**

Cased satin, pink shaded mother-of-pearl Herringbone patt., eight-crimp top, white lining, 4" h. (ILLUS.) . . . . **120 to 170**

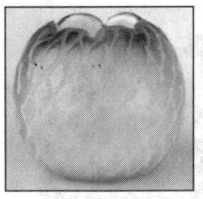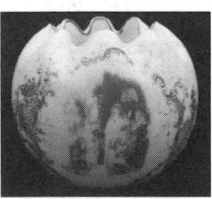

From left: Miniature Mother-of-Pearl Satin Bowl
Custard-colored Decorated Rose Bowl

Cased satin, Rainbow mother-of-pearl Diamond Quilted patt., miniature, six-crimp rin, 2¾" h. (ILLUS.) **600**

Cased satin, shaded blue mother-of-pearl Ribbon patt., irregular ruffled rim, 3" h. **110**

Cased satin, spherical blue mother-of-pearl satin Swirl patt., seven-crimp rim, white lining, 3¼" d., 2¾" h. **265**

Custard-colored, spherical w/eight-crimp rim, creamy ground, enameled w/a group of classical figures in shades of brown, raised scrolls in white w/nutmet staining, 5" h. (ILLUS.) . . . . **175 to 200**

Green, miniature, egg-shaped w/six-crimp rim, dark green decorated around the top w/a wide band of gold w/blue scrolls, gilt scrolls around the lower body, attributed to Moser, ca. 1885, 3" h. (ILLUS.) . . . . . **125 to 175**

 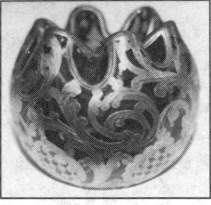

From left: Miniature Green & Gilt Rose Bowl
Rare Miniature Silver-Overlay Bowl

Silver-overlay, miniature, spherical w/six-crimp rim, dark blue overlaid w/elaborate silver scrolls & pierced lattice, probably German, signed "Bailey, Banks & Biddle, Phila.," 2" h. (ILLUS.) .... **200 to 250**

Spangled, heavenly blue Vasa Murrhina overlay, white lining, six-crimp rim, loaded w/mica flakes on the outside, 3⅜" d., 3¾" h. **95**

Spangled, ball-shaped w/six-crimp rim, blue cased in white w/a layer of silver mica flecks, 3⅜" d., 3¾" h. **95**

ROYAL FLEMISH

This ware, made by Mt. Washington Glass Co., is characterized by very heavy enameled gold lines dividing the surface into separate areas or sections. The body, with a matte finish, is variously decorated.

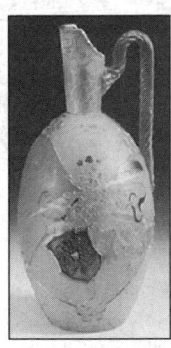 

From left: Rare & Unusual Royal Flemish Ewer
Rose-decorated Royal Flemish Vase

Ewer, slender ovoid body tapering to a slender cylindrical neck w/upright angled spout, high arched applied ropetwist handle, unusual flag staff decoration on segmented stained glass background, w/a fierce rampant lion above the company masthead double eagle emblem shield, 12¼" h. (ILLUS.)......... **$2,990**

Vase, 4½" h., raised rim w/applied angular handles on bulbous transparent colorless glass decorated overall w/gold & silvered metallic coin medallions in quintessential

Royal Flemish motif, raised gold enamel outlines & accents, partial label taped to base................................. **2,645**

Vase, 9½" h., footed ovoid body tapering to a ringed neck & high cupped rim, decorated overall w/trailing enameled roses in shades of pink & green, raised gold enamel outlines on a stylized trellis w/blue spiral accents, marked on base, slight gilt wear, ca. 1894 (ILLUS.) **3,335**

Vase, 13" h., Egyptian scene, classic handled oval body decorated w/gilt enameled panels & medallions centering star-studded scene of camel w/ethnic costumed rider, body guard w/scimitar alongside, Mid-Eastern scrolls & devices at reverse **13,800**

RUBINA CRYSTAL

This glass, sometimes spelled "Rubena," is a flashed ware, shading from ruby to clear. Some pieces are decorated, others are plain.

Bowl, 5¾" d., pressed Hobnail patt. w/upright crimped rim, frosted finish, probably Hobbs, ca. 1890 .... **$35**

Cracker jar, cov., slightly tapering cylindrical optic ribbed body w/enameled floral decoration, silver plate rim, cover & angled bail handle **385**

Salt shaker w/original lid, ring-neck mold **165**

Vase, 6½" h., wide cylindrical form w/an upright ruffled upper half, enameled around the sides w/colorful pansies on green leafy stems, gold rim band, ground pontil, late 19th c....................... **316**

RUBINA VERDE

This decorative glass, popular in the late 19th and early 20th centuries, shades from ruby or deep cranberry to green or greenish-yellow.

Butter dish, cov., the domed mold-blown rubina cover in the Inverted Thumbprint patt. w/a large applied clear knop handle, on a matching clear pressed glass Daisy & Button patt. base, 7" d. **$224**

Celery vase, Inverted Thumbprint patt. **165**

Finger bowl, Inverted Thumbprint patt. **95**

Pitcher, water, bulbous ovoid body w/flaring square mouth, Inverted Thumbprint patt., applied clear twisted & braided collar & handle, rosettes at base of handle, ground pontil........................... **248**

Punch cup, Inverted Thumbprint patt., ... **145**

Punch set: cov. footed punch bowl, ladle & six footed stems; the punch bowl in an optic rib patt. w/a deep ruby cover w/hollow ribbed pale green knop, the wide rounded bowl w/optic ribbing & shading from deep ruby to pale green & raised on a knopped pedestal & round foot, enamel-decorated around the cover & sides w/delicate white & colored floral sprigs, the matching saucer stems on knopped stems w/enamel decoration, Europe, late 19th - early 20th c., bowl 8" h., the set **1,035**

Rubina Verde Vases with Rigaree

Vases, optic-ribbed trumpet-form body w/scalloped rim & flaring cushion foot, applied clear rigaree wrapped around the sides, pr. (ILLUS.) **330**

RUBY-STAINED

This name derives from the color of the glass a deep red. The red staining was thinly painted on clear pressed glass patterns and refired at a low temperature. Many pieces were further engraved as souvenir items and were very popular from the 1890s into the 1920s. This technique should not be confused with "flashed" glass where a clear glass piece is actually dipped in molten glass of a contrasting color. Also see PATTERN GLASS.

Heavy Gothic Ruby-stained Goblet

Creamer, individual, Truncated Cube patt. **$40**
Creamer, Prize patt. **110**
Goblet, Heavy Gothic patt. (ILLUS.) **85**
Relish dish, Box-in-Box patt. **30**

McKee's Majestic Pattern Rose Bowl

Rose bowl, Majestic patt., McKee (ILLUS.) **70**
Spooner, Prize patt. **95**
Syrup pitcher w/original top, Hexagon
  Block patt. **150**

SABINO

Sabino France **SABINO FRANCE**

Sabino Marks

Ernest-Marius Sabino, a French Art Deco glassmaker, began production of art glass in the 1920s. He produced a wide range of items in frosted, colored, opalescent and clear glass in both blown and pressed glass. The Parisian shop closed during World War II and reopened in the 1960s. Earlier works included lamps, vases, figures and other items; after 1960 the production was primarily small birds and nudes. In the 1970s a line of limited edition plates was introduced. Pieces are marked with the name in the mold, an etched signature or both.

Art Deco Sabino Wall Sconce

Figure of a lady, "Nude with Draped Cloak," standing figure w/one arm extended straight out to the side, opalescent vaseline, original paper label reading "Sabino made in France," 7¾" h. **$863**
Figure of Madonna, standing cloaked figure in clear opalescent, signed on the base "Sabino Paris," original paper label "Made in France," 5" h. **201**
Vase, 7" h., Bee patt., footed spherical body w/a small round short neck, opalescent press-molded design of raised

bumblebees clustered on angular honeycomb & floral latticework, engraved mark on base "Sabino Paris" 460

Wall sconces, long arched & gently curved piece in the form of a molded bouquet of flowers on a flared base, metal mounts inscribed "Sabino Paris - Made in France," ca. 1925, 17" w., pr. (ILLUS. of one) 1,380

SATIN

Satin glass was a popular decorative glass developed in the late 19th century. Most pieces were composed of two layers of glass with the exterior layer usually in a shaded pastel color. The name derives from the soft matte finish, caused by exposure to acid fumes, which gave the surface a "satiny" feel. Mother-of-pearl satin glass was a specialized variety wherein air trapped between the layers of glass provided subtle surface patterns such as Herringbone and Diamond Quilted. A majority of satin glass was produced in England, Bohemia and America, but collectors should be aware that reproductions have been produced for many years.

Mother-of-Pearl Satin Creamer

Cologne bottle & stopper, bulbous ovoid body tapering to a small neck w/a sterling silver rim & matching silver mushroom cover, Rainbow mother-of-pearl Diamond Quilted patt., some original gilt sprig decoration, 4⅞" h. $715

Creamer, blue mother-of-pearl Raindrop patt., bulbous base & wide cylindrical neck w/rim spout, applied reeded blue handle, 3⅛" d., 4½" h. (ILLUS.) 195

Pitcher, 5" h., footed wide squatty round body tapering to a short cylindrical neck w/pinched rim spout, frosted clear applied squared handle, Rainbow mother-of-pearl Herringbone patt. 660

Vase, 4¾" h., slightly waisted cylindrical body w/an upright crimped rim, shaded blue to white mother-of-pearl Diamond Quilted patt., overall brightly enameled floral decoration 176

Vase, 4¾" h., 4" d., shaded heavenly blue w/heavy gold floral decoration, red enameled spider web mark on base & capital E for Whitehouse Glass Works, Stourbridge 225

Vase, 6⅞" h., footed spherical bottom below a slender waisted neck w/trumpet rim, applied frosted clear snake wrapped around neck, body shaded orange to white mother-of-pearl Diamond Quilted patt. . . . 143

Vase, 7" h., bulbous teardrop body in deep pink mother-of-pearl Diamond Quilted patt., raised on three applied frosted clear leaf & tab feet, applied around the body w/frosted clear flowering leafy branches, attributed to Webb 275

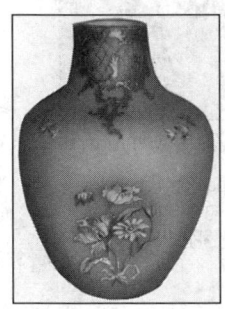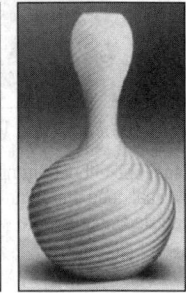

From left: Decorated Blue Satin Vase
Double-Gourd Form Satin Vase

Vase, 7" h., 4½" d., bulbous ovoid body w/dimpled sides, a wide shoulder tapering to a short cylindrical neck, blue decorated around the lower sides w/colorful enameled floral bouquets, the neck w/ornate gilt scroll & lattice decoration, white lining (ILLUS.) 175

Vase, 7⅛" h., double gourd-form w/a spherical base tapering to a slender waist & swelled bulbous neck, shaded light blue mother-of-pearl Swirl patt., yellow interior, attributed to Stevens & Williams (ILLUS.) 316

Vase, 7⅞" h., 6" d., rich blue mother of pearl Raindrop patt., melon sectioned, ruffled top, white lining, frosted top edging, unblemished satin 225

Vase, 8⅛" h. swelled bottom below the wide cylindrical body w/a tricorner flared rim, shaded orange to white mother-of-pearl Swirl patt. 220

Vase, 10" h., double gourd-form, large ovoid bottom tapering to a slender mid-section below the swelled ovoid neck, shaded butterscotch mother-of-pearl Diamond Quilted patt. 182

Vase, 10" h., spherical body below a tall slender 'stick' neck, shaded blue to white mother-of-pearl Diamond Quilted patt. 176

Vase, 7½" h., 3½" d., shaded blue ruffled, enameled cream & blue flowers, grey & white branches, rust colored butterfly, frosted applied three handles on each side, white inside **135**

SILVER DEPOSIT - SILVER OVERLAY

Silver Deposit and Silver Overlay have been made commercially since the last quarter of the 19th century. Silver is deposited on the glass by various means, most commonly by utilizing an electric current. The glass was very popular during the first three decades of this century, and some pieces are still being produced. During the late 1970s, silver commanded exceptionally high prices and this was reflected in a surge of interest in silver overlay glass, especially in pieces marked "Sterling" or "925" on the heavy silver overlay.

Silver Overlaid Round Box

Box, cov., black amethyst, low rounded body w/three interior compartments, the low domed cover w/repeating silver foliate & line designs, silver rim bands on base, fleur-de-lis finial on cover, 7" d., 4½" h. (ILLUS.)...................... **$230**

Perfume bottle w/stopper, squatty spherical teal green body centered by a short, small cylindrical neck w/flattened rim, large mushroom stopper, decorated around the upper body & the stopper w/scrolling flower vines stamped "Sterling," 5½" h. (stopper missing small piece of silver) **345**

Vase, 3 5/8" h., simple shouldered ovoid body w/a short wide flared neck, mold-blown green iridized exterior w/overlaid scroll & floral silver decoration impressed "L Sterling," early 20th c. (design worn, crude).............................. **633**

Vase, 3¾" h., ovoid body tapering to a short flared neck surrounded by four applied teardrop prunts down the sides, iridescent green w/the upper half decorated by silver floral design stamped "patented 3419 - 999/1000 fine" & hallmarked, late 19th c. **633**

Vase, 4¾" h., baluster-form w/ornate silver overlay on a deep rose satin body, late 19th - early 20th c. **546**

Vase, 8¾" h., wide tapering ovoid body w/a wide rounded shoulder centered by a cylindrical neck w/flared rim, amber iridized form overlaid on the front w/pendent berry & leaf silver decoration, leaf impressed "L Sterling," Austria, early 20th c............................. **1,380**

Vase, 10" h., slender baluster-form body in emerald green w/relief-blown oval sections through the ornate pierced sterling silver lattice design of lilies, leaves & vines, silver marked "G3223 - 925 fine" **825**

Vase, 14" h., rose water sprinkler-form, a squatty bulbous base centered by a tall serpentine neck w/a pointed lip, cobalt blue w/silver iridescent butterfly decoration enhance by elaborate overall silver overlay in scrolling foliate designs, apparently unsigned, recessed polished pontil, attributed to Loetz, Austria, early 20th c. (minor damage) **2,415**

SMITH BROTHERS

Smith Brothers Mark

Originally established as a decorating department of the Mt. Washington Glass Company in the 1870s, the firm later was an independent business in New Bedford, Massachusetts. Beautifully decorated opal white glass was their hallmark but they also did glass cutting. Some examples carry their lion-in-the-shield mark.

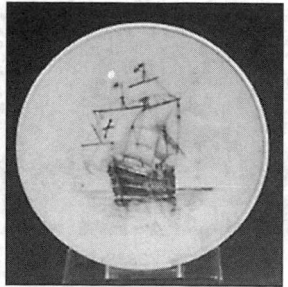

Smith Brothers Santa Maria Plate

Creamer & cov. sugar bowl, each w/a melon-lobed body in white satin decorated w/yellow-centered white daisy-like blossoms & green leaves, each mounted w/ornate silver plate rims w/spout & handle on creamer & lady's profile bust-decorated cover & a bail handle on the sugar, blanks by Mount Washington, 4" h., pr. **$431**

Plate, 8" d., commemorative, satiny white ground decorated the ship Santa Maria, presumably commissioned by Libbey for the Chicago Columbian Exhibition of 1893, ship portrait signed "Copyrighted by A.E. Smith" (ILLUS.) **460**

From left: Smith Brothers Ring-style Vase
Ornately Decorated Smith Bros. Vase

Vase, 6" h., 2½" d., ring-type, cylindrical w/raised rings in white, pink ground enameled in color w/a stork standing among reeds, late 19th c. (ILLUS.) **150**

Vase, 8½" h., wide ovoid double-bulbed lobed body, the bulbous gilt neck molded w/stylized florals, the body h.p. w/chrysanthemum blooms & leaves on a cream & green ground, Smith Brothers trademark on base, late 19th c. (ILLUS.) . . . **1,150**

Smith Bros. Vases with Birds

Vases, 4¼" h., 2¼" d., plain cylindrical body in white enamel-decorated in color w/a white & brown bird on a twig w/red berries & blue & green leaves, late 19th c., pr. (ILLUS.) . . . . **150 to 200**

STEUBEN

Steuben Marks

Most of the Steuben glass listed below was made at the Steuben Glass Works, now a division of Corning Glass, between 1903 and about 1933. The factory was organized by T.G. Hawkes, noted glass designer, Frederick Carder, and others. Mr. Carder devised many types of glass and revived many old techniques.

ACID CUT-BACK

Rare Acid Cut-Back Art Deco Vase

Vase, 7" h., Matsu patt., acid-etched sphere w/Ming trees & stylized clouds, shape No. 6078. . . . . **$690**

Vase, 12" h., tall gently flaring cylindrical body w/a narrow angled shoulder centering the short, wide cylindrical neck, speckled pastel green Cintra in clear & white ground overlaid in Rose & acid-etched twice to shade stylized blossoms & vertical geometric bars, shape No. 3279 (four chips on high blossom petals) . . . **3,450**

Vase, 12" h., 11½" d., bulbous ovoid body w/a deep shoulder to the short flaring neck, double-etched, Mirror Black on Alabaster etched in the Shelton foliate Art Deco patt., shape No. 2683 (ILLUS.) **6,900**

ALABASTER

Centerpiece figure, figure of Kuan Yin, Buddhist goddess depicted in matching two-tier flower arranger, shape No. 6637, 9" h. **439**

Compotes, 7" d., 3" h., open, wide shallow bowl w/Alabaster exterior raised on an applied slender Alabaster stem & round foot, bowl interior lined w/Green Jade, shape No. 3234, pr. (slight variation in color). **489**

Lamp base, squatty bulbous base below a tall slender waisted neck in the white acid-etched glass body, overall design in the Grape patt., mounted on a silvered metal base, shape No. 8006, ca. 1925, glass 14" h. **1,150**

AURENE

Grouping of Steuben Aurene Pieces

Basket, tall waisted cylindrical form w/widely flaring ruffled rim joined w/a high arched applied handle, overall strong blue iridescence, coiled prunts at tips of handles, shape No. 5069, 7" h. (interior staining). **863**

Bowl, 8" d., 4" h., gently flaring deep rounded sides w/a closed rim, overall gold iridescence, signed "Aurene #2687". **440**

Bowl, 12" d., 2¼" h., planter-form w/inward curved rim, reddish gold iridescent surface & interior, polished base inscribed "aurene 2879," shape No. 2879 (wear scratches on base). **403**

Candlestick, disk foot below slender stem w/a swelled twist at the top below the tall cupped socket w/a flattened flared rim, fine overall blue iridescene, shape No. 686, 8¼" h. (ILLUS. far right). **633**

Center Bowl, round w/a wide flattened flanged rim w/eight pointed scallops, amber w/overall blue iridescence, shape No. 158 (?), signed, 10" d., 3" h. (ILLUS. center) **1,035**

Finger bowl & underplate, cylindrical low bowl w/crimped & ruffled flared rim, w/matching underplate, overall gold iridescence, shape No. 171, signed, 5" & 6¼" d., pr. (ILLUS. front left). **690**

Goblets, flared bell-form bowl on stem w/applied twist on disk foot, overall gold Aurene iridescence, signed "Aurene 2361," 6" h., set of 8 . . . . **1,840**

Jar, cov., wide squatty bulbous body, the wide shoulder centered by a flattened domed cover, overall dark blue iridescence w/silver, blue & purple highlights, signed "Aurene #1616," 5" d., 3½" h. **825**

Perfume atomizer, flaring base tapering sharply to a tall slender cylindrical body fitted w/gilt-metal attachment without the bulb, DeVilbiss, some interior stain, surface wear, shape No. 6407, 7½" h. (ILLUS. back right) **345**

Perfume bottle w/stopper, squatty bulbous melon-lobed base tapering ton a short cylindrical neck w/a flattened rim, ball-top bulbous stopper, overall gold iridescence, shape No. 1455, signed on polished pontil, ca. 1910, 6¾" h. (possibly replaced stopper) **633**

Sherbet set: dished underplate w/wide flanged rim & stemmed dish w/bell-form bowl; twelve-ribbed underplate, overall strong purplish blue iridescence, shape No. 2680, each piece signed, 4" & 6¼" d., the set (ILLUS. front right) **518**

Tumbler, cylindrical w/slightly flaring rim, overall gold w/brilliant iridescence, signed "Steuben #2361," 4½" h. **132**

Vase, 4¼" h., millefiore-type, wide ovoid form w/the rounded shoulder centering a small cylindrical neck, ribbed green Aurene cased in white, the exterior decorated w/gold Aurene leaf & vine design & six gold-centered white millefiore "blossoms," inscribed on base "Aurene 550". **4,888**

Vase, 5" h., classic flared ten rib oval body w/fine smooth blue-purple iridescent lustre, mirror bright near base, inscribed "Steuben". **1,093**

Vase, 5" h., footed squatty bulbous ten-ribbed base continuing to widely flaring sides w/a ruffled rim, overall blue iridescence, shape No. 2631, signed on base (ILLUS. back left). **1,093**

Vase, 6¼" h., "tree-trunk" form, three staggered thorny cylindrical holders on a round foot, deep amber w/a golden crimson iridescence, inscribed "STEUBEN Aurene 2744," ca. 1910-20 . . . . . . **862**

Vase, 8" h., ruffled trumpet-form w/strong golden iridescence stretched at rim, inscribed on base "Steuben Aurene 723," shape No. 723 . . . . **748**

Vase, 8⅜" h., jack-in-the-pulpit-form, iridescent amber glass decorated w/pulled silvery-blue feathering, inscribed "Aurene 751," model no. 751, ca. 1910. . . . . . **4,312**

Vase, 9½" h., 'stick'-type, a thin disk foot & a tall slender cylindrical shaft, fine overall blue iridescence, shape No. 2556, signed on pontil (ILLUS. far left) **374**

Vase, 10" h., tall gently swelled cylindrical body w/a narrow angled shoulder & short cylindrical neck w/flared rim, blossom, heart & vine decorated in gold Aurene on an iridescent green body cased in white, shape No. 506, style D, signed "Aurene 506". **5,175**

Vase, 12" h., 11" d., large wide ovoid shouldered form w/a short flaring neck, gold w/yellow, rose & platinum iridescent highlights, incised signature **1,650**

CALCITE

Bowl, 2" h., round w/Calcite exterior & flared & scalloped rim, interior lined in gold Aurene . . **173**

Ceiling light, a round bowl-form fixture w/deep flattened sides & a domed bottom, etched w/a classical foliate design radiating from the center, three sockets & three attached metal hanging hooks, 15¾" d. **690**

Vase, 8¼" h., gold Aurene on Calcite lily form, six scallop rim on trumpet-form w/iridized white calcite exterior, gold within, shape No. 346. . . . . **575**

CELESTE BLUE

Celeste Blue Candlesticks & Bowl

Candlesticks, flaring foot supporting a slender baluster-form stem below a knop & petal-form bobeche & tall cupped sockets, ca. 1920-33, 11½" h., set of 4 (ILLUS. of two, left) **2,300**

Center bowl, applied flared & optic-ribbed low foot supporting a wide swirled optic-ribbed bowl w/rolled rim, polished pontil, shape No. 112, ca. 1925, 16¼" d., 4¼" h. (ILLUS. right) **403**

Finger bowls & underplates, deep cylindrical bowl w/flared flattened rim, molded optic ribbed design on bowls & matching dished underplates, variation of shape No. 2889, ca. 1925, bowl 5" d., underplate 6½" d., eleven bowls & twelve underplates, the set (one bowl chipped) **518**

Plates, 8½" d., luncheon, wide flat border engraved w/a band of leaves & dots, variant of the Kensington patt., set of 12 (one plate chipped). **546**

Stemware, footed, tall flaring bowls w/light optic ribbing on applied round foot, shape No. 5192, eight juice glasses 4½" h., seven iced tea glasses 6¼" h., the set **575**

Vase, 7" h., wide urn-form body w/narrow shoulder to the wide flaring neck, on a small disk foot, optic-ribbed design, recessed polished pontil signed "Steuben" w/fleur-de-lis mark **316**

Vase, 8¼" h., fan-shaped, internal air bubbles & applied glass threading near the rim, on a knopped stem & round foot, unsigned, ca. 1925 . . . . **345**

CLUTHRA

Large Rose Pink Cluthra Vase

Lamp base, large spherical glass body w/flared foot & rim set in an gilt-metal scrolled Oriental-size base & w/top electric fittings, the body in creamy white acid-etched to depict Art Deco-style flowers in a variant of the Moderne patt., ca. 1925, glass 12½" h. **2,070**

Vase, 6¼" h., wide ovoid shouldered body w/a short wide flaring neck, mottled royal blue & white w/small trapped bubbles, polished pontil w/fleur-de-lis mark & "Steuben". **1,035**

Vase, 10½" h., wide bulbous ovoid body tapering to a short wide rolled neck, creamy white & clear w/overall swirled & bubbled effect, shape No. 2683 . . . . **920**

Vase, 10½" h., wide bulbous ovoid body tapering to a short wide rolled neck, rose, white & clear w/overall swirled & bubbled effect, shape No. 2683, slightly irregular rim (ILLUS.) **1,380**

GROTESQUE

Bowl, 6¾" h., three lined pillar-molded form, rounded base w/the high widely flaring clear sides pulled into four points, variation of shape No. 7534 . . . . **230**

Vase, 5½" h., 10" w., deep rounded form w/widely flaring upright randomly ruffled sides w/molded ribs, Ivrene (minor interior stain). **345**

Blue Jade Grotesque Vase

Vase, 6½" h., 6¼ x 12½", deep flaring oblong pillar-ribbed form w/deeply pulled & ruffled sides, dark Blue Jade, signed on pontil (ILLUS.) **3,335**

JADE

Yellow Jade Sculptured Lamp Base

Lamp base, a slender ovoid Green Jade shape w/a bulbed slender neck w/flattened & ruffled rim issuing the electric socket shaft, the glass body applied w/Mirror Black double loop thin side handles, raised on a slender leaftip & beaded ring gilt-metal shaped w/a tall flared leaf cluster on a ringed & beaded round foot w/small ball feet, fittings attributed to Crest Lamp Co., glass 9½" h.. . . . **460**

Lamp base, large ovoid body w/a wide, short cylindrical neck, Plum Jade acid-etched overall in the intricate Belgrade patt., mounted on a high gilt-metal stepped & pierced base w/small bun feet & further fittings at the neck, Shape No. 7001, fittings possibly by Crest Lamp Co., ca. 1925, glass 12" h. (rim chips beneath mountings). **2,415**

Lamp base, upright rectangular Yellow Jade body w/a sculpted leafy blossom stem design, mounted on a footed silvered metal base & harp lamp fittings, shape No. 6199, glass 6" h. (ILLUS.) **518**

Plates, 8½" d., Green Jade, signed, set of 4 . . . . **230**

Sherbet set: serving dish & underplate; each in light Blue Jade, the dish w/a Flint White stemmed base, underplate 6" d., dish 4" d., 3¾" h., the set **575**

Vase, 6" h., footed slender baluster-form, the body in light Blue Jade w/two applied Venetian-style twisted Flint White ring handles, Flint White disk foot, shape No. 2987 (tiny annealing crack in each handle) . . . **403**

Vase, 6" h., upright rectangular form in Yellow Jade, acid-etched bold scroll leaf sprig design, possibly made as a lamp shaft, shape No. 6199 . . . . **805**

Vase, 6¼" h., bulbous ovoid form w/a wide rounded shoulder to a short widely rolled neck, Green Jade, shape No. 2683 . . . . **805**

Vase, 7" h., 8" d., large spherical body w/a closed rim, Green Jade acid-etched overall w/a bold design of chrysanthemum blossoms & leafs, shape No. 6078 . . . . **1,265**

Vase, 10½" h., upright rectangular Green Jade form acid-etched overall w/a large chrysanthemum & leafy stem design, shape No. 6199 . . . . **1,093**

ORIENTAL POPPY

Oriental Poppy Goblet

Goblet, tall bell-form bowl w/optic ribbing in fine opalescent pink, raised on an applied slender Pomona green stem & foot, 8¼" h. (ILLUS.). **489**

Goblets, deep flaring bell-form bowls w/a swirled optic ribbed design in pink opal, raised on a slender opal stem & foot, 5¾" h., pr.. . . . . **575**

Lamp base, the glass shaft of ovoid form tapering to a compressed bulb at the base of the flaring ruffled trumpet neck in rib-molded satin pink-opal, mounted in a gilt-metal decorative ring support on three slender legs w/hoof feet on a tripartite classical foot, complete w/lamp mounts, glass Shape No. 8490, glass 7" h., overall 10¾" h.. . . . . **575**

Vase, 6" h., ovoid body tapering to a short widely flaring neck, pink w/sixteen integrated opal stripes, satin finish, shape No. 650 (two potstone blemishes at side, small chip at rim) **690**

THREADED

Compote, 7" d., 7" h., open shallow flaring colorless bowl decorated w/a band of red threading, raised on a slender baluster-form stem & round foot, shape No. 6886, base marked, ca. 1925. . . . . **316**

Goblets, colored diamond-molded bowls w/Pomona blue threading on an applied Bristol Yellow foot, each stamped "Steuben," 5¾" h., set of 3 . . . . **201**

Plates, 8½" d., luncheon, round colorless crystal w/applied Pomona Green concentric threads around the exterior rim, set of 6. . . . . **230**

VERRE DE SOIE

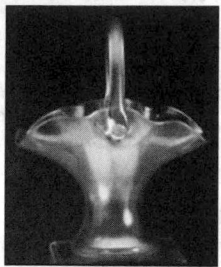

Verre de Soie Basket

Basket, tall waisted cylindrical body w/a widely flaring ruffled rim, applied high arched handle w/a berry prunt at each end, iridized silky finish, shape No. 5069, 10¾" h. (ILLUS.). **920**

Basket, tall waisted cylindrical body w/a widely flaring ruffled rim, applied high arched handle w/a berry prunt at each end, iridized silky finish, shape No. 5069, 14¼" h. **805**

Center bowl, wide flattened bottom on three applied prunt feet, the shallow sides incurved, shape No. 2586 or 3198, 12" d., 2¾" h. **230**

MISCELLANEOUS WARES

Bowls, 7½" d., crystal, deep rounded center w/a wide flattened flanged rim, incised "S" on base, set of 12 (one w/rim chip) **546**

Center bowl, crystal w/a pale rosa pink folded rim, round shallow rib-molded center surrounded by a wide matching flattened rim engraved w/elaborate florals, webbing & scrolled decoration, shape No. 3579, fleur-de-lis mark, 16" d. (some wear scratches). **345**

Cocktail set: six matching handled cups, fleur-de-lis on jug base; colorless crystal w/applied mirror black threads, stopper, jug monogrammed "H.W.N.," shape No. 7056, 9½" h., the set **403**

Goblet, exhibition-type, "Lust," crystal, first in "The Seven Sins" series, engraved w/a woman watched by a man from behind a tree, designed by Sidney Waugh, Shape No. 8212, inscribed on base "Steuben," 7½" h. **1,380**

Model of a fish, crystal, stylized version of an angel fish, design by Frederick Carder & Sidney Waugh, both bases inscribed "Steuben," 10½" h. (minor chips near one base) **1,495**

Model of horse, stylized version of Clydesdale-type horse, rare form from 1930s, base inscribed "Steuben," shape No. 7727, p. 282, designed by Sidney Waugh, 9¾" l., 7" h., ... **1,035**

Model of koala, positioned as pictured in 1976, base inscribed "Steuben," shape No. 8268, designed by Lloyd Atkins, 5¾" h. **1,093**

Models of gazelles or book ends, leaping Art Deco figures raised upon molded rectangular plinth in stylized curvilinear, bases inscribed "Steuben," shape No. 7399, designed by Frederick Carder & Sidney Waugh, 7½" l., 6½" h., pr. **1,438**

Tableware: six 7"d. plates, six stemmed water goblets & six champagnes; crystal, Art Deco style, designed by Bolas Mankowski, w/engraved moon & star motif, bases inscribed "S" or "Steuben," ca. 1934 . . . . **633**

Vase, 7⅜" h., "Wing"-style, colorless crystal w/tall trumpet-form bowl flanked near the bottomm w/small applied clear 'wings' up the sides, raised on a thick tapering cylindrical solid foot, signed, No. SP919, ca. 1957 . . . . **316**

Vase, 12½" h., Paul Revere patt., rare intricately engraved "W138," exhibition piece to commemorate the historic ride in three signettes: Revere standing by his horse, lantern in North Church tower, British soldiers w/bayonet rifles, base inscribed "Steuben," designed by Sidney Waugh, case not available **3,450**

Wines, crystal, the bowls raised on wide angular teardrop stems, designed by Sidney Waugh, shape No. 7737, w/grey fitted Steuben box, 7¼" h., set of 11 . . . . **633**

TIFFANY

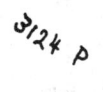 

Various Tiffany Marks

This glassware, covering a wide diversity of types, was produced in glasshouses operated by Louis Comfort Tiffany, America's outstanding glass designer of the Art Nouveau period, from the last quarter of the 19th century until the early 1930s. Tiffany revived early techniques and devised many new ones.

Bowl, 6" d., bi-color, gold-spotted opal w/emerald green & blue border rim & three applied reeded shell feet, button pontil inscribed "L.C. Tiffany - Favrile" **$920**

Bowl, 6¼" d., 2" h., flat bottom w/low cylindrical sides & a widely flaring flattened rim, dark blue 'stretch' border shading to an opalescent optic ribbed interior, signed "L.C. Tiffany, Inc., Favrile #1753" **500**

Candlesticks, mushroom-shaped candle cups of bright iridized pinkish rose above an opal disc stem & conforming foot, inscribed "L.C.T. Favrile 1846," 3½" h., pr. . . **1,610**

Center bowl, ribbed rounded bowl w/wide everted rim, amber w/pink iridescence, signed "L.C. Tiffany - Favrile - 1925," 11½" d. **1,380**

Compote, open, 5¼" d., 4½" h., open, the wide oval bowl w/a five-ruffled rim on white opal decorated w/five green pulled-feathers, gold iridized interior w/stretched rim effect, iridized gold disk foot, inscribed "L.C. Tiffany - Favrile 590E" **1,495**

Cordials, ovoid small body w/a wide flared rim, four pinched-in sides, overall golden iridescence w/amethyst hues, each signed & numbered, 2" h., set of 4 . . . . **660**

Finger bowl & undertray, the squatty wide bowl tapering toward the base & w/a widely flaring flat rim, yellowish amber exterior cased to an opalescent interior in both bowl & tray, each w/a ring of threaded & pulled prunt decoration, undertray w/stretched rim effect, bowl inscribed "L.C.T. B2990," tray inscribed "L.C.T. N9710," tray 7" d., bowl 4" d., the set **1,093**

Flower frogs, cylindrical w/ribbed central section between the two rows of eight loop stem holders, overall gold iridescence, signed, 3" h., pr. **460**

Salt dip, squatty bulbous lightly ribbed body on four small peg feet, wide waisted flaring scalloped rim, overall bluish gold iridescence, signed "L.C.T.," 2⅛" d., 1¼" h. . . **385**

Vase, 2¾" h., 3½" d., spherical form w/short flared rim, overall gold iridescence decorated w/trailing vines w/green heart leaves, inscribed "L.C. Tiffany - Favrile 9044 N1036" **1,035**

Vase, 4½" h., classical urn-form w/wide flat shoulder centering a small flaring cylindrical neck, applied scrolling "shell" shoulder handles, tapering to disk foot, overall golden iridescence w/an intaglio leafy swag design around the middle of the body, inscribed "L. C. Tiffany - Favrile 9719G". **1,840**

Vase, 4¾" h., floriform, a domed ribbed dark greenish amber foot below the swelled slender ovoid body tapering to a flattened mouth, tall green & gold pulled feather designs on an opal ground w/overall iridescence (ILLUS.) **2,464**

From left: Tiffany Floriform Vase
Tiffany Golden Damascene Vase

Vase, 5¼" h., wide swelled ribbed cylindrical lower body w/a wide tapering shoulder w/a short neck & cupped rim, amber w/opalescent vertical stripes & pink & purple iridescent serpentine trailings, inscribed "L.C.T. - 10412" **1,495**

Vase, 5¾" h., "Cypriote," squatty wide bulbous base below a tapering swelled shoulder & small flat mouth, opaque green decorated w/an abstract petal & vine decoration in yellowish gold & red iridescence, remnants of Tiffany Favrile Glass and Decoration paper label, inscribed "M7155," ca. 1902 . . . . **3,737**

Vase, 7" h., bulbous ovoid body tapering to a small flattened rim, black sand-finished ground w/six iridescent gold pulled leaves from the top down, inscribed around prominent pontil button "L.C. Tiffany Favrile 0559" (small bubble in surface) **7,475**

Vase, 8" h., bud-type, tall slender waisted cylindrical form w/widely flaring base, cased opalescent & green w/gold iridescent feather decoration around the foot, signed "L.C. Tiffany - 6817K," ca. 1916. . . . . **1,265**

Vase, 11" h., squatty compressed lower body w/sharply angled shoulder tapering to a tall slender cylindrical neck, opalescent decorated w/pulled feathering in pale yellow & green highlighted w/silvery blue iridescence, inscribed "L.C.T. M7123," ca. 1904 . . . . **2,070**

Vase, 12½" h., flared foot tapering to a tall slender cylindrical body w/a widely flaring ruffled rim, amber w/overall golden iridized Damascene decoration, base inscribed "L.C. Tiffany - Favrile - 329-8242G" (ILLUS.) **1,725**

Vase, 14½" h., floriform on a shaped stem applied to a ribbed, domed foot, amber iridescent, inscribed "L.C.T. Favrile" **1,495**

Vase, 16" h., trumpet-form, tall trumpet on a bulbed stem & domed ribbed foot, amber w/the upper section decorated w/heart &

vine bands in green iridescence on a gold iridescent ground, inscribed "L.C. Tiffany - Favrile 9481K". **6,900**

Wines, bell-shaped bowl raised on a knopped stem & spreading round foot, overall gold iridescence, signed, set of 11 . . **4,025**

TIFFIN

A wide variety of fine glasswares were produced by the Tiffin Glass Company of Tiffin, Ohio. Beginning as a part of the large U.S. Glass Company early in this century, the Tiffin factory continued making a wide range of wares until its final closing in 1984. One popular line is now called "Black Satin" and included various vases with raised floral designs. Many other acid-etched and hand-cut patterns were also produced over the years and are very collectible today. The three "Tiffin Glassmasters" books by Fred Bickenheuser, are the standard references for Tiffin collectors.

Basket, favor-type, No. 310, blue satin **$40**
Basket, favor-type, No. 310, canary. **32**
Basket, favor-type, No. 310, emerald green. **25**
Basket, favor-type, No. 310, rose pink **30**
Basket, Black Satin, No. 9574, 6" h. **85**
Basket, flower, cut Empress patt., No. 6553, green, 13" h. **400**
Candlesticks, double, etched Fuchsia patt., ball center, clear, pr. **150**
Candlesticks, double, etched June Night patt., No. 17392, clear, pr. **80**
Champagne, etched Cherokee Rose patt., No. 15018, clear. **27**
Champagne, etched Cordelia patt. No. 17328, clear **12**
Champagne, etched Empire patt., No. 15018, pink **21**
Champagne, etched Flanders patt., clear **15**
Champagne, etched Flanders patt., No. 15018, yellow. **22**
Champagne, etched Flanders patt., yellow **21**
Champagne, etched June Night patt., clear. **15**
Champagne, etched Persian Pheasant patt., clear. **18**
Claret, etched Bridal patt., No. 15073, green **25**
Claret, etched Empire patt., No. 15018, pink, 4 oz. **45**
Claret, etched Flanders patt., yellow **65**
Claret, etched Persian Pheasant patt., clear **48**
Cocktail, etched Byzantine patt., clear. **15**
Cocktail, etched Byzantine patt., No. 15037, clear **20**
Cocktail, etched Byzantine patt., No. 15048, yellow **15**
Cocktail, etched Cherokee Rose patt., No. 15018, clear. **18**

Cocktail, etched Cordelia patt., No. 17328, clear **12**
Cocktail, etched Flanders patt., No. 15024, pink, 4¾" h. **45**
Cocktail, etched June Night patt., clear, 3½ oz. . . . **16**
Cocktail, etched Persian Pheasant patt., clear **18**
Cocktail, etched Persian Pheasant patt., No. 17358, clear, 4½ oz. **39**
Console bowl, 13" d., rolled edge, etched Flanders patt., pink. **270**
Cordial, Classic (platinum) patt., clear **50**
Cordial, cut Mystic patt., clear **25**
Cordial, etched Cadena patt., yellow **80**
Cordial, etched Cherokee Rose patt., No. 17399, clear. **48**
Cordial, etched Cherokee Rose patt., No. 17403, clear, 1 oz. **55**
Cordial, etched Classic patt., No. 14185, clear . . . **69**
Cordial, etched Flanders patt., pink, 5 1/16" h. . . . **150**
Cordial, etched Persian Pheasant patt., clear **46**
Cornucopia, Twilight cutting, clear. **125**
Creamer, etched Cherokee Rose patt, No. 17399, clear. **22**
Creamer, etched Flanders patt., flat, pink **230**
Creamer & sugar bowl, etched Fuchsia patt., No. 5902, clear, pr. **56**
Creamer & sugar bowl, etched Rosalind patt., No. 5831, mandarin, pr. **110**
Cup & saucer, etched Flanders patt., pink, pr. . . . **120**
Cup & saucer, etched Flanders patt., yellow, pr. **100**
Decanter w/original stopper, Classic (platinum) patt., clear **550**
Decanter w/original stopper, etched Byzantine patt., No. 185, yellow. **600**
Decanter w/original stopper, etched Cadena patt., No. 185, yellow **795**
Decanter w/original stopper, etched Cadena patt., squatty, yellow **373**
Decanter w/original stopper, etched Classic patt., No. 14179, clear, 30 oz. **375**
Decanter w/original stopper, etched Dolores patt., No. 14179, clear, 1 qt. **133**
Decanter w/original stopper, etched Flanders patt., pink w/tall clear stopper **500**
Decanter w/original stopper, etched Flanders patt., round, tall, pink (foot repaired) **450**
Decanter w/original stopper, etched Flanders patt., squatty, yellow **600**
Decanter w/original stopper, etched Thistle patt., No. 17179, clear **160**
Dinner bell, etched June Night patt., No. 1508, clear, (clapper replaced) **75**
Goblet, etched Cadena patt., footed, No. 15065, clear, 5¼" h. **21**
Goblet, etched Classic patt., No. 14185, clear. . . . **33**
Goblet, water, cut Mystic patt., clear **28**

Goblet, water, etched Cherokee Rose,
No. 17403, clear, 9 oz.................... 30

Goblet, water, etched Cherokee Rose patt.,
No. 17403, clear......................... 35

Goblet, water, etched Cordelia patt.,
No. 15048, clear......................... 22

Goblet, water, etched Cordelia patt.,
No. 17328, clear......................... 18

Goblet, water, etched Flanders patt., pink 75

Goblet, water, etched Fuchsia patt.,
No. 15083, clear, 7½" h.................. 27

Goblet, water, etched June Night patt.,
No. 17392, clear......................... 20

Goblet, water, etched Rosalind patt.,
No. 15042, yellow........................ 22

Goblet, water, etched Thistle patt., clear 22

Goblet, water, gold-encrusted Minton patt.,
clear 24

Goblet, water, Wistaria patt., clear 27

Lamp, figural Santa Claus in brick chimney,
ca. 1924-29 2,000

Model of a cat, milk glass & black w/satin
finish.................................. 350

Model of a pheasant, female, head down,
No. 6042, blue, 7½" h., 16" l. 450

Parfait, cut Mystic patt., clear 27

Parfait, etched Classic patt., No. 14185, clear 69

Parfait, etched Rosalind patt., No. 15042, yellow.. 32

Parfait, etched June Night patt., No. 17392,
clear, 4½ oz............................. 28

Pitcher, Classic (platinum) patt., flat, clear...... 225

Pitcher, cov., footed, etched Flanders patt.,
pink, 64 oz. 573

Pitcher, footed, Double Columbine patt., cut
No. 405 design, No. 194, clear w/amber trim.. 170

Pitcher, footed, etched Cadena patt.,
No. 194, clear (no lid)................... 225

Pitcher, footed, etched Rosalind patt.,
No. 128, mandarin 390

Pitcher, milk, Twilight cutting, clear 225

Plate, 6½" d., handled, etched Fuchsia patt.,
No. 5831, clear......................... 23

Plate, 6½" d., handled, etched Cordelia
patt., No. 5831, yellow 22

Plate, 7½" d., Alhambra patt., No. 5831, yellow ... 12

Plate, 7½" d., etched Cadena patt.,
No. 5831, clear.......................... 9

Plate, 7½" d., etched Byzantine patt., yellow 15

Plate, salad, 8" d., etched cherokee Rose
patt., clear............................. 13

Relish, three-part, etched Cherokee Rose
patt., No. 5902, clear, 6½" 35

Rose bowl, footed, Twilight cutting, clear....... 175

Sherbet, etched Byzantine patt., low, clear 12

Sherbet, etched Cadena patt., clear............ 23

Sherbet, etched Cadena patt., low, yellow....... 15

Sherbet, etched Cordelia patt., clear, 3¾" h....... 8

Sherbet, etched Cordelia patt., No. 15048, clear .. 15

Sherbet, etched Flanders patt., low, pink........ 12

Sherbet, etched Fuchsia patt., No. 15083, clear .. 13

Sherbet, pressed King's Crown patt., blue....... 10

Sherbet, Wistaria patt., clear 18

Torchere lamp, No. 16265, clear satin
w/black metal base, bright black glass lid,
13¾" h................................ 390

Tray, center-handled, etched Flanders patt.,
clear 300

Tumbler, flat, etched Rambling Rose patt.,
clear 13

Tumbler, footed, etched Cordelia patt.,
No. 17328, clear, 10 oz. 15

Tumbler, iced tea, etched Cherokee rose
patt., No. 17403, clear 35

Tumbler, iced tea, etched Flanders patt., pink.... 70

Tumbler, juice, footed, etched Byzantine
patt., clear............................. 17

Tumbler, juice, footed, etched Fuchsia patt.,
No. 15083, clear........................ 19

Tumbler, juice, Twilight, No. 17524, clear 34

Tumbler, whiskey, footed, etched Classic
patt., No. 14185, clear, 2 oz. 75

Tumbler, footed, etched Fuchsia patt.,
No. 15083, clear, 6 5/16" h., 12 oz. 32

Tumbler, etched Classic patt., flat, clear, 8 oz. 44

Vase, 5" h., etched Poppy patt., No. 16256, pink .. 55

Vase, 8" h., No. 17430, Wistaria (light pink) 200

Vase, bud, 6" h., etched Cherokee Rose
patt., No. 14185, clear 38

Vase, bud, 8¼" h., etched Fuchsia patt., clear 30

Vase, 8½" h., Poppy patt., black............... 95

Vase, bud, 10½" h., Classic (platinum) patt.,
clear 65

Vase, bud, 11" h., etched Cherokee Rose
patt., No. 17399, beaded, clear 46

Vase, bud, 11" h., etched Rosalind patt.,
yellow w/gold rim 78

Wine, etched Cadena patt., yellow............. 35

Wine, etched Flanders patt., clear 29

Wine, etched Flanders patt., yellow 39

Wine, etched Fuchsia patt., No. 15083,
clear, 5 1/16" h. 1,465

Wine, etched Thistle patt., clear 17

Wine, Pink Rain patt., No. 17477, Wistaria
(light pink)............................. 30

Wine, Twilight cutting, No. 175247, clear 36

VENETIAN

*Venetian glass has been made for six
centuries on the island of Murano, where it
continues to be produced. The skilled glass
artisans developed numerous techniques,
subsequently imitated elsewhere.*

Bowl, 9" d., 3½" h., "inciso," round slightly
irregular thick-walled sharply tapering
body in clear, the interior in brilliant

Heavy Barbini "Inciso" Bowl

reddish orange, the exterior finely carved w/"inciso," unsigned, designed by Alfredo Barbini, ca. 1960 (ILLUS.) **$1,840**

Bowl, 9" d., 3½" h., "inciso," round slightly irregular thick-walled sharply tapering body in clear, the interior in brilliant reddish orange, the exterior finely carved w/"inciso," unsigned, designed by Alfredo Barbini, ca. 1960 (ILLUS.) **$1,840**

Bowl, 9" l., 4" h., "rugiadoso," deep rounded leaf-form w/serrated rim, clear w/applied glass segments on the interior, the surface w/subtle iridescence, designed by Ercole Barovier, Barovier & Toso, ca. 1940 . . . **230**

Bowl, 5½ x 12½", 5½" h., elongated form w/pulled handles, the interior decorated w/gold patches & glass fragments, Barovier and Toso Rugiadoso **258**

Candlesticks, each in pale pink w/gold foil inclusions w/lip wraps in deep cobalt blue, the knop applied w/multi-colored miniature fruit, slender baluster-form stem & flaring round gold foil foot, original paper label "VETRERIA ARTISTICA - BAROVIER & C. - MURANO," ca. 1925, 8½" h., pr. **488**

Figures, an African man & woman in Western attire, each holding a cornucopia, clear trimmed in white & purplish black, ca. 1930, 10½" h., pr. **2,645**

Lamps, table model, blown baluster-form body w/a thick metal base fitting & internal rod to upper electric fittings, the body decorated w/spiraling canes w/white latticino & copper powders, ca. 1950s, 7" d., 20" h., pr. (no shades, some wear to fittings) **121**

Model of a bird, stylized slender J-form body w/a short beak & indentations applied w/glass disk eyes, teal green w/cobalt blue & dark red "murrine" decoration, mounted w/copper legs & feet, designed by Alessandro Pianon for Vistosi, ca. 1962, 11¾" h. **1,725**

Model of a bull, "scavo," highly stylized model of the head down & back arched, tail sticking out, textured grey roughened surface, designed by Alfredo Barbini

for Cenedese, ca. 1948, unsigned, 12" l., 7" h. (minor losses to horns & tip of tail) **977**

Model of a fish, large ovoid ribbed hollow body applied w/specks of white, yellow & green, raised on large wedge-form applied deep amethyst fins w/a serrated fin up the back & a large pointed amethyst mouth, applied yellow & black murrina eyes, attributed to Fratelli Toso, ca. 1930s, 8" h. **385**

Model of a pigeon, "a trina," footed deep rounded body w/upright head & long forked tail, upright pointed wings, clear internally decorated w/white, black & copper-colored aventurine trailings, the figure molded w/ribs, applied beak & crest, designed by Dino Martens, unsigned Aureliano Toso, ca. 1954, 5½" h. **460**

Pitcher, 5½" h., 'Floreale' style, ovoid body tapering to a tricorner rim, applied high looped green handle, the body of clear over green powders & opaque white w/inset murrina flowers, Fratelli Toso **660**

Sculpture, rectangular model of an aquarium, three thick fused sections of marine glass enclosing three whimsical exotic fish composed of red & yellow canes, swimming among emerald green seaweed, designed by Alfredo Barbini, probably for Cenedese, ca. 1950, 2½ x 12½", 8½" h. **2,415**

Vase, 4¾" h., flared cylindrical form, clear, enhanced by gold dust, symmetrical trapped air bubbles & maroon pulled to create a plaid effect, 20th c. **173**

Vase, 9½" h., "Auriliano Toso Oriente," widely flaring trumpet-form body w/a pinched-in rim, clear infused w/patches of orange, black, teal, white, royal & light blue, crimson, plum, copper aventurine & latticino patches w/a large white star murrhina, designed by Dino Martens, ca. 1948. . . . . **9,775**

Vase, 10" h., "sommerso corroso," slender ovoid form on a thick cushion foot, foot & lower body in turquoise blue cased over emerald green above, acid-etched finish, attributed to Seguso Vetri D'Arte, ca. 1960, unsigned **287**

Vase, 12½" h., 'sommerso'-type, tall heavy slightly tapering square from w/heavy clear casing over light over deep blue, ca. 1950s **523**

Vase, 16" h., 'Pezzati' style, tall cylindrical form w/cut flat rim, composed of alternating large patches of translucent blue, amber & opaque white, Barovier & Toso, probably 1950s (some scratches) **1,870**

Vase, 17¼" h., "Aureliano Toso Oriente," rose water sprinkler-form, bulbous base tapering to a tall slender undulating neck w/pointed tip, clear internally decorated w/random patches of black, red, yellow, white & light blue, also w/sections of aventurine inclusions, "zanfirico" threads & a large star "murrhina," designed by Dino Martens, ca. 1950s **4,600**

Rare Large Chalice-form Vase

Vase, 18½" h., chalice-form, the large tall ovoid goblet-form body composed of fused murrine arranged as four golden amber iris blossoms on extended leafy blue stems w/red elements between & against sky blue starry background murrine, all raised on a clear knob w/applied blue prunts & rigaree above the flaring blue funnel foot, attributed to Artisti Barovier, ca. 1920s (ILLUS.) **28,750**

Vase, 19¹⁄₁₆" h., 'Seguso vetri d'Arte,' tall gently flaring cylindrical sides, violet above a layer of crimson & a clear foot, designed by Falvio Poli, ca. 1951, unsigned **1,380**

VENINI

Founded by former lawyer Paolo Venini in 1925, this Venetian glasshouse soon developed a reputation for its fine quality decorative glass and tablewares. Several noted designers have worked for the firm over the years and their unique pieces in the modern spirit, made using traditional techniques, are increasingly popular with collectors today. The factory continues in operation.

Bottle w/original stopper, 'Morandiane' style, tall slender conical body w/flat rim & hollow ball stopper, composed of fine vertical canes of green, white & clear, acid-stamped mark "venini murano ITALIA," designed by Paolo Venini & Fulvio Bianconi, ca. 1950s, 14½" h. **$880**

Bowl, 14" h., free-blown wide form w/high upright sides & a flared rim, pale blue w/an applied deep blue rigaree band around the neck, pointed base pontil, designed by Napoleone Martinuzzi, ca. 1925, unsigned **460**

Chalice, free-blown pale blue w/a wide disk foot w/folded rim supporting an inverted baluster & knop stem below the tall gently flaring bowl w/a wide flattened, flaring rim, possibly designed by Vittorio Zecchin, ca. 1925, unsigned, 14" h. **632**

Compote, 15½" d., 5¾" h., pale blue, a flaring wide funnel pedestal foot w/folded rim supporting the wide bowl w/deep molded ribs in the cavetto below the very wide flattened rim, designed by Napoleone Martinuzzi, ca. 1925, unsigned **977**

Decanter w/stopper, "a canne," stylized female form, deeply waisted w/the flaring upper section w/a flat shoulder centered by a tall narrow cylindrical neck all in dark green, the neck fitted w/a dark blue tall teardrop stopper, the tall lower section composed of a "skirt" w/cane stripes in cobalt blue & emerald green, acid-stamped "VENINI - MURANO," designed by Gio Ponti, executed ca. 1955, 15" h. **4,025**

Venini Clown Figure

Figure of a clown "vurrina arlequino" style seated harlequin's body in blue & white amidst a lavender ground w/silver foil inclusions, applied lattimo glass hands & feet, the face a slice of murrina encompassing eyes, brows, nose & mouth, designed by Fulvio Bianconi, ca. 1950, unsigned, 8" h., 9¾" l. (ILLUS.) . . **25,300**

Venini "Pulegoso" Bird

Model of a bird, "Pulegoso," clear blown
  body w/applied tooled glass wings, pulled
  up at tail & beak, designed by Tyra
  Lundgren, ca. 1950s, acid-stamped
  "VENINI - MURANO - MADE IN ITALY,"
  6¾" h. (ILLUS.). **862**

*From left: Venini Pitcher
Venini Cylindrical Vase*

Pitcher, 9½" h., "a canne" swelled
  cylindrical body tapering to wide
  cylindrical neck w/arched spout, clear
  w/enclosed multi-colored canes in green,
  red, blue, yellow & lavender, designed by
  Gio Ponti, ca. 1952, acid-stamped
  "VENINI - MURANO" (ILLUS.) **4,225**
Vase, 2½" h., 'fazzoletto' handkerchief-form,
  upright pulled & ruffled sides in deep
  green, designed by Fulvio Bianconi, acid-
  stamped mark "venini murano ITALIA,"
  ca. 1950s **121**
Vase, 5½" h., 'soffiati' style, ovoid body
  tapering to a small neck w/flattened rim,
  light green w/six small applied opaque
  white loops around the lower body, acid-
  stamped "venini murano," ca. 1920s **358**
Vase, 7¾" h., "latticino," swelled 'double-
  conical' form in clear decorated w/vertical
  white canes enclosing white threads,
  inscribed "venini - italia," designed by
  Paolo Venini, ca. 1955 . . . . **1,495**
Vase, 8¼" h., "Pezzato," the cylindrical sides
  composed of patchwork squares in
  shades of aubergine, turquoise, smoky
  grey & clear, designed by Fulvio
  Bianconi, ca. 1950, acid-stamped
  "VENINI - MURANO- ITALIA" (ILLUS.) **7,475**
Vase, 9½" h., "fasce verticale," cylindrical
  dimpled form in clear fused w/vertical
  stripes in shades of pale amber, red,
  green & cobalt blue, acid-stamped "venini
  - murano - ITALIA," designed by Fulvio
  Bianconi, ca. 1952. . . . . **7,475**
Vase, 10¾" h., "pezzato," flat flaring sides in
  a compressed cylindrical shape, green
  fused w/patches of red & white tesserae,
  designed by Fulvio Bianconi, ca. 1951 &
  inscribed "venini - italia" (ILLUS.) **5,750**

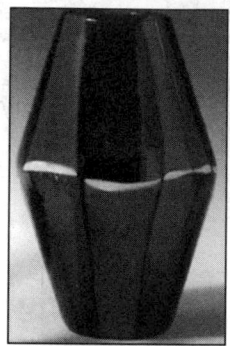

Venini "Pezzato" Vase

Vases, 14¾" h., "Soffiati" style, ovoid
  baluster-form w/flaring neck & thin wafer
  connecting to a round disk foot, rich
  optic ribbed cobalt blue, designed by
  Napoleone Martinuzzi, ca. 1928, stamped
  "venini-murano," pr. **5,175**

WEBB

This glass is made by *Thomas Webb & Sons
of Stourbridge, one of England's most prolific
glasshouses. Numerous types of glass, including
cameo, have been produced by this firm through
the years. The company also produced various
types of novelty and "art" glass during the late
Victorian period. Also see in "Glass"
BURMESE, ROSE BOWLS, and SATIN &
MOTHER-OF-PEARL.*

Cameo vase, 3¼" h., miniature, double-
  gourd form w/a bulbous squatty lower
  body below a bulbous cupped neck,
  bright crimson red overlaid in white &
  cameo etched w/a passion flower designs
  w/pendant leafy vines above & on the
  reverse, late "Webb" on base. **$690**
Cameo vase, 7½" h., footed wide ovoid
  body tapering to a short flaring neck,
  clear overlaid in ruby red & opal white,
  cameo-etched & carved w/narcissus &
  ornamental grasses on the front & back,
  base w/horseshoe-shaped mark "Thos.
  Webb & Sons". **2,760**
Cameo vase, 8" h., flared urn-form body,
  red mother-of-pearl satin Diamond
  Quilted patt. overlaid in opaque white &
  cameo-etched w/an iris & wildflowers,
  base marked "Webb" **575**
Cameo vase, 8½" h., "Old Ivory," urn-form,
  completely cut in an intricate design
  w/mythological bird serpent creatures
  centered in arabesque frames & floral
  backgtrounds, base marked "Thomas
  Webb & Sons," attributed to George
  Woodall **5,175**

Cameo vase, 9¾" h., three-layer, footed wide ovoid body tapering slightly to a wide short cylindrical neck, citron yellow overlaid in bright red & opal white, cameo etched & carved to depict perfect poppy blossoms on leafy stems w/wild grasses at the sides, stepped & angular borders, case marked "Thos. Webb & Sons. Cameo" **4,600**

Cameo vase, 10" h., bud-type, footed slender ovoid body tapering to a tall slender 'stick' neck, light blue overlaid in white & cut w/morning glories & a butterfly between banded borders, ca. 1890, unsigned **2,415**

Tall Webb Cameo Vase

Cameo vase, 18½" h., bottle-form, bulbous base tapering to a tall slender 'stick' neck, yellowish amber overlaid in white, finely carved w/a little bird perched in a flowering prunus branch continuing up around the body w/a variety of flowering plants, unsigned, ca. 1900 (ILLUS.) **9,775**

Cameo vases, 5" h., footed bulbous ovoid body tapering to a short wide cylindrical neck, yellow overlaid in white, one cut w/a pendent branch of bleeding hearts, the other w/a vine of trumpet-form flowers, each cut w/a butterfly between double band borders, impressed "THOMAS WEBB & SONS - CAMEO," ca. 1890, pr. **1,380**

Vase, 12¼" h., footed simple ovoid body tapering to a short flaring neck, colorless body etched overall surfaced & raised enamel-painted iris flowers around a frosted Mallard duck poised for flight, base inscribed "Thomas Webb & Corbett Ltd. - Stourbridge, England," late 19th c. **690**

WESTMORELAND

Westmoreland Marks

Westmoreland Specialty Company was founded in East Liverpool, Ohio in 1889 and relocated in 1890 to Grapeville, Pennsylvania where it remained until its closing in 1985.

During its early years Westmoreland specialized in glass food containers and novelties but by the turn of the century they had a large line of milk white items and clear tableware patterns. In 1925 the company name was shortened to The Westmoreland Glass Company and it was during that decade that more colored glasswares entered their line-up. When Victorian-style milk glass again became popular in the 1940s and 1950s, Westmoreland produced extensive amounts in several patterns which closely resemble late 19th century wares. These and their figural animal dishes in milk white and colors are widely collected today but buyers should not confuse them for the antique originals. Watch for Westmoreland's "WG" mark on some pieces. A majority of our listings are products from the 1940s through the 1970s. Earlier pieces will be indicated.

Animal covered dish, Duck, ruby carnival **$65**

Animal covered dish, Mother Eagle w/chicks, milk white **85**

Animal covered dish, Rabbit, ruby carnival **50**

Banana bowl, bell-footed, Paneled Grape patt., No. 47, milk white, 12" **125**

Basket, Paneled Grape patt., No. 118, milk white, 8" h. **55**

Bonbon, heart-shaped, handled, Waterford patt., No. 36, clear w/ruby stain, 8" **69**

Bowl, 6" d., footed, crimped rim, Paneled Grape patt., milk white **17**

Bowl, 6" d., footed, Old Quilt patt., milk white. **18**

Bowl, 9" d., 6" h., skirted base, Paneled Grape patt., milk glass **45**

Bowl, 9½" d., 3" h., bell-shaped, Paneled Grape patt., milk glass **45**

Bowl, 10" d., footed, lipped rim, Paneled Grape patt., milk glass **77**

Bowl, 12" oval, footed, lipped rim, Paneled Grape, milk white **95**

Bowl, sherbet, Paneled Grape patt., milk glass. **16**

Bowl/nut dish, 6½" oval, Paneled Grape patt., No. 49, milk white **18**

Butter dish, cov., Paneled Grape patt., milk white, ¼ lb. **30**

Cake salver, skirted rim, bell footed,
Paneled Grape patt., No. 59,
milk white, 11" d. **60**

Candelabra, triple branch, skirted, Paneled
Grape patt., No. 90, milk white, pr.......... **500**

Candleholders, Della Robbia patt., clear
w/colored staining, low, pr................. **25**

Candlesticks, Old Quilt patt., milk white,
4" h., pr. **18**

Candy dish, cov., Thousand Eye patt., clear **69**

Candy dish, cov., three-footed, Paneled
Grape patt., No. 103, milk white............ **20**

Candy dish, footed, crimped rim, Waterford
patt., No. 31, clear w/ruby stain **39**

Candy dish, cov., square, Old Quilt patt.,
milk white, 6½" h........................ **27**

Candy jar, cov., footed, Paneled Grape
patt., No. 26, milk white, 6½" h. **26**

Candy jar w/domed cover, footed, Della
Robbia patt., No. 17, milk white,½ lb., 7" h. **42**

Celery vase, footed, pinched rim, Beaded
Grape patt., milk white, 6½" h. **16**

Champagne, Princess Feather patt., pink **18**

Champagne, Thousand Eye patt., clear........ **35**

Cheese dish w/domed cover, Old Quilt
patt., milk white, 4½" h. **45**

Chocolate box, cov., round, Paneled Grape
patt., milk white, 6½" d. **50**

Cocktail, round footed, English Hobnail
patt., clear, 3 oz......................... **8**

Cocktail, square footed, English Hobnail
patt., clear, 3 oz......................... **8**

Compote, footed, crimped & ruffled,
Waterford patt., No. 32, clear w/ruby stain **119**

Compote, open, 6" d., Della Robbia patt.,
clear w/colored staining **25**

Compote, cov., square, low footed, Old
Quilt patt., milk white, 5" h.............. **22**

Compote, open, 4½" d., 6" h., ruffled rim,
Paneled Grape patt., milk white w/pansy
decoration No. 34........................ **30**

Compote, 9" sq., footed, Paneled Grape
patt., milk white......................... **40**

Console set: bowl & pr. of candlesticks;
Thousand Eye patt., clear, 3 pcs........... **145**

Creamer, Paneled Grape patt., milk white **14**

Creamer & cov. sugar bowl, Paneled
Grape patt., milk white, pr................. **45**

Creamer & open sugar bowl, Della Robbia
patt., clear w/colored staining, pr............ **25**

Creamer & open sugar bowl, individual,
Paneled Grape patt., milk white, pr........... **25**

Creamer & sugar bowl, Thousand Eye
patt., clear, pr. **110**

Cruets, English Hobnail patt., milk white,
6½" h., set of 2 .... **30**

Cup & saucer Beaded Edge patt., milk white **12**

Cups & saucers, English Hobnail patt., milk
white, 8 sets **65**

Fruit cocktail w/underplate, Paneled
Grape patt., milk white, 3½", 2 pcs. **18**

Goblet, water, footed, Beaded Grape patt.,
milk white, 9 oz. **11**

Goblet, water, Paneled Grape patt., No. 14,
milk white, 8 oz. **15**

Goblet, wine, Paneled Grape patt., milk white **20**

Goblets, stemmed, Paneled Grape patt.,
milk white, set of 8 .... **80**

Ivy ball vase, footed, cupped rim, Paneled
Grape patt., milk white **38**

Marmalade dish w/ladle, cov., English
Hobnail patt., milk white, 5½", 2 pcs. **25**

Mayonnaise dish, underplate & ladle,
Paneled Grape patt., milk white, 3 pcs. **30**

Mint compote, flat, footed, Waterford patt.,
No. 19, clear w/ruby stain, 5½" d............ **59**

Mint compote, footed, crimped rim,
Waterford patt., No. 34, clear w/ruby stain..... **49**

Model of owl w/glass eyes, dark blue, 5½" h. ... **35**

Model of Pouter Pigeon, apricot mist, 2½" h.... **35**

Model of Pouter Pigeon, crystal, 2½" h........ **25**

Novelty, model of a top hat, English Hobnail
patt., milk white, 3" h..................... **10**

Pitcher, No. 31, Paneled Grape patt., milk
white, 1 pt. **42**

Planter, Paneled Grape patt., milk white, 6 x 9"... **35**

Plate, 7" d., Beaded Edge patt., milk white........ **7**

Plate, 7" d., Beaded Edge patt., No. 64-2
fruit decoration **11**

Plate, 8" d., Princess Feather patt., pink....... **12**

Punch set: 11" d. bowl, base, ladle & 24
cups; Paneled Grape patt., milk white, the set. **550**

Relish dish, three-part, Beaded Grape patt.,
milk white, 9" d. **28**

Salt & pepper shakers, footed, Paneled
Grape patt., milk white, 4¼" h., pr............ **25**

Salt & pepper shakers w/original tops,
Beaded Grape patt., milk white, pr........... **15**

Sherbet, Princess Feather patt., pink opaque **15**

Snack tray, Thousand Eye patt., clear, 2 pcs..... **59**

Sugar bowl, cov., lacy edge, footed,
Paneled Grape patt., No. 45, milk white....... **27**

Sugar bowl/spooner, cov., Paneled Grape
patt., milk glass........................ **43**

Tidbit, two-tier, center-handled, Paneled
Grape patt., milk white **55**

Tumbler, footed, Beaded Edge patt., milk white .. **16**

Tumbler, iced tea, English Hobnail patt.,
clear, set of 3 .... **25**

Tumbler, water, footed, Old Quilt patt., milk
white, 8 oz. **10**

Tumbler, iced tea, Old Quilt patt., milk
white, 5¼" h., 11 oz...................... **16**

Tumbler, 6" h., bell-rimmed, Paneled Grape
patt., milk white......................... **16**

Vase, 9" h., fan-type, octagonal-shaped foot,
Beaded Grape patt., milk white **12**

Vase, 15" h., Paneled Grape patt., milk white..... **26**

GLOBE MAPS

Celestial globe, miniature, globe labeled "New Celestial Globe Pub. by J. & W. Cary, Strand," in a shagreen-covered case fitted w/two clasps, England, first quarter 19th c., globe 3" d. (losses) **$3,450**

Celestial & terrestrial globes, miniature, each small globe fitted in a two-part domed manogany case, marked "Malby's Celestial Globe Showing the Principal Stars of each Constellation. Boughton St. London. March 1, 1844," & "Newton's New & Improved Terrestrial Globe Published by Newton & Son 66 Chancery Lane, London," 19th c., globes 3" d., near pr. (abrasions, losses to globes, repairs to cases) **4,312**

Bardin of London Globe Map

Celestial & terrestrial globes, floor models, each resting on a four-legged turned fruitwood stand w/medial rings, produced by W. & J. H. Bardin of London, the terrestrial globe corrected to 1799, the celestial to 1800, lacking one compass, cracks & minor losses to globes & stands, each 26" h., pr. (ILLUS. of one) **11,500**

Schedler Terrestrial Globe Map

Terrestrial globe, table model, tilted globe raised on a cast-iron base w/a short ringed pedestal above the circular plinth w/floral decoration on leaf-tip cast feet, globe marked "H. Schedler's - Terrestrial - Globe - 12 In. Diameter - Compiled from the latest and most authentic sources including all the recent Georgr. Discoveries - Containing the Principal Lines of Oceanic Steam Communications & Submarine Telegraphs - Pat No. 24751868 Copyright 1889 - USA," late 19th c., globe 12" d. (ILLUS.) **805**

Johnston Terrestrial Globe

Terrestrial globe, floor model, mounted in half round ring on black & red painted spay-legged stand, W. & A.K. Johnston, ca. 1900, 18" d., 43" h. (ILLUS.) **1,610**

Johnston Globe on Iron Stand

Terrestrial globe, floor model, globe on a gilt-metal three-legged stand w/a copper meridian circle & papered horizon ring, the stand w/downswept legs ending in stylized claw-and-ball feet, globe marked "W. & A. Johnston, Geographers, Engravers & Printers to The Queen, 1893, Edinburgh & London," England, late 19th c., restorations, globe 18" d., overall 45" h. (ILLUS.) **4,600**

GRANITEWARE

BLUE & WHITE SWIRL

Baking pan, wire handles, 8¾" w., 12" l. $175
Bowl, mixing, 10" d., 3½" h. 100
Bread raiser, w/tin cover, footed,
 16" d., 9½" h. 475
Chamber pot 10" d., 4¾" h. 125
Coffee biggin, tin biggin & cover, 4" d., 9" h. 800

Blue & White Swirl Lunch Bucket

Lunch bucket, oval, wire & wood handle,
 3 pcs., 9" w., 8¼" l., 7" depth (ILLUS.) 600

Blue & White Swirl Measuring Cup

Measuring cup, 3½" d., 4½" h. (ILLUS.) 500
Muffin pan, 12" l. 250
Mug, miner's, 6" d., 5" h. 140
Pitcher 6" h., 5" d., convex 300

Salt & Pepper Shakers

Salt & pepper shakers, 1½" d., 2½" h., pr.
 (ILLUS.). 2,400
Tea steeper, tin cov., 5" d., 5" h. 225

Teakettle, cov., wood & wire handle,
 10" d., 7" h. 300
Teakettle, cov., wood & wire handle,
 Columbian Ware, 10½" d., 7" h. 625

BLUE DIAMOND WARE
(IRIS BLUE & WHITE SWIRL)

Bowl, mixing, 5" d., 2" h. 75
Cream can, 5" d., 9" h. 575
Funnel, bulbous, 7¼" d., 5" h. 225

Diamond Ware Mustard Pot

Mustard pot, cov., 2¾" d., 4" h. (ILLUS.) 1,000
Platter, oval, 11 x 14" 300
Soup bowl, white interior, 9¼" d., 1½" h. 165

Daimond Ware Teapot

Teapot, cov., bulbous body, 5½" d., 6" h.
 (ILLUS.) 700

BROWN & WHITE SWIRL

Brown Swirl Berlin-style Kettle

Coffeepot, cov., goose neck, 5½" d., 9½" h. **425**
Dish pan, oval, 14" w., 17¾" l., 7" h. **280**
Kettle, cov., Berlin-style, wood & wire
   handle, 6¼" d., 4¼" h. (ILLUS.) **300**
Roaster, cov., round, 12" d., 8½" h. **300**
Spoon, 2¼" d., 13¼" h. **125**
Sugar bowl, cov., 4¼" d., 6" h.. . . . . **900**
Wash basin, 10½" d., 3¼" h. **125**

CHRYSOLITE & WHITE SWIRL
(DARK GREEN & WHITE SWIRL)

Chrysolite Berry Bucket

Berry bucket, cov, wood & wire handle,
   5" d., 5¼" h. (ILLUS.) **375**

Chrysolite Chamber Pot

Chamber pot, cov., 9" d., 6¾" h. (ILLUS.) **300**
Cuspidor, 7½" d., 4¼" h. **400**
Double boiler, cov.. . . . . **50**
Milk pan, 10" d., 2" h.. **75**
Mug, railroad advertisement "C. & N. W.
   Ry.," (Chicago & North Western
   Railroad), 2¾" d., 2¾" h. **200**
Pail, water, 9½" d., 8" h. **225**
Soap dish, hanging, w/insert, 4¼ x 6", 3¼" h. . . . **250**

COBALT BLUE & WHITE SWIRL

Berry bucket, cov., 6" d., 6" h.. . . . . **325**
Coffeepot, cov., wooden handle, 5½" d.,
   9" h. (ILLUS.) **375**
Colander, footed, 9½" d., 3¾" h. **300**
Cup & saucer, cup 2¼" h., 4¼" d.,
   saucer 6" d. **125**

Cobalt Blue Swirl Coffeepot

Cobalt Blue Swirl Dipper

Dipper, windsor, 5¼" d., 9½" handle
   (ILLUS.) **175**

Cobalt Blue & White Swirl Muffin Pan

Muffin pan, eight-cup (ILLUS.). **385**
Pail, water, 11" d., 9" h. **200**
Pie plate **25**
Platter, oval, 8" w., 12" l **275**

EMERALD WARE
(GREEN & WHITE SWIRL)

Emerald Swirl Cream Can

Cream can, cov., wood & wire handle, 5" d.,
   9¼" h. (ILLUS.). **850**
Jelly roll pan, 9" d., 1¼" h.. . . . . **100**
Sauce pan, cov., Berlin-style, 9" d., 6½" h. **250**

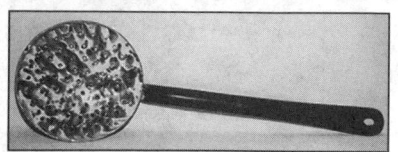

Emerald Swirl Skimmer

Skimmer, 5" d., 11" handle (ILLUS.) **225**

GRAY (MOTTLED)

Mottled Gray Creamer

Candlestick, 6¼" d., 2" h. **280**

Cream can, tin cover, mottled steel ware
w/label, reads "EL-AN-GE," Boston **225**

Creamer, scalloped rim, pewter trim, 3½" d.,
6" h. (ILLUS.) **325**

Measuring cup, embossed "1 quart liquid,"
labeled "Royal Graniteware," 4½" d.,
6¼" h. **200**

Mottled Gray Melon Mold

Melon mold, w/tin cover (ILLUS.). **45**
Milk can, cov. **120**
Salt box w/original cov., hanging-type **245**
Scoop, sugar **45**
Soap dish, hanging, shell-shaped, 5½" w.,
2½" h. **100**
Teakettle, cov., 5¾" d., 4" h. **200**
Teapot, cov., bulbous body, pewter trim &
cover, 7¼" d., 8½" h. **375**

RED & WHITE SWIRL

Red Swirl Coffeepot

Baking pan, 10¼ w., 15¼" l **2,000**
Coffeepot, cov., goose-neck, 5¼" d., 8½" h.
(ILLUS.). **2,000**
Sauce pan, wooden handle, swirl inside &
out, light weight, ca. 1950s, 13" w., 17½" l. . . . **140**
Teakettle, cov., light weight, ca. 1960s,
8" d., 1¼" h., 6" handle. **80**

SOLID COLORS

Berry bucket, cov., cream w/green trim,
4½" d., 5" h. **70**
Coffeepot, cov., cream w/green trim, 5½" d.,
7¾" h. **50**
Colander, footed, solid yellow w/black trim,
10" d., 5" h. **35**
Ladle, white w/black trim & handle, 3" d.,
9" handle **30**
Measuring cup, solid cobalt blue,
3½" d., 4¾" h. **70**
Platter, oval, 10" w., 14" l., cream w/green trim . . . **20**
Teakettle, cov., cream w/green trim,
8" d., 7" h. **80**

CHILDREN'S ITEMS, MINIATURES & SALESMAN'S SAMPLES

Miniature Colanders

Colander, miniature, footed, blue w/white
specks, 2¾" d., 1¼" h. (ILLUS. left) **325**
Colander, miniature, footed, solid blue,
3¼" d., 1¾" h. (ILLUS. right). **325**
Grater, miniature, solid light blue,
1¾" d., 4½" h. **175**
Wash basin, miniature, shaded blue w/floral
design, "Stewart Ware," 4½" d. **125**
Wash basin, salesman's sample, blue &
white swirl, 4½" d.. . . . . **125**
Wash basin, salesman's sample, chrysolite
& white swirl, 3¼" h. **235**

MISCELLANEOUS GRANITEWARE & RELATED ITEMS

Mendets Store Display Box

Bread raiser, tin cover, cobalt & white
mottled, 17¼" d., 11" h. 275

Chamber pot, cov., blue & white mottled,
8" d., 6¾" h. 125

Cookbook, "Granite Iron Ware," dated 1883 200

Hot plate, square, green w/yellow legs,
ca. 1910, 6¼ x 9 x 9 39

Measuring cup, Shamrock Ware, dark
green shading to a lighter green back to
dark green, 3½" d., 4½" h. 200

Mendets box, store display (ILLUS.) 150

Pot scraper, advertising, "Nesco and Pot
Scraper," pictures Nesco boy holding
Royal Granite Enameled Ware,
2⅞" d., 3½" h. 500

Sign, advertising, "Nesco Enameled Ware,"
wooden w/light blue w/cobalt blue
lettering, 34" l., 8½" h. 300

Tea strainer, blue & white mottled, screen
bottom, 4½" d., 6¾" h. 155

Advertising Tray

Tray, advertising, paper tip-type, "To the
Patrons of Granite Iron Ware," copyright
1884, 7" w., 9¾" l. (ILLUS.) 250

HEINTZ ART METAL SHOP WARES

Otto Heintz (Buffalo, N.Y., 1877-1918) changed the name of his Art Crafts Shop to Heintz Art Metal Shop in 1906 as he shifted his focus from copper to machine-formed bronze bodies and from colored enamels to sterling silver overlays as decoration. A patent for the solderless application of the overlays was awarded in 1912, and the diamond mark enclosing the conjoined letters "HAMS" came into use. A series of sophisticated chemical patinas and plated finishes was developed for a line of vases, bowls and book ends. Otto died suddenly in 1918, but the company struggled through the Depression until the end came on Feb. 11, 1930. Values are a function of form, rarity, overlay and originality of patina.

Heintz Art Metal Book Ends

Book ends, No. 7090, flat upright
rectangular side w/brown patina, silver
dogwood decoration, 3 x 5", pr. $265

Book ends, No. 7089, flat rectangular
uprights, green patina, silver bamboo
decoration, 5½ x 6", pr. (ILLUS.) 435

Bowl, No. 3648, brown patina, silver ivy
leaves decoration, 8" d., 4" h. 425

Bowl, No. 1868, footed & two-handled,
brown patina, Greek key silver border
w/factory silver monogram "W," 9" d.,
5" h. 510

Candlestick, No. 3092, turned solid shaft
w/tulip bobeche, brown patina, geometric
silver overlay on saucer base, 14" h. 700

Candlesticks, No. 3125, conical cup
enclosing the bobeche, brown patina,
silver leaves & berries decoration,
4" d., 11" h., pr. 475

Cigar ashtray, No. 2655, round w/two rim
cigar rests & integral matchsafe holder,
glass insert, gold doré finish, Arts &
Crafts geometric silver overlay, 5½ " d. 165

Cigar ashtray, No. 2573, brown patina,
integral matchsafe holder, silver
geometric overlay on rim, 6½ " d. 225

Cigarette box, cov., No. 4090, cedar-lined,
nest of ashtrays inside the cover, green
patina, Art Nouveau style silver scrolling
overlay, 4 x 7", 3" h. (ILLUS.) 525

Heintz Art Metal Cigarette Box

Cigarette box, cov., No. 4081, cedar-lined, green patina, silver birds of paradise design, 3 x 4", 1" h..................... **295**

Cigar humidor, cov., No. 2647, glass liner, brown patina, "Cross" retailer's mark, silver geometric overlay, 5" d., 7" h......... **525**

Desk set, No. 1203, green patina, five pieces w/blotter pad & corners, silver water lilies decoration, the set **450**

Desk set, No. 1182, green patina, inkwell, blotter, pen tray, calendar-letter rack; silver pine needles decoration, the set....... **550**

Heintz Art Metal Lamp

Lamp, table model, domed solid shade w/sloping sides supported on a pair of harp arms, brown patina, stylized silver floral bands on shade & base, 13" h. (ILLUS.)....................... **1,500**

Lamp, boudoir-type, 8½ " d. conical shade w/cut-out design supported on three-arm spider, green patina, silver pine cone & needles design on trumpet-form base, 10½ " h. **900**

Picture frame, rectangular, brown patina, silver holly leaves & berries, opening 4½ x 7", overall 6 x 9" **800**

Vase, No. 3643, swelled cylindrical form w/closed rim, green patina, silver single rose stem decoration, 5" h. (ILLUS.) **345**

Rose Stem on Heintz Art Vase

Goldenrod on Heintz Art Vase

Vase, No. 3622, slender ovoid body tapering to a short, cylindrical neck, brown patina, silver goldenrod decoration around the sides, 12½ " h. (ILLUS.) **725**

Vase, No. 3653, corset-form w/bulbous base, green patina, silver jonquils decoration, 4" h........................ **295**

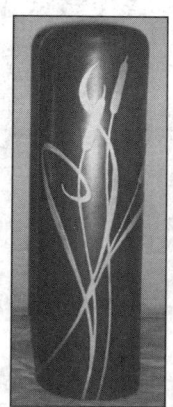

Heintz Art Vase with Cattails

Vase, No. 3608, simple cylindrical form w/closed rim, brown patina, tall silver cattails decoration, 3" d., 10" h. (ILLUS.) **450**

Vase, No. 3744, corset form w/a narrow base diameter, brown patina, silver lovebirds decoration, 8" h. **520**

Vase, No. 3829, pronounced ribbing down the sides, acid-etched silver, poppies decoration, 5" h. **290**

ICART PRINTS

The works of Louis Icart, the successful French artist whose working years spanned the Art Nouveau and Art Deco movements, first became popular in the United States shortly after World War I. His limited edition etchings were much in vogue during those years when the fashion trends were established in Paris. These prints were later relegated to the closet shelves and basements but they have now re-entered the art market and are avidly sought by collectors. Listed by their American titles, those appearing below have been sold within the past eighteen months. All prints are framed unless otherwise noted.

Attic Room (The), 1940, 15 x 17½" **$2,185**
Backstage, 1926, 8 x 11" **977**
Bedtime, 1925, 1825, 14 x 18¼" oval **805**
Bird of Prey, 1918, 12¾ x 18¼" **1,610**
Coursing III, 1930, 16¼ x 26" **3,737**
Fair Model, 1937, unframed, 11⅛ x 19" **2,070**
French Doll, 1926, 14½ x 19¼" oval **920**

Gay Trio

Gay Trio, 1936, 10⅞ x 18⅜" (ILLUS.) **4,428**
Hiding Place (The), 1927, 14½ x 18" **920**
Love's Blossom, 1937, 17 x 25" **1,840**
Madame Bovary, 1929, 16 x 20" oval **920**
Martini, 1932, 12½ x 16⅝" **5,750**

Mockery, Red Screen, 1928, 16¼ x 19" **1,495**
Repose, 1934, 18½ x 45½" **10,350**
Sleeping Beauty, 1927, 15½ x 19½" oval **1,553**
Smoke, 1926, 14 x 19¼" **1,035**
Speed II, 1933, 15½ x 25" **2,530**
Summer Dreams, 1934, 18½ x 20¾" **6,325**

Sweet Mystery

Sweet Mystery, 1935, 16 x 20½" (ILLUS.) **2,300**
Symphony in Blue, 1936, 19½ x 23" **2,300**
Two Beauties, 1931, 24 x 17" **19,550**
Waltz Echoes, 1938, 19 x 19" **1,840**
Werther, 1928, 14 x 21" **1,150**

ICONS

Icon is the Greek word meaning likeness or image and is applied to small pictures meant to be hung on the iconostasis, a screen dividing the sanctuary from the main body of Eastern Orthodox churches. Examples may be found all over Europe. The Greek, Russian and other Orthodox churches developed their own styles, but the Russian contribution to this form of art is considered outstanding.

Rare Large Icon of Christ

Christ Enthroned, large church icon w/central position of the Deisis tier of the iconostasis, powerful image of Christ as the "Lord Almighty," from Yaroslavl-Kostroma region w/Moscow influence, Russia, 17th c., 35½ x 44¼" (ILLUS.) **$14,950**

Christ Pantocrator Icon

Christ Pantocrator, three-quarters length portrait of Christ wearing an emerald green toga over a salmon-colored hiton, delivers blessing w/right hand & holds Gospels w/left hand, dated in lower left "1755," possible monogram signature of Grigorios the Monk, Greece, 28 x 38" (ILLUS.) **5,750**

Christ's Descent into Purgatory, shows Christ lifting Adam & the Prophets, Russia, 18th c., 10½ x 12" (restorations) **489**

Crucifixion (The), finely painted scene w/the addition of the Archangel Michael at top & the corners w/the Four Evangelists & their symbols, panel inset w/an 18th c. gilt-bronze cross, Russia, first half 19th c., 13 x 16" **2,875**

Dormition (The), Abramtservo School, Christ at center in a mandrola receives the soul of his mother in the form of an infant, the 12 Apostles gather around her, the reverse inscribed in Cyrillic script "Abramtsrvo August 15, 1890," Russia, 11 x 14" **1,725**

Head of John the Forerunner (The), polychrome carved relief plaque, inscription at top reads "The Head of Holy John the Forerunner of our Lord," probably southwest Russia, 19th c., 10¼ x 12½" **518**

Hodigitria Mother of God, angels crown Mary as Christ delivers a blessing, in custom-fitted shadowbox kiot w/mother-of-pearl inlays & double-headed eagle at top, Greece, 19th c., 8 x 11½" **1,553**

Image Not Made by Hands (The), face of Christ depicted as it was miraculously transferred to a napkin, overlaid w/a

silver-gilt repoussé & chased riza, hallmarked "84," city mark indistinct, Russia, ca. 1800, 5½ x 7" **546**

Joy to All Who Suffer, Mary shown as intercessor for all those in need, crowned Mother of God in center, the infant Christ on her left arm, a scepter in her right hand, suffering humans & scrolls below, an additional row of saints added, God the Father delivers blessing from above, overlaid w/an elaborate gilt-metal repoussé & chased riza, Russia, 19th c., 12 x 14¼" **1,955**

Kasperovskaya Mother of God, simple metal basma typical of provincial icons, Russia, 19th c., 7½ x 10¾" **489**

The Kazan Mother of God

Kazan Mother of God (The), large church icon, bust of Mary & the Christ Child in the center framed by figures of The Holy Polyect, Patriarch of Constantinople, the Holy Andronik, The Venerable Evdokia & an unidentified female martyr, Russia, 19th c., 28 x 33" (ILLUS.) **3,163**

Kursk Sign Mother of God (The), Old Testament figures including King David, King Solomon, Moses, Daniel, Elijah & others surrounding the central image, overlaid w/a fine silver repoussé & chased riza w/attached halo & porcelain title plaques, riza hallmarked "84," dated "1842," Cyrillic maker's mark for Pavel Nikitin, Moscow, first half 19th c., 9 x 10¾" **3,220**

Lord Almighty (The), overlaid w/an elaborate gilt-metal repoussé & chased riza w/attached halo, Russia, 19th c., 15" sq. **604**

Mother of God of the Passion with Saints (The), top central portion w/a half-length portrait of the Mother of God of the Passion, below are The Holy Abraham the monastic & Miracle Worker & The

The Mother of God of the Passion

Holy Macarius of Zheltov, Miracle Worker of Unzhensk, heavy incised goldleaf ground, Russia, 19th c., 28 x 35" (ILLUS.) **2,990**

Resurrection with Feasts, central panel w/the combined Eastern & Western Resurrection scenes, surrounded by 12 major church feasts, laid down on a goldleaf ground w/faux enamel borders, Russia, ca. 1900, 12¼ x 14" **2,588**

Smolensk Mother of God (The), fine rendering of Hodigitria type, Russia, 19th c., 12¼ x 14" **978**

Sophia, Wisdom of God Icon

Sophia, Wisdom of God, Deisis variant w/Sophia depicted as an aspect of Christ before the Creation, in Eternity, the winged angelic figure w/flame-red face seated on a throne, on the left is Mary, on the right is John the Forerunner, Christ above her & an arch of the heavens w/angels across the top, Russia, 19th c., 12 x 14" (ILLUS.) **2,530**

St. George, the saint w/raised sword riding a white charger, 15th c. style, 18th c. panel overpainted in the 20th c., 10¾ x 12½" **748**

St. Seraphim of Sarov, finely executed, image overlaid w/a fine silver-gilt repoussé & chased riza w/applied multi-colored enamel corner plaques & brilliant multi-color enamel halo, hallmarked "84," Cyrillic mark of Semion Yegornov, Moscow, ca. 1903, 10¾ x 12½" **4,888**

St. Sergius of Radonezh, Sergius was founder of the Holy Trinity Monastery north of Moscow, overlaid w/a superb silver repoussé & chased riza, hallmarked "84" & dated "1849," maker's mark in Cyrillic, Russia, 19th c., 5¾ x 7¼" **690**

The Unburnt Thornbush Mother of God

Unburnt Thornbush Mother of God (The), Mary & the Infant Christ in the center surrounded by various ranks of angels within dark blue & red four-arm stars, the corners w/Old Testament prefigurations of Mary, overlaid w/a chased silver riza, Russia, 18th c., 10½ x 12½" (ILLUS.) **1,265**

Venerable Niphont (The), he holds the Gospels & delivers a blessing, reverse w/dedicatory inscription dated 1903, Russia, ca. 1900, 10½ x 12¼" **460**

INDIAN ARTIFACTS

Items are based on prehistoric stone artifacts of the Northeastern United States. Values are of whole, complete specimens. Breaks would knock prices down. Colorful flint or stone would increase the value as will any item with line designs or effigies involved.

ARROWHEADS

The term "arrowhead" is actually a misnomer. Very few of the items collected were used on arrows. Most were used with spears flung with the atlatl, while most larger specimens were actually knives. Pricing includes arrowheads from 8,000 BC to 1500 AD.

Best, better than average in size,
    workmanship & overall quality. **$10-50**
Better, complete specimens of good quality **2-10**
Grade, broken or slightly damaged,
    most common. **0.75-2**

BASKETRY

Tray, Apache, basketry, tightly & finely
    coiled w/a woven-in concentric design &
    whirling logs, 8½" d. **86**
Tray, Hopi, basketry, coiled in the "Crow
    Mother" design in black, brown & red, 15" d. . . **431**

BEADWORK

Chippewa Beaded Bag

Bag, Chippewa, beaded in purple, green,
    red & white strawberry design on white
    beaded background, leather fringe
    w/hanging beaded strawberry balls,
    ca. 1930s (ILLUS.) **675**

Chippewa Bandoleer Bag

Bandoleer bag, Chippewa, colorful beaded
    floral design w/black trim, ceremonial bag
    (ILLUS.). **1,700**

Menominee Bandoleer Bag

Bandoleer bag, Menominee, loomed,
    beaded on brain-tanned deerskin,
    multicolored floral & geometric designs,
    ca. 1860-70 (ILLUS.) **4,000**

Blackfoot Belt

Belt, Blackfoot, floral beading on white
    beaded background, fringed bottom
    (ILLUS.) **200**
Belt, Plateau, purple, green & white designs
    on white beaded background, ca. 1880s **400**

Cheyenne Doll

Doll, Cheyenne, beaded & fringed buckskin
    dress, high-top beaded moccasins
    w/silver conchos, sinew sewn, includes
    stand, 28" h. (ILLUS.) **2,750**
Holster, Sioux, beaded double rig in blue,
    yellow, green & orange w/leather fringe **350**

Moccasins, Arapaho, blue & white checkered beading w/red & white trim, tin cones on cuff 400

Moccasins, Northern Cheyenne, fully beaded in green, white aqua, yellow & red design, leather cuff, early 450

Northern Cheyenne Moccasins

Moccasins, Northern Cheyenne, fully beaded w/red & blue design on white beaded background (ILLUS.) 450

Moccasins, Sioux, man's, beaded hide, geometric lazy stitched design in light blue, white, red, green & dark blue glass beads, ca. 1930, 11" l., pr. 345

Moccasins, Sioux, man's, beaded hide, lazy stitch diamond design in green, pink, yellow & dark blue, ca. 1910, 11" l., pr. 316

Moccasins, Sioux, man's, beaded hide w/a lazy stitch beadwork design in dark blue, white, red & green, sinew-sewn, ca. 1890, 10" l., pr. 1,035

Pipe bag, Arapaho, beaded & quilled on green beaded background, sinew sewn, ca. 1870-80, 7⅜ x 33" 1,750

Pipe bag, Blackfoot, large red & navy floral beaded design w/white background, long leather fringe, ca. 1880s 2,000

Pipe bag, Northern Cheyenne, beaded tab-style, red & blue diamond design on white beaded background, sinew sewn, ca.1870-80, 7½ x 26" l. 3,000

Pipe bag, Plateau, leather & beaded w/long bottom fringe, ca. 1880-90s (ILLUS.) 1,350

Pipe bag, Sioux, beaded w/extra long quill work, multicolored geometric design on white beaded background, sinew sewn, ca. 1870-80, 7¾ x 40" 3,400

Pouch, Sioux, beaded hide, "strike & light" type, geometric design in white, green, black & red, 4" l. 201

Saddle bag, Sioux, miniature, beaded hide, lazy stitch beadwork in light blue, red, dark blue & yellow, muslin-backed, 12 x 21" . . 920

Trousers, Plains, man's, ringed & beaded hide, decorated w/contour beaded flowers & leaves in red, pink, green, brown & yellow, fringe along entire length of outer seam, ca. 1920s, 38" l. 288

Vest, Blackfoot, man's, fully beaded w/dark purple design on white beaded background 1,400

Vest, Eastern Sioux, child's, beaded hide w/a floral & bird stitched design in dark blue, green, red, white & light blue beads, black cotton cloth back w/blue striped cotton lining, 16 x 16" 1,035

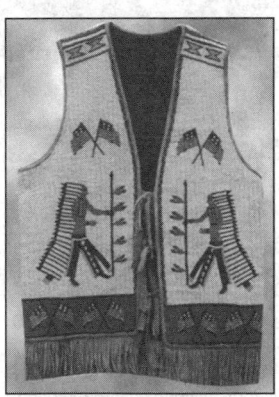

Sioux Indian Vest

Vest, Sioux, man's, fully beaded, pictorial & spiritual markings, front shows headdressed warrior on each side w/crossed flags above, back depicts Indian on horse spearing buffalo, crossed flags in both lower corners & on trim around bottom, white background, leather fringe & front ties (ILLUS.) 650

BONE & ANTLER

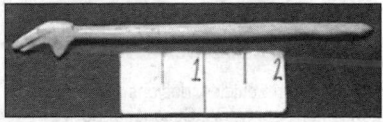

Bone & Antler Awl

Plateau Indian Pipe Bag

Awl, bone, Eastern states, ca. 500-1,500
    AD, 3-7" l. (ILLUS.) **55-350**
Beads, bone, tubular, Eastern states,
    ca. 500-1,500 AD, 1-3" l. **15-50**
Comb, bone, Eastern states, ca. 500-1,500
    AD, 4-6" l. **500-2,000**
Fish hook, bone, Northeastern states,
    ca. 500-1,500 AD, 1-3" l. **150-400**
Flaking tool, antler, Eastern states,
    ca. 500-1,500 AD, 4" l. **75**
Harpoon, antler, Northeastern states,
    ca. 500-1,500 AD, 4-7" l. **150-350**

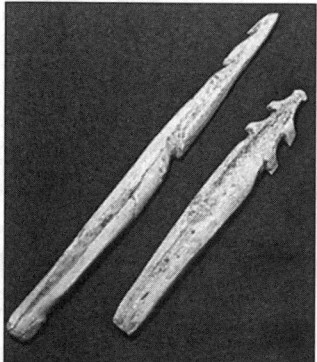

Bone Harpoon

Harpoon, bone, ca. 1000 AD, Pennsylvania
    (ILLUS.). **150-250**

CLAY VESSELS

Large, corded surface, Northeastern states,
    1,000 BC to 1,500 AD, 8" d. **500-1,000**
Medium, incised designs on rim,
    Northeastern states, 1,000 BC to 1,500
    AD, 4-8" d. **500-1,000**
Seed jar, Acoma, pottery, wide squatty
    bulbous form tapering toward the base &
    w/a small top opening, decorated around
    the upper half w/a painted yellow parrot-
    like bird on leafy branch in black on a
    white ground, base signed "Jessie Garcia,"
    Acoma, New Mexico, 10" d., 6½" h. **460**
Small, plain, complete, Northeastern states,
    1,000 BC to 1,500 AD, 2-4" d. **250**

Small Pennsylvania Clay Pots

Small, w/full-form effigies, designs,
    Lancaster County, PA, Susquehannock
    Indians, ca. 1650s (ILLUS.). **250-400**

GROUND SLATE

Point/knife, w/barbed tang, grey,
    Northeasten states, ca. 3,000 BC, 4" l. . . . **200-500**
Ulu, Northeastern states,
    3,000 BC, 6-8" l. **500-1,000**

HISTORICAL ITEMS

Brass kettle, Northeastern states, 8" d. **150-300**
Brass triangles, Northeastern states, 1-2" . . . **15-35**
Catlinite pipe, plain, no stem, Northeastern
    states, ca. late 1880s **250-500**
Glass beads, commons,
    Northeastern states **0.25-5**
Glass beads, rare types,
    Northeastern states. **25-250**

W.A. Jackson Lithograph

Lithograph, "Obtossaway" Chief of the
    Ojibwas by W.A. Jackson, 1903 (ILLUS.) **175**

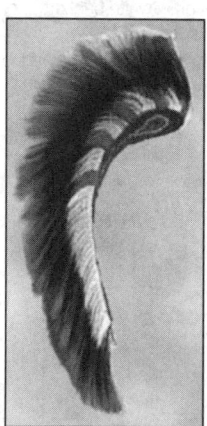

Apache Roach

Roach, Apache, large & colorful w/orangish
    red, black, white & red feathering
    (ILLUS.) **525**

Shell hair pipe bead, Northeastern
states, 4" l. **200-350**
Shell runtee, incised design, Northeastern
states, 1" d. **250-350**

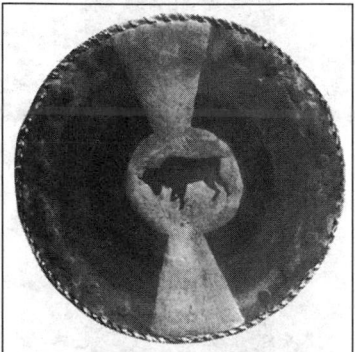

Cheyenne Shield

Shield, Cheyenne, round, painted Buffalo in
center, back reads "Buffalo Bill & Pawnee
Bill's Wild West Circus 1912" (ILLUS.). **650**

JEWELRY

Bear Claw Necklace

Jesuit ring, brass w/design, Northeastern
states. **65-250**
Necklace, bear claw design w/fourteen 4½-
6" long claws, strung w/large Lewis &
Clark Russian blue cut beads, ca. 1880s
(ILLUS.). **6,000**

NATIVE COPPER

Awl, bi-pointed, Great Lakes area, ca. 3,500
BC+, 4" l. **100-300**
Beads, marble size, Great Lakes area,
ca. 3,500 BC+ **5-20**
Celt, Great Lakes area,
ca. 3,500 BC+, 5" l. **300-500**
Spear, socketed, Great Lakes area,
ca. 3,500 BC+, 4" l. **150-350**
Spear, tanged, Great Lakes area, ca. 3,500
BC+, 6" l. **200-400**

OTHER FLINT ITEMS

Drills, 2-4" l. **25-250**
Hafted scrapers, made from tips or bases
of broken points, 1-3" l. **2.50-10**
Hoes & spades, large, Dover or Mill Creek
chert, polished bit, Kentucky & Illinois,
6-13" l. **150-2,000**
Oval blades & knives, 2-4" l. **10-400**
Scrapers, endscrapers & sidescrapers,
½-2" l. **0.25-5**
Scrapers, endscrapers & sidescrapers from
fluted point site,½-2" l. **35**

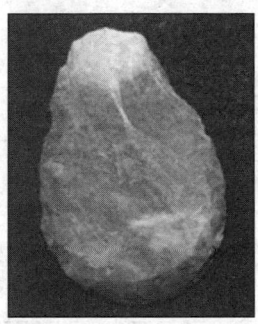

Orange Jasper Scraper

Scrapers, orange jasper endscraper, 2" l.
(ILLUS.). **10-20**

PIPES

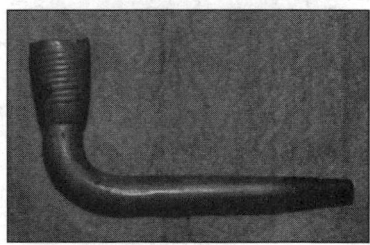

Clay Elbow Pipe

Clay, elbow, effigy, Eastern states, ca. 500
BC to 1,500 AD, 4-6" l. **750-2, 500**
Clay, elbow, plain, Eastern states, ca. 500
BC to 1,500 AD, 3-5" l. **200-300**
Clay, elbow, ring-bowl style, Lancaster, PA,
ca. 1650s, 4-6" l. (ILLUS.). **500-750**
Stone, elbow, plain, Eastern states, ca. 500
BC to 1,500 AD **50-300**
Stone, great pipe, massive, effigy, Eastern
states, ca. 500 BC to 1,500 AD,
8-12" l. **3,500-5,000**
Stone, platform, effigy, Eastern states,
ca. 500 BC to 1,500 AD **2,000-4,000**
Stone, platform, plain, Eastern states,
ca. 500 BC to 1,500 AD **750-1,500**

Tubular Stone

Stone, tube, Eastern states, ca. 500 BC to
1,500 AD, 4-8" l. (ILLUS.). **250-1,500**
Stone, vasiform, effigy, Eastern states,
ca. 500 BC to 1,500 AD **350-1,000**
Stone, vasiform, plain, Eastern states,
ca. 500 BC to 1,500 AD, 2-4" l. **50-250**

SLATE

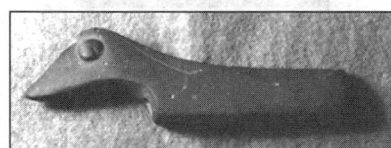

Birdstone

Bannerstone, oval, Eastern & Central
states, 2,000 BC to 1,500 AD, 3" l. **75-200**
Bannerstone, rose quartz, hourglass-type,
Eastern & Central states, 2,000 BC to
1,500 AD, 4" l. **2,000-5,000**
Bannerstone, winged, green-banded,
Eastern & Central states, 2,000 BC to
1,500 AD, 5" l. **400-1,000**
Bar amulet, grey w/drilled ends, Eastern &
Central states, 2,000 BC to 1,500 AD,
4" l. **150-500**
Birdstone, bar-type, green-banded or red,
Eastern & Central states, 2,000 BC to
1,500 AD, 5" l. (ILLUS.). **1,500-3,500**
Boatstone, gouged, drilled, green-banded,
Eastern & Central states, 2,000 BC to
1,500 AD, 4" l. **300-1,000**

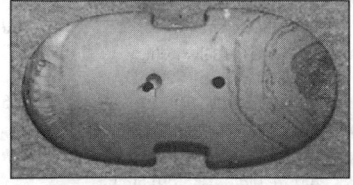

Green Banded Gorget

Gorget, green-banded w/two holes, Central
& Eastern states, 2,000 BC to 1,500 AD,
4" l. (ILLUS.) **75-400**

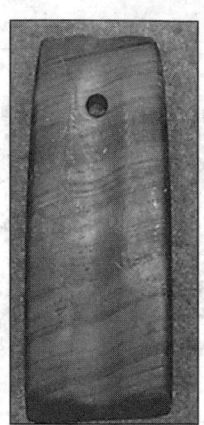

Green Banded Pendent

Pendent, green-banded w/one hole, Central
& Eastern states, 2,000 BC to 1,500 AD,
4" l. (ILLUS.) **75-400**

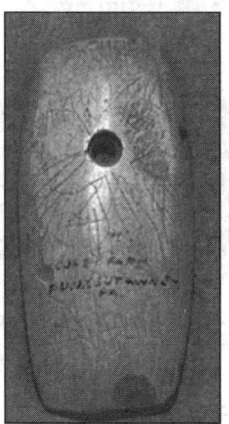

Ohio Pipestone Pendent

Pendent, Ohio pipestone w/incised line
design, Pennsylvania (ILLUS.) **300-500**

SPECIAL PROJECTILES & KNIVES

Adena, Flintridge flint or Indiana
hornstone, Ohio & surrounding areas,
ca. 1,000 BC, 2-4" l. **50-400**
Clovis, fluted point, nice grade flint,
continent-wide distribution,
ca. 8,000 BC, 1-3" l. **100-700**
Columbia River gem points, colorful agate,
Washington & Oregon, ca. 1,000 AD,
½-2" l. **50-250**
Folsom, refined fluted point, agate or flint,
Western states, ca. 7,000 BC, 1-3" l. **500-2,000**

Hardin barbed, Burlington chert, Illinois,
Missouri & surrounding areas, ca. 6,000
BC, 3-5" l. **100-1,000**

Newnan, colorful agatized coral, Florida
area, ca. 4,000 BC, 2-4" l. **200-1,000**

Perkiomen broadpoint, brown jasper,
Pennsylvania, ca. 1,500 BC, 2-4" l. **200-1,500**

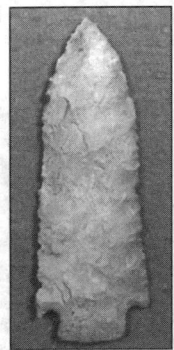

Pinetree Point

Pinetree point, Southcentral states, 4" l.
(ILLUS.). **55-100**

St. Charles dovetail, Flintridge flint, Ohio,
Indiana & surrounding areas, ca. 6,500
BC, 3-5" l. **100-1,500**

Turkeytail, Indiana hornstone, Indiana &
Kentucky, ca. 500 BC, 2-5" l. **100-1,000**

STONE

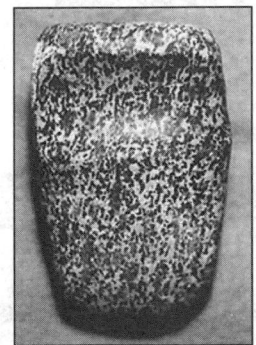

Grooved Stone Ax

Ax, ¾ grooved, ca. 5,000 BC to 1,500 AD,
8" l. (ILLUS.) **150-450**

Ax, fully grooved, ca. 5,000 BC to AD, 6" l. . . . **75-350**

Ax, fully grooved, tomahawk size, ca. 5,000
BC to 1,500 AD, 3" l. **35-150**

Ax, Sioux, stone w/wood, hide & sinew-
sewn handle, 21" l. **230**

Beads, ca. 5,000 BC to 1,500 AD, 1" d. **15-45**

Bowl, ca. 5,000 BC to 1,500 AD, 4" d.,
2" deep **75-150**

Celt, ca. 5,000 BC to 1,500 AD, 1-2" l. **15-50**

Celt, hardstone, ca. 5,000 BC to
1,500 AD, 8" l. **250-350**

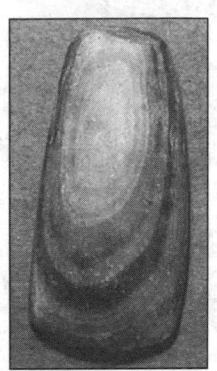

Green-Banded Slate Celt

Celt (skinning tool or ungrooved ax),
green-banded slate, polished, Ohio,
ca. 5,000 BC to 1,500 AD, 4-6" l.
(ILLUS.). **25-100**

Gouge, ca. 5,000 BC to 1,500 AD, 6" l. **200-500**

Mall or hammer, grooved, ca. 5,000 BC to
1,500 AD, 3" l. **15-75**

Mano & metate set, Southwestern states,
ca. 5,000 BC to 1,500 AD **75-200**

Pestle, ca. 5,000 BC to 1,500 AD, 24" l. **250-500**

Pestle, ca. 5,000 BC to 1,500 AD, 8" l. **55-95**

Pestle, w/effigy, ca. 5,000 BC to
1,500 AD **500-1,000**

Sculpture, Inuit, soapstone, a seated
mother coddling her child, finely carved in
greenish black speckled stone, base
inscribed "E91029," ca. 1920, 5" h. **316**

TEXTILES

Navajo Rug

Rug, Navajo, earth-toned feathered pattern
w/diamond trim, 4' x 7' 8" **1,850**

Rug, Navajo, Storm pattern in white, green,
orange & black, 3' 4" x 5' (ILLUS.) **650**

Rug, Navajo, "Yei" design in tan, green,
turquoise & multiple colored accents on
grey, 32 x 53" **201**

Sioux Saddle Blanket

Saddle blanket, Sioux, heavily beaded in red, blue, green & black geometric design on white beaded background, leather center, fringe & red beaded trim, ca. 1880-90, 28 x 62" (ILLUS.) **2,900**

Shirt, Rocky Boy (Chippewa & Cree from North Central Montana), man's long-sleeved, deerskin w/floral & vine beaded design, ca. 1900-20 350

Strike-a-light bag, Kiowa, tin cones & silver conchos on dark green background, ca. 1880s, 3½ x 6" **1,000**

WEAPONS

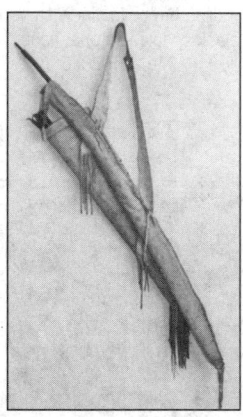

Comanche Bow & Quiver

Bow & quiver, Comanche, four 27" steel-tipped arrows w/red ochre bands in fletching & point of attachment, includes case w/wear on strap & back, ca. 1850s, 46" l. (ILLUS.) **8,000**

Dance club, Sioux, conical w/incised pipestone head, wood & sinew-sewn handle & beaded strip, ca. 1880, 18" l. 259

IVORY

Figure, an elegant standing woman in 18th c. dress w/doves, on a tall turned pedestal base, France, ca. 1880, 7¾" h. (minor losses) **$978**

Figure of a cavalier, standing in elaborate costume w/feathered large hat & hipboots, blowing a trumpet, on a pedestal base, ca. 1880, 6½" h. (minor repair) 546

Carved Ivory Nobleman

Figure of a nobleman, finely carved robed figure holding a scroll, rosewood plinth, Japan, 7½" h. (ILLUS.) 144

Model of an elephant, finely carved & detailed, inlaid w/various colored abalone shell jewels, 5" h. 213

Model of bison, the standing animal finely & realistically carved, Taisho period, Japan, 4½" h.. 403

Model of lion, Okimono of a stalking male lion w/mouth open & roaring, fine details, Taisho period, Japan, 8" l. (cracks) 431

Model of lion, the male animal finely detailed, Taisho period, Japan, 8" l. (lines) . . . 345

Model of the Lion of Lucerne, the recumbent wounded lion lying across oval shields, one w/a cross, France, late 19th c., 3½" l.. 431

Tusk, Narwhal-type, 19th c., 63" l. (tip sanded) **7,475**

Tusk, pierced & carved overall w/foliate designs & a variety of scenes of Oriental figures, China, 19th c., 15" l. (reattached tip) 288

JEWELRY

ANTIQUE (1800-1920)

Citrine Intaglio Bar Pin

Bar pin, citrine & gold, the center prong-set citrine carved in the form of a woman's head, flanked by prong-set round citrines within a 14k yellow gold scrollwork mount (ILLUS.) **$374**

Bracelet, gold (14k yellow), bangle-type, designed as a nail, the head accented w/a bed-set diamond & sapphires, hallmark, stamped "pat. Jan. 28 '08" **748**

Bracelet, gold (18k yellow), diamond & hair, hinged design centered by a crystal plaque over woven hair, w/an applied diamond-set monogram, old mine-cut & rose-cut diamond accents, repoussé & engraved gold mount. **1,840**

Etruscan Revival-style Bracelet

Bracelet, gold & coral, Etruscan Revival-style, centered by a round coral surrounded by a 14k yellow gold openwork design w/applied wiretwist & gold bead detail, flexible mesh bracelet w/floral terminals, Victorian (ILLUS.) **920**

Art Nouveau Pearl Bracelet

Bracelet, gold & pearl, designed as four strands of pearls w/four Art Nouveau-style 18k yellow gold scrolling feather-motif spacers, collet-set diamond & bezel-set ruby & sapphire accents, 6¼" l. (ILLUS. of part) **1,150**

Bracelet, sterling silver & amethyst, Arts & Crafts-style, hammered silver knot motif w/rectangular plaques alternating w/square plaques set w/a faceted amethyst surrounded by applied silver bead detail, hallmark for Theodor Fahrner.... **748**

Flower Brooch

Brooch, diamond, turquoise & coral, flower design w/the flowerhead centered by an oval prong-set turquoise surrounded by bead-set round corals & edged on one side by prong-set round diamonds, gold stem set w/round diamonds, turquoise accents, rose-cut diamond-set leaves mounted in silver-topped 18k yellow gold (ILLUS.). **3,450**

Brooch, gold, Egyptian Revival design w/center turquoise scarab, 14k yellow gold wings w/applied bead & wiretwist detail **230**

Gold & Enamel Portrait Brooch

Brooch, gold & enamel, portrait-type, the oval porcelain plaque painted w/a scene of doves & putti, surrounded by a bow & flower-motif frame in multicolor enamel, 18k yellow gold mount, minor enamel loss, French hallmarks (ILLUS.) **1,955**

Brooch, pearl & diamond, pinwheel design set w/nine round diamonds & seed pearls, 14k yellow gold mount, Krementz hallmark **460**

Brooch, pietra dura, an oval onyx plaque depicting a white rose within an 18k yellow gold frame w/applied bead & wiretwist detail, hallmark **748**

Brooch, porcelain, portrait-type, miniature, the painted porcelain disc depicting the bust of a woman mounted in a diamond-set silver-topped 18k rose gold frame, French hallmarks **690**

Arts & Crafts-style Tourmaline Brooch

Brooch, tourmaline & gold, Arts & Crafts-style circular form w/six bezel-set round green tourmalines framed by 14k yellow gold leaves, hallmark (ILLUS.) **978**

Cameo brooch, agate, depicting three-quarter profile of a woman in high relief, in an 18k rose gold beadwork frame w/foliate cap, Victorian **978**

Cameo Brooch/Pendant

Cameo brooch/pendant, agate, depicting a female bust in profile, framed by seed pearls, 14k yellow gold mount, Victorian (ILLUS.) **1,150**

Chain, gold, the engraved fancy links in 14k rose gold, oval clasp surmounted by a bead-set pearl, Victorian, 15" l. **489**

Floral Link Chain

Chain, silver, Art Nouveau-style, double flowerhead design links, integral shortener, 56" l. (ILLUS. of part) **575**

Chatelaine, silver, Art Nouveau-style, the foliate-motif brooch suspending a pencil case, whistle & pillbox, Wm. B. Kerr & Company hallmark **805**

Cross pendant, shakudo w/18k yellow gold & mixed metal, decorated on one side w/bird & flowering tree design, verso w/floral decoration, Victorian (ILLUS.) **863**

Earrings, gold (14k yellow), wiretwist & beaded spheres w/domed cap, Victorian Revival, pr. **690**

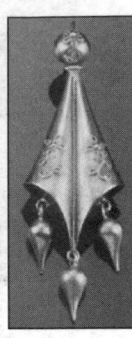

From left: Shakudo Cross Pendant
Gold Victorian Earring

Earrings, gold (15k yellow), round floral terminals suspending a lozenge shape w/three teardrops, Victorian, some dents, pr. (ILLUS. of one) **546**

Lavalier, gold, moonstone & pearl, centrally set w/a large carved moonstone, framed by gold bands set w/seed pearls, seed pearl pendant drops, fine trace link 14k gold chain (minor solder evident to back) **633**

Locket, gold (18k bi-color) & diamond, the shield shape decorated w/five prong-set old mine-cut diamonds & applied wiretwist & gold bead detail, Victorian **978**

Locket, gold (18k yellow), decorated w/the profile of a woman & irises, signed "E. Dropsy," w/French hallmarks, suspended from a 9k yellow gold fancy link chain, 17½" l. **1,725**

Victorian Filigree Necklace

Necklace, gold, emerald & diamond, 14k yellow gold filigree & flowerhead links w/emerald & diamond accents, Victorian, 16" l. (ILLUS. of part) **1,725**

Necklace, tourmaline, Arts & Crafts-style festoon centered by a large cabochon pink tourmaline suspending a cabochon pear-shaped tourmaline drop w/seed pearl accent, fine trace link 14k yellow gold chain **748**

Pendant, silver, chrysoprase & marcasite, openwork design w/center-set oval green chrysoprase surrounded by marcasites & collet-set round chrysoprase, silver scroll-motif mount w/partially obliterated hallmark for Theodor Fahrner, silver reeded trace link chain, ca. 1920s, 16" l. **230**

Arts & Crafts-style Pendant

Pendant, silver, garnet & pearl, Arts & Crafts-style, the scrolled silver openwork centered by a garnet carbuncle w/three blister pearls above & one below, silver bead accents, suspending a garnet cabochon drop, sterling silver paper clip chain w/silver beaded spacers, T-bar closure, signed "F.G. Hale," 16" l. (ILLUS.)............................. **2,300**

Pin, gold, platinum & diamond, Art Nouveau-style chased 18k yellow gold griffin design highlighted by rose-cut diamond wings, mounted in platinum & w/a seed pearl in its mouth, French hallmarks **748**

Art Nouveau Fairy Pin

Pin, gold & plique-a-jour enamel, modeled in the form of a fairy, the veined wings of polychromatic plique-a-jour enamel & set w/round diamond accents, 14k yellow gold mount (ILLUS.) **4,370**

Pin, silver & enamel, a reeded oval silver plaque centered by a quatrefoil design in blue enamel, stamped hallmark for Theodor Fahrner **575**

Ring, carnelian, Arts & Crafts-style w/center oval cabochon foliate-carved carnelian, naturalistic 14k yellow gold mount **403**

Ring, emerald, sapphire & diamond, set w/a pink sapphire & an emerald, each surrounded by rose-cut diamonds, 14k rose gold mount **431**

Ring, gold (18k yellow), designed as entwined snakes, sapphire & diamond accents, Victorian...................... **144**

Ring, pearl & diamond, the center pearl flanked by two collet-set old European-cut diamonds within an openwork diamond-set lozenge shape, platinum-topped 14k yellow gold mount, Edwardian.... **575**

Ring, sapphire & diamond, center collet-set oval sapphire surrounded by rose-cut diamonds within a French-cut sapphire-set rectangular frame, engraved silver-topped 14k yellow gold mount (two sapphires missing) **920**

Watch pin, gold, Art Nouveau-style finely detailed design of a 14k yellow gold dragon w/diamond accent **345**

SETS

Bracelet & pin/pendant, gold (18k yellow) & citrine, semi-rigid band composed of scroll design links, set to the center w/three oval citrines, 14k yellow gold clasp, the pin/pendant of cartouche outline w/center set octagonal-cut citrine, suspending a similarly designed removable pendant, the set.............. **2,070**

Brooch & earrings, gold (14k yellow), the brooch designed w/a circular domed top suspending two bars & graduated batons w/bead terminals, black tracery enamel decoration, w/matching earrings, w/box marked "Bigelow Bros. & Kennard, Boston" Victorian, the set (minor solder, pin stem replaced) **1,035**

Brooch & earrings, gold (18k yellow) & enamel, tiered shield-form plaque suspending a smaller oval plaque w/gold fringe, applied wiretwist & foliate detail, blue & white enamel & seed pearl accents, matching earrings, Victorian, the set **1,955**

Cameo Brooch & Earrings

Cameo brooch & pendant earrings, hardstone, the brooch depicting a l female in profile in a 14k rose gold scroll motif frame w/applied beads, w/matching pendant earrings, in a fitted box marked "Bigelow, Kennard & Co., Boston," Victorian, repair to pin stem, the set (ILLUS.)....................... **1,955**

Amethyst & Diamond Pendant

Earrings & pendant, amethyst & diamond, pendant centered by a faceted oval amethyst, flanked by two collet-set old European-cut diamonds, within an openwork foliate frame set w/rose-cut diamonds, 14⅛" l. 14k yellow gold trace-link chain, together w/similar earrings set w/oval amethysts, silver-topped 14k yellow gold mounts, Russian hallmarks, the set (ILLUS. of pendant) **3,220**

Necklace & earrings, garnet, the 17" l. necklace designed as faceted garnet clusters suspending garnet-set pendant drops w/matching earrings, Victorian, the set. **920**

COSTUME JEWELRY

Costume jewelry, originally made to accessorize dresses and suits in designers' collections, is very collectible today. Fashioned of inexpensive materials and not meant to last any longer than the ensembles it accessorized, it has nonetheless survived and continues to be worn and sought after today. Collectors of costume jewelry value it for its art, design and craftsmanship and as representative of a bygone era. Costume jewelry was affordable in its time and still is for the collector.

Bracelet, Bakelite, bangle-type, amber color, translucent, black "inclusions," carved leaves, ⅞" w. **85**

Bracelet, Bakelite, bangle-type, carved yellow sun motifs, ⅝" w. **45**

Bracelet, charm, enameled romantic motifs on original card. **50**

Bracelet, charm, gold-plated, enamels, rhinestone, Christmas motifs **35**

Bracelet, charm, gold-plated horse motif charms. **30**

Bracelet, gold-filled circles, links alternating w/cabochon open-back set cobalt blue emerald-cut stones, Retro design, ¾" w. **85**

Bracelet, rhinestone, Art Deco, openwork links, pavé set w/clear rhinestones, center larger red marquise rhinestones, clear emerald-cut center stones, ¾" w. (ILLUS. bottom) **85**

Art Deco Bracelet & Dress Clip

Bracelet, silvertone, six rows flat mesh chains, large center leaf shapes set w/Aurora Borealis rhinestones, clear baguette rhinestones, signed "Hobé," 1" w. **75**

Bracelet, sterling, cuff-style, three onyx circles cabochon set in 14k yellow gold, signed "Pierre Cardin Paris, NY.," 1¼" w. **350**

Clip, gold-plated, fur-type, Retro, curved shell-like top, row of blue baguettes center, hanging gold tassel, signed "Kreisler," 3" **95**

Clip, goldtone, fur-type, coil motif set w/clear baguettes, signed "Corocraft," 1½" h. **40**

Clip, goldtone, Renaissance-style florals, leaves, 3" **45**

Clip, rhinestone, Art Deco, red marquise rhinestone floral center, small clear, emerald-cut rhinestone trim, 2" (ILLUS. top w/bracelet). **45**

Clip/locket, glass & metal, fur-type, clip back, black glass cameo in front, space inside for pictures, 1⅝" h. **45**

Clip/lorgnette, sterling silver, folding lorgnette behind white metal marcasite set flower & leaves design **295**

Clips, Bakelite, detailed carved leaves pattern, solid & translucent butterscotch color, 1¾" d., pr. **95**

Clips, goldtone, fur-type, chatelaine-style, two goldtone hearts w/rhinestone-set key on each. **45**

Clips/necklace, goldtone, Art Deco clips connected w/triple gold-plated snakechains. . . . **40**

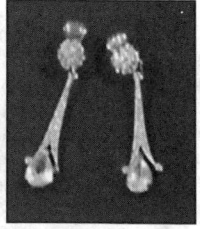

From left: Haskell Earrings & Panetta Earrings

Earrings, crystal & pearl teardrops, clip/screw-on, signed "Miriam Haskell," 2½" l., pr. (ILLUS.) **75**

Earrings, emerald-cut blue stone in gold-plate setting, clip-ons, signed "Givenchy," ⅝", pr. **35**

Earrings, rhinestone, flower w/long rhinestone-set drop, large teardrop bottom, clip-ons, signed "Panetta," 1¾" l., pr. (ILLUS.) 55

Earrings, rhinestone, three unfoiled octagon-shaped butterscotch-colored stones, center citrine-color teardrop topped w/three clear baguettes, slip-ons, signed "Scaasi," 1¼" h., pr. 45

Earrings, sterling, triangle drop, black enamel centers, screw-ons, signed "AAR Mexico," 1⅝" l., pr. 55

Earrings, textured goldtone, three-dimensional flower, clip-ons, signed "Jomaz," 1¼" d., pr. 45

Hatpin, blue rhinestones on antiqued gold circle top, 11" l. 110

Hatpin, enameled blue, white, Columbia University logo, 10½" l. 75

Hatpin, gold-plated openwork enameled Eastern Star motif on top, 7½" l. 70

Hatpin, gold-plated openwork, paperweight top, Scottie inside, ca. 1930s, 4¾" l. 55

Hatpin, green chrysoprase cube inside clear rhinestone frame, 10" l. 75

Hatpin, rhinestone, clear stones hand-set long teardrop, 10½" l. 60

Hatpin, sterling, Art Nouveau design, 12½" l. 150

Hatpin, sterling, embossed Art Nouveau swirls in ball head, signed "Unger Brothers," 9" l. 225

Collectible Lapel Watch

Lapel watch, chrome set in frame of red, blue, green large pear-shaped rhinestones, watch is signed "Pedre" (ILLUS.) 125

Lapel watch, cloisonné enameled gold-filled yellow bow motif w/matching hanging watch pendant, pink roses motif, watch swivels to read time, Crawford 140

Lapel watch, gold-filled, watch in center of bows & ribbons Retro motif, pearl accents, watch signed "Banner" 150

Lapel watch, gold-plated horse head, Retro style, hanging watch, works visible in back, signed "Monocraft" (early Monet) 110

Lapel watch, gold-plated ship's wheel motif hanging from bar pin, signed "Crawford" 65

Lapel watch, sterling, marcasite set, watch hanging from Retro motif bar pin, signed "Croton". 175

Necklace, art glass stones, large blue, alternating w/rhinestones, signed "Kramer" 55

Necklace, Bakelite, green twisted leaves hanging from plastic chain, 15" 125

Necklace, beads, amethyst, small, 31". 45

Necklace, beads, garnet, small, 31" 55

Necklace, enameled white metal, pendant-type, cloisonné enameled white flowers w/black, brown foreground, Japanese-style, signed "de Passillé-Sylvestre," Canada, 24" chain 35

Necklace, gold-filled, pendant-type, octagon-shaped drop w/smoky topaz, signed "Winard," 24". 80

Necklace, gold-plated large heart on large chunky gold-plated chain, signed "Erwin Pearl," heart 2" l., 32" l.. 65

Necklace, goldtone, wide snakechain w/seven very large oval faceted pink Aurora Borealis stones, French-type 125

Mimi di N Collar Necklace

Necklace, green glass beads, collar-style, three rows, large gold-plated openwork metal drops, signed "Mimi di N," ca. 1960s (ILLUS.) 185

Necklace, pearl, double strand, center ornament of baguettes sunburst, around large center pearl, signed "Panetta," 16" 45

Necklace, pewter, pendant-type, medieval-style design, five hanging drops, two red stones, signed "Coro," 32" 35

Reja Daffodil Flower Pin

Pin, enamel iridescent flower spray, daffodil-type, light orange & yellow w/green leaves, rhinestone trim, signed "Reja," 3¼" h. (ILLUS.). **145**

Pin, enamel, rhinestone cherries motif, pavé set red rhinestones, green enamel leaves, stems w/rhinestone trim, 2⅝". **55**

Pin, gold on sterling, flying winged horse (Pegasus) motif, signed "Monet," 2½" **75**

Pin, gold-plated openwork butterfly, pearl head, signed "Jeanne," 4½ x 3¼" **115**

Pin, gold-plated openwork crown set w/pearls & grey rhinestones, diamond-shapd grey stone at top, signed "De Nicola," 2" **125**

Pin, gold-plated seated lion, comic-style, rhinestone eyes, enameled nose & mouth, signed "Jomaz," 1¾" **60**

Pin, gold-plated, stylized starfish motif, signed "Monet," 4¼ x 3¾" **50**

Pin, rhinestone, center deep red raised blown art glass motif, framed by two rows hand-set black comma-shaped rhinestones & deep red long marquise rhinestones in three-dimensional effect, signed "Hattie Carnegie," 2½" d. **175**

Pin, rhinestone, turtle motif, completely set w/large & smaller oval aquamarine unfoiled open-set stones in white metal setting, 3¼" **125**

Pin, sterling, bar-style, four applied abstract cat's faces, signed "Beau," 2¾" w. **30**

Pin, sterling, butterfly, large wings set w/abalone shell & green malachite, Mexico, 2¾" **65**

Pin, sterling, poppy motif, signed "Gumps, Designed by G. Cini," 2". **150**

Pin, wood, carved faux perfume bottle suspended by chains, removable stopper attached by chain, ca. 1940, 3" h. **30**

Pin/pendant, sterling, ornate Renaissance-style design w/four large unfoiled crystals in raised open settings, signed "Cini," 2" **175**

Ring, sterling, gold-washed, blue, green enamel stripes, signed "Jomaz". **65**

Ring, sterling, marcasite set, cabochon amethyst center, 1" w. **65**

Ring, sterling, shell cameo in rhinestone frame, signed "Martelli," adjustable **65**

SETS

Necklace & earrings: enameled rectangular pendant on silver-plated snakechain, silver plaid design on dark blue, matching earrings, clip/screw-ons, signed "Vendome," the set. **40**

Necklace & earrings: gold-plated leaves links, pavé set rhinestone, matching clip earrings, signed "Carnegie," the set. **135**

Corocraft Pin & Earrings Donkeys Set

Pin & earrings: gold on sterling donkey motif, large red marquise stone ears, clear baguettes mane on pin, round rhinestone tails, round rhinestones mane on earrings, signed "Corocraft," ca. 1945, pin 1⅞", screw-on earrings ⅞", the set (ILLUS.) **185**

Pin & earrings: sterling, ornate circle motif, leaf, pear-shaped rhinestones, matching earrings, original box, signed "Carl-Art," pin 1¾" d., the set. **75**

MODERN (1920-1960s)

Diamond & Sapphire Bar Pin

Bar pin, diamond & sapphire, platinum openwork design set w/three round sapphires & further enhanced w/twenty-four round diamonds (ILLUS.). **1,610**

Bar pin, diamond & sapphire, yellow gold base w/silver top, centered w/an old mine diamond, flanked on each side by a line of rose-cut diamonds, each terminal set w/an oval sapphire **805**

Bracelet, aquamarine & zircon, the flowerhead links designed w/prong-set fancy-cut aquamarine petals & bezel-set round blue zircon centers, 14k yellow gold mount, 7½" l. (chip to one aquamarine) . . **575**

Brooch, Bakelite & faux pearl, abstract pineapple design in butterscotch color, set w/twelve faux golden pearls **345**

Brooch, gold (18k yellow), pearl & amethyst, openwork frame w/center bezel-set faceted oval amethyst surrounded by twelve pearls, gold bead & millegrain accents, signed "G no. 12" for Georg Jensen. **460**

Brooch, gold (18k yellow) & tiger's eye, beetle design w/a tiger's-eye shell, textured gold wings & body **288**

Brooch, gold & pearl, the textured 18k yellow gold disc set w/gold beads & twelve black & white pearls **748**

Brooch, gold & rose quartz abstract design centered by an irregular-shaped quartz within an 18k & 24k yellow gold frame, signed "Janiye" **805**

Gold Knot Brooch

Brooch, gold, the double-strand slip knot designed in 18k yellow gold woven wire, hallmark (ILLUS.) **374**

Brooch, ruby & diamond, designed as a holly spray tied w/a bow, the leaves w/forty-nine bead-set rose-cut diamonds mounted in 14k white gold w/black enamel accents, the holly berries w/ten prong-set rubies in 18k yellow gold, w/box **690**

Shell Cameo Bracelet

Cameo bracelet, carved shell, the five oval plaques depicting classical scenes of dancing maidens, engraved gilt metal mount (ILLUS. of part) **748**

Cuff links, gold & enamel, oval plaques in purple guilloche enamel w/a 14k rose gold foliate border, diamond accents, surmounted by a silver crown set w/cabochon rubies, reeded 14k rose gold T-bar accented w/rose-cut diamonds set in silver, Russian hallmarks, pr. **575**

Cuff links, gold, onyx & hematite, the domed oval shape decorated w/intersecting bars of tricolor 18k gold, onyx & hematite, 18k yellow gold mounts, signed "T & Co." for Tiffany & Co., pr. **575**

Poodle Cuff Links

Cuff links, gold, poodle design in 14k yellow gold w/blue stone eyes, signed "Ruser," pr. (ILLUS.) **489**

Cuff links, sterling silver, oval plaque depicting an opossum, hallmark for Unger Brothers, pr. **431**

From left: Rhodalite Garnet Earrings Opal & Diamond Necklace

Earrings, gold (14k yellow) & garnet, three pear-shaped faceted rhodalite garnets on a repoussé shell surmounted by a textured gold leaf, pr. (ILLUS.) **633**

Earrings, gold (18k yellow), five-pointed star design in brushed gold, signed "B.S.K." for Barry Kieselstein, pr. **575**

Necklace, pearl, a double strand of pearls w/brushed 14k white gold clasp set w/round diamonds, can be separated to form two single strands, 14½" & 15½" l. **805**

Necklace, platinum, opal & diamond pendant designed w/an oval opal in a diamond-set pierced platinum frame accented w/collet-set opals suspended from a fine link chain w/four diamond & opal navettes, minor crazing to opal, 17" l. (ILLUS.) **1,725**

Pin, aquamarine & pearl, circular design w/an inner circle of channel-set French-cut aquamarines edged w/seed pearls, 14k yellow gold mount **863**

Pin, Bakelite, designed as a ruler suspending two blue pencils & a red-rimmed slate **345**

Pin, gold, designed w/cluster of five textured 18k yellow gold leaves accented w/rubies, signed "Tiffany & Co.," Italy **374**

Gold & Enamel Bird Pin

Pin, gold & enamel, designed as a bird on a gold branch, textured 18k yellow gold body & polychrome enamel wings & feathered crown, French hallmarks (ILLUS.) . . **460**

Pin, gold, model of a fox, the textured 18k yellow gold body accented by marquise-cut sapphire eyes **288**

Pin, moonstone & sapphire, circular design set w/ten oval moonstones separated by gold bars & an inner circle of ten sapphires, 14k yellow gold frame **518**

Pansy Pin

Pin/pendant, gold (14k yellow) & enamel, naturalistically designed pansy centered by cultured pearl surrounded by gold beads (ILLUS.) **1,610**

Ring, diamond, flower design w/a collet-set old European-cut diamond & two bezel-set pear-shaped diamonds, platinum-topped 18k yellow gold foliate mount **748**

Ring, gold & aquamarine, centered by a platinum prong-set emerald-cut aquamarine, pierced 14k white gold mount . . . **690**

Ring, silver & moonstone, two oval moonstones set vertically & flanked by foliate-motif shoulders, signed "George Jensen, no. 48," designed by Pilstrup **690**

Ring, sterling silver & gold, designed as a circular plaque surmounted by graduated inverted discs in alternating yellow gold & silver, signed "E.R." for Ramosa **230**

Ring, sterling silver, man's, domed shape surmounted by a scarab in gold wash, signed "Tiffany & Co." **374**

Scarf pin, onyx & diamond, a central abstract flame-shaped onyx plaque surrounded by round brilliant-cut diamonds, 18k yellow gold mount **1,380**

Scarf pin, seed pearl, openwork butterfly, 14k yellow gold mount, hallmarks **230**

SETS

Abstract Floral Pin

Brooch & earrings, gold & diamond, designed as a leaf w/folded edge of pavé diamonds w/matching earrings, textured 18k yellow gold, partially obliterated signature for Cherny, the set **805**

Necklace & earrings, pearl & ruby, a 16" l. double-strand pearl necklace w/pearl-set clasp, prong-set ruby accents together w/pearl cluster earrings accented w/bead-set rubies, suspending a pearl drop, 14k white gold mount, the set (one pearl missing from one earring) **805**

Pin & earrings, gold (14k yellow), round abstract floral design w/spiky crossed petals & beaded center, matching earrings, "Preformed Parts" hallmark, the set (ILLUS. of pin) **805**

JUKE BOXES

Introduced in the late 1920s, juke boxes helped to put the "roar" into this era's end. Found mostly in bars and honky tonks, the bulky nickel-play device began mass production by the 1930s. Companies such as Wurlitzer, Seeburg, Rock-Ola and AMI competed in design, sound and bright lights. By the 1940s and 1950s, juke boxes had transformed to more streamlined models and were now found in almost every soda shop and diner in the country. With the coming of the stereo, fast-food establishments and urban renewal during the 1960s, juke box popularity began to decline. Today, the sounds of days gone by may still be heard in some cafes, bars and '50s restaurants. The following information was provided by juke box expert Rick Botts of Des Moines, Iowa.

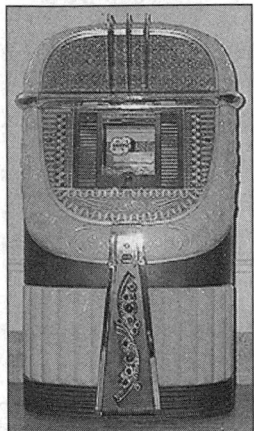

AMI Model A

AMI (Automatic Musical Instrument Co.)
  Model A, 1946-1948, 40-selection,
  unrestored, working (ILLUS.) **$1,200**
AMI Continental, 1961, 200-selection,
  unrestored, working. 1,600
AMI Model D40, 1951, 40-selection,
  unrestored, working 400
Rock-Ola Model 1422, 1946, 20-selection,
  unrestored, working. 2,000
Rock-Ola Model 1426, 1947, 20-selection,
  unrestored, working. 2,100

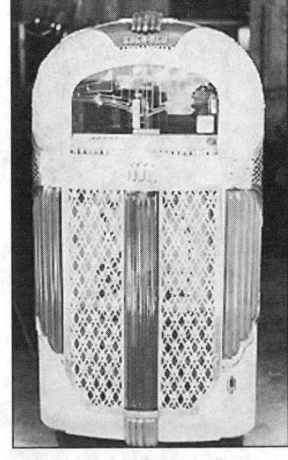

Rock-Ola Model 1428

Rock-Ola Model 1428, 1948, unrestored,
  working (ILLUS.) 2,200

Rock-Ola Model 1454, 1956, 120-selection,
  unrestored, working 800
Rock-Ola Model 1485, 1960, 200-selection,
  unrestored, working. 1,400
Rock-Ola Model 429, 1965, 100-selection,
  unrestored, working 450
Seeburg Model 100A, 1949-50, 100-
  selection, unrestored, working. 1,000
Seeburg Model 100B, 1950-1951, 100-
  selection, unrestored, working. 1,000

Seeburg Model 100C

Seeburg Model 100C, 1952, 100-selection,
  unrestored, working (ILLUS.) 1,500

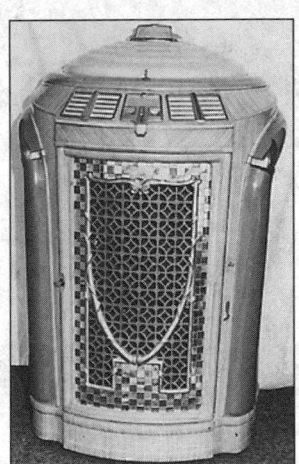

Seeburg Model 148

Seeburg Model 148, 1948, "trash can" style,
  working, unrestored (ILLUS.) 500
Seeburg Model 161, 1958, 160-selection,
  unrestored, working. 1,600
Seeburg Model V-200, 1955, 200-selection,
  unrestored, working. 3,000

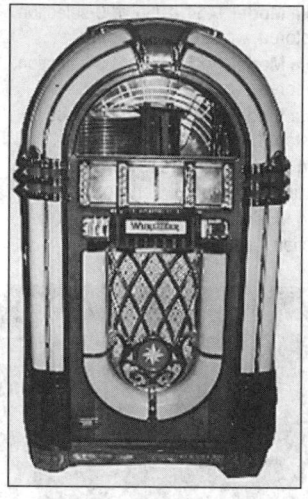

Wurlitzer Model 1015

Wurlitzer Model 1015, 1946-1947, 24-
selection, unrestored, working (ILLUS.) **4,500**
Wurlitzer Model 1050, 1973-74, 100-
selection, unrestored, working............ **2,000**
Wurlitzer Model 2300, 1959, 200-selection,
unrestored, working **800**
Wurlitzer Model 412, 1936, 12-selection,
unrestored, working.................... **1,000**

Wurlitzer Model 416

Wurlitzer Model 416, 1936, 16-selection,
unrestored, working (ILLUS.) **900**
Wurlitzer Model 500, 1938-1939, 24-
selection, unrestored, working........... **1,200**
Wurlitzer Model 600, 1938-1939, 24-
selection, unrestored, working........... **1,000**
Wurlitzer Model 616, 1937, 16-selection,
unrestored, working **600**

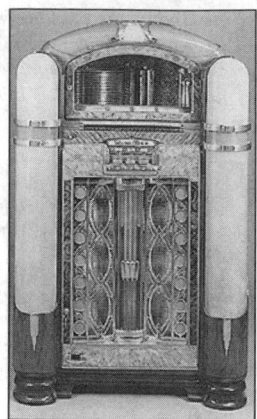

Wurlitzer Model 800

Wurlitzer Model 800, 1940, 24-selection,
unrestored, working (ILLUS.) **4,000**

Wurlitzer Model 81 Counter-top Style

Wurlitzer Model 81, 1942, counter-top style,
12-selection, working, unrestored
(ILLUS.)............................ **6,000**

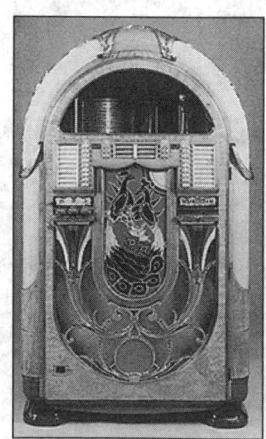

Wurlitzer Model 850

Wurlitzer Model 850, 1941, 24-selection,
unrestored, working (ILLUS.) **12,500**

KEWPIE COLLECTIBLES

Rose O'Neill's Kewpies were so popular in their heyday that numerous objects depicting them were produced and are now collectible. The following represents a sampling.

Cup, child's, porcelain, action Kewpies
  scene, Royal Rudolstadt $75
Doll, composition, Rose O'Neill black
  Kewpie, w/original heart chest sticker, red
  wings, compo. ca. 1930s, 12" h 325
Figure, all bisque action "Kewpie," marked
  "O'Neill," painted eyes to side, open-
  closed mouth, molded & painted tufts of
  hair, molded & painted blue wings,
  unjointed body in sitting position, right leg
  bent & left leg w/foot in air, both hands
  held up, left hand clenched w/hole for bug
  or fly which is missing, 3½" (minor color
  flaws in pupils of eyes) 225
Figure, bisque, Kewpie "Thinker," 4" h. 375
Figures, bisque, huggers, dressed as bride
  & groom, pr. 285

Kewpie Tin Container

Tin container, cov., round, painted in black
  & cream, the cover w/a scene of Kewpies
  on a tightrope, 1 lb., minor scratches &
  wear on edge of cover (ILLUS.) .... **60 to 80**

KITCHENWARES

Also see: GRANITEWARE, METALS, and
WOODENWARES

EGG TIMERS

A little glass tube filled with sand and attached to a figural base measuring between 3" and 5" in height was once a commonplace kitchen item. Many beautiful timers were produced in Germany in the 1920s and later Japan, reaching their heyday in the 1940s. These small egg timers were commonly made in a variety of shapes in bisque, china,
chalkware, cast iron, tin, brass, wood or plastic. Although egg timers were originally used to time a 3-minute egg, some were also used to limit the length of a telephone call as a cost-saving measure.

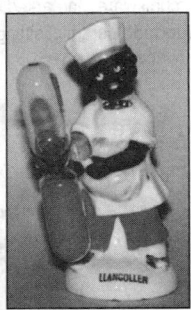

From left: Howling Bear Egg Timer
Souvenir Black Chef Egg Timer

Bear, ceramic, howling, USA (ILLUS.) $95
Bellhop, green, ceramic, Japan, 4½" h. 70
Bellhop on phone, ceramic, Japan, 3" h. 45
Black chef, ceramic, sitting w/arm up
  holding timer, variety of sizes, Germany 100
Black chef, ceramic, standing, marked
  "Llangollen" (ILLUS.) 125
Boy, ceramic, skiing, Germany, 3" h. 75
Boy, Mexican, playing guitar, ceramic,
  German, 3½" h. 55
Cat, ceramic, standing by base of
  grandfather clock, Germany, 4½" h. 75
Chef, holding plate, w/hole to hold timer
  which removes to change, ceramic, Japan 50
Chef, standing in blue w/white apron, towel
  over right arm, timer in jug under left arm,
  Japan, 4½" h. 50

Chef With Cake Egg Timer

Chef with cake, composition, Germany (ILLUS.). . 95
Chicken, wings hold tube, ceramic,
  Germany, 2¾" h. 65
Chimney sweep, ceramic, Goebel,
  Germany.............................. 95
Chimney sweep carrying ladder, ceramic,
  Germany, 3¼" h. 85

Clown on phone, standing, full-figured, Japan . . . 75
Colonial lady with bonnet, ceramic, variety
of dresses & colors, Germany, 3¾" h., each . . . 85
Dog, ceramic, black poodle, sitting, Germany 95
Dutch girl with flowers, walking,
chalkware, unmarked, 4½" h. 75
Elephant, ceramic, sitting w/trunk up,
white, Germany 85

English Bobby Egg Timer

English Bobby, ceramic, Germany (ILLUS.) 95
Goebel, double chefs (man & woman),
ceramic, Germany, 4" h. 100
Goebel, double Mr. Pickwick, green,
ceramic, Germany, 4" h. 165
House with clock face, ceramic, yellow &
gold, Japan. 65

Kitchen Maid Egg Timer

Kitchen Maid, ceramic, w/measuring
spoons (ILLUS.) 75
Lighthouse, ceramic, blue, cream & orange
lustreware, Germany, 4½" h. 95
Little girl on phone, ceramic, sitting w/legs
outstretched, pink dress, Germany 5

Goebel Egg Timer

Little girl with chick on her toes, ceramic,
Goebel, Germany (ILLUS.). 100
Mammy, tin, w/lithographed picture of her
cooking, w/potholder hooks,
unmarked, 7¾" h. 145
Mouse, yellow & green, chalkware, Josef
Originals, Japan, 1970s, 3¼" h. 35
Pixie, ceramic, Enesco, Japan, 5½" h. 40
Rabbit with floppy ears, ceramic, standing,
tan, Germany 100

*From left: Rooster Egg Timer
Squaw Egg Timer*

Rooster, painted cut-out wood, w/sequins
(ILLUS.) 35
Sailboat with sailor, ceramic,
lustreware, Germany 100
Sailor, ceramic, blue, Germany 85
Santa Claus w/present, ceramic, Sonsco,
Japan, 5½" h. 85
Scotsman with bagpipes, plastic,
England, 4½" h. 65
Squaw, plastic, "For boilum egg, just turnum
glass, Watchum sand go down, first
class, when allum sand is onum bottom,
Egg all done take out of potum" (ILLUS.) 35
Telephone, candlestick tube on base w/cup
for timer, wooden, Cornwall Wood
Products, South Paris, Maine. 25
Telephone, ceramic, black, Japan 40
Telephone, black glaze on clay, Japan, 2" h. 25

Tillie Egg Timer

Tillie the Timer, iron, Amish lady on bench
(ILLUS.) 20
Vegetable person, ceramic, Japan 95
Windmill, ceramic, w/dog or pigs on base,
Japan, 3¾" h., each 100

GLASSWARE - MISCELLANEOUS

Juice saver, Fire-King, sapphire blue **145**
Leftover jar lids, for post-production
    decorated jars in Fire King, by Anchor
    Hocking, perhaps a grocery or
    department store promotion, clear, each **3-5**
Leftover jars, cov., Jadeite, w/Philbe design
    embossed, bottom jar w/mismatched
    Sapphire blue lid, Fire King,
    manufactured by Anchor Hocking, early
    1940s, small jar & lid 4½ x 5⅛",
    2⅞" h., each **18-22**

Jeannette Jadeite Two-Cup Measure

Measuring cup, light Jadeite two-cup
    measure, by Jeannette Glass Co., base
    w/a distinctive sunflower design
    Jeannette used (ILLUS.) **20-25**
Mixing bowl, part of three-piece set in
    Sapphire blue Philbe patt., referred to as
    "Utility Bowls" by the company, Fire King
    by Anchor Hocking, 1942-1948,
    innovative rolled rim to decrease or
    prevent rim chips, 6⅞" d. bowl **15-20**
Mixing bowl, part of three-piece set in
    Sapphire blue Philbe patt., referred to as
    "Utility Bowls" by the company, Fire King
    by Anchor Hocking, 1942-1948,
    innovative rolled rim, to decrease or
    prevent rim chips, 8⅜" d. bowl **18-25**

Anchor Hocking Reamer & Pitcher

Reamer & pitcher, green, no markings,
    probably Anchor Hocking (ILLUS.) **15-20**
Refrigerator jar, rectangular, "Fire-King,"
    Jadite w/clear lid. **18**

PYREX Refrigerator Jars

Refrigerator jars, cov.,PYREX,
    manufactured by Corning Glass
    Company, beginning in 1940 & only
    recently discontinued, 1½ quart square
    jars, each (ILLUS. bottom left) **10-15**
Refrigerator jars, cov., PYREX,
    manufactured by Corning Glass
    Company, beginning in 1940 & only
    recently discontinued, 1½ pint oblong
    jars, each (ILLUS. center) **5-10**
Refrigerator jars, cov., PYREX,
    manufactured by Corning Glass
    Company, beginning in 1940 & only
    recently discontinued, smallest 1½ cup
    square jars, each (ILLUS. right) **4-7**
Roaster, cov., Fire-King, sapphire blue,
    8¾" l. **90**
Roaster, cov., Fire-King, sapphire blue,
    10⅜" l. **125**

KITCHEN UTENSILS

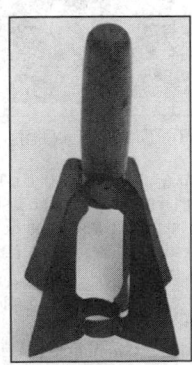

Apple Corer/Segmentor

Apple corer - segmentor, tin apple corer
    w/four-section segmentor, wood handle,
    manufactured, no markings (ILLUS.) **45**
Apple parer, cast iron, "Turntable 98," Goodell . . . **65**

Twisted Wire Basket

Basket, wire w/twisted wire center handle, 7" at widest diameter (ILLUS.) 85

Bisquit pricker tin, 2¼" square x 1½" deep w/handle, top lifts off revealing 9 nails; when attached is combination bisquit cutter/pricker. 55

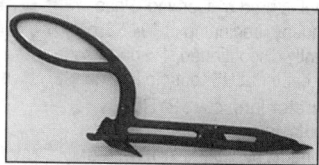

Gun-Style Can Opener

Can opener, cast iron, gun-like structure w/three ways of penetrating can (ILLUS.) 115

Can opener, cast-iron fish form, probably English, 5" l. 85

Cherry pitter, cast iron, "Family Cherrystoner," double. 40

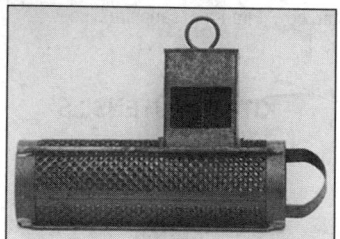

Tin Chocolate Grater

Chocolate grater, tin spring-loaded box which sits on tin grating cylinder & slides back & forth (similar to the Edgar nutmeg grater), marked "The Edgar" Pat. Nov. 10, 1896 (ILLUS.). 350

Chopper, wood handle w/pivoted rotating triangular blade featuring coarse, fine & smooth sides, wooden handle (ILLUS.) 65

Churn, 1 quart Dazey churn marked on the jar w/#10 & "Dazey Churn & Mfg. Co., St. Louis USA" 1,750

Coffee grinder, wooden box type w/pewter hopper & drawer, cast-iron handle marked "Adams," nice detail to wood 195

 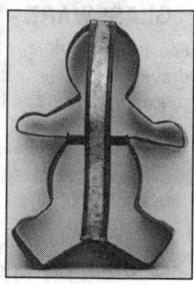

From left: Chopper with Rotating Blade
Gingerbread Cookie Cutter

Cookie or cake cutter, tin, outline of gingerbread man w/strap handle, late (ILLUS.) 18

Cookie or cake cutter, tin, shape of flames advertising "Garland Stoves & Ranges" w/"The World's Best" on the strap handle, manufactured. 275

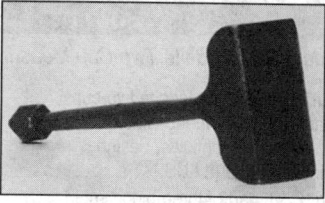

Wrought-Iron Dough Scraper

Dough scraper, wrought iron w/multi-faceted knob, mid-1800s (ILLUS.) 200

Egg beater, metal, "Konvex Mfg. Co. Dayton, Ohio Patented Aug. 23, 1927 & July 24, 1928" marked on wheel, great pivotal action of bowl-shaped beater w/holes at base 425

Egg beater, metal, Ladd #1 churn-mixer, plated top, fluted glass pedestal base 195

New Shaker Flour Sifter

Flour sifter, tin, mesh screen in bottom, shake handle from side to side for action, marked "The New Shaker Sifter, Center Drive, Prevents Tipping, Pat. Applied For," two-cup size (ILLUS.) 35

Flour sifter, wire mesh bowl encompassed by three wire legs w/removable insert of rotating center blade, stamped "Boon, Mills & Co., Pat'd. Jan. 17, 1870," 9" d. 285

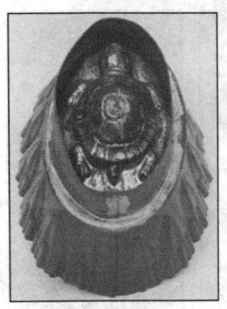 

*From left: Turtle-design Food Mold
Goblet with "Make-Do" Base*

Food mold, tin, oval, mold with turtle on top, 4¼" l., 3¼" h. (ILLUS.) **225**

Fruit jar combination tool, tin funnel w/cast-iron handle, bottom of funnel wide w/collar that unscrews to accept interchangeable disk inserts including fine brass sieve, perforated strainer & narrow tin funnel **45**

Goblet, glass top w/replaced old tin "make-do" base, make-do's becoming very collectible (ILLUS.) **125**

Lemon squeezer, all-glass, hand-held rotation, marked "Little Handy Lemon Squeezer, Silver & Co., New York," 6½" l. (a few chips) **135**

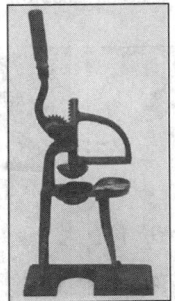

Lemon Squeezer/Slicer

Lemon squeezer/slicer, cast iron, combination cutter & squeezer on wood base w/crank action of handle forcing juice from lemon, inserts often missing, approx. 13" h. (ILLUS.) **175**

Lunch pail, tin, round w/two removable sections & cup on top, wire bail handle **145**

Meat tenderizer, cast iron, handled, w/five toothed rows in rectangular frame, marked "Pat. Applied For" **55**

Nutmeg grater, mahogany & brass, a central square wood block w/grater opening & side handle for mechanism, a cylindrical turned lower section w/a brass cap & a baluster-turned top handle, 19th c., 7⅝" l. (wear) **385**

Nutmeg grater, small perforated cylinder drum w/wire handle at one end, two steel brace sides ending in curve, through center of curve is a rod extending to cylinder w/pressured foot in which nutmeg is placed, Pat. 692926/26, very unusual **800**

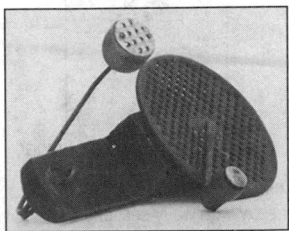

"Common Sense" Nutmeg Grater

Nutmeg grater, wood handle w/tin perforated disk, marked "Common Sense," patented 7/23/1867 by Whitney & Davis of Maine, 5" l. (ILLUS.) **495**

Pie lifter, wood handle w/two long prongs of wire (fork-like) **25**

Pie pan, tin, impressed "Master Supreme" w/star in center **22**

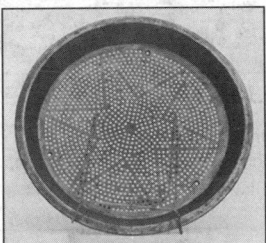

Tin Pie Pan with Star design

Pie pan, tin, pierced star design holes in bottom, used to make crisper crusts (ILLUS.) **45**

Triangular Pot Scraper

Pot scraper, tin, triangular shape w/thumb print center, usually w/advertising, marked around rim "Engman-Matthews - South Bend Ind. - The Range Eternal," used to scrape debris from corners of pots & pans (ILLUS.) **65**

Spring-action Potato Masher

Potato masher, double-spring-action type w/two heavy wire wavy sections, one over the other, turned wooden handle (ILLUS.) **45**

Raisin seeder, shaped wood handle w/seven bent wires protruding from bottom, marked "The Everitt," patented May 8 1893, 3¼" h., ... **65**

Rolling pin, cylindrical, tiger stripe maple **175**

Rolling pin, tin cylinder, two nicely shaped wooden handles, 9¾" l. **350**

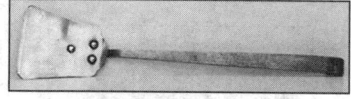

Brass & Iron Marked Spatula

Spatula, wrought-iron handle w/brass spatula blade, marked "F. B. S. Canton, Ohio, Pat. Jan. 26, 1886" (ILLUS) **75**

Cast-iron Advertising Trivet

Trivet, cast iron, advertises "C D Kenny Teas, Coffees, Sugars, 60 Stores," 5" l. (ILLUS.) **125**

NAPKIN DOLLS

These lovely ladies never fail to be the talk of the table. Until about two years ago they were a relatively obscure collectible and those lucky enough to have gotten in on the ground floor will be amazed at their increasing value and desirability. Although most commercially made napkin dolls probably date to the 1950s, they were apparently a popular project in ceramic craft classes from the 1930s through the 1980s.

*From left: Blue Ceramic Napkin Doll
Mexican Woman Napkin Doll*

Ceramic, black model of rooster w/yellow & red trim, 10¼" h. **35**

Ceramic, blue figure of girl holding a bouquet, Holland Mold, ca. 1955, 6½" h. (ILLUS.) .... **65 to 75**

Ceramic, blue Sunbonnet Miss, marked "Holt Howard 1958," 5" h. .... **75 to 95**

Ceramic, blue & white figure of woman clasping hands in front, candleholder in hat, ca. 1954/1955, 13" h. **85 to115**

Ceramic, figure of Mexican woman wearing a sombrero, 9" h. (ILLUS.) .... **95 to 115**

Ceramic, green lustre figure of woman w/floral design, bird perched on extended hand, toothpick tray on head, 10½" ..... **75 to 95**

*From left: Spanish Dancer Napkin Doll
Oriental Woman Napkin Doll*

Ceramic, green & white figure of Spanish dancer holding tambourine, marked "#460 California Originals USA," 8¾" h.-$85, 13" h.-$125, 15" h. (ILLUS.) **150**

Ceramic, pink figure of Oriental woman holding a yellow fan, toothpick holes in peplum, 9¼" h. (ILLUS.) .... **75 to 95**

Ceramic, pink figure of peasant woman w/floral design, wearing head scarf, balancing candleholder on head 8½" h. (ILLUS.) .... **65 to 95**

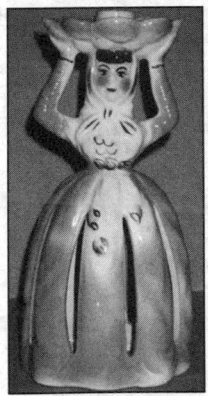 

*From left: Peasant Woman Napkin Doll
Figural Woman Napkin Doll with Candleholder*

Ceramic, pink figure of woman
holding poodle, jewel-decorated,
marked "Kreiss & Co.," hat masks
candleholder, 10¼" h. . . . . **95 to 115**

Ceramic, white figure of woman w/red &
blue trim, candleholder in hat, 12¾" h.
(ILLUS.). . . . . **75 to 95**

Ceramic, yellow figure of Colonial woman
w/4" h. shakers, holding a blue umbrella,
9" h.; shakers $25 to 30 . . . . **110 to 135**

Ceramic and wood, half-figure of Deco-
looking woman w/wood base & wires to
hold napkins, marked "Goebel, W.
Germany," ca. 1957, 8¼" h. . . . . **185 to 225**

Chalkware, beige figure of woman w/lace
skirt & fitted jacket, candleholder in hat,
13" h. . . . . **95 to 125**

Metal, black & gold figure of Deco woman,
8⅞" h. . . . . **100 to 125**

Wood, beige figure of woman on marble
base, "Servy-Etta," marked "U.S.D.
Patent No. 159,005," 11½" h. . . . . **35 to 45**

Wood, figure of black native girl, basket of
fruit on head w/movable arms, 6¾" h. . . . . **65 to 85**

Wooden Figural Chef Napkin Doll

Wood, red half-figure of chef, 12½" h.
(ILLUS.). . . . . **50 to 65**

PIE BIRDS

*A pie bird can be described as a small,
hollow device usually between 3½" to 6" long,
glazed inside and vented from the top. Its
function is to raise the crust of a pie to allow
steam to escape, thus preventing juices from
bubbling over onto the oven floor, while
providing a flaky, dry crust. Originally, in the
1880s, pie birds were funnel-shaped vents used
by the English for their meat pies. Not until the
turn of the century did figurals appear, first in
the form of birds, followed by elephants, chefs,
etc. By the 1930s, many shapes were found in
America. Today the market is flooded with many
reproductions and newly created pie birds,
usually in many whimsical shapes and subjects.
It is best to purchase from knowledgeable dealers
and fellow collectors.*

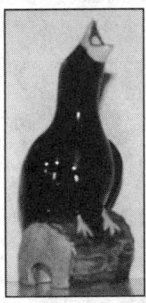 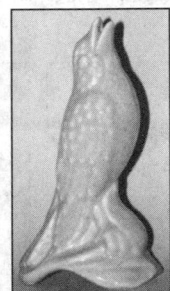

*From left: Bird on Log Pie Bird
Camark Pie Bird*

Bird, black on white base, yellow feet &
beak, Nutbrown, England **50**

Bird, black, perched on log, England (ILLUS.) **95**

Bird, blue, Camark Pottery, USA, 6½" h.
(ILLUS.) **115**

*From left: Royal Worcester Pie Bird
Double-headed Glass Pie Bird*

Bird, brown on white base, Royal
Worcester, England (ILLUS.) **125**

Bird, glass, double-headed, marked
"Scotland" (ILLUS.). **125**

Bird, grey, England. **95**

Bird, on nest w/babies, Artissian Pottery,
USA . . . . **350+**

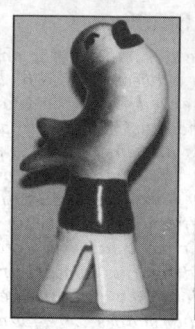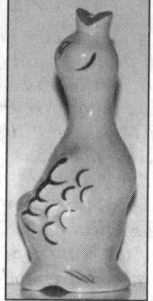

*From left: Bird with Puffed Chest Pie Bird
Decorated Yellow Pie Bird*

Bird, w/puffed chest, dark blue & white, USA
(ILLUS.) **200**
Bird, yellow w/black & red trim, England
(ILLUS.) **85**

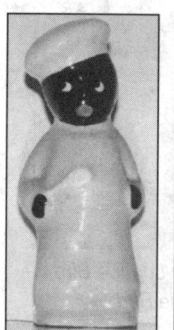

*From left: Black Chef with Blue Smock
"Benny the Baker" Pie Bird*

Black Chef, full-figured, blue smock,
"Pie-Aire," USA (ILLUS.) **150**
Black Chef, full-figured, green smock,
"Pie-Aire," USA....................... **185**
Brown chef, half-figure, England **115**
Chef, "Benny the Baker," w/tools & box,
Cardinal China Co., USA (ILLUS.) **175**

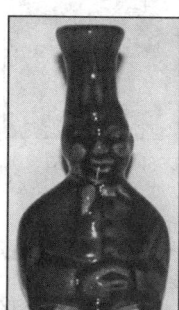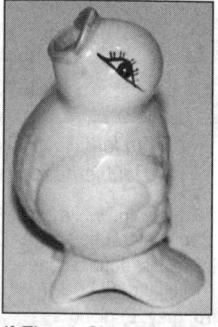

*From left: Brown Half-Figure Chef Pie Bird
Josef Originals Chick Pie Bird*

Chef, half-figure, brown, England (ILLUS.)....... **90**
Chick, w/dust cap, Josef Originals **95**
Chick, yellow w/pink lips, Josef Originals
(ILLUS.) **55**

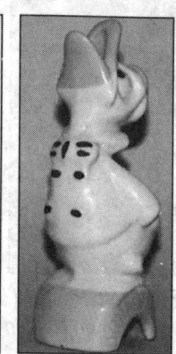

*From left: Dolphin Pie Bird
Rare Donald Duck Pie Bird*

Dolphin, blue, marked "Bermuda" (ILLUS.) **125**
Donald Duck, yellow bill & base, black trim,
USA, rare (ILLUS.)..................... **500+**
Dragon, Creiciau Pottery, United Kingdom **125**
Duck, long neck, blue, pink, or yellow, USA...... **50**

American Full-bodied Duck Pie Birds

Duck, pink, blue or yellow, full-bodied, USA,
each (ILLUS.)......................... **70**
Duck, white w/black detail, yellow beak,
England **100**

English Duck-head Pie Bird

Duck head, tannish grey w/black eyes,
England (ILLUS.) **125**

Nutbrown, England Elephants

Elephant, all-grey w/trunk up, Nutbrown,
England (ILLUS. right) 110
Elephant, all-white w/trunk up, Nutbrown,
England (ILLUS. left) 70
Elephant, grey, Nutbrown, England 100

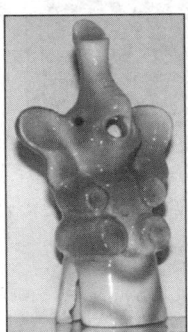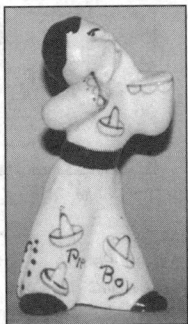

From left: Cardinal China Elephant Pie Bird
"Pie Boy" Pie Bird

Elephant, grey & pink w/swirled pink base,
Cardinal China Co., USA (ILLUS.) 250
Funnel, plain white, England 22
Mammy, outstretched arms, USA. 95
"Patrick," by California Cleminson, many
color variations, USA, each 60
"Pie Boy," by Squire Pottery of California,
USA (ILLUS.) 250
"Pie-Chic," given as premium in Pillsbury
Flour, USA 55

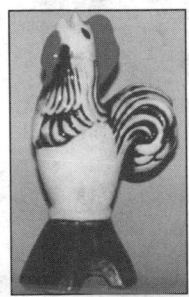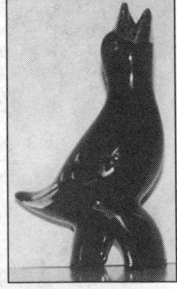

From left: Marion Drake Rooster Pie Bird
LaPere Songbird Pie Bird

Rooster, Marion Drake, white w/black,
red & yellow trim on brown base (ILLUS.) 75

Songbird, beige, blue & pink variations,
USA, each 40
Songbird, black w/gold beak, feet & trim,
LaPere, Ohio, USA (ILLUS.) 125
Walrus, black, ceramic, Japan 125

Walrus Pie Bird

Walrus, black glaze, Japan (ILLUS.) 130

REAMERS

Once a staple in the American household during the 1920s-40s, manual juice reamers have again gained popularity as a hot commodity in today's collectible market. Although some wooden reamers date to the mid-1800s, the majority found today were produced during the reamer's heyday. They range from American-made Depression glass and pottery to exquisitely painted ceramics and uniquely shaped figurals from far-off places like Japan, France, Germany and Czechoslovakia. Lovely silver-plate and sterling examples that once graced elegant Victorian tables now command hefty prices. Even the early electric and Deco chrome models of the 1950s have found a collectible niche.

Figural Clown Head Reamer

Ceramic, clown head in saucer, "Sourpuss,"
4¾" d. (ILLUS.) . . . . 100 to 125
Ceramic, cream w/yellow & purple flowers &
green leaves, two-piece, marked
"Universal Cambridge, Ovenproof,
Made In USA," 9½" . . . . 175 to 195

Ceramic, figure clowns, reamer salt &
pepper shakers, 2½" - 3¾", marked
"Japan" .... 20 to 35

Figural Dog Reamer

Ceramic, figure of dog, marked "Made in
Japan," 4¾" h. (ILLUS.) .... 325 to 350

Ceramic Pitcher Reamer

Ceramic, green pitcher w/blue & green
flowers & brown trim, w/six matching juice
cups, marked "Hand Painted Japan,"
8½" h. (ILLUS.) .... 40 to 60
Ceramic, lustre w/red & yellow flowers, two-
piece, marked "Made in Japan," 2" h.... 95 to 125

Figural Orange Reamer

Ceramic, model of orange w/yellow & blue
flowers & green leaves, "Kiddies Orange
Juice," two-piece, marked "Germany,"
4" h. (ILLUS.) .... 125 to 135
Ceramic, sauce-boat shaped, blue
chintz/multicolored flowers, marked
"Crown Ducal, Made in England,"
3½" h., 8" l. (ILLUS.) .... 350 to 400

Crown Ducal Chintz Reamer

Ceramic, saucer-shaped, cream, tan &
maroon w/blue trim, England, 3¼" d .... 90 to 100
Ceramic, white w/multi-colored flowers &
gold trim, tab handle, 4¾" d .... 185 to 200
Glass, blue w/white opalescent trim, tab
handle, Fry, 4" d.................. 165 to 185

McKee Glass Reamer

Glass, butterscotch, embossed "SUNKIST,"
marked "Pat. No. 18764 Made in USA,"
McKee Glass Co., 6" d. (ILLUS.) 850
Glass, cobalt blue criss-cross, Hazel Atlas
Glass Co., 6⅛" d. .... 275 to 300

McKee Jade-ite Reamer

Glass, Jade-ite, McKee Glass Co.,
6" d. (ILLUS.) .... 25 to 35

Jeannette Glass Reamer with Measure

Glass, Jade-ite, two-piece, two-cup
measure, Jeannette Glass Co.,
6¼" h. (ILLUS.).................... 20 to 25

Metal, one piece w/levered handle, marked
  "Super Juicer," 6" h. . . . . **30 to 40**
Metal, "Seald Sweet Juice Extractor," tilt
  model, w/clamp-on base, 13" h. . . . . **60 to 75**
Metal and glass, amber, "Party Line"
  cocktail shaker, Paden City, 9¼" h. . . . . **95 to 125**
Metal and glass, green bowl & cone,
  "Mount Joy," green metal base w/clamp,
  11" h. . . . . **165 to 185**
Metal & glass, green w/white milk glass
  bowl, ceramic cone, marked "Sunkist
  Jucit Refined," electric, 8¾" h. . . . . **45 to 55**

Silver Plate Reamer

Silver plate, engraved design, marked
  "Apollo, E.P.N.S., Made in USA By
  Bernard Rice's Sons, Inc., 4492,
  Etchardt, Design Pat'd. Apr 22, '24,"
  4¾" d. (ILLUS.) . . . . **125 to 150**

Silver Plate & Wood Reamer

Silver plate & wood, England, 7¾" h.
  (ILLUS.). . . . . **175 to 200**
Wood, hand-held, 6¼" l. . . . . **30 to 40**
Wood, hinged, hand-held, 10" l. . . . . **40 to 50**

SALT & PEPPER SHAKERS

NOVELTY FIGURALS

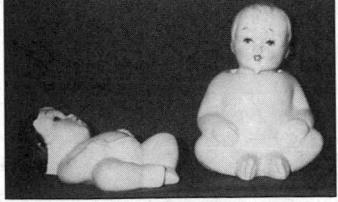

Baby Nodder

Baby nodder, 4" h. (ILLUS.). **38**
Bananas, natural-looking, 4" l **9**
Bears chained to tree, "No Hugging
  Allowed," 4" h. **11**
Binoculars & case, 3½" h. **9**

Black Children Baseball Players

Black children baseball players,
  chalkware, 3" h. (ILLUS.) **48**
Black jazz band, condiment, Germany, 3" h. **250**
Black Jonah sitting on whale, 3½" h. **70**
Blue Bonnet Sue, 5" h. **33**
Bottle of pop & box of popcorn, 2" h. **17**
Bride & groom, Sorcha Boru, 4½" h. **60**
Buffalo, natural-looking, 3" h. **14**
Butcher block & meat cleaver, 2½" h. **17**
Camel w/monkeys nodder, 3¾" h. **213**
Candles w/red tops in holder, bone china, 2" h. . . **9**
Cannon & stack of cannonballs, 2½" h. **9**
Chef standing behind oven w/two pots as
  S&P, condiment, 5½" h. **70**
Chocolate cake & slice, miniature, 1" h. **17**

Miniature Coca-Cola & Hot Dog

Coca-Cola & hot dog, miniature, 1½" h.
  (ILLUS.) **38**
Cow & moon, 3½" h. **18**
Curious George in car, 3½" h. **17**
Dean Martin & Jerry Lewis on tray that
  says "Guess Who?" 3" h. **300**
Declaration of Independence & Liberty
  Bell, miniature, 1" h. **29**
Donald Duck driving speedboat, 3½" h. **150**
Evinrude outboard motors, plastic &
  metal, 3½" h. **150**
Firestone tires, 3" h. **19**
Fish, green & pink, one-piece, 7" l. **33**
Fish in black frying pan, yellow, 2" h. **11**
Fish standing on tails, Ceramic Arts
  Studio, 5" h. **48**
Foxes, natural-looking, 2" h. **19**
Fruit in basket, Occupied Japan, 3½" h. **14**
Fruits & veggies, one-piece, various,
  2½" - 3½" h., each **9**

Girl Exiting Cake

Girl exiting cake, Clay Art, 4" h. (ILLUS.) 23
Graduation hat & diploma, miniature, 1" h. 28
Greyhounds, natural-looking, 1½" h. 33
Halloween Big Boy & friend Dolly, Wolfe
  Studio, 5" h. 63
Halloween Garfield, 2½" h. 28
Hammer & nail, 2½" h. 9
Happy Birthday cake & package, 1" h. 11

Santa & Mrs. Claus Human Beans

Human Beans, dressed like Santa & Mrs.
  Claus, Enesco, 3½" h. (ILLUS.) 19
International kissers, Sweethearts of all
  Nations, 18 different sets, 3" h., each 24
Jack & Jill, Josef Originals, 2¾" h. 70
**Jet airplane condiment w/various tourist
  scenes,** France, 6-7" l. 70
Ken & Barbie chefs, 4" h. 21
King Midas & bag of gold, 3½" h. 83
**Kissing Dutch couple in long common
  white base,** 3¼" h. 80
Lawn mower, red & white, 4" h. 19
Leprechaun kissing Blarney Stone, 2½" h. 17

Loch Ness Monster Condiment

Loch Ness Monster condiment, Sylvac,
  England, 4" h. (ILLUS.) 95
Love Bug, ceramic, Van Tellingen, pr. 45
Margaret Thatcher & Neil Kinnock, 4" h. 48
Matador & bull nodder condiment, 4" h. 113
**Melon-head person in banana boat &
  watermelon whale,** small, 2" h. 58

Mickey Mouse & toy bag in sleigh, 4¼" h. 55
Minnie Mouse w/vanity, 4" h. 19
Model T cars, black & white metal, 1½" h. 14
Oh & Ahhh! couple, 6" h. 38
Oriental lady w/urn, one-piece, 3" h. 19
Pail & brush, 2½" h. 9

Miniature Pancakes & Syrup

Pancakes & syrup, miniature, 1" h. (ILLUS.) 29
Peach-head man w/dark green trousers,
  2½" h. 11
Penguin in car pulling penguin in trailer,
  3" h. 48
Pig w/yellow clothes, stacking condiment,
  5½" h. 43
Pink fish lying on green bowl, Occupied
  Japan, 4" h. 17
Pink Panther, 1981, 3½" h. 213
Porky Pig as cobbler w/boot, 4" h. 55
Rabbit condiment w/ears as S&P, lustre
  glaze, Germany, 4" h. 68

Bone China Rabbits

Rabbits, bone china, 2" h. (ILLUS.) 14

Miniature Rosemeade Raccoons

Raccoons, miniature, Rosemeade, 2" h.
  (ILLUS.) 100
Roller skates, miniature, 1" h. 27
Sailor & mermaid, Van Telligen, 4" h. 138
Salty & Peppy, figural black couple,
  range-size, Pearl China, pr. 145
Santa & snowman w/New Year's toast, 4" h. . . . 28
Scrooge & hat, stacking-type, Fitz and
  Floyd, 3½" h. 33

Space Needle on tray, metal, 5" h. 33
Stanley & Livingston, 5" h. 38
States, two of a kind, various colors, Clay
    Kraft by Milford Pottery, 1½" h.. 11
Steamship condiment w/various tourist
    scenes painted on side, large,
    Germany, 4" h. 80
Sylvester & Tweety on Christmas
    ornaments, 2½" h. 28
Tasmanian Devil NFL San Francisco
    49ers, 3½" h. 19
Tramp, stacking-type, head lifts off body,
    4½" h. 28
Treadle sewing machine, plastic, 3½" h. 19
Turkey in roasting pan, 3" h. 9

Casa Loma Turkey Nodder

Turkey nodder, Casa Loma, 5" h. (ILLUS.) 95
Two peas in a pod, Fitz & Floyd, 2" h.. 53
Umbrella stand, plastic, various colors, 5" h.. 14
Washing machines, black & white metal, 2" h.. . . . 14
White owls, bone china, 1½" h. 9
Windmill S&P w/sugar bowl, blue & white,
    plastic, 6" h. 17

STRING HOLDERS

Before the invention of cellophane tape, string was used to tie up packages in country stores as well as during food preparation in the home kitchen. Today we admire string holders for their decorative nature. Made in cast iron, plaster of Paris (chalkware) and ceramic, many different subjects are depicted.

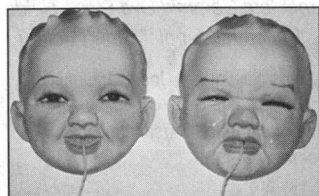

Baby Face String Holders

Apple, chalkware 40
Apple, w/berries, chalkware 35
Apple w/face ceramic, PY 135
Baby Faces, ceramic, Lefton, pair (ILLUS.) 300
Balloon, ceramic, variety of colors, each 75

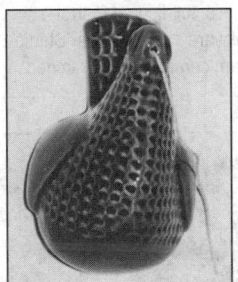

Ceramic Bird String Holder

Bird, ceramic, green, scissors fit in tail,
    Japan (ILLUS.). 38
Bird, ceramic, "String Nest Pull" 45
Bird, chalkware, in birdcage 125
Bird, chalkware, peeking out of birdhouse 175
Bird on Branch, ceramic, Royal Copley 85
Bonzo (dog), w/bee on chest, ceramic 175
Boy w/top hat and pipe, chalkware. 65
Butler, ceramic, full-figured black man 350
Campbell's Soup Boy chalkware, face 350
Cat, ceramic, brown 55

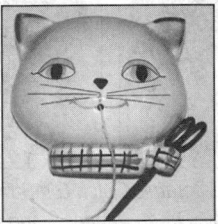

Holt Howard Cat String Holder

Cat, ceramic, Holt Howard (ILLUS.) 40
Cat, on ball of string, chalkware 60
Cat, white face w/pink & black polka dot collar. . . . 50

From left: Light-skinned Chef String Holder
Bunch of Cherries String Holder

Chef, ceramic, full-figure, light-skinned,
    Japan (ILLUS.). 295
Chef, chalkware, baby face w/chef's hat 200
Chef, chalkware, common 60
Cherries, chalkware, bunch (ILLUS.). 150

Clown, ceramic, full-figured Pierrot 85
Clown, chalkware, "Jo-Jo," Miller Studio 200
Deco Woman, ceramic, face w/arched
eyebrows 150

From left: Ceramic Boxer Dog String Holder
Bulldog String Holder

Dog, ceramic, boxer, Japan (ILLUS.) 135
Dog, ceramic, schnauzer 135
Dog, chalkware, bulldog (ILLUS.) 125
Dog, w/chef's hat, chalkware, "Conovers
Original" 175
Dutch Boy, w/cap, chalkware. 125

From left: Ceramic Dutch Girl String Holder
Ceramic Green Pepper String Holder

Dutch Girl, ceramic, head only, Japan (ILLUS.) . . 60
Dutch Girl, chalkware, face, common 45
Elephant, ceramic, yellow, England 75
Funnel, w/thistle or cat & ball, ceramic. 110
Girl in bonnet, chalkware, eyes to side 65
Gourd, chalkware 150
Granny in rocking chair, ceramic, PY 125
Grapes, chalkware, bunch 150
Green pepper, ceramic (ILLUS.) 65
Heart, ceramic, puffed, California Cleminson 75
House, ceramic, Cleminson 125
Humpty Dumpty, sitting on wall, ceramic 125
Indian, w/headband, chalkware 300
Jester, chalkware 95
Kitten w/ball of yarn, ceramic, homemade 40
Kitten w/ball of yarn, chalkware 65
Mammy, ceramic, full-figured, plaid & polka
dot dress. 135
Mammy, chalkware, full-figured, marked
"MAPCO" 275
Mammy, chalkware, head only, w/colored
kerchief (ILLUS.) 225
Man, ceramic, drunk, marked "Elsa" on back . . . 125

From left: Chalk Mammy's Face String Holder
Mexican Woman String Holder

Mexican woman, chalkware, head only,
w/braids & sombrero (ILLUS.) 150

From left: Monkey String Holder
Ceramic Oriental Man String Holder

Monkey, on ball of string, chalkware (ILLUS.) . . . 300
Mouse, sitting, ceramic, Josef Original. 85
Oriental man, w/coolie hat, ceramic,
Abingdon (ILLUS.) 225

From left: Ceramic Owl String Holder
"Prince Pineapple" String Holder

Owl, ceramic, full-figured, Josef Originals
(ILLUS.) 65
Parlor maid, ceramic, "Sarsasparilla" 95
Peach, ceramic. 85
Pear, chalkware 55
Peasant woman, ceramic, full-figured,
knitting sock 175
Penguin, ceramic, full-figured
w/scissors holder 85
Pig, w/flowers, ceramic. 145
Pineapple, chalkware, "Prince Pineapple,"
Miller Studio (ILLUS.) 250

Pirate & gypsy, wood fiber, pr. 150
Prayer lady, ceramic, by Enesco 300
Rooster, ceramic, Royal Bayreuth 350

 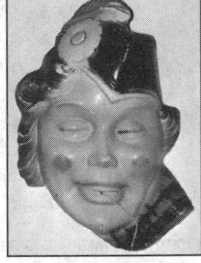

*From left: Chalk Rose String Holder
Scottish Woman String Holder*

Rose, chalkware (ILLUS.). 150
Sailor Boy, chalkware 150
Sailor Girl (Rosie the Riveter), chalkware 150
Scottish woman, chalkware, head only,
    plaid scarf (ILLUS.). 275
Senor, chalkware 65

Ceramic Southern Belle String Holder

Southern Belle lady, ceramic, very full skirt,
    Japan (ILLUS.). 100
Southern Gentleman with ladies, ceramic. 125
Strawberry, chalkware, white flower, green
    leaves & no stem 55
Woman w/turban, chalkware. 150

LAUNDRY ROOM ITEMS

The "good old days" weren't really all that good when Monday "wash day" and Tuesday "ironing day" came around. There was a lot of hard work involved in scrubbing clothes on the washboard and smoothing out the wrinkles with the hefty flatiron or "sadiron" (sad = heavy). Today collectors can look back with some nostalgia on those adjuncts of the laundry room, curious relics of the not-too-distant past.

CLOTHES SPRINKLER BOTTLES

American Bisque Cat Sprinkler Bottles

Cat, black, handmade, ceramic $150
Cat, handmade, ceramic, variety of colors &
    designs, each 100
Cat, Siamese, tan, ceramic. 175
Cat, w/marble eyes, American Bisque,
    ceramic, each (ILLUS.). 300

Ceramic Chinese Man Marked "104"

Chinese Man, marked "104" on bottom,
    handmade, ceramic, all colors, each
    (ILLUS.) 75
Chinese Man, Sprinkle Plenty, white, green,
    & brown, holding iron, ceramic 200
Chinese Man, Sprinkle Plenty, yellow &
    green, Cardinal China Co., ceramic 30

 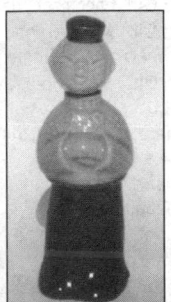

Chinese Man with Removable Head

Chinese Man, w/removable head, ceramic, Japan, each (ILLUS.) 300

Chinese Man, white w/aqua & black trim, ceramic, Cleminson 40

Chinese Man, white w/aqua & black trim, ceramic, w/original shirt tag hanging around neck, Cleminson. 95

Chinese Man, white w/green collar, Chinese writing on chest, holding towel, ceramic 200

Clothespin, red, yellow, or green plastic 25

From left: Clothespin with Smiling Face
Ceramic "Dearie is Weary" by Enesco

Clothespin, w/smiling face, ceramic (ILLUS.) . . . 200

"Dearie is Weary," by Enesco, w/matching salt & pepper, ceramic, the set (ILLUS.) 325

Dutch Boy, green & white, ceramic 200

From left: Handmade Ceramic Dutch Girl
Plastic Dutch Girl

Dutch Girl, handmade, ceramic (ILLUS.). 175

Dutch Girl, white w/green & pink trim, wetter downer, ceramic, mate to Dutch boy 150

Dutch Girl, white w/red & yellow trim, plastic (ILLUS.) 30

Elephant, pink & gray, trunk up, Cardinal China Co., ceramic. 75

Elephant, trunk used for handle, American Bisque, ceramic 300

Elephant, white w/pink & clover on tummy, ceramic. 125

Emperor, handmade, ceramic, Holland Mold, variety of colors & designs, each (ILLUS. of some) 150

Ceramic Holland Mold Emperors

Fireman, ceramic, California Cleminson, rare . . . 500

Iron, blue Delft design, ceramic 150

Iron, green plastic. 25

From left: Ceramic Iron with Farm Couple
Merry Maid Sprinkler Bottle

Iron, illustrated w/farm couple, ceramic (ILLUS.). . 225

Iron, lady ironing, ceramic 65

Iron, souvenir of Aquarena Springs, San Marcos, Texas, ceramic 225

Iron, souvenir of Florida, pink flamingo, ceramic. . 300

Iron, souvenir of Wonder Cave. 300

Iron, white w/embossed rooster, ceramic. 150

Mammy, ceramic 350

Mammy, ceramic, Pfaltzgraff 350

Mary Poppins, ceramic, Cleminson of California 300

Merry maid, all colors, plastic, Reliance. 25

Merry Maid, in a variety of colors, plastic, each (ILLUS.) 75

From left: "Mr. Sprinkle" Sprinkler Bottle
Peasant Woman Sprinkler Bottle

"Mr. Sprinkle," red & white striped plastic
(ILLUS.) 25

Myrtle, ceramic, Pfaltzgraff. 325

Peasant Woman, ceramic, Provincial
Pottery, California (ILLUS.) 300

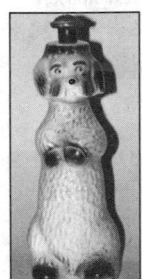

From left: Grey & Black Poodle Bottle
Ceramic Rooster Sprinkler Bottle

Poodle, sitting, grey, pink or white, ceramic,
each (ILLUS.) 250

Prayer Lady, ceramic, by Enesco 500

Queen or king, ceramic, Tilso, Japan 100

Rooster, red, white & green, ceramic (ILLUS.) . . 150

Vase, white w/rose on front & rose sprinkler
top, plastic 35

Watering Can Sprinkling Bottle

Watering Can, ceramic, white w/pink &
green dots (ILLUS.) 225

IRONS

Belgian Box Iron and Trivet

Box iron, brass body, swivel gate, Germany . . . 175

Box iron, brass body w/lift gate & wood
handle, Northern Europe 110

Box iron, iron body w/brass trivet, drop in
slug, wood handle, Belgium (ILLUS.) 750

Box iron, lift-gate, pierced screw secure
uprights, England, 18th c. 150

Horton's Charcoal Iron Model #7

Charcoal iron, cast iron, Horton's Iron
Model #7, patented, late 19th c.
(ILLUS.). . . . . 85 to 100

Charcoal iron, double chimney, marked "Ne
Plus Ultra," pat. by George Finn
July 9, 1902 275

Charcoal iron, marked "Queen Carbon
Sad Iron". 400

Combination iron, cast iron, marked "Acme
Carbon," w/fluter on side of iron, w/wood
handle 350

Combination iron, charcoal w/chimney,
fluter bed on side, unmarked 275

Combination iron, fluter/sadiron w/wire
latch, Charles Anderson Patent 1871 150

Art Deco Electric Iron

Electric iron, Art Deco-style, streamlined
body w/black handle & red & black cord,
marked "Petipoint" (ILLUS.) 175

Electric iron, General Mills w/steam attachment . . 40

"Crown" Fluter

Fluter, crank, cast iron, w/C-clamp, marked "Crown" on base, Pat. Nov. 2, 1875 (ILLUS.) 150

Fluter, crank, marked "American," Pat. Nov. 2, 1875 150

From left: "Geneva Hand Fluter" Early Sears Fuel Iron

Fluter, rocking, cast iron, marked "Geneva Hand Fluter" on rocker, "Heat This Pat'd 1866" on base (ILLUS.) 55

Fuel iron, iron base w/round tank mounted on top of iron, wood handle, Sears (ILLUS.) .. 250

Goffering Iron Set

Goffering iron, cast-iron frame w/double rollers & side crank handle w/wooden grip, includes heating irons, clamp, lead inserts & hand protector, 19th c., the set (ILLUS.)......................... 250 to 275

Little iron, model of a cross rib, 2½" 50

From left: Little Swan Iron "Ferris Cold Handle" Sad Iron

Little iron, cast iron, figure of a swan, 5" l. (ILLUS.)......................... 700

Polisher, cast iron w/embossed star on top of body, marked "Geneva" 65

Sadiron, cast iron, coiled handle, marked "Ferris Cold Handle," Pat. Oct. 6, 1891, St. Louis (ILLUS.)....................... 250

Sadiron, cast iron, w/grid-like design on handle & star embossed on top of body, common 15

Sadiron, detachable handle, bentwood, marked "Bless & Drake" 190

Sadiron, detachable handle, Enterprise, A.C. Williams & others 25

Sadiron, dolphin handle 45

Sleeve iron, 'duck bill' model, marked "Geneva" on body & "GENEVA Pat. applied for" on toe 450

Tailor iron, cast iron, marked "Sensible" w/removable wood & iron handle, 20 lb. 275

Tailor iron, advertising-type, cast iron, embossed "J. A. Griffith & Co. Baltimore," 3½" 250

OTHER ITEMS

Copper Wash Boiler

Wash boiler, cov., copper, deep oval sides w/matching domed cover w/wooden grip, late 19th - early 20th c. (ILLUS.)....... 75 to 100

LIGHTING DEVICES

LAMPS, MISCELLANEOUS

Aladdin Alacite Table Lamps

Aladdin table lamps, squatty bulbous melon-lobed ivory Alacite glass globe mounted on a cast-metal antiqued gold pierced footed base, tall tapering whip-o-lite fluted shades topped by Alacite scroll finials, ca. 1938, 23" h., pr. (ILLUS.)........ $288

Angle kerosene ceiling lamp, three-light, ovoid stamped brass central font suspended from a high arched wire handle, font issuing three short arms w/angled burners fitted w/clear ball gloves & conical milk glass shades, wick adjuster marked "Angle Manufacturing Company, Providence," late 19th - early 20th c. **990**

From left: French Figural Art Deco Lamp Arts & Crafts Student Lamp

Art Deco table lamp, figural, a cast metal figure of a standing nude lady leaning against a rectangular metal frame & swag w/a green patina enclosing a frosted glass panel, a stepped plinth on a black marble base, embossed on the side "Fayral," marked on back "Made in France - Ovington New York," patina wear, 1920s, 16½" h. (ILLUS.) **2,300**

Art Nouveau table lamp, cameo glass & bronzed metal, a 9½" d. wide domical cameo glass shade in mottled green, white & brown overlaid in dark green & cut w/an overall leafy vine decoration, supported on a ring & bronzed metal tree-form pedestal base w/a model of a large elephant at the base, shade attributed to Muller Freres, overall 15" h. (some base flaws, minor flakes to cameo) **1,045**

Arts & Crafts student lamp, two patinated metal conical shades w/ruffled rims & four medallions of caramel & white slag glass, raised on arched arms above a cast patinated metal base w/hammered & studded strapwork detail on a pyramidal base, early 20th c., 20" w., 20¾" h. (ILLUS.) **1,035**

Arts & Crafts table lamp, cast iron & slag glass, the pyramidal pierced iron frame w/lattice top & base trim, each side lined w/green slag glass, raised on a metal spider frame above the pierced iron square pedestal base also lined w/green slag glass panels, on a square black glass foot, early 20th c., overall 20" h. **288**

Arts & Crafts table lamp, hand-hammered copper & mica, the 17" d., conical shade w/a copper framework lined w/four mica panels, raised on a four-socket copper trumpet-form base, by Dirk van Erp, early 20th c.l, overall 20" h. (some modification to sockets, recent mica & patina) **4,950**

Arts & Crafts table lamp, wood & glass, a square oak-framed pyramidal shade fitted w/green slag glass panels around the sides & in the narrow apron, raised on a square oak pedestal pierced for glass panels near the top, resting on a square oak foot, early 20th c., 20¾" h. (some repair to frame, one glass panel w/corner damage) **413**

Astral lamp, gilt-brass, a square C-scroll & foliate-cast foot below the reeded columnar standard w/a scrolled capital below the flaring rounded burner supporting a tall tulip-form shade w/ruffled rim in clear frosted glass engraved w/swags & grape clusters, Cornelius & Co., Philadelphia label, patent-dated April 1, 1843, 26" h. (no burner, minor gilt wear) **1,035**

From left: Fine Glass & Brass Astral Lamp Best Lamp Company Table Lamp

Astral lamp, gilt-brass, glass & marble, the tall slender ribbed standard of opalescent & blue glass w/gilt trim supported by a foliate & scroll gilt-brass base on a square white marble foot, the brass font suspending long triangular prisms & supporting a bulbous vase-form clear & frosted glass shade wheel-cut w/shields, lyres & foliate designs, mid-19th c., 30" h. (ILLUS.) **3,450**

Benedict table lamp, Arts & Crafts style, hand-hammered copper, a sharply tapering baluster-form base w/incised & raised rings & a domed foot, the top fittings supporting a conical copper-framed 20" d. shade w/large mica panels, fine original patina & mica, early 20th c., overall 32" h. **3,575**

Best Lamp Company table lamp, 14" d. domical leaded glass shade composed of repeating panels of geometric blocks above a floral border in shades of pink, green & blue separated by stripes of textured red glass, raised on a patinated metal base w/a twisted vine-form standard on a leafy scroll-cast square foot, raised mark on base "H.A. Best Lamp Co.," Chicago, Illinois, early 20th c., 19½" h. (ILLUS.) **1,725**

Betty lamp, brass, tapering flattened oblong font w/unusual double burner w/two wick supports & brass pick suspended from the curved upright handle & straight iron hanger bar w/hooked end, 19th c., 5" h. plus hanger........................... **193**

Betty lamp, wrought iron, flat-topped oblong oil font w/silhouetted chicken finial, upright end handle w/wire hanging hook & wick pick, pitted, 7¼" h. plus hanger & pick...................... **660**

Betty lamp, wrought iron, low tapering oblong font w/top opening & upright end handle w/chain & pick, 19th c., 4¾" h. **220**

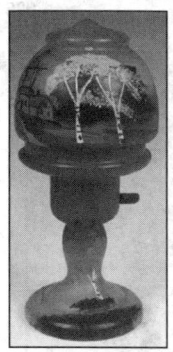

From left: Decorated Czechoslovakian Lamp Leaded Glass Table Lamp

Czechoslovakian boudoir lamp, painted glass, a domed shape shade painted w/a shaded orange to yellow ground decorated w/a primitive country landscape w/windmill & trees in orange, black, green & white, candlestick-form pedestal base w/matching shaded orange to yellow ground & h.p. tree, ca. 1920s, 9" h. (ILLUS.) **248**

Duffner & Kimberly table lamp, 20½" w. square leaded glass shade w/a pattern of cartouches of rose & white striated glass surrounded by scrolling devices in striated shades of amber, brown & white, reserved against a dark blue ground, within pale yellow borders, all above an irregular lower border in striated shades of plum, rose and burgundy, raised on a gilt-bronze base cast w/crests, shade impressed "The Duffner & Kimberly Co. - New York" & "511," ca. 1910, 29" h. (ILLUS.) **21,850**

Rare Duffner & Kimberly Leaded Lamp

Duffner & Kimberly table lamp, 21½" d. domical leaded glass shade in the 'Louis XV' patt., composed of repeating panels of stylized florals separated by raised curved panels in green & amber glass & elaborate gilt-metal overlay, impressed tag "The Duffner & Kimberly Co. New York," raised on a matching slender gilt-bronze base w/cast leafy scrolls & shell-form designs, early 20th c., 28" h. (ILLUS.) **26,450**

Duffner & Kimberly Geometric Lamp

Duffner & Kimberly table lamp, a 19½" d. domical leaded glass shade in geometric green slag glass segments progressively arranged w/tuck-under apron, mounted on a three-socket reeded columnar standard on a stepped round base, crack to one segment, possibly replaced shade cap & finial, early 20th c., 23½" h. (ILLUS.). . **2,185**

Durand table lamp, blue iridescent spherical glass base w/brass fittings & base & two-socket electric fittings, unsigned, 19" h. **275**

Emeralite desk lamp, the long half-round flared glass shade etched w/an overall floral design & a polychrome Arts & Crafts style border, fitted on an adjustable silvered-metal arm on a slender tapering paneled standard & disk foot both w/enameled curvilinear paneled designs, w/original tag, 17" h. (ILLUS.). **920**

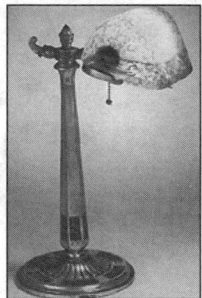

Emeralite Desk Lamp

Fluid-burning lamp, pewter, a domed reeded round base w/a short shaft supporting a cylindrical font w/a squatty bulbous bottom, the tapering shoulder fitted w/a camphene burner, a strap handle from base of font to base, 19th c., 6" h. plus burner **413**

From left: Gone-with-the-Wind Table Lamp
Fine Victorian Hanging Lamp

Gone-with-the-Wind kerosene table lamp, a milk glass ball shade enameled in yellow & painted w/a large stylized leafy flower, stamped brass collar above the matching ovoid glass base raised on a pierced cast brass scrolly footed base, electrified w/font drilled, late 19th c., 23¼" h. (ILLUS.) **303**

Gone-with-the-Wind kerosene table lamp, spherical milk glass globe painted w/red florals on a shaded green ground, brass burner & shoulder fittings above the matching inverted pear-shaped base raised on a gilt-metal scroll-footed base, original burner marked "Fostoria," late 19th c., 20½" h. **325**

Grease lamp, wrought iron, hanging-type, a shallow square pane w/one corner partitioned suspended from a twisted slender post swinging below an adjustable tall racket trammel, early, adjusts from 28¼" h. **303**

Jefferson table lamp, 16" d. scenic domed glass shade w/'pebbled' surface handpainted on interior w/riverside scene including fence & red-roofed buildings, lower edge numbered 2365, mounted on cast metal two-socket ribbed base inscribed "Jefferson" at lower edge, 21½" h. **1,610**

Jefferson table lamp, 18" d. domical reverse-painted shade decorated w/a continuous autumnal landscape w/a winding road passing by a cluster of trees & fall meadows, raised on a slender tall urn-form bronzed metal paneled & ringed pedestal on a flaring dished round foot, original base patina, overall 23" h. **2,420**

Jefferson table lamp, 21" d. flared domical reverse-painted shade decorated w/a lakeside landscape w/summer trees & distant hills, inscribed on lower edge "1972 Jefferson Co.," raised on an assembled lamp base w/new wiring & sockets, overall 16" h. **1,265**

Kerosene parlor hanging lamp, a 14" d. domical open-topped rubina Hobnail patt. glass shade fitted w/a brass crown & jeweled ring suspending prisms & hung from two forked chains joined above to a pierced brass fitting hung from additional chains below the ceiling cap, the lower brass scrolling frame supporting a clear Hobnail & Diamond patt. glass font, late 19th c., overall 40" h. **1,760**

Kerosene parlor hanging lamp, a 17" d. domical open-topped cranberry Hobnail patt. shade w/a brass crown, chains & ring suspending faceted prisms above the pierced leafy nickel-plated support arms & trim around the bulbous brass font, w/original burner, late 19th c. (ILLUS.) **1,650**

Kerosene parlor hanging lamp, a 20" d. open-top domed cranberry mold-blown large Hobnail patt. shade fitted w/a serrated brass crown & fitted into an embossed brass shade ring w/pierced upper rim & hung w/facet-cut prisms, ornate stamped brass framework of pierced leafy scrolling grapevines centering a brass cup holding a clear bulbous oil font, w/clear glass chimney & four delicate brass suspension chains, electrified, ca. 1890 . . . . **1,150**

Kerosene parlor lamp, a 10" d. domed & melon-ribbed open-topped shade in satiny yellow overlaid on white & decorated w/scrolling tan foliage & blue blossoms, brass ring, burner & stamped collar above the matching lobed ovoid glass font on a bronzed metal scrolled foot, Vienna, Austria maker's name on burner & under font, late 19th c., 21" h. (ILLUS.) **2,000**

From left: Fine Viennese Parlor Lamp
Parlor Lamp with Scene of Lions

Kerosene parlor lamp, a domical open-topped milk glass shade decorated in deep red w/a scene of a lion & lioness on a faux mosaic tile ground resting on a three-arm ring suspending facet-cut prisms, brass collar on the tall ovoid glass base w/matching decoration, on a round antiqued brass footed base, unmarked, probably Bradley & Hubbard, turn-of-the-century factory conversion to electric, 29" h. (ILLUS.)........................ **2,070**

Kerosene parlor lamp, Burmese glass, 10" d. domical shade & base handpainted & enameled w/Egyptian decoration of five ibis birds in flight in sunrise sky w/pyramids & palm tree oasis scene, original Burmese glass chimney, gilt metal mounts, not electrified, Mount Washington, late 1890s, 20" h. **10,350**

Lard lamp, cast iron & tin, a low cylindrical font w/small angled wick spout & upright curved handle ending in wire picks, the font raised on a slender cylindrical stem w/a ring strap handle resting in a dished base, brass label marked, w/finial, "S. N. & H.C. Ufford, 113 Court St, Boston, Kinnear's Patent, Feb. 4, 1851" **165**

Lard lamp, tin, a short wide cylindrical font w/two short wick openings raised on a slender cylindrical shaft on a round low domed foot, a C-scroll strap handle from base of font to side of shaft, weighted base, 19th c., 6⅜" h..................... **165**

Leaded glass table lamp, 22" d. domical shade in a hollyhock design, composed of multicolored segments arranged as blossoming red, orange & yellow hollyhock spikes against a white ground above a curved drop apron of lavender & granite textured golden amber border, raised on a slender baluster-form cast-metal three-socket base w/cast foliate decoration down the stem & around the slightly domed foot, attributed to Wilkinson Co., Brooklyn, New York, early 20th c., overall 30" h.................. **6,325**

Unmarked Leaded Glass Lamp

Leaded glass table lamp, a wide domical leaded glass shade in green & white striated tiles w/pink & green flowers above a yellow border w/red, white & green blossoms, raised on a slender patinated metal ribbed standard on a cushion-form base cast w/stylized flower buds on four petal-form feet, greenish brown patina, cracks & losses to shade, early 20th c., 27" h. (ILLUS.) **2,530**

Loetz Shades on Desk Lamp

Loetz glass desk lamp, a pair of small domical open-topped glass shades w/raised gold iridescent festoons on a linen-fold ground, fitted on a two-socket candlestick-form hammered brass base, adjustable standard w/ball finial & shade supports, wide round foot, Austria, late 19th - early 20th c., 17¼" h. (ILLUS.) **1,495**

Longwy Pottery table lamp, cylindrical pottery base w/a well for the kerosene font at the top, decorated in an overall polychrome floral enamel design, w/brass fittings & metal base, France, late 19th c., electrified, 12" h........................ **121**

McKenny and Waterbury Co. boudoir lamp, an 8" d. domical reverse-painted shade decorated w/yellow daffodils & tall green leaves on an amber ground, raised on a patinated metal base w/slender standard on a dished round foot, woven label on base, early 20th c., 13¾" h. (ILLUS.)............................ **1,150**

From left: McKenny & Waterbury Boudoir Lamp
Victorian Organ Lamp

Miller floor lamp, a 21" domical leaded glass shade w/bent panel shoulder in creamy caramel textured slag glass over a wide scalloped slag glass band of light blue & red stylized blossoms, green heart-shaped leaves & orange border, raised on a three-socket slender ringed patinated metal standard on an arched tripod foot, shade w/metal tag stamped "Miller," base also stamped w/name, early 20th c., overall 58½" h. **1,150**

Miller table lamp, Mission-style, four green slag glass panels set in a black scrolled metal framed shade, supported by a rectangular black metal base w/raised & curved armature, w/four applied lion designs, electrified oil canister stamped "Miller - the Juno Lamp - Made in U.S.A.," overall 17¼" h. (black over-painting) **518**

Moe Bridges boudoir lamp, 8" d. domical reverse-painted shade decorated w/an autumnal landscape w/a curving road passing between two tall trees w/hills in the distance, on a slender ring-incised baluster-form bronzed metal pedestal & flaring ringed foot, marked shade, overall 14" h. **990**

Moe Bridges table lamp, 17" d. heavy walled scenic domed glass shade w/'pebbled' surface painted on reverse w/colorful riverside scene of sheep under tall leafy trees, marked "Moe Bridges Milwaukee. San Fran," mounted on two-socket metal vasiform lamp base painted copper color w/green accents, 23" h. (paint chipping) **1,035**

Moe Bridges table lamp, 18" d. domical reverse-painted shade decorated w/a continuous riverside landscape, signed in the lower rim "Moe Bridges Co. 186," mounted on the original gilt-metal base, overall 23" h. (exterior shade stain disappears when lit, sockets replaced, finish seriously worn) **1,610**

Organ floor lamp, a large red globe shade w/worn gilt rampant lion, raised on a burner collar & brass bulbous font fitted in a pierced wrought-iron holder on a tall slender scrolling leaf-trimmed standard surrounded at the base w/a long coiled salamander & flanked by three tall scrolling snake legs w/leafy scroll decoration, marked "R. Hollings & Co. Boston," damage, salamander's feet need repair, late 19th c., 60½" h. (ILLUS.) **715**

Peg lamp, squatty bulbous green iridescent optic ribbed glass font w/a brass collar & kerosene burner w/clear glass burner, fitted into a brass candlestick base w/cylindrical shaft w/ejector & low round dished foot, late 19th c., overall 9¾" h. **110**

Pittsburgh boudoir lamp, 7" w. shade w/four flared panels of ribbed & reverse-painted design, metal shade framework & base enamel-painted w/raised Oriental designs, Pittsburgh Lamp, Brass & Glass Co., ca. 1920, 15" h. (worn finish) **230**

Pittsburgh table lamp, 12" d. scenic domed yellow glass shade painted on surface w/rough-textured green full-length trees & on iron bronzed foliate base marked "PLB & G Co," for Pittsburgh Lamp, Brass & Glass Co., 18" h. **805**

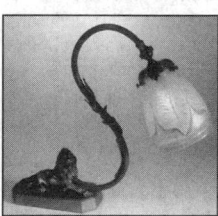

Figural Desk Lamp

Quezal desk lamp, figural, bronze lion reclining on faceted weighted pedestal foot supporting offset curved lamp shaft fitted w/gold, white, & green pulled-feather decorated glass shade inscribed "Quezal," 16" l., 13" h. (ILLUS.) **1,035**

Quezal Figural Table Lamps

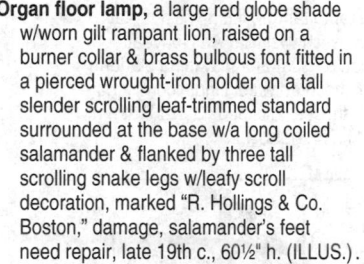

Quezal table lamps, figural cast metal bases, each w/similar Art Nouveau woman on quatraform swirling platform base, mounted w/gold iridescent squared glass shades inscribed "Quezal" at rim, 18½" h., pr. (ILLUS.) 2,530

Slag Glass & Filigree Table Lamp

Slag glass & filigree table lamp, 10½" d. etched metal & green slag glass lamp, beaded metal framework in grapevine pattern on shade, compatible design on base w/fine greenish bronze patina overall, attributed to Riviere Studios, 21" h. (ILLUS.) 1,265

Stickley table lamp, a 13" d. domical woven wicker shade w/a canework design over a paper lining, on a hammered copper frame support above the wooden base composed of four canted square spindles connected by a cross stretcher on a circular base, fine original finish, unsigned Gustav Stickley, Model No. 611, early 20th c., overall 21" h. (restoration to metalwork) 23,100

Stickley table lamp, a 15" w. multi-paneled conical green slag glass shade w/a gently scalloped bottom rim, raised on a hand-hammered copper base w/a cylindrical body & rounded shoulder flanked by large C-scroll strap handles, original patina, impressed Gustav Stickley mark, Model No. 295, 18" h. (minor cracks & glass loss to shade) 3,080

Treen kerosene table lamp, a bulbous ring-turned hardwood font w/a brass collar & tinned interior raised on a slender ring- and knob-turned wood pedestal & square, stepped wood base, 19th c., 8⅜" h. . . 248

U.S. Glass Co. table lamp, figural glass "Parrot" (Cockatoo), red body w/green crest, body on round black base, U.S. Glass Co., ca. 1920s, 13" h. 345

Wall-mounted kerosene lamp, a cranberry Coin Dot patt. ball shade on a brass burner above the large ovoid brass font fitted into an open brass pierced cup

Wall-Mounted Kerosene Lamp

support supported on a cast-brass arm w/pierced scroll bracket & swinging on a cast-brass wall mount hanger, marked "1889 Imperial (Im'pd) Climax," late 19th c., some repair on burner, 14" h. (ILLUS.) 795

Whale oil lamp, tin & glass, a clear cylindrical glass font w/brass collar & two-wick whale burner flanked by upright tin round frames enclosing bull's-eye focusing lenses, all on a slender cylindrical tin shaft & round disk weighted base, old worn black finish, first half 19th c., 8½" h. (old repairs, one lens chipped) 248

Wicker floor lamp, Arts & Crafts style, a 20" d. deep domical wicker shade w/tightly-woven upper & lower bands & a center loosely woven diamond lattice design, cloth-lined, raised on a slender tall slightly tapering tightly woven standard continuing to a domed foot, natural finish, relined shade, early 20th c., overall 63" h. 1,210

HANDEL LAMPS

The Handel Company of Meriden, Connecticut (1885-1936) began as a glass and lamp shade decorating company. Following World War I they became a major producer of decorative lamps which have become very collectible today.

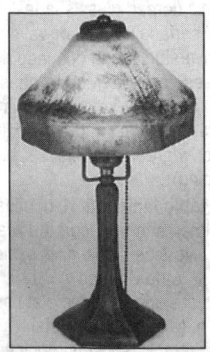

Handel Landscape Boudoir Lamp

Boudoir lamp, 7½" w. paneled conical reverse-painted shade w/a blue background & green & sunset pink, the exterior w/a landscape of leafy trees & water, signed inside "Handel 6232," raised on a slender six-sided metal base flaring at the bottom & w/a greyish green patina, impressed "Handel," cap indented, 14" h. (ILLUS.) **2,185**

Boudoir lamp, 8" d. domical reverse-painted shade decorated w/deep rose blossoms w/yellow centers & green leaves against a shaded blue, yellow & green ground w/three multi-colored butterflies, raised on a slender bronzed metal pedestal base w/round foot, shade signed & numbered, base w/original patina & impressed signature, overall 14" h. **2,970**

Boudoir lamp, 8" d. domical sand-finished reverse-painted shade w/a tree-lined waterfront scene w/a windmill, signed "Handel 6497" on rim, raised on a brown patinated metal flared & ribbed base, overall 15½" h. **1,380**

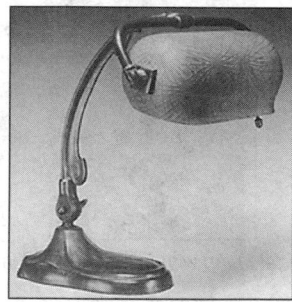

Handel Desk Lamp

Desk lamp, a patinated bronze base w/a naturalistic oblong foot surmounted by an adjustable arched neck mounted w/a scroll & terminating in a green half-round glass shade molded overall w/pine needles, the base w/a Handel fabric label, the shade printed "Handel - Mosserine - 6132½," damage at end of neck, ca. 1910, 11½" h. (ILLUS.) **546**

Desk lamp, the half-round tubular reverse-painted shade w/an acid-textured exterior & the interior painted w/an autumnal landscape, swiveling on a reeded patinated bronze arm & an adjustable curved standard w/scroll decoration on a scallop-cast oval foot, dark brown patina, unsigned, ca. 1915, 12" h. **1,495**

Floor lamp, the domical six-paneled slag glass shade w/pierced metal overlay of water lilies & cattails over red, orange, green & yellow striated glass panels, raised on an adjustable curved arm & a

reeded gilt-metal standard, the base realistically cast w/water lilies & cattails, on four petal feet, base w/fabric label reading "Handel Lamps," ca. 1910, overall 51" h. **3,795**

Floor lamp, 10" d. domical shade w/brown chipped-ice exterior suspended in a shaped bell frame above the tall slender lamp base w/a round, domed foot, bronzed-metal base w/recent patina, shade & base signed, 57" h. **2,530**

Handel Hall Fixture

Hall fixture, 10" d. spherical painted glass shade, grey textured glass internally mottled w/orange & amber & painted on the exterior w/a forest scene w/birds in shades of charcoal, green, yellow, orange & brown, brown-patina, swag tassel, Model 6885, probably painted by Henri Bedigie, ca. 1923, 24" h. (ILLUS.) **11,500**

Table lamp, 14" d. scenic landscape domed shade of Teroma-style textured glass reverse-painted as mountainous scenic view w/leafy trees in foreground, "Handel 7147," raised on copper colored two-socket base w/"Handel" label of felt, 20½" h. (some wear to metal patina, needs rewiring) **4,025**

Table lamp, 12½" d. reverse-painted scenic lamp, flared 'Tam o'Shanter' glass shade w/tall leafy & evergreen trees against pale yellow & sunset pink textured background, rim signed "Handel 2967," raised on spider ring above brass & white columnar base, overall 22½" h. (minor nicks on rim). **1,150**

Table lamp, 14" d. domed textured Teroma-style clear shade reverse-painted w/six red roses on thorny leafy green stems, marked in red "Handel 1521" & "A.C." in the design, mounted on a bronzed metal slender squared two-socket standard on a flaring square foot impressed "Handel," overall 21" h. (rewired, replaced fitter cap) . . **2,300**

Table lamp, 14" d. domical tannish brown textured glass shade w/light reflective opal white interior, a molded basketweave border design w/four drop-ring "buckles" to simulate Mission furniture pulls, mounted on a slender baluster-form copper-finished metal standard w/domed round Handel base, overall 21" h. (base finish worn) **2,300**

Handel Lamp & Paisley-style Shade

Table lamp, 16" d. domical reverse-painted Teroma-style textured glass shade w/a dark tan ground decorated w/a wide border band of colorful paisley-like designs, Model No. 6750, on a slender waisted cast-metal standard w/round foot, (ILLUS.) **9,900**

Table lamp, 16" d. domical shade of Teroma-textured glass reverse-painted wild rose in soft pastel shades of pink, blue, yellow, green as realistic rose blossoms, buds, & leafy stems, inscribed on lower edge "Handel 6422," raised on three-socket ribbed base w/cast "Handel" mark, 21½" h. (some metal patina wear). . . . **6,900**

Handel Lamp with Leaded Shade

Table lamp, 16½" w. paneled domical leaded glass shade composed of small blocks of caramel slag glass w/a patinated metal framework & painted fleur-de-lis border, raised on a slender patinated metal standard w/a raised lapped-leaf design round base on four shaped bracket feet, shade rim tag marked "Handel," 23¼" h. (ILLUS.) **2,070**

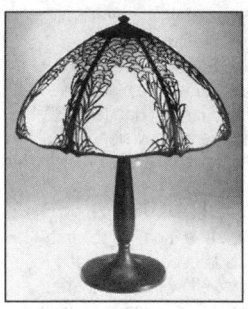

Overlaid Goldenrod Lamp

Table lamp, 17" d. domical leaded glass shade w/seven amber slag glass bent panels framed w/metal overlay to depict field flowers painted yellow, raised on three-socket bronzed base w/Teroma-style texture & molded Handel mark, 22" h., minor damage to metal overlay (ILLUS.) **3,335**

Handel Lamp with Filigree Slag Shade

Table lamp, 17" w. paneled domical slag glass shade, ten sunset orange slag glass bent panels above a shaped green slag border, the panels overlaid w/bronzed metal filigree landscapes of leafy trees, the border w/filigree undulating bands, raised on a bronzed metal tree-form standard w/dark patina, needs rewiring, possible glass restoration, 24½" h. (ILLUS.) **4,025**

Handel Lamp with Moonlit Landscape

Table lamp, 18" d. domical reverse-painted shade decorated w/a riverfront landscape w/a split-rail fence & the moon showing through trees, signed "Handel 8025," raised on a heavy bronze metal base w/four slender scrolled legs around a central shaft above a square platform w/small feet, base unsigned, restored, 23" h. (ILLUS.)...................... **5,175**

Table lamp, 18" d. domical reverse-painted shade decorated w/a silhouetted sunset landscape w/large leafy trees in dark brown against a streaked yellow sky, raised on a tall slender ribbed bronze pedestal swelled at the bottom & resting on a low-footed base ring, shade signed "Handel 6503," overall 24" h............. **4,830**

Rare Floral-decorated Handel Lamp

Table lamp, 18" d. domical reverse-painted shade decorated w/a wide border of pink & white blossoms against a shaded dark green to cream ground, Model No. 6688, raised on a gilt-metal base w/a squatty urn raised on three slender legs ending in scroll feet, three amber teardrop prisms suspended from urn, all on a lappet-bordered round base (ILLUS.)........... **18,150**

Handel Lamp & Overall Floral Shade

Table lamp, 18" d. domical reverse-painted shade decorated w/an overall design of colorful pink, white & red blossoms amid shaded tan & green leafage, Model

No. 6688, raised on a bronzed metal base w/a heavy tapering cylindrical standard cast w/fixed S-scroll handles & ending in a ringed disk foot (ILLUS.)...... **20,350**

Handel Floral Table Lamp

Table lamp, 18" d. domical reverse-painted shade w/sand-finished exterior, painted on interior w/two butterflies w/yellow & orange wings hovering amid a field of wild roses in vivid shades of crimson, pink, dusty rose, lavender & white, w/yellow centers & green leafage, reserved against a pale green ground, patinated-metal base composed of three long slender scrolls joined at the top & raised on a round, stepped foot, w/finial, shade signed in enamel "Handel 6688," upper ring impressed "Handel Lamps," ca. 1915, 23" h. (ILLUS.).............. **16,675**

Fine Handel Exotic Bird Lamp

Table lamp, 18" d. domical reverse-painted shaded decorated w/large long-tailed red & blue exotic birds on gold & black leafy branches against a black ground, signed "Palme," raised on a bronzed metal base w/a squatty urn atop three tall slender legs w/scrolled feet resting on a lappet-bordered round base (ILLUS.)........... **14,300**

Table lamp, 18" d. domical reverse-painted textured shade decorated w/a scene of maroon red & green trees against bluish grey & orange clouds w/sky blue overhead, rim signed "Handel 6937," raised on a three-socket ribbed quatreform bronzed metal standard w/disk foot, overall 22½" h. **5,465**

Table lamp, 18" d. domical textured white-cased shade h.p. on the exterior w/a wide border of delicate repeating foliate designs in the Arts & Crafts style in yellowish amber, inner rim inscribed "Handel 6778 HG," raised on a bronze-finished tall base w/a cupped urn atop three tall slender legs w/scroll feet resting on a round foot w/cast lappet border, overall 22" h. **4,600**

Table lamp, 14 x 20" rectangular pyramidal leaded glass shade w/a Prairie School design w/angled caramel slag top panels within lattice corner bands, a flat base band w/small geometric panels of caramel slag, green & red, on a four-socket bronzed metal pierced double-post base w/a flat rectangular foot, fine original patina, base signed, overall 24" h. **17,600**

PAIRPOINT LAMPS

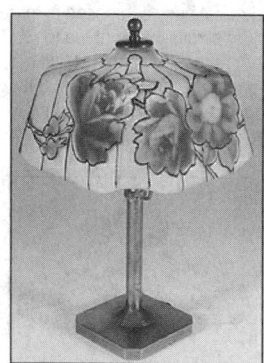

Pairpoint Roses Boudoir Lamp

Boudoir lamp, 8" w. squared domical 'Portsmouth' shade reverse-painted w/large red roses on a pale yellow & white ground, the design outlined in black & black lines on the exterior, raised on a slender cylindrical bronzed metal standard w/a square foot, shade marked "The Pairpoint Corp'n," base marked "Pairpoint" w/logo, 14" h. (ILLUS.) **2,070**

Boudoir lamp, 8½" d. conical reverse-painted shade decorated w/Art Deco stylized large orange roses on green & black leafy stems against a black-streaked ivory ground, raised on a slender nickel-plated bronzed metal slender standard w/a ringed disk foot, base w/impressed mark, shade signed, overall 13½" h. **1,045**

Boudoir lamp, 9¾" d. flaring domical shade in frosted clear painted on the surface w/a continuous band of autumnal leafy trees amid grass w/flowers & butterflies, raised on a slender patinated metal overlapping leaf-cast standard on a round lobed foot, base marked w/raised Pairpoint mark & "C3064," overall 14½" h. . . . **546**

Mantel lamps, two-arm candelabra-form composed of elaborate silver plated metal fittings joined by controlled bubble ball stems & finials, impressed "Pairpoint" marks under candlecups, 10½" w., 14" h., the pair (silver worn, old wiring) **690**

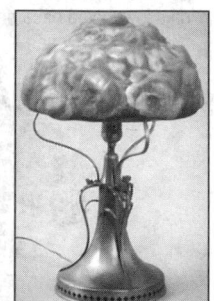

From left: Rare Apple Tree Puffy Pairpoint Lamp Fine Puffy Rose Bouquet Lamp

Table lamp, 12" d. "Puffy" reverse-painted 'Apple Tree' open-topped shade painted w/orangish red, blue & yellow-centered white blossoms against a dark green leafy ground, raised a tree trunk patinated base, rare shade version (ILLUS.) **32,450**

Table lamp, 12" d. "Puffy" reverse-painted 'Azalea' glass shade painted w/white, yellow, peach & red blossoms amid a sea of leafage in various shades of green, yellow & orange, raised on a silver-metal trumpet-form vase w/arched blossom & stem long handles, shade marked "Pat. Applied For," base impressed "Pairpoint Mfg. Co. 8041," overall 19½" h. **17,250**

Table lamp, 12" d. "Puffy" reverse-painted 'Rose Bouquet' closed-top shade decorated w/large red roses against yellow & green leaves on a dark green ground, raised on a bronze metal trumpet-form base w/slender scrolled stem & blossom handles up the sides (ILLUS.) **17,600**

Table lamp, 14" d. conical reverse-painted 'Seville' open-topped shade, decorated w/a monochromatic green ground w/three pairs of long-tailed stylized birds amid scrolling foliage, raised on a bronzed metal base w/a simple cylindrical shaft & a square foot cast w/a Greek key design, 23" h. (ILLUS.). **1,840**

From left: Pairpoint Lamp with Tapestry Shade
Pairpoint Lamp w/Devonshire Shade

Table lamp, 14" d. "Puffy" reverse-painted 'Papillon' glass shade painted on interior w/four butterflies in shades of orange, yellow, brown, blue & black amidst roses in various shades of pink, rose & crimson, w/yellow centers & surrounding leafage in various shades of green & yellow, reserved against a white marbleized ground w/green veining, exterior heightened in gilt, silvered metal handled urn-form base w/brushed silver-finish, w/finial, ca. 1915, 20½" h. **9,200**

Table lamp, 15" d. reverse-painted flared 'Exeter' shade w/two urn & griffin motifs spaced by floral reserves, raised on two-socket baluster-form base, impressed "Pairpoint" & numbered, 20¼" h. (two small rim chips) **1,150**

Table lamp, 15½" d. "Puffy" reverse-painted Floral Garland patt. molded 'Devonshire' glass shade, grey, painted on the interior w/garlands of flowers in various vivid shades of green, pink, yellow, white, purple, burgundy & orange, squared silvered metal baluster-form standard on a squared foot w/incurved edges, base impressed "Pairpoint Mfg. Co. - 3088" w/hallmark, ca. 1915, 21" h. (ILLUS.) **11,500**

From left: Pairpoint Landscape Table Lamp
Oriental Carpet Shade & Lamp

Table lamp, 16" d. domical reverse-painted 'Berkeley' shade, decorated w/a continuous moonlit landscape w/a man in

a rowboat approaching building on a tree-lined shore, signed "C. Durand," raised on a dark gold metal figural three-dolphin base impressed "Pairpoint D3076," 21" h. (ILLUS.) **4,025**

Table lamp, 16" d. reverse-painted 'Chesterfield' lobed drum-form shade, decorated w/an Oriental carpet design in red, green, yellow, white, orange & blue, printed in red "The Pairpoint Corp. - Posted July 9, 1907," the gilt-metal base w/a four-sided baluster-form stem cast & enameled w/foliage on a quatrefoil foot, impressed "Pairpoint Mfg. Co. - B3031" w/logo, shade cracked in half & reglued, wear to base patina, 21¼" h. (ILLUS.) **1,610**

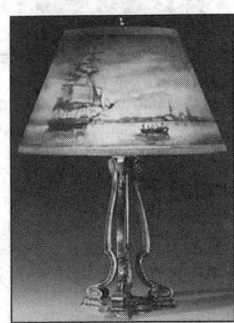

Pairpoint Lamp with Harbor Scene

Table lamp, 16" d. tapering cylindrical reverse-painted 'Lansdowne' open-topped shade, decorated in shades of blue, purple, orange & yellow w/a continuous harbor scene including a rowboat carrying five figures, signed "C. Durand," the gilt-metal base w/a slender central baluster-form shaft surrounded by three slender scroll supports, the tripartite foot cast w/foliage & molded "Pairpoint - 49030" w/logo, 22" h. (ILLUS.) **4,370**

Pairpoint with Grecian Garden Shade

Table lamp, 16" d. tapering cylindrical reverse-painted 'Seville' shade, decorated in shades of yellow, green, rose, brown & blue w/the Greek Garden design, on a patinated metal base w/a squatty urn supported on a central baluster-turned standard flanked by three scroll legs on a tripartite foot, shade unsigned, base signed (ILLUS.) **3,900**

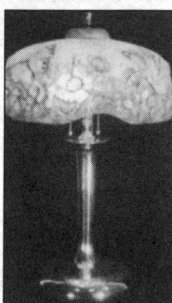

Butterflies & Apple Blossoms Puffy

Table lamp, 16" d. "Puffy" reverse-painted Butterflies & Apple Blossoms design on a 'Papillon' shade, Model No. C-3066, decorated w/white, pink & blue blossoms & green leafage w/pale yellow & blue butterflies against a pale yellow ground, on a simple slender silvered metal base (ILLUS.)............................ **16,500**

Table lamp, 16" d. "Puffy" flat-topped cylindrical 'Hummingbird & Roses' patt. reverse-painted shade, a frosted white ground w/large yellow, red & white roses & green leaves around the lower border w/a colorful hummingbird above, raised on four arms above the gilt-metal slender square pedestal on a flaring, stepped square leaf-cast foot, shade marked, overall 23¼" h........................ **9,775**

Table lamp, 17" w., reverse-painted glass 'Directoire' shade, painted w/landscapes of towns, forests & castles, in shades of green, brown, purple, grey & pink, alternating w/panels centering a stylized flower in green, purple, white & black reserved against yellow ground dappled w/black, silvered metal base impressed "Pairpoint/D 3084," w/finial, ca. 1915, 24½" h. **5,462**

TIFFANY LAMPS

Tiffany October Night Chandelier

Chandelier, "October Night," 27" w. octagonal tapering leaded glass shade w/a design of trelliswork in light green entwined w/vines pendent w/blossoms in shades of blue, rust, yellow, amber & red w/leafage ranging from olive to grass green to emerald green, all reserved against a background of swirled & streaked mauve, white, blue, green, amber & brown glass, bronze hooks & chains w/greenish brown patina, impressed "Tiffany Studios - New York," no electric fittings (ILLUS.) **46,000**

Desk lamp, counter-balance type, a 7" d. domed gold Favrile shade w/damascene decoration w/pink & lavender iridescent highlights on a socket at the end of a slender C-form bronze arm adjusting above a ball & socket bronze base w/round foot, shade signed "L.C.T. Favrile," bronze w/original patina & signed "Tiffany Studios - N.Y. - #416"...... **6,050**

Floor lamp, a 10" d. domed metal shade w/a glass border w/pierced foliate overlay, suspended in an oblong harp on a tall slender fluted gilt-bronze column supported by three legs resting on recumbent figural rams on a tripartite base, stamped mark, 61" h.............. **8,625**

Floor lamp, counter-balance type, a 9" w. tapering cylindrical twelve-sided paneled shade in white & amber glass, stamped "Tiffany Studios N.Y. 1963," raised on a tall slender knopped gilt-bronze standard continuing to a spreading circular base, stamped "Tiffany Studios New York 619," overall 54" h......................... **5,750**

Rare Double Poinsettia Floor Lamp Shade

Floor lamp, "Double Poinsettia," a 22½" d. domical leaded glass shade composed of eight trellised panels, each w/three poinsettia blossoms in striated shades of pink, dusty rose, crimson & mauve w/centers in green, amber & white & surrounding leafage in shades of green, mint green & striated bluish green, all set within green, sky blue & amber trelliswork & reserved against a lime green ground, raised on a bronze standard w/applied stringing cast w/lappets, brown patina, w/finial, shade impressed "Tiffany Studios - New York," base impressed "Tiffany Studios - New York - 379," 64" h. (ILLUS. of shade) **85,000**

Floor lamp, "Poppy," 20" d. domical leaded glass shade w/red blossoms & green leaves w/pierced overlay, against an amber ground, stamped "Tiffany Studios N.Y. 1531," raised on a gilt-bronze slender knopped standard continuing to a spreading round foot, stamped "Tiffany Studios New York 577A," 60" h. **20,700**

Fine Tiffany Student Lamp

Student lamp, bronze base w/brownish green patina, a squatty bulbous ribbed foot centered by a slender turned standard w/two adjustable arched arms ending in sockets fitted w/9" d. green cased over white glass shades, the exterior w/iridescent amber waves, shades signed "L.C.T." & "L.C.T. Favrile," base impressed "Tiffany Studios New York - 316," 26¼" h. (ILLUS.) **37,375**

Table lamp, 22½" d. leaded glass globe shade decorated w/mottled green geometric slag glass segments progressively arranged, stamped "Tiffany Studios" on rim, raised on a four-socket bronze standard on domed, stepped, circular base stamped "Tiffany Studios New York 532," overall 28½" h. **19,550**

Table lamp, a 13¾" d. domical open-topped shade in green cased over white & decorated w/silvery blue iridescent waves, raised on a bronze three-arm base cast w/lappets above a round marble plinth, shade inscribed "L.C.T.," 19¼" h. **5,750**

Table lamp, "Apple Blossom," a 12" d. domical leaded glass shade w/a pattern of apple blossoms in pink & white striated glass w/yellow centers, the surrounding leafage in various mottled & striated shades of green, pendent from white & brown branches, all reserved against an opalescent pale blue ground within green borders, the bronze base w/four upturned support arms on a slender plain standard w/a flaring ribbed round foot, greenish brown patina, shade impressed "Tiffany Studios - New York," base impressed "Tiffany Studios - New York - 11414," 19¾" h. (ILLUS.) **34,500**

From left: Tiffany Apple Blossom Lamp Tiffany Crocus Lamp

Table lamp, "Crocus," 16" d. domical open-topped leaded glass shade w/a repeated pattern of clusters of crocus blossoms in mottled pale yellow & white opalescent, pendent from deep green stems w/leafage in striated green & opalesent white, raised on a slender waisted bronze standard on a domed lightly reeded base w/ball feet, a brownish green patina, shade marked "Tiffany Studios - New York," base impressed "Tiffany Studios - New York - 394 - S197," 23¼" h. (ILLUS.). . **20,700**

Tiffany Daffodil with Dogwood Lamp

Table lamp, "Daffodil with Dogwood Border," 20" d. domical leaded glass shade set w/daffodils on a mottled green ground, edged w/a band of dogwood blossoms, stamped "Tiffany Studios New York 191," raised on a gilt-bronze knobbed & ribbed trumpet-form base, stamped "Tiffany Studios New York 868," 28" h. (ILLUS.). **54,625**

Table lamp, "Gentian," a 17" d. domical shallow leaded glass shade w/a flaring rim, decorated w/stylized blue flowers & green leaves against a rippled white ground, the border set w/'chipped jewels,' stamped "Tiffany Studios New York 1486," raised on a patinated-bronze knopped standard continuing to a spreading round mushroom base, stamped "Tiffany Studios New York 337," 19" h. **25,300**

Tiffany Harvard Table Lamp

Table lamp, "Harvard," 20" w. tapering octagonal leaded glass shade in green blocks, a red & blue shield in green wreath in alternating panels, stamped "Tiffany Studios N.Y. 1914," raised on a slender knopped square bronze standard w/figural relief continuing to a rounded base w/strapwork designs, stamped "Tiffany Studios New York 557," 26" h. (ILLUS.)............................**11,500**

Table lamp, "Heraldic," a 9" w. tapering twelve-paneled leaded glass shade in mottled green glass w/alternating panels depicting shields, stamped "Tiffany Studios N.Y.," the patinated-bronze base w/strapwork designs, stamped "Tiffany Studios New York 690," 18" h. **1,380**

Tiffany Laburnum Table Lamp

Table lamp, "Laburnum," 21" d. domical leaded glass shade composed of yellow cluster blossoms pendent from brown branches w/green leaves against a sky blue background, tagged "Tiffany Studios - New York 1539," mounted on a reticulated gilt-bronze adjustable base impressed "Tiffany Studios - New York 397," 27¾" h. (ILLUS.). **129,000**

Table lamp, "Lily," seven-light, the long gold iridescent Favrile glass trumpet-form lily shades on a clustered stem bronze doré lily pad base, shades signed "L.C. T. Favrile," base impressed "Tiffany Studios - N.Y. - #385," shades 5" l., overall 22" h. . . . **14,300**

Table lamp, "Linenfold," 20¼" d. tapering drum-form shade composed of amber sections of linenfold glass bordered by plain textured amber glass, raised on a simple paneled standard w/wide paneled foot w/an acid-etched medium gold patina, w/finial, shade impressed "Tiffany Studios NY Pat Appl'd for 1952," base impressed "Tiffany Studios - New York - 560," 27½" h. **20,700**

Table lamp, "Poppy," 16½" d. conical leaded glass shade w/a design of poppy blossoms in shades of red & orange striated w/white & amber, overlaid w/bronze filigree, leafage in various shades of green, overlaid on the interior w/bronze filigree reserved against a striated amber ground, intaglio finish, shade impressed "Tiffany Studios - New York - 1401," raised on a gilt-bronze base w/a slender standard on a dished round tab-footed bottom, base impressed "Tiffany Studios - New York - 533," 21" h. . . . **31,050**

Table lamp, "Spider," 15" d. domical leaded glass shade w/a pattern of radiating panels of green & white mottled glass between raised bronze spider legs, raised on a slender bronze inverted mushroom-cast base w/brownish green patina, w/finial, shade impressed "Tiffany Studios - New York," base impressed "Tiffany Studios - 7000," 17½" h. **23,000**

Table lamp, "Tulip," 16" d. domical leaded glass shade decorated w/red & purple tulips against a green & blue shaded ground, stamped "Tiffany Studios New York," raised on a slender gilt-bronze base w/a ring of small scrolls at the top & a ruffled spreading foot w/a further band of scrolls, stamped "Tiffany Studios New York 584," 21" h. **48,875**

OTHER LIGHTING DEVICES

CHANDELIERS

Unique Antler Chandelier

Antler, rustic lodge-style, six-light, a group of entwined large deer antlers w/light sockets inserted at the outer edges, Europe, late 19th - early 20th c., electrified, 50½" w., 44" h. (ILLUS.). **2,070**

Baccarat Crystal Chandelier

Baccarat crystal, eight-light, clear & turquoise cut & molded glass, a central segmented turned standard supporting S-scrolled arms, hung overall w/faceted prisms & chains, unelectrified, late 19th c., 34" h. (ILLUS.) **4,600**

Brass, six-light, the six boldly scrolled brass arms hung w/cut glass chains, each arm ending in a gas socket w/an etched glass shade & blue stained-glass decorative sockets & bobeches, American-made, late 19th c., 38" h. **863**

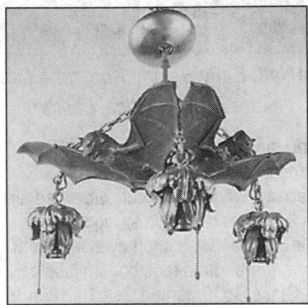

Unique Bronze Bat Chandelier

Bronze, three-light, figural, composed of three large full-bodied spread-winged bats in a triangular formation suspended from bronze chains & a metal ceiling mount, suspending three brass foliate light fixtures, rich brown patina, early 20th c., 21½" h. (ILLUS.). **7,188**

Gilt-metal, Louis XV-Style, 12-light, a tapering & tiered gilt-metal cage w/scrolled candlearms hung overall w/grape-form glass pendants & prisms, hollow glass ball base drop, 19th c., 44" h. . . . **4,600**

Napoleon III Bronze Chandelier

Napoleon III, twelve-light, gilt- and patinated bronze, a central circular tier supporting S-scrolled candlearms modeled w/anthemion & foliage, suspended from flattened oval link chains, France, mid-19th c., 28" d. (ILLUS.). **4,600**

Rare Gustav Stickley Chandelier

Stickley, four-light, Arts & Crafts style, wrought-iron, glass & wood, four square wrought-iron & amber glass lanterns w/six square cut-outs at top suspended from iron flat crossbar w/original chain & canapes suspended from original wooden cross beam, original patina & finish, amber glass replaced, Gustav Stickley Model No. 670, 24" w., 37" h. (ILLUS.). **35,200**

LANTERNS

Barn lantern, pierced tin & blown glass, a metal frame w/the top pierced w/a star & diamond design, the base separates from the removable oil font, mid-19th c., 14¾" h. (very minor dents) **1,955**

Barn lantern, punched tin & glass, a pierced pyramidal cap w/large ring strap handle above a tin framework enclosing panes of glass, one side a door & each side fitted w/wire guards, candle socket inside, 19th c., 11½" h. plus handle (some resoldering on wire guards) **110**

From left: Painted Tin & Glass Barn Lantern
Bronze & Glass Ceiling Lantern

Barn lantern, tin & glass, triangular, two glass panels, one hinged, in a painted tin frame w/angled top & arched heat vent w/a wire bail handle w/wooden grip, hanging loops on the back, interior fitted w/a glass kerosene lamp & chimney, painted brown w/black trim, mid-19th c., no reflector, one hanging loop missing, corrosion & paint wear, 19" h. (ILLUS.) **345**

Bicycle lantern, kerosene-type, nickel-plated brass w/red & green jewels, marked "Jim Dandy," made by The Plume & Atwood Mfg. Co., patent-dated 1896 ...... **154**

Bicycle lantern, miniature, painted tin, a cylindrical dark brown japanned tin case w/a pointed vented top & wire loops at the back, fitted on the front w/revolving red & green interior lenses, late 19th - early 20th c., 4¾" h. **165**

Candle lantern, tin & glass, a pyramidal tin cap pierced w/a star & rayed arch design below the large ring strap handle, tin frame & base enclosing glass sides w/one forming the door opening to a candle socket, marked "Parker's Patent 1859, Proctor'sville, Vt.," 7½" h. plus handle .. **358**

Candle lantern, wood & glass, a primitive wooden framework w/corner posts through the top, wire bail handle & strap heat shield across the top, glass sides & a glazed door opening to a candle socket, 19th c., 9½" h. **413**

Ceiling lanterns, patinated bronze & engraved glass, cylindrical-form, surmounted by crown of five foliate scroll supports w/a mark terminal above a curved clear glass pane engraved w/central star within a stylized floral border, vertical supports cast w/pendant husks, golden brown patina, 28½" h., pr. (ILLUS. of one) **3,162**

Hall lantern, bronze & glass, a squared Arts & Crafts bronze frame set w/four amber iridescent turtle-back tiles in the sides & leaded panels in the base, scroll hooks at top corners & hanging bars & chain, L.C.Tiffany, early 20th c. (ILLUS.) **20,900**

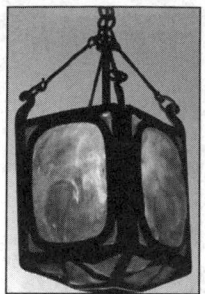

From left: Tiffany Turtle-back Tile Lantern
Arts & Crafts Hall Lantern

Hall lantern, oak & glass, Arts & Crafts style, a carved oak four-sided frame w/peaked top, set w/panels of leaded amber slag glass within arched windows, suspended by a heavy iron link chain, early 20th c., panels loose, some glass cracked, nick in wood, 20" w., 30" h. (ILLUS.) **1,265**

From left: Early Signed Kerosene Lantern
Rare Early Nautical Lantern

Kerosene lantern, brass & glass, a tall clear cylindrical glass globe topped by a pierced cylindrical brass cap w/pierced air holes & a domed top w/a swing strap handle, the base w/a short cylindrical font & burner on a round foot, bottom labeled "N.E. Glass Co. Patented Oct. 24, 1854," 16½" h. plus handle, split in foot, top dented (ILLUS.) **330**

Nautical lantern, tin & glass, a clear glass hexagonal fixed globe in the Beaded Double Bull's-eye patt. fitted w/a cylindrical pierced tin top w/conical cap & ring strap handle, a pierced short cylindrical font base, mid-19th c., corrosion, restoration, 12" h. (ILLUS.) **2,300**

Skater's lantern, tin & glass, a cobalt blue glass pear-shaped globe fitted w/a pierced tin domed cap w/wire bail handle, on a tin burner ring on a domed tin font base, late 19th - early 20th c., 6¾" h. **275**

Beehive Pattern Whale Oil Lantern

Whale oil lantern, glass & tin, a clear mold-blown Beehive patt. glass globe fitted w/a pierced cylindrical top w/conical cap & ring strap handle, pierced cylindrical font base w/flared round foot, mid-19th c., paint loss, minor corrosion, 12½" h. (ILLUS.)....................................**1,035**

SHADES

Art glass, long tapered ruffled bell-form w/intricate gold & green Zipper patt. gold iridescent interior, attributed to Fostoria, 8" h.........................**288**

Art glass, wide squatty bulbous form w/closed pointed top, dark creamy wide ribs alternating w/pale yellow translucent panels, unmarked, probably Fry, 8" d., pr.....**605**

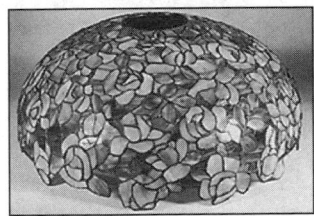

Rare Bigelow Kennard Leaded Shade

Bigelow Kennard-signed, 21¾" d. domical leaded glass shade in a rose design, irregular border, overall trailing yellow & amber rippled glass roses w/striated green leaves on a blue slag ground, embossed metal rim tag "Bigelow Kennard Boston," early 20th c. (ILLUS.)...**14,950**

Bigelow Kennard-signed, leaded glass, a broad parasol form composed of thirty-two bluish green tapering rectangular narrow panels in the Prairie School manner, tagged at the rim "Bigelow Kennard Boston," early 20th c., 24½" d., 5¼" h. (small split in metal rim)...........**1,610**

Handel, domical leaded glass shade composed of red flowers on a green ground, irregular border, 24" d............**5,750**

Handel, leaded glass, domical top above a wide straight skirt, composed of segments forming pink & amber flowers on green leafy vines against a ground of green & white striated tiles, unsigned, ca. 1905, 24" d..........................**8,625**

Large Leaded Glass Handel Shade

Handel-signed, 23" w. squared domical leaded glass shade, shaped edges, decorated around the rim & corners w/clusters of yellow, white, amber & pink blossoms w/green leaves, the sides w/brown trellis reserved against a teal blue ground, molded "Handel," ca. 1910 (ILLUS.)............................**12,650**

Handel-signed, domed acid-etched form in shaded amber, decorated w/bursting fireworks, signed in enamel "HANDEL 5658," ca. 1910, 14" d.................**1,035**

Large Leaded Glass Shade

Leaded glass, 21½" d. domical shaded composed of blocks of mottled butterscotch & creamy slag glass w/a border of butterscotch Xs, early 20th c. (ILLUS.)............................**1,150**

Lotton-signed, slender cylindrical form w/ruffled flaring rim, gold w/pink & platinum iridescent highlights, Charles Lotton, signed & dated "1975," 4½" h., set of 3...............................**176**

Mother-of-pearl satin, ribbed tulip-form w/flaring ruffled & crimped rim, shaded yellow satin exterior, white interior, 8" d., 5" h............................**295**

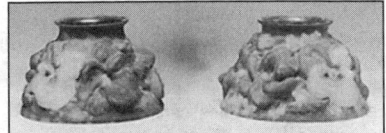

Miniature Puffy Pairpoint Shades

Pairpoint, miniature "Puffy" type, tapering form w/open top, molded & painted w/pansies in purple, red, yellow & brown w/green leaves, against an aqua ground, apparently unmarked, some paint loss, ca. 1920, 5¼" d., pr. (ILLUS.) **2,990**

Pairpoint candleshades, flared colorless glass chimney shades w/'chipped ice' surface & scenic decoration, mounted to gilt metal inserts for sconces or candlesticks, stamped "patented July 19, 1901 The Pairpoint Corp" inside, 9" h. **575**

Quezel-signed, a wide ruffled bottom opening & wide squatty bulbous rim tapering sharply to a ringed fitted neck, creamy white exterior w/gold pulled-feather decoration, gold iridescent interior, signed, 5" h., pr. **605**

Signed Quezel Shade

Quezel-signed, elongated tulip-form ribbed shade in overall gold iridescence, incised signature, 6" h. (ILLUS.) **286**

Quezel-signed, a hipped opal flaring form w/green & gold leaves on white w/gold threading & a gold iridescent interior, signed on inner rim, 5¼" h., set of 5 (minimal thread damage) **748**

Quezel-signed, a swelled cylindrical form w/an upright crimped rim, the exterior w/green & gold pulled-feather design on a creamy white ground, gold iridescent interior, incised signature, 5" h. (small flake on fitter rim) **138**

Quezel-signed, ten-ribbed bell-form w/flared rim, signed on top edge, 4½" h., set of 3 . . . . . **518**

Steuben-signed, ribbed tulip-form in overall gold iridescent Aurene, signed, 5" h., pr. (rim rubs & pinpoints) **330**

Tiffany, high domical blown shade w/eight pinched ruffles, yellow-tinted opalescent w/a damascene gold iridescent wavy exterior decoration, 10" d. **3,737**

Tiffany-signed, conical w/ruffled rim, overall gold iridescence w/green pulled & coiled decoration, stretch iridescence at lower rim, signed "L.C.T.," 7" d., pr. (small chips to top rims) **1,495**

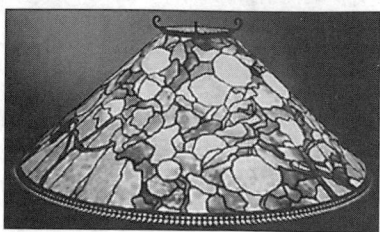

Rare Tiffany Hydrangea Shade

Tiffany-signed, "Hydrangea," 28½" d. conical leaded glass shade w/numerous white mottled blossoms among variegated leaves in shades of green & blue, some in rippled & textured glass on a ground of pale sage green, green-patinated bronze beaded borders at upper & lower rims, rim tag "Tiffany Studios New York," 11" h. (ILLUS.) **68,500**

Tiffany Linenfold Shade

Tifffany-signed, "Linenfold," 19¼" w. twelve-sided conical shade w/amber glass panels bordered by rectangular matching drapery glass, bronze frame impressed "Tiffany Studios New York pat. Applied for 1927," chips & cracks to border panels, 7¼" h. (ILLUS.) **8,625**

LIPSTICK HOLDER LADIES

Collecting items for the woman's vanity has gained much popularity in recent times. There has always been a need to organize all her paraphernalia, whether it be jewelry, perfume, hair accessories or makeup. Everyone knows that the right color lipstick is essential to the outfit one wears. Where do we keep all these different shades of lipstick? In the 1940s through the 1960s the lipstick "lady" seemed to be the answer. What a cute way to have your lipsticks right at hand. These adorable ladies, usually made from some type of ceramic material, seem to have gotten the job done well. Keeping them within reach at your dressing table kept them readily available. Lipstick ladies are not easy to find. Because of their fragile nature, many were relegated to the trash can after use or damage.

From left: "Milady Valet" Lipstick Holder
"Daisy Dorable" Lipstick Holder

Bust of lady, "Milady Valet," by Enesco
(ILLUS.) **$70**
Figure of girl, "Daisy Dorable," standing in
the center of six-lobed holder, by Holt
Howard (ILLUS.). **60**

From left: Flower Child Lipstick Holder
Valentine Girl Lipstick Holder

Figure of girl, Flower Child, girl w/long
blond hair & arms crossed on her chest &
holding flowers, further flowers on her
flaring white gown w/lipstick holes,
Japan (ILLUS.) **75**
Figure of girl, Valentine Girl, seated holding
a valentine w/her wide pink dress
decorated w/hearts & lipstick holes,
Josef Originals (ILLUS.) **75**

Lady at Vanity Lipstick Holder

Figure of lady, seated at vanity applying
makeup, brown hair, pink gown, two
holders behind her, "Pandora Products,"
Japan (ILLUS.). **75**

Lady Beside Mirror Lipstick Holder

Figure of lady, seated beside a large round
vanity mirror, four holders in front
w/applied rose, Japan (ILLUS.) **55**

Lady with "Pond" Dress Holder

Figure of lady, seated beside "pond"
formed by her wide ruffled gown, holding
a blossom, gown decorated w/blossoms,
marked "Whales," Japan (ILLUS.) **70**

From left: Lady Holding Mirror Lipstick Holder
Lady in Short Skirt Lipstick Holder

Figure of lady, seated holding a hand
mirror, brown hair w/ribbon, wide dark
pink dress forms holder, "Original Arnat
Creation," Japan (ILLUS.) **50**
Figure of lady, seated wearing a short skirt
& off-the-shoulder blouse, green hair,
bright yellow base, marked "Our Own
Import" (ILLUS.) **55**
Figure of lady, standing holding baskets,
blond hair, white gown w/gold trim,
unmarked (ILLUS.). **50**

*From left: Lady with Baskets Lipstick Holder
Enesco Lady Lipstick Holder*

Figure of lady, standing holding out her
pink flower-embossed gown, by Enesco
(ILLUS.) **70**

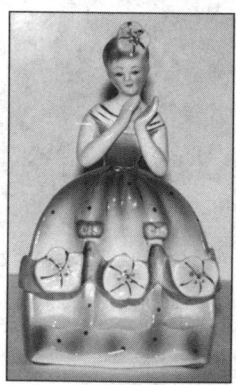

"Miss Pretty Face" Lipstick Holder

Figure of lady, standing w/her arms away &
near her face, wearing a dark green gown
w/large embossed yellow blossoms, large
blossom in her brown hair, "Miss Pretty
Face" (ILLUS.) **55**

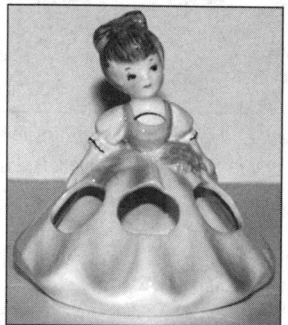

Lady in Yellow Gown Lipstick Holder

Figure of lady, standing wearing widely
flaring ruffled yellow gown & white
blouse, bouquet at her waist, black hair,
marked on base "3409" (ILLUS.) **45**

LUNCH BOXES

*Although there were a few character lunch
boxes before World War II, it was the arrival of
the television age in the 1950s that saw such
boxes proliferate. Most of these vintage boxes
were rectangular metal and included a matching
thermos bottle with both box exterior & thermos
colorfully decorated with a picture relating to the
character and its TV series. Beginning in the
1960s lunch boxes in plastic and vinyl became
popular; these as well as the earlier metal
examples are very collectible today if in top
condition. References on old lunch boxes include
the* Illustrated Encyclopedia of Metal Lunch
Boxes *by Allen Woodall and Sean Brickell
(Schiffer Publishing, 1992) and* Lunch Box: The
Fifties and Sixties *by Scott Bruce (Chronicle
Books, 1988). Prices are for boxes alone unless
otherwise indicated.*

Auto Race, metal, w/thermos, 1967, King
Seeley Thermos **$50**
Battle of the Planets, metal, 1979, King
Seeley Thermos **40**
Charlie's Angels, metal w/thermos,
1978, Aladdin **45**
Cracker Jack, metal w/thermos,
1969, Aladdin **45**
Davy Crocket, w/thermos, very good,
Holtemp Co. **250**
Disney School Bus, metal, dome-type,
orange w/various Disney characters,
Goofy as driver, 1961, Aladdin **40**
Fonz (The), metal w/thermos, 1978, King
Seeley Thermos **45**
Fruit Basket, metal, 1975, Ohio Art **40**
Happy Days, metal, 1977, American
Thermos **40**
Happy Days, metal, 1978, American
Thermos **45**
Hot Wheels, metal, 1969, King Seeley
Thermos **40**
Kung Fu, metal w/thermos, 1974, King
Seeley Thermos **45**
Peanuts, metal w/tan rim, w/thermos, 1966,
King Seeley Thermos **45**
Popeye, metal, 1964, Aladdin. **75**
Six Million Dollar Man, metal w/thermos,
1978, Aladdin **45**
Space 1999, metal w/thermos, 1976, King
Seeley Thermos **45**
Space Shuttle, metal w/thermos, 1977, King
Seeley Thermos **50**
Superman, metal w/thermos, 1978, Aladdin **45**
Tom Corbett Space Cadet, w/original
thermos, good **215**
U.S. Mail, metal, dome-type w/thermos,
1969, Aladdin **45**
Wild Frontier, metal, 1977, Ohio Art **40**

MAGAZINES

The most sought after elements in many of the old magazines (especially pre-1930 issues) are the illustrator/or artists who designed magazine covers, advertisements and story illustrations for numerous periodicals. These are especially apparent in the pre-photographic period, which was from about 1895 to the mid-1930s in general. Most issues that featured movie stars, personalities, sports and specialty articles are in great demand by collectors who have interest in a particular person or subject matter. The most valuable issues are those with multiple value, such as a cover by an important illustrator, auto or other advertising, articles and story illustrations. Most often older issues are parted by dealers for their overall sale content. The magazine values given here are for those sold to the individual who usually only buys 1 or 2 at a time or just those issues in their area of collecting interest. Dealers pay much, much less because they buy in quantity and expect large discounts for doing so. The prices given here are for clean, undamaged and complete magazines. Below are the top-selling American illustrators. Values in general are given here for various magazine illustrations.

MP=Maxfield Parrish (1895-1936) $12 to $200
RA=Rolf Armstrong (1914-32) $8 to $100
E=Erté (1916-36) $12 to $125
GP=Petty (1932-55) $7 to $90
NR=Norman Rockwell (1914-75) $1 to $500
HF=Harrison Fisher (1890-1935) $7 to $70
RO=Rose O'Neill (1896-1935) $4 to $150
VA=Vargas (1920-74) $4 to $175
JCL=J.C. Leyendecker (1896-1954) $4 to $100
FXL=F.X. Leyendecker (1896-1924) $3 to $90
JWS=Jessie Wilcox Smith (1900-34) $4 to $50
CP=Coles Phillips (1907-27) $3 to $50.

General Circulation Magazines, general issues, high and low value range:
Ar=Articles
C=Covers
I=Illustration
A=Advertising
COW=Cream of Wheat ad.

Where there are three columns of values on one line: the first is the value of the average issue, with nothing on cover or within that can be sold to a collector; second column shows values at the lowest level of saleable items; far right column shows the maximum value. V1, first editions always bring a premium value for most publications.

Actual Detective, 1930s-1940s Ar **$6; $10**
Agricultural Digest, 1930s 4; 12; 70
Agricultural Digest, November 1934, MP cover. 75

Air Progress, 1930s-1940s, Ar 8; 60
Air Progress, December 1928, Graf Zeppelin, Ar 16
Airbrush Action, 1980s-1990s, I 3; 13
Airbrush Action, December 1993, Olivia cover. 8
Airbrush Action, March/April 1988, A. Varga, Ar 15
American, October 1934, Henry Ford 8
American Bee Journal, 1860s-1940s, Ar . . 4; 5 ; 40
American Boy, 1899-1930s, Ar, C, I, A, NR, RA, MP, JCL 7; 10; 100
American Boy, August 1916, New Autos 25
American Boy, December 1916, NR cover 105
American Boy, November 1918, H. Cady Cartoon. 15
American Detective, 1930s . . . . 7 ; 10
American Detective, January 1936, V4, #2, Crime Cases. 8
American Druggist, 1900-1950s, Ar, C, I, A 6; 9; 110
American Druggist, April 1932, R. Robinson cover 32
American Druggist, October 1928, 1,000 drinks. . 15
American Girl, 1917-1940, I 4; 6; 30
American Legion, 1920s-1960s, C, A 1; 5; 25
American Legion, April 1931, Ty Cobb Ar 40
American Legion, December 1927, HC Christy cover 28
American Legion, March 23, 1923, John Held cover 25
American Magazine of Art, Teens, I, MP. 9; 10; 100
American Magazine (The), 1920s-1930s Ar, C, I, A 5; 7; 50
American Magazine (The), February 1916, NM cover 32
American Magazine (The), May 1921, NR cover. 65
American Mercury, 1920s-1950s, Ar 3; 25
American Mercury, January 1924, #1 22
American Rifleman, 1920s-1980s, Ar. 1; 3; 8
Antique Automobile, 1940s-1980s. 4; 5; 18
Argosy, 1880s-1970s, Ar, I 6; 8; 40
Arizona Highways, 1920s-1980s, Ar 2; 5; 22
Arizona Highways, March 1935, Turquoise Ar . . . 12
Arizona Highways, November 1980, Schoonover, Wyeth 8
Atlantic Monthly, 1918-1960, C, I, A, MP, NR 3; 7; 100
Atlantic Monthly, Aug. 1973, Marilyn Monroe . . . 12
Atlantic Monthly, November 1933, Wyeth Poster. 22
Audubon, 1890s-1950s, Ar, I. 7; 8; 125
Avante Garde, 1968-1971, Ar 20; 25; 65
Avante Garde, 1969, #8, Picasso 45
Avante Garde, March 1968, #2 Marilyn Monroe 65

Collier's with F.X. Leyendecker Cover

Early Harper's Bazar with Erté Cover

Charming House Beautiful Cover

First Issue of the "New" Life Magazine

Early Puck with Rolf Armstrong Cover

1930s True Confessions Magazine

Charming Early Santa Claus Cover

MELMAC DINNERWARE

Melamine is the actual plastic used by dinnerware manufacturers since its discovery in the late 1930s. Melmac is a trade name used by American Cyanimid Corporation for Melamine they produced. Melmac has become a generic name used in the collectibles field for all Melamine dinnerwares. Full sets of Melmac dinnerware were first available to the American household in 1947. From that year until the mid-1950s, Melmac was available in rich and trendy colors, was styled by "designers" and quite sturdy. By 1955, decals were created, pastel colors dominated and pieces became thinner and less expensive. By the mid-60s, Melmac had become ubiquitous and synonymous with cheap. Vintage Melmac has seen a surge of popularity as a collectible in the last few years. Most desirable are the older solid-colored sets and pieces, followed by 1950s high-style pieces in pink and turquoise. Patterned Melmac pieces are just beginning to catch collectors' attention. Like china and glass, condition is a major factor for Melmac collectors. The above introduction and following price listings were submitted by Michael Goldberg of Portland, Oregon. This selection provides an overall sampling of many popular and hard to find lines of melmac dinnerware.

Russel Wright Residential Line

Ashtray, Branchell, St. Louis, MO, marked
"Kay La Moyne," turquoise $10

Bowl, berry, Holiday by Kenro Co.,
Fredonia, WI, yellow w/red speckling 4

Bowl, berry, Residential, Russel Wright,
Northern Industrial Chemical Co., sea
mist (ILLUS.) 10

Bowl, mixing, Boonton, Boonton Molding
Co., Boonton, NJ, pastel yellow 15

Bowl, mixing, Texas Ware, Plastics
Manufacturing Co., Dallas, TX, marbleized 15

Bowl, serving, Branchell, St. Louis, MO, charcoal. . 10

Bowl, serving, Imperial Ware, rectangular,
pink w/blue speckling 6

Bowl, serving, Meladur, Russel Wright,
American Co., Chicago, IL, divided, forest
green 25

Mallo-Ware Line

Bowl, small, w/tab handle, Mallo-Ware, P.
R. Mallory Plastics Inc., Chicago, IL, pink
(ILLUS.) 3
Bowl, soup, w/tab handle, Watertown
Lifetime Ware, Watertown, CT, brick red 6
Butter dish, cov., Residential, Russel
Wright, Northern Industrial Chemical Co.,
salmon red 25
Butter dish, Rubbermaid, elongated oval, pink . . . 10
Carafe, wine, Flintwood, white & gold swirl, rare . . 25

Brookpark Modern Design

Creamer, Brookpark, Joan Luntz Modern Design,
International Molded Products, Cleveland, OH,
pink (ILLUS. right) 6
Creamer, Capac, pink 3
Creamer, Lucent, yellow 6

Branchell Color-Flyte Creamer

Creamer, w/conical handles, Branchell
Color-Flyte, chartreuse (ILLUS.) 8
Cup & saucer, Aztec, St. Louis. MO,
mustard yellow 4
Cup & saucer, Boontonware, Boonton
Molding Co., Boonton, NJ, turquoise 10

Monterey Melmac

Cup & saucer, Monterey Melmac, brick red
(ILLUS.) 4
Gravy boat, unmarked, w/ponytail handle, pink . . . 4
Plate, child's, Oneida, white w/Hanna
Barbera characters, 1964 15

Sun Petal Design by Lucent

Plate, dinner, Lucent, J. & I. Block Corp.,
Sun Petal patt., translucent (ILLUS.) 8
Plate, dinner, Marcrest, Chicago, IL, aqua 5
Plate, dinner, Northern, Ming Lace patt. 10
Plate, luncheon, Branchell Color-Flyte, charcoal . . . 6
Platter, Florence patt. by Prolon,
Prophylactic Brush Co., Florence, MA, beige. . . 12
Platter, Royalon, Chicago, IL, Rose patt. 5
Platter, Stetson, Contour patt., Stetson
Chemicals, Lincoln, & Chicago, IL, turquoise. . . . 8
Platter, w/wing handles, Boonton, Boonton
Molding Co., Boonton, NJ, powder blue 12
Salad utensils set: 2 pc., Branchell Color-
Flyte, St. Louis, MO, coppertone, the set 20
Salt & pepper shaker set: Boonton,
Boonton Molding Co., Boonton, NJ,
turquoise, the set 15
Salt & pepper shaker set: Brookpark,
International Molded Products,
Cleveland, OH, forest green, the set 20
Sugar bowl, Lucent, J. & I. Block Corp., NY,
pastel blue 15
Sugar bowl, Talk of the Town, Victorian Red. 8
Sugar bowl, unmarked, hot pink, flying
saucer shape 5
Tray, institutional, Brookpark w/Arrowhead
trademark, International Molded
Products, Cleveland, OH, beige, wood-
impregnated 8

Hemcoware Line

Tumbler, Hemcoware, marked "Airline," light
green (ILLUS.) 8
Tumbler, large, Mallo-Ware, P.R. Mallory
Plastics Inc., Chicago, IL, red. 12

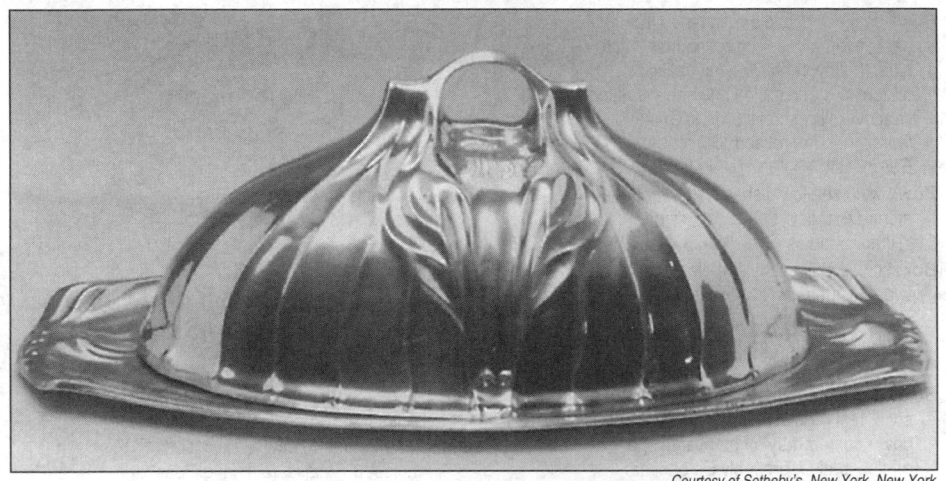

Courtesy of Sotheby's, New York, New York
Pewter Art Nouveau Tray & Cover

METALS

ALUMINUM

Bowl, hammered leaf & acorn decoration,
Continental $20
Lamp, table model, Art Deco style, a 14" d.
conical spun aluminum shade raised on a
slender tall pedestal & round disc foot of
aluminum, manufactured by Soundrite
Co., ca. 1940s, original paper label,
overall 24" h.. 385

BRASS

Early European Brass Basin

Basin on pedestal, the deep rounded bowl
w/a wide flattened rim & flanged base
raised on a funnel-form ringed & tiered
pedestal base, Europe, 18th c., 10¼" d.,
7¾" h. (ILLUS.). 489
Kettle stand, a rectangular scroll-pierced
top above a deep pierced apron w/scroll-
cut edges & upturned end handles, raised

Early Brass Kettle Stand

on two bulbous cabriole brass front legs
& cast iron back legs & apron, probably
England, 19th c., 11½ x 14¾", 13¼" h.
(ILLUS.) 440
Mirror, table model, hand-hammered, a
curved, stepped rectangular frame w/an
attached hinged stand, impressed mark
of Rorag Wien, Vienna, Austria, early
20th c., 12" h. (minor discoloration) 259

BRONZE

European Bronze Sack-form Bowl

Bowl, sack-form, ovoid w/flattened front & back, two handles projecting from each side, the lower half w/a naturalistic texture & green patina, the upper section cast overall w/scrolls & dots, Gustave Gurschner, impressed "Gurschner - 157," Europe, ca. 1900, 6" h. (ILLUS.) **1,610**

Bowl, wide shallow dished form w/flattened etched rim, gold doré finish, signed "Tiffany Studios - New York - #1707," 9" d. . . . **275**

Box, cov., Art Deco style, rectangular w/deep sides, the cover cast in relief w/a scene of a child w/two geese, light patina, attributed to Alice M. Wright, initialed "AMW," 4" l. **201**

Box, cov., hand-hammered, Arts & Crafts style, rectangular w/flat overhanging cover centered by a figural antelope, original patina, probably Europe, early 20th c., 3 x 4" **143**

Cachepot, patinated & parcel gilt in Japanese taste, of deep lobed circular-form, tapering to a ring foot, body applied w/gilt birds in flight or perched on blossoming branches, rim & base also in gilding, 11" d. (some wear) **862**

Candlesticks, Arts & Crafts style, hand-hammered, short baluster-form on stepped round base, unmarked, early 20th c., 2¾" h., pr. **230**

Candlesticks, w/candle cup supported by three arms raised on a slender rod standard above a circular foot, impressed "Tiffany Studios New York D882," brown patina, ca. 1900, 17¾" h. **6,900**

Fine Chinese Bronze Censer

Censer, cov., wide ovoid body tapering to a flared neck w/serrated rim & w/large scrolling zoomorphic head handles, raised on a waisted pedestal base cast w/a finely detailed dragon, the round stepped & vented cover topped by a large Foo dog finial, rich dark brown patina, China, Ching Dynasty, 24½" h. (ILLUS.) **575**

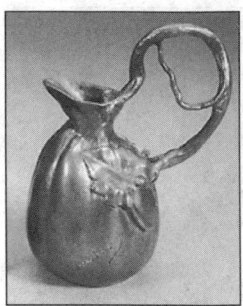

Small French Art Nouveau Ewer

Ewer, Art Nouveau style, ovoid melon-lobed body tapering to a narrow neck w/long pointed rim spout, high arched & looped vine handle w/leaf terminal, signed "P. Loiseau-Rousseau," light gilt patina, France, ca. 1900, small (ILLUS.) **144**

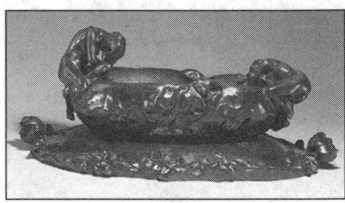

Rare Art Nouveau Bronze Jardiniere

Jardiniere, Art Nouveau style, figural, "Sommeil," a long low oval bowl w/incurved sides cast w/blossoms & leaves & mounted at each end w/a sleepy nude Art Nouveau maiden, raised on a low oblong floral-cast base w/blossoms end handles, inscribed "Vital Cornu - Susse Fres. edt. Paris," France, ca. 1900, 29" l. (ILLUS.) **21,850**

Letter rack, upright backplate w/serpentine rim above three narrow letter pockets on a narrow rectangular base, Zodiac patt., original patina, impressed "Tiffany Studios - New York - #1090," 12½" l., 8½" h. . . . **660**

Table lamp, Art Deco style, ring-turned ovoid standard supported on the back of four stylized lions seated on a reeded-edge square base & four low square feet, brown patina, signed on base "Oscar B. Bach," ca. 1925, 14" h. **3,450**

Umbrella stand, Classical style, a foliate standard surmounted by a crouching elf, the arms formed from snakes, raised on turtle feet, 19th c., 35½" h. **1,092**

Urn, cov., wide ovoid body w/an overall basketweave design, a low cylindrical foot below the wide round body cast in relief w/a mantis & grapevine, the wide angled shoulder also w/grapevine, a short cylindrical neck supporting a domed

From left: Fine Japanese Bronze Urn
Gilt-Bronze Urn

cover w/figural squirrel finial, the sides of the shoulder w/upright looped vine handles, set on a separate stand in the form of clusters of bamboo joined by narrow bamboo vines, stamped "Kosai tsuku-ru," Japan, Meiji Period, 12¼" h. (ILLUS.) **6,325**

Urn, gilt-bronze, ovoid-shape tapering to smaller flared neck, w/two handles, ornately decorated w/flowers & a bee, signed "Leon Lambert," impressed "Siot - Paris - U327," ca. 1900, original liner, 14½" h. (ILLUS.) **6,325**

From left: Fine Neoclassical Bronze Urn
Japanese Bronze Vase

Urns, campana-form, a bulbous base below the high cylindrical sides below the wide rolled rim, the sides cast in high-relief w/a continuous scene of nude classical figures, lappet-cast rim & leafy scroll-cast bottom w/ribbed loop handles, raised on a ringed & reeded flaring pedestal w/square foot, Europe, 19th c., 13½" h., pr. (ILLUS. of one) **5,175**

Vases, tall ovoid body w/a flattened rim, the sides cast in high-relief w/a scene of herons & weeping willow trees w/open branch handles, raised on matching pierced round stands, signed, Japan, late 19th c., 17" h., pr. (ILLUS. of one) **920**

CHROME

Box w/hinged cover, shallow rectangular form w/the flat cover decorated w/a low-relief figure of a walking putti carrying bunches of grapes flanked by small leaping goats, designed by Rockwell Kent, impressed mark "R.K. - Chase - U.S.A.," 5¼ x 6½", 1½" h. **690**

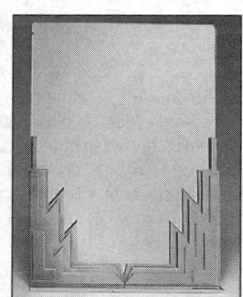

From left: Art Deco Chrome Cocktail Shaker
Rare Art Deco Chrome Mirror

Cocktail shaker, cov., Art Deco style, tapering ovoid rocket-form, standing upright on small fin feet, complete w/all attachments, Baltman & Co., ca. 1930, minute pitting, 3½" d., 12" h. (ILLUS.) **1,610**

Lamp, desk-type, Art Deco style, composed of a horizontal tubular shade pivoting on an angular arm mounted on a rectangular base, ca. 1930, 15" h. **1,035**

Mirror frame, Art Deco style, squared outer border w/inner border of stepped & zigzag cast design, supporting a large rectangular mirror, impressed "Hagenauer - Wien - Made in Austria - Handmade," ca. 1925, 17" h. (ILLUS.) **4,025**

Serving piece, electric, three metal-lidded glass canisters in a circular electric base, signed by Chase, 15" d., 5" h. **115**

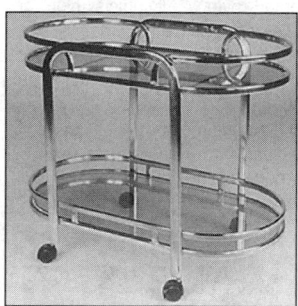

Chrome & Glass Art Deco Tea Cart

Tea cart, Art Deco style, oval metal curvilinear framework w/oblong smoky glass top & lower shelf, on casters, ca. 1930, 18½ x 31½", 25¾" l. (ILLUS.) **805**

COPPER

Candelabra, hand-hammered Arts & Crafts style, a long central stem flanked & joined by U-shaped stem, the whole terminating in crimped edge candle cups, stems joined by scroll openwork decoration, raised on a domed & crimped round base, dark patina, unmarked, ca. 1915, 24" h., pr. **690**

Kettle, deep cylindrical sides, dovetailed construction, iron bail handle, 19th c., 22" d., 13½" h. (battered, iron pitted) **176**

Letter holder, Arts & Crafts style, hand-hammered w/deep original patina, enameled medallion of a sailing ship, inscribed "Twichell," Gertrude Twichell, Boston Society of Arts and Crafts, 1917-26, 5½" w., 4¼" h. **374**

English "Haystack" Measure

Measure, haystack-form, wide flared base below the sharply tapering conical dovetailed body w/a narrow neck & flared rim w/spout, hollow C-form handle, stamped "Gallon," England, 19th c., 12" h. (ILLUS.) **220**

Pitcher, raised foliate design, brass handle & mount, impressed diamond & bird mark of the W.M.F., Germany, early 20th c., polished, 9" w., 17½" h. **230**

Teakettle, cov., wide slightly tapering cylindrical body w/rounded shoulder & low domed cover w/button finial, high arched swing strap handle, swan's-neck spout, dovetailed construction, polished, 6" h. plus handle (dents, pinpoint holes in bottom) **193**

Vase, hand-hammered, tall upright lotus-form w/flaring rim, lobed sides & small flared round foot, impressed "Marie Zimmermann - Maker - 500," w/monogram, ca. 1910-25, 10" h. **3,162**

Hand-made Copper Vase

Vase, patinated ribbed widely flaring oval form w/a scalloped rim, raised on a small oblong foot, dark brown & green patina, inscribed "M. Zimmermann maker - 1463-1915 B" & artist's cipher, Marie Zimmermann, 1915, scratches, 11½" w., 6⅞" h. (ILLUS.) **4,313**

Vase, hand-hammered, Arts & Crafts style, a short flaring round foot below a bulbous flaring vertically lobed lower body w/a wide flattened shoulder centered by a tall gently tapering neck w/a rolled & flattened rim, impressed mark of L. & J.G. Stickley, cleaned patina, early 20th c., 17½" h. (drilled at base, dent on one side) . . **2,200**

Wall plaque, round, raised foliate design around a bust portrait of a woman, impressed diamond w/bird mark of the W.M.F., Germany, early 20th c., polished, 17" d. **173**

IRON

From left: *Rare Victorian Cast-Iron Aquarium Ornate Pierced Iron Candelabrum*

Aquarium, cast, the shell- and foliate-decorated octagonal tank frame w/glass sides centering a rockery-form fountain, raised on a pedestal cast w/figural herons on a molded round base, imperfections, probably J.W. Fiske & Co., New York, last quarter 19th c., 36¾" w., 47¾" h. (ILLUS.) **3,335**

Book ends, cast, model of a ship, 3¼ x 4", pr. **45**

Bootscraper, cast, the center scraper bar raised between two upright addorsed winged griffins w/entwined tails & paw feet, set in the center of an oval drip base w/low upright sides, 19th c., 9½ x 14", 10" h. (slight chip on top corner of scraper bar) **220**

Candelabra, hand-wrought, the flattened upright standard pierced in the form of a stylized flowers w/scrolling leaves within a U-form surround surmounted by an arch & three candle sockets, raised on a double-scroll support & knopped ribbed flaring round foot, impressed "Goberg - Industria - & Eyana(?)," Europe, ca. 1920, 13½" h., pr. (ILLUS. of one). **2,070**

Coffin stand, hand-wrought, American-made, 19th c., 13 x 49¾", 24¼" h. **144**

Door knocker, figural basket of roses, 97% paint **250**

Dough scraper, hand-wrought, heavy tapering round handle forged to curve at right angles into a widely flaring blade pierced w/a small heart opening, 4" l. **248**

Fish broiler, hand-wrought, American, late 18th - early 19th c., 18" l. (corrosion, minor cracks) **173**

Frames, cast, oblong w/oval mirror openings, the ornate border cast w/leafy swags & scrolls w/an American shield at the center bottom & a small medallion at the top center, one medallion w/printed portrait of George Washington, the other w/a portrait of Benjamin Franklin, each w/a gilt spread-winged eagle finial, the shield decorated in red, white & blue, black ground, marked "Design Patented Nov. 25, 1862," 11¾" w., 19¾" h., pr. **550**

Grid iron, hand-wrought, composed of thirteen straight grids on a 13" d. wheel, tripod base, raised handle w/hanging hole, early. **83**

From left: Cast Iron Figural Hitching Post Snake-form Wrought-Iron Holder

Hitching post, cast, figural, a standing black boy wearing a hat, scarf, vest & long pants, his right arm extended w/a closed fist, the hand in his pocket, last half 19th c., repaired, 24½" h. (ILLUS.). **805**

Holder, hand-wrought, figural, a tall upright snake w/a coiled lower body, holding in its open mouth a ball joint w/caliper-form clamp, 19th c., 20¼" h. (ILLUS.) **2,530**

Pipe tongs, hand-wrought, England or America, 18th c., 16½" l. (very minor losses) . . **633**

Shooting gallery target, cast, flat silhouetted figure of a male turkey w/detailed cast feathers, marked "H.C. Evans," traces of green paint, 6¼" h. **116**

Shooting gallery target, cast, flat silhouetted figure of a rooster w/long detailed arched tail, old black paint w/rust, 8" h. **275**

Shooting gallery target, cast, flat silhouetted stylized bear, marked "H.C. Evans & Co.," 5¼" l. **110**

Shooting gallery target, double-type, a flat silhouetted five-point star above a flat silhouetted flying bird, casting numbers on back, 8" h. **171**

Skewer holder & five skewers, hand-wrought, holder w/a pair of curled hooks joined to a short central handle w/small hanging hole, simple detail, 19th c., 14" l., the set. **193**

Skewer holder & six flat skewers, hand-wrought, impressed "RE," 18th c., holder 12¾" l., the set **518**

Trammel, hand-wrought, a long adjustable bar w/heart-shaped finger tab at the top, ending in a four-prong hook, 19th c., adjusts from 13¼" l. **385**

Cast-Iron Classical Urn

Urns, cast, classical-style, the large ovoid body w/a narrow angled shoulder to a wide cylindrical neck w/swelled rim, high arched scroll- and blossom-cast handles from rim to shoulder, the body cast in high-relief w/a continuous band of classical figures, the neck cast w/vines, the ribbed lower body resting on a short domed pedestal w/a square foot, early 20th c., repainted, 32" h., pr. (ILLUS. of one) **2,070**

Utensil rack, hand-wrought, a narrow flat bar w/six applied hooks, the top decorated w/a wavy arched hanging bar enclosing four long slender tight curled bands, 26" l. **248**

Utensil rack, hand-wrought, a slender bar mounted w/six hooks, the center four topped by delicate scrolls below small cut-out chickens, the ends w/scrolls below the arched & shaped hanging bar, 24" w., 16" h. (pitted) **110**

PEWTER

Nathaniel Austin Pewter Basin

Basin, round, eagle touch of Samuel
Danforth, Hartford, Connecticut, 1795-
1816, 8" d., 1⅞" h. (wear, pitting, split in rim)... **165**

Basin, round w/deep sides w/flared rim,
eagle touch of Nathaniel Austin,
Charlestown, Massachusetts, 1763-1807,
wear, corroding, 8" d. (ILLUS.) **193**

Basin, round w/deep slightly flared sides,
eagle touch of Thomas Danforth III,
Philadelphia, Pennsylvania, 1807-13, 7⅞" d... **990**

Basket, Art Nouveau floral relief design,
Kayserzinn, Germany, early 20th c.,
11½" w., 9" h. **259**

Bowl, shallow round form w/flanged rim,
eagle touch of Blakeslee Barn(e)s,
Philadelphia, 1812-17, 11⅛" d.
(wear, scratches) **358**

Candlestick, round stepped foot below the
baluster- and ring-turned standard & tall
cylindrical socket w/flattened wide rim,
unmarked, 19th c., 9⅞" h. **165**

Chamber lamp, lemon-shaped font on a
short stem & dished round base w/side
loop handle, touch mark of Roswell
Gleason, Dorchester, Massachusetts,
1821-71, 4¾" h. (original whale oil burner
w/one loose tube) **198**

Charger, round w/wide flanged rim, crowned
rose touch mark, rim stamped w/initials,
England, late 18th c., 12¼" d. (some wear) ... **275**

Charger, round w/wide flanged rim, crowned
rose touch marks & "London," England,
late 18th c., 15" d. (wear, battering) **330**

Charger, round, wide flanged rim, "Love"
touch, Pennsylvania, ca. 1750-93,
13½" d. (some wear, minor battering) **880**

Charger, wide flanged rim, round, eagle
touch of Thomas Danforth of Hartford,
Connecticut w/"Boardman - Warrented,"
ca. 1820-30, 13½" d. (minor wear &
scratches)........................... **825**

Charger, wide flanged rim, touch of David
Melville, Newport, Rhode Island, 1776-
93, 12¼" d. (wear, scratches)............. **605**

Lamp, whale oil, cylindrical font w/burner
raised on a ring-turned & knopped stem
on a stepped round foot, 19th c., 6" h.
plus burner **165**

Lamp, whale oil, upright disk-form font
w/whale oil burner flanked on each side
by an upright framed bull's-eye focusing
lens, raised on a ring-turned pedestal &
stepped disk foot, unmarked, 19th c.,
9" h. (repair, burner not a good fit) **385**

Measure, ovoid body w/a wide slightly
flaring short neck, C-form strap handle,
attributed to Boardman, 19th c., qt.,
6⅝" h. (dents, wear & repair) **523**

Measure, tankard-form w/tapering cylindrical
sides & S-scroll handle, attributed to
Parks Boyd, Philadelphia, unmarked, late
18th - early 19th c., qt., 5½" h. (repair)....... **550**

Pitcher, cov., tankard-type, slightly tapering
cylindrical body w/flared foot, hinged
stepped & domed cover, deep rim spout,
C-scroll handle, eagle touch of Boardman
& Co., New York, New York, 1825-27,
7⅝" h. (bottom edge damage, spout
battered).............................. **660**

Pitcher, water, bulbous ovoid body w/flat rim
& rim spout, angled handle, faint touch of
Rufus Dunham, Westbrook, Maine, 1837-
60, 6¾" h. (repair, corrosion, battering) **193**

Plaque, Art Nouveau style, oval, decorated
in relief w/maidens, stamped WMF
marks, Germany, ca. 1900, 23" l. **1,840**

Plate, flanged rim, crowned rose touch of
Jacob Whitmore, Middletown,
Connecticut, 1758-90, 8" d. (wear, scratches).. **220**

Plate, flanged rim, eagle touch of Samuel
Danforth, Hartford, Connecticut, 1795-
1816, 7⅞" d............................ **385**

Thomas D. Boardman Plate

Plate, flanged rim, eagle touch of Thomas
Danforth Boardman, Hartford,
Connecticut, early 19th c., wear & pitting,
10¾" h. (ILLUS.)...................... **330**

Plate, flanged rim, eagle touch of Thomas
Danforth III, Philadelphia, 1807-13,
7¾" d. (wear, pitting, small rim split)........ **193**

Plate, flanged rim, "Love" touch,
Pennsylvania, ca. 1750-93, back
w/scratch-engraved initials & "1856,"
8½" d................................ **275**

Plate, flanged rim, "Made in Newp...." touch
of David Melville, Newport, Rhode Island,
1776-93, 8" d. (wear) **358**

Plate, flanged rim, partial eagle touch, probably Parks Boyd, Philadelphia, 1795-1819, 8" d. (worn, battered) **220**

Plate, flanged rim, partial rampant lion touch, probably Thomas Danforth II, Middletown, Connecticut, 1755-82, 8" d. (worn, battered) **193**

Plate, flanged rim, touch mark of Frederick Basset, New York, New York, late 18th c., rare, 8⅜" d. (very worn, battered) **275**

Plate, flanged rim, touch of David Melville, Newport, Rhode Island, 1776-93, 8¼" d. (wear, light pitting) **193**

Plate, flanged rim, touch of Nathaniel Austin, Charlestown, Massachusetts, 1763-1807, stamped initials in rim, 8⅝" d. (wear, pitting) . . **330**

Plate, wide flanged rim, eagle & rectangular touches of Blakeslee Barnes, Philadelphia, 1812-17, 11¼" d. (wear, scratches, edge damage) **303**

Plate, wide flanged rim, "Love" touch, Pennsylvania, ca. 1750-93, 8⅞" d. **231**

Plate, wide flanged rim, touch mark of Jacob Whitmore, Middletown, Connecticut, 1758-90, 8" d. (battering, wear) **138**

Plate, wide flanged rim, touch of Benjamin Harbeson, Philadelphia, ca. 1800, 7⅞" d. (wear, corroded area) **248**

Plate, wide flanged rim, touch of John Danforth, Norwich, Connecticut, 1773-93, 9⅜" d. (wear, scratches) **248**

Plate, wide flanged rim, touch of Roswell Gleason, Dorchester, Massachusetts, 1821-71, 9¼" d. **165**

Plate, impressed "EF" on rim, touch mark of John Skinner, Boston, Massachusetts, 1760-90, 9³⁄₁₆" d. (minor pitting, scratches) **345**

Porringer, cast pierced floral scroll tab handle, anchor touch of William Billings, Providence, Rhode Island, 1791-1806, 5" d. . . **880**

Porringer, cast pierced floral scroll tab handle, eagle touch of Samuel E. Hamlin, Jr., Providence, Rhode Island, 1801-56, 5½" d. **660**

Porringer, cast pierced floral scroll tab handle, eagle touch of William Calder, Providence, Rhode Island, 1817-56, 5" d. (small split in handle) **330**

Porringer, cast pierced floral scrolled tab handle, eagle touch of Thomas Danforth Boardman, Hartford, Connecticut, 1804 - after 1860, 5½" d. **495**

Porringer, cast pierced foliate scroll handle, eagle touch of William Calder, Providence, Rhode Island, 1817-56, minor dents, 5¼" d. (ILLUS.) **660**

Porringer, pierced double-dolphin & shield cast handle, unmarked American, minor pitting, small rim splits, 19th c., 5¾" d. (ILLUS.) **275**

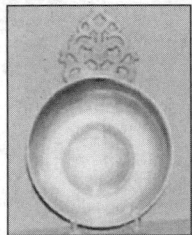

From left: William Calder Porringer
Dolpin-handled Pewter Porringer

Teapot, cov., pear-shaped w/high domed hinged cover, ornate C-scroll handle & swan's-neck spout, attributed to Samuel Pierce, Greenfield, Massachusetts, 1807-31, 7" h. **743**

Teapot, cov., pigeon-breasted body on a short pedestal base w/flaring foot, flared rim & inset domed hinged cover w/wooden blossom finial, ornate C-scroll handle & swan's-neck spout, touch of Roswell Gleason, Dorchester, Massachusetts, 1821-71, 9½" h. (finial repaired) **110**

Teapot, cov., short pedestal base below squatty wide swelled cylindrical body tapering to flared neck w/hinged domed cover, ornate C-scroll handle & swan's-neck spout, Sellew & Co., Cincinnati, 1832-60, 7⅞" h. (repairs) **220**

Teapot, cov., slightly tapering cylindrical body w/hinged pagoda cover w/finial, ornate C-scroll handle & swan's-neck spout, mark of H.B. Ward & Co., Wallingford, Connecticut, ca. 1850s, 10¼" h. (minor dents, soldered repairs) **220**

Teapot, cov., tall footed form w/slightly flaring cylindrical lower body below a tall waisted neck w/flared rim, hinged domed cover w/finial, C-scroll handle & swan's-neck spout, Josiah Danforth, Middletown, Connecticut, 1821-1843, 10¼" h. (some well done soldered repairs, wooden finial reglued) **220**

Teapot, cov., tall footed pigeon-breasted body w/flared rim & hinged domed cover, ornate C-scroll handle & swan's-neck spout, impressed mark of Leonard, Reed & Barton, Taunton, Massachusetts, 1835-40, 12¼" h. **192**

Teapot, cov., tall footed tapering undulating body w/flared rim & domed hinged cover, C-scroll handle & swan's-neck spout, touch of Sellow & Co., Cincinnati, Ohio, 1832-60, 11¼" h. **275**

Teapot, cov., tall lighthouse-style body w/stepped flared base, hinged domed cover, long C-scroll handle, swan's-neck spout, Sellew & Co., Cincinnati, Ohio, 1832-60, 11⅞" h. (repair at base, light pitting) . . **330**

Teapot, cov., tall slightly tapering cylindrical body w/flared foot, hinged domed cover, S-scroll handle, swan's-neck spout, Simpson & Benham, New York, New York, 1845-47, 11" h. (minor soldered repair) . . **385**

Teapot, cov., tapering cylindrical body w/hinged domed cover, ornate C-scroll handle, swan's-neck spout, touch of Morey & Ober, Boston, Massachusetts, 1852-55, 7⅛" h. **385**

Pewter Art Nouveau Tray & Cover

Tray, cov., Art Nouveau style, the shallow dished rectangular tray molded w/stylized scrolling lobes, the matching oval high domed cover w/open handle & molded leaves & engraved w/a monogram, Kayserzinn, Germany, ca. 1900, 21½" l. (ILLUS.) **862**

Art Deco Pewter Vase

Vase, Art Deco style, hand-hammered, the flaring conical body mounted at the rim w/scroll handles, raised on a small domed foot, impressed "M. Daurat" w/artist's monogram, France, ca. 1930, across handles 13¾" w. (ILLUS.) **1,610**

SHEFFIELD PLATE

Sheffield Plate Candelabrum

Candelabra, three-branch, a tall slender ring-turned tapering shaft w/cast scroll bands & a domed foot supporting a foliate-cast section issuing three scrolled upswept slender arms ending in a scroll-cast socket & drip pan, the central shaft w/another socket fitted w/a flame-form finial, England, early 19th c., slight rosing, 25½" h., pr. (ILLUS. of one). **3,220**

Cheese warmer, cov., rectangular w/rounded corners & gadrooned borders, wooden handle, 19th c., 6½" sq. (edge damage on cover, rosing). **115**

Cruet stand & bottles, rectangular form stand w/reticulated design & center handle, square cut glass clear square bottles w/polished plaid design, two w/Sheffield hallmarked covers, Gorham silver mustard spoon, early 19th c., overall 8⁵⁄₁₆" h., the set **805**

Entree dishes, shaped oval, each fluted at the ends, mounted w/foliate & reeded rims, engraved on each cover w/an armorial, mounted w/leaf-capped handles, 12¼" l., the pair **517**

Fine Sheffield Hot Water Urn

Hot water urn, cov., classical urn-form, the round domed base w/beaded rim, the trumpet-form pedestal w/a band of guilloché centered by flowerheads & accented w/husks, the urn-form body w/flat leaf engraving to the bottom w/a wide central band of engraved anthemion, upright angular shoulder handles ending in flat leaves, the tall waisted neck w/a domed cover w/flat-leaf engraving & a foliate baluster finial, w/inner sleeve, Philip Ashberry & Sons, early 19th c., 22¾" h. (ILLUS.) **748**

Plateau, four-part oval, comprising: two rectangular sections & two rectangular sections each w/rounded end, all applied with scrolling acanthus alternating w/leaf-capped shells, fitted w/mirrored plate, on leaf-capped paw feet, each section fitted in a baise-lined wood case, early 19th c., 73" l. **7,187**

Roast cover, oblong domed form w/gadrooned rim, engraved crests, early 19th c., 20⅜" l. **489**

Soup tureen, cov., ovoid body w/applied gadroon & shell border w/two fluted handles w/leaf terminals, on four scroll & flat leaf feet, the domed cover w/reeded band & leaf-form finial, the body & cover w/let-in engraved heraldic device, fitted w/a drop-in liner, early 19th c., 16" l., 10¾" h. (restorations, rosing) **1,725**

Soup tureen, cov., two-handled, mounted w/leaf-capped reeded handles w/lion's mask terminals, gadrooned rims w/acanthus & shells at intervals, on four shell & acanthus-capped claw feet, Matthew Boulton, London, early 19th c., 15¾" l. **1,495**

Vegetable dish, cov., squatty bulbous oval base raised on four knob feet topped by acanthus leaf detail, upturned loop end handles w/acanthus leaf terminals, flared gadrooned rim supporting a stepped & domed cover w/a leaf-cast ring handle, early 19th c., 16" l. (minor wear). **688**

SILVER

AMERICAN (Sterling & Coin)

After dinner coffee service: cov. coffeepot, creamer, sugar & oval tray; each piece w/paneled sides, worked w/stylized floral designs in the Art Deco style, Wm. B. Durgin Co., coffeepot 11½" h., the set **977**

Basket, shallow round form in a basketweave design composed of thin woven silver strips, a high arched & forked strip handle w/a hanging medallion w/initials "SA," John O. Bellis, San Francisco, ca. 1910, 14⅛" d., 9" h. **4,312**

Baskets, openwork woven body w/ropetwist edging & two handles, Howard & Co., ca. 1886, 7" w., 1½" h., pr. **978**

Baskets, two-handled w/ropetwist edging & openwork woven bodies, Howard and Co., New York, New Yori, ca. 1886, 7" w., 1½" h., pr. **978**

Bookweight, rectangular w/shaped top, the front acid-etched w/a scene of men playing lacrosse, the back at top w/crossed ribbon-tied lacrosse sticks, Tiffany & Co., ca. 1875-91, 2 x 11". **460**

Bouillon cups w/liners, sterling frame w/grotesque mask & floral designs, holding Lenox porcelain cups, Gorham Mfg. Co., Providence, Rhode Island, set of 12 . . . . **977**

Bowl, coin, footed paneled octagonal form, Rococo-style feet, engraved decoration & monogram, J. & I. Cox, New York, 1817-35, 5⅛" w., 3⅛" h. **288**

Bowl, Art Nouveau design w/a round form on a flared foot, the shaped rim & base w/applied floral details, Shiebler, ca. 1900, 9⅝" d., 6⅛" h. **1,150**

Bread basket, oval w/reticulated edge & swing center handle, on four scroll feet, monogrammed, Black, Starr & Frost, late 19th - early 20th c., 10¼" l., 8¼" h. **259**

Cake basket, a stepped foot supporting a round body stamped w/scrolls & shells, the edge w/foliate reticulation, upright reticulated handle raised on scrolls, Wm. B. Durgin Co., retailed by Bigelow, Kennard & Co., 20th c., 12½" l., 8¼" h. **690**

Cake basket, oval, the wide spreading foot w/low rounded sides chased w/four grape clusters forming four landscape panels, one each of a windmill, boatmen, a bridge & a watermill, a low grapevine-embossed stem below the wide plain oval bowl w/a wide & deeply rolled rim chased w/bunches of fruit, a center diamond-pierced swing handle, S. Kirk & Son Co., Baltimore, ca. 1905, 14¼" l. **6,325**

Reed & Barton Cake Basket

Cake basket, rectangular w/angled corners, the stepped & flaring rim reticulated w/loop bands, scrolls & chain bands, angled strap handle from end to end also reticulated w/looping bands, cast foliate feet, Reed & Barton, early 20th c., 9⅛ x 12", 5⅜" h. (ILLUS.). **748**

Cake plate, oval w/a low flared foot, Art Nouveau scroll design, monogrammed, Bailey, Banks & Biddle, late 19th c., 9 x 10⅜", 4" h. **460**

Candy dishes, sterling, reticulated rim in a scroll & floral design, on feet, Whiting, late 19th c., 7⅜" d., 1¾" h., pr. **288**

Cann, coin, bulbous form w/molded rim & applied molded circular foot, cast hollow scroll handle w/molded body drop at upper joining, initialed on base "CTL," maker's mark for William Swan, Boston, 1757-74, 5⅛" h. (dents) **1,840**

Center bowl, oval, the everted rim worked in repoussé w/foliage, Gorham Mfg. Co., Providence, Rhode Island, 21½" l. **3,450**

Center bowl, round, w/an undulating rim, the sides worked in repoussé w/floral swags, Black, Starr & Frost, 8½" d. **805**

Centerpiece, a circular base on a low foot supporting two concentric tiers, each w/a trumpet-form base, Tiffany & Co., New York, early 20th c., 10" h. 1,092

Centerpiece, a reticulated trumpet-form silver vase on a stepped foot w/a porcelain cream & gold-rimmed Lenox liner, the base w/three arms, each suspending a reticulated silver basket w/Lenox liner, monogrammed, silver by Gorham Mfg. Co., Providence, Rhode Island, retailed by Smith, Patterson Co., 1911, 10" w., 10¾" h. 1,150

Coffee & tea service: cov. coffeepot, cov. teapot, cov. sugar bowl, creamer & waste bowl; each w/a baluster-form body decorated w/scroll & rib details, ivory heat stops, Gorham Mfg. Co., Providence, Rhode Island, 1901, coffeepot 8" h., the set 1,093

Coffeepot, cov., a rosebud finial on the domed molded hinged cover over a baluster-form body w/a paneled lower portion & applied Greek key banding, elaborately engraved w/Rococo C-scrolls, shells & other foliate devices, the naturalistic C-scroll handle w/rose design, on a circular molded base w/a similar Greek key banding, monogrammed, marked on base by Ball, Black & Co., New York, ca. 1850, 12⅜" h. (very minor dents) 920

Coffeepot, cov., classical urn-form, square foot & tapering round pedestal support the wide urn-form body w/beaded rims & a tapering neck supporting the tapering tall cover w/urn finial, swan's-neck spout, leafy scroll-carved double-scroll wood handle, engraved w/contemporary cypher "JLC," base marked "P.GARRETT" in rectangle, Philip Garrett, Philadelphia, ca. 1790-1800, 15½" h. 10,350

Compote, open, a wide shallow bowl w/a flattened, flaring exterior rim cast w/three scenes, one w/two hounds flanking a trophy of game, one of two leopards flanking a swag of grapes & one of two water birds flanking a trophy of fish, raised on a tall slender pedestal chased w/overlapping leaves & berries on a round domed & reeded foot w/a thin ropetwist rim band, William Forbes for Ball, Black & Co., New York, 950 standard, ca. 1865, 11¾" d. 1,725

Compotes, open, lobed round bowl on a molded base, chased scroll & floral decoration, engraved monogram, Black, Starr & Frost, 1876, 7" d., pr. 690

Compotes, open, shell-shaped, the shell bowl w/a gadrooned border & reticulated edge, w/a cast handle topped w/a caryatid above a design of fish tails,

Shell-shaped Victorian Compote

seaweed & shells, on three dolphin feet, Howard & Co., third quarter 19th c., 8¾ x 10½", 8½" h., pr. (ILLUS. of one) 6,325

Cordials, tapered ovoid bowl on a spreading foot, monogrammed, made for Georg Jensen, Inc., 20th c., 2⅜" h., set of 8 173

Early Richardson Creamer

Creamer, coin, bulbous ovoid body tapering to a scalloped rim & long pointed spout, ornate scroll handle & three applied cast cabriole legs, the body decorated in Rococo style w/C-scrolls & baskets of flowers, Joseph Richardson, Philadelphia, 1711-84, buffed, dents, minor tear, old repair, 4" h. (ILLUS.) 1,495

Creamer, cov., coin, a rosebud finial on a domed, molded hinged cover over a baluster-form body w/paneled lower portion & applied Greek key banding, elaborately engraved w/Rococo C-scrolls, shells & other foliate devices, the naturalistic handle w/rose motif, on a circular molded base w/similar Greek key banding, monogrammed, marked on base by Ball, Black & Co., New York ca. 1850, 9¼" h. (minor dents) 460

Creamer, coin, Classical style, applied reeded bandings & strap handle, monogrammed, Joseph Lownes, Philadelphia, 1758-1820, 4⅞" h. (minor dents) 460

Creamer & open sugar bowl, each w/a tapering ovoid hammered surface also engraved w/a Japanese-style landscape,

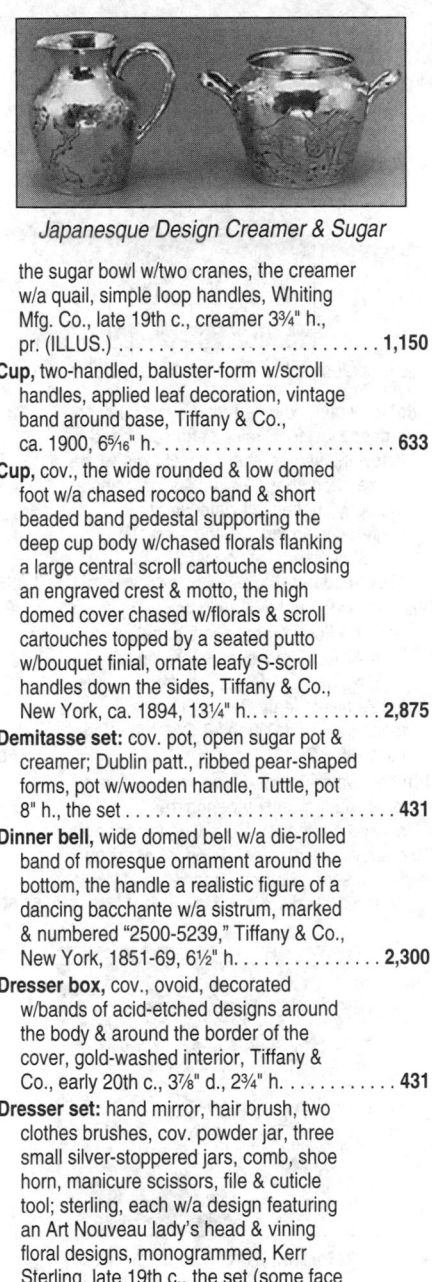

Japanesque Design Creamer & Sugar

the sugar bowl w/two cranes, the creamer w/a quail, simple loop handles, Whiting Mfg. Co., late 19th c., creamer 3¾" h., pr. (ILLUS.) **1,150**

Cup, two-handled, baluster-form w/scroll handles, applied leaf decoration, vintage band around base, Tiffany & Co., ca. 1900, 6⁵⁄₁₆" h. **633**

Cup, cov., the wide rounded & low domed foot w/a chased rococo band & short beaded band pedestal supporting the deep cup body w/chased florals flanking a large central scroll cartouche enclosing an engraved crest & motto, the high domed cover chased w/florals & scroll cartouches topped by a seated putto w/bouquet finial, ornate leafy S-scroll handles down the sides, Tiffany & Co., New York, ca. 1894, 13¼" h. **2,875**

Demitasse set: cov. pot, open sugar pot & creamer; Dublin patt., ribbed pear-shaped forms, pot w/wooden handle, Tuttle, pot 8" h., the set **431**

Dinner bell, wide domed bell w/a die-rolled band of moresque ornament around the bottom, the handle a realistic figure of a dancing bacchante w/a sistrum, marked & numbered "2500-5239," Tiffany & Co., New York, 1851-69, 6½" h. **2,300**

Dresser box, cov., ovoid, decorated w/bands of acid-etched designs around the body & around the border of the cover, gold-washed interior, Tiffany & Co., early 20th c., 3⁷⁄₈" d., 2¾" h. **431**

Dresser set: hand mirror, hair brush, two clothes brushes, cov. powder jar, three small silver-stoppered jars, comb, shoe horn, manicure scissors, file & cuticle tool; sterling, each w/a design featuring an Art Nouveau lady's head & vining floral designs, monogrammed, Kerr Sterling, late 19th c., the set (some face wear, mirror needs resilvering) **431**

Dressing case w/silver fittings: comprising a spirits flask, pair of bottles, talcum powder jar, a toothbrush holder, a shaving brush holder, a folding spoon, a brush box, a cigarette tray, a razor box, two pill boxes, a soap box, two jars, a silver-mounted traveling clock, a hairbrush & a clothes brush; all silver pieces engraved w/initials "C.D.,"

contained in a compartmented leather carrying case w/detachable tray wallets & various loose fittings, silver by Tiffany & Co., ca. 1925, the set (some pieces unmarked, one replacement marked "Cartier") **2,875**

Entree dishes, cov., low oval rounded base w/flattened rim, matching domed cover w/flattened top centered by a detachable finial in the form of a lion holding a shield, the top & base both embossed overall w/flowers in the Kirk style, unmarked, late 19th c., 12¾" l., pr. **3,737**

Fish servers, bas-relief dolphin design handle w/an engraved & reticulated blade & fork, Albert Coles, New York, mid-19th c., pr. **863**

Fruit bowl, Art Nouveau design w/a bas-relief lily rim design, engraved central monogram, Meriden, late 19th c., 11⁵⁄₈" d., 2⅜" h. **345**

Fruit bowl, round w/applied scroll rim & chased roses, engraved monogram, Kirk & Sons, 1896-1925, 9⅛" d., 4" h. **575**

Hip flask, acid-etched Arabesque patt., engraved monogram, 1907-38, 6¼" h. **345**

Ice cream set: six bowls, six ice cream spoons & a serving spoon; sterling, the bowl w/a spherical finial on the hexagonal handle, spoons w/gold-washed engraved bowls, each engraved w/an Old English "T," 1860-70s, the set **489**

Ice spoon, pierced & gold-washed bowl w/three-dimensional polar bear, crossed harpoons form handle, Gorham Mfg. Co., Providence, Rhode Island, 1869, 11⅛" l. **4,313**

Ladle, coin, molded handle w/V-slashed, double molded bowl, marked on handle, monogrammed & dated "1782," Joseph Richardson, Jr. & Nathaniel Richardson, Philadelphia, 1785-91, 13¾" l. **863**

Fine Gorham Loving Cup

Loving cup, wide slightly waisted cylindrical body w/a gently scalloped rim, applied around the top & base w/realistic grapevines which also form three vine feet & three angled vine-covered handles, the side engraved w/a view of a terraced house, Gorham Mfg. Co., Providence, Rhode Island, ca. 1899, 9⅛" h. (ILLUS.) **4,888**

Martini set: cocktail shaker, eight cups & an oval wood tray w/silver gallery; Tiffany & Co., New York, early 20th c., shaker 9½" h., the set **2,990**

Unusual Gorham Montieth

Montieth, the wide gadrooned round foot supporting the deep bowl decorated in the late 17th c. style w/large impressed pairs of V-scrolls w/leaftip ends & a deeply scalloped rim w/putto masks spaced between long horizontal scrolls, bail ring handles at the sides suspended from large grotesque masks, engraved w/the Order of the Thistle, Gorham Mfg. Co., Providence, Rhode Island, late 19th c., 12½" d. (ILLUS.) **4,312**

Mug, coin, baluster-form w/chased overall floral design, S. Kirk & Sons, 1846-61, 4" h. . . **518**

Mug, coin, presentation-type, w/a portrait medallion & a seal, Edward A. Tyler, New Orleans, ca. 1860, 4" h. (minor split in handle, minor dents) **1,610**

Nutmeg grater, shell-form, engraved "Winslow," 19th c., 2⅛" d. (minor loss & corrosion to grater) **316**

Pencil sharpener, on a trumpet foot, w/key twisted & ovoid cover, The Merrill Shops, first quarter 20th c., 4⅝" l., 3½" h. **748**

Pitcher, water, paneled baluster-form, chased decoration, monogrammed, Frank Smith, retailed by Bailey, Banks & Biddle Co., 10" h. **2,645**

Pitcher, water, classical paneled baluster-form w/wide arched spout, angled handle & short pedestal w/rectangular foot, applied & engraved Colonial Revival scroll & floral designs, engraved monogram, Reed & Barton, early 20th c., 10⅜" h. **863**

Pitcher, water, lobed baluster-form, a ropetwist footrim below the bulbous tapering body decorated w/overall undulating horizontal bands & set w/scroll-trimmed cartouches, long narrow spout over large cartouche, high arched ropetwist handle, Tiffany & Co., New York, late 19th c., 10½" h. (ILLUS.) **2,530**

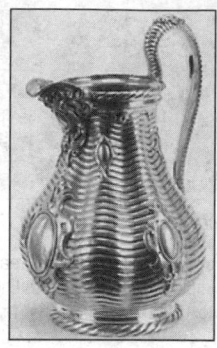

Decorated Tiffany Water Pitcher

Pitcher, water, coin, tapering ovoid body on a ringed low foot, raised shoulder band below the wide cylindrical neck w/a wide, high arched spout & high C-scroll handle, the body chased w/foliate wreath centered w/an inscription dated 1846, Lincoln & Reed, Boston, 1838-48, 10⅝" h. (dents) **1,035**

Pitcher, water, bulbous baluster-form, ringed & floral-embossed foot below the body & neck embossed overall in the Kirk style w/flowers & ferns, wide rolled spout, floral-chased leafy C-scroll handle, monogrammed, Tiffany & Co., New York, ca. 1885, 12¼" h. **3,450**

Pitcher, water, tankard-type, modeled as a tall slender slightly tapering tree trunk applied around the sides w/a wandering grapevine, high arched upright rim spout & long shaped branch handle, R. & W. Wilson, Philadelphia, ca. 1840, 14" h. **5,750**

Gorham Pitcher & Undertray

Pitcher & undertray, rounded rectangular baluster-form body chased w/masks, bands & swags of fruit, high arched spout over grotesque mask, ornate C-scroll handle, raised on four heavy paw feet, on a matching tray w/raised center platform & small bun feet, Gorham Mfg. Co., Providence, Rhode Island, code letters on base of each, ca. 1908, overall 12¼" h. (ILLUS.) **5,462**

Plates, large round dished form w/overall hand-hammered surface & wide flanged rim, base engraved w/an initial, Shreve & Co., early 20th c., 10" d., set of 6 . . . . **1,150**

Porringer, Art Nouveau style, ovoid hammered body w/reticulated foliate handle, early 20th c., 7⅛" l., 1¾" h. **805**

Pot, cov., coin, tapering cylindrical form w/fluted rims & a scroll handle, cover w/a fruit finial, William Adams, 1830s-40s, 5½" h. (monogram erased). **259**

Punch bowl, deep rounded bowl w/rolled & scalloped rim, raised on four cast grapevine feet, the body w/applied swags of grape clusters & leaves between satyrs' heads, engraved monogram "EAW," gilt interior, by George W. Shiebler & Co., New York, retailed by Irwin R. Brayton, ca. 1905, 14½" d., 9¾" h.. . **5,750**

Punch ladle, applied prunus blossoms finial on a vine-wrapped handle, gold-washed bowl, 20th c. **403**

Punch set: bowl & twelve punch cups; the bowl w/a wide domed foot chased w/a continuous floral band, the wide round body chased w/a continuous stylized chinoiserie landscape w/people & buildings, the footed cups w/matching designs on the sides of the bowls, Schofield Co., Baltimore, Maryland, early 20th c., bowl 14⅝" d., the set **4,600**

Simple 20th Century Punch Set

Punch set: punch bowl, 24 cups & round undertray; the bowl & cups w/deep plain gently flaring sides, on shallow round tray, each piece engraved w/the Vanderbilt coat of arms, Graff, Washbourne & Dunn, New York, retailed by Cartier, 20th c., bowl 14" d., undertray 22" d., the set (ILLUS.) **6,612**

Salt dips, figural, in English Regency style, modeled as an argonaut shell supported on the back of a dolphin on an oval wave-chased base, P.L. Krider, Philadelphia, ca. 1870, 3⅝" l., pr. **2,012**

Salt dips & spoons, open oyster shell-form, gold-washed bowl, Gorham Mfg. Co., Providence, Rhode Island, late 19th c., 4⅞" l., pr. **1,495**

Salver, George III-Syle, center engraved w/an armorial, shaped border applied w/intervals of scrolls, on four scroll feet, Howard and Co., New York, New York, ca. 1900, 22½" l. **1,312**

Sauceboats, deep oval body w/a high & wide arched spout & beaded & entrelac rim band, an upright rounded leafy scroll handle, raised on four ram's head & hoofed leg supports, engraved w/a contemporary monogram & dated "June 1st 1859," marked "R & W," retailed by Bigelow Bros. & Kennard, Boston, ca. 1859, 7½" l., pr. **2,300**

Service plates, round w/bas-relief Italian Renaissance border designs, engraved foliate central monogram, Gorham Mfg. Co., Providence, Rhode Island, late 19th c., 10¾" d., set of 12 . . . . **7,763**

Serving dish, modeled as double grape leaves & bunches of grapes w/chased details, Watson Sterling, early 20th c., 10⅝" l. **374**

Serving spoon, coin, bright-cut decoration, monogrammed, George Alexander & Peter Riker, New York, 1797-1800, 12" l. **805**

Shakers, figural, realistically formed as seated pug dogs wearing collars, removable heads pierced on top, each engraved "M.O.R.," Dominick & Haff, New York, marked "D & H Sterling" & date lozenge for 1879, 2¾" h., pr. **4,887**

Sherbet cups w/glass liners, each silver-gilt bowl engraved w/cartouches & floral designs, Gorham Mfg. Co., Providence, Rhode Island, set of 10 . . . . **977**

Soup tureen, cov., oval, the reeded domed oval foot embossed & chased on the top w/flowers, the long rounded body & stepped, domed cover embossed & chased overall in the Kirk style w/flowers & leaves, the cover w/a reeded upright ring handle, gadrooned loop end handles on the body, monogrammed, Tiffany & Co., New York, ca. 1880, overall 13¾" l. **5,750**

Soup tureen, cov., oval, the foot rim w/a die-stamped band, low pedestal supporting a plain squatty bulbous body w/die-stamped rim below the sloping domed cover w/a scroll-pierced & pointed handle w/turned & pointed finial, the long C-scroll end handles topped by figural infant bacchi, partly frosted finish, Wood & Hughes, New York, ca. 1865-70, overall 18½" l. **5,462**

Sugar basket, coin, footed navette form, chased floral leaf decoration, swing handle, monogrammed, Ball, Black & Company, 1850s, 6¾" h., 6" l. **460**

Sugar bowl, cov., round ringed foot supporting a gently flaring hemispherical bowl w/molded rim & domed cover w/wide & low dished round handle, marked "IR" in square, Joseph Richardson Sr., Philadelphia, ca. 1748, 4⅜" d. **20,700**

Sugar bowl, cov., coin, baluster-form body w/applied foliate & star banding, on a square molded base, domed cover w/acorn finial, monogrammed, Thomas Fletcher & Sidney Gardner, Boston, 1808-25, 7" h. (minor dents). **345**

Sugar bowl, cov., coin, a wide round ringed foot w/gadrooned rim band & applied scroll & foliate banding below the squatty bulbous body chased w/long acanthus leaves up the sides below the rolled foliate band rim, domed cover w/strawberry finial, C-scroll handles, monogrammed, Jonathan Stodder & Benjamin Frobisher, Boston, 1816-25, 7¾" h. (minor dents). **403**

Sugar bowl, cov., baluster-form body w/applied rose banding & ram's head mounts on a square molded base, domed cover w/bud finial, keystone touch w/"DH," mid-19th c., 8½" h. **316**

Tankard, cov., footed baluster-form, the round stepped foot w/a gadrooned band, plain body, stepped & domed hinged cover w/gadrooned rim band & pierced shell-form thumbpiece above the double scroll handle w/a heart-shaped endpiece, engraved w/contemporary foliate monogram "BMD," marked three times on base "JA" in script for Joseph Anthony, Jr., Philadelphia, ca. 1785, heavy weight, 9" h. **27,600**

Early 18th Century Tankard

Tankard, cov., tapering cylindrical body w/ringed foot & medial band, stepped domed hinged cover w/short baluster finial, scroll handle w/a convex shield terminal & scroll thumbrest, the side engraved w/a later crest & name, marks of William Cowell, Boston, Massachusetts, ca. 1730, 7½" h. (ILLUS.) . . **7,475**

Tazza, a round shallow bowl w/a flaring arching openwork rim, supported by a figural partly draped putto above a stepped partly fluted flaring round base, Gorham Mfg. Co., Providence, Rhode Island, dated 1871, 12¼" h. **2,300**

Tazze, a shallow flaring squared dish w/rounded corners chased overall w/flowers & ferns, raised on a high domed base of four flaring scroll-embossed legs, S. Kirk & Son, Baltimore, ca. 1880-90, 7" w., pr. **1,725**

Tea & coffee service: cov. coffeepot, cov. teapot, cov. sugar bowl, creamer & waste bowl; each in squatty ovoid form, w/feet & applied rim decoration, scroll finials, engraved monogram inscription, Reed & Barton, 20th c., coffeepot 6¾" h., the set (minor denting) **748**

Tea & coffee service: cov. teapot, cov. coffeepot, cov. sugar bowl, creamer & waste bowl; each of paneled flattened baluster-form, handles w/ivory heat stops, monogrammed, Unger Brothers, early 20th c., coffeepot 5½" h., the set **489**

Tea & coffee service: cov. teapot, cov. coffeepot, tankard-style cov. hot milk pitcher, creamer, cov. sugar bowl, waste bowl & kettle on lampstand base; most pieces w/a squatty bulbous body, each repoussé & chased overall w/flowers & foliage on a textured ground, the finials in the form of blossoms, bases engraved "JK, April 27, 1905," marked by S. Kirk & Son Co., coffeepot 9½" h., the set. **9,775**

American Classical Tea Set

Tea set: cov. teapot, open sugar bowl & creamer; coin, each of classical urn form decorated w/bands of pearls & herringbone design on the foot & shoulder, embossed acanthus leaves, the teapot w/animal head spout & scroll handle, the creamer w/a winged female figure on the scroll handle, the sugar w/applied female masks & laurel leaf handles, teapot & sugar marked, Anthony Rasch & Co., Philadelphia, 1820-30, teapot 9⅜" h., the set (ILLUS.) **2,875**

Tea set: cov. teapot, cov. sugar bowl & creamer; coin, Classical style, each piece w/a ringed pedestal foot supporting a bulbous lobed body below a stepped shoulder w/a scroll-cast band below a smaller leaf band, the domed covers w/leafy scrolls & a knob finial, ornate C-scroll handle, paneled swan's-neck spout on pot, John I. Monell & Charles M. Williams, New York City, ca. 1825, teapot 10⅜" h., the set (very minor dents) **2,185**

Teakettle on lamp stand, the kettle w/a squat round body embellished w/an engraved band of Greek key, raised on a spreading foot similarly engraved, a serpentine spout w/flat leaf detail, domed cover w/Greek key border & corn finial, hinged handle w/ivory heat stops & rams' head terminals, w/a stand, possibly plated, w/scrolled arms & Greek key engraving, on rocaille feet, w/plated burner, Tiffany & Co., New York, 1854-70, kettle 9½" h., the set. **1,380**

Teapot, cov., coin, Classical style, round stepped short pedestal foot below the bulbous squatty oblong body w/two stepped shoulder & cover bands of applied grape & leaf banding, the domed cover w/a basket of fruit finial, ornate C-scroll handle w/insulators & long swan's-neck spout, Henry Ball, Erastus Tompkins & William Black, New York, 1839-51, 10" h. **690**

Teapot, cov., coin, bulbous ovoid body w/applied basket of fruit & flowers banding around the shoulder, raised on a flaring ringed pedestal base, figural serpent & fish-form handles & paneled serpent-form spout, domed cover w/a figural bird finial, marked "L. Allen," second quarter 19th c., 10½" h. (minor dents) . . **978**

Tray, rectangular, shaped rim & chased floral decoration, Durgin, retailed by Bigelow, Kennard and Co., late 19th c., 12" l. . . **489**

Tray, square w/rounded corners, applied scroll border, engraved to center w/a monogram, early 20th c., 12¼" sq. **230**

Tray, oval w/low dished edge & beaded rim, the center engraved w/a crest surrounded by a wide band of grotesque masks & foliage, beaded & turned squared end handles, Tiffany & Co., New York, overall 32½" l. **11,500**

Tumbler, coin, barrel-form w/reeded banding, monogrammed, Asa Blanchard, Lexington, Kentucky, 1818-38, 3⅛" h. (minor dents) **5,463**

Tureen, cov., oval, a stepped oval foot & short pedestal supporting the long squatty bulbous body w/slightly flared rim & large reeded square section end

Large Tiffany Covered Tureen

handles w/a beaded cube in the center & flat leaf terminals, the stepped domed cover w/a scroll-trimmed pierced heart-shaped handle on rayed leaves, monogrammed & dated, Tiffany & Co., New York, 1875- 91, 8½ x 15", 11¼" h. (ILLUS.) **5,175**

Tureen, cover & liner, narrow oval form, domed cover & swelled base each embossed & chased overall w/a scene of a hound flushing game surrounded by flowers & fruit, finial in the figure of a large spread-winged bird perched on a rock, the liner w/hinged ring handles capped by lion masks, A.E. Warner, Baltimore, ca. 1845, 13" l., the set. **2,300**

Urn-vase, cov., silver-gilt, swirl-ribbed domed pedestal foot supports the tall waisted ovoid body chased w/spiral lobes & swirled flowering stems, the domed swirl-ribbed cover w/flame finial, long double C-scroll leafy scroll handles down the sides, engraved w/monograms & dates, Howard & Co., George III-style, New York, 1893, 20" h. **3,450**

Vase, hexagonal trumpet form w/matching domed foot, decorated w/acid-etched Colonial Revival decoration, Tiffany & Co., early 20th c., 11½" h. **920**

Vase, Art Nouveau style, small ringed foot supporting a compressed cushion-form lower body below the tall, slender waisted neck w/a widely flaring rim, long slender curved leaf handles from center body to underside of lower body, lower body w/scrolling chased tulips & leaves, the wide neck chased w/iris blossoms, Dominick & Haff, New York, ca. 1900, 15½" h. **4,025**

Vase, baluster-form w/a tall slightly waisted neck w/a widely rolled rim, the domed pedestal base w/leafy scroll feet, the lower bulbous body chased w/panels of scrolls & floral swags, the neck chased w/scroll-supported urns of flowers alternating w/panels w/applied lion masks & bearded faces, floral swags around the top of neck & scroll bands on the rolled rim, Gorham Mfg. Co., Providence, Rhode Island, special order, 1899, 17½" h. . . . **5,462**

Vase, Art Nouveau style, trumpet-shaped, the base & lower body cast w/openwork caylx of Art Nouveau flowers & tendrils, plain flaring upper body w/small floral clusters around the rim, Whiting Mfg. Co., 1905, 19¼" h. **4,312**

Vase, presentation-type, tall simple classic urn form, domed foot w/chased band supporting the tall body w/an applied girdle of oak branches around the shoulder, the short, wide cylindrical neck w/rolled, beaded rim flanked by high arched leafy scroll slender handles from rim to lower body, the body engraved w/a festoon of shamrock & badge of The Friendly Sons of St. Patrick on one side & presentation panel on the other, Reed & Barton, ca. 1910, 26" h. **6,325**

Vegetable dish, cov., round, the border w/scrolls & foliage, Theodore B. Starr, New York, New York, early 20th c., 10½" d. . . **431**

Wine cooler, simple urn-form body w/an egg-and-dart rim band & twin upright folding rim handle rising from pairs of classical female heads, the body raised on four winged lion monopods w/paw feet, interior fixed cylindrical liner, the side engraved w/contemporary arms, Tiffany & Co., New York, ca. 1865, 13" h. **9,200**

ENGLISH & OTHERS

Bowl, footed, a stepped circular base issuing an openwork berry & foliate stem supports a deep flaring inverted bell-form bowl, George Jensen Silversmithy, Denmark, Pattern No. 17A, 1925-32, 4" h. **690**

Bowl, low round footed form, a French coin set in the bottom, scroll handles, swag & ribbon decoration around the sides, engraved name & date on rim, France, 18th c., 5" d., 4" h. **230**

Bowl, footed, ribbed & fluted deep sides on a low foot, chased swag & ribbon border, engraved inscription under base, Hutton & Sons, Ltd., London, England, 1898-99, 9¼" d., 6¼" h. **748**

Box, cov., in the form of a faux wood cigar box w/labels, Russia, late 19th c., 2¹⁵⁄₁₆ x 5⅛", 1⅝" h. **1,495**

Box, cov., oval, chased scene on the cover depicting a knight bowing to a group of ladies, engraved harbor scenes & floral decoration around the body, Holland, 19th c., 4⅝ x 5⅝", 2½" h. **460**

Box, cov., quatrefoil box w/sides & hinged cover flat-chased w/foliage on a stippled ground, the cover mounted w/five amithystine quartz cabochons, on four ball feet, Germany, ca. 1900, 4¾" l. **517**

Cake basket, footed scalloped round shallow paneled dish w/applied scroll & floral rim, chased floral decoration,

pierced swing handle, monogram & date under base, make "C. & Co.," Sheffield, England, 1864-65, 13" d. **748**

Casters, baluster urn-form, ribbed bands at neck, shoulder & base, Henry Chawner, London, 1791-92, 6⅜" h., pr. **690**

Caudle cup, miniature, of typical form, w/swirled, lobed lower body, mounted w/scroll handles, George I period, London, 1716, 2¾" l. over handles. **460**

Centerpiece, oblong paneled navette form raised on a domed, paneled oblong foot, leafy scroll scalloped rim over gadrooned band, raised & chased side designs, figural child handle at each end, Germany, 19th c., 21¾" l., 12¼" h. **4,025**

Chalice, tall cup form w/chased decoration, engraved inscription, 800 fine, Vienna, Austria, ca. 1897, 15⅝" h. (slight dents) **1,035**

Russian Coffee & Tea Set

Coffee & tea set: cov. coffeepot, cov. teapot, open sugar & creamer; each piece w/a fluted & tapering ovoid form, engraved oval wreath & vining border bands, ivory finials & heat stops, Moscow, Russia, late 19th c., coffeepot 7½" h., the set (ILLUS.). **2,990**

Coffeepot, cov., baluster-form, mounted w/a turned wood side handle, on three pad feet, Francois-Nicolas Rousseau, Paris, 1784, 7" h. **1,150**

George II Coffeepot

Coffeepot, cov., of baluster-form on spreading foot, serpentine spout & fruitwood handle, domed lid w/ovoid finial, body engraved on both sides w/monogram within foliate cartouches, George II period, Richard Gurney & Co., London, 1754, 10½" h. (ILLUS.) **1,840**

Coffeepot, cov., on four ball feet, oval trumpet foot, tapered oblong body, serpentine spout, fruitwood loop handle, domed lid w/oblong finial, George III period, Peter, Ann & William Bateman, London, 1805, 12" l., 11¾" h. (engraving removal to both sides) **1,035**

Creamer, w/rubbed marks for London, scroll handle, square base w/beaded rims, George III period, 1789, 7" h. **460**

Cup, circular base w/wide band of acorns on four leaf-capped claw feet fitted w/a flaring body & wide shoulder, separate collar w/a conforming acorn band, Central European, 5¾" h., 10 ozs. **345**

Demitasse coffee service: Art Deco style, the tall rectangular tapering pot chased & applied w/square strapwork bands & flat cover, long angled handle, ten matching short cup holders fitted w/cobalt blue porcelain liners & a rectangular tray w/curved ends w/rectangular hand hold; Austria, ca. 1930, tray 21½" l., the set. **2,185**

Demitasse set: cov. coffeepot, cov. sugar bowl & creamer; pear-form bodies w/chased Rococo shell & figural decoration, ivory heat stops, flower finials on covers, engraved inscription, Germany, late 19th c., pot 5⅞" h., 3 pcs. **575**

Entree dishes, cov., rectangular w/cut corners, domed cover w/central oval ring handle, gadrooned border on base, engraved crests on cover & interior, John Schofield, England, 1798-99, 10¼" l., pr. . . . **5,750**

Ewer, lobed spherical body, Paul Storr, England, 1831-32, 7⅞" h. **575**

Jardiniere, boat-shaped, w/floral swags & twining ivy, two plain scroll cartouches to either side, copper liner, French, 800 fine, early 20th c., 14" l., 8½" w. **1,380**

Models of lady's shoes, each w/a small flaring heel & a bow on top, repoussé w/cherubs at various pursuits in landscapes, gilded interiors, Europe, late 19th c., 6¾" l. (minor dents) **1,380**

Wang Hing Chinese Silver Mug

Mug, body applied w/lappet panels of bamboo & plum bushes alternating w/figures in gardens or landscapes, on a diaperwork ground, mounted w/a scrolling dragon-form handle, wear to some high spots, Wang Hing, Chinese, late 19th c., 5½" h, 12 ozs. (ILLUS.) **805**

Mug, hunting-style, pyriform body repoussé w/a fox hunting scene, engraved w/a castle, fist & flag crest between leafy trees, w/scroll handle & on spreading circular foot, George III period, Newcastle, 1769, 5½" h. **1,840**

Nutmeg grater, straight-sided oval form, engraved decoration & monogram, "T.W." maker, Birmingham, England, 1799-1800, 1¾" l. **316**

Pitcher, cov., baluster-form w/Huguenot-style cut-work details on cover & bowl, maker "L.G.," England, 1892-94, 9½" h. **1,265**

Salver, center engraved w/small ring of dogwood blossoms within a large band of rose blossoms, everted border cast w/openwork oak leaves & acorns, Portugal, late 19th c. 24" d. **1,840**

Sauceboats, ovoid form w/scroll handle, shell & hoof feet, A. Bros. Ltd., Birmingham, England, 1903-04, 6½" l., pr. **316**

Snuff box, maker's mark "F.B.," w/patent registration mark, Victorian, formed as the head of a dog, the eyes set w/faceted red pastes, London, 1882, 1¾" l. **288**

Snuff box, rectangular, hinged top engraved w/a courting couple, bottom engraved w/foliate pattern on stippled ground, gold-washed interior, Continental, possibly Dutch, 1¼" w., 2" l. **201**

George III Soup Tureen

Soup tureen, cov., rectangular, the domed cover & body chased w/rose foliage & scrolls, centering a cartouche at each side w/one engraved w/an armorial, the cover mounted w/a rose branch-form handle, body w/acanthus & shell-capped handles, on four acanthus-capped scroll feet, Joseph Angel, George III period, England, 1817, cover & body bearing spurious Paul Storr maker's marks, the finial w/Joseph Angel maker's marks, 15" l. (ILLUS.) **5,175**

Spoon, Onslow patt. stem & round scallop-form bowl, George III period, George Smith, London, 1779, 7" l. **144**

Stuffing spoon, front tilt handle, engraved crest on reverse, maker "S.A.," London, 1769-70, 14¼" l. **345**

Sugar basket, navette form, swing handle, rim bands, monogrammed, R. & S. Hennel, England, 1818-19, 7" l. **345**

Hester Bateman Silver Pieces

Table spoon, rounded end back-tipt design, engraved monogram, Hester Bateman, London, England, 1785 (ILLUS. front) **316**

Tea caddy, cov., oval upright form w/stepped, domed cover w/urn finial, the sides engraved w/stylized florette & vine bands & a crest, Hester Bateman, London, England, 1789-90, 5⅝" h. (ILLUS. back) **3,450**

Tea & coffee service: cov. coffeepot, cov. teapot, creamer & cov. two-handled sugar; each of pear form, the flat-domed cover w/a foliate finial, engraved w/monogram, French, early 20th c., coffeepot 8½" h., the set **1,150**

Tea & coffee service: cov. teapot, cov. coffeepot, cov. kettle on lampstand, cov. creamer & cov. two-handled sugar bowl; each of partially reeded, rectangular section, Edwardian period, Birmingham, 1904, kettle on lampstand 12" h. **3,162**

Tea service: cov. teapot, creamer & cov. two-handled sugar bowl; each of bombé rectangular form w/gadrooned rim, on four ball feet, rubbed marks for London, 1814, George III period, England, the set (solder repairs to teapot handle & creamer) . . **1,035**

English Silver Footed Tea Tray

Tea tray, circular on three ball & claw feet, shaped edge w/embossed flowerheads & applied shell & bead border, tray engraved w/scrolling leaves & flower-centered roundels, English, maker's mark "BG," 1921, 18½" d. (ILLUS.) **1,840**

Teapot, cov., squatty bulbous form, faux bamboo finial, spout & handle, ivory heat stops, applied bas-relief prunus & bird decoration on the body, China Trade, China, 20th c., 5½" h. **633**

Teapot & stand, maker's mark "W.F.," ovoid pot, partially reeded, straight spout, wooden ear handle, drop in lid, monogrammed; the tray identically marked, on three ball feet, worn heraldic engraving to center (restorations), George III period, London, 1800, pot 9½" l., 3¾" h. **489**

Toast rack, seven oval loops raised on a rectangular base frame w/small scroll & shell feet & an upright center handle, Hy. Wilkinson & Co., England, 1837, 6½" l., 6¼" h. **345**

Torah shield, rectangular backplate w/shaped surmount, (lacing applied crown), applied w/two columns at each side, each chased w/foliage, centering a pair of applied lions & a pair of shaped rectangular hinged doors, each w/Hebrew inscriptions, all above a long rectangular hinged door w/an open front, Russia, ca. 1890, 12" **2,300**

Tray, rectangular w/rounded ends, gadrooned handles & rim, engraved leafy scroll & crest decoration, marked "W.B." in rectangular cartouche, England, 1813-14, 23⅞" l. **2,300**

Vase, 8¼" h., reticulated silver, trumpet form on domed foot w/repoussé dragon, body pierced w/dragon & foliate panels, w/carved wooden stand, Chinese **259**

Vodka Bucket, tapering circular form w/two bands of reeding & central foliate engraving, swing handle, Russian, mid-late 19th c., 6½" h. **518**

Wine funnel, ribbed flower-form, marked "W.E.T.," Dublin, Ireland, 1820-30, 5⅛" l. **403**

SILVER PLATE (Flatware)

GRAPE (ROGERS)

Berry spoon	55
Butter knife, master	40
Child's fork	30
Cream soup spoon	35
Demitasse spoon	30
Dinner knife, hollow-handled	45
Iced tea spoon	40
Meat fork	45

Salad fork	50
Sugar shell	35
Tablespoon, large	30
Teaspoon	15

GRENOBLE (ROGERS)

Butter knife, master size	8
Butter spreader, individual	9
Cold meat fork	33
Dinner fork	15
Dinner knife	15
Gravy ladle	40
Iced tea spoon	12
Mustard ladle	75
Pastry fork	35
Pie server	50
Salad fork	12
Salad fork	45
Soup spoon, oval bowl	22
Sugar spoon	8
Sugar spoon	22
Teaspoon	8

HANOVER (ROGERS)

Bouillon spoon	7
Butter knife, individual	10
Dinner fork	10
Dinner knife	12
Olive spoon	30
Salad fork	30
Soup ladle	85

MOSELLE (1847 ROGERS)

Beef fork	165
Berry spoon	165
Berry spoon, gold-washed bowl	125
Butter knife, twist handle	33
Cold meat fork	50
Gravy ladle	55
Jelly spoon	95
Luncheon knife, hollow-handled	26
Meat fork, 7½" l.	58
Pickle fork, long handle	112
Soup spoon, oval bowl	38
Teaspoons, set of 12	200 to 250

VINTAGE (ROGERS)

Baby food pusher	82
Berry spoon	66
Bouillion spoon	10
Butter knife, standing	20
Cake server	85
Cake serving fork	45
Cheese scoop, hollow handle	205
Citrus spoon	25
Cold meat fork	35

Cream ladle	40
Cream soup spoon	25
Dessert spoon	38
Dinner fork, hollow-handled	19
Dinner knife	25
Fruit knife	50
Ice cream fork	75
Ice spoon	150
Olive fork	55
Pickle fork, long-handled	38
Pie server	125
Salad fork	39
Soup spoon	11
Sugar spoon	20
Sugar tongs	85
Teaspoon	8
Tomato server	125

SILVER PLATE (Hollowware)

Candelabra, five-light, each modeled as a young girl wearing a flowing robe & supporting a fluted torch issuing four additional scrolling candle arms w/foliate nozzle & bobêche, standing barefoot on a foliate molded capitol surmounting a square base w/fluted & shell molded frieze, a ram's mask in each corner above short hoof feet, 42¼" h., pr. **3,450**

Candelabra, three-light Queen Anne-style, each w/a stepped, octagonal base continuing to a conforming stem & two scrolling candle arms w/faceted candle cup nozzles, 16¼", pr. **690**

Center piece, figural, in the form of a Victorian highwheel 'ordinary' bicycle w/a wire frame around the back holding five clear glass Inverted Thumbprint patt. shot-sized glasses, a dinner bell on the handle bars & fitted w/a figural male bisque uniformed rider, ca. 1890s, the set **303**

Unusual Lobster-footed Chafing Dish

Chafing dish, cover & burner, the slightly flaring deep cylindrical dish w/a straight turned wood side handle raised on a tripod base w/figural upright lobsters forming the legs & joined by cross braces centered by the burner, a domed cover

w/a turned wood knob, impressed "San
Benort," lamp impressed "Lagco" within a
laurel wreath, American, early 20th c.,
wear to high spots, overall 10" h. (ILLUS.) **287**

Cocktail shaker, lighthouse-form, Meriden
Silver Plate, International Silver Co.,
20th c. **1,840**

Coffee service: cov. coffeepot, cov. sugar,
creamer & tray; Art Deco style of
geometric form w/green Bakelite handles,
ca. 1930, coffeepot 8½" h., the set **2,185**

Coffee urn, cov., baluster-form body
w/applied vintage detail & engine-turned
bands, Reed & Barton, late 19th c., 17" h. **230**

Punch set: bowl on fitted stand & six
goblets; each decorated w/flowers,
Meriden Silver Plate Co., ca. 1880, bowl
& stand 16" h., the set **690**

Ornate Silver Plate Sugar & Liner

Sugar bowl, cover & liner, ornate silver
plate stand w/open sides below a
landscape-stamped rim band w/squared
side handles over scrolled panels
alternating w/leaf-stamped scalloped
panels above the scroll-trimmed short
pedestal on a round flared foot, fitted w/a
blue Inverted Thumbprint patt. blown
glass insert fitted w/a domed silver plate
cover w/fanned finial, late 19th c., 5" d.,
8¾" h. (ILLUS.) **395**

Tantalus, marked "Grinsell's Patent," for
three decanters, rectangular tray on four
bun feet, handle w/circular rod supports
w/plain ball knops, inverted thistle-cut
glass decanters w/quadripartite place
neck collars & circular prism-cut stoppers,
w/three associated bottle labels, two
sterling, one plated, late 19th c. (crack to
one decanter) **374**

Tantalus set, a silver plate rectangular tray
on four bun feet, the handle w/circular rod
supports w/plain ball knops, holds three
glass decanters w/inverted thistle-cut
designs & quadripartite plated neck
collars & circular prism-cut stoppers,
w/three associated bottle labels, marked
"Grinsell's Patent," England, late 19th c.,
the set. **489**

Figural Dolphin Toothpick Holder

Toothpick holder, figural, modeled as a
dolphin standing on its tail w/its mouth
wide open, scrolled wave base, late
19th c., 2½" h. (ILLUS.) **235**

Vase, large compressed bottle-form, chased
overall w/large rose blossoms & foliage,
w/gadrooned rim, engraved w/monogram,
ca. 1900, 10" d. (wear to high spots) **345**

Wine coasters, after a Regency design,
oval, each cast & pierced w/bacchanalian
scenes & applied w/a cast grapevine rim,
center w/engine-turned decoration, early
20th c., 10¼" l. **920**

STERLING SILVER (Flatware)

ACORN (GEORG JENSEN)

Baby spoon, curved handle **108**
Berry spoon, pierced **710**
Bonbon spoon **95**
Bouillon spoon **65**
Butter fork **50**
Butter spreader **75**
Cake fork **65**
Cake knife **95**
Canape server, short **238**
Cheese knife **100**
Cheese plane **175**
Cheese scoop **225**
Cheese server **58**
Cheese slicer **68**
Cheese snag **55**
Cherry fork **50**
Citrus spoon **83**
Cocktail fork **60**
Cocktail picks, set of 6 . . . . **240**
Coffee spoon **29**
Cold meat fork, 6⅝" **100**
Cream ladle, 5½" l. **130**
Cream soup spoon **85**
Demitasse spoon **36**
Dessert spoon **85**
Dinner fork, 7¾" **99**
Dinner knife, 9⅞" **112**
Fish knife **115**

Fish server, pierced, 10½" 750
Fish serving fork 90
Food pusher 100
Fruit knife (dinky) 55
Fruit spoon 70
Gravy ladle 275
Hors d'oeuvre fork, 3¾" l. 40
Ice cream fork 93
Iced tea spoon 88
Lemon fork 75
Luncheon fork, 6⅝" 40
Luncheon knife 53
Meat fork, hollow handle, 2-tine 63
Mixing spoon 250
Oyster fork 85
Pastry fork 65
Pickle fork 96
Pie server 292
Pie server, engraved blade 550
Salad fork, 4-tine 103
Salad serving set 567
Salad set, hollow-handle, 8" l. 145
Salad spoon, 8⅞" 325
Salt spoon, individual size 35
Sardine fork 125
Sauce ladle 213
Seafood fork 55
Serving fork 275
Serving spoon 125
Soup spoon, oval bowl 85
Strawberry spoon, pierced, 8⅞" 496
Sugar spoon 95
Sugar tongs 125
Tablespoon, 7½" 130
Tea caddy spoon 225
Teaspoon 69
Tomato server, 6" 323

ALHAMBRA (WHITING MFG. CO.)

Berry spoon, gold-washed bowl 120
Bouillon spoon 6
Cocktail fork 7
Cold meat fork 15
Demitasse spoon 10
Dinner fork 8
Dinner knife, hollow handle 18
Grapefruit spoon 7
Luncheon knife, hollow handle 13
Salad fork 10
Soup ladle 60
Soup spoon 12

CACTUS (GEORG JENSEN)

Berry spoon 275
Bouillon spoon 50
Carving set, roast 300

Cheese plane, stainless blade 140
Cheese server 155
Cheese slice 84
Child's fork 47
Citrus spoon 65
Cocktail fork 95
Cold meat fork, 2-tine 50
Cream ladle 195
Dinner fork 98
Dinner knife, 9" l. 107
Fish fork 75
Fruit knife 80
Gravy ladle 200
Jam spoon 95
Jelly spoon 95
Lemon fork, 2-tine 65
Luncheon fork 95
Luncheon knife 132
Pastry fork, 5⅛" l. 47
Pie server 395
Salad fork 95
Server, flat 95
Sugar scoop 75
Tablespoon 35
Teaspoon 64

CHRYSANTHEMUM (TIFFANY & CO.)

Asparagus tongs 910
Asparagus tongs, individual 375
Berry spoon, kidney-shaped bowl 595
Berry spoon, scalloped, gold washed 450
Berry spoon, shell-shaped bowl 600
Bouillon spoon 80
Breakfast knife, straight blade 125
Butter knife, master 295
Butter serving knife 175
Butter spreader 61
Cheese scoop 375
Citrus spoon 55
Claret ladle, 18" 550
Cocktail fork 73
Cream soup spoon 92
Crumber 650
Demitasse spoon 45
Dessert spoon 88
Dinner fork 105
Dinner fork gold-washed bowl 141
Dinner knife 87
Dinner knives, set of 12 1,380
Dinner service: 18 each dinner knives, fish
  knives, soup spoons, fruit knives,
  demitasse spoons, dinner forks, fish
  forks, dessert spoons, fruit forks &
  12 teaspoons, 1 cold meat fork & 1
  sauce ladle, 176 pcs. (ILLUS. of part, top
  next page) 15,870

Chrysanthemum Pattern

Egg spoon 75
Fish fork............................... 130
Fish forks, set of 10 1,450
Fish knife 90
Fish knife, silver blade................. 185
Fruit knife, sterling blade 95
Fruit spoon 77
Gravy ladle............................ 264
Gumbo spoon 125
Ice cream fork, gold-washed 85
Ice cream server, gold-washed blade 900
Ice cream set: 11¾" ice cream knife & six
    spoons; 7 pcs. 600
Ice cream slice, 11⅜" l................. 798
Ice cream spoon 90
Luncheon fork 80
Luncheon service: 7 each luncheon forks,
    knives, dessert spoons, iced tea spoons,
    cocktail forks; 42 pcs. (in Tiffany
    pouches) 2,750
Mustard ladle.......................... 165
Olive spoon 135
Pastry fork 87
Pie server............................. 225
Pie server, hollow handle.............. 85
Pie server, serrated, pierced 873
Pie server, trowel-shaped 675
Salad fork............................. 92
Serving spoon 175
Soup ladle, fluted bowl 1,200
Stuffing spoon......................... 750
Sugar sifter 375
Tablespoon 133
Tea infuser spoon...................... 495
Teaspoon.............................. 62
Terrapin forks, set of 10 1,500
Waffle server 610
Waffle server, pierced 850

ENGLISH KING (TIFFANY & CO.)

Asparagus fork 750
Berry spoon............................ 175

Berry spoon, conch 495
Berry spoon, gold-washed bowl 350
Bouillon spoon 45
Breakfast knife 58
Butter serving knife 160
Butter spreader, flat................... 48
Butter spreader, hollow handle 60
Cake knife 80
Carving fork, roast.................... 65
Carving set, large, 2 pcs.............. 350
Cheese scoop 295
Chicken tongs 985
Citrus spoon 65
Clam shell spoon 750
Claret spoon, 20" l.................... 425
Cocktail fork 45
Cold meat fork........................ 205
Cream soup spoon 60
Demitasse spoon, gold-washed bowl 50
Dessert spoon......................... 94
Dinner fork........................... 90
Dinner knife.......................... 70
Egg spoon 95
Fish fork............................. 84
Fish knife, hollow handle.............. 50
Fish serving fork 9¼".................. 388
Fish serving knife & fork 785
Fish slice 550
Game knife 1,050
Grapefruit spoon...................... 58
Gravy ladle........................... 285
Ice cream fork 85
Ice tongs 735
Iced tea spoon........................ 65
Lobster fork, gold-washed bowl 400
Luncheon fork 68
Luncheon knife 60
Meat tongs, chicken claw.............. 985
Olive fork 175
Olive spoon 150
Oyster ladle, "Oysters & Sea Weed," lap-
    over edge 1,800
Pastry fork 77
Pickle fork 195
Pie server............................ 669
Pie server, serrated 295
Salad fork............................ 86
Salad set 895
Sauce ladle 130
Seafood fork 45
Serving fork.......................... 195
Serving fork, pierced 245
Soup ladle 961
Stuffing spoon........................ 700
Tablespoon 103
Tea infuser spoon..................... 295

Tea knife. 85
Teaspoon 49
Vegetable spoon 250
Youth fork & knife, pr. 95
Youth set, fork & spoon, pr. 95

GRECIAN (WHITING MFG. CO.)

Berry spoon. 219
Butter, master. 65
Dinner fork, 7⅞" l. 65
Gravy ladle. 138
Ice cream server & 12 spoons 295
Ice tongs 150
Macaroni server. 650
Mustard ladle. 65
Preserve spoon. 250
Salt spoons, master, pr. 85
Sardine fork. 250
Tablespoons, set of 3 200
Teaspoon. 21
Teaspoons, set of 7 150

HYPERION (WHITING MFG. CO.)

Bonbon spoon. 35
Butter, individual. 24
Butter spreader, individual, flat handle 24
Citrus spoon 20
Dinner fork. 47
Fish slice 225
Fruit spoon 30
Fruit spoons, set of 6. 200
Gravy ladle. 150
Ice cream slice. 170
Luncheon fork 30
Nut spoon 40
Punch ladle 425
Salad set, large 350
Sardine fork. 43
Tablespoon, pierced bowl 70
Tea caddy spoon. 75

KING (SAMUEL KIRK & SON)

Baby Fork. 18
Bouillion spoon. 34
Butter server, hollow handle 15
Butter server, individual, hollow-handle. 19
Cocktail fork 175
Cold meat fork, 4-tine 109
Gravy ladle. 77
Luncheon fork 31
Luncheon knife 31
Sugar tongs. 41
Table serving spoon 49
Youth knife. 19

LILY OF THE VALLEY (GORHAM MFG. CO.)

Bonbon spoon. 26
Butter fork 19
Butter serving knife 21
Butter spreader, flat handle. 15
Butter spreader, hollow handle 14
Cocktail fork 18
Cold meat fork, 8" l. 54
Cream soup spoon 17
Demitasse spoon 13
Dinner service for 4, 32 pcs. 640
Gravy ladle. 43
Iced tea spoon. 22
Jelly spoon 20
Lemon fork 20
Luncheon fork 22
Luncheon knife 20
Olive fork 16
Pie server. 275
Pie server, hollow handle. 25
Salad fork. 21
Salad serving fork. 65
Sugar spoon 16
Tablespoon 41
Tablespoon, pierced 53
Teaspoon. 11
Tomato server, pierced 65

OLYMPIAN (TIFFANY & CO.)

Olympian Asparagus Fork

Asparagus fork (ILLUS.) 695
Berry spoon. 795
Berry spoon, conch 895
Berry spoon, kidney-shaped 395
Berry spoon, plated 450
Butter spreader, flat handle. 77
Cake server 68
Carving set, roast, 2 pcs. 440
Cheese knife 275
Chicken tongs 850
Coffee spoon, large. 50
Cream ladle, long handle. 395

Cream ladle, shell bowl 295
Dinner fork 93
Fish knife, hollow handle 125
Fish set 895
Fried egg server 595
Fruit knife, silver blade 95
Grapefruit spoon, gold-washed bowl 155
Gravy ladle 250
Ice cream server 715
Jelly spoon 195
Luncheon fork 69
Luncheon knife 62
Olive fork 125
Oyster ladle 950
Pea server 750
Pie server 800
Punch ladle 1,200
Sandwich tongs 750
Soup ladle, large 813
Soup ladle, swirled bowl 850
Spooner 47
Sugar shell 95
Sugar sifter 263
Sugar spoon 158
Sugar tongs 95
Sugar tongs, shell ends 150
Tablespoon 165
Teaspoon 53
Tomato server 450
Tongs, chicken claw 850
Waffle server 795
Wedding cake knife 79
Youth fork 50

RENAISSANCE (DOMINICK & HAFF)

Berry spoon, 7⅜" l. 235
Butter knife 70
Citrus spoon 24
Citrus spoons, set of 6 255
Claret ladle 185
Cocktail fork 40
Fish serving fork 45
Ice cream fork 45
Jelly cake knife 400
Lettuce fork 145
Luncheon fork 25
Luncheon knife 30
Marrow scoop, gold-washed bowl 175
Punch ladle 625
Salad fork 60
Sardine fork 65
Sauce ladle 450
Soup spoon, oval 45
Strawberry fork 38
Sugar tongs 68
Teaspoon 33

REPOUSSÉ (SAMUEL KIRK & SONS)

Asparagus fork 238
Baby fork 20
Baby fork & spoon set 43
Baby knife, sq. handle, all silver 40
Baby pusher 34
Bacon fork, long-handled 59
Bacon server 175
Baked potato serving fork 32
Berry server, medium 80
Berry spoon, fruit in bowl 126
Berry spoon, fruit in bowl, gold-washed, large . . 212
Berry spoon, oval, large 112
Berry spoon, scalloped 81
Berry spoon, small 50
Berry spoon w/floral edge, large 450
Bonbon server 19
Bonbon spoon 40
Bouillon spoon 22
Butter paddle, hollow handle 20
Butter pick 46
Butter serving knife, flat handle 30
Butter spreader, flat handle 18
Butter spreader, individual, hollow handle 20
Butter spreader, sq. flat handle 40
Cake knife, hollow handle 30
Candle snuffer, hollow handle 36
Carving fork, steak 26
Carving knife, roast 45
Carving set, roast 158
Carving set, steak 103
Casserole spoon 85
Cheese scoop 150
Cheese server 26
Citrus spoon 25
Cocktail fork 20
Cold meat fork, large 82
Corn holder 35
Cream ladle 55
Cream soup spoon 29
Demitasse spoon 15
Dinner bell 33
Dinner fork 59
Dinner knife 33
Fish fork, individual 30
Fish knife, hollow handle, silver blade 27
Fish serving fork 118
Fish set, individual 65
Food pusher, child's 33
Fruit knife, hollow handle 20
Grapefruit spoon 27
Gravy ladle, 6¼" l. 65
Gumbo spoon 43
Hot cake lifter 70
Ice cream fork 30
Ice cream server 150

Iced tea spoon 24
Ice spoon 135
Ice tongs 104
Ice tongs w/chicken claws, large 225
Infant feeding spoon 26
Jelly server 30
Lemon fork 28
Letter opener 43
Lettuce fork, 7¼" l 64
Lobster shears 120
Luncheon fork 28
Luncheon knife 26
Nut spoon 33
Olive fork, 2-tine 23
Olive spoon, pierced 25
Olive spoon, short handle 27
Pea spoon 95
Pickle fork, 3-tine 28
Pie server, all silver 128
Pie/cake server 30
Platter spoon 149
Punch ladle 284
Relish fork 69
Roast beef fork, 2-prong 28
Roast holder 75
Salad fork 30
Salad serving set, 9" l 193
Salad serving spoon 100
Salt spoon, individual 11
Salt spoon, master size 25
Sandwich tongs, 9" l 895
Sauce ladle 34
Serving fork, 6-tine, 9⅞" l 155
Serving spoon, egg-shaped bowl, large, 9½" l . . . 121
Serving spoon, pierced bowl, hollow
   handle, large 48
Sherbet spoon 22
Soup spoon, oval bowl 33
Steak carving set 60
Steak knife 29
Stuffing spoon, 12" l 319
Sugar spoon, fluted 26
Sugar tongs 33
Tablespoon 49
Tablespoon 51
Tablespoon, pear-shaped 63
Tablespoon, pear-shaped, large 82
Tablespoon, pierced bowl 60
Tea knife, all silver, 5¾" l 39
Teaspoon 17
Teaspoon, small 13
Tomato server, 7⅛" l 70
Vegetable serving spoon, oval 78
Youth fork 21
Youth knife 19

WATTEAU (WM. B. DURGIN CO.)

Berry spoon 115
Butter spreader, flat handle 15
Coffee spoon 8
Dinner fork 40
Fish knife 45
Gravy ladle 90
Gumbo spoon 50
Honey spoon 85
Ice cream slice 200
Ice cream spoon 35
Ice tongs 150
Jelly/preserve spoon 60
Luncheon fork 21
Mustard ladle 55
Pastry fork 45
Salad set, long-handled 275
Salt spoon, master 30
Serving fork, 9¼" l 65
Serving spoon 125
Soup spoon, oval bowl 21
Sugar shell 40
Tablespoon 36
Tea strainer 85

TIN & TOLE

Candle box, cov., tin, hanging-type,
cylindrical w/hinged cover & two hanging
straps, scrolled hasp, 19th c., 5¼" d.,
14½" l. 83
Candle mold, tin, eight-tube, loop side
handle, free-standing arched base, 19th c. 94
Candle mold, tin, twelve-tube, loop side
handle, free-standing rectangular base,
19th c. 88

Fancy Tole Chestnut Urn

Chestnut urns, cov., tole, deep rounded
oblong body raised on a square slender
pedestal on a stepped rectangular base,
S-scroll shoulder handles & a waisted
flaring neck supporting a high domed &
stepped cover w/a paneled & pointed gilt
finial, decorated overall w/painted foliage
in gold & sienna on a black ground,
Europe, 19th c., 5 x 9½", 12" h., pr.
(ILLUS. of one) 2,300

Coal scuttle, painted & gilt-stenciled, the black ground decorated w/two panels painted w/harbor scenes, stenciled foliate borders, probably England, late 19th c., 16" h. (wear) **518**

Early Tole Decorated Coffeepot

Coffeepot, cov., tall slightly tapering cylindrical body w/flared foot, low domed hinged cover, strap handle, angled spout, black ground decorated w/colorful florals in red, green, yellow & white, crusty surfaced w/some touch-up repair, interior & bottom rust, some battering,19th c., 9½" h. (ILLUS.) **853**

Tole Coffeepot & Deed Box

Coffeepot, cov., tall tapering cylindrical body w/flared base, hinged domed cover, large strap handle w/grip & angled spout, dark brown japanning decorated w/colorful florals in red, green, brown, blue & yellow, wear, old paint touch-up, repairs,19th c., 10½" h. (ILLUS. left) **495**

Coffeepot, cov., tole, tapering cylindrical form w/hinged domed cover w/finial, crooked spout, reinforced handle w/cover guard, flanged base, painted metallic bronze w/designs of apples & leaves in green & yellow, 19th c., 10½" h. (cover hinge needs repair) **990**

Coffeepot, cov., tin, flared round foot below short ringed lower body & tapering ringed upper body w/a small opening w/fitted low domed cover, reinforced strap handle, angled upright spout, 19th c., 11" h. (ILLUS.) **275**

Early Tin Coffeepot

Coffeepot, cov., tin, tapering cylindrical body w/fitted domed cover & pewter finial, straight angled slender spout & tapering strap side handle, attributed to the Shakers, 12¼" h. **99**

Container, cov., tole, circular, painted black w/red, yellow & green foliate decoration, America, mid-19th c., 8½ d., 8¾" d. (paint wear) **863**

Creamer, cov., tole, tapering cylindrical body w/low domed hinged cover, strap handle, dark brown japanning decorated w/florals in yellow, green, red & white, 19th c., 4¼" h. (some wear) **523**

Deed box, cov., tole, rectangular w/hinged domed cover w/small wire bail handle, dark brown japanned ground decorated w/a band of colored scallops around the cover edge & further scallops around the sides, leafy sprigs on front below a white band painted w/colorful florals in yellow, red, green & black, painter's mark on band, bottom seams loose, minor wear, 19th c., 8¾" l. (ILLUS. right) **825**

Document box, cov., tole, rectangular w/low domed hinged cover w/small wire bail handle, original dark brown japanned ground w/a band of leaf-form dashes around the cover rim & at the sides & below a front wide band in white decorated w/colorful florals in yellow, green, red & black, 19th c., 7" l. (minor wear, hasp incomplete) **330**

Downspout, tin, applied w/cast stars & a spread-winged eagle, dated 1830, American, 25½" w., 23" h. (imperfections) **460**

Drying rack w/drip pan, tin, a top rod to hang candles, the back sheet punch-decorated in the form of ornate geometric trees & initials "L.E." & "M.M.," drip pan extends about 3½", w/two hanging straps, back sheet 13 x 13¾", 19th c. **248**

Tinder box, cov., tin, round, American, late 18th - early 19th c., 4¼" d. (imperfections) **86**

Tray, tole, painted octagonally shaped tray w/stand up rim painted w/a broad border of red, yellow & green flowers & fruit on a black ground, mid-19th c., 12¼" w., 17½" l. (some paint loss & restoration) **1,725**

Tray, tole, rectangular, oval ship portrait depicting the "Houqua" under full sail flying an American flag, border decorated w/ship's identification "'Houqua' 1844 Capt. N.B. Palmer built by Brown and Bell New York," corners w/ship's flag & leafy vines, mid-19th c., 17⅝ x 24" (paint losses, corrosion) **690**

Victorian Tole Decorated Tray

Tray, tole, rectangular w/rounded corners & wide flanged rim w/pierced end handles, the center decorated w/a scene of the Annunciation in color, stylized flowers around border, on a dark ground, losses, wear, Europe, 19th c., 24" l. (ILLUS.) **403**

Tray, tole, decorated w/anthemion leaves, fruit, foliate designs & pinwheels in gold, bronze & red paint on a black ground, probably American, 19th c., 21⅜ x 29¾" (minor areas of repaint, scattered paint loss) **431**

Tray, tole, rectangular, decorated in color w/an allegorical scene representing Time, w/openwork gallery, probably Pontypool, England, late 18th - early 19th c., 21½ x 30" (minor wear & restorations) **1,725**

Wall candle sconce, tin, the back sheet w/a six-point star decoration forming a peak w/a single punched hanging hole, rounded drip pan w/three candle sockets, 19th c., 9¼ x 10¼" **275**

MILITARIA & WARTIME MEMORABILIA

Since the early 19th century, every war that America has fought has been commemorated with a variety of war-related memorabilia often in the form of propaganda items produced during the conflict or as memorial pieces made after the war ended. These materials are today quite collectible and increasingly important for the historic insights they provide. Most common are items dating from World War I and II.

CIVIL WAR

Ambrotype, of a Union sergeant holding a saber **$500**

Belt buckle, Confederate States, brass **750**

Canteen, Model 1858, metal w/wool covering, tin spout w/ring & cork plug, 8" d. (some hole in cloth, later carrying strap) **275**

Carbine, Meriden revolving barrel, issued to a Kentucky unit **800**

Diary, kept by William P. Woodlin, Musician of the 8th Regt. U.S.C.T. 2nd Brigade, Army of the James, begins in November 1863 & ends on October 31, 1864, interesting viewpoint of an African-American soldier **2,200**

Diary, written in German by a member of the 33rd Missouri, kept from 8/2/1862 to 8/12/1865, includes translation **950**

Drum, Civil War era, made by John C. Hayes & Co. of Boston **625**

Civil War Snare Drum

Drum, snare-type, wooden rim, metal body engraved w/a band of five-pointed stars centering a reserve containing the Massachusetts State Seal, heads missing, manufactured by A.H. White, Boston, second quarter 19th c., 17" d., 12½" h. (ILLUS.) **978**

Fife, hickory w/nickel silver ferrules **225**

Frock coat, Georgia 1st Lieutenant, blue grey w/red collar & cuffs & w/Georgia State seal buttons, made in 1861 by Philadelphia tailor **15,000**

General order, issued to the 5th NH Vol. Inf. instructing them to proceed to Washington, DC on 10/26/1862 . . . . **110**

Jacket, Union artillery, w/red piping & collar, made by Scovill & Co. **1,900**

Letters, lot of six, from southwestern New Hampshire towns **400**

Letters, lot of six, written at Ft. Constitution in Portsmouth, New Hampshire **200**

Pennant, Civil War era swallow tail, attributed to a Texan Confederate unit **2,100**

Photograph, cabinet-size, young officer standing wearing uniform, believed to be from Indiana's 53rd Regiment (ILLUS.) **80**

Photograph of Union Officer

Prints, "A History of the Civil War," colorful battle scene prints published by Benson Lossing, 1912, each 8 x 11", set of 7 .... **48**

Revolver, French Drenotte Brevette, w/ivory grip, the grips are engraved w/the name of an officer of the 3rd Louisiana Vol. Inf. (CSA) **2,500**

Revolver, French, marked on barrel "Inv. On E. Lefaucheux Brte Paris" **1,200**

Soldier's pass, from Provost Marshal General Andrews Army of West Mississippi, issued April 25, 1865 in Mobile Alabama, signed by Brig. General L. Andrews **85**

Sword, Model 1840 mounted artillary saber marked "Ames" **924**

Sword, Model 1850 foot officer's model, marked "W. Clauberg - Solingen" **588**

Sword, Model 1860 light cavalry saber, Ames, average condition **756**

Sword, Model 1860 U.S. Navy cutlass, dated 1862 .... **868**

Sword, Union light cavalry, imported from Germany, includes scabbard & buckle, belonging to a member of the 5th Iowa Vol. Cavalry **1,800**

Tintype, full length image of Zouave soldier w/patriotic backdrop **1,300**

Training rifle, Civil War era Springfield, w/wooden barrel **250**

Trephine tool **240**

SPANISH-AMERICAN WAR (1898)

Book, "Harper's Pictorial History of War with Spain," 1899 ediiton, many great prints & pictures, 500 pp **365**

Book, "The Little I Saw of Cuba," 1898 .... **25**

Coat, U.S. Cavalry GT, w/yellow cape, marked "Quartermaster 1898" **1,100**

Program, pictorial souvenir, New York City reception for Admiral Dewey **38**

Stereoview cards, Rough Riders, 1898, set of 3 .... **40**

WORLD WAR I

Book, "The Epic of Vimy," 1936, published by the Canadian Legion of the British Empire Service League, commemorates the dedication of the Monument at Vimy honoring those killed in the battle **100**

Book, "The People' s War Book - History, Cyclopedia and Chronolgy of the Great World War," 1919, James Miller & H.S. Canfield, introductory page features advertisement for selling the book, hundreds of photos, final section the Peace Treaty & outline of the League of Nations **200**

World War I German Imperial Helmet

Helmet, German Imperial-type, black metal dome w/jointed brass chin strap, large gilt-metal imperial eagle on the front, brass spike at top center (ILLUS.) **1,980**

Magazine, "The Cyclone," the battalion journal of the Canadian Corps of Cyclists Battalion Association, only 67 issues printed, rare, each issue **25**

Photograph, Officer Training Camp, Cickamauga Park, Georgia, 1917, 7 x 31" **45**

Pillow shams, satin, various versions indicating where a soldier was stationed, the unit, scenes of battle, etc., in various colors with or without fringe, various sizes, starting at **20**

Pin, metal, Expeditionary Force 6th Division **15**

Postcard, shows Uncle Sam rolling up his shirt sleeves, reads "When the Gentleman Takes Off His Coat He Means Business" **25**

WORLD WAR II

Airplane identification kit, "Official Junior Aircraft Warning Service Kit," includes photos of 32 military planes, large plane I.D. chart & six other items, original illustrated package, the set **18**

Armband, printed fabric, commemorates D-Day airborne invasion, decorated w/the American flag **35**

Book, "Collier's Photographic History of World War II," copyright 1945. . . . . **28**

Book, "United States Sailors in Action," one of a series published by Whitman Publishing Co., Racine, Wisconsin, 1942, color drawings, two-page battle scene spreads, back reads "Buy More War Bonds Now," 24 pp. **25**

Book, "United States Submarines in Action," one of a series published by the Whitman Publishing Co. of Racine, Wisconsin, 1942, full-color cover w/action scene, color drawings, two-page battle scene spread, back page reads "Buy More War Bonds Now," 24 pp. **25**

First aid kit, w/contents, U. S. Army, ca. 1945. . . . **45**

Flight jacket, leather, A-2 pilot's CBI w/large U.S. flag & Chinese chit, three patches on sleeves & chest **975**

Flight jacket, leather A-2 pilot's w/painted cartoon of U.S.S. Hornet on top of Hornet's nest boxing Japanese Zero, front wings denote four kills, marked "Bud" . . **1,450**

Flight jacket, leather, U.S. Navy, M-422A **750**

Flight jacket, pilot's, painted leather, Disney-like hornets boxing Japanese Zero, four rising sun flags on front, together w/silk scarf, size 40 . . . . **1,450**

Machine gun-camera, made to deceive w/lens in barrel, marked "Tokyo Kogaku, F 285.4 mm - 1:11," box w/shipping label from a U.S. captain, Japan, 38" l. **440**

Shell Art Tank Model

Model of a tank, shell art, composed entirely of brass artillery shell casings (ILLUS.) **400**

Ring, Marine Corps, sterling silver **75**

MINIATURES (Paintings)

Bust portrait of a Naval officer, watercolor on ivory, a three-quarter pose of a distinguished middle-aged gentleman wearing a high-colored uniform jacket w/gold epaulets, a double row of brass buttons down the front, stormy sky in background, American School, first half 19th c., in a period shadowbox frame, 2⅝ x 3¼" **$518**

Bust portrait of a young woman, watercolor & pencil on paper, side-parted upswept dark hair w/dark eyes, wearing an off-the-shoulder black dress, black ribbon around neck & hat w/black bow, appears to be original black painted pine frame, stamped "Foster Bros. Boston," J.A. Davis, ca. 1830, 4¾ x 4¼" **2,300**

Fine Rare Miniature of a Girl

Full-length portrait of a young girl, watercolor on ivory, a young girl identified as Frances Pamela Howe, age 3 on paper label, standing w/her hair parted in the center & w/one hand resting on a child's rocker, a cat at her feet, wearing a long white apron over a full knee-length dress & pantaloons, mid-19th c., framed, 3¼ x 4" (ILLUS.) **7,475**

Half-length portrait of a matron, watercolor on ivory, she posed to the right, wearing a high lacy bonnet, a short necklace & white collar w/her low-cut high-bodiced long-sleeved gown, gilt insert, in incomplete leathered case, backing marked "Parcilla Dean, Lynn, Mass. 1778," 2¾ x 3¼" (minor wear) **468**

Half-length portrait of a young lady, watercolor on ivory, seated facing left, her dark hair parted in the center & pulled back, wearing a dark low-cut gown w/lacy collar & a light shawl, framed, unsigned, ca. 1850, 2¾ x 3⅝" (minute pigment loss, damage to case). **920**

Half-length portrait of a young lady, watercolor on ivory, shown facing left, her dark hair pulled up & back into a cluster of curls w/curls framing her face, hazel eyes, wearing a white low-cut Empire-style dress w/long sleeves, in a rectangular flat black lacquered frame w/gilt metal oval liner, ca. 1810-20, 5 x 5½" **275**

Half-length portrait of a young woman, oval, watercolor on ivory, her blonde hair in overall long tight curls, wearing an off-the-shoulder white Empire style gown w/a necklace & blue accessories, in a molded brass narrow oval frame, signed on the back "Painted by Rd. Mills, Birmm. 1829," England, ca. 1830, 3¾ x 4⅜" (minor edge damage) **385**

Half-length portrait of Miss Trumansburg, watercolor on ivory, the young lady facing right, dark center-parted hair off the ears w/sausage curls behind, wearing a dress w/a pleated V-form bodice & narrow lacy collar, a long chain around her neck, identified on label, unsigned, New York, ca. 1850, framed, 2½ x 2¾" (very minor pigment loss, surface grime) **604**

Half-length portraits of a gentleman & lady, watercolor on ivory, he in front view wearing a high-colored coat, vest & large bow tie, she looking to right, her dark hair pulled back into a high chignon, wearing an off-the-shoulder burgundy dress & jewelry, each 1⅝" h., mounted together in a leatherized case w/green velvet lining, ca. 1830, overall 3⅞" l., pr. **1,320**

Half-length portraits of the Morrill Children, watercolor on paper trimmed w/gum arabic, two young men facing left & wearing dark high-collared jackets & white frilled cravats & two young girls facing left & wearing off-the-shoulder dresses w/balloon sleeves, each w/short-cropped hair, in period beveled gilt gesso frames w/top rings, unsigned, ca. 1840, each 2⅝ x 3⅛", set of 4 (toning, fading, minor staining & abrasions) **8,050**

Three-quarter length portrait of a lady, wearing white dress & blue shawl, hair in ringlets, signature right edge, oval & in gilt metal pendant frame, by Laurent Grunbaum, ca. 1840, 4" h. **690**

Three-quarters length portrait of a young woman, watercolor & graphite on paper trimmed w/gum arabic, a primitive portrait of a young lady w/center-parted & pulled-back hair w/a comb, a delicate lacy wide collar & wide ribbon band above her dark balloon-sleeved dress, holding a small book in one hand, in a period beveled veneer frame, unsigned, attributed to Jane A. Davis, ca. 1830-40, 6¼ x 6½" (toning, fading, abrasion losses, very minor staining) **2,300**

MINIATURES (Replicas)

Blanket chest, cherry, rectangular hinged top opening to a well, dovetailed case on short knob-turned legs, lock w/key, old mellow finish, 13½" l. **$358**

Blanket chest, painted wood, six-board construction, rectangular hinged top opening to a well w/a lidded till, dovetailed case w/molded base on short ringed feet w/knob tips, grain painted, 19th c., 11¾ x 16¾", 13⅛" h. (imperfections) **546**

Chest of drawers, pine, a flat thin rectangular top above a case w/two stacks of small square drawers w/tiny brass pulls above a single long drawer at the bottom, arched cut-out side feet, old dark finish, 3¼ x 7¼", 11" h. **275**

Shaker-style Chest of Drawers

Chest of drawers, walnut & poplar, a rectangular top over a dovetailed case w/two rows of small dovetailed drawers over two larger drawers, single board ends w/bootjack feet, attributed to the Shakers, old finish, two bottom drawers rebuilt, replaced porcelain knobs, one missing, late 19th c., 7½ x 15¼", 13½" h. (ILLUS.) **495**

Cupboard, painted pine, a rectangular top above a single door opening to three shelves, on bracket feet, painted red, 19th c., 6 x 12⅝", 22" h. **374**

Dog or pony cart, painted wood, the rectangular box painted green between two large eight-spoked red-painted wheels, black striping, long double tongues at front, 19th c., 24" l., 10" h. (minor losses & paint wear) **489**

Hat, Stetson, in original box **40**

Sad iron, pressed glass, clear, mid-19th c., 1⅜" h. **121**

Secretaire à abattant, gilt-metal mounted hardwood, Empire style, rectangular top overhanging a tall case w/a narrow long drawer over a large rectangular fall-front opening to reveal interior drawers & mirror, over three long drawers flanked by engaged columns topped by metal sphinx heads, each side mounted w/a gilt metal Egyptian-style figure & seated sphinx,

Empire Secretaire à Abattant

pierced gilt-metal mounts on the front, gilt
ball feet, glued construction, France,
19th c., 3¾ x 7½", 10⅞" (ILLUS.) **518**

Trunk, child's, natural pine color, slightly
domed, original hardware & label "M.
Cherry Trunks," New York City, New
York, 18" w., 15" h, 14" deep **395**

MOVIE MEMORABILIA

*Also see: AUTOGRAPHS and PAPER
DOLLS*

BOOKS

"Gone With the Wind," by Margaret
Mitchell, May 1936 first edition,
autographed on inside cover w/pen,
includes slipcover (some tears on
slipcover edges) **$8,625**

"Now I Am Eight," by Shirley Temple,
Saalfield Publishing Co., No. 1766, 1937 . . . . . . **40**

COSTUMES

Al Pacino, "Carlito's Way," 1995, suit, grey
sharkskin, purple cotton dress shirt
w/French cuffs & a diamond pattern grey
tie, custom-made by Carlito Brigante, 3 pcs. . **2,990**

Barbra Streisand, "Funny Lady," 1971,
Fanny Brice's cream satin shirt w/faux
diamond buttons, pique front & wing
collar, together w/bow tie, slacks w/satin
stripe down each leg & hat w/bow, for first
performance of "Crazy Quilt," w/color
photographs featuring Streisand (ILLUS.) . . . **4,600**

*From left: Fanny Brice Tuxedo & Top Hat
Superman Cape*

Charles Boyer, "Conquest," 1937,
Napoleon's costume, dark green wool
cut-away jacket w/red wool cuffs,
mandarin collar & tails w/beige wool at
front closure & cuffs, gold buttons
w/epaulets at shoulders, military medal,
ivory wool britches w/Metro-Goldwyn-
Mayer label marked "D. Coleman 1267
5146 30 36," leather & gold belt & sash,
tan breeches w/similar label marked
"1748214 31-32," includes ruffled jabot
with MGM label & a movie still **5,750**

Christopher Reeve, "Superman," 1978,
Superman's red cape featuring yellow
shield w/Superman "S" outlined in black
thread, two ties at neck w/padding to top
area, marked in ink "No S/6 relined
1/3/78", includes letter of congratulations
to winner co-signed by president & editor
of DC Comics on DC stationery dated
"February 27, 1979" & photocopy of
advertisement for contest (ILLUS.) **19,550**

Dustin Hoffman, "Hook," 1991, Captain
Hook's costume, three-quarter length
coat embellished in pirate's gold thread
w/tassels & buttons, en suite
w/ornamented black long vest & short
pants, silk hose, hoop earrings, coat, vest
& pants w/Barbara Matera label, two
items marked "KT" **6,037**

Freddy Krueger, "Wes Craven's New
Nightmare," 1994, Freddy Krueger's
trademark make-up fashioned pullover
face mask, used in highway scene w/24
other Freddys, marked "11," 13½" **2,300**

John Barrymore, "Marie Antoinette," 1938,
full length robe, deep rose velvet,
embroidered w/gold thread in wheat
pattern bordering front frog closures, fur
cuffs & collar, M-G-M label marked "J.
Barrymore 6-9770 Robe," includes
jeweled jabot w/Western Costume label **6,037**

Johnny Depp, "Don Juan DeMarco," 1995, trademark black mask w/clear plastic insert molded to fit actor's face, includes publicity still from movie **1,150**

Kirk Douglas, "Spartacus," 1960, taupe cotton shorts w/Western Costume label marked "2244-2 Kirk Douglas #2," stamped "Western Costume," w/clipping & movie still featuring Douglas, designed by Bill Thomas. **2,990**

Mask, "Jurassic Park, The Lost World, 1997," head designed to fit over mechanical dinosaur, features tan & beige scales, long carnivorous snout & sinister almond-shaped eyes, 25" l. **2,300**

Military costume, "Planet of the Apes," 1968, futuristic military ape outfit in green w/insert "leather" collar & quasi-military bands on arms, woven inner cuffs extending beyond sleeves, matching pants, ape-like five-toed boots, jacket featuring Western Costume Co. label w/sizes. **1,150**

Robin Williams, "Hook," 1991, Peter Pan's costume for Never Never Land, comprising green suede top w/jagged cut collar & sleeves, fringe tie closure w/matching cotton leggings & arm bands, features a Columbia Studios label w/top marked "Flying R" & shorts marked "Flying K". **3,737**

Sharon Stone, "Diabolique," 1996, sleeveless purple dress w/scoop collar & matching belt, includes publicity featuring Ms. Stone **1,150**

Tom Cruise, "Days of Thunder," 1990, helmet, black w/red & blue accents including two stars, fitted w/communication mouthpiece, marked "Cole Trickle" on front & back, includes padded carrying bag & two video reference prints **3,450**

Captain Kirk's Jacket

William Shatner, "Star Trek II The Wrath of Khan," 1982, Captain Kirk's Starfleet command maroon jacket w/futuristic front closure, foldout cream lapel & black belt

w/Starfleet logo buckle, comes w/letter of authenticity on Paramount stationery from Nicholas Meyer (ILLUS.) **4,312**

LOBBY CARDS

"Battle Cry," starring Tab Hunter & Nancy Olson, 1960 . . . . **65**

"Dino," starring Sal Mineo & Brian Keith,1957. . . **125**

James Bond, lot of 400, German, for various James Bond films **948**

"Off Limits," starring Bob Hope & Mickey Rooney, 1953. . . . . **125**

"The Oklahoman," starring Joel McCrea & Barbara Hale, 1957 . . . . **65**

"Silver Chalice," starring Paul Newman & Virginia Mayo, 1955 . . . . **95**

"Starlift," starring Jane Wyman & Doris Day, 1951. . . . . **75**

"The Day Mars Invaded Earth," starring Kent Taylor & Marie Windsor, 1963 . . . . **125**

"Thunder on the Hill," starring Claudette Colbert & Ann Blyth, 1951 . . . . **75**

"Tripoli," starring John Payne & Maureen O'Hara, 1950 . . . . **65**

"The Vikings," starring Kirk Douglas & Tony Curtis, 1958 . . . . **95**

POSTERS

"A League of Their Own," signed in marker "Geena Davis, Tom Hanks, Love Madonna" & "Penny Marshall," framed, 26 x 39½" **805**

"Star Wars," 1977, designed by Howard Chaykin, "Star Wars" entitled in red, featuring Luke, Leia, Han Solo, Darth Vader, the Death Star & host of interplanetary vehicles, marked "1st Edition Artist: Howard Chaykin, Luke Skywalker The Star Wars Corporation," 20 x 29" **3,162**

"Wanderers West," starring Tom Keen, color lithograph, three-sheet, 1930s. **895**

MISCELLANEOUS

Costume sketch, Ann Miller, "Small Town Girl," 1953, two-piece halter top w/side-slit skirt layered in tangerine, red, yellow & purple, w/attached fabric swatches, watercolor on board, initialed, matted & framed, marked w/film's title & "Ann Miller Gouacho Number Chg #5," 14½ x 21½" **575**

Costume sketch, Grace Kelly, "The Swan," 1956, a bridal gown w/bouquet motif & attached fabric swatch, production information & approval signatures, marked "Grace Kelly, The Swan, 14, Double," initialed lower left, 15 x 22" (stain on right side off image) **1,840**

Costume sketch, Grace Kelly, "The Swan," 1956, depicts Kelly seated wearing blue blouse trimmed in white w/tie closures & white skirt w/matching trim, inscribed "Grace Kelly, The Swan #15," production information & approval signatures on verso including "Hagedon," pencil & watercolor on board, 15 x 22½" **805**

Costume sketch, Joan Crawford, "Mildred Pierce," 1945, features Crawford w/black top trimmed w/fur, hip-hugging black dress cinched at waist, inscribed on verso "1869-638," watercolor & pencil on board, 14 x 21" (some staining & minor creases on border) **1,035**

Costume sketch, Lana Turner, "Diane," 1956, black dress w/matching hood entitled "Dianne Lana Turner #11 teaching prince to dance," production information & approval signatures, including "Hagedon" on verso, watercolor & pencil on board w/attached fabric swatches, 15 x 20" **575**

Costume sketch, Ona Munson, "Gone With the Wind," 1939, drawn for Belle Watling, features a flamboyant gold gown w/ruffled sleeves, swirling swag design & draped scarf, lower right corner signed "Plunkett," 15 x 20" **4,025**

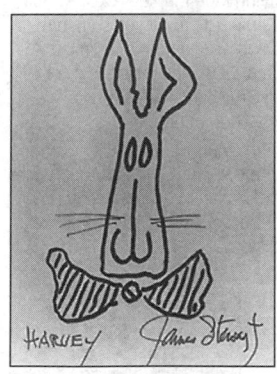

Signed "Harvey" Illustration

Drawing, James Stewart, "Harvey," original bust drawing of Harvey the invisible rabbit w/marker on pale blue paper titled "Harvey," signed by Stewart, matted & framed, 7½ x 9½" (ILLUS.) **4,140**

Fan, w/"I'll Be Seeing You" & showing Shirley Temple holding Royal Crown Cola, ca. 1940s **95**

Goggles, w/original box depicting Johnny Weissmuller & Buster Crabbe **20**

Marilyn Monroe, check, signed & dated October 25, 1957 in blue ink, made out to "New York State Unemployment Insurance Fund," matted w/print photograph of Monroe, 3 x 8" **1,610**

Marilyn Monroe, Marilyn Monroe, "Gentlemen Prefer Blondes," 1953, Twentieth Century Fox, suitcase, faux alligator Travelaire w/fitted brass latches, one marked "TCF 18360," includes photocopy of publicity still, 10 x 18 x 18" **2,300**

Matchbooks, "The Birdcage," 1996, ten white glossy props imprinted in bright green "Birdcage," from fictitious South Beach nightclub owned by Robin Williams & Nathan Lane, the set **747**

Money clip, Frank Sinatra, w/dollar sign, above inscription reads "Thanks, Sinatra," w/original box **690**

Money clip & watch, Louis Armstrong & Bing Crosby, 14k yellow gold, inscribed "To my Friend Satchmo from Poppa Bing," includes auction catalog marked "Property from the Estate of Louis & Lucille Armstrong" **5,175**

Movie contract, James Stewart, "Murder Man," first original contract w/MGM, dated "May 3, 1935," states wages over five years w/rider, signed by Stewart & a vice president for MGM **2,185**

Props from "As Good As It Gets"

Movie prop, "As Good As It Gets," Verdell the dog w/dirty brown faux hair & glass eyes & a purple rubber dog dish inscribed "Verdell," includes two black & white promotional photographs of dog & a copy of the script dated "May 19, 1992" (ILLUS.) . . **1,610**

Movie prop, knife, from James Bond film "On Her Majesty's Secret Service" **1,293**

Movie prop, Oddjob's steel rimmed bowler, from James Bond film "Gold Finger" **93,000**

Movie prop, vodka and caviar set, used in James Bond film "Tomorrow Never Dies" . . . **4,830**

Movie prop, tarantula from "Dr. No," 4½ x 4½" **4,485**

Movie script, Burgess Meredith, "Rocky," 1976, dated November 25, 1975, annotated by Meredith, including "Stolen! Meredith," on cover, title page heavily annotated w/names & numbers of several people involved w/the production, street directions, dates & "This Script Belongs to Burgess Meredith" **2,415**

Note, Katharine Hepburn, thank you typewritten on "Katharine Houghton Hepburn stationery, "Many Thanks - Looks fascinating - Katharine," dated "I-12-1988 (sic)," signed & framed, 6½ x 4½" . . . **316**

Painting, "Doctor Zhivago," 1965, watercolor & oil storyboard, depicts the riot in red square, features people fleeing soldiers on horses, signed "Dukelski" in lower right corner, 12 x 15½" **18,400**

"Home Alone II" Painting

Painting, "Home Alone II," 1992, original for movie poster, by Wil Cormier, featuring Statute of Liberty w/hands framing an open mouth scream, New York skyline in background, acrylic on gessoed rag surface, matted & framed, includes photocopied check to the artist from Twenty Century Fox, 18 x 29" (ILLUS.) **10,350**

Photo I.D., Will Smith, "Men in Black," 1997, Special Agent wallet-style photo I.D., marked "Federal Bureau of Investigation Department of Justice, Badge No. 70482" & "Black," features photo of Will Smith in suit **1,495**

Photograph, Fred Astaire, showing Fred & Adele Astaire, Clifton Webb, Wilda Bennett & ten others in costume, inscribed "Apeda N.Y. 21," signed by all 14 members of cast, ca. 1921, 15 x 17" **1,150**

Photograph, Marilyn Monroe, black & white photo by Sam Shaw depicting Monroe wearing white bathing suit lying in sand as the surf comes in, matted, 11¼ x 17" **460**

Presentation invitation, Katharine Hepburn, "Look Who's Coming to Dinner," 1967, for opening night party billed as tribute to Katharine Hepburn, includes screening of film & her second movie "Morning Glory," 1933, in form of illuminated make-up vanity, black exterior w/lacquer finish, two doors marked w/a star & "Hepburn," white framed interior

w/electric bulbs, glass plate depicting role of film w/scenes from movie, 4½ x 18½ x 36" **805**

Production script, "Citizen Kane," 1941, blue cover marked "Final Script, Citizen Kane, Screenplay by Herman Mankiewicz, Director: Orson Welles, Photography: Gregg Toland," dated "June 18, 1940," w/blue change sheets dated "6/18/40," 214 pp. **3,162**

Shoes, Marilyn Monroe, stilleto-heeled open toed style, black, grey & white, includes monogrammed handkerchief, two black & white photographs of Marilyn & four pieces of documentation **2,990**

Statuette, Columbia Pictures anniversary miniature Oscar, front plaque inscribed, "Academy of Motion Picture Arts and Sciences for the Best Picture of the Year," back plaque marked "15th Anniversary Columbia Pictures 1920-1935," black metal base, 5½" **1,840**

Sunglasses, Lana Turner, trimmed in blue & yellow rhinestones, includes letter concerning the provenance from Eric Root, ca. 1950s **690**

Sunglasses, Tom Cruise, "Days of Thunder," 1990, black lacquer frame w/anti-glare smoked lenses, in case w/identifying tape marked "Cole," w/full color dashboard production sign that reads "Days of Thunder . . . Filming in Charlotte & Daytona," includes color still featuring Cruise in shades & two reference video prints **1,380**

Thermometer, Marilyn Monroe, lithographed tinplate, entitled "Some Like It Hot," w/Marilyn in billowing skirt pose based on movie scene, 13" (some wear & fading) **460**

Harpo Marx Watch

Watch, Harpo Marx, rectangular, figural lighter-form w/rounded sides,14k gold, Dunhill, matte dial w/Arabic numerals & electric blue hands, 15 jewels, three adjustments, engraved vertical striping, plaque inscribed "Harpo," movement signed "J. Schulz," includes letter from Harpo's wife (ILLUS.) **9,775**

MUCHA (Alphonse) ARTWORK

A leader in the Art Nouveau movement, Alphonse Maria Mucha was born in Moravia (which was part of Czechoslovakia) in 1860. Displaying considerable artistic talent as a child, he began formal studies locally, later continuing his work in Munich and then Paris, where it became necessary for him to undertake commercial artwork. In 1894, the renowned actress Sarah Bernhardt commissioned Mucha to create a poster for her play "Gismonda" and this opportunity proved to be the turning point in his career. While continuing his association with Bernhardt, he began creating numerous advertising posters, packaging designs, book and magazine illustrations and "panneaux decoratifs" (decorative pictures).

Mucha Print of Art Nouveau Maiden
Maiden in Field of Iris Print

Advertising print, "Lance Parfum 'Rodo,'" color lithographed on paper by F. Campenois, Paris, seated lady in ruffled robe squirting perfume onto tissue, loose sheet framed, 1896, 12½ x 17½" (time darkened in spots) **$5,176**

Calendar prints, "Tetes Byzantine," color lithographed on paper by F. Champenois, Paris, profiles of Byzantine maidens wearing ornate jeweled hats, two individual prints framed together, 1900, 23 x 33", pr. **13,800**

Calendar prints, "The Seasons," color lithographed on paper, mounted on linen, Art Nouveau maidens in outdoor scenes featuring the four seasons, four individual prints framed together, 1899, 17¼ x 27", the set (minor creases & restorations) **4,887**

Poster, "Flirt - Biscuits Lefevre-Utile," color lithographed by F. Champenois, Paris, scene of young couple flirting in a flower-filled conservatory, laid down, framed, 1899, 11⅝ x 25" **4,312**

Poster, "Imprimerie Cassan Fils...," lithograph printed in colors, advertising around the figure of a seated half-naked Art Nouveau lady holding prints in her lap looking up & talking w/a thoughtful young printer, 1896, framed, 23½ x 63¼" **2,300**

Poster, "Lorenzaccio - Theatre de la Renaissance," color lithographed on linen by F. Champenois, Paris, figure of Sarah Bernhardt in role of "Lorenzaccio," leaning against arched-doorway, framed, 30¾ x 82¾" **11,500**

Print, color lithograph on silk, a scene of a young Art Nouveau maiden w/long brown hair, sitting on a rock w/her feet in a stream, red flowers in her hair, ca. 1896, framed, 18½ x 33½" (ILLUS.) **4,125**

Print, color lithographed on silk, a scene of an Art Nouveau maiden w/long flowing hair standing amid blossoming boughs & holding harp on which are perched five small birds, ca. 1896, framed, 18½ x 33½" **3,850**

Print, color lithographed on silk, a winter scene w/a standing maiden wrapped in a long cloak among snow-covered branches & holding & warming a small bird in her hands, other birds perched in front of her, ca. 1896, framed, 18½ x 33½" **4,125**

Print, color lithographed on silk, an autumn scene w/an Art Nouveau maiden w/wreath of large chrysanthemum blossoms in her long red hair leaning against a rock & picking clusters of large purple grapes w/one hand while holding a white dish in the other, ca. 1896, framed, 18½ x 33½" **4,125**

Prints, color lithograph on paper, one depicting a young Art Nouveau maiden standing in a field of carnations, the other a maiden in a field of iris, late 19th c., one slightly damaged, framed, 16 x 39½", pr. (ILLUS. of one) **4,600**

Prints, "The Seasons," each tall narrow rectangular color lithographed scene w/an Art Nouveau maiden in a seasonal setting, the season name in French at the bottom, 1897, framed, each 17¼ x 26½", the set **10,350**

MUSIC BOXES

Mira disc music box, floor model w/decal designs on the case, plays 18½" discs . . . **$10,500**

Olympia Music Box, Stand & Cabinet

Olympia disc music box, oak lift-top
cabinet w/ornately scroll-carved sides,
the stepped top carved w/a picture of
Admiral Dewey & a battleship, side-crank,
raised on a oak four-legged stand w/pull-
out side ledges & raised on the original
oak upright disc cabinet w/paneled doors
& block feet, w/ten discs, ca. 1900 (ILLUS.). . **8,800**

Polyphon Floor Model Music Box

**Polyphon (Polyphon Musikwerke,
Leipzig, Germany) disc music box,**
coin-operated floor model, tall upright
walnut cabinet w/a high stepped &
molded cornice & frieze band above an
arche glass front flanked by carved,
turned & blocks columns resting on two
turned free-standing column above an
open shelf over the lower cabinet w/a
rectangular top overhanging a paneled
door opening to storage w/eight 19½" d.
discs, working, ca. 1890, 16 x 28", 75" h.
(ILLUS.). **5,175**

Regina disc music box, floor model, case
decorated w/paintings, short bedplate,
plays 15½" discs **8,500**

Regina disc music box, floor model,
curved front cabinet, automatic changer,
plays 15½" discs (restored). **19,500**

Regina disc music box, oak, short
bedplate, double comb, plays 15½" discs
(needs restoration) **4,600**

Reginaphone disc music box, wooden
console w/carved dragons decoration,
double comb, plays 15½" discs. **9,800**

Stella disc music box, carved wood
cabinet, double comb, plays 17¼" discs **4,800**

Swiss cylinder music box, crossbanded
walnut rectangular case, twenty tune
cylinder, single comb, w/original tune
card, attributed to B. H. Abrahams, St.
Croix, ca. 1890, case 24" l. **2,185**

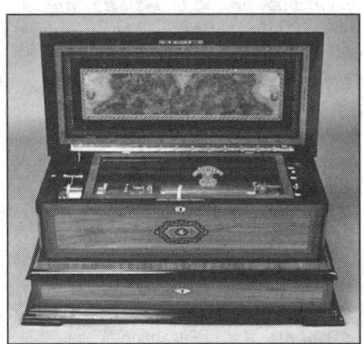

Fine Swiss Cylinder Music Box

Swiss cylinder music box, inlaid
mahogany rectangular cabinet w/burl
panel inside the lid, glass-cover cylinder
mechanism w/interchangeable cylinders,
inlaid banding & central cartouche on
front of the stepped case, late 19th -
early 20th c. (ILLUS.) **6,000**

Swiss cylinder music box, rectangular
walnut case w/floral marquetry on the lid,
double comb, 6" l. cylinder playing four
tunes, late 19th c. **345**

MUSICAL INSTRUMENTS

Dulcimer w/Painted Case

Dulcimer, black painted case w/gilded stylized urn w/flowers, flanked by geometric devices, the interior lined w/blue velvet & fitted with instrument, late 19th c., 3¼" d., 22" l., 14¼" h. (ILLUS.) **$575**

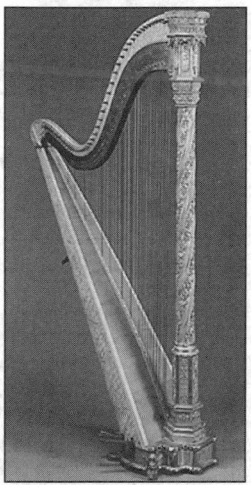

Fine Erard Gothic-style Harp

Harp, floor model, giltwood, a Gothic-style carved post w/spiraling column, bird's-eye maple veneer angled back post, Erard, France, 19th c., 70" h. (ILLUS.) **9,200**

Chickering Reproducing Piano

Piano, baby grand reproducing player-type, Chickering, mahogany case w/old finish, ivory & ebony keys, Ampico reproducing mechanism needs work, Serial No. 13587, early 20th c., w/bench & 210 music rolls, the group (ILLUS.) **5,225**

Piano, baby grand, stained walnut case, the sides carved w/cartouches, Steinway & Sons, Serial No. 283052 . . . . **9,200**

Piano, grand, mahogany case, Steinway & Sons, Serial No. 27452, w/bench, 2 pcs. **11,500**

Francis Guillpoint Violin & Case

Violin, Francis Guillpoint model, dated 1910, w/carrying case (ILLUS.) **95**

NAUTICAL ITEMS

The romantic lure of the sea, and of ships in general, has opened up a new area of collector interest. Nautical gear, especially items made of brass or with brass trim, is sought out for its decorative appeal. Virtually all items that can be associated with older ships, along with items used or made by sailors, are now considered collectible, for technological advances have rendered them obsolete. Listed below are but a few of the numerous nautical items sold in recent months.

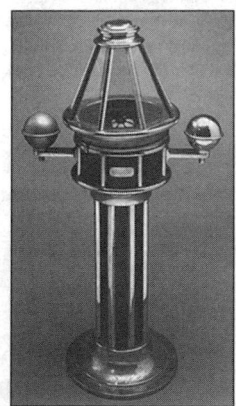

Chrome-plated Yacht Binnacle

Binnacle, chrome-plated, yacht model of small size, a chrome & blackened brass column w/chrome & blackened brass pedestal, a deviastat hand magnetic balance w/compensating balls, w/a John E. Hand & Sons compass model in points & degrees & an octagonal conical glass & chrome dome w/twist lock, ca. 1930, 17" w., 31½" h. (ILLUS.) **$4,025**

Binnacle w/gimballed compass, mahogany & brass, the compass w/points & degrees noted fitted in a brass casement w/rim serial number, the mahogany binnacle w/a brass hood w/opening top vent & compensating ball, the binnacle column composed of slats of wood, by Kelvin & Wilfrid White of Boston & New York, original maker's plate w/an access door & a pedestal w/holes for mounting, 50½" h. **1,840**

Cabin top eagle figure, cast iron, the spread-winged bird perched on a large knob on a square base, primed & painted, base w/mounting holes, from the Tugboat Baltic, made by Philadelphia Shipyards, Camden, New Jersey, late 19th c. **2,760**

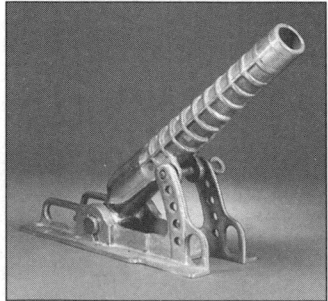

1910 Cunard Line Calendar

Calendar, 1910, lithographed paper in color, advertising the "Cunard Line - Quickest Route to London and Continent Via Fishguard," scene of a large ocean liner in New York harbor w/mention of the Lusitania & Mauritania, after A.G. Bushnell, framed, 14⅞ x 20" (ILLUS.) **1,154**

Bronze Life Saving Cannon

Cannon, life-saving type, solid bronze, used for throwing life-saving lines, w/reinforced barrel, mounted on a sled base

w/maker's plate "model 'F' serial #6906," Philadelphia PA Naval Co., sole patentus B & H Yacht & Hall Lylie pat. ships cannons, bridger, 11 x 25", 39' h. (ILLUS.) .. **2,300**

Clock, ceramic, figural, mantel-type, a model of the ocean liner Normandie under sail, stylized design in black & white w/grey smoke between the three stacks, a small round clock face mounted in the center of the side, on wavy dark blue base, indistinct maker's mark & "France," ca. 1930s, 20" l., 5½" h. **748**

Compass, brass, flat-top model, the brass case w/compass & compass card marked in points & degrees including markings for intermediate points, early flat-top models, John Hand, Philadelphia, ca. 1900, 4¼" d. **173**

Compass, Pex gimballed-style, compass card in points & degrees w/blackened brass ring & milk glass bowl mounted in a brass domed binnacle, John Hand & Sons, ca. 1940s, 4" d. **575**

Decanter set: six-liter size glass bottles w/glass stoppers in a mahogany box w/hinged lid; box lined w/red velvet & brass handles, late 19th - early 20th c., box 8 x 10", 12" h., the set **1,035**

Lithograph, "Remember the Maine," depicts all ships in 1898 U.S. Navy fleet, sepia, 4 x 30" **695**

Marine chronometer, two-day, a gimballed deck clock in a three-tier mahogany box w/silver face, Roman numerals, up & down dial, seconds hand, brass carrying handles, latches & ivory inlay in the box, serial number "2265" & marked on the box "969," all in a mahogany carrying case w/leather strap, by Charles Prodsham, London, England, late 19th c., 8½" sq. **2,185**

Model of a barque, the "Great Republic," four-masted w/full rigging, in a glazed carved walnut case, early 20th c., case 12 x 32½", 23½" h. (minor imperfections) **863**

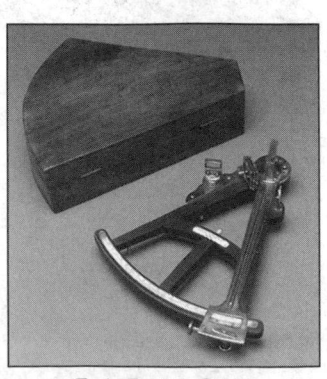

Early English Octant

Octant, brass & ebony, an ebony frame, brass arms & fixtures including filters & sighting hole, ivory scale & ivory-inlaid maker's mark in a mahogany keystone box marked "CH Chappell 1806," Spencer & Barrett Co., London, early 19th c., 4 x 12½ x 13½", 2 pcs.(ILLUS.)...... **690**

Octant, ebony, brass & ivory, by Spencer, Browning & Rust, London, England, ca. 1787-1842, in a painted wood case, 15¾" l. (minor losses, damage & losses to case) ... **575**

Painting, oil on board, "The R.M.S. Aquitania Leaving New York in a Snow Flurry," the black & white ship w/four red smokestacks on dark stormy seas, a smaller vessel in the foreground, signed & dated "Antonio Jacobsen 1914 - 31 Palisade Av. West Hoboken, N.J." in lower left, 21 x 34".................... **16,100**

Sextant, brass & ebony, marked by Spencer, Browning & Co., London, early 19th c., in original fitted mahogany case, 9½" l. (case refinished)................. **863**

Ship Model in Shadowbox Frame

Ship model, a three-masted fully-rigged sailing ship on painted stormy seas within a deep shadowbox frame, no front glass, other minor imperfections, 19th c., 14½ x 29½" (ILLUS.) **633**

Ship model, builder's model of The S.S. Harfleur, a solid hull built up in lifts w/black topside & pink bottom, painted decks & superstructure also of built-up wood, finely detailed, mounted in its original mahogany case w/turned corner columns, original plinth w/molded details & builder's plaque, England, late 19th c., 12½ x 59", 18¼" h.................... **19,550**

Ship model, folk art-style model of the P.S. Columbia, completely made from wood, twin funnels, a wheelhouse, masts w/chain stays, walking beam & original flags, fine detailing w/carved & punched railings, windows, paddle wheels & portholes, tin-covered bottom & under-deck frames, mounted on a mahogany stand & baseboard, late 19th c., 9¼ x 37½", 23½" h.................... **4,600**

Ship model, model of the sailing ship "Flying Cloud," solid hull w/painted black topsides & a painted copper bottom, the exterior w/fine detailing & the deck veneered planking scored & varnished, w/masts & full rigging, early 20th c., cased 16¼ x 42½", 29½" h.......... **2,185**

Ship model, Napoleonic Prisoner of War model of the Minerve, constructed w/a solid hull planked over in bone, pinned in place w/copper pins, numerous details in whale bone & baleen, finely detailed w/the complete masts & rigging, mounted on an inlaid rectangular plinth w/mahogany, boxwood & ebony inlays, all in a mahogany & glass case w/a name board in mahogany w/gold lettering, early 19th c., 6½ x 12", 16" h.............. **13,800**

Ship's telegraph, brass & wood, the casement for the dial of the ship's telegraph of mahogany, the telegraph handles & indicators of brass, a brass lantern mounted to the exterior of the casement to illuminate the dials of the telegraph, the support & pedestal of brass, by Marine Manufacturers & Engineers Corp., New Bedford, Massachusetts, 40" h. **575**

Statue of a sailor, bronze, a standing barefoot sailor holding a strand of rope, from the H.M.S. Excellent, cast by Elkington & Co., stamped "ELKINGTON & CO. COPYRIGHT," brown patina, 15¾" h... **690**

Telescope, brass, single-draw, the brass tube w/the original black leather grip, sliding lens covers, removable lens cap & sliding lens shade, by Bardou Fils et Cie., France, 19th c., closed 2¾" d., 28½" l....... **460**

Thermometer, table model, figural, a marble cylindrical case in the form of a lighthouse composed of alternating red & grey variegated marble sections mounted w/a bone temperature gauge in Fahrenheit & Celsius, mounted on a rockwork stone base, 13½" h. **368**

Yacht binnacle, brass, the pedestal w/six feet w/holes for deck mounting, the base w/a decorative anchor design supporting a fluted column w/three decorative collars, the brass bowl houses a 5" d. Negus compass in points & degrees, compass protected by a heptagonal glazed cone, maker's mark on the top cap of the binnacle & the compass, Negus, New York, New York, early 20th c., 5" d., 31" h. **3,680**

Yacht's wheel & pedestal, a solid brass wheel w/six spokes & handles, the center line marked on one handle w/five engraved bands, the pedestal of typical form w/a flared base & a bowl-shaped top, the maker's mark & serial number stamped on the top of the pedestal, wheel position indicator working & the pedestal is marked at the top w/left & right, Dake Engine Co., Grand Haven, Michigan, early 20th c., 42" d., 35½" h. **1,035**

Yachting trophy, sterling silver, of urn form on a knopped & stepped round foot, the front acid-etched w/a circular building within corded circle, surrounded by the acid-etched inscription "Newport Yacht Racing Association 30 Footers First Place Won by Esperanza August 26th 1909" between two triple-reed bands, three upswept loop handles, maker's mark of Gorham Mfg. Co., also stamped "PVB," 12" h. **920**

NETSUKE

These decorative toggles were used by the Japanese to secure an inro, tobacco pouch or other small personal article by means of a cord slipped through a kimono sash (obi). They are carved of ivory and other materials. There are many reproductions.

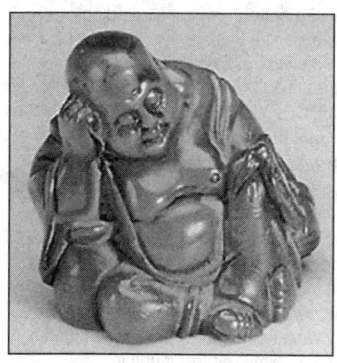

Amber Hotei Netsuke

Amber, figure of a dozing seated rotund Hotei w/fan, covered w/finely aged engravings, signed w/indecipherable character, 19th c., 2" h. (ILLUS.) **$460**

Boxwood, figure of a porter struggling w/a rice bale or koku, good patina, 19th c. **460**

Hardwood, figure group of a seated rakan weaving a giant sandal of straw, finely carved, used as a charm for porters **1,150**

Ivory, figure group of two men locked in combat, a tatooed bandit & an armored samurai, signed "Garaku," 19th c. **863**

Ivory, figure of a bald man clad only in a loincloth kneeling over & holding down a fat badger, 1¾" h. (check on foot of man) **546**

Ivory, figure of a fox disguised as a Buddhist priest, unsigned, 19th c., 3" h. **546**

Netsuke of Dog with Bell

Ivory, model of a dog w/a bell, finely detailed, 19th c., 1¼" h. (ILLUS.) **1,380**

Stylized Phoenix Ivory Netsuke

Ivory, model of a stylized curled phoenix bird, signed, 19th c., 3" l. (ILLUS.) **288**

NUTTING (Wallace) COLLECTIBLES

FURNITURE

Armchair, Carver-type, No. 464 ..... **$650**
Armchair, country Dutch-style, maple, No. 461 .. **750**
Armchair, Wiindsor bowback, No. 420 ..... **500**

Nutting Writing-Arm Windsor

Armchair, Windsor writing arm-type, No. 451 (ILLUS.) **1,600**
Candlestand, cross-based, No. 22 ..... **130**

Chest, one-drawer, oak, No. 909. 1,600
Desk, maple drop front-type, No. 701 1,100
Game table, rotating top. 850
Shelf, hanging wall-type, No. 907 1,300
Side chair, maple four-back-type, No. 392. 300
Side chair, maple slat back-type, No. 374 1,900
Side chair, maple slat back-type, No. 377 525
Side chair, Windsor fan-back, w/comb,
   No. 311 1,100
Stand, three-leg Windsor style, No. 605. 600
Stool, oval, No. 102 250
Stool, Pennsylvania, No. 143. 350
Table, maple drop leaf-type, No. 603 950
Table, maple drop leaf-type, No. 620 1,900
Table, Pembroke, No. 628. 1,600
Table, tavern, No. 660 600
Table, trestle. 350

PRINTS

A Barre Brook, 10 x 16". 70
A Berkshire Brook, 12 x 16" 105
A Berkshire Spring, 7 x 13". 70
A Birch Approach, 13 x 16". 120
A Bit of Sewing, 11 x 14". 75
A Canopied Road, 14 x 17" 80
A Cathedral Brook, 16 x 20" 120
A Chair for John, 16 x 20". 220
A Checkered Road, 9 x 11". 305
A Cottage Kitchen, 9 x 11" 65
A Dahlia Jar, 13 x 16" 550
A Daisy Lawn, 13 x 16". 210
A Delicate Stitch, 18 x 22". 90
A Discovery, 11 x 14" 120
A Dividing Path, 11 x 17". 170

A Fleck of Sunshine

A Fleck of Sunshine, 11 x 17" (ILLUS.) 200
A Formal Call, 11 x 17" 150
A Fruit Luncheon, 14 x 17" 220

A Garden of Larkspur, 16 x 20" 230
A Gettysburg Crossing, 14 x 17" 390
A Home Under Thatch, 11 x 14" 350
A Kennebec Brook, 11 x 13". 240
A Leaf Strewn Brook, 12 x 16" 125
A Listless Day, 14 x 17". 110
A Little River, 11 x 14". 70
A Maple in May, 14 x 17". 100
A Masque Pitcher, 16 x 20". 250
A Meadow Medley 14 x 17". 220
A Memory of Childhood 10 x 12". 170
A Mohonk Drive, 11 x 20" 360
A Montpelior Pool, 10 x 16" 170
A New Hampshire Road, 11 x 17". 110
A New Market Belle, 11 x 17" 110
A Pause at the Bridge, 9 x 11" 310
A Peep at the Hills, 10 x 16" 100
A Pennsylvania Hillside, 13 x 16". 440
A Perkiomen October, 16 x 20" 170
A Perkiomen October, 9 x 11" 210
A Portsmouth Roadside, 9 x 11" 120
A Present of Jewels, 14 x 17". 95
A River in Maine, 12 x 14". 70
A Rug Pattern, 13 x 16". 350
A Sheltered Brook, 16 x 20" 160
A Sheltered Road, 10 x 20" 90
A Sip of Tea, 11 x 14" 120
A Somerton Entrance, 13 x 16" 525
A Spinet Corner, 13 x 16" 100
A Stitch in Time, 11 x 14" 180
A Stone Churn, 11 x 17". 230
A Triple Team, 11 x 13". 725

A Valley in the Pyrenees

A Valley in the Pyrenees, 12 x 14" (ILLUS.) 140
A Warm Spring Day, 11 x 14" 175
A Well Dell, 10 x 13". 35
A Wilkes Barre Brook, 8 x 10" 310
A Woodstock Arch, 12 x 15". 100
Above the Bridge, 13 x 17". 100
Affectionately Yours, 14 x 17" 80
All the Comforts of Home, 13 x 15" 130
All the Comforts of Home, 13 x 15" 130
Among October Birches, 13 x 16" 95
Among October Birches, 13 x 16" 95

Rural Sweetness, 16 x 20" 170
Salem Beautiful, 13 x 16" 130
San Gabriel Stair, 11 x 14" 350
Scotland Beautiful, 13 x 15" 220
Sea Ledges, 13 x 16" 220
Seeking the Shade, 11 x 14" 675
Shadow Bend, 13 x 16" 140
Shadows in the Dell, 16 x 20" 110
Skirting Lake Como, 13 x 16" 425
Skirting Profile Lake, 9 x 11" 50
Soft Summer, 11 x 14" 65
St. Mary's in May, 13 x 16" 105
Swirling Seas, 10 x 12" 160
Tantallon Hold, 7 x 9" 170
Tea for Two, 11 x 14" 110
Tea in Yorktown Parlor, 13 x 15" 260
The Coming Out of Rosa, 13 x 16" 160
The Cottage Beautiful, 12 x 15" 55
The Cottage on the Floss, 11 x 14" 50
The Goose Chase Quilt, 7 x 11" 60
The Gorge of the Penobscot, 13 x 16" 50
The Heart of Maine, 16 x 20" 110
The Isaac Walton Brook, 13 x 16" 350
The Maple Sugar Cupboard, 11 x 16" 80
The Meeting of the Ways, 14 x 17" 170
The Mills at the Turn, 12 x 16" 250
The Nashua Asleep, 13 x 16" 195
The Natural Bridge, 9 x 12" 160
The Nest, 14 x 17" 175
The Olden Time, 10 x 16" 300
The Original Dennison House, 14 x 17" 250
The Pergola Amalfi, 13 x 15" 145
The Pictured Wall, 13 x 16" 200
The Porch Door, 11 x 14" 90
The Quilting Party, 14 x 17" 160
The River of Peace, 12 x 20" 100
The River Song, 15 x 22" 190
The Road to Far Away, 11 x 14" 240
The Rug Maker, 11 x 14" 170
The Shadow Road, 14 x 17" 80
The Silent Shore, 12 x 15" 80
The Stream of Peace, 16 x 20" 250
The Sudbury in October, 13 x 16" 130
The Sweetness of June, 11 x 14" 190
The Swimming Pool, 11 x 14" 90
The Tranquil Vale, 11 x 17" 50
The Treasure Bag, 13 x 15" 130
The Turf Path, 9 x 11 250
The Village Vale, 8 x 12" 120
The Warner Doorway, 9 x 11" 260
The Way It Begins, 11 x 13" 170
The Whirling Candlestand, 11 x 14" 45
The Winding Apple Bough, 10 x 18" 150
The World Beautiful, 10 x 12" 70
Under Curving Hills, 13 x 16" 75
Under the Blossoms, 11 x 14" 130

Under the Yosemite, 9 x 15" 200
Undulating Reflections, 9 x 19" 210
Unt Ancient Stepping Stones, 9 x 12" 35
Upper Winooski, 13 x 16" 140
Vico Esquene, 10 x 13" 600
Vines and Thatch, 11 x 14" 210
Washington Cherry Blossoms, 13 x 16" 170
Water Loving Blooms, 12 x 15" 440
Watersmeet, 13 x 15" 80
Westfield Water, 7 x 13" 65
Where Grandma was Wed, 14 x 20" 190
Whitsunday, 10 x 16" 70
Windsor Blossoms, 14 x 17" 60
Wythe House Williamsburg, 13 x 16" 1,000

WALLACE NUTTING-LIKE PICTURES

CORLOCK

Close-Framed Jefferson Memorial, 8 x 10" 25
The Washington Monument, 8 x 10" 20
Washington Monument, 7 x 11" 20

DAVID DAVIDSON

A Feathery Birch, 7 x 11" 35
A Prize Flock, 10 x 12" 140
A Promise of Harvest, 7 x 9" 50
A Reverie, 13 x 16" 290
A Roadside Mirror, 7 x 9" 20
A Spring Freshet, 13 x 16" 40
A Spring Morning, 5 x 7" 25
Amherst Lake Drive, Plymouth VT, 5 x 7" 40
Arboretum Jewels, 13 x 16" 55
At the Squire's, 5 x 7" 45
Bald Mountain Mohawk Trail, 7 x 9" 35
Benedict Memorial, 12 x 16" 50
Berkshire Sunset, 8 x 11" 55
Blossom Canopy, 7 x 9" 20
Chosen Bonnet, 5 x 7" 40
Contemporary Masterpieces, 5 x 7" 40
Contentment, 8 x 10" 55
Diadem Aisle, 7 x 9" 60
Driving Home the Cows, 11 x 14" 140
Echo Lake Drive, 10 x 12" 50
Four O'Clock Tea, 13 x 16" 65
Franconia Notch, 7 x 11" 30
Golden Sunset, Bar Harbor, 6 x 8" 85
Grandpa's Marguetites, 5 x 7" 50
Her House in Order, 12 x 15" 80
Lamb's May Feast, 5 x 7" 65
Mohawk Elk, 7 x 9" 55
Mt. Washington Goblet, 7 x 9" 45
Portland Head Light, 6 x 8" 65
Pres. Coolidge's Church & Home, 7 x 9" 20
Red Parasol, 5 x 7" 110
Snow Basin, 8 x 12" 65
Snow Bound Brook, 9 x 12" 155

Sunset Point, 12 x 16"...................... 35
The Covered Bridge, 12 x 16"................ 70
The Four Friends, 13 x 16"................. 70
The Heirloom, 5 x 7"...................... 35
The Lambs May Feast, 13 x 15"............. 65
The Pasture Pool, 7 x 9".................. 45
The Rambler Rose, 11 x 14"................ 95
The Road Home, 5 x 7"..................... 45
The Village Belles, 11 x 15"................ 160
The Village Reporters, 5 x 7".............. 65
Three Arches, Mohawk Trail, 10 x 12"........ 50
Wayside Apple, 5 x 7"..................... 25
Wisteria, 5 x 9".......................... 45
Ye Olden Tyme, 10 x 12"................... 35

FRED THOMPSON

A Quiet Autumn Road, 10 x 16".............. 40
Angry Surf, 8 x 15"....................... 40
Apple Tree Bloom, 10 x 16"................ 55
Birchland, 10 x 16"....................... 70
Blossom Time, 8 x 16"..................... 50
Calm of Autumn, 14 x 17".................. 60
Calm of Fall, 7 x 9"...................... 35
Churning Day, 7 x 9"...................... 45
Drifting, 6 x 8" 145
Flower Maid, 7 x 15"...................... 40
Gamecock, 5 x 7".......................... 175
Golden Gate at Sunset, 10 x 16"........... 65
Golden Trail, 7 x 11" 25
Greeting Card, 5 x 7"..................... 160
Lombardy Poplar, 13 x 16" 110
Mountains from Intervale, 14 x 16" 90
Murmuring Waters, 11 x 14"................ 40
October Woods, 7 x 9" 45
Old Mill Dam, 7 x 9"...................... 60
Old Time Flowers, 7 x 9".................. 60
Old Toll Bridge, 7 x 9"................... 45
Pepperrell Hall, 5 x 11".................. 75
Pleasant Lake, 16 x 20"................... 60
Portland Head, 12 x 18"................... 125
Rail Fence, 5 x 7"........................ 50
Silent Stream, 7 x 14" 55
Snuffing the Candle, 10 x 16"............. 85
Spinning Days, 10 x 13"................... 55
Springtime, 13 x 16" 60
Stony Brook, 7 x 9"....................... 55
The Foot Hills, 13 x 16".................. 45
The Minuet, 10 x 13" 95
The Old Toll Bridge, 10 x 16" 70
The Roller, 11 x 22" 110
The Tale of the Kerchief, 12 x 14" 85
Through Autumn Woods, 10 x 20"............ 75
Tranquil Stream, 7 x 12".................. 35
White Head, 12 x 20" 45

GIBSON

A Back Road, 11 x 14"..................... 20
Back Road, 7 x 9"......................... 10
Snow Path, 7 x 9"......................... 50
The Old Homestead, 7 x 8"................. 50

H. MARSHALL GARDINER

Assorted Postcards, set of 9 36
Bermuda, 13 x 16"......................... 60
Bermuda, 13 x 16"......................... 110
Sankaty, 9 x 11".......................... 425

HARRIS

Charlotte Street, Saint Augustine, 13 x 20".... 225
Close-Framed Florida Scene, 6 x 16"......... 55
Florida Wilds, 6 x 10".................... 20

HAYNES

Untitled "Old Faithful," 6 x 9"............... 45
Untitled "Old Faithful," 8 x 13".............. 55
Yellowstone Park Portfolio Set, 10 x 13"....... 60

SAWYER

A Glimpse of the Mountains, 13 x 16"........ 15
Among the New England Hills, 11 x 20" 330
Close-Framed Echo Lake, 10 x 13" 45
Cold Stream, Mohawk Trail, 13 x 16"......... 70
Elephant's Head, 6 x 9"................... 35
Flume Falls, Franconia Notch, 16 x 20"....... 45
Hudson River at the Highlands, 9 x 15"....... 80
Joseph Lincoln's Garden, 8 x 10" 120
Lake Champlain, 10 x 13".................. 20
Lake George, 7 x 9"....................... 50
Lake Louise, 8 x 10" 90
Mackerel Cove, Bailey Island, 8 x 18" 90
Mt. Chocorua, 11 x 14" 45
Mt. Lafayette & Gale River, 8 x 10"......... 35
Nubble Light, 8 x 10"..................... 50
October's Golden Harvest, 16 x 20"......... 155
Plymouth Birches, 8 x 10"................. 150
Rainbow Falls, 8 x 10".................... 35
The Cloister, San Juan Capistrano, 13 x 16"... 150
The Country Highway, 10 x 16" 40
Up Thru Dinville Notch, 13 x 16" 85

PAPER COLLECTIBLES

*Also see: BLACK AMERICANA, CHARAC-
TER COLLECTIBLES, FIRE FIGHTING
COLLECTIBLES, FRATERNAL ORDER
ITEMS, MAGAZINES, MUCHA ARTWORK,
PAPER DOLLS, POLITICAL ITEMS, POP
CULTURE COLLECTIBLES, RADIOS, RADIO
& TELEVISION MEMORABILIA, ROYCROFT
ITEMS, SIGNS & SIGNBOARDS, SPACE AGE*

COLLECTIBLES, STEAMSHIP COLLECT-
IBLES, TOBACCIANA, WESTERN CHARAC-
TER COLLECTIBLES, and WORLD'S FAIR
COLLECTIBLES.

Broadside, "A Traitor's Peace!," from the
New York Workingmen's Democratic
Republican Assoc. in 1864 strongly
opposing any peace settlement between
the United States & the Confederacy
which would prove favorable to the
Confederacy, 11½ x 19" (folded, some
creasing & foxing) **$440**

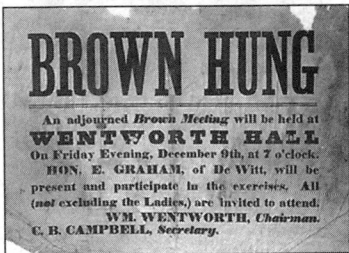

Rare John Brown Broadside

Broadside, "Brown Hung...," announcement
of meeting to be held on December 9th,
probably in upper Midwest, printed shortly
after John Brown's execution in 1859,
creases, edge damage, 7¾ x 10½"
(ILLUS.) **2,640**

Broadside, "John Brown Still Lives!," call for
a special meeting in the upper Midwest
concerning John Brown's raid &
execution, meeting set for Friday
evening, December 30, 1859, 8¼ x 12"
(folds, worn edges, fragile) **5,365**

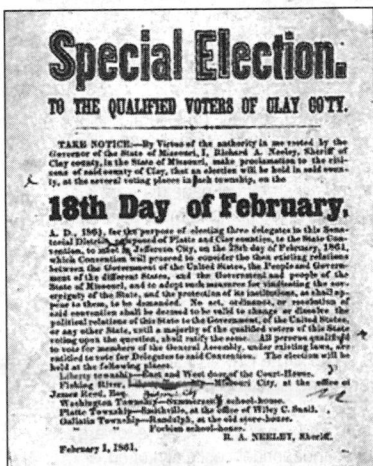

Pre-Civil War Missouri Broadside

Broadside, "Special Election. To The
Qualified Voters of Clay Co'ty," dated
February 1, 1861 for Clay County,
Missouri, issued by "R.A. Neeley, Sheriff,"
concerns electing delegates in Senatorial
district to consider existing relations
between the Government of the United
States & the different states &
Government of Missouri, important notice
just before outbreak of the Civil War,
9¾ x 12½" (ILLUS.) **489**

Cigar labels, group of six unused
Cigarmakers' Union labels, blue, each
w/local factory stamp, ca. early 1880s,
the group **17**

Currency, Colonial-era, 20 shilling note
issued in Pennsylvania on June 18, 1764,
average circulation grade, all signatures
legible **357**

Rare "United States" $6 Bill

Currency, Colonial-era, six dollars, gem
crisp uncirculated bill, the first Continental
Currency issue to use the motto "The
United States," May 20, 1777, brown &
violet ink signatures (ILLUS.) **863**

"The Patterson Steam Engine"

Drawing, "The Patterson Steam Engine,"
pen, ink, & colored pencil on paper,
American School, 19th c., framed,
20 x 35¾" (ILLUS.) **690**

Family register, pen & ink & watercolor on
paper, recording the members of the
McCormick Family, 19th c., framed,
unsigned, 15⅝ x 19⅝" (toning, foxing,
minor staining & tears) **403**

Early N.Y. Fireman's Certificate

Fireman's certificate, New York City Volunteer Fireman's certificate, appoints Moses Dodd a New York City fireman as of March 23, 1829, top & bottom w/elaborate 1807 engravings of firefighters at work, four small tears, repaired w/tape, has been rolled, 12½ x 16" (ILLUS.) **358**

Leaflet, anti-Copperhead sheet from 1864, titled "A Free Pass Entitling holder to tender mercies of the Constitutional Purifying Assoc.....," w/drawings of how the holder can be cleansed of "Copperheadism," 6¼ x 9" (slight bottom tear & foxing spots) **55**

Mezzotint engraving, "Last Words of Captain Nathan Hale - the Hero-Martyr of the American Revolution," scene just before the hanging of Hale, by F.O.C. Darley, ca. 1850s, framed, 9¼ x 11¾" (general soiling, creases, rubbing & spot fading, short edge tears) **207**

Crash of The Hindenburg Report

Newspaper, "Baltimore News-Post," Baltimore, Maryland, May 8, 1937, cover story & dramatic photo of the crash of the "Hindenburg" at Lakehurst, New Jersey, headline reads "Capt. Lehmann Dies - Among 31 Victims of Zep Blast," toned paper, small edge splits, 22 pp., 16¾ x 21¼" (ILLUS.) **230**

Newspaper, "Boston Traveler," Boston, Massachusetts, November 22, 1963, reports death of John F. Kennedy, headline reads "KENNEDY SLAIN," shows "before" and "after" images of presidential limousine, front page only **69**

Newspaper, "The Boston Globe," Boston, Massachusetts, November 23, 1963, complete morning edition w/full news of Kennedy's assassination, front page headline reads "SHOCK-DISBELIEF-GRIEF," picture of Kennedy, the Secret Service man climbing on the back of the presidential limousine & Lyndon Johnson being sworn in as President, etc. **86**

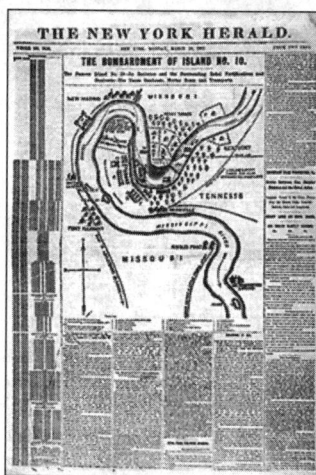

The New York Herald, March 24, 1862

Newspaper, "The New York Herald," New York, New York, March 24, 1862, headline "The Bombardment of Island No. 10" w/large front page diagram & report of Union bombardment of Island No. 10, a Confederate stronghold on the Mississippi at the junction of the Missouri, Tennessee & Kentucky, other war news included, very slightly toned, 8 pp., 15¼ x 22" (ILLUS.) **173**

Newspaper, "The New-Yorker," New York, New York, April 23, 1836, published by H. Greeley & Co., latest reports on the fall of the Alamo & news about move toward Texas independence, lightly toned, occasional dampstaining, disbound, 9½ x 12¼" **114**

Newspaper, "The Pennsylvania Chronicle,
& Extraordinary," Philadelphia,
Pennsylvania, October 12, 1768, includes
news report about the landing of British
troops in Boston in response to Stamp
Act disturbances, disbound, toned pages,
very crisp, minor dampstaining, 9 x 11¼" **259**

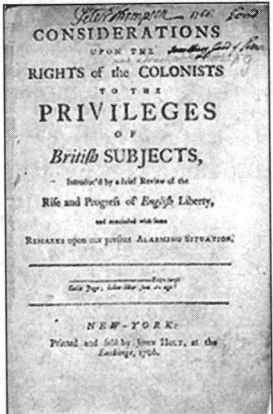

Rare Colonial Pamphlet

Pamphlet, "Considerations Upon the Rights
of the Colonists to the Privileges of British
Subjects...," printed & folded, by John
Holt of New York, 1766, plain paper
covers, 27 pp., 5¼ x 8" (ILLUS.) **1,265**
Program, 1911 Gaiety Theatre, Earl Christy
cover. **25**
Program, bicycle race, "LAW 9th Meet
Baltimore, MD June 18-19-20 1888," fine
bicycle graphics, 48 pp. **149**
Union charter, AFL union charter &
certificate of affiliation, signed by Samuel
Gompers & eight AFL vice-presidents,
dated 1917, framed, certificate 16 x 24" **433**

PAPER DOLLS

MAGAZINE SHEETS

The price stated is for uncut sheets in very good condition, clean and neatly removed from the magazine, properly stored so that there are no raggedy edges. Most of the magazines ran paper dolls in series. A collector is often willing to pay more for "that one sheet which will complete a series." Some of the series ran over a long period of time and the sheet number of sheets can be intimidating. The quality of the artwork and color plays a very big part in the desirability of these sheets. Some seem to be far more rare than others. Yet another factor affecting price is "cross-over" — collectors from

more than one area interested in the same sheet. For example, an avid golfer may buy paper doll sheets showing golfers to frame and use in decorating. The golfer in this case usually is willing to pay more than a paper doll collector would. This is true of all paper dolls. Complete cut sets are worth roughly one fourth as much as uncut sheets.( ) - indicates series

Canadian Home Journal, "Harold and His
Playmates," limited color, June 1929 . . . . **$8**
Child Life, "Let's Play Theater," June 1934 . . . . **8**

"Make-Over Wardrobe for Dollie's Christmas"

Child Life, "Make-Over Wardrobe for
Dollie's Christmas," limited color,
December 1943 (ILLUS.) **8**

"Heidi, A Doll of Switzerland"

Children's Playmate Magazine, "Heidi, A
Doll of Switzerland," by Fern Bisel Peat,
September 1939 (ILLUS.) **6**
Delineator, "Adele," (Carolyn Chester's Full
Base Dolls), February 1912 . . . . **15**
Delineator, "Who Are They?," (Patten Beard
Presents Peter Pan's Movie Contest),
March 1917 . . . . **15**

"Little Louise and Her Pets"

Good Housekeeping, "Little Louise and Her
Pets," patterns for more clothes on back,
February 1909 (ILLUS.) **12**

Good Housekeeping, "Polly Pratt Had a
Valentine," "Every Girl Should Have
One," February 1920, 2 pgs., both **15**

"Polly's Sister Has June Wedding"

Good Housekeeping, "Polly's Sister Has
June Wedding," (Poll Pratt), June 1921
(ILLUS.) **10**

Junior Home Magazine, "Betty in
Bohemian Costume," black & white,
August 1922 . . . . **5**

Ladies' Home Journal, "A Boy and Girl of
the Netherlands," (Lettie Lane Series),
April 1, 1911 . . . . **8**

Ladies' Home Journal, "Betty Bonnet's
Sister's Son," January 1917 . . . . **8**

Ladies' Home Journal, "Children's Cut-out
Paper Parties of the Stories They Love
Best: II Goldilocks," February 1913 . . . . **20**

Ladies' World, "Billie Burke," (Movie Dolls),
black & white, October 1916 . . . . **10**

"Baby Stuart"

Little Folk's Magazine, "Baby Stuart,"
(Paper Dolls from Famous Paintings),
April 1916 (ILLUS.) **15**

McCalls, "Betsy McCall Writes from
Holland," July 1969 . . . . **2**

"Betsy McCall's Best Present"

McCalls, "Betsy McCall's Best Present,"
December 1984 (ILLUS.) **2**

McCalls, "Sister Nell Goes to a Party," by
Nandor Honti, November 1925 . . . . **20**

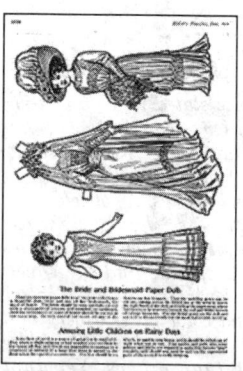

"The Bride and Bridesmaid Paper Dolls"

"Vanity Fair's Own Paper Dolls - no. 7"

PAPERWEIGHTS

Apsley Pellatt "Sulphide Medallion"
  weight, miniature, silhouette cameo of
  Prince Albert, inscribed "H. R. H. Prince
  Albert - Born August 26, 1819 - Married
  February 20, 1840," 1¹⁵⁄₁₆" d. **$468**

Baccarat "Butterfly" weight, insect
  w/flattened millefiori wings, marbled in
  shades of orange, green, blue, yellow &
  red, attached to an eggplant-purple body
  w/black head & antennae & turquoise
  eyes, insect floats over star-cut ground
  inside crystal dome w/six & one
  faceting, 2¹³⁄₁₆" d. **3,025**
Baccarat "Choufleur Carpet Ground"
  weight, w/complex canes in various
  colors, in a sea of twisted lilac &
  lemonade whorls, includes Gridel
  silhouette canes of two moths & a dog &
  a deer & a horse & a rooster & a goat &
  an elephant, w/millefiori flower portrait
  cane w/petals made from arrow canes &
  a center composed of a star cane,
  "B1848" signature/date cane, 3⅛" d. **11,000**
Baccarat "Close Packed Millefiori"
  weight, clear glass set w/two peach
  roses amidst six-pointed star canes,
  whorls, arrow canes, bull's-eye canes,
  shamrock canes, stardust canes,
  quatrefoil canes, fortress canes, trefoil
  canes & cog canes, in various colors, two
  canes appear to have been created
  w/same technique factory used to create
  its pompon blossoms, 2⁹⁄₁₆" d. **1,870**

Baccarat "Double Clematis" Weight

Baccarat "Double Clematis" weight,
  w/double tier of ridged robin's egg blue
  petals around a red & white
  stardust/bull's-eye cane center, on stalk
  w/pair of entwined buds & two types of
  green leaves, over star-cut ground, six &
  one faceting, 2⅝" d. **1,980**
Baccarat "Faceted Macédoine" weight,
  w/pieces of twists & filigree in blue &
  green & red amidst white lace, sides
  of the piece are cut w/geometric
  faceting, 2⅞" d. **385**
Baccarat "Macédoine" weight, including
  several large bull's-eye canes w/pieces of
  twists & filigree in red & blue & green &
  yellow amidst white lace, 2⅞" d. **468**
Baccarat "Pansy" weight, pansy w/deep
  purple upper petals & black-striped
  purple & yellow lower petals, around

stardust/bull's-eye cane, on stalk w/yellow & purple bud & green leaves, in nineteenth-century flower language the pansy symbolized tender thoughts, 3⁹⁄₁₆ d. . . . **1,045**

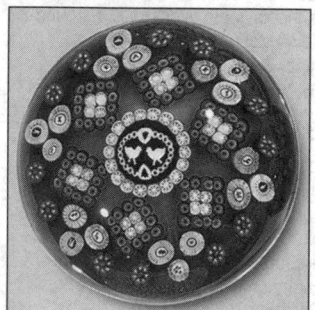

Baccarat Millefiori Lovebirds Weight

Baccarat "Patterned Millefiori" weight, w/large lovebirds silhouette cane surrounded by patterned arrangement of complex canes in cobalt blue & white, including square clusters of canes on translucent green-over-white ground, seventeen other Gridel silhouette canes are composed about edge of weight, signature/date cane, acid etched w/Baccarat insignia, limited edition of 350, 1976, 3⅜" d. (ILLUS.). **660**

Baccarat "Patterned Moth & Shamrock Millefiori" weight, clear glass set w/a large central complex millefiori arrangement composed of seven shamrocks & ruby cogs, surrounded by ring of cobalt blue, ruby & white six-pointed star/arrow canes & a spaced garland of fourteen moth silhouettes, arrangement set on white lace ground, shamrock canes contain annealing cracks an attribute commonly found in this design, 3" d. **3,850**

Baccarat "Rock" Weight

Baccarat "Rock" weight, miniature, also called mountains of the moon & sand dunes, sandy ground flecked w/green glass & mica, 1⅞" d. (ILLUS.) **198**

Baccarat "Scattered Millefiori on Lace" weight, Gridel silhouettes of two moths & a red devil (or clown) & two monkeys & a dog & a goat & an elephant & a rooster & a horse interspersed w/complex cog canes, arrow canes, six-pointed star canes, trefoil canes, shamrock canes, whorl canes, quatrefoil canes & star-shaped canes in various colors, on white lace ground of white filigree & yellow & pink ribbon twists & pieces of filigree, "B1847" signature/date cane, 3⅛"d. **3,300**

Baccarat "Sulphide" weight, silhouette cameo of French King Louis Philippe, on translucent aqua ground, cut w/geometric faceting, 3½" d.. . . . . **825**

Bronze, model of a recumbent lion, original patina, impressed Tiffany Studios mark & "#932," 5" l.. . . . . **440**

Cape Cod Glass Works "Swirl" weight, alternating teal & white swirls, emanating from central pink & green Clichy-type rose, encircled by ring of blue complex cog canes, tiny signature placed in center of rose, 2⅞" d. **220**

Charles Kaziun II "Ruby Crimp Rose" weight, tilted, featuring fifteen-petal crimp rose, cupped inside four green leaves, w/footed crystal pedestal, signed under flowers w/complex K signature cane surrounded by hearts, 3" d. **1,250**

Clichy "Close Concentric Millefiori" weight, w/central pink & green rose surrounded by concentric rows of complex canes, including row of ten white roses alternating w/pink pastry mold canes amidst rows of pastry mold canes, stardust/bull's-eye canes, & florets, in various colors, arrangement set inside turquoise & white stave basket, 2⁵⁄₁₆" d. **2,750**

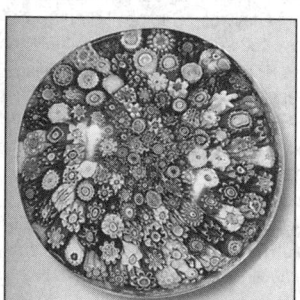

Clichy "Close Packed Millefiori" Weight

Clichy "Close Packed Millefiori" weight, w/nine roses in various colors amidst six-pointed star canes, edelweiss canes, florets, bull's-eye canes, moss, stardust & cog canes in various colors, set in an alternating pink & white stave basket, 3⅛" d. (ILLUS.). **5,225**

Clichy "Spaced Millefiori" weight, opaque cobalt blue ground glass set w/a central pink & green rose amidst pastry mold, edelweiss, stardust, cog & bull's-eye canes, in pink & yellow & cherry & green & white, intriguing pastry mold cane is formed from pressed bull's-eye canes, 2⁹⁄₁₆" d. **2,090**

D'Albret "Sulphide" weight, front-view cameo of Albert Schweitzer renowned philosopher & musicologist, as sculpted by Gilbert Poillerat, on translucent dark purple ground w/diamond-cut base, six & one faceting, dated, limited edition of 1,000, 1969, 2⅞" d. **154**

Edward Rithner "Candy Cane" Weight

Edward Rithner "Candy Cane" weight, w/striped pink & blue & white & aqua rods on spotted ruby ground, ruby ground of this piece is rarely found, minor bruise on underside of weight, 3¹⁄₁₆" d. (ILLUS.) **248**

Footed Pinchbeck weight, w/armed men riding on horseback through wooded area towards young boy leading girl by the arm, copper-zinc alloy popular during the Victorian era for its resemblance to gold, 3¼" d. **660**

James Kontes "Pink Rose" weight, containing pair of pink blossoms w/upright yellow stamens on stalk w/three large buds & green leaves, flowers rest on bed of white lace placed on a translucent cobalt blue ground, signature cane, 3⅛" d. **3,025**

Ken Rosenfeld "Rose Bouquet" weight, featuring furled ruby rose arranged w/three turquoise bell flowers w/green & yellow stamens & white bellflower w/pink & green stamens, on stem w/three white buds & yellow-striped green leaves over star-cut ground, five & one faceting, signature cane, 3³⁄₁₆" d. **1,100**

New England Glass Co. "Open Concentric Millefiori" weight, w/central running rabbit silhouette cane surrounded by a circlet of pink & white star canes & a circlet of complex pink, white & yellow cog canes on white double-swirl latticinio

ground, dome decorated w/elaborate propeller cut encircled by a row of small circular facets & a row of large circular side facets divided by vertical printies, 2⅝" d. (minor chip in the dome) **550**

New England Glass "Fruit Bouquet" Weight

New England Glass Company "Fruit Bouquet" weight, a formal arrangement containing five pears & four cherries, on a bed of green leaves in a white double-swirl latticinio basket, 2¹³⁄₁₆" d. (ILLUS.) **440**

Orient & Flume "Hearts & Vines Surface Design" weight, w/reddish-orange hearts hanging from curling black & yellow vines on iridescent mottled caramel & yellow globe, signed & dated, 1976, 2¹³⁄₁₆" d. **358**

Parabelle Glass "Pink Clematis" Weight

Parabelle Glass "Pink Clematis Paneled Color Ground" weight, the flower w/green moss cane center, encircled by radiating buds & white clematis blossoms w/yellow moss centers, inside garland of complex cog canes in pink & white & yellow & royal blue, arrangement floats over an opaque pink & ruby panel ground inside a pink & ruby stave basket, limited edition of 10, 1993, 3" d. (ILLUS.) **715**

Paul Stankard "Bouquet" weight, w/Saint Anthony's fire, meadowreathe, forget-me-nots, chokeberry blossoms & bellflowers, signature cane, dated, 1978, 2¾" d. **1,980**

Paul Stankard "Faceted Saint Anthony's Fire" weight, flower w/pointed red petals & black-tipped yellow stamens, grown on stem w/trailing root system, pair of seeds sprout next to plant, five & one faceting, signature cane, 1976, 2¹¹⁄₁₆" d. **1,320**

Paul Ysart "Ribbon Bouquet Garland" weight, featuring five flowers in pink & amethyst & Persian blue & baby blue & pistachio, w/opening blue bud, on stems tied w/looped pink ribbon & encircled by garland of complex fuchsia & white cog canes on black ground, signature cane placed in center of one of the flowers, signed, 3" d. **1,045**

Perthshire "Crown" weight, w/blue & red twisted ribbons alternating w/white filigree spokes projecting from complex millefiori cane, first special yearly collection weight produced at Pertshire, signed "P1969" in canes on the base, limited edition of 268, 1969, 3" d. **660**

Perthshire "Golfer" Weight

Perthshire "Golfer" weight, w/central glass transfer of a golfer swinging a club on lace ground, encircled by triple garland of millefiori canes & spiral twists in pink & purple & red & blue, circular top facet, signature/date cane, Perthshire produced golfer designs over several years in edition sizes ranging from 250 to 450, edition size for this weight is not known, 1989, 3⅛" d. (ILLUS.) **440**

Rick Ayotte "Golden-Back Oriole" weight, artist proof, black & yellow South American bird perched on jungle branch w/yellow & green leaves over opaque white ground, signed & dated, 1983, 3⅛" d. . . . **825**

Sandwich Glass Company "Red Poinsettia" weight, w/double tier of five pinkish-red petals around a red & white & green complex cog cane, on stalk w/green leaves over blue & white jasper ground, 3" d. **935**

St. Louis "Amber Ground Bouquet" weight, containing stalks of pink & blue clematis blossoms w/green & white

stardust centers, over diamond-cut amber ground, six & one faceting, signature/date cane, limited edition of 450, 1979, 3" d. **550**

St. Louis "Nosegay" weight, miniature, w/three complex cog & star canes, in blue & salmon & ruby & white on stalk w/spring green leaves, over diamond-cut amber ground, circular top facet w/two rows of circular side facets, 1⅝" d. (small chips to facets). **440**

St. Louis "Pansy & Camomile" Weight

St. Louis "Pansy & Camomile" weight, the pansy w/amethyst upper petals & black-striped amber lower petals around complex cob/six-pointed star cane, in amber & Persian blue & powder blue, w/millefiori cane at center of pansy, flower grows on stalk w/pink camomile blossom composed of recessed C-shaped petals, around pale yellow stamens, on stalk w/emerald green leaves, arranged on white double-swirl latticinio ground, rare, 3⅛" d. (ILLUS.) **8,800**

St. Louis "Pompon" weight, camomile flower w/feathered white petals around a small complex blue & yellow millefiori cane, on a stalk w/white bud & green leaves, over white double-swirl latticinio ground, w/translucent pink glass sandwiched between swirls of filigree, 2¹⁵⁄₁₆" d. **3,575**

Saint Louis "Two-Color Crown" Weight

St. Louis "Two-Color Crown" weight,
w/red & green twists interspersed w/white
latticinio spokes projecting from central
complex six-pointed star/bundled rod
cane, in pink & white & green, 2⅛" d.
(ILLUS.).............................. **1,650**

**William Manson "Green Aventurine
Snake" weight,** reptile w/black & yellow
striped green adventurine coils, slithering
over a sandy ground, five & one faceting,
signed & dated, limited edition of 150, 3⅛" d... **303**

William Manson "Ladybug" weight,
plaque-type, featuring black-spotted red
ladybug crawling on central white
blossom w/yellow millefiori center &
green leaves, inside a spaced garland of
flowers, alternating between amethyst &
turquoise w/yellow millefiori centers &
green leaves, on dark translucent ruby
ground, arrangement displayed in upright
plaque w/tilted window facet, signature
cane, signed & dated, limited edition of
50, 2⅞" d............................... **440**

**Yaffa Sikorsky-Todd & Jeffrey M. Todd
"Wisteria" weight,** featuring a tree
w/vines of hanging purple millefiori
blossoms & green leaves, in grassy field
w/rocks & purple & white millefiori
blossoms, signed & dated, 1995, 3⅛" d...... **468**

PERFUME, SCENT &
COLOGNE BOTTLES

*Decorative accessories from milady's boudoir
have always been highly collectible and in recent
years there has been an especially strong surge of
interest in perfume bottles. Our listings also
include related containers such as pocket bottles
and vials, tabletop containers & atomizers. Most
readily available are examples from the 19th
through the mid-20th century, but earlier
examples do surface occasionally. The myriad
varieties have now been documented in several
recent reference books which should further
popularize this collecting specialty.*

Amethyst glass, cologne, mold-blown
octagonal deeply waisted form w/a tall
slender neck w/flared rim, pontiled base,
probably Boston & Sandwich Glass Co.,
7" h. (hard to find small pot stone crack
on side)................................ **$248**

Amethyst glass, cologne, octagonal bottle-
form w/short flared neck w/tooled rim,
smooth base, probably Boston &
Sandwich Glass Co., 4" h................ **220**

Cameo glass, perfume, lay-down style, ruby
red dagger-shaped overlaid in white,
cameo-etched w/water lilies & water

plants, a butterfly in flight, mounted w/a
monogrammed sterling silver screw-on
cap marked "Gorham," attributed to
Thomas Webb, 10½" l. (interior stain)...... **2,645**

Cameo glass, turquoise blue spherical body
w/raised rim, overlaid in bright white &
cameo-etched in an Oriental flowering
branch design, gilt-metal cap set w/red &
blue stones & Continental hallmarks,
bottle attributed to England, w/original
fitted box, 4½" h...................... **1,955**

Clear glass, scent, free-blown double
gourd-form w/four strips of applied
rigaree, 2½" h......................... **77**

Clear glass, scent, free-blown "sea horse"
form w/curled end, applied rigaree trim,
2¹⁄₁₆" l. (small rim chip)................ **88**

Clear glass, scent, mold-blown, "sea horse"
form w/curled end & twenty-four thin
swirled ribs, 2⅝" l.................... **88**

Clear glass, scent, mold-blown w/twenty-
four fine swirled ribs, flattened ovoid body
w/sheared neck, 3³⁄₁₆" l................ **28**

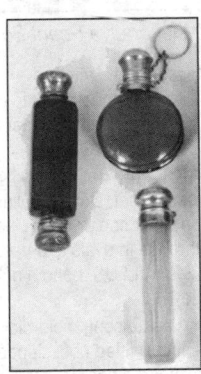

Three Victorian Scent Bottles

Cobalt blue glass, scent, double-ended
cylinder cut w/ten straight panels, one
hinged & one screw-on silver cap,
19th c., some dents in caps, 3⅞" l.
(ILLUS. left) **165**

Cobalt blue glass, scent, mold-blown,
flattened round form w/concentric rings
on both sides, sheared neck, corrugated
edges, early 19th c., 1⅞" w., 2⁷⁄₁₆" l......... **303**

Cobalt blue glass, scent, mold-blown
w/sixteen vertical ribs, narrow tapering
ovoid form w/short sheared neck, slightly
flattened sides, early 19th c., 2¾" l......... **165**

Cranberry glass, scent, double-ended
w/silver center band & silver caps at each
end, silver marked "S. Mordan & Co.
London," England, 19th c., 4¼" l.
(ILLUS. top right, next page) **220**

Cranberry glass, scent, flattened round
form w/hinged brass cap & ring handle,
19th c., 2¾" h. (ILLUS. top right) **165**

Four Decorative Scent Bottles

Cut overlay glass, scent, flattened rectangular form w/cranberry cut to clear in bands of ovals, rounded shoulder & fancy silver collar & cap, 3⅝" l. (ILLUS. bottom right) **193**

Cut-overlay glass, scent, slender cylindrical form w/hinged silver cap, frosted clear exterior cut through in ovals to a vaseline inner layer, 3¾" l. (ILLUS. bottom right, previous page) **175**

Emerald green glass, scent, mold-blown w/twenty-five fine swirled ribs, slender ovoid form w/sheared neck, early 19th c., 3" l.. .... **143**

Emerald green glass, scent, pressed cylindrical form, geometric design of alternating narrow vertical & horizontal ribbing, twist-on pewter cap, first half 19th c., 3⁵⁄₁₆" l. **193**

Emerald green glass, scent, pressed flattened narrow form w/serpentined beveled edges, screw-on pewter cap, first half 19th c., 3⁵⁄₁₆" l. (small chip under cap) **110**

Green glass, green painted & gilded w/a lady's portrait in one oval panel & three other flower-filled panels, Bohemia, 19th c., 10¾" h. (wear) **374**

Light green glass, scent, mold-blown, twenty-four thin swirled ribs, long narrow ovoid body w/sheared neck, slightly flattened sides, early 19th c., 3⁵⁄₁₆" l. **193**

Opaque blue glass, scent, flattened round disk decorated w/gold enameled leaves & white blossoms, brass neck, cap & ring handle, 2¾" l. (ILLUS. top left) **187**

Vaseline to clear glass, scent, pressed long tapering form in a diamond block design, shading from greenish vaseline to clear, silver plate hinged cap & chain handle, 3½" l. (ILLUS. bottom left) **185**

PHONOGRAPHS

Ornate Brunswick Floor Model

Brunswick, disc-type floor model, ornate black-painted upright cabinet w/a flattened domed hinged cover above a case w/an oval front sound panel w/ornate pierced lattice above a pair of tall doors decorated w/ornate painted chinoiserie decoration, molded corner pilasters w/carved scrolls at the top & base, serpentine scrolled front apron, on casters, crackled finish, grill w/glued repairs, ca. 1920, 22¼" sq., 42½" h. (ILLUS.) **$440**

Columbia Grafonola, disc-type, in a special Empire-Style mahogany veneer cabinet, a round top above a deep apron w/a pull-out section housing the player, on a heavy tapering octagonal pedestal resting on a quadripatitie cross-base w/C-scroll feet, original finish & gilt decal label, early 20th c., 31" d., 31½" h. **1,540**

Edison Home Model C with Horn

Edison Home Model C, table top cylinder model, oak case & domed separate cover, floral-painted large morning glory horn, case refinished, 35" h. plus horn (ILLUS.) 523

Rare Miraphone Combination Machine

Miraphone, combination disc music box & disc record player, mahogany case w/hinged lid & applied carving, double-comb music box plays 15½" d. discs, w/a large wooden horn w/phonograph arm & turntable, labeled "Jacot Music Box Co., NY," early 20th c., 18⅝ x 25¼", 12¾" h. plus horn (ILLUS.) 9,900

Victor E Phonograph

Victor E (Monarch Jr.), table-top disc player, oak cabinet w/side crank, large brass & black metal horn w/large label, working, original finish, 21" h. plus horn (ILLUS.) 1,155

Victor Victrola Phonograph

Victor Victrola, table-top disc player, oak cabinet w/internal horn, hinged doors in base, side crank, set on a separate tall oak music cabinet base w/swelled corners & a pair of tall doors above the serpentine apron & small bracket feet, phonograph 11¾" h., cabinet, 34½" h., 2 pcs. (ILLUS.) 275

PHOTOGRAPHIC ITEMS

Albumen print, oval studio pose of two fisherman w/their poles & equipment, Edward Miller & Francis Myers, on a scroll-stamped rectangular cardboard mount, Elizabeth, New Jersey, dated May 30, 1872, 5¼ x 7½" $127

Cute Ambrotype of Little Boy on Horse

Ambrotype, sixth plate, adorable portrait of a young boy about 2-3 years old seated on a painted rocking horse, wearing a tasseled hat, short-sleeved jacket, long pants & boots, unhappy expression, w/old glass protector, stamped ornate mat, old seal, lightly tinted cheeks (ILLUS.) 300

Ambrotype, sixth plate image of a Confederate sergeant, shown half-length in uniform, purchased in North Carolina, in case w/broken spine 396

Ambrotype, a uniformed Victorian gentleman w/his highwheel bicycle, open case, mid-19th c., 2¾ x 3⅛" (minor imperfections) 88

Ambrotype, cased ninth plate image of a young man, inside of case inscribed "Thomas D. Saunders, Lexington MO. Dec 5, '58." 88

Ambrotype, cased sixth plate, a father tenderly holding & looking down upon his "sleeping" - (deceased) child, leather case . . . 248

Ambrotype, cased sixth plate image of a young woman w/wedding ring, leather case w/embossed metal mat of Military motif . . . 66

Ambrotype, cased sixth plate of a seated Civil War Union Cavalry non commissioned officer (lid missing from leather case) **236**

Cabinet photo, girl w/wicker doll carriage w/doll, standing wearing a white dress w/a studio landscape backdrop, by Wells, Canton, New York, ca. 1890s (slight soiling) . . . **28**

Cabinet photo, patriotic photo of a young lady standing wearing a horizontally-striped dress & holding an American flag, studio pose by Krahmer, Butler, New York (slight soiling) **31**

Duck Hunter Cabinet Photo

Cabinet photo, studio shot of a duck hunter, a man wearing a hat seated in a prop boat & holding his rifle, a dog w/him & dead game birds behind him, light yellow mount, by W. H. Fermann, Stoughton, Wisconsin, soiling, small stain (ILLUS.) **50**

Cabinet photo, studio shot of two gamblers, the men seated at a small table smoking & holding hands of cards, money & a pistol on the table, ivory mount, by Wood of Carthage, ca. 1890 (light soil & wear, small crease) **47**

Camera, Beau Brownie No. 2A, Art Deco design face in mauve & black enamel, black leatherette over aluminum body, designed by Walter D. Teague, w/original box & manual, ca. 1930s, 3¼ x 5", 5" h., the set **176**

Camera, Kodak #3-A Autographic Model C, original leather case **50**

Camera, No. 1A Gift Kodak, folding-type, Art Deco design face in brown, red & cocoa enamel, brown leather case, designed by Walter D. Teague, ca. 1930s, 5 x 8", 3½" h. . . **209**

Carte de visite, Civil War Union soldier, verso w/blue 2¢ tax stamp, "Wolff's Gallery Alexandria VA" **88**

Carte de visite, Confederate General Stonewall Jackson **59**

Carte de visite, Edwin M. Stanton standing studio portrait, by Anthony from a Brady negative, Lincoln's Secretary of War

Stanton Carte de Visite

standing beside a table, corners clipped, light foxing, 1860s (ILLUS.) **121**

Carte de visite, exterior photo of a marble works, shows tow men, horses, wagon, marble monuments & a building in the background w/signage "Brown Marble Works," reverse w/pencil inscription reading "Brown Marble Yard, Schoharie, NY," original negative blemish in lower right corner **69**

Carte de visite, exterior photo of the Cincinnati & Covington Bridge, the suspension bridge over the Ohio River linking the two cities, taken from the Covington side, the reverse w/bridge data (slight soiling) **91**

Carte de visite, General George B. McClellan. . . . **69**

Carte de visite, John Wilkes Booth, Lincoln assassin seated in a large Gothic Revival armchair, head leaning on one arm, by J. Cady, Brandon, Vermont, probably copied from a Brady shot (soil around edges, small spot on image) **114**

Carte de visite, of a seated Civil War Union Office (appears to be a 1st Lt.), verso w/blue 2 cent tax stamp, also marked "Photographed by J.W. Stevens, Craftsbury VT" **110**

Early Carte de Visite Street Scene

Carte de visite, outdoor scene of inter-racial street vendors in Saratoga, New York, shows a cook, a man w/a small wagon to carry the floor-model scale w/its sign "Tray Your Weight," two black men also shown, fine detail, by P.H. McKernon, Saratoga Springs, New York (ILLUS.) 433

Carte de visite, portrait of Jean Louis Rodolphe Agassiz (1807-73), noted Swiss-born naturalist & glaciologist, standing at a blackboard drawing a sea urchin (light soiling & foxing, a few spots) 42

Carte de visite, seated Civil War Union soldier brandishing a Colt revolver & wearing an oval "US" belt plate, verso inscribed "E.W. Rozell 68 Inf. Vol. Chatanouga, Tenn." 165

Carte de visite, Sergeant Boston Corbett, 16th N.Y. Cavalry, credited w/shooting John Wilkes Booth 193

Carte de visite, standing Civil War Union Cavalry Office, wearing full uniform, including gloves, holstered pistol, sash, belt & officer's belt-plate, long coat & sword, verso inscribed "Yours Truly. A. Downing 1st Lieut. Co. D. 7th Kansas Cav. husband of Martha Gibson," photographers mark of A.C. Nichols, Leavenworth, Kansas. 187

Carte de visite, studio shot of a live puma reclining at ease on the floor, by A.S. Hayward, Chester, Vermont, cream mount w/white border & red trim, ca. 1860s (light soil, foxing, original negative flaw in corner). 162

Carte de Visite of Lady Chess Players

Carte de visite, women playing chess, studio view w/a lady seated on each side of a table w/the chess board, by D. Clark, New Brunswick, New Jersey, two cent tax stamp, Civil War era, light browning (ILLUS.) 91

Daguerreotype, sixth plate, half-length portrait of a seated young man holding his walking stick, tranquil pose, noted behind image "Rudolf S....., 1847," early mat style (minor tarnish spots) 88

Daguerreotype, sixth plate post-mortem, young child about one year old shown three-quarters length laid on cloth, paper note states "Ellen Windale (?) in her coffin,"1850s (no seal, light tarnish) 385

Daguerreotype, sixth plate, bust portrait of a beautiful young girl, posed w/both hands to side of face, her hair fashioned in cascading ringlets, brooch neck jewelry & interesting sunburst effect to backdrop, leather case w/grape design 220

Daguerreotype, sixth plate three-quarter image of middle age woman w/hands clasped at the waist, calling card beneath image inscribed "Julie Ann Budlong born 1820 died 1884 at Campbell NB. Taken Oct. 25, 1860 at Blue Grass Iowa" 55

Daguerreotype, sixth plate image of a well-dressed seated man wearing a top hat & holding a book in his left hand, plate marked "L. B. Binsse & Co. NY," leather case. . 121

Daguerreotype, fourth plate, three-quarter length portrait of a seated well-dressed gentleman, leather case 250

Daguerreotypes, cased ninth plate images depicting an elderly woman & man (presumably husband & wife), woman w/bonnet & rectangular glasses, in L.P. & Co. Union Case "A Family Party," w/note apparently w/instructions to artist of how to paint these images, pr. (chipped lip to case) 165

Fine Victorian Photo Album

Photo album on stand, celluloid covers decorated on the front w/a color scene of a late Victorian couple in bicycle riding attire stopped for a picnic along a country lane, their safety bicycles parked against a split rail fence, on original album stand w/drawer, ca. 1890s, 2 pcs. (ILLUS.) 523

Photograph, a group portrait of the Chicago bicycle racing club taken at a board track, signed "Spandau & Coultry Photo 117 N. Dearborn St. Chicago July 2, 1915," in period frame, 8 x 10" 193

Photograph, Army Balloon Corps, long panoramic shot showing six observation balloons & their crews at base somewhere near Los Angeles, ca. 1915, by Huddleston Photo Co., Los Angeles, 10 x 43½" (rolled causing serious creases, tear in lower right corner) **330**

First Flag Raising on Iwo Jima

Photograph, Iwo Jima flag raising, first flag raised on Mt. Suribachi, February 23, 1945, inscribed & signed by the photographer "1st Flag Raising, Feb. 23, 1945 - Mt. Suribachi, Iwo Jima - With best wishes - Lou Lowery," later that day another photographer & other Marines raised a larger flag which was snapped & became the famous shot, black & white, 8 x 10" (ILLUS.) **605**

Photograph, occupational, women in factory, marked on front mount "Taken Dec. 14, 1899, Rec'd Dec. 19, 1899. Taken in Button Room of B.M. & Co.'s factory," reverse marked "Glove factory, Gloversville, NY," photo 5 x 7" on 8 x 10" mount (soiled mount, photo foxed) **94**

Photograph, outdoor scene of the Providence, Rhode Island bicycle club w/uniformed wheelmen posed on a cliff w/five highwheel bicycles, late 19th c., 7½ x 9¼" (some minor imperfections) **248**

Photograph, the Titanic setting out from New York harbor, black & white glossy print from International News Photos, Inc., shows the Titanic & another ship w/a small tugboat, a detailed label on the reverse describes the sinking of the Titanic four days after this photo was shot, 8 x 10" (slight soiling, tiny corner bend) . . **242**

Tintype, sixth plate, studio shot of a standing lumberjack, wearing work clothes & holding an ax across one shoulder, late 19th - early 20th c. (very minor scratches) **36**

Tintype of Confederate Ranger

Tintype, ninth plate image of a seated Confederate soldier, Napoleon Ruff - Confederate Ranger, New Boston, Texas, member of Lane's Rangers, shown clutching a canteen w/shoulder strap, a small pistol tucked in his belt, in full thermoplastic case (ILLUS.) **1,650**

Tintype, sixth plate, Union sergeant in a non-regulation uniform, possibly a Zouave-type, standing wearing a knife in his belt, puttees on shoes, braidwork on sleeves, plate marked "Melainotype - Neff's pat. '56," oval mark from metal mat frame, probably early in the Civil War **200**

Tintype, fourth plate of elegantly dressed woman w/highlighted gold earrings, cameo broach & ring, plate marked "Melainotype Plate - Porneff's Pat 19 Feb 46," domed glass, leather case **55**

Tintype, fourth plate of infant propped up on a pillow (possibly a post-mortem), slightly tinted, contained in a Union case marked "Littlefield, Parsons & Co." **250**

Tintype, maids, a group of woman each wearing an apron & two w/brooms, one pointing at an open book held by another, studio shot (light bends, some scratches) **44**

Tintype, sixth plate image of a very plump midget, perhaps a famous side-show star **61**

Tintype, sixth plate of man, "Catching Butterflies," L. P. & Co. Union case **55**

Tintype, small studio shot of a seated smiling late Victorian lady dressed in an American flag outfit & holding two slender crossed flag poles w/American flags, 2½ x 3¼" (some small scratches) **110**

Token, bronze-copper, round, obverse w/a central eagle clutching arrow & olive branch & "Root & Co. Daguerreian Gallery, 363 Broadway, NY," reverse w/a laurel wreath & "First premium awarded to Root & Co. for best Daguerreotypes," 1" d. (one spot, slight wear) **110**

PLAYING CARDS

The following prices are a composite of recent sales and auctions for the more "findable" playing card decks. Decks listed are complete with original boxes and no serious defects. Condition is excellent, showing only light wear. For decks in better or worse condition, substantial adjustments may be necessary. Mint decks may be 25-75% higher, rough decks 25-75% lower. Missing jokers or original boxes may reduce value 25% or more. The more rare the deck, the less important condition is to the value, and even a missing card or two for an important deck will not deter a collector. Collectors would like to find all their decks in mint condition, but we have to be realistic when it comes to rare material. The mint-condition mid-1880s rare deck may command a price in the thousands. On the other hand, age alone does not determine rarity or value to a collector. Decks from the turn of the century, which are standard and not rare or highly collectible, may be worth very little.

The following listings indicate the deck name, manufacturer, date, type of deck or design, and the number of cards and joker. "EC" means "extra card."

Reference material recommended: Encyclopedia of American Playing Cards, Hochman, 6 vols., soft-cover, 1976-1982. The Bible for American deck collectors. Playing Cards of the Fournier Museum, Vol. 1, Fournier, Vitoria, Spain, 1982. Valuable for identifying foreign decks. Cary Collection of Playing Cards, 4 vols., Keller, Yale University Library, New Haven, 1981. Excellent, expensive set for identifying worldwide cards. Scott Specialized Catalog of U.S. Stamps, Scott Publ. Co., Sidney, Ohio. Reference for U.S. revenue playing card stamps.

Playing card collector clubs: 52 Plus Joker, The American Antique Deck Collector's Club, Rhonda Hawes, Sec./Treas., 204 Gorham Ave., Hamden, CT 06514. www.52plusjoker.org. Write or call for information. Club was founded in 1985 and has 500 members worldwide. It furnishes a quarterly publication and member directory, and offers several auctions yearly in addition to conventions and free appraisals for members. International Playing Card Society, Mike Tregear, 34 Guest Rd., Prestwich, Manchester, M25 3DL, England. Founded in 1972 and international in scope, this club is heavily into research and learned articles about playing cards.

Airplane Spotter, USPC, 1943, plane silhouettes, 52+J+EC, (ILLUS. left) **$40**
Apollo, Nat'l. Card Co., 1890, 52+J (ILLUS. right) **100**

Bicycle #808, USPC Co., 1895, Wheel #1, 52+J (ILLUS. left) **60**
C & O, USPC, 1900, railroad, photos each card, 52+J (ILLUS. right) **75**

Century of Progress, WPCC, 1933, photos, narrow, 52+J+EC (ILLUS. left) **25**
Coke, Brown & Bigelow, 1943, advertising, girl & leaves, 52+J+EC (ILLUS. right) **100**

Columbian Exposition, Winters, 1893, drawn pictures, 52+J+EC (ILLUS.).......... **100**

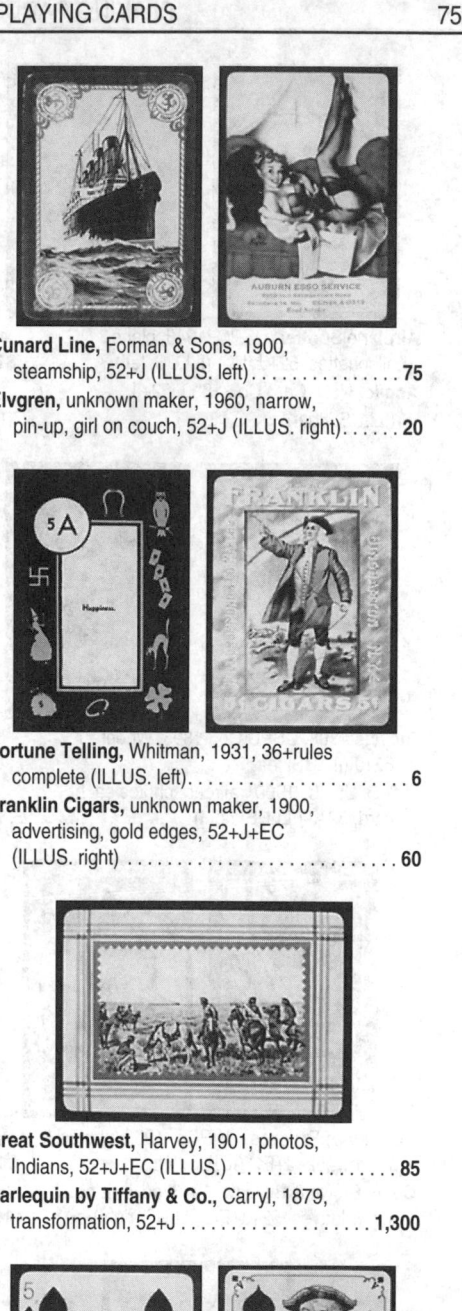

Cunard Line, Forman & Sons, 1900,
steamship, 52+J (ILLUS. left) 75
Elvgren, unknown maker, 1960, narrow,
pin-up, girl on couch, 52+J (ILLUS. right) 20

Fortune Telling, Whitman, 1931, 36+rules
complete (ILLUS. left). 6
Franklin Cigars, unknown maker, 1900,
advertising, gold edges, 52+J+EC
(ILLUS. right) 60

Great Southwest, Harvey, 1901, photos,
Indians, 52+J+EC (ILLUS.) 85
Harlequin by Tiffany & Co., Carryl, 1879,
transformation, 52+J 1,300

Hustling Joe, USPC Co., 1895,
semi-transformation, 52+J (ILLUS. left) 800

Jack Daniel's, ca. 1970, advertising, unique
design & courts 6
Jeu Louis XV, Grimaud, France, 1890,
52+EC (ILLUS. right) 75

Kennedy Kards, Humor House, 1963,
caricature courts, 52+JJ (ILLUS. left) 15
New York World's Fair, 1964-65, color
drawings of fair on each card, 52+JJ 9
Olea, Spanish, ca. 1900, Spanish suits,
square corners, 48 complete 51
Rubberset, unknown maker, 1920,
advertising, 52, missing joker (ILLUS. right 15

Swiss Costumes #174, Dondorf, Germany,
1906, 52+J (ILLUS. left) 75
Trumps Long Cut, 1886, tobacco insert,
drawn early pin-ups, black back, hard
tofind in good condition, 52+J, no box
(ILLUS. right) 1,500
TWA Lockheed 749, USPC, 1970,
standard, 52+JJ 4
Van Camp's, ca. 1911, advertising deck
w/colorful back, unusual ace of spades &
joker, 52+J 85

Yellowstone, Haynes, 1925, photos,
narrow, common, 52+J (ILLUS.) 20

POLITICAL & CAMPAIGN ITEMS

CAMPAIGN

License Plate Attachments

Auto license plate attachment, 1924 campaign, Calvin Coolidge, rectangular, marked "Vote For Coolidge" (ILLUS.) **$65-75**
Auto license plate attachment, 1928 campaign, Al Smith, rectangular,marked "Boost Al Smith for President" (ILLUS.) .. **100-125**
Auto license plate attachment, 1932 campaign, Herbert Hoover, oval marked "Hoover" (ILLUS.) **45-50**
Auto license plate attachment, 1936 campaign, Alfred Landon "Man of the People, Landon for President" w/bust above (ILLUS.) **75**
Auto license plate attachment, 1948 campaign, Thomas Dewey, marked "I'm For Dewey" w/bust of Dewey above (ILLUS.).. **75-80**

William McKinley Top Hat

Campaign hat, 1900 campaign, William McKinley, top hat w/pinback & rosette (ILLUS.) **100-125**

Effigy Canes

Effigy cane, 1888 campaign, Benjamin Harrison (ILLUS.) **125-150**
Effigy cane, 1888 campaign, Grover Cleveland (ILLUS.) **125-150**
Effigy cane, 1896 campaign, William Jennings Bryan (ILLUS.) **100-125**
Effigy cane, 1896 campaign, William McKinley (ILLUS.) **100-125**

Lincoln Campaign Flag

Flag, 1864 campaign, "Ohio Union Lincoln" in white stenciled lettering on heavy lilac-colored cotton, dark stains & hole, 13 x 13¾" (ILLUS.) **1,840**

Rare 1912 Bullmoose Party Flag

Flag, 1912 campaign, Theodore Roosevelt Bullmoose Party rectangular flag in red & blue, a woven design w/a bust portrait of Roosevelt in the center flanked by geometric designs & four small blocks each w/a moose, outer border bands framing the words "Progressive Party - Prosperity," stapled to a 30" l. stick, slight top stain, tiny nick at bottom, 11½ x 18" (ILLUS.) **3,025**
Flag, 1936 campaign, Alfred Landon & Frank Knox, miniature cotton flag w/blue wording on yellow, stitched to a small 11" h. gold-painted wood stand w/round base, printed "Landon and Knox," flag 3½ x 5" **64**
Noisemaker, 1896 campaign, William McKinley horn, marked "Protection Prosperity" (ILLUS.) **55-65**
Noisemaker, 1948 campaign, "True Blue Truman" siren whistle **85-95**
Noisemaker, 1968 campaign, Richard Nixon, clicker, marked "Click With Dick" **12-15**

William McKinley Horn

Paper lantern, 1872 campaign, Ulysses S.
Grant, eight-paneled w/red & green
scrolled design on white background,
center images of Grant in uniform,
cats, dogs, farm girls, a boy w/flute,
mountain scene w/river & young
woman playing a game, manufactured
by Prague & French, Norwalk, Ohio,
7 x 23½" (ILLUS.) **432**

Ulysses S. Grant Paper Lantern

Pinback button, 1896 campaign, (R)
William McKinley-Garrett Hobart, jugate-
style, cross furled flags, shield w/oval
portraits, red, white blue, black, grey, 1½".. **300-325**

Pinback button, 1900 campaign, (D)
William Jennings Bryan, "Clock" single
portrait image, dial set a "16 to 1," red,
white & blue, brown, 1¼". **150-175**

Pinback button, 1900 campaign, (R)
William McKinley-Theodore Roosevelt,
jugate-style, "Musical Notes," red, white &
blue, black, gold, 1½" horizontal oval **650-700**

Pinback button, 1900 campaign, William
McKinley-William Jennings Bryan, jugate-
style, "Partial Eclipse Will Be Total in
November," brown-tone, 1¼" **600-650**

Pinback button, 1908 campaign, (R)
William Howard Taft-James Sherman,
jugate-style, "Elephant Ears," red, black,
brown, yellow, 1¼" **850-900**

Pinback button, 1904 campaign, Roosevelt
portrait in shield w/three stars on each side. . **12-15**

Pinback button, 1904 campaign, Theodore
Roosevelt single portrait **8-10**

Pinback button, 1912 campaign, cartoon,
Theodore Roosevelt, "I Feel Like A
Bull Moose" **12-15**

Pinback button, 1912 campaign, (D)
Woodrow Wilson-Thomas Marshall,
"I Wood-Row Wilson," visual pun of
candidates in rowboat w/Capitol in
background, multicolor, 1¼" **2,500-3,000**

Pinback button, 1916 campaign, (R)
Charles Hughes-Charles Fairbanks,
jugate-style, sepia-tone in brass frame,
1¼" **750-800**

Pinback button, 1916 campaign, (R) Chas.
Hughes-Chas. Fairbanks, Edge (Gov.) &
Frelinghuysen (Sen.), coattail pin, portraits
in four leaf clover, green, black & white, 1" . . **200-250**

Pinback button, 1920 campaign, (R)
Warren Harding-Calvin Coolidge, jugate-
style, conjoining portraits, no lettering,
sepia-tone, ⅞" **600-650**

Pinback button, 1924 campaign, (D) John
Davis, "Honest Days With Davis," cartoon
of Teapot Dome, black & white, ⅞" **650-700**

Pinback button, 1924 campaign, (R) Calvin
Coolidge, single portrait, "Our
President/Deeds Not Words," brown-
tone, 3¾" **500-550**

Pinback button, 1924 campaign, (R) Calvin
Coolidge-Charles Dawes, jugate-style,
black & white, 1¾" **425-450**

Pinback button, 1928 campaign, (D) Al
Smith-Joseph Robinson, jugate-style,
multicolor, ⅞" **150-175**

Pinback button, 1928 campaign, (R)
Herbert Hoover-Charles Curtis, jugate-
style, brown-tone, ⅞" **150-175**

Pinback button, 1928 campaign, (R)
Herbert Hoover-Charles Curtis, jugate-
style, "My Country Tis of Thee," Statue of
Liberty, multicolor, 1¼" **2,000-2,500**

Pinback button, 1932 campaign, (D)
Franklin Roosevelt-John Garner, jugate-
style, "For Repeal and Prosperity," red,
white & blue, black, gold, 1¼" **400-425**

Pinback button, 1932 campaign, (R)
Herbert Hoover-Charles Curtis, jugate-
style, black & white, ⅞" **50-75**

Pinback button, 1936 campaign, (D)
Franklin Roosevelt-John Garner, jugate-
style, "Return Our Country to the People,"
black & white, ⅞" **900-1,000**

Pinback button, 1936 campaign, (R) Alfred
Landon-Frank Knox, jugate-style, red,
white & blue, 1¼" **85-100**

Pinback button, 1940 campaign, (D)
Franklin Roosevelt-Henry Wallace,
jugate-style, brown, red, white & blue, 1¼".. **40-50**

Pinback button, 1940 campaign, Wendell
Wilkie-Charles McNary, jugate-style, red,
white & blue, ⅞" **175-200**

Pinback button, 1944 campaign, (D) Franklin Roosevelt-Harry Truman, jugate-style, sepia-tone **125-150**

Pinback button, 1944 campaign, (R) Thomas Dewey-John Bricker, jugate-style, red, white & blue, ¾" **225-250**

Pinback button, 1948 campaign, (D) Harry Truman-Alban Barkley, black & white, ⅞" . . **200-225**

Pinback button, 1948 campaign, (R) Thomas Dewey-Earl Warren, jugate-style, black & white, 1¼" **25-30**

Adlai Stevenson Pinback Button

Pinback button, 1952 campaign, Adlai Stevenson, cartoon, Bill Maulden's "Willie" from popular WWII "Up Front" series w/"I Like Stevenson" above (ILLUS.) . . **8-10**

Pinback button, 1952 campaign, (D) Adlai Stevenson-John Sparkman, jugate-style, "Vote Straight Democratic," red, white & blue, 4" **300-325**

Pinback button, 1952 campaign, (R) Dwight Eisenhower-Richard Nixon, small elephant, black & white, 4" **80-85**

Pinback button, 1956 campaign, (D) Adlai Stevenson-Estes Kefauver, jugate-style, four leaf clover design, "Adlai and Estes Are Best For You/Right Will Prevail," green, white, 2¼" **400-425**

Pinback button, 1960 campaign, (D) John F. Kennedy, jugate-style, "Leaders Of Our Country & A Friendly World," red, white & blue, 3½" **40-50**

Pinback button, 1960 campaign, (R) Richard Nixon-Henry Lodge, jugate-style, "Experience Counts/Vote For A Better America," red, white & blue, black & white 2½". **500-525**

Anti-Goldwater Pinback Button

Pinback button, 1964 campaign, cartoon, anti-Barry Goldwater, nuclear cloud & marked "Go With Goldwater" (ILLUS.) **10-12**

Pinback button, 1964 campaign, cartoon, anti-Lyndon Johnson, marked "Kill For Peace" w/bust of L.B.J. **10-12**

Pinback button, 1968 campaign, (AI) George Wallace, cartoon, Wallace leaning against school bus, red, white & blue, black & white, 1¾" **10-12**

Anti-Humphrey Pinback Button

Pinback button, 1968 campaign, cartoon, anti-Humphrey, depicts Humphrey w/large cowboy hat marked "LBJ" (ILLUS.) . . **10-12**

Pinback button, 1968 campaign, (D) Hubert Humphrey, cartoon, "HHH Fills the Prescription," Humphrey as druggist, blue, black & white, 1½" **18-20**

Pinback button, 1968 campaign, Richard Nixon-Spiro Agnew, jugate-style, red, white & blue, 1½" **10-12**

Pinback button, 1972 campaign, (D) George McGovern, cartoon, pictorial "Robin McGovern," anti-McGovern depicting McGovern as Robin Hood, green, black, white **100-110**

Pinback button, 1976 campaign, (R) Gerald Ford-Robert Dole, jugate-style w/eagle, red, white & blue, yellow, 1¾" **12-15**

Pinback button, 1984 campaign, (D) Walter Mondale-Geraldine Ferraro, jugate-style w/capitol building, multicolor, 2½" **7-10**

Pinback button, 1984 campaign, (R) Ronald Reagan-George Bush, jugate-style, "Reelect Ron and George," black & white, red, white & blue, 2¼". **7-10**

Pinback button, McKinley-Theodore Roosevelt, jugate-style w/ribbon design, 2" d. **250-300**

Pinback button, McKinley-Theodore Roosevelt "lunch pail" pin, marked "A Full Dinner Bucket" above & "Sound Money-Good Market" below portraits **45-55**

Pinback button, Theodore Roosevelt-Charles Fairbanks "Teddy bear" cartoon pin, black & white, 1¼" (ILLUS.) **2,200-2,500**

Pinback button, Vermont Republican Convention badge w/ribbon, marked "Republican State Convention Montpelier, Vt. June 29, 1904". **100-125**

"Teddy Bear" Pinback Button

Rare 1912 Bullmoose Party Postcard

Postcard, 1912 campaign, Theodore Roosevelt Bullmoose party, a vertical style w/a large head of a moose supporting the U.S. Capitol between its horns below the word "Progress," below the moose the inscription "Be A Progressive - Progressiveness indicates activity of mind and heart. A progressive citizen is usually a patriotic citizen. Compliments of ....," postmarked "Chicago - Oct. 30, '12" (ILLUS.) **242**

1912 Taft Political Postcard

Postcard, 1912 campaign, William H. Taft, comic scene of a large elephant labeled "GOP" racing toward the White House, a pointed upright protruding spring forming the elephant's tail, printed "Has He Got

Enough Steam?" at center bottom, a round vignette at left of a steam roller w/"The Steam Roller," & second portrait vignette of Taft in the bottom right corner, unused, small crease in upper corner (ILLUS.) **65**

Sheet music, 1904 campaign, Theodore Roosevelt, "The Man of the Moment - Teddy Will Carry It Through," cover w/oval reserve w/standing photo of Roosevelt, first song by James Swope, second song by Emma Cornic & Anna Carlson, 1903, 6 pp. (soil, wear) **67**

Slogan pinback button, 1924 campaign, Calvin Coolidge "Let's Go With Coolidge" . . **10-12**

Anti-F.D.R. Pinback Button

Slogan pinback button, 1940 campaign, Wendell Wilkie anti-F.D.R., marked "No Third Term" (ILLUS.) **8-10**

Slogan pinback buttons, 1952 campaign, Dwight Eisenhower, "I Like Ike" & "Ike Likes Me," Eisenhower variants, each **10-12**

Spare Tire Cover

Spare tire cover, 1932 campaign, Franklin Roosevelt, oilcloth, marked "Franklin D. Roosevelt President" w/picture of Roosevelt in center, black & white (ILLUS.) **500-550**

Stickpin Theodore Roosevelt-Fairbanks, brass eye-glass stickpin w/individual portrait of Fairbanks in one lens & Roosevelt in the other **200-250**

Toy, 1952 campaign, Dwight Eisenhower, elephant marked "I Like Ike," grey w/blue blanket, battery operated, Line Mar (ILLUS.) **200-225**

Ike Toy Elephant

NON-CAMPAIGN

Baseball, George Bush, signed & inscribed "To Rich, G Bush," housed in clear display case w/miniature molded plastic gold-painted glove, "Official Size & Weight" baseball signed in black felt pen, includes "Operation Desert Shield" trading card w/color photo of President Bush on obverse, short description of January 1991 war w/Iraq on verso, made by Pacific Trading Cards, Inc., Lynwood, Washington, display case 5½ x 7 x 8" **403**

Book, "An American Life" by Ronald Reagan, signed "Ronald Reagan" in black marker on bookplate w/Presidential Seal affixed to inside page, cloth hardcover w/gilt-lettered spine & original dust jacket, 748 pgs., Simon & Schuster, 1990, 6½ x 9⅛" **380**

"Presidents of the United States" Book

Book, "Presidents of the United States" by Richard O'Neill & Antonia Bryan, signed by Presidents Gerald R. Ford, Jimmy Carter & George Bush, 64 pgs., Smithmark Books, 1992, 9 x 12" (ILLUS.) **345**

Calling card, Sarah C. Polk, signed "Mrs. James K. Polk, Polk Place, Nashville, Tenn., Jan'y 10, 1888," folded 6 x 9½" w/stamped signature of James K. Polk in middle section, signature below **547**

Document, Thomas Jefferson, signed "Th Jefferson" w/counter-signature by Secretary of State James Madison, land

grant to Elijah Austin of Fairfield County, Ohio for quarter lot in Chillicothe, Land Office seal in lower left corner, 8 x 14¼" (light wrinkling w/a few creases, pinholes & small paper loss upper right corner) **3,450**

Golf ball, Gerald R. Ford, signed "Jerry Ford" in blue ink along one side & printed in black capital letters along ball top, donated by Ford to charity auction **220**

Letter, Abraham Lincoln, signed "A Lincoln" as President on Executive Mansion letterhead, addressed to Genl. Montgomery Cunningham Meigs/U.S.A., dated May 13, 1862, 5¾ x 9¾" (faint vertical runs through "L" on bold Lincoln signature) **8,165**

Mourning ribbon, silk, bust of Ulysses S. Grant above facsimile signature, printed by L.H. Hall's Sons, New York, ca. 1885, 4¾ x 5¾" (minor creasing to corners & edges)............................. **317**

Photograph, Grover Cleveland, cabinet photo signed "Grover Cleveland, Feb. 11, 1897" in black fountain pen, bust-length profile in brown on white, embossed card by "C. M. Bell" of Washington, D.C., 4¼ x 6½" **920**

Photograph, Harry S Truman, black & white head & shoulders portrait in matte finish, signed & inscribed "Best of luck and a happy life to Mike Stein, from - Harry Truman - 6/15/64," includes transmittal letter from Truman's secretary, 8 x 10" (diagonal crease through center) **317**

Photograph, John F. Kennedy, signed "Best - John Kennedy," shows JFK at podium giving speech, back stamped "Newsweek Photo by Tony Rollo" w/penciled notation, photo was taken September 25, 1961 during U.N. speech, black & white, 8 x 10" (creases at corners) **1,984**

Photograph, William McKinley, sepia-tone cabinet card, bust profile & marked "Launey, Hon. William McKinley, New York," dated "July 22, 1896" in ink, signed & inscribed in pencil on verso "With cordial regards W McKinley," 6½ x 4¼" card .. **345**

Photograph, Woodrow Wilson, signed "Woodrow Wilson" on blank mounting board below head & shoulder portrait, imprinted "1908," photo by B. F. McManus, 8 x 11" (slight loss at upper edge).......... **460**

Plaque, Theodore Roosevelt, bronze, marked "Aggressive Fighting for the Right Is the Noblest Sport the World Affords" beneath bust, sculpted by James Earle Frazer w/raised letter signature & "19@20" in upper right corner, 9½ x 12½" (some scratches) **690**

Portrait, John F. Kennedy, Norman Rockwell No. 1545/2500 Limited Edition, published 1976 by American Heritage

JFK Norman Rockwell Portrait

Graphics, Los Angeles, Cal., includes story of painting & Certificate of Authenticity from the Jeffries Company, 20 x 15" color portrait in 20¾ x 14¾" gilt-lettered portfolio (ILLUS.) **892**

1917 Political Poster

Poster, "The Man of the Hour," red, blue, gold, black & aqua, features black & white portraits of Woodrow Wilson, George Washington & Abraham Lincoln beneath two large flags, "What We Fought For in '76, In God We Trust, The Stars and Stripes Forever, First, Last and All The Time" above flags, Wilson's portrait titled "The Man of the Hour," 1776, 1917 & 1862 below Washington, Wilson & Lincoln respectively, W. M. Gibson Co., Philadelphia, Pa., designed by Louis A. Spiro, ca. 1917, 12 x 16" (ILLUS.) . . **433**

Print, "Death Bed of Abraham Lincoln" by J.L. Magee, Philadelphia, Pa., uncolored lithograph on toned brown sheet, depicts deathbed scene of Lincoln w/several cabinet members, Mary Lincoln, Robert Lincoln & Rev. Doctor Gurley on knees praying w/Bible in hand, image framed by mourning veil, not dated, 15½ x 18¼" (a few minor age stains) **345**

Print, "Martha Washington" by Caldwell & Co., NY, uncolored oval bust w/Martha Washington in her bonnet, soiling in margins, a few short tears, ca. 1850s (ILLUS.) . . **345**

Martha Washington Print

Print, Nathaniel Currier's "Washington, First in War, First in Peace and First in the Hearts of His Countrymen," full length portrait of Washington holding a sword in front of a study window, hand-colored in red, blue, green & yellow tones, 15½ x 19½" **288**

Signature, John F. Kennedy, signed "John Kennedy, 1960," 1¾ x 2½" sheet **690**

Snuff box, Abraham Lincoln, dark brown & black carved horn, lid features portrait of young, beardless Lincoln, 2" w., 3¾" l., 1" deep (portions of image torn) **692**

POP CULTURE COLLECTIBLES

The collecting of pop culture memorabilia is not a new phenomenon; fans have been collecting music-related items since the emergence of rock and roll in the 1950s. But it was not until the 'coming of age' of the post-war generation that the collecting of popular culture memorabilia became a recognized movement. The most sought-after items are from the 1960s, when music, art, and society were at their most experimental. This time period is dominated by artists such as The Beatles, The Rolling Stones and Bob Dylan, to name a few. From the 1950s, Elvis Presley is the most popular. Below we offer a cross-section of popular culture collectibles ranging from the 1950s to the present day.

American Bandstand earrings, goldtone, 1950s, very fine, pr. **$25**

American Bandstand tie-clip, 1950s, very fine **20**

Beach Boys guitar, Franciscan acoustic model, natural finish, twenty fret fingerboard w/dot inlays, pin bridge, black pickguard, signed in blue ink on the body by all four recent members of the group,

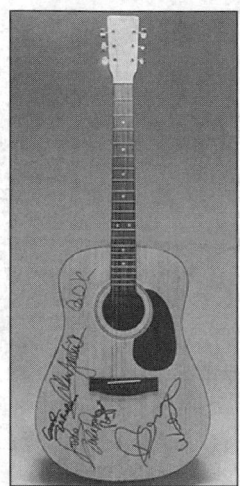

Beach Boys-signed Acoustic Guitar

in black gig bag, accompanied by two photographs of Love & Bruce Johnston posing w/the guitar after signing, the group (ILLUS.)........................ **3,450**

Beatles autographed album, "Sgt. Peppers Lonely Hearts Club Band" album opened to the color photos of the group & signed by each member above their head, includes special presentation inscription, ca. late 1967, overall 21¾ x 24" **57,500**

Beatles autographs, signed in blue ballpoint pen on a pink piece of paper, matted w/a color-tinted photograph of the group, ca. 1963, overall 17¾ x 21¾"....... **2,587**

Beatles "On Stage" diorama, plastic, 1960s, very fine **60**

Big Brother & the Holding Company concert poster, printed in black & white w/photographs taken by Linda Eastman of each band member including Janis Joplin, also notes "Tim Buckley, Albert King & the Joshua Light Show," Fillmore East, March 8, 1968, designed by Charles Brandwynn, 15 x 21½"........... **1,265**

Bob Marley autographed album cover, for "Exodus" album, signed on the front in blue felt pen "Rasta Live Bob Marley," matted & framed, 18½" sq. **3,162**

Bruce Springsteen guitar, electric American Standard Fender Stratocaster, Serial No. N8332110, cream finish, double cutaway body, twenty-two fret fingerboard w/dot inlays, three rotary controls & white pickguard, signed by Springsteen in black felt pen, in black hardshell case, w/a promotional poster for the album "Greetings from Asbury Park, N.Y.," matted w/a copy of the album cover & three corresponding 'silver' copies of the album, framed, the group..... **1,150**

Bruce Springsteen harmonica, Hohner Marine Band model, E key, matted w/an album cover for "Darkness on the Edge of Town," signed by Springsteen in black felt pen, overall 17 x 24" **1,955**

Buffalo Springfield award, special citation of achievement for the the the single "For What It's Worth," presented by Broadcast Music, Inc., to Ten East Music for achieving over one million broadcast performances, 12" sq. **575**

Mint in Box Dave Clark 5 Figures

Dave Clark 5 figures, plastic, Remco, 1960s, together w/a master shipping case from the factory, mint in original box, box 6 x 9½" (ILLUS.)........................ **770**

Deborah Harry photograph, black & white shot of Harry posing w/arms raised w/the Hollywood sign in the background, signed & inscribed at the bottom by the photographer, Chris Stein, & also Harry, ca. early 1980s, 11¾ x 17¼"............. **1,035**

Dick Clark doll, vinyl, 1950s, near mint, 26" h. . . . **634**

Elton John autographed CD insert, from "Candle In The Wind," signed & inscribed in black ink "With love, Elton," matted w/a black & white machine print photograph of Princess Diana, overall 15 x 19"......... **345**

Rare Elvis Presley Doll

Elvis Presley doll, vinyl & cloth, life-like Elvis head on body dressed in a plaid shirt & blue pants, w/original box, Acme, 1957, 18" h. (ILLUS.).................. **2,145**

Early Elvis Presley Jacket

Elvis Presley jacket, black wool woven w/a repeating pattern of white thread w/red & blue flecks, labeled inside right pocket "Lansky Brothers Corner Beale and 2nd Memphis Tenn.," accompanied by a typescript letter, signed, from Bill Black, dated March 17 1962 giving background on the jacket, w/three black & white photos of Presley wearing the jacket at his first recording session at RCA, January 10, 1956 (printed later) & a copy of a video "Elvis '56 In The Beginning," the group (ILLUS.)................... **59,700**

Elvis Presley set list, handwritten in all capitals in blue ink on yellow lined paper, comprising twenty songs, dated "Aug 20th Las Vegas," 1974, matted & framed w/a color machine print of Presley performing on stage & descriptive plaque, accompanied by letter concerning provenance, list 8½ x 11", the group (ink smeared in places, circular beverage mark on side)....................... **8,625**

Janis Joplin necklace, cast metal in the form of a coiled dragon, w/link chain (replaced), accompanied by a color snapshot of Joplin wearing an identical necklace & a letter concerning provenance, dragon 5¾" l. **11,500**

Jim Morrison autograph, signed "Morrison" in black ballpoint pen on a blue album page, matted w/a 'gold' copy of the signed "Light My Fire" & a black & white photo of Morrison, overall 15¼ x 21" **977**

Jim Morrison self-published book, "An American Prayer," limited edition, original red morocco boards w/title stamped in gilt, 1970 .... **2,300**

Jimi Hendrix autograph, black ink on a piece of paper, matted w/a black & white machine print photograph of Hendrix, framed, ca. 1968, 15½ x 19½" **1,035**

Jimi Hendrix concert poster, printed in dark shades of red on cream, psychedelic design w/"In Person - Jimi Hendrix -

Jimi Hendrix Concert Poster

Experience," across the top, performance at the Merriweather Post Pavillion, Columbia, Maryland, August 16, 1968, also notes "England's Underground Sensation - The Soft Machine," designed by D.W. Beeghly, 22¼ x 28" (ILLUS.)............................. **2,300**

Jimi Hendrix Vest

Jimi Hendrix vest, military-style, ivory brushed cotton, hook closures on front, two side pockets, detailed w/metal braid thread, metal weave braid trim on front closure & bottom edge, metal button on left shoulder (right side button missing), labeled "Charles Chrisdie & Co.," matted w/a black & white machine print photograph of Hendrix & a letter concerning provenance (ILLUS.)............................. **3,450**

John Lennon autographed album cover, for "Imagine," signed & inscribed in blue ballpoint pen on the front cover "To Sheryl love John Lennon 76" w/a self-portrait caricature of Lennon's smiling face, additionally annotated at lower right corner w/a doodle of a couple looking up at a four-legged animal standing on a cloud (ILLUS.) **8,050**

John Lennon-signed Album Cover

John Lennon & Yoko Ono recording, one-
sided acetate, of "Sunday, Bloody
Sunday," 45 r.p.m. w/"The Master Cutting
Room" white label w/typed details, dated
"2/24/72," inscribed by Lennon at the
bottom, accompanying sleeve also
inscribed, matted w/color machine print
photograph of Lennon, overall 15 x 24". **1,092**

John Lennon's spectacles, wire-rimmed,
prescription lens, matted in a shadowbox
frame w/a color machine print photograph
of Lennon wearing a similar pair,
accompanied by a letter concerning the
provenance, overall 11½ x 16½" **25,875**

John Mellencamp painting, oil on canvas,
a row of half-length portraits of three
people, two women flanking a
moustached man, signed & dated in
lower right "Mellencamp 88," framed,
43½ x 55½" **4,600**

Kiss Viewmaster reel set, 1970s, sealed, mint. . . **25**

Madonna bustier & hat, from the "Who's
That Girl" tour, gold lurex bustier w/zip-up
fastening & shoulder straps, decorated on
the front & back w/brightly colored
sequins, scarlet & fuschia silk flowers &
many novelties & charms including a
plastic lobster, a Kewpie doll & a pair of
slinky eyes, etc., signed in black felt pen
on the bottom edge "Love Madonna," the
hat in blue covered w/fuschia polyester &
similar novelties to the bustier, 1987,
2 pcs. **12,650**

Mick Jagger unpublished song lyrics,
handwritten, nine lines in blue ballpoint
pen on a sheet of lined notebook paper,
ca. 1965, matted & framed w/a machine
print photograph of Jagger, 18½" sq. **1,610**

Ringo Starr doll, w/drum, Remco, 1964,
near mint **75**

Rolling Stones guitar, electric Fender
Telecaster, Serial No. 539064, white
finish, single cutaway body, twenty-one
fret fingerboard w/dot inlays, two rotary
controls, tremolo bridge/tailblock & black
pickguard, signed on the body in blue felt

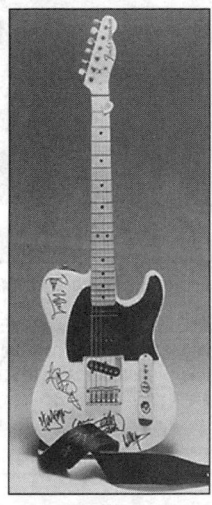

Autographed Rolling Stones Guitar

pen by all five recent members of the
group, additionally inscribed on the back,
brown leather guitar strap signed in silver
felt pen by Keith Richards, w/two guitar
picks & perspex display case, the group
(ILLUS.). **4,600**

Rolling Stones Autographed Photo

Rolling Stones photograph, black &
white machine print autographed in
blue or red ballpoint pen by all five
original members of the group
including Brian Jones, matted &
framed, 5 x 5¼" (ILLUS.). **2,300**

Stevie Nicks tee shirt, sky blue cotton
w/white trim, the back w/navy printed
lettering "Tusk Fleetwood Mac World
Tour '79-'80," worn on stage, matted
w/color photo of Nicks, 1979, overall
24 x 32" **575**

The Doors presentation disc, gold disc for
the album "Strange Days," presented to
Jim Morrison, R.I.A.A. certified, white
matte format, framed, 17½ x 2 ¾" **7,475**

Yellow Submarine Bicycle

Yellow Submarine bicycle, lady's model, Huffy, three-speed, yellow painted frame, seat decorated w/printed design featuring the submarine, based on the Beatles movie, ca. late 1960s (ILLUS.) **2,587**

POSTCARDS

Advertising, Campbell's Soup, horizontal . . . **$35-45**
Advertising, Campbell's Soup, vertical. **100-200**
Advertising, Coca-Cola, H. King **800-1000**
Artist, Ellen Clapsaddle, signed **75-100**
Artist, Francis Brundage, signed. **45-65**
Artist, Gene Carr. **8-15**
Artist, Raphael Kirchner **85-150**
Artist, Samuel Schmucker **100-500**
Artist, Tom Browne **6-10**
Aviation, Tuck. **12-20**
Bilikens. **6-10**
Bilikens, political **200-300**
Boy Scouts, mottos **10-15**
Colonial Heros **8-12**
Comics, by Dwig. **5-15**
Days of the Week **6-10**
Dolls **5-15**
Elves & Fairies **5-15**
Expositions, California Mid-Winter **150-300**
Expositions, Cotton States. **200-300**
Expositions, Trans-Mississippi. **65-95**
Expositions, World Columbian **20-30**
Ginks. **8-12**
Golligwoggs **20-45**
Holidays, Patriotic. **4-10**
Holidays, Saint Patrick's Day **3-7**
Holidays, Thanksgiving. **3-7**
Holidays, Valentines **3-9**
Homes of the Presidents. **5-8**
Installment sets **100-300**
Leather political **7-10**
Lord's Prayer **5-12**
Mechanicals **25-35**
Metal **5-7**
Mickey Mouse. **25-45**
Moons **6-12**

Mushrooms. **5-12**
Native Americans, not photo **10-15**
Novelty, metal/cloth attachments **7-15**
Patriographics **7-10**
Political, 1900 . . . . **75-200**
Political, 1908 . . . . **25-50**
Political, 1912. . . . . **35-50**
Political, Socialist Party, early. **300-700**
Prohibition, comic. **5-15**
Quaddy, by Cady **65-75**
Real hair **15-35**

Cracker Jack Salesmen Photo Card

Real photo, advertising, "Cracker Jack" salesmen, row of men standing under a large tent behind a long table w/full glasses of soda & blocks of ice, banner on table reads "CRACKER JACK - The More You Eat - the More You Want," unused, very small bend in upper left corner, tiny spots (ILLUS.) **78**

Barnum & Bailey Commissary Wagon

Real photo, circus, circus mailman at his post in a covered wagon w/wording on side "Barnum & Bailey Commissary," various men waiting for the mail, ca. 1910-20, unused, slight center blemish, inked name bleeding through in corner (ILLUS.). **67**
Real photo, delivery wagon & furniture store, buckboard delivery wagon w/driver in front of row of buildings, the center one w/an awning sign "Thos. E. Drake," store markings also on wagon, Prospect, Ohio, 1907, nice sepia tones, used (very light soil & minor corner dings). **44**

Real photo, gas station, "The Mission"
Texaco station, small rural building
w/Coca-Cola signs, large frame house in
right background, written in white ink
across the bottom "The Mission, Rte. 50,"
ca. 1920s, unused (slight soil & faint
white lines) 86

Ice Cream Delivery Wagon

Real photo, ice cream delivery wagon,
horse-drawn covered & open-sided
wagon w/driver seated inside, wagon
marked for W.B. Smith Ice Cream Cones,
unknown location, image a little light in
spots, unused (ILLUS.). 209
Real photo, "Public Square, Dushore, Pa.,"
ca. 1910 18
Real photo, shop interiors 35-100
Real photo, steam shovel, at an excavation
site w/five workers shown, marked on the
side "Marion Shovel Model 36," unused
(slight soiling) 25
Real photo, studio shots 6-10
Real photo, telephone linemen, three
linemen on wires above the street flanked
by buildings, one man working, two
relaxing, used, postmarked 1911 (small
bend & slight damage in upper left) 33
Roosevelt Bears, No. 1-16 20-30
Santa, hold-to-light 125-500
Santa, Uncle Sam, hold-to-light 3000-4000
Snowmen, ... 10-25

Rare Suffrage Postcard

Suffrage, Christmas greeting w/red & green
cartoon view of Santa Claus loaded down
w/a large bag full of boxes w/"Votes For
Women," hand-written "Merry Christmas
To All," postmarked "Dec. 17, '15 -
Saginaw, Michigan," slightly soiled (ILLUS.) . . 275
Teddy Bears, ... 5-15

Transportation, steamships, non-Titanic 10-45
Transportation, trains, printed 5-15
Transportation, trains, real photo 10-25
University Girls 8-15
Views, churches, schools, banks 5-10
Views, parks 1-2
Wiener Werkstaette 100-300
Wire Tail, animals 8-10
Wire Tail, animals-political 100-200
WWI-Propaganda 10-25
Yellow Kid, calendar card 65-100
Zodiac 4-10

POSTERS

*Also see: MOVIE MEMORABILIA, DISNEY
COLLECTIBLES & POP CULTURE.*

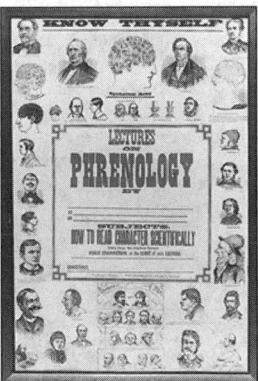

Advertising Poster "Lectures on Phrenology..."

Advertising, rectangular paper, "Lectures
on Phrenology from Phrenological
Magazines Fowler & Wells Co. 18 E.
22nd Street, New York. Know Thyself,"
shows several bust illustrations of the
men & women, some showing surface of
the brain divided into areas, w/"Lectures
on Phrenology..." in center & "Know
Thyself" at top, 19th c., 29½ x 19¾"
(ILLUS.) $805
Chocolate, "Chocolat Klaus," Art Nouveau
design of a woman riding a horse,
France, early 20th c., framed, 48¼ x 66¾" . . . 805
Concert, "Judy Garland - Lincoln Center
Philharmonic Hall - Sunday Feb. 25, 8:30
PM - One Performance Only," large
caricature drawing of Judy holding a
microphone, blue, green & red on white,
art by Seymour Chwast, late 1960s, 23 x 37" . . 164
Gasoline, "Gulf," rectangular, printed in
color w/a dark blue ground & orange &
blue swirls of thin ribbon & dots w/large

Gulf Gasoline New Year's Poster

white wording "Happy New Year" above
"Gulf" logo in circle in orange, blue &
white, archival backing, w/notice for
posting between December 31 - January
15, 1940, minor edge wear & soiling,
27¾ x 42" (ILLUS.)...................... **94**

Motor oil, "Golden Shell Motor Oil,"
rectangular paper, shows large can of oil
in light & dark orange w/large shell logo &
wording "Golden Shell Motor Oil," black
background w/an orange dot to right
below the can reading in black "25¢ A
Quart," large white wording across the
bottom "Reduces Engine Wear," archival
backing, 39¼ x 55" (minor edge wear &
soiling, small edge tears & background
touch-up) **132**

From left: *Early Moving Pictures Poster*
Nazi Anti-Semitic Poster

Moving pictures, "The Pastime Moving
Picture Show...," printed in red, blue &
cream, two turn-of-the-century bathing
beauties posed on a rock above the
description box, late 19th - early 20th c.,
linen-backed, 21 x 28" (ILLUS.) **275**

Propaganda, German anti-Semitic design,
black & white photo montage of strange
or evil looking laughing Jews, printed in
German in the center "When Jews
Laugh" & across the bottom in German
"Read the latest edition of Der Sturmer
(Nazi paper)," 1930s, slightly browned &
soiled, 12 x 17" (ILLUS.)................ **646**

Toy shop, "Paris - Montpellier - Jouets," a
scene of a rider on a rocking horse,
printed in red & black, France, dated
1906, framed, 46½ x 66¾" **1,035**

Traveling show, "Jessie James" lithograph
for traveling show, 1905 .... **675**

World War I, "Road to France," shows
Navy, Army & gunner, by James M.
Flagg, black & white, 18½ x 24½" **275**

World War II, "Back 'Em Up - Buy Extra
Bonds!," scene w/General Eisenhower,
20 x 28" **95**

POWDER HORNS & FLASKS

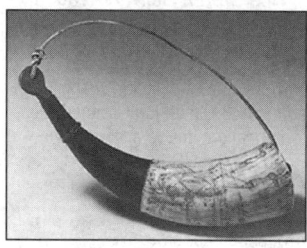

Engraved Powder Horn

Horn, curved horn w/stylized engraved
figures of Indian brave holding spear &
knife, gentleman w/pistol, & lady in long
dress, inscribed "Alex Coth(?) his horn
F.R. Stouth June 23, 1778," tapered
spout carved w/ring, small crack & chip
to edge of butt, 11" l. (ILLUS.)........... **$1,495**

Horn, incised decoration of various stags,
foliate & geometric designs & the name
"Samuel Evens," late 18th - early 19th c.,
11¼" l. (minor cracks & losses)........... **633**

Horn, sailor's, engraved w/a whale, kettle,
harpoons, hooks & "E. Pyne of New
Bedford," early wrought-iron hook, good
patina, dated 1848, 8¼" l. (minor rim chips)... **550**

Decorated Horn Dated 1831

Horn, engraved w/a foliated border, hearts,
star & a patriotic banner, the rounded
plug decorated w/hearts centering an
inset brass button depicting an eagle

surrounded by stars, also inscribed
"E.K.G. 1831 Horn NH," metal pouring tip,
6½" l. (ILLUS.) **1,955**

Horn, engraved w/a scene of a two-story
building w/the inscription "Meeting
House," also a ship w/an American flag
titled "Ship Rochester," 19th c., 9¼" l.
(crack in end w/plug, tip trimmed) **825**

Ornately Engraved Powder Horn

Horn, ornately engraved w/reserves on a
crosshatched field of ships at sea &
Charleston Harbor, w/the arms of Spicer
of Exeter or Weare of Devon, inscribed
"South Carolina made in Charlestown
Amerique 1764," Charleston, South
Carolina, minor imperfections, 9½" l.
(ILLUS.) **6,325**

Horn, engraved w/various designs including
buildings, animals, birds & the date
"1822," metal tip & rounded plug end,
good color, 11" l. (some old surface chips) .. **1,595**

Horn, plain curved horn w/good color, a
ring-turned wooden screw tip & domed
turned & carved end plug, 19th c., 11½" l. **275**

Horn, engraved w/floral & geometric
designs, initialed & dated "AB 1807," 13" l. ... **978**

Horn, engraved w/the inscription "Daniel
Chase his horn made in August ye
1786," decorated w/the British coat-of-
arms, a townscape, a hunt scene & a
reserve of a gentleman, 13" l. (minor
cracks & flaking) **1,035**

Horn, decorated w/various incised Masonic
designs, a ship flying the American flag,
the name "J. McIntire" & other patriotic
symbols within a scrolling border, 19th c.,
15" l. (faded, crack, minor losses) **173**

Horn, cannon supply-type, long twisted curl,
w/brass end fittings, American-made,
early 19th c., 26½" l. (cracks) **1,725**

PRINT ARTISTS - EARLY
20TH CENTURY

BESSIE PEASE GUTMANN

A Chip of the Old Block, 14 x 18" **$310**
A Little Bit of Heaven, 14 x 18" **75**
Bed Time, 7 x 9" **50**

Candle Making, 7 x 9" **75**
Contentment, 4 x 8" **60**
In the Library, 10 x 13" **50**
Introducing Baby, 8 x 12" **80**

Gutmann 'Lorelei' Print

Lorelei, 14 x 18" (ILLUS.) **1,300**
Tea for Two, 10 x 12" **50**
The Fairest of the Flowers, 14 x 18" **450**
The Family Album, 11 x 14" **10**
The New Bonnet, 7 x 9" **50**
The Patchwork Quilt, 11 x 14" **80**
To Love and To Cherish, 14 x 20" **300**
Untitled Butterflies & Daisies, 5 x 6" **50**

G.B. FOX

Awaiting the Call, 5 x 7" **15**
Majestic Mountains, 7 x 10" **10**
Majestic Nature, 7 x 9" **10**
So Sweet the Dreams, 7 x 9" **25**
The Champion, 9 x 12" **20**

HARRISON FISHER

Baby Mine, 9 x 12" **70**
For You A Rose, 11 x 14" **65**
Untitled Girl in Chair, 5 x 7" **35**
Untitled Girl with Black Hat, 5 x 8" **30**
Untitled Girl with Blue Bow in Hair, 5 x 8" **30**

MAXFIELD PARRISH

Atlas, 11 x 14" **120**
Buds Below the Roses, 8 x 14" **130**
Canyon (The), 12 x 15" **170**
Centaur (The), 9 x 11" **55**
Circe's Palace, 9 x 11" **55**
Community Plate Ad, 5 x 7" **40**
Contentment, 14 x 20" **365**
Daybreak, 10 x 18" **275**
Daybreak, 6 x 10" **95**
Dinkey Bird (The), 11 x 15" **70**
Dreamlight, 14 x 23" **425**
Evening Shadows, 11 x 14" **105**

Garden of Allah (The), 15 x 30"............ 200
Golden Age (The) 45
Golden Hours, 14 x 18"................... 300
King of the Black Isles (The), 9 x 11"......... 50
Landing of the Brazen Boatsman, 9 x 11"..... 105
Lute Players (The), 10 x 18"............... 300
New Hampshire - Land of Scenic, 18 x 22"..... 50
Peaceful Valley, 12 x 17".................. 160

Sing A Song of Six Pence Print

Sing A Song of Six Pence, P.F. Collier &
  Son, 1911, original oak frame, 9 x 21"
  (ILLUS.)............................. 2,200
Sunrise, 7 x 9"......................... 130
Thy Templed Hills, 12 x 16"............... 155
Twilight, 8 x 11"....................... 130
Valley of the Diamonds (The), 10 x 15"........ 30
Village Brook (The), 8 x 11".............. 180
Wild Geese, 12 x 15"..................... 270

PHILIP BOILEAU

Anticipation, 13 x 20"................... 260
Mother's Love, 10 x 16".................. 100
The Twins, 4 x 6"....................... 50
Untitled Mother & Daughter, 6 x 8".......... 135

R. ATKINSON FOX

A Sheltering Bower, 6 x 8"................ 45
A Sheltering Bower, 9 x 12"............... 20
A Song of Evening, 9 x 16"................ 40
After the Storm, 10 x 16"................. 55
An Old Fashioned Garden, 14 x 17".......... 55
An Old Fashioned Garden, 14 x 18".......... 60
An Old Oak, 10 x 16".................... 50
At the Foothills of Pike's Peak, 7 x 9"........ 20
Battle of the Wild, 5 x 7"................. 25
Clipper Ship, 12 x 16"................... 35
Dawn, 8 x 14".......................... 35
Garden of Contentment, 10 x 18"........... 135
Garden of Hope puzzle, 9 x 15"............ 35
Garden of Love, 10 x 18".................. 70
Garden of Romance, 12 x 19"............... 60
Glorious Vista, 10 x 14".................. 20
Going to the Sun Mountain, 5 x 7"........... 20
Great Falls of Yosemite, 7 x 9"............. 35
Heart's Desire, 14 x 22"................. 100
In Pastures, 4 x 10"..................... 45

Inspiration Inlet, 10 x 18" 55
Love's Paradise, 8 x 14".................. 50
Memories of Childhood Days, 14 x 18"........ 95
Music of the Waters, 3 x 4"................ 30
Nature's Charms, 14 x 22"................ 115
Nature's Grandeur, 14 x 22"............... 120
Nature's Grandeur, 6 x 8"................. 25
Neath Sunset Skies, 6 x 8"................ 40
Old Old Oak, 10 x 16" 75
Out of the Sky He Comes, 5 x 7"............ 35
Paradise, 7 x 9"......................... 30
Playmate Guardian, 8 x 10"................ 75
Poppies, 14 x 20"....................... 80
Poppies, 18 x 30"....................... 575
Romance Canyon, 12 x 15"................. 85
Rose Bower, 10 x 16" 65
Russet Gems, 7 x 11" 30
Silent Rockies, 6 x 8".................... 50
The Answering Call, 8 x 10" 25
The Approaching Storm, 4 x 9" 40
The Grandeur of Summer, 10 x 14" 65
The Magic Pool, 10 x 15".................. 205
The Old Mill, 7 x 10"..................... 35
The Snow-Capped Mountain, 7 x 10"......... 25
Thoroughbreds, 6 x 8".................... 200
Two Medicine River Falls, 7 x 9" 45
Where Nature Beats in Perfect Tune, 10 x 12" .. 25

PURSES & BAGS

From left: *Glass Beaded Purse*
Enameled Mesh Purse

Beaded, scenic reticule, ca. 1850............ $88
Beaded, glass, overall beading w/scroll
  design on green ground, ca. 1920,
  probably Czechoslovakian, 15" l. (ILLUS.).... 110
Enameled mesh, Art Deco style w/diamond
  design & scallop design on bottom, metal
  frame & chain, turquoise, pink & black,
  ca. 1920, marked "Whiting - Davis,"
  7" l. (ILLUS.)........................... 121

Goldtone mesh, armor-style, gilt metal embossed frame, knob clasp, taffeta-lined, snake handle, Whiting - Davis, 6¼ x 8¾" **75**

Mesh, white enamel decoration w/gold-colored clasp & chain, Whiting-Davis **65**

Ornate Silver Purse

Russian silver, rectangular form w/novelty chain & bead handle, bas-relief double lion swag, ribbon & floral design on cover w/green cabochon stone clasp, fitted maroon silk interior, late 19th - early 20th c., 7¾" l., 3¼" w. (ILLUS.) **863**

Velvet, clutch-type, Moroccan black velvet w/silver embroidery **40**

RADIO & TELEVISION MEMORABILIA

Not long after the dawning of the radio age in the 1920s, new programs were being aired for the entertainment of the national listening audience. Many of these programs issued premiums and advertising promotional pieces which are highly collectible today. With the arrival of the TV age in the late 1940s, the tradition of promotional items continued and in addition to advertising materials, many toys and novelty items have been produced which tie-in to popular shows. Below we list alphabetically a wide range of items relating to classic radio and television. Some of the characters originated in the comics or on the radio and then found new and wider exposure through television. We include them here because they are best known to today's collectors because of television exposure.

Addams (The) family bank, "The Thing" w/original box **$95**

Baby Snooks (radio) doll, composition, all original, ca. 1939, 12" h. **95**

Barney Rubble (The Flintstones) toy, windup tin, a figure of Barney w/large feet, walks when wound, Marx, 1960s, very good (ILLUS.) **303**

Barney Rubble Windup Toy

Batman (TV) button, Crimefighter, lithographed metal, 1⅜" d. **12**

Beverly Hillbillies card game, ca. 1963 . . . . **25**

Captain Kangaroo tablecloth, in original package, 1950s **30**

Captain Midnight decoder pin, metal, 1946 . . . . . **75**

Charlie McCarthy bank, still-type, white metal w/movable wood jaw, depicts Charlie seated on suitcase, Vanio, US 938, pristine, 5½" h. **275**

Charlie McCarthy pin, shirt-type, plastic, bust of Charlie wearing tuxedo, top hat & monocle, moveable mouth, black & white w/natural-colored face, premium, ca 1930s, 1⅜" h. **66**

Charlie McCarthy toy, windup tin, color lithographed, Charlie walker, very good, Louis Marx **308**

From left: Charlie McCarthy & His Benzine Buggy, Charlie McCarthy Dummy

Charlie McCarthy toy, windup tin, color lithographed, Charlie McCarthy & His Benzine Buggy, Louis Marx, excellent, 7" l. (ILLUS.) . . . . **475 to 575**

Charlie McCarthy toy, windup tin, color lithographed, Charlie as a drummer, Louis Marx, excellent, 9" l. **935**

Charlie McCarthy ventriloquist dummy, composition & cloth, the composition head w/hinged mouth, composition hands & feet, straw-filled body, wearing original black & white tuxedo & top hat, all original, ca. 1930s, 41" h. (ILLUS.) **413**

Charlie McCarthy & Mortimer Snerd toy,
windup tin, color lithographed, private car,
side of car inscribed "We'll Mow You
Down," ca. 1930, Louis Marx, excellent,
15" l. **3,520**
**Daniel Boone (Fess Parker) (TV) magic
slate,** 1964, Saalfield **48**

Scarce Dino the Dinosaur Toy

Dino the dinosaur (The Flintstones) toy,
windup tin & plastic, Dino peddling a
tricycle w/a domed bell on the back,
Marx, very good, 1960s (ILLUS.) **495**

Donnie & Marie Coloring Book

Donnie & Marie coloring book, color cover
w/photos of the Osmonds, two paper
dolls on the back cover, Osmond
Productions, 1977, uncut & uncolored (ILLUS.). . **40**

Flub-A-Dub Marionette

Flub-A-Dub (Howdy Doody) marionette,
composition & cloth, the character w/a
yellow & blue head, red body, black cloth
ears & flippers & orange blanket, 1950s,
no wear (ILLUS.) **193**
Fred Flintstone (The Flintstones) toy,
battery-operated, metal & plush, Fred
sitting atop his large dinosaur worker,

dinosaur w/purple plush body w/black
spots, Marx, 1960s, very good **303**
Fred Flintstone (The Flintstones) toy,
windup tin, "Flintstone Flivver," Fred
driving the stone age auto w/the name on
the side, Marx, 1960s, works well, 7" l. **413**

Fred Flintstone Windup Toy

Fred Flintstone (The Flintstones) toy,
windup tin & plastic, color lithographed,
Fred peddling a tricycle w/a domed bell at
the back, Marx, 1960s, excellent (ILLUS.) **385**

George Jetson Windup Toy

George Jetson (The Jetsons) toy, windup
tin, color lithographed figure of George
Jetson w/large feet for walking when
wound, Marx, very good, 1960s (ILLUS.) **220**
Howdy Doody birthday cake decorations,
pink, on original card, mint condition **75**
Howdy Doody bowling game, in original
box, Parker Bros. **98**
Howdy Doody Christmas light, wall-type. **125**
Howdy Doody flasher rings, set of 8 . . . . **155**

Howdy Doody's T.V. Game

Howdy Doody game, "Howdy Doody's T.V.
Game," board-type, colorful box, Milton
Bradley, 1950s, mint in box (ILLUS.). . . . . . . **45 to 65**

Lucille Ball Ceramic Bank

I Love Lucy bank, ceramic, realistic bust portrait of Lucille Ball, Vandor, 1996 (ILLUS.) .. **35**

Jetson Family Bank

Jetsons bank, ceramic, globe-form w/the Jetson family riding in their spacecraft, hand-colored, probably Vandor, ca. 1990 (ILLUS.) **175**

Jetsons Bed-shaped Bank

Jetsons bank, ceramic, modeled in the form of a bed w/Elroy & Astro asleep, hand-colored, probably Vandor, ca. 1990 (ILLUS.) .. **125**

Laverne & Shirley Coloring Book

Laverne & Shirley coloring & activity book, blue cover w/white & gold lettering, large color photo of the characters taken during the episode about Shirley's wedding, copyright 1983 by Paramount Pictures Corp., published by Playmore Publishing & Waldman Publishing Co., uncolored (ILLUS.) **15**

From left: *Laverne & Shirley Coloring Book Lum & Abner Horlick's Mixer*

Laverne & Shirley coloring & activity book, orange cover w/blue & black lettering, large color photo of the characters in their room & the heads of the stars shown below, copyright 1983 by Paramount Pictures Corp., published by Playmore Publishing & Waldman Publishing Co., uncolored (ILLUS.) **15**

Lum & Abner Horlick's mixer, cov., glass & metal, the tall cylindrical glass base printed in blue w/portraits of the radio characters & "Horlick's - Lum - Abner," domed screw-on metal cover w/a looped twist handle, cover marked "Horlick's Malted Milk Mixer Pat. Pend.," ca. 1930s, 12 oz., overall 9" h. (ILLUS.) **40**

Mighty Mouse Tennis Shoes

Mighty Mouse tennis shoes, child's, white cloth w/rubber soles, Mighty Mouse logo on sides, never worn, w/original black, yellow & red box w/top missing, 1950s, pr. (ILLUS.)............................. **231**

Milton Berle toy, windup tin crazy car, Louis Marx, 6" l., near mint w/original box......... **418**

Mortimer Snerd Walker Toy

Mortimer Snerd (Charlie McCarthy) toy, windup tin, color lithographed, Mortimer walker, standing holding bunch of flowers & box of candy, Marx, 1939, excellent condition, 8¾" h. (ILLUS.) **853**

Mortimer Snerd (Charlie McCarthy) toy, windup tin, color lithographed, Mortimer in a car, Louis Marx, very good, 7¼" l....... **462**

Mortimer Snerd Windup toy

Mortimer Snerd toy, windup tin, "Mortimer Snerd's Home Town Band," figure of Mortimer pushing a large drum on a wheeled base, Marx, 1930s, 8¾" l. (ILLUS.) .. **975**

Mr. Bluster Marionette

Mr. Bluster (Howdy Doody) marionette, composition & cloth, the character w/hinged mouth, red-painted hat & shoes, blue jacket & pale lavender pants, some paint missing on left hand, 1950s, 16" h. (ILLUS.) **138**

Orphan Annie Code Captain belt, adjustable red, white & blue band w/brass buckle, "Official Code Captain Secrets," red, white & blue box w/picture of Annie, 1940, never played w/in original package **286**

Orphan Annie Sun-Watch & Compass, metal, never played w/in original mint box, the group,.......................... **77**

Quick Draw McGraw Toy

Quick Draw McGraw toy, friction-type, tin & plastic, Quick Draw seated in a small tin auto, Marx, 1960s, 4" l. (ILLUS.) **165**

Rin Tin Tin playset, Fort Apache Series 500, Marx, excellent **125**

Romper Room tambourine, ca. 1950s **55**

Sonny & Cher dolls, ca. 1976, mint in matching boxes, pr. **100**

Waltons (The) color & activity book, red cover w/yellow & black wording & black & white photos of the characters & color

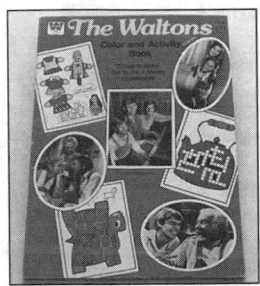

The Waltons Coloring-Activity Book

activity sheets, copyright 1975 by Lorimar
Productions, Whitman, uncolored
(ILLUS.) **25**

Yogi Bear in Car Toy

Yogi Bear toy, friction-type, tin & plastic,
Yogi Bear seated in a small car, head
moves, Marx, 1960s, 4" l. (ILLUS.) **149**

RAILROADIANA

Badge, "Union Pacific Railroad" guard,
ca. 1900. .... **$135**
Bowl, small, "Missouri Pacific Railroad,"
china, "The Eagle patt." **75**
Butter pat, "St. Louis & San Francisco
Railway," silver plate, by International Silver .. **100**
Butter warmer, "Missouri Pacific Railroad,"
silver plate, by International Silver **50**
Calendar, "Great Northern Railway," 1945,
"Custer's Last Fight," decorated
w/American Indian **575**

1956 Pennsylvania RR Calendar

Calendar, "Pennsylvania Railroad," 1956,
colorful landscape scene of trains
passing on tracks, calendar pad below,
signature of agent at top corner of
calendar, write-up about the "Truck Train"
on the back, framed, scratches at top,
overall creases, minor frame wear,
30½" sq. (ILLUS.) **275**
Cap badge, "Chesapeake & Ohio Railway,"
metal, conductor **50**
Cap badge, "Minneapolis, St. Paul & Sault
Ste. Marie Railway," (Soo Line) metal,
brakeman **95**

Early Locomotive Carte de Visite

Carte de visite photo, Smith, Dawson &
Bailey Locomotives, nice shot of an early
engine & wood car w/buildings in the
background, promotion for Pittsburgh
machinists, boiler makers, founders &
locomotive makers, side of locomotive
marked "B.B. & St. L. RR.," wood car
marked on side "Newton," sharp image,
corners trimmed, ink doodles at left not
on image (ILLUS.) **272**
Coffeepot, cov., "Chicago & Northwestern
Railway," silver plate, International Silver **65**
Cup & saucer, "Union Pacific Railroad,"
china, "Winged Streamliner" patt. **20**
Demitasse cup & saucer, "Canadian
National Railway," china, "Queen
Elizabeth" patt. **50**
Engine builder's plate, brass, oval,
"American Loco. Co. Schenectady H3-
1912 50627," 8 x 11½" **875**
Engine builder's plate, brass, rectangular,
"American Locomotive Co. 38921
Pittsburg Works January 1906," 7½ x 14" **550**
Engine builder's plate, brass, diamond-
shaped, "Lima Locomotive Works
Incorporated 8-1937 J7660," 9 x 16" **900**
Glass, juice, "Missouri, Kansas & Texas Railway".. **70**
Gravy boat, "Missouri, Kansas & Texas
Railway," silver plate, by R. Wallace **120**
Hat, brakeman, "Rock Island Lines" **120**
Hat, conductor, "St. Louis & San Francisco
Railway" **190**
Key, switch-type, "Atchison, Topeka &
Santa Fe Railway" **35**
Key, switch-type, "Illinois Central Railroad" **25**
Key, switch-type, "Union Pacific Railroad" **75**

Lantern, "Buffalo, Rochester & Pittsburgh Railroad," tall globe, bell-bottom style, clear globe w/raised lettering **160**

Lantern, "Burlington Route," tall globe-type, clear globe w/raised lettering **95**

Lantern, "Chicago, Milwaukee, St. Paul & Pacific Railroad," short globe-type, clear globe w/raised lettering **50**

Lantern, "Chicago, St. Paul , Minneapolis & Omaha Railway," tall globe-type, Dietz barn-style frame, red globe w/raised lettering "C.S.T.P. M. & O." **400**

Lantern, "Colorado & Southern Railway," tall globe, bell-bottom style, red unmarked globe **200**

Lantern, "Delaware, Lackawanna & Western Railroad," tall globe-type, clear globe w/raised wording "Safety First" **90**

Lantern, "Florida East Coast Railway," short globe-type, Adlake mark on frame, cobalt blue globe w/MacBeth mark **95**

Lantern, "Great Northern Railway," tall globe-type, red globe w/raised lettering **210**

Lantern, "Minneapolis, St. Paul & Sault Ste. Marie Railway" (Soo Line), short globe-type, cobalt blue etched globe **105**

Lantern, "Missouri, Kansas & Texas Railway," tall globe, bell-bottom brass top type, clear globe w/raised lettering **625**

Lantern, "Northern Pacific Railroad," tall globe-type, clear globe w/raised lettering **210**

Lantern, "Northwestern Pacific Railroad," short globe-type, red etched globe **65**

Lantern, "Pacific Electric Railway," tall globe-type, etched clear globe **75**

Lantern, presentation-type, all-brass, bell bottom style, red & clear tall globe, presentation inscription on globe "D.A. Kendall, Pine Bluff, Ark.," Handlan Co. **950**

Lantern, presentation-type, all-brass, bell bottom style, tall clear unmarked globe w/unique copper arm lens protectors, Geo. M. Clark Co. **300**

Lantern, presentation-type, chrome-plated, cobalt blue & clear globe etched w/initials "F.D. ORR," Adams & Westlake Co. **2,000**

Lantern, "Reading Railway," tall globe-type, frame marked "LO CO DEPT," clear unmarked globe **100**

Lantern, "Rutland Railroad," short globe-type, red etched globe **90**

Lantern, "Southern Pacific Company," tall globe-type, clear globe w/raised lettering **160**

Lantern, "St. Louis & San Francisco Railroad," tall globe-type, Adlake Reliable frame w/bamboo handle, clear globe w/raised wording "Frisco" & "Safety First" **260**

Lantern, "Wabash Railroad," tall globe, bell-bottom brass top type, clear globe w/raised wording "Wabash Banner Flag" **385**

Mayonnaise bowl, "Missouri Pacific Railroad," china, "The Eagle" patt. **75**

Plate, "Denver & Rio Grande Western Railroad," luncheon, china, "Prospector" patt. . . **95**

Plate, "Great Northern Railway," bread & butter, china, "Glory of the West" patt. **45**

Plate, "Union Pacific Railroad," china, "Circus" patt., scene of monkey w/pipe, 8¼" d. . **95**

Platter, "Denver & Rio Grande Western Railroad," oval, china, "Prospector" patt. **25**

Platter, "Northern Pacific Railway," china, small oval, "Monad" patt. **60**

Platter, "Union Pacific Railroad," china, oval, "Harriman Blue" patt., 6¼ x 9" **50**

Platter, "Chicago, Milwaukee, St. Paul Pacific Railroad," china, oval, "Traveler" patt., 8 x 10" **85**

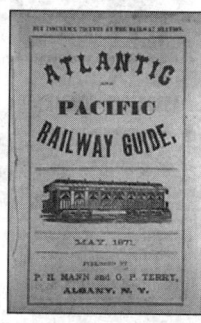

Early Railway Guide

Railway guide, "Atlantic and Pacific Railway Guide - May 1871," sketch of Pullman Car on the cover, nice illustrations inside, various timetables, string-bound, 24 pp., 5¾ x 9¼", spine wear, light soiling, erased writing on the cover (ILLUS.) **138**

Service plate, "Baltimore & Ohio Railroad," china, "Centenary" patt. **75**

Service plate, "Missouri Pacific Railroad," china, "State Flower" patt. **190**

Service plate, "Pennsylvania Railroad," china, "Gotham" patt. **90**

Service plate, "Southern Railway," china, "Peach Blossom" patt. **30**

Serving set: "Atchison, Topeka & Santa Fe Railway," open serving dish, bowl w/handled cover & tray; silver plate; the set. . . **275**

Foreign Railroad Sign

Sign, embossed self-framed porcelain w/black silhouetted engine on a yellow ground, foreign-made, one-sided, Neuhas Paris, Vitracier Japy, rust spotting, scratches & soiling, triangular, 37" w., 36½" h. (ILLUS.)................... 149

Sign, "North Carolina Railroad," round, "Seaboard Coast Line" in black on yellow ground, 22" d. (minor scratches) 77

Soup bowl, "St. Louis & San Francisco Railway," china, "Denmark" patt.................... 35

Step stool, "Northern Pacific," metal 375

Step stool, "Texas & Pacific Railroad," metal.... 425

Tablecloth, "Rock Island Lines," linen 40

Tablecloth, "St. Louis & San Francisco Railway," linen 80

Teapot, cov., "Missouri Pacific Railroad," "The Eagle" patt., silver plate 75

Time table, "Denver & Rio Grande Railroad," 1929........................ 35

Torch can, "Atchison, Topeka & Santa Fe Railway," metal........................ 150

Tumbler, "Chesapeake & Ohio Railroad," glass... 11

Tumbler, "Missouri, Kansas & Texas Railway," glass........................ 70

ROYCROFT ITEMS

Elbert Hubbard, eccentric entrepreneur of the late 19th century, founded Roycroft Shops and established a craft community in East Aurora, New York in 1895. Individuals were trained in the trades of bookbinding, leather tooling and printing. Craft-style furniture in the manner of Gustav Stickley and known as "Aurora Colonial" furniture was produced. A copper workshop, begun in 1908, turned out numerous items. All of these, along with those pieces of Buffalo Pottery china which were produced exclusively for use at the Roycroft Inn and carry the Roycroft symbol, constitute a special category associated with the Arts and Crafts movement.

Roycroft Andirons

Andirons, wrought iron, each formed w/pierced scrolled standard continuing to scrolled feet & surmounted w/spiral-twist finials, square log bar extending behind, ca. 1910, wear, 35" h., pr. (ILLUS.)....... **$4,025**

Book, "An American Bible" by Alice Hubbard, copyright 1918, embossed leather cover, 5 x 7½".................... 22

Book, "The Motto Book" by Fra Elbertus, copyright 1920, limp suede cover, 5½ x 8"..... 50

Book, "Little Journeys - English authors, Alfred Tennyson," signed & numbered "362, Elbert Hubbard," illuminated title page, copyright 1899, limp suede cover, 6 x 8" 55

Book ends, hand-hammered copper, high arched backplate w/notches at top, hammered ground centered by a long raised oval decorated w/a leafy floral scroll outlined w/a dotted border highlighted w/orange enamel, impressed logo on base, 4¾" h., pr. 299

Book stand, oak, for the "Little Journey's" book series, a rectangular top over two shelves w/two vertical slats & double keyed tenons on a shoefoot, original finish, metal orb tag, early 20th c., 14 x 26", 26" h........................ 660

Books, "Little Journeys," volume one through fourteen, various titles, leather-bound, good condition, the set............ 110

Bowl, hand-hammered copper, low rounded sides w/closed rim, original patina, impressed mark, 6" d., 3" h................ 523

Bowl, hand-hammered copper, rounded w/three feet, original patina, early impressed mark, 7" d., 4" h. 1,100

Fruit tray, hand-hammered copper, round w/a stylized rim decoration, No. 805, ca. 1918, 9¾" d. (some pitting)............ 518

'Goodie' box, cov., mahogany w/hammered metal latch, trim & handles, rectangular, orb signature, early 20th c., 26" l., 9" h. (slightly worn original finish, minor split in top) 770

Lamp, table model, helmet-style, hand-hammered copper w/a domed shade w/flared rim raised on a cupped socket holder on a slender ringed cylindrical standard on a flaring round foot, medium patina, No. 906, ca. 1919, 14¼" h. (minor dents & scratches).................... 1,840

Library table, oak, rectangular top over a lower stretcher shelf w/a mousehole cut-out & double-keyed tenons, fine original finish, orb signature, Model No. 072, 33 x 50", 30" h........................ 6,050

Vase, hand-hammered copper, "American Beauty" type, footed half-round lower base w/an angled shoulder tapering sharply to the tall ringed cylindrical neck w/a flaring rim, original patina, impressed mark, 18½" h. 5,500

RUGS - HOOKED & OTHER

HOOKED

Cat & Birds Hooked Rug

Cat & birds, central diamond-form reserve of a seated cat w/perched bird spandrels, worked in gold, terra-cotta, taupe, red & light grey on a black & grey field, American, late 19th - early 20th c., mounted, minor hole, fading, 24½ x 43" (ILLUS.). **$1,265**

Cat & kitten, black animals on white center, surrounded by floral design in black, white, green, yellow, red, blue & brown, backed for hanging, faded colors, wear & repair, 24" w., 29½" h. **605**

Centennial designs, dated 1776-1876, the variegated scrolling border enclosing a foliate reserve, worked in blue, red, brown, camel, taupe, green, purple & grey, backed, 38 x 70½" (minor repairs, staining & fading) **460**

Cottage scene, a white cottage w/green shutters, signed "1936 Gussman's Essex N.Y.," worked in green, white, sage, yellow, orange, red & blue yarns, 26½ x 35½" (some fading) **173**

Dog, rectangular w/center off-white oval w/standing black Scottie dog wearing a collar, surrounded by a scalloped black border w/stylized red, blue & green floral spray in each corner, 20 x 31½" **413**

Dog sled scene, rectangular snowy landscape w/two people w/a dog sled team, Grenfell label on reverse, Newfoundland or Labrador, early 20th c., 27¼ x 39" (minor fading, staining, very minor losses). **2,185**

Hearts & Floral Hooked Rug

Hearts & floral, heart border enclosing field of large stylized floral design w/a heart in each corner, centering "Hattie," worked in red, sage, taupe, brown, cream & pink yarns on a black field, American, late 19th - early 20th c., minor losses, repairs, minor staining, dry areas, 31½ x 52" (ILLUS.). **1,150**

Horse, central oval reserve w/horse figure worked in beige & brown standing in a grassy green area near a picket fence, blue sky background, surrounded by ivory border w/oak leaves in brown & green, minor wear, 23½ x 37" **275**

Horse & carriage, scene of horse-drawn open carriage & driver w/footman assisting a lady passenger w/parasol, polychrome w/blues & greens, black scalloped border, 27 x 48" (some wear & minor damage) **440**

Leopard Hooked Rug

Leopard, the spotted animal standing in a grassy landscape w/stylized leafage, worked in shades of brown, green & beige fabrics, American, late 19th c., mounted on a stretcher, 26 x 46½" (ILLUS.). . **1,380**

Three Bears, the Three Bears, Papa, Mama & Baby, marching in a row dressed in human clothing & carrying their bowl of porridge, multicolored on a beige ground w/black border, 24 x 40" (minor wear) **550**

Tiger & Foliage Hooked Rug

Tiger, central reserve showing a running tiger w/band borders & surrounded by a striated field w/foliate devices & band borders, worked in green, burnt orange, sage, ecru, red & plum yarns, American, late 19th - early 20th c., backed, minor splits, losses & repairs, very minor wear, 45 x 82" (ILLUS.). **2,415**

OTHER

Braided rug, rectangular w/shaped edges, diamond, heart & circle designs worked in pale blue, teal blue, pink & black, 20th c., 41 x 80" (minor wear) 460

Drugget-style, rectangular, Arts & Crafts style w/a Native American design w/a stepped diamond in green, orange & black in the center & matching triangular corner designs at each end all on an oatmeal ground, fringed ends, early 20th c., 51 x 83" 143

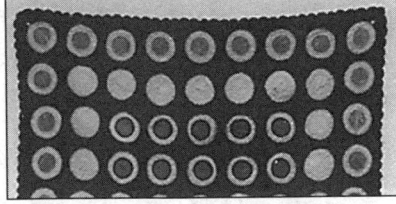

Appliqued Wool Penny Rug

Penny rug, a scalloped border on the rectangular rug, black wool w/chenille background decorated w/appliqued circles of red & pale grey wool & olive velvet highlighted w/black & yellow embroidery, wear to scalloped edge, small holes & wear, 24½ x 35½" (ILLUS. of part) 193

Woven rag, long runner of multicolored thin stripes predominantly blue, brown & white, Pennsylvania, unused, 38½ x 506" 330

Woven rag runner, composed of strips sewn together in a plaid cross-form design in red, blue, green & gold, unused, 14½ x 164" 523

SCIENTIFIC INSTRUMENTS

Hydraulic Air Pump and Bell Jar

Air pump w/bell jar, hydraulic-type, glass, oak & brass w/paint-decorated lever, marked "W.A. Olmstead Chicago," tubing needs reattaching at base of glass cylinder, late 19th - early 20th c., 11¼ x 26", 26" h. (ILLUS.) $303

Barometer, banjo-style, inlaid mahogany, a round top w/an inlaid sunburst above the slender neck w/an inset thermometer flanked at the bottom by inlaid seashells above the round silvered metal dial, slender rounded base drop w/inlaid sunburst, G. Caprani & Co., Norwich, England, late 18th - early 19th c., 36" h. 1,200

Barometer, banjo-style, inlaid mahogany, the broken arch pediment above a panel w/an inlaid urn design above the slender shaped neck w/an inset thermometer over another inlaid panel over the white painted dial labeled "Taylor Instrument Companies, Rochester, N.Y. 1927," shaped base pendent drop w/vine & urn inlay, early 20th c., 28" h. 303

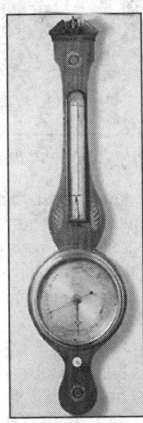

English Mahogany Barometer

Barometer, banjo-style, inlaid mahogany, the broken-arch pediment centering an acorn finial above an inlaid rosette, the tall slender neck w/a glazed thermometer (broken) flanked by inlaid seashells, the lower circular silvered metal dial above a bone adjustment wheel & another inlaid rosette, Piotti, Hull, England, 19th c., some alterations, 10" w., 38½" h. (ILLUS.) 1,380

Barometer, banjo-style, inlaid mahogany, the pointed pediment crest above an inlaid rosette above the slender neck w/inset thermometer panel above inlaid seashells above the round silvered metal dial & rounded base drop, F. Amadio & Sons, London, England, late 18th - early 19th c., 38½" h. (broken thermometer panel) 800

Book, "Nineteenth Century Scientific Instruments" by Gerarde L'E. Turner, copyright 1983, hardcover w/dust jacket **94**

Coal testing machine, a blown glass cylinder fitted in a dovetailed mahogany case, includes handwritten document on New Central Coal Companies letterhead w/recipe for testing coal, 19th c., case, 6¾ x 12½", 15¼" h., the set **215**

Colorimeter, brass w/a steel base, signed by "J. Dubosco & P. Pellin, Paris," also label of "Arthur Thomas, Phila.," France, late 19th - early 20th c., 15½" h. (minor base surface rust). **385**

Hydrometer, Sikes-type, in inlaid mahogany case labeled "Re-adjusted by W. R. Loftus, Ltd., London," case 2 x 4 x 8" (missing plate from exterior lid) **110**

Three Early Scientific Instruments

Magnifying glass, table model, round lens mounted in a square cherry frame flanked by small colonettes w/ball finials & above a block- and baluster-turned crossbar, raised on a slender turned adjustable pedestal on a domed turned foot, 19th c., 22⅝" h. (ILLUS. left) **385**

Microscope, brass & iron, double adjustable lens on pedestal base w/"U"-form foot, marked "Ed. Messter," Berlin, Germany, ca. 1910 . . . . **226**

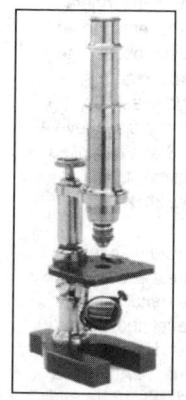

From left: Early French Microscope
Early Viennese Microscope

Microscope, brass & iron, single adjustable lens on pedestal base w/"U"-form foot, marked "E. Hartnack & A. Prasmowski, Paris," France, ca. 1870 (ILLUS.). **171**

Microscope, brass & iron, single adjustable lens on pedestal base w/"U"-form foot, marked "C. Reichart, Wien," Vienna, Austria, ca. 1880 (ILLUS.) **246**

Victorian English Microscope

Microscope, brass & lacquered metal, the single lens upper adjustable platform on flat curved brass supports above the black lacquered metal outcurved long feet, by W. Watson & Sons, England, ca. 1870 (ILLUS.) **308**

Microscope, enameled brass & steel body, w/a three-lens revolving turret, Spencer, 13" h. (minor wear to table) **193**

Microscope, lacquered brass on an enameled metal base, three-lens, marked "Spencer Lens, Buffalo, N.Y.," w/original booklet & case, the set (ILLUS. right w/magnifying glass) **193**

Microscope, painted metal, adjustable top w/three revolving lenses, on a raised base w/"U"-form foot, marked "Spencer, Buffalo - USA," ca. 1925 (some finish wear) **150**

Microscope, w/four additional eyepieces & three-power revolving turret, Bausch & Lomb, w/case, 13¾" h. **165**

Ophthalmoscope, cast iron & brass, the ornate curved & footed iron base supporting a shielded projecting lens at one end, F.A. Hardy, electric-powered, 22½ x 25" (ILLUS. center w/magnifying glass) **165**

Spectroscope, brass tubes on a base, signed "James Queen, Philadelphia," 9¼" h. (some areas of corrosion on tubes) . . . **220**

Surveyor's chain, linked metal chain, geodectic model, ca. 1891 . . . . **239**

Surveyor's compass, walnut, the long
rectangular wood frame w/end uprights
centered by the flat round dial, compass
rose engraved "Made & Sold by John
Dupee ye North Side Swingbridge Boston
New Eng.," w/protective cover, Boston,
mid-18th c., 14" l. (very minor losses &
staining to rose engraving) **1,955**

Surveyor's level, brass & enameled brass,
engine-turned rings for the sighting tube,
w/a mahogany case, Bausch, Lomb &
Saegmuller, case 8⅜ x 21" (some wear) **303**

Surveyor's level, brass, W. & L.E. Gurley,
w/original carrying case & tripod, case
6⅜ x 11¼", the set (some case wear) **303**

Surveyor's tool, metal w/lacquered brass
finish, signed "Keuffer & Esser, N.Y.," cased . . **193**

Demonstration-type Telegraph Key

Telegraph keyboard, demonstration model,
metal mechanism on rectangular wood
base, by Max Ohl A.G., Germany,
ca. 1910 (ILLUS.) **274**

Telescope w/tripod, brass, 40½" l. brass
tube on an oak tripod base w/decorative
turned legs, signed "M. Jaggli, Zurich,"
Switzerland, tripod 59" h. (some dents in
tube, age cracks in legs) **633**

SCRIMSHAW

*Scrimshaw is a folk art by-product of the
19th century American whaling industry.
Intricately carved and engraved pieces of
whalebone, whale's teeth and walrus tusks were
produced by whalers during their spare time at
sea. In recent years numerous fine grade hard
plastic reproductions have appeared on the
market so the novice collector must use caution
to distinguish these from the rare originals.*

Baleen corset busk, long flat slender form
engraved w/various geometric designs,
plants & a three-masted sailing ship,
19th c., 12¾" l. (crack, minor chips, minor
insect damage) **$144**

Bodkin, carved whale ivory w/openwork
heart-form finial, 19th c., 4½" l. (minor
age crack) **1,495**

Busk, whalebone, polychrome decorated
w/a floral bouquet, potted plant, ship at
sea & a basket of fruit & foliage initialed
"H.D.R.," heightened w/red, blue, yellow,
& green colors, 19th c., 13⅛" l. **920**

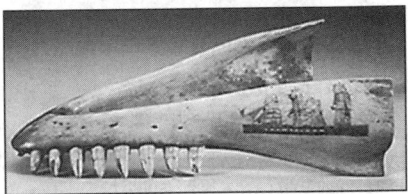

Scrimshaw Dolphin Jawbone

Dolphin jawbone, one side decorated
w/engraved scene of an approaching
whale boat, the other side w/two
whaleships, one w/boats aboard & the
other ship coming about, decorated by
two different artists, 19th c., minor losses,
particularly to the teeth, 10½" w., 16" l.
(ILLUS.) **1,610**

Jagging wheel, whalebone & walrus tusk,
double wheel, w/three-tined crimper,
baleen spacers, 19th c., 7¾" l. (age crack) . . **1,840**

Jagging wheel, carved whalebone, shaped
open carved handle, 19th c., 7½" l.
(losses to wheel) **978**

Pie crimper, whale ivory, stylized carved
figure of seahorse w/incised & painted
black mane grasping wheel in its
forelegs, mid 19th c., 6" l. (age crack) **7,475**

Swift, whalebone & ivory, clothespin-type,
turned shaft & cup, mounted on a turned
mahogany base, 19th c., 19½" h.
(minor losses) **3,450**

Ornate Scrimshaw Walrus Tusks

Walrus tusks, one engraved on front
w/"Walrus" & images of cannons, a ship
& an eagle over a series of American
flags, the reverse w/engraved images of

two different types of whales & a whaleboat, the second tusk is engraved on the front w/"Tusks," images of crossed swords, a ship, an eagle w/standard & flags, a horse & rider w/the reverse engraved w/two different types of whales, each on circular stepped wooden base, late 19th - early 20th c., approximately 13" h., pr. (ILLUS.) **3,450**

Whale pan bone, rectangular plaque engraved w/a British whaling ship under sail & four whaleboats w/nine whales, supported on a mahogany stretcher, 19th c., 9 x 12¾" (some old splits & cracks) **5,750**

Whale's tooth, decorated w/urn of flowers, 19th c., 7½" l. **1,840**

Whale's tooth, decorated w/whaling scene depicting the vessel working on a pod of whales, two boats away, 19th c., 8" l. (surface wear, minor chips) **2,415**

Whale's tooth, engraved w/an elegant lady, mid-19th c., 7" l. (very minor cracks & chips) **920**

Whale's tooth, obverse decorated w/a framed vignette of a whaling scene w/boats in pursuit, reverse depicting an American whaleship, 19th c., 9" l. (surface wear) **1,725**

Whale's tooth, obverse depicting a ship under sail, reverse w/a flamed scene inscribed "Pacific in a Hurricane" above a leafy garland, 19th c., 8¾" l. (age crack) **2,300**

Whale's tooth, obverse w/English ship under full sail, reverse w/a three-masted ship flanked by two entwined leafy borders, & a geometric border around base, 19th c., 6⅞" l. **1,265**

Whale's tooth, polychrome decorated, obverse depicting a bosun blowing his whistle, reverse depicting a British vessel entering an American port, heightened with red, blue, black & flesh tone colors, 19th c., 8" l. **12,650**

Whale's tooth, polychrome tooth, obverse depicting a woman among crossed flags & a memorial portrait, flanked by flowers, reverse w/an American eagle & banner above a warship flying an American flag, 19th c., 3½" w., 6¼" l. **1,495**

Whale's tooth, snuff box w/brass lid, obverse decorated w/crossed British flags & anchor above a full-rigged sailing ship, reverse depicts a rural village scene, 5" l. **513**

Whale's tooth, decorated w/reserves of a church & a three-masted ship under sail, 19th c., 5" l. (minor cracks, very minor chip) .. **690**

Whale's tooth, decorated w/an engraved figure of Lady Liberty holding an American eagle & an American flag w/the

Whale's Tooth with Lady Liberty

anchor of hope resting at her feet & a garland of leaves encircling the top of the tooth, American, 19th c., 6¼" h. (ILLUS.) ... **1,380**

Whale's tooth, polychrome decorated w/"The Mother of Washington Receiving Marquis LaFayette," early 20th c., 6½" l. **690**

Scrimshaw Whalebone Ditty Box

Whalebone ditty box, oval, wooden top & base w/eight-finger construction, brass tack decoration, 19th c., minor wear, 3⅜ x 6⅛ x 8¼" (ILLUS.) **3,105**

Whalebone swift, a bone clamp engraved w/a star & floral design, w/adjustable sliding throat & screw lock, the top of an egg cup design & w/a star & floral design, pieces bound together w/brass pins & cuttyhunk ties (modern), w/a carrying box, polychrome decoration, 19th c., box 3¾ x 3⅞ x 29", 2 pcs. **1,380**

SEWING ADJUNCTS

With sewing tools and accessories so popular, collectors in the United States, Canada and England actively search for these small antiques. The wide variety available gives buyers a good selection from which to choose - and allows for plenty of different price ranges too. Be cautious of reproductions - Victorian and Georgian styled sterling thimbles and needlecases marked "Thailand" are found frequently and new pewter thimble holders are sometimes sold as old. A good reference book on sewing tools and accessories is Gay Ann Rogers' An Illustrated History of Needlework Tools, which can be found in many bookstores. All items listed below are in good condition, minor wear and with no missing parts.

Bodkin, bone, simply turned, handmade, no
  design, 3" l............................ **$21**

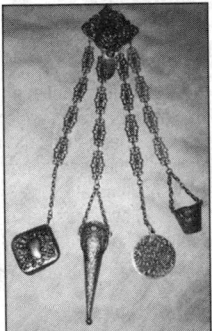

Victorian White Metal Chatelaine

Chatelaine, white metal, four-section
  w/thimble basket, tape measure, scissors
  holder & pin disc, France, late 19th c.
  (ILLUS.)............................. **595**
Crochet hook, brass, retractable hook in
  decorative case, England, ca. 1870s......... **48**
Crochet hook, turned bone, 1880s............ **18**
Darner, black egg shape on sterling handle,
  Art Nouveau design, ca. 1920s............ **75**
Darner, blown glass, common shoe form,
  blue, ca. 1900........................... **65**
Darner, Shaker, mushroom-shaped,
  checkerboard style design in maple,
  cherry & walnut.......................... **98**
Darner, Shaker, wood ball in socket style,
  late 19th c., rare....................... **245**
Emery, sterling silver, double-ended
  cylinder, English hallmarks, floral design,
  ca. 1880s............................... **125**
Emery, strawberry-shaped, plaid orange
  fabric w/hand-stitched seeds, ca. 1890s...... **55**
Hem gauge, sterling silver, complete
  w/sliding marker, Art Nouveau design,
  ca. 1920s............................... **95**
Knitting sheath, wood, goose-wing styling,
  carved initials "T.C.," ca. 1850, 9" l......... **275**
Knitting sheath, wood, hand-carved date of
  "1822" near top w/crosshatched design
  on lower half, England................... **350**
Lace bobbin, bone w/brass wire-wrapped
  shaft, England, 1860s.................... **89**
Lace bobbin, bone w/pewter "dots" inlaid in
  shaft (leopard design), England, 1840s....... **98**
Lace bobbin, solid brass in lathe-turned
  form, England, 1890s, uncommon.......... **85**

Lace bobbin, wood w/pewter-banded shaft,
  England, ca. 1840...................... **48**
Lace pricking, heavy parchment used for
  lace pattern, simple design for 1" wide
  lace, England, 1840s, 12" l............... **39**
Needlecase, bone cylinder w/overall beaded
  design, England, 1840s................. **145**
Needlecase, bone, simple lathe-turned
  form, England, 1880s.................... **50**
Needlecase, bone, Stanhope-type, opening
  showing multiple views from the 1878
  Paris Exhibition........................ **145**
Needlecase, bone, umbrella-form w/fist
  handle, England, 1870s................. **165**
Needlecase, figural, wood, carved as man
  w/a fish tail, probably Austrian, late
  19th c., rare........................... **195**
Needlecase, ivory, carved overall
  w/dragons, China, ca. 1840.............. **115**
Needlecase, sterling silver, fleur-de-lis
  designs on embossed case, France, 1920s.... **90**
Needleholder, brass, engraved "Stella,"
  Avery, 1870s.......................... **425**
Needleholder, brass, marked "The Unique,"
  folding-type, Avery, 1870s.............. **485**
Needleholder, brass, quadruple casket
  form, leaf design on front, Avery, 1880s..... **285**
Needleholder, figural, brass, butterfly form,
  Avery, 1880s.......................... **750**
Needleholder, figural, brass, model of a
  wheelbarrow, Avery, 1870s.............. **950**
Netting clamp, steel, heart-shaped
  thumbscrew, England, 1850s............. **150**
Pin disc, cardboard rectangle, advertising-
  type for Prudential Insurance, scene of
  mother w/child......................... **12**
Pin disc, cardboard rectangle, scene of
  children & dog, ca. 1880............... **120**
Pin disc, Tartanware, heart-shaped,
  Scottish, ca. 1880s, 1½" d.............. **325**
Pin disc, Tartanware, heart-shaped,
  Scottish, ca. 1880s, 2" d............... **450**
Pincushion, figural, brass, model of a
  rabbit, ca. 1900, 3" h.................. **130**

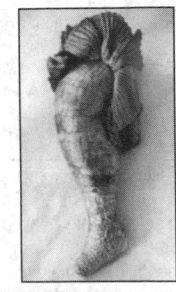

Lady's Leg Pincushion

Pincushion, lady's leg-style, brown fabric,
  England, late Victorian, 9" l. (ILLUS.)......... **56**

Scissors, gilt over white metal, figural stork, Germany, 1920s **39**

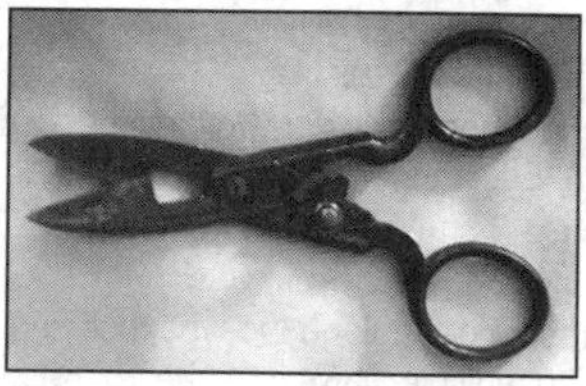

Early Steel Button Hole Scissors

Scissors, steel, button hole-type, rachet mechanism, England, 1860s (ILLUS.) **38**

Scissors, steel, figural owl, Germany, 1920s **49**

Scissors, steel, marked "Sheffield," England, late 19th c., w/leather case, matching set of 3 . . . . **245**

Scissors, steel, w/embroidered silk case, China, 1920s **48**

Early Patented Sewing Bird

Sewing bird, brass, 1853 patent date on wing edge, originally w/two pincushions (ILLUS. w/top cushion missing) **375**

Sewing bird, silver plated brass, 1853 patent date on edge of wing, one pincushion . . **335**

Sewing bird, steel, simple streamlined form without detail, 1850s **265**

Two-tier Inlaid Sewing Box

Sewing box, bird's-eye maple & inlaid walnut, two-tiered rectangular form w/pointed corner finials & inlaid corner blocks, drawer in lower tier, American-made, mid-19th c., minor surface imperfections, very minor losses to finials, 6¾ x 9½", 7¾" h. (ILLUS.) **374**

Miniature Sewing Chest of Drawers

Sewing box, inlaid walnut, model of a chest of drawers, rectangular top w/molded rim topped by two small heart-inlaid drawers w/pincushion finials, the case w/three long drawers w/small metal knobs & inlaid letters flanked by bands of inlaid hearts, presentation item made in 1868 in Concord, New Hampshire, 8¼" w., 12" h. (ILLUS.) **3,500**

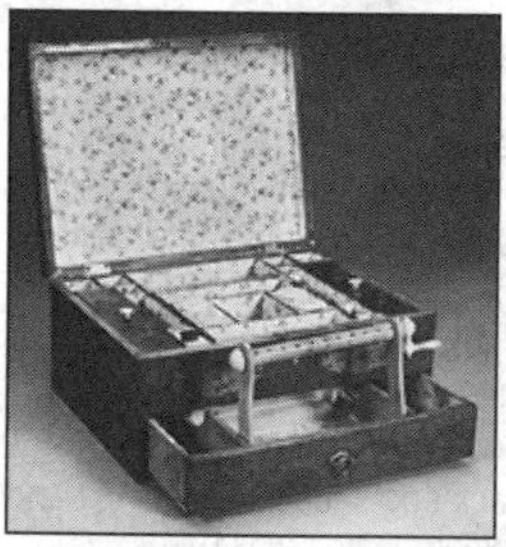

English Lady's Sewing Box

Sewing box, inlaid wood, rectangular w/hinged paper-lined lid opening to a compartmented interior w/wooden & ivory sewing implements, the lower drawer opening to a compartmented interior w/additional implements, case refinished, very minor losses, England, early 19th c., 9 x 12", 5⅝" h. (ILLUS.) **1,610**

Shell Art Sewing Box

Sewing box, sailor's shell art-type, rectangular, old cigar box w/the top inlaid w/varied large & small seashells surrounding a central pink silk pincushion, small shells form banding on cover & base, American-made, ca. 1910, 6 x 9", 6" h. (ILLUS.) **140**

Sewing clamp, steel, simple rachet-type 95

Sewing clamp, wood, Tunbridge ware
w/ivory trim, England, ca. 1850, 9" l. 265

Sewing kit, Shaker, folding style, silk,
pockets for needle packets, ca. 1920 60

Silk winder, glass, medical use, England,
1860s, 2" d. 44

Silk winder, mother-of-pearl, pillow-shaped,
England, 2½" l. 65

Silk winder, Tartanware, cross-form,
Scotland, 1860s, 2½" d. 225

Stiletto, sterling silver handle w/steel shaft,
Art Nouveau design, American-made,
ca. 1920s 65

Tape measure, brass, figural, model of a
shoe, marked "Three feet in one shoe,"
American-made, ca. 1900 165

Tape measure, celluloid, figural, model of a
basket w/painted flowers, spring-wind,
probably German, 1920s 145

Tape measure, copper & brass, figural,
ornate model of a coffee grinder, manual-
wind, Europe, ca. 1900. 300

Tape measure, vegetable ivory, pierced
design, manual-wind, England, 1860-1890 . . . 125

Tape measure, vegetable ivory w/bone
winder, model of a crown, England, 1860s . . . 130

Tape measure, white metal, figural, model
of a clam, marked "A clam w/three feet,"
ca. 1900 195

Tatting shuttle, celluloid, pink & green
pearlized, American-made, 1930s 65

Tatting shuttle, sterling silver, Art Nouveau
floral design, American-made, ca. 1920s 235

Thimble, 14k gold, Ketcham & McDougall,
engraved scrolls w/carved rim, early 1900s . . . 155

Thimble, gold, heavily carved narrow band,
Simons Bros., 1890s 195

Thimble, gold, plain band, unmarked 145

Thimble, sterling sandwiched over steel,
band decorated w/geometric designs,
marked "Dorcas," 1860s. 75

Thimble, sterling sandwiched over steel,
plain band, marked "Dorcas," England, 1860s. . 50

Thimble, sterling silver, coral cabochons
around rim, unmarked American, early 1900s. . 185

Thimble, sterling silver, impressed florals on
band, Simons, ca. 1900 45

Thimble, sterling silver, "Salem Witch,"
Ketcham & McDougall, 19th c. 575

Thimble, sterling silver, souvenir-type,
marked "The Spa," England, ca. 1870s 60

Thimble, sterling silver, souvenir-type,
Washington, D.C. & the Capitol Building,
Ketcham & McDougall, early 20th c. 460

Thimble, sterling silver w/pale blue
enameled band w/florals, red stone in
top, ca. 1900, unusual 195

Thimble holder, Mauchline ware, top w/oval
photographic print titled "View of
Marblehead Massachusetts," made in
Scotland, 1860s 190

Thimble holder, mother-of-pearl, purse-
form w/brass chain, England, ca. 1860s 90

Basket-form Thimble Holder

Thimble holder, velvet, model of a basket in
red w/a white arched handle, paper label
on the base marked "The Fairy,"
English, 1860s (ILLUS.) 145

Ivory Winding Clamp

Winding clamp, carved ivory, spool top
w/netting knob, Asian, ca. 1840 (ILLUS.) 345

SHAKER ITEMS

*The Shakers, a religious sect founded by Ann
Lee, first settled in this country at Watervliet,
New York, near Albany, in 1774. By 1880 there
were nine settlements in America. Workmanship
in Shaker crafts is an extension of their religious
beliefs and features plain and simple designs
reflecting a chaste elegance that is now much
in demand though relatively few early items
are common.*

Berry baskets, splint & tin, wide splints
angled slightly & flared, joined at the top
& base by narrow tin rims, quart, 6⅜" d.,
3½" h., pr. **$242**

Blanket, woven wool, finely woven charcoal w/white & grey wide border stripes, fringed, Sister Mildred Barber, Sabbathday Lake, Maine, 64 x 134"........ **523**

Box maker's mold, hardwood, a heavy central split post w/side screw clamp handle, one end carved w/a round mold, the other w/an oval mold, old patina, 14¾" h........................ **413**

Buck saw, wood & metal, a wooden H-form frame w/turned wood handles at lower corners, wire brace at the top & thin sawblade at the bottom, old patina, Union Village, Ohio, 26" l..................... **330**

Bucket, cov., stave construction w/three metal bands, tapering cylindrical form in old blue paint & black bands, black stenciled "28" on side & bottom, the fitted cover w/rounded edges & small turned center knob, interior w/worn light green paint, wire bail handle w/turned wood hand grip, 11" h. **2,860**

Candlestand, cherry w/old dark red finish, round top on a turned tapering columnar standard on a tripod base w/three flattened cabriole legs ending in snake feet, Mount Lebanon, 19th c., 16½" d., 24¼" h. (repaired crack in top) **3,080**

Carpenter's scribe gauge, all-wood w/slender turned long end handles, 24½" l..... **61**

Cheese colander, tin, wide flat-bottomed pan w/shallow flared sides w/rim handles, the bottom pierced overall w/large drainage holes, 22" d. (split at rim).......... **72**

Cloak cabinet, walnut, a flat rectangular top above a tall case w/a four-panel tall door opening to interior shelves repainted grey over a short lower two-panel door, slightly scalloped apron & simple cut-out feet, chamfered corners, refinished, Union Village, Ohio, 13½ x 37", 77" h. (repairs, feet have lost height, bottom door replaced, top door repaired) **2,750**

Cloak w/hood, child's, blue wool, machine-sewn, 25" l. (minor moth damage, some wear & soiling) **468**

Coffee boiler, cov., tin, large tapering cylindrical body w/large rim spout & strap handle w/grip on opposite rim, a swing strap handle across the top, 16" h. plus swing handle (rust damage, repair) **165**

Cradle, adult-type, painted pine & maple, long rectangular form w/low gently canted sides w/higher sides & headboard at one end, original red wash, dovetailed & nailed construction, possibly Harvard, Massachusetts, 19th c., 33 x 78¾", headboard 23½" h..................... **978**

Cupboard over chest of drawers, refinished pine, rectangular top w/a molded cornice over a pair of paneled

Shaker Canterbury Cupboard-Chest

cupboard doors w/simple wooden knobs above a case of six long graduated drawers w/wooden knobs, plinth base, Canterbury, New Hampshire, 19th c., 20 x 39¾", 72" h. (ILLUS.)............. **17,600**

Shaker Deaconess' Desk

Desk, deaconess', butternut & tiger stripe maple, a low backrail over the hinged angled lift top w/molded edges opening to a desk box raised on a simple turned pedestal on a tripod base w/flattened cabriole legs, refinished, Enfield, Connecticut, ca. 1830, 17 x 21½", 29" h. (ILLUS.)............................ **6,900**

Drying rack, walnut, tall rectangular uprights supported on shaped shoe feet & joined by three long rectangular rails, mortised construction, old worn finish, 28" w., 39" h. (one foot replaced).......... **165**

Dust pan, floor-type, tin & wood, the wide, flat U-form tin bottom w/conforming high tapering upright sides w/a slender turned wood upright handle at the back, 34½" l. (some soldered & glued repairs) **330**

Foot warmer, wood & punched tin, oval board top & base w/cylindrical tin sides punched w/pinwheel designs, attributed to Elder Abraham Perkins of the Church family, Enfield, New Hampshire, old tag "Leavitt Collection," 11" l. **798**

Grain shovel, wood w/some curl, a wide blade w/squared rim trimmed w/tin edging & rounded upturned back w/long extended handle w/cut-out hand grip, old patina, impressed initials "GMW" for George M. W. Wichersham (1806-88), Mount Lebanon cabinetmaker, 44" l. (rusted tin edge repair) 385

Harvest table, walnut, long two-board top overhanging a mortised & pinned deep apron on square tapering legs, old soft finish, Union Village, Ohio, 24 x 77", 28½" h. 2,530

Hearth brush, a long slender turned handle w/acorn terminal, thick short wood crossbar w/long black bristles, old worn finish, 21½" l. (bristles incomplete) 72

Jug, stoneware, cylindrical lower white body w/cylindrical dark brown shoulder & small neck w/loop strap handle, the body w/a blue transfer-printed label "Shaker Brand Ketchup—E.D. Pettengill Co. Portland, ME.," 14" h. (minor chips) 880

Magazines, "The Manifesto," Canterbury, New Hampshire, Vol. XIII, 12 issues, 1893, the set. 105

Measuring stick, walnut, long slender flat stick w/turned oblong knob handle, marked off in 4½" intervals & scratch-carved ¼", ½", 9" & 18", old patina, overall 39" l. 165

Rocking chair w/arms, child's, turned back stiles w/turned pointed finials flanking the replaced red tape back, open shaped arms w/mushroom hand grips on the baluster-turned arm supports over the replaced red tape seat, simple turned legs w/inset rockers, double front & side rungs, single rear rung, old but not original dark finish, Mount Lebanon, 28½" h. . . 550

From left: Mt. Lebanon Rocker with Arms
Early Shaker Armless Rocker

Rocking chair w/arms, maple, a slender shawl rail across the top of the tall back above four gently arched slats between simple turned stiles, flattened curved open arms w/mushroom hand rests over simple baluster-turned arm supports above the replaced splint seat, simple turned legs inset into rockers & joined by

double stretchers at the front & sides, Mt. Lebanon, New York, 1880-1930, repair to two legs, 42½" h. (ILLUS.). 1,265

Rocking chair w/arms, painted wood, ladder-back style w/four wide gently arched slats & a shawl bar at the top joining the turned stiles, shaped flat arms w/mushroom hand grips above baluster-turned arm supports, replaced blue & grey tape seat, worn down to original finish, No. 7, 40" h. 825

Rocking chair without arms, maple, the tall back w/three gently arched slats joining simple turned stiles w/pointed knob finials above the replaced tape seat, legs inset into rockers & joined by double stretchers at the front & sides, old refinishing, Canterbury, New Hampshire, 1830-40, 40" h. (ILLUS.) 690

Rug, hooked rag, rectangular w/multi-colored speckled design w/a red & olive green border, attributed to Canterbury, New Hampshire, 23 x 38" 220

Scarf, silk, square of fine grey silk outlined in a bright blue stripe, Pleasant Hill & South Union Communities, Kentucky, mid-19th c., framed, 30" sq. 1,093

Sewing box, brown leather, rectangular small box w/brown silk binding & interior, includes steel scissor, silver closure shows three Shaker sisters in relief, 4¼" l. 72

Sewing box, cover w/cloth pincushion, oval bentwood, two finger lappets in the base & one in the cover, the cover w/domed pincushion covered in worn & tattered white & black plaid silk over homespun, light natural varnish finish, Canterbury, New Hampshire, 3¾" l. 1,045

Early Shaker Sewing Steps

Sewing steps, pine & poplar, two steps w/arched sides & a varnished stain, New Lebanon, New York, 1850-75, 13⅛ x 15¾", 15¼" h. (ILLUS.). 2,645

Shawl, woven wool, tiny plaid design in charcoal grey & white w/fringe, Ethel Hudson, Canterbury, New Hampshire, 36 x 74" 66

Side chair, maple, ladder-back style w/three arched slats between the turned stiles w/ovoid finials, woven tape faded green & tan seat, simple turned legs w/double stretchers at the front & sides, single one at the back, back legs w/tilters, Canterbury, New Hampshire, refinished, 41¼" h............................ **1,320**

Side chair, the tall back w/three gently arched slats between the turned stiles w/oblong turned finials, a replaced tape seat in mauve, yellow & sage green, simple turned legs w/double front & side stretchers & a single rear stretcher, old finish, Perkins Barlow, Mount Lebanon, New York, 40¾" h...................... **770**

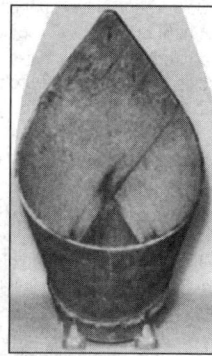

Kentucky Shaker Sieve

Sieve, bentwood, rounded shape w/tall pointed back & woven horsehair sieve, old patina, attributed to Pleasant Hill, Kentucky, 9" h. (ILLUS.)................. **358**

Stand, cherry, nearly square two-board top w/molded edges widely overhanging a narrow apron w/a single drawer w/turned wood knob, slender tall round turned legs, old dark varnish stain finish, 19th c., 18½ x 18¾", 27" h. (minor age cracks, one front post w/nailed repair) **330**

Storage box, cov., oval bentwood, three finger lappets in base & one in cover, copper tacks, old refinishing, 9½" l. (minor edge damage on cover) **275**

Storage box, cov., oval bentwood, three finger lappets in base & one in cover w/tack construction, old forest green paint, Sabbathday Lake, Maine, 10¾" l. **2,035**

Storage box, cov., oval bentwood, three finger lappets on base & one on the lid, copper tacks, old white repaint over grey, 12" l. (minor age cracks in cover, one w/old plastic wood repair)................ **495**

Sugar bucket, cov., stave construction w/two interlaced wooden bands, arched bentwood swing handle, old yellow paint, Watervliet, New York, 12½" d., 12½" h. **605**

Tea table, maple, round wide top tilting above a turned tapering pedestal on a tripod base w/flat cabriole legs ending in snake feet, wrought-iron catch, top of column threaded to screw into hinge block, old refinishing, attributed to Watervliet, New York, 19th c., 36" d., 26¾" h...................... **2,310**

Shaker Painted Wall Cupboard

Wall cupboard, painted pine, rectangular top w/rounded edges slightly overhangs the case w/a single wide flat door w/wooden thumb latch & small wooden knob opening to a single shelf all above a single long narrow bottom drawer, old red translucent stain, minor imperfections, mid-19th c., 8 x 12", 16¾" h. (ILLUS.)...... **1,093**

Wall cupboard, painted pine, rectangular top above a case w/a tall recessed panel door opening to two shelves, original turned wood pull & original bittersweet orange wash, Mt. Lebanon, New York, 1830-40, 18¼ x 25", 41¾" h. (imperfections)...................... **3,220**

Wardrobe, painted wood, rectangular top w/narrow coved cornice above a tall, narrow two-panel door flanked by wide side boards, interior shelves, on simple bracket feet, original bright red wash, probably Canterbury, New Hampshire, third quarter 19th c., 17½ x 48", 83½" h. (hardware changes, only one shelf original) **5,175**

Work table, poplar, wide rectangular three-board top widely overhanging the deep apron, on turned tapering legs w/square top posts, mortised & pinned apron, cleaned down to traces of old white paint, Union Village, Ohio, 36 x 61", 28¼" h...................... **2,200**

Yarn reel, wooden, table-clamp base w/slender central shaft supporting an expandable crisscross slat framework, small cup finial, old yellow varnish, Hancock, Massachusetts, 19th c., 20" h. (one member w/damage, one retied) **143**

SHEET MUSIC

"Adventures Of Icabod And Mr. Toad (The)," Disney movie, VG $25

"Amazonenritt," ca. 1900, published by Leipzip (GV) 12

"Angel Face," 1905, cover depicts black female w/wings, added bonus photo of Chris Smith, Billy & Estelle Johnson (VG-) 33

Any Old Place In Yankee Land...

"Any Old Place In Yankee Land Is Good Enough For Me," 1908, words by Alex Rogers, music by Will Marion Cook & Chris Clark (ILLUS.) 27

"Biggest Thing In A Soldier's Life (The)," 1918, WWI, large (G+) 10

"Blue Blazes Rag," 1919, by Arthur Sizemore, published by Kremer, large size (VG) 326

"Circus Parade," 1914, cover by E.T. Paull (EX) . . 45

"Der Faderland For Mine," 1907, from comic show "About Town"(VG-) 16

Do Ya, Dontcha, Wontcha?

"Do Ya, Dontcha, Wontcha?," 1930, words by Bernie Grossman, music by Lou Handman, from movie "See America Thirst" (ILLUS.) 40

"Glokenspiel Gavotte," ca. 1900, male angel & lady butterfly w/bells on cover, full color litho (VG) 8

"Goodbye My Soldier Boy, God Bless You," by IULA, WWI, large size (VG-) 11

How Sorry You'll Be

"How Sorry You'll Be (Wait'll You See)," by Bert Kalmar & Harry Ruby (ILLUS.) 30

"I Ain't Got Enough To Pass Around," 1921, by Fred Johnson & J. Branneb (VG) 22

"I Want To Be Loved By A Soldier," WW1, by Abner Silver (EX) 10

"In Love With Love, The Stepping Stones," 1923, Raggedy Ann and Andy on cover, rough edges on inside page (VG) 12

"India Rubber, A Slow Drag," 1913, by "Duke" Baiers (VG+) 15

"It's A Helluva, Swelluva, Helluva Life, In The Army," WWII, by Pvt. J. C. Lewis (G) 10

The Jelly Roll Blues

"Jelly Roll Blues (The)," 1915, by Ferd Morton,VG- (ILLUS.) 39

"Liberty & Union," by J.T. Wamelink, patriotic cover design w/the American eagle above crossed flags & a vignette of Liberty, published in Pittsburgh, 1864, 6 pp., 10¼ x 13¼" (disbound, slight soiling) 54

"Lost On The Lady Elgin," 1860, by Henry C. Work (VG-) 20

"Mickey Mouse's Birthday Party,"" 1936, cover depicts Disney characters playing on cake (VG+) 65

John Philip Sousa's Exposition March

The Teenie Weenie Waltz

Trouble Darktown Worries

SIGNS & SIGNBOARDS

*Also see: ADVERTISING ITEMS,
BREWERIANA, COCA-COLA COLLEC-
TIBLES, DRUGSTORE & PHARMACY ITEMS
and TOBACCIANA.*

Budweiser Poster

Beer, "Budweiser" poster, framed lithograph
entitled "Custer's Last Fight," depicts
battle scene w/company logos at each
bottom corner w/"Anheuser-Busch, St.
Louis Missouri, U.S.A. - World's Largest
Brewery - Home of Budweiser & Other
Anheuser-Busch Fine Beers" (ILLUS.) $300

Bootmaker, trade sign, carved wood large model of a high-top boot, tin weather cap, old gold repaint w/red & blue, from Ohio shoe store, 27¾" h. (age cracks, weathering, glued repair). **2,200**

Fleers Gum Sign

Chewing gum, "Fleers Bubble Gum," lithographed tin, red w/black & white package marked "Fleers Dubble Bubble Gum - 1¢," in center w/"Thanks! - Call again for ---" above & "Fleers Dubble Bubble Gum" below, few dents & scratches around edges, 3¾ x 6⅞" (ILLUS.) . . **143**

Chewing gum, "Oh Boy Gum," tin, color lithographed w/a half-length 'fade-away' portrait of a smiling young boy against a black background, a small elf whispering in his ear while he holds a selection of the gums in one hand, yellow lettering at bottom "It's Pure!," scratches, 8 x 16" **286**

"Missing Miss" Cigar Sign

Cigars, "Missing Miss," tin octagonal sign w/rolled edge, entitled "Viola," lithographed bust portrait of beautiful young woman w/long brown hair, wearing a low-cut dress w/red scarf draped over shoulder, reading "Missing Miss" at the top w/"5¢" on each side & "Cigar - Tony Bennauer Mfr., Mendota, Ill.," dated 1908, by Meek Co., minor flaking & surface rust, 14½" (ILLUS.). **661**

Cigars, "Petoskey Chief 5¢ Cigar," lithographed paper, a bust portrait of a Native American chief w/feathered headdress, an expansive landscape in the distance, reads "Try A Petoskey Chief - Our Best 5¢ Cigar," wide flat wood frame, repaired tear in lower corner, overall soiling, 27½ x 36". **3,795**

City limits, "City of Ardmore," one-side oval porcelain, dark green ground w/outer band printed in black on white "City of Ardmore" w/stars, a central oval w/scenic vignettes in brown, white & green showing a steer, oil rigs & a motor boat, 10½ x 16" (chips at grommet holes). **303**

"Piley's Cream Station" Sign

Cream station, "Piley's Cream Station," porcelain, two-sided, rectangular, dark blue ground w/white lettering reading "Piley's Cream Station," two holes at top, 17 x 22" (ILLUS.) **165**

Rare "Keen Kutter" Sign

Cutlery/tools, "Keen Kutter," porcelain, flat two-sided sign reading "E. C. Simmons - KEEN KUTTER - Cutlery and Tools," white letters on red ground, several edge & hole chips, 11 x 14" (ILLUS.) **440**

Fire extinguishers, "Pyrene," die-cut color lithographed cardboard, color nighttime scene w/an open early auto hood w/the engine ablaze standing out from background to form 3-D effect, a young father using a fire extinguisher on the fire w/his wife & baby standing behind him,

Early Pyrene Fire Extinguisher Sign

oval in upper corner contains wording "Pyrene Kills Auto Fires," ca. 1920s, soiling, creases, 21" w., 32½" h. (ILLUS.) **825**

Flour, "Pillsbury's," copper self-framed lithographed metal, leafy-scroll embossed flanged self-frame around a rectangular color sign w/a large spread-winged eagle w/banner in its beak atop a large flour barrel w/a busy port in the background & above a vignette factory scene, reads "Chas. A. Pillsbury & Co. - Merchant Millers - America's Finest - Pillsbury's Best, Minneapolis, Minn. (on barrel) - For Sale Here," minor water spotting in corner, 24 x 30" **4,675**

Mobil Gasoline Flange-type Sign

Gasoline, Mobil gasoline, flange-type, two-sided porcelain, a die-cut figure of the red Pegasus logo mounted in an angled iron bracket w/scrolling ends, touch-up to overall chips, some fading, water stain, soiling & scratches, 32½ x 40½" (ILLUS.)... **1,760**

Gasoline, "Phillips 66," two-sided shield-shaped porcelain, red lettering on black at top & black & red below, "SPS 57" at bottom, 29½" w., 29½" h. (chip to numeral each side, minor edge chipping) **495**

Gasoline, "Red Crown Gasoline," round two-sided porcelain, white ground w/an outer ring w/the wording in red, the center

circle w/a large red, white & blue crown symbol, 42" d. (slight touch-up to ground, minor scratches & soiling) **715**

Gasoline, "Shell Gasoline," two-sided die-cut porcelain, shell-shaped, orange w/red lettering, 24½" w., 24½" h. (minor chips, scratches, soiling)..................... **660**

Ground oats, "'Meckumfat' Regd. Sussex Ground Oats" color lithographed paper on cardboard, rectangular, advertising above & below a colorful farmyard scene showing various types of fowl including ducks, chickens & turkeys, "To Be Obtained From All High Class Shops" across the bottom, 14½ x 18¾" **275**

Ice cream, "North Pole Real Ice Cream," neon-type, green neon lettering against a black background, soiling, 7" deep, 12 x 26" .. **231**

Ink, "Sanford's Inks," embossed tin, rectangular, a large central display of various ink products below the wording "Faultless: Sanford's Inks and Mucilage," wooden framed w/stamped brass corner trim, some in-painting, overall scratching & chipping, 19½ x 26" **2,990**

Motor oil, "Mobiloil," porcelain standing curb-type, the sign w/a rounded upper portion w/the red flying Pegasus logo on white, the lower narrow rectangular portion w/"Mobiloil" in white on a black ground, raised on a slender iron post w/a round foot, 30½" w., 64" h. (minor touch-up, scratches & water stain, hole at bottom where sign meets post) **770**

Die-cut Shell Motor Oil Sign

Motor oil, "Shell Motor Oil," two-sided porcelain die-cut, in the shape of an upright rectangular can, grey top, side in black w/yellow-outlined red lettering & large shell logo in the center, "Shell-Mex Ltd." & London address at the bottom, minor chips on graphic & edges, ragged edges & part of one grommet hole missing, 15¾ x 20" (ILLUS.).............. **660**

Motor oil, "Pennzoil, Outboard Motor Oil, 100% Pure Pennsylvania, Safe Lubrication," porcelain sign above cast-iron lollipop base, curb-type, marked "Ing Rich Beaver Falls, PA.," 32" w., 46½" h. (repainted base, minor chips & scratches) **358**

Motor supplies, "Bure Power Carburetor Center," plastic & metal, electric, rectangular w/yellow, red & black on white background, 2½ x 24¼", 11¾" h. **242**

Optometrist sign, polychrome & gilt-decorated zinc, double-sided model of large spectacles w/a arched banner below w/worn lettering reading "C.F. Hussey Optometrist," late 19th c., 41" l., 12½" h. (imperfections) **2,645**

Outboard motors, "Evinrude and Elto," embossed tin, rectangular reading "Evinrude and Elto Outboard Motors - Hooded Power - Floated in Rubber - Bruce L. Pierce, Lake Tippecanoe, Leesburg, Ind.," orange, black & white, 11¾ x 23¾" **479**

Pocket Watch Trade Sign

Pocket watch, trade-type, carved & painted wood & metal, flattened silhouetted form painted on both sides w/white face & black Roman numerals, gold rim, suspended between two brackets, late 19th c., 27" h., 18" w. (ILLUS.) **3,450**

"Snoboy" Fruits & Vegetables Sign

Produce, "Snoboy," porcelain, round w/central logo of snowman wearing red mittens & earmuffs & "Snoboy - 'Picked for flavor' - Fresh Fruits and Vegetables"

in yellow & white letters, ca. 1940s, bright colors & luster finish, several small chips, 20" d. (ILLUS.) **168**

Salt, "Diamond Crystal Shaker Salt," easel-backed color lithographed cardboard, rectangular, an orange background w/two hands holding a can of the product & filling a salt shaker, black wording reads "Ask For Diamond Crystal - Diamond Crystal Shaker Salt," reverse dated "4/22," rounded corner, 10¼ x 15" **303**

Scales, "Fairbanks-Morse," porcelain, black w/white letters reading "Fairbanks-Morse Scales," by Burdick, Chicago, Illinois, bright luster finish, 9 x 50" **77**

Shotgun shells, "Remington/UMC," embossed tin, rectangular featuring "Nitro Club Shotshell" box & reads "Arms & Ammunition - Complete Stocks - High Quality - Low Prices - Soo Hdw. Co. 300-302 Ashmun St. - Sault Sainte Marie, Mich.," lithographed by American Art Works, Coshocton, Ohio, 9⅝ x 27½" **380**

Winchester Shell Sign

Shotgun shells, "Winchester," case insert string-hung paper on cardboard lithograph w/colorful graphic of pheasant w/wings & tail feathers spread against a blue background & product container w/"Winchester Repeater Paper Shot Shells - Smokeless Powder" on top & "24 Winchester 12 Ga. Repeater Paper Shot Shells...." w/large W superimposed on front above two shells, by American Litho Co., New York, 9¼ x 13¾" (ILLUS.) **2,530**

Shotgun shells, "Dead Shot," lithographed paper w/original metal bands at top & bottom, scene of a large falling mallard drake w/hunter in bottom distance, reads "Smokeless - Black" at the bottom, some minor creasing, minor edge tears, wide flat frame, 24 x 33" **3,508**

Soap, "White King Washing Soap," tin lithographed sign depicting the product box on a red ground w/"Granulated" in white letters in upper corner, "White King Washing Machine Soap" on box w/logo & "It Takes So Little And It Goes So Far," 10 x 14" (few minor dings in outside border) .. **259**

"Salada" Tea Curb Sign

Tea, "Salada," die-cut porcelain, two-sided, model of a stylized teapot in orange w/black wording "'Salada' Tea Served Here," curb-type w/cast-iron base, minor edge chips, 42" w., 29½" h. (ILLUS.) **793**

Michelin Tire Sign

Tires, "Michelin," one-sided porcelain, rectangular w/pointed bottom edge, dark blue ground w/yellow name at the top & running white Michelin man w/black tire, new old stock, 27 x 31½" (ILLUS.) **330**

Early Pennsylvania Tire Sign

Tires, "Pennsylvania Oilproof Vacuum Cup Tires," color lithographed paper, a half-length portrait of a lovely young lady wearing a pale green dress & a large straw hat w/green trimmings, portrait titled "Euphemia," advertising in lower section, also printed "Pennsylvania

Rubber Company, Jeannette, Pa. U.S.A.," early 20th c., in a narrow oak frame, minor frame wear, 25¼ x 35½" (ILLUS.) **440**

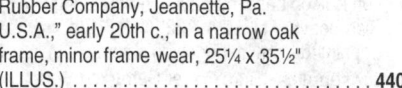

Model Smoking Tobacco Sign

Tobacco, "Model Smoking Tobacco," porcelain, rectangular w/white lettering on a red ground, depicts bald gentleman w/ large mustache holding a smoking pipe w/"Yes, I said 10¢ MODEL Smoking Tobacco," chipping near hanging holes (ILLUS.) **160**

Fordson Tractors Sign

Tractor, "Fordson Tractors" porcelain, two piece, black w/white lettering reading "Service Fordson" w/"Tractors" on a smaller sign suspended by chains (ILLUS.) . . . **375**

Truck, "GMC General Motors Trucks," round neon, wall-type, glass & metal, orange, black & white decoration & lettering, 18" d. (new face w/original face included) **633**

Truck dealer, "GMC Trucks," two-sided porcelain, long rectangular form w/rounded lower corners, light & dark green w/"GMC" in a small circle above "Trucks" in large letters, 24 x 48" (minor scratches & edge chips) **572**

"Jas.E.Pepper" Whiskey Advertising Sign

Whiskey, "Jas.E.Pepper & Co.," reverse painting on glass w/center scene of the Pepper distillery buildings w/"Jas.E.Pepper & Co. - Pepper Distillery - Lexington, KY." above flanked by shield forms reading "'Pepper' Distillery Hand Made Sour Mash Jas.E.Pepper & Co. Distillers Lexington, KY." & "The Oldest and Best Brand of Whiskey - Made in Kentucky," w/wide ornate frame (ILLUS.) **4,000**

Whiskey, "Pride of Kentucky Whiskey," lithographed paper, a colorful scene of a wide landscape w/the distillery in the distance & a lovely lady in riding habit w/a handsome horse in the right foreground beside a large barrel of whiskey, advertising across the top & bottom, copyrighted in 1896, molded giltwood frame, some border spotting, staining & soiling, 39 x 51". **2,875**

Carrollton Woolen Mills Advertisement

Woolen mill, "Carrollton Woolen Mills," lithographed paper w/bust portrait of pretty young blonde girl wearing a ruffled red & white bonnet tied under her chin, reading "Compliments of Carrollton Woolen Mills - Our Brands of Jeans - 'Eagle Valley' - 'Garlands' - 'Port William'" & "Jeans and Jeans Pants - Double Seamed - Patent Machine Tacked and Warranted to Stand the Storm - Brands of Pants - Carrollton Eagle Valley No. 10," framed (ILLUS.) **45**

SILHOUETTES

These cut-out paper portraits in profile were named after Etienne de Silhouette, Louis XV's unpopular minister of finance and an amateur profile cutter. As originally applied, the term was synonymous with cheapness, or anything reduced to its simplest state. These substitutes for the more expensive oil painting or miniatures

were popular from about 1770 until 1850 when daguerreotype images replaced the vogue. Silhouettes may be either hollow-cut, with the head cut away leaving the white paper frame for mounting against a dark background, or the profile itself may be cut from black paper and pasted to a light background.

Bust portrait of a young woman, hollow-cut & backed w/black cloth, facing left w/her hair pulled up & curls over her forehead, wearing a high-waisted dress w/a high ruffled collar, in a small molded pine frame, 4½ x 6¼" **$94**

Bust portrait of an Officer in Uniform, miniature, ink & watercolor on paper, wearing a red tunic & gold braided epaulettes, oval, signed in lower right by Robert Norman, Anglo-American, first half 19th c., framed, 3 x 4" (toning, creases,minor staining & pigment loss) **460**

Bust portraits of a young man & woman, hollow-cut paper, double-style, the facing pair each within a black & gilt-trimmed eglomisé glass mat w/oval openings, she w/her hair pulled up in back & held by a tall comb, he w/a high white shirt collar, one w/ink detail, the other w/pencil detail, in a narrow molded giltwood frame, first half 19th c., 8¼" w., 5½" h. (eglomisé wear) . . **468**

Bust profile of a man, hollow-cut, shown facing right wearing a high-collared coat, traces of gilded detail & embossed gilded paper oval liner, flat rectangular black lacquered frame w/oval brass-trimmed opening & gilded fitings, first half 19th c., 4¾ x 5½" **165**

Full-length portrait of a seated lady w/a letter, miniature, ink & watercolor on paper w/polychrome & bronzed highlights, unsigned, first half 19th c., framed, 7¼ x 9½" (toning, staining, minor foxing, minor pigment loss) **546**

Full-length Gentleman's Silhouette

Full-length portrait of gentleman, cut profile of the man facing right wearing a long-tailed frock coat & holding a top hat & cane, mounted on a black & white lithographed landscape background w/a rail fence, identified on the back as "William Ingold Schermerharn," lithograph glued on a backing w/stains & damage, in a beveled pine frame, first half 19th c., silhouette 10 x 12⅛ (ILLUS.) **440**

Group of eight portraits, hollow-cut, composed of four facing pairs of men & women, each woman w/her hair pulled up & held by a comb, each man wearing a high collar & narrow tie, cut-out fanned designs in each corner & leafy vertical bands between the groups of portraits, probably Pennsylvania, first half 19th c., in original molded wood frame, unsigned, 7⅛ x 9⅛" (toning staining, minor losses, minor insect damage to backing) **575**

Silhouette of Young Lady

Half-length profile of young lady, hollow-cut, portrait of dark-haired young lady holding a rose & book, watercolor, pen & ink on paper, American School, ca. 1830, 4¼ x 3¼" (ILLUS.) **345**

SODA FOUNTAIN COLLECTIBLES

The neighborhood ice cream parlor and drugstore fountain are pretty much a thing of the past as fast-food chains have sprung up across the country. Memories of the slower-paced lifestyle represented by the rapidly disappearing local soda fountain have spurred the interest of many collectors today. Anything relating to the soda fountains of old and the delicious concoctions they dispensed are much sought-after.

Three Soda Fountain Glasses

Glass, "Orange-Julep," flaring clear glass w/orange printing (ILLUS. left) **$44**

Glass, "Peerless - High Grade Soda Water," clear cylindrical glass w/red wording (ILLUS. center) **25**

Glass, "Suncrush Orange," tall slender waisted clear glass w/orange sun face & wording (ILLUS. right) **64**

XXX Cola Fountain Glass

Glass, "XXX Cola," clear flared glass w/orange printing (ILLUS.) **22**

Ice cream scoop, Gilchrist No. 31 w/wooden handle **35**

Heart-shaped Ice Cream Scoop

Ice cream scoop, heart-shaped, wooden handle, in original box, 11" l. (ILLUS.) **15,400**

Malted milk jar, "Borden's," aluminum **100**

Milk shake mixer, Hamilton Beach, green porcelain, triple head **500**

Sign, "Captain Kidd Beverages," lithographed tin, rectangular w/black border & narrow orange border around center scene of pirate on shore & galleon

Fine Captain Kidd Beverages Sign

offshore, printed in black, orange & white,
banner across top w/brand & further
wording below (ILLUS.) **1,650**

Sign, "Borden," one-sided tin, shows large
ice cream cone, Dairy Products
Advertising, Weston-Ontario, scratches,
soiling, bent corners, 24" w., 36" h. **127**

Richardson Root Beer Dispenser

Soda dispenser, "Richardson Root Beer,"
large wooden keg w/steel bands & double
spigots & drip tray at the front, on metal
feet, lift-off top, red & white applied sign
on side reads "RICHardson - Root Beer
- Rich in flavor," ca. 1950s (ILLUS.) **425**

World Record Hires Syrup Dispenser

Syrup dispenser, "Drink Hires 5¢," pottery,
tall slender waisted pedestal base w/long
metal spigot support bulbous bowl-form
top w/domed cover w/pointed knob finial,
green banding & black wording w/full-

color pictures of the Hires boy around the
body, Mettlach pottery, early 20th c.,
world record, 11" d., 14" h. (ILLUS.) **107,250**

Syrup dispenser, "Drink Hires It Is Pure"
front & back, ceramic, hour-glass shape
w/top pump, 11" h. without pump,
(hairline crack above "H" on one side) **805**

Syrup dispenser, "Drink Hires Root Beer,"
blue china, multiple images of
trademarked boy pointing & holding
mug w/"Drink Hires 5 cents" between
images, spigot base reads "America's
Health Drink Hires Rootbeer" &
"Hires Rootbeer is luscious and pure,"
Mettlach, Germany, 10½" d., 19" h. **48,300**

Orange-Crush Syrup Dispenser

Syrup dispenser, "Ward's Orange-Crush,"
pottery, large figural orange on rounded
green leaf-molded base w/white
blossoms, metal cap & pump spigot on
top, early 20th c. (ILLUS.) **1,500**

SPACE AGE COLLECTIBLES

*Although fiction novels about space
exploration have been around since the 19th
century, and such space fantasies as "Flash
Gordon" and "Buck Rogers" were popular in the
1930s, the modern Space Age started after World
War II. There have been dozens of space science
fiction movies and television shows produced
since the early 1950s when Russia and the
United States were locked in the "Space Race."
Our listings include items which were produced
to tie-in to all the movies, TV shows and works of
fiction released since the early 1950s. These
'fantasy' listings are arranged alphabetically by
the name of the character, show or movie. Also
see: CHARACTER COLLECTIBLES, TOYS and
LUNCH BOXES.*

Buck Rogers pocket watch, 1935, very
good, Ingraham **$900**

Buck Rogers Rocket Police Patrol spaceship, good, Marx 500

Buck Rogers "Solar Scout" badge 85

Buck Rogers Sonic Ray gun, w/original box, ca. 1952 185

Buck Rogers space racer, Wyandotte 160

Darth Vader head bank, ceramic, Roman Ceramics, ca. 1977, 6 x 6" 95

Lost In Space robot, good w/good box, Remco, 1966 375

Lost In Space robot model kit, Aurora, mint in box, never assembled. 190

Space Patrol "Space-O-Phone," w/original string attached, Ralston premium, 1950s...... 85

Tom Corbett Atomic Pistol

Tom Corbett, Space Cadet Atomic Pistol, plastic, blue body w/red trigger & clear lens cap on flashlight tip, Marx, w/original box, 1950s, excellent condition (ILLUS.) 468

Yoda Ceramic Bank

Yoda (Star Wars) bank, ceramic, figural, painted green, white & brown, Sigma (ILLUS.). . 85

SPORTS MEMORABILIA

BASKETBALL

Jersey, Larry Bird game-worn model, green w/black "Follow Through" patch on left shoulder, "Celtics 33" & "Bird 33" in white, original tagging sewn into bottom, 1989-90 (light wear) $2,385

Jersey, Larry Johnson game-worn model, greenish blue w/dark & light blue pinstripes, "Charlotte 2" on front in white, "Johnson" across shoulders, NBA insignia on upper left chest, original tags on tail, 1992-93, size 50" 2,443

Ticket, printed paper, first Chicago Bulls game, October 18, 1966, game against the San Francisco Warriors in Chicago, red & green on white, excellent unused condition 495

Trophy, gilt metal, 1960 Duke Championship model, detailed figure of player shooting at top, round black base w/gold band reading "Champions 1960" & raised ACC crest in center, 13" h. 1,030

Uniform, Philadelphia Sphas ABL type, off-white cotton knit w/blue stripe & "Philadelphia" sewn in felt across the chest & "8" on the back, includes navy shorts w/belt clasp, Spalding tag on jersey & John Wanamaker tag on shorts, 1930s, the set........................ 400

Usher's cap, Cincinnati Royals, royal blue w/wicker face & celluloid pin w/"USHER" in gilt-metal frame, white bill under clear plastic, worn at Cincinnati Gardens........ 1,761

BOXING

Book, "Fights For the Championship and Celebrated Prize Battles," 1855, hardcover, anthology of boxing fights compiled by the editor of "Bell's Life In London" (partially split at spine) 190

Boxing gloves, fight-worn gloves for Gene Tunney, supple red leather, worn at exhibition fight at Stanford University, original black laces, Spalding, 1920s, pr. 3,367

Broadside, Joe Louis, "Roar of the Crowd," two-sided, nine illustrations 65

Cabinet photograph, John L. Sullivan, late 19th c. 150

Magazine, 1975 "Victory Sports," special edition on Muhammad Ali, very good condition 20

Sugar Ray Robinson Passport

Passport, Sugar Ray Robinson, U.S. passport issued to "Walker Smith known as Sugar Ray Robinson," dated April 25, 1958, nice photo of Robinson w/signature above (ILLUS.) **2,712**

Photograph, Sonny Liston, black & white posed shot in boxing stance, facsimile signature reads "Best wishes from World Heavyweight Champion, Sonny Liston," his real autograph just below, 3½ x 6" **460**

Poster, Ali vs Frazier fight, on-site promotional billboard in cardboard, yellow ground printed w/standing photos of each fighter below black & red wording reading "Fight II...The Big Fight Everyone Is Waiting To See - Madison Sq. Garden - Mon. Jan. 28th - Main Event - 12 Rounds - Joe Frazier vs Muhammed Ali...," 1974, 23 x 30" **2,463**

Poster, side-show type, "In Person ... Jack Johnson - X Heavyweight Champion of the World!...,"cardboard, printed in red & black on white, shows a young Johnson in the lower corner, produced in 1941 while Johnson was appearing at a circus-type museum, autographed by Johnson, 14 x 22" **2,436**

Recruiting poster, World War II-type, features Joe Louis in uniform against a blue ground, black on white wording reads "Pvt. Joe Louis Says... "We're going to do our part...and we'll win because we're on God's side," 1942, 7 x 10" . . **983**

Stereo view card, Sullivan vs Kilrain, 1899, by Geo. Barker, Niagara Falls, New York, shows Kilrain knocked through the ropes by Sullivan, orange border **505**

Ticket stub, "Jeffries vs Sharkey," October 27, 1899, Heavyweight Championship, $20 ticket, Coney Island, New York, excellent condition, 2⅝ x 3⅝" **536**

FOOTBALL

Charm bracelet, enameled gold plate, 1910 Notre Dame, two miniature footballs attached to heavy chain, one 14k gold ball engraved "1910" & inlaid w/blue enamel w/ "ND" for Notre Dame, very light wear **903**

Countertop advertising display, "Chesterfield Cigarettes," die-cut cardboard printed in color, an open pack of cigarettes above a brown football printed in white w/"Winning on Mildness," 1950s, 16 x 23". **127**

Football, 1959 Baltimore Colts team-signed ball, white w/black bands, signed by 32 members of the team, slightly deflated, overall excellent condition **661**

Jersey, Buffalo Bills, blue cloth, game-worn by Art Baker, three-year style w/grey wording on front "Baker - 33," & "Baker" on the back, marked "Rawlings 44" & wash tags sewn-in, 1960-61 . . . . **1,794**

Magazine, "Life," September 29, 1947, Johnny Lujack on cover **20**

Pinback button, souvenir-type, printed metal w/blue ground centered by a narrow yellow oval w/full-length image of football player, printed in red across the top "ILLINOIS," across the bottom in yellow & red "Captain Red Grange - 1925" (blue slightly faded) **633**

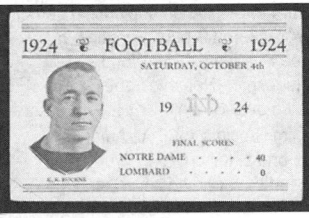

Early Knute Rockne Postcard

Postcard, souvenir-type, Knute Rockne, bust photo of "K.K. Rockne" in lower left, white printed in blue & pale green, top front w/"1924 - Football - 1924" over "Saturday, October 4th - 1924" over "Final Scores - Notre Dame...40 - Lombard...0," reverse postmarked "Notre Dame" & inscribed "Hello Katy. This sure was a good game, for Notre Dame, Bill" (ILLUS.) **1,094**

Program & ticket voucher, Rose Bowl, 1937, Washington vs Pittsburgh, cover in red & blue lettering on white above a black ground w/red & blue players, blue wording on white across bottom, lists both rosters & photomontages of the teams, matching student voucher filled out in pencil, 2 pcs. **1,072**

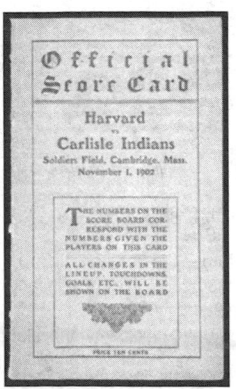

Early Harvard Program-Score Card

Program-scorecard, "Official Score Card - Harvard vs Carlisle, Indiana... November 1, 1902...," pale green printing on cream paper, near mint (ILLUS.) **222**

Sheet music, "Maybe It's Love," 1930, w/All-American football team pictured on cover **85**

Souvenir book, January 1939 (50th anniversary) Pasadena "Tournament of Roses," w/Shirley Temple on cover as Grand Marshall **150**

Ticket, "Super Bowl VI," 1972, full ticket, in New Orleans, Miami Dolphins vs Dallas Cowboys, printed in color, punch holes for entry, near mint, 2⅝ x 6½" **986**

Ticket stub, 1958 NFL championship game, pink w/black, red & purple printing, reads "Yankee Stadium - 1958 World's Championship - Reserve $150," Baltimore over New York **616**

Trophy, Jim Brown's 1956 All-American trophy, brass, tall urn-form w/upturned loop handles & domed cover, stepped foot on cylindrical black base w/plaque inscribed "Jim Brown - All-American half-back at Syracuse University - Holder of Athlete of the Year Award in Syracuse for 1956," cup itself engraved "Herald Journal Ninth Annual Award," 26" h. **2,226**

Usher's cap, "Green Bay Packers," green w/yellow printing & black bill, 1930s-40s, minor wear **383**

GOLF CLUBS

WOODEN SHAFTED

Abercrombie & Fitch, mid iron, model WG5, marked "Burke Monel" **60**

Abercrombie & Fitch, putter, model WH10, Burke Monel **60**

Aitken (Alex), brassie, splice head (S) **300**

Alloway Putter

Alloway, putter, oval head w/red guttie face insert (ILLUS.) **3,500**

Anderson (James), lofting iron, slightly dished smooth face, thick hosel, dark stained shaft, ca. 1890 . . . . **400**

Anderson (James), cleek, long thin blade, smooth face, 4½" hosel w/deep nicking, ca. 1875 . . . . **500**

Anderson (Jamie), putter, ca. 1880 (L) **4,800**

Anderson & Sons Iron

Anderson & Sons (R.), iron, crescent-shaped center shaft head (ILLUS.) **1,500**

Auchterlonie (D. & W.), driver, splice head, shaft stamp, ca. 1910 . . . . **150**

Ayers, (F.H.), iron, P.A. Vaile model, swan neck hosel, dot face (B) **600**

B. G. I. Company, brassie niblick, No. 97, New model, splice head **500**

B. G. I. Company, brassie, No. 92, straight face, splice head **225**

B. G. I. Company, driver, No. 500, one piece, straight face, B **1,500-2,000**

B. G. I. Company (Bridgeport Gun Implement, Co.) driver, No. 41, Simpson model, socket head **150**

Burke Golf Company, driver, Grand Prize series, No. 90, long narrow head **100**

Burke Golf Company, spoon, Grand Prize series, No. 67, Victory model **125**

Carrick (F. & A.), cleek, long face, 4½-5" hosel, straight line name stamp, cross cleek mark, ca. 1880 . . . . **650**

Dunn (Wm. Jr.), driver, short splice head, NY markings, dark color **550**

Fairfield, driver, No. 290, straight face, splice head **250**

Fairfield, gooseneck putting cleek, No. 202 . . . . . **125**

Forgan & Son (Robert), lofter, Prince of Wales plume mark, smooth face, long blade, ca. 1890 . . . . **150-300**

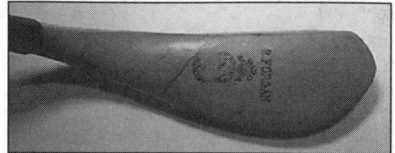

Forgan & Son Play Club

Forgan & Son (Robert), play club, long head, Prince of Wales plume mark over warrant cleek mark, ca. 1880 (ILLUS.) **5,000**

Gibson & Company (William), cleek,
leather face copied after Nicoll **1,800**

Gibson & Company (William), mashie,
Fairlie model (anti-shank) B **150**

Gibson & Co. Mashie Niblick

Gibson & Company (William), mashie
niblick, Dead'un model, drilled face holes,
star cleek mark, D (ILLUS.) **650**

Gibson & Company (William), medium
iron, Smith model (anti-shank), smooth
face (B). **200**

Golf Goods Manufacturing Company,
driver, model 104, splice head **500**

Hagen (Walter), putter, wood mallet
Gassiat-type, name in script. **400**

Hagen (Walter), woods, "WH" series, splice
head, brass face. **200**

Halley & Company (J.B.), putter, gun
metal, small mallet head, shell cleek mark. . . . **125**

Hendry & Bishop, niblick, Archie Compston
model, smooth concave face **350**

Hendry & Bishop, putter, Per Whit model,
round blade, hollow back (B) **400**

Holmac Putter

Holmac, Inc., putter, rudder pudder, T-
shaped brass, U (ILLUS.) **3,000**

Imperial Golf Company, putter, model 1, (A, S) . . **250**

Kempshall Manufacturing Company,
putter, Dunn model, black pyralin square
head, center shaft, brass face (U) **400**

Kroydon Golf Company, niblick, R 2, 50
degree, vertical lines on face **250**

Kroydon Golf Company, putter, S 32,
center shafted (A). **150**

Lee Company (Harry C.), driver,
dreadnought model, socket head, name
in script. **100**

MacGregor, bobby iron, Perfection series,
model B4, Maxwell style, full stagdot
face, round back. **125**

MacGregor, brassie, model 17, dot face (A) **250**

MacGregor, driving niblick, gun metal head,
name in oval, smooth face **750**

MacGregor, niblick, marked Willie Dunn,
smooth face, small head, Dunn "bowtie"
cleek mark **450**

Martin & Kirkaldy, baffy, splice head, full
sole plate **225**

Martin & Kirkaldy, driver, Andrew Kirkaldy
autograph model, dreadnought socket head . . **175**

McEwan & Son, niblick, guttie ball period,
medium size head, smooth face, Stewart
serpent cleek mark. **275**

McEwan & Son, play club, feather
ball period, large thistle stamp,
ca. 1780 (L). **25,000-30,000**

Morris (Tom), niblick, guttie ball period,
smooth face, small head **450**

Tom Morris Putter

Morris (Tom), putter, guttie ball period,
cylindrical iron head (ILLUS.) **2,500**

Nicoll, George, niblick, small head, name in
arc, before 1898. . . . . **350**

O-V-B, cleek, model 731, Carruthers hosel **100**

Ogilvie (Dave), spoon, pick-up model **400**

Park & Son (William), play club, Willie Sr.,
long head (L). **3,000-7,000**

Patrick & Son (A.), brassie, Perfector
model, triangle face insert, 20th C. **200**

Paxton (Peter), lofter, smooth face,
Eastbourne address, made by W. Wilson **750**

Reach Company (A.J.), driver, model 56R,
splice head, Keystone cleek mark **100**

Reach Company (A.J.), wood set, model 598. . . **325**

Ross (Donald), brassie, socket head,
crossed-clubs cleek mark. **150**

Sayers (Bernard), driver, light colored head,
ca. 1885 (S) **400**

Sayers (Bernard), putter, Benny model,
grooved sole, stainless. **150**

Scott (A.H.), driver, fork-splice head (B) **400**

Scott (A.H.), putter, Stymie model, concave
face. **150**

Simpson (Robert), driver, Bulger splice
head, ash shaft (S). **900**

Simpson (Robert), driver, marked
"Compressed" (B)...................... 350
Slazenger & Sons, putter, gun metal blade,
marked "Slazenger & Sons" 175
Spalding & Brothers Company (A.G.),
driver, Clan series, splice head 450
Spalding & Brothers Company (A.G.), mid
iron, Gold Medal series, fitted w/lard
perforated metal shaft (U) 4,000
Spalding & Brothers Company (A.G.),
putter, Clan series, iron blade 400
St. Andrew Golf Company, brassie, socket
head, patented Grypta grip............... 300
St. Andrew Golf Company, driver, HBC
model, stripe top, ivory face & backweight.... 200
Standard Golf Company, duplex club, RL2
model, 2-sided head..................... 600
Standard Golf Company, putter, KL model,
extra long nose (L) 400
Stewart (Thomas), niblick, giant
head, line face........................ 1,600

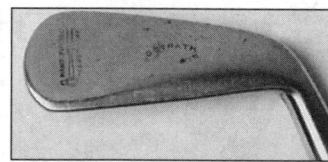

Strath Driving Iron

Strath (George), driving iron, Spalding Gold
Medal series, smooth face (ILLUS.)......... 100

Skyes Mid Iron

Sykes (William), mid iron, The Select,
Gourlay moon & star cleek mark, dot face
(ILLUS.) 60
Tucker (William), driving cleek, Defiance
brand, smooth face..................... 150
Winchester Arms Company, putter, model
6682, gun metal, flange sole 250
Winton Company (W.M.), mashie, model
42, Smith model (anti-shank) 175
Wright & Ditson, brassie, model XBE,
socket head, ivorine insert w/nine plugs...... 100

HOCKEY

Hockey stick, early miniature wood stick
w/varnished finish & black wrapping,
signed on both sides by members of the
1933 Stanley Cup teams, the Toronto
Maple Leaves & Boston Bruins, 39

names in all, top reads "Maple Leafs
Played Boston To 1-0 Win For NHL Title
April 3 '33...Worlds Record Overtime 105
Minutes," 44" l. (some cracks in varnish).... 1,643
Postcard, early color-tinted photo shot of
the 1906 Ottawa Silver Seven Stanley
Cup Champions, posing w/the Stanley
Cup & wearing red, black & white-striped
jerseys, blank back..................... 253

HORSE RACING

1980s Belmont Stakes Glasses

Belmont Stakes glass, 1985, clear frosted
cylindrical form printed in brown, green &
yellow (ILLUS. left)..................... 100
Belmont Stakes glass, 1989, frosted clear
cylindrical form printed in green, black &
red (ILLUS. right) 82
Kentucky Derby glass, frosted clear
cylindrical form, brown head portrait of
the 1948 winner 'Citation'................. 12

STATUARY - BRONZE, MARBLE & OTHER

*Bronzes and other statuary are increasingly
popular with today's collectors. Particularly
appealing are works by "Les Animaliers,"
the 19th-century French school of sculptors
who turned to animals for their subject matter.
These, together with figures in the Art Deco and
Art Nouveau taste, are common in a wide
price range.*

BRONZE

"Maiden with Pheasant"

Alliot, Lucien, figure of "Maiden with Pheasant," reclining female nude leaning back on one arm w/pheasant perched on other hand, patinated bronze, inscribed "L. Alliot," late 19th c., France, 34½" h. (ILLUS.) **$4,312**

Bareau, Georges, figure group, female nude holding a bow in one hand w/other arm outstretched, seated on large eagle, domed octagonal base, brown patina, inscribed "Georges-Bareau," 31½" h. **10,925**

Barrias, Louis Ernest, "Nature Revealing Herself to Science," figure of a robed semi-nude female w/arms stretched out to sides, gilt-bronze, inscribed "E. Barrias" & "Susse Fres Edtrs" w/circular foundry mark, mid19th - early 20th c., 23" h. **9,200**

Bofill, Antoine, "Le Travail," figure of a semi-nude male holding a tool in one hand, the other resting on a plow, brown patina, inscribed "Bofill" & square stepped base set w/a plaque inscribed "Le Travail - Par Bofill - Exp.on Des Beaux Arts Paris," early 20th c., 30" h. **2,875**

Bronze Figure of a Farm Girl

Boucher, Alfred, figure of a farm girl wearing a long skirt, weskit & head scarf, leaning on her pitchfork, medium brown patina, incised "Alfred Boucher" w/foundry mark "Doin de Cauville, Paris," mid 19th - early 20th c., 17¼" h. (ILLUS.) **920**

Charpentier, Alexandre, figure of nude female laying face down on a rock by a pool, head hanging over edge w/arms & hair touching the water, unpatinated, "Alexandre Charpentier," early 20th c., 6¾" h. **1,035**

Couston, Guillaume, "The Marly Horse Groups," rearing horses w/grooms, brownish black patination, after the

"The Marly Horse Groups"

original by Guillaume Couston, the Elder, signed "Couston," late 19th c., France, 20" h., 16½" l., pr. (ILLUS.) **2,070**

Dubucand, figural group of horse & rider, brown patina, inscribed "Dubucand," 19th c., 21" h. **4,025**

Bronze Bust of a Male Elf

Egaze, Emile, bust of a male elf w/beard, pointed ears, medium brown patina, bronze socle, signed & dated 1880, France, 15" h. (ILLUS.) **1,955**

Fournier, Paul, figure of a musician w/long hair, wearing jacket, fitted pants & hat, seated on a pillar & playing a lute, brown patina, inscribed "Paul Fournier," late 19th c., France, 28" h. **2,875**

Fremiet, Emmanuel, model of a standing mouse, gilt patinated, signed,19th c., France, 3" h. **748**

Figure of a Hound by Fremiet

Fremiet, Emmanuel, model of a standing
hound, brownish black patina,
signed,19th c., France, 9¼" h.,
10" l. (ILLUS.) **2,760**

Fremiet, Emmanuel, model of a recumbent
setter dog, on a molded oval base,
signed "E. Fremiet," dark brown &
blackish patina, France, ca. 1860-80, 9" l. **748**

Fugère, Henry, "Dancer," figure of a young
female posed on tip-toe w/other leg
raised, one arm out to the side & the
other raised, wearing a flaring skirt &
a short sleeveless bodice, carved ivory
torso w/gilt-bronze attire, inscribed
"H. Fugère" & stamped "4055," late
19th - early 20th c., France, 16¼" h. **5,750**

Gaudez, Adrien Etienne, figure of a female
in draped robe playing a stringed
instrument, dark brown patina, inscribed
"A. Gaudez - sc.," late 19th - early
20th c., 40" h. **6,900**

German bronze, model of two wrestling
lions, one recumbent, w/the other
standing over, dark brown patina on
marble base, signed "W.G." & stamped
"Guss V. Pierner & Franz, Dresden,"
early 20th c., 21" l. **2,530**

Caesar Crossing the Rubicon

Gerome, Jean Leon, figure group, depicting
Caesar on horseback, crossing the
Rubicon, after a model by Jean Leon
Gerome, 20" l. (ILLUS.) **3,737**

Gory, A., figure, depicting a partially clad
Middle Eastern maiden drawing a scarf
over her head, signed, 13½" h. **460**

Gilt-bronze & Marble Bust by Gory

Gory, Affortunato, bust of young lady,
carved marble face & hair, gilt-bronze
bonnet w/tie under chin & jacket, raised
on a green marble pedestal, signed
"A. Gory," ca. late 19th - mid 20th c.,
16" h. (ILLUS.). **5,175**

Guillemin, Emile Corioian Hippolyte,
figure of an Egyptian female wearing
loose flowing robe & long scarf on head,
large earrings, necklace & bracelets, one
arm raised & holding a scepter, gilt-
bronze, golden brown patina, inscribed
"E. Guillemin" & "F. Barbedienne.
Fondeur" w/foundry mark, mid-19th -
early 20th c., 29" h. **11,500**

Joan of Arc on Horseback

Huntington, Anna Hyatt, figure group,
depicting Joan of Arc wearing helmet &
armor on horseback w/sword raised aloft,
signed & stamped "Gorham Co.
Founders 0502," 18" h. (ILLUS.) **4,600**

Bronze German Shepherd

Joire, Jean model of a recumbent German
shepherd dog wearing a studded
collar, greenish black patination, signed
"J. Joire" & "Susse Freres" foundry mark,
ca. 1910, France, 11¼" l. (ILLUS.). **690**

Kauba, Carl, "St. George & the Dragon,"
figure of St. George seated on a rearing
horse above the dragon he has slain,
shaded brown patina, on a marble base,
America, late 19th - early 20th c., 15" h. . . . **5,750**

Kaube, C., figure, depicting an Indian
in buckskin w/head feathers &
elaborate chest protector, holding

From left: Polychrome Bronze Indian Figure
Figure of "Danseuse"

a rifle across one knee resting on
a rock, polychrome bronze, signed,
18" h. (ILLUS.)........................ **4,887**

Lenordey, Pierre, figure of a gladiator, titled
"Gladiateur," dark brown patination,
signed "P. Lenordey" & "V. Boyer,"
France, ca. 1870, 16" l................. **1,725**

Leonard, Agathon, "Danseuse," figure
of a female, her head tilted to the side,
her arms extended, wearing a long
flowing gown, gilt-bronze, inscribed
"A. Leonard - Sclp." & impressed "Susse
Frères Editeurs Paris - M.," late 19th -
early 20th c., France, 19½" h. (ILLUS.)..... **8,625**

Lorenzl, Josef, figure of a woman,
"Dancer," posed on tip-toe w/one arm
bent toward the body & the other raised
toward her shoulder, carved ivory head,
hair & hands w/floral design cold-painted
bronze close-fitting body suit & long
flowing neck scarf, green stone base,
inscribed "Lorenzl - Austria" & signed in
enamel "Crejo," ca. 1920s, 14¼" h........ **5,750**

Malissard, George, figure of a military
officer in uniform on horseback, medium
brown patina, on green marble base,
signed & dated "1927," w/foundry seal "A.
Valsuani, France," 22" h................ **1,725**

Marioton, Claudius, "Le Travail," figure of a
blacksmith holding tools, light brown
patina, inscribed "Marioton - sc," title
plaque inscribed "Le Travail," mid-19th -
early 20th c., 30" h.................... **2,300**

Martell, K.L., model of a seated bulldog,
wearing a studded collar, medium brown
patina, marble base, incised "K.L.
Martell," 9½" h. **1,610**

Mene, Pierre Jules, model of a whippet,
standing w/left front leg raised, looking at
a ball laying nearby, flat round base,
brownish black patina, signed, early - late
19th c., France, 6" h., 7" l. **863**

Moigniez, Jules, model group, crouching
whippet & spaniel dog on hind legs
playing w/a glove held in the whippet's
mouth, brown patina, signed, ca. 1880,
11½" l.............................. **2,415**

Moreau, Mathurin, figure of a barefoot girl
wearing a cap & peasant blouse & skirt &
carrying a basket on her back, resting
near a tree trunk, brown patina, inscribed
"Moreau Mathurin Hors Concours," mid-
19th - early 20th c., 27" h............... **3,162**

Moreau, Mathurin, figure of "Poesie,"
female wearing loose robe & holding an
open book on one hand, the other holding
a pen, brown patina, circular wooden
base set w/title plaque, inscribed "Math
Moreau," "copyright 1904 - By Lapointe" &
impressed "Medaille D'Honeur," 27½" h..... **2,875**

Moreau, Mathurin, figure group, winged
victory w/laurel branch, behind & above
standing semi-nude youth holding lute,
golden brown patina, inscribed "Mathurin
Moreau H*****" & impressed "Medaille
D'Honeur," mid-19th - early 20th c., 38" h. ... **11,500**

Omerth, figure group, standing man wearing
hat & long coat w/cape & holding aloft a
cane w/an angled handle, carved ivory
face, hair & hands, a seated dog looking
up at him, golden patina, square onyx
base, signed "Omerth" & "7464," 15" h..... **2,300**

Parsons, Edith Barretto, model of a small
standing dog, looking backward, greenish
brown patina, incised "Edith Barretto
Parsons," stamped "Gorham Co.
Founders," 4½" h., 7" l. **805**

"Rahda" Figure by Philippe

Philippe, Paul, "Rahda," figure of an exotic
female dancer on her toes w/head thrown
back & both arms raised, bandeau top &
ruffled sarong skirt swirling about her
knees, cold-painted bronze, inscribed "P.
Philippe" & stamped "JDA 133," ca.
1920s, France, 22" h. (ILLUS.) **4,025**

From left: Mother & Child Figure Group
Bronze Figure of Scottish Soldier

Plé, Henri-Honoré, figure group, a young mother wearing a long full skirt & laced bodice guides her infant son in learning to walk by holding a cloth wrapped around his chest w/one hand & his arm w/the other, brown patina, raised on a fluted green marble columnar pedestal, inscribed "Henri Plé," mid-19th - early 20th c., 32" h., the group (ILLUS.) **16,100**

Pollet, Joseph Michel Ange, "The Night," figure of a nude female standing w/one leg raised slightly, head back w/arms raised & behind head, inscribed "Pollet," 19th c., 39" h. **5,750**

Rhind, William Birnie, figure of a standing Scottish soldier in full uniform, both hands on the barrel of a rifle on the ground before him, medium brown patina, signed "Birnie Rhind," ca. 1920, Scotland, 22¾" h. (ILLUS.) **1,495**

Richard, A., figure group, standing saddled camel w/young man wearing shirt & short pants standing alongside, cold-painted bronze, brown patina, signed "A. Richard," 19" h. **4,887**

Rispal, Jules-Louis, figure group, nude female w/arms holding head & shoulders of young deer, gilt-bronze, inscribed "J. Rispal - 1903," 25" h. **4,025**

Salmson, Jean Jules, figure of Pandora wearing a robe, looking down, seated on a broken column w/right arm resting on the column & left arm over her chest, green to brown patina, incised "Jean Jules Salmson," 19th c., 22" h. **2,990**

Simone, E., model of a recumbent hound, medium brown patina, incised "E. Simone" & dated "1-2-20," France, 7¾" h., 16" l. **1,150**

Van der Straeten, Georges, bust of a young lady, a smiling face looking to her right, her hair tied in a topknot w/curls on either side of her face, wearing a décolleté dress w/gathered shoulders & tied w/a bow, red & brown patina, signed w/Société des bronzes de Paris seal, Belgian, ca. 1895, 15¾" **977**

Vienna bronze, figure of a Native American baby asleep in a cradle board, after Carl Kauba, cold-painted, early 20th c., 8" l. **863**

Vienna bronze, miniature model of an alligator w/head raised, realistic cold-painting, early 20th c., 7" l. **546**

Vienna bronze, model of a lobster, realistic cold-painting, early 20th c., 5½" l. **316**

Vienna bronze, small figure of a young Pan seated playing his pipes at the base of a large ovoid classical urn, cold-painted, ca. 1920, 5½" h. **633**

Vienna bronze, model group, depicting a mummy case opening to reveal a gilt nude maiden, cold-painted bronze, after a model by Namgreb, signed, 8" h. **1,955**

Vienna Bronze Elephant Figure

Vienna bronze, figure depicting an elaborately caparisoned elephant & rider, cold-painted bronze, 9½" h. (ILLUS.) **3,737**

Zocchi, Arnaldo, figure of Christopher Columbus, standing, wearing a hat & long coat, arms in front w/hands holding scrolled map, dark brown patina, on marble base, incised signature on base w/foundry mark for J. Mazzucchelli B.saires, Italy, late 19th - early 20th c., 16¼" h. **1,380**

MARBLE

Bust of a Renaissance maiden, shown w/a laurel wreath in her long hair, wearing a pendent necklace & a dress w/a Renaissance-style bodice, on a brick-colored rectangular base w/chamfered corners, Italy, ca. 1880, 16½" h. (chips) **1,035**

Figure group, depicting two semi-draped bacchic youths standing on a rocky base, further raised on a marble plinth, 21" h. **6,900**

Marble Figure Group by Gory

Gory, Affortunato, figure group, three
    putti sitting on waves & playing various
    musical instruments, inscribed "A. Gory,"
    late 19th - early 20th c., some repairs,
    31" h. (ILLUS.)...................... **8,050**

Marble Figure by Lapini

Lapini, Cesare, white marble figure of a
    young girl w/short hair, a sheer flowing
    gown swirling about her legs, one hand
    near the hip & the other arm held in
    front of her, inscribed "Lapini Firenze
    108," late 19th c., Italy, restorations,
    33" h. (ILLUS.)...................... **3,450**
Lazzerini, Pietro, figure group, a young girl
    wearing a short dress, hair tied back & a
    young semi-nude boy, their arms about
    each other, inscribed "Prof Pietro
    Lazzerini ***8," late 19th c., 38" h........ **17,250**
Milano, D. Varcaglia, figure of a young boy
    seated on a bench, marble, signed,
    w/pedestal base, 32½" h., 2 pcs.......... **6,325**
Rossi, E., bust of a young crying boy
    wearing a cap & holding a bird in one
    hand & bust of a young girl w/long wavy
    hair holding needlework in her hands,
    circular socles, signed "Prof E. Rossi -

Marble Busts of Young Boy & Girl

Studio ......," 19th c., Italy, together w/two
    unrelated black marble pedestals,
    the group (ILLUS.)................... **9,775**
Vichi, F., figure of Andromeda, the nude
    maiden chained to a large rock, waves
    crashing over her lower body, inscribed
    "Vichi," raised on an octagonal pedestal,
    Italy, late 19th c., 57" h............... **17,250**

OTHER

Alabaster, bust of a lovely young woman
    w/an intricate coiffure, raised on a
    square base, Europe, late 19th - early
    20th c., 26" h. **1,955**

Alabaster Figure Group

Alabaster, De Cori, A., allegorical figure
    group w/semi-draped maiden w/a floral
    crown in hair & holding flowers above her
    head, a putto near her feet, inscribed "A.
    De Cori - Studio Romanelli - Firenze,"
    some restorations (ILLUS.) **4,312**
Alabaster, figure of a classical semi-nude
    female w/her arms crossed in front,
    looking back over one shoulder, on a
    round foot, Italy, ca. 1880, 32" h. (repairs,
    minor loss) **978**

Alabaster, Saccardi, A., figure of an Egyptian beauty, the young woman standing, leaning on a square column decorated w/hieroglyphics & holding a water urn, wearing a pigeon-form headdress, a halter & a long flowing skirt, all on a chamfered rectangular "tile" base, Italy, early 20th c., signed, 19" h. **1,380**

Alabaster, figure depicting Dante, the standing figure w/a rolled manuscript in his hand, 19½" h. **805**

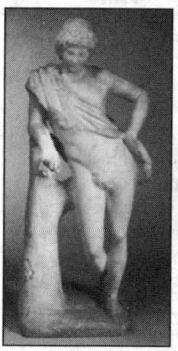
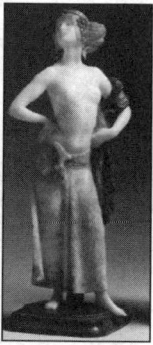

*From left: Alabaster Figure of Apollo
Figure of "Salome"*

Alabaster, figure of Apollo, leaning against a tree stump, after the antique, ca. 1880, repairs, minor loss, 29" h. (ILLUS.) **978**

Alabaster, carved figure of Venus, the standing figure at her bath, 33" h. **2,530**

Mixed materials, Ernst Seger, "Salome," figure of a semi-nude female standing w/hands on her hips, white marble torso w/shaded tan onyx scarf draped around the waist & gilt & cold-painted bronze scarf over one arm, glass bead band in her hair, green stone base, inscribed "E. Seger" w/"RKB" foundry stamp, early 20th c., Germany, 13" h. (ILLUS.) **5,750**

Terra Cotta Figure Group by Blondat

Terra cotta, figure group, "Les Enfants aux Grenouilles" or "Jeunesses," modeled in high-relief w/three nude children atop a cascade of water & peering into the basin below mounted w/three frogs, inscribed "Max-Blondat" & impressed "MB cartouche - 21," ca. 1907, 13 x 15", 14" h. (ILLUS.) **2,875**

STEIF TOYS & DOLLS

From a felt pincushion in the shape of an elephant, a world-famous toy company emerged. Margarete Steiff (1847-1909), a polio victim as a child and confined to a wheelchair, planned a career as a seamstress and opened a shop in the family home. However, her plans were dramatically changed when she made the first stuffed elephant in 1880. By 1886 she was producing stuffed felt monkeys, donkeys, horses and other animal forms. In 1893 an agent sold her toys at the Leipzig Fair. This venture was so successful that a catalog was printed and a salesman hired. Margarete's nephews and nieces became involved in the business, assisting in its management and the design of new items. Through the years, the Steiff Company has produced a varied line including felt or plush animals including Teddy bears, gnomes, elves, felt dolls with celluloid heads, Kewpie dolls and even radiator caps with animals or dolls attached as decoration. Descendants of the original family members continue to be active in the management of the company still adhering to Margarete's motto "For our children, the best is just good enough."

Bear on wheels, brown mohair, embroidered nose, excelsior stuffing, steel frame & wheels, early 20th c., 9¼" l., 6½" h. (eyes & button missing, fur loss on muzzle & front feet, nose embroidery worn) **$201**

Bear on wheels, grey mohair w/glass eyes & leather collar, standing on a steel frame w/cast-iron wheels, unmarked, 22" l., 14" h. (wear) **825**

Bear on wheels, large standing animal w/brown mohair coat & glass eyes, mounted on a steel frame w/sheet metal wheels w/black rubber treads, ring pull voice box, added leather collar & rope pull, button in ear w/ribbon, 31" l., 24" h. **2,090**

Dog, seated, yellow mohair, glass eyes, black embroidered nose, mouth & claws, 1913, 5½" h. (spotty fur loss, button missing) . . **173**

Dog on rockers, St. Bernard, synthetic dark brown & white fur, plastic eyes, black embroidered nose, ear button, steel frame & rocker base, mid-20th c., 50" l., 23" h. (fur matted on back) **173**

Dog on wheels, cream & ginger fur, embroidered nose & mouth, cast iron frame & wheels, ca. 1910, 13" l., 10" h. (extensive fur loss) **86**

Doll, "Hellen" or "Helma," center face seam, black steel eyes, light brown hair, original Dutch costume w/Dutch cap, ca. 1913, 13¾" h. (slight fabric fading, back of left sabot damaged, button missing) **1,150**

Donkey, standing, tan body w/black trim, original red leather harness, button in ear, mint, 5" h. **88**

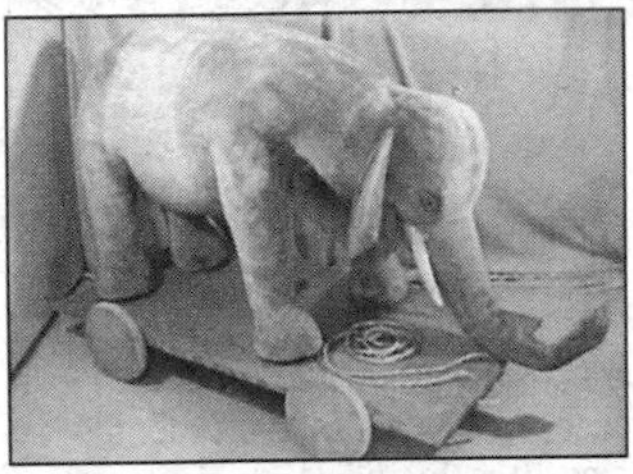

Large Steiff Elephant on Platform

Elephant on platform, large grey mohair elephant w/long curved trunk standing on a rectangular wooden platform w/wooden wheels, original button in the ear, small repair to back of head, overall 9" l., 3½" h. (ILLUS.) **385**

Giraffe, button in ear & tag,11" h. **633**

Steiff Wittie Owl

Owl, "Wittie," dark brown & black plush, large green glass eyes, felt talons, original tag, very good condition, 4" h. (ILLUS.) **33**

Palomino colt, standing, blond mohair, button in ear, 11" h. (wear) **330**

Steiff Peggy Penguin

Penguin, "Peggy," black & white plush w/orange bill & yellow & black head, 19" h. (ILLUS.) **242**

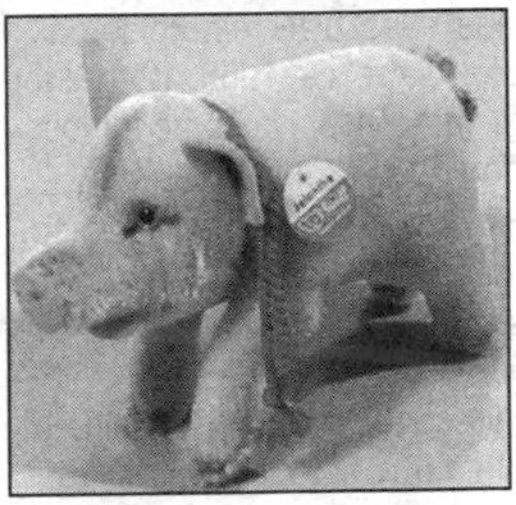

Steiff Jolanthe the Pig

Pig, "Jolanthe," plush, tan w/glass eyes, red cord around neck, original tag, mint, 6" l. (ILLUS.) **94**

Rabbit, tan plush, mother rabbit standing wearing a green felt dress w/red buttons & white apron, original tag, excellent condition, 10" h. **110**

Wolf hand puppet, tan mohair w/black highlights, glass eyes, red tongue, excellent condition, 10" l. **83**

TEDDY BEARS

Teddy bear, blonde mohair, fully jointed, black steel eyes, brown embroidered nose, mouth & claws, felt pad, blank ear button, right foot pad autographed by Steiff executive, "J.R. Junginger" (spotty fur loss, slight fiber loss) **863**

Steiff Teddy Bear with Long Ear Button

Teddy bear, brown mohair w/felt paws, glass eyes, jointed, long ear button, early, excellent condition, 10" h. (ILLUS.) **193**

Teddy bear, marked w/silver button w/raised script in left ear, beige mohair body w/swivel head, excelsior stuffing, brown glass eyes, shaved muzzle w/dark brown floss nose & mouth, felt pads, 11" h. **225**

Teddy bear, blonde mohair, fully jointed, black steel eyes, very pointed nose, yellow felt pads, embroidered claws, excelsior stuffing, ca. 1907, 12" h. (traces

of nose embroidery, some moth damage
& fiber loss, excelsior needs replacing on
left leg, button missing) **288**

Teddy bear, ginger mohair, fully jointed,
black steel eyes, black embroidered
features & claws, ca. 1905, 12" h. (needs
stuffing, pads replaced, some fur loss,
fabric damaged on muzzle) **288**

Teddy bear, golden mohair, fully jointed,
black embroidered nose, mouth & claws,
black steel eyes, blank button, felt pads,
excelsior stuffing, ca. 1905-09, 14" h.
(spotty fur loss mostly on back side of
bear & head) **1,380**

Teddy bear, golden mohair, fully jointed,
brown embroidered nose, mouth &
claws, felt pads, black steel eyes,
excelsior stuffing, ca. 1905, 16" h.
(button missing, spotty fur & fiber
loss, left ear needs restitching) **1,955**

Teddy bear, cinnamon mohair, plush swivel
head w/center seam, black shoebutton
eyes, black floss nose & mouth, excelsior
stuffing, felt pads on paws, four black
floss claws on each paw, 17" h. **7,200**

Teddy bear, golden mohair, fully jointed,
black embroidered nose, mouth & claws,
black steel eyes, felt pads, excelsior
stuffing, ear button, growler, ca. 1905,
17" h. (moth damage) **2,990**

Steiff Golden Teddy Bear

Teddy bear, pale golden mohair, plush
swivel head w/center seam, black
shoebutton eyes, black floss mouth &
nose w/vertical stitching, excelsior
stuffing, applied ears, jointed shoulders &
hips, felt pads on paws, four black
claws, hump on back, marked w/blank button in
left ear, 17" h. (ILLUS.) **7,000**

Teddy bear, "Heins," light yellow mohair,
fully jointed, black embroidered nose,
mouth & claws, glass eyes, excelsior
stuffing, ear button, ca. 1920s, 24" h.
(slight fiber loss, pads replaced) **2,760**

Teddy bears, twin light yellow mohair, fully
jointed, black steel eyes, tan embroidered
nose, mouth & claws, cream pads,

Twin Steiff Teddy Bears

excelsior stuffing, ca. 1905, moth
damage, spotty fur loss, ear buttons
missing,10" h., pr. (ILLUS.) **2,530**

STEINS

*From left: Porcelain Bismarck Stein
Porcelain Indian Stein*

Character, "Bismarck," porcelain, marked
"Musterschutz," small hairline crack on
helmet, ½ liter (ILLUS.). **$350**

Character, "Indian," porcelain, by E. Bohne
Sohne, ½ liter (ILLUS.). **700**

Character, "Iron Maiden," stoneware,
marked "T.W.," ½ liter. **350**

Character, "Mephisto," porcelain, marked
"Musterschutz," by Schierholz, ½ liter **2,500**

Character, "Monk" pottery, marked
"M.W.G.," ½ liter **250**

Character, "Nun," pottery, marked "M.W.G.,"
½ liter **250**

Character, "Owl," stoneware, marked
"M.W.G.," ½ liter. **220**

Character, "Singing Pig," porcelain, marked
"Musterschutz," by Schierholz, ½ liter **450**

Character, "Skull," porcelain, by E. Bohne
Sohne, ½ liter **600**

Character, "Von Moltke," porcelain, marked "Musterschutz," by Schierholz, ½ liter **1,000**

Character, "Munich Child," pottery, stout child w/long robe holding embossed large stein marked "HB - Munchen" & radishes, base impressed "Reinemann - Munchen," twin tower pewter thumblift, 1 liter, 10" h. **375**

Glass, blown, inscribed "Ulan Regt. Nr. 6, 1873-1883," pewter lid w/Ulan helmet finial, ½ liter **300**

Glass, blown, red flashed, engraved, stag, clear glass inlaid lid, ½ liter. **400**

Glass, blown, yellow flowers, etched, clear glass inlaid lid, ½ liter **300**

Glass Beer Stein

Glass, blue shaded to clear threaded glass w/embossed pewter hinged lid & base, clear applied handle, 3⁄10 liter (ILLUS.) **165**

Glass, cylindrical clear body decorated w/a painted drinking scene, hinged pewter lid, early 20th c., ¼ liter, 7¼" h. **288**

Mettlach, No. 1154, etched four-panel scenes of hunters, inlaid lid, 1 liter **600**

Mettlach, No. 1527, etched, four men drinking, brown background, signed "Warth," inlaid lid, 1 liter **600**

Mettlach, No. 1566, etched, man on high-wheel bicycle, signed "Gorig" inlaid lid, ½ liter. **1,000**

Mettlach, No. 1786, etched, lid w/relief scene of Munich, St. Florian putting out fire, dragon handle, ceramic dragon's head thumblift, pewter lid, ½ liter **700**

Mettlach, No. 1818, etched, tavern scene, pewter lid, signed "Gorig," 6⅕ liters. **1,800**

Mettlach, No. 1821, relief, musician w/guitar, inlaid lid, 3⅕ liters **350**

Mettlach, No. 1909, colorful transfer-printed design of a man smoking a pipe while sitting at a tavern table w/stein, artist signed, verse on reverse by B. Auerbach, inlaid pewter lid, ½ liter (chip beneath base of thumblift cover) **175**

Mettlach, No. 2001A, relief-molded in the form of hand-painted books of law, inlaid pewter lid, ½ liter **575**

Mettlach, No. 2024, etched 'Berlin' design w/shield of the city of Berlin, inlaid lid, ½ liter . . **550**

Mettlach, No. 2035, etched Bacchus carousing, inlaid lid, ½ liter. **450**

Mettlach, No. 2038, decorated relief, town of Rodenstein, houses & towers on inlay, inlaid lid, 3⅗ liters **3,800**

Mettlach, No. 2049, etched, chess stein, chessboard, inlaid lid, ½ liter **2,500**

Mettlach, No. 2090, etched club stein, man at table w/his club smoking pipe, signed "Schlitt," inlaid lid, ½ liter. **550**

Mettlach, No. 2100, etched, Prosit stein, knight w/stein & man w/fur clothing, signed "Schlitt," inlaid lid, ½ liter **1,100**

Mettlach, No. 2106, decorated relief, monkeys in cage, monkey handle, inlaid lid, ½ liter. **4,500**

Mettlach, No. 2126, etched symphonia stein, composers, signed "Schlitt," pewter lid, 5½ liters **6,500**

Mettlach, No. 2136, etched, Anheuser Busch Brewery, inlaid lid, ½ liter **2,500**

Mettlach, No. 2219, relief, dancing & musical scenes, three panels, inlaid lid, 3⅒ liters. **500**

Mettlach, No. 2235, etched scene of a barmaid holding steins, targets in the background, pewter lid, ½ liter **460**

Mettlach, No. 2277, etched scene of Nurnberg, inlaid lid, ½ liter **525**

Mettlach, No. 24, relief, figures on four separate panels, inlaid lid, 1 liter **300**

Mettlach, No. 2401, etched decoration of Tannhauser titled "Tannhauser in the Venusberg," inlaid lid, 1 liter. **345**

Mettlach, No. 2402, etched, the courting of Siegried, inlaid lid, ½ liter **900**

Mettlach, No. 2520, etched, student & barmaid, signed "Schlitt," inlaid lid, 1 liter. **700**

Mettlach, No. 2580, etched, Die Kannenburg stein, knight in castle, signed "Schlitt," conical inlaid lid, ½ liter **700**

Mettlach, No. 2722, etched, occupational, shoemaker, inlaid lid, ½ liter **1,500**

Mettlach, No. 2782, Rookwood-style, h.p. bust portrait of a Cavalier drinking, hinged pewter lid, 17¾" h., 4½ liter **489**

Mettlach, No. 3236, etched Art Nouveau design in blue & white, inlaid lid, ½ liter **575**

Mettlach, No. 3395, Cameo style, footed spherical body w/a cylindrical neck & rim spout w/mask, molded C-form handle, inlaid lid, the body w/a wide blue band decorated w/white relief peasant figures drinking, tenpin & vine design on blue neckband, 7" d., 12" h. **385**

Mettlach, No. 485, relief, musicians & dancers on blue background, inlaid lid, 1 liter . . **350**

Mettlach, No. 5001, faience-type, printed-under-glaze coat of arms, pewter lid, 4.6 liters. . **850**

Mettlach, No. 954 (2176), PUG, knight drinking, signed "Schlitt," pewter lid, 2⅒ liters. . **600**

Mettlach Drinking Gnomes

Mettlach, No. 966 (2184), PUG, drinking gnomes, by Schlitt, inlaid lid, ½ liter (ILLUS.) . . **300**

Porcelain, Royal Vienna-type, h.p., marked w/beehive, "Urtheil des Paris" scenes inside & outside inlaid lid, ¼ liter **1,800**

Porcelain, cylindrical, depicting a frieze of stags, repoussé molded silver cover, Europe, 19th c., 5½" h. **690**

Porcelain w/lithophane base, h.p. floral decoration & name banner on front, pewter fixtures, ½ liter **110**

Pottery, etched, marked "1339," by J.W. Remy, inlaid lid, 1½ liters **200**

Pottery, etched, marked "HR, 441," by Hauber & Reuther, pewter lid, ½ liter **250**

Pottery, etched, marked "M.W.G.," pewter lid, ½ liter **200**

German Pottery Stein

Pottery, relief, decorated w/faces of German composers, inlaid lid, ½ liter (ILLUS.) **200**

Regimental, "2. Comp., Inft. Regt. Nr. 100, Dresden, 1909-1911," four side scenes, roster, Saxon thumblift, porcelain, ½ liter, 11.8" h. **425**

Regimental, "2. Comp., Train Battl. Nr. 13, Ludwigsburg, 1908-1909," two side scenes, roster, Wurtten thumblift, porcelain, ½ liter, 12" h. **700**

Regimental, "3. Comp., Inft. Regt., Nr. 118, Worms, 1906-1908," two side scenes, roster, eagle thumblift, porcelain, ½ liter, 12.4" h. **400**

Regimental, "3. Komp., Pionier Batl. Nr. 16, Metz, 1908-1910," four side scenes, roster, eagle thumblift, porcelain, ½ liter, 11.7" h. **700**

Regimental, "8. Battr., Fuss Artl. Regt. Nr. 14, Strassburg, 1911-1913," four side scenes, roster, griffin thumblift, porcelain, ½ liter, 12.2" h. **550**

Regimental, "8. Comp., 19. Bayr. Inft. Reg., Erlangen, 1912-1914," four side scenes, roster, lion thumblift, porcelain, ½ liter, 12.2" h. **450**

Stoneware, painted under glaze w/a colorful scene of a young bicycle racer in uniform standing triumphantly in front of his highwheel bicycle below a banner w/a German inscription & surrounded by a floral wreath, molded upper & lower bands, high domed hinged pewter lid w/eagle finial & griffins thumblift, Germany, ca. 1900, 3½ liter, 18¾" h. **1,348**

Stoneware, decorated w/colorful h.p. image of a royal mounted guard above a polychrome embossed base, artist-signed "S.H. 1892" & "RH Germany 1191" impressed on base, 5 liter, 19½" h. **385**

STEREOSCOPES & STEREO VIEWS

Hand stereoscope viewers with an adjustable slide may be found at $30 to $50 each in good condition. Elaborate table models are priced much higher. Prices of view cards depend on the subject material and range from less than $1 to $10 or more.

STEREOSCOPES

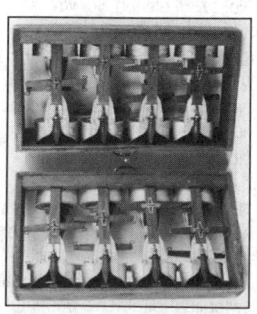

Drawers of Stereopticans

Stereopticans, three drawers each containing 20 aluminum & wood turn-of-the-century viewers from a educational facility, the set (ILLUS. of two drawers). . . . **$1,100**

Stereopticon, sheet metal & cast-iron w/old black enamel, coin-operated, a large cylindrical drum-form w/a bracket control handle at the front side & a raised viewing window at the top, marked "The American Novelty Co., Cincinnati," 14" h. (some rust & modifications) **193**

STEREO VIEWS

Alma, Colorado placer miners, quarry mining scene w/a crane & miners at work w/spraying hoses, by T.C. Miller, Alma Park, Colorado, cabinet size, buff mount (soiling, mount wear, center bend) **146**

Early Billiard Parlor View

Billiard parlor, cabinet-size view showing a woman & four men around an early billiard table, billiard rack, photos & guns mounted on background walls, very light soiling (ILLUS.) **248**

Early Blake St., Denver Stereo View

Blake Street, Denver, Colorado, panorama street view w/many store signs, wagons & horses, etc., yellow mount, very light soil & faint foxing, minor edge wear (ILLUS.) **163**

Chinese cook, "Our Cook," young Chinese man seated wearing traditional dress, crude studio background, purple mount, by E. J. Hayward, Santa Barbara, California, late 19th - early 20th c. (some soil spots, mount wear) **162**

Erie Canal Locks, Lockport, New York, shows locks going through town w/canal boat at bottom left, orange mount, by F.B. Clench, detailed (light soiling, edge wear, bend on one side). **35**

General U.S. Grant at Cold Harbor, Virginia . . . **200**

Klondike Gold Rush, "Prospectors Preparing Camp," view of tenting in the bush country, Keystone View Co., Meadville, Pennsylvania, No. 11547, 1899. . . . . **26**

Klondike Gold Rush, steamboats scene, "The 'Dora Bluhm' at Port of St. Michaels, Alaska," steamboats docked in background, tents in the foreground, Keystone View Co., Meadville, Pennsylvania, No. 9355, 1898 . . . . **33**

Klondike Gold Rush, "Two of a Kind," view of two fisherman standing by water & comparing two fish while two dogs look on, Keystone View Co., Meadville, Pennsylvania, No. 11532, 1899 . . . . **22**

Leadville, Colorado Mine Scene

Leadville Mine, miners pose w/mine cars at the mine entrance, reverse labeled "This is most important mining camp in Col. Has pop. of over 20,000, although but 2 yrs. old," by L.K. Oldroyd, published in Colorado Springs, soiling spots (ILLUS.) **220**

Minnesota Logging Scene

Logging scene, Upton, Minnesota titled "Winter in the Pine Forests," cookboat on water in foreground surrounded by floating logs, late 1860s, slight soiling & mount wear, spot in upper left original (ILLUS.) **48**

Native American scene, Chief Sharp Nose & family, F.J. Haynes, Northern Pacific Views No. 1718, Chief wearing a military

View of Chief Sharp Nose & Family

jacket sitting outside his canvas lodge
w/his family, scuff at left mount edge, light
soiling (ILLUS.). **234**

Native American scene, Navajos, larger
size, shows five people outside a hogan,
chief's blanket over the door, E. & H. T.
Anthony, soiling, edge wear, foxing, print
damaged & lifted along bottom **74**

Native American scene, Watkins, Indian
Camp, Yosemite, No. 1064, shows a
woman w/child on cradle board in a brush
shelter w/baskets, original negative flaws,
creases & edge wear **92**

New York City elevated railroad, train in
subway station, car marked "Long Island" **30**

Prison scene, marble quarries at Sing Sing
Prison, shows convicts at work, No. 4298
of Sing Sing Prison Views, by E. & H.
Anthony, label gives details on the prison,
yellow mount (light soil & foxing,
corner dings) **39**

Pullman Car interior, view down the aisle
of an early ornate passenger car, by
O.C. Smith, No. 20, yellow mount
(very light soil) **157**

Railroad yard, titled "Altoona R.R. works -
the Furnace preparing to pour," shows
workers, molds & furnaces, No. 504 of
Penn Central series by E. Anthony, 501
Broadway, yellow mount (some soiling
& light foxing, edge wear). **56**

Silver bullion, outdoor shot of 65 tons of
silver bullion & 10 tons of silver ore
stacked in bars at Platte Station,
Colorado, Gurnsey's Rocky Mountain
Views #87, published in Colorado Springs
(soil spots) **109**

View of Steamer "Nipsic"

Steamer "Nipsic," from the Darien
Expedition, the ship shown in Columbia
Bay, personal family inscription on the
reverse, yellow stock, original negative
flaws, glue streaks, E. & H. Anthony (ILLUS.) . . **112**

Wood train & Chinamen in Bloomer Cut,
open train cars in a narrow pass
w/several Chinese workers on top in
the foreground & others in the distance,
by Thomas Hous.eworth of San
Francisco, Central Pacific Railroad
series No. 1351, orange mount (some
soil & mount wear, light bend) **138**

STOVES

*Over the past several years, much renewed
interest in antique stoves has surfaced. From the
coveted base-burner beauties to "pot-bellies,"
steel-jacketed "oak" stoves, cooking stoves,
heaters and laundry stoves, these handsome
"heavies" are in demand. Like many areas of
antiques and collectibles, the market for stoves is
thin. It is almost impossible to designate some
particular "worth" without several considerations such as economic status, demographics,
artistic value, type and age. And although these
factors may play a roll in determining a final
sale, they do not necessarily "set" the price on a
particular stove. Antique stove expert Clifford
Boram has supplied us with the following
pricing information and photographs.*

*From left: Art Westminster Base Burner
Imperial Universal Base Burner*

Base burner, 1890 Art Westminster
No. 404, Rathborne-Sard, Albany, N.Y.,
all cast iron w/mica windows & large
rectangular majolica tile on three sides,
13" firepot (ILLUS.) **$22,000**

Base burner, 1911 Wehrle 100, restored,
18" firepot **9,000**

Base burner, 1911 Wehrle 100, The Wehrle
Co., Newark, Ohio, restored, 14" firepot **4,000**

Base burner, 1913 Imperial Universal 50,
Cribben & Sexton, Chicago, all cast iron
w/mica windows on three sides, nickel
plating, restored, 15" firepot (ILLUS.) **4,000**

Base burner, Art Garland 250, ca. 1920,
restored **1,250**

Base burner, Art Garland 58, Michigan
Stove Co., Detroit, ca. 1910, restored **8,000**

Base burner, Noble Crown, ca. 1920,
restored (dismounted from base) **1,300**

Base burner, Radiant Stewart 34, Fuller &
Warren, Milwaukee, ca. 1900, restored **5,000**

Coal range, 1917 Brilliant Universal, blue
cast iron w/high closet, no reservoir, good
original condition **200**

Combination range, 1928 Kalamazoo
Peerless, grey & white, good original
condition **875**

Combination range, Globe, grey, Kokomo,
Ind., ca. 1925, good original condition **150**

Cook stove, 1872 Governor 8, Chicago
Stoves Wks., reservoir & low closet, good
original condition **325**

Cottage parlor stove, 1842 E. Ripley's
Patent Hinge 2 .... **850**

Gas heater, Jewel, twelve-tube radiator, no
low radiant chamber, ca. 1889, restored **500**

Gas range, 1924 Quick Meal, grey four-
burner w/canopy & high closet, unrestored
& apart **375**

Gas range, 1929 Magic Chef 39 (Jonquil),
four-burner, good original condition **250**

Gas range, 1929 Roper, four-burner, one-
oven, unrestored **20**

1938 Magic Chef Gas Range

Gas range, 1938 Magic Chef, white
porcelain on sheet iron, chrome trim, six-
burner, two-oven w/high closet, restored
(ILLUS.) **1,025**

Gas range, 1938 Magic Chef, white
six-burner, two-oven w/high closet,
unrestored & apart **725**

Gas range, Chambers, white four-burner,
ca. 1949, good original condition **250**

Gas range, Eagle, low-oven style w/wood
side, cream & green, ca. 1929, unrestored ... **150**

Gas range, O'Keefe & Merritt, four-burner
w/cabinet base, ca. 1929, good original
condition **110**

Gas range, Quick Meal, blue four-burner
cabinet, ca. 1919, good original condition **925**

Oak stove, 1925 Ideal Heater 417, Gem
City Mfg. Co., Quincy, Ill., good original
condition **175**

Oak stove, American Oak 214, Keokuk
Stove Wks., ca. 1895, restored **300**

1933 Magic Chef Gas Range

Gas range, 1933 Magic Chef, American
Stove Co., St. Louis & Cleveland,
white porcelain on sheet iron, six-
burner, two-oven w/high closet, black
Bakelite knobs & handles, good original
condition (ILLUS.) **800**

From left: Peoria Oak Stove
Round Oak Stove

Oak stove, Peoria Oak 160, Culter &
Proctor, ca. 1905, restored (ILLUS.) **600**

Oak stove, Retort 218, Marion, Ind., cased
oak w/three mica doors, ca. 1905,
restored **2,400**

Round Oak 18-T-31, 1940, good original
condition. **225**
Round Oak D-18, 1901, complete, unrestored . . **300**
Round Oak D-18, 1904, extra half section,
restored, missing standing Indian from
top, 18" firepot (ILLUS.) **325**

Superb Peninsular Steel Range

Steel range, 1907 Superb Peninsular
w/reservoir & high closet, restored (ILLUS.) . . **2,000**

Templar 27 Todd Stove

Todd stove, 1878 Templar 27, Wm. Resor,
Cincinnati, all cast iron w/two mica
windows in feed door & side door,
incomplete, 27" firebox (ILLUS.). **25**
Todd stove, 1908 Acme Wildwood w/sheet-
iron jacket, Wehrle/Sears, unrestored
condition (no hearth) **60**

Magee 88 Range

Wood-burning range, 1880 Magee 88,
Magee Furnace Co., Boston, double
oven, eight-hole cast iron w/high closet,
8" lids, no reservoir, restored (ILLUS.) **5,500**
Wood-burning range, 1927 Home Comfort
AC, high closet, no reservoir, unrestored. **50**
Wood- & coal-burning base heater, Ideal
Garland 220, ca. 1898, restored (no urn) . . . **1,300**
Wood- & coal-burning range, 1910
Glenwood F 107, cast iron w/high
shelf, restored **1,100**
Wood- & coal-burning range, 1925
Universal, blue, gas sidecar, unrestored **200**
Wood- & coal-burning range, Alpine Bride,
black cast iron, ca. 1920, restored **300**

TEA CADDIES

Boullework, brass & tortoiseshell,
rectangular w/a serpentine front, scrolled
inlay w/a rosewood interior, lock signed
"Tahan, Paris," Louis Philippe-style,
ca. 1870, 9" l. **$1,150**
Fruitwood, model of a large apple w/top
section opening to a foil-lined interior,
golden yellow color, England, ca. 1790,
4½" d., 4½" h. **1,150**
Inlaid mahogany, rectangular, the inlaid w/a
shell design, opening to two interior
lidded compartments, early 19th c.,
England, 7½" l. **230**
Lacquer, oblong w/wide beveled corners &
serpentine borders, black w/gilt trim &
panels w/Chinese scenes, raised on gilt
dragon head feet, Chinese Export, mid-
19th c., 8½" l., 5½" h. (wear, cracks) **288**

Fine Mahogany Tea Caddy

Mahogany, Chippendale style, rectangular
dovetailed case w/stepped hinged cover
w/pierced butterfly bracket & bail handle,
butterfly pierced keyhole escutcheon on
the front, molded base on scroll-cut
bracket feet, late 18th c. (ILLUS.) **1,650**

Marquetry-inlaid rosewood, rectangular, inlaid w/foliage & a sheet of music on the cover, Europe, 19th c., 9" l. **259**

Papier-maché, nearly square upright box w/low hinged lid, stenciled w/anthemion borders & mounted on the front w/oval painted & inset plaques, ring handle on lid, England, ca. 1790, 3¾ x 4", 4½" h. **575**

Satinwood veneer, oval w/the fitted top banded w/inlay, the interior w/a mahogany divider & lids w/turned ivory knobs, England or America, early 19th c., 4¼ x 7⅝", 5" h. (losses to leaded paper, cracks, inlay loss) **1,265**

Tortoiseshell, deep oblong cushion shape w/hinged lid, two interior lidded compartments, England, early 19th c., 8¼" l. (losses) **1,265**

Walnut & ivory, trunk-form w/a domed cover, inlaid rows of rectangular ivory plaques alternating w/large brass tacks & attached w/smaller tacks, cloud-form ivory inlaid lid panel & keyhole escutcheon, opens to two lidded wells, England, mid-19th c., 9" l., 5" h. **259**

1920s Mohair Teddy Bear

Early German Teddy Bear

TEDDY BEAR COLLECTIBLES

Theodore (Teddy) Roosevelt had become a national hero during the Spanish-American War by leading his "Rough Riders" to victory at San Juan Hill in 1898. He became the 26th president of the United States in 1901 when President McKinley was assassinated. The gregarious Roosevelt was fond of the outdoors and hunting. Legend has it that while on a hunting trip, soon after becoming President, he refused to shoot a bear cub because it was so small and helpless. The story was picked up by a political cartoonist who depicted President Roosevelt, attired in hunting garb, turning away and refusing to shoot a small bear cub. Shortly thereafter, toy plush bears began appearing in department stores labeled "Teddy's Bear" and they became an immediate success. Books on the adventures of "The Roosevelt Bears" were written and illustrated by Paul Piper under the pseudonym of Seymour Eaton and this version of the Teddy Bear became a popular decoration on children's dishes.

Postcard, Roosevelt Bears at the Boston Public Library **$20**

Teddy bear, brown short mohair stuffed w/straw, jointed limbs, hump on back, glass eyes, ca. 1920s, 20" h. (ILLUS.) **330**

Teddy bear, straw-filled tan mohair, button eyes, fully jointed, tail moves the head, Germany, early 20th c., very good condition, 10" h. (ILLUS.) **605**

Teddy bear, golden mohair, embroidered nose & mouth, arm jointed at shoulders, red felt beret & trousers, black metal feet, includes key, Schuco "dancing bear," ca. 1930, 5" (slight fur loss) **288**

Teddy bear, light golden mohair, felt pads, black embroidered nose & mouth, dark brown claws, excelsior stuffing, unmarked, 10" (spotty overall fur loss) **748**

Teddy bear, golden mohair, black shoe button eyes, black embroidered nose, mouth & claws, beige pads, jointed excelsior stuffing, Ideal Toy Co., ca. 1910, 10½" (remnants of red felt tongue, minor fur loss) **403**

Teddy bear, brown woven mohair, black shoe button eyes, embroidered nose, mouth & claws, fully jointed, felt pads, 11" (some fur wear, moth damage) **115**

Teddy bear, blond mohair, black shoe button eyes, embroidered nose & mouth, fully jointed, excelsior stuffing, ca. 1910, 12" (extensive fur loss) **259**

Teddy bear, blond mohair body w/swivel head, excelsior stuffing in arms & legs, beige felt pads, kapok stuffing in torso, squeaker, unmarked, 12" 130

Teddy bear, white mohair, black shoe button eyes, tan embroidered nose, mouth & claws, felt pads, fully jointed, includes pink dress & floral coat, ca. 1905, 12" (wear, two replaced pads) 575

Teddy bear, black mohair body w/swivel head, excelsior stuffing, amber glass eyes, shaved muzzle w/black floss nose & mouth, beige felt pads, fully jointed, unmarked, 13" 400

Teddy bear, golden mohair body w/swivel head, excelsior stuffing, white shoe button eyes w/metal centers, black floss pointed nose, low applied ears, squeeze-type squeaker, long felt pads, floss claws, fully jointed, unmarked, 14" 230

Teddy bear, blond mohair, black steel eyes, embroidered nose, mouth & claws, felt pads, fully jointed, ca. 1910, 17" (spotty fur loss, arms damaged at shoulders) 518

Teddy bear, golden mohair body w/swivel head, excelsior stuffing, brown glass eyes, shaved muzzle w/black floss nose, long arms w/felt pads & threes floss claws, large oversized feet w/felt pads, & three floss claws, fully jointed, unmarked, 17" 325

Teddy bear, yellow long mohair, glass eyes, embroidered nose & mouth, felt pads, kapok stuffing, fully jointed, 1930s, England, 17" (some fiber loss & moth damage) 200

Teddy bear, blond mohair, shoe button eyes, black embroidered nose, mouth & claws, felt pads, excelsior stuffing, fully jointed, possibly Ideal, ca. 1910, 18" (small patches of fur loss, loose joints) 1,035

Teddy bear, light golden long mohair, swivel head, large brown glass eyes, black floss nose, black floss mouth, excelsior stuffing in head & body, fully jointed, small lump on back, mohair pads on paws, unmarked, 18" 365

Teddy bear, beige mohair w/dark brown tips, swivel head w/excelsior stuffing, dark brown glass eyes, red felt open-close mouth, black floss claws, unmarked, 19" 110

Teddy bear, ginger mohair, fully jointed, black shoe button eyes, black embroidered nose, mouth & claws, excelsior stuffing, felt pads, ca. 1919, 20" h. (some pad damage, slight fur loss mostly on face) 460

Teddy bear, golden mohair body w/swivel head, excelsior stuffing, glass eyes, brown floss nose, shaved muzzle, large oversized ears, cloth pads, no stitched claws, fully jointed, unmarked, 23" 295

Teddy bear, dark golden mohair, fully jointed, shoe button eyes, hump on back, possibly early Ideal, 24" 875

Teddy bear, light yellow mohair, black shoe button eyes, brown knit fabric nose, embroidered mouth & claws, felt pads, fully jointed, ca. 1905, w/provenance & early photo, Ideal Toy Co., 25" (some pad damage & fur loss, left ear needs reattaching, fur somewhat greyed) 10,925

Teddy bear, golden mohair, glass eyes, tan felt pads, fully jointed, excelsior stuffing, detached partial cloth label, pink silk & mohair jacket, early Bruin, 28" (traces of nose, mouth & claw embroidery, slight fur loss, settled stuffing in limbs) 6,325

Teddy bear on wheels, ginger mohair, black embroidered nose, mouth & claws, glass eyes, steel frame, solid wooden wheels, ca. 1920s, 17" l. (some spotty fur loss) 748

Teddy bear on wheels, light brown mohair, glass eyes, open mouth, remnants of embroidered nose, felt pads, excelsior stuffing, metal frame & cast iron wheels, ca. 1913, 20½" l. (wear around mouth & nose) 230

TELEVISION SETS

Admiral Table Top TV

Admiral, 7" Bakelite table top from 1948, uncracked (ILLUS.) $125

Admiral 17T11, 7" Bakelite table top from 1948, no cracks 125

Admiral 20X122, 10" Bakelite console, 30" high, 1948, no cracks 200

Admiral C2516, 24" console from 1954, simple styling 15

Andrea CO-VJ12, late 1940s console with 12" picture tube 55

Andrea KTE-5, 1938 5" assembled kit television, 2-channel, complete with all original parts 2,500

Andrea 1938 Kit TV

Andrea KTE-5, 1938 kit TV with 5" CRT,
  all original (ILLUS.) **2,500**
Andrea T-VK12, heavy wooden table top,
  1948 continuous tuning set **75**
Automatic, TV-490, cloth-covered 7"
  portable with built-in magnifier **350**
Automatic TV-707, unusual blond wooden
  1948 table top with 7" screen in center of
  front **200**
CBS Columbia 10FM, 1948 wooden table
  top with rounded edges **150**
CBS Columbia 12CC2, experimental
  color-drum set, ca. 1951, very rare **3,000**
CBS Columbia 205C1, 1955 color TV with
  19" round CRT **200**
CBS Columbia 22CO5, 1955 B&W console
  with 21" picture tube **20**
DuMont 180, 1937 pre-war with 14" CRT
  and 4-channel tuner, rare, over **3,000**

DuMont 1948 Chatham

DuMont 1948 Chatham, 12" set with good
  knobs and trim (ILLUS.) **175**
DuMont RA-102, 1947 12" console with
  very unusual styling **650**
DuMont RA-103 Chatham, trapezoidal-
  shaped 12" table top from 1947, clean
  and complete **175**
DuMont RA-103 D3, square version of 12"
  table top **20**
DuMont RA-115, large-screen console,
  beautiful double-door set **25**
DuMont RA-119 Royal Sovereign,
  surprisingly large 30" console from 1952 . . . . **400**

General Electric Bakelite TV

General Electric, 10" Bakelite table top
  from 1948, streamlined, unbroken (ILLUS.) . . . **250**
General Electric 10T1, Bakelite 10" table
  top from 1948, streamlined and unusual **250**
General Electric 12T1, 1949 12" wooden
  table top with very square corners **25**
General Electric 801, 1947 10" console,
  screen and large AM dial behind small
  doors **100**
General Electric 806, 10" table top, tall with
  glass front plate **65**
General Electric 901, very large and heavy
  projection set from 1947, complete **200**
General Electric HM-171, 5" table top from
  1938, 3-channel (push buttons below the
  screen), sight only, no speaker, excellent
  cosmetics **3,000**
General Electric Hotpoint, painted metal,
  mid-1950s portables, nice colors, clean, each . . **50**
Jenkins Model 100, 1932 scanning-disc TV,
  complete with motor, disc and neon
  assembly on original board **1,500**
Jenkins Model R-400, scanning-disc TV
  with lens projecting image on ground,
  glass screen, over **2,500**
JVC 3100D Video Capsule, 1970s pyramid-
  shaped white plastic table top, clean and
  working **400**
JVC 3240 Video Sphere, spherical plastic
  TV with chain on top and square plastic
  base **200**

JVC Video Sphere

JVC Video Sphere Model 3240, in white or
  red, working (ILLUS.) **200**

Motorola 19CT1, 1954 color console with
original 19" round CRT, clean with raster..... **400**

Motorola 19P1, early, large portable
transistor TV, 1954...................... **85**

Motorola 21C2, mid-1950s 21" wooden
console............................... **25**

Motorola VT-105, 10" wooden table top
from 1948, stepped top **250**

Motorola VT-71, 7" wooden table top from
1947, suprisingly common set **150**

Motorola Wooden Table Top TV

Motorola VT-71, common wooden 7" table
top from 1948 (ILLUS.).................. **150**

Panasonic TR-005, flying saucer-shaped
early 1970s mini table top, over **500**

Panasonic "Flying Saucer"

Panasonic TR-005, small silver "Flying
Saucer" from 1970s (ILLUS.) **500**

Philco 48-700, 1948 heavy wooden table
top with 7" screen, very clean............. **200**

Philco Table Top TV

Philco 49-1001, 10" table top from 1949
with offset CRT (ILLUS.) **85**

Philco 49-1240, 12" console from 1949........ **25**

Philco Predicta console, Barber Pole, flat
front on 3 small feet, mahogany, as found **400**

Philco Predicta table top, clean and
complete, working condition.............. **500**

Philco Predicta Tandem, 2-pc. set, 21"
CRT on a long white cord, as found......... **400**

Philco-48-100, stepped top 10" table top
from 1948............................ **250**

Pilot TV-37

Pilot TV-37, 3" 1947 cheaply made set,
clean cabinet (ILLUS.) **200**

RCA 21-CT-55, 1955 color TV with 21"
round tube, clean with raster **150**

RCA 630-TS, RCA's first 10" post-war table
top, 1946 set, clean and complete **200**

RCA 721-TS, small 10" table top from 1947,
clean and complete, as found **100**

RCA 9PC41, 1949 pop-up screen projecting
set, buffet-style........................ **65**

RCA CT-100, first mass-produced 1954
color TV with 15" CRT, as found **450**

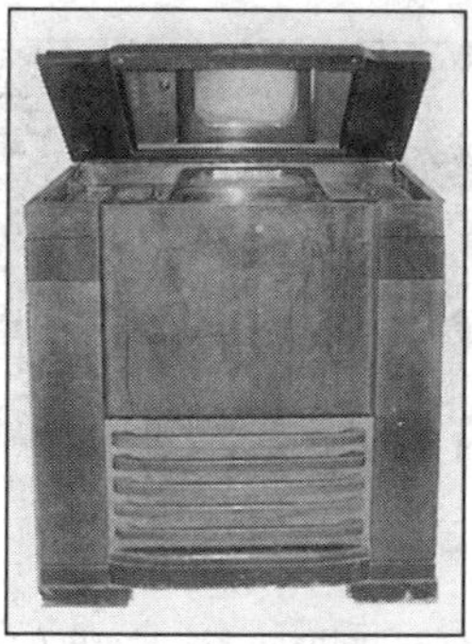

RCA TRK-12

RCA TRK-12, 5-channel 1939, 12"
mirror-in-lid TV (ILLUS.) **3,000**

RCA TRK-12, mirror-in-lid 1939 console,
original-5 channel tuner, good top and
veneer, as found **3,000**

RCA TT5, 5" table top, 5-channel tuner, ca.
1939, clean and complete **3,000**

Sparton, 10" combination TV-radio-phone,
clean and complete **75**

Zenith, 16" "porthole" console, ca. 1950,
clean and complete **125**

Appliqued & Embroidered Table Rug

TEXTILES

BEDSPREADS

Rare Crewel-embroidered Bedspread

Crewel-embroidered linen, large rectangular center panel w/pleated side & end panels, embroidered overall w/scrolled flowering vine design on a linen ground, worked in green, salmon, yellow, navy blue & purple yarns, initialed & dated "E.H. 1804," American, toning, scattered staining, minor fiber loss & wear, 98 x 104" (ILLUS.) **$6,900**

Hooked bed rug, loose weave butternut-dyed wool ground w/hooked wool floral design in green, cerise & coral, probably northern New England, minor losses, tears, repairs, 70 x 80" (ILLUS.) **575**

Early New England Bed Rug

COVERLETS

Jacquard, single weave, one piece, central medallion w/foliage borders, red, olive green, greyish blue & natural white, bottom edge labeled "M. by H. Stager, Mount Joy, Lancaster Co. Pa. Warranted Fast Colors No. 1," 78 x 83" (wear, stains) **275**

Jacquard, single weave, two-piece, large floral medallions, a vintage grape border, corners labeled "W. in Mt. Vernon, Knox County Ohio by Jacob and Michael Ardner, 1854," reds, gold, navy blue & natural white, 74 x 80" (overall & edge wear, minor stains) **358**

Jacquard, single weave, one-piece, large four-rose center clusters surrounded by a large leafy scroll medallion within a scroll edging & spread-winged eagle spandrels, leafy scroll border w/stylized pineapples

in each corner, edge label "Manuf. by
H.F. Stager & Son, Fast Colors, Mount
Joy, Lancaster County, Penn.," green,
navy blue, red & natural white, 76 x 80"
(minor stains) **550**

Large Medallions w/Pinwheel Borders

Jacquard, double woven, two-piece, leafy
stars within scalloped medallions,
pinwheel & foliate border, red on white,
signed "Berlin - Holmes Co. 1845"
w/roosters in corners, minor staining,
fiber wear, 66½ x 82" (ILLUS.) **230**

Jacquard, single weave, two-piece, bands
of vintage grape design across the
center, tulip borders at ends & leafy vines
along sides, corners labeled "Jacob
Snyder, Stark Co., Ohio, 1850," navy
blue, pink, olive yellow & natural white,
74 x 82" (edge & overall wear, some
fringe missing) **495**

Florals with Eagle Border Coverlet

Jacquard, double woven, two-piece, large
four-blossom clusters w/pairs of leaves
alternating w/smaller blossomheads,
eagle & foliate border, blue & natural
white, signed "Caroline L. Mott 1835.
French Weaver Waterville," New York,
fiber wear, minor repairs & staining,
83" sq. (ILLUS.) **920**

Jacquard, double woven, two-piece, large
four-rose medallions & a double vintage
border, tomato red, navy blue & natural
white, 76 x 84" (top edge worn, light stains) . . . **220**

Jacquard, double woven, one-piece, rows
of large leafy rose blossoms alternating
w/bands of small starbursts, leaf &
blossom border band, navy blue & natural
white, attributed to Enon Valley,
Pennsylvania, 19th c., 76 x 86" **165**

Jacquard, single weave, one-piece, central
medallion w/corner designs w/horses,
eagles, dogs, bust of Grant & "Liberty,
Virtue, 1869," wine red & natural white
w/an olive green warp in the reds,
76 x 86" (wear, wool yarn missing in
some areas) **605**

Daniel Bury Jacquard Coverlet

Jacquard, single weave, two-piece, large
star & flower medallions w/wide borders
of peacocks standing on domes marked
"North America" & "E Pluribus Unum"
alternating w/vintage grape borders &
baskets of fruit, corners w/stars & signed
"Daniel Bury" (1842-47), navy blue &
natural white, minor wear & stains,
60 x 88" (ILLUS.) **715**

Dated Coverlet with Urns & Birds

Jacquard, double woven, two-piece, large
urns of fruits & flowers & birds feeding
young surrounded by leafy scrolls in the
center, a Christian & heathen border,
border marked "Piqua 1846," natural
white, tomato red, navy blue & royal blue,
minor stains, end binding w/wear,
76 x 88" (ILLUS.) **1,540**

Jacquard, double woven, two-piece,
geometric floral center medallion,
floral border, all corners labeled "J. Craig

2 miles N. East of Greensburg, D.C., IA. 1855," 78½ x 90½" (stains, wear, fringe on one edge) **578**

Jacquard, single weave, two-piece, rows of large oval delicate blossoms surrounded by long serrated leaves & alternating w/small starburst, zigzag blossomhead border, signed "Michael Ruth - John Kaufman - 1838," navy blue, red & natural white, Bucks County, Pennsylvania, sewn-on fringe, 76 x 96" (minor wear & stains) **358**

Jacquard, double woven, one-piece, a central floral medallion w/a vintage border, large floral clusters & long-tailed birds in the corners, narrow scroll & blossom border, corners dated "1852," tomato red & natural white, 89 x 98" (wear, stains & some edge damage) **220**

Overshot, double woven, two-piece, summer-winter type, Optical patt. w/Pine Tree border, navy blue & natural white, 75 x 92½" (stains, some wear, no fringe) **275**

Overshot, double woven, two-piece, summer-winter type, Snowflake & Pine Tree patt., navy blue & natural white, 19th c. (wear, stains, some edge wear & fringe loss) **330**

Overshot, Rob Peter to Pay Paul, Orange Peel patt., indigo, white wool & linen, 19th c., 77 x 79½" **173**

Overshot, two panels sewn together, woven w/cloverleaf and checkerboards, fringed border, 19th c., 74 x 68" **460**

LINENS & NEEDLEWORK

Blanket, twill-woven wool plaid, initialed & dated "M.M. March the 10 1840," worked in green, rust, sage & yellow yarns, 70 x 81½" **805**

Blanket, twill-woven wool plaid, initialed "MDC," worked in navy blue & cream yarns, 19th c., 75 x 97" **374**

Needlework family register, silk thread on linen, rectangular w/a wide stylized floral vine border w/the names of the parents & date of marriage in panels at the top above a three-section rectangular register w/columns titled "Names," "Births," & "Deaths," pious verse below w/a one-story house flanked by leafy trees at the bottom, begins w/the marriage of Amaziah Phillips & Lucy Bates in 1809, probably Beverly, Massachusetts, vibrant colors, unframed, 17 x 25" (minor toning, very minor staining) **4,600**

Pillowcases, cotton w/tiny cross-stitching, monogrammed "H.H.F." & dated "1852," 16 x 41", pr. **65**

Pillowcases, embroidered cotton & linen w/crocheted & tatted trim, single size, set of 12 . . . . **40**

Pillowcases, white, monogramed "H," pr. **18**

Sheet set, padded satin, red couching, "CC," monogram, 108 x 120", together w/four 33 x 42" pillow shams, eyelet trim, 5 pcs. **195**

Sheet set, white padded satin stitch "CC" monogram, Buretto petals, handmade eyelet trim, 96 x 104", together w/four matching pillow cases, 5 pcs. **150**

Sheet set, white w/blue Madeira cut work & embroidery, 88 x 102", together w/four matching pillow cases, 5 pcs. **150**

Table rug, appliqued & embroidered, rectangular, composed of thirty-two tan & black blocks in a checkerboard design using colored appliques of birds & flowers, framed by flowers & hearts, New England, mid-19th c., minor imperfections, 39½ x 74½" (ILLUS. beginning of category) **4,025**

Early Embroidered Table Rug

Table rug, appliqued, pieced & embroidered wool, the thirteen panel design decorated w/various embroidered & appliqued foliate designs worked in red, green, purple, blue, sage, taupe & white on a black field, New England, first half 19th c., very minor losses, scattered minor fiber wear, minor fading, 30¾ x 50¾" (ILLUS.) **2,645**

Table runner, linen, 6" ecru crocheted edge, 12" corners, 18 x 68" **35**

Tablecloth, ecru filet lace, 72 x 84" **55**

Tablecloth, extremely fine drawn work, embroidered dragons center, 80 x 88" **245**

Tablecloth, hand-crocheted white lace composed of squares w/pineapples & fans in each corner, made up of 475 small three inch squares, never used, 72 x 90" **85**

Tablecloth, double damask, woven Blue Willow patt., 92" **75**

Towel, embroidered woven linen, initialed & dated "BC 1828," red embroidery on a cream ground, probably Pennsylvania, 16½ x 56" **86**

NEEDLEWORK PICTURES

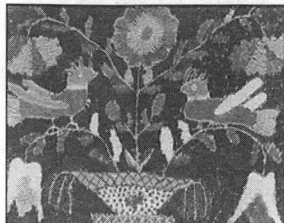

Urn with Flowers & Birds Embroidery

Birds & urn of flowers, wool & silk embroidery w/a large stylized urn at the bottom issuing stems w/drooping tulips & a large top sunflower flanked by arched stems w/blossoms, a pair of large colorful birds on the branches, worked in green brown & rose wool & blue, white, pink & yellow sink on a linen ground, probably Pennsylvania, late 18th - early 19th c., 7 x 8½" (ILLUS.) **2,300**

Landscape, scene of musicians & two dancing couples in 18th c. dress in a landscape of trees, an oak tree, flowers, a dog, birds & the sun, all petit-point in intricate stitches in shades of grey, blue, gold, brown, black, white & red, good colors, original pine stretcher & molded walnut arch-topped frame, 18th c., 25½ x 35½" (age cracks in frame). **1,210**

Detailed English Landscape Scene

Landscape scene, needlepoint embroidery on linen w/a detailed landscape showing a lady picking fruit from a tree in the front left, a lady riding in a small open cart in the center, animals, trees, houses, a windmill & a mansion in the distance, all within a leaf border, George III period, England, framed, 33 x 37½" (ILLUS.) **3,450**

Moses in the Bullrushes, silk needlework & painting on silk, embroidered in gold, green, blue & brown threads on a painted silk ground w/two maidens & the infant Moses on the seashore & New Haven, Connecticut harbor in the background, in original giltwood & gesso framed w/original reverse-painted black mat

Fine Moses in the Bullrushes Picture

w/gilt border & stars & title at the bottom, paper label from back reads "Maria Van Wyck's journal, Litchfield, Conn. June 1808 'spent the day in Embroidery,' Maria Van Wyck born 1794 d. Dec 8, 1831 m. Tunis Brinckerhoff 1814," Miss Patten's School, Hartford, Connecticut, 19¼ x 24" (ILLUS.) **23,000**

Fine Detailed Mourning Picture

Mourning picture, silk embroidery on painted silk, worked in shades of green, yellow, beige, cream & blue silk in a variety of stitches including split, satin & chain stitch & French knots w/watercolor on silk figures of two maidens in Neoclassical gowns flanking a vine-draped monument atop a plinth inscribed "Sac. to the Memory of Capt. Mayo Gerrish born Nov. 15, 1768 died March 28, 1809 age 41," in original black reverse-painted mat w/gilt trim, Newburyport, Massachusetts, ca. 1818, 17 x 23" (ILLUS.). **13,800**

Needlework embroidery on silk scene, an oval reserve w/a scene of a woman kneeling in prayer amid neoclassical urns & columns, a brass sequin border, flowering vine outer border, water-color highlights, early 19th c., framed, 13½ x 16½" (toning, minor fiber wear & sequin loss) **259**

Peacocks on flowering vines, Arts & Crafts style, silk needlework on linen, a facing pair of detailed long-tailed peacocks perched on forked branches of a tree w/large blossoms & leaves, worked in shades of cream, tan, brown, green, & dark blue, framed, three small tears, early 20th c., 52 x 59" **550**

QUILTS

Fine Appliqued Album Quilt

Appliqued Album patt., composed of nine large sections each w/stylized flowering vines or urns of flowers in green & pink calico w/solid red & goldenrod, large leafy blossom stems around border, blind-stitched & whip-stitched w/floss w/some floss embroidery on stems, overall wear, stains, 75 x 80" (ILLUS.) **2,035**

Appliqued crib quilt, Oak Leaf variant patt., worked in red, green & yellow calicos on a white ground, 19th c., 28¾ x 36" **575**

Appliqued Floral Medallion Quilt

Appliqued Floral Medallion patt., composed of six large four-arm stylized floral medallions across the center in pink & green calico w/delicate running flowering vine border, well-quilted white ground, 20th c., 80 x 96" (ILLUS.) **550**

Appliqued Flowerhead & Blossom Sprig patt., composed of an arrangement of five large floral clusters w/a large central blossom issuing four blossoms & leaf sprigs, running floral vine border, in olive green calico & solid red & yellow on a quilted white ground, embroidered date & initials "E.S.E. 1855," 85" sq. (overall wear, minor stains) **798**

Appliqued Oak Leaf patt., worked in green on a white quilted field, mid-19th c., 61 x 81" (fading, staining, toning) **316**

Appliqued Princess Feather patt., four large eight-arm pinwheels in salmon pink alternating w/teal green, separated by striped bands & star blocks on a white ground, 75 x 82" (overall wear, some fading & color loss, stains) **303**

Rose of Sharon Appliqued Quilt

Appliqued Rose of Sharon patt., composed of eight large floral clusters alternating w/crossed branch & heart clusters on a white ground, running vine border, worked in green calico & red cotton, second half 19th c., toning, minor fading, very minor staining, 82½ x 84" (ILLUS.) **805**

Appliqued Rose Wreath patt., rose wreath clusters in the center framed by similar running borders, cut corners, worked in red & teal green, mid-19th c., 82 x 84" (fading, very minor staining) **230**

Appliqued Sunburst & Eagle patt., worked in green, terra cotta & red on a white quilted field, mid-19th c., 88 x 90" (fading, staining, minor areas of fiber wear) **230**

Appliqued Sunburst & Rose of Sharon patt., four large scalloped sunbursts w/blossom centers centered by a rose cluster & vining blossom border, four birds on sprigs around the border, worked in red, green & terra cotta on a white quilted ground, mid-19th c., 83½" sq. (very minor staining on back) **2,415**

Simple Tulips in Pots Appliqued Quilt

Appliqued Tulips in Pots patt., a simple arrangement of nine large three-blossom tulips in small pots in dark green, red & goldenrod on a finely feathered wreath-quilted white ground (ILLUS.) **600**

Ornate Tulips in Pots Quilt

Appliqued Tulips in Pots patt., composed of an arrangement of sixteen blocks w/large three-blossom tulips in small pots all enclosed by sawtooth borders within a wide outer border of birds on branches, trees & stars all on a white ground, in green & red calico, 19th c., minor staining, scattered fiber wear, 92½ x 94½" (ILLUS.) **978**

Pieced Barn Raising patt., Log Cabin variant, composed of various calico & other materials, late 19th c., 68 x 69½" (fading, minor fiber wear) **374**

Pieced Bowtie patt., composed of multi-colored blocks in prints & calico in shades of brown, blue, red & beige on a red dotted ground, 65 x 71" (overall wear & minor stains) **358**

Fine Centennial Pieced Quilt

Pieced Centennial patt., the center w/four large printed fabric reserves w/scenes of various exhibition halls at the 1876 Centennial Exposition, bordered by pairs of American flags & bands of white stars worked in red, white, blue & black, wide border bands, staining, 74½ x 83" (ILLUS.) **748**

Pieced Double Irish Chain patt., composed of blue & pink calico w/a sawtooth border on white, 72 x 80" (wear, small stains, some edge wear & fading to binding) **495**

Pieced Grandmother's Flower Garden patt., composed of multi-color print & solid color blocks on a white & yellow ground, 78 x 92" (very minor stains) **248**

Pieced Lone Star patt., composed of blocks of goldenrod, yellow & white sateen, 82 x 84" (minor stains) **330**

Pieced Miniature Nine Patch patt., composed of small patches in pink, green calico & multi-colored prints on a navy blue ground, 64" sq. (stains, wear, some edge damage) **358**

Pieced Monkey Wrench patt., worked on multi-colored print blocks on a diamond-quilted white ground, machine-sewn banding, 72 x 84 (overall wear & stains) **193**

Sawtooth Design Quaker-made Quilt

Pieced Sawtooth Border patt., wide bands of blue & amethyst w/white sawtooth borders on a khaki field, signed & dated on reverse "Mary Anne Wisner 1841," Pennsylvania, Quaker-made, fading, staining, losses, 95½ x 100½" (ILLUS.) **690**

Pieced Star Medallion patt., composed of nine large star medallions worked in blocks of red, yellow & teal green on a white quilted ground w/a red border band, 75" sq. (overall wear, light stains, small hole in backing) **435**

Early Chintz Trapunto Quilt

Pieced Stars in Hexagons patt., composed of chintz pieces arranged in stars in hexagons forming concentric hexagonal rings, white ground, trapunto technique, blue & red chintz binding, ca. 1850 (ILLUS.) **6,325**

Amish Sunshine & Shadow Quilt

Pieced Sunshine & Shadow patt., a large
central square composed of multi-colored
blocks of wool, crepe, knit, etc., all within
a wide purple border, made by Mrs.
Hannah King, 1930, Amish, moth
damage, spotted fading in border, 80" sq.
(ILLUS.) **357**

Trapunto quilt, white on white, embroidered
feather border centers a reserve of a
basket of fruit & flowers, surrounded by
foliate banding, fruit, birds & corner fans,
signed "Mary E. Tuutenberg, 1873,"
81½ x 83" (old repairs, fiber wear,
scattered minor stains & toning). **748**

SAMPLERS

Early Rhode Island Sampler

Alphabet, pious verse & inscription,
upper bands of alphabet separated by
bold vining bands from the short pious
verse above another vining band & the
lower inscription reading "Ann Cushing is
my name with my needle I wrought the
same in the 9 year of my age July the 10
1748," Newport, Rhode Island, framed,
7⅝ x 10¾" (ILLUS.). **1,955**

Alphabets above birds, wreaths & urns, a
long rectangular form w/wool needlepoint
& silk cross-stitch on woven mesh, a top
series of alphabets in various sizes above

a lower band of large baskets & urns of
flowers, wreaths & a pair of facing birds,
signed "Mary J. Mathers," in green, golds,
brown, red, blue, purple & yellow, framed,
14¾ x 18¼" (alphabets faded, stains,
some added or repaired wool stitches) **1,045**

Alphabets, inscription & pious verse, the
upper two-thirds composed of rows of
alphabets above the inscription "Huldah
F. Hopkins, Sampler Wrought in the 8th
year of her age, Stockbridge July 1812,"
a short pious verse at the bottom, silk
threads in shades of blue, brown & white
on a coarse tow linen ground, framed,
American, 13 x 18" **468**

Detailed Early Massachusetts Sampler

**Alphabets, numerals, pious verse &
landscape,** the upper panel of various
sizes of alphabets over a row of numerals
above the pious verse in tiny letters
above the lower panel composed of
scrolling grapevines, birds, trees &
flowers, a narrow geometric border on
three sides all within a wider running bold
flowering vine border, signed "Haverhill
August 29 Betsey Gage Plummer Born
AD 1782 this wrought in the 14 year of
her age...," Massachusetts, framed,
toning, tack holes, minor staining,
15¾ x 19⅜" (ILLUS.) **10,925**

Alphabets & pious verse, an upper panel
of alphabets & a pious verse above a
lower panel of geometric designs &
flowering plants, a geometric floral
border, signed "Harriet French AE7 at
Miss Hammonds School Boston," on
linen, framed, 11⅜ x 11⅞" (toning, fading,
scattered staining). **1,150**

**Alphabets, pious verse over birds &
flowers,** the upper panel of alphabets
over a pious verse above the large lower
panel centered by a large vase w/tall
flowering vines flanked by parrots &
various fruit, flower & animal designs, all
within a running geometric leaf border,
signed "Mary Greenleaf born in July the

Ornate Early American Sampler

16 1786," Newbury or Newburyport area, Massachusetts, unframed, toning, fading, minor staining, very minor fiber wear, 16¼ x 21⅛" (ILLUS.)................. **10,925**

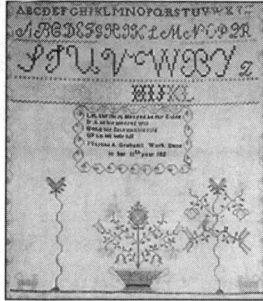

Early Unfinished Sampler

Alphabets & pious verse over florals, the top w/graduated bands of alphabets over a small pious verse & inscription in a running vine box above a pair of tall-stalked plants flanking a central basket of flowers, a tiny dog in each corner, a narrow running vine outer border, unfinished, signed "Martha A. Grahams Work Done in her 11th years 182...," toning, fading, minor losses & staining, framed, 16¼ x 18⅝" (ILLUS.).............. **805**

Alphabets & pious verse over flowers, three alphabet panels above a pious verse w/trees, lower panel of birds & floral devices, three sides bordered w/a band of narrow geometric stylized flowers, "Rizpah Farmer born Sept the 26 1797 aged 13 years," mounted on fabric, framed, 17¾ x 18½" (toning, fading)....... **1,955**

Flowering vine, potted plants & inscription, upper panel of flowering vine w/bow above a lower panel of a potted flowering plant & flowering vine w/bow flanked by foliate designs, flowering vine border on a dark ground, signed "Lucy

Deweys sampler wrought in the eleventh year of her age 1794," unfished, unframed, 15½ x 17" (toning, fading) **2,070**

Landscape, pious verse & other devices, the upper panel w/various foliate, fruit, animal & regalia designs above a middle panel w/a pious verse, the lower panel w/a scene of a brick house & fence flanked by soldiers, trees & flowering plants, geometric floral border, signed "Eliza matilda Excell AD 13 Pear street 1839," framed, 12 x 15⅞" (toning, minor fading & staining, scattered minor holes) ... **1,495**

Pious verse above large building, the two portions flanked by scattered trees, flowers, butterflies & bee skeps, all within an geometric running floral border, silk threads in green, gold, blue, pink, brown, black & white on a homespun linen ground, signed "Emma Husselbee, Brierly Hill, June 18th, 184...," old frame, 21½ x 22" (minor stains, several holes) **935**

Pious verse & floral & bird panel, the upper panel w/a long pious verse above a lower panel w/flowering leafy vines above birds perched on flowering trees, all within a foliate & butterfly border, signed "Jane Oliver 1825 aged 13 years," probably England, framed, 12⅞ x 19⅛" (toning, fading, minor staining)............. **546**

TAPESTRIES

Aubusson Floral Decorated Tapestry

Aubusson, tall rectangular form w/a central long arched & scroll-trimmed panel decorated in peonies, roses & dahlias in earth tones of blues, browns & taupe, France, 1830, 52" l., 126" h. (ILLUS.) **6,038**

Aubusson panel, depicting a panoramic 18th c. landscape scene w/figures among ancient ruins & a tower, 19th c., 32 x 58" (brittle, minor fabric loss) **805**

Beer & Ale, "Budweiser," "Anheuser-Busch,
Champion Clydesdale Horses" on back,
blank saddle, color drawing of 8-horse
team on front, red, green, brown, black &
white, forty-strike size, royal flash 8-16

Beer & Ale, "Coors" on back, "Coors Export
Lager" on saddle, "The Brass Rail, 1518
Champa Street, Denver, Colo." on front,
colorful waterfall scene w/can & short-
necked bottle inside, yellow, red, blue &
white, forty-strike size, royal flash 10-12

Beer & Ale, "Falstaff" shield logo
w/"America's Premium Quality Beer" on
front & back, "Falstaff Brewing Corp. St.
Louis, MO." on saddle, white, red, yellow
& black 5-8

Beer & Ale, "Hamm's Beer.... from the land
of sky blue waters" on front, "Refreshingly
yours" on saddle, ad on back, stock
design in white, blue & red 5-8

Beer & Ale, "Heileman's Old Style Lager, G.
Heileman Brewing Co., La Crosse,
Wisconsin" on back, "Aged Longer Than
Any Other Beer" on saddle, "Cavalier" on
front, white, green & yellow 6-12

Beer & Ale, "Michelob..., period" w/Busch
logo on front, "Anheuser-Busch, Inc." on
saddle, Michelob shield on back, black,
red, white & gold, thirty-strike size 5-10

Beer & Ale, "Olympia Beer It's the Water"
on front & back, "It's the Water"
on saddle, "makes the difference"
w/"Olympia Brewing Co., Tumwater,
Wash., U.S.," on back, black, orange & white . . 5-8

Pabst Breweries Matchcover

Beer & Ale, "Pabst Breweries" logo
w/"Houtz Tobacco Company, Phone 534,
Sunbury, Penna" on front, can w/glass &
"Pabst TapaCan" on back, three cans
w/"Pabst TapaCan" across sticks, "Pabst
TapaCan, Brewery Goodness, Sealed
Right In" on inside, dark blue, light blue,
red & white (ILLUS.) 25-40

Beer & Ale, "Rainier Beer, Mountain Finest"
on front & back, blank saddle, white,
yellow & red, back striker 5-10

Beer & Ale, "Red Ribbon Beer" w/bottle &
sandwich on back, "Famous Since 1870"
on saddle, ad on front, stock design in
black, red, silver, yellow & white 8-16

Beer & Ale, "Schlitz, The Beer that made
Milwaukee Famous" on front & back,
blank saddle, brown, white, blue & green,
front or back striker 6-11

Beer & Ale, "Schmidt's Beer, The Brew that
grew with the Great Northwest" on front &
back, "Jacob Schmidt Brewing Co., St.
Paul, Minn" on saddle, white, red & blue 6-12

Beer & Ale, "Stroh's & Stroh Light, Official
Beers 1982 World's Fair" on front back,
red, white & blue, back striker & thirty-
strike size 5-10

Beer & Ale, "Stroz, The Orchid of Beers"
on back, "Since 1876" on saddle, ad on
front, stock design in white, red, pink &
brown 5-10

Blacks, "Coon Chicken Inn, 2950 Highland
Drive, Salt Lake City, Phone 7-1062" on
back, black bellhop on front, "Famous
Coast to Coast" on saddle, gold, red,
black, white & pink 28-30

Blacks, "Cotton Patch, 2720 Midway Drive,
San Diego, California" w/mammy on
front, "AC. 3-8316" on saddle, "The
Bayou Room" on back, map inside, red,
white & black 12-18

Black Matchcover

Blacks, "Frostop, 22nd Ave & 64th St,
Kenosha, Wis" & depicting stylized black
face w/large lips w/few teeth & "Man dat
sho is good!" on forehead on front, "Star
Match Co., St. Louis, MO," black, red &
white (ILLUS.) 23-28

Blacks, "Hotel Barlow, D.M. Floyd,
Manager, Hope Arkansas" on front, "Air
Cooled...," on saddle, name w/black man

& watermelon w/"Down Where The Watermelon Grow" on back, red, green, white & black 18-23

Blacks, "Mammy's Chicken Farm 60, W 52nd St, New York" & depicting mammy w/chicken dinner on back, gold, black, red & white 5-8

Blacks, "Mammy's" on footer, "Black Mammy" on front & back, "HI. 5-4948" on saddle, "Fine Foods, Cocktails, Capitol Drive at Teutonia, Milwaukee" on back, map inside, white, black, red & yellow, thirty-strike size, back striker 15-20

Blacks, "Picaninny, Famous for Barbecued Food" & depicting black child w/red lips & name on front, addresses on back, gold, black & red, Lion Match Corporation 18-23

Blacks, "Sambo's Pancakes" on footer, Indian boy w/tiger on front & back, "they're delightful" on saddle, city list inside, white, red, yellow, green & pink, front or back striker 10-12

Candy, "Reese's Peanut Butter Cups 1¢" on front, "H.B. Reese Candy Co., Hershey, PA." on saddle, box of 1¢ candies on back, orange, green, white & black 5-8

Candy, "Tootsie Rolls, America's Favorite Chewy Chocolate Candy" w/boy & girl riding on roll, "Over 240 Million sold last year 1¢ and 5¢ rolls," dark blue, light blue, red, white & brown, full length 7-10

Double Mint Gum Matchcover

Chewing gum, "Buy Wrigley's Double Mint Quality Gum," w/dark green arrow, orange, yellow & white, full length (ILLUS.) . . . 5-8

Girlie, Girlie Matchcover Catalog, No. 200, Marilyn Monroe, drawing on front, thirty-strike size, back striker 17-23

Girlie, Girlie Matchcover Catalog, No. 247, Domino Club, San Francisco w/reclining nude "Evelyn" on back, blank saddle, thirty-strike size 10-12

Girlie, Girlie Matchcover Catalog, No. 405, Girlie, black & white photo by Ray Schulz, ca. 1989, giant, full-length 11-20

Girlie set, Arrow Match Company, Set No. 2 of 5, "Scotty Says!: Go West Young Man," "Always Vote!" "Support The Community That Supports You," "Drive Safely," "Salute America See It First!" drawings, ad on front, Girlie Matchcover Catalog p. 2, ca. 1950, the set 28-30

Girlie set, Playboy 25th Anniversary, Set of 11, back striker 8-16

Girlie set, Playboy Club, Set of 17, 20th Anniversary, silver, cities on footer, ca. 1980, back striker 19-25

Girlie set, Playboy Club, Set of 19, "1961 HMH Publishing Co." on back, back striker, the set 16-25

Girlie set, Superior Match Co. (Elvgren), Set No. 1 of 5, "A Good Hook Up," "A Live Wire," "Doctor's Orders," "Man's Best Friend," "Sure Shot," ad on front, Girlie Matchcover Catalog p. 26, ca. 1938, the set 20-25

Political, "Bush for President" w/photo on front, dated Nov. 8, 1988, thirty-strike size, back striker 3-6

From left: Wendell Willkie Pop-up Matchcover Pepsi-Cola Matchcover

Political, "Elect Willkie [pop-up], Preserve Your Freedom, Be Thankful You Can Still Do It" on front, blank saddle, "Win with Wendell Willkie" on back, red, white & blue (ILLUS., left) 14-25

Political, "Goldwater in '64" on front back, white & blue. 7-10

Political, "I Like Ike" on front, "Delaware Citizens for Eisenhower-Nixon, 613 Orange St., Wilmington, Delaware" on back, blank saddle, red, white & blue 15-18

Political, "Kennedy for President" w/photo on front, "Johnson for Vice President" w/photo on back, "Vote Democratic" on saddle, red, white & blue. 8-17

Political, "Nixon Agnew" on front in red & white lettering, elephant on back, thirty-strike size 8-13

Political, "Ross Perot for President, 1992" on back, "Elect" on saddle, photo of Perot on front, "Vote Nov. 3rd" on footer, red, white & blue. 3-5

Political, "Truman/Barkley Inaugural Dinner" w/photos of both on front, U.S. Seal on back, Mayflower Hotel & names inside, dated January 19, 1949 35-4

Political, "Win With Wallace" on front, blank
saddle, "Vote Independent American
Party" on back, white & dark blue 8-14
Railroad, "Chicago Great Western Railroad"
logo on front, blank saddle, "Ship Via
Chicago Great Western Ry." w/circular
map on back, red, white, gold & black or
black, white, gold & red 5-8
Railroad, "Litchfield & Madison Railway,
The St. Louis Gateway Route" on front,
blank saddle, "L&M Engine 201"
w/drawing on back, "Daily Co-ordinate
Through...," on inside, red, white,
gold & black. 10-12
Railroad, "Milwaukee (The) Road, Out in
Front" on front, blank saddle, "Route of
the Hiawathas" w/photo of electric
locomotive on back, "Travel with
Pleasure" inside, white, orange, blue,
maroon & black 5-8
Railroad, "Milwaukee (The) Road, Ship and
Travel via..." on front, blank saddle, "The
Milwaukee Road, America's Resourceful
Railroad" w/trains on back, yellow, white,
red & black 4-7
Railroad, "Pennsylvania Railroad"
w/streamlined train & "Serving the Nation"
on back, "Shortest East West Route" on
saddle, "Travel Luxury at Low Fares"
w/"The Great All-Weather Fleet" &
drawing on front, black, red & white 7-10
Railroad, "Reading Lines, The Wall Street,
A Smart..., Modern..., Colorful..., Train...,"
on front, "The Crusader" w/silver train &
"Stainless Steel" on back, "between
Philadelphia and New York" on saddle,
"Two Famous Reading....," inside, blue,
yellow, silver & white. 8-13
Railroad, "Union Pacific Railroad" shield on
back, "Dependable Transportation"
w/train on front, red, white, blue & yellow 5-8
Soda Pop, "7UP" w/small bottle on front,
"Take Some Home" on saddle, "Fresh
UP..., 7 UP..., It Likes You" on back,
green, red, white & black. 9-15
Soda Pop, "Drink Coca-Cola" w/lollipop logo
on front, "Drink Coca-Cola" on saddle,
"Take home a carton, Get that Refreshing
New Feeling" w/a six pack on back,
yellow, red, green & brown 8-14
Soda pop, "Pepsi-Cola, 5¢ Bigger
Drink/Better Taste" on front back, "More
Bounce to the Ounce!" on saddle, "Say
Pepsi...," inside, dark blue, light blue, red
& white (ILLUS., previous page) 8-13
World's Fair, Knoxville, Tenn., 1982,
"Stroh's Light, Official Beer 1982 World's
Fair" on front & back, blue, red, yellow &
white, thirty-strike size, back striker 6-10
World's Fair, New York, 1939-40, "Don't
Mark Time, 4 Minute Crossings," colorful 7-11

World's Fair set, Seattle, 1962, Century 21,
Boulevards of the World, Coliseum 21,
The Gayway, Monorail, Mt. Rainier,
United States Science Pavilion, set of six . . . 25-30

SNUFF BOTTLES & BOXES

BOTTLES

Agate, brown w/the lighter brown skin
cleverly carved in the form of a foo dog
incense burner, China 489
Agate, moss agate of pebble-form carved
w/double-gourds in the darker brown of
the stone, well hollowed out, green jade
branch-form top, China, late 19th c. 920
Agate, patterned grey & white stone, well-
hollowed, stopper of coral-colored Peking
glass, China, late 19th c. 633
Bamboo, carved in the form of a pair of
peaches, China, 20th c. (no stopper) 201
Burnt jade, well-hollowed, fine deep amber
tone, China, late 19th c. 173
Lacquer, cinnabar lacquer carved deeply
w/a landscape scene w/children,
China, 19th c. 86
Peking glass, coral color carved w/a dragon
& phoenix, green jade stopper, China 345
Porcelain, covered w/a yellow glaze over
an underglaze-iron red landscape,
molded lion mask handles & a coral-
glazed porcelain stopper, fake Ch'ien
lung mark, China 288
Porcelain, model of a crab claw covered in
an orange glaze, China 115
Porcelain, white enameled w/a cricket on
each side, Tao Kuang mark & period, China . . 575
Soapstone, carved in high-relief w/a pine
tree & a horse, China 115
Soapstone, carved in the form of a
Buddha's hand citron w/fine markings in
scarlet & black, stopper of coral carved in
a foliate form, China, 19th c. 690

BOXES

Tortoiseshell, carved & decorated
w/Chinese figures, early 19th c.,
⅝ x 1½ x 2½" (some chips & losses) 374

MISCELLANEOUS

Cigar box, Safety brand, wooden box w/a
fine gilded lithographed label inside the
lid, a colorful scene of a uniformed male
racer & his safety bicycle, exterior sides
also illustrated, dated 1901, fair condition 154
Cigar lighter, cast white metal, figural, a
figure of a stocky gentleman wearing a
top hat & resembling W.C. Fields stands
besides a stone bucket for matches, oil
burner in the top hat, on a stepped
oblong base, traces of gilt, 5¼" h. 413

Cigarette case, sterling silver, obverse enamel decorated w/nautical flags of the alphabet, reverse w/a monogram encircled by a wreath, dated "July 4, 1903," 3 x 3½" (wear, scratches) **920**

"Federal-Style Humidor"

Humidor, cov., inlaid mahogany, Federal-Style, rectangular form w/locked cover over two drawers w/brass hardware, ca. 1900 (ILLUS.) **1,150**

Pipe, carved wood, figural, in the form of two faces, decorated in red, yellow & black paint, late 19th - early 20th c., 24" l. (minor cracks)........................ **173**

Tobacco box, cov., brass, long narrow oval shape w/two hinged flat covers, a short end one & a long lengthwise one, long cover engraved " E. Ingham 1860," footed, 6 7/8" l. (one foot bent)............ **193**

Tobacco canister, cov., bentwood, cylindrical w/fitted flat cover, the sides w/the original red paper label printed in black & gold "Velocipede Tobacco Fine Cut" surrounding a scene of a couple on velocipedes, tax stamp for 1868, 10 lbs., 12" h., (some paper loss) **935**

Tobacco cutter, cast iron, counter-type, "Brighton," elf thumbing his nose on handle **175**

Tobacco cutter, cast iron, counter-type, model of a dog **450**

TOOLS

Grandfather's old tool belt is no longer just a dust collector in the garage. From the wrenches, hammers and screwdrivers found inside to the catalog used to order them, tools and related items have become highly sought-after collectibles. Descriptions, pricing and photographs were supplied by Martin J. Donnelly Antique Tools.

Angle divider, Stanley Rule & Level, No. 30, pat. Oct. 27, 1903, original box, 7½" l. (ILLUS.) **$165**

Stanley Angle Divider

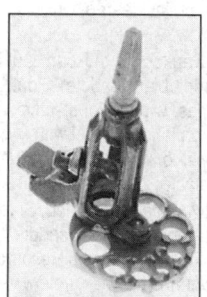

Cast Iron Auger

Auger, unmarked, cast iron, hollow w/pivoting head, ¾" to 1" stock, 6" l. (ILLUS.) **115**

Axe, Kelley-How-Thomson Co., Duluth, Minn., marked w "Hickory" logo, 36" l. **245**

Axe, Mann (William), Lewistown, Penn., No. 93, double bit post mortise, 20" l......... **125**

Axe, Plumb (Fayette R.), Philadelphia, official Kaw Indian single bit belt style w/embossed logos, original paint, 15" l....... **675**

Axe, Vaughn & Bushnell, Chicago, Ill., child's size hand style w/fawn foot handle, 10" l........................... **75**

Axe, White (H.G.), claw felling style w/original handle, 34" l. **285**

Beam compass, B. & J. Mfg. Co., Detroit, Mich., original box marked "Schieber Beam Compass For Yard Sticks," 4½" l. **45**

Bench hook, Millers Falls Company, No. 56, screw adjust w/red Japan infill, 2½" l...... **55**

Bevel, Hall & Knapp, New Britain, Conn., rosewood & brass, Stanley precursor, 8" l. ... **295**

Bevel, St. Johnsbury Tool Co., rosewood & steel, pat. June 14, 1870, 15" l. **895**

Bit brace, Shepardson, Shelburne Falls, Mass., pat. March 1, 1870, 12½" l.......... **265**

Brace, Askham (J.), Sheffield (England), beech & brass, mushroom chuck, ebony head,13½" l............................ **185**

Brace, Fenn (J.), Newgate St. (London), turned rosewood head, lady's size, 13" l...... **695**

Brace, Marples, William, Hibernia Works, ebony "Ultimatum," w/Royal Crest, 14½" l. (ILLUS.) **795**

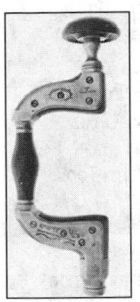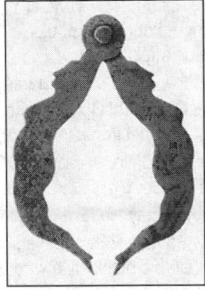

From left: Ebony "Ultimatum" Brace
Hand-made Caliper

Brace, Moulson Brothers, Union Works,
solid ebony w/brass plating, 13¾" l. **550**

Brace, Stanley Rule & Level, No. 8, fray
type, cast iron, marked "Ord. Dept.
U.S.A.," 11" l. **125**

Caliper, Spiers, Stewart, Ayr, Scotland,
machinist's double w/"Spiers/Ayr" imprint,
dated "1917," 5" l. **175**

Caliper, Starrett Co., L.S Athol, Mass.,
double-joint w/divider legs, 6½" l. **45**

Caliper, unmarked, full-body w/faces, 3" l.
(ILLUS.) **495**

Carpenter's slick, Greenlee Tool Co.,
Rockford, Ill., 3" blade, turned beech
handle, 29" l. **225**

Chisel, Buck Brothers, crank-neck type,
1¾" w., 15½" l. **85**

Chisel, Watts (L.H.), 85 Avenue D, New
York, early, hand-forged, 1½" size, 15½" l. **65**

Chisel, Witherby (T.H.), heavy corner socket
type, ¾" w., 14½" l. **95**

Countersink, Smith (Otis A.), Rockfall,
Conn., pat. Oct. 6, 1885, 1" l. **115**

Crate openers: Murcott (John H.), Inc., St.
Albans, No. 76, "Baby Terrier" hammer-
style, original box, 7" l., set of 6 . . . . **155**

Goodell-Pratt Company Drill

Drill, Goodell-Pratt Company No. 101,
hardwood head, pat. Aug. 13, 1895,
16½" l. (ILLUS.) **85**

Drill, Millers Falls Company, cast iron, early
chuck hand-style, 13½" l. **115**

Drill, Vail & Co., G., Morris Co., N.J., early
ratcheting hand-style, "Speedwell Iron
Wks," 14½" l. **385**

Ear punch, Stearns & Co., E.C., Syracuse,
N.Y., cast iron w/heart-shaped cutter, 11" l. . . . **55**

Gauge, Adjustable Gauge Co., Lexington,
Kentucky, angle divider, pat.
Aug. 11, 1908, 8" l. (missing fixing screw) **85**

Circular Wire Gauge

Gauge, Brown (J.R.) & Sharpe, circular wire
gauge w/eagle stamp, 3¼" l. (ILLUS.) **55**

Gauge, Stanley Rule & Level, No. 85½,
rosewood panel marking gauge
w/"Sweetheart" trademark, 21" l. **245**

Gauge, Starrett Co. (The L.S.S.), Athol, Ma.,
No. 269 A, graduated tapering style
w/multiple leaves, 2½" l. **45**

Hammer, Alta Tool Co., Newark, N.J.,
No. 553, nail-holding type w/horseshoe
trademark, 12½" l. **245**

Hammer, Anderson (Solomon S.), New
Berlin, N.Y., No. 4, 155, "wraparound"
claw style, pat. Aug. 20, 1845, 14" l. **895**

Hammer, Blodgett Edge Tool Manufacturing
Co., extra deep hollowing adze, early
handle, New Hampshire, 33" l. **225**

Hammer, Germantown Tool Works,
Philadelphia, Penn., claw style in small
size, 10" l. **45**

Hammer, Nelson (A.T.), Wilton, Iowa, pat.
July 28, 1903, 11" l. **85**

Hammer, Osborne (C.S.) & Co., Newark,
N.J., No. 5, rosewood handle, 11" l. **125**

Hammer, Stanley Rule & Level, No. 5,
saddler's w/original nickel finish, patent
granted to Thomas Conklin Dec. 10,
1867, offered by Stanley from
1872-1898, 12" l. **95**

Hammer, Vaughn & Bushnell, Chicago, Ill.,
No. 11½, curved claw type w/original
label, 12½" l. **85**

Hatchet, Acme, carpenter's w/original
labels, 15" l. **95**

Hatchet, Marble's Arms & Mfg. Co., No. 2P,
folding camp style w/rare "pick" feature,
pat. 1900, 10½" l. **695**

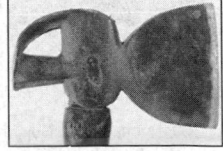

Early Hatchet/Hammer

Hatchet & hammer, Simonds (George),
Boston, Mass., pat. June 11, 1889,
13½" l. (ILLUS.) **345**

Inclinometer level, Helb, Edward, Railroad, Penna., pat. July 12, 1904, 99% original finishes, 24" l. **950**

Inclinometer level, Robinson (M.W.), Brooklyn, N.Y., No. 49, L.L. Davis pat., 24" l. . . **550**

Level, Davis Level & Tool Co, No. 1 "mantel clock," double screw adjustor, 99% original black Japanned finish & gold pinstriping, Springfield, Mass., post-American Civil War, 6" l. **745**

Level, Disston (Henry) & Sons, Philadelphia, Penn., brass bound mahogany, pat. Oct. 29, 1912, 12" l. **255**

Hight Micrometer Level

Level, Hight Micrometer, Pat. Apld For, plumb & level vials, turnscrew adjustment & central semicircular protractor, includes fitted wooden case, Toledo, Ohio, ca. early 1900s, 24" l. (ILLUS.) **3,695**

Level, Stanley Rule & Level, No. 36, double plumb, 9" l. **65**

Level, Stanley Rule & Level, No. 40, cast iron pat., 3" l. **45**

Level, Stanley Rule & Level, No. 98, 99% of original finish, "Sweetheart" trademark, top plate embossed, 9" l. **975**

Level, Stratton Brothers, Greenfield Mass., No. 10, rosewood w/full brass bound, 10" l. . . . **950**

Micrometer, Goodell-Pratt Company, No. 20, 1" to 2" w/original box, 7" l. **45**

Plane, 16" jack, 2" iron, ca. 1875, "Ensenore Wrks, New York" **30**

Plane, 8" coffin-shaped smooth, 2" double iron, ca. 1828, "Union Factory, Warranted, H. Chapin" (mark B). **30**

Bailey's "The Victor" Plane

Plane, Bailey (L.), Boston, Mass., No. 14, light duty plow metallic, "Victor" brand, pat. July 6, 1875, 8" l. (ILLUS.) **5,250**

Plane, coachmaker door check, 2" iron, iron sole, ca. 1854, "H. Barrus & Co., Goshen, MA" **35**

Plane, Fulton, New York, N.Y., No. 55334, midget knuckle-joint block, pat. Feb. 3, 1891, original box, 7" l. **125**

Plane, low angle block, Stanley No. 60½ **45**

Plane, Ohio Tool Co., Columbus, Ohio, No. 08, cast iron jointer, metallic, 24" l. **365**

Plane, round No. 2, ca. 1851, "Ohio Tool Co." (mark C6) **25**

Plane, Stanley No. 3 w/original decal on handle . . **35**

Plane, Stanley Rule & Level, No. 220, adjustable block style w/rosewood knob, original box, 7" l. **55**

Pliers w/wrench, Diamond Horseshoe Caulk Co., No. DH 16, combination pliers & wrench w/screwdriver, 6" l. **65**

Early Steel Plumb Bob

Plumb bob, Bergen Tool Co., Batavia, Ill., early steel bob w/original fitted wooden-spindle case, 4¾" l. (ILLUS.) **395**

Plumb bob, Keuffel & Esser Co., New York, No. 83 0006, brass, unused in original case, 5" l. **85**

Plumb bob, Kuker-Ranken Inc., Seattle, Washington, No. K32, solid brass, original box, No. 2 size, 9¼" l. **225**

Plumb bob, Stanley Rule & Level, No. 5, cast iron nickel plated w/internal reel, 4½" l. . . **275**

Protractor, Chevallier, brass body, France, 6" l. **285**

Protractor, Roessler (Paul), New Haven, Conn., early brass, marked "Engl.," 4¾" l. **85**

Router, Millers Falls Company, No. 77, closed-throat, all original irons & box, 9" l. **145**

Early Caliper Rule

Rule, Brown & Sharpe Manufacturing Providence, w/caliper, pat. June 14, 1892, 3" l. (ILLUS.). **95**

Rule, D.B. & S., Providence, R.I., triangular,
steel, 6" l. 75

Rule, Lufkin Rule Co. (The), No. 1106, steel
zig-zag folding type w/embossed
numbers, 72" l. 15

Rule, Lufkin Rule Co. (The), No. 780, two-
fold, full bound, narrow, 24" l. 85

Rule, Stanley Rule & Level, No. 38, one-
fold, ivory w/caliper, 6" l. 375

Rule, Stanley Rule & Level, No. 57, four-fold
w/arch joint, unbound, 36" l. 165

Rule, Stanley Rule & Level, No. 65, four-fold
w/square joint, unbound, 12" l. 85

Rule, Tiffany & Co., sterling silver, pointer
w/pencil, 12" l. 275

Rule & level, Stanley Rule & Level, No. 424,
aluminum, zig-zag folding type, 48" l. 75

Patternmaker's Saw

Saw, Atkins (E.C.) & Co., Indianapolis, No.
26, patternmaker's saw, original "Keeper,"
11" l. (ILLUS.) 115

Saw, Booth (John) & Son, Philadelphia,
Penn., beechwood handle pad saw,
7½" l. (missing blade) 65

Saw, Disston (Henry), Philadelphia, No. 25,
Jackson-Gorham patent, pat. May 12,
1856, combination level, rule, square &
saw, 29" l. 1,695

Saw, Jacobs, buck saw, cast-iron corner
brackets, pat. Sept. 4, 1894, 29" l. 145

Saw, Millers Falls Company (The), hack
saw, marked "Keyhole Hack Saw" on
original card, for wood or metal,
ca. 1930s, 10½" l. 35

Screwdriver, Brown & Co., R.H., Westville,
Conn, early combination w/all original bits
in hardwood box, 8" l. 295

Screwdriver, Millers Falls Company, No.
850, No. 4 size, Phillips head w/8" blade,
original box, 14½" l. 45

Scroll saw, Sutton (Delay F.), Rochester,
N.Y., elaborately decorated flywheel,
detailed lathe & spindle attachments,
original patent office tag marked "March
30, 1880," 9" l. 3,650

Slide rule, Tavella Sales Co., New York,
circular, original pouch, Copyright 1936, 4" l. . . . 45

Spoke shave, Stanley Rule & Level, No. 84,
narrow boxwood w/"Sweetheart"
trademark, narrow boxwood, 11½" l. 195

Spring winder, Hjorth Lathe And Tool
Company, No. 1, "Perfection" spring
winder, pat. July 30, 1907, original box, 5" l. . . . 125

Square, Lufkin Rule Co. (The), Saginaw,
Mich., No. 166, machined steel, 4½" l. 45

Tack puller, Buffum Tool Co., Louisiana,
Missouri, forged steel w/"Swastika"
logo, 7½" l. 115

Tack puller, McGillis, Brown & Pratt Co., old
hardware stock w/original handbill, "The
Perfection Tack Puller," 6" l. 55

Tape measure, Lukin Rule Co. (The),
round, Art Deco style marked "M.I.T.
Reunion Banquet June 11, 1925," 1½" d. 225

Tape measure, Stanley Rule & Level, No.
6386, casing marked "Direct Reading" on
blue finish, 72" l. 65

Cast Bronze Trammels

Trammels, unmarked, cast bronze w/shield
cut-outs, 6" l., pr. (ILLUS.) 225

Wrench, Atwater's Tiger Wrench, Brazilian
rosewood handle, 80% original shiny
nickel plating, Utility Wrench Co. of New
York City, pat. Aug. 18, 1878, 4½" l. 545

Wrench, Bemis & Call Co., Springfield,
Mass., No. 75, crescent style, w/straight
handle, 6" l. 55

Early "Monkey" Wrench

Wrench, Coes (L.) & Co., Worcester,
Mass., early "monkey" wrench,
pat. March 29, 1869, 6½" l. (ILLUS.) 55

Wrench, Hall (Chas. E.) Co. (The), Buffalo,
N.Y. No. 15, dual-function nut wrench
w/hook end, full nickel plating, 7" l. 110

Hewett Wrench

Wrench, Hewett, pat. June 27, 1840, 10" l.
(ILLUS.) **335**

Wrench, Irland Pipe Wrench Co., Boston,
Mass., quick-adjust pipe wrench w/spring
lever, pat. Sept. 22, 1903, 11" l. **85**

Wrench, Simmons Hardware Co., St. Louis,
adjustable alligator wrench, marked
w/"K.K." logo, pat. May 23, 1903, 7" l. **85**

Wrench, Simplex Manufacturing Co. (The),
New York, "Anderson Turn-More," pat.
Oct. 30, 1906, 10" l. **145**

TOYS

Friction-Powered F-51 Airplane

Accordion, paper w/three reeds, colorful
scene of a carnival & a clown playing an
accordion, marked "Made in Germany,"
6¼" l. **$33**

Airplane, die-cast metal, P-38 fighter, #81,
folding wheels, yellow & green combat
camouflage, Hubley Mfg. Co. (Lancaster,
Pennsylvania). **248**

Airplane, friction-type, lithographed tin,
F-51, single engine war plane, Japan,
ca. 1950s, very good in original box,
6¾" l. (ILLUS.) **83**

Airplane, lithographed tin, Pan American
Airways, four engine propeller model,
Louis Marx & Co., 27" wingspan **187**

Keystone Airmail Airplane

Airplane, pressed steel, airmail model,
single-engine, dark yellow body w/red
metal wheels & red tail fin, complete,
good labels, Keystone Mfg. Co.
(Boston, Massachusetts), ca. 1930,
24" wingspan (ILLUS.) **963**

Airplane, pressed steel, Super Titan Liner,
four-engine, silver & blue body,
Wyandotte Toys **303**

Airplane, windup tin, "Wood's Mechanical
Airplane," silver body on yellow wheels,
single-engine monoplane, Girard-Marx,
ca. 1930, excellent condition w/box, 12" l. **605**

Army lift truck, pressed steel, Structo Mfg.
Co., (Freeport, Illinois),12" l. (repainted) **28**

Army mobile search light, pressed steel,
Louis Marx & Co., ca. 1950, 12" l. **55**

Army troop carrier, pressed steel,
complete, Louis Marx & Co., ca. 1950, 18" l. . . **165**

Texaco Service Station Boxed Set

Auto service station set, "Texaco Service
Station - Steel with Plastic Accessories,"
color box cover w/red, white & blue
house-form station w/vehicles & pumps, a
young boy at one end, all on a greenish
yellow ground, Tag No. 856, never out of
box, minor box wear, the set (ILLUS.) **385**

Automobile, 1930s Coupe, pressed steel,
Wyandotte Toys, 13" (repainted) **77**

1958 AMT Edsel Promo Car

Automobile, 1958 Edsel convertible promo
car, plastic, pale green w/dark green trim,
black & white wheels, AMT (Japan), mint
in mint box (ILLUS.) **248**

Automobile, boat-tailed racer, cast iron,
orange w/chrome driver & wheel front
axle, 6" l. (2 rubber tires missing). **165**

Automobile, coupe, cast iron, w/chrome
rumble seat, rubber tires, painted red,
Kenton Hardware (Kenton, Ohio), 7" l. **330**

Automobile, Model T 4-door sedan, cast
iron, Arcade Mfg. Co.(Freeport, Illinois),
6¼" l. (some rust, 1 wheel replaced) **220**

Automobile, Model T Ford, cast metal,
original black paint in excellent condition,
red & silver metal wheels, sticker on
the bottom, Buddy L (Moline Pressed
Steel Co., E. Moline, Illinois), minimal
wear (ILLUS.) **1,128**

Buddy L Model T Ford

The Mattel Dream Car

Automobile, "The Mattel Dream Car," friction-type, plastic, blue & silver plastic body w/clear bubble top, Mattel, 1950s, w/original box (ILLUS.) **220**

Automobile, Volkswagon, pressed steel, Tonka Mfg., ca. 1950s, 9" **11**

Automobile set, "Build and Paint Auto Set," three pot metal cars & paints, Barclay Mfg. Co. (Hoboken, New Jersey), 1930s, original box **110**

Balance toy, w/aluminum cowboy on horse, weight at end of bent rod, c.1940s, 24" l. **77**

Battery-operated, boat, outboard motorboat, cruiser-type w/canvas top, front light, motor in box, Schuco Toy Co. (Nuremberg, Germany), motor in box **175**

Battery-operated, Charlie Weaver bartender, mixes drinks, smoke comes out his ears, mint on box **95**

Battery-operated, "Electro Submarino," Schuco, w/original instructions, in original rare box **250**

Battery-Operated Fishing Bear

Battery-operated, "Fishing Bear," seated furry bear w/pink straw hat & blue & black checked outfit holding a fishing pole, w/original box w/small tear in front, Japan, ca. 1950s (ILLUS.) **330**

Rare Battery-Operated Santa Toy

Battery-operated, "Santa Claus Phone Bank," cloth & plastic Santa seated at a tin desk w/a phone, connected to a wall-style phone-bank, never used, w/original box, ca. 1950s (ILLUS.) **605**

Windy Elephant Battery-Operated Toy

Battery-operated, "Windy - Juggling Elephant," grey plush rearing elephat w/a tin umbrella above his trunk, atop a square tin base, T.N. (Japan), ca. 1950s, mint toy in original box (ILLUS.) **176**

BB gun, Daisy Model 25, pump w/plastic grip & forearm, w/operation manual, original box **50**

Beetle, molded plastic, antenna moves up & down when rolled **17**

Beetle, windup tin, "A Souvenir from the Universal Theatres Concession CO. Chicago, Ill.," made in Germany, "GRDM," legs move when pulled or pushed, 2½" l. **99**

Bell ringer toy, tin & cast metal, four-wheeled platform w/each wheel mounted w/three round bells, pulled by two running horses on small wheels, late 19th c.,11" l. **193**

Blocks, educational-type, lithographed paper on wood, one side features animals & letters of the alphabet, the other side shows various horse-drawn early fire vehicles, one end features a fireman, the other end shows soldiers, very good condition, late 19th c., each block 2½ x 4", set of 12 413

Late Victorian Picture Puzzle Blocks

Blocks, puzzle-type, each side produces a different view, one shows a large reclining white & black dog, matching view on box cover, late 19th c., minor wear, original box, each block 1¾" sq., set of 20 (ILLUS.) 165

Blocks, puzzle-type, lithographed paper on wood, "The Young Ship Builder's Picture Puzzle Blocks," makes eight different early ship scenes, McCloughlin Brothers, 1892, near mint in near mint box, each block 2½" sq., set of 12 600

Boat, battery-operated, plastic, "Lang Craft Powered Model Boat," cabin cruiser in brown, red & white, includes original box & outboard motor box, 1950s, mint toy, 13" l. 193

The Marlin Cabin Cruiser Toy

Boat, plastic, "Fleet Line Speedboats - The Marlin," cabin cruiser in brown & white w/greey Star Flite Evinrude motor, w/original red & blue box, never played with, 1950s, 18½" l. (ILLUS.) 825

Britain's (soldiers) set, "Britain's Historical Series - Her Majesty's State Coach," No. 9401, cast metal, coach w/six-horse team, drivers & passengers, England, 1950s, never removed from box, box 8 x 18¼", the set 495

Britain's (soldiers) set, cast metal, Canadian Mounted Police, set of six w/one horse, mint in original box, ca. 1950-60, the set 99

Bulldozer, pressed steel, Tonka Mfg., ca. 1950s, 12" l. 110

Bus, cast iron, 1933 Century of Progress Greyhound bus, repaint on cab, 10½" l. (one tire replaced, broken axle frame on cab) 110

Arcade Double-Decker Bus

Bus, cast iron, double-decker, green w/silver metal trim & black & silver tires, original sticker intact, Arcade Mfg. Co. (Freeport, Illinois), very good condition, 7¾" l. (ILLUS.) . . 330

Bus, cast iron, Faegol, "Made by Arcade, mfg. Freeport, Ill.," steel wheels (repaint) 220

Wanamaker's Toy Store Bus

Bus, friction-type, sight-seeing style, pressed steel, long flat-topped model w/projecting hood, metal wheels w/hard rubber tires, dark yellow body & black roof, red & gold oval "Wanamaker's Toy Store" decal on the side, paint chips & scratches, mechanism not working ca. 1930s, 26" l. (ILLUS.) 1,320

Camper, pressed steel, "Winnebago Indian," Tonka Mfg., 23" l. 44

Cane, wooden, cap firing w/lead weight on bottom holding firing points, black & gold cast metal duck head handle, 34" l. 105

Small Victorian Cap Pistol

Cap pistol, cast iron, one side marked "Pluck," the other side w/"Patent March 22nd 1880 - June 17th 1898," 3½" l. (ILLUS.) 50

Cap pistol, cast iron & plastic, "The American," metal body w/white plastic molded grips, leather holster, Kilgore Mfg.

Co. (Westerville, Ohio), No. 105,
complete w/original box, very good
condition, gun 10" l. (small chip on right
handle, box flaps loose) 385

Rare Stevens & Brown Clockwork Toy

Clockwork mechanism, buckboard,
painted tin, red wagon w/driver pulled by
a black horse, most original paint,
Stevens & Brown (New York, New York),
late 19th c., works (ILLUS.) **2,420**

Clockwork mechanism, figure of gardener
pushing cart, black face, probably
Lehman, late 19th - early 20th c. **440**

Early Clockwork Velocipede Toy

Clockwork mechanism, girl on velocipede,
papier-maché, cloth & tin, the rider w/a
papier-maché head & jointed cloth body
pedaling a velocipede, Stevens & Brown,
girl's head missing paint, clothes soiled &
tattered, ca. 1880, 10¾" l. (ILLUS.) **1,485**

Clockwork mechanism, touring car
w/driver, lithograhed tin, doors open,
adjustable steering, Bing (Germany) **523**

Clockwork mechanism, truck, "Kingsbury
Army Truck USA Defense" on original
canvas cover, Kingsbury Mfg. Co.
(Keene, New Hampshire), ca. 1930s-40s,
14" l. **160**

Clown, roly-poly, composition material, blue
& white, early 20th c., 4½" h. **138**

Coloring book, "Spot Planes," Merrill
Publishing Co., 1944 10 x 15" **17**

Combine, die-cast metal, John Deere Turbo
Combine w/yellow cab, Ertl Toy Co.
(Dyersville, Iowa), 15" l. **22**

Combine, pressed steel, John Deere model,
green w/yellow trim, black rubber tires,
Eska, ca. 1950s, w/original slightly
damaged box, excellent condition **303**

Cow, nodder-type, composition, model of a
realistic cow w/worn brown & white hide
covering, small natural horns & glass
eyes in nodding head, late 19th c., 12" l.
(some wear & damage, tail missing) **193**

Drum, metal, w/parchment top & bottom,
Ohio Art Co., 10" h. (some rust spots) **17**

Earthmover, pressed steel, Heiliner
Earthmover, William Doepke Mfg. Co., 29" l. . . . **143**

Erector Master Builder Set

Erector set, "Erector Master Builder Set
#10092," metal carrying case, overall
excellent (ILLUS.). **770**

Erector set, Gilbert Model #4-1/2,
w/manual, 1951, original box **22**

Farm set: wooden barn & nine pieces of
livestock; "Red Robin Farm," sliding
doors, stenciled brick front & ends, 18" l.,
17" h., the set **220**

Fire aerial ladder truck, pressed steel, red
cab & trailer w/adjustible silver ladder,
black rubber wheels, "S.M.F.D." on side,
Smith-Miller Toy Co. (Los Angeles,
California), ca. 1950s, toy excellent,
original box very good **825**

Fire hook & ladder truck, pressed steel,
Wyandotte Toys, ca. 1950, 25" l **83**

Fire ladder truck, pressed steel, William
Doepke Mfg. Co., ca. 1950s, 33" l. **242**

Fire pumper, cast iron, chrome & red paint,
unmatched, two-horse hitch w/gold
trimmed harness, connecting rods
simulate a gallop, early 20th c., 15" l. **770**

Early Cast Iron Fire Pumper

Fire pumper, cast iron, steam-type, worn
red paint on body & driver, silver metal
wheels, early 20th c., 5" l. (ILLUS.) **182**

Fire snorkel truck, pressed steel, Tonka
Mfg., ca. 1950s, 17" **66**

Fire water tower truck, pressed steel, red chassis w/open cab, long adjustable crane in back, black rubber tires w/red hubs, American LaFrance model, all decals, minimal paint wear, Sturditoys (Sturdy Corp., Providence, Rhode Island), 1920s, 34" l. **1,073**

Forklift, pressed steel, Tonka Mfg., ca. 1950s, 16" l. (repainted) **22**

Gravity toy, lithographed tin & wood, two blades mounted on a wire spiral, one blade w/a lithographed tin boy at each end & the other w/wood & paper fans, wood & metal stand on each end of the wire, the blades rotate as they descend, early 20th c. **220**

Gyrocopter, pressed steel, Wyandotte Toys, ca. 1930s, 12½" wingspan (one blade missing) **127**

Hay loader, pressed steel, "Barber-Greene" high capacity loader, William Doepke Mfg. Co., 22" l. (repainted) **187**

Horse & cart, windup tin, driver in open cart, wire spoke wheels, trotting horse, paint excellent, early 20th c., 9" l. **743**

Hunter on hoseback, rider wearing green hat & red jacket, pointing his rifle, brown horse on narrow rectangular base, Elastolin, early, 5¼" h. **44**

Jeep, "G.I. Joe Desert Patrol Attack Jeep," plastic, includes Jeep, machine gun & ring, portable radio, Hasbro Mfg., original box, ca. 1960s, 20" l. (missing antenna) **649**

Jig toy, painted wood, early flat hinged figure of Harlequin in a costume painted in red, blue & yellow triangles, tall rounded dark paper hat, reverse painted green, yellow & cream, pull string to move arms & legs, composition collar, hand-written on the back "Harry K. 1876," 12" h. **121**

Kaleidoscope, Steven, original box, ca. 1950s **14**

"Favorite" Toy Kitchen Range

Kitchen range, cast iron, "Favorite," greenish blue paint & nickel trim, warming oven above, complete w/skillet, pot &

coal bucket, small break where top hooks into bottom, good paint, early 20th c., 8" w., 9½" h. (ILLUS.) **259**

Machine gun, lithographed tin, "No.100 "Mac" Machine Gun," shoots paper, McDowell, ca. 1920s, original box **44**

Magic lantern, "Triumph Lantern Magic" metal, bulbous lens section on a flaring metal base, w/six slides & paper describing it, made in Germany, original box, early 20th c. **165**

Marionette, carved wood & stuffed cloth, the realistically-carved man's head w/articulated mouth & glass eyes, carved wood torso, stuffed cloth arms & carved wood hands, jointed carved wood legs w/painted shoes, remnants of wig, 25" h. **495**

Marionette, carved wood & stuffed cloth, the wooden head carved realistically as a dark-haired man w/mustache, the waisted body of straw-stuffed cloth, cloth upper arms & carved wood lower arms, jointed carved wood legs w/carved & painted boots, undressed, includes a "Theatrical Date Book - 1886-87-88" also signed "Lew Morton of Three Ronaldos," marionette 33" h., the group **715**

Microscope set, includes accessories & handbooks, A.C. Gilbert Co., 1948, original carrying case **39**

Monkey, lithographed tin, string climbing-type, marked "Made in USA," 5½" l. **39**

Hubley "Indian Crash Car" Motorcycle

Motorcycle, cast iron, three-wheeled "Indian Crash Car," red body & driver, gold wheels, Hubley Mfg. Co. (Lancaster, Pennsylvania), ca. 1930s, 80% paint, 6½" l. (ILLUS.) **330**

Motorcycle, cast metal w/rider, blue paint w/gold accent, rubber tires, Champion Hardware Co.(Geneva, Ohio), 7" l. **385**

Harley-Davidison Friction Motorcycle

Motorcycle, friction-type, lithographed tin, black w/white trim & "Harley-Davidson" on the side, working pistons, perfect working order, Japan, ca. 1950s, 9" l. (ILLUS.) **605**

Moving van, painted metal, GMC semi, "Mayflower," Nylint, boxed, modern, 22" l. **44**

Keystone Moving Van

Moving van, pressed steel, worn orange-painted van w/applied oval label reading "Keystone Moving Van - Long Distance Moving," black cab w/moving steering wheel, orange metal wheels w/rubber tires, back door opens, stop signal flag, springs at back wheels, paint chips & scratches, Keystone Mfg. Co. (Boston, Massachusetts), large (ILLUS.) **1,100**

Music box, model of a televison set, TV & clock music box plays as couple dance in TV screen, jewel musical alarm, Bradley Time of Germany, ca. 1950s, original box (back needs three small screws) **39**

Super-Sonic Jet Pedal Toy

Pedal airplane, "Super-Sonic Jet," pressed steel w/rubber-rimmed tires, white & red, all-original, even overall wear, Murray, ca. 1950s (ILLUS.) **1,430**

Early Eska John Deere Pedal Tractor

Pedal vehicle, tractor & wagon, pressed steel, John Deere model, green w/yellow wheels & trim, Eska, purchased ihn 1955, original receipt included, old repaint, 2 pcs. (ILLUS.) **1,128**

Penny toy, lithographed tin, flatbed truck, yellow cab & flatbed on red frame w/red tin wheels, Germany, early 20th c., very good condition, 4" l. **275**

Nylint U-Haul Pick-up and Trailer

Pick-up truck & trailer, pressed steel, orange & white, original "U-Haul" stickers on each, Nylint, Model 4100, w/original box, very good condition, 2 pcs. (ILLUS.) **303**

Hubley Pirate Pistol

Pistol, "The Hubley Pirate Pistol," metal long-barreled antique-style w/ivory-colored plastic grips, marked on handle, w/original box w/colorfully printed picture of a pirate & treasure map, No. 265, Hubley Mfg. Co. (Lancaster, Pennsylvania), minor rust on pistol, flap on box torn off by present, pistol 9" l. (ILLUS.). . **94**

Early Tootsietoy Playtime Set

Play set, "Playtime," set of original cast metal vehicles & airplanes, all mint in original colorful box, Tootsietoy, ca. 1930s, 10 pcs. (ILLUS.) **633**

Pop-up toy, cat, black w/white face, pull rings to make it stand up, Fisher-Price (East Aurora, New York), ca. 1950s..........50

Pull toy, airplane, pressed steel, single engine plane, two decals "Little Jim Playthings," Army Airforce signs on wings, clicker, J.C. Penney, Steel Craft #NX107, 22½" wing span (gearing for propeller missing)......................550

Pull toy, Bunny Cart, No. 472, Fisher-Price......99

Pull toy, horse on platform, the body covered in real horse hair, straw-filled, most of leather briddle & harness remains, on a rectangular red board wheeled base, late 19th c., 9½" l., 9" h.............495

Pull toy, lion, molded tin body in gold on green platform, early 20th c., 4½" l..........121

Rare Santa & Sleigh Pull Toy

Pull toy, Santa Claus in sled w/reindeer, cast iron, Santa dressed in red sitting in a fancy white sleigh pulled by two white reindeer on a red wheel, late 19th - early 20th c., excellent paint, 16½" l. (ILLUS.)....**1,925**

Puppet, Joe Louis hand puppet, vinyl head & gloves, cloth costume, JVZ Co., 10" l. (small hole in one glove) 72

Early Cat Push Toy

Push-type, painted wood & cast iron, a flat grey-painted model of a jointed cat raised on a two-wheeled base, wooden push rod behind, late 19th c., cat 10" l. (ILLUS.).......358

Record player, windup tin, "Bing Pygmy Phone," tin horn above the rectangular box holding the works, the base in green printed in red, white & black around the sides w/figures of the Seven Dwarfs, a black child, Little Red Riding Hood & the Big Bag Wolf, Bing (Germany), works well, early 20th c. 413

Riding toy, horse, pressed metal, push down on stirrups & he walks, painted, Mobo, ca. 1950s......................132

Rifle, "My Pet Sparking Rifle," metal rifle in original cardboard long box printed on the top w/a color scene of the Cavalry chasing Indians, Model No. 2731, Made in Japan, ca. 1950s, 27" l. 44

Road construction set, cast iron, miniature vehicles & signs, Arcade Mfg. Co., ca. 1950s, near mint original box 605

Road grader, pressed steel, Tonka Mfg., ca. 1950s, 18" l. (repainted) 11

Robot, batter-operated, "Roto-Robot," open door, shooting & blinking guns, rotating body, walks, mint in box 145

Rare Mechanized Robot Toy

Robot, battery-operated, "Mechanized Robot," lithographed tin w/black body, red arms & feet & domed clear plastic over the head, T.N. (Japan), ca. 1950s, near mint w/damaged box, robot 13" h. (ILLUS.).............................**1,843**

Robot, battery-operated, "Mr. Atom - The Electronic Walking Robot," angular silver & red body, excellent condition w/original box, ca. 1950s 825

Robot, battery-operated, Piston robot, see-through body w/lighted pistons, realistic sounds, mint in box 145

TV Robot Toy

Robot, battery-operated, "TV Robot," the squared torso in the form of a TV screen, battery compartment clean, 11½" h. (ILLUS.) 248

Robot, "Mego Man," windup, Sy, Japan, 7" l. (windup not working) 193

Rocking horse on platform, carved & painted wood, the horse painted brown w/leather saddle & ears, glass eyes, on cast iron rockers & painted stand, 19th c., 37" l., 28" h. (paint wear, losses) 345

Rocking horse on rockers, carved & painted wood, the well-carved horse in white w/original leather saddle & collar, long curved red-painted rockers, mid-19th c., 65" l., 34" h. (saddle slightly deteriorated) 2,750

Russian peasant woman, roly-poly, painted wood, Russia, pre-War, 3½" h. 22

Sand loader, pressed steel, Tonka Mfg., ca. 1950s, 11". 28

Sand toy, painted tin, hand-cranked wire chain belt carries six buckets that dump into bin cart which dumps when full, painted red & green, ca. 1930s, small 242

Friction Toy Animal Satellite

Satellite, friction-type, lithographed tin, a spherical form in grey w/red trim & a design of a dog on the side, a little dog pops out of the top, marked "MS-7" on side, Japan, 1950s, excellent condition, 4¼" d. (ILLUS.). 165

Seesaw, painted tin, boy & girl wire frame mounted on a wooden base, 7" h. (minor paint loss on figures) 121

The American Girl Toy Sewing Machine

Sewing machine, "The American Girl," cast metal, black body w/nickel plate trim, National Sewing Machine Company, w/original box, very good condition, early 20th c. (ILLUS.) 138

Ship building set, "Kidstruction Ship Builder," plastic, builds 25 big ships, Lee Craft, ca. 1950s, original box........... 22

Skidder, pressed steel, John Deere, #590, Ertl Toy Co., 16" l. 72

Sled, child's size, painted wood, the platform painted red w/a stag & foliage decoration, on metal runners, probably northern Europe, 19th c., 12⅛ x 45" (paint wear, surface abrasion) 173

Early Elastolin Solider on Horse

Soldier on horseback, figure wearing khaki uniform & helmet, naturally painted hands & face, on brown horse w/black harness, on narrow rectangular base, Elastolin, early, 5½" h. (ILLUS.)................... 55

Soldiers, marching platoon, khaki uniforms, painted faces, Elastolin, ca. 1930s, each 3¾" h., set of 14 138

Steam roller, pressed steel, Tonka Mfg., ca. 1950s, 15" l. 17

Early Tonka Steam Shovel

Steam shovel, pressed steel, red body & platform w/black wheels, adjustable blue digging arm, Model 50, Tonka, excellent condition (ILLUS.)....................... 248

Stuffed cloth, monkey, brown body w/tan & brown head & orange cap, w/built-in noise makers, glass eyes, early 20th c. 72

Tank, pressed steel, hand-crank rotating orange turret w/firing noise, sheet metal body w/ten metal wheels, green body, decals on both sides, Structo Mfg. Co., 12" l... 407

Victorian Ten Pins Set

Ten pins set, turned wood, the tall tapering
& pointed wood pins w/pointed tops,
black trim bands, original turned balls,
late 19th c., excellent condition, each
pin 12" h., the set (ILLUS.) 220

Arcade Fordson Tractor

Tractor, cast iron, Fordson model, green
chassis & driver, red metal wheels, never
played with, Arcade, ca. 1930, 6" l. (ILLUS.) . . **297**

Massey-Harris Scale Model Tractor

Tractor, cast metal, Massey-Harris scale
model, red chassis w/silver driver, black
rubber tires w/yellow hubs, mint in
original box (ILLUS.). **303**
Tractor, pressed steel, International 6388
2+2, 15" l. **66**
Train car, caboose w/bay window, Chessie
System, No. 16518, 1990. . . . . **45**
Train car, car hauler, Johnny Lightning, No.
16757, uncatalogued 1996. . . . . **100**
Train car, gondola w/coil covers, "Lionel
Visitor's Center," No. 19955,
uncatalogued 1998. . . . . **35**

Train car, refrigeration car, Lionel Lines,
No. 214R, standard gauge, 1929-40 . . . . **800**
Train engine, Chesapeake & Ohio GP-7
locomotive, No. 2347, uncatalogued
1965 . . . . **3,000**
Train engine, Joshua Lionel Cowen 4-6-4
Hudson locomotive, No. 8210, 1982 . . . . **375**
Train engine, Lackawanna FM TrainMaster
locomotive, No. 2321, 1954-56 . . . . **550**
Train engine, Lionel Lines 2-4-2 locomotive,
No. 390/390E, standard gauge, 1929-33 . . . . **800**
Train engine, Lionel Lines 2-6-2 locomotive,
No. 2025, 1947-49, 1952 . . . . **150**
Train engine, Lionel Lines 2-6-4 locomotive,
No. 2037, 1953-64 . . . . **125**
Train engine, Lionel Lines 2-8-4 Berkshire
locomotive, No. 736, 1955-66 . . . . **300**
Train engine, Lionel Lines locomotive,
No. 256, "O" gauge, electric, 1924-30 . . . . . . **800**
Train engine, Lionel Lines locomotive, No.
8/8E, standard gauge, electric, 1925-32 . . . . . **250**

American Flyer Engine No. 3116

Train engine, lithographed tin, electric,
American Flyer Model 3116, complete,
very good condition (ILLUS.) **248**
Train set, "American Flyer," Burlington
Zephyr 9900, original box, the set **110**
Train set, lithographed tin, Ives electric
Standard guage, engine No. 3242,
club car No. 184, parlor car No. 185,
observation car No. 186, complete
w/track & box, all-original, ca. 1930s,
the set **1,430**
Train set, pressed steel, "Buddy L," 26" l.
engine, 18" l. coal car, two 20" l. cattle
cars & 19" l. caboose, original paint
except on coal car, caboose marked
"Built by Moline Pressed Steel Co., East
Moline, Ill.," each piece marked w/"Buddy
L," the set (paint chips, scratches, ragged
edges on bottom of caboose) **3,685**
Trencher-backhoe, pressed steel, #2534,
Tonka Mfg., boxed, ca. 1950s, 18" l. **14**
Truck, auto carrier, lithographed tin, Japan,
ca. 1950s, 13" l. **22**
Truck, coal delivery-type, pressed steel, red,
white & black paint w/the deep back
marked "Glen Dale Coal Company,"
Marx, ca. 1950, 12" l. (ILLUS.) **248**

Marx Coal Delivery Truck

Tootsietoy Delivery Van

Truck, delivery moving van, cast metal, red cab & red & silver trailer, black wheels, "Tootsietoys - Coast to Coast," Tootsietoy (Dowst Bros., Chicago, Illinois), excellent condition, 9¼" l. (ILLUS.) **110**

Truck, delivery, pressed steel, "Hiway Express" on sides, Marx, ca. 1930s, 16" l. **165**

Large Buddy L Dump Truck

Truck, dump, pressed steel, black cab & red rear box, red & black tires, complete w/all stickers, Buddy L, ca. 1930s, 24" l. (ILLUS.) **2,475**

Wyandotte Flatbed Truck

Truck, flatbed-type, pressed steel, red chassis w/gold grill, blue flatbed w/yellow interior, w/tilting ramp, Wyandotte, very good condition, ca. 1930s, 18" l. (ILLUS.) **506**

Truck, gasoline tanker, pressed steel, "Texaco" on sides, ca. 1950s, Buddy L, 23" l. **187**

Truck, low-boy type, pressed steel, "Coast to Coast" on sides, Marx, ca. 1950, 25" l. **110**

Truck, low-boy type, pressed steel, Smith-Miller Toy Co., 23" l. (repainted). **248**

Kenton Oil & Gas Tank Truck

Truck, oil & gas tanker, cast iron, painted green w/raised words "Oil" & "Gas" along the sides in gold w/further gold trim, solid stamped steel wheels, minor painted chips, minor surface rust on wheel, missing driver, Kenton Hardware, 10" h., 4¾" h. (ILLUS.). **2,750**

Truck, semi w/trailer, pressed steel, "Kroehler Semi," Structo Mfg. Co., ca. 1950s, 23" l. **55**

Truck, stack-type, cast iron, marked on cab "5 Ton Truck," Hubley Mfg. Co., 16" l. (old replacement driver & headlight) **1,760**

Dinky ABC-TV Truck

Truck, van-style, cast metal, pale blue over silver w/red band & logo, "ABC-TV" over front, Dinky Toy (Meccano, Liverpool, England), very good condition, 4½" l. (ILLUS.) **193**

Wagon, coaster-type, steel, "My Pal," oval shallow carriage on four metal wheels w/hard rubber rims & high half-round modernistic hub caps, long hinged handle w/grip, worn dark red paint on body & wheels, marked "Manufactured in U.S.A. Pines Winterfront Co. Chicago, Ill.," 23½" l. (minor denting, rust spotting, scratches & soiling) **1,210**

Wagon, painted wood, rectangular platform painted red on mustard yellow wheels, black lettering on the sides "The Flyer," 19th c., 22" l., 8" h. (paint wear, repairs) **173**

Water pump & round tank, cast iron, gold pump, blue tank, Arcade Mfg. Co., early 20th c., 8½" h. **138**

Windup celluloid & tin Mary & her little lamb, the celluloid figure of Mary in a long blue dress & bonnet standing on a metal wheeled platform above the mechanism, the lamb on a smaller wheeled platform pulled behind, Japan, excellent condition **605**

Windup Celluloid Occupied Japan Toy

Windup celluloid & tin traveling boy, celluloid figure of a boy w/pink cap & blue jacket w/hinged arms & legs on a crank shaft extending from a rectangular tin suitcase, made in Occupied Japan, ca. 1950, excellent working condition, 4" h. (ILLUS.) **138**

Mr. Machine Windup Toy

Windup plastic "Mr. Machine," flattened plastic sections w/hinged head & arms, on mechanized base, red & yellow, w/original box, 1960s, excellent working condition, Ideal (ILLUS.) **413**

Windup tin aquaplane, color lithographed monoplane in silver, blue & red w/a large red propeller, on oblong half-round red & green pontoons, No. 38, J. Chein, mint toy w/original box **385**

Windup tin "Herculese Ferris Wheel," color lithographed, six gondolas in double wheels above a rectangular base, J. Chein, complete w/original box, excellent condition **495**

Windup tin "Marx Merrymakers," upright piano w/four Mickey Mouse-like mice around it, original marquee on the top, Marx, 1930s (ILLUS.) **1,760**

Fine Marx Merrymakers Toy

Windup tin "Whoopie Car," comic character driving a jalopy, orange chassis w/black wording, Marx, Model No. 150, rarer version, works well, complete w/box, 1930s. **935**

Early Steelcraft Zeppelin

Zeppelin, pressed steel, red body & red metal wheels, "Graf Zeppelin" on side & Sundial Shoes decal advertisement on the top front, Steelcraft, ca. 1930s, very good condition, 26" l. (ILLUS.) **770**

TRADE CATALOGS

Beach Co., sawing machines, 1910 . . . . **$35**

Bicycles, A.G. Spalding & Bros., Sporting Goods, illustrates ordinaries, "cripper" tricycle, velocipedes & accessories, 1886 . . . . **182**

Bicycles, Warwick Bicycles Mfg. Co., Springfield, Massachusetts, 1894 . . . . **50**

Brunswick, billiard supplies & equipment, 1954, 16 pp. **35**

Channon (H.) Co., machinery & tools, Chicago, Illinois, 1910 . . . . **65**

Crescent, woodworking machines, 1912 . . . . **45**

Goldswaiate's Drug Store, w/several shaker ads, 1898 . . . . **20**

Keating Bicycles, superb cover art, 1897-98 . . . . **50**

Manhattan Electric, supplies, medical apparatus, etc., 1913 . . . . **40**

Morgan Woodwork Co., woodworking machines, 1923 . . . . **150**

Olympia Music Box Catalog

Olympia Music Boxes, black & white cover illustration of a disk music box, titled "The Olympia Self-Playing Music Box," & "Plays Over A Thousand Tunes," oval vignette portrait of Admiral Dewey & the Battleship Olympia, ca. 1900, 40 pp. (ILLUS.) 72

Peerless Folding Furniture, illustrated, Art Deco cover, 1936 39

Rogers Peet Co., Fall, men's fashions, 1928 35

Streeter Brothers Shoes, illustrated, 1903 28

United Dairy Cream Separators, illustrated, 1935 35

TRAMP ART

Tramp art flourished in the United States from about 1875 into the 1930s. These chip-carved woodenwares, mostly in the form of boxes or other useful items, were made mainly from old cigar boxes although fruit and vegetable crates were also used. The wood is predominately edge-carved and subsequently layered to create a unique effect. Completed items were given an overall stained finish which was sometimes further enhanced with painted highlights. Though there seems to be no written record of the artists, many of whom were itinerants, there is a growing interest in collecting this ware.

Box, double-pedestal box-on-box, smaller top section w/lift-off top, bottom compartment surrounded by arrowhead-like points, ca. 1910, 8" h., 10" w., 5⅜" deep $350

Box, octagonal shape on pedestal, rounded base, pyramid sides w/scored top layer, velvet lining, ca. 1930, 9" h., 7" w., 7" deep 225

Box, single circular pedestal w/hinged top, flat top layers on pyramids, mirror under lid, ca. 1890, 10" h., 8" w., 6½" deep 500

Box, simple singular pyramid top on hinges, lined w/blue velvet, six secret compartments slide open on sides & top, ca. 1920, 14" h., 17" w., 13" deep 850

Sewing Box

Box, sewing, painted red, white & blue, over-painted detailing on pyramid tops, pincushion top, printed cigar box label under fabric-lined lid, ca. 1890, 19½" h., 16½" w., 11½" deep (ILLUS.) **4,200**

Box, center-type, the ten-sided top on a pedestal & four shaped legs w/overall chip-carved raised panel decoration, northeastern United States, late 19th c., 33½" w., 30" h. (imperfections) **1,265**

Boxes, two pagoda-shaped boxes w/several stacking sections, painted sandpaper windows, unique notching style w/pyramids attached & line-scored, ca. 1910, 12" h., 11" w., 8" deep, pr. 650

Clock, architectural case w/mirrored & pyramid-topped wings, flat layering on spire column, small clock over archway in center, ca. 1900, 40" h., 23" w., 15" deep ... **4,000**

Clock case, miniature house w/chimney, clock on top, curtains & crepe flowers in pots below, light & dark woods, ca. 1930, 13½" h., 15¾" w., 5¾" deep 850

Doll furniture, miniature dresser w/seven drawers, glass knobs, top mirror, signed & dated 1889, 17" h., 9" w., 7" deep. 675

Lamp, table-style, octagonal top w/marquetry design, apron & center column display different designs on each side, ca. 1910, 34" h., 32" w., 32" deep..... **4,800**

Picture frame, double-cross corner, crate wood w/light stain, 9" h., 7⅜" w.............. 75

Picture frame, cross-corner style w/distinctive double notched top layers, cigar box wood on crate wood base, ca. 1940, 12" h., 14" w................... 385

Picture frame, crown of thorns made from small whittled pieces of wood, assembled without glue or nails, ca. 1890, 12" h., 16" w................... 750

Picture frame, polychrome finish w/mirror & round crest, two layers, ca. 1940, 19" h., 11" w. (many losses) 350

Picture frame, double oval opening on rectangular backing, painted top layers, ca. 1910, 14" h., 22" w................... 300

Picture frame, hearts in each corner w/pyramids in shape of diamonds on all sides, painted gold, ca. 1920, 22" h., 25½" w. **1,600**

Picture frame, block corner style, velvet liner & brass tack decoration, ca. 1925, 25" h., 29" w. **1,125**

Picture frame, steps & whittled posts, stars & rosettes covering outside walls, open back for access ca. 1920, 29" h. 24" w., 14" deep **2,000**

Picture frame, gold painted w/fretwork liner of carved hearts & Polish lettering, bits of mirror in top pyramids, ca. 1915, 32" h., 27½" w. **1,900**

Picture frame, topped w/painted gold cross, top of pyramids highlighted w/gold paint, contains religious print, ca. 1910, 33" h., 22" w. **550**

Wall pocket, polychromed-finish mirror above, drawer & pocket below, star & rosette accent, ca. 1880, 23" h., 10½" w., 5" deep **695**

TRAYS - SERVING & CHANGE

Both serving and change trays once used in taverns, cafes and the like and usually bearing advertising for a beverage maker are now being widely collected. All trays listed are heavy tin serving trays, unless otherwise noted.

Edelweiss Beer Tray

Bakery & Confectionery Workers Union tip tray, round w/a black & gold design, the center w/a copy of the union label, the gold border printed in black "Eat only bread bearing the union label," made in Coshocton, Ohio, early 20th c., 4¼" d. (scratches) **$72**

Century of Progress tip tray. **60**

De Laval tip tray, tin, round w/lithograph scene of woman using a cream separator, her small child standing in the doorway, "De Laval Cream Separators - The World's Standard" in gold letters around rim, 4¼" d. (rust spotting) **165**

Edelweiss Beer, round, metal lithographed bust portrait of smiling young woman surrounded by floral border w/"Edelweiss - the Peter Schoenhofen Brewing Co., Chicago" & "Copyright 1913" minor crazing, scratches, soiling & staining, minor paint chips on edges, 13½" d. (ILLUS.) **165**

Excelsior Brewing Company Tray

Excelsior Brewing Company, oval, tin w/lithographed illustration of lady holding glass of beer & flanked by bottle of Excelsior beer, marked in bottom rim "Compliments of The Excelsior Brewing Co - Brooklyn, N.Y.," some touch up to paint chips to edges & filed, crazing & soiling, 16¾" w., 13¾" h. (ILLUS.) **396**

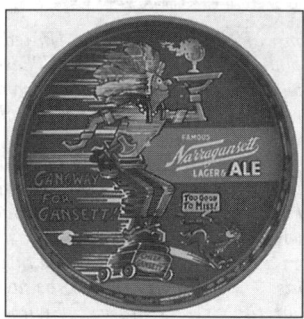

Narragansett Lager & Ale Tray

Famous Narragansett Lager & Ale, round, tin, vibrantly colored lithographed "Dr. Seuss" scene of Indian wearing headdress speeding forward on wheeled cart, holding aloft a tray w/glass of beer, a cat running alongside w/"Too Good To Miss," also marked "Famous Narragansett Lager & Ale" & "Gangway For Gansett!," wheat & leaf design around inside edge, minor paint chips around edges, soiling & minor scratches overall, small scuff marks on Indian's stomach, scratch above headdress, 12" d. (ILLUS.) **116**

Fehr's Famous F.F.X.L. Beers, round, tin lithographed outdoor scene of an embracing couple, the woman w/long blonde hair & flowing robes, the dark-haired man wearing a red cloak, "Fehr's Famous F.F.X.L. Beers - None Purer None Better - Frank Fehr Brewing Co., Incorporated Louisville, KY.," around rim, 13" d. (minor scratches & markings from glasses, small nail hole at top center) **451**

Golden West Brewing Co. Tray

Golden West Brewing Co., tin, round w/colorful scene of factory, wagons & trolley below logo & "Golden West Brewing Co. - Oakland, Cal." around rim, ca. 1911-20, American Art Works, few scratches, 13" d. (ILLUS.) **550**

Green River Whiskey Tray

Green River Whiskey, round, tin, lithograph scene of black man w/horse & marked "She was Bred in Old Kentucky," minor scratches, 24" d. (ILLUS.) **468**

Iroquois Indian Head Beer, round, tin w/lithograph of Indian in full headdress in center, "Iroquois Indian Head Beer" above & "Iroquois Ale" below, bordered by two red lines, w/"Iroquois Beverage Corp. Buffalo, N.Y. - Am. Can Co. N.Y. & Chgo." in rim, 12" d. (minor yellowing, scratches & soiling, paint chips, bubbling & rust to bottom) **61**

Jesse L. Ross & Company, oval, metal w/full color illustration of a woman in flowing white gown w/red scarf & cupid figure playing a flute, ornate scrolled border, marked "Jesse L. Ross & Co. Druggists, Waynesburg, PA" & "The H.D. Beach Co., Coshocton, Ohio No. 1," 13¾" w., 16¾" l. (minor rust & paint chips). . . . **248**

Josephine Baker Follies Bergeres, tin, female dancer in scanty costume w/"L' acquario Milano" at bottom center, signed "Walery Paris," France, 12" d. (scratches & minor rust spotting) **550**

Kenny's Teas Coffees tip tray, tin w/multicolored lithograph bust portrait of beautiful woman w/roses in her long dark hair & holding roses, "Drink And Enjoy - Teas - Kenny's - Coffees" around rim, 4¼" d. (edge wear, scratches, soiling & minor rust spotting) **165**

Meine Milch Tray

Meine Milch, oval, porcelain, young girl holding bottle of milk depicting robotic mouse carrying two bottles of milk, "Meine Milch aus der Meierei-Zentrale - Milchlieferungs - Ger. - Berlin," & stamped on reverse "DRGM Frankfurter Emaillir - Werke Neu-Isenburg," minor chips to edges & scratches, 1½ x 7½", 11½" l. (ILLUS.) **204**

Monticello Whiskey tip tray **200**

National Cigar Stands tip tray **80**

Orange-Julep Tray

Orange-Julep, rectangular, tin w/lithographed scene of girl in green bathing suit sitting on the beach holding a colorful umbrella in one hand & glass in the other w/"Drink Orange-Julep" at top & bottom & "American Art Works Inc. Coshocton Ohio" in bottom right corner, few minor paint chips around edges, soiling, scratches on lower right side of umbrella, 10¼" w., 13¼" l. (ILLUS.) **165**

Pulver's Cocoa Tip Tray

Pulver's Cocoa tip tray, round, tin w/center illustration of cocoa box portrait of woman & "Pulver's Cocoa," rim marked "Pulver's Cocoa Purity Itself - Mayer & Lavenson Co. N.Y.," minor scratches, fading & staining, 4½" d. (ILLUS.) **138**

Queen Quality tip tray, round, metal w/lithograph bust portrait of woman w/red ribbon in long dark hair & wearing low-cut gown, "Queen Quality - Proprietors Cleveland - Incandescent Mantles," Lockwood Taylor Hardware Co., 4¼" d. (minor rust spotting, scratches & soiling) **44**

Robert Burns Cigar tip tray **70**

Sparrow's Chocolates, rectangular, tin w/metal hanger, scene depicts little girl climbing up on table for candy, tray is also shown hanging on wall of the room, colorful geometric design border, marked "Sparrow's" at top & "Chocolates" at the bottom, 6¼" w., 8 1/8" l. (very minor paint chips, crazing, scratches, denting, soiling & some paint loss on face) **77**

Squirt Tray

Squirt, oval, tin w/lithograph of little boy w/lasso & bottle of Squirt w/"Squirt The Drink with the Happy Taste," soiling & small scratches overall, paint wear to edges, 11½" w., 14½" l. (ILLUS.) **281**

White Rock Tip Tray

White Rock tip tray, round, metal w/lithograph scene of lady in transparent gown kneeling on rock near water w/"White Rock - the World's Best Table Water" in red & black letters around rim & marked "Chas. W. Shone Co., Litho., Chicago. 6-497," edge wear, scratches & soiling, 4¼" d. (ILLUS.) **198**

Wieland's Beer, rectangular, tin, illustration of lady sitting near a table w/vase of roses & reading a letter, Wieland logo & "Brewery's Own Bottling - Copyright 1909," Wieland Brewery, San Francisco, California, 10½" w., 13¼" l. **171**

Yosemite Lager - Enterprise Brewing Co., color center scene of three workmen sitting & standing near a workbench & each enjoying a glass of beer, printing around the rim, dated 1905, 13" d. **144**

Zobelein's Eastside Zest tip tray, oval, metal, "Zobelein's Eastside Zest - Non - Intoxicating - Pure and Healthful - Cereal Beverage - Eastside Brewing Co., Los Angeles, Cal.," 4½" w., 6" l. (minor rust spotting, scratches & soiling) **50**

TRUMP INDICATORS

A trump indicator is a device that was placed on the table during card games such as Whist and its successor, Bridge. They were to remind the players what the trump suit was. The earlier trump indicators from the 19th century, used in the game of Whist, had only the four suits of hearts, spades, diamonds and clubs. Later, in the game of Bridge, "No Trump" was added. These gadgets are difficult to find and appear in many forms: people, animals, buildings, useful objects, etc. Some are made of beautiful porcelain while others are crudely made from metal and wood. The ones made from celluloid can be dated from the first half of the 20th century. One thing trump indicators all have in common is their movable pointer or spinner displaying what card suit is trump. As with so many items from the past, their usefulness has become outdated. In the modern game of Bridge, a player would probably be reminded "If you can't remember what the trump is, you shouldn't be playing Bridge." But, as gaming collectibles increase in popularity, the desirability of trump indicators will continue to score high.

Devil Trump Indicator

Celluloid, devil, red figure w/hinged arm & tail pointers & curved end uprights (ILLUS.) **$225**

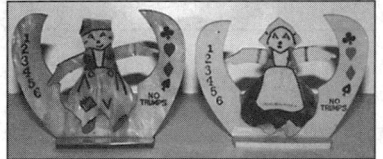

Dutch Boy & Girl Trump Indicators

Celluloid, Dutch Boy, stylized figure w/hinged arms as pointers, curved uprights at sides (ILLUS. left) **60**
Celluloid, Dutch Girl, stylized figure w/hinged arms as pointers, curved uprights at sides (ILLUS. right) **60**

Ship's Wheel Trump Indicator

Copper & wood, model of a ship's wheel, rotates to show suits, copper on half-round black-painted wooden base (ILLUS.) **75**

Figural Dog Trump Indicator

Metal, model of a dog, cast metal painted black, white & red, seated beside metal board w/paper card indicators (ILLUS.) **185**

Rotating Clown Trump Indicator

Porcelain, figure of a clown rotating to show suits, perched on the rim of a fanned ashtray base, Germany (ILLUS.) **250**

Clown Indicator and Card Deck Holder

Porcelain, figure of a clown, seated holding disk w/hand as indicator, painted red & black, beside an upright rectangular card deck holder (ILLUS.) **150**

Clown & Bass Suit Indicator

Porcelain, figure of a clown standing beside & playing a bass, rotating paper card inside instrument indicates suit, Germany (ILLUS.) 125

Porcelain, figure of a clown, standing holding a round disk w/suit indicator, on rim on round ashtray w/iridized gold finish, Japan 125

Comical Dog Trump Indicator

Porcelain, model of a bulldog, seated comical dog w/crossed eyes & mouth open w/rotating card to indicate trump suit, Germany (ILLUS.). 150

Dachshund Trump Indicator

Porcelain, model of a dog, dachshund w/flattened body printed w/suit above an arrow indicator, stands on the rim of an oblong ashtray, Germany (ILLUS.). 100

Wooden Barrel Trump Indicator

Wooden, model of a barrel, pencil holders at top, suit marked around the base (ILLUS.) 95

Wooden, model of a bird, stylized bird w/long beak & forked tail, body hinged to indicate suit on curved upright bar at side, painted black, dark green, white & red, on brown base (ILLUS.) 85

Stylized Bird Trump Indicator

Wooden Souvenir Trump Indicator

Wooden, souvenir-type, walnut upright holder w/a round photograph w/souvenir inscription, encloses a round disk indicating the suit (ILLUS.) 50

VALENTINES

Honeycomb Valentine

Fold-out type, honeycomb tissue & heart w/portrait of young girl in center surrounded by a border of gold-trimmed red hearts, white ruffles & lace, w/"My Sweet Valentine," 4" (ILLUS.). $5

Sailor's valentine, hinged octagonal segmented cases enclosing shell-arranged designs, one half w/a blossom-form design w/ring of shells enclosing "To One I Love" in center, the other half w/rings of various shells & center heart design, 19th c., 9" w. (ILLUS.). 2,185

Sailor's Shell Valentine

Fraktur Labyrinth "Valentine"

Water-color & pen & ink on paper,
inscribed labyrinth w/flowers & hearts,
orange, yellow & green, American
School, 1824, 13 x 12½" (ILLUS.) **4,600**

Bookmark/Valentine Heart

Water-color & pen & ink on paper,
bookmark/valentine, large red & yellow
inscribed heart w/floral designs in
corners, attributed to "The Engraver
Artist," ca. 1791-1805, probably Berks
County, Pennsylvania, American
School, 3¼ x 4" (ILLUS.) **3,162**

Cutwork Floral Valentine

Water-color & pen & ink on paper, cutwork
w/red, yellow & green lovebirds, tulips &
inscribed hearts in the boughs of a
flowering plant, American School, 19th c.,
framed, 6 x 8" (ILLUS.) **7,475**

VENDING & GAMBLING DEVICES

Mills' "Dewey" Double Slot Machine

Candy vendor, "Dairy Maid" painted green
metal, rectangular w/rounded top, marked
"Candies 1¢" & "1¢ Dairy Maid 1¢"
w/various flavors of the chocolate-
covered candy listed below, "Mfg. by
Burrel & King Pat. 1995273 3-19-35,"
4½ x 5¼, 37" h. **$231**

Gambling, Jennings' "Standard Chief"
countertop slot machine, 10-cent play,
ca. 1946 (usual wear, lock restored) **1,210**

Gambling, Mills' "Dewey" double upright
musical floor model 5¢ or 25¢ play,
ca. 1903-16, nicely restored, 21 x 52 x
69" (ILLUS.). **25,000**

Rare "Pay-out" Slot Machine

Gambling, Mills' "Pay-out" countertop slot
machine w/gumball front, jackpot &
fortune reel strips, 1-cent play, ca. 1933,
26½" h. (ILLUS.) . . . . **1,800 to 2,500**

"Pay-out" Slot Machine with Baseball Scene

Gambling, Watling's "Pay-out" countertop
slot machine, enameled baseball scene,
paid mint & money, 5-cent play ... **2,500 to 3,000**

Watling's "Rol-A-Top" Slot Machine

Gambling, Watling's "Rol-A-Top" countertop
slot machine, 5-cent-25-cent play, back
will not open, ca. 1935 (ILLUS.) **2,420**

Watling's "Treasury" Slot Machine

Gambling, Watling's "Treasury" countertop
slot machine, 25-cent play, ca. 1935
(ILLUS.)............................ **2,600**

From left: Master No. 2 Gum Vendor
Pulver Gum Vendor

Gum vendor, "Master No. 2" (gooseneck
master), metal & porcelain cabinet, lid &
base, marked "Pat. Aug. 14, 1923 Oct. 7,
1924," Norn's Mfg. Co. Ca. 1925, 16" h.
(ILLUS.) **385**
Gum vendor, "Pulver" red porcelain
countertop model, marked "Pulver
Chewing Gum - One Cent Delivers A
'Tasty Chew'" in white letters, animated
clown inside, 4½ x 9", 20½" h. (no key,
rust to metal on back, soiling & a few
chips to porcelain) **715**
Gum vendor, "Pulver" yellow porcelain,
wrinkle finish, Daffy Duck figure on inside,
signed "Walter Lantz Copyright," N.O.S.
in original cardboard box w/keys,
4½ x 8½", 20" h. (ILLUS.) **1,760**

From left: Stoner Gum Vendor
Advertising Match Vendor

Gum vendor, rectangular, red metal, "Fresh
Gum" in red & white script letters on glass
front, w/key, Stoner Mfg. Corp, Aurora,
Illinois, denting, minor rust spotting,
scratches & soiling, 19" h. (ILLUS.) **165**
Match vendor, cast iron & metal rectangular
dispenser reading "Diamond Book
Matches - 2 for 1¢" on original wood
crate, w/set of instructions, 5 x 6", 13" h.
(paint loss, fading, paint drops) **501**

Match vendor, cylindrical metal w/glass display area w/"5¢ Peace Time" & "Joe Anderson Havana Cigars" on front, further paper advertising for Peace Time Cigars, Lyra Cigars, by Universal Match Corporation, edge wear, rust spotting, scratches & soiling, 9" d., 14½" h. (ILLUS.) ... **880**

From left: Quizette Card Vendor
Roulette Wheel

Quiz card vendor/napkin dispenser, tapering square metal form w/napkin holder on each side, 1-cent play, machine accepts penny & dispenses a quiz card, 10-15 cards inside, plaque on front shows circle w/an owl & "Wise Owl Quizette" in border w/"Drop Coin - Pull Lever Down" next to coin slot & "Test Your I Q - Can You Answer This Question" above dispenser slot, Continental Service & Equipment Co., some chips to finish, repainted, 5" w., 10" h. (ILLUS.) **88**

Razor blade vendor, "Gillette" rectangular tapering metal form w/paper label reading "Buy Now - look sharp feel sharp be sharp! - Gillette - 5 for 25¢," made by Modern Merchandising Corp., St. Louis, Missouri, 2½" w., 4½" l., 19" h. (scuffs, paint drops, label peeling at edges, no key) **94**

Roulette wheel, nickel plated cast steel & wood, the flat disc decorated w/mirrors & glass w/red, white, blue & black paint, mounted on a wooden column on a tripod base w/flat cabriole legs & topped by a metal eagle finial, late 19th - early 20th c., 32½" d., 50½" h. (column w/some glued cracks) **990**

Roulette wheel, w/five segments containing reverse painted scenes on glass of race horses, ca. 1880s-1890s (ILLUS.) **5,225**

Spark plug gasket vendor, hanging-type, tin, reads "Cleaned Spark Plugs Need New Gaskets - for Perfect Compression Seal and to Avoid Overheating - AC Spark Plug Gaskets - One Cent Each," 3 x 4", 6½" h. (paint loss, edge wear). **116**

Stamp vendor, metal body w/white porcelain front, "Stamps" painted in white letters on red ground down each side,

front w/blue border & white stars, 5¢ & 10¢ coin slots in top corners, "U.S. Postage Stamps" above likeness of Uncle Sam, marked "Federal Dispenser Corporation, Los Angeles, 28, CAL," N.O.S., 4½ x 8", 20" h. **160**

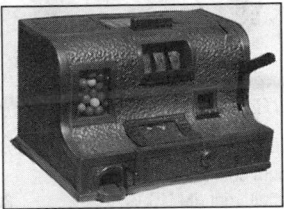

"Baby Vendor" Trade Stimulator

Trade stimulator, "Baby Vendor" cast aluminum countertop model, 1-cent play w/gumball front (ILLUS.) .... **400 to 600**

"The Target" Trade Stimulator

Trade stimulator, Jennings' "The Target" trade stimulator, aluminum countertop model, Western decoration, 1-cent play, ca. 1926-32 (ILLUS.) .... **450 to 750**

"Little Perfection" Trade Stimulator

Trade stimulator, Mills' "Little Perfection" rectangular wood casing countertop model, horseshoe on front, metal frame on top w/playing instructions, 1-cent play, ca. 1901-33 (ILLUS.). .... **600 to 850**

"Royal Reels" Trade Stimulator

Trade stimulator, "Royal Reels" cast aluminum countertop model w/gumball front (ILLUS.) . . . . **300 to 600**

"Triple-L-Jax" Trade Stimulator

Trade stimulator, "Trip-L-Jax" wood & cast aluminum, 1-cent play (ILLUS.) . . . . . . **400 to 600**

WATCHES

POCKET WATCHES

Howard & Co. Pocket Watch

Hunting case, Lady Waltham, American Waltham, 6 size, 14k gold, 16 jewel **$400-450**
Hunting case, lady's, lapel-type, Henry Courvoisier & Cie., 18k gold case w/black enamel & green leaves set w/16 diamond chips **350**

Hunting case, man's, American Waltham,14 size repeater, five-minute, stem wind, lever set, 14k gold **4,500-6,500**
Hunting case, man's, Howard (E.) & Co., No. 301286, white dial w/black Roman numerals, subsidiary seconds dial, chased & engraved case, 18k yellow gold, minor cracks to dial (ILLUS.) **920**
Hunting case, man's, Illinois, Bunn Special, 18 size, adjusted, five positions, gold jewel settings, stem wind, lever set, gold-faced case, 21 jewel **400-500**
Open-face, man's, American Waltham, Riverside model, 16 size, double roller, pendant set, 14k gold, 15 jewel **350-400**

Ami Bourquin Pocket Watch

Open-face, man's, Ami Bourquin, No. 30993, Locle, key wind, white porcelain dial, black Roman numerals, subsidiary seconds dial, engraved case decorated w/blue & black enamel accented w/rose-cut diamonds, fitted wooden box w/inlaid decoration, 18k gold (ILLUS.) **1,095**
Open-face, man's, "Howard" Keystone model, 18k gold case w/23-jewel movement . . **850**
Open-face, man's, open face, Illinois, Burlington Special, 0 size, gold-filled case, 15 jewel **150-200**
Open-face, man's, South Bend, size 16, silveroid case, stem wind, 17 jewel **90-125**

WRISTWATCHES

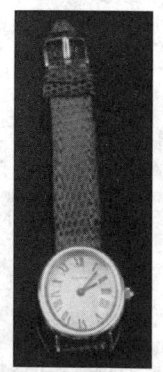

Lady's Cartier Wristwatch

Boucheron, man's, No. A250/565, tank-style w/reeded bezel, goldtone reeded dial, invisible clasp at lugs, black leather & exchangeable ostrich skin Boucheron straps, French hallmarks, 18k yellow gold .. **2,530**

Cartier, lady's, Swiss movement, manual wind, domed bezel, goldtone dial, black Roman numerals, hallmark, leather strap, 18k yellow gold (ILLUS.) **920**

Concord Watch Co., lady's, Art Deco, diamond-set rectangular form w/convex sides & flaring lugs, black Arabic indicators, engraved sides, black grosgrain band, 14k gold-filled clasp **575**

Gruen, curvex, gold-filled w/long rectangular case, original leather band, 17 jewel, ca. 1940s........................ **350-500**

Hamilton Diamond Wristwatch

Hamilton, lady's, diamond, silvertone dial, black Arabic numerals, diamond-set frame & bracelet, platinum mount (ILLUS.).. **2,415**

Ingersoll, Mickey Mouse, embossed "Mickey's" on metal band, fair condition, originally priced $2.95, ca. 1933 .... **225-300**

Le Coultre, Memivox, date, self-winding, black dial, stainless steel case, slammer movement **600-850**

Lucien Piccard, lady's, mother-of-pearl dial w/Arabic numeral & abstract indicators, framed in channel-set rubies, circular link bracelet centered by gold discs framed in rubies, 14k yellow gold, boxed **978**

Nardin, lady's, bi-colored gold, stylized buckle motif accented w/calibre-cut rubies & diamonds, snake link bracelet, slight dial discoloration **2,185**

Pulsar, digital, magnet set w/magnet & box, stainless steel, ca. 1973 .... **150-200**

Rolex, man's, Oyster Perpetual, goldtone dial, abstract indicators, sweep seconds hand, ostrich strap, slight spotting to dial, 14k yellow gold (ILLUS.) **805**

Rolex, No. 1016, Explorer, hack, 26 jewel, ca. late 1960s-80s............... **2,600-3,200**

Rolex, No. 3599, stainless steel, hooded lugs, bubble-back, ca. 1938 ...... **20,000-28,000**

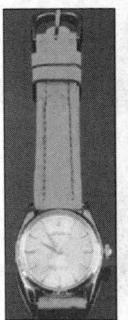

From left: Rolex "Oyster Perpetual" Wristwatch Tag Heuer Wristwatch

Tag Heuer, man's, Chronograph 2000, silvertone dial, abstract black & cream colored indicators, date, silvertone subsidiary dials & bracelet, boxed (ILLUS.)............................ **1,095**

Tiffany & Co., lady's, white square dial w/black Arabic numerals & applied gold indicators, domed crystal, flanked by ten diamonds & two aquamarines, completed by two rectangular link chains, 14k gold **1,035**

Tiffany & Co., man's, lapis lazuli color dial, stepped bezel, black crocodile strap **633**

U.S. Time, Babe Ruth w/original baseball box, Babe on dial, leather strap, ca. 1948 .... **800-1,000**

Universal, man's, Geneve, Uni-Compax, two-dial chronograph w/silver-tone dial, sweep seconds hand, black lizard strap, 18k yellow gold........................ **980**

Vacheron & Constantin, chronograph, 2 reg., 18k pink gold,19 jewel, ca. 1942 .... **9,000-13,500**

Vacheron & Constantin, man's, Geneve, black dial, goldtone abstract & Araic numeral indicators, subsidiary seconds dial, black leather strap, 18k yellow gold.... **1,725**

WEATHERVANES

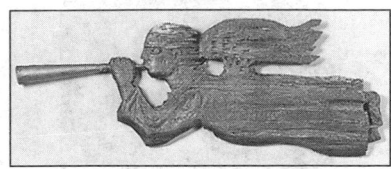

Angel Gabriel Weathervane

Angel Gabriel, carved & gilded pine, flat board carved w/the horizontal figure of a winged angel blowing a long sheet metal trumpet, new gilding, late 19th c., 45¼" l., 15½" h. (ILLUS.) **$4,600**

Arrow bannerette, fashioned from two thicknesses of sheet metal w/feathered scrolls, pierced stars & a lyre-form body, w/cast-zinc arrowhead & star terminus, painted yellow over gilding, late 19th c., 62" l., 13" h. **9,200**

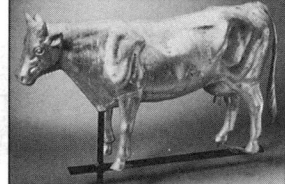

Fine Bull Weathervane

Bull, molded & applied copper, full-bodied standing animal w/tall upright horns, fine verdigris, bullet holes, minor dents, seam splits, loss to half of one leg & balls on horns, possibly A. L. Jewell & Co., Waltham, Massachusetts, last quarter 19th c., 42" l., 30⅛" h. (ILLUS.). **34,500**

Codfish, molded copper & zinc, full-bodied, realistically molded w/zinc head & serrated sheet-copper fins & tail, weathered to an overall verdigris, mounted on a rod & metal base, late 19th c., 33" l., 10" h. **8,625**

Long-horned Cow Weathervane

Cow, molded copper, standing animal w/head raised, long curled horns, weathered gilt verdigris surface, attributed to Harris & Co., Boston, Massachusetts, late 19th c., 8 x 33", 21" h. (ILLUS.). **23,000**

Short-horned Cow Weathervane

Cow, molded gilt copper, standing animal w/head slightly lowered & looking straight ahead, short horns, minor dents, gilt loss, late 19th c., 28" l. (ILLUS.) **2,185**

Eagle, molded copper, earlier molded copper arrow & architectural wrought-iron & copper stand supporting the full-bodied bird w/raised spread wings & molded feather detail, early 20th c., eagle 36" w., 28" h., overall 104" h. (imperfections) **1,725**

Eagle, sheet iron, silhouetted figure w/raised wings fashioned from two sheets of sheet iron, painted yellow gold, ca. 1900, 22" l., 12" h. **1,035**

Fox, running, cast & gilded zinc, swell-bodied animal w/head up, ears pricked & tail back, retains traces of gilding, mounted on a rod & metal base, late 19th c., 28½" l., 14½" h. **4,887**

Fine Leaping Horse Weathervane

Horse, leaping, gilt molded & applied copper, stylized full-bodied animal w/elongated body, flaring mane & upright serrated tail, front legs folded under, old painted surface, repair to tail, other minor imperfections, probably A.L. Jewell & Co., Waltham, Massachusetts, second half 19th c., 36½" l., 18" h. (ILLUS.). **23,000**

Horse, prancing, molded copper, hackey-style w/raised head & neck, upright bobbed tail, sheet copper ears & mane, weathered to an overall verdigris w/traces of gilding, late 19th c., 31" l., 22½" h. **16,100**

Horse, running, molded & gilded copper & zinc, full-bodied animal w/head & neck stretched forward, tail straight out, cast zinc head, sheet-copper ears & serrated mane & tail, retains worn gilding, mounted on a metal rod & base, J. Howard & Company, Bridgewater, Massachusetts, late 19th c., 36½" l., 17" h.. . **9,775**

Horse, sheet iron, silhouetted figure of galloping horse painted black & red, ca. 1900, 43" l., 19½" h. **2,587**

Horse "Blackhawk" Weathervane

Horse, trotting, "Blackhawk," gilded molded copper, the animal w/an upright neck & downturned head, tail arched & out, fine verdigris, gilt loss, minor seam splits, losses, late 19th c., 25" l., 17" h. (ILLUS.)... **3,105**

Horse, trotting, gilt molded copper, full-bodied w/head held high & tail straight back, old painted surface, late 19th c., 32½" l., 17¼" h. (very minor seam splits, gilt loss) **1,035**

Locomotive, sheet iron, silhouetted steam locomotive painted dark green, late 19th c., 15" l., 20½" h. **920**

Rattlesnake, carved wood in the form of a curled serpent painted red w/yellow markings, late 19th c., 35½" l............. **6,612**

Fighting Cock Rooster Weathervane

Rooster, molded copper, fighting cock-style w/swelled body w/molded eye & feather detail & a ridged sheet copper tail, worn to an overall verdigris w/traces of gilding, mounted on a rod & later white metal base, small hole on one side, some splits in rod, third quarter 19th c., 16½" l., 318½" h. (ILLUS.) **3,737**

Whale, wood, silhouetted body w/a hinged tail at right angles to the body, simple carved mouth & tack eyes, old worn & weathered repaint w/traces of gilding, old hardware, late 19th - early 20th c., 30" l. (split at mouth)....................... **1,650**

WESTERN CHARACTER COLLECTIBLES

Since the closing of the Western frontier in the late 19th century the myth of the American cowboy has loomed large in popular fiction. With the growth of the motion picture industry early in this century, cowboy heroes became a mainstay of the entertainment industry. By the 1920s major Western heroes were a big draw at the box office and this popularity continued with the dawning of the TV age in the 1950s. We list here a variety of collectibles relating to all American Western personalities popular this century.

Annie Oakley badge, Post cereal premium..... **$18**

Annie Oakley lunch box & thermos, steel, Aladdin Industries, 1955, the set **160**

Annie Oakley & horse figures, hard plastic, Hartland, pr...................... **275**

Brave Eagle & horse figures, hard plastic, Hartland, pr............................. **250**

Buck Jones pinback button, tin, club member-type, figural horseshoe............ **45**

Buffalo Bill Cody Cabinet Photo

Buffalo Bill Cody cabinet photo, half-length portrait w/Buffalo Bill seated looking to the right & wearing elaborate Western outfit, his name & nickname stamped in ink at the bottom, on grey board, slight soil spots, edge dinged, ca. 1900 (ILLUS.)....................... **399**

Buffalo Bill's Wild West Song Book

Buffalo Bill Cody song book, "Special Song Book of the Buffalo Bill's Wild West Combined with Great Pawnee Bill's Far East," seventeen songs copyrighted between 1908 & 1912, illustrated cover, 18 pp., 10 x 14" (ILLUS.) **244**

Buffalo Bill's Wild West invitation, printed paper from "Messrs. Cody & Salsbury" to the annual opening of the show at New York City's Madison Square Garden on April 20, 1900, 5 x 8" (horizontal fold, slight soiling)........................... **220**

Bullet (Roy Rogers' dog) figure, molded plastic, Hartland, 1950s **65**

Dale Evans wristwatch 140

Gabby Hayes accessory set, set of
handcuffs, jailer keys & badge on original
graphic display card, the set. 125

Gene Autry bicycle horn, pistol-
shaped,"Rootin' Tootin' Pistol Horn,"
metal flaring barrel w/handlebar
attachment & rubber squeeze handle,
1950s, boxed, 7" l. 95

Gene Autry billfold, picture of Gene &
Champ on the front & Gene playing guitar
on the back, original star badge inside 120

Gene Autry game, board-type, "Bandit
Trail" 138

Gene Autry gold washed pistol, MIB,
Leslie Henry 550

Gene Autry guitar, Emenee, 1950s,
w/original decorative box, near mint,
2 pcs. 200

Gene Autry handkerchief 32

Gene Autry photograph & letter, written to
a fan, signed by Autry as Technical
Sergeant in U.S. Army Air Forces, 1940s,
photo 5 x 7", 2 pcs. 45

Gene Autry ring, advertising premium. 40

Gene Autry songbook, "The Oklahoma
Yodeling Cowboy," 28 cowboy songs &
mountain ballads, great cover graphics,
1934 45

General Custer & horse figures, hard
plastic, Hartland, pr. 200

"Gunsmoke" book, 1963, contains 8
stories w/text, cartoon strip & James
Arness pictures, hard cover, colored,
93 pp. 60

Hopalong Cassidy bedspread, full-size,
chenille, scene of Hoppy riding Topper,
beige,1950s 175

Hopalong Cassidy bedspread & curtain
panels, chenile, 3 pcs. 250

Hopalong Cassidy Binoculars

Hopalong Cassidy binoculars, black
w/yellow decal of Hoppy on horseback,
original yellow, red & black box marked
"Hopalong Cassidy Field Glasses," mint
toy in excellent box, ca. 1940 (ILLUS.). 330

Hopalong Cassidy camera, box-style
w/flash attachment, black w/silver front
printed w/pictures of Hoppy & his
facsimile signature, ca. 1950s, very good
condition (ILLUS.). 193

Hopalong Cassidy Camera

Hopalong Cassidy Canasta Set, very good
w/good box. 90

Hopalong Cassidy coloring book, 1951,
8½ x 11" 55

Hopalong Cassidy compass, wrist watch-
style w/round compass decorated
w/Hoppy's face on top & two crossed
guns on the bottom, original black leather
band w/Hoppy & Western scenes, mint 195

Very Rare Hoppy Gun & Holster Set

Hopalong Cassidy gun & holster set, a
pair of cast metal gold-washed revolvers,
black leather holster, pair of spurs &
booklet, mint in original box w/some tape
damage, the set (ILLUS.) 2,750

Hoppy Wyandotte & R & S Holster Set

Hopalong Cassidy gun & holster set, pair
of cast-metal revolvers w/white plastic
grips by Wyandotte, in black leather
holsters w/silvered metal trim w/jewels
by R & S Toy Company, in original box
w/picture of Hoppy & Topper & "Hopalong
Cassidy - Genuine Leather Holster Set,"
mint toys in excellent box, the set
(ILLUS.). 1,540

Hopalong Cassidy hair barrette. 75

Hopalong Cassidy Night Light

Hopalong Cassidy night light, plastic, cylindrical body w/domed red top & red ringed base, clear sides around color-printed inner cylinder that turns as the light bulb heats up, scenes of Hoppy riding w/signpost "Hopalong Cassidy Bar 20 Ranch," 1950s, 9" h. (ILLUS.) **825**

Hopalong Cassidy pen knife, miniature, black plastic handle w/his name on one side & picture of Hoppy & Topper on the other side, single blade, end ring, excellent condition, extended 3¾" l **77**

Hopalong Cassidy pennant, triangular felt, black w/plcture of Hoppy & Topper & a rope-style Hopalong facsimile signature, Casey Premium Merchandise Company, Chicago, mint **75**

Hopalong Cassidy pocket knife, three-blade, black & white sides w/picture of Hoppy & Topper, steel ends & ring, very good condition, closed 3½" l **127**

Hopalong Cassidy puzzle set, jigsaw-type, three different color scenes of Hoppy & Topper, Milton Bradley, Set No. 4025, 1950-52, assembled in original color illustrated box, the set **95**

Hopalong Cassidy record & story album, "Hopalong Cassidy and the Square Dance Holdup," two-record set w/story & photos, the set . . . . **75 to 100**

Hopalong Cassidy record & story album, "Hopalong Cassidy & the Singing Bandit" . . . . **75 to 100**

Hopalong Cassidy ring, advertising premium **40**

Hopalong Cassidy ring, w/compartment, advertising premium **50**

Hopalong Cassidy Rug

Hopalong Cassidy rug, chenille, white ground w/outlined colored horsehead & fence w/"Hopalong Cassidy" in thin colored letters, ca. 1950s, very good condition (ILLUS.) **66**

Hopalong Cassidy toy, Shooting Gallery, wind-up, Automatic Toy Co., in original decorated box, the set **295**

Hopalong Cassidy Tumbler

Hopalong Cassidy tumbler, milk glass, gently flaring cylindrical sides, black printed half-length picture of Hoppy w/a lasso above his name, ca. 1950s, 5" h. (ILLUS.) **33**

Hopalong Cassidy woodburning set, electric burning tool & wooden plaques, American Toy Co., Chicago, 1950, complete in original box **275**

Lone Ranger belt & holster, leather **85**

Lone Ranger boots, child's, brown leather **175**

Lone Ranger card game, ca. 1938 . . . . **87**

Large Lone Ranger Doll

Lone Ranger doll, composition w/cloth cowboy hat & outfit including shirt, vest, scarf, badge, chaps & cuffs, minor rub on nose, 20" h. (ILLUS.) **688**

Lone Ranger figure, chalkware **78**

Lone Ranger lunch box **58**

Lone Ranger pencil box **88**

Lone Ranger pinback button, celluloid, red, white & black round picture of the Lone Ranger & Silver in the center, white

border w/black wording "The Lone
Ranger - Sunday Herald and Examiner,"
newspaper premium, ca. 1930s, excellent
condition 28

Lone Ranger play suit, w/original box,
unused, size 12 110

Lone Ranger pressbook, 1938 serial 900

Lone Ranger school bag, green fabric &
vinyl, colorful flap scene of the Lone
Ranger & Tonto on horseback,
w/shoulder strap, 1950s, 10½ x 12" 175

Lone Ranger star badge, Safety Bread
Club 38

Lone Ranger & Silver figures, hard plastic,
rearing horse, ca. 1960s, Hartland, pr. 250

Lone Ranger & Silver toy, windup tin, the
Lone Ranger riding a rearing Silver, a
lariat in one hand, L. Marx, good
condition 495

Rare Photo of Lone Star Harry

Lone Star Harry cabinet photo, bust
portrait of long-haired sharpshooter
w/cowboy hat & early outfit, the back
w/identification & notation "Champion 6
Shooter Manipulator," marked on front
"Wendt Photo Artist 229 Bowery N.Y.,"
slight soiling & damage to top corner, one
corner bent (ILLUS.) 935

**Paladin (Have Gun - Will Travel, TV)
figure,** hard plastic, Hartland 350

Roy Rogers alarm clock, very good,
Ingraham 170

Roy Rogers bath towel 125

Roy Rogers billfold, leather, zip-around
closure, scene of Roy on rearing
Trigger, mint 145

Roy Rogers cap gun with holster 275

Roy Rogers curtains, scenes of Roy, Dale
Evans & Pat Brady, grey ground, two
panels, the set 225

Roy Rogers game, "Horseshoe Set," two tin
targets w/sticks & four vinyl horseshoes,
Ohio Art Co., 7¼ x 14" box. 175

Roy Rogers Lantern

Roy Rogers lantern, "Roy Rogers Ranch
Lantern," lithographed tin, battery-
operated, red, blue & yellow, wire bail
handle, Ohio Art Co., mint original box,
12" h. (ILLUS.) 275

Roy Rogers lunch box, saddle bag 157

Roy Rogers token, round copper-tone
metal, "Roy Rogers Riders Lucky Piece" 25

Roy Rogers - Dale Evans Lunch Box

**Roy Rogers & Dale Evans lunch box &
thermos,** pressed steel, box-style, color
picture of Roy on rearing Trigger on one
side, vignette scenes on the other side,
"Roy Rogers and Dale Evans - Double R
Bar Ranch," red border band, some paint
wear on edges, American Thermos, 1955
(ILLUS.) 220

**Roy Rogers, Dale Evans w/Trigger
coloring book,** 1951, 64 pp., 2 pages
slightly colored in, excellent condition 125

Roy Rogers & Trigger figures, hard
plastic, Hartland, pr. 140

Hubley Model of Silver

Silver (Lone Ranger's horse) model, hard
plastic, jointed standing figure w/separate
harness, color insert card of the Lone
Ranger & Silver, mint condition in mint
box, Hubley, 1950s (ILLUS.) 110

Spurs, child's, ca. 1950s, Kilgore, mint in
box, pr. 95
Texan, Jr. cap gun, ca. 1950s 55
Tom Mix good luck spinner, Ralston
premium 50
Tom Mix magnet ring 45

Tom Mix Premium Set

Tom Mix secret manual & decoder badge,
original Ralston premium set also
including booklet titled "The Life of Tom
Mix," mint & unused in original mailing
envelope, the set (ILLUS.) 66
Tonto & Scout figures, hard plastic,
Hartland, pr. 210
**Topper (Hopalong Cassidy's horse) soap
figure,** "Hopalong Cassidy's Horse
"Topper" in Pure Castile Soap," figure in
rectangular box w/illustrated cover
featuring a cardboard cut-out of a
Hopalong gun on the lid & bottom &
targets, Daggett & Ramsdell, complete in
original box, the set 95
Ward Bond & horse figures, hard plastic,
Hartland, pr. 225
Wild Bill Hickok badge, Post Raisin Bran 18
Wild Bill Hickok outfit, child's, ca. 1950s,
mint in box 95
Wyatt Earp & horse figures, hard plastic,
Hartland, pr. 200

WITCH BALLS

Clear w/heavy white loopings, free-blown,
open pontil, 4" d. $715
Clear w/white loopings, free-blown, open
pontil, 5" d. 303
Golden amber, free blown, probably New
England, 5¼" d. (small pot stones &
scratches). 165
Light vaseline w/white loopings, free-
blown, large open pontil, 4½" d. 110
Red, white & blue loopings, free-blown,
open pontil, 5½" d. (minor pontil chips) 990
**White w/heavy overall reddish pink &
some spots of light blue fragments,**
free-blown, open pontil, 4¼" d. (few
'pops' & pontil chip) 165

WOOD SCULPTURES

*American folk sculpture is an important part
of the American art scene today. Skilled wood
carvers turned out ship's figureheads, cigar store
figures, plaques and carousel animals of stylized
beauty and great appeal. The wooden
shipbuilding industry, which had originally
nourished this folk art, declined after the Civil
War and the talented carvers then turned to
producing figures for tobacconist's shops,
carousel animals and show figures for circuses.
These figures and other early ornamental
carvings that have survived the elements and
years are eagerly sought.*

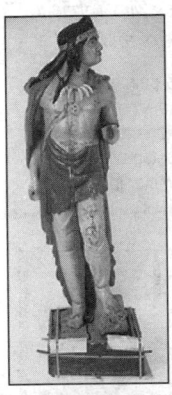

*From left: Cigar Store Indian Brave
Indian Princess with Cigars & Leaves*

Cigar store figure of Indian brave,
standing looking to the side, wearing a
cape, breeches & loincloth, extended arm
missing, fine carving, good paint, late
19th c., 88" h. (ILLUS.) $24,150
Cigar store figure of Indian Princess,
standing wearing a colorful skirt, sash &
breeches, high colorful feathered
headdress, holding a roll of cigars in one
hand & holding aloft a bunch of tobacco
leaves in the other, on original base,
repainted, found in Rhode Island, late
19th - early 20th c., over 7' h. (ILLUS.) 18,700
Cigar store figure of Indian Princess,
standing wearing colorful buckskin skirt,
one leg raised resting on rock, one arm
raised holding a cut plug of tobacco, tall
flared headdress, trimmed in red, green,
yellow, blue & brown, late 19th c. (ILLUS.) .. 5,500
Figure of a European soldier, carved &
painted, the stylized standing figure in
uniform w/a domed helmet, one arm to
his side, the other meant to hold a lance,
a rifle slung over his shoulder, leather
medal & shoulder straps, light painted
jacket & dark pants, velvet bed roll, early
20th c.,22½" h. (minor imperfections)........ 374

From left: Indian Princess with Tobacco Plug
European Figure of an Angel

Figure of an angel, carved & painted
stylized figure wearing an off-the-
shoulder gown & drapery, one arm aloft
w/hole for a missing trumpet, probably
northern Europe, 19th c., minor losses,
repairs, 28" h. (ILLUS.) **2,185**

From left: Carved Figure of Father Time
European Female Saint Carving

Figure of Father Time, stylized carved
giltwood figure of an emaciated elderly
man wearing a toga-like robe, one arm
aloft holding an hourglass, standing on an
oblong mound base, American,
mid-19th c., old repaint, repair to ankles,
paint loss, loss of headdress, minor
insect damage in base, 16" h. (ILLUS.) **460**

Figure of female saint, carved standing &
wearing classical robes, one hand
holding a long sword upright, naturalistic
coloring on face & hands, golden paint on
robes, Europe, 18th c. (ILLUS.). **6,037**

Figure of Madonna & Child, carved oak
architectural-type figure of Madonna of
the Sea, standing w/a rose wreath on her
head, holding the Infant Jesus in one

From left: Figure of Madonna of the Sea
Crowned Madonna & Child Figures

hand, supporting an anchor w/the other,
Europe, late 19th c., age cracks, some
losses, 51" h. (ILLUS.). **3,450**

Figure of Madonna & Child, carved &
painted figures w/the Madonna wearing a
red robe & brown gold-trimmed cloak &
w/a tall flaring ornate gold crown, holding
the crowned Infant Jesus w/gold globe in
one hand & holding a sceptre in the
other, on an ornate scroll- and angel-
carved base, Europe, 18th or 19th c.,
30" h. (ILLUS.). **5,060**

Figure of mermaid, gilded wood, carved
buxom female figure wearing a diadem
w/tail curled, mounted on rod attached to
shaped painted wood base, 19th c.,
15 x 16½" **1,495**

Carved Model of a Chamois

Model of a chamois, the standing animal
w/the front legs resting on a raised
rock, a tree stump support, its head
erect w/upright short curled horns,
polychrome decoration, Europe, 19th c.,
contemporary base, minor cracks, paint
loss, craquelure, repair to antler, 24½" h.
(ILLUS.). **1,150**

Model of a dog, carved wood, recumbent figure of dog w/head up, inset glass eyes & tail back, painted black & brown, ca. 1900, 8⅛" l., 3" h. **1,035**

Model of a horse, carved full-bodied figure of brown horse, free standing w/white 'stockings' & horsehair tail, late 19th c., 26" l., 23" h. **6,325**

Model of a monkey, carved & painted seated on a tall columnar rockwork base, wearing a large red hat & yellow & red smock, holding out in one hand a shallow round red dish, brown fur & green base, probably France, late 19th c., 65" h. (minor imperfections). **10,925**

Wall plaque, carved & painted eagle wall plaque w/attenuated wings grasping a long banner w/stars in its beak, ca. 1900, 43" l., 8¼" h. **14,950**

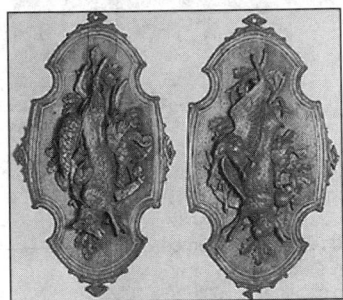

Ornate Carved Wall Plaques

Wall plaques, carved limewood, oblong cartouche form carved in full-relief w/hanging game trophies, one w/a hare, birds, leaves & powder horn, the other w/a fox, birds, leaves & a powder horn, molded edges, minor damage, probably Europe, late 19th c., 24 x 42", pr. (ILLUS.) . . **3,450**

Whirligig, carved & painted wood, flattened bearded figure of sailor boy w/rotating arms held straight out from his sides, wearing a blue shirt w/white collar & white trousers w/red belt, ca. 1900, 14¼" h. **517**

Whirligig, carved & painted wood, mustached Hussar figure dressed in full uniform, fitted w/rotating paddle arms, painted black, blue, white & gold, mounted on wood base, 13½" h. (one arm loose) **3,450**

WOODENWARES

The patina and mellow coloring, along with the lightness and smoothness that come only with age and wear, attract collectors to old woodenwares. The earliest forms were the simplest and the shapes of items whittled out in the late 19th century varied little in form from those turned out in the American colonies two centuries earlier. A burl is a growth, or wart, on some trees in which the grain of the wood is twisted and turned in a manner which strengthens the fibers and causes a beautiful pattern to be formed. Treenware is simply a term for utilitarian items made from "treen," another word for wood. While maple was the primary wood used for these items, they are also abundant in pine, ash, oak, walnut, and other woods. "Lignum Vitae" is a species of wood from the West Indies that can always be identified by the contrasting colors of dark heartwood and light sapwood and by its heavy weight, which caused it to sink in water. Also see KITCHENWARES.

Two Early Burl Bowls

Bowl, burl, deep rounded sides on small footring, refinished, 4¼" d., 1¾" h. (ILLUS. right) **$193**

Bowl, turned burl, of circular form w/incised top & sides, old mellow surface, America, 19th c., 5½" d., 3½" h. **374**

Bowl, ash burl, oval w/well-shaped cut-out rim handles, good figure, thin sides, old finish, dark stain, age crack & wear in bottom, 7⅞ x 8⅞", 2¾" h. (ILLUS. left) **2,640**

Bowl, burl, simple deep rounded sides w/a dark finish rubbed to a mottled shine, 9" d., 3¾" h. **330**

Bowl, turned & painted, an incised 1¼" rim band & beaded sides, incised line at base, original red-painted surface, 19th c., 12¾" d., 4¼" h. (minor imperfections). **920**

Bowl, ash burl, good figure & soft varnish finish, pronounced rim w/irregular notch w/worn edges, minor hairline crack, 13½" d., 6" h. **660**

Bowl, turned burl, large deep oblong form, 19th c., 13 x 16", 6" h. (rim losses). **230**

Bowl, burl, deep-sided oblong form w/recessed hand holds, ca. 1900, 17" l., 4" h. **3,450**

Bowl, ash burl, widely flaring rounded sides, worn patina, 17¼" d., 4¾" h. (small holes at flaws in burl) **605**

Bowl, turned, sharply tapering flaring sides w/small round bottom, exterior w/old worn light blue paint, interior heavily worn, 16¾ x 17½", 5¾" h. **358**

Bowl, burl, 19th c., 19⅝" d., 6¾" h. (crack, minor rim chips). **1,265**

Bowl, turned maple, wide w/incised rim & base, painted ivory, American, 18th c., 25⅛" d., 9¼" h. (minor rim chips & paint wear)........................... **1,955**

Bucket, stave construction, cylindrical form w/two wide bentwood bands w/finger lappets, natural patina, old ink inscription on bottom "Given to Gertrude H. Taylor by Augusta Bates Taylor in the Spring of 1922," 11½" d., 8¼" h. **165**

Bucket, stave construction w/two black steel bands, the exterior w/worn red graining, white interior, wire bail handle w/diamond attachments & a turned wood hand grip, 7½" d., 6" h. (bottom steel band replaced) **220**

Butter churn, stave construction, painted blue, late 18th - early 19th c., 8¾" d., 26" h. (paint wear) **374**

Butter paddle, ash burl, one-piece w/flat tapering handle w/end hook & wide shallow angled oval bowl, scrubbed finish, 9" l. **369**

Butter paddle, burl, bird's head handle, wear & handle has glued break, 8½" l. **160**

Cake board, carved walnut, three lozenge-shaped molds of a dog, a soldier on horseback & a flower-filled vase, impressed mark of J. Conger, New York, 19th c., 13 x 17" **805**

Cake box, cov., maple, circular form w/inset lid & handle stenciled w/a band of stylized flowers & leafage on yellow ground, together w/a copper milk pail molded w/figure of a standing cow............ **2,070**

Candle dryer on stand, painted, the stand w/two carved arms w/carved drying holes on the vase- and ring-turned pedestal, on a carved round base, original bluish green paint, New England, 19th c., 22" h. (minor paint wear) **575**

Carrier, octagonal, painted red w/four hexagonal compartments & one central square shape, shaped fixed handle, late 19th c., 12½" d., 4" h. (minor paint loss)...... **575**

Compote, inlaid pierced wood, staved construction w/turned & carved decoration w/brass bands, 8½" d., 8" h. **633**

Cookie board, cherry, rectangular, chip-carved w/a walking bear in a landscape, branded "B.R.," inscribed in ink "B. Raber," 5 x 7⅞" **193**

Cornucopia, wood, carved spiraling & graduated turned horn w/rope-twist border painted a red-gold color, late 19th c., 13½" l., 12" h. **460**

Corset busk, carved, the long flat board decorated on one side w/pinwheels, hearts & geometric designs, the reverse inscribed "Mary Harlow," 19th c., 13½" l. (minute cracks & a chip)................ **201**

Cuspidor, turned wood w/incised line decoration, 15¼" h. (damage, repairs)....... **403**

Dipper, bentwood, deep wide slightly tapering cylindrical sides w/copper tacks at the side seam, inset angled baluster-turned pointed side handle, old brown finish, 7½" d. plus handle **193**

Dough box on legs, rectangular deep box w/canted sides & a one-board top, raised on an inset canted apron w/corner blocks continuing to canted ring- and rod-turned legs w/knob feet, poplar w/cherry finish, 19th c., 20¾ x 35¾", 27½" h. **413**

Early Dough Box on Stand

Dough box on stand, pine & ash, a rectangular lift-off top w/braces above a deep canted dovetailed box w/a mid-molding over the base w/arched canted apron & four block-turned legs, old refinish, possibly New England, late 18th c., imperfections, 22 x 45", 25" h. (ILLUS.)............................ **1,840**

Drying rack, painted poplar, three-section, three flat slender rails joining the tall flat uprights, old worn greyish yellow repaint, attributed to the Shakers, 19th c., each section 35" w., 56" h. **193**

Flagon, cov., painted maple & elm, cylindrical stave construction w/sapling binding, the lid w/a locking mechanism, probably northern Europe, early 19th c., 13½" h. (paint wear, minor losses, insect damage)........................ **805**

Rare Turned & Incised Wood Goblet

Goblet, turned & decorated, the wide bell-shaped bowl w/molded rim, on a bulbous knop stem & round disk foot, heavily incised decoration w/panels of animals & Royal crest between religious verses, England, late 18th - early 19th c., 8¼" h. (ILLUS.) 9,200

Grain measure, cylindrical stave-constructed double-type w/two replaced metal rings, old sage green paint, 10¾" h. 99

Grain measure, round bentwood, steel bands w/cast-iron handles, old patina, branded "Danial Cragin...Wilton, N.H.," 14½" d., 8" h. 83

Pease Turned Wood Jar

Jar, cov., bulbous tapering flat-bottomed container w/a short flared neck & low domed cover w/acorn finial, curly wood w/old finish, attributed to Pease of Ohio, late 19th c., minor age cracks, 6½" h. (ILLUS.) 825

Knife box, bentwood, ash & chestnut, the low rectangular form w/rounded corners & center divider w/raised turned handhold, old varnish finish, 8½ x 13" 138

Knife box, inlaid rosewood, rectangular w/canted shallow sides inlaid w/ivory bands up each corner & w/an inlaid ivory rectangular panel centering a large diamond on the long sides, deeply scalloped central dividing handle topped by an arched ivory grip, probably New England, 19th c., 13⅛" l., 5¼" h. (very minor cracks, minor inlay loss) 2,300

Rare Decorative Knife Box

Knife box, inlaid walnut, a deep canted rectangular base w/inlaid band, teardrops & center stars fitted w/an end drawer w/ivory pull below the dovetailed upper tray w/canted sides & a scalloped rim, arched center divider w/turned bar over cut-out hand hole, old soft finish, 19th c., 9¾ x 14", 8" h. (ILLUS.) 5,060

Knife box, mahogany, rectangular w/canted sides & dovetailed corners, center divider w/a high scroll-cut handle w/oblong cut-out hand hole, old finish, 10 x 14½" 358

Leather worker's vise, chestnut, the base w/a tapering rectangular block supporting flattened uprights on two sides which curve at the top to form the vise, one side w/inset handle for adjusting vise opening, old patina, Shaker, Union Village, Ohio, 28" h. 116

Pantry box, cov., round w/nailed construction & swing handle, original red-painted surface, 19th c., 10⅞" d., 7" h. (chip on top & bottom, paint wear) 546

From left: Fine Mahogany Pipe Box
Early European Spoon Rack

Pipe box, mahogany, hanging-type, tall slender form w/high arched backboard w/hanging hole above the shaped rim & front w/a large heart cut-out, a small drawer at the bottom, molded base, late 18th c., American, imperfections, 18" h. (ILLUS.) 1,380

Pitcher, cov., painted fir, cylindrical stave construction, sapling-bond, the cover w/a locking mechanism, painted red, probably northern Europe, early 19th c., 13½" (imperfections) 1,380

Spice chest, butternut & poplar, w/arched back for hanging, eight drawers w/recessed circular knobs, ca. 1870, 5 x 11", 18" h. 350

Spoon rack, painted pine, hanging-type, the tall backboard w/a peaked cut-out top & cut-out zigzags down the sides flanking two pierced bands for spoons above a slant-lidded lower compartment w/cotter pin hinges, old dark green paint, probably Europe, late 18th c., together w/six pewter spoons, rack 5⅝ x 11½", 24¾" h., the group (ILLUS.) 920

Large Bentwood Storage Box

Storage box, cov., bentwood, painted
pine, oval w/deep sides & finger lappet
construction, upright rounded end
handles, flat board top w/central brace
w/cut-out hand hole, American, 19th c.,
cracks, minor losses, paint wear,
19¾ x 26¾", 14⅜" h. (ILLUS.)...........**1,495**

Sugar bucket, cov., stave construction
w/tapering cylindrical sides w/two wooden
bands, flat fitted cover & bentwood swing
handle, worn old red repaint over brown,
14" d., 14" h..............................**385**

Sugar bucket, cov., stave construction
w/two tacked wooden bands, alternating
staves of dark walnut & light pine, flat
fitted cover, wire bail handle w/turned
hand grip, old patina, 6⅝" h..............**193**

Tea bin, cov., painted poplar, the hinged
cover w/canted corners above a
conforming box, old red paint & transfer
w/"A&P" logo & Greek key border, late
19th c., 17 x 18", 30" h. (imperfections)......**403**

Tub, stave constructed, low cylindrical sides
wrapped w/two wide pointed lappet
bands, painted w/two shades of old green
paint, impressed mark "C. Whitney,"
19th c., 17" d., 6" h. **220**

Watch hutch, carved & decorated, a D-form
shelf w/a stepped & scalloped edge
supporting a miniature tall-case clock
case w/short legs w/claw-and-ball feet
supporting a projecting base below the
tall rectangular box w/a painted
rectangular reserve on the lower front
below the round watch face opening
decorated w/delicate notch-carving below
a crest w/a pair of pierced turret finials
flanking a spread-winged eagle on ball,
painted blue & grey w/gilt highlights,
Europe, 19th c., 3⅜ x 12", 10" h.
(no backboard, paint wear).............**1,265**

Watch hutch, inlaid mahogany, Federal
style, a tall flattened baluster-form case
w/molded inlaid base & edge banding,
the lower front inlaid w/a large paterae,
the upper case w/a round opening
surrounded by inlaid starburst rays,
molded small top w/inlaid semi-circle &
spearpoints, hanging loop at top, minor
edge damage & veneer loss, early
19th c., 11¼" h. (ILLUS.)...............**3,575**

Rare Inlaid Watch Hutch

Yarn swift, wooden table clamp-on style, a
wrought-iron thumbscrew supporting a
slender central shaft w/expanded
crisscrossed slats & small cup top finial,
old dark brown patina, 19th c., 20" h.........**193**

Yarn winding reel, floor model, hard & soft
woods, splayed simple turned legs
supporting a heavy rectangular block
supporting a tall slender tapering post
w/four long lower crossbars & four short
upper crossbars, the bars each joined
by angled pairs of long slats, old black
paint, 54¾" h...........................**220**

WORLD'S FAIR COLLECTIBLES

*There has been great interest in collecting
items produced for the great fairs and
expositions held through the years. During the
1970s, there was particular interest in items
produced for the 1876 Centennial Exhibition and
now interest is focusing on those items associated
with the 1893 Columbian Exposition. Listed
below is a random sampling of prices asked for
items produced for the various fairs.*

1893 COLUMBIAN EXPOSITION

Brochure, booklet-type, seashell-shaped,
"Gas Engine & Power Co.," cover
w/scene of two boats & reads "The Only -
Napthia Launch," 4⅔ x 4¾" (minor wear).....**$55**

Hatchet, glass, souvenir, embossed portrait
of George Washington, marked "Worlds
Fair 1893, Libbey Glass Co. Toledo,
Ohio," 8" l. (minor flakes) ....**25 to 50**

Model of a lady's hightop shoe, metal,
open top, dated **75**

Needle case, paper, illustrated w/figures of
Brownies...............................**35**

Pennant, cloth, small **14**

Punch cup, pressed frosted glass, gold
highlighted rim w/black inscription, Libbey
Glass Co. 14

Purse, change-type, mother of pearl, depicts
arrival of Christopher Columbus. 125

Puzzle, "Picture Puzzle of the World's Fair,"
lithographed paper on board, complete,
Parker Bros., 1893, boxed, 12¾ x 20¾"
(some wear, damage to edge of cover) 230

**Salt & pepper shakers w/original metal
lids,** egg-shaped, angled position w/a
flattened base section, one w/a pink
ground, the other w/a white ground, each
enameled in color w/"Columbian
Exposition 1893," marked by Libbey,
2¾" h., pr. 385

Souvenir spoon, ship depicted in bowl,
ornate handle w/image of Columbus 35

Stevengraph, woven silk scene of the
"Declaration of Independence". 225

Toothpick holder, cranberry-stained,
signed on back "John Ortgen" 75

1901 PAN AMERICAN EXPOSITION

Lapel pin, figural buffalo below "Pan
American Exposition" 65
Plate, Kitten patt., frosted w/open edge 65

1904 ST. LOUIS WORLD'S FAIR

Plate, 10¼" d., blue transfer scene showing
Main Entrance Palace of Art. 22
Postcard, hold-to-light-type, color scene of
the Palace of Machinery, large size 30
Sketch book. 15

1933-34 CHICAGO "CENTURY OF PROGRESS"

Century of Progress 1934 Map

Bank, tin, lithographed cylindrical shape
w/fair scenes 37
Envelope, w/Zeppelin stamp 60
Fan, paper, advertising "A&P Stores," 1933 50
Gearshift knob. 89

Map, "Pure Oil Pathfinder Map of A
Century of Progress Exposition," color
cover w/scenes of exposition, blue
& white back cover, 1934, excellent
condition, 8 x 9" (ILLUS.) 22

1939-40 GOLDEN GATE INTERNATIONAL EXPOSITION

Ashtray, china, Homer Laughlin China
center logo & date, near mint 70

1939-40 NEW YORK WORLD'S FAIR

The Middleton Family Advertisement

Advertisements, from "Life," featuring
Camel, Lucky Strike, the Middleton family
& other products (ILLUS.) . . . . 15 to 40

Crosley Arrow Automobile

Automobile, Crosley Arrow (ILLUS.) 50,000

World's Fair Banner & Guide's Uniform

Banner, "Welcome to World's Fair"
(ILLUS. left). 1,000

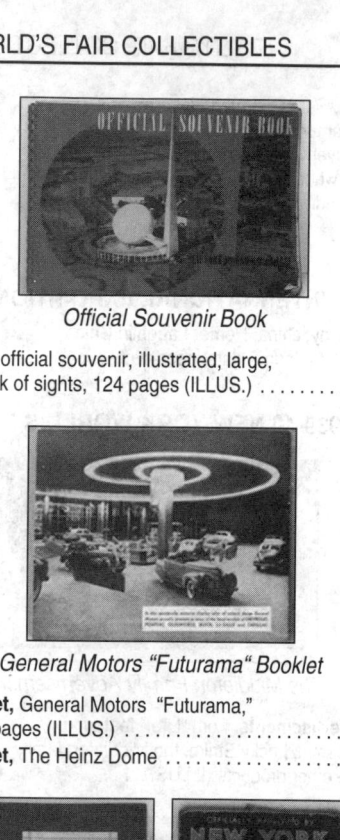

Official Souvenir Book

Book, official souvenir, illustrated, large,
book of sights, 124 pages (ILLUS.) **80**

General Motors "Futurama" Booklet

Booklet, General Motors "Futurama,"
20 pages (ILLUS.) **30**
Booklet, The Heinz Dome **10**

*From left: "The Story of Lucky Strike" Booklet
New York World's Fair Commemorative Coin*

Booklet, "The Story of Lucky Strike," by Roy
C. Flannagan, brown cover w/Trylon &
Perisphere embossed on it (ILLUS.) **80**
Booklet, "Yours Today -The Foods of
Tomorrow," from Birdseye Foods, printed
in red, white & blue **10**
Broadside, printed paper, advertising "Billy
Rose's Aquacade," w/illustrated
endorsement for Arco skates, 1940, 8 x 11" . . . **12**
Button, "Asbury Park Day at the World's
Fair," May 18, 1939, very rare **175**
Button, picturing George Washington, 1940,
very rare, 1¼" d. **100**
Coasters, glass, depicting Trylon &
Perisphere, original Holland label, set of 6. . . . **120**
Coin, bronze, commemorative, scene of
Trylon & Perisphere on one side
w/George Washington on the reverse
side, in original cardboard package (ILLUS.) . . . **75**

Coin, metal, World's Fair design. **35**
Comics, 2nd edition. **13,000**
Compact, enameled metal, by Gwenda,
cover w/a scene of fair **180**
Cuff links, metal, w/Trylon & Perisphere **50**
Films, boxed, movie views of the fair, the set. **70**
Game, "Build Your Own New York Fair
Playset," by Standard Toykraft
Products, rare **350**
Guide book, 1st edition **35**

*Various Guide Books from the 1939
New York World's Fair*

Guide books, various, notice how the
themes changed on the 1940 one in the
middle, more of American centered &
theme changed, each (ILLUS.) . . . . **25+**
Hot plate, silvered metal, w/scene of
fairgrounds, several different ones, each **20**
Ice bucket, clear cylindrical glass w/central
cylindrical shaft, exterior color-printed
w/green landscape vignettes of the fair &
red or yellow wording around the bottom
edge "New York World's Fair" **75**
Jacket, guide's **125**

Life Magazine with Girl Guide On Cover

Pictorial Map by Tony Sarg

Magazine, "Life," w/the World's Fair Girl Guide on cover (ILLUS.) . . . . **25 to 50**

Map, pocket-sized, Trylon & Perisphere illustrated against bird's-eye view of the fairgrounds, printed in black, yellow & cream **30**

Map, "The New York 1939 Official World's Fair Pictorial Map," created by Tony Sarg (ILLUS.) **50**

Nut set: master dish & four side dishes; lithographed metal, advertising Planters Peanuts w/Mr. Peanut logo & Trylon & Perisphere in center of each, the set **98**

Satin Pillow Sham

Pillow case, satin, orange, w/scenes of the fair (ILLUS.) **30**

Pin, figural, Heinz Pickle **15**

Plate, ceramic, white w/red border, color scene of Trylon & Perisphere in center **50**

Various World's Fair Postcards

1940 New York World's Fair Poster

Postcards, subjects pictured include Lagoon of Nations, Hall of Communications, RCA Bldg., hundreds of different ones, price each (ILLUS.) . . . . . **3 to 10**

Poster, color-printed paper, vertical comic-style scene of a family racing to the fair, the man on a highwheel bicycle, the girl on a scooter, a boy on a bicycle & a lady pushing a baby in a carriage, in color on a dark blue & white ground, reads "Go by all means - World's Fair in New York - 1940 - Admission Fifty Cents," artwork by S. Ekman, good condition, 20 x 30" (ILLUS.) . . **132**

Poster of the Entire Grounds at the New York World's Fair

Poster, printed in color, bird's-eye view of the entire grounds, includes Lagoon of Nations & Constitution Mall (ILLUS.) **300**

1940 Poster

Poster, printed in color w/an oversized statue of George Washington & the flags of several nations above crowds at the fairgrounds, "For Peace and Freedom - World's Fair of 1940 - New York" (ILLUS.) **300**

Poster, Trylon & Perisphere, by Joseph Binder, 20" x 30" **225**

Program, from opening day - April 30, 1939, in orange & blue colors of the fair, with the Trylon & Perisphere (ILLUS.) **200**

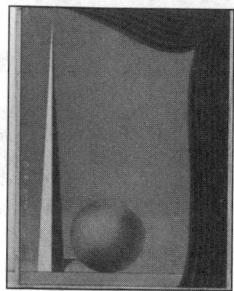

*1939 New York World's Fair
Opening Day Program*

Salt & pepper shakers, Bakelite, in the shape of the Trylon & Perisphere, two sets, one in orange w/blue base & one in blue w/orange base, each 30

Set of Poster Stamps

Set of poster stamps, issued for the fair, featured various sights, the set (ILLUS.) 250
Snow globe, Trylon & Perisphere inside 70

Kitchen Table & Chair Set

Belgian Tapestry of New York World's Fair

Table and chair set, kitchen-type, Art Deco style, white ground w/red & black logos of Trylon & Perisphere, the set (ILLUS.) **4,000**
Tapestry, in full color, featuring the Trylon & Perisphere, Federal Building, Administration Building,Constitution Mall & Lagoon of Nations, made in Belgium, Lic. #839 (ILLUS.) 350
Teapot, cov., white pottery, Trylon & Perisphere embossed on side & tinted in blue, green & tan 100

1939 RCA Television

Television set, early floor model, wooden case, 1939 RCA (ILLUS.) **2,500**
Thermometer, tin, round, fair designs 25
Toy bus, cast iron, Arcade Greyhound, "New York World's Fair" painted on the roof .. 150
Toy catalog, Arcade catalog, cover shows Trylon & Perisphere, 1940 60
Tray, lithographed metal, scenes of the fair 50
Tumblers, glass, juice, w/various scenes, including Administration Building, Theme Center & Transportation Building & two others, 5 oz., set of 5 125
Tumblers, glass, water, w/1939 Fair band at bottom & various Fair buildings at top, including Amusement, Aviation, Fountain-Lagoon & five others, set of 8 275
Uniform, guide's (ILLUS., right w/banner)..... **3,000**
View-Master, w/World's Fair reels, the set....... 50

New York World's Fair Child's Wagon

Wagon, child's, pressed steel, "Western Flyer," red body on white & red metal wheels, 5" l. (ILLUS.) 66

1962 SEATTLE WORLD'S FAIR

Tumbler, glass, scenes of fair **12**

1964-65 NEW YORK WORLD'S FAIR

Glass Ashtrays

Ashtray, glass, square, various color
scenes, one w/the Unisphere & New York
Skyline, 2¼" x 2¼", price each (ILLUS.). **5**

From left: White China Ashtray
Black Ashtray

Ashtray, china, round, white w/color scenes,
gold border & trim, made in Japan, 4½" d.
(ILLUS.) **10**
Ashtray, glass, rectangular, five color
scenes in black, white, blue, red & silver,
4" x 4¾" (ILLUS.) **10**

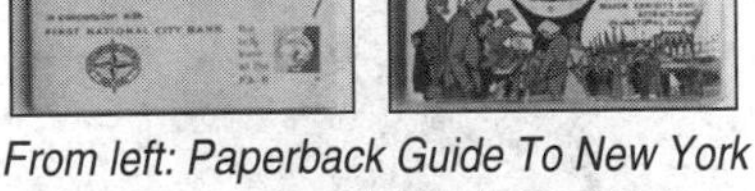

From left: Paperback Guide To New York
Official Souvenir Flash Card Set

Book, paperback, "New York: A Practical
Guide to Hotels, Restaurants, Night
Spots, Shopping & Sightseeing" by Arthur
Frommer, printed in cooperation w/The
First National Bank, the only bank at the
Fair (ILLUS.). **25**
Book, pop-up type **35**
Booklet, "Triumph of Man," by Travelers
Insurance Company **15**

Card set, color cardboard, produced by Ed-
U-Cards, marked "The Official Souvenir
Flash Card Set," the front features a color
painting of an exhibit at the fair, back
describes the front view in English,
French & Spanish, some of the scenes
pictured include Bell Telephone Pavilion,
Plaza of the Astronauts & the Kodak
Pavilion, boxed 28 pc. set (ILLUS.) **40**

Coaster

Coaster, metal, color view of Unisphere in
center, black border, description on the
back side, 4" d. (ILLUS.). **5**

Panoramic Film Tour

Film, "A Panoramic Film Tour of the World's
Fair" by Castle Films, the 8mm film about
four minutes long, in original box (ILLUS.) **50**

Film of "N.Y. World's Fair From the Air"

Film, "The New York World's Fair From the
Air!" by Castle Films, the 8mm film about
four minutes long, in original box (ILLUS.) **50**
Gift box, white box w/red figures of
Unisphere, other tourist sites of New York
City, from Macy's Department Store,
various sizes produced for the period of
the World's Fair, each **20**

From left: Jelly Tumbler
Popular Science Magazine

Jelly tumbler, clear glass, each featured
transfer scene of a site on the front in red,
5½" h., each (ILLUS. of one) **15**

License plate, automobile, 1964 New York
State, orange & black, 5 x 12" **75**

Magazine, "Popular Science," October,
1963, the new autos pictured inside are
on various under construction sites at the
fair (ILLUS.) **40**

Mug, ceramic, various sizes & colors, each **20**

Newspaper, front page from The Herald
Tribune Newspaper, for $1 you could
have produced the front page of The
New York Tribune on the day that the
individual was born, each **30**

Pennant, felt, orange & blue w/white
letters, 27" l. **35**

Gold Flowered Plate

Plate, white w/gold flowered border, various
color scenes of the fair in the center, 10" d.
(ILLUS.) **45**

Puzzle, jigsaw-type **20**

Road Map

Road map, from Atlantic Imperial, "New
York World's Fair & Metropolitan New
York City," complete map inside &
pictures, 4¼ x 9" (ILLUS.) **25**

Ship "Santa Maria"

Ship model, Santa Maria, wooden ship
painted in colors, on a stepped black
base marked "Santa Maria - New York
World's Fair 64-65," 5" h. (ILLUS.) **25**

World's Fair First Day of Issue Postal

Stamped cover, first day of issue
cancelation of U. S. five cent stamp
issued for the fair's opening, features the
Unisphere & the Plaza of Astronauts (ILLUS.). . **10**

Stamped envelope, U. S. five cent stamped
envelope issued for the fair **10**

Toy Televison Viewer

Television viewer toy, orange & blue
plastic, contains eight different scenes of
the fair, 1½" x 2¼" (ILLUS.) **35**

Toy, windup tin, color lithographed,
Greyhound Bus Glide-A-Ride toy,
guide vehicle pulling passenger
cards, made in Japan, rare. **550**

Black Plastic World's Fair Tray

Tray, black plastic, round, various color scenes pictured including Lunar Fountain, General Motors, Ford Motor, Swiss Sky Ride, "Peace Through Understanding" at bottom, 10½" d. (ILLUS.) **35**

Frosted Tumbler

Tumbler, frosted glass, many different designs in the set, front features scenes such as The Unisphere, Pool of Industry, Port Authority Building, World's Fair Circus, w/the painted image on front & a description on the back, 6½" h., each (ILLUS. of one) **15**

Unisphere model, official replica, manufactured by Topping Inc. of Elyria, Ohio, displayed in an open box w/the fair colors, rare **100**

WRITING ACCESSORIES

Early writing accessories are popular collectibles and offer a wide variety to select from. A collection may be formed around any one segment pens, letter openers, lap desks or inkwells or the collection may revolve around choice specimens of all types. Material, design and age usually determine the value. Pen collectors like the large fountain pens developed in the 1920s but also look for pens and mechanical pencils that are solid gold or gold-plated. Also see: BOTTLES & FLASKS

FOUNTAIN PENS

Carter, hard rubber, black w/gold cap band, early model, 5¾" l. (shows wear) **$50**

Carter, hard rubber, red & black w/ring in top & gold band, 4" l. vest size **60**

Carter, hard rubber, red w/small lever & gold trim, 5" l. **100**

Carter, plastic, blue green w/gold ringed cap, 6⅞" l., NM **200**

Conklin, "Conklin Chicago," red w/black stripes . . . **35**

Conklin, Crescent Filler, hard rubber, black, chevron-swirl design, gold cap band & nib, No. 3 on bottom of barrel & nib **65**

Conklin, Crescent Filler, hard rubber, black, chevron-swirl design, No. 5 on bottom of barrel & nib (shows wear) **50**

Conklin, Crescent Filler, hard rubber, black, chevron-swirl design, gold cap band, No. 4 on bottom of barrel & nib, 5½" l. **80**

Conklin, lever filler w/black chevrons on golden plastic, good nib, 7" l. **149**

Diamond Point, black & blue marbleized w/white streak, 5⅞" l. **95**

Diamond Point, red & white marbleized w/gold nib & pocket clip, cap ring, 5⅞" l. (some discoloring) **135**

Eversharp, "5th Avenue," burgundy barrel, goldwashed cap & gold nib **45**

Eversharp, "64," burgundy barrel with 1/10 gold overlay cap, gold tip on barrel end, 5¾ to 6" l. **75**

Eversharp, "64," solid gold cap, original pen from radio show "64 Dollar Question" of 1940s, recipient's name on barrel side **200**

Eversharp, Coronet, gold clad w/"Corinthian" striping in gold, Art Deco styling w/tiny blue or red triangles at top of cap, lever filled, 5⅞" **400**

Eversharp, Doric, desk style w/stand, w/12-sided barrel & cap **180**

Eversharp, Doric, w/12-sided barrel & cap, gold seal in cap above clip **190**

Eversharp, Doric, w/12-sided barrel, marbleized color, gold nib, cap band & pocket clip, NM **200**

Eversharp, Skyline, striped bottom, solid cap in blue-silver **50**

Lipic, No. 5, blue, green & white marbleized, gold cap band, nib marked w/#5 . . . . **60**

Lipic, No. 5, red, brown, black & white marbleized, gold cap band, nib marked w/#5, 6¾" l. **100**

Mont Blanc, grey silver w/silver cap, gold nib, clean color **200**

Mont Blanc, No. 452, black w/white "flower" on tip of cap, very large **140**

Morrison, No. 6, hard rubber, black, chevron-swirl design, gold nib, cap band, nib marked w/#6 . . . . **60**

Parker, desk pen, green, blue & black marbleized, gold band, ea. 8" l. **175**

Parker, Duofold, hard rubber, red, gold nib & ring top, vest size **80**

Parker, Duofold, large, blue w/tiny specks of black & white in deep blue, gold cap band, pocket clip, large nib, 7" l. **500**

Parker, Duofold, large, hard rubber, red, gold cap band & pocket clip, marked w/large "Parker" imprint on barrel side, no discoloration **300**

Parker, Duofold "True Blue," blue & white marbleized w/gold cap band & pocket clip (no stains, little yellowing to white) **200**

Parker, Duofold, yellow w/gold cap band & ring top, good nib **165**

Parker, gold filigree "lace" over black hard rubber base, floral design, 5⅓". **200**

Parker, No. 21, blue w/silvery stainless steel cap . . **20**

Parker, No. 32, silver filigree lace over black hard rubber, floral or scroll design, marked "32" & "sterling," gold nib, 6½" (some discoloration) **295**

Parker, No. 51, burgundy red barrel, silver striped cap w/grey pearl at tip, gold diamond on pocket clip. **110**

Parker, No. 51, gold striped cap design w/grey pearl at tip of cap, blue diamond on pocket clip **140**

Parker, No. 51, grey plastic, smooth barrel, silvery cap & hooded nib, marked "51" at barrel top just beneath cap fitting, NM **75**

Parker, No. 61, red w/silver cap, arrow clip **100**

Parker Gold Pen & Pencil Set

Parker set, w/matching pencil, gold solid sheath in floral relief, slim, gold nib & unusual clip, the set (ILLUS.) **300**

Sheaffer, No. 5, grey & white marbleized w/thin bright red "vein" running through pattern, gold nib, cap band, clip marked w/#5 . . **80**

Sheaffer, sheathed in gold, striped pattern, ring top, ca. late 1920s **75**

Sheaffer set, w/matching pencil, large "cigar" shape, plastic, red w/black striping, gold nib, cap band & pocket clip, the set. **200**

Swan, large colorful marble w/gold nib & No. 7, cap band & pocket clip. **180**

Swan, red & black marbleized, tiny swan on gold plate at top of cap, gold nib, marked w/name "E Martin" on side, nice clear color . . . **110**

Wahl-Eversharp, desk style, gold-clad w/gold nib, includes holder, 8½" l. **240**

Wahl-Eversharp, desk style, green w/sparkly gold dust veins, gold nib & band, black tip on rear, no pen holder **250**

Wahl-Eversharp, hard rubber, black, lever, gold cap ring & nib, 6" l. **75**

Marbleized Pen & Pencil Set with Chevron Design

Wahl-Eversharp set, w/matching pencil, black & white marbleized, gold nib & cap band w/chevron design, no discoloring or cracks in cap, 7" l., the set (ILLUS.) **400**

Pen & Pencil Set in Greek Key Style

Wahl-Eversharp set, w/matching pencil, green & gold marbleized w/Greek-key cap band, pellet present under nib, very NM color, 7⅛" l., the set (ILLUS.). **350**

Waterman, Ideal, hard rubber, black, chevron-swirl design, gold nib, cap band & applied pocket clip, marked "Waterman's Ideal, 1902" **150**

Waterman, No. 4, greenish gold clad w/striping cap & barrel, gold clip, nib marked w/#4, 1924. . . . . **225**

Waterman, No. 452, silver "lace" over black hard rubber, "sterling" floral swirl design filigree, "452" on barrel bottom, 5½" l. **205**

Waterman's Patrician

Waterman, Patrician, marbleized color, gold plate on top of cap w/world globe design, gold nib, marked "Patrician," large (ILLUS.) . . . **500**

Waterman, "Waterman Ideal," repoussé sterling silver case, early 20th c., 5½" l. **259**

INKWELLS

For the last 7,000 years, mankind's history has been written in ink of one kind or another. The continuing fascination with containers designed to hold this essential fluid has escalated greatly during the past twenty years. Inkwells of all types, designs and makers have become increasingly difficult to find as collectors discover the immensely wide variety of inkwells, inkstands and ink containers. Entire collections may be formed of a particular type such as figurals featuring a human, insect or animal figures. Many collectors specialize in glass, wood or bronze while others seek the elusive pewter or art glass well, travel well or perhaps the most difficult category, the tiny, miniature wells designed for the desk of a child. Pricing of the following inkwells and stands is drawn from flea markets, antiques shops and auctions.

Bronze stand, bronze, an oval figural rockwork base w/a realistic figure of a partridge standing atop one end, a round cov. inkwell at the other end, a dished pen tray in the front base, brown & multi-colored patina, Europe, early 20th c., 14" l. 345

Bronze well, a squatty bulbous form tapering to a low hinged cover, Oriental design of overall cast stylized dragons in endless loops, inside of cover marked "MF & Co. Viking," Marshall Field & Co., Chicago, early 20th c., 3¾" h. (no liner) 98

Cameo glass well, domed straight sided yellow glass container overlaid in white & cut w/a design of wheat & small five-petaled flowers on leafy stems, applied silver collar & compressed spherical silver monogrammed cover marked by Gorham Mfg. Co., glass probably by Stevens & Williams, ca. 1890, 4½" h. 1,150

Staffordshire earthenware, white head painted black w/numbered sections above three wells surrounded by blue scrolls, rectangular base stamped "By F. Bridges, Phrenologist," 19th c., 5½" h. 747

LAP DESKS & WRITING BOXES

Fine Mahogany Writing Box

Lap board, pine & walnut, portable rectangular board w/a half-round cut-out for the user's waist, the board composed of alternating strips of pine & walnut w/an impressed rule, strips mounted on a paper backing so it can be rolled up for storage, side braces w/brass clips keep it rigid when in use, old shipping label on the back reads "U.S. & Canada Express - 112 Canal St. - From Boston, Mass.," attributed to the Shakers, 19½ x 36" 220

Writing box, mahogany, rectangular case w/hinged slant lid opening to a compartmented two-drawer interior w/whalebone & ivory pulls, applied carved base band, old surface, minor cracks, 19th c., 14¼ x 17½", 7" h. (ILLUS.) . . . 920

LETTER OPENERS

Commercial Aluminum Letter Opener

Aluminum, anodized, commercial design w/company name, blue, 7" l. (ILLUS.) 5

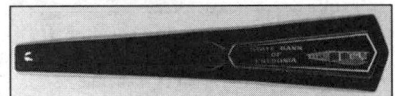

Commercial Aluminum Letter Opener

Aluminum, commercial design w/bank building in relief, "State Bank of Fredonia," 7½" l. (ILLUS.). 10

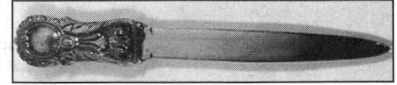

Brass Letter Opener

Brass, Art Nouveau style w/sun & flower design, 8" l. (ILLUS.) 100
Brass, commercial design, blade embellished w/measurement in inches, 7½" l. . . . 29

Brass Curved-Handled Letter Opener

Brass, curved "S" handle which may be monogrammed, 6" l. (ILLUS.). 45

Brass Letter Opener

Brass, deep relief of peasant woman whose skirt is pulled by a dog, unique w/back turned, 8⅛" l. (ILLUS.) **90**

Brass, head of woman in oval, coated, 6⅔" l. **17**

Brass, open-worked sculpture of woman wearing unusual short bolero jacket & large hat, probably European, 7½" l. **90**

Brass, sharp worked handle, eagle wings flank laurel wreath w/"RGMA" beneath, appears to be military, European, 5½" l. **75**

Brass, snake swallowing another w/design coiling up handle, possibly medical brass, 6⅞" l. **85**

Brass, w/heraldic design, royal lion on globe, 5½" l. **80**

Brass, w/swirled rose, accompanied desk set, 7" l. **36**

Brass & steel, Art Nouveau style w/flower handle, 7" l. **60**

Brass & steel, embossed w/dolphin motif on handle, 7¾" l. **105**

Bronze, deep relief of iris w/leaves, Tiffany, 9" l. . . **450**

Bronze, lion inset in pot metal (damage along blade) **20**

Bronze, pine needle design w/green Art Glass under filigree handle, marked "Tiffany Studios, NY", 9" l. **490**

Ancient Bronze Seal Opener

Bronze, seal opener, slightly curved blade w/hilt featuring medieval knight in prayer, ancient type brought from Holy Land centuries ago, from period between daggers & letter openers, 6⅞" l. (small pits in bronze) (ILLUS.) **2,500**

Bronze, w/fused logo in coin-like shape in handle, 6⅞" l. **35**

Bronze Gemmed-Handled Letter Opener

Bronze, w/inlaid wire & cabochon gems on handle, simple idea & unusual manufacture, 7⅞" l. (ILLUS.) **95**

Celluloid, carved w/elephant parade design, Asian, ca. 1930s, undervalued **25**

Celluloid, w/figure of Apostle, called "French Ivory" **20**

Horn, w/steel blade, earlier style, 8" l. **60**

Iron, commercial design, enameled company name, 6⅛" l. **20**

Iron, worked simple type, die-stamped design, ca. 1800s, 7" l. **30**

Papier-maché, floral design, France, ca. late 1800s, unusual, 6¾" l. **70**

Plastic, plastic bubble handle w/architectural feature, a "double" collectible . . . **20**

Plastic, souvenir type, top/bubble showing sailboat, ca. 1930s **25**

Plastic, souvenir type, top/bubble w/real 4-leaf clover underneath, ca. 1930s **30**

Plastic, swirled opaque w/octagon in handle, commercial, 6" l. **5**

Plastic, transparent red w/business building in relief on handle **10**

Plastic, w/ruler on side of blade, 6½" l. **15**

Pot Metal, heavily imprinted w/Liberty Bell in handle, stiletto, 7" l. **9**

Silver plate, floral handle in deep relief, 6½" l. **75**

Steel, commercial gift style w/bank logo & message, 8½" l. **25**

Steel, inset w/letters & numbers in copper w/logo, 5⅛" l. **25**

Steel Multipurpose Handled Letter Opener

Steel, w/multi-purpose handle concealing two knife blades & scissors & nail file, "Evelyn Knok" on blade, Switzerland possibly origin of Swiss army knife idea, 9" l. (ILLUS.) **115**

Pearl-Type Handled Letter Opener

Steel, w/pearl-type handle concealing knife blade, another transition between wax seals & envelopes (ILLUS.) **110**

Steel, w/seal or distillery, a "double" collectible, 8" l. **70**

White-gold, delicate flower in handle, special make, Cartier, 7⅞" l. **350**

Wood, carved rosewood, w/head of Amerindian brave in war bonnet. **100**

Wood, cookie press design in handle, similar to Amish style, 6" l. **40**

Wood, handcarved, Folk Art w/peasant woman, from Ozark region, ca. 1950s, 5½" l. . . **45**

Wood, South Seas TIKI idol figure, inset w/abalone eyes, Polynesia, 6" l. **90**

Wood, w/leather & bone insets, pharmaceuticals company, 6½" l. **55**

INDEX